GENERAL MOTORS CADILLAC 1967-89 REPAIR MANUAL

CHILTON'S

Covers all U.S. and Canadian models of Cadillac DeVille, Eldorado, Fleetwood and Seville

by **Tony Tortorici**, A.S.E., S.A.E.

CHILTON *Automotive Books*

PUBLISHED BY **HAYNES NORTH AMERICA, Inc.**

AUTOMOTIVE PARTS & ACCESSORIES ASSOCIATION MEMBER

Manufactured in USA
© 1994 Haynes North America, Inc.
ISBN 0-8019-8587-0
Library of Congress Catalog Card No. 98-071964
0123456789 9876543210

Haynes Publishing Group
Sparkford Nr Yeovil
Somerset BA22 7JJ England

Haynes North America, Inc
861 Lawrence Drive
Newbury Park
California 91320 USA

ABCDE
FGHIJ

Contents

Contents

SAFETY NOTICE

Proper service and repair procedures are vital to the safe, reliable operation of all motor vehicles, as well as the personal safety of those performing repairs. This manual outlines procedures for servicing and repairing vehicles using safe, effective methods. The procedures contain many NOTES, CAUTIONS and WARNINGS which should be followed, along with standard procedures to eliminate the possibility of personal injury or improper service which could damage the vehicle or compromise its safety.

It is important to note that repair procedures and techniques, tools and parts for servicing motor vehicles, as well as the skill and experience of the individual performing the work vary widely. It is not possible to anticipate all of the conceivable ways or conditions under which vehicles may be serviced, or to provide cautions as to all possible hazards that may result. Standard and accepted safety precautions and equipment should be used when handling toxic or flammable fluids, and safety goggles or other protection should be used during cutting, grinding, chiseling, prying, or any other process that can cause material removal or projectiles.

Some procedures require the use of tools specially designed for a specific purpose. Before substituting another tool or procedure, you must be completely satisfied that neither your personal safety, nor the performance of the vehicle will be endangered.

Although information in this manual is based on industry sources and is complete as possible at the time of publication, the possibility exists that some car manufacturers made later changes which could not be included here. While striving for total accuracy, the authors or publishers cannot assume responsibility for any errors, changes or omissions that may occur in the compilation of this data.

PART NUMBERS

Part numbers listed in this reference are not recommendations by Haynes North America, Inc. for any product brand name. They are references that can be used with interchange manuals and aftermarket supplier catalogs to locate each brand supplier's discrete part number.

SPECIAL TOOLS

Special tools are recommended by the vehicle manufacturer to perform their specific job. Use has been kept to a minimum, but where absolutely necessary, they are referred to in the text by the part number of the tool manufacturer. These tools can be purchased, under the appropriate part number, from your local dealer or regional distributor, or an equivalent tool can be purchased locally from a tool supplier or parts outlet. Before substituting any tool for the one recommended, read the SAFETY NOTICE at the top of this page.

ACKNOWLEDGMENTS

Portions of materials contained herein have been reprinted with the permission of General Motors Corporation, Service Technology Group.

1

GENERAL INFORMATION AND MAINTENANCE

HOW TO USE THIS BOOK

This Chilton's Total Car Care manual is intended to help you learn more about the inner workings of your Cadillac while saving you money on its upkeep and operation.

The beginning of the book will likely be referred to the most, since that is where you will find information for maintenance and tune-up. The other sections deal with the more complex systems of your vehicle. Systems (from engine through brakes) are covered to the extent that the average do-it-yourselfer can attempt. This book will not explain such things as rebuilding a differential because the expertise required and the special tools necessary make this uneconomical. It will, however, give you detailed instructions to help you change your own brake pads and shoes, replace spark plugs, and perform many more jobs that can save you money and help avoid expensive problems.

A secondary purpose of this book is a reference for owners who want to understand their vehicle and/or their mechanics better.

Where to Begin

Before removing any bolts, read through the entire procedure. This will give you the overall view of what tools and supplies will be required. So read ahead and plan ahead. Each operation should be approached logically and all procedures thoroughly understood before attempting any work.

If repair of a component is not considered practical, we tell you how to remove the part and then how to install the new or rebuilt replacement. In this way, you at least save labor costs.

Avoiding Trouble

Many procedures in this book require you to "label and disconnect . . ." a group of lines, hoses or wires. Don't be think you can remember where everything goes—you won't. If you hook up vacuum or fuel lines incorrectly, the vehicle may run poorly, if at all. If you hook up electrical wiring incorrectly, you may instantly learn a very expensive lesson.

You don't need to know the proper name for each hose or line. A piece of masking tape on the hose and a piece on its fitting will allow you to assign your own label. As long as you remember your own code, the lines can be reconnected by matching your tags. Remember that tape will dissolve in gasoline or solvents; if a part is to be washed or cleaned, use another method of identification. A permanent felt-tipped marker or a metal scribe can be very handy for marking metal parts. Remove any tape or paper labels after assembly.

Maintenance or Repair?

Maintenance includes routine inspections, adjustments, and replacement of parts which show signs of normal wear. Maintenance compensates for wear or deterioration. Repair implies that something has broken or is not working. A need for a repair is often caused by lack of maintenance. for example: draining and refilling automatic transmission fluid is maintenance recommended at specific intervals. Failure to do this can shorten the life of the transmission/transaxle, requiring very expensive repairs. While no maintenance program can prevent items from eventually breaking or wearing out, a general rule is true: MAINTENANCE IS CHEAPER THAN REPAIR.

Two basic mechanic's rules should be mentioned here. First, whenever the left side of the vehicle or engine is referred to, it means the driver's side. Conversely, the right side of the vehicle means the passenger's side. Second, screws and bolts are removed by turning counterclockwise, and tightened by turning clockwise unless specifically noted.

Safety is always the most important rule. Constantly be aware of the dangers involved in working on an automobile and take the proper precautions. Please refer to the information in this section regarding SERVICING YOUR VEHICLE SAFELY and the SAFETY NOTICE on the acknowledgment page.

Avoiding the Most Common Mistakes

Pay attention to the instructions provided. There are 3 common mistakes in mechanical work:

1. Incorrect order of assembly, disassembly or adjustment. When taking something apart or putting it together, performing steps in the wrong order usually just costs you extra time; however, it CAN break something. Read the entire procedure before beginning. Perform everything in the order in which the instructions say you should, even if you can't see a reason for it. When you're taking apart something that is very intricate, you might want to draw a picture of how it looks when assembled in order to make sure you get everything back in its proper position. When making adjustments, perform them in the proper order. One adjustment possibly will affect another.

2. Overtorquing (or undertorquing). While it is more common for overtorquing to cause damage, undertorquing may allow a fastener to vibrate loose causing serious damage. Especially when dealing with aluminum parts, pay attention to torque specifications and utilize a torque wrench in assembly. If a torque figure is not available, remember that if you are using the right tool to perform the job, you will probably not have to strain yourself to get a fastener tight enough. The pitch of most threads is so slight that the tension you put on the wrench will be multiplied many times in actual force on what you are tightening.

There are many commercial products available for ensuring that fasteners won't come loose, even if they are not torqued just right (a very common brand is Loctite®). If you're worried about getting something together tight enough to hold, but loose enough to avoid mechanical damage during assembly, one of these products might offer substantial insurance. Before choosing a threadlocking compound, read the label on the package and make sure the product is compatible with the materials, fluids, etc. involved.

3. Crossthreading. This occurs when a part such as a bolt is screwed into a nut or casting at the wrong angle and forced. Crossthreading is more likely to occur if access is difficult. It helps to clean and lubricate fasteners, then to start threading the bolt, spark plug, etc. with your fingers. If you encounter resistance, unscrew the part and start over again at a different angle until it can be inserted and turned several times without much effort. Keep in mind that many parts have tapered threads, so that gentle turning will automatically bring the part you're threading to the proper angle. Don't put a wrench on the part until it's been tightened a couple of turns by hand. If you suddenly encounter resistance, and the part has not seated fully, don't force it. Pull it back out to make sure it's clean and threading properly.

Be sure to take your time and be patient, and always plan ahead. Allow yourself ample time to perform repairs and maintenance.

TOOLS AND EQUIPMENT

♦ See Figures 1 thru 15

Without the proper tools and equipment it is impossible to properly service your vehicle. It would be virtually impossible to catalog every tool that you would need to perform all of the operations in this book. It would be unwise for the amateur to rush out and buy an expensive set of tools on the theory that he/she may need one or more of them at some time.

The best approach is to proceed slowly, gathering a good quality set of those tools that are used most frequently. Don't be misled by the low cost of bargain tools. It is far better to spend a little more for better quality. Forged wrenches, 6 or 12-point sockets and fine tooth ratchets are by far preferable to their less expensive counterparts. As any good mechanic can tell you, there are few worse experiences than trying to work on a vehicle with bad tools. Your monetary savings will be far outweighed by frustration and mangled knuckles.

Begin accumulating those tools that are used most frequently: those associated with routine maintenance and tune-up. In addition to the normal assortment of screwdrivers and pliers, you should have the following tools:

- Wrenches/sockets and combination open end/box end wrenches in sizes 1/8–3/4 in. and/or 3mm–19mm 13/16 in. or 5/8 in. spark plug socket (depending on plug type).

➡ **If possible, buy various length socket drive extensions. Universal-joint and wobble extensions can be extremely useful, but be careful when using them, as they can change the amount of torque applied to the socket.**

- Jackstands for support.
- Oil filter wrench.
- Spout or funnel for pouring fluids.

• Grease gun for chassis lubrication (unless your vehicle is not equipped with any grease fittings)

• Hydrometer for checking the battery (unless equipped with a sealed, maintenance-free battery).

• A container for draining oil and other fluids.

• Rags for wiping up the inevitable mess.

In addition to the above items there are several others that are not absolutely necessary, but handy to have around. These include an equivalent oil absorbent gravel, like cat litter, and the usual supply of lubricants, antifreeze and fluids. This is a basic list for routine maintenance, but only your personal needs and desire can accurately determine your list of tools.

After performing a few projects on the vehicle, you'll be amazed at the other tools and non-tools on your workbench. Some useful household items are: a large turkey baster or siphon, empty coffee cans and ice trays (to store parts), a ball of twine, electrical tape for wiring, small rolls of colored tape for tagging lines or hoses, markers and pens, a note pad, golf tees (for plugging vacuum lines), metal coat hangers or a roll of mechanic's wire (to hold things out of the way), dental pick or similar long, pointed probe, a strong magnet, and a small mirror (to see into recesses and under manifolds).

A more advanced set of tools, suitable for tune-up work, can be drawn up easily. While the tools are slightly more sophisticated, they need not be outrageously expensive. There are several inexpensive tach/dwell meters on the market that are every bit as good for the average mechanic as a professional model. Just be sure that it goes to a least 1200–1500 rpm on the tach scale and that it works on 4, 6 and 8-cylinder engines. The key to these purchases is to make them with an eye towards adaptability and wide range. A basic list of tune-up tools could include:

• Tach/dwell meter.

• Spark plug wrench and gapping tool.

• Feeler gauges for valve adjustment.

• Timing light.

The choice of a timing light should be made carefully. A light which works on the DC current supplied by the vehicle's battery is the best choice; it should have a xenon tube for brightness. On any vehicle with an electronic ignition sys-

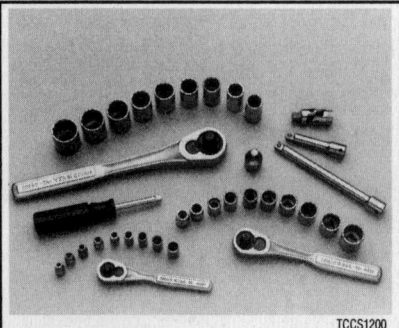

Fig. 1 All but the most basic procedures will require an assortment of ratchets and sockets

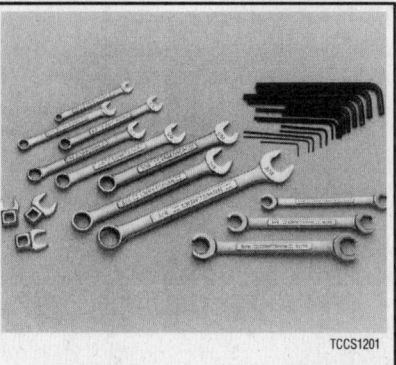

Fig. 2 In addition to ratchets, a good set of wrenches and hex keys will be necessary

Fig. 3 A hydraulic floor jack and a set of jackstands are essential for lifting and supporting the vehicle

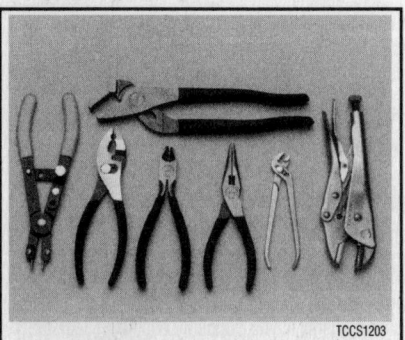

Fig. 4 An assortment of pliers, grippers and cutters will be handy for old rusted parts and stripped bolt heads

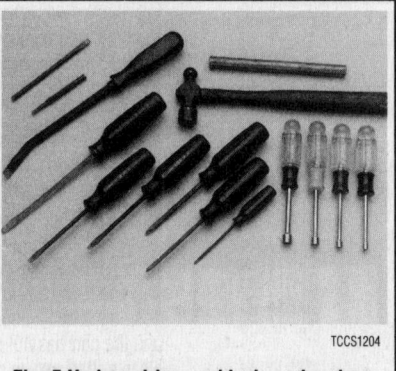

Fig. 5 Various drivers, chisels and prybars are great tools to have in your toolbox

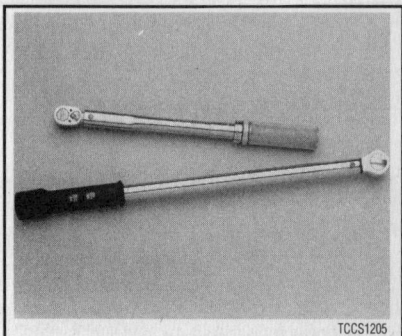

Fig. 6 Many repairs will require the use of a torque wrench to assure the components are properly fastened

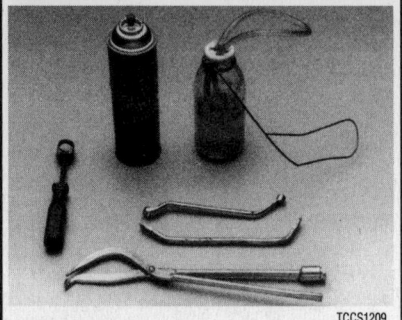

Fig. 7 Although not always necessary, using specialized brake tools will save time

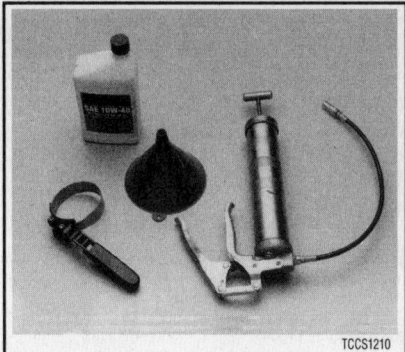

Fig. 8 A few inexpensive lubrication tools will make maintenance easier

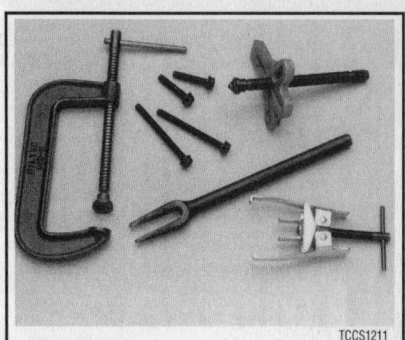

Fig. 9 Various pullers, clamps and separator tools are needed for many larger, more complicated repairs

Fig. 10 A variety of tools and gauges should be used for spark plug gapping and installation

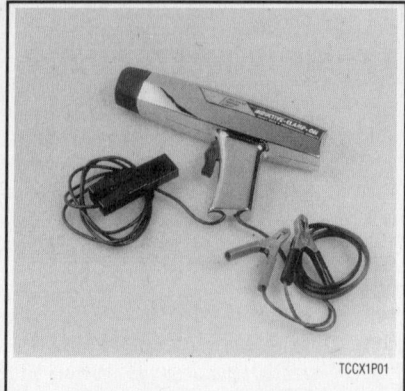

Fig. 11 Inductive type timing light

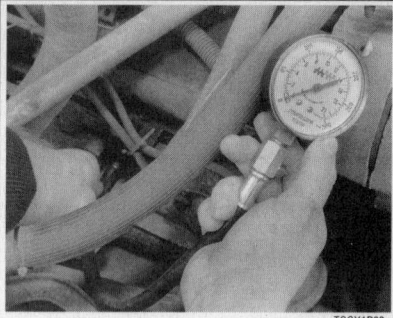

Fig. 12 A screw-in type compression gauge is recommended for compression testing

Fig. 13 A vacuum/pressure tester is necessary for many testing procedures

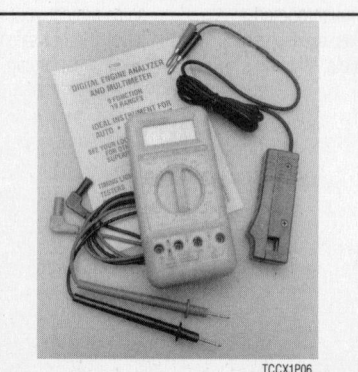

Fig. 14 Most modern automotive multimeters incorporate many helpful features

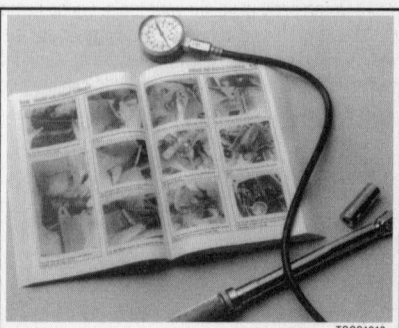

Fig. 15 Proper information is vital, so always have a Chilton Total Car Care manual handy

tem, a timing light with an inductive pickup that clamps around the No. 1 spark plug cable is preferred.

In addition to these basic tools, there are several other tools and gauges you may find useful. These include:

• Compression gauge. The screw-in type is slower to use, but eliminates the possibility of a faulty reading due to escaping pressure.
• Manifold vacuum gauge.
• 12V test light.
• A combination volt/ohmmeter
• Induction Ammeter. This is used for determining whether or not there is current in a wire. These are handy for use if a wire is broken somewhere in a wiring harness.

As a final note, you will probably find a torque wrench necessary for all but the most basic work. The beam type models are perfectly adequate, although the newer click types (breakaway) are easier to use. The click type torque wrenches tend to be more expensive. Also keep in mind that all types of torque wrenches should be periodically checked and/or recalibrated. You will have to decide for yourself which better fits your pocketbook, and purpose.

Special Tools

Normally, the use of special factory tools is avoided for repair procedures, since these are not readily available for the do-it-yourself mechanic. When it is possible to perform the job with more commonly available tools, it will be pointed out, but occasionally, a special tool was designed to perform a specific function and should be used. Before substituting another tool, you should be convinced that neither your safety nor the performance of the vehicle will be compromised.

Special tools can usually be purchased from an automotive parts store or from your dealer. In some cases special tools may be available directly from the tool manufacturer.

SERVICING YOUR VEHICLE SAFELY

♦ **See Figures 16, 17 and 18**

It is virtually impossible to anticipate all of the hazards involved with automotive maintenance and service, but care and common sense will prevent most accidents.

The rules of safety for mechanics range from "don't smoke around gasoline," to "use the proper tool(s) for the job." The trick to avoiding injuries is to develop safe work habits and to take every possible precaution.

Do's

• Do keep a fire extinguisher and first aid kit handy.
• Do wear safety glasses or goggles when cutting, drilling, grinding or prying, even if you have 20–20 vision. If you wear glasses for the sake of vision, wear safety goggles over your regular glasses.

• Do shield your eyes whenever you work around the battery. Batteries contain sulfuric acid. In case of contact with, flush the area with water or a mixture of water and baking soda, then seek immediate medical attention.
• Do use safety stands (jackstands) for any undervehicle service. Jacks are for raising vehicles; jackstands are for making sure the vehicle stays raised until you want it to come down.
• Do use adequate ventilation when working with any chemicals or hazardous materials. Like carbon monoxide, the asbestos dust resulting from some brake lining wear can be hazardous in sufficient quantities.
• Do disconnect the negative battery cable when working on the electrical system. The secondary ignition system contains EXTREMELY HIGH VOLTAGE. In some cases it can even exceed 50,000 volts.
• Do follow manufacturer's directions whenever working with potentially hazardous materials. Most chemicals and fluids are poisonous.

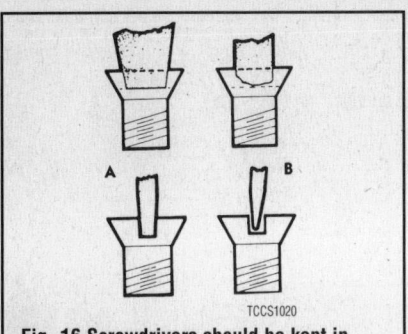

Fig. 16 Screwdrivers should be kept in good condition to prevent injury or damage which could result if the blade slips from the screw

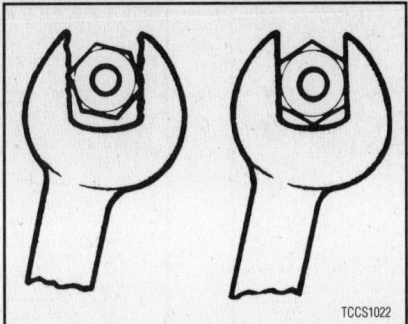

Fig. 17 Using the correct size wrench will help prevent the possibility of rounding off a nut

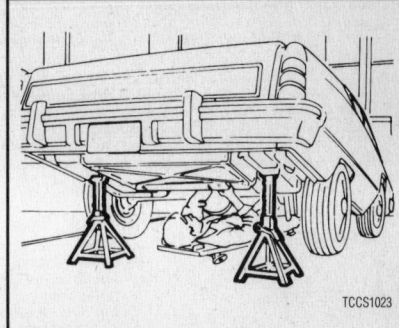

Fig. 18 NEVER work under a vehicle unless it is supported using safety stands (jackstands)

• Do properly maintain your tools. Loose hammerheads, mushroomed punches and chisels, frayed or poorly grounded electrical cords, excessively worn screwdrivers, spread wrenches (open end), cracked sockets, slipping ratchets, or faulty droplight sockets can cause accidents.

• Likewise, keep your tools clean; a greasy wrench can slip off a bolt head, ruining the bolt and often harming your knuckles in the process.

• Do use the proper size and type of tool for the job at hand. Do select a wrench or socket that fits the nut or bolt. The wrench or socket should sit straight, not cocked.

• Do, when possible, pull on a wrench handle rather than push on it, and adjust your stance to prevent a fall.

• Do be sure that adjustable wrenches are tightly closed on the nut or bolt and pulled so that the force is on the side of the fixed jaw.

• Do strike squarely with a hammer; avoid glancing blows.

• Do set the parking brake and block the drive wheels if the work requires a running engine.

Don'ts

• Don't run the engine in a garage or anywhere else without proper ventilation—EVER! Carbon monoxide is poisonous; it takes a long time to leave the human body and you can build up a deadly supply of it in your system by simply breathing in a little at a time. You may not realize you are slowly poisoning yourself. Always use power vents, windows, fans and/or open the garage door.

• Don't work around moving parts while wearing loose clothing. Short sleeves are much safer than long, loose sleeves. Hard-toed shoes with neoprene soles protect your toes and give a better grip on slippery surfaces. Watches and jewelry is not safe working around a vehicle. Long hair should be tied back under a hat or cap.

• Don't use pockets for toolboxes. A fall or bump can drive a screwdriver deep into your body. Even a rag hanging from your back pocket can wrap around a spinning shaft or fan.

• Don't smoke when working around gasoline, cleaning solvent or other flammable material.

• Don't smoke when working around the battery. When the battery is being charged, it gives off explosive hydrogen gas.

• Don't use gasoline to wash your hands; there are excellent soaps available. Gasoline contains dangerous additives which can enter the body through a cut or through your pores. Gasoline also removes all the natural oils from the skin so that bone dry hands will suck up oil and grease.

• Don't service the air conditioning system unless you are equipped with the necessary tools and training. When liquid or compressed gas refrigerant is released to atmospheric pressure it will absorb heat from whatever it contacts. This will chill or freeze anything it touches.

• Don't use screwdrivers for anything other than driving screws! A screwdriver used as an prying tool can snap when you least expect it, causing injuries. At the very least, you'll ruin a good screwdriver.

• Don't use an emergency jack (that little ratchet, scissors, or pantograph jack supplied with the vehicle) for anything other than changing a flat! These jacks are only intended for emergency use out on the road; they are NOT designed as a maintenance tool. If you are serious about maintaining your vehicle yourself, invest in a hydraulic floor jack of at least a 1½ ton capacity, and at least two sturdy jackstands.

FASTENERS, MEASUREMENTS AND CONVERSIONS

Bolts, Nuts and Other Threaded Retainers

▶ See Figures 19 and 20

Although there are a great variety of fasteners found in the modern car or truck, the most commonly used retainer is the threaded fastener (nuts, bolts, screws, studs, etc.). Most threaded retainers may be reused, provided that they are not damaged in use or during the repair. Some retainers (such as stretch bolts or torque prevailing nuts) are designed to deform when tightened or in use and should not be reinstalled.

Whenever possible, we will note any special retainers which should be replaced during a procedure. But you should always inspect the condition of a retainer when it is removed and replace any that show signs of damage. Check all threads for rust or corrosion which can increase the torque necessary to achieve the desired clamp load for which that fastener was originally selected. Additionally, be sure that the driver surface of the fastener has not been compromised by rounding or other damage. In some cases a driver surface may become only partially rounded, allowing the driver to catch in only one direction. In many of these occurrences, a fastener may be installed and tightened, but the driver would not be able to grip and loosen the fastener again.

If you must replace a fastener, whether due to design or damage, you must ALWAYS be sure to use the proper replacement. In all cases, a retainer of the

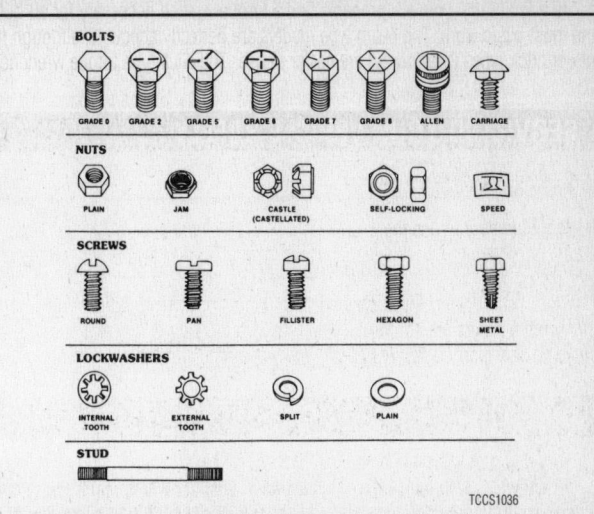

Fig. 19 There are many different types of threaded retainers found on vehicles

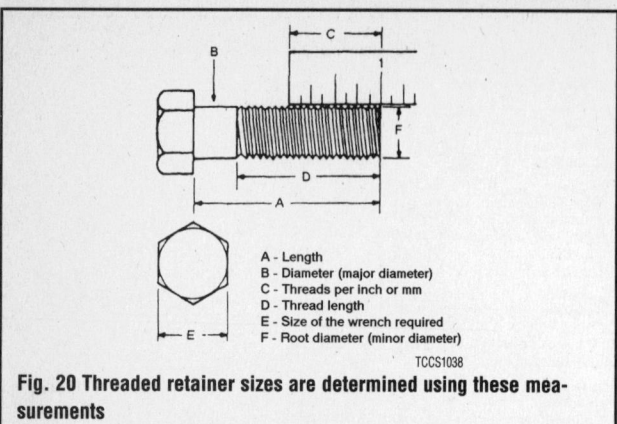

A - Length
B - Diameter (major diameter)
C - Threads per inch or mm
D - Thread length
E - Size of the wrench required
F - Root diameter (minor diameter)

TCCS1038

Fig. 20 Threaded retainer sizes are determined using these measurements

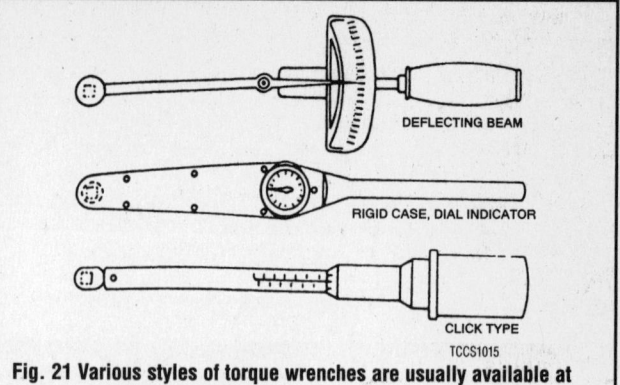

DEFLECTING BEAM

RIGID CASE, DIAL INDICATOR

CLICK TYPE

TCCS1015

Fig. 21 Various styles of torque wrenches are usually available at your local automotive supply store

same design, material and strength should be used. Markings on the heads of most bolts will help determine the proper strength of the fastener. The same material, thread and pitch must be selected to assure proper installation and safe operation of the vehicle afterwards.

Thread gauges are available to help measure a bolt or stud's thread. Most automotive and hardware stores keep gauges available to help you select the proper size. In a pinch, you can use another nut or bolt for a thread gauge. If the bolt you are replacing is not too badly damaged, you can select a match by finding another bolt which will thread in its place. If you find a nut which threads properly onto the damaged bolt, then use that nut to help select the replacement bolt.

✳✳ WARNING

Be aware that when you find a bolt with damaged threads, you may also find the nut or drilled hole it was threaded into has also been damaged. If this is the case, you may have to drill and tap the hole, replace the nut or otherwise repair the threads. NEVER try to force a replacement bolt to fit into the damaged threads.

Torque

Torque is defined as the measurement of resistance to turning or rotating. It tends to twist a body about an axis of rotation. A common example of this would be tightening a threaded retainer such as a nut, bolt or screw. Measuring torque is one of the most common ways to help assure that a threaded retainer has been properly fastened.

When tightening a threaded fastener, torque is applied in three distinct areas, the head, the bearing surface and the clamp load. About 50 percent of the measured torque is used in overcoming bearing friction. This is the friction between the bearing surface of the bolt head, screw head or nut face and the base material or washer (the surface on which the fastener is rotating). Approximately 40 percent of the applied torque is used in overcoming thread friction. This leaves only about 10 percent of the applied torque to develop a useful clamp load (the force which holds a joint together). This means that friction can account for as much as 90 percent of the applied torque on a fastener.

TORQUE WRENCHES

♦ See Figure 21

In most applications, a torque wrench can be used to assure proper installation of a fastener. Torque wrenches come in various designs and most automotive supply stores will carry a variety to suit your needs. A torque wrench should be used any time we supply a specific torque value for a fastener. Again, the general rule of "if you are using the right tool for the job, you should not have to strain to tighten a fastener" applies here.

Beam Type

The beam type torque wrench is one of the most popular types. It consists of a pointer attached to the head that runs the length of the flexible beam (shaft) to a scale located near the handle. As the wrench is pulled, the beam bends and the pointer indicates the torque using the scale.

Click (Breakaway) Type

Another popular design of torque wrench is the click type. To use the click type wrench you pre-adjust it to a torque setting. Once the torque is reached, the wrench has a reflex signaling feature that causes a momentary breakaway of the torque wrench body, sending an impulse to the operator's hand.

Pivot Head Type

♦ See Figure 22

Some torque wrenches (usually of the click type) may be equipped with a pivot head which can allow it to be used in areas of limited access. BUT, it must be used properly. To hold a pivot head wrench, grasp the handle lightly, and as you pull on the handle, it should be floated on the pivot point. If the handle comes in contact with the yoke extension during the process of pulling, there is a very good chance the torque readings will be inaccurate because this could alter the wrench loading point. The design of the handle is usually such as to make it inconvenient to deliberately misuse the wrench.

➡ **It should be mentioned that the use of any U-joint, wobble or extension will have an effect on the torque readings, no matter what type of wrench you are using. For the most accurate readings, install the socket directly on the wrench driver. If necessary, straight extensions (which hold a socket directly under the wrench driver) will have the least effect on the torque reading. Avoid any extension that alters the length of the wrench from the handle to the head/driving point (such as a crow's foot). U-joint or wobble extensions can greatly affect the readings; avoid their use at all times.**

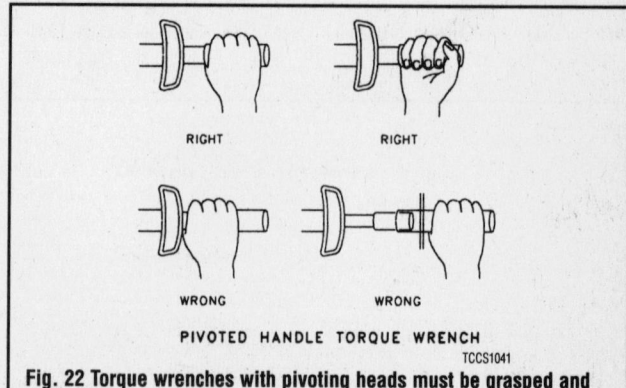

RIGHT   RIGHT

WRONG   WRONG

PIVOTED HANDLE TORQUE WRENCH

TCCS1041

Fig. 22 Torque wrenches with pivoting heads must be grasped and used properly to prevent an incorrect reading

Rigid Case (Direct Reading)

A rigid case or direct reading torque wrench is equipped with a dial indicator to show torque values. One advantage of these wrenches is that they can be held at any position on the wrench without affecting accuracy. These wrenches are often preferred because they tend to be compact, easy to read and have a great degree of accuracy.

TORQUE ANGLE METERS

Because the frictional characteristics of each fastener or threaded hole will vary, clamp loads which are based strictly on torque will vary as well. In most applications, this variance is not significant enough to cause worry. But, in certain applications, a manufacturer's engineers may determine that more precise clamp loads are necessary (such is the case with many aluminum cylinder heads). In these cases, a torque angle method of installation would be specified. When installing fasteners which are torque angle tightened, a predetermined seating torque and standard torque wrench are usually used first to remove any compliance from the joint. The fastener is then tightened the specified additional portion of a turn measured in degrees. A torque angle gauge (mechanical protractor) is used for these applications.

Standard and Metric Measurements

▸ **See Figure 23**

Throughout this manual, specifications are given to help you determine the condition of various components on your vehicle, or to assist you in their installation. Some of the most common measurements include length (in. or cm/mm), torque (ft. lbs., inch lbs. or Nm) and pressure (psi, in. Hg, kPa or mm Hg). In most cases, we strive to provide the proper measurement as determined by the manufacturer's engineers.

Though, in some cases, that value may not be conveniently measured with what is available in your toolbox. Luckily, many of the measuring devices which are available today will have two scales so the Standard or Metric measurements may easily be taken. If any of the various measuring tools which are available to you do not contain the same scale as listed in the specifications, use the accompanying conversion factors to determine the proper value.

The conversion factor chart is used by taking the given specification and multiplying it by the necessary conversion factor. For instance, looking at the first line, if you have a measurement in inches such as "free-play should be 2 in." but your ruler reads only in millimeters, multiply 2 in. by the conversion factor of 25.4 to get the metric equivalent of 50.8mm. Likewise, if the specification was given only in a Metric measurement, for example in Newton Meters (Nm), then look at the center column first. If the measurement is 100 Nm, multiply it by the conversion factor of 0.738 to get 73.8 ft. lbs.

CONVERSION FACTORS

LENGTH–DISTANCE

Inches (in.)	x 25.4	= Millimeters (mm)	x .0394	= Inches
Feet (ft.)	x .305	= Meters (m)	x 3.281	= Feet
Miles	x 1.609	= Kilometers (km)	x .0621	= Miles

VOLUME

Cubic Inches (in3)	x 16.387	= Cubic Centimeters	x .061	= in3
IMP Pints (IMP pt.)	x .568	= Liters (L)	x 1.76	= IMP pt.
IMP Quarts (IMP qt.)	x 1.137	= Liters (L)	x .88	= IMP qt.
IMP Gallons (IMP gal.)	x 4.546	= Liters (L)	x .22	= IMP gal.
IMP Quarts (IMP qt.)	x 1.201	= US Quarts (US qt.)	x .833	= IMP qt.
IMP Gallons (IMP gal.)	x 1.201	= US Gallons (US gal.)	x .833	= IMP gal.
Fl. Ounces	x 29.573	= Milliliters	x .034	= Ounces
US Pints (US pt.)	x .473	= Liters (L)	x 2.113	= Pints
US Quarts (US qt.)	x .946	= Liters (L)	x 1.057	= Quarts
US Gallons (US gal.)	x 3.785	= Liters (L)	x .264	= Gallons

MASS–WEIGHT

Ounces (oz.)	x 28.35	= Grams (g)	x .035	= Ounces
Pounds (lb.)	x .454	= Kilograms (kg)	x 2.205	= Pounds

PRESSURE

Pounds Per Sq. In. (psi)	x 6.895	= Kilopascals (kPa)	x .145	= psi
Inches of Mercury (Hg)	x .4912	= psi	x 2.036	= Hg
Inches of Mercury (Hg)	x 3.377	= Kilopascals (kPa)	x .2961	= Hg
Inches of Water (H2O)	x .07355	= Inches of Mercury	x 13.783	= H2O
Inches of Water (H2O)	x .03613	= psi	x 27.684	= H2O
Inches of Water (H2O)	x .248	= Kilopascals (kPa)	x 4.026	= H2O

TORQUE

Pounds-Force Inches (in-lb)	x .113	= Newton Meters (N·m)	x 8.85	= in-lb
Pounds-Force Feet (ft-lb)	x 1.356	= Newton Meters (N·m)	x .738	= ft-lb

VELOCITY

Miles Per Hour (MPH)	x 1.609	= Kilometers Per Hour (KPH)	x .621	= MPH

POWER

Horsepower (Hp)	x .745	= Kilowatts	x 1.34	= Horsepower

FUEL CONSUMPTION*

Miles Per Gallon IMP (MPG)	x .354	= Kilometers Per Liter (Km/L)	
Kilometers Per Liter (Km/L)	x 2.352	= IMP MPG	
Miles Per Gallon US (MPG)	x .425	= Kilometers Per Liter (Km/L)	
Kilometers Per Liter (Km/L)	x 2.352	= US MPG	

*It is common to covert from miles per gallon (mpg) to liters/100 kilometers (1/100 km), where mpg (IMP) x 1/100 km = 282 and mpg (US) x 1/100 km = 235.

TEMPERATURE

Degree Fahrenheit (°F)	= (°C x 1.8) + 32
Degree Celsius (°C)	= (°F – 32) x .56

TCCS1044

Fig. 23 Standard and metric conversion factors chart

SERIAL NUMBER IDENTIFICATION

Vehicle Identification Number Plate

▸ **See Figures 24 thru 32**

The Vehicle Identification Number (VIN) is important in ordering parts and for servicing. The 1967–70 models used an eight digit Vehicle Identification Number. The 1971–80 models used a thirteen digit VIN number and the 1981 and later models use a seventeen digit VIN number. All VIN plates are attached to the cowl bar in the lower left hand corner of the windshield where it is visible from outside the car.

➡**Model years appear in the VIN as the last digit of each particular year (6 is 1976, 8 is 1978, etc.), until 1980 (which is A). This is the final year under the thirteen digit code. The seventeen digit VIN begins with 1981 (B), and continues 1982 (C), 1983 (D) . . . with the exception of any letter which might be mistaken for a number such as I or O, which are skipped.**

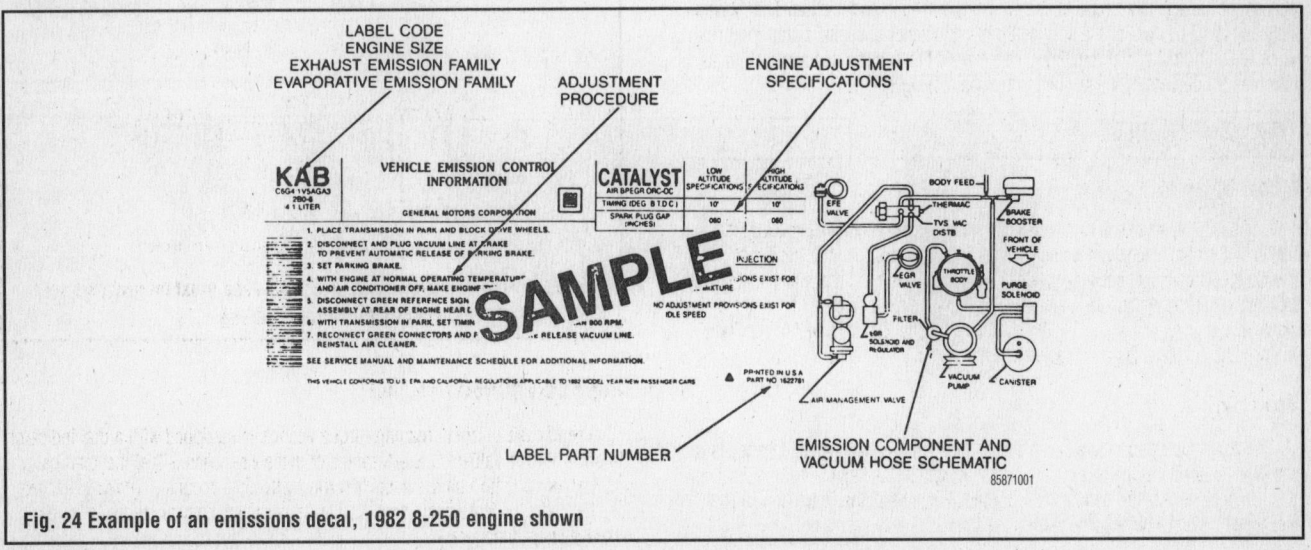

Fig. 24 Example of an emissions decal, 1982 8-250 engine shown

ENGINE IDENTIFICATION CHART

Engine No. Cyl Displ. Cu. In. (L)	Eng. Mfg.	Bbl.	'67	'68	'69	'70	'71	'72	'73	'74	'75	'76	'77	'78	'79	'80	'81	'82	'83	'84	'85	'86	'87	'88	'89
8-250	Cad.	DFI																8	8	8	8	8	8		
8-273	Cad.	DFI																						5	5
6-252	Buick	4														4	4	4							
8-307	Olds.	4																				Y	Y	Y	Y
8-350	Olds.	EFI									R	R	B	B	B										
8-350	Olds.	Diesel												N	N	N	N	N	N	N					
8-368	Cad.	4														6	6	6	6	6					
8-368	Cad.	DFI														9	9	9	9	9					
8-425	Cad.	4											S	S	S										
8-425	Cad.	EFI											T	T	T										
8-429	Cad.	4	*																						
8-472	Cad.	4		*	*	*	R	R	R	R															
8-500	Cad.	4				*	S	S	S	S	S														
8-500	Cad.	EFI									S	S													

EFI-Electronic Fuel Injection System
DFI-Digital Electronic Fuel Injection System

85871003

Fig. 25 Engine Identification Codes

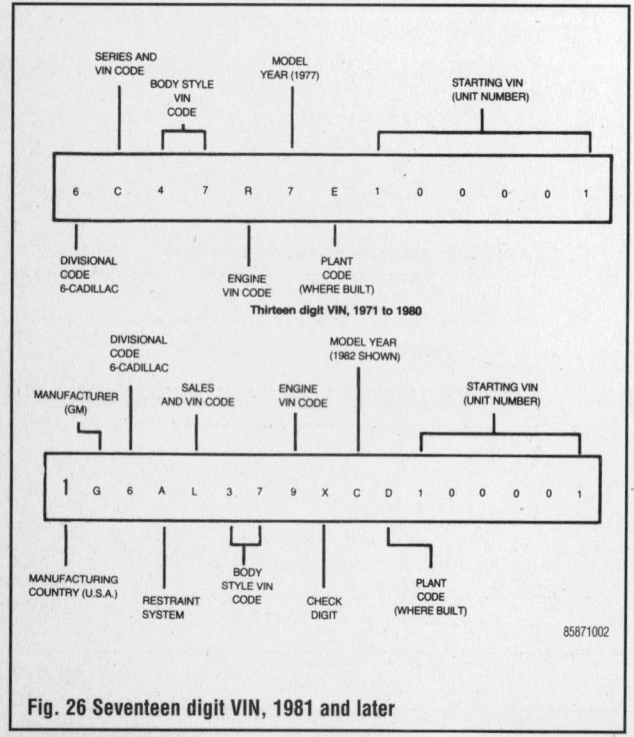

Fig. 26 Seventeen digit VIN, 1981 and later

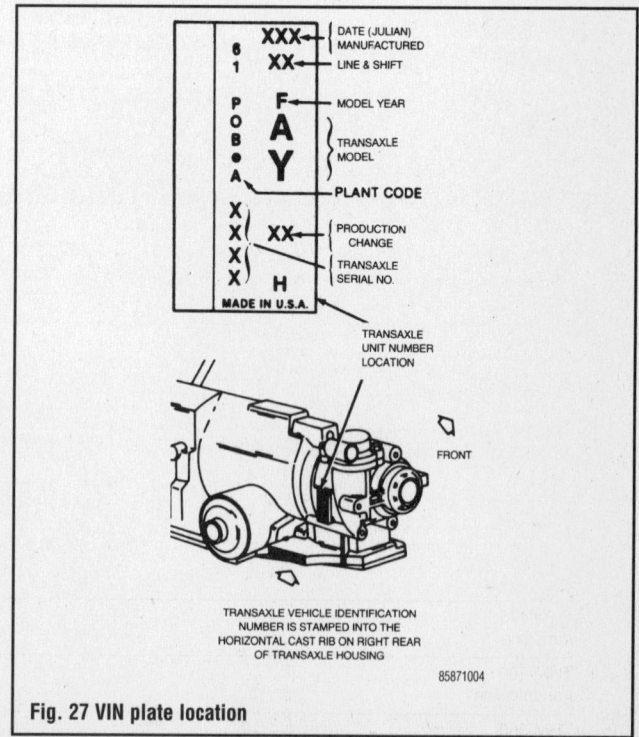

Fig. 27 VIN plate location

Fig. 28 View of the VIN plate

Fig. 29 Vehicle Emission Control Information

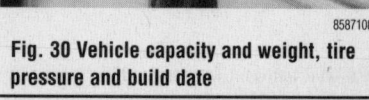

Fig. 30 Vehicle capacity and weight, tire pressure and build date

Fig. 31 View of the engine compartment

Fig. 32 A/C service information label on compressor

Automatic Transmission/Transaxle Identification

⬧ See Figures 33, 34, 35, 36 and 37

All Cadillac models covered in this guide use various GM Turbo Hydra-Matic (THM) automatic transmissions and transaxles. Transmission identification numbers are found on either side of the transmission case, depending on

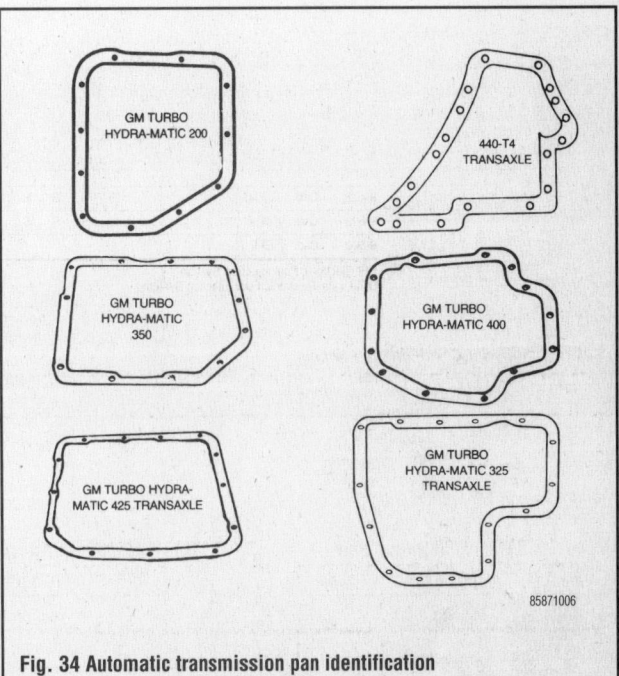

Fig. 34 Automatic transmission pan identification

AUTOMATIC TRANSMISSION/TRANSAXLE IDENTIFICATION CHART

Transmission	'67	'68	'69	'70	'71	'72	'73	'74	'75	'76	'77	'78	'79	'80	'81	'82	'83	'84	'85	'86	'87	'88	'89
Turbo Hydra-matic transmission	*	*	*	*	*	*	*	*	*	*													
Turbo Hydra-matic transaxle	*	*	*	*	*	*	*	*	*	*													
THM 440-T4 transaxle																				*	*	*	*
THM 425 transaxle											*		*		*								
THM 400 transmission											*	*	*	*	*	*	*	*					
THM 350 transmission															*								
THM 350C transmission															*								
THM 325 transaxle															*	*	*						
THM 325-4L																*	*	*					
THM 200 transmission													*	*									
THM 200C transmission														*	*								
THM 200-4R transmission															*	*	*	*	*	*	*	*	*

THM—Turbo hydra-matic

Fig. 33 Automatic Transmission Identification Chart

model. Some models also have I.D. numbers stamped on the governor cover or the number may be ink stamped on the bell housing. The Eldorado and Seville front wheel drive models (through 1985) have the identification numbers to the rear of the vertical cast rib on the left hand side of the transaxle housing. For 1986, the transaxle identification number is stamped into the horizontal cast rib on the right rear of the transaxle housing.

Cadillac rear wheel drive models may be equipped with any of the following: THM400, THM350, THM350C, THM200, THM200-4R and the THM200C transmissions. Cadillac Eldorado and Seville models use the THM440-T4, THM425, THM325, and the THM325-4L transaxles.

A quick and easy way to identify the transmissions/transaxles is to look at the shapes of the pans. Use the illustrations of the pan gaskets to help determine your particular transmission/transaxle.

Vehicle Emission Control Information Label

◆ See Figures 38 and 39

The Vehicle Emission Control Information (VECI) label is located in the engine compartment (fan shroud, radiator support, hood underside, etc.) of every vehicle produced by General Motors. The label contains important emissions specifications and setting procedures, as well as a vacuum hose schematic with various emissions components identified.

When servicing your Cadillac this label should always be checked for up-to-date information pertaining specifically to your car.

➡Always follow the timing procedures on this label when adjusting ignition timing.

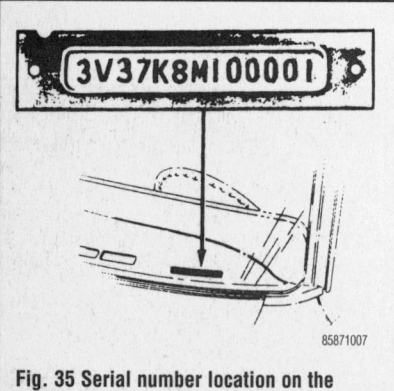

Fig. 35 Serial number location on the Turbo Hydra-Matic 350 and 350C

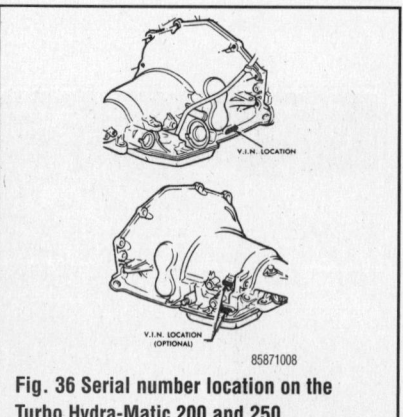

Fig. 36 Serial number location on the Turbo Hydra-Matic 200 and 250

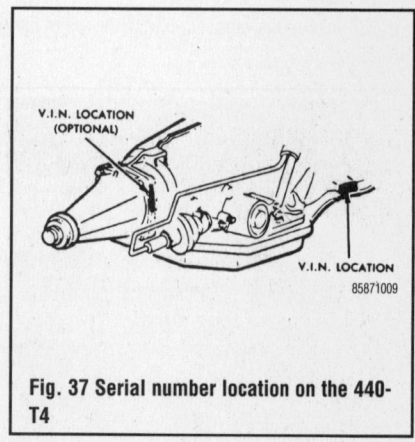

Fig. 37 Serial number location on the 440-T4

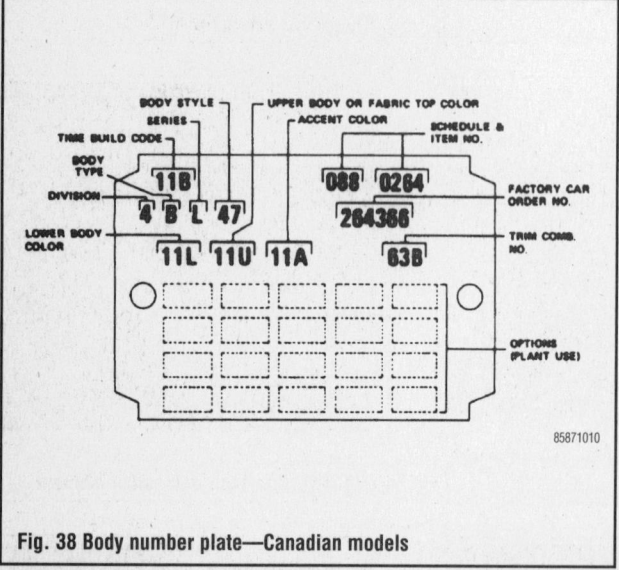

Fig. 38 Body number plate—Canadian models

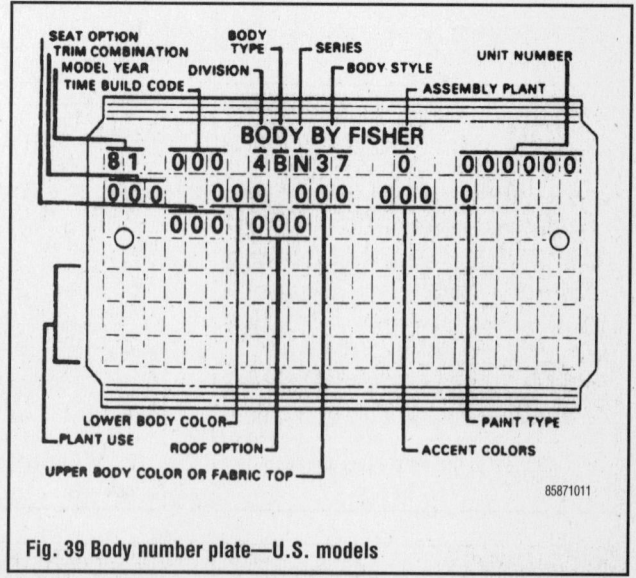

Fig. 39 Body number plate—U.S. models

ROUTINE MAINTENANCE AND TUNE-UP

Proper maintenance and tune-up is the key to long and trouble-free vehicle life. Studies have shown that a properly tuned and maintained vehicle can achieve better gas mileage than an out-of-tune vehicle. As a conscientious owner and driver, set aside a Saturday morning, say once a month, to check or replace items which could cause major problems later. Keep your own personal log to jot down which services you performed, how much the parts cost you, the date, and the exact odometer reading at the time. Keep all receipts for such items as engine oil and filters, so that they may be referred to in case of related problems or to determine operating expenses. As a do-it-yourselfer, these receipts are the only proof you have that the required maintenance was performed. In the event of a warranty problem, these receipts will be invaluable.

The literature provided with your vehicle when it was originally delivered includes the factory recommended maintenance schedule. If you no longer have this literature, replacement copies are usually available from the dealer.

Air Cleaner

All engines are equipped with dry type air cleaners which use replaceable air filter elements. The positive crankcase ventilation system (PCV) air filter element on gasoline engine is also found in the air filter housing (usually mounted on the inside of the housing rim). Both of these filter elements should be replaced at 30,000 mile or 1½ year intervals, unless the vehicle is driven in extremely dusty or smoggy conditions where replacement should be much more frequent.

Never remove the air cleaner from a diesel with the engine running. The intake vacuum is very great and dirt, wingnuts, etc. will be sucked directly into the combustion chambers, causing major engine damage.

AIR CLEANER ELEMENT AND CRANKCASE BREATHER REPLACEMENT

▶ **See Figures 40 thru 50**

➡ The filter element used on all Cadillacs is of the dry, disposable type. It should never be washed, soaked or oiled.

1. Remove the wing nut(s) from the top of the air cleaner assembly and lay it aside.

2. Remove the air cleaner cover and gently lift the air cleaner element out of the housing without knocking any dirt into the carburetor.

3. Pull the crankcase breather out of the valve cover or remove the clip and remove it from the air cleaner (if so equipped).

To install:

4. Wipe the inside of the air cleaner housing with a paper towel or clean rag.

5. Install a new crankcase breather.

6. Install a new air cleaner element.

7. Replace the air cleaner cover and install the wing nut(s).

Fuel Filter

CARBURETED ENGINES

The gasoline engine fuel filter should be replaced every year or 15,000 miles or more often if necessary.

Fig. 40 Removing the air cleaner lid

Fig. 41 View of the air cleaner assembly lid

Fig. 42 Removing the air filter

Fig. 43 View of the air cleaner breather hose

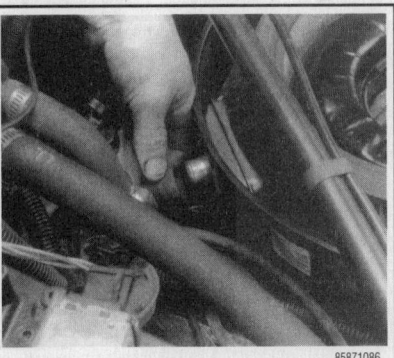

Fig. 44 Removing the air cleaner breather hose

Fig. 45 Removing the breather element

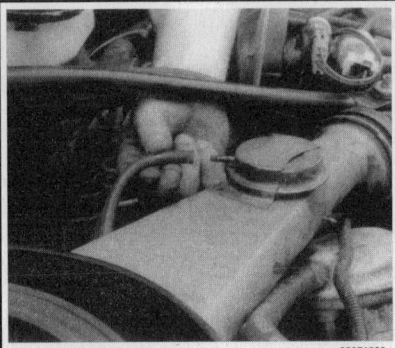

Fig. 46 Removing the vacuum hose from the top of the air cleaner

Fig. 47 Removing the intake air duct hose

Fig. 48 Removing the vacuum hose from the bottom of the air cleaner

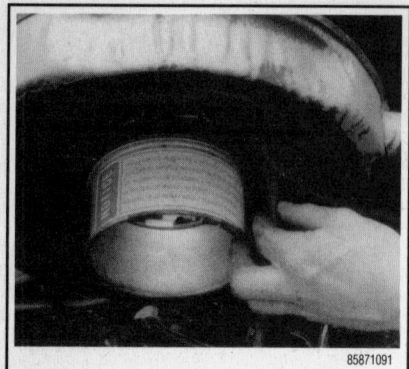

Fig. 49 Removing the air cleaner assembly

Fig. 50 Installing the air cleaner assembly

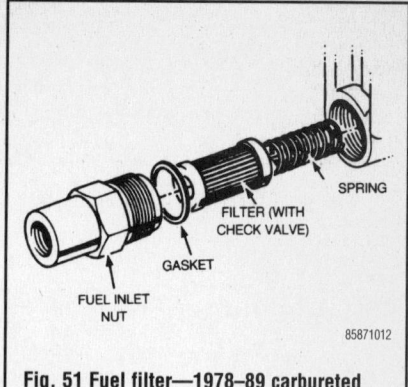

Fig. 51 Fuel filter—1978–89 carbureted engines

On 1967–74 models the fuel filter is mounted inside the fuel pump. From 1975 and later the filter is located in the carburetor behind the fuel inlet nut. Beginning in 1976, a check valve is included in the fuel filter.

1967–74 Vehicles

To replace the inlet (located at the fuel pump) fuel filter:
1. Jack up the car and support on jackstands.
2. Place some absorbent rags under the fuel fittings to catch any fuel which may spill, when the fitting is removed.
3. Clamp closed the fuel inlet hose on the fuel pump.
4. Disconnect the fuel pump outlet line at the fuel pump.
5. Remove the fuel outlet nut and remove the fuel filter.

➥Use two wrenches to prevent loosening of the nut welded to the pump cover.

6. To install, reverse the above procedure.

1975–89 Vehicles

◆ See Figure 51

To replace the inlet (carburetor body) fuel filter:
1. Place some absorbent rags under the fuel fittings to catch the gasoline which will spill out when the lines are loosened.
2. Disconnect the fuel line connection at the intake fuel filter nut. Plug the opening to prevent loss of fuel.
3. Remove the intake fuel filter nut from the carburetor with a box wrench or socket.
4. Remove the filter element and spring.

To install:
5. The filter element can be cleaned in solvent and blown dry. However, for the low cost of a new filter it is more advisable to simply install a new element.
6. Install the element spring, then the filter element in the carburetor.
7. Install a new gasket on the intake fuel nut, then install the nut in the carburetor body and tighten securely.
8. Install the fuel line and tighten the connector. Check for leaks at all fittings with the engine idling.

FUEL INJECTED ENGINES

◆ See Figures 52 thru 57

The fuel filter on fuel injected vehicles may be located in one of two locations. On all 1976–79 vehicles except the Seville, the filter is mounted in the engine compartment near the fuel pump. On the 1976–79 Seville, and all 1980–85 vehicles, the fuel filter is located on the left side of the chassis just ahead of the rear axle. On 1986–89 vehicles, the filter can be found near the frame, in back of the left front wheel. There are two types of fuel filters used on the gasoline fuel injected vehicles, the one-piece disposable inline filter, used on all 1982–86 250 and 1988–89 273 V8 engines, and the replaceable element type filter used on all the other engines.

✳✳ CAUTION

Fuel is under high pressure: if the steps below are not followed, the fuel could spray out and result in a fire hazard and possible injury.

1. Disconnect the negative battery terminal.
2. Release the pressure from the fuel system:
• Without pressure fitting: Cars without a pressure fitting in the fuel line, cover the fitting to be removed with a shop towel while loosening so that fuel will be absorbed. Dispose of gasoline properly.
• With pressure fitting: Locate the pressure fitting in the fuel line and remove the protective cap. Loosely install a special valve depressor (G.M. tool no. J-5420) on the fitting. Wrap a towel around the fitting to block any spray and slowly tighten the tool until the pressure has been relieved.
3. Replace the filter as follows:
a. On the replaceable element type filter; the fuel filter element is replaced by unscrewing the bottom cover and removing the filter element. Replace the element and gasket with an AC type GF 157 or equivalent. Hand tighten the bottom cover.

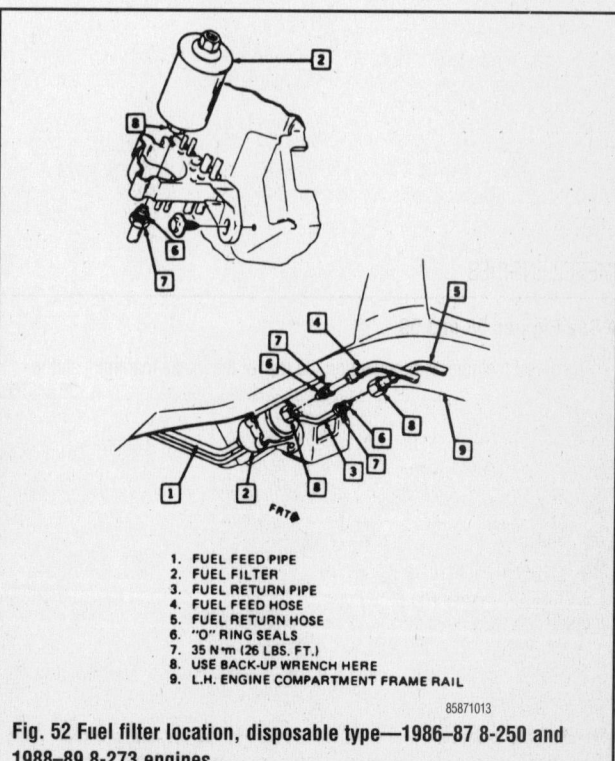

1. FUEL FEED PIPE
2. FUEL FILTER
3. FUEL RETURN PIPE
4. FUEL FEED HOSE
5. FUEL RETURN HOSE
6. "O" RING SEALS
7. 35 N·m (26 LBS. FT.)
8. USE BACK-UP WRENCH HERE
9. L.H. ENGINE COMPARTMENT FRAME RAIL

Fig. 52 Fuel filter location, disposable type—1986–87 8-250 and 1988–89 8-273 engines

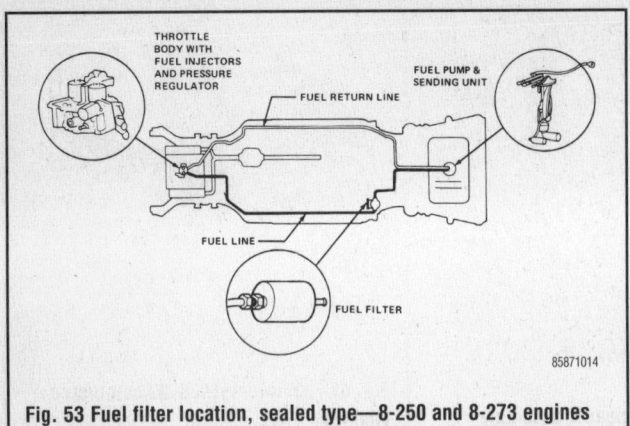

Fig. 53 Fuel filter location, sealed type—8-250 and 8-273 engines

Fig. 54 Common fuel filter location—lower right corner

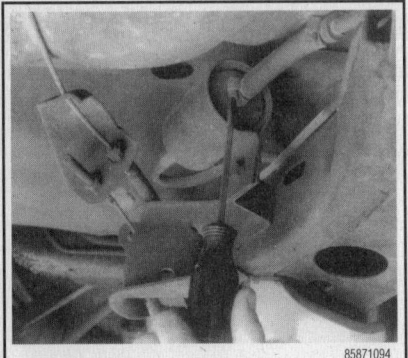

Fig. 55 Removing the fuel filter hose clamp

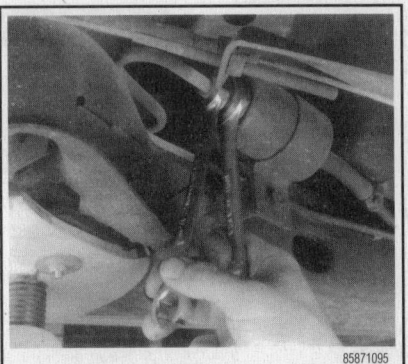

Fig. 56 Removing fuel filter lines—always use a back-up wrench

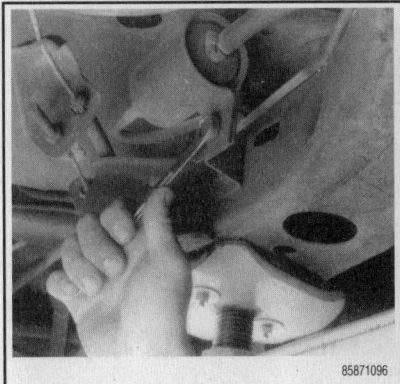

Fig. 57 Removing fuel filter mounting

b. On the in-line disposable type filter; the fuel filter canister is replaced by loosening the fitting on the end of the filter, then use a pair of pliers to expand the clamp on the other end and slide it down past the point where the hose extends over the inlet of the filter. Gently twist and remove the hose, unscrew and remove the fitting. Remove and discard the old filter. Install the new filter into the hose and replace the clamp. Reinstall the fitting, and check for leaks with the engine idling.

➡A dry fuel system on cars equipped with EFI/DFI may require a substantial cranking period before starting. Be sure to crank the engine in short bursts, allowing time for the starter motor to cool between each burst.

DIESEL ENGINES

▶ See Figures 58 and 59

The diesel fuel filter is mounted on the rear of the intake manifold, and is larger than that on a gasoline engine because diesel fuel generally is dirtier (has more suspended particles) than gasoline.

The diesel fuel should be changed every 30,000 miles or two years.

To install a new filter:

1. With the engine cool, place absorbent rags underneath the fuel line fittings at the filter.
2. Disconnect the fuel lines from the filter.
3. Unbolt the filter from its bracket.
4. Install the new filter. Start the engine and check for leaks. Run the engine for about two minutes, then shut the engine off for the same amount of time to allow any trapped air in the injection system to bleed off.

The GM diesel cars also have a fuel filter inside the fuel tank which is maintenance-free.

➡If the filter element ever becomes clogged, the engine will stop. This stoppage is usually preceded by a hesitation or sluggish running. General Motors recommends that after changing the diesel fuel filter, the Housing Pressure Cold Advance be activated manually, if the engine

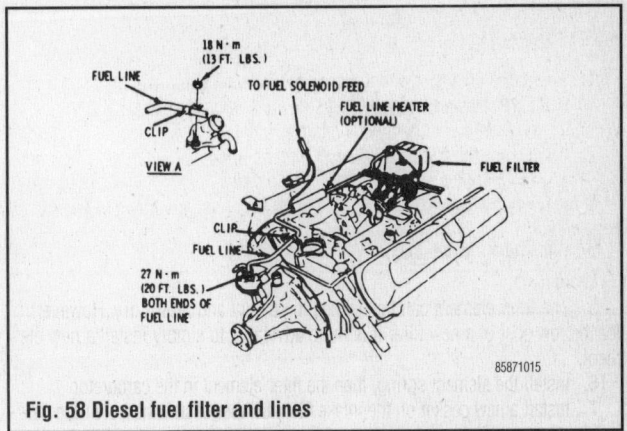

Fig. 58 Diesel fuel filter and lines

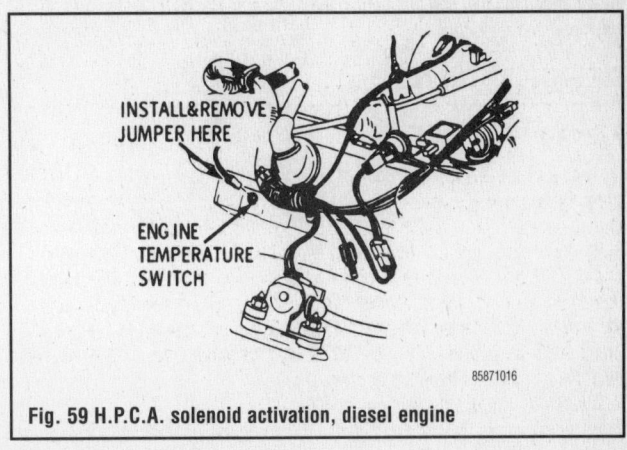

Fig. 59 H.P.C.A. solenoid activation, diesel engine

temperature is above 125°F (52°C). Activating the H.P.C.A. will reduce engine cranking time. To activate the H.P.C.A. solenoid, disconnect the two lead connector at the engine temperature switch and bridge the connector with a jumper. After the engine is running, remove the jumper and reconnect the connector to the engine temperature switch. When the new filter element is installed, check for leaks.

Positive Crankcase Ventilation (PCV Valve)

♦ **See Figures 60 thru 65**

All gasoline engines covered in this guide are equipped with a closed crankcase emission control system (see Section 4) featuring a vacuum-operated Positive Crankcase Ventilation valve (PCV). A faulty PCV valve or clogged hoses to and from the valve can cause a rough idle, oil leaks, or excessive oil sludging. Check the system at least once a year and replace the valve at least every 30 months or 30,000 miles. A general test is to remove the PCV valve from the valve cover and shake it. If a rattle is heard, the valve is usually OK.

A more positive test is:

1. Remove the PCV valve from the rocker arm cover or intake manifold.
2. Connect a tachometer to the engine and run the engine at idle.
3. Check the tachometer reading, then place your thumb over the end of the valve. You should feel a suction.
4. Check the tachometer again. The engine speed should have dropped at least 50 rpm. It should return to a normal idle when you remove your thumb from the end of the valve.
5. If the engine does not change speed or if the change is less than 50 rpm, the hose is clogged or the valve defective. Check the hose first-if it is not clogged, replace the PCV valve. Test the new valve in the same way.

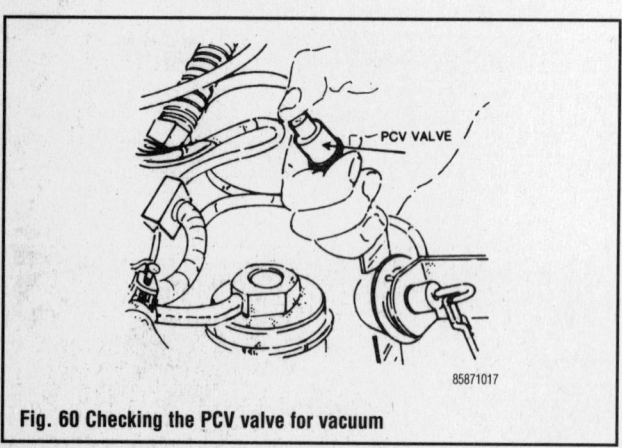

Fig. 60 Checking the PCV valve for vacuum

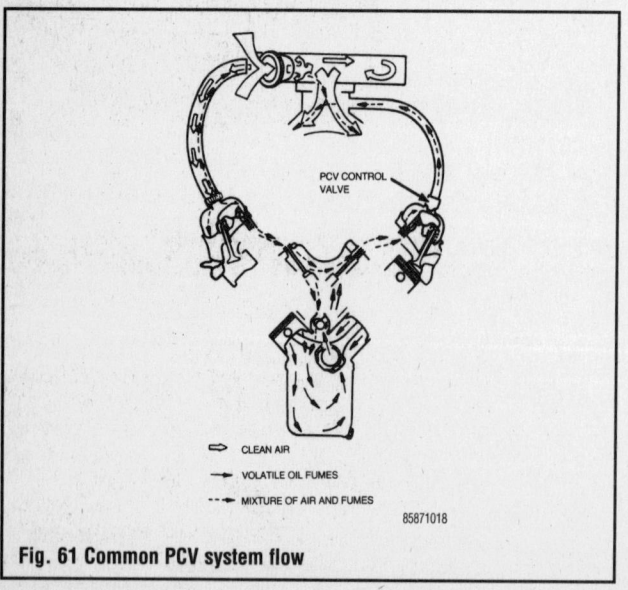

Fig. 61 Common PCV system flow

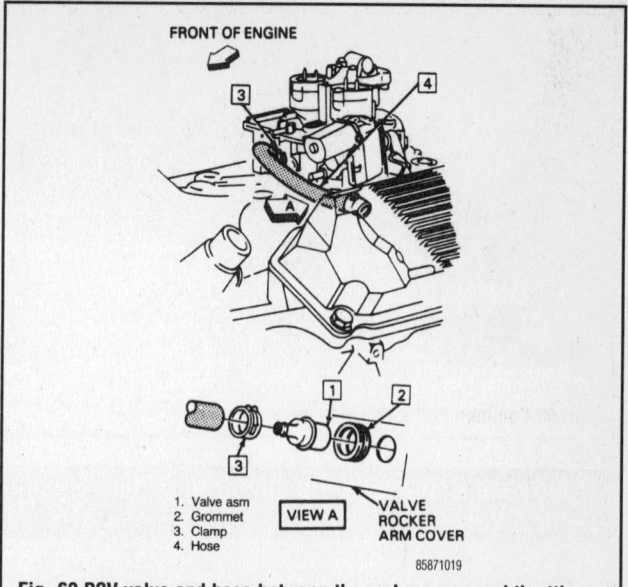

1. Valve asm
2. Grommet
3. Clamp
4. Hose

VIEW A — VALVE ROCKER ARM COVER

Fig. 62 PCV valve and hose between the rocker cover and throttle body—1986–89 Eldorado and Seville

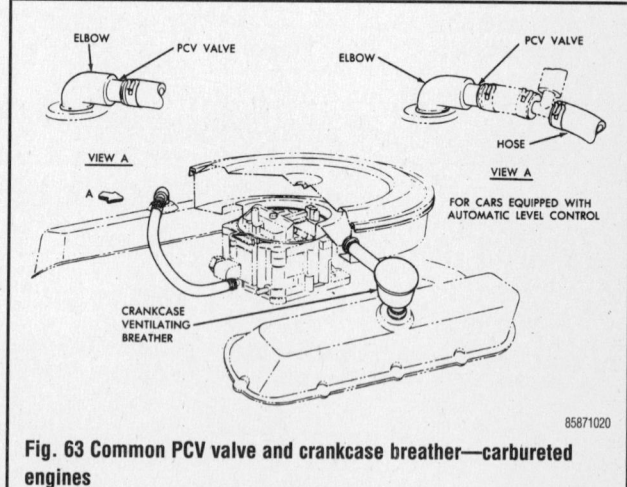

Fig. 63 Common PCV valve and crankcase breather—carbureted engines

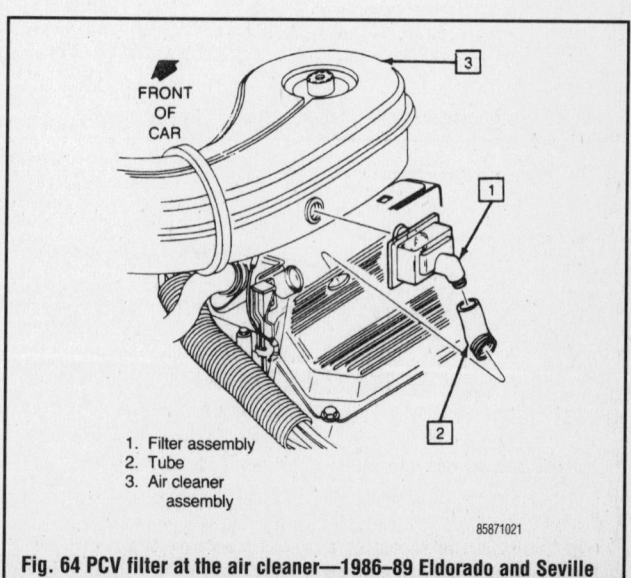

1. Filter assembly
2. Tube
3. Air cleaner assembly

Fig. 64 PCV filter at the air cleaner—1986–89 Eldorado and Seville

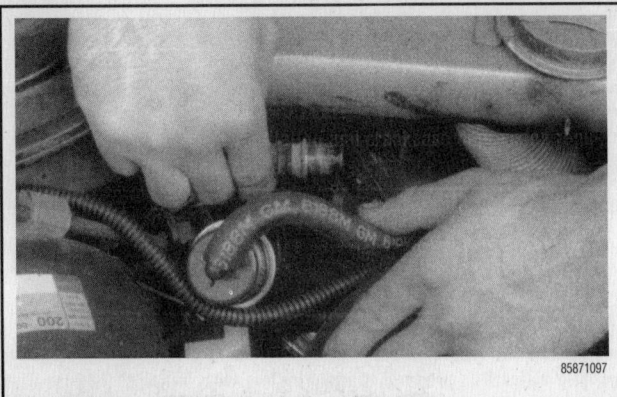

Fig. 65 Common PCV location in the valve cover

Crankcase Depression Regulator and Flow Control Valve

350 CU. IN. DIESEL ENGINES

▶ **See Figures 66 and 67**

The Crankcase Depression Regulator (CDR), found on 1981 and later diesels, and the flow control valve used from 1978 to 1980, are designed to scavenge crankcase vapors in basically the same manner as the PCV valve on

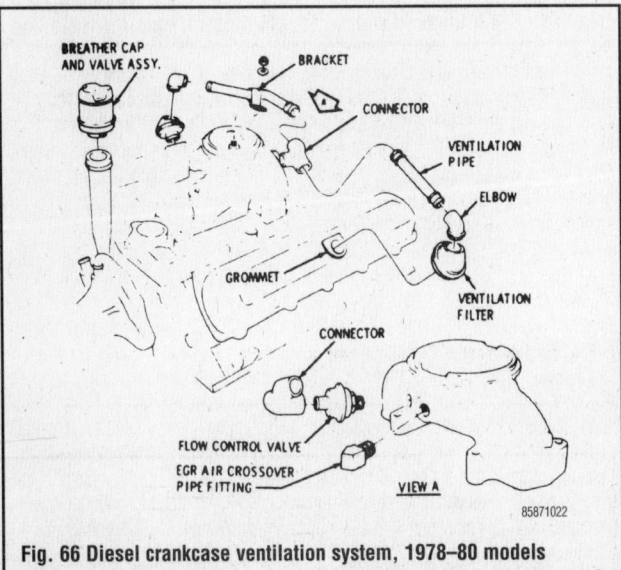

Fig. 66 Diesel crankcase ventilation system, 1978–80 models

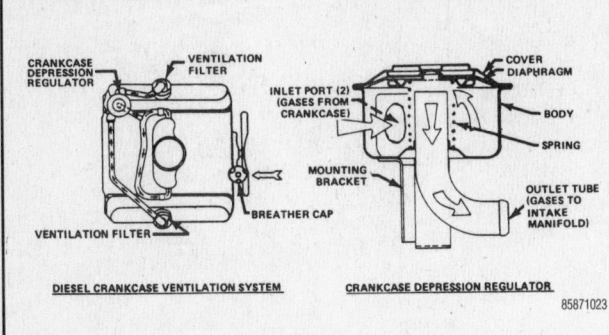

Fig. 67 Diesel crankcase ventilation and crankcase depression regulator cutaway, 1981 and later models

gasoline engines. The valves are located either on the left rear corner of the intake manifold (CDR), or on the rear of the intake crossover pipe (flow control valve). On each system there are two ventilation filters, one per valve cover.

The filter assemblies should be cleaned every 15,000 miles by simply prying them carefully from the valve covers (be aware of the grommets underneath), and washing them out in solvent. The ventilation pipes and tubes should also be cleaned. Both the CDR and flow control valves should also be cleaned every 30,000 miles (the cover can be removed from the CDR; the flow control valve can simply be flushed with solvent). Dry each valve, filter, and hose with compressed air before installation.

➡ **Do not attempt to test the crankcase controls on these diesels. Instead, clean the valve cover filter assembly and vent pipes and check the vent pipes. Replace the breather cap assembly every 30,000 miles. Replace all rubber fittings as required every 15,000 miles.**

Evaporative Canister

▶ **See Figure 68**

The evaporative canister, sometimes referred to as a charcoal canister, is mounted inside the engine compartment. The canister and its filter are part of the evaporative emissions system (see Section 4) and work to eliminate the release of unburned fuel vapor into the atmosphere. The vapor is absorbed by the carbon in the canister and stored until manifold vacuum, when the engine is running, draws the vapors into the engine for burning.

The filter in the bottom of the canister is replaceable on all models through 1989 except the 1986–89 Seville and Eldorado which uses a different design. Change the filter every two years or 24,000 miles, or more often under extremely dusty or smoggy conditions.

To change the filter, proceed as follows:
1. Tag and disconnect all hoses connected to the evaporative canister.
2. Loosen the retaining clamps and then lift out the canister.
3. Grasp the filter element in the bottom of the canister with your fingers and pull it out. Replace it with a new element.
4. Replace the canister in the clamps and reconnect all hoses. If any of the hoses are brittle or cracked, replace them only with fuel-resistant replacement hose marked **EVAP**.

Fig. 68 View of the evaporative canister

Battery

PRECAUTIONS

Always use caution when working on or near the battery. Never allow a tool to bridge the gap between the negative and positive battery terminals. Also, be careful not to allow a tool to provide a ground between the positive cable/terminal and any metal component on the vehicle. Either of these conditions will cause a short circuit, leading to sparks and possible personal injury.

Do not smoke or all open flames/sparks near a battery; the gases contained in the battery are very explosive and, if ignited, could cause severe injury or death.

All batteries, regardless of type, should be carefully secured by a battery hold-down device. If not, the terminals or casing may crack from stress during vehicle operation. A battery which is not secured may allow acid to leak, making it discharge faster. The acid can also eat away at components under the hood.

Always inspect the battery case for cracks, leakage and corrosion. A white corrosive substance on the battery case or on nearby components would indicate a leaking or cracked battery. If the battery is cracked, it should be replaced immediately.

GENERAL MAINTENANCE

Always keep the battery cables and terminals free of corrosion. Check and clean these components about once a year.

Keep the top of the battery clean, as a film of dirt can help discharge a battery that is not used for long periods. A solution of baking soda and water may be used for cleaning, but be careful to flush this off with clear water. DO NOT let any of the solution into the filler holes. Baking soda neutralizes battery acid and will de-activate a battery cell.

Batteries in vehicles which are not operated on a regular basis can fall victim to parasitic loads (small current drains which are constantly drawing current from the battery). Normal parasitic loads may drain a battery on a vehicle that is in storage and not used for 6–8 weeks. Vehicles that have additional accessories such as a phone or an alarm system may discharge a battery sooner. If the vehicle is to be stored for longer periods in a secure area and the alarm system is not necessary, the negative battery cable should be disconnected to protect the battery.

Remember that constantly deep cycling a battery (completely discharging and recharging it) will shorten battery life.

BATTERY FLUID

♦ See Figure 69

Check the battery electrolyte level at least once a month, or more often in hot weather or during periods of extended vehicle operation. On non-sealed batter-

ies, the level can be checked either through the case (if translucent) or by removing the cell caps. The electrolyte level in each cell should be kept filled to the split ring inside each cell, or the line marked on the outside of the case.

If the level is low, add only distilled water through the opening until the level is correct. Each cell must be checked and filled individually. Distilled water should be used, because the chemicals and minerals found in most drinking water are harmful to the battery and could significantly shorten its life.

If water is added in freezing weather, the vehicle should be driven several miles to allow the water to mix with the electrolyte. Otherwise, the battery could freeze.

Although some maintenance-free batteries have removable cell caps, the electrolyte condition and level on all sealed maintenance-free batteries must be checked using the built-in hydrometer "eye." The exact type of eye will vary. But, most battery manufacturers, apply a sticker to the battery itself explaining the readings.

➡**Although the readings from built-in hydrometers will vary, a green eye usually indicates a properly charged battery with sufficient fluid level. A dark eye is normally an indicator of a battery with sufficient fluid, but which is low in charge. A light or yellow eye usually indicates that electrolyte has dropped below the necessary level. In this last case, sealed batteries with an insufficient electrolyte must usually be discarded.**

Checking the Specific Gravity

♦ See Figures 70, 71 and 72

A hydrometer is required to check the specific gravity on all batteries that are not maintenance-free. On batteries that are maintenance-free, the specific gravity is checked by observing the built-in hydrometer "eye" on the top of the battery case.

❋❋ CAUTION

Battery electrolyte contains sulfuric acid. If you should splash any on your skin or in your eyes, flush the affected area with plenty of clear water. If it lands in your eyes, get medical help immediately.

The fluid (sulfuric acid solution) contained in the battery cells will tell you many things about the condition of the battery. Because the cell plates must be kept submerged below the fluid level in order to operate, the fluid level is extremely important. And, because the specific gravity of the acid is an indication of electrical charge, testing the fluid can be an aid in determining if the battery must be replaced. A battery in a vehicle with a properly operating charging system should require little maintenance, but careful, periodic inspection should reveal problems before they leave you stranded.

At least once a year, check the specific gravity of the battery. It should be between 1.20 and 1.26 on the gravity scale. Most auto stores carry a variety of inexpensive battery hydrometers. These can be used on any non-sealed battery to test the specific gravity in each cell.

The battery testing hydrometer has a squeeze bulb at one end and a nozzle at the other. Battery electrolyte is sucked into the hydrometer until the float is lifted from its seat. The specific gravity is then read by noting the position of the float. If gravity is low in one or more cells, the battery should be slowly charged and checked again to see if the gravity has come up. Generally, if after charging, the specific gravity between any two cells varies more than 50 points (0.50), the battery should be replaced, as it can no longer produce sufficient voltage to guarantee proper operation.

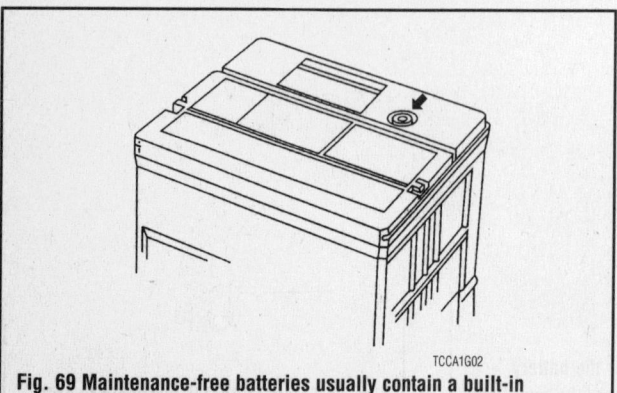

TCCA1G02

Fig. 69 Maintenance-free batteries usually contain a built-in hydrometer to check fluid level

TCCA1P07

Fig. 70 On non-sealed batteries, the fluid level can be checked by removing the cell caps

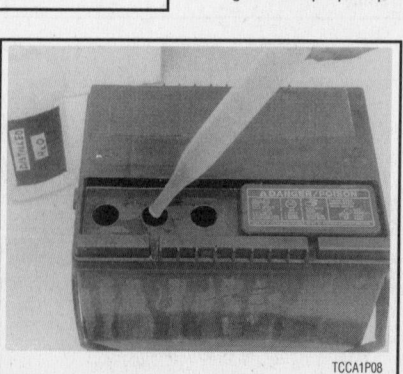

TCCA1P08

Fig. 71 If the fluid level is low, add only distilled water until the level is correct

TCCA1P09

Fig. 72 Check the specific gravity of the battery's electrolyte with a hydrometer

CABLES

▶ **See Figures 73, 74, 75 and 76**

Once a year (or as necessary), the battery terminals and the cable clamps should be cleaned. Loosen the clamps and remove the cables, negative cable first. On top post batteries, the use of a puller specially made for this purpose is recommended. These are inexpensive and available in most parts stores. Side terminal battery cables are secured with a small bolt.

Clean the cable clamps and the battery terminal with a wire brush, until all corrosion, grease, etc., is removed and the metal is shiny. It is especially important to clean the inside of the clamp thoroughly (an old knife is useful here), since a small deposit of oxidation there will prevent a sound connection and inhibit starting or charging. Special tools are available for cleaning these parts, one type for conventional top post batteries and another type for side terminal batteries. It is also a good idea to apply some dielectric grease to the terminal, as this will aid in the prevention of corrosion.

After the clamps and terminals are clean, reinstall the cables, negative cable last; DO NOT hammer the clamps onto battery posts. Tighten the clamps securely, but do not distort them. Give the clamps and terminals a thin external coating of grease after installation, to retard corrosion.

Check the cables at the same time that the terminals are cleaned. If the cable insulation is cracked or broken, or if the ends are frayed, the cable should be replaced with a new cable of the same length and gauge.

CHARGING

> ⁂ **CAUTION**
>
> **The chemical reaction which takes place in all batteries generates explosive hydrogen gas. A spark can cause the battery to explode and splash acid. To avoid personal injury, be sure there is proper ventilation and take appropriate fire safety precautions when working with or near a battery.**

A battery should be charged at a slow rate to keep the plates inside from getting too hot. However, if some maintenance-free batteries are allowed to discharge until they are almost "dead," they may have to be charged at a high rate to bring them back to "life." Always follow the charger manufacturer's instructions on charging the battery.

REPLACEMENT

When it becomes necessary to replace the battery, select one with an amperage rating equal to or greater than the battery originally installed. Deterioration and just plain aging of the battery cables, starter motor, and associated wires makes the battery's job harder in successive years. This makes it prudent to install a new battery with a greater capacity than the old.

Belts

INSPECTION

▶ **See Figures 77, 78, 79, 80 and 81**

Inspect the belts for signs of glazing or cracking. A glazed belt will be perfectly smooth from slippage, while a good belt will have a slight texture of fabric visible. Cracks will usually start at the inner edge of the belt and run outward. All worn or damaged drive belts should be replaced immediately. It is best to replace all drive belts at one time, as a preventive maintenance measure, during this service operation.

CHECKING TENSION AND ADJUSTING

▶ **See Figures 82 thru 89**

Inspect your car's drive belts every 7,500 miles or six months for evidence of wear such as cracking, fraying, and incorrect tension. Replace the belts at a maximum of 30,000 miles, even if they still look acceptable.

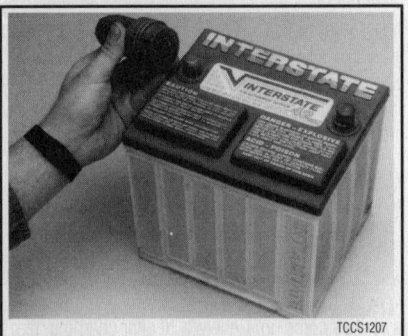

Fig. 73 The underside of this special battery tool has a wire brush to clean post terminals

TCCS1207

Fig. 74 Place the tool over the battery posts and twist to clean until the metal is shiny

TCCS1208

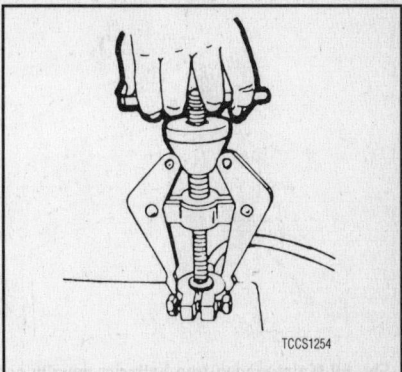

Fig. 75 A special tool is available to pull the clamp from the post

TCCS1254

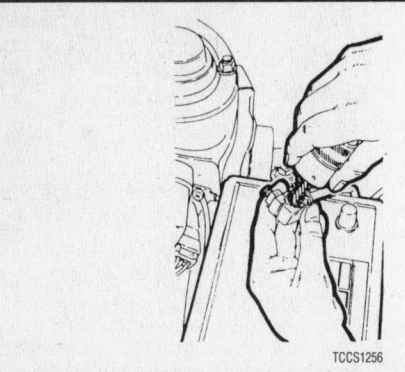

Fig. 76 The cable ends should be cleaned as well

TCCS1256

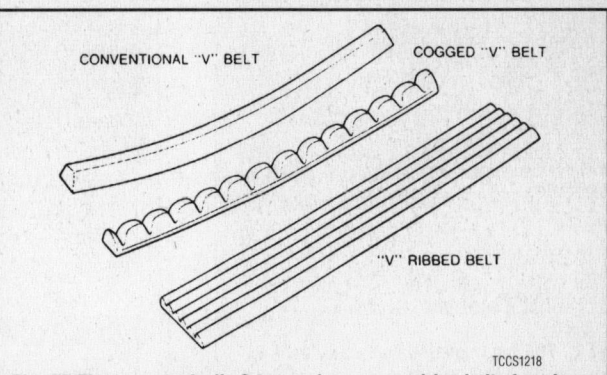

Fig. 77 There are typically 3 types of accessory drive belts found on vehicles today

TCCS1218

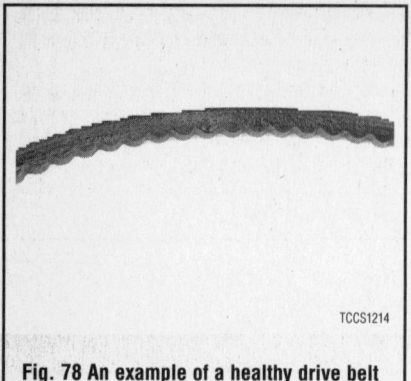

TCCS1214

Fig. 78 An example of a healthy drive belt

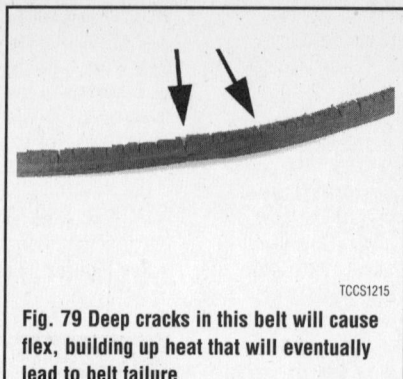

TCCS1215

Fig. 79 Deep cracks in this belt will cause flex, building up heat that will eventually lead to belt failure

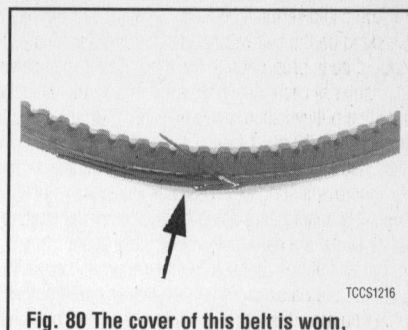

TCCS1216

Fig. 80 The cover of this belt is worn, exposing the critical reinforcing cords to excessive wear

TCCS1217

Fig. 81 Installing too wide a belt can result in serious belt wear and/or breakage

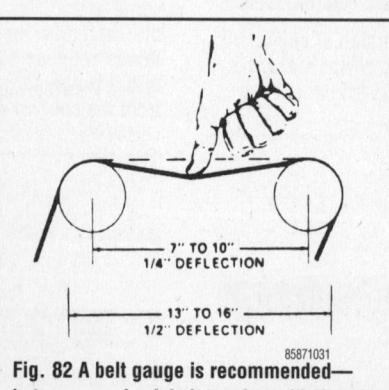

7" TO 10"
1/4" DEFLECTION

13" TO 16"
1/2" DEFLECTION

85871031

Fig. 82 A belt gauge is recommended—but you can check belt tension with thumb pressure

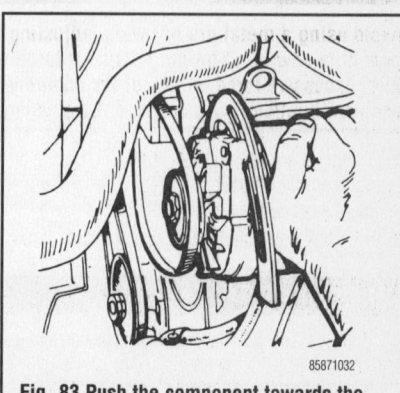

85871032

Fig. 83 Push the component towards the engine and slip off the belt

85871033

Fig. 84 Slip the new belt over the pulley

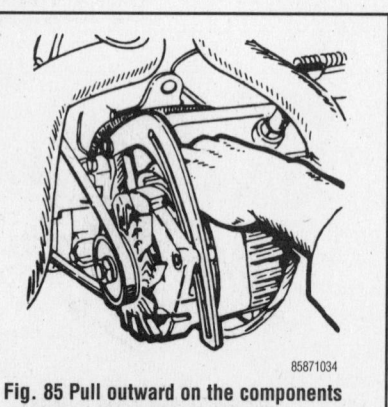

85871034

Fig. 85 Pull outward on the components and tighten the mounting bolts

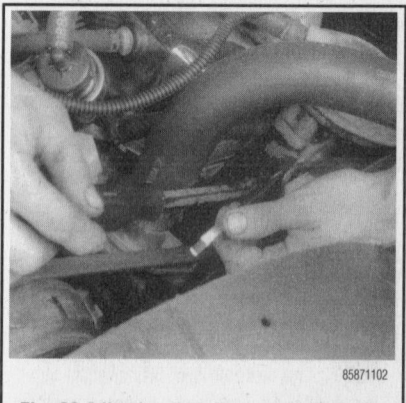

85871102

Fig. 86 Adjusting the alternator drive belt

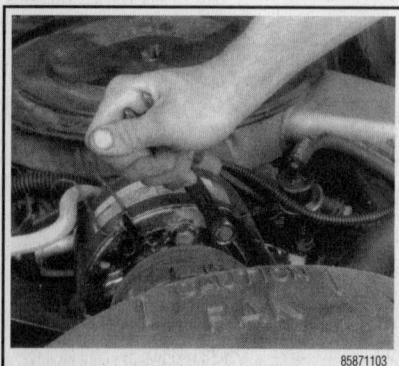

85871103

Fig. 87 Loosen the A/C compressor mounting bolt before adjusting belt tension

85871104

Fig. 88 Adjusting the A/C compressor drive belt

85871105

Fig. 89 A view of properly installed drive belts—always note belt routing before removal

You can determine belt tension at a point halfway between the pulleys by pressing on the belt with moderate thumb pressure. The amount of deflection should be in proportion to the length of the belt between pulleys (measured from the center of each pulley). For example, a belt stretched 13–16 in. (330–406mm) between pulleys should deflect ½ in. (13mm) at the halfway point; a belt stretched 7–10 in. (178–250mm) should deflect ¼ in. (6mm), etc. If the deflection is found to be too little or too tight, an adjustment must be made.

Before adjusting any of your engine's drive belts, clean all mounting bolts on the component being adjusted and apply penetrating oil if necessary on those bolts which are hard to reach-which may be many if your car has a V8 with lots of power options. Loosen the mounting and adjusting bolts of whichever component (alternator, air pump, air conditioner compressor, power steering pump, etc.) you are adjusting. Pull outward, away from the engine, on the component until the belt seems tight. Temporarily snug up on the adjusting bolt and check belt deflection; if it is OK, tighten the mounting bolts and adjusting bolt.

⁂ WARNING

Avoid using a metal pry bar when adjusting belt tension of any component; a sawed-off broom handle or large wooden dowel rod works fine. Excessive force on any of the component housings (which are usually aluminum) will damage the housings.

To replace a belt, follow the above procedure for belt adjustment to the point of loosening the adjusting bolt. Push the component in towards the engine; this should give enough slack in the belt to remove it from the pulleys. Tighten the new belt in the normal manner.

Hoses

INSPECTION

▶ See Figures 90, 91, 92 and 93

Upper and lower radiator hoses, along with the heater hoses, should be checked for deterioration, leaks and loose hose clamps at least every 15,000 miles (24,000 km). It is also wise to check the hoses periodically in early spring and at the beginning of the fall or winter when you are performing other maintenance. A quick visual inspection could discover a weakened hose which might have left you stranded if it had remained unrepaired.

Whenever you are checking the hoses, make sure the engine and cooling system are cold. Visually inspect for cracking, rotting or collapsed hoses, and replace as necessary. Run your hand along the length of the hose. If a weak or swollen spot is noted when squeezing the hose wall, the hose should be replaced.

REMOVAL & INSTALLATION

▶ See Figures 94 and 95

1. Remove the radiator pressure cap.

⁂ CAUTION

Never remove the pressure cap while the engine is running, or personal injury from scalding hot coolant or steam may result. If possible, wait until the engine has cooled to remove the pressure cap. If this is not possible, wrap a thick cloth around the pressure cap and turn it slowly to the stop. Step back while the pressure is released from the cooling system. When you are sure all the pressure has been released, use the cloth to turn and remove the cap.

2. Position a clean container under the radiator and/or engine draincock or plug, then open the drain and allow the cooling system to drain to an appropriate level. For some upper hoses, only a little coolant must be drained. To remove hoses positioned lower on the engine, such as a lower radiator hose, the entire cooling system must be emptied.

⁂ CAUTION

When draining coolant, keep in mind that cats and dogs are attracted by ethylene glycol antifreeze, and are quite likely to drink any that is left in an uncovered container or in puddles on the ground. This will prove fatal in sufficient quantity. Always drain coolant into a sealable container.

TCCS1219

Fig. 90 The cracks developing along this hose are a result of age-related hardening

TCCS1220

Fig. 91 A hose clamp that is too tight can cause older hoses to separate and tear on either side of the clamp

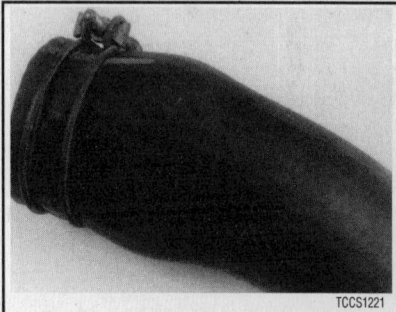

TCCS1221

Fig. 92 A soft spongy hose (identifiable by the swollen section) will eventually burst and should be replaced

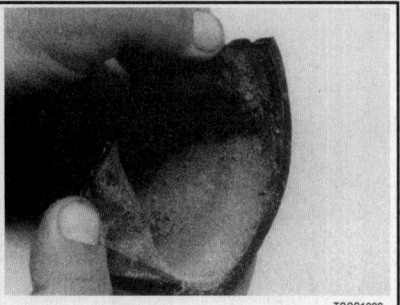

TCCS1222

Fig. 93 Hoses are likely to deteriorate from the inside if the cooling system is not periodically flushed

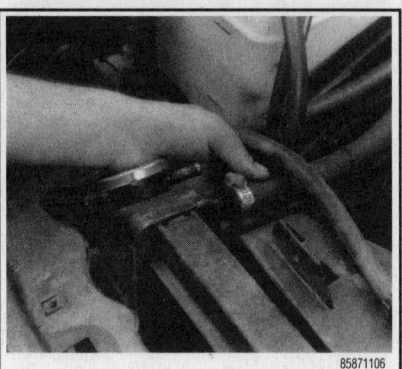

85871106

Fig. 94 Removing the heater hose

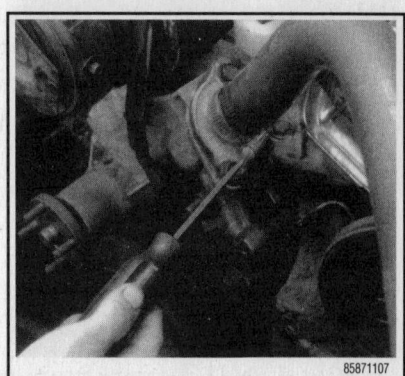

85871107

Fig. 95 Removing the radiator hose

3. Loosen the hose clamps at each end of the hose requiring replacement. Clamps are usually either of the spring tension type (which require pliers to squeeze the tabs and loosen) or of the screw tension type (which require screw or hex drivers to loosen). Pull the clamps back on the hose away from the connection.

4. Twist, pull and slide the hose off the fitting, taking care not to damage the neck of the component from which the hose is being removed.

➡ **If the hose is stuck at the connection, do not try to insert a screwdriver or other sharp tool under the hose end in an effort to free it, as the connection and/or hose may become damaged. Heater connections especially may be easily damaged by such a procedure. If the hose is to be replaced, use a single-edged razor blade to make a slice along the portion of the hose which is stuck on the connection, perpendicular to the end of the hose. Do not cut too deep so as to prevent damaging the connection. The hose can then be peeled from the connection and discarded.**

5. Clean both hose mounting connections. Inspect the condition of the hose clamps and replace them, if necessary.

To install:

6. Dip the ends of the new hose into clean engine coolant to ease installation.

7. Slide the clamps over the replacement hose, then slide the hose ends over the connections into position.

8. Position and secure the clamps at least ¼ in. (6.35mm) from the ends of the hose. Make sure they are located beyond the raised bead of the connector.

9. Close the radiator or engine drains and properly refill the cooling system with the clean drained engine coolant or a suitable mixture of coolant and water.

10. If available, install a pressure tester and check for leaks. If a pressure tester is not available, run the engine until normal operating temperature is reached (allowing the system to naturally pressurize), then check for leaks.

❄❄ CAUTION

If you are checking for leaks with the system at normal operating temperature, BE EXTREMELY CAREFUL not to touch any moving or hot engine parts. Once temperature has been reached, shut the engine OFF, and check for leaks around the hose fittings and connections which were removed earlier.

Air Conditioning System

SYSTEM SERVICE & REPAIR

➡ **It is recommended that the A/C system be serviced by an EPA Section 609 certified automotive technician utilizing a refrigerant recovery/recycling machine.**

The do-it-yourselfer should not service his/her own vehicle's A/C system for many reasons, including legal concerns, personal injury, environmental damage and cost.

According to the U.S. Clean Air Act, it is a federal crime to service or repair (involving the refrigerant) a Motor Vehicle Air Conditioning (MVAC) system for money without being EPA certified. It is also illegal to vent R-12 and R-134a refrigerants into the atmosphere. State and/or local laws may be more strict than the federal regulations, so be sure to check with your state and/or local authorities for further information.

➡ **Federal law dictates that a fine of up to $25,000 may be levied on people convicted of venting refrigerant into the atmosphere.**

When servicing an A/C system you run the risk of handling or coming in contact with refrigerant, which may result in skin or eye irritation or frostbite. Although low in toxicity (due to chemical stability), inhalation of concentrated refrigerant fumes is dangerous and can result in death; cases of fatal cardiac arrhythmia have been reported in people accidentally subjected to high levels of refrigerant. Some early symptoms include loss of concentration and drowsiness.

➡ **Generally, the limit for exposure is lower for R-134a than it is for R-12. Exceptional care must be practiced when handling R-134a.**

Also, some refrigerants can decompose at high temperatures (near gas heaters or open flame), which may result in hydrofluoric acid, hydrochloric acid and phosgene (a fatal nerve gas).

It is usually more economically feasible to have a certified MVAC automotive technician perform A/C system service on your vehicle.

R-12 Refrigerant Conversion

If your vehicle still uses R-12 refrigerant, one way to save A/C system costs down the road is to investigate the possibility of having your system converted to R-134a. The older R-12 systems can be easily converted to R-134a refrigerant by a certified automotive technician by installing a few new components and changing the system oil.

The cost of R-12 is steadily rising and will continue to increase, because it is no longer imported or manufactured in the United States. Therefore, it is often possible to have an R-12 system converted to R-134a and recharged for less than it would cost to just charge the system with R-12.

If you are interested in having your system converted, contact local automotive service stations for more details and information.

PREVENTIVE MAINTENANCE

Although the A/C system should not be serviced by the do-it-yourselfer, preventive maintenance should be practiced to help maintain the efficiency of the vehicle's A/C system. Be sure to perform the following:

• The easiest and most important preventive maintenance for your A/C system is to be sure that it is used on a regular basis. Running the system for five minutes each month (no matter what the season) will help ensure that the seals and all internal components remain lubricated.

➡ **Some vehicles automatically operate the A/C system compressor whenever the windshield defroster is activated. Therefore, the A/C system would not need to be operated each month if the defroster was used.**

• In order to prevent heater core freeze-up during A/C operation, it is necessary to maintain proper antifreeze protection. Be sure to properly maintain the engine cooling system.

• Any obstruction of or damage to the condenser configuration will restrict air flow which is essential to its efficient operation. Keep this unit clean and in proper physical shape.

➡ **Bug screens which are mounted in front of the condenser (unless they are original equipment) are regarded as obstructions.**

• The condensation drain tube expels any water which accumulates on the bottom of the evaporator housing into the engine compartment. If this tube is obstructed, the air conditioning performance can be restricted and condensation buildup can spill over onto the vehicle's floor.

SYSTEM INSPECTION

Although the A/C system should not be serviced by the do-it-yourselfer, system inspections should be performed to help maintain the efficiency of the vehicle's A/C system. Be sure to perform the following:

The easiest and often most important check for the air conditioning system consists of a visual inspection of the system components. Visually inspect the system for refrigerant leaks, damaged compressor clutch, abnormal compressor drive belt tension and/or condition, plugged evaporator drain tube, blocked condenser fins, disconnected or broken wires, blown fuses, corroded connections and poor insulation.

A refrigerant leak will usually appear as an oily residue at the leakage point in the system. The oily residue soon picks up dust or dirt particles from the surrounding air and appears greasy. Through time, this will build up and appear to be a heavy dirt impregnated grease.

For a thorough visual and operational inspection, check the following:

• Check the surface of the radiator and condenser for dirt, leaves or other material which might block air flow.

• Check for kinks in hoses and lines. Check the system for leaks.

• Make sure the drive belt is properly tensioned. During operation, make sure the belt is free of noise or slippage.

• Make sure the blower motor operates at all appropriate positions, then check for distribution of the air from all outlets.

→Remember that in high humidity, air discharged from the vents may not feel as cold as expected, even if the system is working properly. This is because moisture in humid air retains heat more effectively than dry air, thereby making humid air more difficult to cool.

Windshield Wipers

ELEMENT (REFILL) CARE & REPLACEMENT

♦ See Figures 96, 97 and 98

For maximum effectiveness and longest element life, the windshield and wiper blades should be kept clean. Dirt, tree sap, road tar and so on will cause streaking, smearing and blade deterioration if left on the glass. It is advisable to wash the windshield carefully with a commercial glass cleaner at least once a month. Wipe off the rubber blades with the wet rag afterwards. Do not attempt to move wipers across the windshield by hand; damage to the motor and drive mechanism will result.

To inspect and/or replace the wiper blade elements, place the wiper switch in the **LOW** speed position and the ignition switch in the **ACC** position. When the wiper blades are approximately vertical on the windshield, turn the ignition switch to **OFF**.

Examine the wiper blade elements. If they are found to be cracked, broken or torn, they should be replaced immediately. Replacement intervals will vary with usage, although ozone deterioration usually limits element life to about one year. If the wiper pattern is smeared or streaked, or if the blade chatters across the glass, the elements should be replaced. It is easiest and most sensible to replace the elements in pairs.

If your vehicle is equipped with aftermarket blades, there are several different types of refills and your vehicle might have any kind. Aftermarket blades and arms rarely use the exact same type blade or refill as the original equipment.

Regardless of the type of refill used, be sure to follow the part manufacturer's instructions closely. Make sure that all of the frame jaws are engaged as the refill is pushed into place and locked. If the metal blade holder and frame are allowed to touch the glass during wiper operation, the glass will be scratched.

Tires and Wheels

Common sense and good driving habits will afford maximum tire life. Make sure that you don't overload the vehicle or run with incorrect pressure in the tires. Either of these will increase tread wear. Fast starts, sudden stops and sharp cornering are hard on tires and will shorten their useful life span.

→For optimum tire life, keep the tires properly inflated, rotate them often and have the wheel alignment checked periodically.

Inspect your tires frequently. Be especially careful to watch for bubbles in the tread or sidewall, deep cuts or underinflation. Replace any tires with bubbles in the sidewall. If cuts are so deep that they penetrate to the cords, discard the tire. Any cut in the sidewall of a radial tire renders it unsafe. Also look for uneven tread wear patterns that may indicate the front end is out of alignment or that the tires are out of balance.

TIRE ROTATION

♦ See Figure 99

Tires must be rotated periodically to equalize wear patterns that vary with a tire's position on the vehicle. Tires will also wear in an uneven way as the front steering/suspension system wears to the point where the alignment should be reset.

Rotating the tires will ensure maximum life for the tires as a set, so you will not have to discard a tire early due to wear on only part of the tread. Regular rotation is required to equalize wear.

When rotating "unidirectional tires," make sure that they always roll in the same direction. This means that a tire used on the left side of the vehicle must not be switched to the right side and vice-versa. Such tires should only be rotated front-to-rear or rear-to-front, while always remaining on the same side of the vehicle. These tires are marked on the sidewall as to the direction of rotation; observe the marks when reinstalling the tire(s).

Some styled or "mag" wheels may have different offsets front to rear. In these cases, the rear wheels must not be used up front and vice-versa. Furthermore, if these wheels are equipped with unidirectional tires, they cannot be rotated unless the tire is remounted for the proper direction of rotation.

→The compact or space-saver spare is strictly for emergency use. It must never be included in the tire rotation or placed on the vehicle for everyday use.

TIRE DESIGN

♦ See Figure 100

For maximum satisfaction, tires should be used in sets of four. Mixing of different brands or types (radial, bias-belted, fiberglass belted) should be avoided. In most cases, the vehicle manufacturer has designated a type of tire on which the vehicle will perform best. Your first choice when replacing tires should be to use the same type of tire that the manufacturer recommends.

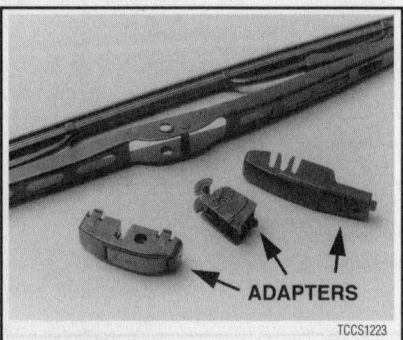

TCCS1223

Fig. 96 Most aftermarket blades are available with multiple adapters to fit different vehicles

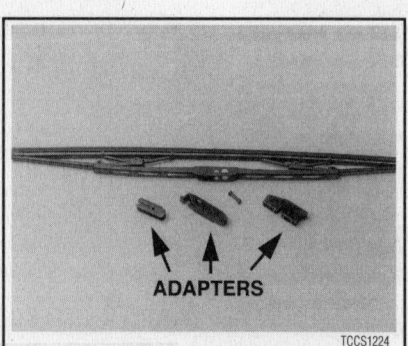

TCCS1224

Fig. 97 Choose a blade which will fit your vehicle, and that will be readily available next time you need blades

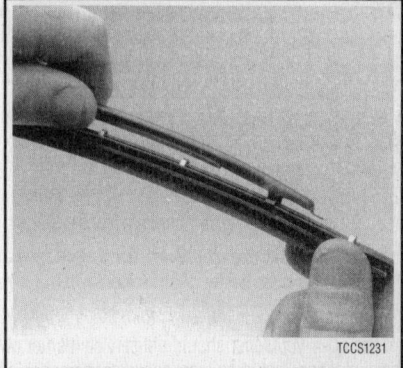

TCCS1231

Fig. 98 When installed, be certain the blade is fully inserted into the backing

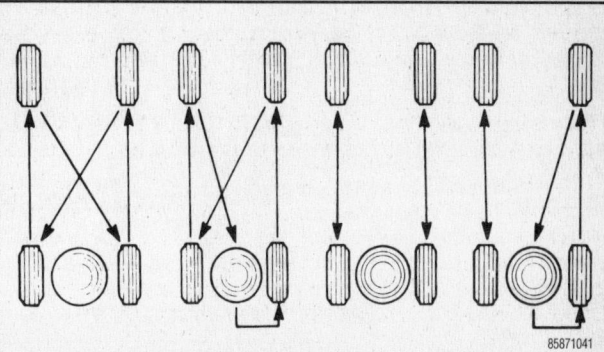

85871041

Fig. 99 Tire rotation patterns acceptable for both bias-ply and radial tires

When radial tires are used, tire sizes and wheel diameters should be selected to maintain ground clearance and tire load capacity equivalent to the original specified tire. Radial tires should always be used in sets of four.

✳✳ CAUTION

Radial tires should never be used on only the front axle.

When selecting tires, pay attention to the original size as marked on the tire. Most tires are described using an industry size code sometimes referred to as P-Metric. This allows the exact identification of the tire specifications, regardless of the manufacturer. If selecting a different tire size or brand, remember to check the installed tire for any sign of interference with the body or suspension while the vehicle is stopping, turning sharply or heavily loaded.

Snow Tires

Good radial tires can produce a big advantage in slippery weather, but in snow, a street radial tire does not have sufficient tread to provide traction and control. The small grooves of a street tire quickly pack with snow and the tire behaves like a billiard ball on a marble floor. The more open, chunky tread of a snow tire will self-clean as the tire turns, providing much better grip on snowy surfaces.

To satisfy municipalities requiring snow tires during weather emergencies, most snow tires carry either an M + S designation after the tire size stamped on the sidewall, or the designation "all-season." In general, no change in tire size is necessary when buying snow tires.

Most manufacturers strongly recommend the use of 4 snow tires on their vehicles for reasons of stability. If snow tires are fitted only to the drive wheels, the opposite end of the vehicle may become very unstable when braking or turning on slippery surfaces. This instability can lead to unpleasant endings if the driver can't counteract the slide in time.

Note that snow tires, whether 2 or 4, will affect vehicle handling in all non-snow situations. The stiffer, heavier snow tires will noticeably change the turning and braking characteristics of the vehicle. Once the snow tires are installed, you must re-learn the behavior of the vehicle and drive accordingly.

➡Consider buying extra wheels on which to mount the snow tires. Once done, the "snow wheels" can be installed and removed as needed. This eliminates the potential damage to tires or wheels from seasonal removal and installation. Even if your vehicle has styled wheels, see if inexpensive steel wheels are available. Although the look of the vehicle will change, the expensive wheels will be protected from salt, curb hits and pothole damage.

TIRE STORAGE

If they are mounted on wheels, store the tires at proper inflation pressure. All tires should be kept in a cool, dry place. If they are stored in the garage or basement, do not let them stand on a concrete floor; set them on strips of wood, a mat or a large stack of newspaper. Keeping them away from direct moisture is of paramount importance. Tires should not be stored upright, but in a flat position.

INFLATION & INSPECTION

♦ See Figures 101 thru 106

The importance of proper tire inflation cannot be overemphasized. A tire employs air as part of its structure. It is designed around the supporting strength of the air at a specified pressure. For this reason, improper inflation drastically reduces the tire's ability to perform as intended. A tire will lose some air in day-to-day use; having to add a few pounds of air periodically is not necessarily a sign of a leaking tire.

Two items should be a permanent fixture in every glove compartment: an accurate tire pressure gauge and a tread depth gauge. Check the tire pressure (including the spare) regularly with a pocket type gauge. Too often, the gauge on the end of the air hose at your corner garage is not accurate because it suffers too much abuse. Always check tire pressure when the tires are cold, as pressure increases with temperature. If you must move the vehicle to check the tire inflation, do not drive more than a mile before checking. A cold tire is generally one that has not been driven for more than three hours.

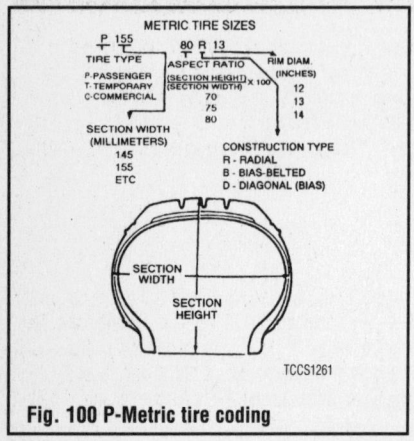

Fig. 100 P-Metric tire coding

Fig. 101 Tires with deep cuts, or cuts which bulge, should be replaced immediately

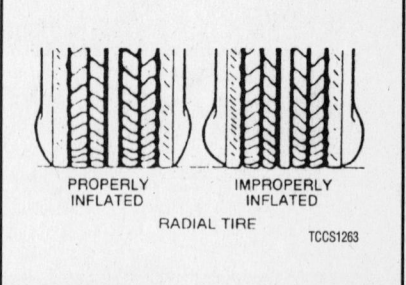

Fig. 102 Radial tires have a characteristic sidewall bulge; don't try to measure pressure by looking at the tire. Use a quality air pressure gauge

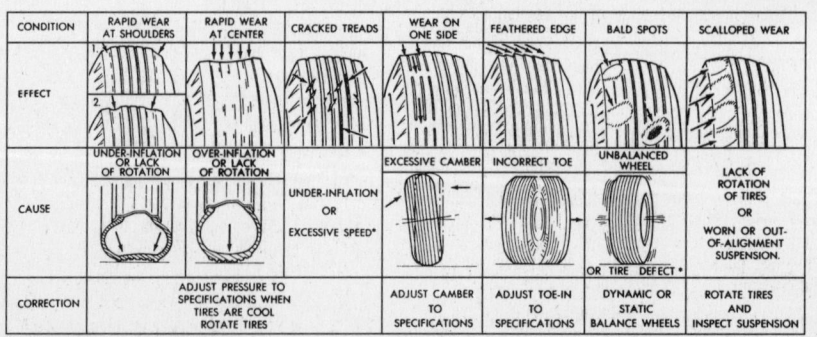

Fig. 103 Common tire wear patterns and causes

Fig. 104 Tread wear indicators will appear when the tire is worn

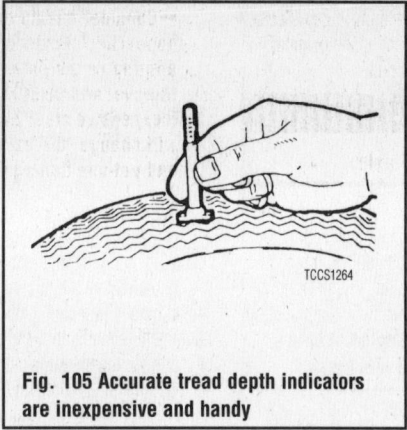

Fig. 105 Accurate tread depth indicators are inexpensive and handy

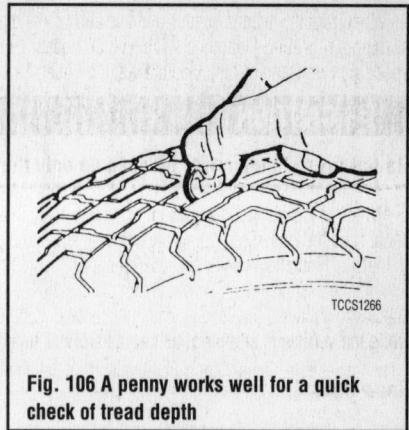

Fig. 106 A penny works well for a quick check of tread depth

A plate or sticker is normally provided somewhere in the vehicle (door post, hood, tailgate or trunk lid) which shows the proper pressure for the tires. Never counteract excessive pressure build-up by bleeding off air pressure (letting some air out). This will cause the tire to run hotter and wear quicker.

✳✳ CAUTION

Never exceed the maximum tire pressure embossed on the tire! This is the pressure to be used when the tire is at maximum loading, but it is rarely the correct pressure for everyday driving. Consult the owner's manual or the tire pressure sticker for the correct tire pressure.

Once you've maintained the correct tire pressures for several weeks, you'll be familiar with the vehicle's braking and handling personality. Slight adjustments in tire pressures can fine-tune these characteristics, but never change the cold pressure specification by more than 2 psi. A slightly softer tire pressure will give a softer ride but also yield lower fuel mileage. A slightly harder tire will give crisper dry road handling but can cause skidding on wet surfaces. Unless you're fully attuned to the vehicle, stick to the recommended inflation pressures.

All automotive tires have built-in tread wear indicator bars that show up as ½ in. (13mm) wide smooth bands across the tire when ⅟₁₆ in. (1.5mm) of tread remains. The appearance of tread wear indicators means that the tires should be replaced. In fact, many states have laws prohibiting the use of tires with less than this amount of tread.

You can check your own tread depth with an inexpensive gauge or by using a Lincoln head penny. Slip the Lincoln penny (with Lincoln's head upside-down) into several tread grooves. If you can see the top of Lincoln's head in 2 adjacent grooves, the tire has less than ⅟₁₆ in. (1.5mm) tread left and should be replaced. You can measure snow tires in the same manner by using the "tails" side of the Lincoln penny. If you can see the top of the Lincoln memorial, it's time to replace the snow tire(s).

FLUIDS AND LUBRICANTS

Fluid Disposal

Used fluids such as engine oil, transmission fluid, antifreeze and brake fluid are hazardous wastes and must be disposed of properly. Before draining any fluids, consult with your local authorities; in many areas, waste oil, antifreeze, etc. is being accepted as a part of recycling programs. A number of service stations and auto parts stores are also accepting waste fluids for recycling.

Be sure of the recycling center's policies before draining any fluids, as many will not accept different fluids that have been mixed together.

Fuel and Engine Oil Recommendations

FUEL

Gasoline Engines

It is important that you use fuel of the proper octane rating in your car. Octane rating is based on the quantity of anti-knock compounds added to the fuel and it determines the speed at which the gasoline will burn. The lower the octane, the faster the gas burns. The higher the octane, the slower the fuel burns and a greater percentage of compounds in the fuel prevent spark ping (knock), detonation and pre-ignition, and post-ignition (dieseling).

All 1971 and later models covered in this guide will perform happily on unleaded regular gasoline. Owners of 1967–70 Cadillac cars may opt for unleaded premium fuel of at least 91 octane to protect against detonation. Since many factors such as altitude, terrain, air temperature, and humidity affect operating efficiency, knocking may result even though the recommended fuel grade is being used. If persistent knocking occurs, it may be necessary to switch to a higher grade of fuel. Continuous or heavy knocking may result in engine damage.

➡ **Your engine's fuel requirement can change with time, mainly due to carbon buildup, which will in turn change the compression ratio. If your** engine pings, knocks, or diesels (runs with the ignition off) switch to a higher grade of fuel. Sometimes just changing brands will cure the problem. If it becomes necessary to retard the timing from the specifications, don't change it more than a few degrees. Retarded timing will reduce power output and fuel mileage, in addition to making the engine run hotter.

Diesel Engines

▶ **See Figure 107**

Fuel makers produce two grades of diesel fuel, No. 1 and No. 2, for use in automotive diesel engines. Generally speaking, No. 2 fuel is recommended over No. 1 for driving in temperatures above 20°F (−7°C). In fact, in many areas, No. 2 diesel is the only fuel available. By comparison, No. 2 diesel fuel is less volatile than No. 1 fuel, and gives better fuel economy. No. 2 fuel is also a better injection pump lubricant.

Two important characteristics of diesel fuel are its cetane number and its viscosity.

The cetane number of a diesel fuel refers to the ease with which a diesel fuel ignites. High cetane numbers mean that the fuel will ignite with relative ease or that it ignites well at low temperatures. Naturally, the lower the cetane number, the higher the temperature must be to ignite the fuel. Most commercial fuels have cetane numbers that range from 35–65. No. 1 diesel fuel generally has a higher cetane rating than No. 2 fuel.

Viscosity is the ability of a liquid, in this case diesel fuel, to flow. Using straight No. 2 diesel fuel below 20°F (−7°C) can cause problems, because this fuel tends to become cloudy, meaning wax crystals begin forming in the fuel (20°F/−7°C is often called the cloud point for No. 2 fuel). In extreme cold weather, No. 2 fuel can stop flowing altogether. In either case, fuel flow is restricted, which can result in a no start condition or poor engine performance. Fuel manufacturers often winterize No. 2 diesel fuel by using various fuel additives and blends (No. 1 diesel fuel, kerosene, etc.) to lower its winter-time viscosity. Generally speaking, though, No. 1 diesel fuel is more satisfactory in extremely cold weather.

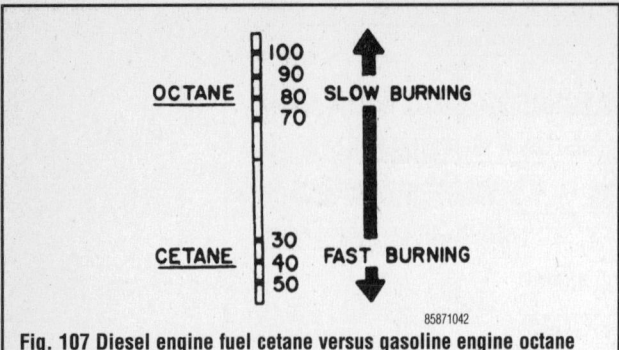

Fig. 107 Diesel engine fuel cetane versus gasoline engine octane ratings—the higher the cetane number the faster the fuel burns

➡No. 1 and No. 2 diesel fuels will mix and burn with no ill effects, although the engine manufacturer will undoubtedly recommend one or the other. Consult the owner's manual for information.

Depending on local climate, most fuel manufacturers make winterized No. 2 fuel available seasonally.

Many automobile manufacturers (Cadillac for example) have published pamphlets giving the locations of diesel fuel stations nationwide. Contact the local dealer for information if they are still available.

Do not substitute home heating oil for automotive diesel fuel. While in some cases, home heating oil refinement levels equal those of diesel fuel, many times they are far below diesel engine requirements. The result of using dirty home heating oil will be a clogged fuel system, in which case the entire system may have to be dismantled and cleaned.

One more word on diesel fuels. Don't thin diesel fuel with gasoline in cold weather. The lighter gasoline, which is more explosive, will cause rough running at the very least, and may cause extensive damage if enough is used.

It is normal that the engine noise level is louder during the warm-up period in winter. It is also normal that whitish-blue smoke may be emitted from the exhaust after starting and during warm-up. The amount of smoke depends upon the outside temperature.

OIL

Gasoline Engines

♦ See Figures 108 and 109

When adding oil to the crankcase or changing the oil or filter, it is important that oil of an equal quality to original equipment be used in your car. The use of inferior oils may void the warranty, damage your engine, or both.

The Society of Automotive Engineers (SAE) grade number of oil indicates the viscosity of the oil (its ability to lubricate at a given temperature). The lower the SAE number, the lighter the oil; the lower the viscosity, the easier it is to crank the engine in cold weather but the less the oil will lubricate and protect the engine at high temperatures. This number is marked on every oil container.

Oil viscosities should be chosen from those oils recommended for the lowest anticipated temperatures during the oil change interval. Due to the need for an oil that embodies both good lubrication at high temperatures and easy cranking in cold weather, multigrade oils have been developed. Basically, a multigrade oil is thinner at low temperatures and thicker at high temperatures. For example, a 10W-40 oil (the W stands for winter) exhibits the characteristics of a 10 weight (SAE 10) oil when the car is first started and the oil is cold. Its lighter weight allows it to travel to the lubricating surfaces quicker and offer less resistance to starter motor cranking than, say, a straight 30 weight (SAE 30) oil. But after the engine reaches operating temperature, the 10W-40 oil begins acting like straight 40 weight (SAE 40) oil, its heavier weight providing greater lubrication with less chance of foaming than a straight 30 weight oil.

The API (American Petroleum Institute) designation, also found on the oil container, indicates the classification of engine oil used under certain given operating conditions. Only oils designated for use Service SF or SG should be used in your Cadillac. Oils of this type perform many functions inside the engine besides their basic lubrication. Through a balanced system of metallic detergents and polymeric dispersants, the oil prevents high and low temperature deposits and also keeps sludge and dirt particles in suspension. Acids, particularly sulfuric acid, as well as other by-products of engine combustion are neutralized by the oil. If these acids are allowed to concentrate, they can cause corrosion and rapid wear of the internal engine parts.

☀☀ WARNING

Non-detergent or straight mineral oils should not be used in your GM engine.

Diesel Engines

♦ See Figure 110

Diesel engines require different engine oil from those used in gasoline engines. Besides performing the same functions as gasoline engine oil, diesel oil must also deal with increased engine heat and the diesel blow-by gases, which create sulfuric acid, a high corrosive.

Under the American Petroleum Institute (API) classifications, gasoline engine oil codes begin with an **S** and diesel engine oil codes begin with a **C**. This first letter designation is followed by a second letter code which explains what type of service (heavy, moderate, light) the oil is meant for. For example, the top of a typical oil can will include: API SERVICES SC, SD, SE, CA, CB, CC. This means the oil in the can is a good, moderate duty engine oil when used in a diesel engine.

Recommended Lubricants

Item	Lubricant
Engine Oil (Gasoline)	API "SF", "SF/CC" or "SF/CD"
Engine Oil (Diesel)	API "SF/CC", "SF/CD"
Automatic Transmission/Transaxle	DEXRON® II AFT
Rear Axle-Standard/Final Drive	SAE 80W GL-5 or SAE 80W/90 GL-5
Positraction/Limited Slip	GM Part #1052271 or 1052272
Power Steering Reservoir	DEXRON® AFT—1967–76 Power Steering Fluid—1977 and later
Brake Fluid	DOT 3
Antifreeze	Ethylene Glycol
Front Wheel Bearings	GM Wheel Bearing Grease
Hood and Door Hinges	Engine Oil
Chassis Lubrication	NLGI #1 or NLGI #2
Lock Cylinders	WD-40 or Powdered Graphite

Fig. 108 Recommended Lubricants

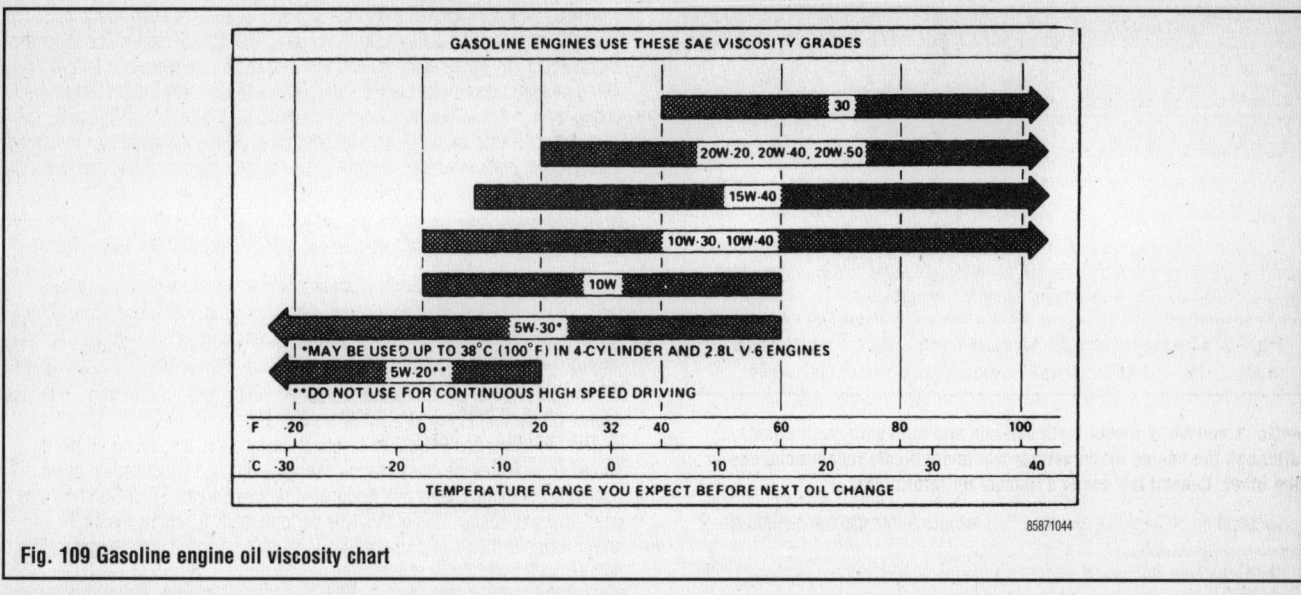

Fig. 109 Gasoline engine oil viscosity chart

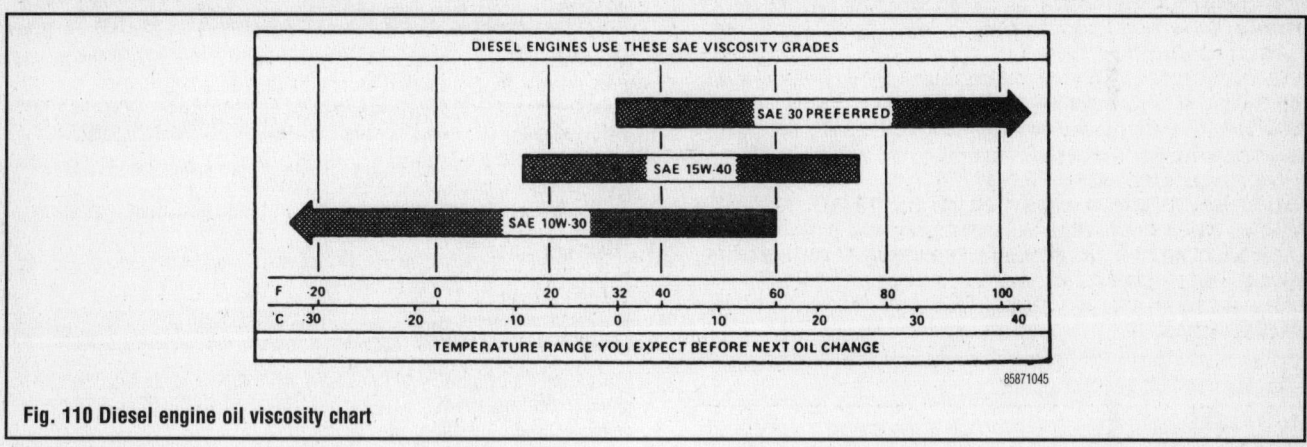

Fig. 110 Diesel engine oil viscosity chart

It should be noted here that the further down the alphabet the second letter of the API classification is, the greater the oil's protective qualities are (CD is the severest duty diesel engine oil, CA is the lightest duty oil, etc.) Similarly, for gasoline engine oil classifications the second letter indicates the protective qualities (SF is the severest duty gasoline engine oil, SA is the lightest duty oil, etc.).

Many diesel manufacturers recommend an oil with both gasoline and diesel engine API classifications. Consult the owner's manual for specifications.

The top of the oil bottle will also contain a Society of Automotive Engineers (SAE) designation, which gives the oil's viscosity. A typical designation will be: SAE 10W-30, which means the oil is a winter viscosity oil, meaning it will flow and give protection at low temperatures.

On the diesel engine, oil viscosity is critical, because the diesel is much harder to start (due to its higher compression) than a gasoline engine. Obviously, if you fill the crankcase with a very heavy oil during the winter (SAE 20W-50, for example), the starter is going to require a lot of current from the battery to turn the engine. And, since batteries don't function well in cold weather in the first place, you may find yourself stranded some morning. Consult the owner's manual for recommended oil specifications for the climate you live in.

➡ Single-grade (straight weight) oils such as SAE 30 are more satisfactory than multi-viscosity oils for highway driving in diesel engines.

Synthetic Oil

There are excellent synthetic and fuel-efficient oils available that, under the right circumstances, can help provide better fuel mileage and better engine protection. However, these advantages come at a price, which can be three or four times the price per quart of conventional motor oils.

Before pouring any synthetic oils into your car's engine, you should consider the condition of the engine and the type of driving you do. Also, check the car's warranty conditions regarding the use of synthetics.

Generally, it is best to avoid the use of synthetic oil in both brand new and older, high mileage engines. New engines require a proper break-in, and the synthetics are so slippery that they can prevent this; most manufacturers recommend that you wait at least 5,000 miles before switching to a synthetic oil. Conversely, older engines are looser and tend to use more oil; synthetics will slip past worn parts more readily than regular oil, and will be used up faster. If your car already leaks and/or uses oil (due to worn parts and bad seals or gaskets), it will leak and use more with a slippery synthetic inside.

Consider your type of driving. If most of your accumulated mileage is on the highway at higher, steadier speeds, a synthetic oil will reduce friction and probably help deliver better fuel mileage. Under such ideal highway conditions, the oil change interval can be extended, as long as the oil filter will operate effectively for the extended lift of the oil. If the filter can't do its job for this extended period, dirt and sludge will build up in your engine's crankcase, sump, oil pump and lines, no matter what type of oil is used. If using synthetic oil in this manner, you should continue to change the oil filter at the recommended intervals.

Cars used under harder, stop-and-go, short hop circumstances should always be serviced more frequently, and for these cars synthetic oil may not be a wise investment. Because of the necessary shorter change interval needed for this type of driving, you cannot take advantage of the long recommended change interval of most synthetic oils.

Finally, some synthetic oils are not compatible with conventional oils and cannot be added to them. This means you should always carry a couple of quarts of synthetic oil with you while on a long trip, as not all service stations carry this oil.

Engine

OIL LEVEL CHECK

▶ **See Figures 111, 112 and 113**

✳ CAUTION

Prolonged and repeated skin contact with used engine oil, with no effort to remove the oil, may be harmful. Always follow these simple precautions when handling used motor oil:

- Avoid prolonged skin contact with used motor oil.
- Remove oil from skin by washing thoroughly with soap and water or waterless hand cleaner. Do not use gasoline, thinners or other solvents.
- Avoid prolonged skin contact with oil-soaked clothing.

Every time you stop for fuel, check the engine oil as follows:

1. Make sure the car is parked on level ground.
2. When checking the oil level it is best for the engine to be at normal operating temperature, although checking the oil immediately after stopping will lead to a false reading. Wait a few minutes after turning off the engine to allow the oil to drain back into the crankcase.
3. Open the hood and locate the dipstick which will be on either the right or left side depending upon your particular engine. Pull the dipstick from its tube, wipe it clean and then reinsert it.
4. Pull the dipstick out again and, holding it horizontally, read the oil level. The oil should be between the **FULL** and **ADD** marks on the dipstick. If the oil is low, add oil of the proper viscosity through the capped opening in the top of the cylinder head cover. See the Oil Recommendations chart in this section for the proper viscosity and rating of oil to use.
5. Replace the dipstick and check the oil level again after adding any oil. Be careful not to overfill the crankcase. Approximately one quart of oil will raise the level from the **ADD** mark to the **FULL** mark. Excess oil will generally be consumed at a faster rate.

OIL AND FILTER CHANGE

▶ **See Figures 114 thru 120**

The oil in the engine of your Cadillac should be changed every six months or 7,500 miles, whichever comes first (except diesels). If you live in an extremely dusty or smoggy area, change your car's oil more frequently. A new filter should be installed with every oil change, and the used oil put into a suitable container and taken to a collection or reclamation point for recycling (many garages and gas stations have storage tanks for this purpose).

➡ **Change the oil in diesel cars every 5,000 miles.**

The oil drain plug is located on the bottom, rear of the oil pan (bottom of the engine, underneath the car).

The mileage figures given are the Cadillac recommended intervals assuming normal driving and conditions. If your car is being used under dusty, polluted or off-road conditions, change the oil and filter more frequently than specified. The same goes for cars driven in stop-and-go traffic or only for short distances. Always drain the oil after the engine has been running long enough to bring it to normal operating temperature. Hot oil will flow easier and more contaminants will be removed along with the oil than if it were drained cold. To change the oil and filter:

1. Run the engine until it reaches normal operating temperature.
2. Put the transmission in Park, set the parking brake, and jack up the front of the car. Support the front end with jackstands.

✳ CAUTION

The EPA warns that prolonged contact with used engine oil may cause a number of skin disorders, including cancer! You should make every effort to minimize your exposure to used engine oil. Protective gloves should be worn when changing the oil. Wash your hands and any other exposed skin areas as soon as possible after exposure to used engine oil. Soap and water, or waterless hand cleaner should be used.

3. Slide a drain pan of at least 6 quarts capacity under the engine oil pan.
4. Loosen the drain plug. Turn the plug out slowly by hand, keeping an inward pressure on the plug as you unscrew it so the hot oil will not escape until the plug is completely removed.

✳ WARNING

When you are ready to release the plug, pull it away from the drain hole quickly, to avoid being burned by the hot oil.

5. Allow the oil to drain completely and then install the drain plug. DO NOT OVERTIGHTEN the plug, or you will strip the threads in the drain hole and you'll have to buy a new pan or a trick replacement plug.
6. Using an oil filter strap wrench, remove the oil filter. Keep in mind that it's holding about a quart of dirty, hot oil.
7. As soon as you remove the oil filter, hold it upright until you can empty it into the drain pan. Dispose of the filter.

✳ WARNING

Prolonged and repeated skin contact with used engine oil, with no effort to remove the oil, may be harmful. Follow these simple precautions when handling used motor oil.

- Avoid prolonged skin contact with used motor oil.
- Remove oil from skin by washing thoroughly with soap and water or waterless hand cleaner. Do not use gasoline, thinners or solvents.

8. Using a clean rag, wipe off the filter mounting adaptor on the engine block. Be sure that the rag doesn't leave any lint which could clog an oil passage.
9. Wipe a coating of clean engine oil on the rubber gasket of the new filter. Spin it onto the engine by hand—DO NOT use the strap wrench. When the gasket starts to snug up against the adaptor surface, give it another ½–¾ turn by hand. Don't turn it any more, or you'll squash the gasket and the filter may leak.

Fig. 111 Checking the oil level—note location of oil dipstick

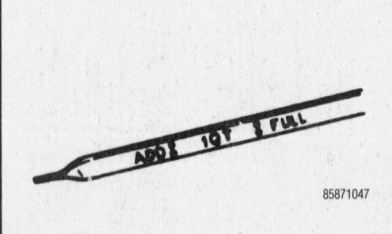

Fig. 112 The oil level should show between the ADD and FULL marks on the dipstick

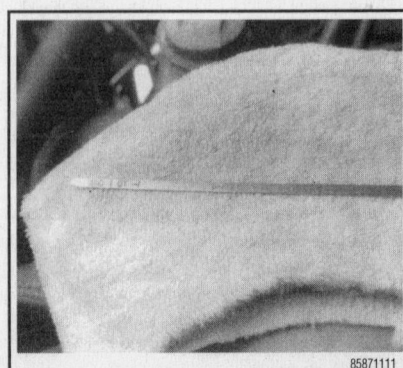

Fig. 113 Always check the oil level while holding the dipstick horizontally

10. Refill the engine with the correct amount of fresh oil through the valve cover cap, or breather tube (diesels). See the Capacities chart in this section.

11. Check the oil level on the dipstick. It is normal for the oil level to be slightly above the full mark right after an oil change. Start the engine and allow it to idle for a few minutes.

✳✳ WARNING

Do not run the engine above idle speed until the oil pressure light (usually red) goes out, indicating the engine has built up oil pressure.

12. Shut off the engine and allow the oil to drain back down for a few minutes before checking the dipstick again. Check for oil leaks around the filter and drain plug.

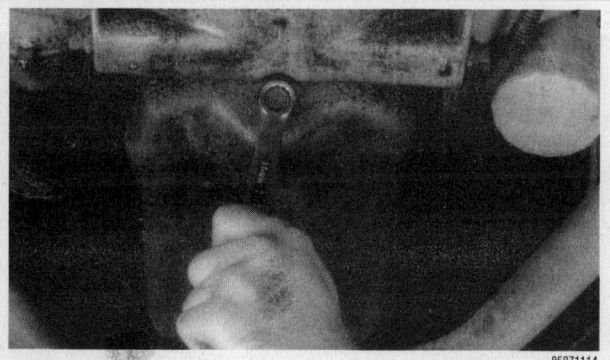

Fig. 114 Engine oil plug location

Automatic Transmission/Transaxle

FLUID RECOMMENDATION

Use only a high quality Dexron®II automatic transmission fluid. The use of other types of fluid may cause severe damage to the transmission.

FLUID LEVEL CHECK

♦ See Figures 121, 122, 123 and 124

Check the automatic transmission fluid level at least every 7,500 miles. The dipstick can be found in the rear of the engine compartment. The fluid level should be checked only when the transmission is hot (normal operating temperature). The transmission is considered hot after about 20 miles of highway driving.

1. Park the car on a level surface with the engine idling. Shift the transmission into Neutral and set the parking brake.

➡ On models using the 440-T4 transaxle (1986 Eldorado and Seville), the transmission must be in Park.

2. Remove the dipstick, wipe it clean and then reinsert it firmly. Be sure that it has been pushed all the way in. Remove the dipstick again and check the fluid level while holding it horizontally. With the engine running, the fluid level should be between the second notch and the **FULL HOT** iine. If the fluid must be checked when it is cool, the level should be between the first and second notches.

3. If the fluid level is below the second notch (engine hot) or the first notch (engine cold), add automatic transmission fluid through the dipstick tube. This is easily done with the aid of a funnel. Check the level often as you are filling the transmission. Be extremely careful not to overfill it. Overfilling will cause slippage, seal damage and overheating. Approximately one pint of ATF will raise the fluid level from one notch/line to the other.

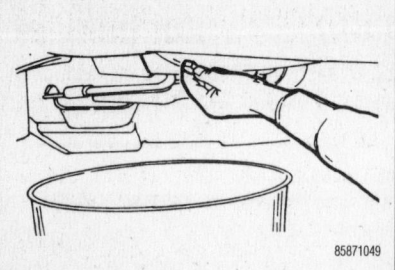

Fig. 115 By keeping an inward pressure on the plug as you unscrew it, oil won't escape past the threads

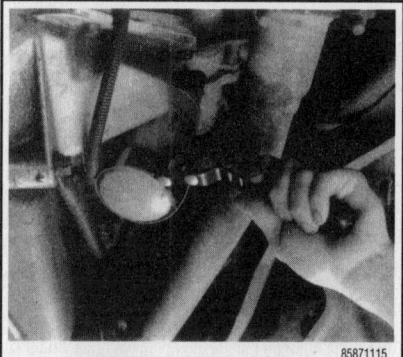

Fig. 116 Removing the oil filter with oil filter wrench

Fig. 117 Before installing a new oil filter, lightly coat the rubber gasket with clean oil

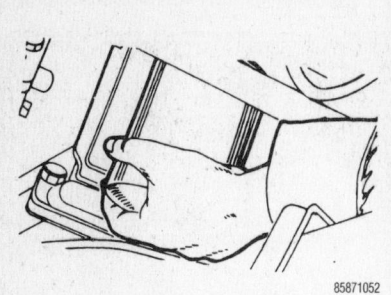

Fig. 118 Install the new filter by hand only—DO NOT USE TOOL TO TIGHTEN OIL FILTER IF POSSIBLE

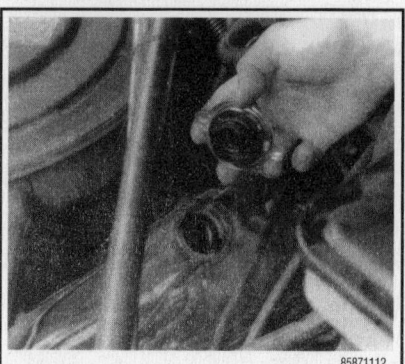

Fig. 119 Removing the oil cap on the valve cover

Fig. 120 Adding oil to the engine

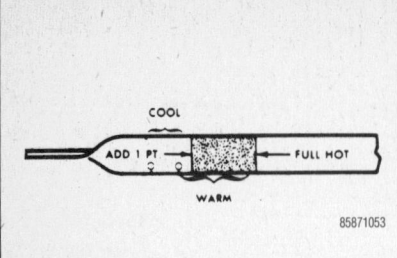

Fig. 121 On the automatic transmission dipstick—the proper level is within the shaded marks

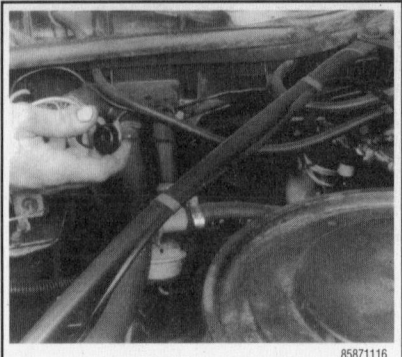

Fig. 122 Automatic transmission dipstick location

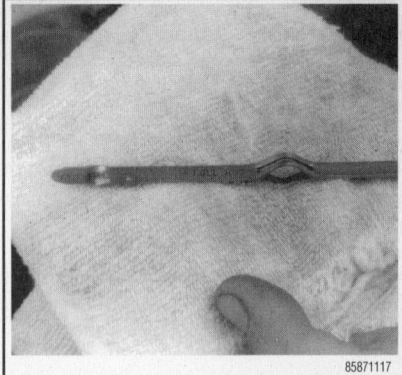

Fig. 123 Automatic transmission dipstick

Fig. 124 Adding automatic transmission fluid

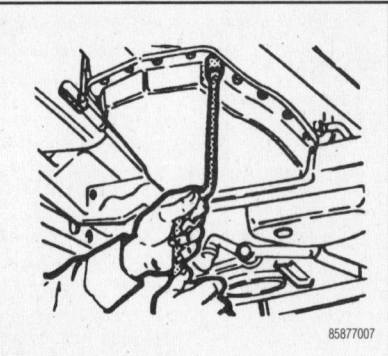

Fig. 125 Removing the pan on the automatic transmission

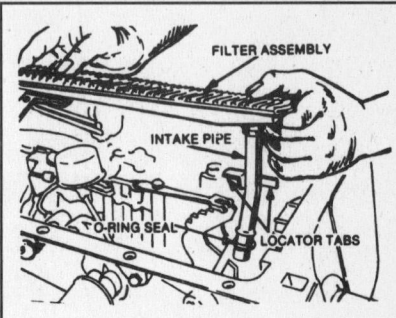

Fig. 126 Removing the filter, intake pipe and O-ring on a Turbo Hydra-Matic 325, 400 or 425

➡ **Always use DEXRON®II ATF. The use of any other fluid will cause severe damage to the transmission.**

The fluid on the dipstick should always be a bright red color. If it is discolored (brown or black), or smells burnt, serious transmission troubles, probably due to overheating, should be suspected. The transmission should be inspected by a qualified technician to locate the cause of the burnt fluid.

FLUID DRAIN AND REFILL (AND PAN AND FILTER SERVICE)

◆ **See Figures 125 thru 135**

The fluid should be changed with the transmission warm. A 20 minute drive at highway speeds should accomplish this.
1. Raise and support the vehicle, preferably in a level attitude.
2. If the crossmember prevents removal of the pan, support the transmission and remove the support crossmember.

3. Place a large pan under the transmission pan. Remove all the front and side pan bolts. Loosen the rear bolts about four turns.
4. Pry the pan loose and let it drain.
5. Remove the pan and gasket. Clean the pan thoroughly with solvent and air dry it. Be very careful not to get any lint from rags in the pan.

➡ **It is normal to find a SMALL amount of metal shavings in the pan. An excessive amount of metal shavings indicates transmission damage.**

6. Remove the strainer to valve body screws, the strainer, and the gasket. Most 350 transmissions will have a throw-away filter instead of a strainer. On the 325, 400 and 425 transmissions, remove the filter retaining bolt, filter, and intake pipe O-ring.
To install:
7. If there is a strainer, clean it in solvent and air dry.
8. Install the new filter or cleaned strainer with a new gasket. Tighten the screws to 12 ft. lbs. (16 Nm). On the 325, 400 and 425, install a new intake pipe O-ring and a new filter, tightening the retaining bolt to 10 ft. lbs. (14 Nm).

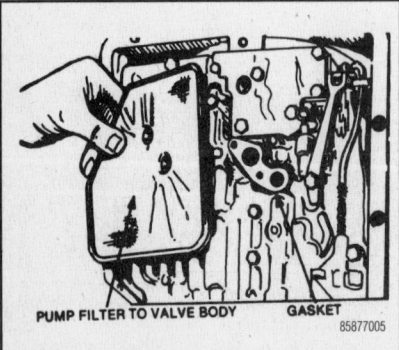

Fig. 127 Removing the filter and gasket on a Turbo Hydra-Matic 200 or 350

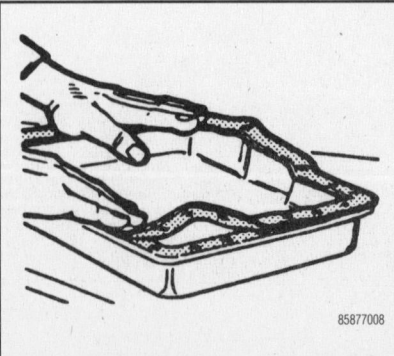

Fig. 128 Always replace the gasket when installing the pan

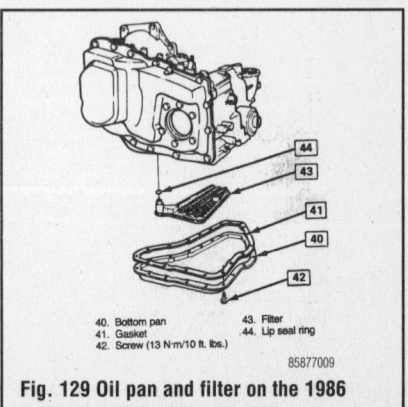

Fig. 129 Oil pan and filter on the 1986 Eldorado and Seville (440-T4)

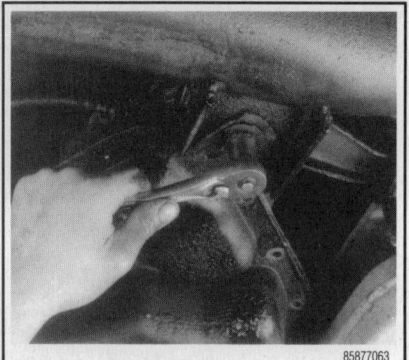

Fig. 130 Removing all necessary bracket bolts for transmission oil pan removal

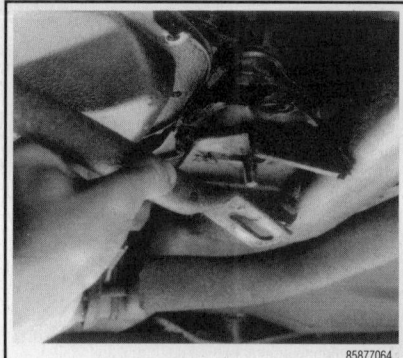

Fig. 131 Removing all necessary brackets for transmission oil pan

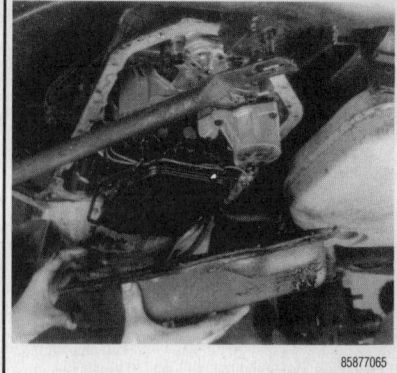

Fig. 132 Removing transmission oil pan

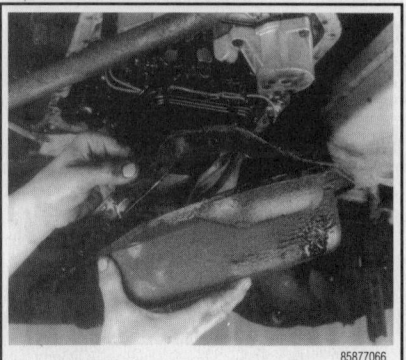

Fig. 133 Removing the gasket from the transmission oil pan

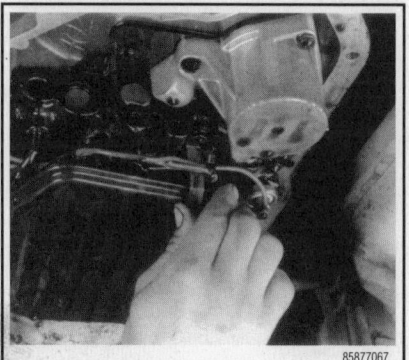

Fig. 134 Removing transmission filter retaining bracket

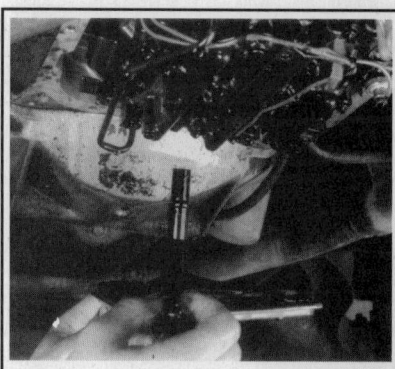

Fig. 135 Removing transmission oil filter

9. Install the pan with a new gasket. Tighten the bolts evenly to 12 ft. lbs. (16 Nm) on most models except the 440-T4 which should be 10 ft. lbs. (14 Nm).

10. Lower the car and add the proper amount of DEXRON®II automatic transmission fluid through the dipstick tube.

11. Start the engine in Park and let it idle. Do not race the engine. Shift into each shift lever position, shift back into Park, and check the fluid level on the dipstick. The level should be ¼ in. below **ADD**. Be very careful not to overfill. Recheck the level after the car has been driven long enough to thoroughly warm up the transmission. Add fluid as necessary. The level should then be at **FULL**.

Rear Axle

FLUID LEVEL CHECK

♦ See Figures 136, 137, 138, 139 and 140

➡This procedure applies to rear wheel drive models only.

The oil in the differential should be checked at least every 7,500 miles.

1. Park the car on a level surface and remove the filter plug from the front side of the differential.

2. If the oil begins to trickle out of the hole when the plug is removed, the differential is full. If no lubricant trickles out, carefully insert your finger (watch out for sharp threads) into the hole and check that the oil is up to the bottom edge of the filler hole.

3. If not, add oil through the hole until the level is at the edge of the hole. Most gear oils come in a plastic squeeze bottle with a nozzle end, which makes adding lubricant simple. You can also use a common turkey baster for this job. Use only standard GL-5 hypoid-type gear oil-SAE 80W or SAE 80W/90.

➡On all models equipped with a positraction/limited slip differential, GM recommends that you use only special GM lubricant available at your local Cadillac parts department.

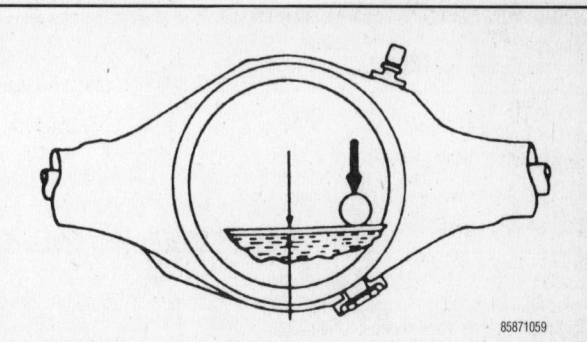

Fig. 136 The fluid level in the differential should be up to the edge of the filler hole (large arrow)

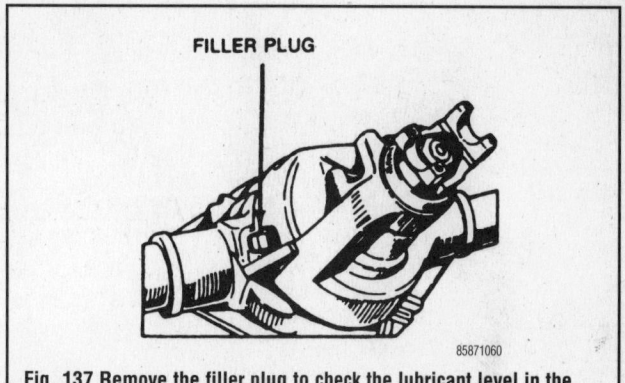

Fig. 137 Remove the filler plug to check the lubricant level in the rear axle

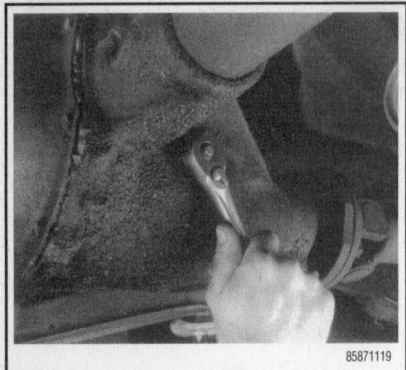

Fig. 138 Removing the filler plug in the rear axle with tool

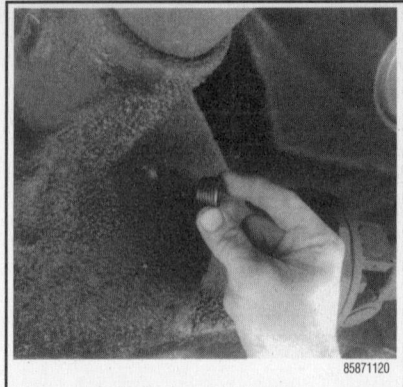

Fig. 139 Removing the filler plug

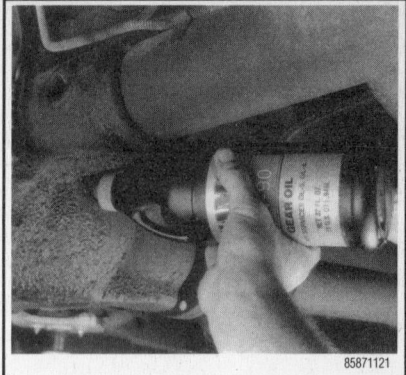

Fig. 140 Adding rear axle fluid

DRAIN AND REFILL

There is no recommended change interval for the rear axle lubricant, but it is always a good idea to change the lube if you have purchased the car used or if it has been driven in water high enough to reach the axle.

1. Park the car on a level surface and set the parking brake.
2. Remove the rear axle filler plug on the front side of the differential housing.
3. Place a large drain pan underneath the rear axle.
4. Unscrew the retaining bolts and remove the rear axle cover. The axle lubricant will now be able to drain into the container.
5. Using a new cover gasket and sealant, install the axle cover. Tighten the retaining bolts in a crisscross pattern.
6. Refill the axle with the proper quantity (see Capacities chart in this section) of SAE 80W or SAE 80W-90 GL-5 gear lubricant. Replace the filler plug, take the car for a short ride and check for any leaks around the plug or rear cover.

Cooling System

FLUID RECOMMENDATION

Coolant mixture in Cadillac is 50-50 ethylene glycol and water for year round use. Use a good quality antifreeze with water pump lubricants, rust inhibitors and other corrosion inhibitors along with acid neutralizers.

FLUID LEVEL CHECK

▶ **See Figures 141, 142, 143 and 144**

It is best to check the coolant level when the engine and radiator are cool. Cadillac models covered in this guide are equipped with coolant recovery tanks connected by hoses to the radiator and mounted on the inner fender skirt. If the coolant level is at or near the **FULL COLD** (engine cold) or the **FULL HOT** (engine hot) lines on the tank, the level is satisfactory.

✳ WARNING

Never add coolant to a hot engine unless it is running; if it is not running, you risk cracking the engine block. The coolant recovery tank is the only accurate place to check the coolant level; however, coolant can be added to either the tank or directly to the radiator.

If you find the coolant level low, add a 50/50 mixture of ethylene glycol-based antifreeze and clean water. Do not add straight water unless you are out on the road and in emergency circumstances; if this is the case, drain the radiator and replenish the cooling system with an ethylene glycol mix at the next

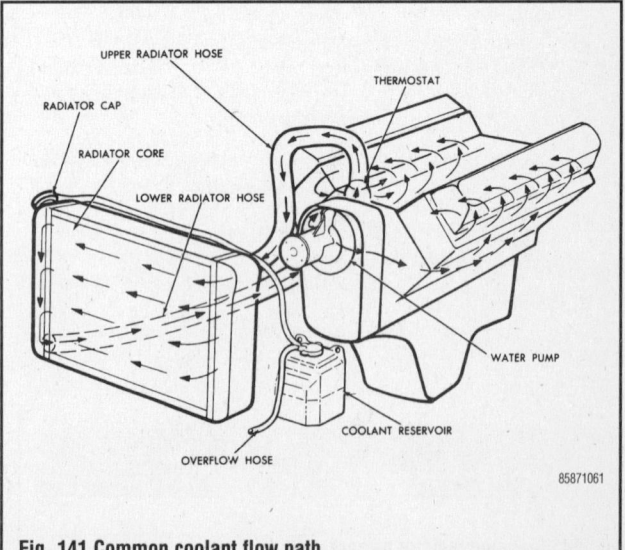

Fig. 141 Common coolant flow path

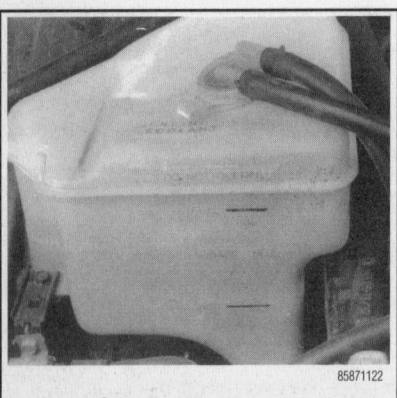

Fig. 142 Engine coolant reservoir

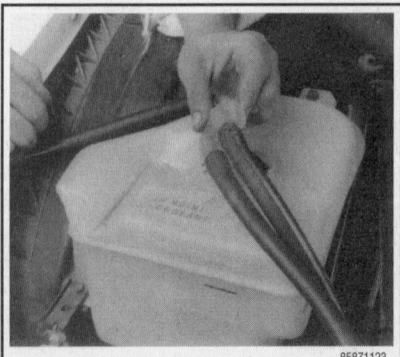

Fig. 143 Removing the engine coolant reservoir cap

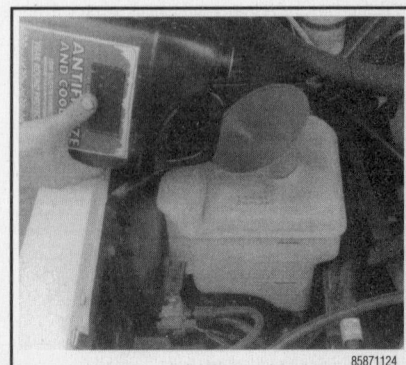

Fig. 144 Adding engine coolant to reservoir

opportunity. Modern ethylene glycol antifreezes are special blends of anti-corrosive additives and lubricants that help keep the cooling system clean and help lubricate water pump bearings, which is why they are recommended by the manufacturers.

DRAINING, FLUSHING AND TESTING THE COOLING SYSTEM

▶ **See Figures 145 and 146**

The cooling system in your car accumulates some internal rust and corrosion in its normal operation. A simple method of keeping the system clean is known as flushing the system. It is performed by circulating a can of radiator flush through the system, and then draining and refilling the system with the normal coolant. Radiator flush is marketed by several different manufacturers, and is available in cans at auto departments parts stores, and many hardware stores. This operation should be performed every 30,000 miles or once a year.

To flush the cooling system:

1. Drain the existing anti-freeze and coolant. Open the radiator and engine drain petcocks (located near the bottom of the radiator and engine block, respectively), or disconnect the bottom radiator hose at the radiator outlet.

➡**Before opening the radiator petcock, spray it with some penetrating oil. Be aware that if the engine has been run, the coolant emptied will be HOT. DO NOT attempt to drain the cooling system until the temperature drops to a safe level.**

2. Close the petcock or re-connect the lower hose and fill the system with water-hot water if the system has just been run.

※ CAUTION

When draining the coolant, keep in mind that cats and dogs are attracted by the ethylene glycol antifreeze, and are quite likely to drink any that is left in an uncovered container or in puddles on the ground. This will prove fatal in sufficient quantity. Always drain the coolant into a sealable container. Coolant should be reused unless it is contaminated or several years old.

3. Add a can of quality radiator flush to the radiator or recovery tank, following any special instructions on the can.

4. Idle the engine as long as specified on the can of flush, or until the upper radiator hose gets hot.

5. Drain the system again. There should be quite a bit of scale and rust in the drained water.

6. Repeat this process until the drained water is mostly clear.

7. Close all petcocks and connect all hoses.

8. Flush the coolant recovery reservoir with water and leave empty.

9. Determine the capacity of your car's cooling system (see Capacities specifications in this guide). Add a 50/50 mix of ethylene glycol antifreeze and water to provide the desired protection.

10. Run the engine to operating temperature, then stop the engine and check for leaks. Check the coolant level and top up if necessary.

11. Check the protection level of your antifreeze mix with an antifreeze tester (a small, inexpensive syringe-type device available at any auto parts store). The tester has five or six small colored balls inside, each of which signify a certain temperature rating. Insert the tester in the recovery tank and suck just enough coolant into the syringe to float as many individual balls as you can (without sucking in too much coolant and floating all the balls at once). A table supplied with the tester will explain how many floating balls equal protection down to a certain temperature. For example, three floating balls might mean the coolant will protect your engine down to 5°F (−15°C).

CHECKING THE RADIATOR CAP

▶ **See Figure 147**

Anytime you check the coolant level, check the radiator cap as well. A worn or cracked gasket can mean improper sealing, which can cause lost coolant, lost pressure, and engine overheating (the cooling system is pressurized and the radiator cap has a pressure rating above the pressure of the system).

A worn cap should be replaced with a new one. Make sure the new cap has the proper pressure rating for your car's system; this is usually marked on the standard factory cap. You may want to go a few pounds per-square-inch over this rating, but never buy a cap having a rating less than the pressure of your car's system.

CLEANING THE RADIATOR OF DEBRIS

▶ **See Figure 148**

The efficiency of the radiator can be seriously impaired by blockage of the radiator fins. Leaves, insects, road dirt, paper-all are common obstacles to fresh air entering your radiator and doing its job.

Large pieces of debris, leaves and large insects can be removed from the fans by hand. The smaller pieces can be washed out with water pressure from a garden hose. This is often a neglected area of auto maintenance, so do a thorough job.

Bent radiator fins can be straightened carefully with a pair of needle-nose pliers. The fins are soft, so don't wiggle them, move them ONCE.

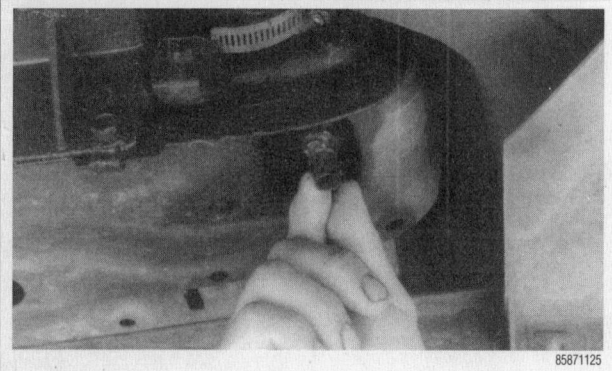

Fig. 145 Common radiator petcock

Fig. 146 Washer fluid reservoir location— DO NOT PUT ENGINE COOLANT IN THIS RESERVOIR

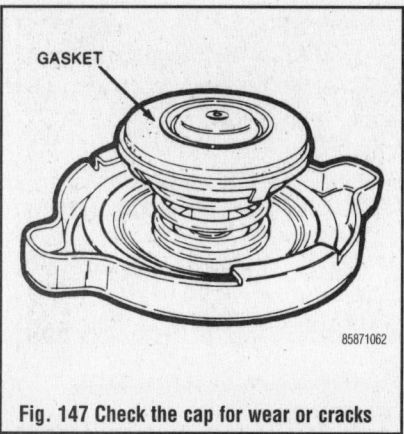

Fig. 147 Check the cap for wear or cracks

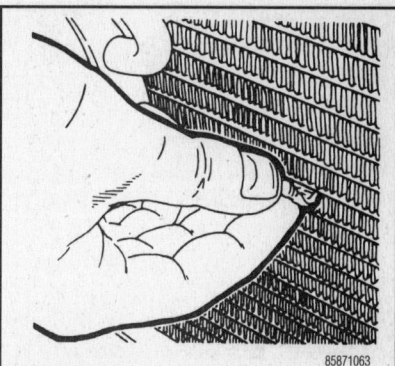

Fig. 148 Keep the radiator fins clear of dirt and bugs for maximum cooling

Brake Master Cylinder

FLUID RECOMMENDATION

Fill the master cylinder with a good quality Heavy-Duty Dot 3 Brake Fluid.

LEVEL CHECK

▶ **See Figures 149, 150, 151 and 152**

The brake master cylinder is located under the hood, in the left rear section of the engine compartment. It is divided into two sections (reservoirs) and the fluid must be kept within ¼ in. (6mm) of the top edge of both reservoirs. The level should be checked at least every 7,500 miles.

➡ **Any sudden decrease in the level of fluid indicates a possible leak in the system and should be checked out immediately.**

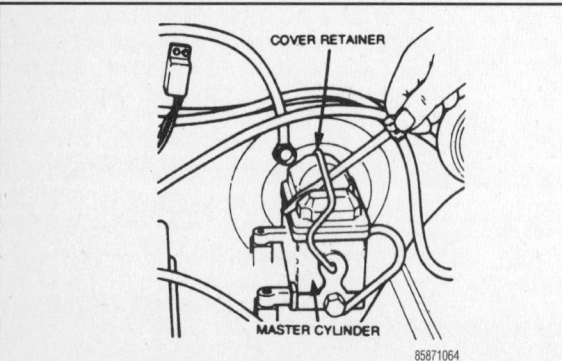

Fig. 149 Pry off the retaining bail to check the master cylinder level on earlier models

To check the fluid level, simply pry off the retaining bar and then lift off the top cover of the master cylinder. When making additions of brake fluid, use only fresh, uncontaminated brake fluid which meets or exceeds DOT 3 standards (as stated on the container). Be careful not to spill any brake fluid on painted surfaces, as it eats paint. Do not allow the brake fluid container or the master cylinder reservoir to remain open any longer than necessary; brake fluid absorbs moisture from the air, reducing its effectiveness and causing corrosion in the lines.

➡ **The reservoir cover on some later models (1978–86) may be without a retaining bail. If so, simply pry the cover off with your fingers.**

Power Steering Reservoir

FLUID RECOMMENDATION

The power steering reservoir uses Dexron II® Automatic Transmission Fluid on all 1967–76 models. All 1977 and later models require GM power steering fluid, available at any Cadillac dealer or your local auto parts store.

LEVEL CHECK

▶ **See Figures 153, 154 and 155**

Power steering fluid should be checked at least every 7,500 miles. The power steering pump is belt driven and has the dipstick built into the filler cap. To prevent possible overfilling, check the fluid level only when the fluid has warmed up to operating temperature and with the front wheels turned straight ahead. If the level is low, fill the pump reservoir until the fluid level measures full on the reservoir dipstick. When the fluid level is low, there is usually a moaning sound coming from the pump as the front wheels are turned, especially when standing still or parking. The steering wheel will also be more difficult to turn when fluid level in the pump reservoir gets low.

Fig. 150 Master cylinder fluid level locations

Fig. 151 Removing the top of the master cylinder

Fig. 152 Adding brake fluid to the master cylinder

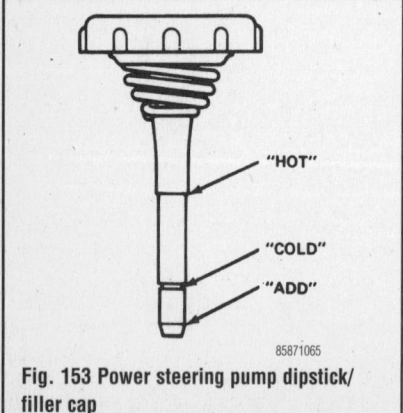

Fig. 153 Power steering pump dipstick/filler cap

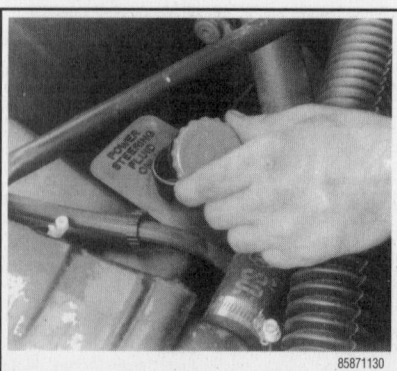

Fig. 154 Power steering pump dipstick/filler cap location

Fig. 155 Check the power steering fluid by holding the dipstick level

Chassis Greasing

FRONT SUSPENSION

▶ **See Figure 156**

Every year or 7,500 miles the front suspension ball joints, both upper and lower on each side of the car, must be greased. Most cars covered in this guide should be equipped with grease nipples on the ball joints, although some may have plugs which must be removed and nipples fitted.

Jack up the front end of the car and safely support it with jackstands. Block the rear wheels and firmly apply the parking brake. If the car has been parked in temperatures below 20°F (–7°C) for any length of time, park it in a heated garage for an hour or so until the ball joints loosen up enough to accept the grease.

Depending on which front wheel you work on first, turn the wheel and tire outward, either full-lock right or full-lock left. You now have the ends of the upper and lower suspension control arms in front of you; the grease nipples are visible pointing up (top ball joint) and down (lower ball joint) through the end of each control arm. If the nipples are not accessible enough, remove the wheel and tire. Wipe all dirt and crud from the nipples or from around the plugs (if installed). If plugs are on the car, remove them and install grease nipples in the holes (nipples are available in various thread sizes at most auto parts stores). Using a hand operated, low pressure grease gun loaded with a quality chassis grease, grease the ball joint only until the rubber joint boot begins to swell out.

> **✳ WARNING**
>
> **Do not pump so much grease into the ball joint that excess grease squeezes out of the rubber boot. This destroys the watertight seal.**

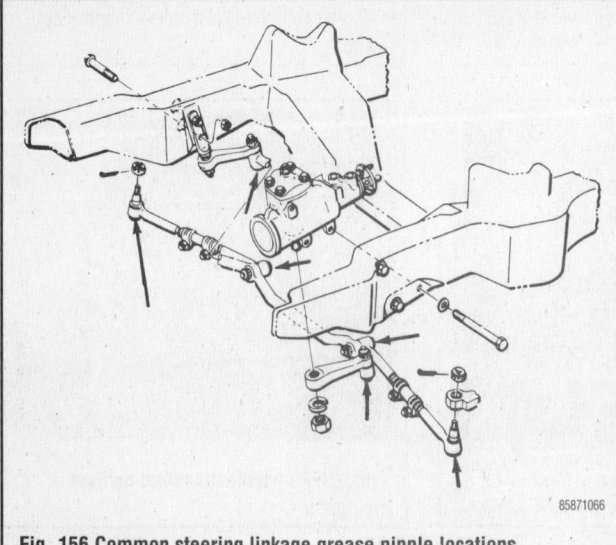

Fig. 156 Common steering linkage grease nipple locations

STEERING LINKAGE

The steering linkage should be greased at the same interval as the ball joints. Grease nipples are installed on the steering tie rod ends on most models. Wipe all dirt and crud from around the nipples at each tie rod. Using a hand-operated, low pressure grease gun loaded with a suitable chassis grease, grease the linkage until the old grease begins to squeeze out around the tie rod ends. Wipe off the nipples and any excess grease. Also grease the nipples on the steering idle arms.

PARKING BRAKE LINKAGE

Use chassis grease on the parking brake cable where it contacts the cable guides, levers and linkage.

AUTOMATIC TRANSMISSION LINKAGE

Apply a small amount of clean engine oil to the kickdown and shift linkage points at 7,500 mile intervals.

Body Lubrication

HOOD LATCH AND HINGES

Clean the latch surfaces and apply clean engine oil to the latch pilot bolts and the spring anchor. Also lubricate the hood hinges with engine oil. Use a chassis grease to lubricate all the pivot points in the latch release mechanism.

DOOR HINGES

▶ **See Figure 157**

The gas tank filler door, car doors, and trunk lid hinges should be wiped clean and lubricated with clean engine oil once a year. Use engine oil to lubricate the trunk lock mechanism and the lock bolt striker. The door lock cylinders and latch mechanisms should be lubricated periodically with a few drops of graphite lock lubricant or a few shots of silicone spray.

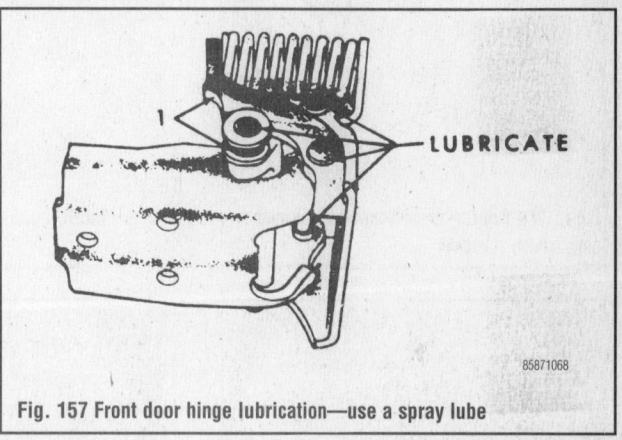

Fig. 157 Front door hinge lubrication—use a spray lube

Wheel Bearings

REPLACEMENT

▶ **See Figures 158 thru 167**

1. Remove the front brake caliper.
2. Remove the hub and outer bearing assembly.
3. Carefully pry the seal from the hub, then remove the inner bearing assembly.
4. If necessary, remove the outer bearing brace.
5. Wash all parts in clean solvent and either blow dry with compressed air or let air dry. Check bearings for cracked cages and worn or pitted rollers. Check the bearing races for cracks, scores, or brinelling.

To install:

6. To install the new bearings, drive or press the outer braces into the hub (if removed). A large socket (preferably one that's already beat up) can be used with a rubber hammer to drive the bearing in place.
7. Thoroughly clean the hub and spindle with clean solvent.
8. Apply a thin wipe of quality, high temperature wheel bearing grease to the spindle at the outer bearing seat, along with the inner bearing seat, shoulder and seal seat.
9. Apply a small wipe of grease inboard of each bearing cup in the hub. Pack the bearing cone and roller assemblies full of grease by hand, working the grease thoroughly into the bearings between the rollers, cone, and cage.
10. Place the inner bearing cone and roller assembly in the hub. Then, using your finger, put an additional wipe of grease outboard on the bearing.

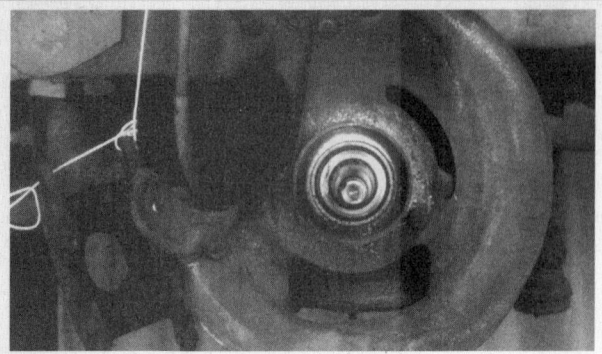

Fig. 158 Position the brake caliper out of the way

11. Install a new grease seal, using a flat place to seat the seal flush, into the hub. Lubricate the seal lip with a thin layer of grease.

12. Carefully install the hub and rotor assembly. Place the outer bearing cone and roller assembly in the outer bearing cup. Install the washer and nut. Initially tighten the nut to 12 ft. lbs. (16 Nm) while turning the wheel assembly forward by hand. Put another wipe of grease outboard of the bearing. This will give the bearings extra grease.

13. Install the brake caliper, then the wheel assembly.

ADJUSTMENT

Tapered Roller Bearings

The proper functioning of the front suspension cannot be maintained unless the front wheel tapered roller bearings are correctly adjusted. Cones must be a slip fit on the spindle and the inside diameter of cones should be lubricated to

Fig. 159 Cleaning the wheel bearing dust cap

Fig. 160 Removing the wheel bearing dust cap

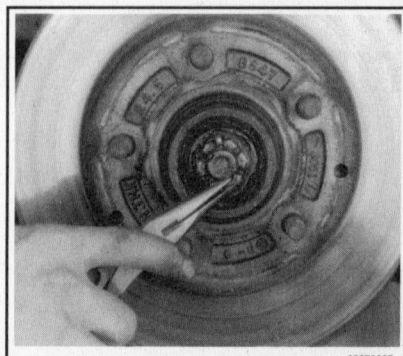

Fig. 161 Removing the wheel bearing cotter pin

Fig. 162 Removing the wheel bearing cotter pin with tool

Fig. 163 Removing the wheel bearing lock

Fig. 164 Removing the wheel bearing washer

Fig. 165 Removing the wheel bearing

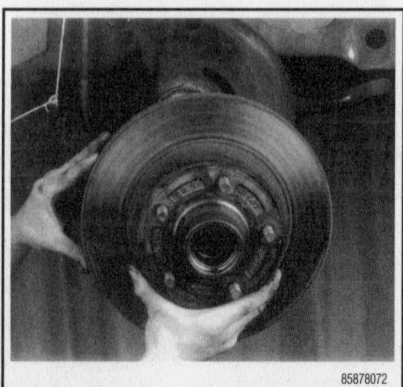

Fig. 166 Removing the disc/hub assembly

Fig. 167 View of wheel bearing dust cap, cotter pin, adjusting nut, washer and wheel bearing (left to right)

insure that the cones will creep. Spindle nut must be a free-running fit on threads.

1. Remove cotter pin from spindle and spindle nut.

2. Tighten the spindle nut to 12 ft. lbs. (16 Nm) while turning the wheel assembly forward by hand to fully seat the bearings. This will remove any grease or burrs which could cause excessive wheel bearing plate later.

3. Back off the nut to the just loose position.

4. Hand tighten the spindle nut. Loosen spindle nut until either hole in the spindle lines up with a slot in the nut (not more than ½ flat).

5. Install new cotter pin. Bend the ends of the cotter pin against nut. Cut off extra length to ensure ends will not interfere with the dust cap.

6. Measure the looseness in the hub assembly. There will be from 0.001-0.005 in. (0.025–0.130mm) end play when properly adjusted.

7. Install dust cap on hub.

Bolt-On Type Bearings

Most 1981 and later models have front and rear sealed wheel bearings. The bearings are pre-adjusted and require no lubrication maintenance or adjust-ment. There are darkened areas on the bearing assembly. These darkened areas are from a heat treatment process and do not indicate a need for bearing replacement.

PACKING

Clean the wheel bearings thoroughly with solvent and check their condition before installation.

❊❊ WARNING

Do not blow the bearing dry with compressed air as this would allow the bearing to turn without lubrication.

Apply a sizable daub of lubricant to the palm of one hand. Using your other hand, work the bearing into the lubricant so that the grease is pushed through the rollers and out the other side. Keep rotating the bearing while continuing to push the lubricant through it.

JUMP STARTING A DEAD BATTERY

♦ See Figure 168

Whenever a vehicle is jump started, precautions must be followed in order to prevent the possibility of personal injury. Remember that batteries contain a small amount of explosive hydrogen gas which is a by-product of battery charging. Sparks should always be avoided when working around batteries, especially when attaching jumper cables. To minimize the possibility of accidental sparks, follow the procedure carefully.

❊❊ CAUTION

NEVER hook the batteries up in a series circuit or the entire electrical system will go up in smoke, including the starter!

Jump Starting Precautions

- Be sure that both batteries are of the same polarity (have the same terminal, in most cases NEGATIVE grounded).
- Be sure that the vehicles are not touching or a short could occur.
- On non-sealed batteries, be sure the vent cap holes are not obstructed.
- Do not smoke or allow sparks anywhere near the batteries.
- In cold weather, make sure the battery electrolyte is not frozen. This can occur more readily in a battery that has been in a state of discharge.
- Do not allow electrolyte to contact your skin or clothing.

Jump Starting Procedure

SINGLE BATTERY GASOLINE AND DIESEL ENGINE MODELS

1. Make sure that the voltages of the 2 batteries are the same. Most batteries and charging systems are of the 12 volt variety.

2. Pull the jumping vehicle (with the good battery) into a position so the jumper cables can reach the dead battery and that vehicle's engine. Make sure that the vehicles do NOT touch.

3. Place the transmissions/transaxles of both vehicles in **Neutral** (MT) or **P** (AT), as applicable, then firmly set their parking brakes.

➡ If necessary for safety reasons, the hazard lights on both vehicles may be operated throughout the entire procedure without significantly increasing the difficulty of jumping the dead battery.

4. Turn all lights and accessories OFF on both vehicles. Make sure the ignition switches on both vehicles are turned to the **OFF** position.

5. Cover the battery cell caps with a rag, but do not cover the terminals.

6. Make sure the terminals on both batteries are clean and free of corrosion for good electrical contact.

7. Identify the positive (+) and negative (-) terminals on both batteries.

8. Connect the first jumper cable to the positive (+) terminal of the dead battery, then connect the other end of that cable to the positive (+) terminal of the booster (good) battery.

9. Connect one end of the other jumper cable to the negative (-) terminal on the booster battery and the final cable clamp to an engine bolt head, alternator bracket or other solid, metallic point on the engine with the dead battery. Try to pick a ground on the engine that is positioned away from the battery in order to minimize the possibility of the 2 clamps touching should one loosen during the procedure. DO NOT connect this clamp to the negative (-) terminal of the bad battery.

❊❊ CAUTION

Be very careful to keep the jumper cables away from moving parts (cooling fan, belts, etc.) on both engines.

10. Check to make sure that the cables are routed away from any moving parts, then start the donor vehicle's engine. Run the engine at moderate speed for several minutes to allow the dead battery a chance to receive some initial charge.

11. With the donor vehicle's engine still running slightly above idle, try to start the vehicle with the dead battery. Crank the engine for no more than 10 seconds at a time and let the starter cool for at least 20 seconds between tries. If the vehicle does not start in 3 tries, it is likely that something else is also wrong or that the battery needs additional time to charge.

12. Once the vehicle is started, allow it to run at idle for a few seconds to make sure that it is operating properly.

13. Turn ON the headlights, heater blower and, if equipped, the rear defroster of both vehicles in order to reduce the severity of voltage spikes and subsequent risk of damage to the vehicles' electrical systems when the cables are disconnected. This step is especially important to any vehicle equipped with computer control modules.

14. Carefully disconnect the cables in the reverse order of connection. Start with the negative cable that is attached to the engine ground, then the negative

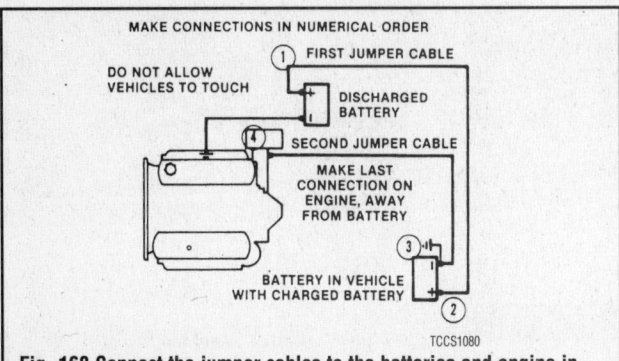

MAKE CONNECTIONS IN NUMERICAL ORDER

DO NOT ALLOW VEHICLES TO TOUCH

① FIRST JUMPER CABLE

DISCHARGED BATTERY

SECOND JUMPER CABLE

MAKE LAST CONNECTION ON ENGINE, AWAY FROM BATTERY

BATTERY IN VEHICLE WITH CHARGED BATTERY

TCCS1080

Fig. 168 Connect the jumper cables to the batteries and engine in the order shown

cable on the donor battery. Disconnect the positive cable from the donor battery and finally, disconnect the positive cable from the formerly dead battery. Be careful when disconnecting the cables from the positive terminals not to allow the alligator clips to touch any metal on either vehicle or a short and sparks will occur.

DUAL BATTERY DIESEL MODELS

▶ **See Figure 169**

Some diesel model vehicles utilize two 12 volt batteries, one on either side of the engine compartment. The batteries are connected in a parallel circuit (positive terminal to positive terminal and negative terminal to negative terminal). Hooking the batteries up in a parallel circuit increases battery cranking power without increasing total battery voltage output. The output will remain at 12 volts. On the other hand, hooking two 12 volt batteries in a series circuit (positive terminal to negative terminal and negative terminal to positive terminal) increases the total battery output to 24 volts (12 volts plus 12 volts).

✳✳ WARNING

Never hook the batteries up in a series circuit or the entire electrical system will be damaged, including the starter motor.

In the event that a dual battery vehicle needs to be jump started, use the following procedure:
1. Turn the heater blower motor **ON** to help protect the electrical system from voltage surges when the jumper cables are connected and disconnected.
2. Turn all lights and other switches **OFF**.

➡**The battery cables connected to one of the diesel vehicle's batteries may be thicker than those connected to its other battery. (The passenger side battery often has thicker cables.) This set-up allows relatively high jump starting current to pass without damage. If so, be sure to connect the positive jumper cable to the appropriate battery in the disabled vehicle. If there is no difference in cable thickness, connect the jumper cable to either battery's positive terminal. Similarly, if the donor vehicle also utilizes two batteries, the jumper cable connections should be made to the battery with the thicker cables; if there is no difference in thickness, the connections can be made to either donor battery.**

JACKING

▶ **See Figures 170, 171 and 172**

Your vehicle was supplied with a jack for emergency road repairs. This jack is fine for changing a flat tire or other short term procedures not requiring you to go beneath the vehicle. If it is used in an emergency situation, carefully follow the instructions provided either with the jack or in your owner's manual. Do not attempt to use the jack on any portions of the vehicle other than specified by the vehicle manufacturer. Always block the diagonally opposite wheel when using a jack.

A more convenient way of jacking is the use of a garage or floor jack. You may use the floor jack at the frame contact points shown in the accompanying illustration.

Never place the jack under the radiator, engine or transmission components. Severe and expensive damage will result when the jack is raised. Additionally, never jack under the floorpan or bodywork; the metal will deform.

Whenever you plan to work under the vehicle, you must support it on jackstands or ramps. Never use cinder blocks or stacks of wood to support the vehicle, even if you're only going to be under it for a few minutes. Never crawl under the vehicle when it is supported only by the tire-changing jack or other floor jack.

➡**Always position a block of wood or small rubber pad on top of the jack or jackstand to protect the lifting point's finish when lifting or supporting the vehicle.**

Small hydraulic, screw, or scissors jacks are satisfactory for raising the vehicle. Drive-on trestles or ramps are also a handy and safe way to both raise and support the vehicle. Be careful though, some ramps may be too steep to drive your vehicle onto without scraping the front bottom panels. Never support the vehicle on any suspension member (unless specifically instructed to do so by a repair manual) or by an underbody panel.

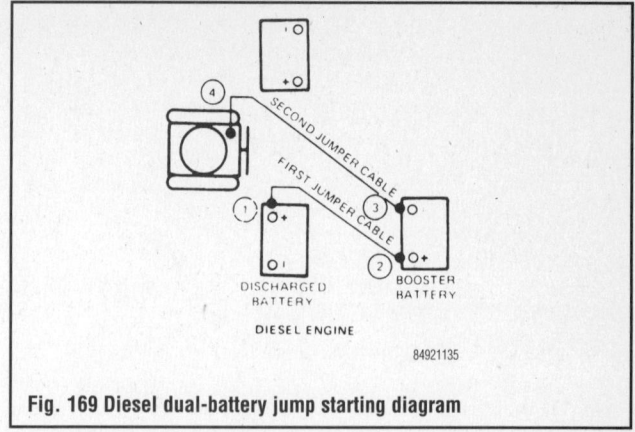

Fig. 169 Diesel dual-battery jump starting diagram

3. Connect the end of a jumper cable to one of the disabled diesel's positive (+) battery terminals, then connect the clamp at the other end of the same cable to the positive terminal (+) on the jumper battery.
4. Connect one end of the other jumper cable to the negative battery terminal (-) on the jumper battery, then connect the other cable clamp to an engine bolt head, alternator bracket or other solid, metallic point on the disabled vehicle's engine. DO NOT connect this clamp to the negative terminal (-) of the disabled vehicle's battery.

✳✳ CAUTION

Be careful to keep the jumper cables away from moving parts (cooling fan, belts, etc.) on both engines.

5. Start the engine on the vehicle with the good battery and run it at a moderate speed.
6. Start the engine of the vehicle with the discharged battery.
7. When the engine starts on the vehicle with the discharged battery, remove the cable from the engine block before disconnecting the cable from the positive terminal.

Jacking Precautions

The following safety points cannot be overemphasized:
• Always block the opposite wheel or wheels to keep the vehicle from rolling off the jack.
• When raising the front of the vehicle, firmly apply the parking brake.
• When the drive wheels are to remain on the ground, leave the vehicle in gear to help prevent it from rolling.
• Always use jackstands to support the vehicle when you are working underneath. Place the stands beneath the vehicle's jacking brackets. Before climbing underneath, rock the vehicle a bit to make sure it is firmly supported.

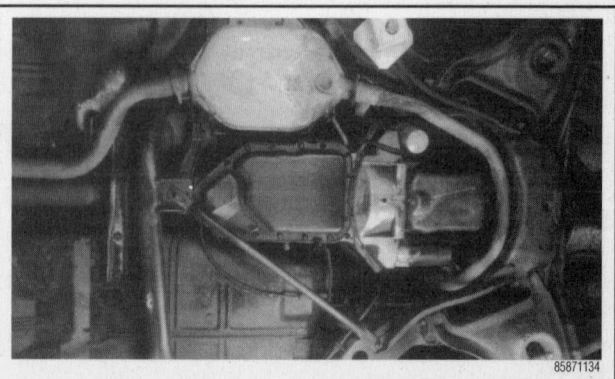

Fig. 170 Vehicle front lift point—note the lift arms

Fig. 171 Vehicle rear lift point—note the lift arms

85871135

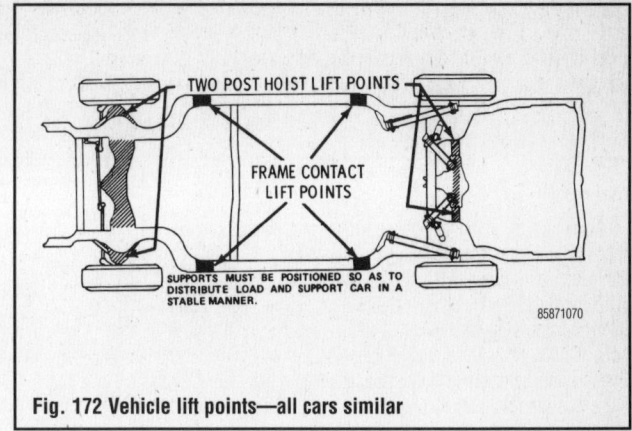

TWO POST HOIST LIFT POINTS

FRAME CONTACT LIFT POINTS

SUPPORTS MUST BE POSITIONED SO AS TO DISTRIBUTE LOAD AND SUPPORT CAR IN A STABLE MANNER.

85871070

Fig. 172 Vehicle lift points—all cars similar

MAINTENANCE SCHEDULE FOR DIESEL — FUELED CADILLACS

WHEN TO PERFORM SERVICES (MONTHS OR MILES WHICHEVER OCCURS FIRST)	SERVICES (FOR DETAILS, SEE NUMBERED PARAGRAPHS)	5,000 (8 000 km)	10,000 (16 000 km)	15,000 (24 000 km)	20,000 (32 000 km)	25,000 (40 000 km)	30,000 (48 000 km)	35,000 (56 000 km)	40,000 (64 000 km)	45,000 (72 000 km)
SECTION A — LUBRICATION AND GENERAL MAINTENANCE										
EVERY 5,000 MILES (8 000 km)	•ENGINE OIL CHANGE	X	X	X	X	X	X	X	X	X
	•OIL FILTER CHANGE	X	X	X	X	X	X	X	X	X
	•CHASSIS LUBRICATION	X	X	X	X	X	X	X	X	X
	•FLUID LEVELS CHECK	X	X	X	X	X	X	X	X	X
SEE EXPLANATION	TIRE ROTATION	X				X		X		
	REAR AXLE OR FINAL DRIVE LUBE CHECK	X		X	X	X		X	X	X
EVERY 12 MONTHS OR 15,000 MILES (24 000 km)	•COOLING SYSTEM CHECK				X		X			X
	•CRANKCASE VENTILATION SYSTEM SERVICE				X		X			X
EVERY 30,000 MILES (48 000 km)	WHEEL BEARING REPACK ①						X			
	FINAL DRIVE BOOTS AND SEALS CHECK						X			
SEE EXPLANATION	AUTO. TRANSMISSION FLUID & FILTER CHANGE									
SECTION B — SAFETY MAINTENANCE										
AT FIRST 5,000 MILES (8 000 km) THEN AT 15,000/30,000/45,000 MILES	•EXHAUST SAFETY CHECKS SEE EXPLANATION	X		X			X			X
EVERY 12 MONTHS OR 10,000 MILES (16 000 km)	OWNER SAFETY CHECKS SEE EXPLANATION		X		X		X		X	
	TIRE, WHEEL AND DISC BRAKE CHECK		X		X		X		X	
	SUSPENSION AND STEERING CHECK		X		X		X		X	
	BRAKE AND POWER STEERING CHECK		X		X		X		X	
EVERY 5,000 MILES (8 000 km)	•DRIVE BELT CHECK	X	X	X	X	X	X	X	X	X
EVERY 12 MONTHS OR 15,000 MILES (24 000 km)	DRUM BRAKE AND PARKING BRAKE CHECK				X		X			X
	THROTTLE LINKAGE CHECK				X		X			X
	BUMPER CHECK				X		X			X
EVERY 24 MONTHS OR 30,000 MILES (48 000 km)	FUEL CAP, FUEL LINES AND FUEL TANK						X			
SECTION C — EMISSION CONTROL MAINTENANCE										
AT FIRST 5,000 MILES (8 000 km) THEN AT 15,000/30,000/45,000 MILES	EXHAUST PRESSURE REGULATOR VALVE (IF EQUIPPED)	X		X			X			X
AT FIRST 5,000 MILES (8 000 km) THEN AT 30,000 MILES (48 000 km)	ENGINE IDLE SPEED ADJUST.	X					X			
EVERY 30,000 MILES (48 000 km)	AIR CLEANER REPLACEMENT						X			
	FUEL FILTER REPLACEMENT						X			

OWNER'S SERVICE LOG — MILES (km)
INSERT MONTH, DAY, AND MILEAGE (km) (i.e. MAY 5-9612) IN COLUMN CLOSEST TO MILEAGE (km) WHEN SERVICE IS PERFORMED

THE CADILLAC SERVICE RECOMMENDATIONS CONTAINED IN THIS MAINTENANCE SCHEDULE UP TO 45,000 MILES (72 000 km) ARE TO BE PERFORMED AFTER 45,000 MILES (72 000 km) AT THE SAME SERVICE INTERVAL FREQUENCY.

• ALSO A SAFETY SERVICE   • ALSO AN EMISSION CONTROL SERVICE   ① NOT REQUIRED ON FRONT WHEEL DRIVE MODELS

85871D11

Gasoline-Engined Cars Maintenance Intervals

When to Perform Services (Months or Miles, Whichever Occurs First)	Services
Every 12 months or 7,500 miles (12 000 km)	●CHASSIS-Lubricate
	●FLUID LEVELS-Check
	CLUTCH PEDAL FREE TRAVEL-Check/Adjust
	FINAL DRIVE BOOTS AND SEALS (Eldorado & Seville F.W.D.) Check condition
See Explanation of Maintenance Schedule	*ENGINE OIL-Change
	*ENGINE OIL FILTER-Replace
	TIRES-Rotation (Radial Tires)
	REAR AXLE OR FINAL DRIVE-Check lube
Every 12 months or 15,000 miles (24 000 km)	*COOLING SYSTEM-See Explanation of Maintenance Schedule
Every 30,000 miles (48 000 km)	WHEEL BEARINGS-Repack (Rear wheel drive cars only)
	CLUTCH CROSS SHAFT-Lubricate
See Explanation	AUTOMATIC TRANSMISSION-Change fluid and service

SAFETY MAINTENANCE

When to Perform Services	Services
Every 12 months or 7,500 miles (12 000 km)	TIRES, WHEELS AND DISC BRAKES-Check condition
	*EXHAUST SYSTEM-Check condition
	SUSPENSION & STEERING SYSTEM-Check condition
	BRAKES AND POWER STEERING-Check all lines and hoses
Every 12 months or 15,000 miles (24 000 km)	*DRIVE BELTS-Check condition and adjustment (1)
	DRUM BRAKES AND PARKING BRAKE-Check condition of linings; adjust parking brake
	THROTTLE LINKAGE-Check operation and condition
	BUMPERS-Check condition
	*FUEL CAP, TANK AND LINES-Check

EMISSION CONTROL MAINTENANCE

When to Perform Services	Services
At first 6 Months or 7,500 Miles (12 000 km)—Then at 24-Month/30,000 Mile (48 000 km) Intervals as Indicated in Log, Except Choke Which Requires Service at 45,000 Miles (72 000 km)	CARBURETOR CHOKE & HOSES-Check (2)
	ENGINE IDLE SPEED-Check adjustment (2)
	EFE SYSTEM-Check operation (if so equipped)
	CARBURETOR OR THROTTLE BODY MOUNTING-Torque attaching bolts or nuts to manifold (2)
Every 30,000 miles (48 000 km)	THERMOSTATICALLY CONTROLLED AIR CLEANER-Check operation
	VACUUM ADVANCE SYSTEM AND HOSES-Check (3)
	SPARK PLUG WIRES-Check
	IDLE STOP SOLENOID AND/OR DASH POT OR ISC-Check operation
	SPARK PLUGS-Replace (2)
	ENGINE TIMING ADJUSTMENT AND DISTRIBUTOR-Check
	AIR CLEANER AND PCV FILTER ELEMENT-Replace (2)
	PCV VALVE-Replace
	EGR VALVE-Service

85871C01

CAPACITIES

Year	Engine No. Cyl. Displ. Cu. In. (L)	Engine Crankcase Add 1 Qt For New Filter*	Transmission (Pts To Refill After Draining) Automatic	Drive Axle (pts)	Fuel Tank (gals)	Cooling System (qts) With Heater	Cooling System (qts) With A/C	Heavy Duty Cooling
1967	8-429 (7.0)	4	24/26	5/4.5	26/24	18/17	18/17	19.5
1968–71	8-472 (7.7)	4/5	25/26	5/4.5	26	21	21	25
	8-500 (8.2)	5	26	4.5	24	20	20	22
1971–73	8-472 (7.7)	4	8	5	27.5	21.3	21.3	21.8
	8-500 (8.2)	5	11.9	4	27.5	21.3	21.3	21.8
1974	8-472 (7.7)	4	8	5	27.5	21.3	21.3	23.8
	8-500 (8.2)	5	11.9	4	27.5	21.3	21.3	21.8
1975–76	8-350 (5.7)	4	8	5	21	18.9	18.8	—
	8-500 (8.2)	4/5	8/10	5/4	27/5	21.3/23	21.3/23	25.8
1977	8-350 (5.7)	4	8	5	21	17.2	17.2	—
	8-425 (7.0)	4/5	8/10	5/4	24.5/27.5	21/26	21/26	—
1978	8-350 (5.7)	4	8	4.3	21	18.9	18.9	—
	8-350 (5.7) Diesel	6	6	4.3	21	18.9	18.9	—
1979	8-425 (7.0)	4/5	8/10	4.3/3.4	24/27.5	19.8/24.3	19.8/24.3	—
	8-350 (5.7)	4	9/10	4.3/3.2	19.6	17.2	17.2	—
	8-425 (7.0)	4	9	4.25	25	21	21	—
1980	6-252 (4.1)	4	10	3.25	20	13.6	13.6	14.1
	8-350 (5.7)	4	10	3.25	21	15.5	15.5	—
1981	8-350 (5.7) Diesel	6	6	4.25	27	23.7	23.7	—
	8-368 (6.0)	4	8	4.25	25	21.4	21.4	—
	6-252 (4.1)	4	8	4.25	25	18.2	18.2	—
	8-350 (5.7) Diesel	6	6	4.25	27	23.7	23.7	—
	8-368 (6.0)	4	8	4.25	25	21.4	21.4	—
1982	6-252 (4.1)	4	8	4.25/3.25	25/21	10.8/6.25	10.8/6.26	18.2
	8-350 (5.7) Diesel	6	6	4.25/3.25	27	23.7	23.7	23.7
	8-368 (6.0)	4	8	4.25	25	21.4	21.4	21.4
1983	8-250 (4.1)	4	10	4.25/3.25	24/21	11	11	—
	8-350 (5.7) Diesel	6	10	4.25/3.25	26/21	23/18	23	—
	8-368 (6.0)	4	8	4.25	25	21.4	21.4	—
1984	8-250 (4.1)	4	10	4.25/3.25	24/21	11	11	—
	8-350 (5.7) Diesel	6	10	4.25/3.25	26/21	23/18	23	—
	8-368 (6.0)	4	8	4.25	25	21.4	21.4	—
1985	8-250 (4.1)	4	10	3.5/3.2	24.5/20.3	11	11	—
	8-350 (5.7) Diesel	6	10	3.5/3.2	26.0/22.8	23.7/18.4	23.7/18.4	—
1986	8-250 (4.1)	5⊙	13	—	18.0	12.6	12.6	—
	8-307 (5.0)	4	10.6	3.6	24.5	15.3	15.3	—
1987	8-250 (4.1)	5⊚	13	—	18.0	12.6	12.6	—
	8-307 (5.0)	4	10.6	3.5	20.7	15.3	15.3	—
1988–89	8-273 (4.5)	5⊙	13	—	18.8	12.1	12.1	—
	8-305 (5.0)	4	10.6	4.25	25.0	15.2	15.2	15.6

NOTE: Where two figures appear with a slash (/), the first is the rear wheel drive Cadillac, and the second is the Eldorado or the 1982 and later Seville. These differences only appear where the same engine is used in two different models.
⊙ With or without filter change
⊚ 5.5 with oil filter change

85871C02B

2

ENGINE PERFORMANCE AND TUNE-UP

EMISSION CONTROLS

TUNE-UP PROCEDURES

The tune-up is a routine maintenance procedure which is essential for the efficient and economical operation of your car's engine. Regular tune-ups will also help prolong the life of the engine.

The interval between tune-ups is a variable factor which depends upon the way you drive your car, the conditions under which you drive it (city versus highway, weather, etc.), and the type of engine installed. A complete tune-up should be performed on your Cadillac at least every 15,000 miles or one year, whichever comes first. 1981 and later cars have an increased tune-up interval of 30,000 miles.

This interval should be halved if the car is operated under severe conditions such as trailer towing, prolonged idling (a common occurrence in the city), start and stop driving, or if starting and running problems are noticed. It is assumed here that the routine maintenance described in Section 1 has been followed, as this goes hand-in-hand with the recommended tune-up procedures. The end result of a tune-up can only be the sum of all the various steps, so every step applicable to the tune-up should be followed.

If the specifications on the underhood sticker in the engine compartment of your car disagree with the Tune-Up Specifications chart in this section the figures on the sticker must be used. The sticker often reflects changes made during the production run, or displays specifications that apply only to your particular engine.

The replaceable parts involved in a tune-up include the spark plugs, air filter, distributor cap, rotor, and the spark plug wires. In addition to these parts and the adjustments involved in properly installing them, there are several adjustments of other parts involved in completing the job. These include carburetor idle speed and air/fuel mixture, ignition timing, and valve clearance adjustments.

➡**This section gives specific procedures on how to tune-up your Cadillac, and is intended to be as complete and basic as possible. For an explanation of computer trouble codes which help diagnose problems on sophisticated electronic fuel injection and electronic engine control systems, refer to Section 5.**

✳✳ CAUTION

When working with a running engine, make sure that there is proper ventilation. Also make sure that the transmission is in Park (unless otherwise specified) and the parking brake is fully applied. Always keep hands, clothing and tools well clear of the hot exhaust manifolds and radiator and especially the belts and fan. Remove any wrist or long neck jewelry or ties before beginning any job, and tuck long hair under a cap. When the engine is running, do not grasp ignition wires, distributor cap or coil wires as a shock in excess of 50,000 volts may result. Whenever working around the distributor, make sure the ignition is OFF.

HEI System Tachometer Hookup

There is a terminal marked TACH on the distributor cap. Connect one tachometer lead to this terminal and the other lead to a ground. On some tachometers, the leads must be connected to the TACH terminal and to the battery positive terminal.

✳✳ WARNING

Never ground the TACH terminal; serious module and ignition coil damage will result. If there is any doubt as to the correct tachometer hookup, check with the tachometer manufacturer.

Diesel Engine Precautions

1. Never run the engine with the air cleaner removed: if anything is sucked into the inlet manifold it will go straight to the combustion chambers, or jam behind a valve.
2. Never wash a diesel engine: the reaction of a warm fuel injection pump to cold (or even warm) water can ruin the pump.

3. Never operate a diesel engine with one or more fuel injectors removed unless fully familiar with injector testing procedures: some diesel injection pumps spray fuel at up to 1400 psi-enough pressure to allow the fuel to penetrate your skin.
4. Do not skip engine oil and filter changes.
5. Strictly follow the manufacturer's oil and fuel recommendations as given in the owner's manual.
6. Do not use home heating oil as fuel for your diesel unless it's a dire emergency.
7. Most manufacturers caution against using starting fluids in the automotive diesel engine, as it can cause severe internal engine damage.
8. Do not run a diesel engine with the Water in Fuel warning light on in the dashboard. See Section 5 for water purging procedure.
9. If removing water from the fuel tank yourself, use the same caution you would use when working around gasoline engine fuel components.
10. Do not allow diesel fuel to come in contact with rubber hoses or components on the engine, as it can damage them.

TACHOMETER HOOKUP—DIESEL ENGINE

A magnetic pick-up tachometer is necessary for diesel work because of the lack of an ignition system. The tachometer probe is inserted into the hole in the timing indicator.

Spark Plugs

⯈ **See Figures 1 and 2**

A typical spark plug consists of a metal shell surrounding a ceramic insulator. A metal electrode extends downward through the center of the insulator and protrudes a small distance. Located at the end of the plug and attached to the

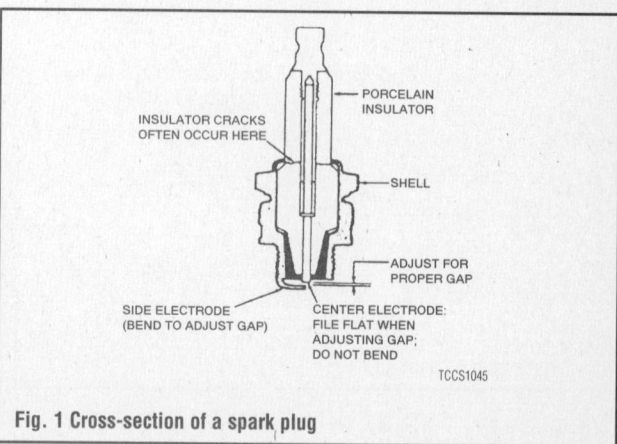

Fig. 1 Cross-section of a spark plug

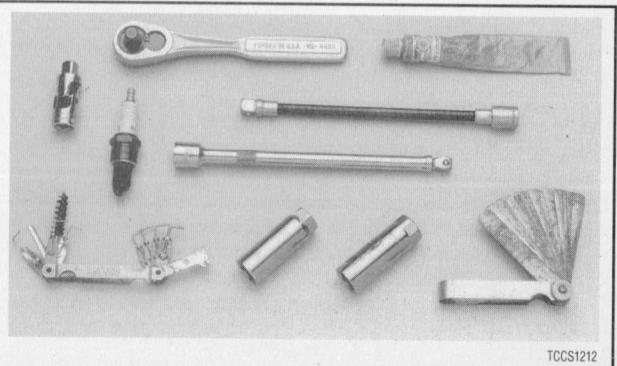

Fig. 2 A variety of tools and gauges are needed for spark plug service

side of the outer metal shell is the side electrode. The side electrode bends in at a 90⁻ angle so that its tip is just past and parallel to the tip of the center electrode. The distance between these two electrodes (measured in thousandths of an inch or hundredths of a millimeter) is called the spark plug gap.

The spark plug does not produce a spark, but instead provides a gap across which the current can arc. The coil produces anywhere from 20,000 to 50,000 volts (depending on the type and application) which travels through the wires to the spark plugs. The current passes along the center electrode and jumps the gap to the side electrode, and in doing so, ignites the air/fuel mixture in the combustion chamber.

SPARK PLUG HEAT RANGE

♦ See Figure 3

Spark plug heat range is the ability of the plug to dissipate heat. The longer the insulator (or the farther it extends into the engine), the hotter the plug will operate; the shorter the insulator (the closer the electrode is to the block's cooling passages) the cooler it will operate. A plug that absorbs little heat and remains too cool will quickly accumulate deposits of oil and carbon since it is not hot enough to burn them off. This leads to plug fouling and consequently to misfiring. A plug that absorbs too much heat will have no deposits but, due to the excessive heat, the electrodes will burn away quickly and might possibly lead to preignition or other ignition problems. Preignition takes place when plug tips get so hot that they glow sufficiently to ignite the air/fuel mixture before the actual spark occurs. This early ignition will usually cause a pinging during low speeds and heavy loads.

The general rule of thumb for choosing the correct heat range when picking a spark plug is: if most of your driving is long distance, high speed travel, use a colder plug; if most of your driving is stop and go, use a hotter plug. Original equipment plugs are generally a good compromise between the 2 styles and most people never have the need to change their plugs from the factory-recommended heat range.

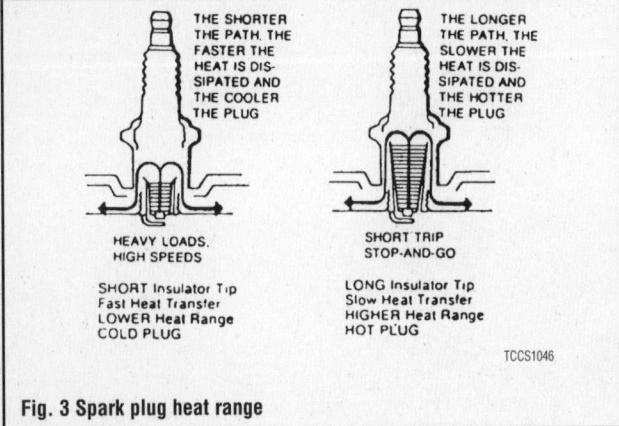

Fig. 3 Spark plug heat range

REMOVAL & INSTALLATION

A set of spark plugs usually requires replacement after about 20,000–30,000 miles (32,000–48,000 km), depending on your style of driving. In normal operation plug gap increases about 0.001 in. (0.025mm) for every 2500 miles (4000 km). As the gap increases, the plug's voltage requirement also increases. It requires a greater voltage to jump the wider gap and about two to three times as much voltage to fire the plug at high speeds than at idle. The improved air/fuel ratio control of modern fuel injection combined with the higher voltage output of modern ignition systems will often allow an engine to run significantly longer on a set of standard spark plugs, but keep in mind that efficiency will drop as the gap widens (along with fuel economy and power).

When you're removing spark plugs, work on one at a time. Don't start by removing the plug wires all at once, because, unless you number them, they may become mixed up. Take a minute before you begin and number the wires with tape.

1. Disconnect the negative battery cable, and if the vehicle has been run recently, allow the engine to thoroughly cool.

2. Carefully twist the spark plug wire boot to loosen it, then pull upward and remove the boot from the plug. Be sure to pull on the boot and not on the wire, otherwise the connector located inside the boot may become separated.

3. Using compressed air, blow any water or debris from the spark plug well to assure that no harmful contaminants are allowed to enter the combustion chamber when the spark plug is removed. If compressed air is not available, use a rag or a brush to clean the area.

➡Remove the spark plugs when the engine is cold, if possible, to prevent damage to the threads. If removal of the plugs is difficult, apply a few drops of penetrating oil or silicone spray to the area around the base of the plug, and allow it a few minutes to work.

4. Using a spark plug socket that is equipped with a rubber insert to properly hold the plug, turn the spark plug counterclockwise to loosen and remove the spark plug from the bore.

✳✳ WARNING

Be sure not to use a flexible extension on the socket. Use of a flexible extension may allow a shear force to be applied to the plug. A shear force could break the plug off in the cylinder head, leading to costly and frustrating repairs.

To install:
5. Inspect the spark plug boot for tears or damage. If a damaged boot is found, the spark plug wire must be replaced.
6. Using a wire feeler gauge, check and adjust the spark plug gap. When using a gauge, the proper size should pass between the electrodes with a slight drag. The next larger size should not be able to pass while the next smaller size should pass freely.
7. Carefully thread the plug into the bore by hand. If resistance is felt before the plug is almost completely threaded, back the plug out and begin threading again. In small, hard to reach areas, an old spark plug wire and boot could be used as a threading tool. The boot will hold the plug while you twist the end of the wire and the wire is supple enough to twist before it would allow the plug to crossthread.

✳✳ WARNING

Do not use the spark plug socket to thread the plugs. Always carefully thread the plug by hand or using an old plug wire to prevent the possibility of crossthreading and damaging the cylinder head bore.

8. Carefully tighten the spark plug. If the plug you are installing is equipped with a crush washer, seat the plug, then tighten about ¼ turn to crush the washer. If you are installing a tapered seat plug, tighten the plug to specifications provided by the vehicle or plug manufacturer.
9. Apply a small amount of silicone dielectric compound to the end of the spark plug lead or inside the spark plug boot to prevent sticking, then install the boot to the spark plug and push until it clicks into place. The click may be felt or heard, then gently pull back on the boot to assure proper contact.

INSPECTION & GAPPING

♦ See Figures 4, 5, 6 and 7

Check the plugs for deposits and wear. If they are not going to be replaced, clean the plugs thoroughly. Remember that any kind of deposit will decrease the efficiency of the plug. Plugs can be cleaned on a spark plug cleaning machine, which can sometimes be found in service stations, or you can do an acceptable job of cleaning with a stiff brush. If the plugs are cleaned, the electrodes must be filed flat. Use an ignition points file, not an emery board or the like, which will leave deposits. The electrodes must be filed perfectly flat with sharp edges; rounded edges reduce the spark plug voltage by as much as 50%.

Check spark plug gap before installation. The ground electrode (the L-shaped one connected to the body of the plug) must be parallel to the center electrode and the specified size wire gauge (please refer to the Tune-Up Specifications chart for details) must pass between the electrodes with a slight drag.

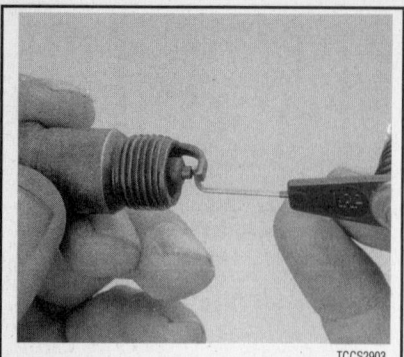

Fig. 4 Checking the spark plug gap with a feeler gauge

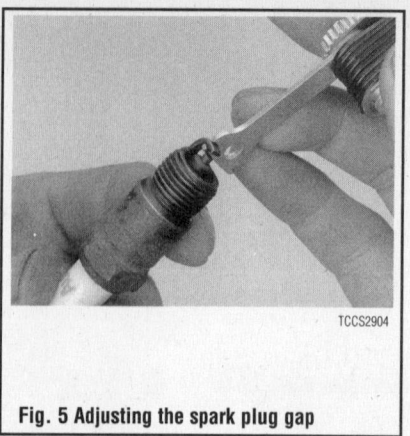

Fig. 5 Adjusting the spark plug gap

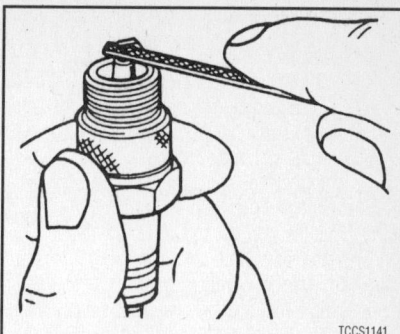

Fig. 6 If the standard plug is in good condition, the electrode may be filed flat—WARNING: do not file platinum plugs

A **normally worn** spark plug should have light tan or gray deposits on the firing tip.

A **carbon fouled** plug, identified by soft, sooty, black deposits, may indicate an improperly tuned vehicle. Check the air cleaner, ignition components and engine control system.

This spark plug has been **left in the engine too long,** as evidenced by the extreme gap- Plugs with such an extreme gap can cause misfiring and stumbling accompanied by a noticeable lack of power.

An **oil fouled** spark plug indicates an engine with worn poston rings and/or bad valve seals allowing excessive oil to enter the chamber.

A **physically damaged** spark plug may be evidence of severe detonation in that cylinder. Watch that cylinder carefully between services, as a continued detonation will not only damage the plug, but could also damage the engine.

A **bridged or almost bridged** spark plug, identified by a build-up between the electrodes caused by excessive carbon or oil build-up on the plug.

Fig. 7 Inspect the spark plug to determine engine running conditions

➡**NEVER adjust the gap on a used platinum type spark plug.**

Always check the gap on new plugs as they are not always set correctly at the factory. Do not use a flat feeler gauge when measuring the gap on a used plug, because the reading may be inaccurate. A round-wire type gapping tool is the best way to check the gap. The correct gauge should pass through the electrode gap with a slight drag. If you're in doubt, try one size smaller and one larger. The smaller gauge should go through easily, while the larger one shouldn't go through at all. Wire gapping tools usually have a bending tool attached. Use that to adjust the side electrode until the proper distance is obtained. Absolutely never attempt to bend the center electrode. Also, be careful not to bend the side electrode too far or too often as it may weaken and break off within the engine, requiring removal of the cylinder head to retrieve it.

Spark Plug Wires

CHECKING AND REPLACEMENT

▸ **See Figure 8**

Every 10,000 miles, inspect the spark plug wires for burns, cuts, or breaks in the insulation. Check the boots and the nipples on the distributor cap. Replace any damaged wiring.

Every 30,000 miles or so, the resistance of the wires should be checked with an ohmmeter. Wires with excessive resistance will cause misfiring, and may make the engine difficult to start in damp weather. Generally, the useful life of the cables is 45,000-60,000 miles.

To check resistance, remove the distributor cap, leaving the wires in place. Connect one lead of an ohmmeter to an electrode within the cap; connect the other lead to the corresponding spark plug terminal (remove it from the spark plug for this test). Replace any wire which shows a resistance over 30,000 ohms. The following chart gives resistance values as a function of length. Generally speaking, however, resistance should not be considered the outer limit of acceptability.

• 0-15 inches: 3,000-10,000 ohms

Fig. 8 Always mark spark plug wires before removing from distributor cap

• 15-25 inches: 4,000-15,000 ohms
• 25-35 inches: 6,000-20,000 ohms
• Over 35 inches: 25,000 ohms

It should be remembered that resistance is also a function of length; the longer the wire, the greater the resistance. Thus, if the wires on you vehicle are longer than the factory originals, resistance will be higher, quite possibly outside these limits.

When installing new wires, replace them one at a time to avoid mix-ups. Start by replacing the longest one first. Install the boot firmly over the spark plug. Route the wire over the same path as the original. Insert the nipple firmly onto the tower on the distributor cap, then install the cap cover and latches to secure the wires.

FIRING ORDERS

▸ **See Figures 9, 10, 11, 12 and 13**

➡**To avoid confusion, remove and tag the spark plug wires one at a time, for replacement.**

If a distributor is not keyed for installation with only one orientation, it could have been removed previously and rewired. The resultant wiring would hold the correct firing order, but could change the relative placement of the plug towers in relation to the engine. For this reason it is imperative that you label all wires before disconnecting any of them. Also, before removal, compare the current wiring with the accompanying illustrations. If the current wiring does not match, make notes in your book to reflect how your engine is wired.

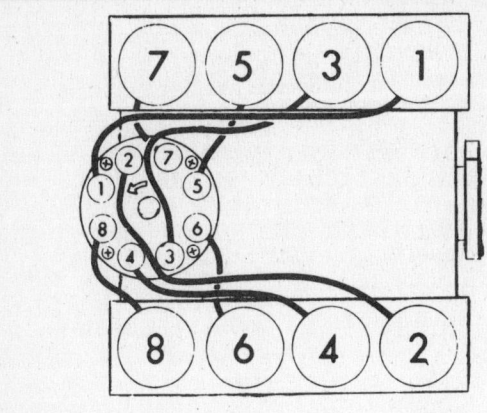
Fig. 9 GM (Cadillac) 250 (4.1L) V8
GM (Cadillac) 273 (4.5L) V8
Engine firing order: 1-8-4-3-6-5-7-2
Distributor rotation: counterclockwise

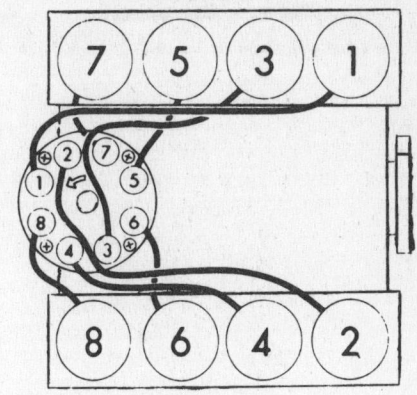
Fig. 10 GM (Oldsmobile) 307 (5.0L) V8
GM (Oldsmobile) 350 (5.7L) V8 w/EFI
Engine firing order: 1-8-4-3-6-5-7-2
Distributor rotation: counterclockwise

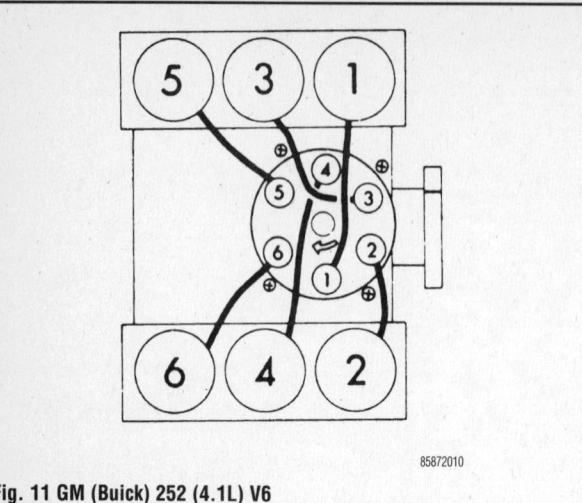

Fig. 11 GM (Buick) 252 (4.1L) V6
Engine firing order: 1–6–5–4–3–2
Distributor rotation: clockwise

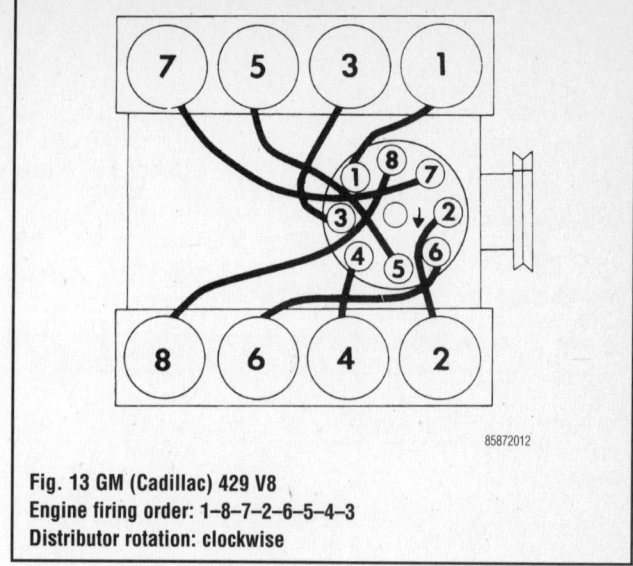

Fig. 13 GM (Cadillac) 429 V8
Engine firing order: 1–8–7–2–6–5–4–3
Distributor rotation: clockwise

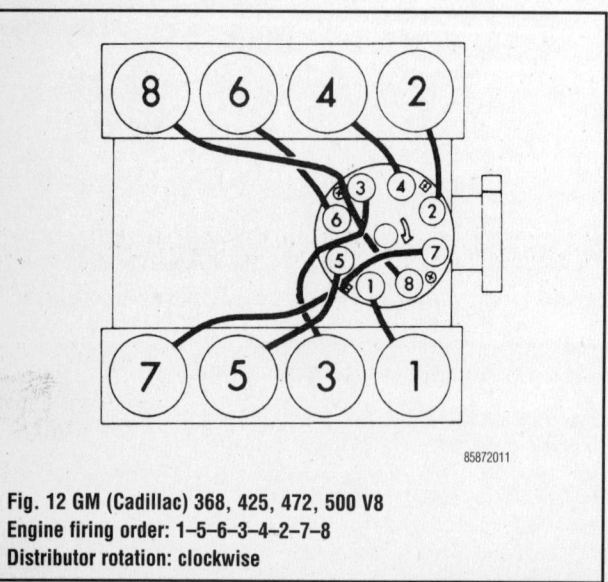

Fig. 12 GM (Cadillac) 368, 425, 472, 500 V8
Engine firing order: 1–5–6–3–4–2–7–8
Distributor rotation: clockwise

POINT TYPE IGNITION

Breaker Points and Condenser

The points function as a circuit breaker for the primary circuit of the ignition system. The ignition coil must boost the 12 volts supplied by the battery to as much as 25,000 volts in order to fire the plugs. To do this, the coil depends on the points and the condenser to make a clean break in the primary circuit.

The coil has both primary and secondary circuits. When the ignition is turned ON, the battery supplies voltage through the coil and onto the points. The points are connected to ground, completing the primary circuit. As the current passes through the coil, a magnetic field is created in the iron center core of the coil. When the cam in the distributor turns, the points open, breaking the primary circuit. The magnetic field in the primary circuit of the coil then collapses and cuts through the secondary circuit windings around the iron core. Because of the physical principle called electromagnetic induction, the battery voltage is increased to a level sufficient to fire the spark plugs.

When the points open, the electrical charge in the primary circuit tries to jump the gap created between the two open contacts of the points. If this electrical charge were not transferred elsewhere, the metal contacts of the points would start to change rapidly.

The function of the condenser is to absorb excessive voltage from the points when they open and thus prevent the points from becoming pitted or burned.

If you have ever wondered why it is necessary to tune-up your engine occasionally, consider the fact that the ignition system must complete the above cycle each time a spark plug fires. On a four-cylinder, four-cycle engine, two of the four plugs must fire once for every engine revolution. If the idle speed of your engine is 800 revolutions per minute (800 rpm), the breaker points open and close two times for each revolution. For every minute your engine idles, your points open and close 1,600 times (2 x 800=1,600). And that is just at idle. What about at 60 mph?

There are two ways to check breaker point gap: with a feeler gauge or with a dwell meter. Either way you set the points, you are adjusting the amount of time (in degrees of distributor rotation) that the points will remain open. If you adjust the points with a feeler gauge, you are setting the maximum amount the points will open when the rubbing block on the points is on a high point of the distributor cam. When you adjust the points with a dwell meter, you are measuring the number of degrees (of distributor cam rotation) that the points will remain closed before they start to open as a high point of the distributor cam approaches the rubbing block of the points.

If you still do not understand how the points function, take a friend, go outside, and remove the distributor cap from your engine. Have your friend operate the starter (make sure that the transmission is not in gear) as you look at the exposed parts of the distributor.

There are two rules that should always be followed when adjusting or replacing points. The points and condenser are a matched set; never replace one without replacing the other. If you change the point gap or dwell of the engine, you also change the ignition timing. Therefore, if you adjust the points, you must also adjust the timing.

REMOVAL & INSTALLATION

1967–74 Models

▶ **See Figures 14, 15, 16, 17 and 18**

The usual procedure is to replace the condenser each time the point set is replaced. Although this is not always necessary, it is easy to do at this time and the cost is negligible. Every time you adjust or replace the breaker points, the ignition timing must be checked and, if necessary, adjusted. No special equipment other than a feeler gauge is required for point replacement or adjustment, but a dwell meter is strongly advised. A magnetic screwdriver is handy to prevent the small points and condenser screws from falling down into the distributor.

Point sets using the push-in type wiring terminal should be used on those distributors equipped with an R.F.I. (Radio Frequency Interference) shield (1970–74). Points using a lockscrew-type terminal may short out due to contact between the shield and the screw.

1. Push down on the spring-loaded distributor cap retaining screws and give them a half-turn to release. Remove the cap. You might have to unclip or detach some or all of the plug wires to remove the cap. If so, number the wires and the cap for removal.

2. Clean the cap inside and out with a clean rag. Check for cracks and carbon paths. A carbon path shows up as a dark line, usually from one of the cap sockets or inside terminals to a ground. Check the condition of the carbon button inside the center of the cap and the inside terminals. Replace the cap as necessary. Carbon paths cannot usually be successfully scraped off. It is better to replace the cap.

3. Remove the two screws and lift the round rotor off. There is less danger of losing the screws if you just back them out all the way and lift them off with the rotor. Clean off the metal outer tip if it is burned or corroded. Don't file it. Replace the rotor as necessary or if one came with your tune-up kit.

4. Remove the radio frequency interference shield if your distributor has one. Watch out for those little screws! The factory says that the points don't need to be replaced if they are only slightly rough or pitted. However, sad experience shows that it is more economical and reliable in the long run to replace the point set while the distributor is open, then to have to do this at a later (and possible more inconvenient) time.

5. Pull off the two wire terminals from the point assembly. One wire comes from the condenser and the other comes from within the distributor. The terminals are usually held in place by spring tension only. There might be a clamp screw securing the terminals on some older versions. There is also available a one-piece point/condenser assembly. The radio frequency interference shield isn't needed with this set. Loosen the point set hold-down screw(s). Be very careful not to drop any of these little screws inside the distributor. If this happens, the distributor will probably have to be removed to get at the screw. If the hold-down screw is lost elsewhere, it must be replaced with one that is no

longer than the original to avoid interference with the distributor workings. Remove the point set, even if it is to be reused.

6. If the points are to be reused, clean them with a few strokes of special point file. This is done with the points removed to prevent tiny metal filings from getting into the distributor. Don't use sandpaper or emery cloth; they will cause rapid point burning.

7. Loosen the condenser hold-down screw and slide the condenser out of the clamp. This will save you a struggle with the clamp, condenser, and the tiny screw when you install the new one. If you have the type of clamp that is permanently fastened to the condenser, remove the screw and the condenser. Don't lose the screw.

To install:

8. Attend to the distributor cam lubricator. If you have the round kind, turn it around on its shaft at the first tune-up and replace it at the second. If you have the long kind, switch ends at the first tune-up and replace it at the second.

➡**Don't oil or grease the lubricator. The foam is impregnated with a special lubricant.**

If you didn't get any lubricator at all, or if it looks like someone took it off, don't worry. You don't really need it. Just rub a matchhead size dab of grease on the cam lobes.

9. Install the new condenser. If you left the clamp in place, just slide the new condenser into the clamp.

10. Replace the point set and tighten the screws. Replace the two wire terminals, making sure that the wires don't interfere with anything. Some distributors have a ground wire that must go under one of the screws.

11. Check that the contacts meet squarely. If they don't, bend the tab supporting the fixed contact.

12. Turn the engine until a high point on the cam that opens the points contacts the rubbing block on the point arm. You can turn the engine by hand if you can get a wrench on the crankshaft pulley nut, or you can grasp the fan belt and turn the engine with the spark plugs removed.

✲✲ CAUTION

If you try turning the engine by hand, be very careful not to get your fingers pinched in the pulleys.

Another alternative is to bump the starter switch or use a remote starter switch.

13. On the V8 engine, simply insert a ⅛ in. Allen wrench into the adjustment screw and turn. The wrench sometimes comes with a tune-up kit.

14. Insert the correct size feeler gauge and adjust the gap until you can push the gauge in and out between the contacts with a slight drag, but without disturbing the point arm. This operation takes a bit of experience to obtain the correct feel. Check by trying the gauges 0.001-0.002 in. (0.025–0.050mm) larger and smaller than the setting size. The larger one should disturb the point arm, while the smaller one should not drag at all. Recheck the gap, because if often changes when the screw is tightened.

15. After all the point adjustments are complete, pull a white index card through (between) the contacts to remove any traces of oil. Oil will cause rapid contact burning.

16. Replace the radio frequency interference shield, if any. You don't need it

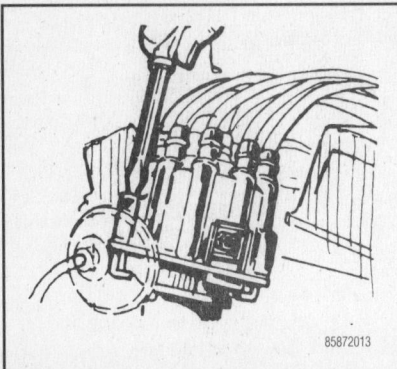

Fig. 14 Distributor cap spring latch locations

Fig. 15 The rotor is held on by 2 screws

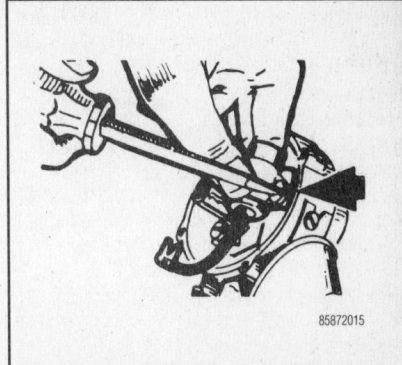

Fig. 16 The condenser is held in place by a screw and a clamp

85872016

Fig. 17 Install the point set on the breaker plate and then attach the wires

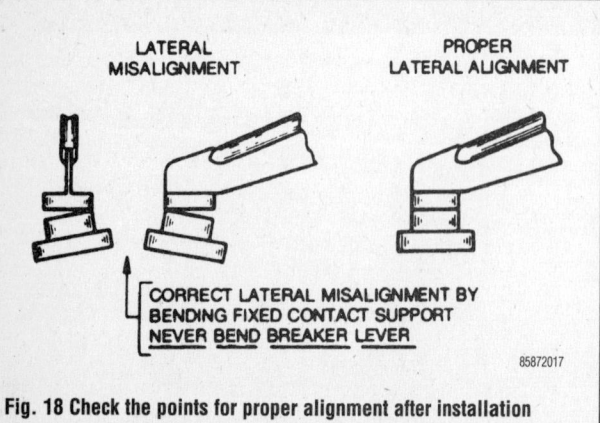

LATERAL MISALIGNMENT

PROPER LATERAL ALIGNMENT

CORRECT LATERAL MISALIGNMENT BY BENDING FIXED CONTACT SUPPORT NEVER BEND BREAKER LEVER

85872017

Fig. 18 Check the points for proper alignment after installation

if you are installing the one-piece point/condenser set. Push the rotor firmly down into place. It will only go on one way. Tighten rotor screws. If the rotor is not installed properly, it will probably break when the starter is operated.

17. Replace the distributor cap.

18. If a dwell meter is available, check the dwell.

➡This hookup may not apply to electronic, capacitive discharge, or other special ignition systems. Some dwell meters won't work at all with such systems.

1975 and Later Models

These engines use the breakerless HEI (High Energy Ignition) system. Since there is no mechanical contact, there is no wear or need for periodic service. There is an item in the distributor that resembles a condenser; it is a radio interference suppression capacitor which requires no service.

Dwell Angle

Dwell angle is the amount of time (measured in degrees of distributor cam rotation) that the contact points remain closed. Initial point gap determines dwell angle. If the points are set too wide they open gradually and dwell angle (the time they remain closed) is small. This wide gap causes excessive arcing at the points and, because of this, point burning. This small dwell doesn't give the coil sufficient time to build up maximum energy and so coil output decreases. If the points are set too close, the dwell is increased, but the points may bounce at higher speeds and the idle becomes rough making starting harder. The wider the point opening, the smaller the dwell. The smaller the gap, the larger the dwell. Adjusting the dwell by making the initial point gap setting with a feeler gauge is sufficient to get the car started but a finer adjustment should be made. A dwell meter is needed to check the adjustment.

Connect the red lead (positive) wire of the meter to the distributor primary wire connection on the positive (+) side of the coil, and the black ground (negative) wire of the meter to a good ground on the engine. The dwell angle may be checked either with the engine cranking or running, although the reading will be more accurate if the engine is running. With the engine cranking, the reading will fluctuate between 0 dwell and the maximum figure for that angle. While cranking, the maximum figure is the correct one.

Dwell angle is set electronically on HEI distributors, requiring no adjustment or checking.

ADJUSTMENT

1967–74 Models

◆ See Figures 19 and 20

Dwell can be checked with the engine running or cranking. Decrease dwell by increasing the point gap; or increase dwell by decreasing the gap. Dwell angle is simply the number of degrees of distributor shaft rotation during which the points stay closed. Theoretically, if the point gap is correct, the dwell should also be correct or nearly so. Adjustment with a dwell meter produces more exact, consistent results since it is a dynamic adjustment. If dwell varies more than 3 degrees from idle speed to 1,750 engine rpm, the distributor is worn.

1. Open the metal window on the distributor and insert a ⅛ in. Allen

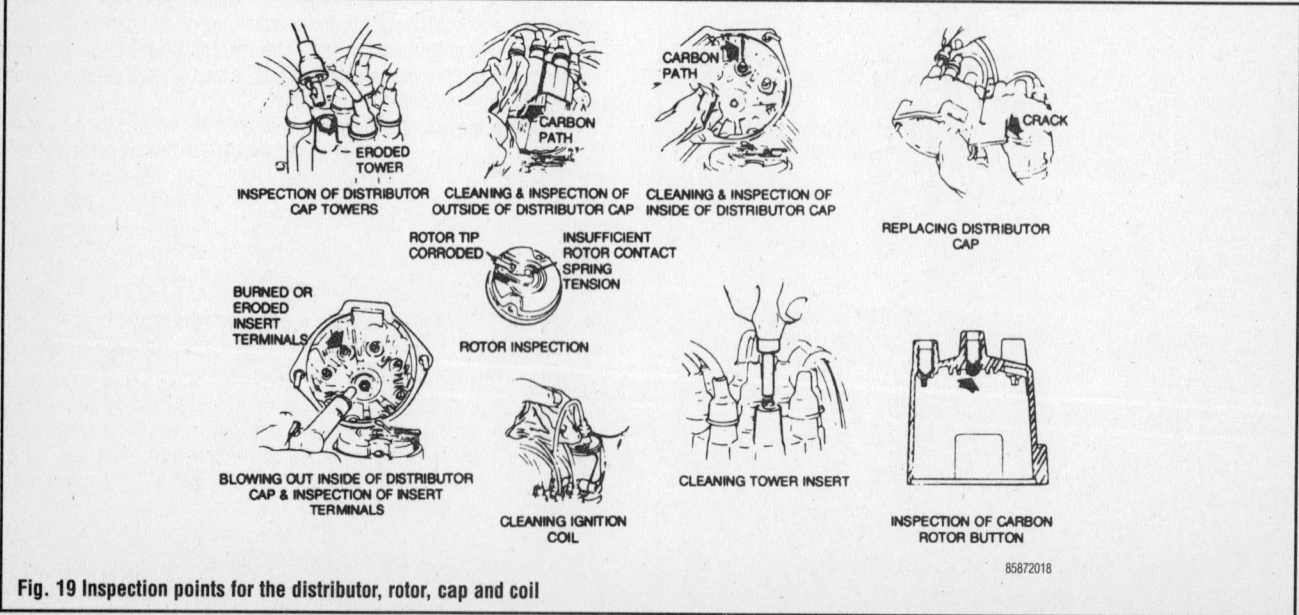

INSPECTION OF DISTRIBUTOR CAP TOWERS — ERODED TOWER

CLEANING & INSPECTION OF OUTSIDE OF DISTRIBUTOR CAP — CARBON PATH

CLEANING & INSPECTION OF INSIDE OF DISTRIBUTOR CAP — CARBON PATH

REPLACING DISTRIBUTOR CAP — CRACK

ROTOR TIP CORRODED   INSUFFICIENT ROTOR CONTACT SPRING TENSION

BURNED OR ERODED INSERT TERMINALS

ROTOR INSPECTION

BLOWING OUT INSIDE OF DISTRIBUTOR CAP & INSPECTION OF INSERT TERMINALS

CLEANING IGNITION COIL

CLEANING TOWER INSERT

INSPECTION OF CARBON ROTOR BUTTON

85872018

Fig. 19 Inspection points for the distributor, rotor, cap and coil

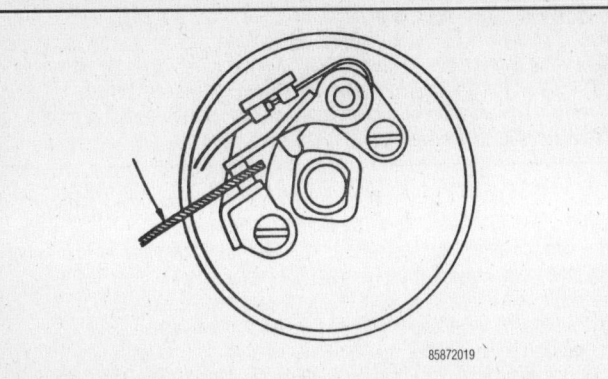

Fig. 20 The arrow indicates the feeler gauge used to check the point gap

wrench. Turn until the meter shows the correct reading. Be sure to snap the window closed.

2. An approximate dwell adjustment can be made without a meter. Turn the adjusting screw clockwise until the engine begins to misfire, then turn it out ½ turn.

3. If the engine won't start, check:
   a. That all the spark plug wires are in place.
   b. That the rotor has been installed.
   c. That the two (or three) wires inside the distributor are connected.
   d. That the points open and close when the engine turns.
   e. That the gap is correct.

4. After the first 200 miles or so on a new set of points, the point gap often closes up due to initial rubbing block wear. For best performance, recheck the dwell (or gap) at this time. This quick initial wear is the reason the factory recommends 0.003 in. (0.08mm) more gap on new points.

5. Since changing the gap affects the ignition timing, the timing should be checked and adjusted as necessary after each point replacement or adjustment.

HIGH ENERGY IGNITION (HEI) SYSTEM

▶ **See Figure 21**

The High Energy Ignition system was optional in 1974 and became standard equipment in 1975. The HEI system consists of an ignition coil, electronic module and a magnetic pick-up assembly all within the distributor.

Starting 1978, an electronic spark selection system was introduced on the 350 V8. The system continuously and automatically controls ignition system spark advance (or retard) to improve fuel economy, reduce emissions, and aid hot starting.

The distributor, in addition to housing the mechanical and vacuum advance mechanisms (1975 through 1980), contains the ignition coil, the electronic control module, and the magnetic triggering device. The magnetic pick-up assembly contains a permanent magnet, a pole piece with internal teeth, and a pick-up coil (not to be confused with the ignition coil).

The 1981 and later HEI distributors are equipped with Electronic Spark Control (EST). This system uses a one piece distributor, with the ignition coil mounted in the distributor cap similar to the earlier system. For more information on EST, refer to Section 4.

All spark timing changes in the 1981 and later distributors are performed electronically by the Electronic Control Module (ECM), which monitors information from various engine sensors, computes the desired spark timing and then signals the distributor to change the timing accordingly. No vacuum or mechanical advance units are used.

In the HEI system, as in other electronic ignition systems, the breaker points have been replaced with an electronic switch-a transistor-which is located within the control module. This switching transistor performs the same function the points did in older conventional ignition systems; it simply turns coil primary current on and off at the correct time. So, electronic and conventional points-type ignition systems operate on the same basic principle.

The module which houses the switching transistor is controlled (turned on and off) by a magnetically generated impulse, induced in the pick-up coil. When the teeth of the rotating timer align with the teeth of the pole piece, the induced voltage in the pick-up coil signals the electronic module to open the coil primary circuit. The primary current then decreases, and a high voltage is induced in the ignition coil secondary windings which is then directed through the rotor and spark plug wires to fire the spark plugs.

In essence, the pick-up coil module system simply replaces the conventional breaker points and condenser. The condenser found within the distributor is for radio suppression purposes only and has nothing to do with the ignition process. The module automatically controls the dwell period, increasing it with increasing engine speed. Since dwell is automatically controlled, it cannot be adjusted. The module itself is non-adjustable and non-repairable and must be replaced if found defective.

Electronic Spark Selection

Electronic spark selection is used on 1978 Cadillac Sevilles along with all 1979 Seville, Eldorado, Limousine, Commercial Chassis and carbureted standard Cadillac models. In 1980 it can be found on most Cadillac models except diesels. The system advances or retards ignition timing according to conditions. Timing is retarded during starting to reduce the load on the starter. By delaying ignition until the piston is nearly at TDC, the piston is not forced downward prematurely. Timing is also retarded on California cars when coolant temperature is below 130°F. This reduces catalyst warm-up time. Spark timing is advanced during high engine vacuum/high engine rpm conditions (highway cruise) to increase efficiency and fuel economy.

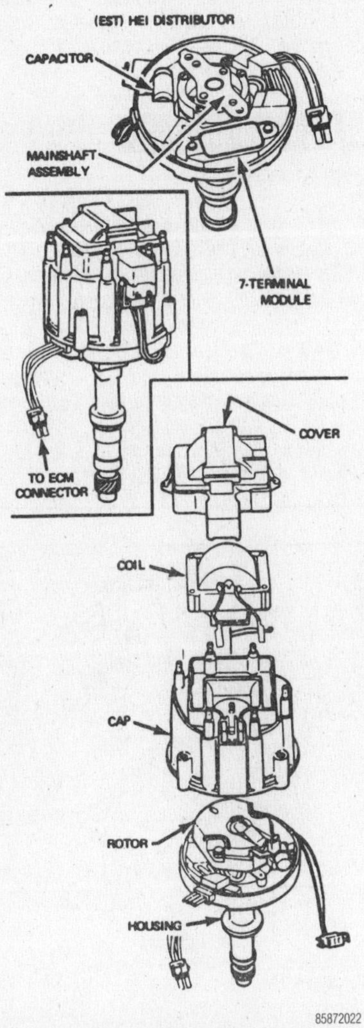

Fig. 21 HEI distributor components when equipped with EST—note the absence of the vacuum advance unit

Components used in addition to the G.M. HEI system are an electronic decoder and a five-pin distributor module. Some 1980 models use a seven-pin distributor module. The HEI pick-up coil sends its signal to the decoder to provide engine speed and ignition timing information. The decoder signal sends its information on through the connector. The signal either delays or does not delay coil primary current shut down. Coolant temperature on California models is sensed at the EGR solenoid except on 1980 carbureted models, which are equipped with a three-way coolant temperature switch instead. This system is not serviceable without special diagnostic tools. This system was not used after 1980.

HEI System Precautions

Before going on to troubleshooting, it might be a good idea to take note of the following precautions:

TIMING LIGHT USE

Inductive pick-up timing lights are the best kind to use with HEI. Timing lights which connect between the spark plug and the spark plug wire occasionally (not always) give false readings.

SPARK PLUG WIRES

The plug wires used with HEI systems are of a different construction than conventional wires. When replacing them, make sure you get the correct wires, since conventional wires won't carry the voltage. Also, handle them carefully to avoid cracking or splitting them and never pierce them.

TACHOMETER USE

Not all tachometers will operate or indicate correctly when used on a HEI system. While some tachometers may give a reading, this does not necessarily mean the reading is correct. In addition, some tachometers hook up differently from others. If you can't figure out whether or not your tachometer will work on your car, check with the tachometer manufacturer. Dwell readings, of course, have no significance at all.

HEI SYSTEM TESTERS

Instruments designed specifically for testing HEI systems are available from several tool manufacturers. Some of these will even test the module itself. However, the tests given in the following section will require only an ohmmeter and a voltmeter.

Troubleshooting the HEI System

The symptoms of a defective component within the HEI system are exactly the same as those you would encounter in a conventional system. Some of these symptoms are:
- Hard or no starting
- Rough idle
- Poor fuel economy
- Engine misses under load or while accelerating

If you suspect a problem in your ignition system, there are certain preliminary checks which you should carry out before you begin to check the electronic portions of the system. First, it is extremely important to make sure the vehicle battery is in a good state of charge. A defective or poorly charged battery will cause the various components of the ignition system to read incorrectly when they are being tested. Second, make sure all wiring connections are clean and tight, not only at the battery, but also at the distributor cap, ignition coil, and at the electronic control module.

Since the only change between electronic and conventional ignition systems is in the distributor component area, it is imperative to check the secondary ignition circuit first. If the secondary circuit checks out properly, then the engine condition is probably not the fault of the ignition system. To check the secondary ignition system, perform a simple spark test. Remove one of the plug wires and insert some sort of extension in the plug socket. An old spark plug with the ground electrode removed makes a good extension. Hold the wire and extension (using a suitable insulated tool) about ¼ in. (6mm) away from the block and crank the engine. If a normal spark occurs, then the problem is most likely not in the ignition system. Check for fuel system problems, or fouled spark plugs.

If, however, there is no spark or a weak spark, then further ignition system testing will have to be done. Troubleshooting techniques fall into two categories, depending on the nature of the problem. The categories are (1) Engine cranks, but won't start or (2) Engine runs rough or cuts out.

ENGINE FAILS TO START

If the engine won't start, perform a spark test as described earlier. This will narrow the problem area down considerably. If no spark occurs, check for the presence of normal battery voltage at the battery (BAT) terminal in the distributor cap. The ignition switch must be in the **ON** position for this test. Either a voltmeter or a test light may be used for this test. Connect the test light wire to ground and the probe end to the BAT terminal at the distributor. If the light comes on, you have voltage to the distributor. If the light fails to come on, this indicates an open circuit in the ignition primary wiring leading to the distributor. In this case, you will have to check wiring continuity back to the ignition switch using a test light. If there is battery voltage at the BAT terminal, but no spark at the plugs, then the problem lies within the distributor assembly. Go on to the distributor components test section.

ENGINE RUNS ROUGH OR CUTS OUT

1. Make sure the plug wires are in good shape first. There should be no obvious cracks or breaks. You can check the plug wires with an ohmmeter, but do not pierce the wires with a probe. Check the chart for the correct plug wire resistance.

2. If the plug wires are OK, remove the cap assembly and check for moisture, cracks, chips, or carbon tracks, or any other high voltage leaks or failures. Replace the cap if any defects are found. Make sure the timer wheel rotates when the engine is cranked. If everything is all right so far, go on to the distributor components test section following.

Distributor Components Testing

▶ See Figures 22, 23 and 24

If the trouble has been narrowed down to the units within the distributor, the following tests can help pinpoint the defective component. An ohmmeter with both high and low ranges should be used. These tests are made with the cap assembly removed and the battery wire disconnected. If a tachometer is connected to the TACH terminal, disconnect it before making these tests.

1. Connect an ohmmeter between the TACH and BAT terminals in the distributor cap. The primary coil resistance should be less than one ohm.

2. To check the coil secondary resistance, connect an ohmmeter between the rotor button and the BAT terminal. Note the reading. Connect the ohmmeter between the rotor button and the TACH terminal. Note the reading. The resistance in both cases should be between 6,000–30,000 ohms. Be sure to test between the rotor button and both the BAT and TACH terminals.

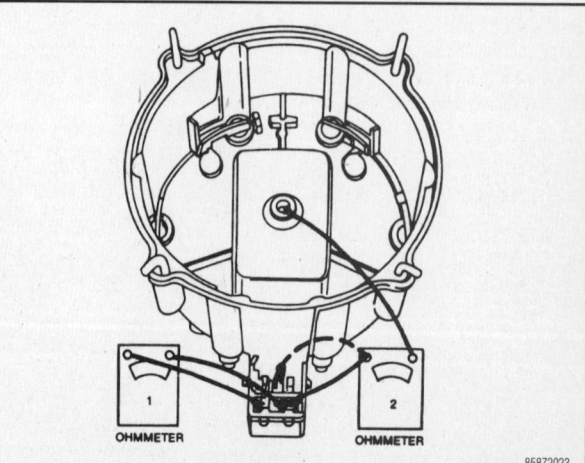

85872023

Fig. 22 Checking coil resistance—Ohmmeter 1 shows primary coil resistance connection—Ohmmeter 2 shows the secondary resistance connection (1980 shown, others similar)

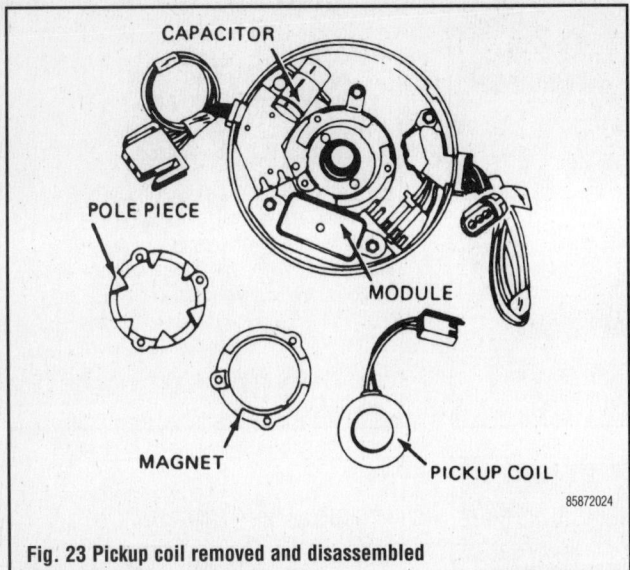

Fig. 23 Pickup coil removed and disassembled

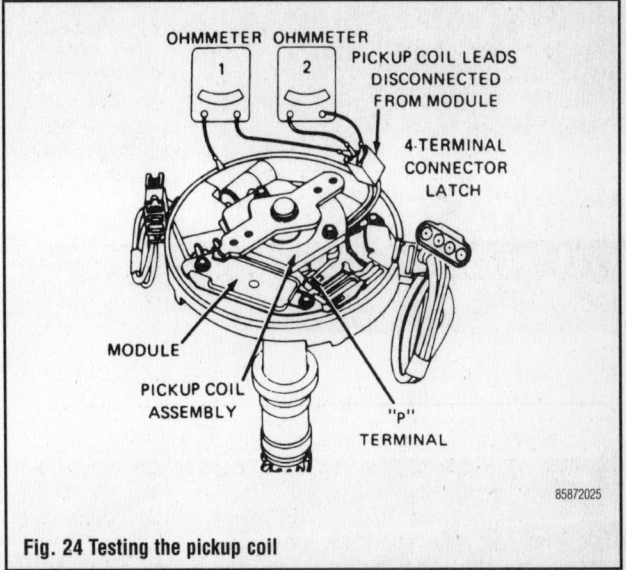

Fig. 24 Testing the pickup coil

3. Replace the coil only if the readings in Step 1 and Step 2 are infinite.

➥These resistance checks will not disclose shorted coil windings. This condition can only be detected with scope analysis or a suitably designed coil tester. If these instruments are unavailable, replace the coil with a known good coil as a final coil test.

4. To test the pick-up coil, first disconnect the white and green module leads. Set the ohmmeter on the high scale and connect it between a ground and either the white or green lead. Any resistance measurement less than infinity requires replacement of the pick-up coil.

5. Pick-up coil continuity is tested by connecting the ohmmeter (on low range) between the white and green leads. Normal resistance is between 650–850 ohms, or 500–1500 ohms on 1977 and later models. Move the vacuum advance arm while performing this test. This will detect any break in coil continuity. Such a condition can cause intermittent misfiring. Replace the pick-up coil if the reading is outside the specified limits.

6. If no defects have been found at this time, and you still have a problem, then the module will have to be checked. If you do not have access to a module tester, the only possible alternative is a substitution test. If the module fails the substitution test, replace it.

HEI System Maintenance

Except for periodic checks of the spark plug wires, and an occasional check of the distributor cap for cracks (see Steps 1 and 2 under Engine Runs Rough or Cuts Out for details), no maintenance is required on the HEI System. No periodic lubrication is necessary; engine oil lubricates the lower bushing, and an oil-filled reservoir lubricates the upper bushing.

Component Replacement

♦ See Figures 25 thru 38

INTEGRAL IGNITION COIL

1. Disconnect the feed and module wire terminal connectors from the distributor cap.
2. Remove the ignition set retainer.
3. Remove the 4 coil cover-to-distributor cap screws and the coil cover.
4. Remove the 4 coil-to-distributor cap screws.
5. Using a blunt drift, press the coil wire spade terminals up out of distributor cap.
6. Lift the coil up out of the distributor cap.
7. Remove and clean the coil spring, rubber seal washer and coil cavity of the distributor cap.
8. Coat the rubber seal with a dielectric lubricant furnished in the replacement ignition coil package.
9. Reverse the above procedures to install.

DISTRIBUTOR CAP

1. Remove the feed and module wire terminal connectors from the distributor cap.
2. Remove the retainer and spark plug wires from the cap.
3. Depress and release the 4 distributor cap-to-housing retainers and lift off the cap assembly.
4. Remove the 4 coil cover screws and cover.

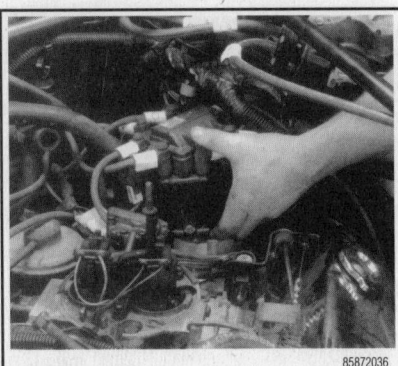

Fig. 25 Removing the HEI distributor cap assembly

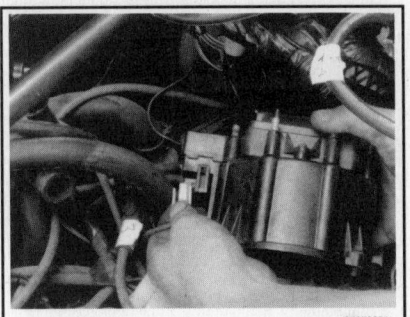

Fig. 26 Removing the HEI distributor cap to-engine (white connector) wiring connection

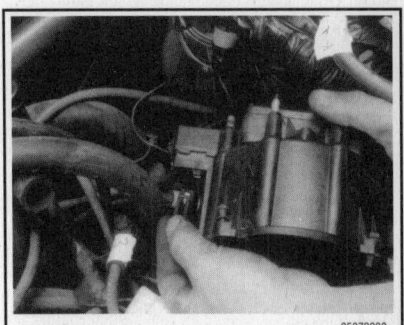

Fig. 27 Removing the HEI distributor cap-to-engine (black connector) wiring connection

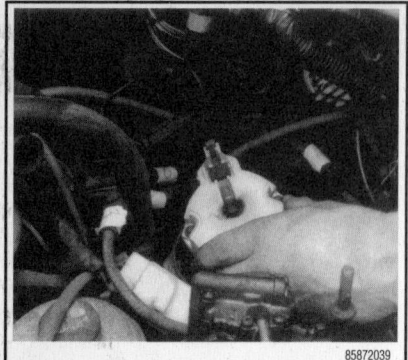

Fig. 28 View of the HEI distributor rotor

Fig. 29 View of the HEI distributor wiring

Fig. 30 View of the HEI distributor cap assembly

Fig. 31 Inside view of the HEI distributor cap—note the carbon build up—this cap should be replaced

Fig. 32 Outside view of the HEI distributor cap—note the electrical connections

Fig. 33 Removing the HEI distributor cap assembly cover

Fig. 34 Removing the HEI distributor ignition coil spade terminals

Fig. 35 Removing the HEI distributor ignition coil

Fig. 36 Installing the HEI distributor ignition coil spring—note correct position

Fig. 37 Installing the HEI distributor ignition coil rubber seal washer

Fig. 38 View of the HEI distributor ignition coil spring and rubber seal washer

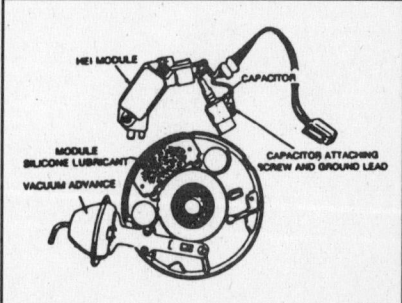

Fig. 39 Be sure to coat the mating surface with silicone lubricant when replacing the HEI module

5. Using a finger or a blunt drift, push the spade terminals up out of the distributor cap.

6. Remove all 4 coil screws and lift the coil, coil spring and rubber seal washer out of the cap coil cavity.

7. Using a new distributor cap, reverse the above procedures to assemble being sure to clean and lubricate the rubber seal washer with dielectric lubricant.

ROTOR

1. Disconnect the feed and module wire connectors from the distributor.
2. Depress and release the 4 distributor cap-to-housing retainers and lift off the cap assembly.
3. Remove the two rotor attaching screws and rotor.
4. Reverse the above procedure to install.

VACUUM ADVANCE (1975–80 Models)

1. Remove the distributor cap and rotor as previously described.
2. Disconnect the vacuum hose from the vacuum advance unit.

3. Remove the two vacuum advance retaining screws, pull the advance unit outward, rotate and disengage the operating rod from its tang.
4. Reverse the above procedure to install.

MODULE

▶ **See Figure 39**

1. Remove the distributor cap and rotor as previously described.
2. Disconnect the harness connector and pick-up coil spade connectors from the module. Be careful not to damage the wires when removing the connector.
3. Remove the two screws and module from the distributor housing.
4. Coat the bottom of the new module with dielectric silicone lubricant supplied with the new module. Reverse the above procedure to install.

✳✳ WARNING

The silicone lubricant supplied with new modules must be applied, as it serves as a heat insulator and aids in module cooling. The module will "cook" itself without the lubricant.

IGNITION TIMING

▶ **See Figures 40, 41, 42, 43 and 44**

Ignition timing is the measurement, in degrees of crankshaft rotation, of the point at which the spark plugs fire in each of the cylinders. It is measured in degrees before or after Top Dead Center (TDC) of the compression stroke.

Because it takes a fraction of a second for the spark plug to ignite the mixture in the cylinder, the spark plug must fire a little before the piston reaches TDC. Otherwise, the mixture will not be completely ignited as the piston passes TDC and the full power of the explosion will not be used by the engine.

The timing measurement is given in degrees of crankshaft rotation before the piston reaches TDC (BTDC). If the setting for the ignition timing is 5 degrees BTDC, the spark plug must fire 5 degrees before each piston reaches TDC. This only holds true, however, when the engine is at idle speed.

As the engine speed increases, the pistons go faster. The spark plugs have to ignite the fuel even sooner if it is to be completely ignited when the piston reaches TDC. To do this, the distributor has various means of advancing the timing of the spark as the engine speed increases. On older vehicles, this is accomplished by centrifugal weights within the distributor and a vacuum diaphragm mounted on the side of the distributor. Newer models are equipped with EST and all spark timing changes are controlled electronically.

If the ignition is set too far advanced (BTDC), the ignition and expansion of the fuel in the cylinder will occur too soon and tend to force the piston down while it is still traveling up. This causes engine ping. If the ignition spark is set too far retarded, after TDC (ATDC), the piston will have already passed TDC and started on its way down when the fuel is ignited. This will cause the piston to be forced down for only a portion of its travel. This will result in poor engine performance and lack of power.

Timing marks consist of a notch on the rim of the crankshaft pulley and a scale of degrees attached to the front of the engine. The notch corresponds to the position of the piston in the number 1 cylinder. A stroboscopic (dynamic) timing light is used, which is hooked into the circuit of the No. 1 cylinder spark plug. Every time the spark plug fires, the timing light flashes. By aiming the timing light at the timing marks, the exact position of the piston within the cylinder can be read, since the stroboscopic flash makes the mark on the pulley appear to be standing still. Proper timing is indicated when the notch is aligned with the correct number on the scale.

There are three basic types of timing lights available. The first is a simple neon bulb with two wire connections (one for the spark plug and one for the plug wire, connecting the light in series). This type of light is quite dim, and must be held closely to the marks to be seen, but it is quite inexpensive. The second type of light operates from the car's battery. Two alligator clips connect to the battery terminals, while a third wire connects to the spark plug with an adapter. This type of light is more expensive, but the xenon bulb provides a nice bright flash which can even be seen in sunlight. The third type replaces the battery source with 110 volt house current. Some timing lights have other functions built into them, such as dwell meters, tachometers, or remote starting switches. These are convenient, in that they reduce the tangle of wires under the hood, but may duplicate the functions of the tools you already have.

If your car has electronic ignition, you should use a timing light with an inductive pickup. This pickup simply clamps onto the No. 1 spark plug wire, eliminating the adapter. It is not susceptible to crossfiring or false triggering, which may occur with a conventional light, due to the greater voltages produced by electronic ignition.

➡ **If timing procedures on the underhood tune-up sticker differ from these, always follow the underhood tune-up label when adjusting the timing.**

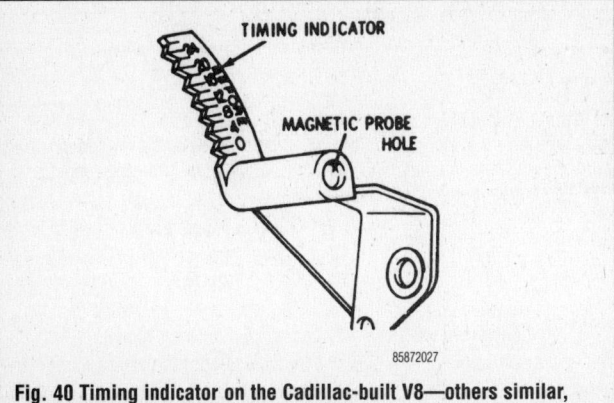

Fig. 40 Timing indicator on the Cadillac-built V8—others similar, timing mark is on the harmonic balancer

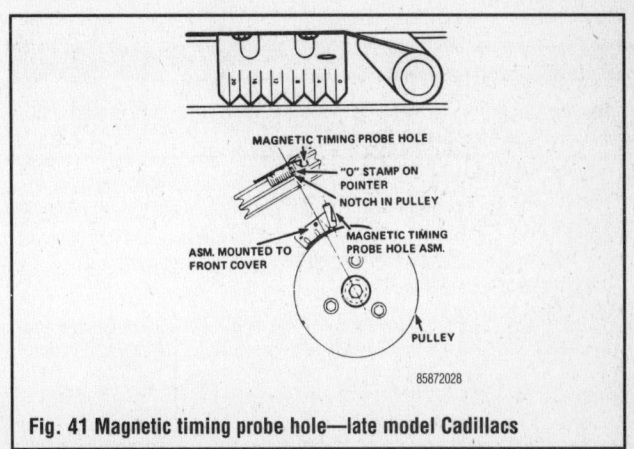

Fig. 41 Magnetic timing probe hole—late model Cadillacs

Fig. 42 Checking ignition timing with timing light

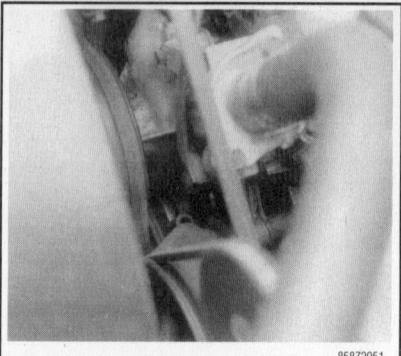

Fig. 43 The timing indicator may be difficult to see if it is not cleaned and marked

Fig. 44 Close-up view of the timing indicator and magnetic probe hole

Checking and Adjustment

EXCEPT 4.1L, 4.5L AND 5.0L ENGINES

1. Warm the engine to normal operating temperature. Shut off the engine and connect the timing light to the No. 1 spark plug (left front).

✳✳ WARNING

DO NOT, under any circumstances, pierce a spark plug wire to hook up the light. Once the insulation is broken, voltage will jump to the nearest ground, and the spark plug will not fire properly.

2. Clean off the timing marks and mark the pulley or damper notch and the timing scale with white chalk or paint. The timing notch on the damper or pulley can be elusive. Bump the engine around with the starter or turn the crankshaft with a wrench on the front pulley bolt to get it to an accessible position.

3. Disconnect and plug the vacuum advance hose at the distributor, to prevent any distributor advance. The vacuum line is the rubber hose connected to the metal cone-shaped canister on the side of the distributor. A short screw, pencil, or a golf tee can be used to plug the hose.

➡ 1981 and later models with Electronic Spark Timing have no vacuum advance, therefore you may skip the previous step, but you must disconnect the four terminal EST connector before proceeding.

4. Start the engine and adjust the idle speed to that specified in the Tune-Up Specifications chart. Some cars require that the timing be set with the transmission in Neutral, You can disconnect the idle solenoid, if any, to get the speed down. Otherwise, adjust the idle speed screw. This is to prevent any centrifugal advance of timing in the distributor.

On 1975–77 HEI systems, the tachometer connects to the TACH terminal on the distributor and to a ground. For 1978 and later models, all tachometer connections are to the TACH terminal. Some tachometers must connect to the TACH terminal and to the positive battery terminal. Some tachometers won't work at all with HEI. Consult the tachometer manufacturer if the instructions supplied with the unit do not give the proper connection.

✳✳ WARNING

Never ground the HEI TACH terminal; serious system damage will result, including module burnout.

5. Aim the timing light at the timing marks. Be careful not to touch the fan, which may appear to be standing still. Keep your clothes and hair, and timing light wires clear of the fan, belts, and pulleys. If the pulley or damper notch isn't aligned with the proper timing mark (see the Tune-Up Specifications chart), the timing will have to be adjusted.

➡ TDC or Top Dead Center corresponds to 0; B, or BTDC, or Before Top Dead Center, may be shown as BEFORE; A, or ATDC, or After Top Dead Center, may be shown as AFTER.

6. Loosen the distributor base clamp locknut. You can buy special wrenches which make this task a lot easier.

7. Turn the distributor slowly to adjust the timing, holding it by the body and not the cap. Turn the distributor in the direction of rotor rotation (found in the Firing Order illustration) to retard, and against the direction to advance.

8. Tighten the locknut. Check the timing, in case the distributor moved as you tightened it.

9. Connect the distributor vacuum hose or engage the EST connector, as applicable. Check for the proper idle speed and, adjust as applicable.

10. Shut off the engine and disconnect the light.

4.1L (V6) ENGINE

1. Connect a timing light to the No. 1 spark plug wire according to the light manufacturer's instructions. DO NOT pierce the spark plug wire to connect the timing light.

2. Set the parking brake and position the transaxle in the **PARK** position.

3. Turn the **ON** and allow it to reach normal operating temperatures. Be sure the air cleaner is installed and the air conditioning turned **OFF**.

4. Inspect the instrument panel to be sure the **CHECK ENGINE** light is turned **OFF**.

5. Disconnect the 4-wire terminal connector from the distributor. See the Underhood sticker for identification. The **CHECK ENGINE** light will turn **ON**.

6. If necessary, loosen the distributor hold-down bolt and turn the distributor until the specified timing is obtained.

➡ All V6 engines harmonic balancers have 2 timing marks, 1 measuring 1/8 in. (3mm) wide and 1 measuring the normal 1/16 in. (1.5mm) wide. The smaller mark is used for setting the timing with a hand held timing light. The 1/8 in. (3mm) wide mark is required when using magnetic timing equipment. All engines have a mounting bracket on the front cover which will accept a magnetic timing pick-up probe.

7. Tighten the mounting bolt and recheck timing to see if it changed during tightening.

8. Reconnect the electrical connector to the distributor.

9. Stop the engine, then, temporarily disconnect the negative battery terminal to cancel any stored trouble codes.

4.1L AND 4.5L (V8) ENGINES

▸ See Figure 45

➡ The engine incorporates a magnetic timing probe hole for use with special electronic timing equipment. Consult manufacturer's instructions before using this system. The following procedure is for use with the HEI—EST distributor.

1. Connect a timing light to the No. 1 spark plug wire according to the light manufacturer's instructions. DO NOT pierce the spark plug wire to connect the timing light.

2. Set the parking brake and position the transaxle in the **PARK** position.

3. Follow the instructions on the emission control label located in the engine compartment.

➡ DO NOT attempt to time the engine if it is operating on 7 cylinders for damage to the catalytic converter may occur.

4. On the 4.5L (273 cu. in.) engine, connect a jumper wire between pins **A** (ground) and **B** of the Assembly Line Data Link (ALDL) connector (located near the parking brake pedal under the dash).

➡️**By jumping the Assembly Line Data Link (ALDL) connector, the ECM will command the BCM to display a SET TIMING message on the Climate Control Driver Information Console (CCDIC). The engine will now operate at base timing. The timing can now be checked with a standard timing light at 10 degrees BTDC at 900 rpm or less.**

5. Start the engine and run it at idle speed until normal operating temperatures are reached.

6. Aim the timing light at the degree scale just over the harmonic balancer; the line on the pulley should align with the mark on the timing plate.

7. If necessary to adjust the timing, use the Distributor Wrench tool No. J–29791 or equivalent, to loosen the hold-down clamp, then, rotate the distributor until the desired ignition advance is achieved. When the correct timing is set, torque the hold-down clamp nut/bolt to 20 ft. lbs. (27 Nm).

➡️**To advance the timing, rotate the distributor opposite the normal direction of rotor rotation. Retard the timing by rotating the distributor in the normal direction of rotor rotation.**

5.0L (V8) ENGINE

◆ **See Figure 45**

1. Connect a timing light to the No. 1 spark plug wire according to the light manufacturer's instructions. DO NOT pierce the spark plug wire to connect the timing light.

2. Set the parking brake and position the transaxle in the **PARK** position.

3. Turn the engine **ON** and allow it to reach normal operating temperatures.

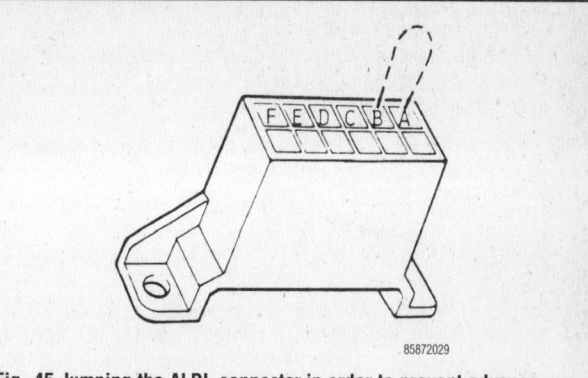

Fig. 45 Jumping the ALDL connector in order to prevent advance while setting base ignition timing

Make sure the choke is **FULLY OPEN** and the air conditioning turned **OFF**. Connect a jumper wire between pins **A** (ground) and **B** of the Assembly Line Data Link (ALDL) connector (located near the parking brake pedal under the dash).

4. Aim the timing light at the timing plate. If necessary, loosen the distributor hold-down nut and rotate the distributor until the specified timing adjustment is obtained.

5. While the engine is still operating, remove the ground wire from the diagnostic terminal.

➡️**If the ground wire is removed before the engine is turned OFF, no trouble codes will be stored.**

6. Remove the timing light.

DIESEL INJECTION TIMING

Checking and Adjustment

5.7L (V8) DIESEL ENGINE

The engine is properly timed when the injection pump timing mark is aligned between the edges of the pump adapter. If the engine is not aligned, perform the following procedures:

1. Loosen the injection pump-to-bracket nuts.

2. Turn the injection pump to align the timing marks with the adapter. Torque the injection pump-to-bracket nuts to 18 ft. lbs. (24 Nm).

➡️**Using a ¾ in. wrench on the boss at the front of the injection pump will aid in the rotation of the pump.**

3. If necessary, check and/or tighten the fuel lines. Adjust the throttle linkage. Start the engine and check the operation.

VALVE LASH

All engines covered in this guide are equipped with hydraulic valve lifters. Engines so equipped operate with zero clearance in the valve train; because of this the rocker arms do not require periodic adjustment. Initial adjustment is required, however, upon assembly of components. The hydraulic lifters themselves do not require any adjustment as part of the normal tune-up, although they occasionally become noisy (especially on high-mileage engines) and need to be replaced. Hydraulic lifter service is covered in Section 3.

IDLE SPEED AND MIXTURE ADJUSTMENTS

◆ **See Figure 46**

Idle mixture and idle speed adjustments are critical aspects of engine tune and exhaust emission control. It is important that all tune-up instructions be carefully followed to ensure good engine performance and minimum exhaust pollution. Through the succeeding model years covered in this guide, the different combinations of emissions systems on different engine models have resulted in a wide variety of tune-up specifications. See the Tune-Up Specifications chart in this section. Some models covered here have an emissions information sticker placed within easy sight in the engine compartment, giving timing, carburetor adjustment and other important tune-up information. If there is any difference between the specifications listed in this guide and those on your car's emissions sticker, always follow the specs on the sticker.

The following carburetor adjustment procedures are listed by year. Other carburetor adjustments and maintenance are found in Section 5.

➡️**If the idle mixture screws have been reset and capped at the factory, the caps should be removed only in the case of major carburetor overhaul, or if all other possible causes of poor idle have been thoroughly checked. If you must adjust the idle mixture, have the carbon monoxide (CO) concentration checked at a professional shop equipped with a CO** meter. **Mixture adjustments are included only where it is possible for the owner/mechanic to perform them.**

Carbureted Engines

1967–74 MODELS

➡️**Adjust with the air cleaner removed.**

Idle speed is adjusted at an anti-dieseling solenoid. The throttle must be opened slightly to allow the plunger to move out all the way, then it must be closed against the now-extended solenoid plunger before making the idle speed adjustment. The solenoid plunger will retract when the ignition is shut off.

1. Disconnect and plug the distributor vacuum advance hose and parking break vacuum hose (at the release cylinder). If equipped with self-leveling, remove and plug the air leveling compressor hose at the air cleaner. Remove the air cleaner but keep the vacuum hoses connected.

2. Connect a tachometer and set the parking brake with transmission in Neutral.

3. Turn in the mixture screws until they seat gently, then turn the screws out approximately 6 turns through 1973 or 4 turns for 1974.

4. Start the engine and allow it to warm up. Make sure the choke is off, the parking brake is firmly set and the drive wheels are blocked.

5. Place the car in Drive with A/C off.

➡**Press down on the hot idle compensator pin while making adjustments to Fleetwood 75 and Commercial models only.**

6. Set idle speed to 550 rpm 1967–69, 620 rpm 1970–1973 or 640 rpm for 1974 by adjusting the anti-dieseling solenoid.

7. Turn each mixture screw clockwise ¼ turn at a time alternately until an idle speed of 600 rpm is obtained.

8. Install the limiter caps, then disconnect the wire that energizes the solenoid. The plunger should retract to allow a slower idle speed of 350–400 rpm.

9. Shut off the engine, disconnect the tach, connect the vacuum lines and solenoid wire and install the air cleaner.

1975–76 MODELS

➡**Adjust with the air cleaner removed.**

Normal engine idle speed is adjusted with the idle speed screw located at the throttle lever side of the carburetor.

1. Disconnect and plug the distributor vacuum advance hose and parking brake vacuum hose (at the release cylinder). Disconnect the air leveling compressor hose at the air cleaner and plug it. Remove the air cleaner, but keep the vacuum hoses connected.

2. Connect a tachometer to the engine, set the parking brake, and block the wheels. Place the transmission in Neutral.

3. Turn in the mixture screws until they seat gently, then turn them out 5 turns.

4. Start and warm the engine to normal operating temperature. Be sure that the choke is off and that the throttle level stop tang is contacting the carburetor idle speed screw (slow idle position).

5. Place the transmission in Drive with A/C off.

6. Set the idle speed to the higher of the two figures on the underhood sticker by adjusting the idle speed screw located at the throttle level side of the carburetor.

➡**Do not depress the brake pedal on cars equipped with the Hydro-boost brake system as engine speed will be decreased.**

7. Alternately turn each mixture screw inward ¼ turn at a time until 600 rpm is reached.

8. Install replacement mixture screw limiter caps and recheck idle speed.

9. Stop the engine, remove the tachometer, connect all vacuum lines, and install the air cleaner.

1977 MODELS

➡**Adjust with the air cleaner removed.**

Normal engine idle speed is adjusted with the idle speed screw located at the throttle level side of the carburetor.

1. Disconnect and plug the distributor vacuum advance hose and parking brake vacuum hose (at the release cylinder). Disconnect the air leveling compressor hose at the air cleaner and plug it. Remove the air cleaner, but keep the vacuum hoses connected.

2. Connect a tachometer to the engine, set the parking brake, and block the wheels. Place the transmission in Neutral.

3. Turn in the mixture screws until they seat gently, then turn them out 5 turns.

4. Start and warm the engine to normal operating temperature. Be sure that the choke is off and that the throttle lever stop tang is contacting the carburetor idle speed screw (slow idle position).

5. Place the transmission in Drive with A/C off.

6. Set the idle speed to the higher of the two figures on the underhood sticker by adjusting the idle speed screw located at the throttle lever side of the carburetor.

➡**Do not depress the brake pedal on cars equipped with the Hydro-boost brake system as engine speed will be decreased.**

7. Alternately turn each mixture screw inward ¼ turn at a time until 675 rpm is reached.

8. Install replacement mixture screw limiter caps and recheck idle speed.

9. Stop the engine, remove the tachometer, connect all vacuum lines, and install the air cleaner.

1978 AND LATER MODELS

Changes have been made in the carburetors for these model years that make idle speed and mixture adjustments impossible without the use of a propane enrichment system which is not readily available to the general public.

Most 1979 and later carburetors have mixture needles concealed under staked-in screws. Mixture adjustments are possible only during carburetor overhaul.

➡**Vehicles equipped with the Computer Command Control System can't use the propane enrichment or lean drop methods of idle mixture adjustment.**

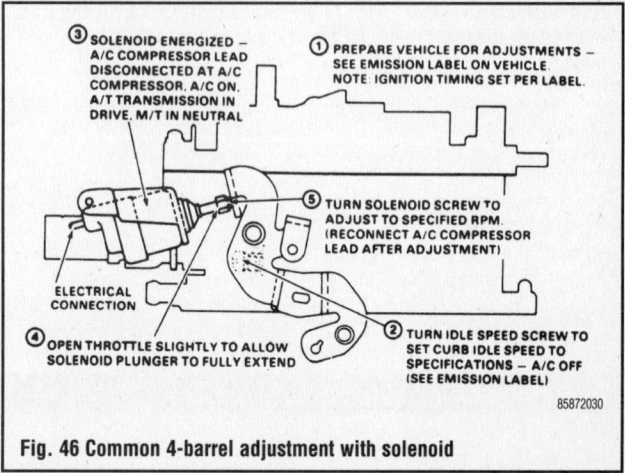

Fig. 46 Common 4-barrel adjustment with solenoid

Fuel Injected Engines

➡**Idle speed adjustment is not required unless throttle body parts have been replaced, the Throttle Position Sensor (TPS) and/or the Idle Speed Control (ISC) have been adjusted. Before performing the minimum idle speed adjustment, visually inspect the vacuum hoses for leaks, splits or cuts, the throttle body and intake manifold for vacuum leaks. Vacuum leaks can cause the engine(s) to run at a high rpm.**

ELECTRONIC FUEL INJECTION

1. Using a scratch awl, pierce and pry the idle speed screw plug from the throttle body; it can be discarded and not replaced.

2. Connect a tachometer to the engine. Set the parking brake, place the transaxle in the **PARK**, position the steering wheel in the **STRAIGHT AHEAD** position and turn **OFF** the air conditioning and all accessories.

3. Operate the engine until normal operating temperatures are reached.

4. Check and/or adjust the timing.

5. On the Climate Control Driver Information Console (CCDIC), press the "COOLER" button and wait for at least 20 seconds; this will cause the ISC motor plunger to retract. Once the motor has retracted, inspect the throttle lever to make sure it is resting on the minimum idle speed screw.

6. If the minimum idle speed it too high, use a T–20 Torx® Driver to adjust the minimum idle speed screw. The minimum idle speed should be 450–550 rpm (0–500 miles) or 450–600 rpm (above 500 miles).

7. After adjustment, disconnect the test equipment and turn the ignition switch **OFF** for 10 seconds.

8. Turn the engine **ON**, check the ISC operation and inspect the ECM and/or BCM readout for stored codes or telltale lights. Perform the diagnostics.

9. Disconnect the negative battery cable for 10 seconds; this will reset the TPS learned value in the ECM.

DIGITAL FUEL INJECTION (DFI)

1. Connect a tachometer to the engine. Set the parking brake, place the transaxle in the **PARK**, position the steering wheel in the **STRAIGHT AHEAD** position. Turn **OFF** the air conditioning and all accessories. Ground the green test connector located near the alternator.

2. Start and run the engine until normal operating temperatures are reached.

3. Check and/or adjust the timing.

4. Remove the air cleaner and plug the THERMAC vacuum tap.

5. To retract plunger of the ISC motor, perform the following procedures.

   a. Disengage the ISC connector, then engage a jumper harness to the ISC.

   b. Connect the jumper wire leading to the ISC terminal **C** to 12V at the battery or junction block.

   c. Apply finger pressure to the ISC plunger (close the throttle switch). Touch the jumper wire connected to the ISC terminal **D** to ground until the ISC plunger retracts fully and stops; DO NOT allow the ground wire to be connected for longer than necessary or damage to the ISC motor can result.

➡️**Never connect a voltage source to the ISC motor terminals A and B as damage to the internal throttle switch contacts will result.**

   d. Once the motor has retracted, inspect the throttle lever to make sure it is resting on the minimum idle speed screw.

6. If the minimum idle speed it too high, adjust the minimum idle speed screw. The minimum idle speed should be 375–500 rpm (0–500 miles) or 475–550 rpm (above 500 miles).

7. After adjustment, disconnect the test equipment and turn the ignition switch **OFF** for 10 seconds.

8. Turn the engine **ON**, check the ISC operation and inspect the ECM and/or BCM readout for stored codes or telltale lights. Perform the diagnostics.

9. Disconnect the negative battery cable for 10 seconds; this will reset the TPS learned value in the ECM.

Diesel Engines

▶ **See Figure 47**

A special tachometer with an RPM counter suitable for the 350 V8 diesel is necessary for this adjustment; a standard tach suitable for gasoline engines will not work.

1. Place the transmission in Park, block the rear wheels and firmly set the parking brake.

2. If necessary, adjust the throttle linkage as described in Section 5.

3. Start the engine and allow it to warm up for 10–15 minutes.

4. Shut off the engine and remove the air cleaner.

5. Clean off any grime from the timing probe holder on the front cover; also clean off the crankshaft balancer rim.

6. Install the magnetic probe end of the tachometer fully into the timing

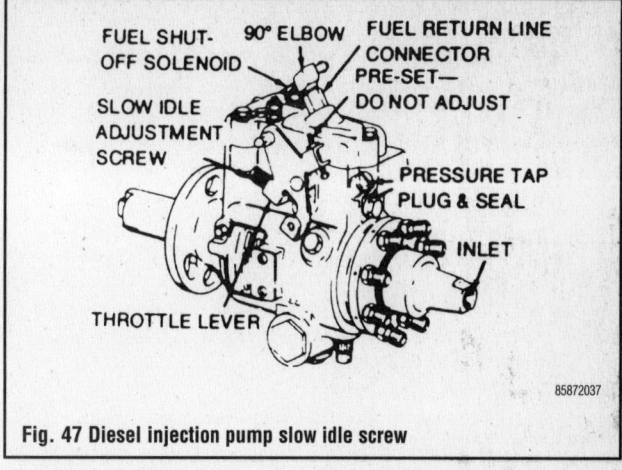

FUEL SHUT-OFF SOLENOID — 90° ELBOW — FUEL RETURN LINE CONNECTOR PRE-SET—DO NOT ADJUST — SLOW IDLE ADJUSTMENT SCREW — PRESSURE TAP PLUG & SEAL — INLET — THROTTLE LEVER

85872037

Fig. 47 Diesel injection pump slow idle screw

probe holder. Complete the remaining tachometer connections according to the tach manufacturer's instructions.

7. Disconnect the two-lead connector from the generator.

8. Make sure all electrical accessories are OFF.

➡️**At no time should either the steering wheel or the brake pedal be touched.**

9. Start the engine and place the transmission in Drive (after first making sure the parking brake is firmly applied).

10. Check the slow idle speed reading against the one printed on the underhood emissions sticker. Reset if necessary.

11. Unplug the connector from the fast idle cold advance (engine temperature) switch, and install a jumper wire between the connector terminals.

❄️❄️ WARNING

DO NOT allow the jumper to ground.

12. Check the fast idle speed and, if necessary, reset according to the specification printed on the underhood emissions sticker.

13. Remove the jumper wire and reconnect it to the temperature switch.

14. Recheck the slow idle speed and reset if necessary.

15. Shut off the engine.

16. Reconnect the leads at the generator and A/C compressor.

17. Disconnect and remove the tachometer.

18. If the car is equipped with cruise control, adjust the servo throttle rod to minimum slack, then put the clip in the first free hole closest to the bellcrank or throttle lever.

19. Install the air cleaner.

GASOLINE ENGINE TUNE-UP SPECIFICATIONS

(When analyzing compression test results, look for uniformity among cylinders rather than specific pressures)

Year	Engine V.I.N. Code	Engine No. Cyl. Displ. Cu. In. (L)	Fuel Delivery	Engine Manufacturer	Spark Plugs Orig. Type	Spark Plugs Gap (in.)	Distributor Point Dwell (deg.)	Distributor Point Gap (in.)	Ignition Timing (deg. B.T.D.C.) Automatic Transmission	Intake Valve Opens (B.T.D.C.)	Fuel Pump Pressure (psi)	Idle Speed (rpm) Automatic Transmission
1967	*	8-429 (7.0)	4 bbl	Cad.	44	0.035	30°	0.016	5B	39	5¾	500
1968-69	*	8-472 (7.7)	4 bbl	Cad.	44N	0.035	30°	0.016	5B	18	5¾	550
1970-71	R	8-472 (7.7)	4 bbl	Cad.	R46N	0.035	30°	0.016	8B	18	6	600
	S	8-500 (8.2)	4 bbl	Cad.	R46N	0.035	30°	0.016	7½B	18	6	600
1972-73	R	8-472 (7.7)	4 bbl	Cad.	R46N	0.035	30°	0.016	8B	34	5¼-6½	600/400
	S	8-500 (8.2)	4 bbl	Cad.	R46N	0.035	30°	0.016	8B	34	5¼-6½	600/400
1974	R	8-472 (7.7)	4 bbl	Cad.	R45NS	0.035	30°	0.016	10B	21	5¼-6½	600/400
	S	8-500 (8.2)	4 bbl	Cad.	R45NS	0.035	30°	0.016	10B	21	5¼-6½	600/400
	S	8-500 (8.2)	4 bbl	Cad.	R45NS	0.035	Electronic		10B	21	5¼-6½	600/400
1975	S	8-500 (8.2)	4 bbl	Cad.	R45NSX	0.060	Electronic		6B	21	5¼-6½	600/400
	S	8-500 (8.2)	EFI	Cad.	R45NSX	0.060	Electronic		12B	21	39 min.	600
1976	R	8-050 (5.7)	4 bbl	Olds.	R46SX	0.080	Electronic		10B (6B)	22	5¼-6½	600
	S	8-500 (8.2)	4 bbl	Cad.	R45NSX	0.060	Electronic		6B	21	5¼-6½	600
	S	8-500 (8.2)	EFI	Cad.	R45NSX	0.060	Electronic		12B	21	39 min.	600
1977	R	8-050 (5.7)	4 bbl	Olds.	R47SX	0.060	Electronic		10B (6B)	22	5¼-6½	650
	S	8-425 (7.0)	4 bbl	Cad.	R45NSX	0.060	Electronic		10B @ 1400	21	5¼-6½	675
	T	8-425 (7.0)	EFI	Cad.	R45NSX	0.060	Electronic		18B @ 1400	21	39 min.	675
1978	B	8-350 (5.7)	EFI	Olds.	R47SX	0.060	Electronic		10B (8B)	22	5¼-6½	600
	S	8-425 (7.0)	4 bbl	Cad.	R45NSX	0.060	Electronic		18B @ 1400	21	5¼-6½	650
	T	8-425 (7.0)	EFI	Cad.	R45NSX	0.060	Electronic		18 @ 1400	21	39 min.	650
1979	B	8-350 (5.7)	EFI	Olds.	R47SX	0.060	Electronic		10B	22	5¼-6½	600
	S	8-425 (7.0)	4 bbl	Cad.	R45NSX	0.060	Electronic		23B	21	5¼-6½	600
	T	8-425 (7.0)	EFI	Cad.	R45NSX	0.060	Electronic		18B	21	39 min.	600
1980	4	6-252 (4.1)	4 bbl	Buick	R45TSX	0.060	Electronic		15B	16	4¼-5½	550
	6	8-368 (6.0)	4 bbl	Cad.	R45NSX	0.060	Electronic		18B	11	5½-6½	575
	9	8-368 (6.0)	DFI	Cad.	R45NSX	0.060	Electronic		10B	11	12-14	575
1981	4	6-252 (4.1)	4 bbl	Buick	R45TSX	0.060	Electronic		15B	16	4¼-5¾	550 ②
	6	8-368 (6.0)	4 bbl	Cad.	R45NSX	0.060	Electronic		18B	11	5½-6½	575
	9	8-368 (6.0)	DFI	Cad.	R45NSX	0.060	Electronic		10B	16	12-14	470 ③
1982	8	8-250 (4.1)	DFI	Cad.	R43NTS6	0.060	Electronic		①	37	12-14	450
	4	6-252 (4.1)	4 bbl	Buick	R45TSX	0.060	Electronic		①	16	4¼-5¾	550 ②
	6	8-368 (6.0)	4 bbl	Cad.	R45NSX	0.060	Electronic		18B	11	5½-6½	575
	9	8-368 (6.0)	DFI	Cad.	R45NAX	0.060	Electronic		①	11	12-14	450
1983	8	8-250 (4.1)	DFI	Cad.	R43NTS6	0.060	Electronic		①	37	12-14	①
	6	8-368 (6.0)	4 bbl	Cad.	R45NSX	0.060	Electronic		18B	11	5½-6½	575
	9	8-368 (6.0)	DFI	Cad.	R45NAX	0.060	Electronic		①	11	12-14	①
1984	8	8-250 (4.1)	DFI	Cad.	R43NTS6	0.060	Electronic		①	37	12-14	①
	6	8-368 (6.0)	4 bbl	Cad.	R45NSX	0.060	Electronic		18B	11	5½-6½	575
	9	8-368 (6.0)	DFI	Cad.	R45NAX	0.060	Electronic		①	11	12-14	①

85872C01

GASOLINE ENGINE TUNE-UP SPECIFICATIONS

(When analyzing compression test results, look for uniformity among cylinders rather than specific pressures)

Year	Engine V.I.N. Code	Engine No. Cyl. Displ. Cu. In. (L)	Fuel Delivery	Engine Manufacturer	Spark Plugs Orig. Type	Spark Plugs Gap (in.)	Distributor Point Dwell (deg.)	Distributor Point Gap (in.)	Ignition Timing (deg. B.T.D.C.) Automatic Transmission	Intake Valve Opens (B.T.D.C.)	Fuel Pump Pressure (psi)	Idle Speed (rpm) Automatic Transmission
1985	8	8-250 (4.1)	DFI	Cad.	R42CLTS6	0.060	Electronic		①	①	12-14	①
1986	8	8-250 (4.1)	DFI	Cad.	R44LTS6	0.060	Electronic		①	①	12-14	①
	Y	8-307 (5.0)	4 bbl	Olds.	FR3LS6	0.060	Electronic		①	①	5½-6½	①
1987	8	8-250 (4.1)	DFI	Cad.	R44LTS6	0.060	Electronic		①	①	12-14	①
	Y	8-307 (5.0)	4 bbl	Olds.	FR3LS6	0.060	Electronic		①	①	5½-6½	①
1988-89	5	8-273 (4.5)	DFI	Cad.	R44LTS6	0.060	Electronic		①	①	12-14	①
	Y	8-307 (5.0)	4 bbl	Olds.	FR3LS6	0.060	Electronic		①	①	5½-6½	①

*Set timing with carburetor adjustment to 1100 rpm. unless sticker specifies otherwise.
B—Before Top Dead Center
Part numbers in this chart are not recommendations by Chilton for any product by brand name.
① See underhood sticker
② In Drive: A/C 680
③ Drive or Neutral

85872C1A

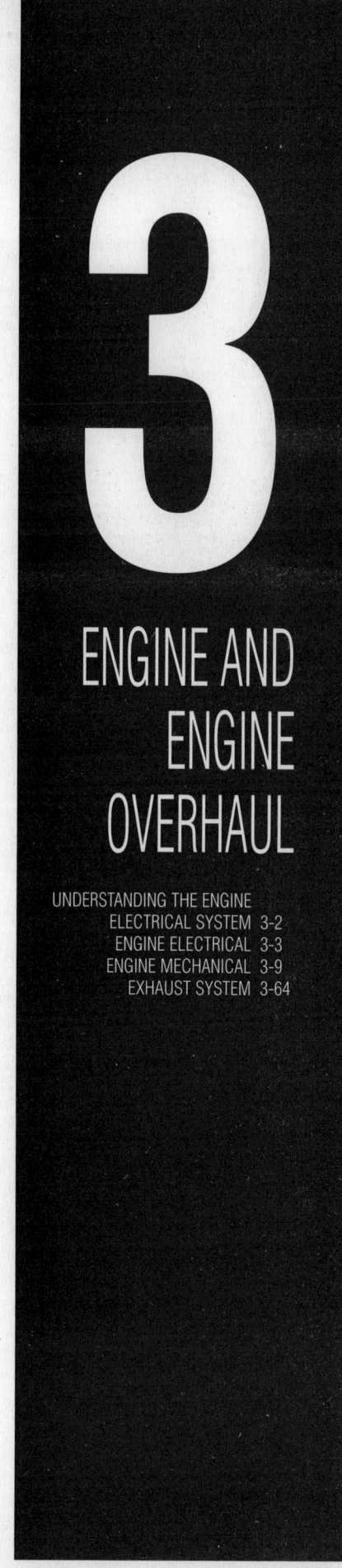

3

ENGINE AND ENGINE OVERHAUL

UNDERSTANDING THE ENGINE ELECTRICAL SYSTEM

The engine electrical system can be broken down into three separate and distinct systems:
1. The starting system
2. The charging system
3. The ignition system

Battery and Starting System

The battery is the first link in the chain of mechanisms which work together to provide cranking of the automobile engine. In most modern cars, the battery is a lead-acid electro-chemical device consisting of six two-volt (2V) subsections connected in series so the unit is capable of producing approximately 12V of electrical pressure. Each subsection, or cell, consists of a series of positive and negative plates held a short distance apart in a solution of sulfuric acid and water. The two types of plates are of dissimilar metals. This causes a chemical reaction to be set up, and it is this reaction which produces current flow from the battery when its positive and negative terminals are connected to an electrical appliance such as a lamp or motor. The continued transfer of electrons would eventually convert the sulfuric acid in the electrolyte to water, and make the two plates identical in chemical composition. As electrical energy is removed from the battery, its voltage output tends to drop. Thus, measuring battery voltage and battery electrolyte composition are two ways of checking the ability of the unit to supply power. During the starting of the engine, electrical energy is removed from the battery. However, if the charging circuit is in good condition and the operating conditions are normal, the power removed from the battery will be replaced by the generator (or alternator) which will force electrons back through the battery, reversing the normal flow, and restoring the battery to its original chemical state.

The battery and starting motor are linked by very heavy electrical cables designed to minimize resistance to the flow of current. Generally, the major power supply cable that leaves the battery goes directly to the starter, while other electrical system needs are supplied by a smaller cable. During the starter operation, power flows from the battery to the starter and is grounded through the car's frame and the battery's negative ground strap.

The starting motor is a specially designed, direct current electric motor capable of producing a very great amount of power for its size. One thing that allows the motor to produce a great deal of power is its tremendous rotating speed. It drives the engine through a tiny pinion gear (attached to the starter's armature), which drives the very large flywheel ring gear at a greatly reduced speed. Another factor allowing it to produce so much power is that only intermittent operation is required of it. Thus, little allowance for air circulation is required, and the windings can be built into a very small space.

The starter solenoid is a magnetic device which employs the small current supplied by the starting switch circuit of the ignition switch. This magnetic action moves a plunger which mechanically engages the starter and electrically closes the heavy switch which connects it to the battery. The starting switch circuit consists of the starting switch contained within the ignition switch, a transmission neutral safety switch and the wiring necessary to connect it with the starter solenoid or relay.

A pinion, which is a small gear, is mounted to a one-way drive clutch. This clutch is splined to the starter armature shaft. When the ignition switch is moved to the **START** position, the solenoid plunger slides the pinion toward the flywheel ring gear via a collar and spring. If the teeth on the pinion and flywheel match properly, the pinion will engage the flywheel immediately. If the gear teeth butt one another, the spring will be compressed and will force the gears to mesh as soon as the starter turns far enough to allow them to do so. As the solenoid plunger reaches the end of its travel, it closes the contacts that connect the battery and starter and then the engine is cranked.

As soon as the engine starts, the flywheel ring gear begins turning fast enough to drive the pinion at an extremely high rate of speed. At this point, the one-way clutch begins allowing the pinion to spin faster than the starter shaft so that the starter will not operate at excessive speed. When the ignition switch is released from the starter position, the solenoid is de-energized, and a spring contained within the solenoid assembly pulls the gear out of mesh and interrupts the current flow to the starter.

Some starters employ a separate relay, mounted away from the starter, to switch the motor and solenoid current on and off. The relay thus replaces the solenoid electrical switch, but does not eliminate the need for a solenoid mounted on the starter used to mechanically engage the starter drive gears. The relay is used to reduce the amount of current the starting switch must carry.

The Charging System

The automobile charging system provides electrical power for operation of the vehicle's ignition and starting systems as well as all electrical accessories. The battery serves as an electrical surge or storage tank, storing (in chemical form) the energy originally produced by the engine-driven generator. The system also provides a means of regulating generator output to protect the battery from being overcharged and to avoid excessive voltage to the accessories.

The storage battery is a chemical device incorporating parallel lead plates in a tank containing a sulfuric acid-water solution. Adjacent plates are slightly dissimilar, and the chemical reaction of the two dissimilar plates produces electrical energy when the battery is connected to a load such as the starter motor. The chemical reaction is reversible, so that when the generator is producing a voltage (electrical pressure) greater than that produced by the battery, electricity is forced into the battery, and the battery is returned to its fully charged state.

The vehicle's generator is driven mechanically, through V-belts, by the engine crankshaft. It consists of two coils of fine wire, one stationary (the stator), and one movable (the rotor). The rotor may also be known as the armature, and consists of fine wire wrapped around an iron core which is mounted on a shaft.

The electricity which flows through the two coils of wire (provided initially by the battery in some cases) creates an intense magnetic field around both rotor and stator, and the interaction between the two fields creates voltage, allowing the generator to power the accessories and charge the battery. There are two types of generators; the earlier is the direct current (DC) type. The current produced by the DC generator is generated in the armature and carried off the spinning armature by stationary brushes contacting the commutator. The commutator is a series of smooth metal contact plates on the end of the armature. The commutator plates, which are separated from one another by a very short gap, are connected to the armature circuits so that current will flow in one direction only in the wires carrying the generator output. The generator stator consists of two stationary coils of wire which draw some of the output current of the generator to form a powerful magnetic field and create the interaction of fields which generates the voltage. The generator field is wired in series with the regulator.

Newer automobiles use alternating current generators or alternators because they are more efficient, can be rotated at higher speeds, and have fewer brush problems. In an alternator, the field rotates while all the current produced passes only through the stator windings. The brushes bear against continuous slip rings rather than a commutator. This causes the current produced to periodically reverse the direction of its flow. Diodes (electrical one-way switches) block the flow of current from traveling in the wrong direction. A series of diodes is wired together to permit the alternating flow of the stator to be converted to a pulsating, but unidirectional flow at the alternator output. The alternator's field is wired in series with the voltage regulator.

The regulator consists of several circuits. Each circuit has a core, or magnetic coil of wire, which operates a switch. Each switch is connected to ground through one or more resistors. The coil of wire responds directly to system voltage. When the voltage reaches the required level, the magnetic field created by the winding of wire closes the switch and inserts a resistance into the generator field circuit, thus reducing the output. The contacts of the switch cycle open and close many times each second to precisely control voltage.

While alternators are self-limiting as far as maximum current is concerned, DC generators employ a current regulating circuit which responds directly to the total amount of current flowing through the generator circuit rather than to the output voltage. The current regulator is similar to the voltage regulator except that all system current must flow through the energizing coil on its way to the various accessories.

SAFETY PRECAUTIONS

Observing these precautions will ensure safe handling of the electrical system components, and will avoid damage to the vehicle's electrical system:
• Be absolutely sure of the polarity of a booster battery before making connections. Connect the cables positive-to-positive, and negative-to-negative. Connect positive cables first and then make the last connection to a ground on the body of the booster vehicle so that arcing cannot ignite hydrogen gas that may have accumulated near the battery. Even momentary connection of a booster battery with the polarity reversed will damage alternator diodes.

- Disconnect both vehicle battery cables before attempting to charge a battery.
- Never ground the alternator or generator output or battery terminal. Be cautious when using metal tools around a battery to avoid creating a short circuit between the terminals.
- Never ground the field circuit between the alternator and regulator.
- Never run an alternator or generator without load unless the field circuit is disconnected.
- Never attempt to polarize an alternator.

- Keep the regulator cover in place when taking voltage and current limiter readings.
- Use insulated tools when adjusting the regulator.
- Wherever DC generator-to-regulator wires have been disconnected, the generator must be repolarized. To do this with an externally grounded, light duty generator, momentarily place a jumper wire between the battery terminal and the generator terminal of the regulator. With an internally grounded heavy duty unit, disconnect the wire to the regulator field terminal and touch the regulator battery terminal with it.

ENGINE ELECTRICAL

General Information

The point type ignition system was used on the vehicles covered in this manual, until 1974. The Delco-Remy High Energy Ignition (HEI) System is a breakerless, pulse triggered, transistor controlled, inductive discharge ignition system available as an option in 1974 and as standard equipment after 1975.

There are only nine external electrical connections; the ignition switch feed wire, and the eight spark plug leads. On eight cylinder models through 1977, and all 1978 and later models, the ignition coil is located with the distributor cap, connecting directly to the rotor.

The magnetic pick-up assembly located inside the distributor contains a permanent magnet, a pole piece with internal teeth, and a pick-up coil. When the teeth of the rotating timer core and pole piece align, an induced voltage in the pick-up coil signals the electronic module to open the coil signal primary circuit. As the primary current decreases, a high voltage is induced in the secondary windings of the ignition coil, directing a spark through the rotor and high voltage leads to fire the spark plugs. The dwell period is automatically controlled by the electronic module and is increased with increasing engine rpm. The HEI System features a longer spark duration which is instrumental in firing lean and EGR diluted fuel/air mixtures. The condenser (capacitor) located within the HEI distributor is provided for noise (static) suppression purposes only and is not a regularly replaced ignition system component.

As already noted in Section 2, 1981 and later models continue to use the HEI distributor although it now incorporates on Electronic Spark Timing System (for more information on EST, please refer to Section 4). With the new EST system, all spark timing changes are performed by the Electronic Control Module (ECM) which monitors information from various engine sensors, computes the desired spark timing and then signals the distributor to change the timing accordingly. Because all timing changes are controlled electronically, no vacuum or mechanical advance systems are used whatsoever.

Ignition Coil

TESTING

1967–74 Vehicles

PRIMARY CIRCUIT WITH VOLTMETER

A quick, tentative check of the 12 volt ignition primary circuit (including ballast resistor) can be made with a simple voltmeter, as follows:

1. With engine at operating temperature, but stopped, and the distributor side of the ignition coil grounded with a jumper wire, hook up a voltmeter between the ignition coil (switch side) and a good ground.
2. Jiggle the ignition switch (switch on) and watch the meter. An unstable needle will indicate a defective ignition switch.
3. With ignition switch on (engine stopped) the voltmeter should read 5.5–7 volts for 12 volt systems.
4. Crank the engine. Voltmeter should read at least 9 volts during cranking period.
5. Now remove the jumper wire from the coil. Start the engine. Voltmeter should read from 9.0–11.5 volts (depending upon generator output) while running.

PRIMARY CIRCUIT WITH OHMMETER

To check ignition coil resistance, primary side, switch ohmmeter to low scale. Connect the ohmmeter leads across the primary terminals of the coil and read the low ohms scale.

Coils requiring ballast resistors should read about 1.0Ω resistance. 12 volt coils, not requiring external ballast resistors, should read about 4.0Ω resistance.

SECONDARY CIRCUIT WITH OHMMETER

To check ignition coil resistance, secondary side, switch ohmmeter to high scale. Connect one test lead to the distributor cap end of the coil secondary cable. Connect the other test lead to the distributor terminal of the coil. A coil in satisfactory condition should show between 4KΩ and 8KΩ on the scale. Some special coils (Mallory, etc.) may show a resistance as high as 13KΩ. If the reading is much lower than 4KΩ, the coil probably has shorted secondary turns. If the reading is extremely high (40KΩ or more) the secondary winding is either open, there is a bad connection at the coil terminal, or resistance is high in the cable.

If both primary and secondary windings of the coil test good, but the ignition system is still unsatisfactory, check the system further.

1975–89 Vehicles

▶ See Figures 1 and 2

An ohmmeter with both high and low ranges should be used. These tests are made with the cap assembly removed and the battery wire disconnected. If a tachometer is connected to the **TACH** terminal, disconnect it before making these tests.

1. Connect an ohmmeter between the **TACH** and **BAT** terminals in the distributor cap. The primary coil resistance should be less than 1Ω.
2. To check the coil secondary resistance, connect an ohmmeter between the rotor button and the **BAT** terminal. Note the reading. Connect the ohmmeter between the rotor button and the **TACH** terminal. Note the reading. The resistance in both cases should be between 6KΩ and 30KΩ. Be sure to test between the rotor button and both the **BAT** and **TACH** terminals.
3. Replace the coil only if the readings in Step 1 and Step 2 are infinite.

➡ **These resistance checks will not disclose shorted coil windings. This condition can only be detected with scope analysis or a suitable designed coil tester. If these instruments are unavailable, replace the coil with a known good coil as a final coil test.**

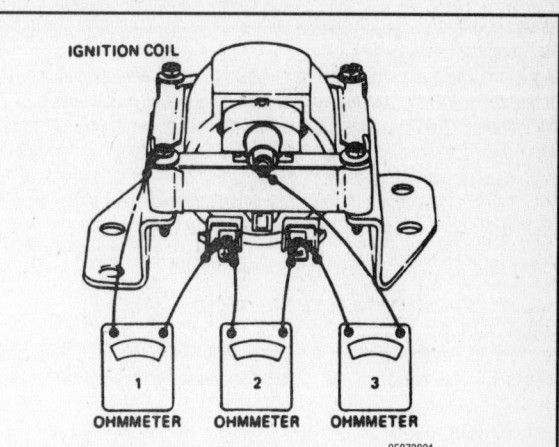

85873001

Fig. 1 Testing the external HEI ignition coil— Test 1: use high scale, reading should be very high or infinite. Test 2: use low scale, reading should be very low or zero. Test 3: use high scale, reading should not be infinite

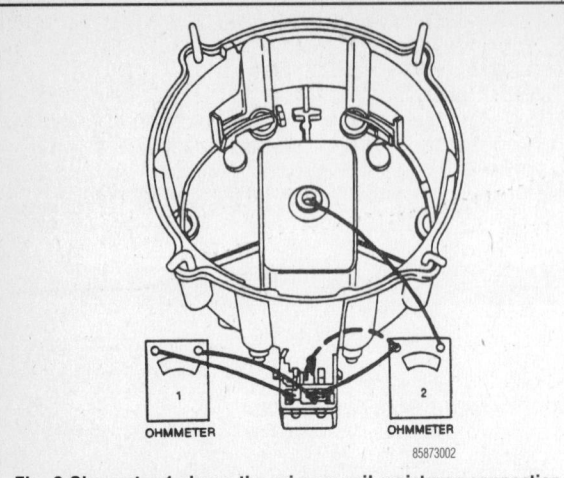

Fig. 2 Ohmmeter 1 shows the primary coil resistance connection. Ohmmeter 2 shows the secondary resistance connection (1980 shown, most models similar)

REMOVAL & INSTALLATION

1967–74 Vehicles

1. Remove the ignition switch-to-coil lead from the coil.
2. Unfasten the distributor leads from the coil.
3. Remove the screws which secure the coil to the engine and lift it off.
4. Installation is the reverse of removal.

1975–89 Vehicles

1. Disconnect the feed and module wire terminal connectors from the distributor cap.
2. Remove the ignition wire set retainer.
3. Remove the 4 coil cover-to-distributor cap screws.
4. Using a blunt drift, press the coil wire spade terminals up out of distributor cap.
5. Lift the coil up out of the distributor cap.
6. Remove and clean the coil spring, rubber seal washer and coil cavity of the distributor cap.
7. Reverse the above procedures to install.

Ignition Module

REMOVAL & INSTALLATION

▶ **See Figures 3 and 4**

1. Remove the distributor cap and rotor as previously described.
2. Disconnect the harness connector and pick-up coil spade connectors from the module (note their positions).
3. Remove the two screws and module from the distributor housing.
4. Coat the bottom of the new module with silicone dielectric compound.

➡**If a five terminal or seven terminal module is replaced, the ignition timing must be checked and reset as necessary.**

5. To install, reverse the removal procedures.

Distributor

REMOVAL & INSTALLATION

Point Type Ignition

1. Remove the distributor cap and position it out of the way.
2. Disconnect the primary coil wire and the vacuum advance hose.

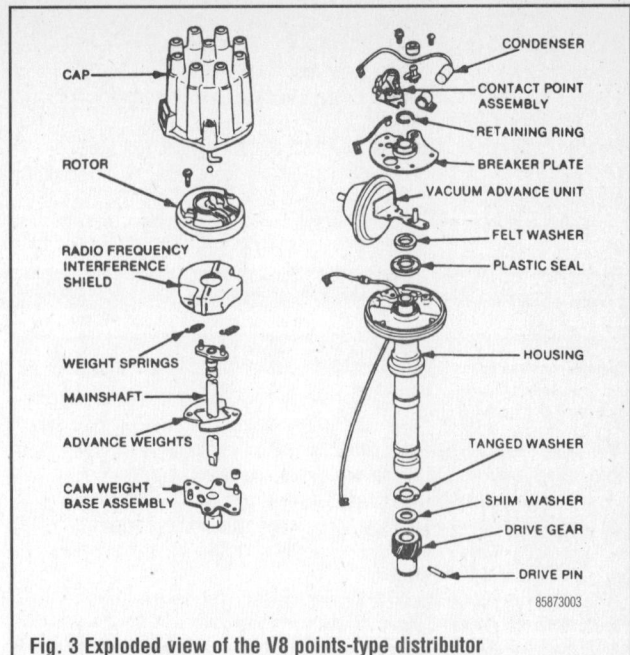

Fig. 3 Exploded view of the V8 points-type distributor

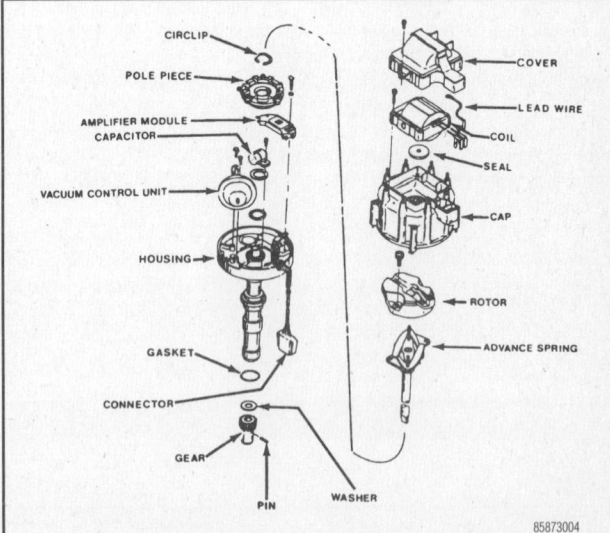

Fig. 4 Exploded view of the HEI distributor (1981 and later models have no vacuum advance unit)

3. Scribe a mark on the distributor body and the engine block showing their relationship. Mark the distributor housing to show the direction in which the rotor is pointing. Note the positioning of the vacuum advance unit.
4. Remove the hold-down bolt and clamp and remove the distributor.
To install the distributor with the engine undisturbed:
5. Reinsert the distributor into its opening, aligning the previously made marks on the housing and the engine block.
6. The rotor may have to be turned either way a slight amount to align the rotor-to-housing marks.
7. Install the retaining clamp and bolt. Install the distributor cap, primary wire or electrical connector, and the vacuum hose.
8. Start the engine and check the ignition timing.
To install the distributor with the engine disturbed:
9. Turn the engine to bring the No. 1 piston to the top of its compression stroke. This may be determined by inserting a clean rag into the No. 1 spark plug hole and slowly turning the engine over. When the timing mark on the crankshaft pulley aligns with the 0 on the timing scale and the rag is blown out by compression, the No. 1 piston is at top dead center (TDC).

10. Install the distributor to the engine block so that the vacuum advance unit points in the correct direction.

11. Turn the rotor so that it will point to the No. 1 terminal in the cap.

12. Install the distributor into the engine block. It may be necessary to turn the rotor a little in either direction in order to engage the gears.

13. Tap the starter a few times to ensure that the oil pump shaft is mated to the distributor shaft.

14. Bring the engine to No. 1 TDC again and check to see that the rotor is indeed pointing toward the No. 1 terminal of the cap.

15. After correct positioning is assured, turn the distributor housing so that the points are just opening. Tighten the retaining clamp.

16. Install the cap and primary wire. Check the ignition timing. Install the vacuum hose.

HEI Distributor

▶ **See Figures 5, 6 and 7**

➡ **On DFI systems (Digital Fuel Injection), the malfunction trouble codes must be cleared after removal or adjustment of the distributor. This is accomplished by removing battery voltage to terminal "R" for 10 seconds. See the CCC system in Section 4.**

1. Disconnect the ground cable from the battery.

2. Tag and disconnect the feed and module terminal connectors from the distributor cap.

3. Disconnect the hose at the vacuum advance (1975–80 only).

4. Depress and release the 4 distributor cap-to-housing retainers and lift off the cap assembly.

11. Connect the feed and module connectors to the distributor cap.

12. Connect a timing light to the engine and plug the vacuum hose.

13. Connect the ground cable to the battery.

14. Start the engine and set the timing.

15. Turn the engine off and tighten the distributor clamp bolt. Disconnect the timing light and unplug and connect the hose to the vacuum advance.

Alternator

▶ **See Figures 8 and 9**

ALTERNATOR PRECAUTIONS

To prevent serious damage to the alternator and the rest of the charging system, the following precautions must be observed:

1. When installing a battery, make sure that the positive cable is connected to the positive terminal and the negative to the negative.

2. When jump-starting the car with another battery, make sure that like terminals are connected. This also applies when using a battery charger.

3. Never operate the alternator with the battery disconnected or otherwise on an uncontrolled open circuit. Double check to see that all connections are tight.

4. Do not short across or ground any alternator or regulator terminals.

5. Do not try to polarize the alternator.

6. Do not apply full battery voltage to the field (brown) connector.

7. Always disconnect the battery ground cable before disconnecting the alternator lead.

Fig. 5 Remove all electrical connections before removing the distributor assembly

Fig. 6 Removing distributor assembly hold-down bolt—note special wrench is used

Fig. 7 Removing the distributor assembly

5. On EFI cars, disconnect the speed sensor connector at the distributor trigger.

6. Using crayon or chalk, make locating marks on the rotor and module and on the distributor housing and engine for installation purposes.

➡ **On the 4.1L-250 and 4.5L-273 cu. in. V8 engines a special tool No. J-29791 is used to loosen the hold-down nut. Also on these engines, a thrust washer is used between the distributor drive gear and the crankcase. This washer may stick to the bottom of the distributor as it is removed. Make sure this washer is at the bottom of the distributor bore before installation.**

7. Loosen and remove the distributor clamp bolt and clamp, and lift the distributor out of the engine. Noting the relative position of the rotor and module alignment marks, make a second mark on the rotor to align it with the mark on the module.

To install:

8. With a new O-ring on the distributor housing and the second mark on the rotor aligned with the mark on the module, install the distributor, taking care to align the mark on the housing with the one on the engine. It may be necessary to lift the distributor and turn the rotor slightly to align the gears and the oil pump driveshaft.

9. With the respective marks aligned, install the clamp and bolt finger-tight.

10. Install and secure the distributor cap.

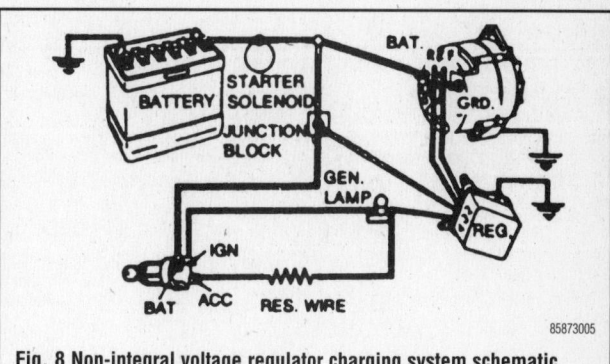

Fig. 8 Non-integral voltage regulator charging system schematic

REMOVAL

▶ **See Figure 10**

1. Disconnect the battery ground cable to prevent diode damage.

2. Tag and disconnect the alternator wiring.

3. Remove the alternator brace bolt. If the car is equipped with power steering loosen the pump brace and mount nuts. Detach the drive belt(s).

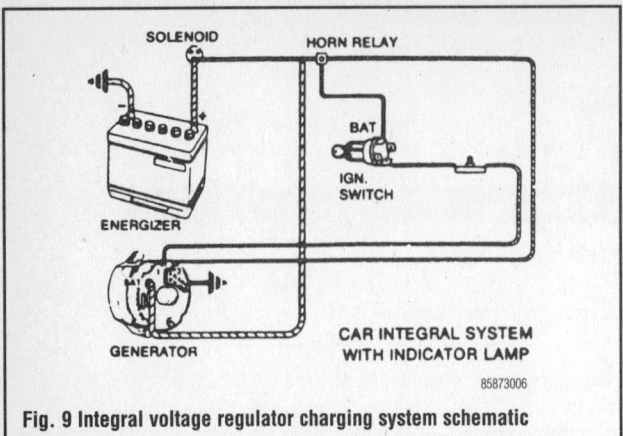

Fig. 9 Integral voltage regulator charging system schematic

4. Support the alternator and remove the mount bolt(s). Remove the unit from the vehicle.

INSTALLATION AND BELT ADJUSTMENT

➤**On Heavy Duty Alternator ONLY (100/145 amp with external voltage adjuster): after connecting the negative cable, momentarily connect a jumper wire between "Bat" and "R" alternator terminals to polarize the charging system. Start the engine and run it at fast idle for ten seconds; the charge light should go out.**

To install, reverse the above removal procedure. Alternator belt tension is quite critical. A belt that is too tight may cause alternator bearing failure; one that is too loose will cause a gradual battery discharge. For details on correct belt adjustment, see Drive Belts in Section 1.

Regulator

The voltage regulator combines with the battery and alternator to comprise the charging system. Just as the name implies, the voltage regulator controls (regulates) the alternator voltage output to a safe amount. A properly working regulator prevents excessive voltage from burning out wiring, bulbs, or contact points, and prevents overcharging of the battery. Mechanical adjustments (air gap, point opening) must be followed by electrical adjustments and not vice versa.

Since 1973 all GM cars have been equipped with alternators which have built-in solid state voltage regulators. The regulator is in the end frame (inside) of the alternator and requires no adjustment. The following adjustments apply to pre-1973 units.

➤**Although standard since 1973, this integral alternator/regulator has been available as an option since 1971.**

REMOVAL & INSTALLATION

1. Disconnect the battery ground cable.
2. Disconnect the wiring harness from the regulator.
3. Remove the mounting screws and remove the regulator.

To install:

4. Make sure that the regulator base basket is in place before installation.
5. Clean the attaching area for proper grounding.
6. Install the regulator. Do not overtighten the mounting screws, as this will cancel the cushioning effect of the rubber grommets.

ADJUSTMENT

▸ **See Figures 11, 12, 13 and 14**

The external regulators found on these vehicles from 1967–72 are the only regulators which are adjustable. The internal regulators found later (and on some 1971 and 1972 vehicles) are non-adjustable and must be replaced if found faulty. The standard voltage regulator is the conventional double contact type; however, an optional transistorized regulator was available in 1967–70. Voltage adjustment procedures are the same for both except for the adjustment points. The double contact adjustment screw is under the regulator cover, the 1967–70 transistorized regulator is adjusted externally after removing an Allen screw from the adjustment hole.

Field Relay Mechanical Adjustments

As explained earlier, mechanical adjustments must be made first and then followed by electrical adjustments.

POINT OPENING

Using a feeler gauge, check the point opening as illustrated. To change the opening, carefully bend the armature stop. The point opening for all regulators should be 0.014 in. (0.35mm).

AIR GAP

Check the air gap with the points just touching. The gap should be 0.060 in. (1.5mm). If the point opening setting is correct, then the relay will operate OK even if the air gap is off. To adjust air gap, bend the flat contact spring.

Voltage (Electrical) Adjustment

1. Connect a ¼Ω, 25 watt fixed resistor (a knife blade switch using a ¼ ohm resistor) into the charging circuit (as illustrated) at the battery positive ter-

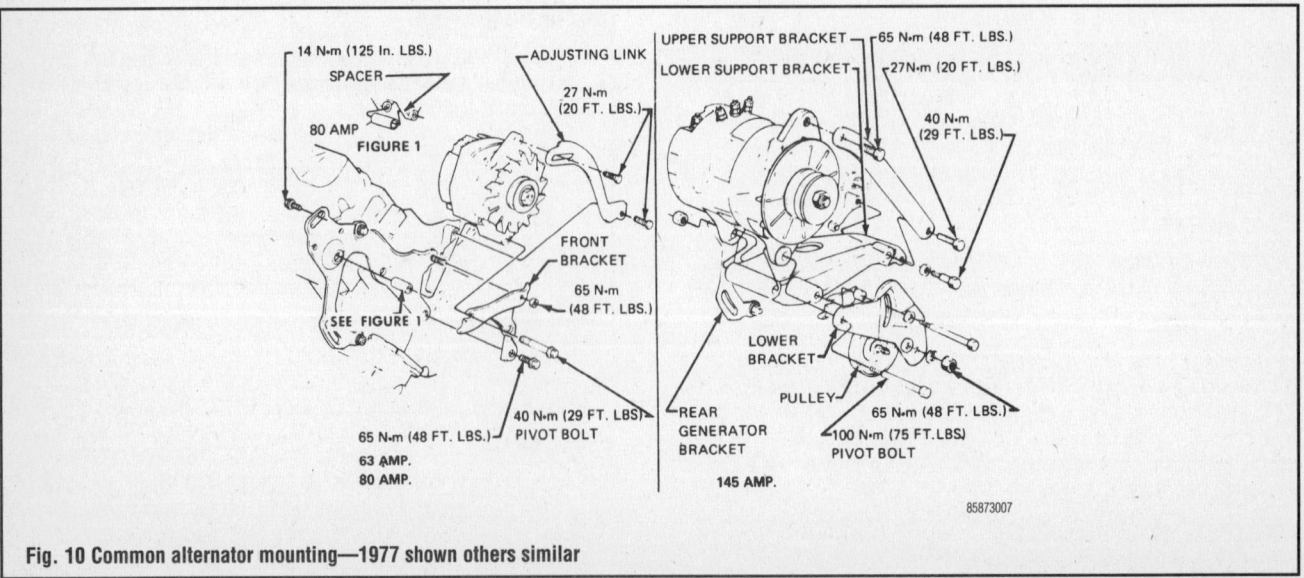

Fig. 10 Common alternator mounting—1977 shown others similar

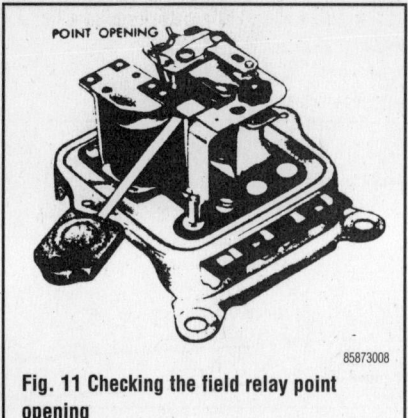

Fig. 11 Checking the field relay point opening

Fig. 12 Checking the air gap in the field relay

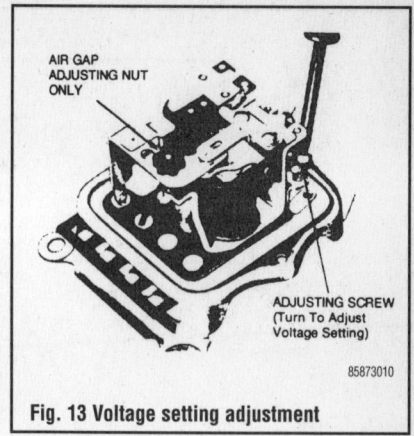

Fig. 13 Voltage setting adjustment

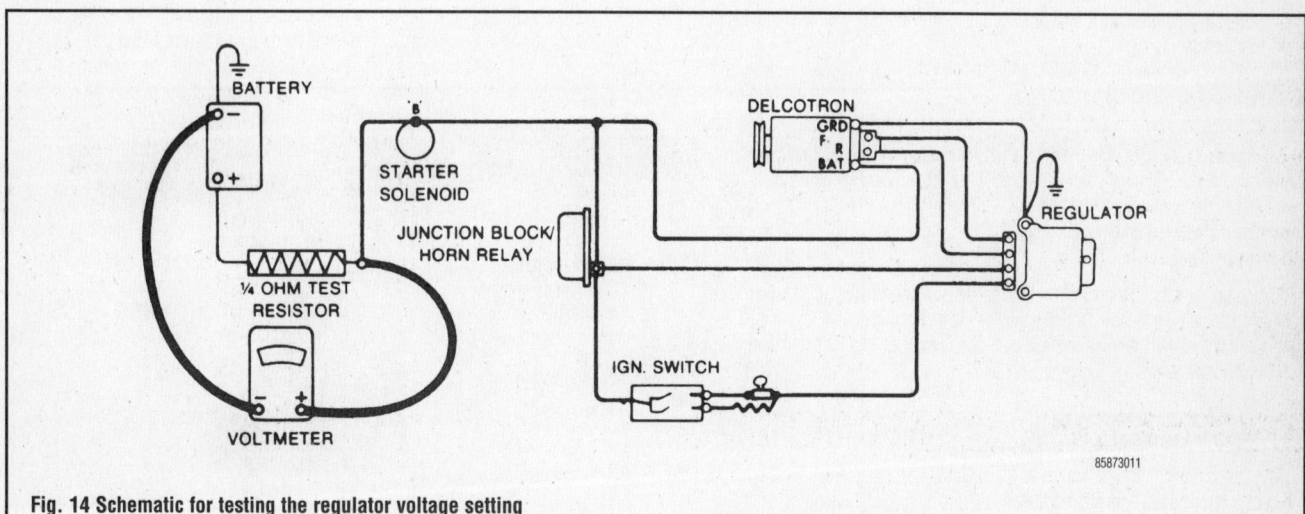

Fig. 14 Schematic for testing the regulator voltage setting

minal. One end of the resistor connects to the battery positive terminal while the other connects to the voltmeter.

2. Operate the engine at 1,500 rpm or more for at least 15 minutes. Disconnect and reconnect the regulator connector and read the voltage on the voltmeter. If the regulator is functioning properly, the reading should be 13.5–14.4V. If the reading is not within this range, keep the engine running at 1,500 rpm and do the following:

    a. Disconnect the terminal connector (four terminal connector) and remove the regulator cover. Reconnect the connector and adjust the voltage to 14.2–14.6 by turning the adjusting screw.

✳✳ WARNING

When removing the regulator cover ALWAYS disconnect the connector first to prevent regulator damage by short circuit.

    b. Disconnect the connector, install the cover, and reconnect the connector.

    c. Increase the regulator temperature by running the engine at 1,500 rpm for 10 more minutes.

    d. Disconnect and reconnect the connector and read the voltmeter. A reading of 13.5–14.4 indicates a good regulator.

Starter

REMOVAL & INSTALLATION

◆ **See Figures 15, 16, 17 and 18**

➡**The starters on some engines require the addition of shims to provide proper clearance between the starter pinion gear and the flywheel.**

These shims are available in 0.015 in. sizes from Cadillac dealers. Flat washers can be used if shims are unavailable.

1. Disconnect the battery cable.
2. Raise the car to a convenient working height.
3. Disconnect all wiring from the starter solenoid. Replace each nut as the connector is removed, as thread sizes differ from connector to connector. Note or tag the wiring positions for installation.

➡**On some models it may be necessary to remove the crossover pipe to complete this procedure.**

4. Remove the front bracket from the starter and the two mounting bolts. On engines with a solenoid heat shield, remove the front bracket upper bolt and detach the bracket from the starter.

5. Remove the front bracket bolt or nut. Lower the starter front end first, and then remove the unit from the car.

6. Reverse the removal procedures to install the starter. Tighten the two mounting bolts.

SHIMMING THE STARTER

◆ **See Figures 19 and 20**

Starter noise during cranking and after the engine fires is often a result of too much or too little distance between the starter pinion gear and the flywheel. A light pitched whine during cranking (before the engine fires) can be caused by the pinion and flywheel being too far apart. Likewise, a whine after the engine starts (as the key is released) is often a result of the pinion-flywheel relationship being too close. In both cases flywheel damage can occur. Shims are available in 0.015 in. sizes to properly adjust the starter on its mounts. You will also need a flywheel turning tool, available at most auto parts stores or from any auto tool store or salesperson.

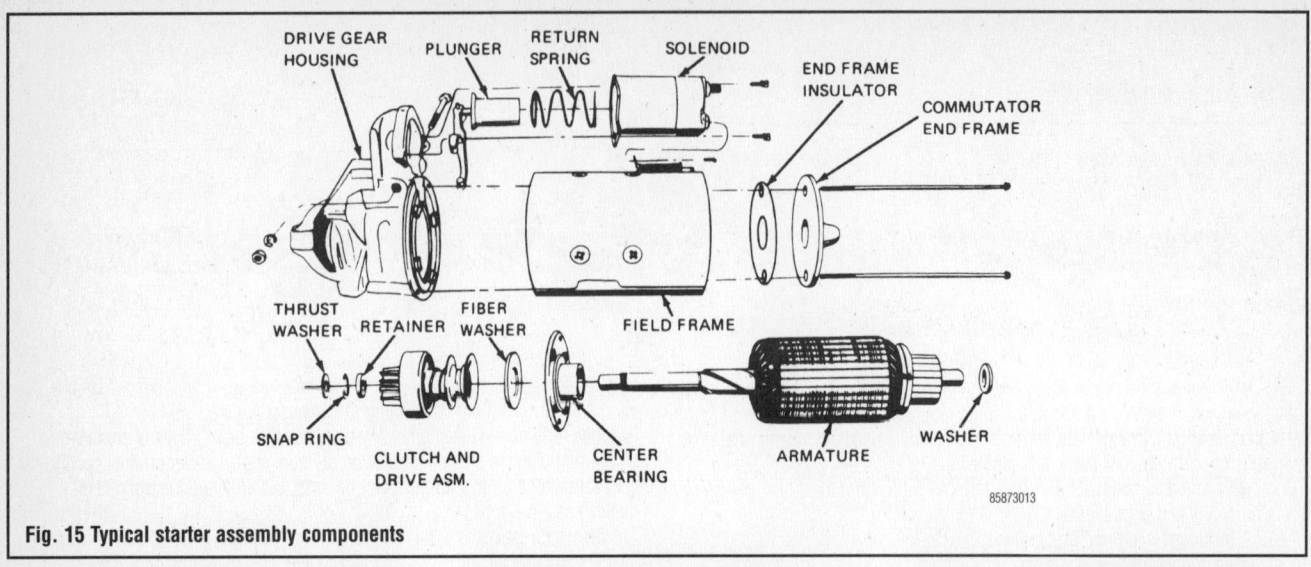

Fig. 15 Typical starter assembly components

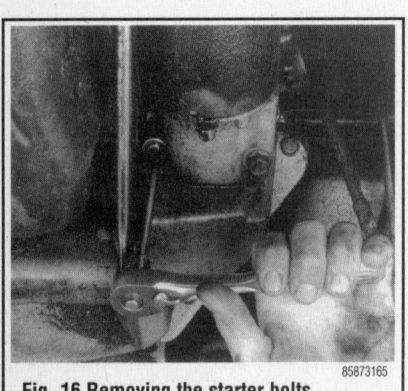

Fig. 16 Removing the starter bolts

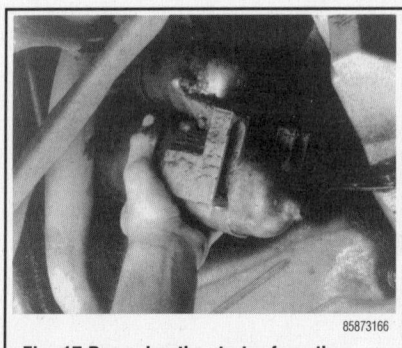

Fig. 17 Removing the starter from the vehicle

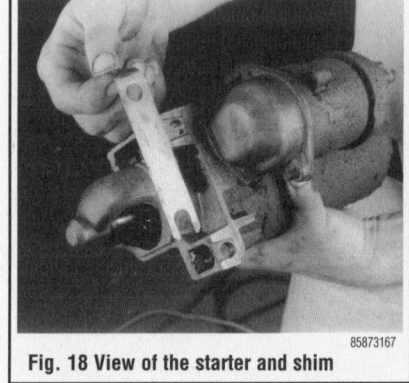

Fig. 18 View of the starter and shim

If your car's starter emits the above noises, follow the shimming procedure below:

1. Disconnect the negative battery cable.
2. Remove the flywheel inspection cover on the bottom of the bellhousing.
3. Using the flywheel turning tool, examine the flywheel teeth, turning the wheel to check its entire circumference. If damage is evident, the flywheel should be replaced.
4. Insert a screwdriver into the small hole in the bottom of the starter and move the starter pinion and clutch assembly so the pinion and flywheel teeth mesh. If necessary, rotate the flywheel so that a pinion tooth is directly in the center of the two flywheel teeth and on the centerline of the two gears, as shown in the accompanying illustration.
5. Check the pinion-to-flywheel clearance by using a 0.020 in. (0.5mm) wire gauge (a spark plug wire gauge may work here, or you can make your

own). Make sure you center the pinion tooth between the flywheel teeth and the gauge — NOT in the corners, as you may get a false reading! If the clearance is under this minimum, shim the starter away from the flywheel by adding shim(s) one at a time to the starter mount. Check clearance after adding each shim.

6. If the clearance is a good deal over 0.020 in. (0.5mm), in the vicinity of 0.050 in. (1.3mm) plus, shim the starter towards the flywheel. Broken or severely mangled flywheel teeth are also a good indicator that the clearance here is too great. Shimming the starter towards the flywheel is done by adding shims to the outboard starter mounting pad only. Check the clearance after each shim

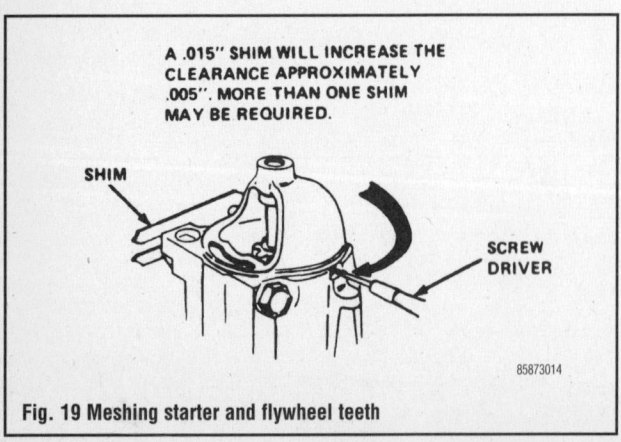

Fig. 19 Meshing starter and flywheel teeth

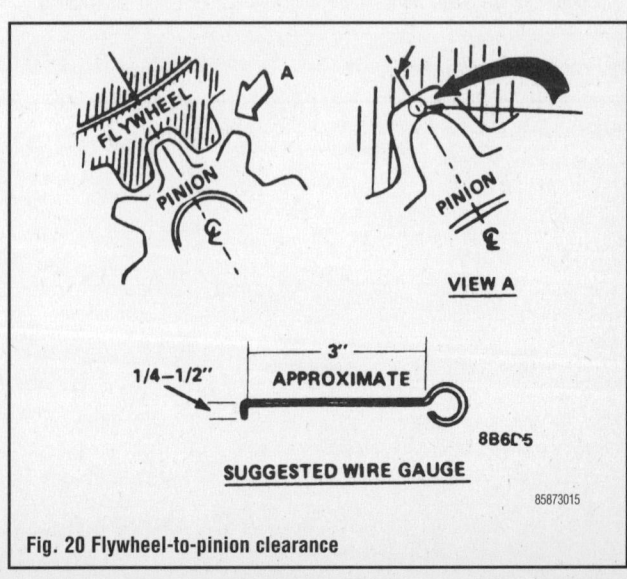

Fig. 20 Flywheel-to-pinion clearance

is added. A shim of 0.015 in. at this location will decrease the clearance about 0.010 in. (0.25mm).

SOLENOID REPLACEMENT

1. Remove the screw and washer from the motor connector strap terminal.

2. Remove the two solenoid retaining screws.
3. Twist the solenoid housing clockwise to remove the flange key from the keyway in the housing. Then remove the housing.
4. To re-install the unit, place the return spring on the plunger and place the solenoid body on the drive housing. Turn counterclockwise to engage the flange key. Place the two retaining screws in position and install the screw and washer which secures the strap terminal. Install the unit on the starter.

ENGINE MECHANICAL

Engine Overhaul

Most engine overhaul procedures are fairly standard. In addition to specific parts replacement procedures and complete specifications for your individual engine, this section also is a guide to accepted rebuilding procedures. Examples of standard rebuilding practice are shown and should be used along with specific details concerning your particular engine.

Competent and accurate machine shop services will ensure maximum performance, reliability and engine life.

In most instances it is more profitable for the do-it-yourself mechanic to remove, clean and inspect the component, buy the necessary parts and deliver these to a shop for actual machine work.

On the other hand, much of the rebuilding work (crankshaft, block, bearings, pistons, rods, and other components) is well within the scope of the do-it-yourself mechanic.

TOOLS

The tools required for an engine overhaul or parts replacement will depend on the depth of your involvement. With a few exceptions, they will be the tools found in a mechanic's tool kit (see Section 1). More in-depth work will require any or all of the following:
- a dial indicator (reading in thousandths) mounted on a universal base
- micrometers and telescope gauges
- jaw and screw-type pullers
- scraper
- valve spring compressor
- ring groove cleaner
- piston ring expander and compressor
- ridge reamer
- cylinder hone or glaze breaker
- Plastigage
- engine stand

Use of most of these tools is illustrated in this section. Many can be rented for a one-time use from a local parts jobber or tool supply house specializing in automotive work.

Occasionally, the use of special tools is called for. See the information on Special Tools and the Safety Notice in the front of this book before substituting another tool.

INSPECTION TECHNIQUES

Procedures and specifications are given in this section for inspecting, cleaning and assessing the wear limits of most major components. Other procedures such as Magnaflux and Zyglo can be used to locate material flaws and stress cracks. Magnaflux is a magnetic process applicable only to ferrous materials. The Zyglo process coats the material with a fluorescent dye penetrant and can be used on any material. Check for suspected surface cracks can be more readily made using spot check dye. The dye is sprayed onto the suspected area, wiped off and the area sprayed with a developer. Cracks will show up brightly.

OVERHAUL TIPS

Aluminum has become extremely popular for use in engines, due to its low weight. Observe the following precautions when handling aluminum parts:
- Never hot tank aluminum parts (the caustic hot-tank solution will eat the aluminum)
- Remove all aluminum parts (identification tag, etc.) from engine parts prior to hot-tanking.

- Always coat threads lightly with engine oil or anti-seize compounds before installation, to prevent seizure.
- Never over-torque bolts or spark plugs, especially in aluminum threads. Stripped threads in any component can be repaired using any of several commercial repair kits (Heli-Coil® Microdot® Keensert®, etc.)

When assembling the engine, any parts that will be in frictional contact must be pre-lubricated to provide lubrication at initial start-up. Any product specifically formulated for this purpose can be used, but engine oil is not recommended as a pre-lube.

When semi-permanent (locked, but removable) installation of bolts or nuts is desired, threads should be cleaned and coated with Loctite or other similar, commercial non-hardening sealant.

REPAIRING DAMAGED THREADS

▶ See Figures 21 thru 26

Several methods of repairing damaged threads are available. Heli-Coil® (shown here), Keenserts and Microdot are among the most widely used. All involve basically the same principle drilling out stripped threads, tapping the hold and installing a pre-wound insert, making welding, plugging and oversize fasteners unnecessary.

Two types of thread repair inserts are usually supplied — a standard type for most Inch Coarse, Inch Fine, Metric Coarse and Metric Fine thread sizes and a spark plug type to fit most spark plug port sizes. Consult the individual manufacturer's catalog to determine exact applications. Typical thread repair kits will contain a selection of pre-wound threaded inserts, a tap (corresponding to the outside diameter threads of the insert) and an installation tool. Spark plug inserts usually differ because they require a tap equipped with pilot threads and a combined reamer/tap section. Most manufacturers also supply blister-packed thread repair inserts separately in addition to a master kit containing a variety of taps and inserts plus installation tools.

Before effecting a repair to a threaded hole, remove any snapped, broken or damaged bolts or studs. Penetrating oil can be used to free frozen threads; the offending item can be removed with locking pliers or with a screw or stud extractor. After the hole is clear, the thread can be repaired.

Checking Engine Compression

A noticeable lack of engine power, excessive oil consumption and/or poor fuel mileage measured over an extended period are all indicators of internal engine wear. Worn piston rings, scored or worn cylinder bores, blown head gaskets, sticking or burnt valves and worn valve seats are all possible culprits here. A check of each cylinder's compression will help you locate the problems.

As mentioned in the Tools and Equipment information of Section 1, a screw-in type compression gauge is more accurate than the type you simply hold against the spark plug hole. Although it takes slightly longer to use, it's worth it to obtain a more accurate reading.

GASOLINE ENGINES

▶ See Figure 27

1. Warm up the engine to normal operating temperature.
2. Remove all spark plugs.
3. Disconnect the high tension lead from the ignition coil.
4. On carbureted cars, fully open the throttle either by operating the carburetor throttle linkage by hand or by having an assistant floor the accelerator pedal. On fuel injected cars, disconnect the cold start valve and all injector connections.
5. Screw the compression gauge into the No. 1 spark plug hole until the fitting is snug.

Standard Torque Specifictions and Fastener Markings

In the absence of specific torques, the following chart can be used as a guide to the maximum safe torque of a particular size/grade of fastener.

- There is no torque difference for fine or coarse threads.
- Torque values are based on clean, dry threads. Reduce the value by 10% if threads are oiled prior to assembly.
- The torque required for aluminum components or fasteners is considerably less.

U.S. Bolts

SAE Grade Number	1 or 2			5			6 or 7		
Number of lines always 2 less than the grade number.									
Bolt Size (Inches)—(Thread)	Maximum Torque			Maximum Torque			Maximum Torque		
	Ft./Lbs.	Kgm	Nm	Ft./Lbs.	Kgm	Nm	Ft./Lbs.	Kgm	Nm
¼—20	5	0.7	6.8	8	1.1	10.8	10	1.4	13.5
—28	6	0.8	8.1	10	1.4	13.6			
5/16—18	11	1.5	14.9	17	2.3	23.0	19	2.6	25.8
—24	13	1.8	17.6	19	2.6	25.7			
3/8—16	18	2.5	24.4	31	4.3	42.0	34	4.7	46.0
—24	20	2.75	27.1	35	4.8	47.5			
7/16—14	28	3.8	37.0	49	6.8	66.4	55	7.6	74.5
—20	30	4.2	40.7	55	7.6	74.5			
½—13	39	5.4	52.8	75	10.4	101.7	85	11.75	115.2
—20	41	5.7	55.6	85	11.7	115.2			
9/16—12	51	7.0	69.2	110	15.2	149.1	120	16.6	162.7
—18	55	7.6	74.5	120	16.6	162.7			
5/8—11	83	11.5	112.5	150	20.7	203.3	167	23.0	226.5
—18	95	13.1	128.8	170	23.5	230.5			
¾—10	105	14.5	142.3	270	37.3	366.0	280	38.7	379.6
—16	115	15.9	155.9	295	40.8	400.0			
7/8— 9	160	22.1	216.9	395	54.6	535.5	440	60.9	596.5
—14	175	24.2	237.2	435	60.1	589.7			
1— 8	236	32.5	318.6	590	81.6	799.9	660	91.3	894.8
—14	250	34.6	338.9	660	91.3	849.8			

Metric Bolts

Relative Strength Marking	4.6, 4.8			8.8		
Bolt Markings						
Bolt Size Thread Size x Pitch (mm)	Maximum Torque			Maximum Torque		
	Ft./Lbs.	Kgm	Nm	Ft./Lbs.	Kgm	Nm
6 x 1.0	2–3	.2–.4	3–4	3–6	.4–.8	5–8
8 x 1.25	6–8	.8–1	8–12	9–14	1.2–1.9	13–19
10 x 1.25	12–17	1.5–2.3	16–23	20–29	2.7–4.0	27–39
12 x 1.25	21–32	2.9–4.4	29–43	35–53	4.8–7.3	47–72
14 x 1.5	35–52	4.8–7.1	48–70	57–85	7.8–11.7	77–110
16 x 1.5	51–77	7.0–10.6	67–100	90–120	12.4–16.5	130–160
18 x 1.5	74–110	10.2–15.1	100–150	130–170	17.9–23.4	180–230
20 x 1.5	110–140	15.1–19.3	150–190	190–240	26.2–46.9	160–320
22 x 1.5	150–190	22.0–26.2	200–260	250–320	34.5–44.1	340–430
24 x 1.5	190–240	26.2–46.9	260–320	310–410	42.7–56.5	420–550

85873021

Fig. 21 Standard torque specifications and fastener markings

Be careful not to crossthread the plug hole. On aluminum cylinder heads use extra care, as the threads in these heads are easily ruined.

6. Ask an assistant to depress the accelerator pedal fully on both carbureted and fuel injected cars. Then, while you read the compression gauge, ask the assistant to crank the engine two or three times in short bursts using the ignition switch.

7. Read the compression gauge at the end of each series of cranks, and record the highest of these readings. Repeat this procedure for each of the engine's cylinders. Compare the highest reading of each cylinder to the compression pressure specifications in the Tune-Up Specifications chart in Section 2. The specs in this chart are maximum values.

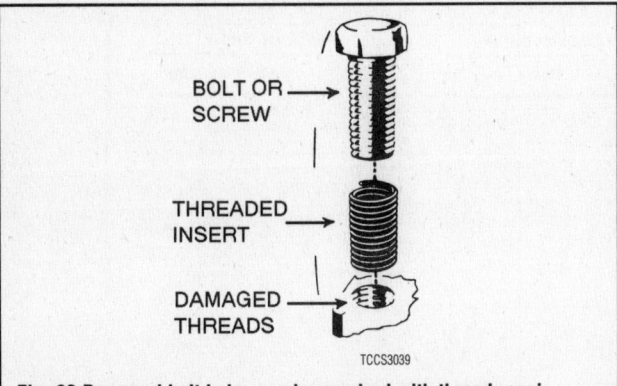

Fig. 22 Damaged bolt holes can be repaired with thread repair inserts

A cylinder's compression pressure is usually acceptable if it is not less than 80% of maximum. The difference between each cylinder should be no more than 12–14 pounds.

8. If a cylinder is unusually low, pour a tablespoon of clean engine oil into the cylinder through the spark plug hole and repeat the compression test. If the compression comes up after adding the oil, it appears that that cylinder's piston rings or bore are damaged or worn. If the pressure remains low, the valves may not be seating properly (a valve job is needed), or the head gasket may be blown near that cylinder. If compression in any two adjacent cylinders is low, and if the addition of oil doesn't help the compression, there is leakage past the head gasket. Oil and coolant water in the combustion chamber can result from this problem. There may be evidence of water droplets on the engine dipstick when a head gasket has blown.

DIESEL ENGINES

▶ **See Figure 28**

Checking cylinder compression on diesel engines is basically the same procedure as on gasoline engines except for the following:

1. A special compression gauge adaptor suitable for diesel engines (because these engines have much greater compression pressures) must be used.

2. Remove the injector tubes and remove the injectors from each cylinder.

Don't forget to remove the washer underneath each injector; otherwise, it may get lost when the engine is cranked.

3. When fitting the compression gauge adaptor to the cylinder head, make sure the bleeder of the gauge (if equipped) is closed.

4. When reinstalling the injector assemblies, install new washers underneath each injector.

Fig. 23 Standard thread repair insert (left) and spark plug thread insert (right)

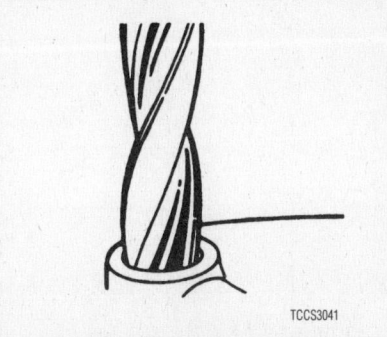

Fig. 24 Drill out the damaged threads with specified drill—drill completely through the hole or to the bottom of a blind hole

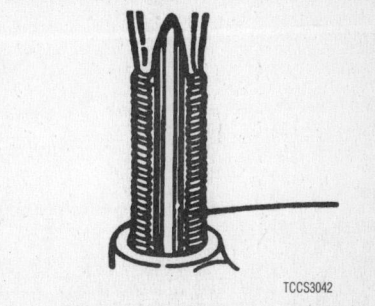

Fig. 25 With the tap supplied, tap the hole to receive the thread insert—keep the tap well oiled and back it out frequently to avoid clogging the threads

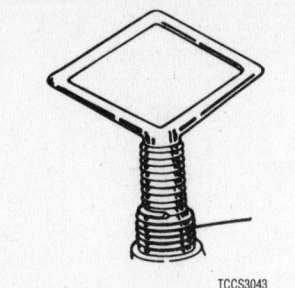

Fig. 26 Screw the threaded insert onto the installation tool until the tang engages the slot—screw the insert into the tapped hole until it is 1/4–1/2 turn below the top surface—after installation, break off the tang with a hammer and punch

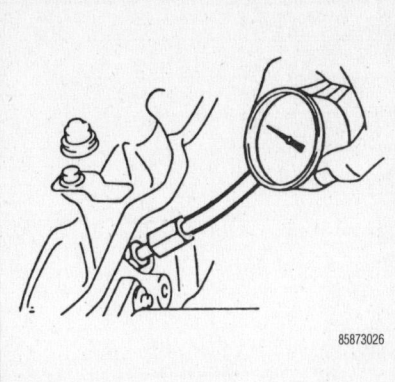

Fig. 27 The screw-in type compression gauge is more accurate

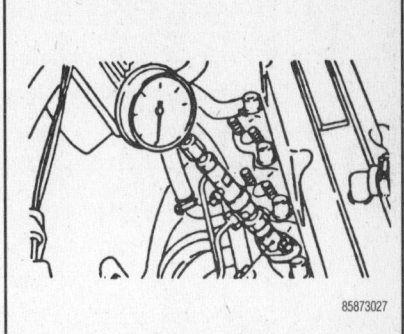

Fig. 28 Diesel engines require a special compression gauge adaptor

CRANKSHAFT AND CONNECTING ROD SPECIFICATIONS

Year	Engine No. Cyl. Displ. Cu. In. (L)	Main Brg. Journal Dia.	Main Brg. Oil Clearance	Shaft End-play	Thrust on No.	Connecting Rod Journal Diameter	Connecting Rod Oil Clearance	Connecting Rod Side Clearance
1967	8-429 (7.0)	3.000	0.0003–0.0026	0.002–0.012	3	2.2494	0.0013	0.006–0.016
1968-73	8-472 (7.7)	3.250	0.0003–0.0026	0.002–0.012	3	2.5000	0.0005–0.0028	0.008–0.016
	8-500 (8.2)	3.250	0.0003–0.0026	0.002–0.012	3	2.5000	0.0005–0.0028	0.008–0.016
1974	8-472 (7.7)	3.250	0.0013–0.0026	0.002–0.012	3	2.5000	0.0005–0.0028	0.011–0.021
	8-500 (8.2)	3.250	0.0003–0.0026	0.002–0.012	3	2.5000	0.0005–0.0028	0.011–0.021
1975-79	8-350 (5.7)	2.4985–2.4995	0.0005–0.0021②	0.004–0.014	3	2.1238–2.1248	0.0005–0.0026	0.006–0.020
	8-350 (5.7) Diesel	2.9993–3.0003	0.0005–0.0021③	0.004–0.014	3	2.1238–2.1248	0.0005–0.0026	0.008–0.020
	8-425 (7.0)	3.250	0.0001–0.0026	0.002–0.012	3	2.5000	0.0005–0.0028	0.008–0.020
	8-500 (8.2)	3.250	0.0001–0.0026	0.002–0.012	3	2.5000	0.0005–0.0028	0.008–0.020
1980	6-252 (4.1)	2.4995	0.0003–0.0018	0.003–0.009	2	2.2487–2.2495	0.0005–0.0026	0.006–0.023
	8-350 (5.7)	2.4985–2.4995③	0.0005–0.0021③	0.004–0.014	3	2.1238–2.1248	0.0005–0.0026	0.006–0.020
	8-350 (5.7) Diesel	2.9993–3.0003	0.0005–0.0021③	0.004–0.014	3	2.1238–2.1248	0.0005–0.0026	0.006–0.020
	8-368 (6.0)	3.250	0.0001–0.0026	0.002–0.012	3	2.5000	0.0005–0.0028	0.008–0.020
1981-82	8-250 (4.1)	2.640	0.0004–0.0030	0.001–0.007	3	1.9300	0.0005–0.0028	0.008–0.020
	6-252 (4.1)	2.4995	0.0003–0.0018	0.003–0.009	2	2.2487–2.2495	0.0005–0.0026	0.006–0.023
	8-350 (5.7) Diesel	2.9993–3.0003	0.0005–0.0021③	0.004–0.014	3	2.1238–2.1248	0.0005–0.0026	0.006–0.020
	8-368 (6.0)	3.250	0.0001–0.0026	0.002–0.012	3	2.5000	0.0005–0.0028	0.008–0.020
1983-86	8-307 (5.0)	2.4988–2.4998④	0.0005–0.0021④	0.0035–0.0135	3	2.052–2.054	0.0005–0.0028	0.008–0.020
	8-250 (4.1)	2.640	0.0004–0.0027	0.001–0.007	3	2.052–2.054	0.0005–0.0028	0.008–0.020
	8-350 (5.7) Diesel	2.9993–3.0003	0.0005–0.0021③	0.004–0.014	3	2.1238–2.1248	0.0005–0.0026	0.006–0.020
	8-368 (6.0)	3.250	0.0001–0.0026	0.002–0.012	3	2.5000	0.0005–0.0028	0.008–0.020
1987	8-250 (4.1)	2.6374–2.6384	0.0016–0.0039	0.0010–0.0070	3	2.052–2.054	0.0005–0.0028	0.008–0.020
	8-307 (5.0)	2.4988–2.4998④	0.0005–0.0021	0.0035–0.0135	3	2.1238–2.1248	0.0004–0.0033	0.006–0.020
1988-89	8-273 (4.5)	2.6776–2.6786	0.0016–0.0039	0.0010–0.0070	3	2.052–2.054	0.0005–0.0028	0.008–0.020
	8-307 (5.0)	2.4988–2.4998④	0.0005–0.0021	0.0035–0.0135	3	2.1238–2.1248	0.0004–0.0033	0.006–0.020

① No. 1: 2.4988–2.4998 in.
② No. 5: 0.0015–0.0031 in.
③ No. 2, 3, 4, 5: 2.4985–2.4995
④ No. 5: 0.0015–0.0031
⑤ No. 1: 0.0008–0.0031

85873C4B

GENERAL ENGINE SPECIFICATIONS

Year	Engine V.I.N. Code	Engine No. Cyl. Displ. Cu. In. (L)	Engine Manufacturer	Carb Type	Horsepower @ rpm ①	Torque @ rpm (ft. lbs.) ①	Bore × Stroke (in.)	Compression Ratio	Oil Pressure (psi @ rpm)
1967	*	8-429 (7.0)	Cad.	4 bbl	340 @ 4600	480 @ 3000	4.125 × 4.000	10.5:1	33
1968-69	*	8-472 (7.7)	Cad.	4 bbl	375 @ 4400	525 @ 3000	4.300 × 4.060	10.5:1	35-40
1970	R	8-472 (7.7)	Cad.	4 bbl	375 @ 4400	525 @ 3000	4.300 × 4.060	10.0:1	35-40
	R	8-500 (8.2)	Cad.	4 bbl	400 @ 4400	550 @ 3000	4.300 × 4.304	10.0:1	34-40
1971	R	8-472 (7.7)	Cad.	4 bbl	375 @ 4400	525 @ 3000	4.300 × 4.060	8.5:1	35-40
	S	8-500 (8.2)	Cad.	4 bbl	365 @ 4400	535 @ 2800	4.300 × 4.304	8.5:1	35-40
1972-73	R	8-472 (7.7)	Cad.	4 bbl	220 @ 4000	365 @ 2400	4.300 × 4.060	8.5:1	35
	S	8-500 (8.2)	Cad.	4 bbl	235 @ 3800	385 @ 2400	4.300 × 4.304	8.5:1	35
1974	R	8-472 (7.7)	Cad.	4 bbl	220 @ 4000	365 @ 2400	4.300 × 4.060	8.25:1	35
	S	8-500 (8.2)	Cad.	4 bbl	210 @ 3600	380 @ 2000	4.300 × 4.304	8.25:1	35
1975	S	8-500 (8.2)	Cad.	4 bbl	210 @ 3600	380 @ 2000	4.300 × 4.304	8.25:1	35
	S	8-350 (5.7)	Olds.	EFI	180 @ 4400	275 @ 2000	4.057 × 3.385	8.0:1	35
1976	R	8-500 (8.2)	Cad.	EFI	190 @ 3600	360 @ 2000	4.300 × 4.304	8.5:1	35
	S	8-350 (5.7)	Olds.	4 bbl	215 @ 3600	275 @ 2000	4.057 × 3.385	8.5:1	35
1977	R	8-425 (7.0)	Cad.	EFI	180 @ 4000	320 @ 2000	4.082 × 4.060	8.0:1	35
	S	8-350 (5.7)	Olds.	4 bbl	215 @ 3600	275 @ 2000	4.057 × 3.385	8.0:1	40
1978	B	8-425 (7.0)	Cad.	EFI	170 @ 4200	270 @ 2000	4.057 × 3.385	8.0:1	35
	N	8-350 (5.7)	Olds.	4 bbl	180 @ 4400	320 @ 2000	4.082 × 4.060	8.2:1	35
	S	8-350 (5.7)	Olds.	EFI	180 @ 3600	260 @ 2000	4.057 × 3.385	8.0:1	40
1979	B	8-350 (5.7)	Olds.	4 bbl	215 @ 3600	260 @ 2000	4.057 × 3.385	8.0:1	35
	N	8-350 (5.7)	Olds.	Diesel	120 @ 3600	220 @ 1800	4.057 × 3.385	22.0:1	35
	S	8-425 (7.0)	Cad.	EFI	180 @ 4400	260 @ 2000	4.082 × 4.060	8.0:1	40
	T	8-350 (5.7)	Olds.	4 bbl	120 @ 3600	260 @ 2000	4.057 × 3.385	8.5:1	35
1980	4	6-252 (4.1)	Buick	EFI	185 @ 3800	265 @ 1600	3.965 × 3.400	8.2:1	37
	8	8-350 (5.7)	Olds.	4 bbl	125 @ 3800	205 @ 2000	4.057 × 3.385	8.1:1	35
	N	8-350 (5.7)	Olds.	Diesel	160 @ 4400	265 @ 1600	4.057 × 3.385	8.0:1	40
	S	8-425 (7.0)	Cad.	4 bbl	150 @ 3800	206 @ 1600	4.082 × 4.060	22.5:1	35
1981-82	4	8-368 (6.0)	Buick	EFI	105 @ 3200	190 @ 2000	3.800 × 4.060	8.2:1	40
	8	6-252 (4.1)	Buick	4 bbl	145 @ 3800	265 @ 1600	3.965 × 3.400	8.2:1	37
	6	8-350 (5.7)	Olds.	DFI	125 @ 3800	210 @ 2000	4.057 × 3.385	8.0:1	35
	9	8-350 (5.7)	Olds.	Diesel	150 @ 3800	205 @ 1600	4.057 × 3.385	22.5:1	40
1983	4	8-368 (6.0)	Cad.	4 bbl	105 @ 3200	190 @ 2000	3.800 × 4.060	8.2:1	35
	8	8-250 (4.1)	Cad.	DFI	135 @ 4400	265 @ 1400	3.465 × 3.307	22.5:1	40
	6	8-350 (5.7)	Olds.	Diesel	105 @ 3200	200 @ 2200	4.057 × 3.385	8.2:1	30
	9	8-368 (6.0)	Cad.	4 bbl	150 @ 3800	205 @ 1600	3.800 × 4.060	8.5:1①	40
1984-85	8	8-368 (6.0)	Cad.	DFI	105 @ 3200	190 @ 2000	3.800 × 4.060	8.2:1	35
	N	8-250 (4.1)	Cad.	Diesel	140 @ 3800	265 @ 1400	3.465 × 3.307	8.2:1	30
	6	8-350 (5.7)	Olds.	DFI	140 @ 4200	200 @ 2200	4.057 × 3.385	22.7:1	35
	9	8-368 (6.0)	Cad.	4 bbl	130 @ 4200	198 @ 2200	3.800 × 4.060	8.2:1	35
1986	8	8-368 (6.0)	Cad.	DFI	130 @ 4200	200 @ 2200	3.800 × 4.060	8.5:1	35
	N	8-307 (5.0)	Olds.	4 bbl	140 @ 3800	255 @ 2000	3.465 × 3.307	8.2:1	30
	6	8-250 (4.1)	Cad.	Diesel	140 @ 4200	200 @ 2200	4.057 × 3.385	9:1	40
1987	8	8-305 (5.0)	Olds.	DFI	140 @ 3200	240 @ 2800	3.800 × 3.385	22.7:1	30
	Y	8-273 (4.5)	Cad.	DFI	140 @ 3200	255 @ 2000	3.622 × 3.307	8.2:1	37③
1988-89	8	8-307 (5.0)	Olds.	DFI	155 @ 4200	240 @ 2800	3.800 × 3.385	7.9:1	37③
	Y	8-305 (5.0)	Olds.	DFI	140 @ 3200	255 @ 2000	3.800 × 3.385	9:1	30-45③

NOTE: Horsepower and torque are SAE net figures. They are measured at the rear of the transmission with all accessories installed and operating. Since the figures vary when a given engine is installed in different models, some are representative rather than exact.
① @ rpm
② 9.1 with Swirl Cylinder Heads
③ @ 1500 RPM

85873C3B

PISTON AND RING SPECIFICATIONS

Year	Engine No. Cyl. Displ. Cu. In. (L)	Piston-Bore Clearance	Ring Side Clearance Top Compression	Ring Side Clearance Bottom Compression	Ring Side Clearance Oil Control	Ring Gap Top Compression	Ring Gap Bottom Compression	Ring Gap Oil Control
1967	8-429 (7.0)	0.0005-0.0007	0.0022-0.0035	0.0022-0.0035	None⊙	0.013-0.030	0.013-0.030	0.015-0.161
1968-74	8-472 (7.7)	0.0006-0.0010	0.0017-0.0040	0.0017-0.0040	None⊙	0.013-0.025	0.013-0.025	0.015-0.055
	8-500 (8.2)	0.0006-0.0010	0.0017-0.0040	0.0017-0.0040	None⊙	0.013-0.025	0.013-0.025	0.015-0.055
1975-79	8-350 (5.7)	0.0010-0.0020	0.0020-0.0040	0.0020-0.0040	0.0006-0.0098	0.010-0.023	0.010-0.023	0.015-0.055
	8-350 (5.7) Diesel	0.0005-0.0006	0.005-0.007	0.0018-0.0038	0.0078 max.	0.015-0.025	0.015-0.025	0.015-0.055
	8-425 (7.0)	0.0006-0.0014	0.0017-0.0040	0.0017-0.0040	None⊙	0.013-0.023	0.013-0.023	0.015-0.055
	8-500 (8.2)	0.0006-0.0010	0.0017-0.0040	0.0017-0.0040	None⊙	0.013-0.025	0.013-0.025	0.015-0.055
1980-82	6-252 (4.1)	0.0013-0.0035	0.0030-0.0050	0.0030-0.0050	0.0035 max.	0.013-0.023	0.013-0.023	0.015-0.035
	8-250 (4.1)	0.0010-0.0018	0.0016-0.0037	0.0016-0.0037	None⊙	0.009-0.020	0.009-0.020	0.010-0.050
	8-350 (5.7)	0.0010-0.0020	0.0020-0.0040	0.0020-0.0040	0.0006-0.0096	0.010-0.023	0.010-0.023	0.015-0.055
	8-350 (5.7) Diesel	0.0005-0.0006	0.005-0.007	0.0018-0.0038	0.0078 max.	0.015-0.025	0.015-0.025	0.015-0.055
	8-368 (6.0)	0.0006-0.0014	0.0017-0.0040	0.0017-0.0040	None⊙	0.013-0.023	0.013-0.023	0.015-0.055
1983-86	8-250 (4.1)	0.0008	0.0016-0.0037	0.0016-0.0037	None⊙	0.015-0.025	0.015-0.025	0.010-0.050
	8-350 (5.7) Diesel	0.0035-0.0045	0.005-0.007	0.003-0.005	0.001-0.005	0.019-0.027	0.013-0.023	0.015-0.055
	8-368 (6.0)	0.0006-0.0014	0.0017-0.0040	0.0017-0.0040	None⊙	0.013-0.023	0.013-0.023	0.015-0.055
	8-307 (5.0)	0.0008-0.0018	0.0020-0.0040	0.0020-0.0040	0.0010-0.0050	0.009-0.019⊙	0.009-0.019⊙	0.010-0.055
1987	8-250 (4.1)	0.0008	0.0016-0.0037	0.0016-0.0037	None⊙	0.015-0.024	0.015-0.024	0.010-0.050
	8-307 (5.0)	0.00075-0.00175	0.0018-0.0038	0.0018-0.0038	0.001-0.005	0.009-0.019	0.009-0.019	0.015-0.055
1988-89	8-273 (4.5)	0.0008	0.0016-0.0037	0.0016-0.0037	None⊙	0.015-0.024	0.015-0.024	0.010-0.050
	8-307 (5.0)	0.00075-0.00175	0.0018-0.0038	0.0018-0.0038	0.001-0.005	0.009-0.019	0.009-0.019	0.015-0.055

⊙ Side sealing
⊙ With TRW rings: 0.010-0.025

85873C05

VALVE SPECIFICATIONS

Year	Engine No. Cyl. Displ. Cu. In. (L)	Seat Angle (deg.)	Face Angle (deg.)	Spring Test Pressure (lbs. @ in.)	Spring Installed Height (in.)	Stem-to-Guide Clearance (in.) Intake	Stem-to-Guide Clearance (in.) Exhaust	Stem Diameter (in.) Intake	Stem Diameter (in.) Exhaust
1967	8-429 (7.0)	45	44	160 @ 1.50	1 15/16	0.0005-0.0025	0.0010-0.0025	0.3415-0.3425	0.3415-0.3420
1968-71	8-472 (7.7)	45	44	160 @ 1.50	1 15/16	0.0005-0.0025	0.0010-0.0025	0.3415-0.3425	0.3415-0.3420
	8-500 (8.2)	45	44	160 @ 1.50	1 15/16	0.0005-0.0025	0.0010-0.0025	0.3415-0.3425	0.3415-0.3420
1972-73	8-472 (7.7)	45	44	160 @ 1.50	1 15/16	0.0010-0.0027	0.0012-0.0027	0.3420	0.3418
	8-500 (8.2)	45	44	168 @ 1.50	1 15/16	0.0010-0.0027	0.0012-0.0027	0.3418	0.3416
1974	8-472 (7.7)	45	44	168 @ 1.50	1 15/16	0.0010-0.0027	0.0016-0.0027	0.3420	0.3418
	8-500 (8.2)	45	44	168 @ 1.50	1 15/16	0.0010-0.0027	0.0012-0.0029	0.3418	0.3416
1975-78	8-350 (5.7) E.F.I.	⊙	⊙	187 @ 1.27	1 43/64	0.0010-0.0027	0.0015-0.0032	0.3429	0.3424
	8-350 (5.7) Diesel	⊙	⊙	151 @ 1.30	1 43/64	0.0010-0.0027	0.0015-0.0032	0.3429	0.3424
	8-425 (7.0)	45	44	160 @ 1.50	1 15/16	0.0010-0.0027	0.0010-0.0027	0.3416	0.3416
	8-500 (8.2)	45	44	160 @ 1.50	1 15/16	0.0010-0.0027	0.0010-0.0027	0.3416	0.3416
1979	8-350 (5.7) E.F.I.	⊙	⊙	187 @ 1.27	1 43/64	0.0010-0.0027	0.0015-0.0032	0.3429	0.3424
	8-350 (5.7) Diesel	⊙	⊙	151 @ 1.30	1 43/64	0.0010-0.0027	0.0015-0.0032	0.3429	0.3424
	8-425 (7.0)	45	44	162 @ 1.50	1 15/16	0.0010-0.0027	0.0012-0.0029	0.3416	0.3435
1980	6-252 (4.1)	45	44	164 @ 1.34 ⊙	1 11/32	0.0015-0.0035	0.0015-0.0032	0.3412	0.3412
	8-350 (5.7) E.F.I.	⊙	⊙	187 @ 1.27	1 43/64	0.0010-0.0027	0.0015-0.0032	0.3429	0.3424
	8-350 (5.7) Diesel	⊙	⊙	152 @ 1.30	1 43/64	0.0010-0.0027	0.0015-0.0032	0.3429	0.3424
	8-368 (6.0)	45	44	160 @ 1.50	1 15/32	0.0010-0.0027	0.0012-0.0029	0.3420	0.3418
1981	6-252 (4.1)	45	44	164 @ 1.34 ⊙	1 11/32	0.0015-0.0035	0.0015-0.0032	0.3412	0.3412
	8-350 (5.7) Diesel	⊙	⊙	210 @ 1.30	1 43/64	0.0010-0.0027	0.0015-0.0032	0.3429	0.3424
	8-368 (6.0)	45	44	160 @ 1.50	1 15/32	0.0010-0.0027	0.0012-0.0029	0.3410	0.3417

85873C06

VALVE SPECIFICATIONS

Year	Engine No. Cyl. Displ. Cu. In. (L)	Seat Angle (deg.)	Face Angle (deg.)	Spring Test Pressure (lbs. @ in.)	Spring Installed Height (in.)	Stem-to-Guide Clearance (in.) Intake	Stem-to-Guide Clearance (in.) Exhaust	Stem Diameter (in.) Intake	Stem Diameter (in.) Exhaust
1982	8-250 (4.1)	45	44	182 @ 1.28	1 43/64	0.0010-0.0030	0.0010-0.0030	0.3413-0.3420	0.3411-0.3418
	6-252 (4.1)	45	44	164 @ 1.34[1]	1 11/32	0.0015-0.0035	0.0015-0.0032	0.3412	0.3412
	8-350 (5.7) Diesel	[2]	[3]	210 @ 1.30	1 43/64	0.0010-0.0027	0.0015-0.0032	0.3429	0.3424
	8-368 (6.0)	45	44	160 @ 1.50	1 15/32	0.0010-0.0027	0.0010-0.0027	0.3417	0.3417
1983-86	8-250 (4.1)	45	44	167 @ 1.34	1 43/64	0.0010-0.0030	0.0010-0.0030	0.3413-0.3420	0.3411-0.3418
	8-350 (5.7) Diesel	[2]	[3]	210 @ 1.22	1 43/64	0.0010-0.0027	0.0015-0.0030	0.3425-0.3432	0.3420-0.3427
	8-368 (6.0)	45	44	160 @ 1.50	1 15/32	0.0010-0.0027	0.0010-0.0032	0.3417	0.3417
	8-307 (5.0)	45[1]	46[1]	187 @ 1.27	1 47/64	0.0010-0.0027	0.0015-0.0032	0.3425-0.3432	0.3420-0.3427
1987	8-250 (4.1)	45	44	[2]		0.0010-0.0030	0.0010-0.0030	0.3410-0.3420	0.3410-0.3420
	8-307 (5.0)	45[1]	44[1]	187 @ 1.27		0.0010-0.0027	0.0010-0.0030	0.3425-0.3432	0.3420-0.3427
1988-89	8-273 (4.5)	45	44	[2]		0.0010-0.0030	0.0010-0.0030	0.3410-0.3420	0.3410-0.3420
	8-307 (5.0)	45[1]	44[1]	187 @ 1.27		0.0010-0.0027	0.0015-0.0032	0.3425-0.3437	0.3420-0.3427

[1] Exhaust valve seat: 31°
[2] Exhaust valve face: 30°
[3] Intake: 45°; exhaust: 31°
[4] Intake: 44°; exhaust: 30°
[5] Exhaust: 59°
[6] Exhaust: 60°
[7] Intake 212 @ 1.28
216 @ 1.28

TORQUE SPECIFICATIONS
All readings in ft. lbs.

Year	Engine No. Cyl. Displ. Cu. In. (L)	Cylinder Head Bolts	Rod Bearing Bolts	Main Bearing Bolts	Crankshaft Damper or Pulley Bolt	Flywheel to Crankshaft Bolts	Manifold Intake	Manifold Exhaust
1967	8-429 (7.0)	60	40-45	90-100	65-70	75-80	25-30	25-30
1968-74	8-427 (7.7)	115	40	90	Press fit	75	30	35
	8-500 (8.2)	115	40	90	Press fit	75	30	35
1975-79	8-350 (5.7)	85[1]	42	80[1]	310	60	40	25
	8-350 (5.7) Diesel	130[2]	42	120	200-310	60	40[2]	25
1980-85	8-425 (7.0)	90	40	90	Press fit	75	30	35
	8-500 (8.2)	115	40	90	Press fit	75	30	25
	6-252 (4.1)	80	40	100	225	60	45	25
	8-250 (4.1)	[1]	20	85	Press fit	20	[1]	20
	8-350 (5.7)	85[1]	42	80[2]	310	60	40	25
	8-350 (5.7) Diesel	130[2]	42	120	200-310	60	40[2]	25
1986	8-368 (6.0)	95[4]	40	90	Press fit	75,	30	
	8-250 (4.1)	125[4]	22	85	Press fit	37	[1]	18
	8-307 (5.0)	125[4]	42	80[4]	200-310	60	40	25
1987	8-250 (4.1)	[1]	22	85	Press fit	37	[1]	18
	8-307 (5.0)	130[4]	48	80[4]	200-310	60	40	25
1988-89	8-273 (4.5)	[1]	22	85	Press fit	70	40	18
	8-307 (5.0)	130[4]	18[1]	80[4]	200-310	60	40	25

[1] 130—1977 and later
[2] 120 ft. lbs. on No. 5
[3] Long bolt: 35, Short bolt: 12
[4] Tighten all bolts in sequence to 45 ft. lbs., then in sequence to 90 ft. lbs.
[5] Tighten bolts 1, 2, 3, 4 in sequence to 11–15 ft. lbs.; tighten bolt 5 thru 16 to 18–22 ft. lbs.; retighten all bolts in sequence to 18–22 ft. lbs.
[6] Dip bolt in oil before tightening
[7] Tighten all bolts in sequence to 38 ft. lbs., then in sequence to 68 ft. lbs.; then bolts 1, 3, 4 to 90 ft. lbs.
[8] See text
[9] Rear main: 120
[10] Plus rotate 70°

85873C06A

85873C07

Engine

REMOVAL & INSTALLATION

Except Eldorado and Seville

1967–71 VEHICLES

The engine is removed together with the transmission.

1. Place the car on jackstands and drain the cooling system, crankcase, and transmission.

✳✳ CAUTION

When draining the coolant, keep in mind that cats and dogs are attracted by the ethylene glycol antifreeze, and are quite likely to drink any that is left in an uncovered container or in puddles on the ground. This will prove fatal in sufficient quantity. Always drain the coolant into a sealable container. Coolant should be reused unless it is contaminated or several years old.

2. Disconnect the battery cables.
3. Take a scribe and carefully mark the position of the hood hinges where they mount to the fender apron, and remove the hood complete with its hinge mechanism.
4. Disconnect the generator and remove the radiator core, fan and lower pulley.
5. Disconnect the lines from the power steering pump at the pump.
6. Disconnect the refrigerator lines (refer to the necessary service procedures) on models with air conditioning, take out the heater hoses, the power brake vacuum line, the carburetor air cleaner, the carburetor and its linkage.
7. Remove the transmission gravel deflector and disconnect the levers and speedometer at the transmission, disconnect the fuel lines, take off the battery ground straps, the primary ignition wire, the oil pressure and cooling system temperature switch wires.
8. Remove the ignition coil and take off the wires to the ignition resistor, disconnect the vacuum hoses to the manifold and windshield wipers.
9. Split the rear universal joint and slide the driveshaft from the back of the transmission.
10. Remove the frame intermediate support, disconnect the starter and disconnect the exhaust pipe at the exhaust manifolds.
11. Remove the bolts that hold the front motor supports at the frame and then take off the idler arm support screws and lower the idler arm and steering connecting link.
12. Attach a lifting device and take up the slack until the lifting device has a little load on it.
13. Disconnect and remove the rear engine support bracket from the frame. Carefully lift the engine with its transmission out of the car.
14. It may be necessary to support the transmission on some sort of movable floor jack so that it can be kept in a downward position and yet guided out easily.

To install:

15. Installation of the engine is the reverse of the removal procedures.

1972–85 VEHICLES

▶ See Figures 29, 30, 31 and 32

1. Disconnect the negative battery cable.
2. Remove hood, after scribing hood hinge outline for proper alignment.
3. Remove air cleaner and heat shroud.
4. Drain cooling system. Unfasten the fender struts from the radiator shroud.
5. Remove radiator hose bracket, radiator cover and fan.
6. Remove upper radiator hose.
7. Disconnect throttle and cruise control linkage at carburetor.
8. Disconnect the brake vacuum hose from the vacuum pipe. Remove the cruise control power unit on cars so equipped.
9. Disconnect power steering pump bracket and swing pump out of way with hoses still connected. Position power steering fluid cooler out of the way.
10. Remove air conditioning compressor bracket bolts and swing compressor out of way with hoses still connected. Do not discharge system.
11. Disconnect temperature sender wire, idle speed-up wire (if so equipped), ignition primary wire, downshift switch wire, S.C.S. solenoid (if so equipped) and anti-dieseling solenoid wires, electronic ignition connector, block temperature sender lead, and all ground straps. On fuel injection engines, disconnect the EFI manifold harness and move it out of the way.
12. Bend back clips and position wiring harness out of the way.
13. Disconnect all vacuum hoses, and purge hose from E.L.C. canister. Disconnect the automatic level control line, on models so equipped.
14. Disconnect alternator, heater switch and oil pressure sender wires.
15. Remove wiring harness from clips.
16. Remove water hose from fitting at rear of right hand cylinder head.
17. Loosen and remove alternator and A.I.R. pumps and remove belts.

Fig. 29 View of the engine compartment—mark all hoses, lines and wiring before engine removal

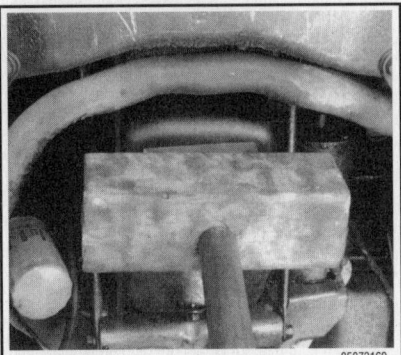

Fig. 30 Support the engine assembly before removing the motor mount bolts

Fig. 31 Use a wrench to loosen . . .

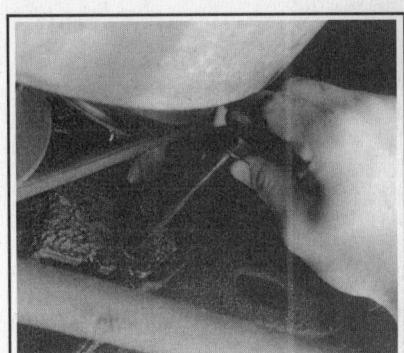

Fig. 32 . . . then remove the motor mount bolts

18. Disconnect the struts and swing out of the way.

19. Jack up the car and support on jackstands. On 1977 and later models, remove the six engine-to-transmission bolts and remove each engine mount through bolt.

20. Relieve fuel pressure on fuel injected cars as outlined in the Fuel Pump Removal in Section 5.

21. Support the engine and transmission with separate jacks.

22. Remove starter motor, then disconnect exhaust pipes from manifolds.

23. Remove the four bolts attaching the flywheel inspection cover to the transmission and remove the cover.

24. Remove the bolts attaching the flywheel to the converter.

25. Disconnect and plug the fuel line and the vapor return line at the fuel pump.

26. Lower the car to the ground.

27. Connect a lifting bracket to the engine.

28. Support transmission with a wood-padded floor jack.

29. Raise engine slightly and pull forward to disengage from transmission, then pull engine up and out.

To install:

30. Install the engine into the vehicle by reversing the removal procedure.

1986–89 VEHICLES

1. Disconnect the negative battery cable.
2. Drain the cooling system.
3. Remove the air cleaner.
4. Disconnect the hot air pipe.
5. Remove the hood and mark the position for reassembly.
6. Disconnect the ground cable at the inner fender panel.
7. Disconnect the ground cable from the right head to the cowl.
8. Remove the upper radiator support and fan.
9. Remove the drive belts.
10. Remove the radiator hoses.
11. Disconnect the automatic transmission collar lines.
12. Remove the radiator and heater hoses.
13. Disconnect all the vacuum hoses and apply tape to each hose to identify for assembly.
14. Remove the power steering pump with the hoses attached.
15. Remove the air conditioning compressor with the brackets and the hoses attached.
16. Disconnect the fuel hose from the fuel line.
17. Disconnect the engine electrical harness from the engine, except at the starter.
18. Disconnect the accelerator control and transmission throttle valve cables.
19. Disconnect the AIR pipe to the catalytic converter.
20. Raise and support the car safely. Refer to Section 1.
21. Disconnect the exhaust and crossover pipes at the manifold.
22. Remove the torque converter cover, mark the relationship of the flywheel to the converter and remove the three converter to flywheel bolts.
23. Remove the engine mount bolts or nuts.
24. Disconnect the starter with the wires attached and support the starter to the frame.
25. Remove the five engine to transmission bolts. Leave the lower left.
26. Lower the car and secure a lift chain to the engine.
27. Place a board on top of the jack and slightly raise the transmission.
28. Remove the remaining engine to transmission bolt and remove the engine.

To install:

29. Installation is the reverse of removal but please note the following important steps.

30. When attaching the transmission to the engine, locate the engine dowels into the transmission and position the through bolts into the mounts and torque to 75 ft. lbs. (102 Nm).

31. Observe the flywheel to torque converter marks made during disassembly and line up in the original position. Make sure the weld nuts on the torque converter are flush with the flywheel. Test for freedom of rotation.

32. Install the three converter to flywheel bolts finger tight, then tighten to 46 ft. lbs. (62 Nm). Retighten the first bolt tightened.

Eldorado

1967–71 VEHICLES

1. Disconnect the negative battery terminal.
2. Match mark the hood hinges for reassembly. Remove the hood.

3. Remove the two nuts holding the cowl rods at the wheel and pivot rods up from the cowl.

4. Remove the air cleaner.

5. Drain the cooling system.

6. Disconnect wires from alternator.

7. On cars equipped with Automatic Climate Control (ACC), partially remove compressor.

8. Disconnect transmission cooler line at left front of final drive by removing the screw that holds attaching clip.

9. Remove the heater hoses at the engine and at the water control valve.

10. Remove the left and right shrouds by removing the four screws that attach each shroud.

11. Remove the four screws holding the fan assembly to water pump pulley and remove as an assembly.

➡**Fan clutches used on air conditioned cars are always to be in an in-car position. When removed from car, support the assembly to keep clutch disc in a vertical plane to keep silicone fluid from leaking from clutch mechanism.**

12. On cars equipped with Automatic Climate Control (ACC), disconnect the vapor return line near fuel pump and remove clamp holding vacuum hoses to steel vapor return.

13. On cars equipped with exhaust emission control systems, remove the air pump.

14. Disconnect the fuel line at the fuel pump and plug the end of the line.

15. Remove the power steering pump bracket-to-cylinder block screws and position pump and bracket to one side. Remove the pump belt. Do not disconnect the power steering hoses.

16. Disconnect the accelerator linkage at the carburetor.

17. Disconnect the wiring connectors at the transmission downshift switch.

18. Disconnect the positive terminal wiring at coil and remove harness from two retaining clips on the left valve cover.

19. If the car is equipped with cruise control, disconnect the wiring connector at the power unit. Remove cotter pin securing accelerator linkage to exterior arm, remove washer and separate linkage from exterior arm. Also disconnect two cables at power unit.

20. Disconnect the oil pressure switch connector at rear of engine.

21. Disconnect all the vacuum hoses leading from intake manifold and carburetor.

22. Remove the two nuts that hold left exhaust clamp to the exhaust manifold and disconnect pipe.

23. Remove the four upper transmission to adapter screws.

24. Remove the right output shaft (drive axle) as described in later paragraph.

25. Disconnect the starter motor retainer clamps by removing one screw at the bearing support and one screw at the engine mounting bracket.

26. Disconnect the wiring at starter solenoid and remove two screws holding the starter motor to the engine and remove the starter.

27. Remove the one screw at the brace at the final drive.

28. Remove the two nuts holding the right exhaust pipe clamp at the exhaust manifold.

29. Remove the four screws holding the transmission front cover to the transmission.

➡**The upper left screw is accessible with an extension and universal socket.**

30. Remove the three converter-to-flexplate attaching screws.

➡**This is done by removing the cork in the harmonic balancer and inserting a screw in the balancer. Rotate the screw to gain access to flexplate-to-converter screws. Do not pry on the flexplate ring gear to rotate the converter.**

31. Remove the vacuum modulator line at transmission and at engine.

32. Working through the center crossmember, loosen, but do not remove, the two transmission mounting nuts.

33. Remove the two nuts and washers holding the engine mounting studs to front frame crossmember.

➡**There is one bolt left holding the final drive housing to the engine support bracket and two screws holding the transmission to the spacer to the engine.**

Do not proceed further until chain hoist is connected to the engine, because the engine may shift!

34. Attach the chain hoist and take up slack.
35. Remove the lower right and left transmission-to-adapter-to-cylinder block screws.
36. Place the small jack under the final drive housing to support the final drive and transmission.
37. Remove the bolt and lockwasher holding final drive housing to engine support bracket.
38. Remove the engine by pulling it slightly forward to disengage it from transmission and up from engine compartment. Turn the engine slightly clockwise while removing to assist in clearing engine compartment.
39. Secure the converter holding strap J-21366 to transmission case using a suitable nut, because the converter is now free.

To install:
40. Installation of the engine is the reverse of the removal procedure but please note the following important steps.
41. Lower the engine in the chassis on an angle that matches the position of the transmission. Install the two top bolts securing the engine to the transmission.
42. Lower the engine completely, seating the left hand mount first and then the right.
43. Tighten all remaining bolts securing the engine to the transmission to 35 ft. lbs. (47 Nm).
44. Tighten the three screws securing the convertor to the flexplate to 30 ft. lbs. (41 Nm).
45. Tighten the two screws securing the front engine mount to the crossmember to 35 ft. lbs. (47 Nm).
46. Attach all electrical connections that were disconnected, solenoids, temperature sensor, generator, switches etc.

1972–78 VEHICLES

※ **CAUTION**

If it is necessary to reposition the air conditioner compressor or the lines, do not disconnect the lines!

1. Matchmark the hood hinges for reassembly. Remove the hood.
2. Drain the cooling system.
3. Disconnect the battery cables and remove the battery.
4. Remove the air cleaner.
5. Remove the upper radiator hose at the thermostat housing.
6. Remove the radiator cover screws.
7. Remove the fan blade assembly by loosening the alternator and rotating the fan to gain access to each screw.
8. Disconnect the wiring from the alternator, starter motor, and compressor. Disconnect the water control valve at the rear of the block.
9. Remove the power steering pump and position it out of the way. Do not detach any of the hoses.
10. Disconnect the air conditioning compressor mounts and position it out of the way. Do not disconnect any of the lines.
11. Disconnect the vacuum lines, cruise control and throttle linkage at the carburetor.
12. Remove the left exhaust manifold flange nuts. Also remove the cooler line bracket screw and the filler pipe nut from the exhaust manifold.
13. Remove the upper screw attaching the steering gear coupling shroud to the frame.
14. Raise the car on a hoist.
15. Remove the remaining screw from the steering gear shroud and remove the shroud.
16. Remove the final drive bracket-to-motor mount attaching screw.
17. Disconnect and plug the fuel lines.
18. Remove the front engine mounts.
19. Remove the lower radiator hose.
20. Remove the right exhaust manifold flange nuts.
21. Remove the starter motor.
22. Remove the flywheel inspection cover and the flywheel-to-converter screws.

23. Remove two transmission-to-engine bolts.
24. Remove the right side output shaft bolts.
25. Remove the two output shaft bracket-to-block bolts and the screw attaching the bracket to the final drive.
26. Loosen the right side shock lower mounting bolt and position the shock outward on the stud.
27. Move the drive axle as far back as possible and remove the output shaft.
28. Lower the car and remove the four transmission-to-engine attaching bolts.
29. Install a lifting chain and remove the engine.

To install:
30. Installation of the engine is the reverse of removal but please pay special attention to the following steps.
31. Lower the engine into position.

➡ **Use of longer transmission to engine bolts will simplify engine locating. Install these two bolts in the top two holes. Use of a long pry bar will provide pressure at the appropriate points.**

32. Tighten the nuts with washers to the engine mount studs to 52 ft. lbs. (70 Nm).
33. When installing the power steering pump, use a 7/16 inch flexible socket and a 9 in. extension for easier bolt installation.

1979 VEHICLES

1. Matchmark the hood hinges for reassembly.
2. Drain the cooling system.
3. Disconnect the battery cables and remove the battery.
4. Remove the air cleaner.
5. Loosely install a special valve compressor tool on the EFI line pressure fitting. Place a towel around the fitting to catch any spray. Slowly tighten the tool to relieve pressure.
6. Raise the car on a hoist and remove the exhaust pipe flange bolts from the manifolds. Separate the left side pipe from the Y pipe and remove the exhaust pipe from the car.
7. Disconnect the shift linkage from the transmission.
8. Disconnect the flexible fuel line from the main fuel pipe. Use a new clamp on installation.
9. Remove the six drive axle-to-output shaft attaching screws from each side.
10. Remove the nuts from the engine and transmission mounts.
11. Remove the lower fan shroud attaching screws and disconnect the lower radiator hose.
12. Lower the car and disconnect the upper radiator hose and the transmission cooler lines.
13. Remove the radiator upper cover and remove the radiator.
14. Remove the four clutch fan nuts and the fan shroud.
15. Disconnect the power steering hoses at the steering gear. Cap the ends to prevent entry of dirt.
16. Disconnect the flexible fuel line from the pressure regulator fuel return pipe. Use a new clamp on installation.
17. If equipped with cruise control, disconnect the vacuum lines from the power unit. Pull the hoses out of the tie-down straps and position them out of the way.
18. Disconnect:
   a. the canister hose
   b. canister vacuum supply hose
   c. throttle cable from the throttle body
   d. heater hoses at the water valve and the water pump
   e. brake vacuum line at the brake pipe
   f. speedometer at the transmission
   g. engine wiring harness at the center bulkhead connector
   h. distributor wiring
   i. heater wire from the water valve
   j. wiring at the windshield wiper motor and the washer bottle
   k. engine ground strap from the cowl
   l. wiring at the air conditioning compressor
19. Remove the coolant reservoir tank.
20. Loosen the A.I.R. pump and remove the belt from the air conditioning compressor.
21. Remove the compressor-to-bracket screws and position the compressor out of the way. Do not disconnect any of the lines.

22. Install a lifting chain.
23. Remove the engine, transmission and final drives as a unit.
To install:
24. Installation of the engine into the vehicle is the reverse of removal but please note the following important steps.
25. When lowering the engine, transmission and final drive assembly into the chassis. Align the engine and transmission mounts, right and left drive axle to output flanges, and right exhaust pipe to manifold before fully seating engine assembly into chassis, the remove the engine lifting chain.
26. Tighten the engine mount nuts to 65 ft. lbs. (88 Nm), and the transmission mount nuts to 48 ft. lbs. (65 Nm).
27. Tighten the six drive axle-to-output shaft attaching screws to 60 ft. lbs. (81 Nm).
28. When connecting the flexible fuel line to the main fuel pipe, use a new clamp.
29. Tighten the exhaust pipe flange—to-manifold bolts to 22 ft. lbs. (30 Nm).

1980–85 VEHICLES

1. Disconnect the negative battery cable.
2. Remove hood, after scribing hood hinge outline for proper alignment.
3. Remove air cleaner and heat shroud.
4. Drain cooling system. Unfasten the fender struts from the radiator shroud.
5. Remove radiator hose bracket, radiator cover and fan.
6. Remove upper radiator hose.
7. Tag and disconnect all electrical wires and leads which may interfere with engine removal. Position them out of the way.
8. Tag and disconnect the accelerator, cruise control and transmission TV cables.
9. Disconnect the cruise control diaphragm and its bracket and position them out of the way.
10. Disconnect the oil and transmission cooler lines and position them out of the way.
11. With the lines intact, partially remove the air conditioning compressor and move out of the way.
12. Release the fuel system pressure and disconnect the fuel inlet and return lines at the throttle body.
13. Remove the six screws securing the transmission to the engine.
14. Raise and safely support the car.
15. Remove the two nuts securing the front engine mounts to the frame crossmember.
16. Remove the flywheel inspection cover.
17. Remove the screws securing the flywheel to the converter.
18. Disconnect the oil pressure switch.
19. Disconnect the wiring at the starter motor.
20. Remove the exhaust pipes from the exhaust manifolds.
21. Lower the car and support the transmission to be independent of the engine.
22. With a lifting chain correctly attached, raise the engine slowly and pull forward to disengage the transmission.
23. Raise the engine and remove from the car.
To install:
24. Installation of the engine is the reverse of removal but please note the following important steps.
25. Lower the engine into the chassis on an angle matching the transmission. Make sure that the mating dowels on the block mate with the transaxle case.

➡**Make sure that the converter is properly positioned to the flexplate and engaged to the front pump of the transaxle.**

26. Tighten the mount-to-frame nuts to 65 ft. lbs. (88 Nm).
27. Tighten the six screws securing the engine to transmission 35 ft. lbs. (47 Nm).
28. Tighten the three screws securing the flywheel to the converter to 30 ft. lbs. (41 Nm).

1986–89 VEHICLES

1. Tag and disconnect the battery cables (negative cable first) and then remove the battery.
2. Drain the cooling system.
3. Remove the air cleaner.

4. Matchmark the hood hinges for reassembly and then remove the hood.
5. Remove the cooling fan and the accessory drive belts.
6. Disconnect the upper radiator hose and heater hose at the thermostat housing.
7. Tag and disconnect all electrical wires and leads which may interfere with engine removal. Position them out of the way.
8. Tag and disconnect the accelerator, cruise control and transmission TV cables.
9. Disconnect the cruise control diaphragm and its bracket and position them out of the way.
10. Disconnect the oil and transmission cooler lines and position them out of the way.
11. Remove the radiator.
12. Disconnect the oil cooler lines at the oil filter adapter and remove them.
13. Remove the air cleaner mounting bracket.
14. Remove the oil filter housing adapter.
15. Disconnect the A.I.R. tubes at the diverter valve.
16. Remove the front right and rear cross braces.
17. Remove the right front heater hose.
18. Remove the coolant recovery tank.
19. Remove the A.I.R. air filter box and its bracket.
20. Remove the idler pulley.
21. Remove the power steering line brace on the right cylinder head. Remove the power steering and tensioner assembly and position it out of the way.
22. Discharge the air conditioning system (refer to the necessary service procedures) and remove the lines to the accumulator and condenser.

➡**Carefully bleed the fuel pressure at the fuel line Schrader valve using a suitable tool and container or rag to catch excess fuel.**

23. Disconnect the fuel lines at the throttle body. Disconnect the fuel line bracket at the transmission and move the lines out of the way.
24. Remove the EGR lines and brackets.
25. Disconnect the vacuum modulator line and the fuel air filter. Position them out of the way.
26. Raise the front of the car and support it on safety stands. Support the engine/transaxle assembly with floor jacks.
27. Remove the starter heat shield. Tag and disconnect the cables at the starter and the engine ground strap. Remove the exhaust crossover pipe and then remove the starter motor.
28. Remove the two flexplate covers. Remove the three flexplate-to-converter bolts.
29. Remove the air conditioning compressor lower dust shield.
30. Remove the right front wheel.
31. Remove the right rear transmission-to-engine mounting bolt.
32. Remove the lower engine damper nut.
33. Remove the front engine mount nuts and the right rear transaxle mounting bolts.
34. Remove the right side engine brace.
35. Lower the car (and the jacks supporting the engine/transaxle assembly!) and remove the top five engine-to-transaxle mounting bolts.
36. Install an engine lifting chain/hoist and remove the engine from the vehicle.
To install:
37. Installation of the engine is the reverse of removal but please pay special attention to the following steps.
38. Raise the transaxle with a separate jack far enough to engage with the engine. Lower the engine into the chassis at the same angle as the transaxle. Make sure that the mating dowels on the block mate with the transaxle case.

➡**Make sure that the converter is properly positioned to the flexplate and engaged to the front pump of the transaxle.**

Seville

1976–79 VEHICLES

1. Disconnect the negative battery cable. On the diesel, remove the rear battery and the engine vacuum pump.
2. Drain the cooling system.

✳✳ CAUTION

When draining the coolant, keep in mind that cats and dogs are attracted by the ethylene glycol antifreeze, and are quite likely to

drink any that is left in an uncovered container or in puddles on the ground. This will prove fatal in sufficient quantity. Always drain the coolant into a sealable container. Coolant should be reused unless it is contaminated or several years old.

3. Remove the hood. Scribe marks on the hinges and their mounting points for installation.
4. Remove the air cleaner assembly.
5. Remove the struts from both right and left wheelhousings.
6. Remove the radiator cover.
7. Disconnect the power brake hose at the point where it joins the steel tube to the rear of the left cylinder head.
8. Disconnect the left and right side sections of the wiring harness and position them out of the way.
9. Disconnect the heater hose from the rear of the intake manifold.
10. Disconnect the upper and lower radiator hoses from the engine and remove the fan assembly from the water pump.
11. Remove the distributor cap and spark plug wires.
12. Disconnect the two ground wires from the compressor bracket and position the harness out of the way.
13. Disconnect the accelerator linkage and vapor canister hose from the throttle body.
14. Relieve fuel pressure on EFI cars as outlined in the Chassis Mounted Fuel Pump Removal section.
15. Disconnect the fuel inlet line from the fuel rail and plug the line.
16. Remove the power steering hoses at the steering gear and plug the hoses and gear. Secure hoses to engine.
17. Disconnect the fuel return line from the pressure regulator outlet fitting.
18. Remove the air conditioner compressor from the engine without disconnecting the refrigerant lines and move it out of the way.
19. Raise the car on a hoist.
20. Disconnect the exhaust pipe and exhaust crossover pipe from the exhaust manifolds.
21. Remove the torque converter cover.
22. Remove the starter motor.
23. Remove the screw and clip securing the transmission oil cooler lines to the engine oil pan.
24. Remove the three bolts securing the flexplate to the converter.
25. Remove the through-bolt from each engine mount.
26. Remove the bolts holding the engine and transmission together.
27. Lower the car.
28. Remove the bolts securing the heater water valve to the evaporator and move the valve out of the way.
29. Support the transmission with a jack and a block of wood placed between the jack and the transmission case.
30. Install a suitable lifting device on the engine and raise the engine off the motor mounts. Reposition the transmission support.
31. Raise the engine carefully, pull it forward and lift it from the car.

To install:

32. Installation of the engine is the reverse of removal but please note the following steps during installation.
33. Raise the transmission as high as possible using a floor jack and a block of wood.
34. Lower the engine in the chassis at an angle that matches the transmission. Engage the engine to transmission and loosely install the two engine to transmission mounting bolts.
35. Lower the engine completely allowing it to seat on its mounts.
36. Tighten the engine mount through-bolts to 30 ft. lbs. (41 Nm).
37. When connecting the fuel inlet line to the fuel rail, use a back-up wrench and tighten the flare nut to 15–20 ft. lbs. (20–27 Nm).

1980–85 VEHICLES

1. Disconnect the negative battery cable.
2. Remove hood, after scribing hood hinge outline for proper alignment.
3. Remove air cleaner and heat shroud.
4. Drain cooling system. Unfasten the fender struts from the radiator shroud.
5. Remove radiator hose bracket, radiator cover and fan.
6. Remove upper radiator hose.
7. Tag and disconnect all electrical wires and leads which may interfere with engine removal. Position them out of the way.

8. Tag and disconnect the accelerator, cruise control and transmission TV cables.
9. Disconnect the cruise control diaphragm and its bracket and position them out of the way.
10. Disconnect the oil and transmission cooler lines and position them out of the way.
11. With the lines intact, partially remove the air conditioning compressor and move out of the way.
12. Release the fuel system pressure and disconnect the fuel inlet and return lines at the throttle body.
13. Remove the six screws securing the transmission to the engine.
14. Raise and safely support the car.
15. Remove the two nuts securing the front engine mounts to the frame crossmember.
16. Remove the flywheel inspection cover.
17. Remove the screws securing the flywheel to the converter.
18. Disconnect the oil pressure switch.
19. Disconnect the wiring at the starter motor.
20. Remove the exhaust pipes from the exhaust manifolds.
21. Lower the car and support the transmission to be independent of the engine.
22. With a lifting chain correctly attached, raise the engine slowly and pull forward to disengage the transmission.
23. Raise the engine and remove from the car.

To install:

24. Installation of the engine is the reverse of removal but please pay special attention to the following steps.
25. Raise the engine to engage the transmission with a separate jack.
26. Lower the engine into the chassis on an angle matching the transmission. Make sure that the mating dowels on the block mate with the transaxle case.

➡**Make sure that the converter is properly positioned to the flexplate and engaged to the front pump of the transaxle.**

27. Tighten the mount-to-frame nuts to 65 ft. lbs. (88 Nm).
28. Tighten the six screws securing the engine to transmission to 35 ft. lbs. (47 Nm).
29. Tighten the three screws securing the flywheel to the converter to 30 ft. lbs. (41 Nm).

1986–89 VEHICLES

1. Tag and disconnect the battery cables (negative cable first) and then remove the battery.
2. Drain the cooling system.
3. Remove the air cleaner.
4. Matchmark the hood hinges for reassembly and then remove the hood.
5. Remove the cooling fan and the accessory drive belts.
6. Disconnect the upper radiator hose and heater hose at the thermostat housing.
7. Tag and disconnect all electrical wires and leads which may interfere with engine removal. Position them out of the way.
8. Tag and disconnect the accelerator, cruise control and transmission TV cables.
9. Disconnect the cruise control diaphragm and its bracket and position them out of the way.
10. Disconnect the oil and transmission cooler lines and position them out of the way.
11. Remove the radiator.
12. Disconnect the oil cooler lines at the oil filter adapter and remove them.
13. Remove the air cleaner mounting bracket.
14. Remove the oil filter housing adapter.
15. Disconnect the A.I.R. tubes at the diverter valve.
16. Remove the front right and rear cross braces.
17. Remove the right front heater hose.
18. Remove the coolant recovery tank.
19. Remove the A.I.R. air filter box and its bracket.
20. Remove the idler pulley.
21. Remove the power steering line brace on the right cylinder head. Remove the power steering and tensioner assembly and position it out of the way.
22. Discharge the air conditioning system and remove the lines to the accumulator and condenser.

➡Carefully bleed the fuel pressure at the fuel line Schrader valve using a suitable tool and container or rag to catch excess fuel.

23. Disconnect the fuel lines at the throttle body. Disconnect the fuel line bracket at the transmission and move the lines out of the way.

24. Remove the EGR lines and brackets.

25. Disconnect the vacuum modulator line and the fuel air filter. Position them out of the way.

26. Raise the front of the car and support it on safety stands. Support the engine/transaxle assembly with floor jacks.

27. Remove the starter heat shield. Tag and disconnect the cables at the starter and the engine ground strap. Remove the exhaust crossover pipe and then remove the starter motor.

28. Remove the two flexplate covers. Remove the three flexplate-to-converter bolts.

29. Remove the air conditioning compressor lower dust shield.

30. Remove the wheels.

31. Remove the right rear transmission-to-engine mounting bolt.

32. Remove the lower engine damper nut.

33. Remove the front engine mount nuts and the right rear transaxle mounting bolts.

34. Remove the right side engine brace.

35. Lower the car (and the jacks supporting the engine/transaxle assembly!) and remove the top five engine-to-transaxle mounting bolts.

36. Install an engine lifting chain/hoist and remove the engine from the vehicle.

To install:

37. Installation of the engine is the reverse of removal but please note the following steps.

38. Raise the transaxle with a separate jack far enough to engage with the engine. Lower the engine into the chassis at the same angle as the transaxle. Make sure that the mating dowels on the block mate with the transaxle case.

➡Make sure that the converter is properly positioned to the flexplate and engaged to the front pump of the transaxle.

Cylinder Head Cover

REMOVAL & INSTALLATION

▶ **See Figures 33 and 34**

6-Cylinder Engines

1. Remove air cleaner.

2. Disconnect and reposition as necessary any vacuum or PCV hoses that obstruct the valve covers.

➡It may be necessary to reposition the air conditioning refrigerant hoses out of the way of the valve cover, however do not disconnect the lines from the compressor.

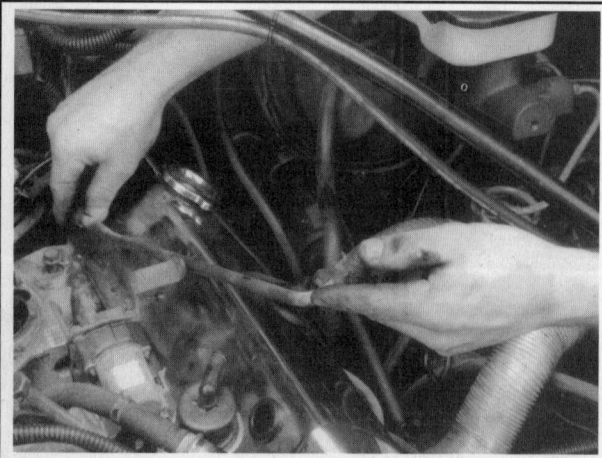

Fig. 33 Remove all necessary brackets prior to valve cover removal

Fig. 34 Removing the valve cover—always replace the gasket

3. Disengage the necessary electrical wiring (spark plug, etc.) from the valve cover clips.

4. Unbolt and remove the valve covers.

➡Do not pry the covers off if they seem stuck. Instead, gently tap around each cover with a rubber mallet until the old gasket or sealer breaks loose.

To install:

5. Use a new valve cover gasket or RTV (or any equivalent) sealer. If using sealer, follow directions on the tube. Install valve cover and tighten cover bolts to 36 in. lbs. (4 Nm).

6. Connect and reposition all vacuum and PCV hoses, and reconnect electrical and/or spark plug wires at the cover clips. Install the air cleaner.

V8 Gasoline Engines Except 8-250, 8-273 and 8-307

RIGHT SIDE

1. Disconnect the negative battery cable. Remove the air cleaner.

2. On the 1985–86 models, disconnect the CCC harness from the intake manifold and the oxygen sensor.

3. At the exhaust manifold, disconnect the AIR hose.

4. Disconnect the wires from the alternator, the choke and the spark plugs, then the harness from the rocker cover (lay it aside).

5. Remove the EGR valve.

6. Remove the rocker arm cover bolts and the cover.

7. Using a putty knife, clean the gasket mounting surfaces.

8. To install, use a new gasket or sealant and reverse the removal procedures. Start the engine and check for leaks.

LEFT SIDE

1. Disconnect the negative battery cable. Remove the air cleaner.

2. Disconnect the power brake pipe from the carburetor and the booster.

3. Disconnect the AIR hose from the exhaust manifold.

4. At the rocker arm cover, remove the PCV valve.

5. Disconnect the wire from the oxygen sensor.

6. Remove the rocker arm cover bolts and the cover.

7. Using a putty knife, clean the gasket mounting surfaces.

8. To install, use a new gasket or sealant and reverse the removal procedures. Start the engine and check for leaks.

8-250 Engine

1982–85 LEFT SIDE

1. Remove the air cleaner.

2. Remove the spark plug wires and retainers from the lower valve cover studs.

3. Disconnect the accelerator, transmission downshift, and cruise control cables. Remove the bracket.

4. Remove the PCV valve from the cover grommet.

5. Remove the seven attaching studs and screws and remove the cover.

To install:

6. Installation is the reverse of removal but please note the following steps.

7. Apply RTV sealant to the two short edges where the cylinder head and intake manifold meet at the front and rear of the cylinder head. Install new triangular seals in position.

8. Reseal the rocker arm cover with gasket part No. 1627340 or apply a continuous bead 3–4mm in diameter of RTV sealant to the sealing flange of the cover. Do not use RTV on gasket.

9. Position the cover to the cylinder head and install the screws. Torque to 4 ft. lbs. (5 Nm). Do not slide the cover around to align screws.

1982–85 RIGHT SIDE

1. Disconnect the negative battery cable.

2. Remove the air cleaner. Carefully loosen screws securing A/C hose to rear of compressor. DO NOT DISCHARGE THE SYSTEM. Pivot hose to allow cover removal.

3. Disconnect two clips holding wiring harness to EGR valve shield and EGR solenoid bracket.

4. Remove the spark plug wires and retainers from the lower valve cover studs.

5. Remove the AIR management valve.

6. Remove vacuum line from the throttle body to vacuum pump.

7. Remove the EGR valve and heat shield.

8. Remove the seven attaching screws and studs and remove the cover. Remove and discard triangular end seals and clean RTV from the engine surfaces.

To install:

9. Inspect sealing flange. Apply RTV sealer to engine surface. Install new triangular seals.

10. Install and fully seat rocker arm cover gasket in cover. Do not use RTV on gasket.

11. Carefully position cover to cylinder head and install screws. Torque evenly to 8 ft. lbs. (11 Nm).

12. Install the remaining components.

8-273 Engine

1986–89 LEFT SIDE

▶ **See Figure 35**

1. Disconnect the negative battery cable.

2. Remove the air cleaner.

3. Remove the accessory drive belt.

4. Loosen the two lower power steering pump bracket nuts.

5. Remove the power steering pump, belt tensioner and bracket assembly and position out of the way toward the front of the engine.

6. Disconnect the left side spark plug wires and conduit.

7. Disconnect the throttle spring and CC rod.

8. Remove the PCV valve.

9. Remove the seven rocker arm cover attaching screws and remove the rocker arm cover.

10. Remove the cover seal and the triangular seals and discard.

To install:

11. Install new triangular seals and a new molded seal into the groove in the cover.

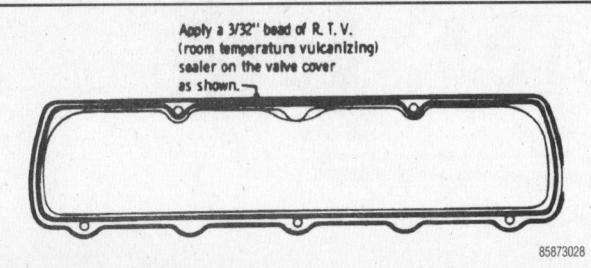

Fig. 35 Apply sealer to the valve cover before assembling—common cover shown, bolt holes may vary

12. Tighten the attaching screws to 96 in. lbs. (11 Nm).

13. Install all remaining components in the reverse order of removal.

1986–89 RIGHT SIDE

1. Disconnect the negative battery cable.

2. Remove the air cleaner.

3. Remove the heater hose bracket and vacuum lines from the valve cover.

4. Disconnect the right side spark plug wires and conduit.

5. Disconnect all electrical connections positioned over the valve cover.

6. Remove the seven rocker arm cover attaching screws and remove the rocker arm cover.

7. Remove the cover seal and the triangular seals and discard.

To install:

8. Install new triangular seals and a new molded seal into the groove in the cover.

9. Tighten the attaching screws to 96 in. lbs. (11 Nm).

10. Install the remaining components.

8-307 Engine

LEFT SIDE

1. Disconnect the negative battery cable.

2. Disconnect the spark plug wires.

3. Disconnect the air cleaner to crankcase inlet pipe and filter.

4. Disconnect the following wires:

• ILC anti-dieseling solenoid

• RVB/ILC/EGR solenoid assembly

• Oil pressure sensor

• Temperature sensor

• Coolant sensor

• Alternator

5. Remove the ILC anti-dieseling solenoid.

6. Remove the alternator drive belt and rear bracket.

7. Loosen the exhaust manifold upper shroud only.

8. Remove the EGR valve.

9. Remove the oil level indicator.

10. Remove the valve cover screws nuts.

11. Install tool BT-8315 or J-34144 midway between the ends of the valve cover, on the upper side. Tighten the screw to apply a load on the cover.

12. Using a rubber mallet, strike on the side of the valve cover, above where the tool is installed.

✳✳ WARNING

Use a cloth to absorb the blow of the mallet or damage to the cover may result.

To install:

13. Installation is the reverse of removal but please note the following steps.

14. Clean the valve cover and head mating surfaces.

15. Apply a ¼ in. (6mm) bead of RTV sealant on the valve cover.

➡**The RTV sealer must be wet to the touch at the time of valve cover attachment to the cylinder head.**

16. Install the valve cover and tighten the attaching screws/nuts to 90 in. lbs. (10 Nm).

RIGHT SIDE

1. Disconnect the negative battery cable.

2. Disconnect the spark plug wires.

3. Disconnect the PCV valve and hose.

4. Reposition the heater hoses and move aside.

5. Disconnect the ILC anti-dieseling solenoid and hoses.

6. Disconnect the following wires:

• ILC anti-dieseling solenoid

• AIR

• Oxygen sensor

7. Disconnect the canister purge hose.

8. Remove the following on the AIR system:

• AIR hoses to the AIR switching valve and catalytic converter pipe

• AIR switching valve

- AIR/air conditioning drive belt
- AIR pump pulley
9. Disconnect the air conditioning compressor rear bracket.
10. Remove the valve cover screws nuts.
11. Install tool BT-8315 or J-34144 midway between the ends of the valve cover, on the upper side. Tighten the screw to apply a load on the cover.
12. Using a rubber mallet, strike on the side of the valve cover, above where the tool is installed.

✳✳ WARNING

Use a cloth to absorb the blow of the mallet or damage to the cover may result.

To install:
13. Clean the valve cover and head mating surfaces.
14. Apply a ¼ in. (6mm) bead of RTV sealant on the valve cover.

➡The RTV sealer must be wet to the touch at the time of valve cover attachment to the cylinder head.

15. Install the valve cover and tighten the attaching screws/nuts to 90 in. lbs. (10 Nm).
16. Install the remaining components in the reverse order of removal.

V8 Diesel Engines

♦ See Figure 36

1. Refer to the Injection Lines, removal and installation procedures, under the Diesel Fuel System in Section 5, then remove the fuel injection lines.

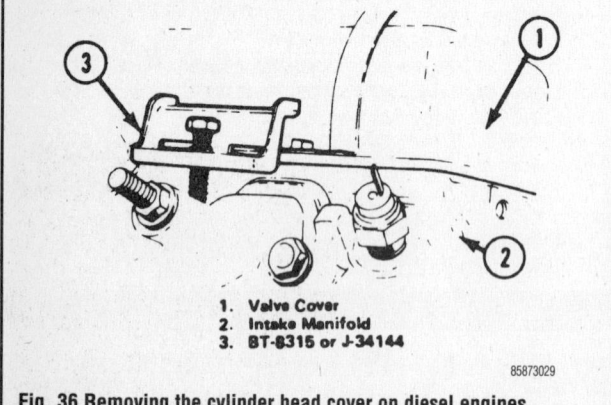

1. Valve Cover
2. Intake Manifold
3. BT-8315 or J-34144

85873029

Fig. 36 Removing the cylinder head cover on diesel engines

2. Remove the rocker arm cover-to-cylinder head screws and any accessory mounting brackets (if necessary).
3. Using the Valve Cover Removal tool No. J-34144 or BT-8315, place it midway between the ends of the valve cover (on the upper side), then tighten the screw to lift the rocker arm cover.
4. Using a rubber mallet and a shop cloth (placed on the rocker arm cover above the removal tool to absorb the blow), strike the cover to complete remove it.
5. Using a putty knife, clean the gasket mounting surfaces.
6. Using RTV sealant, apply a ¼ in. (6mm) bead to the rocker arm cover.

➡When installing the rocker arm cover, the sealant must be wet to the touch.

7. To install, reverse the removal procedures. Start the engine and check for leaks.

Rocker Arm Shaft Assembly

➡All engines except the 6-252 and the 8-429 use rocker arms instead of rocker arm assemblies, please refer to Rocker Arm for procedures.

REMOVAL & INSTALLATION

6-252 and 8-429 Engines

♦ See Figures 37, 38 and 39

1. Remove the valve covers.
2. Remove the rocker arm shaft assembly bolts.
3. Remove the rocker arm shaft assembly and place it on a clean surface.
4. To remove the rocker arms from the shaft assembly use the procedure given below.

DISASSEMBLY AND ASSEMBLY

6-252 Engine

1. To remove the rocker arms from the shaft, you must first remove the nylon arm retainers. These can be removed with by prying them out with locking jaw pliers or breaking them by hitting them below the head with a chisel.
2. Remove the rocker arms from the shaft. Make sure you keep them in order. Also note that the external rib on each arm points away from the rocker arm shaft bolt located between each pair of rocker arms.
3. If you are installing new rocker arms, note that the replacement rocker arms are marked **R** and **L** for right and left side installation. Do not interchange them.
4. Install the rocker arms on the shaft and lubricate them with oil.

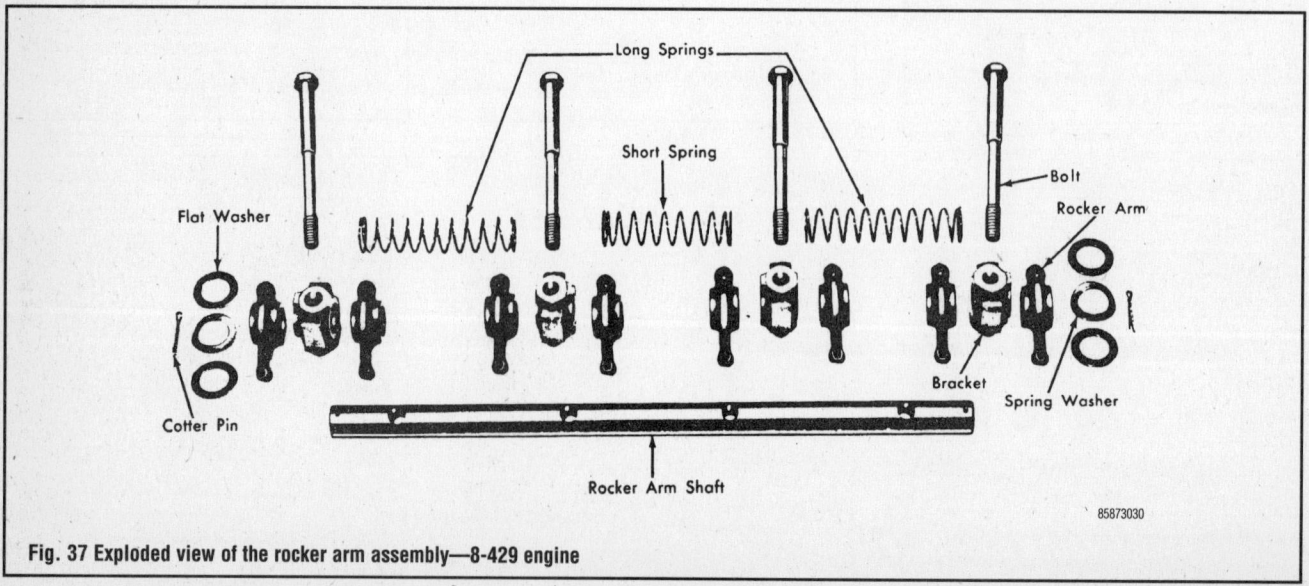

Fig. 37 Exploded view of the rocker arm assembly—8-429 engine

➡Install the rocker arms for each cylinder only when the lifters are off the cam lobe and both valves are closed.

5. Center each arm on the ¼ in. (6mm) hole in the shaft. Install new nylon rocker arm retainers in the holes using a ½ in. drift.

6. Locate the push rods in the rocker arm cups and insert the shaft bolts. Tighten the bolts a little at a time to 30 ft. lbs. (41 Nm).

7. Install the valve covers using sealer or new gaskets.

8-429 Engine

1. Remove the cotter pin from the end of the rocker shaft (end with chamfered edge) and remove the washer, spring, and second washer. Discard the cotter pin.

2. Remove the rocker arms, brackets, and springs from the shaft, keeping them in order so that they can be installed in the exact same position.

3. Measure the rocker shaft in center of the rocker arm wear pattern. If this diameter is more than 0.003 in. (0.08mm) smaller than the diameter of the shaft in the adjacent, unworn section, the shaft should be replaced.

To assemble:

4. If a new rocker shaft is necessary, install a new cotter pin on end of shaft (end without chamfered edge).

5. Install the washer, spring washer, and second washer over the shaft.

6. Install the rocker arms, brackets, and springs on shaft as shown in the illustration.

➡The oil grooves in the rocker shaft should face downward toward the cylinder head and the notches in ends of shaft should face the engine when the assembly is installed on cylinder head.

7. Install the washer, spring washer, and second washer on the shaft and secure with a new cotter pin.

➡The thinner end of the rocker shaft brackets should be against the heads of screws.

8. Reinstall the rocker arm shaft on the cylinder head.

Rocker Arms

REMOVAL & INSTALLATION

➡The 6-252 and the 8-429 engines use a rocker arm shaft assembly. For these procedures refer to the Rocker Arm Shaft Assembly.

Except 8-250, 8-273, 8-307, 8-368 MD, and 8-350 Diesel

▶ See Figures 40, 41, 42 and 43

1. Remove the valve cover.
2. Remove the rocker arm flanged bolts, and remove the rocker pivots.
3. Remove the rocker arms.

➡Remove each set of rocker arms (one pair per cylinder) as a unit.

4. To install, position a set of rocker arms (for one cylinder) in the proper location.

➡Install the rocker arms for each cylinder only when the lifters are off the cam lobe and both valves are closed.

5. Coat the replacement rocker arm and pivot with SAE 90 gear oil and install the pivots.

6. Install the flanged bolts and tighten alternately to specifications.

1981 and Later 8-368 Modulated Displacement (MD) Engine

▶ See Figure 44

These engines feature a modulated displacement design that can operate eight, six or four cylinders depending on driving requirements. The selective operation of the number of cylinders is controlled by a microprocessor that operates four engine valve selector units. The selector units are electromechanical devices which can deactivate both the intake and the exhaust valve of a cylinder.

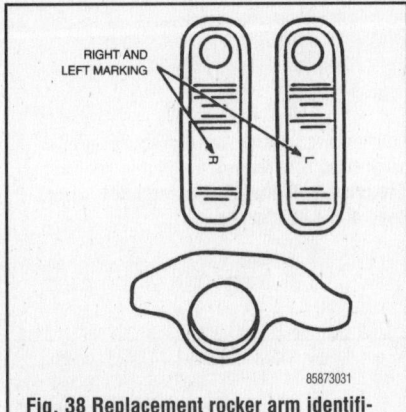

Fig. 38 Replacement rocker arm identification—6-252 engine

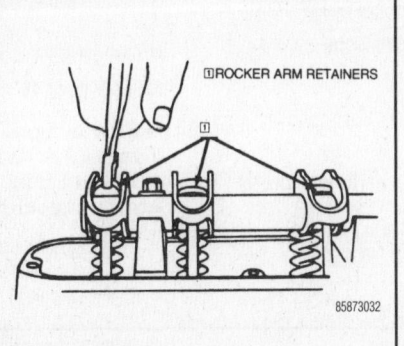

Fig. 39 Removing the nylon retainer—6-252 engine

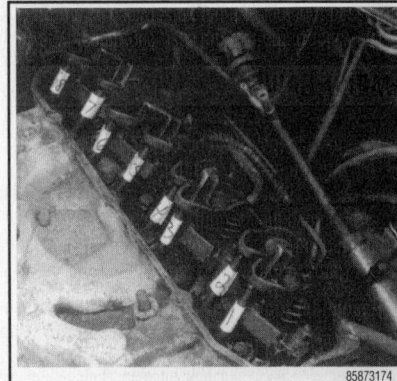

Fig. 40 Mark all pushrods before removal—keep rocker arms in order

Fig. 41 Removing the rocker arm pivot—keep components in order

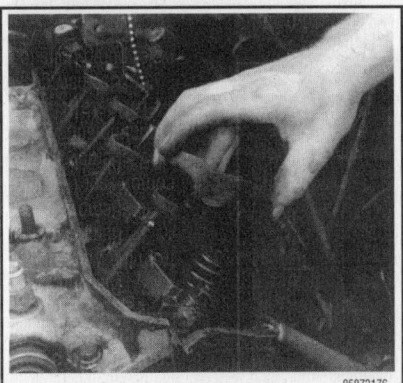

Fig. 42 Removing the rocker arm

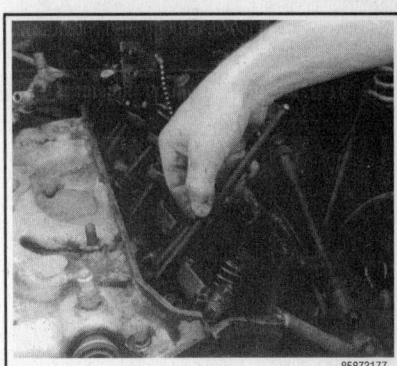

Fig. 43 Removing the pushrods—keep pushrods in order

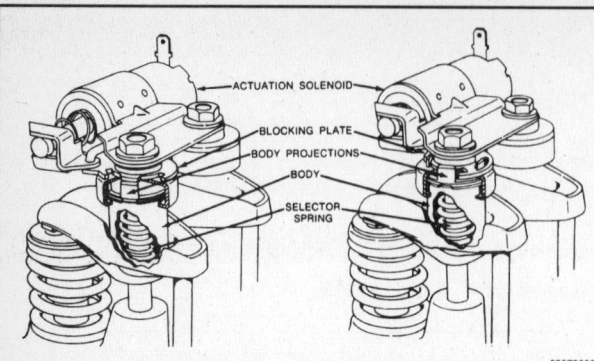

Fig. 44 Modulated displacement valve train details: on the left, the selector body is prevented from moving upward by contact between the projections on the body and the blocking plate above it, allowing normal valve operation. On the right, the solenoid has rotated the blocking plate, aligning the windows with the body projections. As the rocker arm rises, the fulcrum rides up the stud and lifts the body. The rocker pivots about the tip of the valve, which remains closed.

Because of the complexity of this system it is suggested that any service of the rocker arms be performed by an authorized Cadillac dealer.

8-250 and 8-273 Engines

▶ See Figures 45 and 46

1. Remove the valve cover.
2. Remove the five nuts from the stud-headed bolts, then remove the valve train support with the rocker arms and pivots attached as an assembly.

➡This method is preferred as the pivot assemblies may be damaged if the pivot bolt torque is not removed evenly against the valve spring pressure.

3. Place the support in a vise, then remove the rocker arms and pivots in pairs for each cylinder.
To install:
4. Position the rocker arms and pivots to the valve train support and loosely install the pivot bolts. Torque the pivot bolts to 20 ft. lbs. (27 Nm).

➡When installing new parts, thoroughly lubricate all parts with SAE 90 gear oil.

5. Position the valve train support with the rocker arms and pivots installed over the five stud headed head bolts.
6. Position the pushrod into the seat of each rocker arm and loosely install the five retaining nuts. Tighten the five nuts alternately and evenly while check-

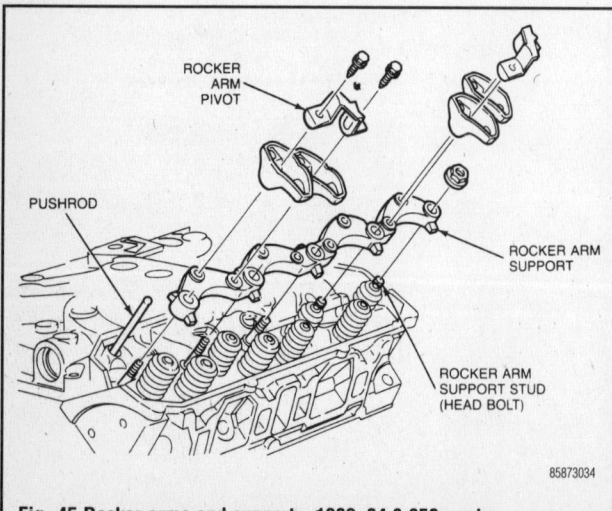

Fig. 45 Rocker arms and support—1982–84 8-250 engine

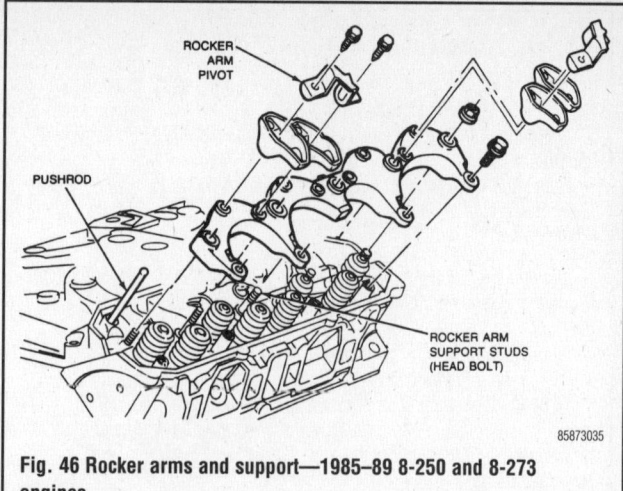

Fig. 46 Rocker arms and support—1985–89 8-250 and 8-273 engines

ing the positioning of the push rods. When the nuts are all the way down, tighten to 35 ft. lbs. (47 Nm).
7. Install the valve cover.

8-307 Engine

▶ See Figure 47

1. Remove the valve covers.
2. Remove the rocker arm bolts.
3. Remove the pivot.
4. Remove the rocker arms.
To install:
5. Lubricate the wear points with engine oil.
6. Install the pivot and rocker arms and tighten the bolts to 22 ft. lbs. (30 Nm).
7. Install the valve covers.

Diesel Engine

▶ See Figure 48

➡When the diesel engine rocker arms are removed or loosened, the lifters must be bled down to prevent oil pressure buildup inside each lifter, which could cause it to raise up higher than normal and bring the valves within striking distance of the pistons.

1. Remove the valve cover.
2. Remove the rocker arm pivot bolts, the bridged pivot and rocker arms.
3. Remove each rocker set as a unit.
4. To install, lubricate the pivot wear points and position each set of rocker arms in its proper location. Do not tighten the pivot bolts for fear of bending the valves when the engine is turned.

DIESEL ENGINE BLEED-DOWN

1. Before installing any removed rocker arms, rotate the crankshaft so that No. 1 cylinder is 32 degrees BTDC. This is 50mm (2 in.) counterclockwise from the **0** pointer on the timing indicator on the front of the engine. If only the right valve cover was removed, remove the glow plug from No. 1 cylinder to determine if the piston is in the correct position. If the left valve cover was removed, rotate the crankshaft until the No. 5 cylinder intake valve pushrod ball is 7mm (0.275 in.) above the No. 5 cylinder exhaust valve pushrod ball.

✴✴ WARNING

In order to avoid pushrod damage, use only hand wrenches to torque the rocker arm pivot bolts.

2. If the No. 5 cylinder pivot and rocker arms were removed, install them. Torque the bolts alternately between the intake and exhaust valves until the intake valve begins to open, then stop.
3. Install the remaining rocker arms except No. 3 and No. 8 intake valves, if these rockers were removed.

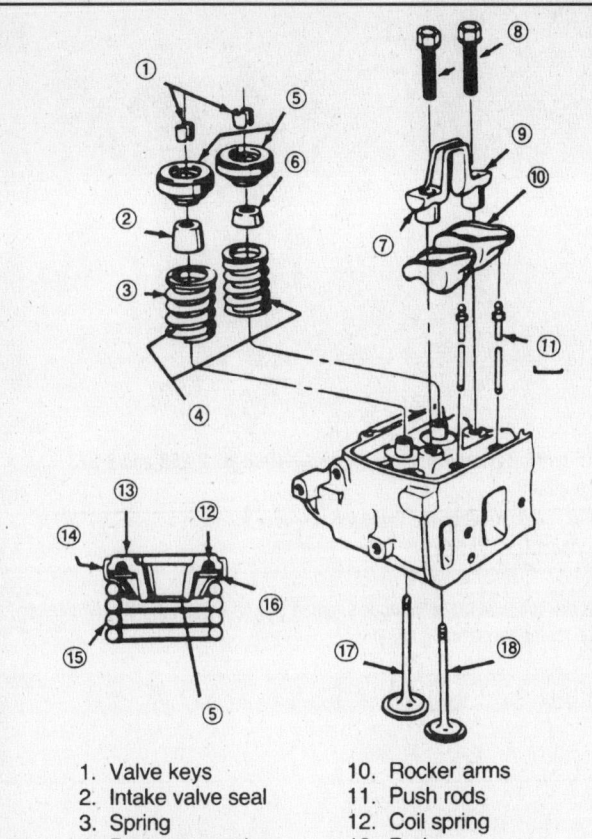

1. Valve keys
2. Intake valve seal
3. Spring
4. Dampener spring
5. Valve rotator
6. Exhaust valve seal
7. Identification pad
8. 34 N·m (25 lbs. ft.)
9. Rocker arm pivot
10. Rocker arms
11. Push rods
12. Coil spring
13. Body
14. Collar
15. Valve spring
16. Flat washer
17. Intake valve
18. Exhaust valve

85873036

Fig. 47 Disassembled view of the rocker arm and springs—8-307 engine

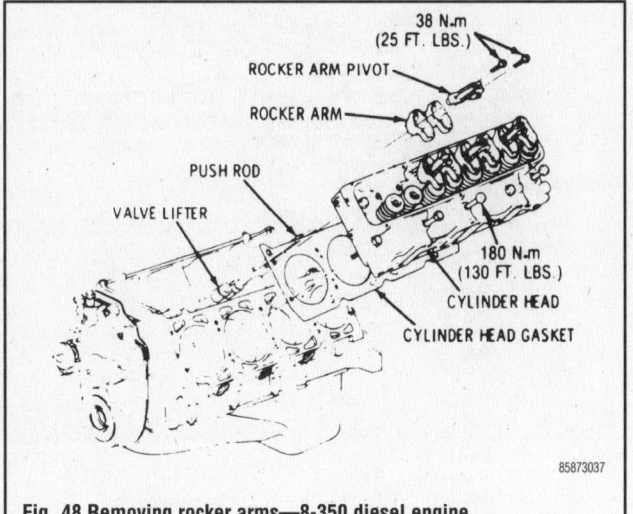

85873037

Fig. 48 Removing rocker arms—8-350 diesel engine

4. If removed, install but do not torque the No. 3 valve pivots beyond the point that the valve would be fully open. This is indicated by a strong resistance while still turning the pivot retaining bolts. Going beyond this will bend the pushrod. Torque the bolts slowly, allowing the lifter to bleed down.

5. Finish torquing the No. 5 cylinder rocker arm pivot bolt slowly. Do not go beyond the point that the valve would be fully open. This is indicated by a strong resistance while still turning the pivot retaining bolts. Going beyond this will bend the pushrod.

6. DO NOT turn the engine crankshaft for at least 45 minutes, allowing the lifters to bleed down. This is important.

7. Finish reassembling the engine as the lifters are being bled.

Thermostat

REMOVAL & INSTALLATION

▶ **See Figures 49 thru 54**

1. Drain the radiator until the level is below the thermostat level (below the level of the intake manifold).

2. Remove the water outlet elbow assembly from the engine. Remove the thermostat from inside the elbow.

3. Install new thermostat in the reverse order of removal, making sure the spring side is inserted into the manifold. Clean the gasket surfaces on the water outlet elbow and the intake manifold. Use a new gasket when installing the elbow to the manifold. Refill the radiator to approximately 2½ in. (63.5mm) below the filler neck.

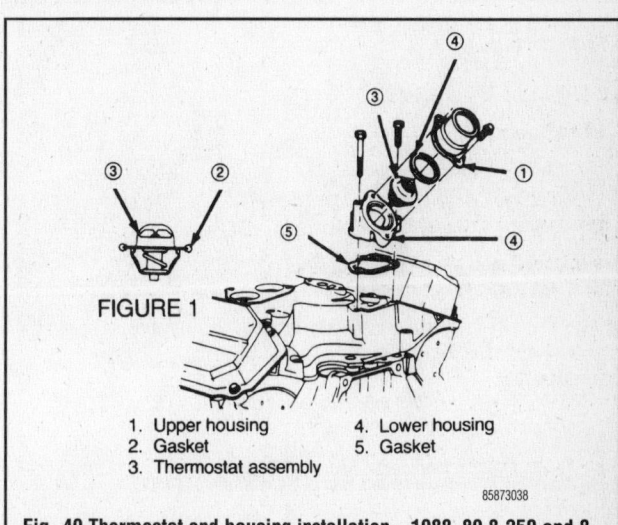

FIGURE 1

1. Upper housing
2. Gasket
3. Thermostat assembly
4. Lower housing
5. Gasket

85873038

Fig. 49 Thermostat and housing installation—1988–89 8-250 and 8-273 engines

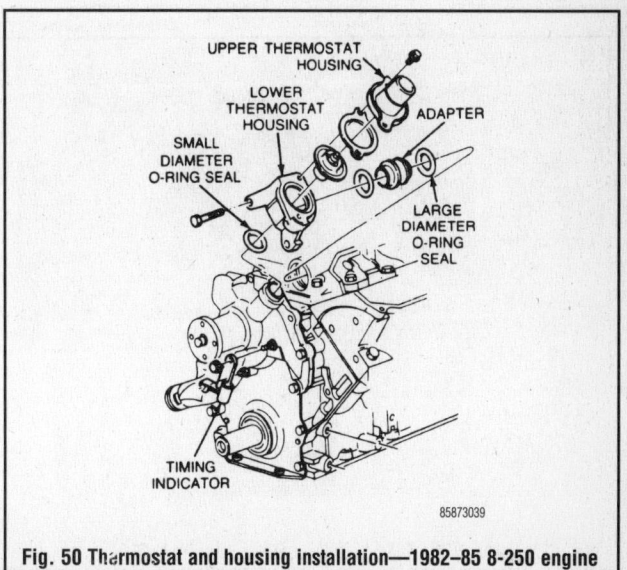

85873039

Fig. 50 Thermostat and housing installation—1982–85 8-250 engine

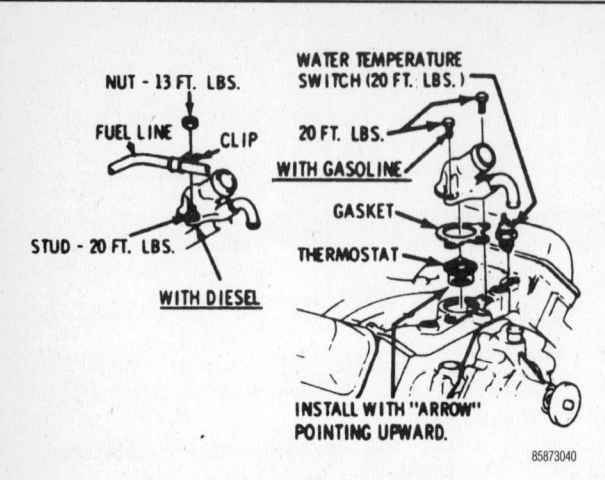

Fig. 51 Thermostat and housing installation—8-307 and 8-350 engines

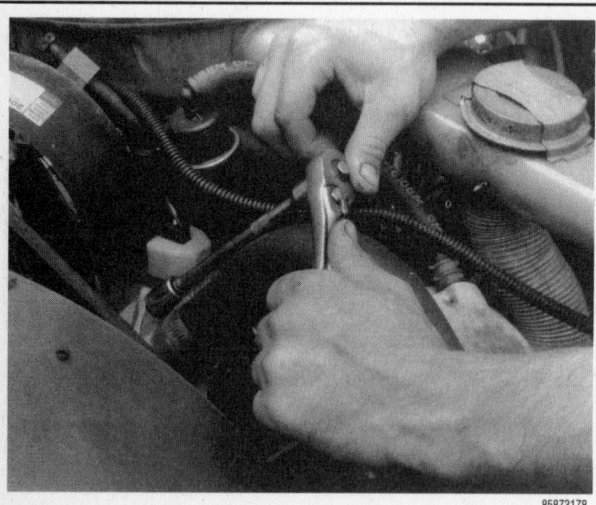

Fig. 52 Removing the thermostat housing bolts

Fig. 53 Removing the thermostat housing

Fig. 54 Removing the thermostat—note position of thermostat for correct installation

➡If the thermostat is equipped with a pin hole, be sure to install pin side facing upwards.

Intake Manifold

REMOVAL & INSTALLATION

Carbureted Engines

◗ **See Figures 55, 56, 57 and 58**

1. Remove the negative battery terminal, air cleaner, heat tube and PCV valve.
2. Disconnect the throttle and cruise control linkages.

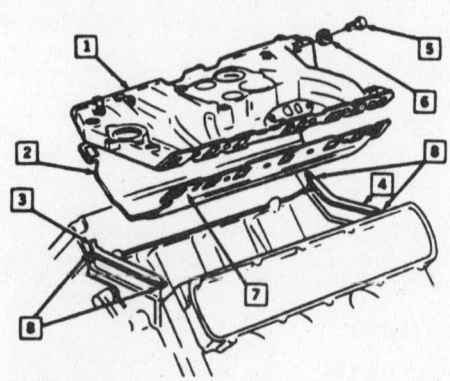

1. Manifold
2. Gasket
3. Front seal
4. Rear seal

Both seals are to be positioned under cylinder heads at each end
5. Bolt (lubricate entire intake manifold bolt with engine oil)
6. Washer
7. 1050026 or equivalent sealer, apply around all port areas of cylinder head side of intake manifold gasket
8. Apply 1052915, GE 1673 or equivalent sealer to both ends of intake manifold seals

Fig. 55 Intake manifold gaskets and seals—8-307 engine

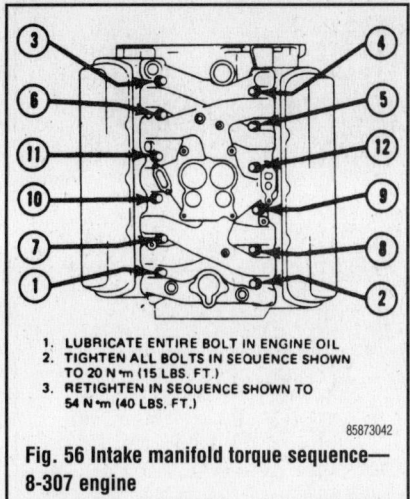

Fig. 56 Intake manifold torque sequence—8-307 engine

1. LUBRICATE ENTIRE BOLT IN ENGINE OIL
2. TIGHTEN ALL BOLTS IN SEQUENCE SHOWN TO 20 N·m (15 LBS. FT.)
3. RETIGHTEN IN SEQUENCE SHOWN TO 54 N·m (40 LBS. FT.)

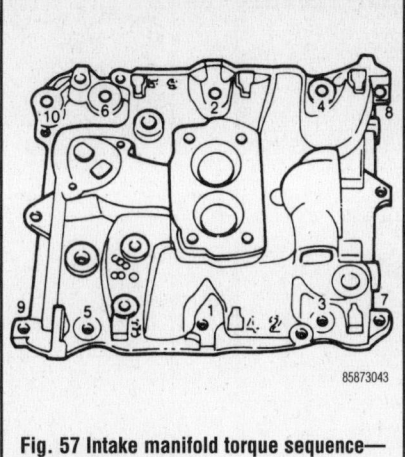

Fig. 57 Intake manifold torque sequence—6-252 engine

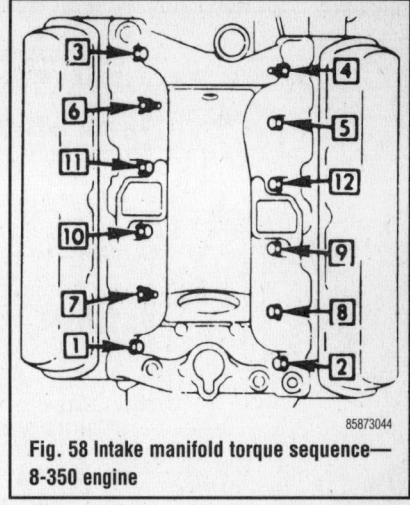

Fig. 58 Intake manifold torque sequence—8-350 engine

3. Remove the coil wires or HEI electrical connector from the distributor.

4. Remove the distributor cap and the ignition wires. Mark the position of the rotor and the wires for reinstallation.

5. Disconnect the temperature sending unit and the electrical connection from the air conditioning compressor. Remove the SCS solenoid (if so equipped).

6. Disconnect the two wires from the downshift switch. On 1977 and later models disconnect the throttle return spring and downshift switch bracket. Disconnect the electrical choke (if so equipped).

7. Remove the plug from the anti-dieseling solenoid and any other necessary electrical connection.

8. Disconnect the power brake booster vacuum line and the modulator vacuum line.

9. Disconnect the fuel line from the carburetor.

10. Disconnect the vacuum advance line (if so equipped) and the canister purge hoses and position them out of the way.

11. Remove the air conditioning compressor and position it out of the way. DO NOT disconnect the refrigerant lines.

12. Disconnect the coolant by-pass hose at the manifold (if so equipped).

13. Remove the carburetor.

14. Remove the manifold bolts and remove the manifold.

15. Installation is the reverse of removal, taking note of the following:

   a. Coat the ends of the new rubber end seals with RTV sealer. Place the seals on the front and rear of the engine block. Position the seal tabs in the hole provided. Tuck the beveled ends of the seals under the edge of the cylinder head.

   b. Apply a thin layer of graphite along both sides of the top fiber part of the intake gasket.

   c. Position the intake manifold on the cylinder heads by lowering it straight down. The manifold is centered evenly by tightening the third bolt from each side. Tighten all the mounting bolts to the specifications listed in the Torque Specification Chart.

Fuel Injected Engines

▶ See Figures 59 thru 67

EXCEPT 8-250 AND 8-273 ENGINES

1. Disconnect the negative battery cable and remove the air cleaner and crankcase filter.

2. Disconnect the throttle cable and cruise control linkage at the throttle body. Remove the cable from the bracket and move it aside.

3. Disconnect the coolant temperature switch wire, the HEI wire, speed sensor wire, downshift switch wire, and the injector wiring harness from the fuel rail brackets and move the harness out of the way.

4. Disconnect the two vacuum hoses from the throttle body to the thermal vacuum switch (TVS).

5. Disconnect the vacuum hoses and power brake pipe from the rear of the throttle body.

6. Bleed the pressure from the fuel delivery system, as outlined in the Fuel Pump Removal section in Section 5. Using a back-up wrench to avoid kinking the fuel line, disconnect the fuel line from the fuel rail.

7. Disconnect the EGR solenoid wires, air temperature sensor wire and the MAP sensor vacuum hose.

8. Remove the PCV valve from the rocker cover and move it out of the way.

9. Remove the spark plug wires and the distributor cap.

10. On the 425 and 500 engines, disconnect the front fuel rail. Be careful not to kink any of the lines. On the 350 and 368 engine, drain the radiator, disconnect the upper radiator hose, the thermostat bypass hose and the heater hose at the rear of the manifold.

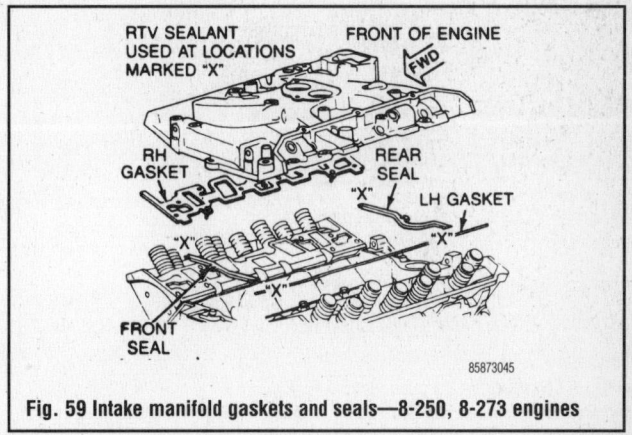

Fig. 59 Intake manifold gaskets and seals—8-250, 8-273 engines

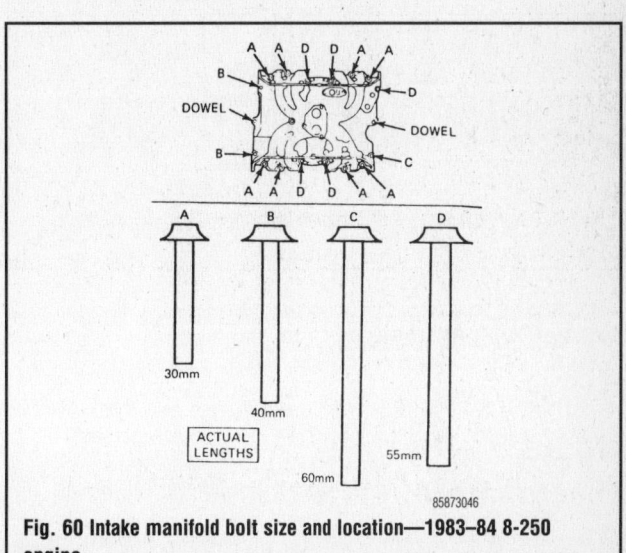

Fig. 60 Intake manifold bolt size and location—1983–84 8-250 engine

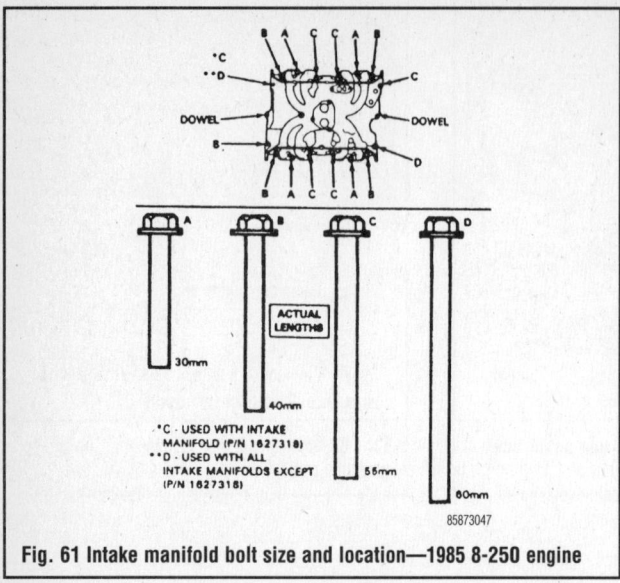

Fig. 61 Intake manifold bolt size and location—1985 8-250 engine

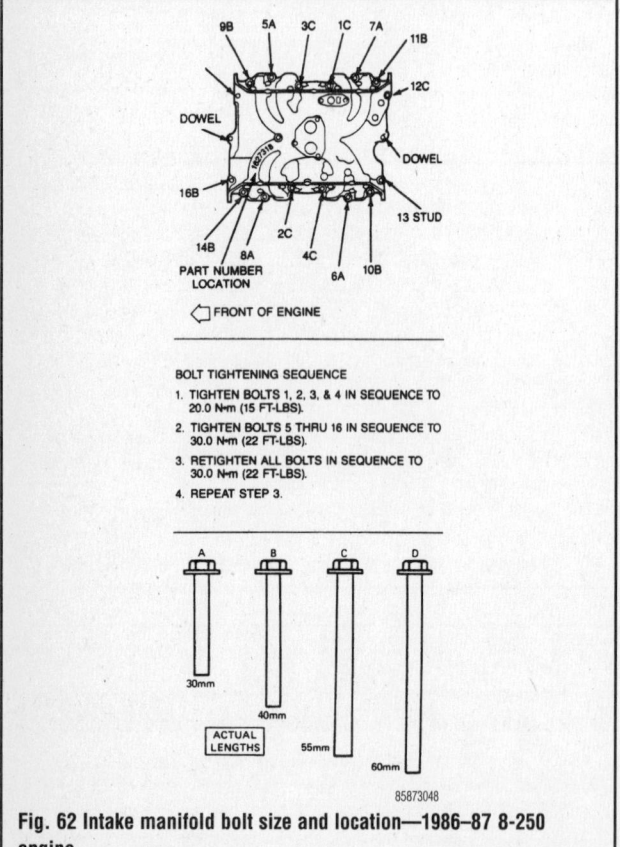

Fig. 62 Intake manifold bolt size and location—1986–87 8-250 engine

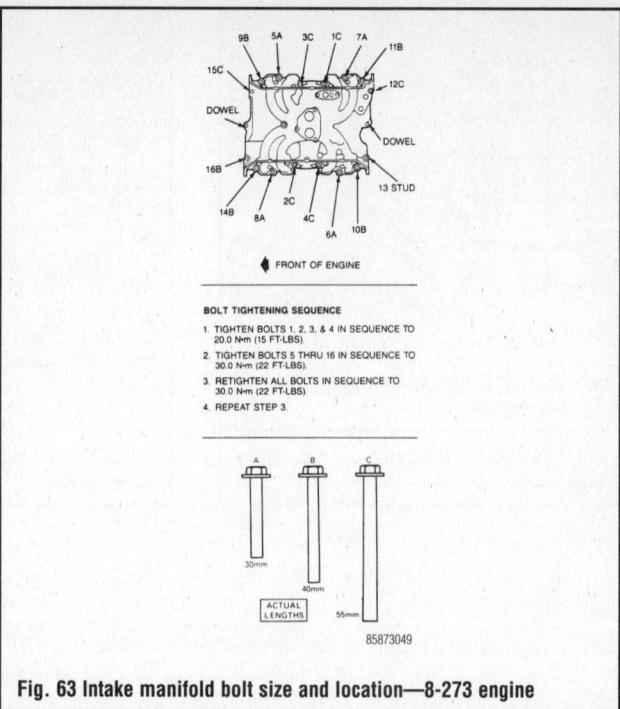

Fig. 63 Intake manifold bolt size and location—8-273 engine

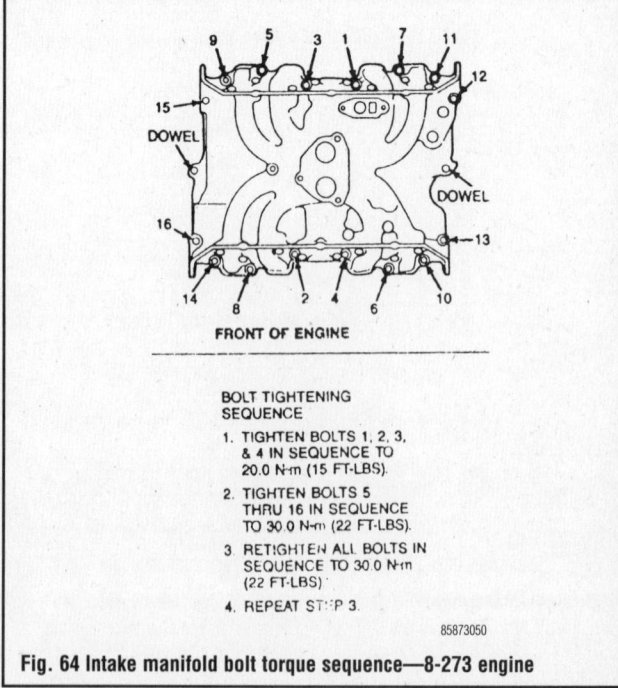

Fig. 64 Intake manifold bolt torque sequence—8-273 engine

11. Remove the air conditioning compressor and tie it out of the way. Do not disconnect the refrigerant lines.

12. Remove the fuel feel (DFI) and return hose from the fuel pressure regulator.

13. Remove the intake manifold retaining screws and remove the manifold. Do not pry or lift the manifold by the fuel rails or their mounting brackets.

To install:

14. Clean all gasket material from the mating surfaces of the manifold, cylinder heads and block.

15. Place new rubber intake manifold seals over the rails at the front and rear of the cylinder block. The tabs on the gasket should be positioned in the holes in the rails and the beveled ends of the gasket tucked into the slot at the mating of the head and rail.

➡**For the 8-368 cu. in. engine proceed to Steps 19–21.**

16. Apply gasket sealer to the sheet metal gasket-shield on the engine. The holes in the gasket should engage the dowel pins on the cylinder heads. Be careful not to use too much sealer near the injector tips.

17. Carefully position the manifold on the top of the engine. Install and tighten the intake manifold retaining screws to the specified torque.

18. Assemble and install the remaining components in the reverse order of removal.

➡**To insure a leak free installation the following steps should be taken on the 8-368 cu. in. engine.**

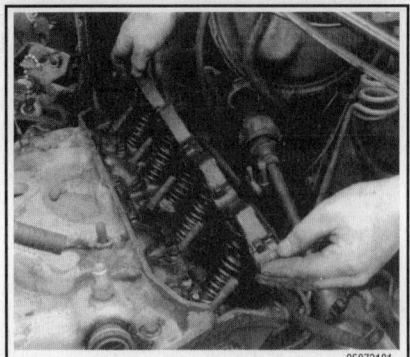

Fig. 65 View of the rocker arm support and intake manifold

Fig. 66 Removing the intake manifold

Fig. 67 View of the engine assembly with the intake manifold removed

19. Coat the ends of the new rubber end seals with RTV sealer. Place the seals on the front and rear of the cylinder block. Position the seal tabs in the holes provided. Tuck the beveled ends of the seals under the edge of the cylinder head.

20. Apply a thin layer of graphite along both sides of the top fiber part of the intake gasket. Install intake gasket.

21. Position the intake manifold on the cylinder heads by lowering straight down. The manifold is centered evenly by tightening the third bolt from each side. Tighten all mounting bolts to 30 ft. lbs. (41 Nm).

1982–85 8-250 ENGINE

1. Drain the coolant from the radiator and disconnect the upper radiator hose from the upper thermostat housing.

2. Disconnect the electrical connections from the following: Coolant sensor, MAT sensor, throttle position sensor, the 12 volt feed wire and the 4 way connector, ISC motor and the injectors.

3. Disconnect the heater hose from the rear of the intake manifold.

4. Disconnect the fuel lines from the throttle body.

5. Mark and remove the distributor assembly.

6. Remove the rocker arm covers then remove the rocker arm support with the rocker arms intact by removing the five nuts which attach the support to the stud-headed head bolts. Keep the pushrods in sequence so they may be reassembled in their original position.

7. Partially disconnect the air conditioning compressor and move to one side without discharging the air conditioning system.

8. Remove the vacuum harness connections from the TVS at the rear of the intake manifold.

9. Remove the 16 intake manifold bolts and remove the two bolts securing the lower thermostat housing to the front cover.

10. Bend the front and rear engine lift brackets out of the way then remove the intake manifold and lower thermostat housing as an assembly by lifting straight up.

To install:

11. Position new gaskets to the cylinder head and crankcase.

➡The right intake manifold gasket for 1984–85 models contains a restrictor which controls the flow of exhaust gas into the intake manifold. The manifold gasket with the restrictor has "RIGHT BANK" printed on it to aid in identification. It is important to use the correct gasket.

12. Apply RTV sealant to the four corners where the end seals will meet the side gaskets, place the end seals into position, then again apply RTV sealant at the four corners.

13. Using new O-rings, assemble the lower thermostat housing and water transfer pipe to the intake manifold.

14. Lightly coat a new water pump to thermostat O-ring with chassis grease and position the O-ring the water pump outlet. Do not insert the O-ring into the thermostat housing bore.

15. Carefully lower the intake manifold/thermostat housing assembly straight down onto the engine so that the dowel pins in the crankcase engage the intake manifold and the thermostat housing is positioned over the water pump outlet.

16. Loosely install the 16 intake manifold bolts. Four different length bolts are used. Engine lift hooks are installed under the front right and left rear mounting screws. Bolt lengths may differ on earlier years, use the correct bolts. Torque the bolts to values and the sequence shown in the illustrations.

➡Final intake manifold torque must not exceed 22 ft. lbs. (30 Nm).

17. Secure the thermostat housing to front cover with the two bolts. Tighten the stud headed bolt to 30 ft. lbs. (41 Nm) and the tapping screw to 8 ft. lbs. (11 Nm).

18. Connect the water hose to the nipple at the rear of the intake manifold.

19. Connect the upper radiator hose and refill the cooling system.

20. Install the distributor as outlined earlier in this section.

21. Install the air conditioning compressor.

22. Install the pushrods in the positions from which they were removed. Make sure they are fully seated in their valve lifters. Since this cannot be seen, the feel for this condition must be developed.

23. Position the valve train support with the rocker arms and pivots installed over the five stud-headed head bolts. Carefully position the pushrod into the seat in each rocker arm and loosely install the five remaining nuts, recheck the pushrods for correct position and tighten the retaining nuts alternately and evenly checking the position of the pushrods from time to time. When the nuts are all the way down, tighten to 35 ft. lbs. (47 Nm).

24. Install both rocker arm covers.

25. Make all vacuum connections.

26. Connect the electrical connections to the following: Coolant sensor, MAT sensor, throttle position sensor, the 12 volt feed wire and the 4 way connector, ISC motor and the injectors.

27. Start the engine and adjust the ignition timing as necessary. Check for leaks.

1986–89 8-250 AND 8-273 ENGINES

1. Disconnect the negative battery cable.

2. Remove the air cleaner assembly.

3. Drain the engine coolant.

✳✳ CAUTION

When draining the coolant, keep in mind that cats and dogs are attracted by the ethylene glycol antifreeze, and are quite likely to drink any that is left in an uncovered container or in puddles on the ground. This will prove fatal in sufficient quantity. Always drain the coolant into a sealable container. Coolant should be reused unless it is contaminated or several years old.

4. Remove the right side cross brace.

5. Remove the coolant recovery tank.

6. Remove the drive belts.

7. Remove the idler pulley assembly.

8. Remove the power steering line brace connected to the right cylinder head.

9. Disconnect the power steering pump and tensioner bracket assembly and position it toward the front of the engine.

10. Tag and disconnect the electrical leads at the alternator and then remove the alternator.

11. Disconnect the cruise control and its bracket. Disconnect the TV cables. Position both assemblies out of the way.

12. Tag and disconnect all wires, hoses and lines which might interfere with manifold removal.

13. Disconnect the upper radiator and heater hoses.

14. Disconnect the spark plug wire protectors, remove the distributor cap and position the cap and wire assembly out of the way.

15. Mark the position of the distributor rotor and remove the distributor.

➡Never rotate the engine with the distributor removed.

16. Bleed the fuel pressure at the fuel line Schrader valve as detailed in Section 4 and then disconnect the fuel and vacuum lines at the throttle body.

17. Disconnect the vacuum supply solenoid and its lines.

18. Remove the valve covers and the rocker arms and pushrods.

➡The pushrods should be marked so that they may be installed in their original sequence.

19. Remove the mounting bolts and remove the intake manifold.

To install:

20. Remove all traces of old gasket and/or sealant material.

21. Install new end seals. Apply RTV sealant to the ends that will meet with the side gaskets.

22. Install new manifold gaskets and position the manifold.

23. Tighten the manifold bolts in the order shown in the illustration, to the proper torque. Refer to the Torque Specification Chart.

24. Install the pushrods in the positions from which they were removed. Make sure they are fully seated in their valve lifters. Since this cannot be seen, the feel for this condition must be developed.

25. Position the valve train support with the rocker arms and pivots installed over the five stud-headed head bolts. Carefully position the pushrod into the seat in each rocker arm and loosely install the five remaining nuts, recheck the pushrods for correct position and tighten the retaining nuts alternately and evenly checking the position of the pushrods from time to time. When the nuts are all the way down, tighten to 35 ft. lbs. (47 Nm).

26. Install the remaining components in the reverse order of removal.

Diesel Engines

▶ **See Figures 68 and 69**

1. Remove the air cleaner.

2. Drain the radiator. Loosen the upper bypass hose clamp, remove the thermostat housing bolts, and remove the housing and the thermostat from the intake manifold.

3. Remove the breather pipes from the rocker covers and the air crossover. Remove the air crossover.

4. Disconnect the throttle rod and the return spring. If equipped with cruise control, remove the servo.

5. Remove the hairpin clip at the bellcrank and disconnect the cables. Remove the throttle cable from the bracket on the manifold; position the cable away from the engine. Disconnect and label any wiring as necessary.

6. Remove the alternator bracket if necessary. If equipped with air conditioning, remove the compressor mounting bolts and move the compressor aside, without disconnecting any of the hoses. Remove the compressor mounting bracket from the intake manifold.

7. Disconnect the fuel line from the pump and the fuel filter. Remove the fuel filter and bracket.

8. Remove the fuel injection pump and lines. See Section 5, Fuel System, for procedures.

9. Disconnect and remove the vacuum pump or oil pump drive assembly from the rear of the engine.

10. Remove the intake manifold drain tube.

11. Remove the intake manifold bolts and remove the manifold. Remove the adapter seal. Remove the injection pump adapter.

To install:

12. Clean the mating surfaces of the cylinder hears and the intake manifold using a putty knife.

13. Coat both sides of the gasket surface that seal the intake manifold to the cylinder heads with G.M. sealer #1050026 or the equivalent. Position the intake manifold gaskets on the cylinder heads. Install the end seals, making sure that the ends are positioned under the cylinder heads.

14. Carefully lower the intake manifold into place on the engine.

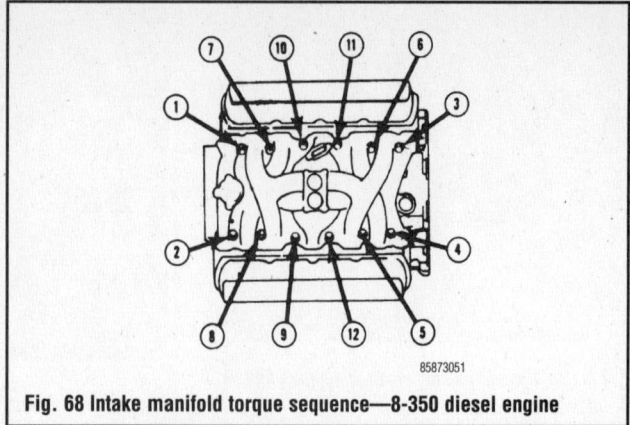

Fig. 68 Intake manifold torque sequence—8-350 diesel engine

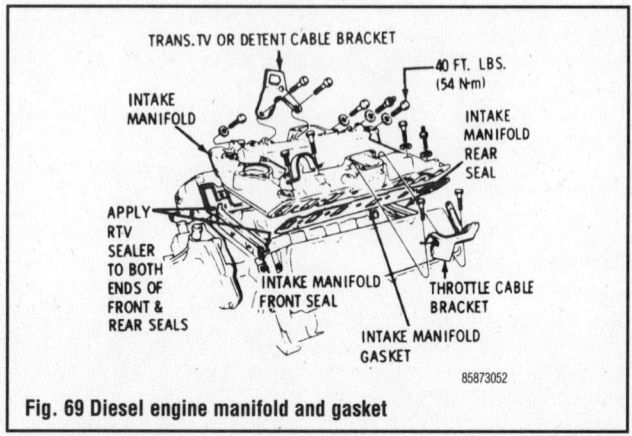

Fig. 69 Diesel engine manifold and gasket

15. Clean the intake manifold bolts thoroughly, then dip them in clean engine oil. Install the bolts and tighten to 15 ft. lbs. (20 Nm). in the sequence shown. Next, tighten all the bolts to 30 ft. lbs. (41 Nm), in sequence, and finally tighten to 40 ft. lbs. (54 Nm) in sequence.

16. Install the intake manifold drain tube and clamp.

17. Install injection pump adapter. See Section 5. If a new adapter is not being used, skip steps 4 and 9.

Exhaust Manifold

REMOVAL & INSTALLATION

▶ **See Figures 70 thru 80**

Except 6-252, 8-250, 8-307 and 8-350 Engines

➡Before attempting this procedure it may be easier to remove the crossover pipe. On California emission equipped cars the Oxygen sensor and the A.I.R. hoses must be removed before removal of the exhaust manifold.

1. In order to remove the left exhaust manifold, remove the air cleaner assembly and the heat duct. Remove the nuts from the no. 2 and no. 8 cylinder (no. 2 and no. 6 on the Eldorado) manifold studs and heat shroud from around the manifold.

2. Unfasten the nuts which secure the downpipe to either manifold. Remove the two studs retaining the EFE valve to the right side manifold and remove the EFE valve. EFI equipped cars have a spacer in place of the EFE valve.

3. Remove the bolts which secure the manifold to the cylinder heads. If working on the left manifold on the Eldorado, also remove the clip securing the dipstick tube.

➡It may not be possible to remove the fifth bolt from the front of the cylinder heads on some Cadillac engines. Back the bolt all the way out and remove it with the manifolds.

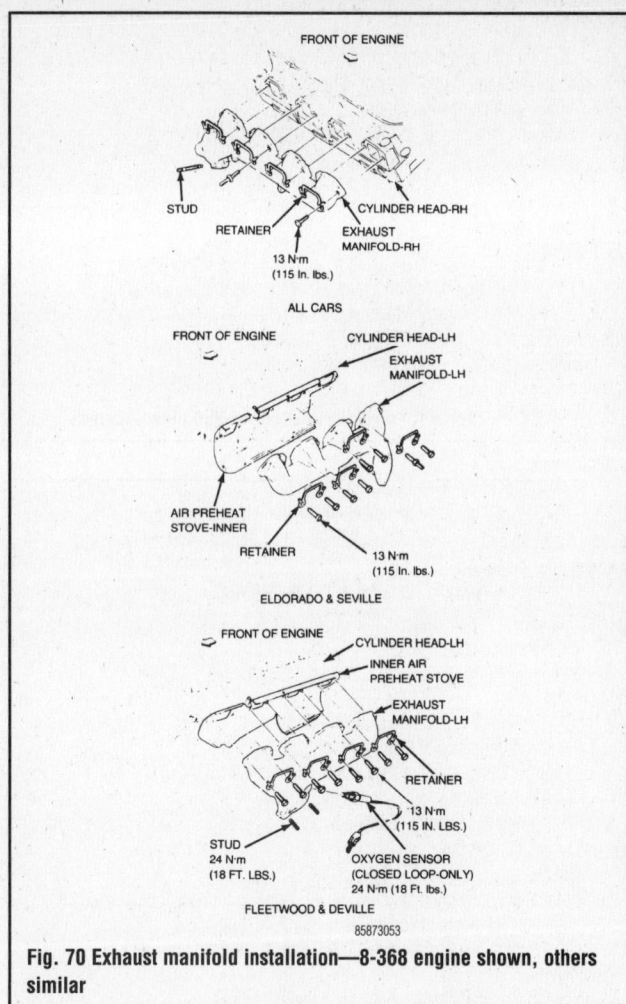

Fig. 70 Exhaust manifold installation—8-368 engine shown, others similar

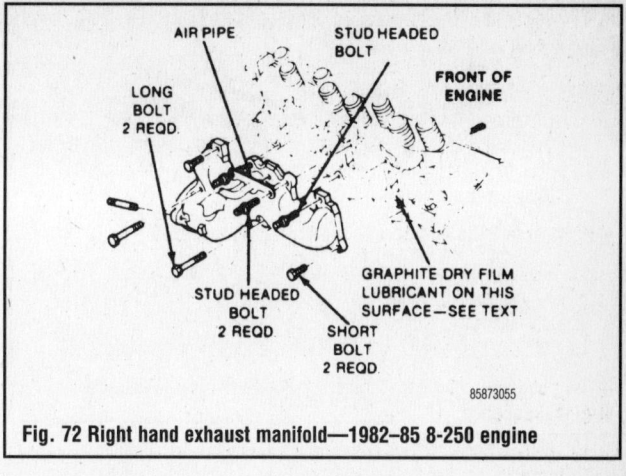

Fig. 72 Right hand exhaust manifold—1982–85 8-250 engine

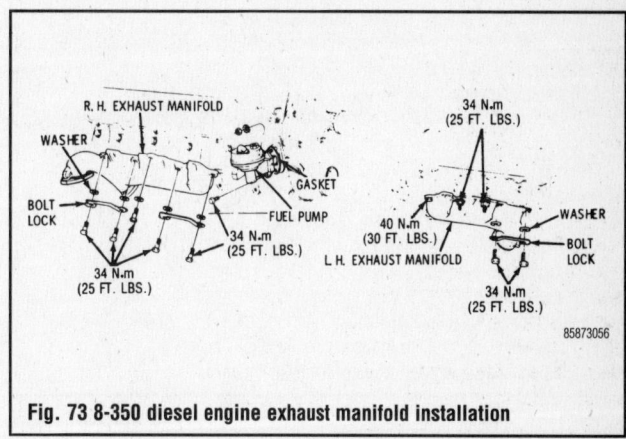

Fig. 73 8-350 diesel engine exhaust manifold installation

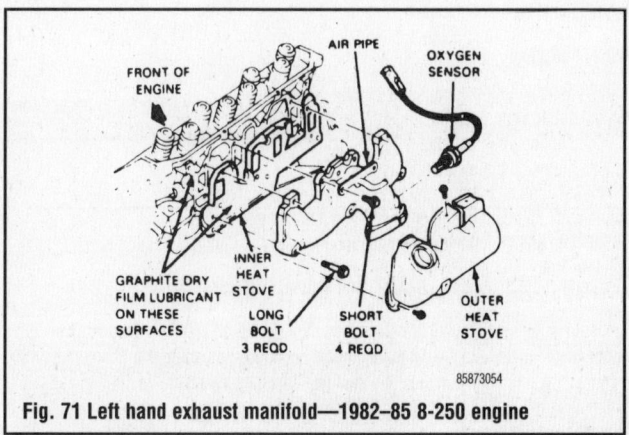

Fig. 71 Left hand exhaust manifold—1982–85 8-250 engine

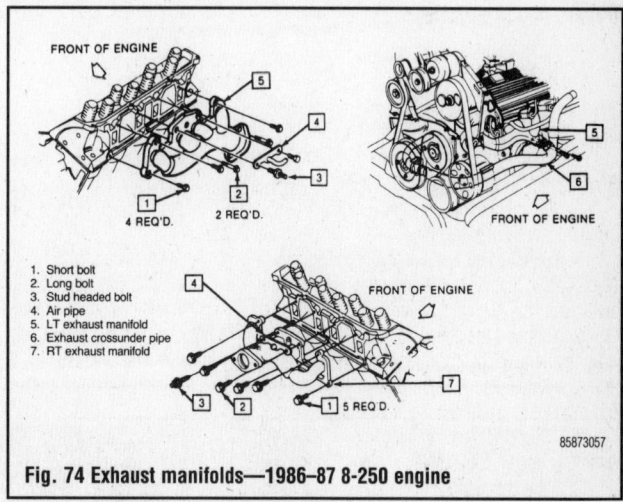

Fig. 74 Exhaust manifolds—1986–87 8-250 engine

4. Lift the manifold out of the engine compartment.

5. Installation is the reverse of removal. Lubricate the cylinder head installation surface with moly grease. Install the fifth bolt from the front prior to installing the manifold. Tighten the bolts to specifications. On the right manifold, position the EFE valve (spacer on EFI equipped cars) on the manifold with the actuator toward the engine block. Tighten the two stud bolts.

6-252 Engine

1. Remove the three upper exhaust manifold bolts. Be careful not to break the spark plug noise suppression bracket.

2. Raise the car and safely support it on jackstands.

3. Disconnect the exhaust crossover pipe.

4. Disconnect the EFE pipe on the left side and remove the EFE valve.

5. Remove the two lower exhaust manifold-to-cylinder head bolts.

6. Carefully lower the exhaust manifold and remove from beneath the car.

7. Installation is the reverse of removal

8-350 EFI and Diesel Engines

LEFT SIDE

1. Remove the air cleaner.

2. Remove the lower alternator bracket.

3. Raise the car and support on jackstands. Disconnect the crossover pipe.

4. Lower the car and remove the manifold from above.

5. Installation is the reverse of the removal.

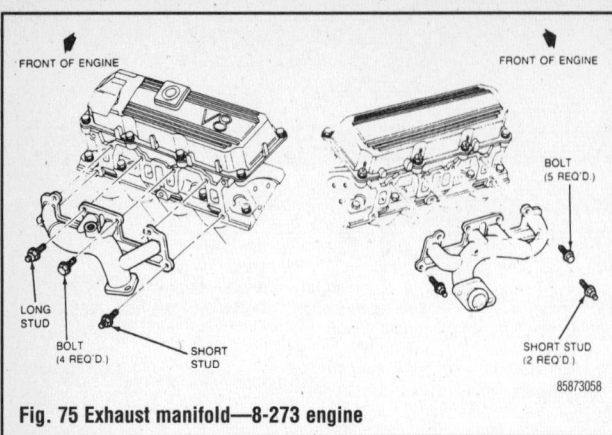

Fig. 75 Exhaust manifold—8-273 engine

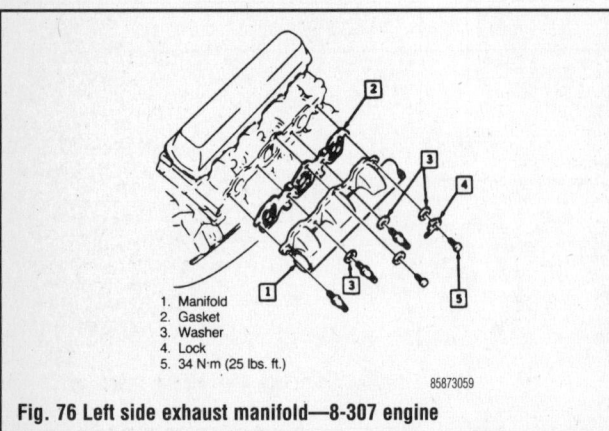

1. Manifold
2. Gasket
3. Washer
4. Lock
5. 34 N·m (25 lbs. ft.)

Fig. 76 Left side exhaust manifold—8-307 engine

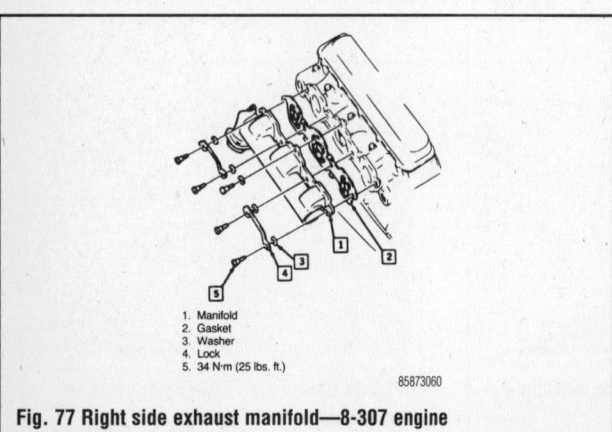

1. Manifold
2. Gasket
3. Washer
4. Lock
5. 34 N·m (25 lbs. ft.)

Fig. 77 Right side exhaust manifold—8-307 engine

RIGHT SIDE

1. Raise the car and support on jackstands.
2. Disconnect the crossover and exhaust pipes.
3. Remove the right front wheel.
4. Remove the exhaust manifold from under the car.
5. Installation is the reverse of the removal.

8-250 and 273 Engines

LEFT SIDE

1. Remove the air cleaner and tube assembly from the preheat stove.
2. Remove the one screw securing the oil dipstick tube to the preheat stove.
3. Remove the preheat stove from the manifold.
4. Disconnect the Y-pipe from the exhaust manifold.
5. Remove the oxygen sensor using a 1 inch box end wrench.
6. Remove the exhaust manifold retaining bolts and remove the exhaust manifold from the car.

   To install:
7. Installation is the reverse of removal. Apply a thin layer of graphite dry film lubricant to the areas of the exhaust manifold which will contact the cylinder head and heat stove. Failure to do this may result in exhaust manifold cracking after prolonged driving.
8. Tighten the manifold bolts to 18 ft. lbs. (24 Nm).

RIGHT SIDE

1. Remove the nut securing the transmission cooler line bracket to the exhaust manifold.
2. Remove the two nuts retaining the air valve bracket to the manifold.
3. Remove the upper exhaust manifold to head bolts.
4. Jack up the car and safely support with jackstands.
5. Remove the lower exhaust manifold to head bolts.
6. Disconnect the exhaust Y-pipe from the manifold and remove the exhaust manifold from the engine.

   To install:
7. Installation is the reverse of removal. Apply a thin layer of graphite dry film lubricant to the areas of the exhaust manifold which will contact the cylinder head. Failure to do this may result in exhaust manifold cracking after prolonged driving.
8. Tighten the manifold bolts to 18 ft. lbs. (24 Nm).

8-307 Engine

RIGHT SIDE

1. Disconnect the negative battery cable.
2. Raise and support the vehicle on jackstands.
3. Remove the exhaust pipe bolts, then lower the vehicle.
4. Remove the air cleaner.
5. Disconnect the spark plug wires from the spark plugs, the vacuum hoses from the carbon canister and the AIR hose(s).
6. Loosen the alternator belt, then remove the lower alternator bracket and the AIR valve.
7. Disconnect the converter's AIR pipe from the back of the manifold.

Fig. 78 Removing the heat shield— exhaust manifold removal

Fig. 79 Remove all necessary components—common exhaust manifold removal

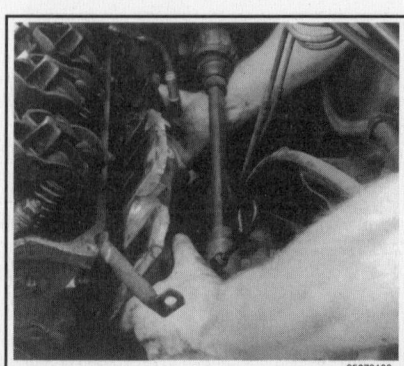

Fig. 80 Removing the exhaust manifold— always replace the gasket

8. Remove the exhaust manifold bolts and the manifold.
9. Using a putty knife, clean the gasket mounting surfaces.
10. To install, use new gaskets and reverse the removal procedures. Adjust the drive belts. Start the engine and check for leaks.

LEFT SIDE

1. Disconnect the negative battery cable.
2. Raise and support the vehicle on jackstands.
3. Remove the exhaust pipe from the manifold, then lower the vehicle.
4. Disconnect the AIR hose.
5. If equipped with air conditioning, loosen the bracket at the front of the head, then remove the rear bracket and the compressor.
6. If equipped with power steering, remove the power steering pump and the lower adjusting bracket.
7. Remove the exhaust manifold bolts, the wire loom holder at the valve cover and the manifold.

8. Using putty knife, clean the gasket mounting surfaces.
9. To install, use new gaskets and reverse the removal procedures. Adjust the drive belts. Start the engine and check for leaks.

Radiator

REMOVAL & INSTALLATION

▶ See Figures 81 thru 91

➡ On the 8-250 and 8-273 engines use only a coolant solution specifically designed for use in aluminum engines.

1. Disconnect the battery ground cable.
2. Drain the cooling system.

Fig. 81 Removing the support mounting bolt

Fig. 82 Removing the support

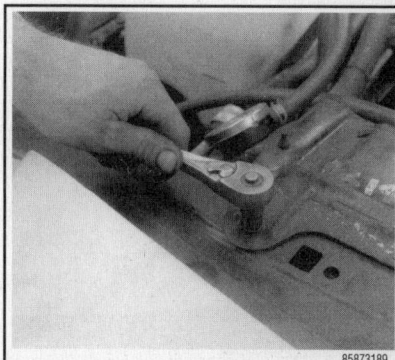
Fig. 83 Removing the radiator metal cover bolt

Fig. 84 Removing the radiator metal cover

Fig. 85 Detaching the radiator overflow hose

Fig. 86 Unfastening the transmission oil cooler lines

Fig. 87 Removing the radiator

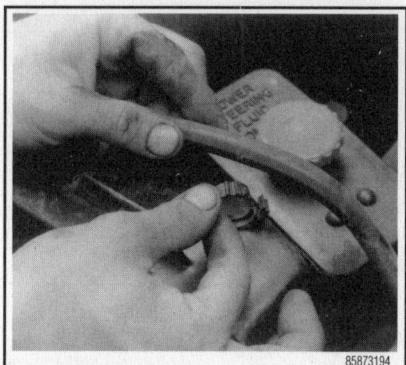
Fig. 88 Removing the hose from the radiator fan shroud

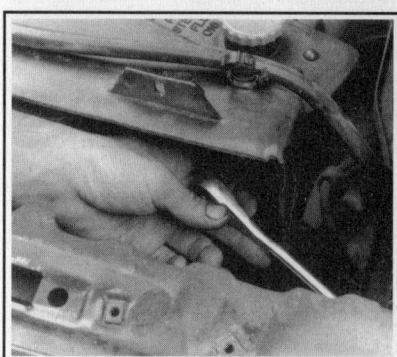
Fig. 89 Removing the power steering tank bolts from the radiator fan shroud

Fig. 90 Removing the power steering tank from the radiator fan shroud

Fig. 91 Removing a common radiator fan shroud

3. Disconnect the air conditioning compressor, if so equipped, and position it out of the way without disconnecting the hoses.

4. Remove the clamp that holds the air conditioning high pressure vapor line to the cradle.

5. Loosen the hose clamps and disconnect the upper and lower radiator hoses.

6. Disconnect the two transmission cooler lines and plug them.

➡**Disconnect the heater return hose, if so equipped.**

7. Remove the two top radiator cradle clamps, straps or sheet metal cover and the fan shroud. Disconnect the reservoir hose from the filler neck.

8. Remove the vacuum hoses, if so equipped. Mark them for proper installation.

9. Pull the radiator straight up and out of the car.

10. Reverse the above procedure for installation.

Water Pump

The water pump is a die cast, centrifugal type with sealed bearings. Since it is pressed together, it must be serviced as a unit.

REMOVAL & INSTALLATION

▶ **See Figures 92 thru 102**

Except Diesel Engine

1. Disconnect the negative battery cable and drain the cooling system.

2. If necessary, remove the fan shroud or the upper radiator support.

3. Remove the necessary drive belts.

4. Remove the fan and water pump pulley.

5. Remove the alternator and the power steering pump (if equipped) brackets, then move the units aside.

6. Remove the heater hose and the lower radiator hose from the pump.

7. Remove the water pump retaining bolts and the pump. Clean the gasket mounting surfaces.

➡**Use an anti-seize compound on the water pump bolt threads.**

To install:

8. Use new gaskets and reverse the removal procedures. Torque the water pump, the alternator and the power steering (if equipped) mounting bolts to 30 ft. lbs. (41 Nm). Adjust the drive belts and fill the cooling system.

➡**If a belt tensioning gauge is available, adjust the belts to 100–130 lbs. of tension on new belts or to 70 lbs. on used belts. If the gauge is not available, adjust the belts so that a ¼–½ inch (6–13mm) deflection can be made on the longest span of the belt under moderate thumb pressure.**

Diesel

1. Disconnect the negative battery cable and drain the cooling system.

✳✳ CAUTION

When draining the coolant, keep in mind that cats and dogs are attracted by the ethylene glycol antifreeze, and are quite likely to drink any that is left in an uncovered container or in puddles on the ground. This will prove fatal in sufficient quantity. Always drain the coolant into a sealable container. Coolant should be reused unless it is contaminated or several years old.

2. Disconnect the lower radiator hose, the heater hose and the by-pass hose from the water pump.

3. Remove the fan assembly, the drive belts and the water pump pulley.

4. Remove the alternator, the power steering pump and the air conditioning compressor (if equipped) brackets, then move the units aside.

5. Remove the water pump mounting bolts and the pump. Clean the gasket mounting surfaces.

To install:

6. Use new gaskets, sealant and reverse the removal procedures. Torque the water pump bolts to 22 ft. lbs. (30 Nm). Adjust the belts and refill the cooling system.

➡**Apply sealer to the lower water pump bolts.**

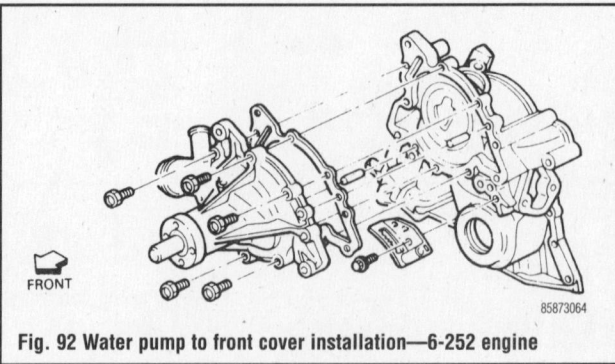

Fig. 92 Water pump to front cover installation—6-252 engine

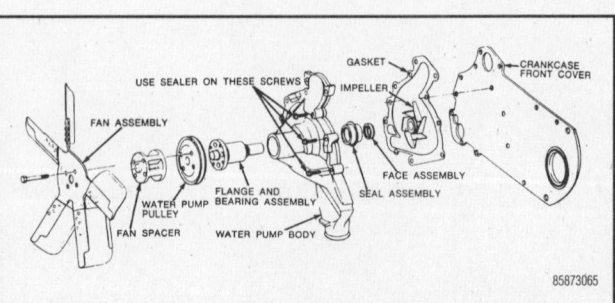

Fig. 93 Water pump exploded view—8-368, 425, 472 and 500 engines

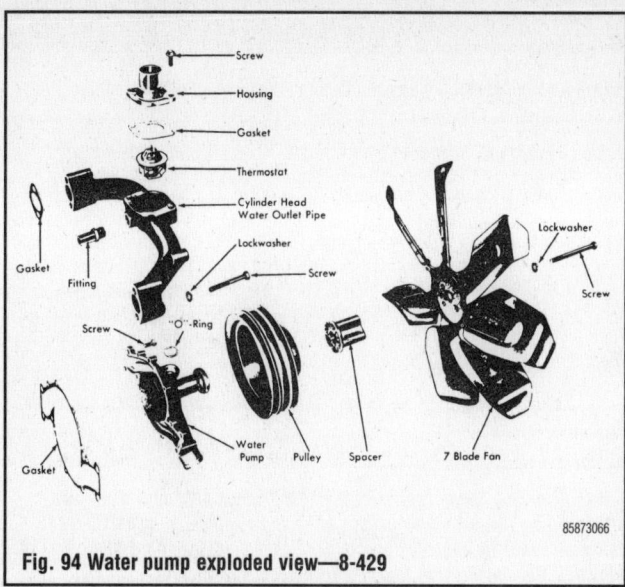

Fig. 94 Water pump exploded view—8-429

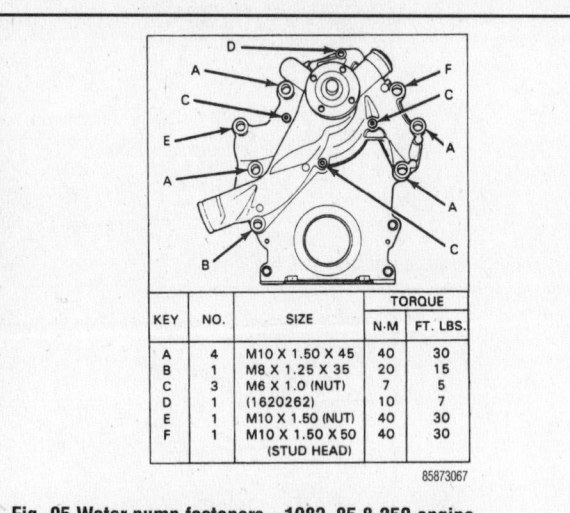

KEY	NO.	SIZE	TORQUE	
			N·M	FT. LBS.
A	4	M10 X 1.50 X 45	40	30
B	1	M8 X 1.25 X 35	20	15
C	3	M6 X 1.0 (NUT)	7	5
D	1	(1620262)	10	7
E	1	M10 X 1.50 (NUT)	40	30
F	1	M10 X 1.50 X 50 (STUD HEAD)	40	30

Fig. 95 Water pump fasteners—1982–85 8-250 engine

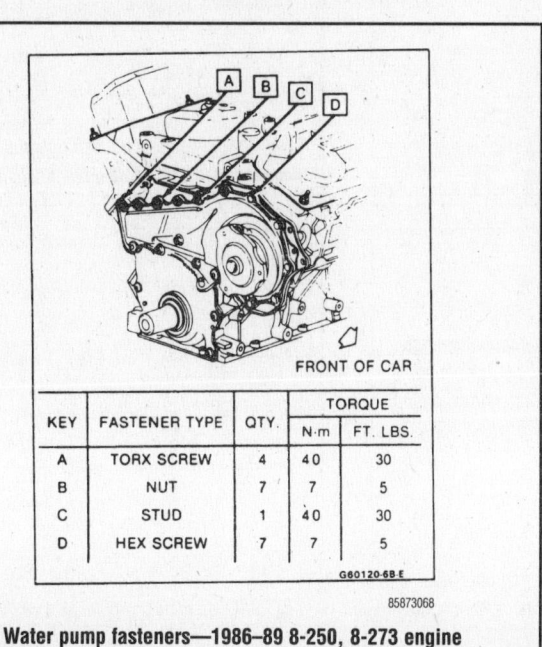

FRONT OF CAR

KEY	FASTENER TYPE	QTY.	TORQUE	
			N·m	FT. LBS.
A	TORX SCREW	4	40	30
B	NUT	7	7	5
C	STUD	1	40	30
D	HEX SCREW	7	7	5

Fig. 96 Water pump fasteners—1986–89 8-250, 8-273 engine

Fig. 97 Removing the cooling fan retaining nuts

Fig. 98 Remove the clutch fan assembly

Fig. 99 Remove the water pump pulley

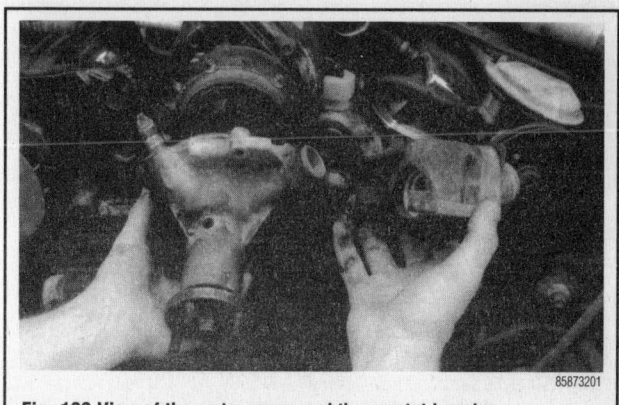

Fig. 100 View of the water pump and thermostat housing

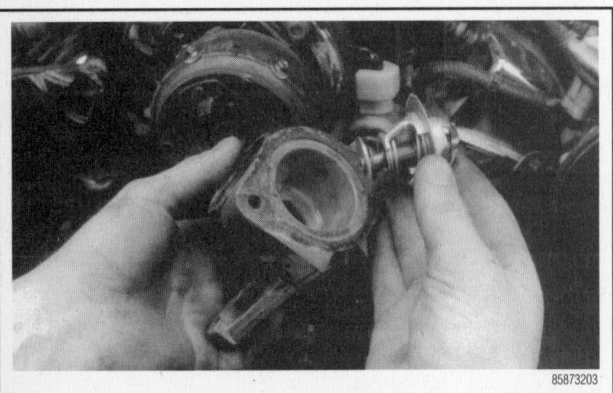

Fig. 101 Removing the thermostat housing—always replace the gasket

Fig. 102 Removing the thermostat—always replace the gasket

Cylinder Head

REMOVAL & INSTALLATION

♦ See Figures 103 thru 112

➥ Care must be used when replacing Cadillac engine cylinder head bolts. They are different lengths. Mark them during removal so they may be installed in their original position.

Most engines described in this book use hydraulic lifters, which require no periodic adjustment. In the event of cylinder head removal or any operation that requires disturbing the rocker arms, the rocker arms will have to be adjusted. Refer to Valve Lash Adjustment later in this section.

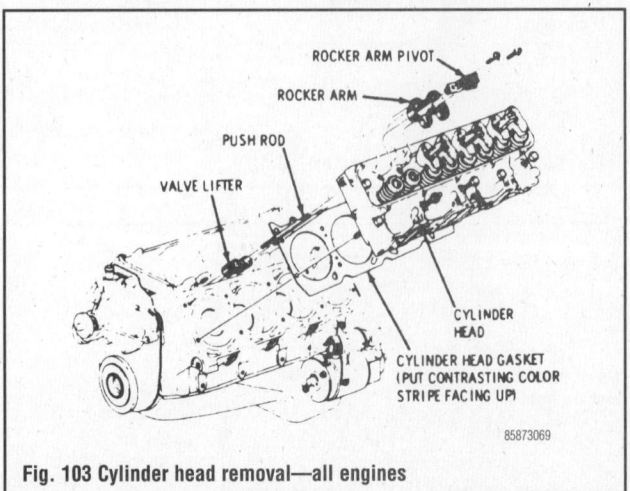

Fig. 103 Cylinder head removal—all engines

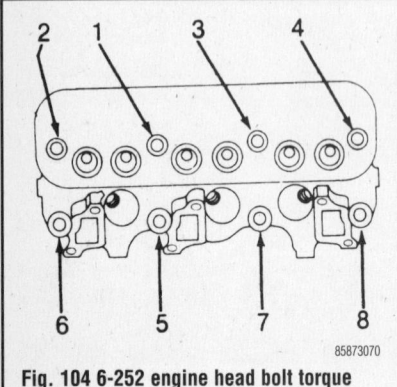

Fig. 104 6-252 engine head bolt torque sequence

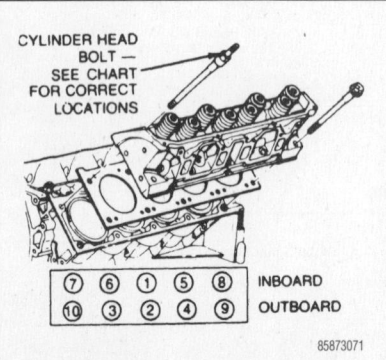

Fig. 105 Cylinder head bolt tightening sequence—1982–85 8-250

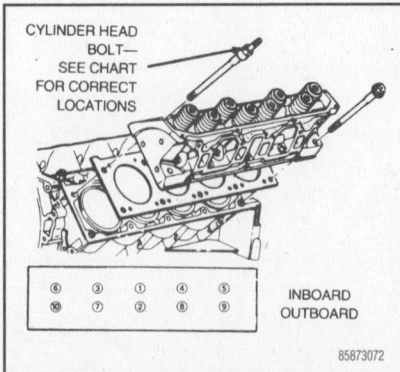

Fig. 106 Cylinder head bolt tightening sequence—1986–89, 8-250, 8-273 engine

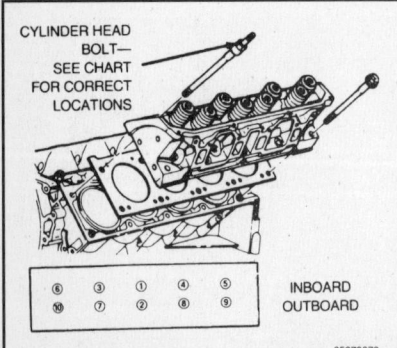

Fig. 107 Cylinder head bolt tightening sequence—8-307, 8-350 (gas engine)

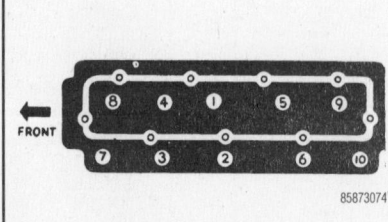

Fig. 108 Cylinder head bolt tightening sequence—8-368, 425, 429, 472 and 500 cu. in. engines

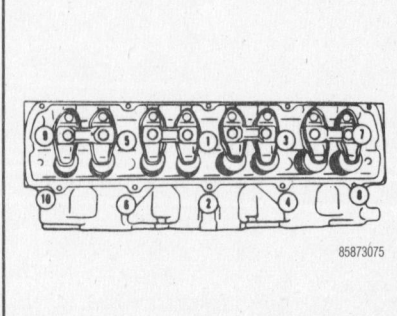

Fig. 109 Cylinder head bolt tightening sequence—8-350 diesel engine

Fig. 110 Removing the cylinder head assembly

Fig. 111 Removing cylinder head gasket— always replace

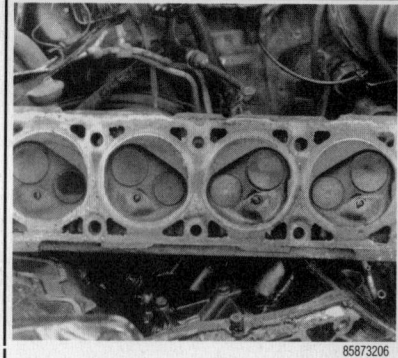

Fig. 112 View of the underside of a common cylinder head

V8 Engines Except 8-307 Eldorado and Seville with 8-250 and 8-273 Engines

1. Disconnect the battery.
2. Drain the coolant and save it if still fresh.
3. Remove the air cleaner.
4. Remove the air conditioning compressor, but do not disconnect any air conditioning lines. Secure the compressor to one side.
5. Disconnect the AIR hose at the check valve.
6. Remove the intake manifold.
7. When removing the right cylinder head, loosen the alternator belt, disconnect the wiring and remove the alternator.
8. When removing the left cylinder head, remove the dipstick, power steering pump and air pump if so equipped.
9. Label the spark plug wires and disconnect them.
10. Disconnect the exhaust manifold from the head being removed.
11. Remove the valve cover. Scribe the rocker arms with an identifying mark for reassembly; it is important that the rocker assembly is reinstalled in the same position as it was removed. Remove the rocker arm bolts, rocker arms and pivots or rocker arm assemblies.
12. Take a piece of heavy cardboard and cut 16 holes (or 8 holes if you are only removing one head) in it the same diameter as the pushrod stem. Number the holes in relation to the pushrods being removed. This cardboard holder will keep the pushrods in order (and hopefully out of harm's way) while they are out of the engine. Remove the pushrods.

➡ Pushrods MUST be returned to their original locations.

13. Install two ⁷⁄₁₆–14 x 6 in. bolts to be used as lifting handles in two of the rocker arm support screw holes.
14. Remove the cylinder head bolts, noting the different sizes and locations and remove the cylinder head and gasket. If the head seems stuck to the block, gently tap around the edge of the head with a rubber mallet until the joint breaks.

To install:

15. Using a putty knife, clean the gasket mounting surfaces.
16. Position the cylinder head gasket over the dowels on the cylinder block.
17. Position the cylinder head on the block.
18. Install the cylinder head bolts finger tight in all locations. Tighten the bolts in sequence and to the torque value in the Torque Specification Chart.
19. Remove the two ⁷⁄₁₆–14 x 6 in. lifting bolts.
20. Install the pushrods through the openings in the cylinder head. The bottom of the pushrod must be seated in the hydraulic valve lifter cup.
21. Install the rocker arm assemblies on the cylinder heads in the same positions as found during disassembly and tighten the retaining screws to 60 ft. lbs. (81 Nm).
22. Install the remaining components in the reverse order of removal.
23. Install the intake and exhaust manifolds as described earlier.

6-250 Engine

1. Disconnect the negative battery cable.
2. Remove the intake manifold-to-engine bolts and the manifold as outlined earlier.
3. Loosen and remove the drive belt(s).

4. When removing the left cylinder head, remove the oil dipstick, the air pump (if equipped) with the mounting bracket and move it aside with the hoses attached.
5. When removing the right cylinder head, remove the alternator, disconnect the power steering gear pump and the brackets.
6. Label and disconnect the spark plug wires; remove the spark plug wire clips from the rocker arm cover studs.
7. Remove the exhaust manifold-to-cylinder head bolts.
8. Using an air hose and/or cloths, clean the dirt from the cylinder head and adjacent area to avoid getting dirt into the engine.
9. Remove the rocker arm cover and the rocker arm/shaft assembly from the cylinder head. Lift out the push rods.
10. Loosen the cylinder head-to-engine bolts, then, remove the bolts and the cylinder head.

To install:

11. Using a putty knife, clean the gasket mounting surfaces.
12. Apply graphite lubricant to the exhaust manifold faces of the cylinder head.
13. Install a new head gasket over the dowels on the cylinder block.
14. Install the cylinder head bolts finger tight with the stud-headed bolts in the upper row and the conventional bolts in the lower row. Torque the bolts in the sequence shown and to the value listed in the Torque Specification Chart.
15. Reinstall the intake and exhaust manifolds

Eldorado and Seville With 8-250 Engine

1982–87 VEHICLES

1. Disconnect the negative battery cable. Drain the engine coolant.
2. Remove the intake and exhaust manifolds.
3. Disconnect all electrical and ground connections from the cylinder head.
4. When removing the left cylinder head, partially remove the power steering pump.
5. When removing the right cylinder head, remove the alternator and the heater hose from the rear of the head.
6. Remove the air pump, if equipped.
7. Remove bolts holding the rocker arm cover to the heads and remove the cover.
8. Remove nuts holding the rocker arm support to cylinder head, then remove the support and rocker arm assemblies. Store these assemblies so that they may be reinstalled in their correct locations.
9. Remove the pushrods and store them with their respective rocker arm assemblies.
10. Remove the cylinder head bolts.
11. Lift the cylinder head off of the block.

➡ Install cylinder liner holders to prevent loss of the bottom seal.

To install:

12. Using a putty knife, clean the gasket mounting surfaces.
13. Apply graphite lubricant to the exhaust manifold faces of the cylinder head.
14. Install a new head gasket over the dowels on the cylinder block.
15. Install the cylinder head bolts finger tight. Torque the bolts in the sequence shown and to the value listed in the Torque Specification Chart.
16. Install the remaining components in the reverse order of removal.

Eldorado and Seville with 8-250 and 8-273 Engines

1988–89 VEHICLES—LEFT SIDE

1. Disconnect the negative battery cable.
2. Drain the cooling system.
3. Remove the rocker arm covers.
4. Remove the intake manifold-to-engine bolts and intake manifold.
5. Disconnect the exhaust manifold crossover pipe, the exhaust pipe-to-exhaust manifold bolts, the exhaust manifold-to-cylinder head bolts and the exhaust manifold.
6. Remove the engine lifting bracket and the dipstick tube.
7. Remove the AIR bracket-to-engine bolts and move the bracket aside.
8. Remove the cylinder head-to-engine bolts and the cylinder head.

To install:

9. Using a putty knife, clean the gasket mounting surfaces.
10. Install a new head gasket over the dowels on the cylinder block use sealant (if necessary).
11. Apply GM lubricant No. 1052356 or equivalent, to the cylinder head bolt threads and install the cylinder head bolts finger tight. Torque the cylinder head bolts (in sequence) using three steps: 1st to 38 ft. lbs. (51 Nm), 2nd to 68 ft. lbs. (92 Nm) and 3rd to 90 ft. lbs. (122 Nm) for bolts No.1, 3 & 4. Check the Torque Specification Chart.
12. To complete the installation, reverse the removal procedures. Start the engine, allow it to reach normal operating temperatures and check for leaks.

1988–89 VEHICLES—RIGHT SIDE

1. Remove negative battery cable.
2. Drain the cooling system.
3. Remove the rocker arm covers.
4. Remove the intake manifold-to-engine bolts and intake manifold.
5. Disconnect the exhaust manifold crossover pipe, the exhaust pipe-to-exhaust manifold bolts, the exhaust manifold-to-cylinder head bolts and the exhaust manifold.
6. Remove the engine lifting bracket.
7. Remove the AIR bracket-to-engine bolts and move the bracket aside.
8. Remove the cylinder head-to-engine bolts and the cylinder head.

To install:

9. Using a putty knife, clean the gasket mounting surfaces.
10. Install a new head gasket over the dowels on the cylinder block use sealant (if necessary).
11. Apply GM lubricant No. 1052356 or equivalent, to the cylinder head bolt threads and install the cylinder head bolts finger tight. Torque the cylinder head bolts (in sequence) using three steps: 1st to 38 ft. lbs. (51 Nm), 2nd to 68 ft. lbs. (92 Nm) and 3rd to 90 ft. lbs. (122 Nm) for bolts No.1, 3 & 4. Check the Torque Specification Chart.
12. To complete the installation, reverse the removal procedures. Start the engine, allow it to reach normal operating temperatures and check for leaks.

8-307 Engine

> ✳✳ **CAUTION**
>
> **Do not disconnect the air conditioning lines. Severe personal injury could result!**

1. Drain the cooling system.

> ✳✳ **CAUTION**
>
> **When draining the coolant, keep in mind that cats and dogs are attracted by the ethylene glycol antifreeze, and are quite likely to drink any that is left in an uncovered container or in puddles on the ground. This will prove fatal in sufficient quantity. Always drain the coolant into a sealable container. Coolant should be reused unless it is contaminated or several years old.**

2. Remove the intake manifold and carburetor as an assembly.
3. Remove exhaust manifolds.
4. Loosen or remove any accessory brackets which interfere.
5. Remove the valve cover(s). Loosen any accessory brackets which are in the way.

6. Remove the battery ground strap from the cylinder head.
7. Remove cylinder head bolts and cylinder head(s).
8. Install in the reverse order of removal. It is not recommended that sealer be used on the new head gasket. Dip head bolts in oil before installing and allow them to drain so oil will not fill the threads and interfere with proper torquing. Tighten all head bolts in the correct sequence to 90 ft. lbs. (122 Nm), then torque, again in sequence, to 130 ft. lbs. (176 Nm) Retorque the bolts after engine is warmed up.

8-350 Diesel Engine

1. Remove the intake manifold, using the procedure outlined above.
2. Remove the rocker arm cover(s), after removing any accessory brackets which interfere with cover removal.
3. Disconnect and label the glow plug wiring.
4. If the right cylinder head is being removed, remove the ground strap from the head.
5. Remove the rocker arm bolts, the bridged pivots, the rocker arms, and the pushrods, keeping all the parts in order so that they can be returned to their original positions. It is a good practice to number or mark the parts to avoid interchanging them.
6. Remove the fuel return lines from the nozzles.
7. Remove the exhaust manifold(s), using the procedure outlined above.
8. Remove the engine block drain plug on the side of the engine from which the cylinder head is being removed.
9. Remove the head bolts. Remove the cylinder head.

To install:

10. Clean the mating surfaces thoroughly. Install new head gaskets on the engine block. Do NOT coat the gaskets with any sealer. The gaskets have a special coating that eliminates the need for sealer. The use of sealer will interfere with this coating and cause leaks. Install the cylinder head onto the block.
11. Clean the head bolts thoroughly. Dip the bolts in clean engine oil and install into the cylinder block until the heads of the bolts lightly contact the cylinder head.
12. Tighten the bolts, in the sequence illustrated, to 100 ft. lbs. (136 Nm). When all bolts have been tightened to this figure, begin the tightening sequence again, and torque all bolts to 130 ft. lbs. (176 Nm).
13. Install the engine block drain plugs, the exhaust manifolds, the fuel return lines, the glow plug wiring, and the ground strap for the right cylinder head.
14. Install the valve train assembly. Refer to the Diesel Engine Rocker Arm Replacement in this section for the valve lifter bleeding procedures.
15. Install the intake manifold.
16. Install the valve covers. These are sealed with Room Temperature Vulcanizing (RTV) silicone sealer instead of a gasket. Use GM #1052434 or an equivalent. Install the cover to the head within 10 minutes, while the sealer is still wet.

CYLINDER HEAD CLEANING & INSPECTION

➡ **Any diesel cylinder head work should be handled by a reputable machine shop familiar with diesel engines. Disassembly, valve lapping, and assembly can be completed by following the gasoline engine procedures.**

Gasoline Engines

▶ **See Figures 113, 114 and 115**

Once the complete valve train has been removed from the cylinder head(s), the head itself can be inspected, cleaned and machined (if necessary). Set the head(s) on a clean work space, so the combustion chambers are facing up. Begin cleaning the chambers and ports with a hardwood chisel or other non-metallic tool (to avoid nicking or gouging the chamber, ports, and especially the valve seats). Chip away the major carbon deposits, then remove the remainder of carbon with a wire brush fitted to an electric drill.

➡ **Be sure that the carbon is actually removed, rather than just burnished.**

After decarbonizing is completed, take the head(s) to a machine shop and have the head hot tanked. In this process, the head is lowered into a hot chemi-

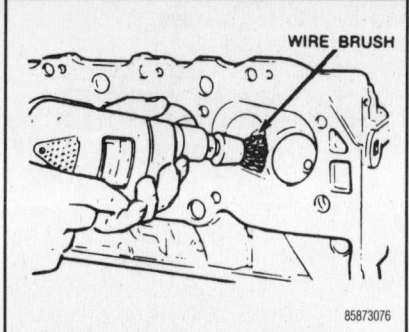

Fig. 113 Use a wire brush and electric drill to remove carbon from the combustion chambers and exhaust ports

Fig. 114 Use a gasket scraper to remove the bulk of the old head gasket from the mating surface

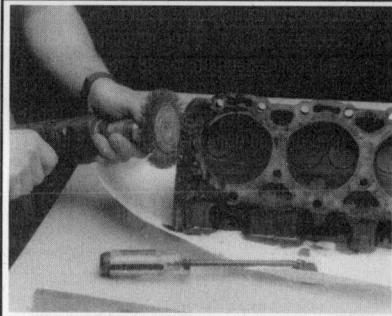

Fig. 115 An electric drill equipped with a wire wheel will expedite complete gasket removal

cal bath that very effectively cleans all grease, corrosion, and scale from all internal and external head surfaces. Also have the machinist check the valve seats and re-cut them if necessary. When you bring the clean head(s) home, place them on a clean surface. Completely clean the entire valve train with solvent.

CHECKING FOR HEAD WARPAGE

◆ See Figures 116, 117 and 118

Lay the head down with the combustion chambers facing up. Place a straightedge across the gasket surface of the head, both diagonally and straight across the center. Using a flat feeler gauge, determine the clearance at the center of the straightedge. If warpage exceeds 0.003 in. (0.08mm) in a 6 in. (152mm) span, or 0.006 in. (0.15mm) over the total length, the cylinder head must be resurfaced (which is akin to planning a piece of wood). Resurfacing can be performed at most machine shops.

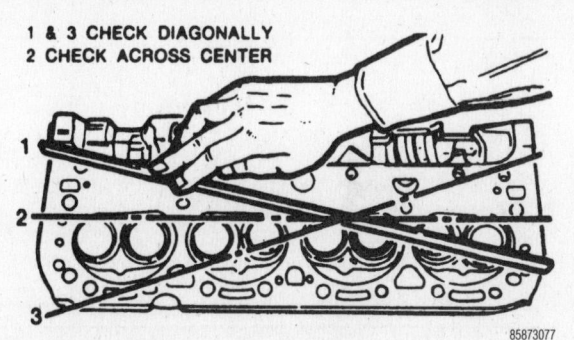

Fig. 116 Check the cylinder head mating surface for warpage with a precision straightedge

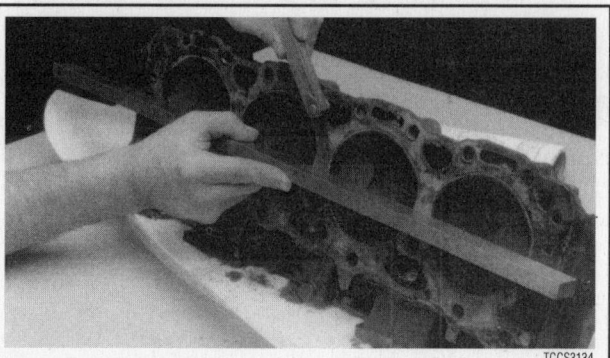

Fig. 117 Check the cylinder head for warpage along the center line using a straightedge and feeler gauge

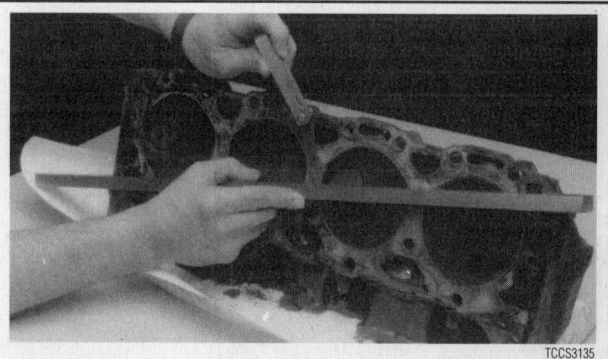

Fig. 118 Be sure to check for warpage across the cylinder head at both diagonals

➡ When resurfacing the cylinder head(s) of V6 or V8 engines, the intake manifold mounting position is altered, and must be corrected by machining a proportionate amount from the intake manifold flange.

Valves and Springs

REMOVAL

◆ See Figures 119 thru 126

1. Remove the head(s), and place on a clean surface.
2. Using a suitable spring compressor (for pushrod type overhead valve engines), compress the valve spring and remove the valve spring cap key.

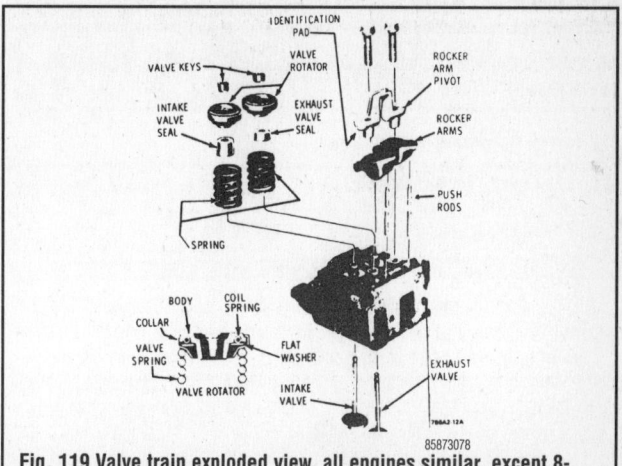

Fig. 119 Valve train exploded view, all engines similar, except 8-429 and 6-252 engines (with rocker shafts)

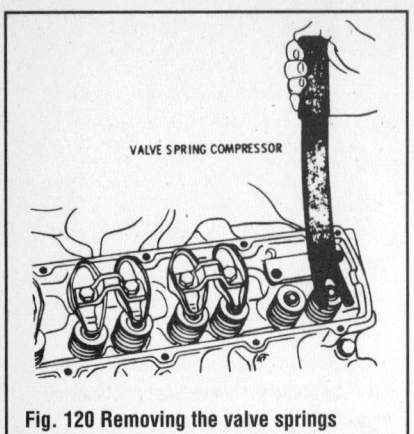

Fig. 120 Removing the valve springs

Fig. 121 Compressing the valve spring with tool

Fig. 122 Removing the valve keys

Fig. 123 Removing the valve rotator

Fig. 124 Removing the valve spring

Fig. 125 Removing the valve

Fig. 126 Removing the valve seal

Release the spring compressor and remove the valve spring and cap (and valve rotator on some engines).

➡**Use care in removing the keys; they are easily lost.**

3. Remove the valve seals from the intake valve guides. Throw these old seals away, as you'll be installing new seals during reassembly.
4. Slide the valves out of the head from the combustion chamber side.
5. Make a holder for the valves out of a piece of wood or cardboard, as outlined for the pushrods in Cylinder Head Removal. Make sure you number each hole in the cardboard to keep the valves in proper order. Slide the valves out of the head from the combustion chamber side; they MUST be installed as they were removed.

INSPECTION

◆ **See Figures 127 thru 133**

Inspect the valve faces and seats (in the head) for pits, burned spots and other evidence of poor seating. If a valve face is in such bad shape that the head of the valve must be ground in order to true up the face, discard the valve because the sharp edge will run too hot. The correct angle for valve faces is 45 degrees. We recommend the re-facing be done at a reputable machine shop.

Check the valve stem for scoring and burned spots. If not noticeably scored or damaged, clean the valve stem with solvent to remove all gum and varnish. Clean

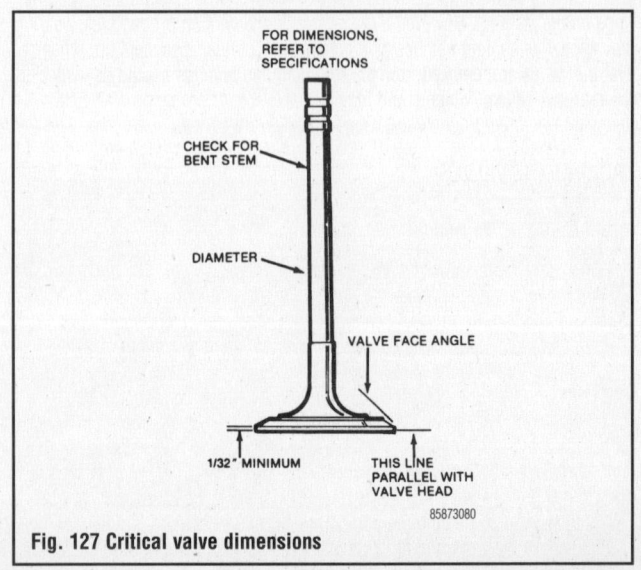

Fig. 127 Critical valve dimensions

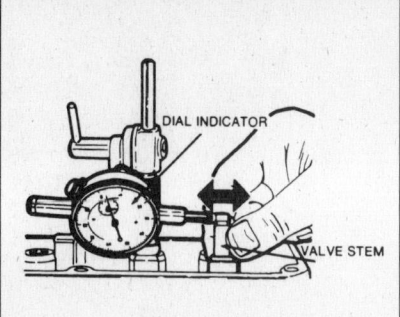

Fig. 128 Checking the valve stem-to-guide clearance

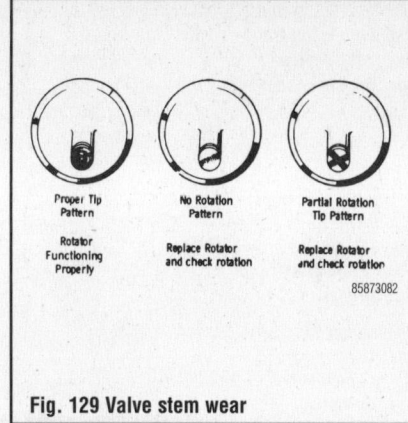

Fig. 129 Valve stem wear

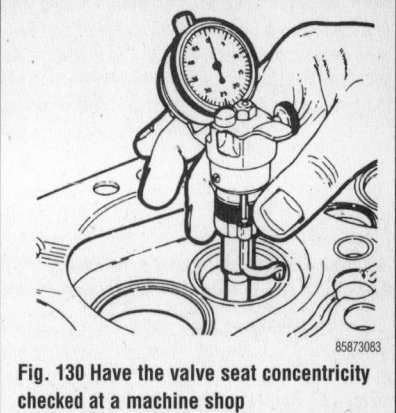

Fig. 130 Have the valve seat concentricity checked at a machine shop

Fig. 131 A dial gauge may be used to check valve stem-to-guide clearance

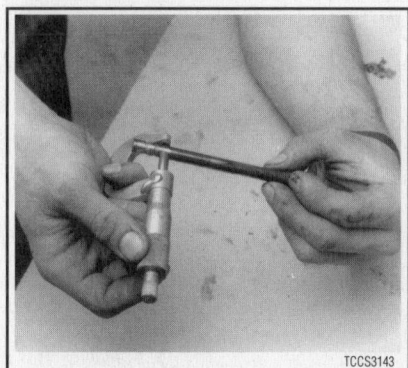

Fig. 132 Use a micrometer to measure the valve stem diameter

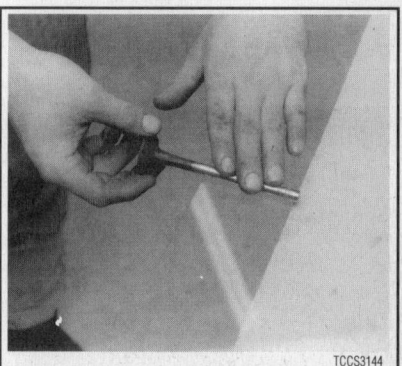

Fig. 133 Valve stems may be rolled on a flat surface to check for bends

the valve guides using solvent and an expanding wire-type valve guide cleaner. If you have access to a dial indicator for measuring valve stem-to-guide clearance, mount it so that the stem of the indicator is at 90 degrees to the valve stem, and as close to the valve guide as possible. Move the valve off its seat, and measure the valve guide-to-stem clearance by rocking the stem back and forth to actuate the dial indicator. Measure the valve stems using a micrometer, and compare the specifications to determine whether stem or guide wear is responsible for the excess clearance. If a dial indicator and micrometer are not available to you, take your cylinder head and valves to a reputable machine shop for inspection.

Some of the engines covered in this guide are equipped with valve rotators, which double as valve spring caps. In normal operation the rotators put a certain degree of wear on the tip of the valve stem; this wear appears as concentric rings on the stem tip. However, if the rotator is not working properly, the wear may appear as straight notches or X patterns across the valve stem tip. Whenever the valves are removed from the cylinder head, the tips should be inspected for improper pattern, which could indicate valve rotator problems. Valve stem tips will have to be ground flat if rotator patterns are severe.

LAPPING THE VALVES

▶ **See Figures 134 and 135**

When valve faces and seats have been re-faced and re-cut, or if they are determined to be in good condition, the valves must be lapped in to ensure efficient sealing when the valve closes against the seat.

1. Invert the cylinder head so that the combustion chambers are facing up.
2. Lightly lubricate the valve stems with clean oil, and coat the valve seats with valve grinding compound. Install the valves in the head as numbered.
3. Attach the suction cup of a valve lapping tool to a valve head. You'll probably have to moisten the cup to securely attach the tool to the valve.
4. Rotate the tool between the palms, changing position and lifting the tool often to prevent grooving. Lap the valve until a smooth, polished seat is evident (you may have to add a bit more compound after some lapping is done).
5. Remove the valve and tool, and remove ALL traces of grinding compound with solvent-soaked rag, or rinse the head with solvent.

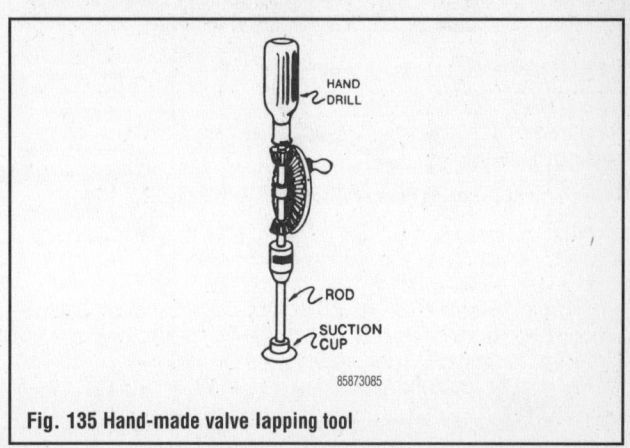

Fig. 134 Lapping the valves by hand

Fig. 135 Hand-made valve lapping tool

➡Valve lapping can also be done by fastening a suction cup to a piece of drill rod in a hand eggbeater type drill. Proceed as above, using the drill as a lapping tool. Due to the higher speeds involved when using the hand drill, care must be exercised to avoid grooving the seat. Lift the tool and change direction of rotation often.

INSTALLATION

▶ **See Figure 136**

➡Before installing the valves, be sure to check the valve springs as described later in this section. Replace springs if necessary.

New valve seals must be installed when the valve train is put back together. Certain seals slip over the valve stem and guide boss, while others require that the boss be machined. In some applications Teflon guide seals are available. Check with a machinist and/or automotive parts store for a suggestion on the proper seals to use.

➡Remember that when installing valve seals, a small amount of oil is able to pass the seal to lubricate the valve guides; otherwise, excessive wear will result.

To install the valves and rocker assembly:
1. Lubricate the valve stems with clean engine oil.
2. Install the valves in the cylinder head, one at a time, as numbered.
3. Lubricate and position the seals and valve springs, again a valve at a time.
4. Install the spring retainers, and compress the springs.
5. With the valve key groove exposed above the compressed valve spring, wipe some wheel bearing grease around the groove. This will retain the keys as you release the spring compressor.
6. Using needlenose pliers (or your fingers), place the keys in the key grooves. The grease should hold the keys in place. Slowly release the spring compressor; the valve cap or rotator will raise up as the compressor is released, retaining the keys.
7. Install the rocker assembly, and install the cylinder head(s).

VALVE LASH ADJUSTMENT

All engines described in this book use hydraulic lifters, which require no periodic adjustment. In the event of cylinder head removal or any operation that requires disturbing the rocker arms, the rocker arms will have to be adjusted.

Initial Adjustment

1. Remove the cylinder head covers and gaskets.
2. Adjust the valves as follows:
   a. Crank the engine until the mark on the damper aligns with the **TDC** or **0** mark on the timing tab and the engine is in the No. 1 firing position. This can be determined by placing the fingers on the No. 1 cylinder valves as the marks align. If the valves do not move, it is in the No. 1 firing position. If the valves move, it is in the No. 6 firing position (No. 4 and V6) and the crankcase should be rotated one more revolution to the No. 1 firing position.
   b. Back out the adjusting nut until lash is felt at the pushrod, then turn the adjusting nut in until all lash is removed. This can be determined by checking pushrod end-play while turning the adjusting nut. When all play has been removed, turn the adjusting nut in 1 full turn.

   c. With the engine in the No. 1 firing position, the following valves can be adjusted:
   • V8 Exhaust: 1, 3, 4, 8
   • V8 Intake: 1, 2, 5, 7
   • V6 Exhaust: 1, 5, 6
   • V6 Intake: 1, 2, 3
   d. Crank the engine 1 full revolution until the marks are again in alignment. This is the No. 6 firing position (No. 4 and V6). The following valves can now be adjusted:
   • V8 Exhaust: 2, 5, 6, 7
   • V8 Intake: 3, 4, 6, 8
   • V6 Exhaust: 2, 3, 4
   • V6 Intake: 4, 5, 6
3. Reinstall the rocker arm covers using new gaskets or sealer.
4. Install the distributor cap and wire assembly.
5. Adjust the carburetor idle speed, if necessary.

Valve Guides

SERVICING

▶ **See Figure 137**

The V6 and V8 engines covered in this guide use integral valve guides; that is, they are a part of the cylinder head and cannot be replaced. The guides can, however, be reamed oversize if they are found to be worn past an acceptable limit. Occasionally, a valve guide bore will be oversize as manufactured. These are marked on the inboard side of the cylinder heads on the machined surface just above the intake manifold.

If the guides must be reamed (this service is available at most machine shops), then valves with oversize stems must be fitted. Valves are usually available in 0.001 in., 0.003 in. and 0.005 in. stem oversizes. Valve guides which are not excessively worn or distorted may, in some cases, be knurled rather than reamed. Knurling is a process in which the metal on the valve guide bore is displaced and raised, thereby reducing clearance. Knurling also provides excellent oil control. The option of knurling rather than reaming valve guides should be discussed with a reputable machinist or engine specialist.

Valve Springs

HEIGHT AND PRESSURE CHECK

▶ **See Figures 138, 139, 140 and 141**

1. Place the valve spring on a flat, clean surface next to a square.
2. Measure the height of the spring, and rotate it against the edge of the square to measure distortion (out-of-roundness). If spring height varies between springs by more than 1/16 in. (1.5mm) or if the distortion exceeds 1/16 in. (1.5mm), replace the spring.

A valve spring tester is needed to test spring pressure, so the valve springs must usually be taken to a professional machine shop for this test. Spring pressure at the installed and compressed heights is checked, and a tolerance of plus or minus 5 lbs. is permissible on the springs covered in this guide.

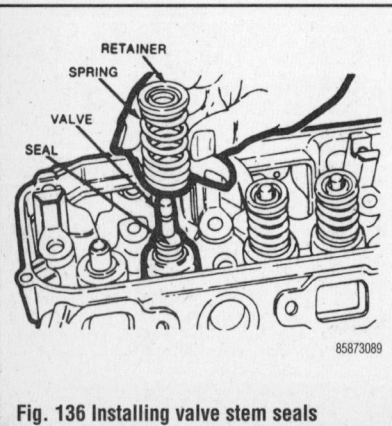

Fig. 136 Installing valve stem seals

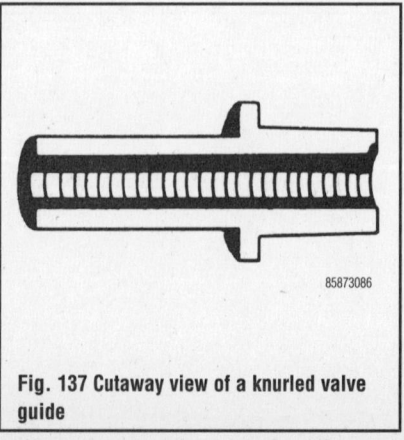

Fig. 137 Cutaway view of a knurled valve guide

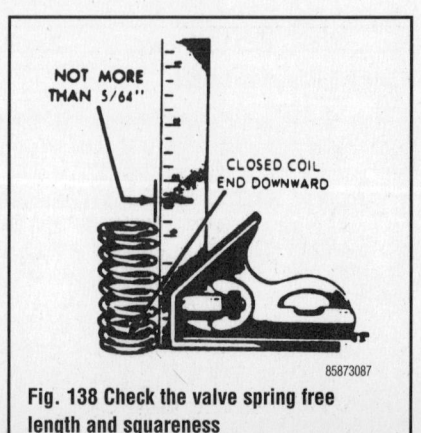

Fig. 138 Check the valve spring free length and squareness

Valve Lifters

REMOVAL & INSTALLATION

▶ **See Figures 142, 143, 144, 145 and 146**

Gasoline and Diesel Engines

➡ **Valve lifters and pushrods should be kept in order so they can be reinstalled in their original position. Some engines will have both standard**

size 0.010 in. (0.25mm) and oversize valve lifters as original equipment. The oversize lifters are etched with an O on their sides; the cylinder block will also be marked with an O if the oversize lifter is used.

1. Remove the intake manifold and gasket.
2. Remove the valve covers, rocker arm assemblies and pushrods.
3. If the lifters are coated with varnish, apply carburetor cleaning solvent to the lifter body. The solvent should dissolve the varnish in about 10 minutes.
4. Remove the lifters. On diesels, remove the lifter retainer guide bolts, and remove the guides. A special tool for removing lifters is available, and is helpful for this procedure.

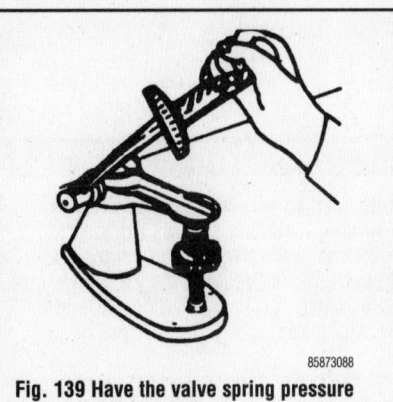

Fig. 139 Have the valve spring pressure checked professionally

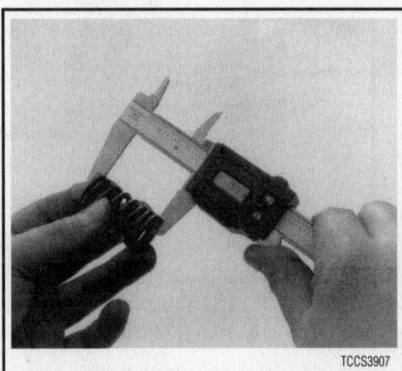

Fig. 140 Use a caliper gauge to check the valve spring free-length

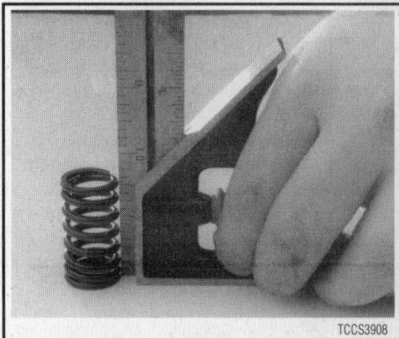

Fig. 141 When checking the spring for squareness use a carpenter's square and a flat surface

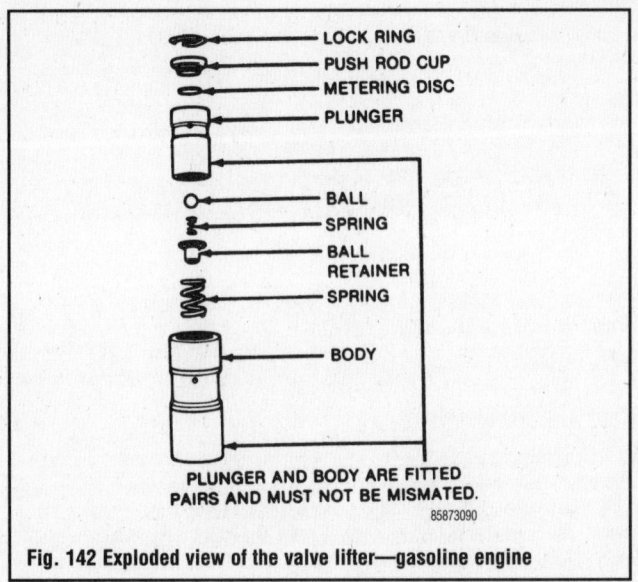

Fig. 142 Exploded view of the valve lifter—gasoline engine

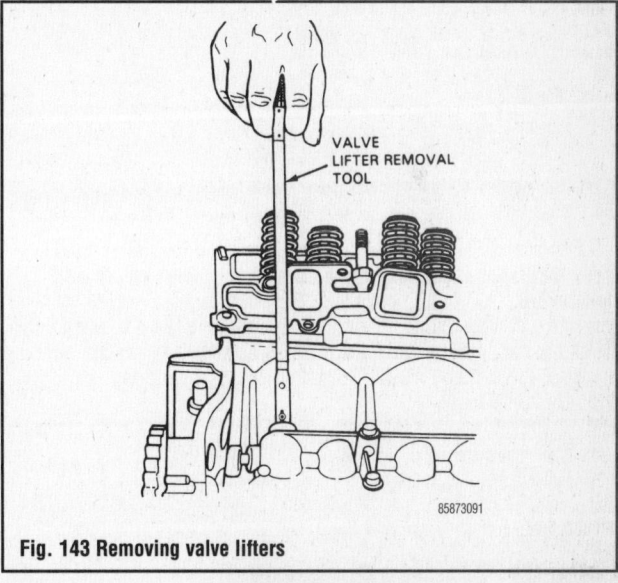

Fig. 143 Removing valve lifters

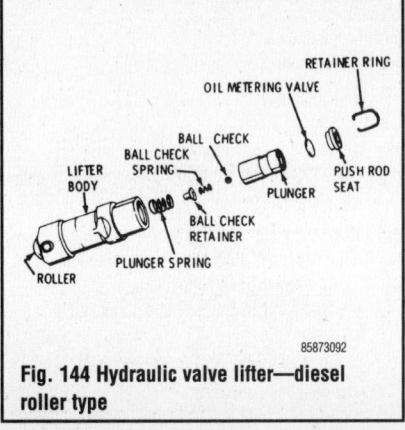

Fig. 144 Hydraulic valve lifter—diesel roller type

Fig. 145 Oversize valve lifter bore marking

Fig. 146 Removing the valve lifter—intake manifold removed

To install:

5. New lifters must be primed before installation, as dry lifters will seize when the engine is started. On the diesel lifters, submerge the lifters in clean diesel fuel or kerosene and work the lifter plunger up and down to prime. On gasoline engine lifters, submerge the lifters in SAE 10 oil, which is very thin. Carefully insert the end of a ⅛ in. (3mm) drift into the lifter and push down on the plunger. Hold the plunger down while the lifter is still submerged; do not pump the plunger. Release the plunger. The lifter is now primed.

6. Coat the bottoms of the gasoline engine lifters, and the rollers of the diesel engine lifters with Molykote or an equivalent molybdenum-disulfide lubricant before installation. Install the lifters and pushrods into the engine in their original order. On diesels, install the lifter retainer guide.

7. Install the intake manifold gaskets and manifold.

8. Position the rocker arms, pivots and bolts on the cylinder head. On the 252 V6, position and install the rockers and rocker shafts. Refer to the Rocker Arm removal and installation procedure in this section for lifter bleed-down. New lifters must be bled down; valve-to-piston contact could occur if this procedure is neglected.

9. Install the valve covers, connect the spark plug wires and install the air cleaner assembly.

➡An additive containing EP lube, such as EOS, should always be added to crankcase oil for break-in when new lifters or a new camshaft is installed. This additive is generally available in automotive parts stores.

Oil Pan

REMOVAL & INSTALLATION

◆ **See Figures 147, 148, 149 and 150**

Except Eldorado and 1980–89 Seville

6-252 ENGINE

1. Raise the vehicle and support on jackstands.
2. Drain the engine oil and remove the oil filter.

✳✳ **CAUTION**

The EPA warns that prolonged contact with used engine oil may cause a number of skin disorders, including cancer! You should make every effort to minimize your exposure to used engine oil. Protective gloves should be worn when changing the oil. Wash your hands and any other exposed skin areas as soon as possible after exposure to used engine oil. Soap and water, or waterless hand cleaner should be used.

3. Remove the flywheel cover and the exhaust crossover pipe.
4. Raise the engine, remove the oil pan bolts and lower the oil pan.
5. To install reverse the removal procedure. Clean the gasket surface of the pan and block and use a new gasket.

8-250 ENGINE

1. Disconnect the negative battery cable.
2. Jack the car up and support it with jackstands.
3. Drain the engine oil and remove the oil filter.

✳✳ **CAUTION**

The EPA warns that prolonged contact with used engine oil may cause a number of skin disorders, including cancer! You should make every effort to minimize your exposure to used engine oil. Protective gloves should be worn when changing the oil. Wash your hands and any other exposed skin areas as soon as possible after exposure to used engine oil. Soap and water, or waterless hand cleaner should be used.

4. Remove the flywheel inspection cover and support struts.
5. Disconnect the exhaust Y-pipe at the exhaust manifolds and remove the one bolt at the catalytic converter bracket.
6. Remove the oil pan screws, lower the exhaust pipe, and remove the oil pan.

➡If the pan is difficult to remove, lightly tap the edges of the pan with a plastic hammer.

7. Seal the oil pan to the block with RTV sealant.
8. Tighten the oil pan retaining screws and nuts to 11 ft. lbs. (15 Nm).
9. The remainder of the installation is the reverse of removal.

8-307 ENGINE

1. Disconnect the negative battery cable.
2. Remove the oil level indicator, and the fan shroud.
3. Raise and support the vehicle on jackstands. Drain the oil from the engine.

✳✳ **CAUTION**

The EPA warns that prolonged contact with used engine oil may cause a number of skin disorders, including cancer! You should make every effort to minimize your exposure to used engine oil. Protective gloves should be worn when changing the oil. Wash your hands and any other exposed skin areas as soon as possible after exposure to used engine oil. Soap and water, or waterless hand cleaner should be used.

4. Remove the flywheel cover.
5. Remove the exhaust crossover pipe from the manifold and the catalytic converter.

➡It may be necessary to remove the starter.

6. Cadillac recommends installing an engine support and adapter under the engine.
7. Remove front engine mounts.
8. Raise the front of the engine as high as possible.
9. Remove the oil pan bolts and lower the pan.
10. Using a putty knife, clean the gasket mounting surfaces.
To install:
11. Apply sealer to both sides of the gasket.
12. Install the oil pan gasket.
13. Apply G.E.1673 or equivalent RTV sealer to both oil pan seals. Install the oil pan. Torque the oil pan bolts to 10 ft. lbs. (14 Nm), nuts to 17 ft. lbs. (23 Nm).
14. Lower the engine and install the mounts. Torque to 75 ft. lbs. (102 Nm).
15. Install the remaining components in the reverse order of removal.

8-350 AND 368 ENGINES

1. Remove the wheel housing struts from the fenders. Disconnect the negative battery terminal.
2. Remove the 3 screws from the upper radiator shroud, two securing the shroud, and one securing the top radiator hose. Drill out the rivets securing the upper shroud to the lower one and remove the shroud. Use bolts and nuts to replace the rivets when reinstalling the shroud.
3. Loosen the drive belts and remove the crankshaft pulley.
4. Jack up your car and support it with jackstands.
5. Remove the through-bolt from each motor mount.
6. Remove the crossover pipe and the converter as an assembly.
7. Remove the starter.
8. Remove the torque converter cover.
9. Drain the oil pan.

✳✳ **CAUTION**

The EPA warns that prolonged contact with used engine oil may cause a number of skin disorders, including cancer! You should make every effort to minimize your exposure to used engine oil. Protective gloves should be worn when changing the oil. Wash your hands and any other exposed skin areas as soon as possible after exposure to used engine oil. Soap and water, or waterless hand cleaner should be used.

10. Using a jack, with a block of wood on top, place it under the crankshaft hub. Jack up the engine, remove the pan bolts and the pan.

11. Clean all the gasket material from the pan and the block mating surfaces. Use a new gasket kit and sealer. Make sure the seals are firmly positioned on the flange surfaces with each seal properly located in the cut-out notches of the pan gasket.

12. Installation is the reverse of removal. Torque the pan bolts to 10 ft. lbs. (14 Nm).

8-425, 429, 472 AND 500 ENGINES

1. Drain engine oil and disconnect negative battery cable.

✳✳ CAUTION

The EPA warns that prolonged contact with used engine oil may cause a number of skin disorders, including cancer! You should make every effort to minimize your exposure to used engine oil. Protective gloves should be worn when changing the oil. Wash your hands and any other exposed skin areas as soon as possible after exposure to used engine oil. Soap and water, or waterless hand cleaner should be used.

2. Disconnect exhaust crossover pipe at exhaust manifolds.

3. Disconnect exhaust support bracket at transmission extension housing, and position exhaust system to one side.

4. Remove starter motor.

5. Remove two idler arm support mounting screws from frame side member, and lower support.

6. Disconnect pitman arm at drag link, and lower steering linkage.

7. Remove the transmission lower cover.

8. Remove engine oil pan.

9. When reinstalling, reverse above procedure and torque oil pan screws and nuts to 10 ft. lbs. (14 Nm). The transmission cover screws should be torqued to 20 ft. lbs. (27 Nm).

1967–78 Eldorado

1. Remove engine as previously described in Engine removal and installation.

2. Drain engine oil.

✳✳ CAUTION

The EPA warns that prolonged contact with used engine oil may cause a number of skin disorders, including cancer! You should make every effort to minimize your exposure to used engine oil. Protective gloves should be worn when changing the oil. Wash your hands and any other exposed skin areas as soon as possible after exposure to used engine oil. Soap and water, or waterless hand cleaner should be used.

3. Remove the transmission lower cover.

4. Remove nuts and cap screws that hold oil pan to cylinder block and engine front cover, then remove the oil pan.

5. Remove side gaskets and rubber front and rear seals from oil pan. Discard the gaskets and seals.

6. Install by reversing the removal procedure. Torque to 10 ft. lbs. (14 Nm). Use sealer in the corner notch openings.

1979–85 Eldorado and 1980–85 Seville

1. Disconnect the negative battery cable.

2. Raise the car on a hoist.

3. Remove the frame brace front attaching bolts from both sides and pivot the braces outward.

4. Remove the six securing bolts from the drive axle to the output shaft on both sides. Separate the flanges of the output shafts and drive axles to gain clearance for removal with the shafts attached.

5. Remove the battery cable-to-output shaft retaining screws and remove the two screws securing the support to the engine block.

6. Remove the final drive-to-transmission screw that holds the front of the shield. Remove the shield.

7. Remove the remaining final drive-to-transmission bolts.

8. Remove the final drive support bracket-to-engine block screw.

9. Using a puller, separate the steering linkage intermediate shaft from the pitman arm and the idler arm. Push the linkage toward the front of the car.

10. With the aid of a helper, slide the final drive assembly forward, off the transmission splined shaft, and remove the unit with the output shaft attached. Do not use the shafts as handles, as damage to the seals will occur.

11. Remove the battery cable and the wiring harness connectors from the starter solenoid BAT terminal.

12. Remove the harness connector from the solenoid S terminal.

13. Remove the harness from the clip on the solenoid and position it out of the way.

14. On some earlier years it may be necessary to remove the starter motor attaching bolts and remove the starter.

15. Drain the engine oil.

✳✳ CAUTION

The EPA warns that prolonged contact with used engine oil may cause a number of skin disorders, including cancer! You should make every effort to minimize your exposure to used engine oil. Protective gloves should be worn when changing the oil. Wash your hands and any other exposed skin areas as soon as possible after exposure to used engine oil. Soap and water, or waterless hand cleaner should be used.

16. On the 8-250 engine, it is necessary to raise the engine 1–2 in. Do not lift on the oil pan or the crankshaft. Use a 2 x 4 block of wood against the cylinder head ledge of the crankcase or against the cylinder head. Prop the engine up in this position.

17. Remove the oil pan attaching screws and remove the oil pan.

➡ On cars equipped with diesel engines it is necessary to loosen the motor mounts and jack up the engine slightly to remove the oil pan.

18. Reverse to install. Observe the following torques:
- oil pan screws: 10 ft. lbs. (14 Nm)
- engine-to-frame crossmember nuts: 65 ft. lbs. (88 Nm)
- final drive-to-transmission bolts: 30 ft. lbs. (41 Nm)
- front support bracket-to-block: 50 ft. lbs. (68 Nm)
- output shaft-to-drive axle: 60 ft. lbs. (81 Nm)
- steering linkage intermediate shaft-to-pitman arm: 60 ft. lbs. (81 Nm)

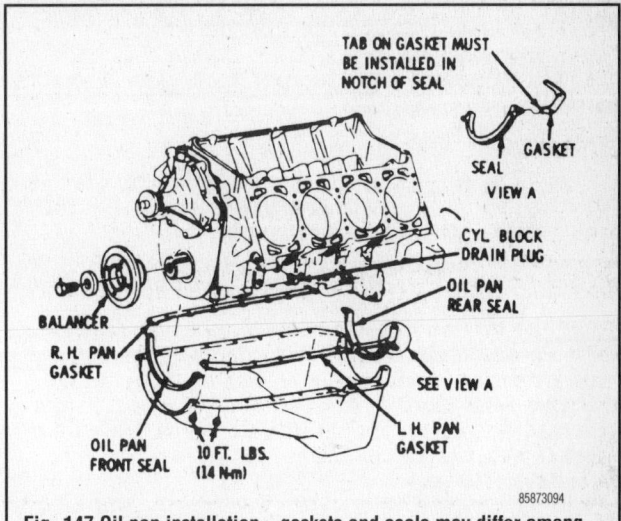

Fig. 147 Oil pan installation—gaskets and seals may differ among engines

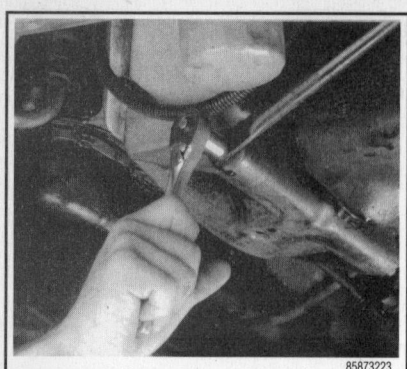

Fig. 148 Removing the support—common oil pan removal

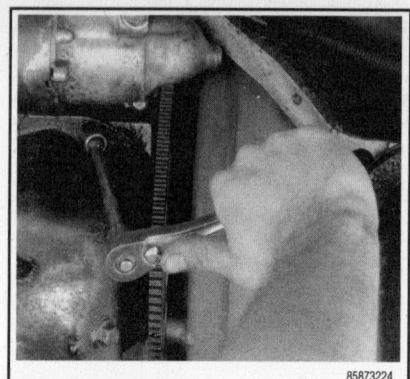

Fig. 149 Removing oil pan bolts

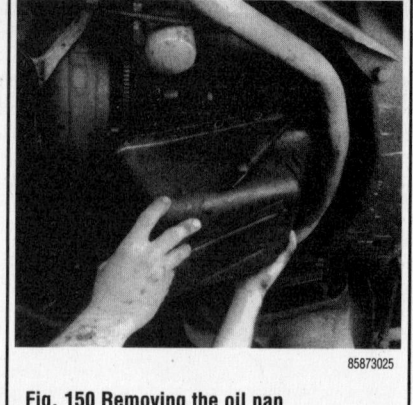

Fig. 150 Removing the oil pan

1986–89 Eldorado and Seville

1. Disconnect the negative battery cable.
2. Raise the front of the vehicle and support it with safety stands.
3. Remove the oil pan drain plug and drain the oil.

❋❋ CAUTION

The EPA warns that prolonged contact with used engine oil may cause a number of skin disorders, including cancer! You should make every effort to minimize your exposure to used engine oil. Protective gloves should be worn when changing the oil. Wash your hands and any other exposed skin areas as soon as possible after exposure to used engine oil. Soap and water, or waterless hand cleaner should be used.

4. Remove both flywheel covers.
5. Disconnect the crossover pipe for the exhaust system and position it out of the way.
6. Starting at the middle of each side and working out, remove the oil pan mounting bolts and nuts.
7. Remove the oil pan.

To install:

8. Clean the oil pan and cylinder block mating surfaces thoroughly.
9. Apply a ¼ in. (6mm) bead of RTV sealant at the rear main bearing cap and the front cover-to-cylinder block joints.
10. Install the oil pan and tighten the mounting bolts and nuts to 12 ft. lbs. (16 Nm).
11. Install the remaining components.

Oil Pump

REMOVAL & INSTALLATION

6-252 and 8-429 Engines

The 6-252 and the 8-429 engine oil pump housing is an integral part of the engine front cover. Whenever the oil pump components require service, the engine front cover must be removed from the engine.

To remove the oil pump follow the front cover removal procedures outlined earlier in this section. The overhaul and disassembly procedures are outlined in the following section under Overhaul.

8-250 and 8-273 Engine

1. Jack up the car and support on jackstands.
2. Remove the oil pan following the procedures outlined earlier in this section.
3. Remove the two screws and one nut securing the oil pump to the engine.
4. To install, engage the driveshaft to the distributor gear. Tighten the nut to 22 ft. lbs. (30 Nm) and the two screws to 15 ft. lbs. (20 Nm).
5. Install the oil pan and lower the car.

8-307 and 8-350 Engines

▶ See Figure 151

1. Drain the crankcase oil and remove the oil pan following the procedures previously described in this section.

❋❋ CAUTION

The EPA warns that prolonged contact with used engine oil may cause a number of skin disorders, including cancer! You should make every effort to minimize your exposure to used engine oil. Protective gloves should be worn when changing the oil. Wash your hands and any other exposed skin areas as soon as possible after exposure to used engine oil. Soap and water, or waterless hand cleaner should be used.

2. Remove the oil pump-to-rear main bearing cap attaching bolts and remove the oil pump and driveshaft extension.
3. To install, reverse the removal procedure. The end of the driveshaft extension nearest the washer is inserted into the driveshaft. Torque the bolts to 35 ft. lbs. (47 Nm).

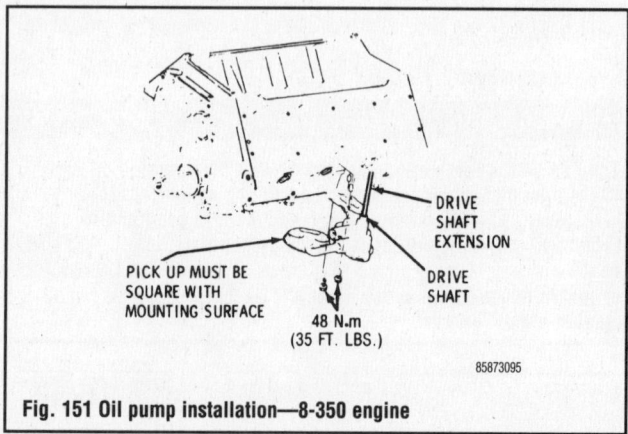

Fig. 151 Oil pump installation—8-350 engine

8-368, 425, 472, and 500 Engines

1. Jack up the car and support on jackstands.
2. Remove the oil filter.
3. Remove the five capscrews that secure the oil pump to the engine.

➡**Remove the screw nearest the pressure regulator last.**

To install:

4. Use a new gasket and engage the pump driveshaft with the distributor drive.
5. Install the screw nearest the pressure regulator first, then install the remaining screws and tighten to 15 ft. lbs. (20 Nm).

6. Install the oil filter and add one quart of oil to the engine.

7. Run the engine, check for leaks, stop the engine and check the oil level.

Timing Chain, Cover and Front Oil Seal

REMOVAL & INSTALLATION

Except 6-252, 8-250, 8-308 and 8-350 EFI and Diesel Engines

▶ See Figures 152 thru 160

➡ On 8-368 cu. in. engines with nylon oil pans, the pan must be removed from the engine, not just loosened.

1. Disconnect negative battery cable and drain cooling system.

2. Detach upper radiator hose retainer from cradle and position hose out of the way.

3. Remove the fan, alternator and power steering belts.

4. Remove four capscrews that secure crank pulley to harmonic balancer, then remove the pulley.

5. Remove the plug from the end of the crankshaft. Install the puller and remove the harmonic balancer.

6. Drain the engine oil. Loosen the oil pan bolts enough to allow the front of the oil pan to drop slightly.

✳✳ CAUTION

The EPA warns that prolonged contact with used engine oil may cause a number of skin disorders, including cancer! You should make every effort to minimize your exposure to used engine oil. Protective gloves should be worn when changing the oil. Wash your hands and any other exposed skin areas as soon as possible after exposure to used engine oil. Soap and water, or waterless hand cleaner should be used.

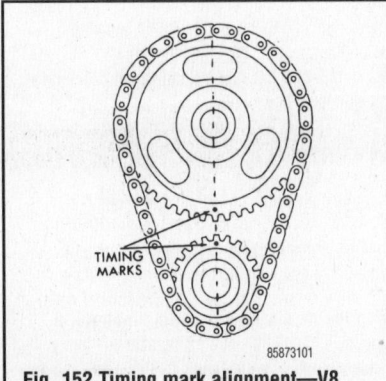

Fig. 152 Timing mark alignment—V8 engines

Fig. 153 Remove all necessary brackets—timing cover removal

Fig. 154 Access holes are often provided for hard to reach bolts

Fig. 155 Removing the crankshaft pulley bolts

Fig. 156 Removing the crankshaft pulley

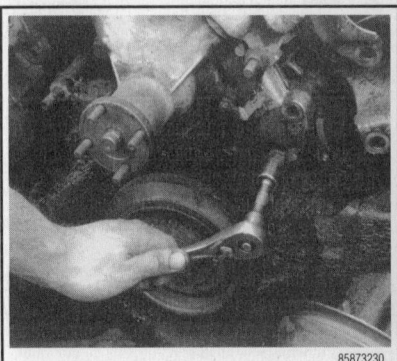

Fig. 157 Removing the timing case cover bolts

Fig. 158 Removing the timing mark indicator

Fig. 159 Removing the timing chain cover

Fig. 160 Make sure the timing marks are properly aligned if the timing chain is to be removed

➡️**It may be necessary to remove the starter to gain access to the bolts that are directly behind it.**

7. Disconnect lower radiator hose from water pump, then remove the screws that hold front cover to engine. Remove cover with water pump attached.

8. With a suitable tool, pry out front cover oil seal.

9. Lubricate new oil seal with wheel bearing grease. Position the seal on the end of the crankshaft with the garter spring side toward the engine.

10. Using a seal installer, drive the front seal into the front cover until it bottoms.

11. Remove distributor and fuel pump.

12. Remove oil slinger and fuel pump eccentric.

13. Remove capscrews that secure camshaft sprocket.

14. Remove camshaft sprocket along with timing chain.

To install:

15. Reverse removal procedure. Mount the timing chain over the camshaft and the crankshaft sprocket, then start the camshaft sprocket over the shaft. Make certain the aligning dowel is in a position where it will enter the hole in the camshaft freely. Make certain that the timing marks on the sprockets are in line between shaft centers.

16. Camshaft sprockets are a tight fit. However, a comparatively easy way to install a tight-fitting sprocket is to draw it on carefully with two bolts somewhat longer than the regular mounting bolts. By drawing alternately against each bolt, and tapping gently with a plastic hammer, even a very tight camshaft gear sprocket can be installed.

17. When the camshaft is secured, turn the engine two full revolutions until the timing marks again assume the original position. Check to make certain that the punch marks, which are stamped into the front face of the sprockets, are in line between the shaft centers.

6-252 Engine

♦ **See Figure 161**

1. Drain the cooling system.

2. Remove the radiator, fan, pulley and belt.

3. Remove the fuel pump and alternator, if necessary to remove cover.

4. Remove the distributor. If the timing chain and sprockets will not be disturbed, note the position of the distributor for installation in the same position.

5. Remove the thermostat bypass hose.

6. Remove the harmonic balancer.

7. Remove the timing chain-to-crankcase bolts.

8. Remove the oil pan-to-timing chain cover bolts and remove the timing chain cover.

9. Using a punch, drive out the old seal and the shedder toward the rear of the seal.

10. Coil the new packing around the opening so the ends are at the top. Drive in the shedder using a punch. Properly size the packing by rotating a hammer handle around the packing until the balancer hub can be inserted through the opening.

11. Align the timing marks on the sprockets.

12. Remove the camshaft sprocket bolt without changing the position of the sprocket. Remove the oil pan.

13. Remove the front crankshaft oil slinger.

14. Remove the camshaft sprocket bolts.

15. Using a suitable tool, carefully pry the camshaft sprocket and the crankshaft sprocket forward until they are free. Remove the sprockets and the chain.

To install:

16. Make sure, with sprockets temporarily installed, that No. 1 piston is at top dead center and the camshaft sprocket O-mark is straight down and on the centerline of both shafts.

17. Remove the camshaft sprocket and assemble the timing chain on both sprockets. Then slide the sprockets-and-chain assembly on the shafts with the O-marks in their closest together position and on a centerline with the sprocket hubs.

18. Assemble the slinger on the crankshaft with I.D. against the sprocket, (concave side toward the front of engine). Install the oil pan, if removed.

19. Install the camshaft sprocket bolts.

20. Install the distributor drive gear.

21. Install the drive gear and eccentric bolt and retaining washer. Torque to 40–55 ft. lbs. (54–75 Nm).

22. Install the timing case cover. Install a new seal by lightly tapping it in place. The lip of the seal faces inward. Pay particular attention to the following points.

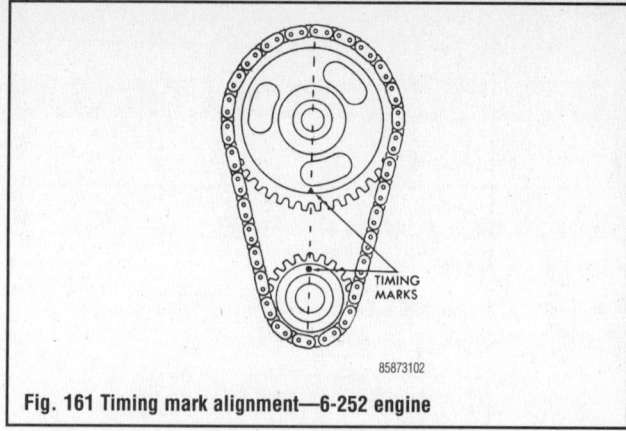
Fig. 161 Timing mark alignment—6-252 engine

a. Remove the oil pump cover and pack the space around the oil pump gears completely full of petroleum jelly. There must be no air space left inside the pump. Reinstall the pump cover using a new gasket.

b. The gasket surface of the block and timing chain cover must be clean and smooth. Use a new gasket correctly positioned.

c. Install the chain cover being certain the dowel pins engage the dowel pin holes before starting the attaching bolts.

d. Lube the bolt threads before installation and install them.

e. If the car has power steering the front pump bracket should be installed at this time.

f. Lube the O.D. of the harmonic balancer hub before installation to prevent damage to the seal when starting the engine.

➡️**The V6 engine has two timing marks on the harmonic balancer. A 1 in. (25mm) long, thin scribe mark is used for strobe light timing. Another mark, 4 in. (101mm) back, has a wider slot and is about ½ in. (13mm) long. This mark is used for magnetic pick-up timing.**

8-250 and 8-273 Engines

1982–85 VEHICLES

♦ **See Figures 162 and 163**

1. Disconnect the negative battery cable and drain the radiator.

2. On the Fleetwood and Seville models, remove the two screws on each side of the radiator securing the support rod. Move the support rods out of the way.

3. Remove the wiring harness from the upper fan shroud clamps.

4. Remove the power steering pump reservoir from the upper radiator shroud.

5. Remove the upper fan shroud from the lower fan shroud by removing the staples.

6. Remove the clutch fan assembly.

7. Remove the generator, A.I.R. pump, vacuum pump, and air conditioning pump drive belts.

8. Partially remove the air conditioning compressor from the engine mounting brackets without discharging the system.

9. Remove the alternator and support bracket from the engine.

10. Loosen the clamp and disconnect the coolant reservoir-to-water pump hose at the pump.

11. Disconnect the inlet and outlet hoses at the water pump.

12. Drain the crankcase by either removing the crankcase plugs (one on each side) or by elevating the rear wheels. This will prevent coolant from draining into the oil pan as the front cover is removed.

13. Remove the water pump and crankcase pulleys.

14. Remove the air conditioning bracket at the water pump.

15. Remove the timing mark tab from the front cover.

16. Remove the crankcase pulley-to-hub bolts and separate the pulley from the hub.

17. Remove the plug from the end of the crankshaft. Install a puller and remove the hub or balancer.

18. Remove the remaining front cover attaching screws and remove the cover with the water pump and lower thermostat housing as an assembly.

19. With a suitable tool, pry out front cover oil seal.

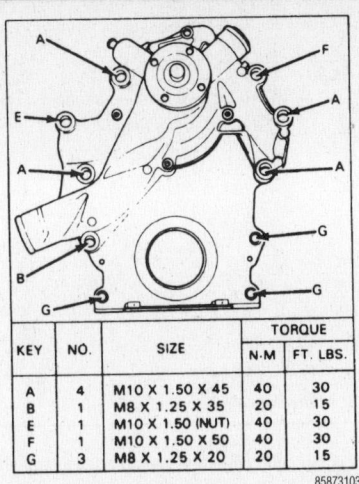

KEY	NO.	SIZE	TORQUE	
			N·M	FT. LBS.
A	4	M10 X 1.50 X 45	40	30
B	1	M8 X 1.25 X 35	20	15
E	1	M10 X 1.50 (NUT)	40	30
F	1	M10 X 1.50 X 50	40	30
G	3	M8 X 1.25 X 20	20	15

85873103

Fig. 162 Front cover screw location and torque specifications— 1982–85 8-250 engine

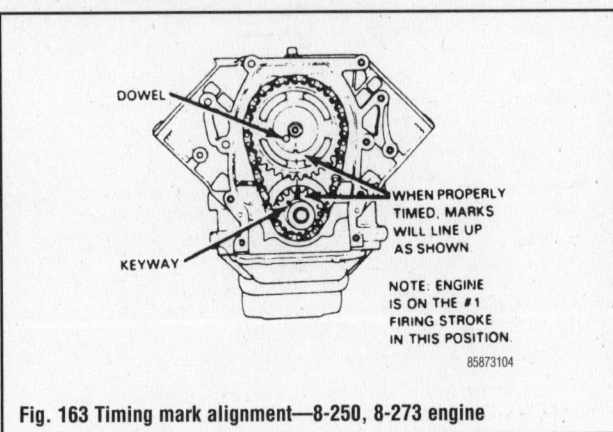

85873104

Fig. 163 Timing mark alignment—8-250, 8-273 engine

20. Lubricate new oil seal with wheel bearing grease. Position the seal on the end of the crankshaft with the garter spring side toward the engine.

21. Using a seal installer, drive the front seal into the front cover until it bottoms.

22. The timing chain and sprocket may now be removed as follows:

a. Remove the oil slinger from the crankshaft.

b. Rotate the engine and line up the timing marks as shown in the illustration.

c. Remove the screw securing the camshaft sprocket to the camshaft, then remove the camshaft and crankshaft sprocket with the chain attached.

To install:

23. Installation is the reverse of removal. After installing the timing chain over the camshaft sprocket rotate the crankshaft until the timing mark on the crank sprocket is positioned straight up.

24. While holding the timing chain by the cam sprocket, position the chain over the crankshaft so that the timing marks are aligned as in the illustration.

25. Hold the camshaft sprocket in position against the end of the camshaft and press the sprocket on the camshaft by hand. Make sure the index pin the camshaft is lined up with the index hole in the sprocket.

26. If necessary, keep the engine from rotating while torquing the camshaft sprocket screw to 37 ft. lbs. (50 Nm).

➡ Engine timing has been set so that the No. 1 cylinder is in the T.D.C. firing position. If for some reason the distributor was removed make sure the rotor is set so that cylinder No. 1 is in the firing position.

27. Install the oil slinger on the crankshaft with the smaller end of the slinger against the crankshaft sprocket.

28. Install the engine front cover by reversing the above removal procedure.

1986–89 VEHICLES

◆ See Figures 164 and 165

1. Disconnect the negative battery cable.

2. Place a clean drain pan under the radiator, open the drain cock and drain the engine coolant. Remove the air cleaner and move it aside.

3. Remove the serpentine belt.

4. Label and disconnect the alternator wiring. Remove the alternator and the alternator bracket.

5. Remove the air conditioner accumulator from the bracket and move it aside; DO NOT disconnect the fittings on the accumulator.

6. Remove the water pump pulley bolts and the pulley. If necessary, remove the idler pulley.

7. Raise and support the front of the vehicle on jackstands.

8. Remove the crankshaft pulley-to-crankshaft pulley bolt. Using the Puller tool No. J–24420–B or equivalent, attach it to the crankshaft pulley; using the center bolt, press the crankshaft pulley from the crankshaft. Remove the woodruff key from the crankshaft.

9. Remove the front cover-to-engine bolts, the oil pan-to-front cover bolts and the front cover.

10. Remove the oil slinger from the crankshaft. Rotate the crankshaft and align the timing marks to **TDC**.

11. Remove the camshaft sprocket-to-camshaft screw, the camshaft and crankshaft sprockets with the chain attached.

To install:

12. Reverse the removal procedures. After installing the timing chain over the camshaft sprocket rotate the crankshaft until the crankshaft sprocket timing mark is positioned **STRAIGHT UP**.

13. Install the cam sprocket and timing chain over the crankshaft so that the timing marks are aligned.

14. Hold the camshaft sprocket in position against the end of the camshaft and press the sprocket on the camshaft by hand. Make sure the camshaft index pin is align with the sprocket index hole.

15. If necessary, keep the engine from rotating while torquing the camshaft sprocket screw to 37 ft. lbs. (50 Nm).

➡ Engine timing has been set so that the No. 1 cylinder is in the TDC firing position. If the distributor was removed make sure the rotor is positioned on the No. 1 cylinder firing position.

16. Install the oil slinger on the crankshaft with the smaller end of the slinger against the crankshaft sprocket.

17. Using a putty knife, clean the gasket mounting surfaces.

18. Using a small pry bar, pry the oil seal from the front cover (discard it).

19. Clean the oil seal mounting surface. Lubricate the new seal with engine oil.

20. Using a hammer and the Oil Seal Installation tool No. J–29662 or equivalent, drive the new oil seal in to the front cover until it seats.

21. To complete the installation, use a new gasket, RTV sealant (on the oil pan lip) and reverse the removal procedures. Torque the front cover-to-engine bolts to 15 ft. lbs. (20 Nm), the crankshaft pulley-to-crankshaft bolt to 18 ft. lbs. (24 Nm).

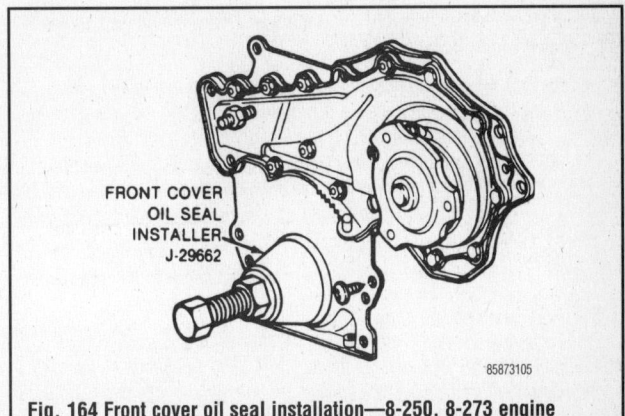

85873105

Fig. 164 Front cover oil seal installation—8-250, 8-273 engine

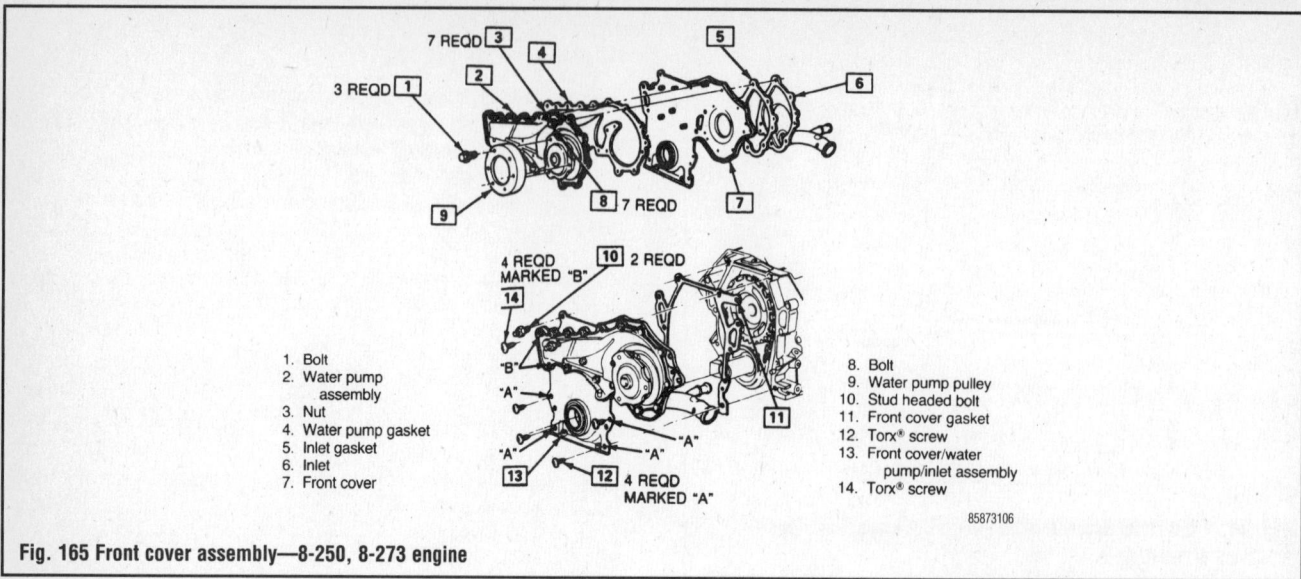

1. Bolt
2. Water pump assembly
3. Nut
4. Water pump gasket
5. Inlet gasket
6. Inlet
7. Front cover

8. Bolt
9. Water pump pulley
10. Stud headed bolt
11. Front cover gasket
12. Torx® screw
13. Front cover/water pump/inlet assembly
14. Torx® screw

85873106

Fig. 165 Front cover assembly—8-250, 8-273 engine

5.0L Engine

▶ **See Figures 166 and 167**

1. Disconnect the negative battery cable. Drain the cooling system into a suitable drain pan.

> ✳✳ **CAUTION**
>
> **When draining the coolant, keep in mind that cats and dogs are attracted by the ethylene glycol antifreeze, and are quite likely to drink any that is left in an uncovered container or in puddles on the ground. This will prove fatal in sufficient quantity. Always drain the coolant into a sealable container. Coolant should be reused unless it is contaminated or several years old.**

2. Remove the drive belts and accessory belts. Remove the fan assembly and fan pulley. Using Hub Balancer Puller J–8614 or equivalent remove the hub balancer.

3. On vehicles equipped with air conditioning, remove the rear air conditioning compressor braces and lower the air conditioning mount bolts. Remove the compressor bracket and nuts at the water pump. Slide the mounting bracket forward and remove the compressor mount bolt. Disconnect the wires at the compressor and lay the unit aside. Disconnect the air injection hose at the right exhaust manifold.

4. Remove the compressor mount bracket. Remove the upper air injection pump bracket with the power steering reservoir. Remove the lower air injection pump bracket.

5. Disconnect the heater and radiator hoses to the water pump. Remove the water pump. Remove the front cover retaining bolts, timing indicator, front cover and old gasket.

➡ **It may be necessary to grind a flat surface on the dowel pins to aid in the removal of the front cover.**

6. Remove the crankshaft oil slinger, camshaft thrust button and spring.

7. Crank the engine until the No. 1 piston is at TDC and the timing marks on the camshaft and crankshaft sprockets are aligned (No. 4 firing).

8. Remove the fuel pump, gasket and fuel pump eccentric. Remove the camshaft sprocket bolts and remove the camshaft sprocket and chain.

➡ **The sprocket is a tight fit on the camshaft. If the sprocket does not come off easily, use a plastic mallet and strike the lower edge of the sprocket. This should dislodge the sprocket allowing it to be removed from the shaft.**

9. To remove the crankshaft gear, first remove the crankshaft key, then using puller tools BT-6812, or J-25287 and J-21052-2 or equivalent. Remove the crankshaft sprocket.

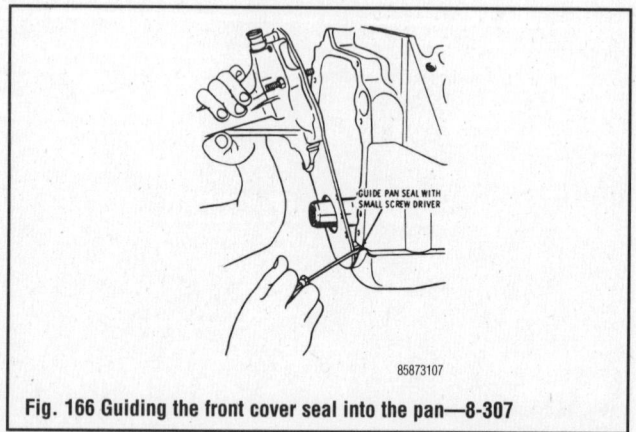

85873107

Fig. 166 Guiding the front cover seal into the pan—8-307

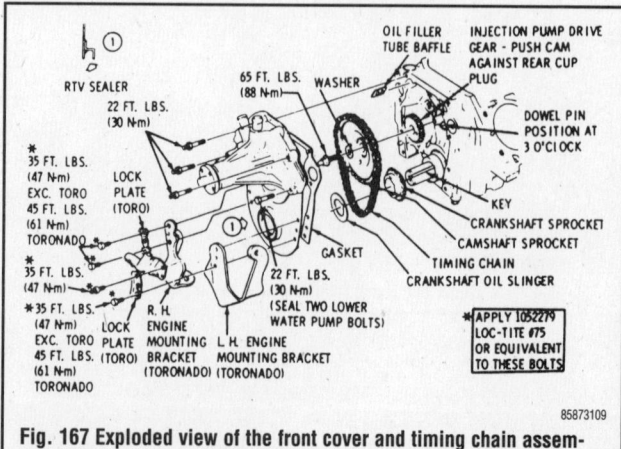

85873109

Fig. 167 Exploded view of the front cover and timing chain assembly—8-350 and 8-307 similar

To install:

10. Insert the camshaft sprocket and crankshaft sprocket into the timing chain, with the timing marks aligned. Lube the thrust surface with Molykote or equivalent.

11. Grasp both sprockets and the timing chain together and put them into their prospective places.

12. Rotate the camshaft sprocket and engage it on the camshaft. Install the fuel pump eccentric, flat side toward the engine.

13. Install the camshaft sprocket bolt finger tight. Rotate the crankshaft until the keyways are aligned. Install the crankshaft sprocket key, tap it in with a brass hammer until the key bottoms.

14. When the timing marks are in alignment, the number six cylinder should be at top dead center. When both timing marks are on the top, the number one cylinder is at top dead center of the compression stroke.

15. Slowly and evenly draw the camshaft sprocket onto the camshaft using the mounting bolt and torque the bolt to 65 ft. lbs. (88 Nm).

16. Lubricate the timing chain and finish the installation by reversing the order of the removal procedure.

17. When installing the front cover, apply a suitable RTV sealant around the coolant holes of the new front cover. Be sure to trim the ends of the oil pan seal and install the seal onto the timing chain cover.

8-350 EFI and Diesel Engines

♦ **See Figures 168, 169 and 170**

1. Drain the cooling system and disconnect the radiator hoses.
2. Remove all belts, fan and pulley, crankshaft pulley and balancer, using a balancer puller.

❊❊ WARNING

The use of any other type of puller, such as a universal claw type which pulls on the outside of the hub, can destroy the balancer. The outside ring of the balancer is bonded in rubber to the hub. Pulling on the outside will break the bond.

The timing mark is on the outside ring. If it is suspected that the bond is broken, check that the center of the keyway is 16 degrees from the center of the timing slot. If addition, there are chiseled aligning marks between the weight and the hub.

3. Unbolt and remove the cover, timing indicator and water pump.
4. It may be necessary to grind a flat on the cover for gripping purposes.
5. To replace the timing sprocket or chain use the following procedure:
   a. Remove the camshaft gear.

➡ **The fuel pump operating cam is bolted to the front of the camshaft sprocket and the sprocket is located on the camshaft by means of a dowel.**

   b. Remove the oil slinger, timing chain, and the camshaft sprocket. If the crankshaft sprocket is to be replaced, remove it also at this time. Remove the crankshaft key before using the puller. If the key can not be removed, align the puller so it does not overlap the end of the key, as the keyway is only machined part of the way into the crankshaft gear.

   c. Reinstall the crankshaft sprocket being careful to start it with the keyway in perfect alignment since it is rather difficult to correct for misalignment after the gear has been started on the shaft. Turn the timing mark on the crankshaft gear until it points directly toward the center of the camshaft. Mount the timing chain over the camshaft gear, then start the camshaft gear up on to its shaft with the timing marks as close as possible to each other and in-line between the shaft centers. Rotate the camshaft to align the shaft with the new gear.

   d. Install the fuel pump eccentric with the flat side toward the rear.
   e. Drive the key in with a hammer until it bottoms.
   f. Install the oil slinger.

➡ **Any time the timing chain and gears are replaced on the diesel engine it will be necessary to retime the engine. Refer to the paragraph on Diesel Engine Injection Timing in Section 5.**

To install:

6. Grind a chamfer on one end of each dowel pin.
7. Cut the excess material from the front end of the oil pan gasket on each side of the block.
8. Clean the block, oil pan and front cover mating surfaces with solvent.
9. Cut about ⅛ in. (3mm) off each end of a new front pan seal.
10. Install a new front cover gasket on the block.
11. With a suitable tool, pry out front cover oil seal.
12. Lubricate new oil seal with wheel bearing grease. Position the seal on the end of the crankshaft with the garter spring side toward the engine.
13. Using a seal installer, drive the front seal into the front cover until it bottoms.
14. Apply sealer to the gasket around the coolant holes.
15. Apply sealer to the block at the junction of the pan and front cover.
16. Place the cover on the block and press down to compress the seal. Rotate the cover left and right and guide the pan seal into the cavity using a small screwdriver. Oil the bolt threads and install two bolts to hold the cover in place. Install both dowel pins (chamfered end first), then install the remaining front cover bolts.
17. Apply a lubricant, compatible with rubber, on the balancer seal surface.
18. Install the balancer and bolt. Torque the bolt to 200–300 ft. lbs. (271-407 Nm).
19. Install the other parts in the reverse order of removal.

Camshaft

REMOVAL & INSTALLATION

♦ **See Figures 171 and 172**

Except 6-252, 1986 8-250, 307 and 8-350 EFI and Diesel Engines

➡ **If equipped with air conditioning, the system must be discharged before the camshaft is removed (refer to Section 1). The condenser must also be removed from the car.**

1. Disconnect the battery.
2. Drain and remove the radiator.
3. Disconnect the fuel line at the fuel pump. Remove the pump on carbureted models.
4. Disconnect the throttle cable and the air cleaner.
5. Remove the alternator belt, loosen the alternator bolts, and move the alternator to one side.
6. Remove the power steering pump from its brackets and move it out of the way.

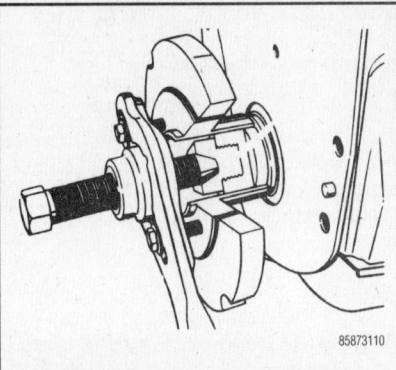

Fig. 168 Removing the harmonic balancer using a puller

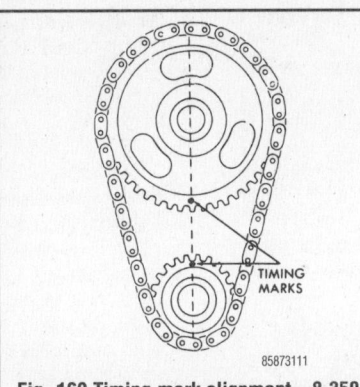

Fig. 169 Timing mark alignment—8-350 engines

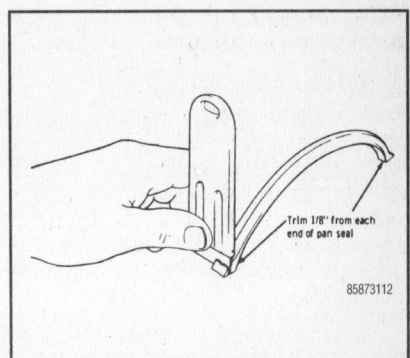

Fig. 170 Trimming the pan seal with a razor blade

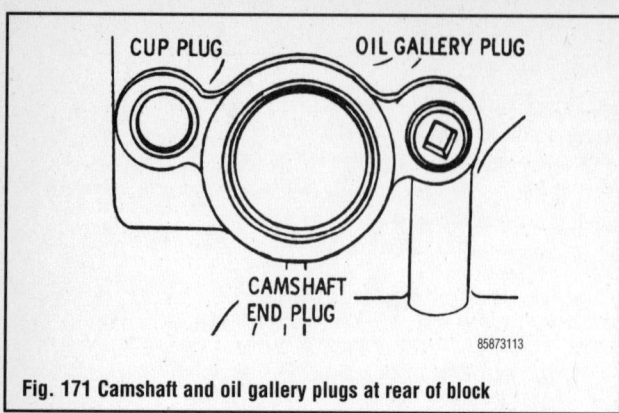

Fig. 171 Camshaft and oil gallery plugs at rear of block

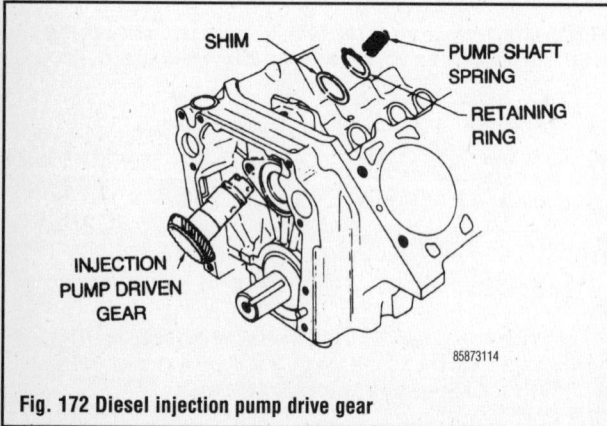

Fig. 172 Diesel injection pump drive gear

7. Remove the air conditioning compressor from its brackets and move the compressor out of the way without disconnecting the lines.
8. Disconnect the hoses from the water pump.
9. Disconnect the electrical and vacuum connections.
10. Mark the distributor as to location in the block. Remove the distributor. Remove the crankshaft pulley and the hub attaching bolt. Remove the crankshaft hub.
11. Remove the engine front cover.
12. Remove the valve covers.
13. Remove the intake manifold.
14. Mark the lifters, pushrods, and rocker arms as to location so that they may be installed in the same position. Remove these parts.
15. If the car is equipped with air conditioning, discharge the air conditioning system and remove the condenser.
16. Remove the fuel pump eccentric, camshaft gear, oil slinger, and timing chain. Remove the camshaft thrust plate (on front of camshaft) if equipped.
17. Carefully remove the camshaft from the engine.

To install:
18. Inspect the shaft for signs of excessive wear or damage.
19. Liberally coat camshaft and bearings with heavy engine oil or engine assembly lubricant and insert the cam into the engine.
20. Align the timing marks on the camshaft and crankshaft gears. See Timing Chain Replacement and Valve Timing for details.
21. Install the distributor using the locating marks made during removal. If any problems are encountered, see Distributor Installation.
22. Reverse the removal procedure but pay attention to the following points:
  a. Install the timing indicator before installing the power steering pump bracket.
  b. Install the flywheel inspection cover after installing the starter.
  c. Replace the engine oil and radiator coolant.

6-252 Engine

1. Remove intake manifold.
2. Remove valve covers.
3. Remove rocker arm and shaft assemblies, push rods and valve lifters. Mark parts as necessary and keep pushrods in order for later assembly.

4. Remove timing chain cover, timing chain and sprocket.
5. Carefully slide camshaft forward, out of the bearing bores, working slowly to avoid marring the bearing surfaces. Remove camshaft.

To install:
6. Liberally coat the entire cam with a heavy engine oil or a lubricant specially formulated for engine rebuilding. Slowly slide the camshaft into the engine block, exercising extreme care not to damage the cam bearings.
7. Reassemble the engine in the reverse order of removal.

1986 8-250 Engine

1. Remove the engine from the vehicle as detailed earlier in this section.
2. Remove the front cover and timing chain assembly.
3. Remove the valve lifters.
4. Grasp the end of the camshaft and carefully slide it forward until it clears the engine.

➡ **Threading a large bolt into the end of the camshaft will facilitate removal.**

✳ WARNING

Extreme care must be exercised to prevent the camshaft lobes from scratching the bearings!

To install:
5. Inspect the camshaft and its bearing for excessive wear, flaking or scoring.

➡ **If a new camshaft is required, the valve lifters and the driveshaft driven gear must be replaced also.**

6. Coat the camshaft, bearing journals and distributor drive gear with engine oil.
7. Carefully slide the camshaft back into the cylinder block.
8. Install the timing chain and the valve lifters. Install the front cover and related components.
9. Install the engine into the vehicle.

8-307 Engine

1. Drain the engine coolant.
2. Remove the upper radiator baffle. Disconnect the upper radiator hose at the water outlet and position it out of the way. Remove the upper radiator hose support clamp.
3. Disconnect the transmission cooler lines at the radiator and position them out of the way.
4. Remove the upper radiator support and then remove the radiator.
5. Remove the air cleaner.
6. Tag and disconnect the throttle cable.
7. Remove the drive belts and then remove the A.I.R. pump pulley. Remove the fan, fan clutch and the water pump pulley.
8. Loosen the alternator bracket and swivel the alternator over and out of the way.
9. With the hydraulic lines still attached, remove the power steering pump and position it out of the way.
10. Move the air conditioning compressor mounting bracket. With the lines still attached, move the compressor aside far enough to provide access to the front of the cylinder block.
11. Disconnect and remove the thermostat bypass hose.
12. Tag and disconnect all electrical leads and vacuum lines which may interfere with camshaft removal.
13. Remove the A.I.R. pump.
14. Remove the distributor as detailed previously in this section. Leave the cap and wires attached and just move it aside.
15. Remove the crankshaft pulley and hub.
16. Remove the fuel pump.
17. Remove the front cover.
18. Remove the cylinder head covers.
19. Remove the intake manifold complete with its gasket and seals.
20. Remove all cylinder head valve train components. Remove the valve lifters, guides and retainer.
21. Discharge the air conditioning system as outlined in Section 1 and remove the condenser.

22. Remove the camshaft thrust button and spring.

23. Remove the fuel pump eccentric.

24. Remove the camshaft timing gear along with the timing chain.

25. Remove the camshaft retaining plate and the flange adapter.

26. Carefully slide the camshaft out from the cylinder block.

To install:

27. Coat the camshaft and bearing journals with clean engine oil.

28. Replace the oil filter.

29. Slide the camshaft into the cylinder block. Install the flange adapter and retainer plate.

30. Install the timing chain and sprockets as detailed earlier in this section.

31. Installation of the remaining components is in the reverse order of removal. Road test the vehicle and check for leaks.

8-350 EFI and Diesel Engine

➡**If equipped with air conditioning, the system must be discharged before the camshaft is removed (refer to Section 1). The condenser must also be removed from the car.**

Removal of the camshaft on the diesel also requires removal of the injection pump drive and driven gears, removal of the intake manifold, disassembly of the valve lifters, and retiming of the injection pump.

1. Disconnect the negative battery cables. Drain the coolant. Remove the radiator.

2. Remove the intake manifold and gasket and the front and rear intake manifold seals. Refer to the Intake Manifold removal and installation procedure.

3. Remove the balancer pulley and the balancer. See Caution under Diesel Engine Front Cover removal and installation, above. Remove the engine front cover using the appropriate procedure.

4. Remove the valve covers. Remove the rocker arms, pushrods and valve lifters; see the procedure earlier in this section. Be sure to keep the parts in order so that they may be returned to their original positions.

5. Remove the camshaft sprocket retaining bolt, and remove the timing chain and sprockets, using the procedure outlined earlier.

6. Position the camshaft dowel pin at the 3 o'clock position.

7. Push the camshaft rearward and hold it there, being careful not to dislodge the oil gallery plug at the rear of the engine. Remove the fuel injection pump drive gear by sliding it from the camshaft while rocking the pump driven gear.

8. To remove the fuel injection pump driven gear, remove the pump adapter, the snapring, and remove the selective washer. Remove the driven gear and spring.

9. Remove the camshaft by sliding it out the front of the engine. Be extremely careful not to allow the cam lobes to contact any of the bearings, or the journals to dislodge the bearings during camshaft removal. Do not force the camshaft, or bearing damage will result.

10. If either the injection pump drive or driven gears are to be replaced, replace both gears.

To install:

11. Coat the camshaft and the cam bearings with a heavyweight engine oil, GM lubricant #1052365 or the equivalent.

12. Carefully slide the camshaft into position in the engine.

13. Fit the crankshaft and camshaft sprockets, aligning the timing marks as shown in the timing chain removal and installation procedure, above. Remove the sprockets without distributing the timing.

14. Install the injection pump driven gear, spring, shim, and snapring. Check the gear end play. If the end play is not within 0.002–0.006 in. (0.05–0.15mm) through 1979, and 0.002–0.015 in. (0.05–0.38mm) on 1980 and later, replace the shim to obtain the specified clearance. Shims are available in 0.003 in. increments, from 0.080 in. to 0.115 in.

15. Position the camshaft dowel pin at the 3 o'clock position. Align the zero marks on the pump drive gear and pump driven gear. Hold the camshaft in the rearward position and slide the pump drive gear onto the camshaft. Install the camshaft bearing retainer.

16. Install the timing chain and sprockets, making sure the timing marks are aligned.

17. Install the lifters, pushrods and rocker arms. See Rocker Arm Replacement, Diesel Engine for lifter bleed down procedures. Failure to bleed down the lifters could bend valves when the engine is turned over.

18. Install the injection pump adapter and injection pump. See the appropriate sections under Fuel System above for procedures.

19. Install the remaining components in the reverse order of removal.

CAMSHAFT INSPECTION

Completely clean the camshaft with solvent, paying special attention to cleaning the oil holes. Visually inspect the cam lobes and bearing journals for excessive wear. If a lobe is questionable, have the cam checked at a reputable machine shop; if a journal or lobe is worn, the camshaft must be reground or replaced. Also have the camshaft checked for straightness on a dial indicator.

➡**If a cam journal is worn, there is a good chance that the bearings are worn as well.**

CAMSHAFT BEARINGS REMOVAL & INSTALLATION

◆ **See Figures 173 and 174**

If excessive camshaft wear is found, or if the engine is being completely rebuilt, the camshaft bearings should be replaced.

➡**The front and rear bearings should be removed last, and installed first. Those bearings act as guides for the other bearings and pilot.**

1. Drive the camshaft rear plug from the block.

2. Assemble the removal puller with its shoulder on the bearing to be removed. Gradually tighten the puller nut until the bearing is removed.

3. Remove the remaining bearings, leaving the front and rear for last. To remove these, reverse the position of the puller, so as to pull the bearings towards the center of the block. Leave the tool in this position, pilot the new front and rear bearings on the installer, and pull them into position.

4. Return the puller to its original position and pull the remaining bearings into position.

➡**Ensure that the oil holes align when installing the bearings. This is very important! You can make a simple tool out of a piece of ³⁄₃₂ in. brass rod to check alignment. See the illustration.**

5. Replace the camshaft rear plug, and stake it into position.

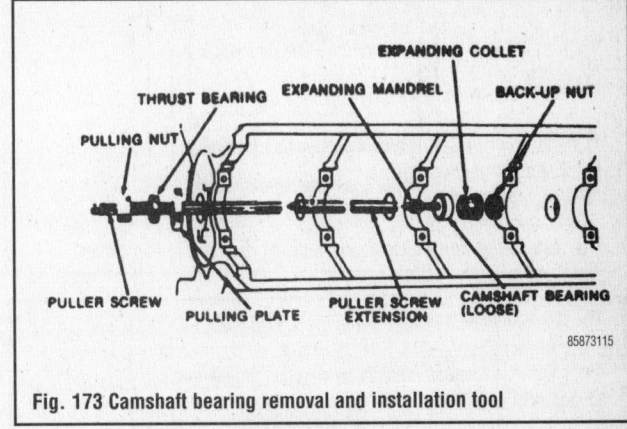

Fig. 173 Camshaft bearing removal and installation tool

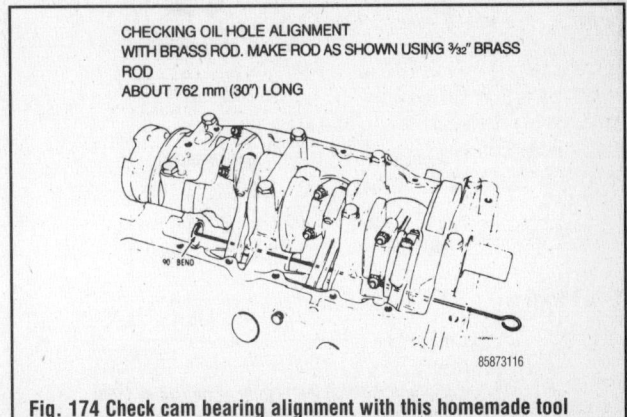

Fig. 174 Check cam bearing alignment with this homemade tool

Pistons and Connecting Rods

REMOVAL & INSTALLATION

♦ **See Figures 175 thru 184**

Before removing the pistons, the top of the cylinder bore must be examined for a ridge. A ridge at the top of the bore is the result of normal cylinder wear, caused by the piston rings only travelling so far up the bore in the course of the piston stroke. The ridge can be felt by hand; it must be removed before the pistons are removed.

A ridge reamer is necessary for this operation. Place the piston at the bottom of its stroke, and cover it with a rag. Cut the ridge away with the ridge reamer, using extreme care to avoid cutting too deeply. Remove the rag, and remove the cuttings that remain on the piston with a magnet and a rag soaked in clean oil. Make sure the piston top and cylinder bore are absolutely clean before moving the piston.

1. Remove intake manifold and cylinder head or heads.
2. Remove oil pan.
3. Remove oil pump assembly if necessary.
4. Matchmark the connecting rod cap to the connecting rod with a scribe; each cap must be reinstalled on its proper rod in the proper direction. Remove the connecting rod bearing cap and the rod bearing. Number the top of each piston with silver paint or a felt-tip pen for later assembly.

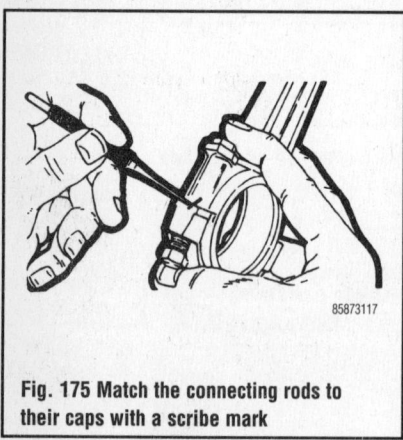

Fig. 175 Match the connecting rods to their caps with a scribe mark

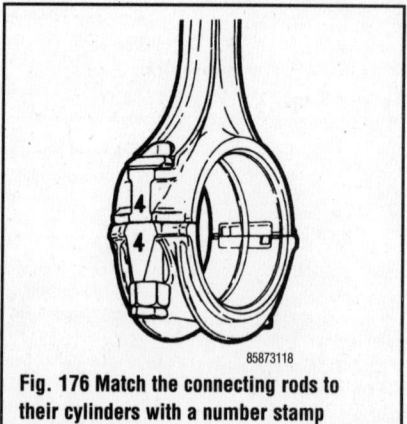

Fig. 176 Match the connecting rods to their cylinders with a number stamp

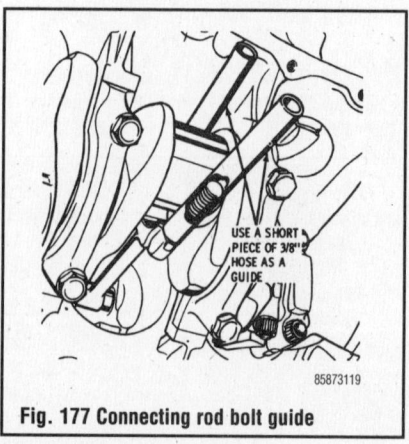

Fig. 177 Connecting rod bolt guide

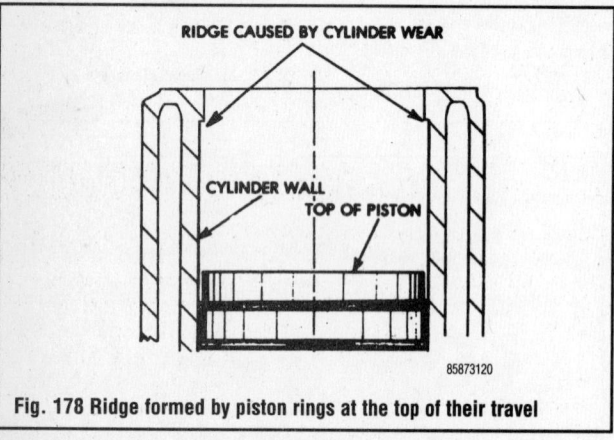

Fig. 178 Ridge formed by piston rings at the top of their travel

Fig. 179 Push the piston and rod out with a hammer handle

5. Cut lengths of ⅜ in. diameter hose to use as rod bolt guides. Install the hose over the threads of the rod bolts, to prevent the bolt threads from damaging the crankshaft journals and cylinder walls when the piston is removed.
6. Squirt some clean engine oil onto the cylinder wall from above, until the wall is coated. Carefully push the piston and rod assembly up and out of the cylinder by tapping on the bottom of the connecting rod with a wooden hammer handle.
7. Place the rod bearing and cap back on the connecting rod, and install the nuts temporarily. Using a number stamp or punch, stamp the cylinder number on the side of the connecting rod and cap this will help keep the proper piston and rod assembly on the proper cylinder.

➡On V6 engines, starting at the front the cylinders are numbered 2–4–6 on the right bank and 1–3–5 on the left. On all 8-250, 273, 307, 350 and 429 engines, starting at the front the right bank cylinders are 2–4–6–8 and the left bank 1–3–5–7. On all other V8s, starting at the front the left bank cylinders are 2–4–6–8 and the right bank 1–3–5–7.

8. Remove remaining pistons in similar manner.
On all engines, the notch on the piston will face the front of the engine for assembly. The chamfered corners of the bearing caps should face toward the front of the left bank and toward the rear of the right bank, and the boss on the

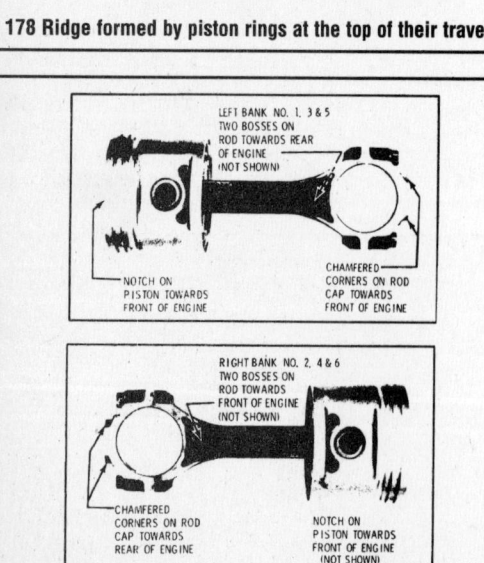

Fig. 180 Piston to connecting rod positioning—6-252 engine

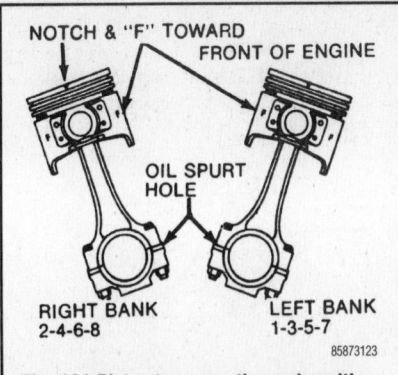

Fig. 181 Piston to connecting rod positioning—8-250, 307, 350 and 429 engines

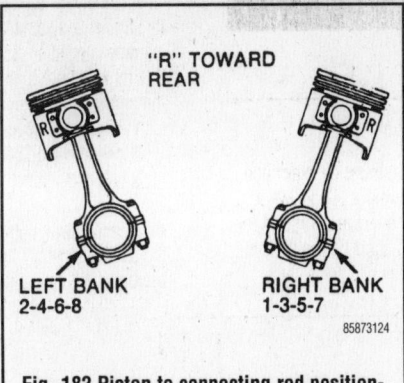

Fig. 182 Piston to connecting rod positioning—8-368, 425, 472 and 500 engines

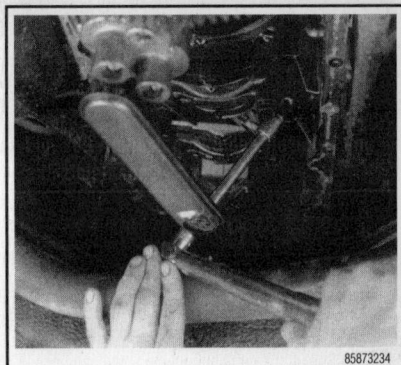

Fig. 183 Removing the connecting rod cap bolts

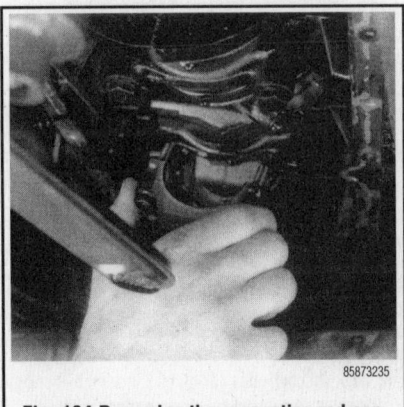

Fig. 184 Removing the connecting rod cap

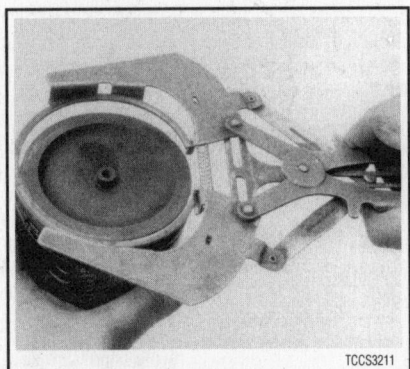

Fig. 185 Use a ring expander tool to remove the piston rings

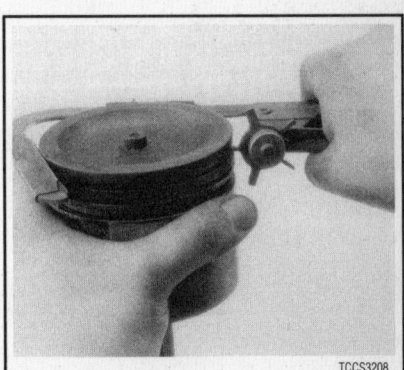

Fig. 186 Clean the piston grooves using a ring groove cleaner

connecting rod should face toward the front of the engine for the right bank and to the rear of the engine of the left bank.

On various engines, the piston compression rings are marked with a dimple, a letter **T**, a letter **O**, **GM** or the word **TOP** to identify the side of the ring which must face toward the top of the piston.

CLEANING AND INSPECTING

▶ **See Figures 185 thru 191**

A piston ring expander is necessary for removing piston rings without damaging them; any other method (screwdriver blades, pliers, etc.) usually results in the rings being bent, scratched or distorted, or the piston itself being damaged. When the rings are removed, clean the ring grooves using an appropriate ring groove cleaning tool. Take care not to cut too deeply. Thoroughly clean all carbon and varnish from the piston with solvent.

✳✳ WARNING

Do not use a wire brush or caustic solvent (acids, etc.) on piston. Inspect the pistons for scuffing, scoring, cranks, pitting, or excessive ring groove wear. If these are evident, the piston must be replaced.

The piston should also be checked in relation to the cylinder diameter. Using a telescoping gauge and micrometer, or a dial gauge, measure the cylinder bore diameter perpendicular (90%) to the piston pin, 2½ in. (63.5mm) below the cylinder block deck (surface where the block mates with the heads). Then, with the micrometer, measure the piston perpendicular to its wrist pin on the skirt. The difference between the two measurements is the piston clearance.

If the clearance is within specifications or slightly below (after the cylinders have been bored or honed), finish honing is all that is necessary. If the clearance is excessive try to obtain a slightly larger piston to being clearance to within specifications. If this is not possible obtain the first oversize piston and hone (or

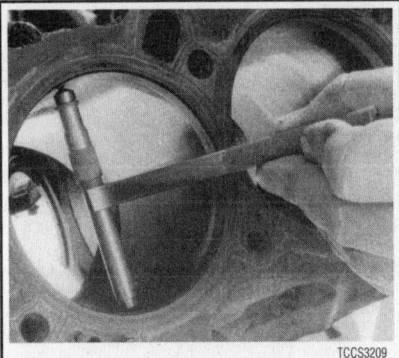

Fig. 187 A telescoping gauge may be used to measure the cylinder bore diameter

Fig. 188 Measure the piston's outer diameter using a micrometer

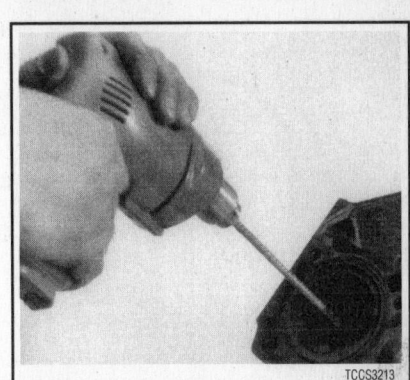

Fig. 189 Removing cylinder glazing using a flexible hone

Fig. 190 A properly cross-hatched cylinder bore

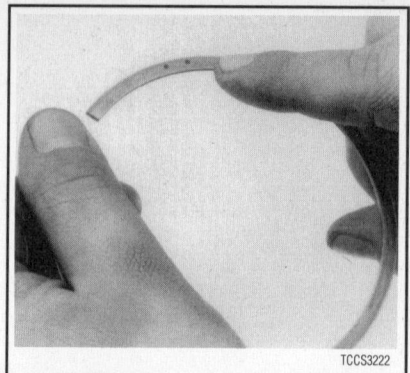

Fig. 191 Most rings are marked to show which side should face upward

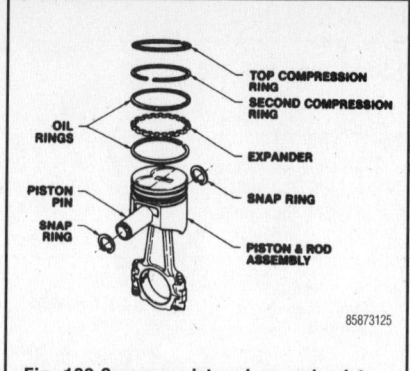

Fig. 192 Common piston rings and wrist pin

if necessary, bore) the cylinder to size. Generally, if the cylinder bore is tapered 0.005 in. (0.13mm) or more or is out-of-round 0.003 in. (0.08mm) or more, it is advisable to rebore for the smallest possible oversize piston and rings. After measuring, mark pistons with a felt-tip pen for reference and for assembly.

➡Cylinder block boring should be performed by a reputable machine shop with the proper equipment. In some cases, cleanup honing can be done with the cylinder block in the car, but most excessive honing and all cylinder boring must be done with the block stripped and removed from the car.

Piston Ring and Wrist Pin

♦ See Figures 185, 186, 188, 192 thru 196

REMOVAL

Some of the engines covered in this guide utilize pistons with pressed-in wrist pins; these must be removed by a special press designed for this purpose. Other pistons have their wrist pins secured by snaprings, which are easily removed with snapring pliers. Separate the piston from the connecting rod.

A piston ring expander is necessary for removing piston rings without damaging them; any other method (screwdriver blades, pliers, etc.) usually results in the rings being bent, scratched or distorted, or the piston itself being damaged. When the rings are removed, clean the ring grooves using an appropriate ring groove cleaning tool, using care not to cut too deeply. Thoroughly clean all carbon and varnish from the piston with solvent.

✳✳ WARNING

Do not use a wire brush or caustic solvent (acids, etc.) on pistons.

Inspect the pistons for scuffing, scoring, cracks, pitting, or excessive ring groove wear. If these are evident, the piston must be replaced.

The piston should also be checked in relation to the cylinder diameter. Using a telescoping gauge and micrometer, or a dial gauge, measure the cylinder bore

diameter perpendicular (90%) to the piston pin, 2½ in. (63.5mm) below the cylinder block deck (surface where the block mates with the heads). Then, with the micrometer, measure the piston perpendicular to its wrist pin on the skirt. The difference between the two measurements is the piston clearance. If the clearance is within specifications or slightly below (after the cylinders have been bored or honed), finish honing is all that is necessary. If the clearance is excessive, try to obtain a slightly larger piston to bring clearance to within specifications. If this is not possible, obtain the first oversize piston and hone (or if necessary, bore) the cylinder to size. Generally, if the cylinder bore is tapered 0.005 in. (0.13mm) or more or is out-of-round 0.003 in. (0.08mm) or more, it is advisable to rebore for the smallest possible oversize piston and rings.

After measuring, mark pistons with a felt-tip pen for reference and for assembly.

➡Cylinder honing and/or boring should be performed by a reputable, professional mechanic with the proper equipment. In some cases, clean-up honing can be done with the cylinder block in the car, but most excessive honing and all cylinder boring must be done with the block stripped and removed from the car.

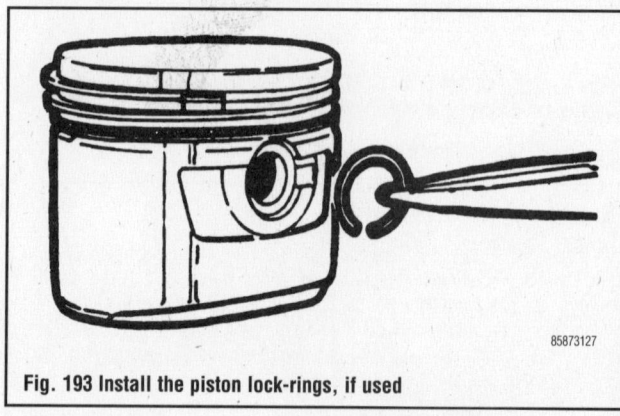

Fig. 193 Install the piston lock-rings, if used

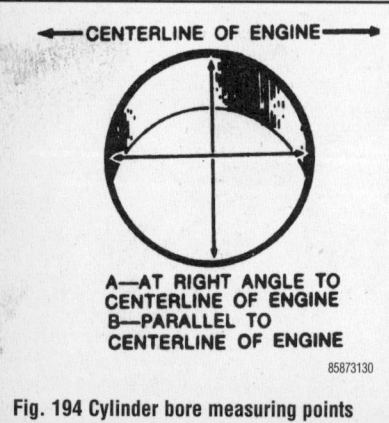

Fig. 194 Cylinder bore measuring points

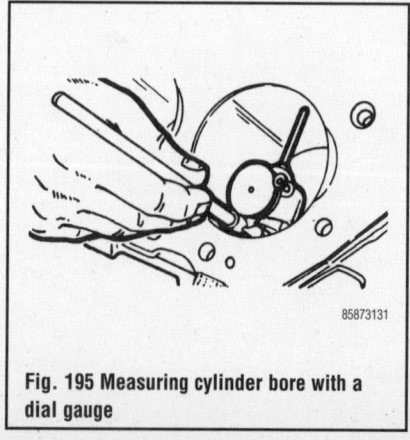

Fig. 195 Measuring cylinder bore with a dial gauge

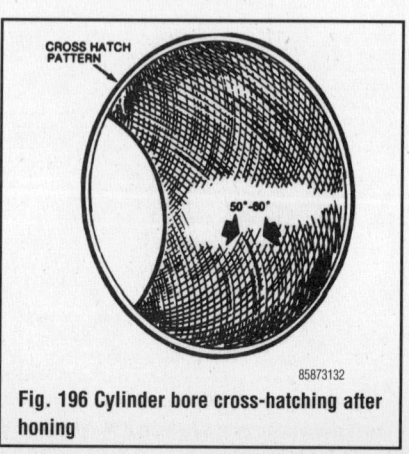

Fig. 196 Cylinder bore cross-hatching after honing

PISTON RING END GAP

▶ **See Figures 197, 198 and 199**

Piston ring end gap should be checked while the rings are removed from the pistons. Incorrect end gap indicates that the wrong size rings are being used; ring breakage could occur.

Compress the piston rings to be used in a cylinder, one at a time, into that cylinder. Squirt clean oil into the cylinder, so that the rings and the top 2

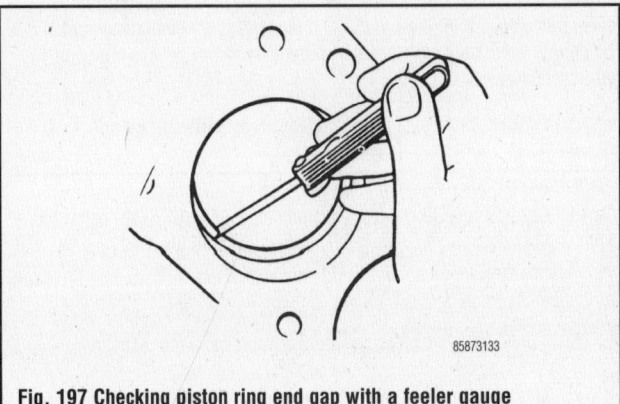

Fig. 197 Checking piston ring end gap with a feeler gauge

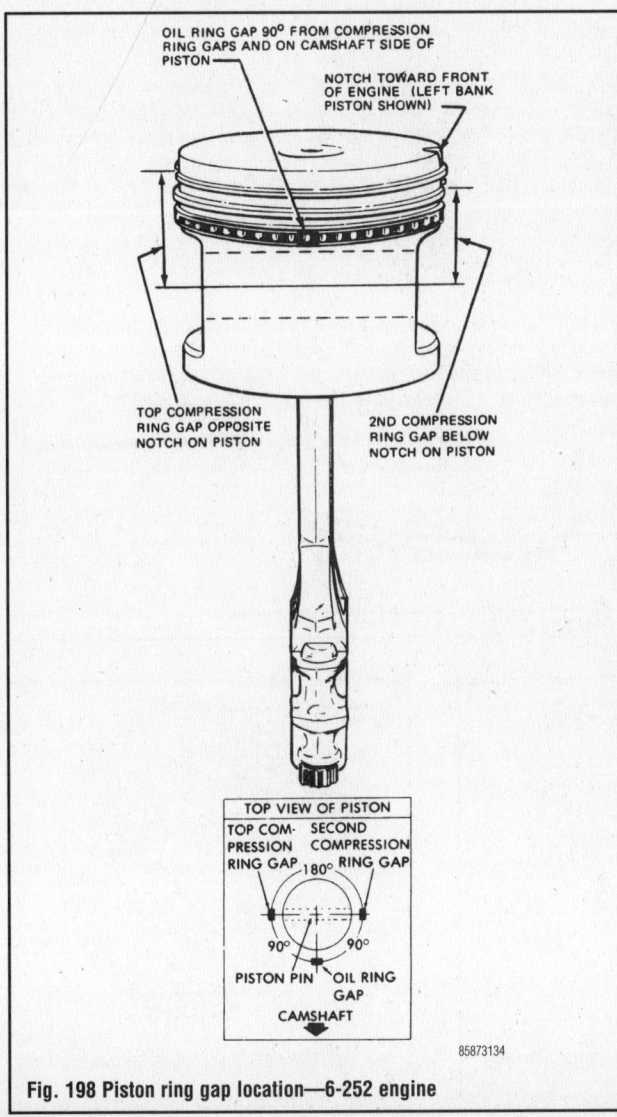

Fig. 198 Piston ring gap location—6-252 engine

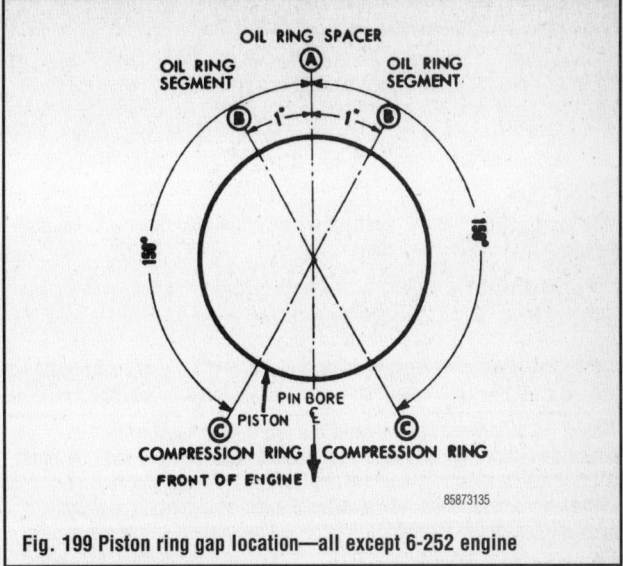

Fig. 199 Piston ring gap location—all except 6-252 engine

in. (50mm) of cylinder wall are coated. Using an inverted piston, press the rings approximately 1 in. (25mm) below the deck of the block (on diesels, measure ring gap clearance with the ring positioned at the bottom of ring travel in the bore). Measure the ring end gap with a feeler gauge, and compare to the Ring Gap chart in this section. Carefully pull the ring out of the cylinder and file the ends squarely with a fine file to obtain the proper clearance.

PISTON RING SIDE CLEARANCE CHECK & INSTALLATION

▶ **See Figure 200**

Check the pistons to see that the ring grooves and oil return holes have been properly cleaned. Slide a piston ring into its groove, and check the side clearance with a feeler gauge. On gasoline engines, make sure you insert the gauge between the ring and its lower land (lower edge of the groove), because any wear that occurs forms a step at the inner portion of the lower land. On diesels, insert the gauge between the ring and the upper land. If the piston grooves have worn to the extent that relatively high steps exist on the lower land, the piston should be replaced, because these will interfere with the operation of the new rings and ring clearances will be excessive. Piston rings are not furnished in oversize widths to compensate for ring groove wear.

Install the rings on the piston, lowest ring first, using a piston ring expander. There is a high risk of breaking or distorting the rings, or scratching the piston, if the rings are installed by hand or other means.

Position the rings on the piston as illustrated; spacing of the various piston ring gaps is crucial to proper oil retention and even cylinder wear. When installing new rings, refer to the installation diagram furnished with the new parts.

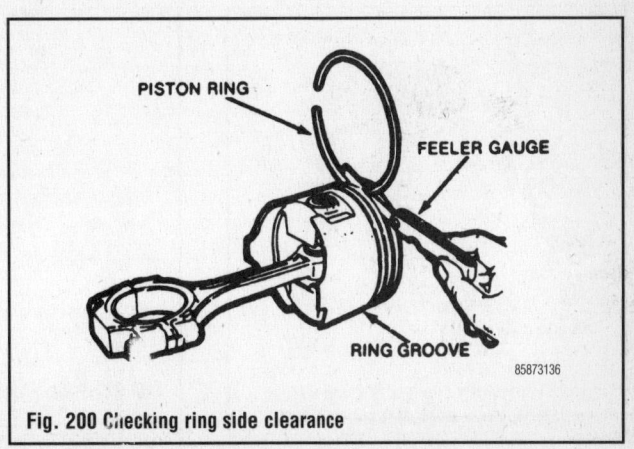

Fig. 200 Checking ring side clearance

Connecting Rod Bearings

Connecting rod bearings for the engines covered in this guide consist of two halves or shells which are interchangeable in the rod and cap. When the shells are placed in position, the ends extend slightly beyond the rod and cap surfaces so that when the rod bolts are torqued the shells will be clamped tightly in place to insure positive seating and to prevent turning. A tang holds the shells in place.

➡**The ends of the bearing shells must never be filed flush with the mating surface of the rod and cap.**

If a rod bearing becomes noisy or is worn so that its clearance on the crank journal is sloppy, a new bearing of the correct undersize must be selected and installed since there is no provision for adjustment.

❋❋ WARNING

Under no circumstances should the rod end or cap be filed to adjust the bearing clearance, nor should shims of any kind be used.

Inspect the rod bearings while the rod assemblies are out of the engine. If the shells are scored or show flaking, they should be replaced. If they are in good shape check for proper clearance on the crank journal (see below). Any scoring or ridges on the crank journal means the crankshaft must be replaced, or reground and fitted with undersized bearings.

CHECKING CLEARANCE & REPLACING BEARINGS

▶ **See Figure 201**

➡**Make sure connecting rods and their caps are kept together, and that the caps are installed in the proper direction. On some engines like the Buick-built 350 V8, the caps can only be installed one way.**

Replacement bearings are available in standard size, and in undersizes for reground crankshafts. Connecting rod-to-crankshaft bearing clearance is checked using Plastigage at either the top or bottom of each crank journal. The Plastigage has a range of 0.001–0.003 in. (0.025–0.080mm).

1. Remove the rod cap with the bearing shell. Completely clean the bearing shell and the crank journal, and blow any oil from the oil hole in the crankshaft; Plastigage is soluble in oil.
2. Place a piece of Plastigage lengthwise along the bottom center of the lower bearing shell, then install the cap with shell and torque the bolt or nuts to specification. DO NOT turn the crankshaft with Plastigage in the bearing.
3. Remove the bearing cap with the shell. The flattened Plastigage will be found sticking to either the bearing shell or crank journal. Do not remove it yet.
4. Use the scale printed on the Plastigage envelope to measure the flattened material at its widest point. The number within the scale which most closely corresponds to the width of the Plastigage indicates bearing clearance in thousandths of an inch.
5. Check the specifications chart in this section for the desired clearance. It is advisable to install a new bearing if clearance exceeds 0.003 in. (0.08mm);

however, if the bearing is in good condition and is not being checked because of bearing noise, bearing replacement is not necessary.

6. If you are installing new bearings, try a standard size, then each undersize in order until one is found that is within the specified limits when checked for clearance with Plastigage. Each undersize shell has its size stamped on it.
7. When the proper size shell is found, clean off the Plastigage, oil the bearing thoroughly, reinstall the cap with its shell and torque the rod bolt units to specification.

➡**With the proper bearing selected and the nuts torqued, it should be possible to move the connecting rod back and forth freely on the crank journal as allowed by the specified connecting rod end clearance. If the rod cannot be moved, either the rod bearing is too far undersize or the rod is misaligned.**

PISTON/CONNECTING ROD ASSEMBLY & INSTALLATION

▶ **See Figures 202, 203, 204 and 205**

Install the connecting rod to the piston, making sure piston installation notches and any marks on the rod are in proper relation to one another. Lubricate the wrist pin with clean engine oil, then install the pin into the rod and piston assembly, either by hand or by using a wrist pin press as required. Install snaprings if equipped, and rotate them in their grooves to make sure they are seated. To install the piston and connecting rod assembly:

1. Make sure connecting rod big-end bearings (including end cap) are of the correct size and properly installed.
2. Fit rubber hoses over the connecting rod bolts to protect the crankshaft journals, as in the Piston Removal procedure. Coat the rod bearings with clean oil.
3. Using the proper ring compressor, insert the piston assembly into the cylinder so that the notch in the top of the piston faces the front of the engine (this assumes that the dimple(s) or other markings on the connecting rods are in correct relation to the piston notch(s).
4. From beneath the engine, coat each crank journal with clean oil. Pull the connecting rod, with the bearing shell in place, into position against the crank journal.
5. Remove the rubber hoses. Install the bearing cap and cap nuts and torque to specification.

➡**When more than one rod and piston assembly is being installed, the connecting rod cap attaching nuts should only be tightened enough to keep each rod in position until all have been installed. This will ease the installation of the remaining piston assemblies.**

6. Check the clearance between the sides of the connecting rods and the crankshaft using a feeler gauge. Spread the rods slightly with a screwdriver to insert the gauge. If clearance is below the minimum tolerance, the rod may be machined to provide adequate clearance. If clearance is excessive, substitute an unworn rod, and recheck. If clearance is still outside specifications, the crankshaft must be welded and reground, or replaced.
7. Replace the oil pump, if removed, then install the oil pan.
8. Install the cylinder head(s) and intake manifold.

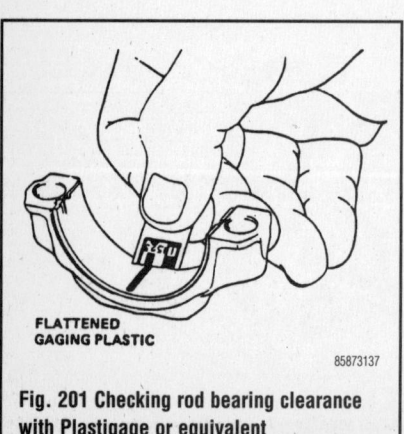

FLATTENED
GAGING PLASTIC

85873137

Fig. 201 Checking rod bearing clearance with Plastigage or equivalent

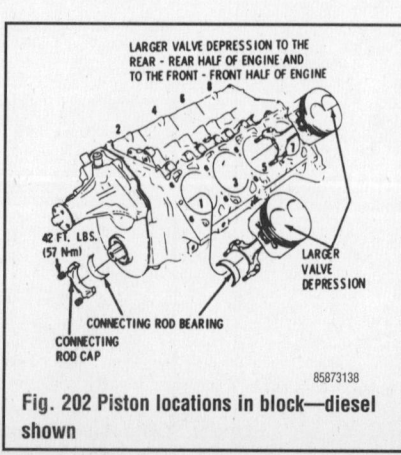

LARGER VALVE DEPRESSION TO THE
REAR - REAR HALF OF ENGINE AND
TO THE FRONT - FRONT HALF OF ENGINE

42 FT. LBS.
(57 Nm)

LARGER
VALVE
DEPRESSION

CONNECTING ROD BEARING
CONNECTING
ROD CAP

85873138

Fig. 202 Piston locations in block—diesel shown

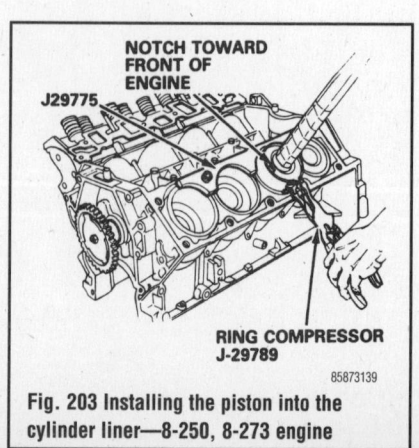

NOTCH TOWARD
FRONT OF
ENGINE

J29775

RING COMPRESSOR
J-29789

85873139

Fig. 203 Installing the piston into the cylinder liner—8-250, 8-273 engine

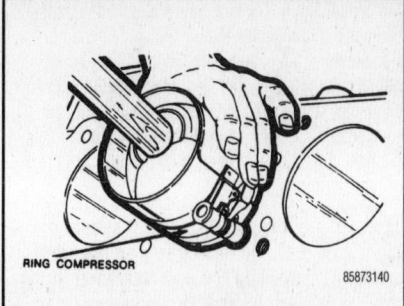

Fig. 204 Using a wooden hammer handle, tap the piston down through the ring compressor and into the cylinder

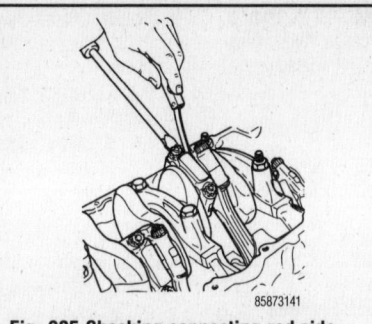

Fig. 205 Checking connecting rod side clearance with a feeler gauge—use a small pry bar to carefully spread the connecting rods

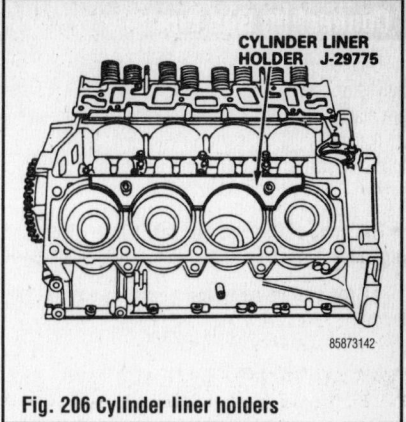

Fig. 206 Cylinder liner holders

Cylinder Liners

REMOVAL & INSTALLATION

◆ **See Figures 206, 207, 208 and 209**

8-250 and 8-273 Engines

➡This procedure requires special tools; J-29775 cylinder liner holder, and J-29776 cylinder liner gauge. Also this is a complex procedure and is not recommended for the novice mechanic.

1. Remove the cylinder heads and install the cylinder liner holders J-29775.
2. Remove the oil pan and then remove the pistons as previously described.

➡Since the cylinder liners are removable it is necessary to keep the liner matched with the appropriate piston. Ink mark these assemblies as they are removed. Do not stamp liners with a punch stamp. Since it is possible (but not advisable) to install the liners without regard to orientation, liners which will be reinstalled should be ink marked with their original position so that this orientation may be maintained during installation.

3. To remove the liners, remove the holder J-29775 and pull the liners from their position in cylinder block. Discard the O-ring from bottom of the cylinder liner.

To install:

4. Inspect the mating surfaces of the cylinder block and liner to be sure they are clean and free of nicks or burrs. Minor blemishes should be polished out with crocus cloth (fine emery cloth).

5. If liners are being installed in their original positions in the original block, it will not be necessary to gauge their height as this process was done on a select-fit basis during manufacturing. In this situation, install a new, lightly oiled O-ring seal on the liner and position the liner in its original position and with its original orientation in the block. Repeat this procedure for each liner removed. Install liner clamp J-29775.

➡Engines that have experienced overheating must be measured upon reassembly.

6. If a new piston/liner assembly is to be installed, proceed as follows:

   a. Position the new liner in its position in the block without the O-ring installed.

   b. Lay the cylinder liner gauge J-29776 on a flat surface such as the cylinder deck face or a piece of glass and zero the dial indicator. Only moderate pressure on the gauge is needed to zero the indicator. Excessive pressure will cause the gauge to bend creating a false zero.

   c. Measure the liner height by inserting the spring loaded guide pins into the liner so that the machined pads rest on the edge of the liner and the dial indicator pointer contacts the block's deck face. Apply moderate pressure to the gauge until the pointer stops moving.

   d. Read and record the dial reading. If this reading is on the (+) side of the dial, the cylinder liner is higher than the block face by the indicated amount. If this reading is on the (−) side of the dial, the cylinder liner is below the block face.

   e. Repeat steps C and D at two more locations as shown.

   f. Take the average of the three readings as the actual value for liner height. For example if reading #1 is + 5 (0.05mm), Reading #2 is + 7 (0.07mm) and Reading #3 is + 3 (0.03mm). then the total (15) divided by 3 is + 5.

   g. Correct liner height is +0.01mm to +008mm above cylinder deck face. If any liner is below +0.01mm (0.00 or a − value) or above +0.08mm, the liner must be replaced with another new assembly. Liners may be rotated in the block to obtain proper liner height. This orientation must be noted and re-established for final assembly.

   h. If liner height is within the range of +0.01mm to +0.08mm, the liner-to-liner dimension must also be established before assembly is attempted.

   i. To gauge liner-to-liner height, install the adjacent liner(s) in their original position and orientation without the O-ring. Using gauge J-29776 gauge between the liners while holding the second liner firmly in place with your free hand. This reading must be within plus or minus 0.05mm (plus or minus on gauge). Ink mark the liner orientation once it is established.

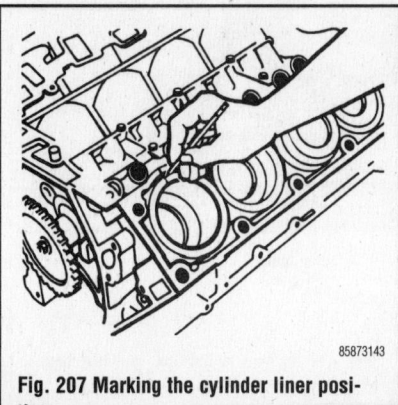

Fig. 207 Marking the cylinder liner position

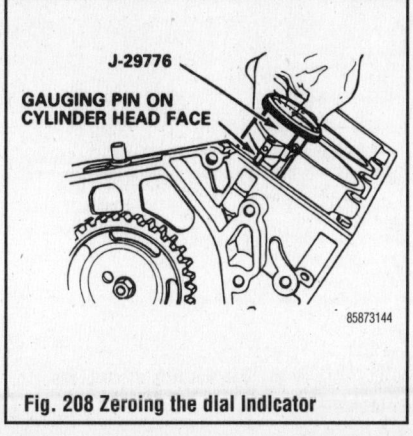

Fig. 208 Zeroing the dial indicator

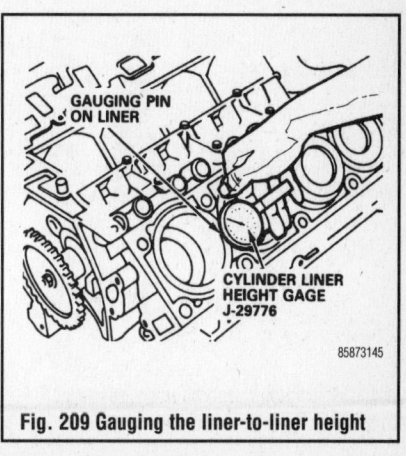

Fig. 209 Gauging the liner-to-liner height

7. Once the gauging operation is completed on all the new liner assemblies, liners should be installed in their respective positions using a new, lightly oiled, O-ring on each liner. Liners must be installed in the position and orientation in the block for which they have been gauged.

8. Install liner holders J-29775.

Rear Main Oil Seal

REMOVAL & INSTALLATION

Except 6-252, 1986–89 8-250, 8-273, 8-307 and 8-350 Engines

♦ See Figures 210 thru 220

1. Remove the oil pan.
2. Remove the rear main bearing cap and loosen the bolts holding the other four bearings about three turns each. Remove the old rear main bearing seals.

To install:

3. Clean the groove in the cap and in the block. Lubricate seals with engine oil.
4. Make an installation tool.
5. Start the upper half into the groove in the block with the lip facing forward and rotate it into position, using the tool as a guide. Press firmly on both ends to be sure it is protruding uniformly on each side.
6. Install the lower half of the seal into the bearing cap with the lip facing forward and one end of the seal over the ridge and flush with the split line. Hold one finger over this end to prevent it from slipping, and push the seal into seated position by applying pressure to the other end. Be sure the seal is firmly seated and protrudes evenly on each side. Do not apply pressure to the lip. This may damage the effectiveness of the seal.

➡ On vehicles equipped with neoprene type seals, make sure that the seal is flush at the split line to avoid leaks.

7. Apply rubber cement to the mating surfaces of the block and cap being careful not to get any cement on the bearing, the crankshaft or the seal. The cement coating should be about 0.010 in. (0.25mm) thick.
8. Tighten the bearing bolts to 89 ft. lbs. (121 Nm) for the 250 and 90–100 ft. lbs. (122–136 Nm) for all others. Be sure to tighten the bolts of the other four bearings also. Rotate the crankshaft one full turn to check for binding.
9. Reinstall the oil pan.

6-252 Engine

On the 6-252 engine, the factory recommends removing the crankshaft to replace the upper seal, but the seal can be replaced using the method below.

1. Remove the oil pan and the rear main bearing cap.
2. Loosen the rest of the crankshaft main bearings slightly and allow the crankshaft to drop about 1/16 in. (1.5mm), no more.
3. Remove the old upper half of the oil seal.
4. Wrap some soft copper wire around the end of the new seal and leave about 12 in. (305mm) on the end. Lubricate the new seal generously with clean oil.
5. Slip the free end of the copper wire into the oil

seal groove and around the crankshaft. Pull the wire until the seal protrudes an equal amount on each side. Rotate the crankshaft as the seal is pulled into place.

6. Remove the wire. Push any excess seal that may be protruding back into the groove.
7. Before tightening the crankshaft bearing caps, visually check the bearings to make sure they are in place. Torque the bearing cap bolts to specification. Make sure there is no oil on the mating surfaces.
8. To replace the seal in the main bearing cap, remove the old seal and place a new seal in the groove with both ends projecting above the mating surface of the cap.
9. Force the seal into the cap groove by rubbing down on it with a hammer handle or other smooth round tool, until the seal projects above the groove not more than 1/16 in. (1.5mm). Using a razor blade, cut the ends off flush with the surface of the cap.
10. Place new neoprene seals in the grooves in the sides of the bearing caps after soaking the seals in kerosene for two minutes.

➡ The neoprene seals will swell up once exposed to the oil and heat. It is normal for the seals to leak for a short time, until they become properly seated. The seals must NOT be cut to fit.

11. Reverse the above procedure for installation. Use a small bead of sealer on the outer edge of the bearing cap mating surface.
12. Install the oil pan. Run the engine at low rpm for the first few minutes of operation.

1986–89 8-250 and 8-273 Engines

➡ To perform this procedure, use a Seal Removal tool No. J–26868 or equivalent, and a Seal Installer tool No. J–34604 or equivalent.

1. Remove the transaxle.
2. Unbolt and remove the flexplate from the rear end of the crankshaft.
3. Using a Seal Removal tool No. J–26868 or equivalent, remove the old seal. Thoroughly clean the seal bore of any leftover seal material with a clean rag.
4. Lubricate the lip of a new seal with wheel bearing grease. Position it over the crankshaft and into the seal bore with the spring facing inside the engine.
5. Using a Seal Installer tool No. J–34604 or equivalent, press the seal into place. The seal must be square (this is the purpose of the installer) and flush with the block to 1mm indented.
6. To complete the installation, reverse the removal procedures. Torque the flexplate-to-crankshaft bolts to 37 ft. lbs. (50 Nm). Refill the crankshaft. Operate the engine and check for leaks.

8-307, 8-350 Gasoline and Diesel Engines

The crankshaft need not be removed to replace the rear main bearing upper oil seal. The lower seal is installed in the bearing cap.

1. Drain the crankcase oil and remove the oil pan and rear main bearing cap.

✳✳ CAUTION

The EPA warns that prolonged contact with used engine oil may cause a number of skin disorders, including cancer! You should

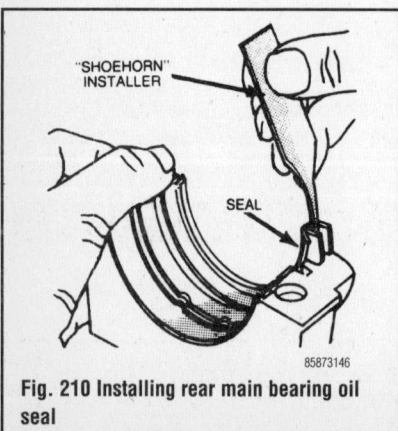

Fig. 210 Installing rear main bearing oil seal

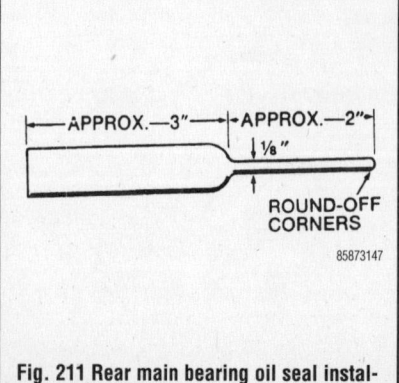

Fig. 211 Rear main bearing oil seal installation tool

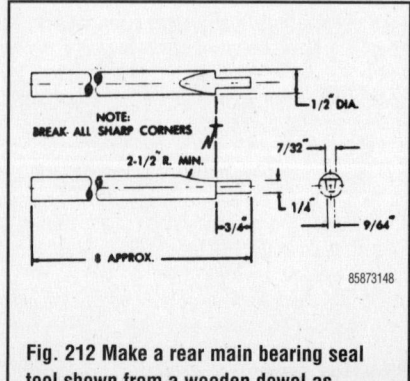

Fig. 212 Make a rear main bearing seal tool shown from a wooden dowel as shown

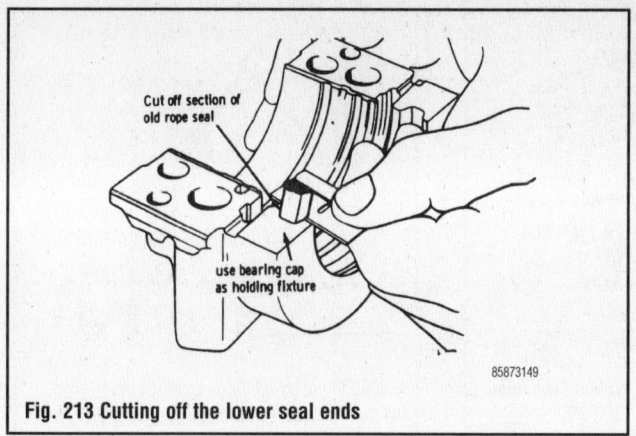

Fig. 213 Cutting off the lower seal ends

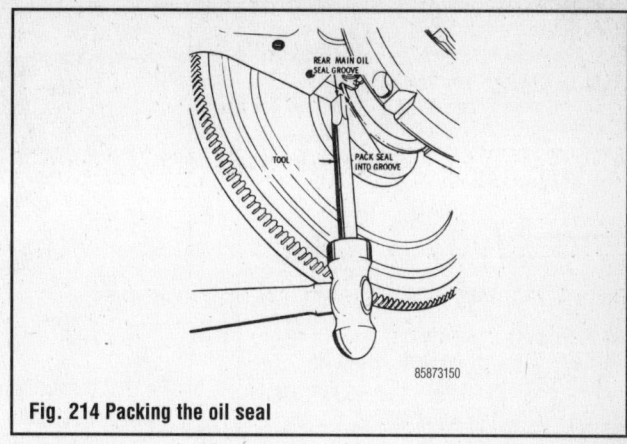

Fig. 214 Packing the oil seal

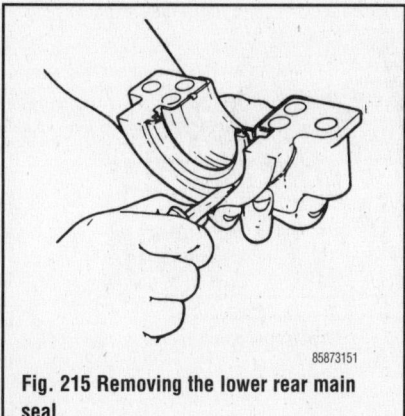

Fig. 215 Removing the lower rear main seal

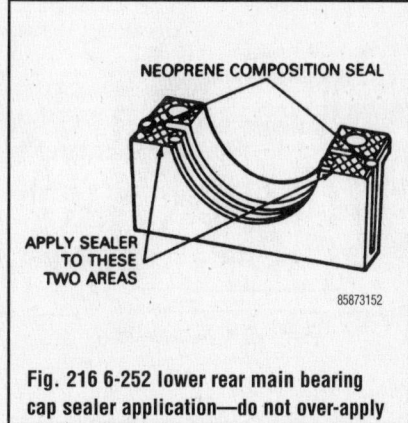

Fig. 216 6-252 lower rear main bearing cap sealer application—do not over-apply

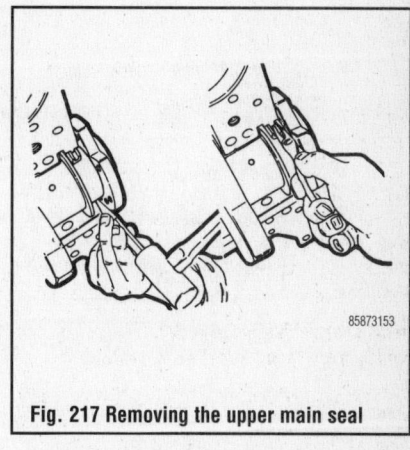

Fig. 217 Removing the upper main seal

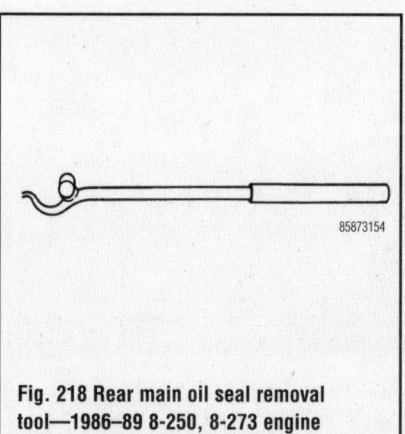

Fig. 218 Rear main oil seal removal tool—1986-89 8-250, 8-273 engine

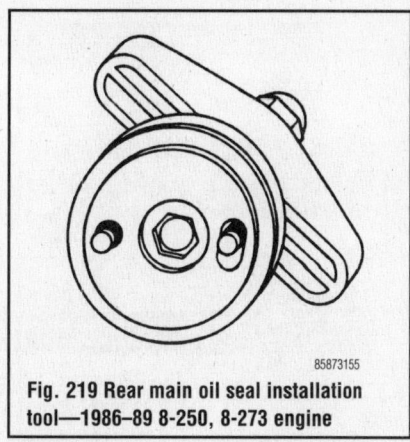

Fig. 219 Rear main oil seal installation tool—1986-89 8-250, 8-273 engine

Fig. 220 Rolling the new front seal into position

make every effort to minimize your exposure to used engine oil. Protective gloves should be worn when changing the oil. Wash your hands and any other exposed skin areas as soon as possible after exposure to used engine oil. Soap and water, or waterless hand cleaner should be used.

2. Using a special main seal tool or a tool that can be made from a dowel (see illustration), drive the upper seal into its groove on each side until it is tightly packed. This is usually ¼-¾ in. (6-19mm).

3. Measure the amount the seal was driven up on one side; add ¹⁄₁₆ in. (1.5mm), then cut this length from the old seal that was removed from the main bearing cap. Use a single-edge razor blade. Measure the amount the seal was driven up on the other side; add ¹⁄₁₆ in. (1.5mm) and cut another length from the old seal. Use the main bearing cap as a holding fixture when cutting the seal as illustrated. Carefully trim protruding seal.

4. Work these two pieces of seal up into the cylinder block on each side with two nailsets or small screwdrivers. Using the packing tool again,

pack these pieces into the block, then trim them flush with a razor blade or hobby knife as shown. Do not scratch the bearing surface with the razor.

5. Install a new seal in the rear main bearing cap. Run a ¹⁄₁₆ in. (1.5mm) bead of sealer onto the outer mating surface of the bearing cap. Assemble the cap to the block and torque to specifications.

Crankshaft and Main Bearings

◆ See Figures 221 thru 229

CRANKSHAFT REMOVAL

1. Drain the engine oil and remove the engine from the car. Mount the engine on a workstand in a suitable working area. Invert the engine, so the oil pan is facing up.

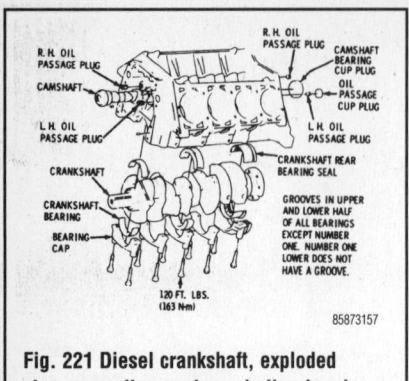

Fig. 221 Diesel crankshaft, exploded view—gasoline engines similar, bearing configuration may differ among engines

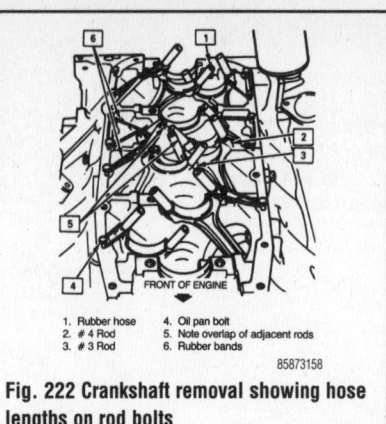

1. Rubber hose
2. # 4 Rod
3. # 3 Rod
4. Oil pan bolt
5. Note overlap of adjacent rods
6. Rubber bands

Fig. 222 Crankshaft removal showing hose lengths on rod bolts

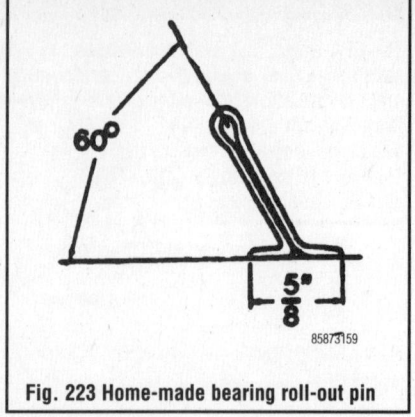

Fig. 223 Home-made bearing roll-out pin

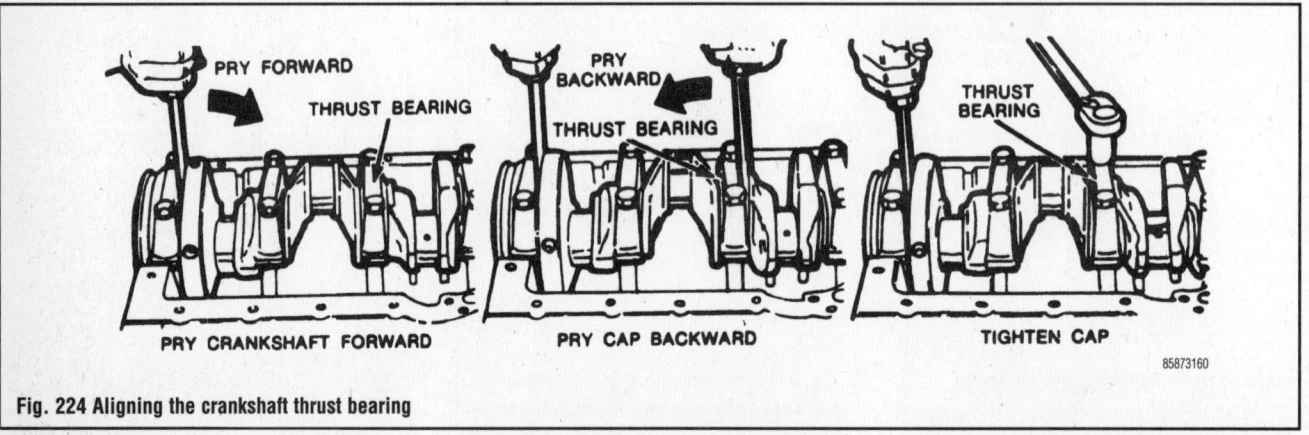

Fig. 224 Aligning the crankshaft thrust bearing

Fig. 225 View of the crankshaft and main bearings

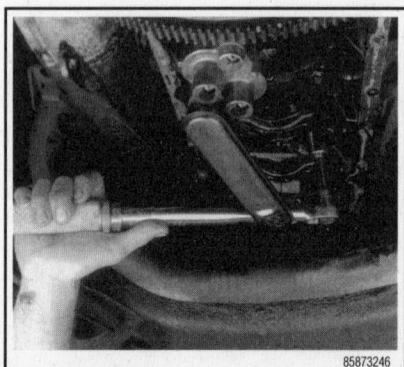

Fig. 226 Removing the main bearing cap bolts

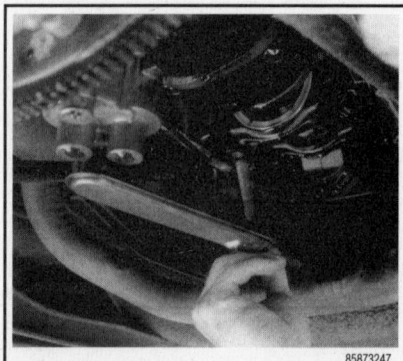

Fig. 227 View of the main bearing cap bolts

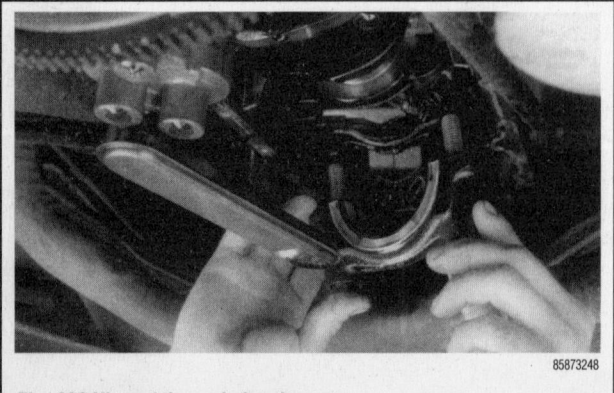

Fig. 228 View of the main bearing cap

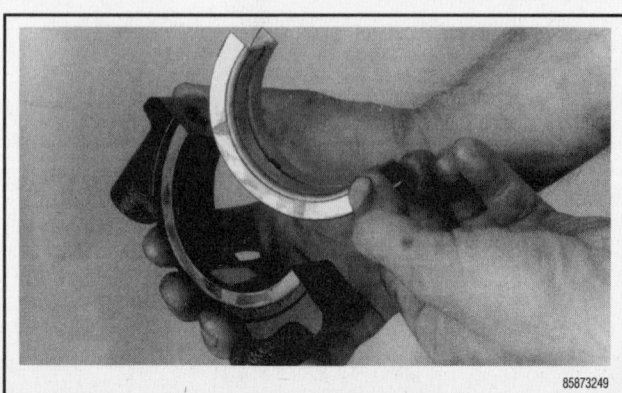

Fig. 229 Common main bearing cap and thrust bearing

2. Remove the engine front (timing) cover.
3. Remove the timing chain and gears.
4. Remove the oil pan.
5. Remove the oil pump.
6. Stamp the cylinder number on the machined surfaces of the bolt bosses of the connecting rods and caps for identification when reinstalling. If the pistons are to be removed eventually from the connecting rod, mark the cylinder number on the pistons with silver paint or felt-tip pen for proper cylinder identification and cap-to-rod location.
7. Remove the connecting rod caps. Install lengths of rubber hose on each of the connecting rod bolts, to protect the crank journals when the crank is removed.
8. Mark the main bearing caps with a number punch or punch so that they can be reinstalled in their original positions.
9. Remove all main bearing caps.
10. Note the position of the keyway in the crankshaft so it can be installed in the same position.
11. Install rubber bands between a bolt on each connecting rod and oil pan bolts that have been reinstalled in the block (see illustration). This will keep the rods from banging on the block when the crank is removed.
12. Carefully lift the crankshaft out of the block. The rods will pivot to the center of the engine when the crank is removed.

MAIN BEARING INSPECTION & REPLACEMENT

Like connecting rod big-end bearings, the crankshaft main bearings are shell-type inserts that do not utilize shims and cannot be adjusted. The bearings are available in various standard and undersizes; if main bearing clearance is found to be too sloppy, a new bearing (both upper and lower halves) is required.

➡ Factory-undersized crankshafts are marked, sometimes with a 9 and/or a large spot of light green paint; the bearing caps also will have the paint on each side of the undersized journal.

Generally, the lower half of the bearing shell (except No. 1 bearing) shows greater wear and fatigue. If the lower half only shows the effects of normal wear (no heavy scoring or discoloration), it can usually be assumed that the upper half is also in good shape conversely, if the lower half is heavily worn or damaged, both halves should be replaced. Never replace one bearing half without replacing the other.

CHECKING CLEARANCE

♦ See Figures 230 and 231

Main bearing clearance can be checked both with the crankshaft in the car and with the engine out of the car. If the engine block is still in the car, the crankshaft should be supported both front and rear to remove clearance from the upper bearing. Total clearance can then be measured between the lower bearing and journal. If the block has been removed from the car, and is inverted, the crank will rest on the upper bearings and the total clearance can be measured between the lower bearing and journal. Clearance is checked in the same manner as the connecting rod bearings, with Plastigage.

➡ Crankshaft bearing caps and bearing shells should NEVER be filed flush with the cap-to-block mating surface to adjust for wear in the old bearings. Always install new bearings.

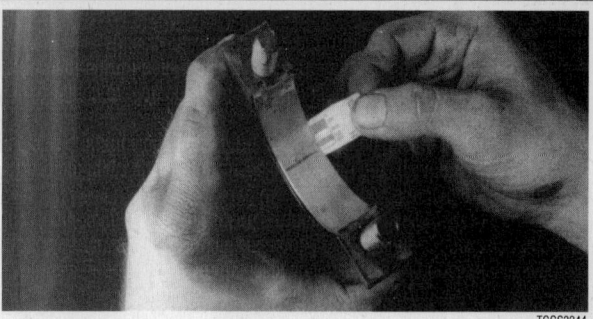

Fig. 230 As with the connecting rod bearings, remove the cap and compare the gauging material to the provided scale in order to determine clearance

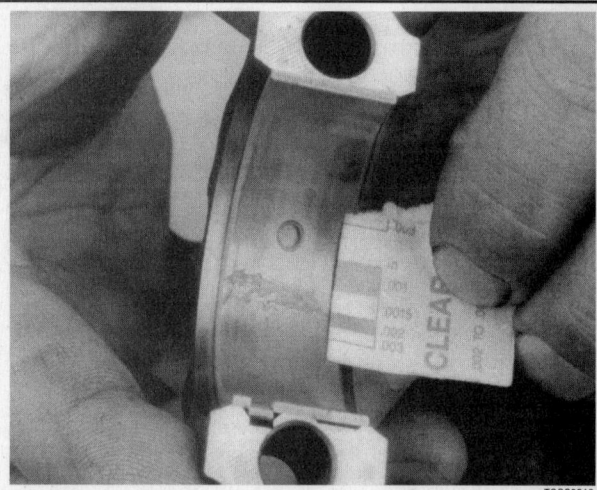

Fig. 231 After the bearing cap has been removed, use the gauge supplied with the gauge material to check bearing clearance

1. If the crankshaft has been removed, install it (block removed from car). If the block is still in the car, remove the oil pan and oil pump. Starting with the rear bearing cap, remove the cap and wipe all oil from the crank journal and bearing cap.
2. Place a strip of Plastigage the full width of the bearing, (parallel to the crankshaft), on the journal.

✳✳ WARNING

Do not rotate the crankshaft while the gaging material is between the bearing and the journal.

3. Install the bearing cap and evenly torque the cap bolts to specification.
4. Remove the bearing cap. The flattened Plastigage will be sticking to either the bearing shell or the crank journal.
5. Use the graduated scale on the Plastigage envelope to measure the material at its widest point.

➡ If the flattened Plastigage tapers towards the middle or ends, there is a difference in clearance indicating the bearing or journal has a taper, low spot or other irregularity. If this is indicated, measure the crank journal with a micrometer.

6. If bearing clearance is within specifications, the bearing insert is in good shape. Replace the insert if the clearance is not within specifications. Always replace both upper and lower inserts as a unit.
7. Standard 0.001 or 0.002 in. undersize bearings should produce the proper clearance. If these sizes still produce too sloppy a fit, the crankshaft must

be reground for use with the next undersize bearing. Recheck all clearances after installing new bearings.

8. Replace the rest of the bearings in the same manner. After all bearings have been checked, rotate the crankshaft to make sure there is no excessive drag. When checking the No. 1 main bearing, loosen the accessory drive belts (engine in car) to prevent a tapered reading with the Plastigage.

MAIN BEARING REPLACEMENT

Engine Out of Car

1. Remove and inspect the crankshaft.
2. Remove the main bearings from the bearing saddles in the cylinder block and main bearing caps.
3. Coat the bearing surfaces of the new, correct size main bearings with clean engine oil and install them in the bearing saddles in the block and in the main bearing caps.
4. Install the crankshaft. See Crankshaft Installation.

Engine in Car

1. With the oil pan, oil pump and spark plugs removed, remove the cap from the main bearing needing replacement and remove the bearing from the cap.
2. Make a bearing roll-out pin, using a bent cotter pin as shown in the illustration. Install the end of the pin in the oil hole in the crankshaft journal.
3. Rotate the crankshaft clockwise as viewed from the front of the engine. This will roll the upper bearing out of the block.
4. Lube the new upper bearing with clean engine oil and insert the plain (unnotched) end between the crankshaft and the indented or notched side of the block. Roll the bearing into place, making sure that the oil holes are aligned. Remove the roll pin from the oil hole.
5. Lube the new lower bearing and install the main bearing cap. Install the main bearing cap, making sure it is positioned in proper direction with the matchmarks in alignment.
6. Torque the main bearing cap bolts to specification.

➡ **See Crankshaft Installation for thrust bearing alignment.**

CRANKSHAFT END PLAY & INSTALLATION

When main bearing clearance has been checked, bearings examined and/or replaced, the crankshaft can be installed. Thoroughly clean the upper and lower bearing surfaces, and lube them with clean engine oil. Install the crankshaft and main bearing caps.

Dip all main bearing cap bolts in clean oil, and torque all main bearing caps, excluding the thrust bearing cap, to specifications (see the Crankshaft and Connecting Rod chart in this section to determine which bearing is the thrust bearing). Tighten the thrust bearing bolts finger tight. To align the thrust bearing, pry the crankshaft the extent of its axial travel several times, holding the last movement toward the front of the engine. Add thrust washers if required for proper alignment. Torque the thrust bearing cap to specifications.

To check crankshaft end-play, pry the crankshaft to the extreme rear of its axial travel, then the extreme front of its travel. Using a feeler gauge, measure the end-play at the front of the rear main bearing. End play may also be measured at the thrust bearing. Install a new rear main bearing oil seal in the cylinder block and main bearing cap. Continue to reassemble the engine.

Flywheel and Ring Gear

REMOVAL & INSTALLATION

The ring gear is an integral part of the flywheel and is not replaceable.
1. Remove the transmission.
2. Remove the six bolts attaching the flywheel to the crankshaft flange. Remove the flywheel.
To install:
3. Inspect the flywheel for cracks, and inspect the ring gear for burrs or worn teeth. Replace the flywheel if any damage is apparent. Remove burrs with a mill file.
4. Install the flywheel. The flywheel will only attach to the crankshaft in one position, as the bolt holes are unevenly spaced. Install the bolts and torque to specification.

EXHAUST SYSTEM

Inspection

▶ See Figures 232 thru 238

➡ **Safety glasses should be worn at all times when working on or near the exhaust system. Older exhaust systems will almost always be covered with loose rust particles which are more than a nuisance and could injure your eye.**

❊❊ CAUTION

DO NOT perform exhaust repairs or inspection with the engine or exhaust hot. Allow the system to cool completely. Exhaust systems are noted for sharp edges, flaking metal and rusted bolts. Gloves and eye protection are required. A healthy supply of penetrating oil and rags is highly recommended.

Your vehicle must be raised and supported safely at four points to inspect the exhaust system properly. Start the inspection at the exhaust manifold where the header pipe is attached and work your way to the back of the vehicle. On dual exhaust systems, remember to inspect both sides of the vehicle. Check the complete exhaust system for open seams, holes, loose connections, or other deterioration which could permit exhaust fumes to seep into the passenger compartment. Inspect all mounting brackets and hangers for deterioration, some may have rubber O-rings that can become overstretched and non-supportive (and should be replaced if worn). Many technicians use a pointed tool to poke up into the exhaust system at rust spots to see whether or not they crumble. Most models have heat shield(s) covering certain parts of the exhaust system, it is often necessary to remove these shields to visually inspect those components.

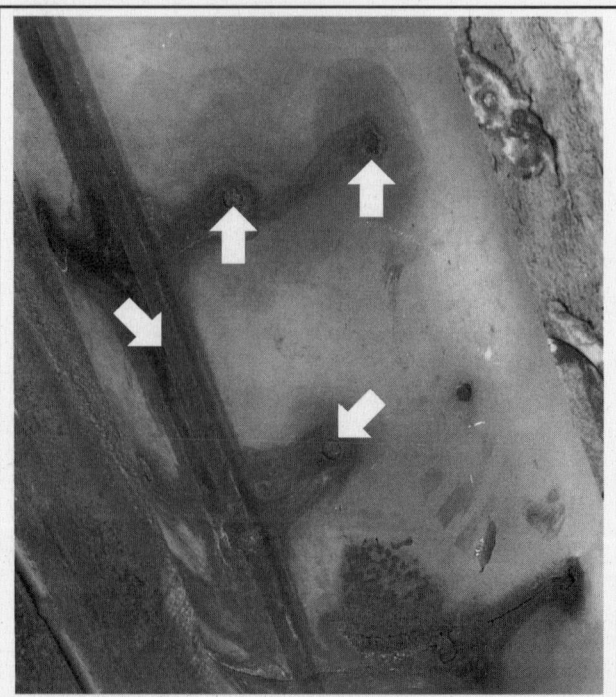

TCCA3P74

Fig. 232 Check the muffler for rotted spot welds and seams

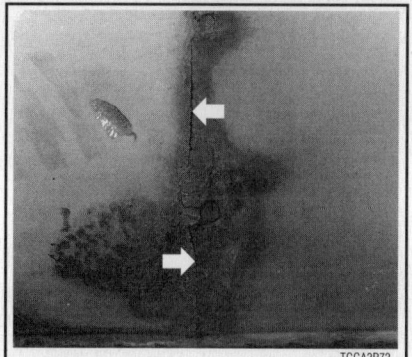

Fig. 233 Cracks in the muffler are a guaranteed leak

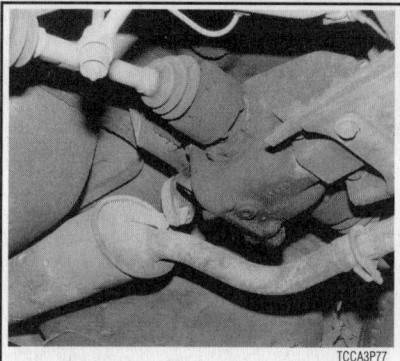

Fig. 234 Make sure the exhaust does contact the body or suspension

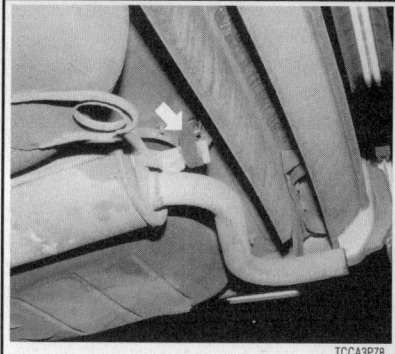

Fig. 235 Check for overstretched or torn exhaust hangers

Fig. 236 Example of a badly deteriorated exhaust pipe

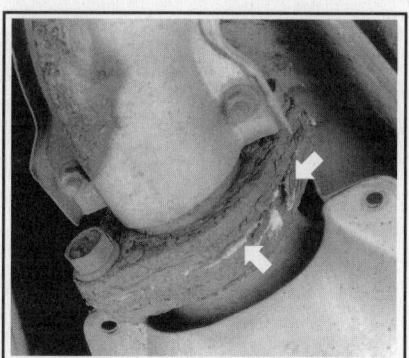

Fig. 237 Inspect flanges for gaskets that have deteriorated and need replacement

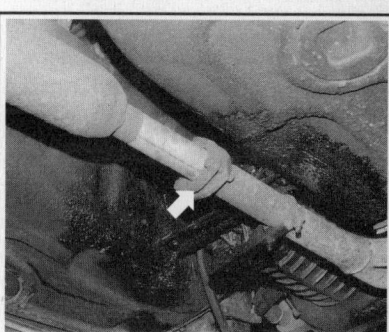

Fig. 238 Some systems, like this one, use large O-rings (donuts) in between the flanges

REPLACEMENT

♦ See Figures 239, 240 and 241

There are basically two types of exhaust systems. One is the flange type where the component ends are attached with bolts and a gasket in-between. The other exhaust system is the slip joint type. These components slip into one another using clamps to retain them together.

✳ CAUTION

Allow the exhaust system to cool sufficiently before spraying a solvent exhaust fasteners. Some solvents are highly flammable and could ignite when sprayed on hot exhaust components.

Before removing any component of the exhaust system, ALWAYS squirt a liquid rust dissolving agent onto the fasteners for ease of removal. A lot of knuckle skin will be saved by following this rule. It may even be wise to spray the fasteners and allow them to sit overnight.

✳ CAUTION

Do NOT perform exhaust repairs or inspection with the engine or exhaust hot. Allow the system to cool. Exhaust systems are noted for sharp edges, flaking metal and rusted bolts. Gloves and eye protection are required.

1. Raise and support the vehicle safely, as necessary for access. Remember that some longer exhaust pipes may be difficult to wrestle out from under the vehicle if it is not supported high enough.
2. If you haven't already, apply a generous amount of penetrating oil or solvent to any rusted fasteners.
3. On flange joints, carefully loosen and remove the retainers at the flange. If bolts or nuts are difficult to break loose, apply more penetrating liquid and

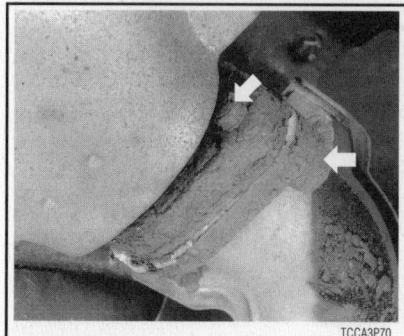

Fig. 239 Nuts and bolts will be extremely difficult to remove when deteriorated with rust

Fig. 240 Example of a flange type exhaust system joint

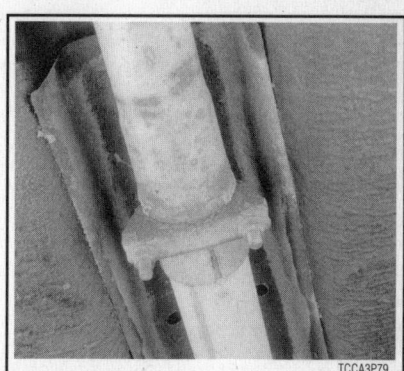

Fig. 241 Example of a common slip joint type system

give it some additional time to set. If the fasteners still will not come loose an impact driver may be necessary to jar it loose (and keep the fastener from breaking).

➡**When unbolting the headpipe from the manifold, make sure that the bolts are free before trying to remove them. If you snap a stud in the exhaust manifold, the stud will have to be removed with a bolt extractor, which often means removal of the manifold itself.**

4. On slip joint components, remove the mounting U-bolts from around the exhaust pipe you are extracting from the vehicle. Don't be surprised if the U-bolts break while removing the nuts.

5. Loosen the exhaust pipe from any mounting brackets retaining it to the floor pan and separate the components. Slight twisting and turning may be required to remove the component completely from the vehicle. You may need to tap on the component with a rubber mallet to loosen it. If all else fails, use a hacksaw to separate the parts. An oxy-acetylene cutting torch may be faster but the sparks are DANGEROUS near the fuel tank, and at the very least, accidents could happen, resulting in damage to the under-vehicle parts, not to mention yourself.

6. When installing exhaust components, you should loosely position all components before tightening any of the joints. Once you are certain that the system is run correctly, begin tightening the fasteners at the front of the vehicle and work your way back.

TORQUE SPECIFICATIONS

Component	US	Metric
Air cleaner to carburetor stud	62 inch lbs.	7 Nm
AIR manifold to cylinder head	20 ft. lbs.	27 Nm
Carburetor to intake manifold	12 ft. lbs.	16 Nm
Coolant outlet to intake manifold	20 ft. lbs.	27 Nm
Coolant pump to front cover	11 ft. lbs.	14 Nm
Crankshaft balancer to crankshaft	255 ft. lbs.	345 Nm
Distributor clamp to cylinder block bolt	26 ft. lbs.	35 Nm
EGR valve to intake manifold	20 ft. lbs.	27 Nm
Engine mount to cylinder block	75 ft. lbs.	100 Nm
Engine mount to bracket	55 ft. lbs.	73 Nm
Fan driven pulley to water pump hub bolts	20 ft. lbs.	27 Nm
Fan driven pulley to balancer bolts	28 ft. lbs.	40 Nm
Flywheel to converter	46 ft. lbs.	63 Nm
Flywheel to crankshaft	60 ft. lbs.	81 Nm
Front cover to block	35 ft. lbs.	47 Nm
Fuel pump to block	25 ft. lbs.	34 Nm
Fuel pump eccentric to camshaft	65 ft. lbs.	88 Nm
Oil pan bolts	10 ft. lbs.	14 Nm
Oil pan nuts	17 ft. lbs.	24 Nm
Oil pan drain plug	30 ft. lbs.	41 Nm
Starter to block	20 ft. lbs.	27 Nm
Transmission to block	35 ft. lbs.	47 Nm
Valve cover to cylinder head nuts/bolts	90 inch lbs.	10 Nm
Valve lifter guide retainer bolt	82 inch lbs.	9 Nm

85873C08

4

EMISSION CONTROLS

GASOLINE ENGINE EMISSION CONTROLS

In its normal operation, the internal combustion engine releases several compounds into the atmosphere. Since most of these compounds are harmful to our health if inhaled or ingested in sufficient quantity for long periods of time, the Federal Government has placed a limit on the quantities of the three main groups of compounds: unburned hydrocarbons (HC); carbon monoxide (CO); and oxides of nitrogen (NOx).

The emissions systems covered in this section are designed to regulate the output of these noxious fumes by your car's engine and fuel system. Three areas of the automobile are covered, each with its own anti-pollution system or systems: the engine crankcase, which emits unburned hydrocarbons in the form of oil and fuel vapors; the fuel storage system (fuel tank and carburetor), which also emits unburned hydrocarbons in the form of evaporated gasoline; and the engine exhaust. Exhaust emissions comprise the greatest quantity of auto emissions, in the forms of unburned hydrocarbons, carbon monoxide, and oxides of nitrogen. Because of this, there are more pollution devices on your car dealing with exhaust emissions than there are dealing with the other two emission types.

Positive Crankcase Ventilation

OPERATION

All engines covered in this guide are equipped with a positive crankcase ventilation (PCV) system to control crankcase blow-by vapors. The system functions as follows:

When the engine is running, a small portion of the gases which are formed in the combustion chamber leak by the piston rings and enter the crankcase. Since these gases are under pressure, they tend to escape from the crankcase and enter the atmosphere. If these gases are allowed to remain in the crankcase for any period of time, they contaminate the engine oil and cause sludge to build up in the crankcase. If the gases are allowed to escape into the atmosphere, they pollute the air with unburned hydrocarbons. The job of the crankcase emission control equipment is to recycle these gases back into the engine combustion chamber where they are reburned.

The crankcase (blow-by) gases are recycled in the following way: as the engine is running, clean, filtered air is drawn through the air filter and into the crankcase. As the air passes through the crankcase, it picks up the combustion gases and carries them out of the crankcase, through the oil separator, through the PCV valve, and into the induction system. As they enter the intake manifold, they are drawn into the combustion chamber where they are reburned.

The most critical component in the system is the PCV valve. Located in the valve cover or intake manifold, this valve controls the amount of gases which are recycled into the combustion chamber. At low engine speeds, the valve is partially closed, limiting the flow of the gases into the intake manifold. As engine speed increases, the valve opens to admit greater quantities of the gases into the intake manifold. If the valve should become blocked or plugged, the gases will be prevented from escaping from the crankcase by the normal route. Since these gases are under pressure, they will find their own way out of the crankcase. This alternate route is usually a weak oil seal or gasket in the engine. As the gas escapes by the gasket, it also creates an oil leak. Besides causing oil leaks, a clogged PCV valve also allows these gases to remain in the crankcase for an extended period of time, promoting the formation of sludge in the engine. See Section 1 for PCV valve replacement intervals.

SERVICE

▶ **See Figures 1 thru 6**

Slow, unstable idling, frequent stalling, oil leaks, and oil in the air cleaner are all signs that the PCV valve may be clogged or faulty. Follow the PCV valve testing procedure in Section 1 and replace the valve if necessary. Check the valve at every tune-up. Remove the valve by gently pulling it out of the valve cover or manifold, then open the clamp on the hose end with a pair of pliers. Hold the clamp open while sliding it an inch or two down the hose (away from the valve), and then remove the valve. If the end of the hose is hard or cracked where it holds the valve, it may be feasible to cut the end off if there is plenty of extra hose. Otherwise, replace the hose. Replace the grommet in the valve cover if it is cracked or hard, and replace the clamp if it is broken or weak. In replac-

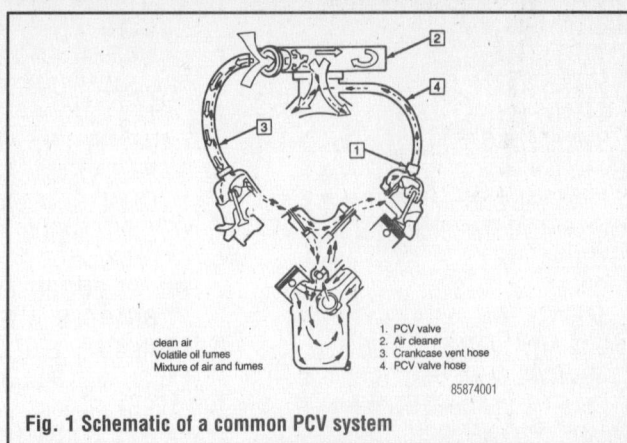

clean air
Volatile oil fumes
Mixture of air and fumes

1. PCV valve
2. Air cleaner
3. Crankcase vent hose
4. PCV valve hose

85874001

Fig. 1 Schematic of a common PCV system

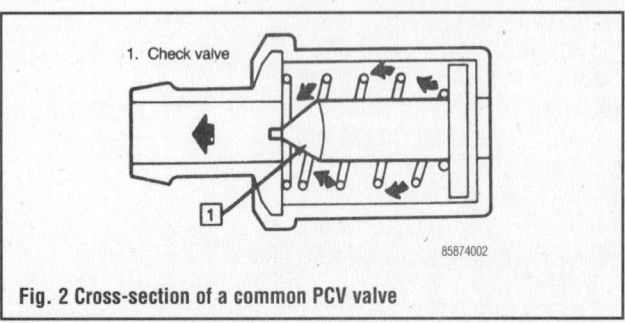

1. Check valve

85874002

Fig. 2 Cross-section of a common PCV valve

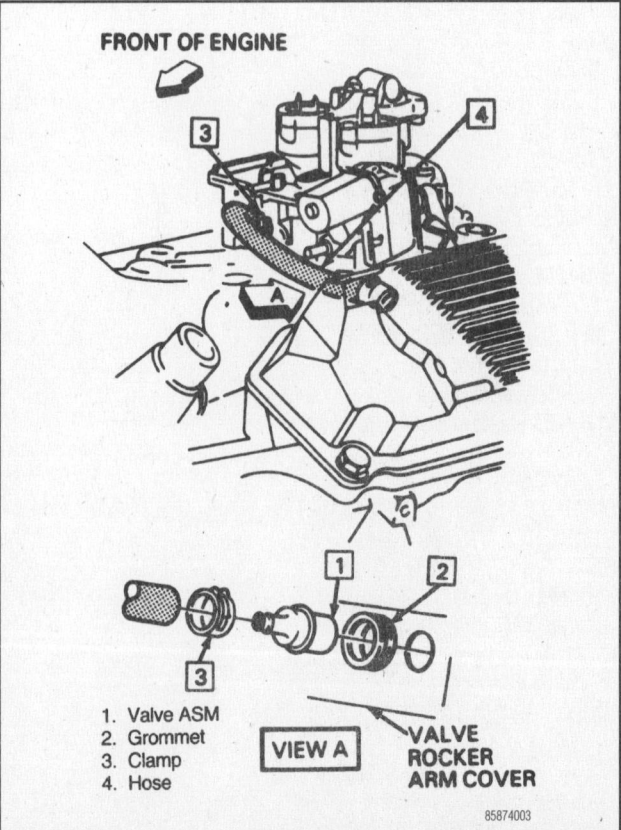

FRONT OF ENGINE

1. Valve ASM
2. Grommet
3. Clamp
4. Hose

VIEW A

VALVE ROCKER ARM COVER

85874003

Fig. 3 PCV valve and hose between the rocker cover and throttle body—1986–89 Eldorado and Seville

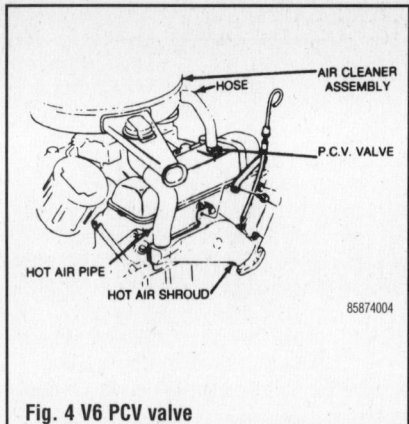

Fig. 4 V6 PCV valve

Fig. 5 View of a related emission hose—note the PCV valve is installed in the valve cover

Fig. 6 Removing the PCV valve from the valve cover

ing the valve, make sure it is fully inserted in the hose, that the clamp is moved over the ridge on the valve so that the valve will not slip out of the hose, and that the valve is fully inserted into the grommet in the valve cover.

PCV Filter

REMOVAL & INSTALLATION

1. Slide the rubber coupling that joins the tube coming from the valve cover to the filter off the filter nipple. Then, remove the top of the air clearer. Slide the spring clamp off the filter, and remove the filter. See illustration in Section 1.

2. Inspect the rubber grommet in the valve cover and the rubber coupling for brittleness and cracking. Replace parts as necessary.

3. Insert the new PCV filter through the hole in the air cleaner with the open portion of the filter upward (See illustration in Section 1). Make sure that the square portion of filter behind the nipple fits into the (square) hole in the air cleaner.

4. Install a new spring clamp onto the nipple. Make sure the clamp goes under the ridge on the filter nipple all the way around. Then, reconnect the rubber coupling and install the air cleaner cover.

Evaporative Emission Control System

OPERATION

This system reduces the amount of escaping gasoline vapors. Float bowl emissions are controlled by internal carburetor modifications. Redesigned bowl vents, reduced bowl capacity, heat shields, and improved intake manifold-to-carburetor insulation reduced vapor loss into the atmosphere. The venting of fuel tank vapors into the air has been stopped by means of the carbon canister storage method. This method transfers fuel vapors to an activated carbon storage device which absorbs and stores the vapor that is emitted from the engine's induction system while the engine is not running. When the engine is running, the stored vapor is purged from the carbon storage device by the intake air flow and then consumed in the normal combustion process. As the manifold vacuum reaches a certain point, it opens a purge control valve atop the charcoal storage canister. This allows air to be drawn into the canister, thus forcing the existing fuel vapors back into the engine to be burned normally.

On 1981 and later V6s, the purge function is electronically controlled by a purge solenoid in the line which is itself controlled by the Electronic Control Module (ECM). While the system is in the Open Loop mode, the solenoid valve is energized, blocking all vacuum to the purge valve. When the system is in the Closed Loop mode, the solenoid is de-energized, thus allowing existing vacuum to operate the purge valve. This releases the trapped fuel vapor and it is forced into the induction system.

Most carbon canisters used are of the Open design, meaning that air is drawn in through the bottom (filter) of the canister. Some 1981 and later V6 canisters are of the Closed design, which means that the incoming air is drawn directly from the air cleaner.

SERVICE

▶ See Figures 7, 8 and 9

The only service required for the evaporative emissions system is the periodic replacement of the charcoal canister filter (if so equipped). If the fuel tank cap on your car ever requires replacement, make sure that it is of the same type as the original.

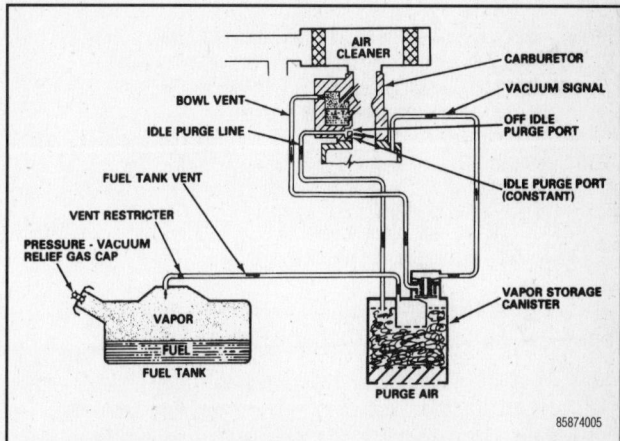

Fig. 7 Open canister evaporative emission control system (EECS)—this system is more common than the closed system

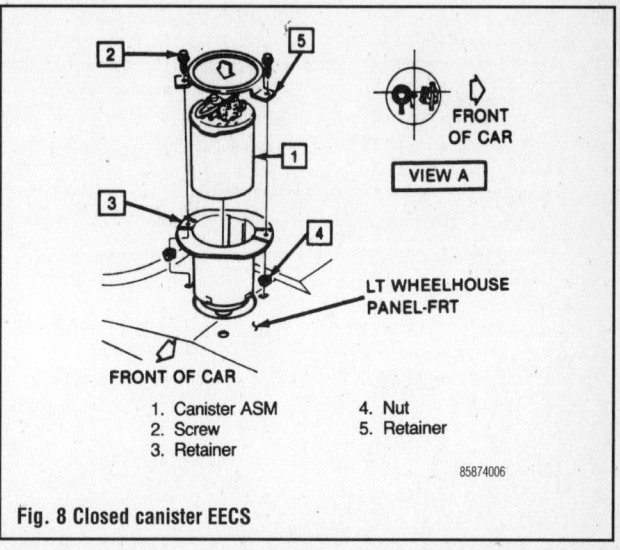

1. Canister ASM
2. Screw
3. Retainer
4. Nut
5. Retainer

Fig. 8 Closed canister EECS

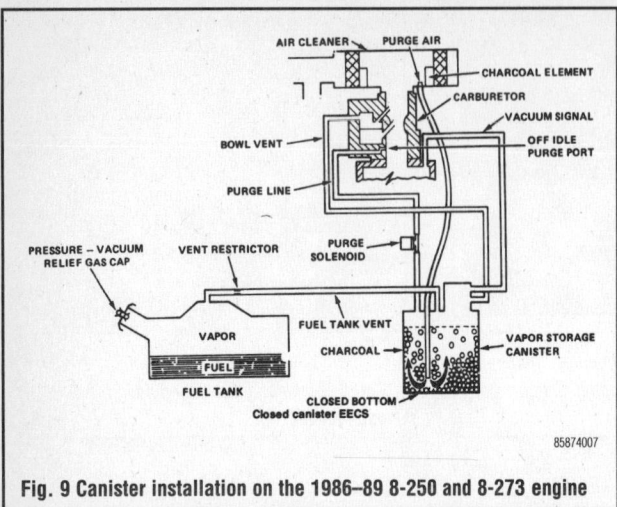

Fig. 9 Canister installation on the 1986–89 8-250 and 8-273 engine

Evaporative Canister

REMOVAL & INSTALLATION

All Engines Except 8-250

1. Loosen the screw holding the canister retaining bracket.
2. Rotate the canister retaining bracket and remove the canister.
3. Tag and disconnect all hoses leading from the canister.
4. Installation is in the reverse order of removal.

8-250 Engines

1. Remove the relay center cover.
2. Remove the two relay center bracket bolts.
3. Remove the clip holding the canister purge lines to the relay center bracket.
4. Disconnect the electrical connectors at the canister and then position the center relay bracket away from the top of the canister.
5. Tag and disconnect all vacuum hoses at the canister; position them out of the way.
6. Remove the two canister mounting bolts and then lift out the canister.
To install:
7. Install the canister in the bracket as shown in the illustration.
8. Install the retainer and the two bolts.
9. Installation of the remaining components is in the reverse order of removal.

FILTER REPLACEMENT

1. Remove the vapor canister.
2. Pull the filter out from the bottom of the canister.
3. Install a new filter and then replace the canister as previously detailed.

Exhaust Gas Recirculation (EGR) System

All 1973 and later engines covered in this guide are equipped with exhaust gas recirculation (EGR). This system consists of a metering valve, a vacuum line to the carburetor, and cast-in exhaust gas passages in the intake manifold. The EGR valve is controlled by carburetor vacuum, and accordingly opens and closes to admit exhaust gases into the fuel/air mixture. The exhaust gases lower the combustion temperature, and reduce the amount of oxides of nitrogen (NOx) produced. The valve is closed at idle between the two extreme throttle positions.

In most installations, vacuum to the EGR valve is controlled by a thermal vacuum switch (TVS). The TVS, which is installed into the engine block, shuts off vacuum to the EGR valve until the engine is hot. This prevents the stalling and lumpy idle which would result if EGR occurred when the engine was cold.

EGR VACUUM CONTROL SOLENOID

▶ **See Figures 10 thru 16**

To regulate EGR flow on 1981 and later models, a solenoid is used in the vacuum line, and is controlled by the Electronic Control Module (ECM). The ECM uses information from the coolant temperature, throttle position, and manifold pressure sensors to regulate the vacuum solenoid. When the engine is cold, a signal from the ECM energizes the EGR solenoid, thus blocking vacuum to the EGR valve. (The solenoid is also energized during cranking and wide-open throttle.) When the engine warms up, the EGR solenoid is turned off by the ECM, and the EGR valve operates according to normal ported vacuum and exhaust backpressure signals.

As the car accelerates, the carburetor throttle plate uncovers the vacuum port for the EGR valve. At 3–5 in. Hg, the EGR valve opens and then some of the exhaust gases are allowed to flow into the air/fuel mixture to lower the combustion temperature. At full-throttle the valve closes again.

Some California engines are equipped with a dual diaphragm EGR valve. This valve further limits the exhaust gas opening (compared to the single diaphragm EGR valve) during high intake manifold vacuum periods, such as high speed cruising, and provides more exhaust gas recirculation during acceleration when manifold vacuum is low. In addition to the hose running to the thermal vacuum switch, a second hose is connected directly to the intake manifold.

For 1977, all California models and cars delivered in areas above 4000 ft. are equipped with back pressure EGR valves. This valve is also used on all 1978–81 models. The EGR valve receives exhaust back pressure through its hollow shaft. This exerts a force on the bottom of the control valve diaphragm, opposed by a light spring. Under low exhaust pressure (low engine load and partial throttle), the EGR signal is reduced by an air bleed. Under conditions of high exhaust pressure (high engine load and large throttle opening), the air bleed is closed and the EGR valve responds to an unmodified vacuum signal. At wide open throttle, the EGR flow is reduced in proportion to the amount of vacuum signal available.

1979 and later models have a ported signal vacuum EGR valve. The valve opening is controlled by the amount of vacuum obtained from a ported vacuum source on the carburetor and the amount of backpressure in the exhaust system.

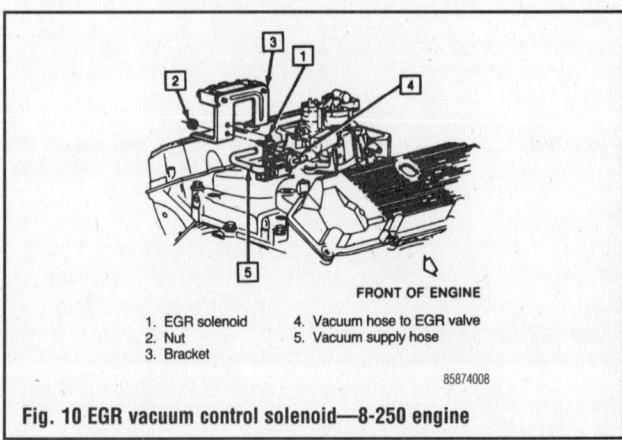

1. EGR solenoid
2. Nut
3. Bracket
4. Vacuum hose to EGR valve
5. Vacuum supply hose

Fig. 10 EGR vacuum control solenoid—8-250 engine

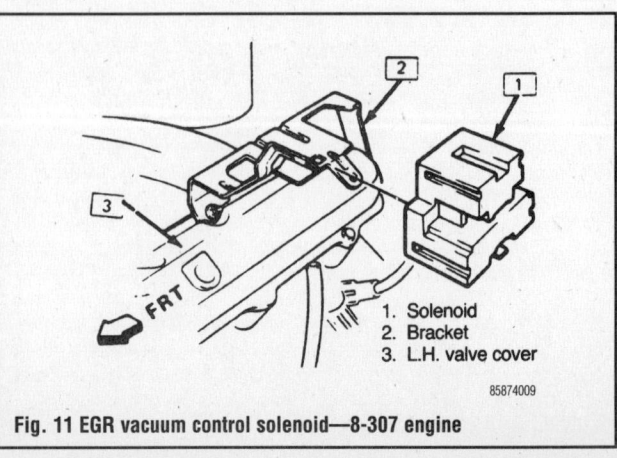

1. Solenoid
2. Bracket
3. L.H. valve cover

Fig. 11 EGR vacuum control solenoid—8-307 engine

FAULTY EGR VALVE SYMPTOMS

▶ **See Figure 17**

An EGR valve that stays open when it should be closed causes weak combustion, resulting in a rough-running engine and/or frequent stalling. Too much EGR flow at idle, cruise, or when cold can cause any of the following:

- Engine stopping after a cold start
- Engine stopping at idle after deceleration
- Surging during cruising
- Rough idle

An EGR valve which is stuck closed and allows little or no EGR flow causes extreme combustion temperatures (too hot) during acceleration. Spark knock (detonation or pinging), engine overheating and excess engine emissions can all be a result, as well as engine damage. See the accompanying EGR system diagnosis chart for possible cause and correction procedures.

EGR Valve

REMOVAL & INSTALLATION

▶ **See Figure 18**

1. Detach the vacuum lines from the EGR valve.
2. Unfasten the two bolts or bolt and clamp which attach the valve to the manifold. Withdraw the valve.

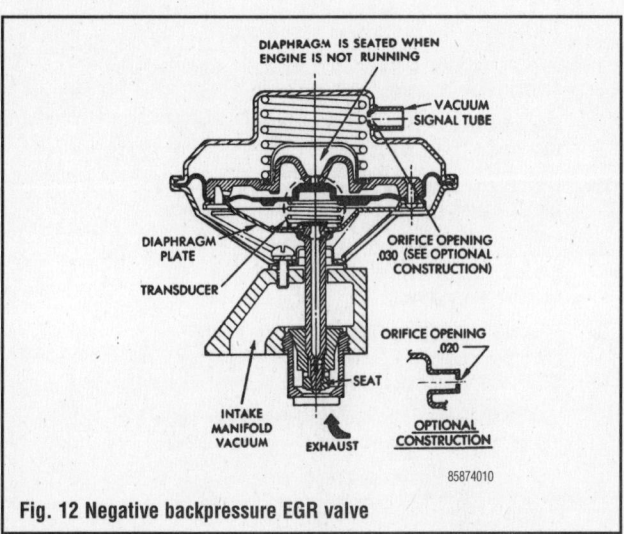

Fig. 12 Negative backpressure EGR valve

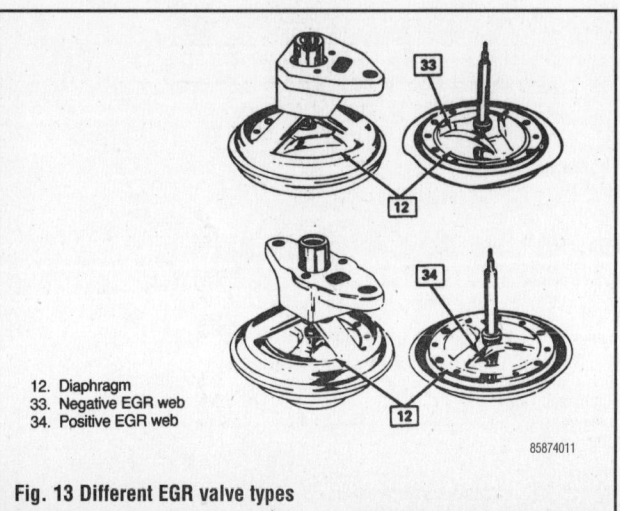

12. Diaphragm
33. Negative EGR web
34. Positive EGR web

Fig. 13 Different EGR valve types

3. Installation is the reverse of removal. Always use a new gasket between the valve and the manifold. On dual diaphragm valves, attach the carburetor vacuum line to the tube at the top of the valve, and the manifold vacuum line to the tube at the center of the valve.

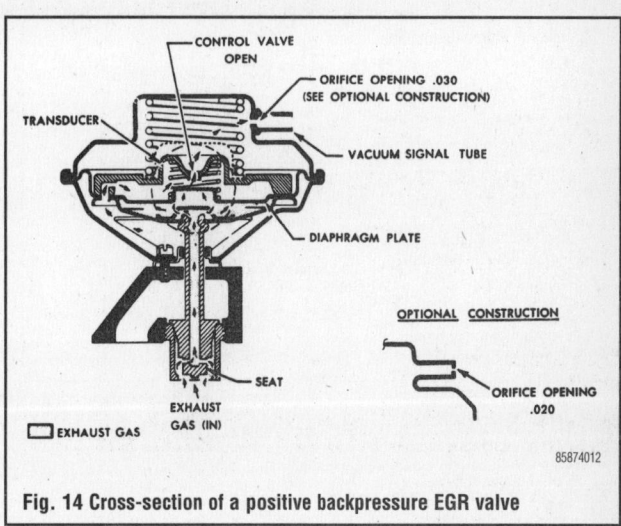

Fig. 14 Cross-section of a positive backpressure EGR valve

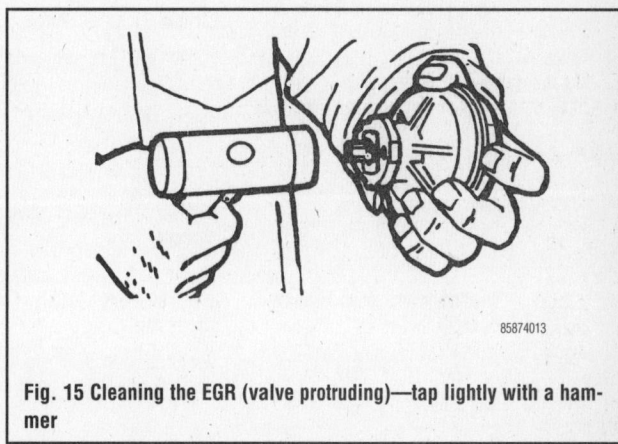

Fig. 15 Cleaning the EGR (valve protruding)—tap lightly with a hammer

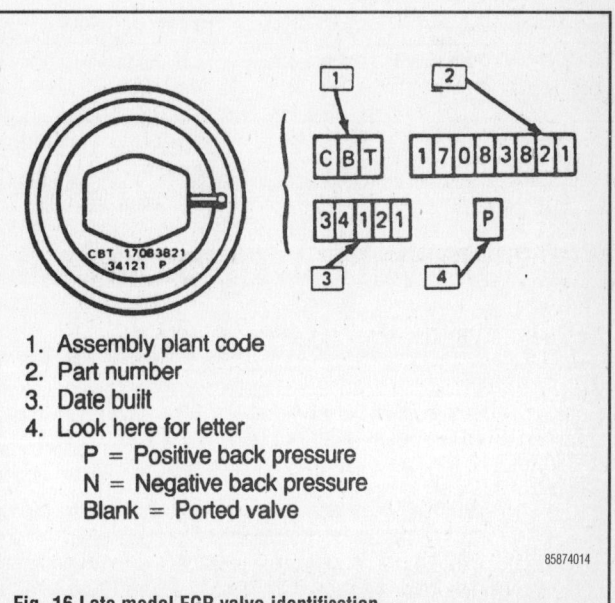

1. Assembly plant code
2. Part number
3. Date built
4. Look here for letter
   P = Positive back pressure
   N = Negative back pressure
   Blank = Ported valve

Fig. 16 Late model EGR valve identification

EGR System Diagnosis

Condition	Possible Cause	Correction
Engine idles abnormally rough and/or stalls.	EGR valve vacuum hoses mis-routed.	Check EGR valve vacuum hose routing. Correct as required.
	Leaking EGR valve.	Check EGR valve for correct operation.
	EGR valve gasket failed or loose EGR attaching bolts.	Check EGR attaching bolts for tightness. Tighten as required. If not loose, remove EGR valve and inspect gasket. Replace as required.
	EGR control solenoid.	Check vacuum into control solenoid from carburetor EGR port with engine at normal operating temperature and at curb idle speed. Then check the vacuum out of the EGR control solenoid to EGR valve. If the two vacuum readings are not equal within ± 1/2 in. Hg. (1.7 kPa), then problem could be within EGR solenoid or ECM unit.
	Improper vacuum to EGR valve at idle.	Check vacuum from carburetor EGR port with engine at stabilized operating temperature and at curb idle speed. Vacuum should not exceed 1.0 in. Hg. If vacuum exceeds this, check carburetor idle.
Engine runs rough on light throttle acceleration and has poor part load performance.	EGR valve vacuum hose misrouted.	Check EGR valve vacuum hose routing. Correct as required.
	Check for loose valve.	Torque valve.
	Failed EGR control solenoid.	Same as listing in "Engine Idles Rough" condition.
	Sticky or binding EGR valve.	Clean EGR passage of all deposits.
		Remove EGR valve and inspect. Replace as required.
	Wrong or no EGR gasket(s) and/or Spacer.	Check and correct as required. Install new gasket(s), install spacer (if used), torque attaching parts.
Engine stalls on decelera-tions.	Control valve blocked or air flow restricted.	Check internal control valve function per service procedure.
	Restriction in EGR vacuum line or control solenoid signal tube.	Check EGR vacuum lines for kinks, bends, etc. Remove or replace hoses as required. Check EGR control solenoid function.
		Check EGR valve for excessive deposits causing sticky or binding operation. Replace valve.
	Sticking or binding EGR valve.	Remove EGR valve and replace valve.
Part throttle engine detona-tion.	Control solenoid blocked or air flow restricted.	Check control solenoid function per check chart.
	Insufficient exhaust gas recircula-tion flow during part throttle accel-erations.	Check EGR valve hose routing. Check EGR valve operation. Repair or replace as required. Check EGR control solenoid as listed in "Engine Idles Rough" section. Check EGR passages and valve for excessive deposit. Clean as required.

(NOTICE: Non-Functioning EGR valve could contribute to part throttle detonation.)

Check EGR per service procedure.

(NOTICE: Detonation can be caused by several other engine variables. Perform ignition and carburetor related diagnosis.)

Engine starts but immediately stalls when cold.	EGR valve hoses misrouted.	Check EGR valve hose routings.
	EGR control solenoid system mal-functioning when engine is cold.	Perform check to determine if the EGR sole-noid is operational. Replace as required.

(NOTICE: Stalls after start can also be caused by carburetor problems.)

85874015

Fig. 17 EGR system diagnosis

Fig. 18 Removing the EGR valve

CLEANING

Valves That Protrude From Mounting Face

> ☀ **WARNING**
>
> **Do not wash the valve assembly in solvents or degreasers—permanent damage to the valve diaphragm may result.**

1. Remove the vacuum hose from the EGR valve assembly. Remove the two attaching bolts, remove the EGR valve from the intake manifold and discard the gasket.
2. Holding the valve assembly in hand, tap the valve lightly with a small plastic hammer to remove exhaust deposits from the valve seat. Shake out any loose particles. DO NOT put the valve in a vise.
3. Carefully remove any exhaust deposits from the mounting surface of the valve with a wire wheel or putty knife. Do not damage the mounting surface.
4. Depress the valve diaphragm and inspect the valve seating area through the valve outlet for cleanliness. If the valve and/or seat are not completely clean, repeat Step 2.
5. Look for exhaust deposits in the valve outlet, and remove any deposits with an old screwdriver.
6. Clean the mounting surfaces of the intake manifold and valve assembly. Using a new gasket, install the valve assembly to the intake manifold. Torque the bolts to 25 ft. lbs. (34 Nm). Connect the vacuum hose.

Shielded Valves or Valves That Do Not Protrude

1. Clean the base of the valve with a wire brush or wheel to remove exhaust deposits from the mounting surface.
2. Clean the valve seat and valve in an abrasive-type spark plug clean-ing machine or sandblaster. Most machine shops provide this service. Make sure the valve portion is cleaned (blasted) for about 30 seconds, and that the valve is also cleaned with the diaphragm spring fully compressed (valve unseated). The cleaning should be repeated until all deposits are removed.
3. The valve must be blown out with compressed air thoroughly to ensure all abrasive material is removed from the valve.
4. Clean the mounting surface of the intake manifold and valve assembly. Using a new gasket, install the valve assembly to the intake manifold. Torque the bolts to 25 ft. lbs. (34 Nm). Connect the vacuum hose.

TVS Switch

REMOVAL & INSTALLATION

1. Drain the radiator.
2. Disconnect the vacuum lines from the switch noting their locations. Remove the switch.
3. Apply sealer to the threaded portion of the new switch, and install it, torquing to 15 ft. lbs. (20 Nm).
4. Rotate the head of the switch to a position that will permit easy hookup of vacuum hoses. Then install the vacuum hoses to the proper connectors.

Thermostatic Air Cleaner (TAC or THERMAC)

All 1970 and later engines covered in this guide utilize the TAC/THERMAC system. This system is designed to warm the air entering the carburetor when underhood temperatures are low, and to maintain a controlled air temperature into the carburetor at all times. By allowing preheated air to enter the carburetor, the amount of time the choke is on is reduced, resulting in better fuel economy and lower emissions. Engine warm-up time is also reduced.

The Thermac system is composed of the air cleaner body, a filter, sensor unit, vacuum diaphragm, damper door, and associated hoses and connections. Heat radiating from the exhaust manifold is trapped by a heat stove and ducted to the air cleaner in order to supply heated air to the carburetor. A movable door in the air cleaner case snorkel allows air to be drawn in from the heat stove (cold operation) or from underhood air (warm operation). The door position is controlled by the vacuum motor, which receives intake manifold vacuum as modulated by the temperature sensor.

SYSTEM CHECKS

▶ **See Figure 19**

1. Check the vacuum hoses for leaks, kinks, breaks, or improper connections and correct any defects.
2. With the engine off, check the position of the damper door within the snorkel. A mirror can be used to make this job easier. The damper door should be open to admit outside air.
3. Apply at least 7 in. Hg of vacuum to the damper diaphragm unit. The door should close. If it doesn't, check the diaphragm linkage for binding and correct hookup.
4. With vacuum still applied and the door closed, clamp the tube to trap the vacuum. If the door doesn't remain closed, there is a leak in the diaphragm assembly.

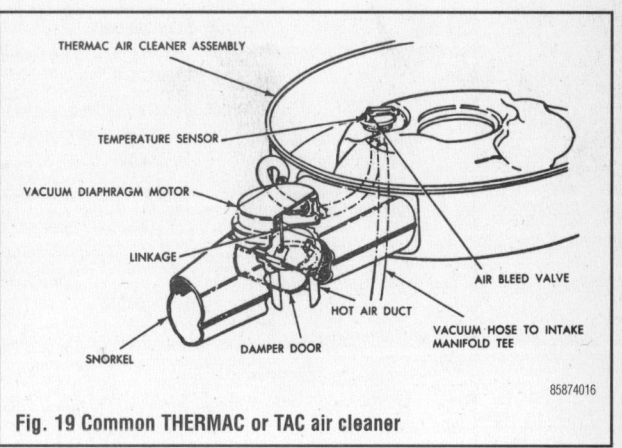

Fig. 19 Common THERMAC or TAC air cleaner

REMOVAL & INSTALLATION

▶ **See Figure 20**

Vacuum Motor

1. Remove the air cleaner.
2. Disconnect the vacuum hose from the motor.
3. Drill out the spot welds with a ⅛ in. bit (1/16 in. on later models), then enlarge as necessary to remove the retaining strap.
4. Remove the retaining strap.
5. Lift up the motor and cock it to one side to unhook the motor linkage at the control damper assembly.

To install:

6. To install the new vacuum motor, drill a 7/64 in. hole in the snorkel tube as the center of the vacuum motor retaining strap.

7. Insert the vacuum motor linkage into the control damper assembly.
8. Use the motor retaining strap and a sheet metal screw to secure the retaining strap and motor to the snorkel tube.

➡ **Make sure the screw does not interfere with the operation of the damper assembly. Shorten the screw if necessary.**

Temperature Sensor

▶ **See Figures 21 and 22**

1. Remove the air cleaner.
2. Disconnect the hoses at the air cleaner.
3. Pry up the tabs on the sensor retaining clip and remove the clip and sensor from the air cleaner.
4. Installation is the reverse of removal.

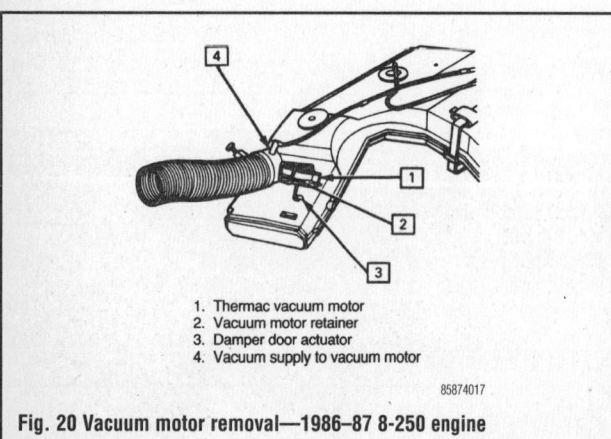

1. Thermac vacuum motor
2. Vacuum motor retainer
3. Damper door actuator
4. Vacuum supply to vacuum motor

85874017

Fig. 20 Vacuum motor removal—1986–87 8-250 engine

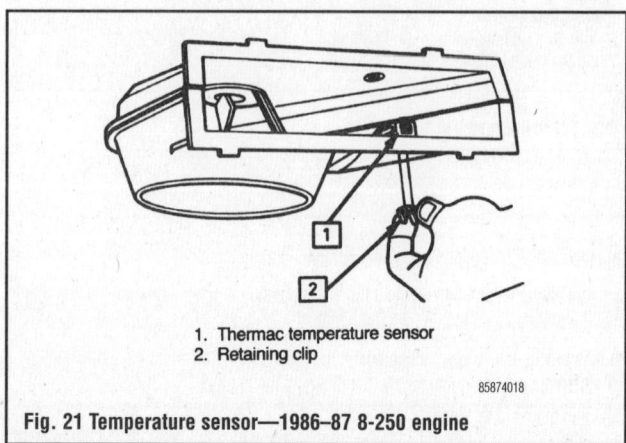

1. Thermac temperature sensor
2. Retaining clip

85874018

Fig. 21 Temperature sensor—1986–87 8-250 engine

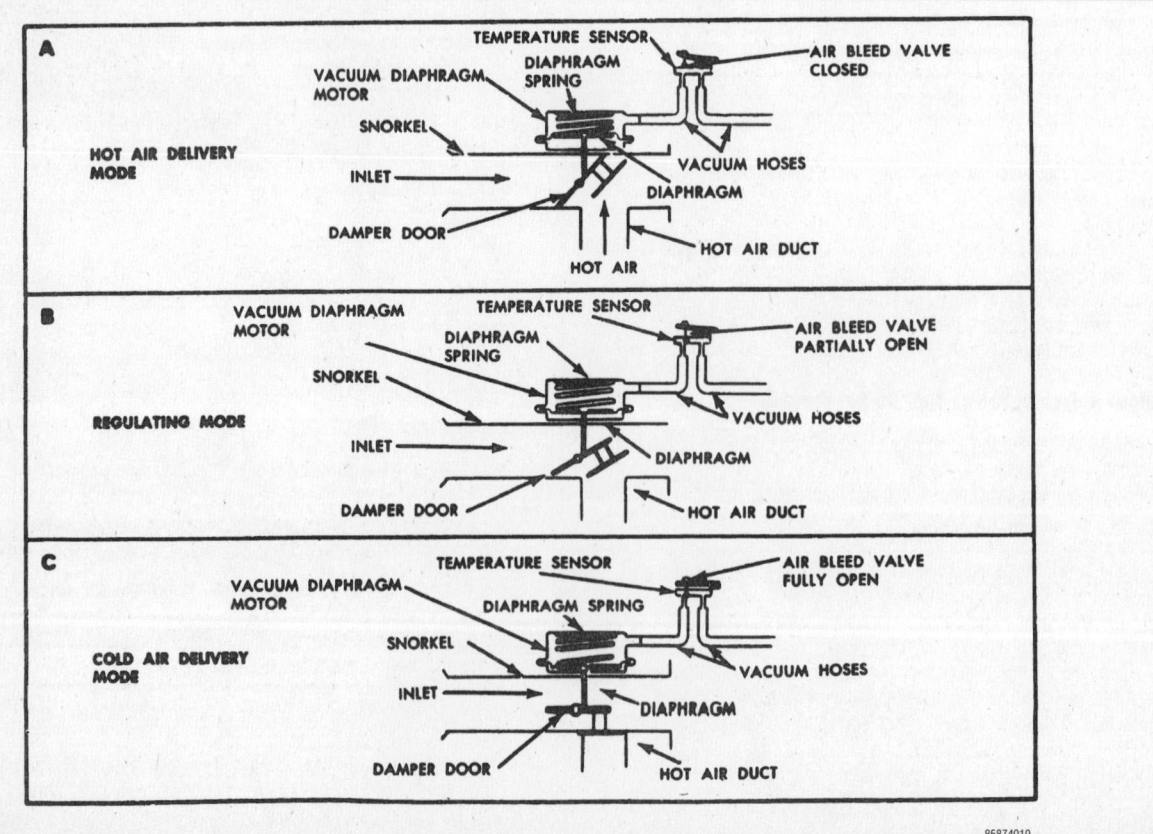

85874019

Fig. 22 Schematic of the vacuum motor operation

Air Injection Reactor (AIR) System

The AIR system injects compressed air into the exhaust system, near enough to the exhaust valves to continue the burning of the normally unburned segment of the exhaust gases. To do this it employs an air injection pump and a system of hoses, valves, tubes, etc., necessary to carry the compressed air from the pump to the exhaust manifolds. Carburetors and distributors for AIR engines have specific modifications to adapt them to the air injection system; those components should not be interchanged with those intended for use on engines that do not have the system.

A diverter valve is used to prevent backfiring. The valve senses sudden increases in manifold vacuum and ceases the injection of air during fuel-rich periods. During coasting, this valve diverts the entire air flow through the pump muffler and during high engine speeds, expels it through a relief valve. Check valves in the system prevent exhaust gases from entering the pump.

➡The AIR system on the V6 engines is slightly different, but its purpose remains the same.

SERVICE

▶ See Figure 23

The AIR system's effectiveness depends on correct engine idle speed, ignition timing, and dwell. These settings should be strictly adhered to and checked frequently. All hoses and fittings should be inspected for condition and tightness of connections. Check the drive belt for wear and tension every 12 months or 12,000 miles.

COMPONENT REMOVAL & INSTALLATION

Air Pump

▶ See Figures 24, 25 and 26

✴ WARNING

Do not pry on the pump housing or clamp the pump in a vise: the housing is soft and may become distorted.

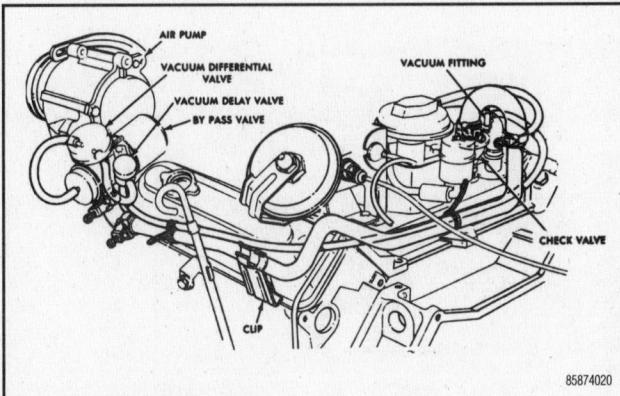

Fig. 23 AIR system—V6 engine

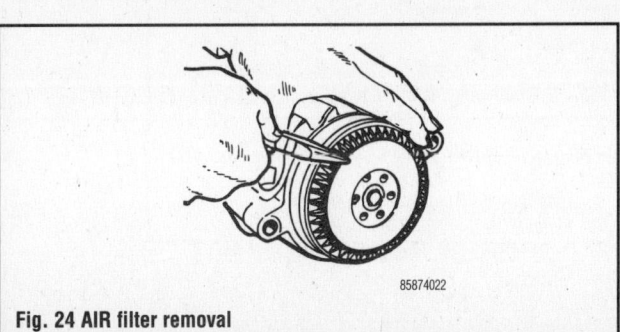

Fig. 24 AIR filter removal

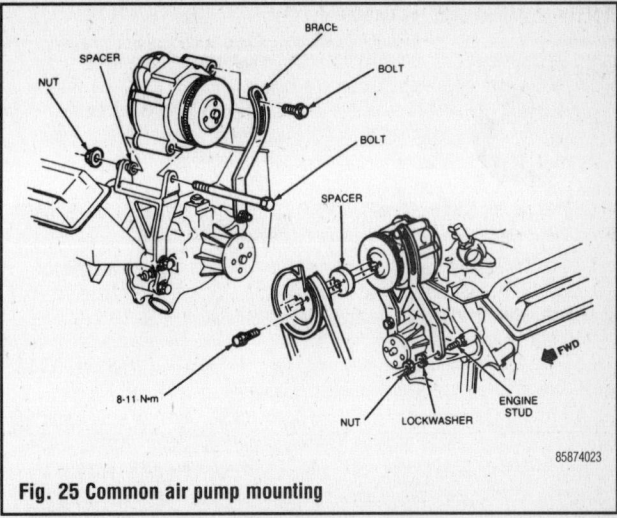

Fig. 25 Common air pump mounting

Fig. 26 Checking the air pump drive belt

1. Disconnect the air hoses at the pump.
2. Hold the pump pulley from turning and loosen the pulley bolts.
3. Loosen the pump mounting bolt and adjustment bracket bolt. Remove the drive belt.
4. Remove the mounting bolts, and then remove the pump.
5. Install the pump using a reverse of the removal procedure.

Pump Filter

1. Remove the drive belt and pump pulley.
2. Using needle-nose pliers, pull the fan from the pump hub.

✴ WARNING

Use care to prevent any dirt or fragments from entering the air intake hole. DO NOT insert a screwdriver between the pump and the filter, and do not attempt to remove the metal hub. It is seldom possible to remove the filter without destroying it.

3. To install a new filter, draw it on with the pulley and pulley bolts. Do not hammer or press the filter on the pump.
4. Draw the filter down evenly by torquing the bolts alternately. Make sure the outer edge of the filter slips into the housing. A slight amount of interference with the housing bore is normal.

➡The new filter may squeal initially until the sealing lip on the pump outer diameter has worn in.

Diverter (Anti-Afterburn) Valve

1. Detach the vacuum sensing line from the valve.
2. Remove the other hose(s) from the valve.
3. Unfasten the diverter valve from the elbow or the pump body.
4. Installation is performed in the reverse order of removal. Always use a new gasket. Tighten the valve securing bolts to 85 inch lbs. (10 Nm).

Air Management System

The Air Management System is used on 1981 and later to provide additional oxygen to continue the combustion process after the exhaust gases leave the combustion chamber; much the same as the AIR system described earlier in this section. Air is injected into either the exhaust port(s), the exhaust manifold(s) or the catalytic converter by an engine driven air pump. The system is in operation at all times and will bypass air only momentarily during deceleration and at high speeds. The bypass function is performed by the Air Management Valve, while the check valve protects the air pump by preventing any backflow of exhaust gases.

The AIR system helps to reduce HC and CO content in the exhaust gases by injecting air into the exhaust ports during cold engine operation. This air injection also helps the catalytic converter to reach the proper temperature quicker during warm-up. When the engine is warm (closed loop), the AIR system injects air into the beds of a three-way converter to lower the HC and CO content in the exhaust.

The Air Management System utilizes the following components:
1. An engine driven air pump.
2. Air management valves (Air Control and Air Switching).
3. Air flow and control hoses.
4. Check valves.
5. A dual-bed, three-way catalytic converter. The belt driven, vane-type air pump is located at the front of the engine and supplies clean air to the system for purposes already stated. When the engine is cold, the Electronic Control Module (ECM) energizes an air control solenoid. This allows air to flow to the air switching valve. The air switching valve is then energized to direct air into the exhaust ports.

When the engine is warm, the ECM de-energizes the air switching valve, thus directing the air between the beds of the catalytic converter. This then provides additional oxygen for the oxidizing catalyst in the second bed to decrease HC and CO levels, while at the same time keeping oxygen levels low in the first bed, enabling the reducing catalyst to effectively decrease the levels of NOx.

If the air control valve detects a rapid increase in manifold vacuum (deceleration), certain operating modes (wide open throttle, etc.) or if the ECM self-diagnostic system detects any problems in the system, air is diverted to the air cleaner or directly into the atmosphere.

The primary purpose of the ECM's divert mode is to prevent backfiring. Throttle closure at the beginning of deceleration will temporarily create air/fuel mixtures which are too rich to burn completely. These mixtures will become burnable when they reach the exhaust if they are combined with injection air. The next firing of the engine will ignite the mixture causing an exhaust backfire. Momentary diverting of the injection air from the exhaust prevents this.

The Air Management System check valves and hoses should be checked periodically for any leaks, cracks or deterioration.

REMOVAL & INSTALLATION

▶ See Figures 27, 28, 29, 30 and 31

Air Pump

1. Remove the valves and/or adapter at the air pump.
2. Loosen the air pump adjustment bolt and remove the drive belt.
3. Unscrew the three mounting bolts and then remove the pump pulley.
4. Unscrew the pump mounting bolts and then remove the pump.
5. Installation is in the reverse order of removal. Be sure to adjust the drive belt tension after installing it.

Check Valve

1. Release the clamp and disconnect the air hoses from the valve.
2. Unscrew the check valve from the air injection pipe.
3. Installation is in the reverse order of removal.

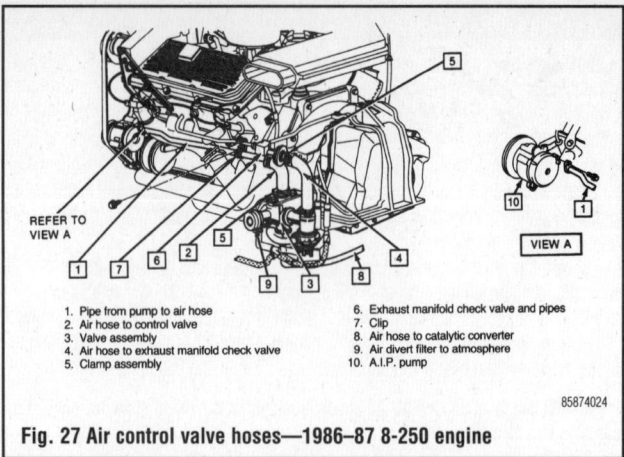

1. Pipe from pump to air hose
2. Air hose to control valve
3. Valve assembly
4. Air hose to exhaust manifold check valve
5. Clamp assembly
6. Exhaust manifold check valve and pipes
7. Clip
8. Air hose to catalytic converter
9. Air divert filter to atmosphere
10. A.I.P. pump

85874024

Fig. 27 Air control valve hoses—1986–87 8-250 engine

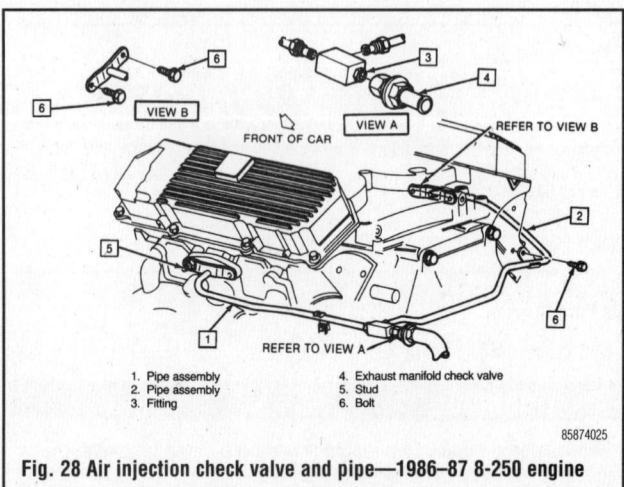

1. Pipe assembly
2. Pipe assembly
3. Fitting
4. Exhaust manifold check valve
5. Stud
6. Bolt

85874025

Fig. 28 Air injection check valve and pipe—1986–87 8-250 engine

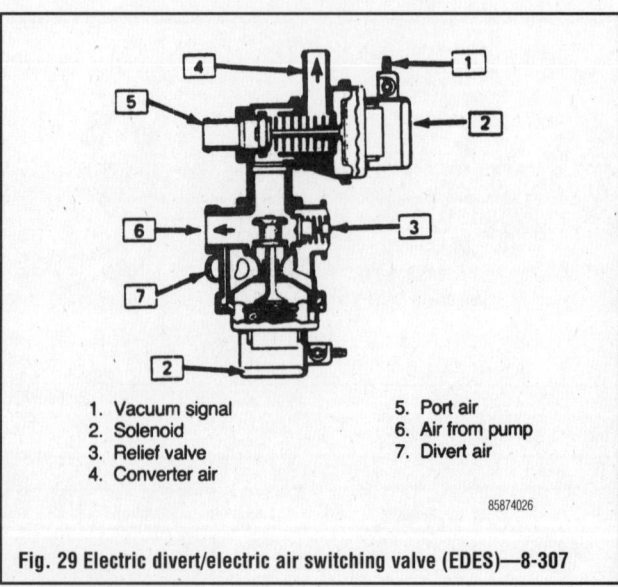

1. Vacuum signal
2. Solenoid
3. Relief valve
4. Converter air
5. Port air
6. Air from pump
7. Divert air

85874026

Fig. 29 Electric divert/electric air switching valve (EDES)—8-307

Air Management Valve

1. Disconnect the negative battery cable.
2. Remove the air cleaner.
3. Tag and disconnect the vacuum hose from the valve.

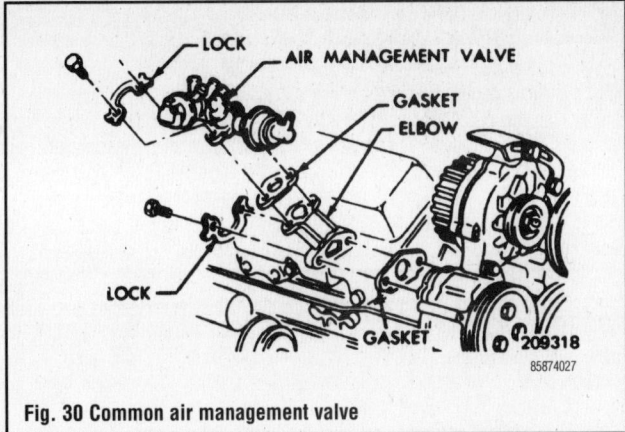

Fig. 30 Common air management valve

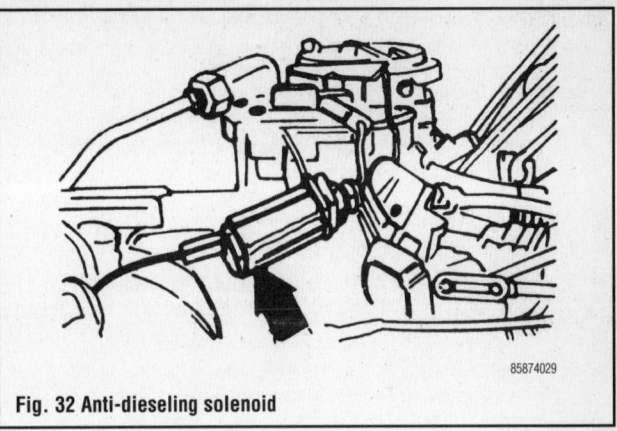

Fig. 32 Anti-dieseling solenoid

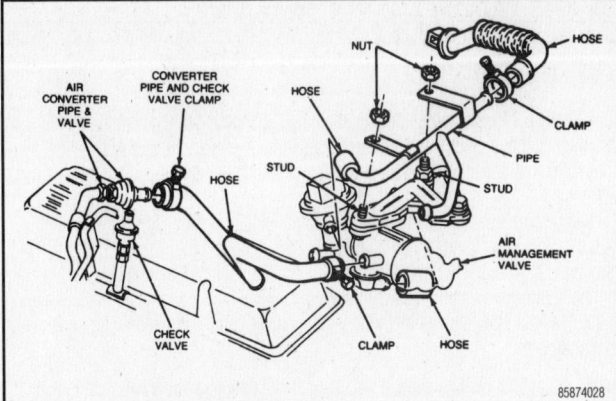

Fig. 31 Check valve and hoses—1981 and later air management system except 8-250 and 8-273 engines

4. Tag and disconnect the air outlet hoses from the valve.

5. Bend back the lock tabs and then remove the bolts holding the elbow to the valve.

6. Tag and disconnect any electrical connections at the valve and then remove the valve from the elbow.

7. Installation is in the reverse order of removal.

Anti-Dieseling Solenoid

♦ **See Figure 32**

Some carbureted models have idle solenoids. Due to the leaner carburetor settings required for emission control, the engine may have a tendency to diesel or run-on after the ignition is turned off. The carburetor solenoid, energized when the ignition is on, maintains the normal idle speed. When the ignition is turned off, the solenoid is de-energized and permits the throttle valves to fully close, thus preventing run-on. For adjustment of carburetors with idle solenoids see the carburetor adjustments later in this section.

Early Fuel Evaporation (EFE) System

♦ **See Figures 33, 34 and 35**

Two types of EFE have been used on the engines covered in this guide. Both provide quick heat to the induction system, which helps evaporate fuel (reducing emissions) when the engine is cold and aids cold driveability. The Vacuum Servo EFE system uses a valve between the exhaust manifold and exhaust pipe, operated by vacuum and controlled by either a thermal vacuum valve or electric solenoid. The valve causes hot exhaust gas to enter the intake manifold heat riser passages, heating the incoming fuel mixture. The Heated-type EFE uses a ceramic heater plate located under the carburetor, controlled through the ECM. The vacuum-type EFE should be checked for proper operation at every tune-up.

➡ **On 1981 and later V6 engines, the EFE system is controlled by the ECM.**

To check the valve:

1. Locate the EFE valve on the exhaust manifold and note the position of the actuator arm. On some cars, the valve and arm are covered by a two-piece cover which must be removed for access. Make sure the engine is overnight cold.

2. Watch the actuator arm when the engine is started. The valve should close when the engine is started cold; the actuator link will be pulled into the diaphragm housing.

3. If the valve does not close, stop the engine. Remove the hose from the EFE valve and apply 10 in. of vacuum by hand pump. The valve should close and stay closed for at least 20 seconds (you will hear it close). If the valve opens in less than 20 seconds, replace it. The valve could also be seized if it does not close; lubricate it with spray-type manifold heat valve lube. If the valve does not close when vacuum is applied and when it is lubricated, replace the valve.

4. If the valve closes, the problem is not with the valve. Check for loose,

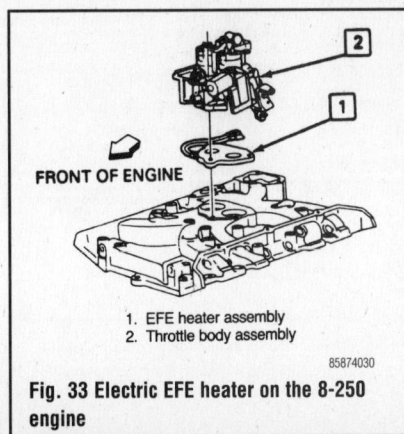

1. EFE heater assembly
2. Throttle body assembly

Fig. 33 Electric EFE heater on the 8-250 engine

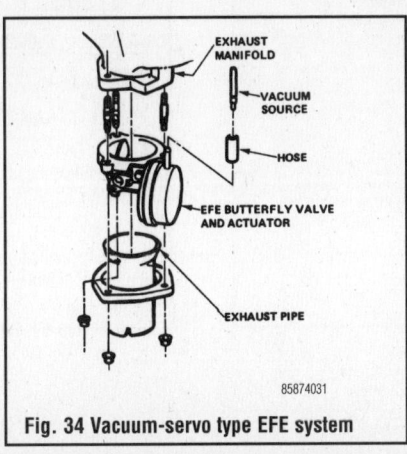

Fig. 34 Vacuum-servo type EFE system

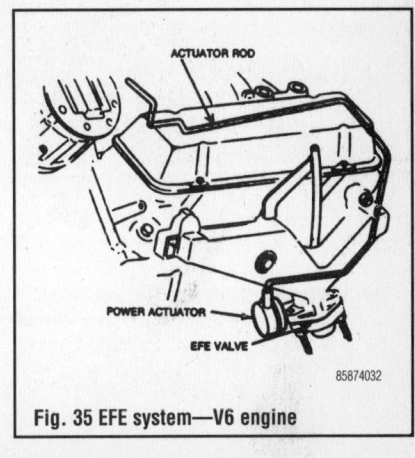

Fig. 35 EFE system—V6 engine

cracked, pinched or plugged hoses, and replace as necessary. Test the EFE solenoid (located on the valve cover bracket); if it is working, the solenoid plunger will emit a noise when the current is applied.

5. Warm up the engine to operating temperature.

6. Watch the EFE valve to see if it has opened. It should now be open. If the valve is still closed, replace the solenoid if faulty, and/or check the engine thermostat-the engine coolant may not be reaching normal operating temperature.

EFE VALVE REPLACEMENT

➡**If the car is equipped with an oxygen sensor, it is located near the EFE valve. Use care when removing the EFE valve as not to damage the oxygen sensor.**

1. Disconnect the vacuum hose at the EFE valve.

2. Remove the exhaust pipe-to-manifold nuts, and the washers and tension springs if used.

3. Lower the exhaust crossover pipe. On some models, complete removal of the pipe is not necessary.

4. Remove the EFE valve.

5. To install, reverse the removal procedure. Always install new seals and gaskets.

EFE SOLENOID REPLACEMENT

1. Disconnect the battery ground.

2. Remove the air cleaner assembly if necessary.

3. Disconnect and tag all electrical and vacuum hoses as required.

4. Remove the screw securing the solenoid to the valve cover bracket and remove the solenoid.

5. Installation is reverse of removal.

ELECTRIC-TYPE EFE REPLACEMENT

◆ **See Figure 36**

1. Remove the air cleaner.

2. Disconnect all vacuum, electrical and fuel connections from the carburetor.

3. Disconnect the EFE heater electrical connector.

4. Remove the carburetor.

5. Remove the EFE heater insulator (plate) assembly.

6. Installation is the reverse of removal.

Controlled Combustion System

The CCS system relies upon leaner air/fuel mixtures and altered ignition timing to improve combustion efficiency. A special air cleaner with a thermostatically controlled opening is used on most CCS equipped models to ensure that air entering the carburetor is kept at 100°F (38°C). This allows leaner carburetor settings and improves engine warm-up. A higher temperature thermostat is employed on CCS cars to further improve emission control.

SERVICE

Since the only extra component added with a CCS system is the thermostatically controlled air cleaner, there is no additional maintenance required; however, tune-up adjustments such as idle speed, ignition timing, and dwell become much more critical. Care must be taken to ensure that these settings are correct, both for trouble-free operation and a low emission level.

Computer Controlled Catalytic Converter System (C-4)

◆ **See Figure 37**

The C-4 System, installed on certain 1979 and all 1980 carbureted cars, is an electronically controlled exhaust emissions system. The purpose of the system is to maintain the ideal air/fuel ratio at which the catalytic converter is most effective.

Major components of the system include an Electronic Control Module (ECM), an oxygen sensor, an electronically controlled carburetor, and a three-way oxidation reduction catalytic converter. The system also includes a maintenance reminder flag connected to the odometer which becomes visible in the instrument cluster at regular intervals, signaling the need for oxygen sensor replacement.

➡**To reset the maintenance warning flag, remove the lower steering column cover. The sensor reset cable is located to the left of the speedometer cluster. Pull on the sensor reset cable lightly to reset. Reinstall the lower steering cover.**

The oxygen sensor, installed in the exhaust manifold, generates a voltage which varies with exhaust gas oxygen content. Lean mixtures (more oxygen) reduce voltage; rich mixtures (less oxygen) increase voltage. Voltage output is sent to the ECM.

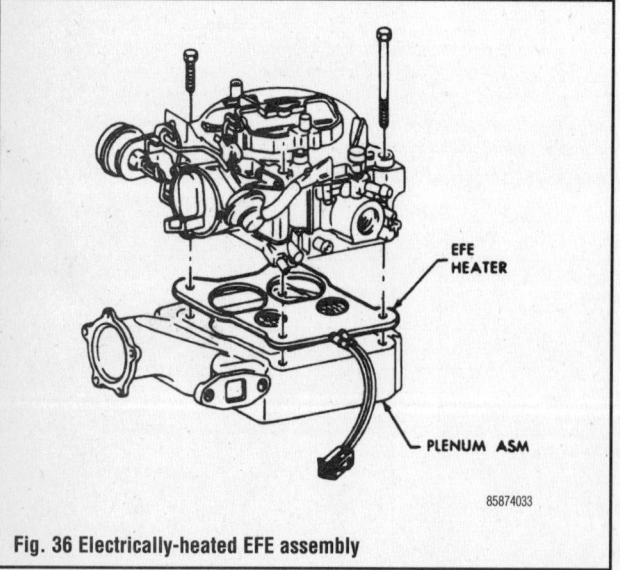

Fig. 36 Electrically-heated EFE assembly

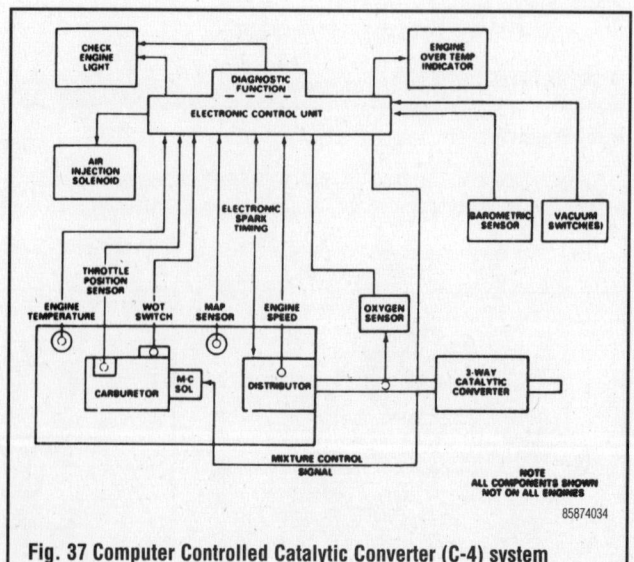

Fig. 37 Computer Controlled Catalytic Converter (C-4) system schematic

An engine temperature sensor installed in the coolant outlet monitors temperatures of the engine cooling system. Vacuum control switches and throttle position sensors also monitor engine conditions and supply signals to the ECM.

The Electronic Control Module receives input signals from all sensors. It processes these signals and generates a control signal sent to the carburetor. The control signal cycles between on (lean command) and off (rich command). The amount of on and off time is a function of the input voltage sent to the ECM by the oxygen sensor.

E4ME carburetors are used with the C-4 System. Basically, an electrically operated mixture control solenoid is installed in the carburetor float bowl. The solenoid controls the air/fuel mixture metered to the idle and main metering systems. Air metering to the idle system is controlled by an idle air bleed valve. It follows the movement of the mixture solenoid to control the amount of air bled into the idle system, enriching or leaning out the mixture as appropriate. Air-fuel mixture enrichment occurs when the fuel valve is open and the air bleed valve is closed. All cycling of this system, which occurs ten times per second, is controlled by the ECM. A throttle position switch informs the ECM of open or closed throttle operation. A number of different switches are used, varying with application. When the ECM receives a signal from the throttle switch, indicating a change of position, it immediately searches its memory for the last set of operating conditions that resulted in an ideal air/fuel ratio, and shifts to that set of conditions. The memory is continually updated during normal operation.

A Check-Engine light is included in the C-4 System installation. When a fault develops, the light comes on, and a trouble code is set into the ECM memory. However, if the fault is intermittent, the light will go out, but the trouble code will remain in the ECM memory as long as the engine is running. The trouble codes are used as a diagnostic aid, and are pre-programmed.

Unless the required tools are available, troubleshooting the C-4 System should be confined to mechanical checks of electrical connectors, vacuum hoses and the like. All diagnosis and repair should be performed by a qualified mechanic.

Computer Command Control System

▶ **See Figures 38, 39, 40 and 41**

The Computer Command Control System, installed on all 1981 and later carbureted cars, is basically a modified version of the C-4 system. Its main advantage over its predecessor is that it can monitor and control a larger number of interrelated emission control systems.

➡ **For information regarding computer control/troubleshooting of the Electronic and Digital fuel injected vehicles, please refer to Section 5 of this manual.**

This new system can monitor up to 15 various engine/vehicle operating conditions and then use this information to control as many as 9 engine related systems. The System is thereby making constant adjustments to maintain good vehicle performance under all normal driving conditions while at the same time allowing the catalytic converter to effectively control the emissions of NOx, HC and CO.

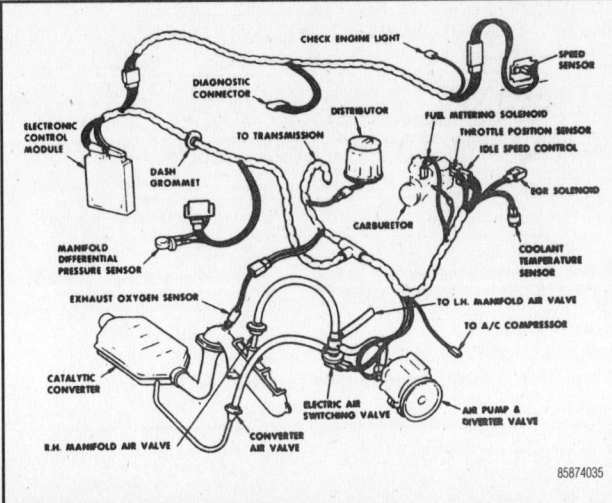

Fig. 38 Computer Command Control (CCC) system schematic

In addition, the System has a built in diagnostic system, that recognizes and identifies possible operational problems and alerts the driver through a Check Engine light in the instrument panel. The light will remain ON until the problem is corrected. The System also has built in back-up systems that in most cases of an operational problem will allow for the continued operation of the vehicle in a near normal manner until the repairs can be made.

The CCC system has some components in common with the C-4 system, although they are not interchangeable. These components include the Electronic Control Module (ECM), which, as previously stated, controls many more functions than does its predecessor, an oxygen sensor system, an electronically controlled variable-mixture carburetor, a three-way catalytic converter, throttle position and coolant sensors, a Barometric Pressure Sensor (BARO), a Manifold Absolute Pressure Sensor (MAP) and a Check Engine light in the instrument panel.

Components unique to the CCC system include the Air Injection Reaction (AIR) management system, a charcoal canister purge solenoid, EGR valve controls, a vehicle speed sensor (in the instrument panel), a transmission converter clutch solenoid (only on models with automatic transmission), idle speed control and Electronic Spark Timing (EST).

The ECM, in addition to monitoring sensors and sending out a control signal to the carburetor, also controls the following components or sub-systems: charcoal canister purge control, the AIR system, idle speed, automatic transmission converter lock-up, distributor ignition timing, the EGR valve, and the air conditioner converter clutch.

The EGR valve control solenoid is activated by the ECM in a fashion similar

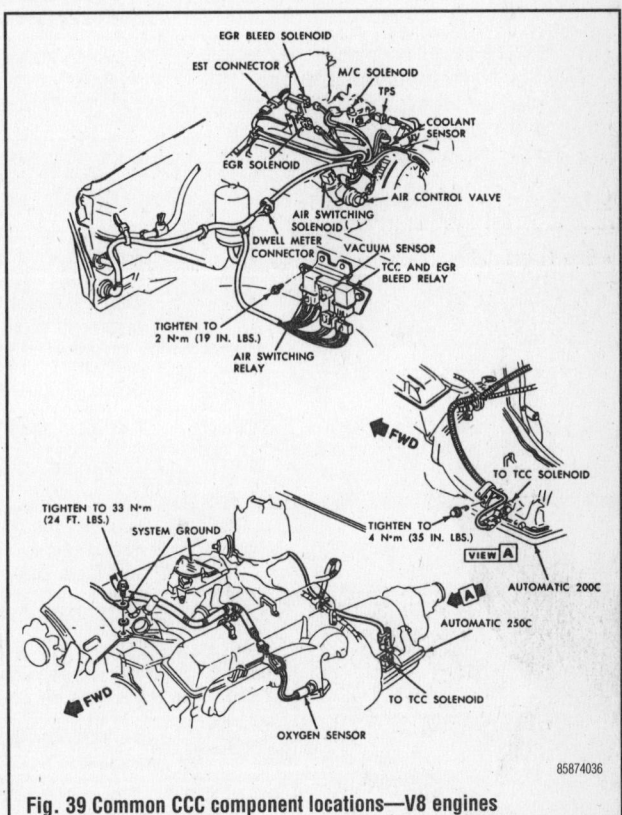

Fig. 39 Common CCC component locations—V8 engines

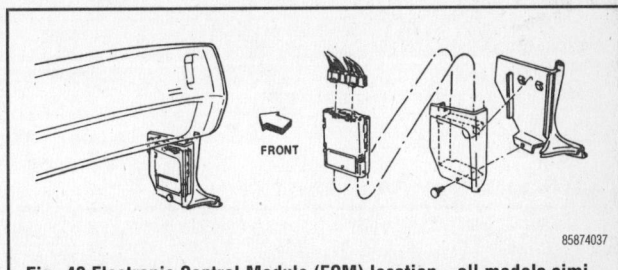

Fig. 40 Electronic Control Module (ECM) location—all models similar

Trouble Code Identification Chart

NOTE: *Always ground the test lead/terminal AFTER the engine is running*

Trouble Code	Applicable System	Possible Problem Area
12	C-4, CCC	No reference pulses to the ECM. This is not stored in the memory and will only flash when the fault is present (not to be confused with the Code 12 discussed earlier).
13	C-4, CCC	Oxygen sensor circuit. The engine must run for at least 5 min. at part throttle before this code will show.
13 & 14 (at same time)	C-4	See code 43.
13 & 43 (at same time)	C-4	See code 43.
14	C-4, CCC	Shorted coolant sensor circuit. The engine must run 2–5 min. before this code will show.
15	C-4, CCC	Open coolant sensor circuit. The engine must run for at least 5 min. before this code will show.
21	C-4	Shorted wide open throttle switch and/or open closed-throttle switch circuit (when used).
	C-4, CCC	Throttle position sensor circuit. The engine must run for at least 10 sec. (25 sec.—CCC) before 800 rpm before this code will show.
23	C-4, CCC	Open or grounded carburetor mixture control (M/C) solenoid circuit.
24	CCC	Vehicle speed sensor circuit. The engine must run for at least 5 min, at normal speed before this code will show.
32	C4, CCC	Barometric pressure sensor (BARO) circuit output is low.
32 & 55 (at same time)	C-4	Grounded +8V terminal or V(REF) terminal for BARO sensor, or a faulty EMC.
34	C-4	Manifold absolute pressure sensor (MAP) output is high. The engine must run for at least 10 sec. below 800 rpm before this code will show.
	CCC	Maniford absolute pressure sensor (MAP) circuit or vacuum sensor circuit. The engine must run for at least 5 min. below 800 rpm before this code will show.
35	CCC	Idle speed control circuit shorted. The engine must run for at least 2 sec. above ½ throttle before this code will show.
42	CCC	Electronic spark timing (EST) bypass circuit grounded.
43	C-4	Throttle position sensor adjustment. The engine must run for at least 10 sec. before this code will show.
44	C-4, CCC	Lean oxygen sensor indication. The engine must run for at least 5 min. in closed loop (oxygen sensor adjusting carburetor mixture) at part throttle under load (drive car) before this code will show.
44 & 55 (at same time)	C-4, CCC	Faulty oxygen sensor circuit.
45	C-4, CCC	Rich oxygen sensor indication. The engine must run for at least 5 min. before this code will show (see 44 for conditions).
51	C-4, CCC	Faulty calibration unit (PROM) or improper PROM installation in the ECM. It will take at least 30 sec. before this code will show.
52 & 53	C-4	"Check Engine" light off: intermittant ECM problem. "Check Engine" light on: faulty ECM—replace.
52	C-4, CCC	Faulty ECM.
53	CCC	Faulty ECM.
54	C-4, CCC	Faulty mixture control solenoid circuit and/or faulty ECM.
55	C-4	Faulty throttle position sensor or ECM.
	CCC	Grounded +8V supple (terminal 19 on ECM connector), grounded 5V reference (terminal 21 on ECM connector), faulty oxygen sensor circuit or faulty ECM.

NOTE: *Not all codes will apply to every model.*

85874038

Fig. 41 Trouble Code Identification Chart

to that of the charcoal canister purge solenoid described earlier in this section. When the engine is cold, the ECM energizes the solenoid, which blocks the vacuum signal to the EGR valve. When the engine is warm, the ECM de-energizes the solenoid and the vacuum signal is allowed to reach and then activate the EGR valve.

The Transmission Converter Clutch (TCC) lock is controlled by the ECM through an electrical solenoid in the automatic transmission. When the vehicle speed sensor in the dash signals the ECM that the car has attained the pre-determined speed, the ECM energizes the solenoid which then allows the torque converter to mechanically couple the engine to the transmission. When the brake pedal is pushed, or during deceleration or passing, etc., the ECM returns the transmission to fluid drive.

The idle speed control adjusts the idle speed to all particular engine load conditions and will lower the idle under no-load or low-load conditions in order to conserve fuel.

➡Not all engines use all systems. Control applications may differ.

BASIC TROUBLESHOOTING

▶ See Figures 42, 43 and 44

➡The following explains how to activate the Trouble Code signal light in the instrument cluster.

Before suspecting the C-4 or CCC system, or any of its components as being faulty, check the ignition system (distributor, timing, spark plugs and wires). Check the engine compression, the air cleaner and any of the emission control components that are not controlled by the ECM. Also check the intake manifold, the vacuum hoses and hose connectors for any leaks. Check the carburetor mounting bolts for tightness.

➡For information regarding computer control/troubleshooting of the Electronic and Digital fuel injected vehicles, please refer to @TX:The following symptoms could indicate a possible problem area with the C-4 or CCC systems:

1. Detonation
2. Stalling or rough idling when the engine is cold
3. Stalling or rough idling when the engine is hot
4. Missing
5. Hesitation
6. Surging
7. Poor gasoline mileage
8. Sluggish or spongy performance
9. Hard starting when engine is cold
10. Hard starting when the engine is hot
11. Objectionable exhaust odors
12. Engine cuts out
13. Improper idle speed (CCC only).

As a bulb and system check, the Check Engine light will come on when the ignition switch is turned to the ON position but the engine is not started.

The Check Engine light will also produce the trouble code/codes by a series of flashes which translate as follows: When the diagnostic test lead (C-4) or terminal (CCC) under the instrument panel is grounded, with the ignition in the

ON position and the engine not running, the Check Engine light will flash once, pause, and then flash twice in rapid succession. This is a Code 12, which indicates that the diagnostic system is working. After a long pause, the Code 12 will repeat itself two more times. This whole cycle will then repeat itself until the engine is started or the ignition switch is turned OFF.

When the engine is started, the Check Engine light will remain on for a few seconds and then turn off. If the Check Engine light remains on, the self-diagnostic system has detected a problem. If the test lead (C-4) or test terminal (CCC) is then grounded, the trouble code will flash (3) three times. If more than one problem is found to be in existence, each trouble code will flash (3) three times and then change to the next one. Trouble codes will flash in numerical order (lowest number to highest). The trouble code series will repeat themselves for as long as the test leads or terminal remains grounded.

A trouble code indicates a problem with a given circuit. For example, trouble code 14 indicates a problem in the cooling sensor circuit. This includes the coolant sensor, its electrical harness and the Electronic Control Module (ECM).

Since the self-diagnostic system cannot diagnose every possible fault in the system, the absence of a trouble code does not necessarily mean that the system is trouble-free. To determine whether or not a problem with the system exists that does not activate a trouble code, a system performance check must be made. This job should be left to a qualified service technician.

In the case of an intermittent fault in the system, the Check Engine light will go out when the fault goes away, but the trouble code will remain in the memory of the ECM. Therefore, if a trouble code can be obtained even though the Check Engine light is not on, it must still be evaluated. It must be determined if the fault is intermittent or if the engine must be operating under certain conditions (acceleration, deceleration, etc.) before the Check Engine light will come on. In some cases, certain trouble codes will not be recorded in the ECM until the engine has been operated at part throttle for at least 5–18 minutes.

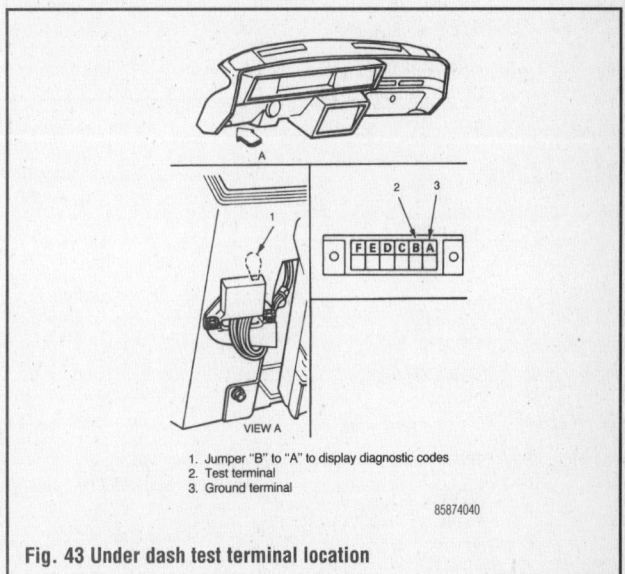

1. Jumper "B" to "A" to display diagnostic codes
2. Test terminal
3. Ground terminal

85874040

Fig. 43 Under dash test terminal location

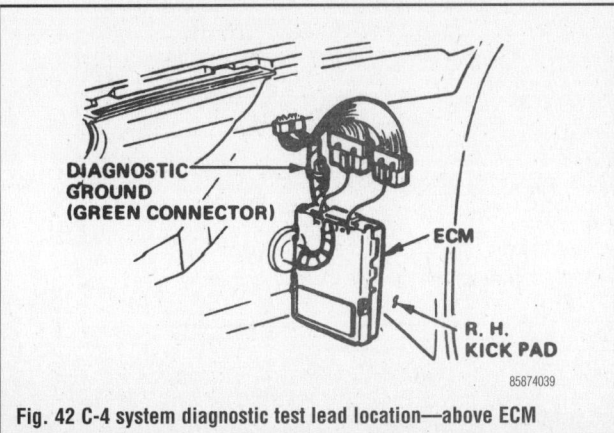

85874039

Fig. 42 C-4 system diagnostic test lead location—above ECM

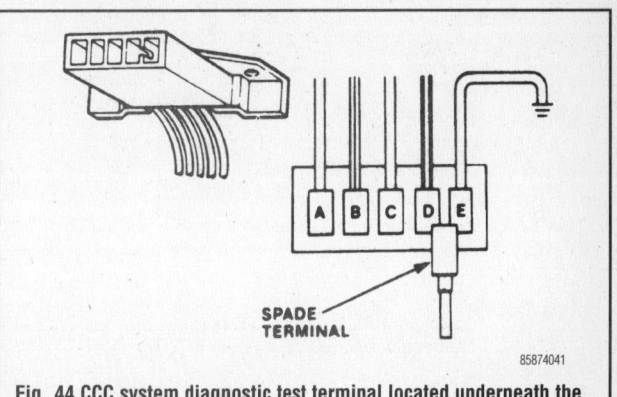

85874041

Fig. 44 CCC system diagnostic test terminal located underneath the left side of the instrument panel

On the C-4 system, the ECM erases all trouble codes every time that the ignition is turned off. In the case of intermittent faults, a long term memory is desirable. This can be produced by connecting the orange connector/lead from terminal **S** of the ECM directly to the battery (or a hot fuse panel terminal). This terminal must always be disconnected immediately after diagnosis as it puts an undue strain on the battery.

On the CCC system, a trouble code will be stored until the terminal **R** at the ECM has been disconnected from the battery for at least 10 seconds.

ACTIVATING THE TROUBLE CODE DISPLAY

On the C-4 system, activate the trouble code by grounding the trouble code test lead. Use the illustrations to help you locate the test lead under the instrument panel (usually a white and black wire with a green connector). Run a jumper wire from the lead to a suitable ground.

On the CCC system, locate the test terminal under the instrument panel (see illustration). Use a jumper wire and ground only the lead.

➡ Ground the test lead/terminal according to the instructions given previously in the Basic Troubleshooting section.

MIXTURE CONTROL SOLENOID (M/C)

The fuel flow through the carburetor idle main metering circuits is controlled by a mixture control (M/C) solenoid located in the carburetor. The M/C solenoid changes the air/fuel mixture to the engine by controlling the fuel flow through the carburetor. The ECM controls the solenoid by providing a ground. When the solenoid is energized, the fuel flow through the carburetor is reduced, providing a leaner mixture. When the ECM removes the ground, the solenoid is de-energized, increasing the fuel flow and providing a richer mixture. The M/C solenoid is energized and de-energized at a rate of 10 times per second.

THROTTLE POSITION SENSOR (TPS)

◗ **See Figure 45**

1980 and Later

The throttle position sensor is mounted in the carburetor body and is used to supply throttle position information to the ECM. The ECM memory stores an average of operating conditions with the ideal air/fuel ratios for each of those conditions. When the ECM receives a signal that indicates throttle position change, it immediately shifts to the last remembered set of operating conditions that resulted in an ideal air/fuel ratio control. The memory is continually being updated during normal operations.

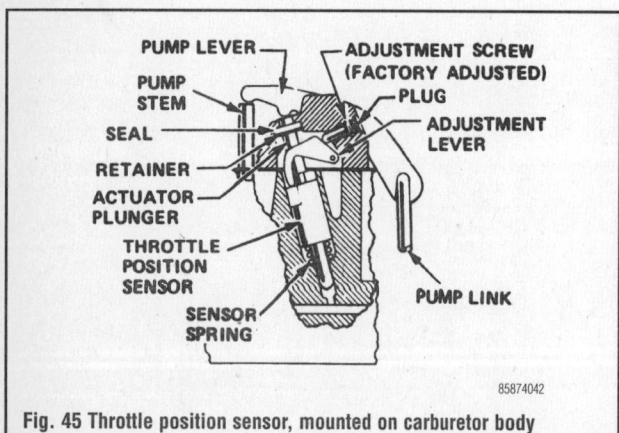

Fig. 45 Throttle position sensor, mounted on carburetor body

IDLE SPEED CONTROL (ISC)

◗ **See Figure 46**

The idle speed control does just what its name implies-it controls the idle. The ISC is used to maintain low engine speeds while at the same time prevent-

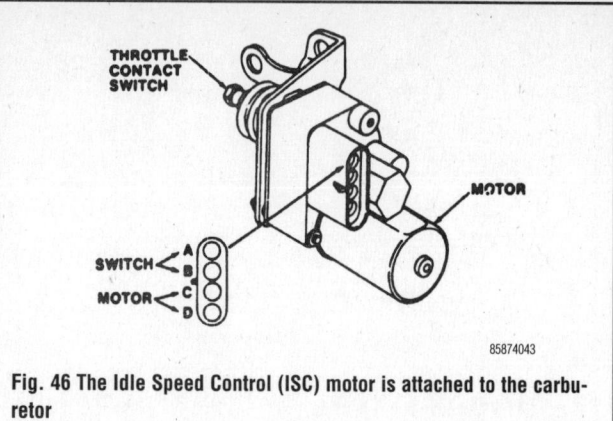

Fig. 46 The Idle Speed Control (ISC) motor is attached to the carburetor

ing stalling due to engine load changes. The system consists of a motor assembly mounted on the carburetor which moves the throttle lever so as to open or close the throttle blades.

The whole operation is controlled by the ECM. The ECM monitors engine load to determine the proper idle speed. To prevent stalling, it monitors the air conditioning compressor switch, the transmission, the park/neutral switch and the ISC throttle switch. The ECM processes all this information and then uses it to control the ISC motor which in turn will vary the idle speed as necessary.

Electronic Spark Timing (EST)

◗ **See Figures 47, 48, 49 and 50**

All 1981 and later models use EST. The EST distributor, as described in an earlier section, contains no vacuum or centrifugal advance mechanism and uses a seven terminal HEI module. It has four wires going to a four terminal connector in addition to the connectors normally found on HEI distributors. A reference pulse, indicating engine rpm is sent to the ECM. The ECM determines the

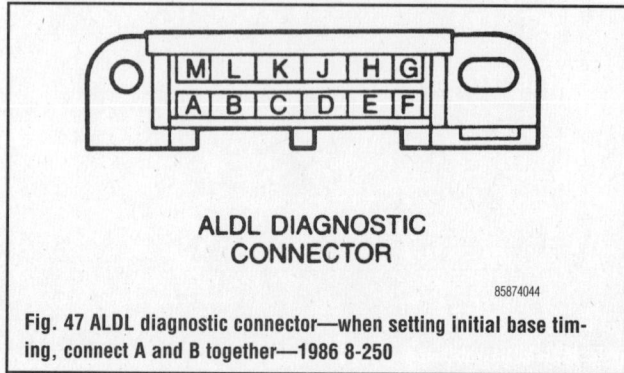

Fig. 47 ALDL diagnostic connector—when setting initial base timing, connect A and B together—1986 8-250

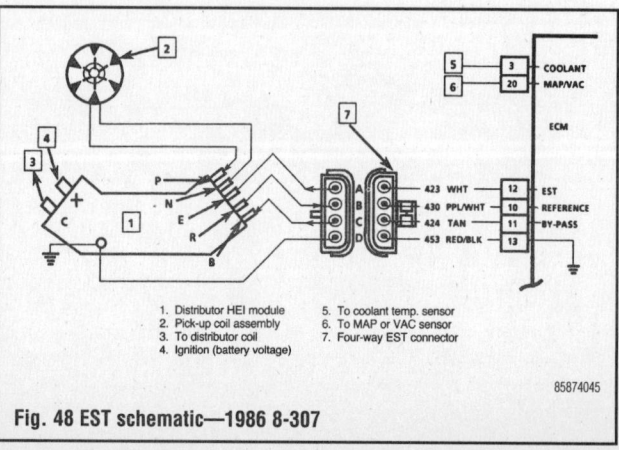

1. Distributor HEI module
2. Pick-up coil assembly
3. To distributor coil
4. Ignition (battery voltage)
5. To coolant temp. sensor
6. To MAP or VAC sensor
7. Four-way EST connector

Fig. 48 EST schematic—1986 8-307

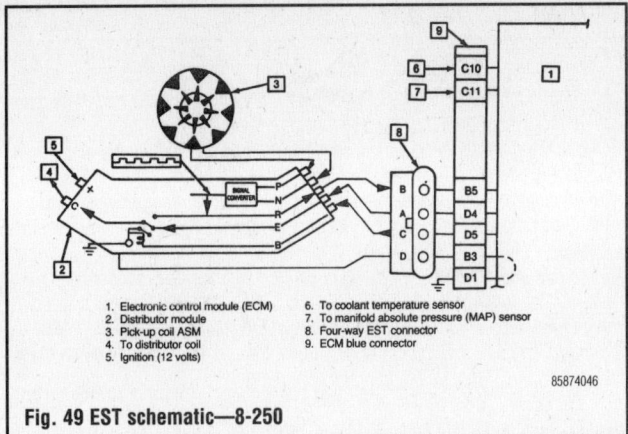

1. Electronic control module (ECM)
2. Distributor module
3. Pick-up coil ASM
4. To distributor coil
5. Ignition (12 volts)
6. To coolant temperature sensor
7. To manifold absolute pressure (MAP) sensor
8. Four-way EST connector
9. ECM blue connector

85874046

Fig. 49 EST schematic—8-250

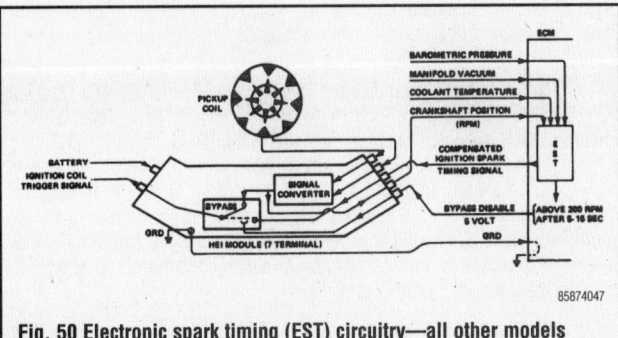

85874047

Fig. 50 Electronic spark timing (EST) circuitry—all other models

proper spark advance for the engine operating conditions and then sends an EST pulse back to the distributor.

Under most normal operating conditions, the ECM will control the spark advance. However, under certain operating conditions such as cranking or when setting base timing, the distributor is capable of operating without ECM control. This condition is called BYPASS and is determined by the BYPASS lead which runs from the ECM to the distributor. When the BYPASS lead is at the proper voltage (5), the ECM will control the spark. If the lead is grounded or open circuited, the HEI module itself will control the spark. Disconnecting the 4-terminal EST connector will also cause the engine to operate in the BYPASS mode.

On 1986–87 models with the 8-250 engine, the initial timing is set by running a jumper wire between pins A and B on the ALDL diagnostic connector while it is NOT in the display mode. After bridging the two pins, initial timing may be set to specifications as shown on the underhood specifications sticker. Bridging the two pins together will cause a SET TIMING message to appear on the CCDIC. This indicates an ECM command for initial base timing.

Electronic Spark Control (ESC) System

GENERAL INFORMATION

252 V6 Engine

The Electronic Spark Control (ESC) system is a closed loop system that controls engine detonation by adjusting the spark timing. There are two basic components in this system, the controller and the detonation sensor.

The controller processes the sensor signal and modifies the EST signal to the distributor to adjust the spark timing. The process is continuous so that the presence of detonation is monitored and controlled. The controller is not capable of memory storage.

The sensor is a magneto-restrictive device, mounted in the engine block that detects the presence, or absence, and intensity of detonation according to the vibration characteristics of the engine. The output is an electrical signal which is sent to the controller.

Transmission Converter Clutch (TCC)

‣ See Figure 51

All 1986–89 models with an automatic transmission or transaxle utilize TCC. The ECM controls the converter by means of a solenoid mounted in the transmission. When the vehicle speed reaches a certain level, the ECM energizes the solenoid and allows the torque converter to mechanically couple the transmission to the engine. When the operating conditions indicate that the transmission should operate as a normal fluid coupled transmission, the ECM will de-energize the solenoid. Depressing the brake will also return the transmission to normal automatic operation.

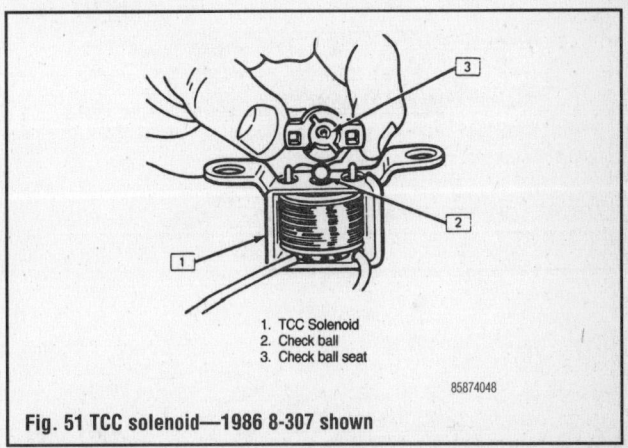

1. TCC Solenoid
2. Check ball
3. Check ball seat

85874048

Fig. 51 TCC solenoid—1986 8-307 shown

Catalytic Converter

‣ See Figures 52, 53 and 54

The catalytic converter is a muffler-like container built into the exhaust system to aid on the reduction of exhaust emissions. The catalyst element consists of individual pellets or a honeycomb monolithic substrate coated with a metal such as platinum, palladium, rhodium or a combination. When the exhaust gases come into contact with the catalyst, a chemical reaction occurs which will reduce the pollutants into harmless substances like water and carbon dioxide.

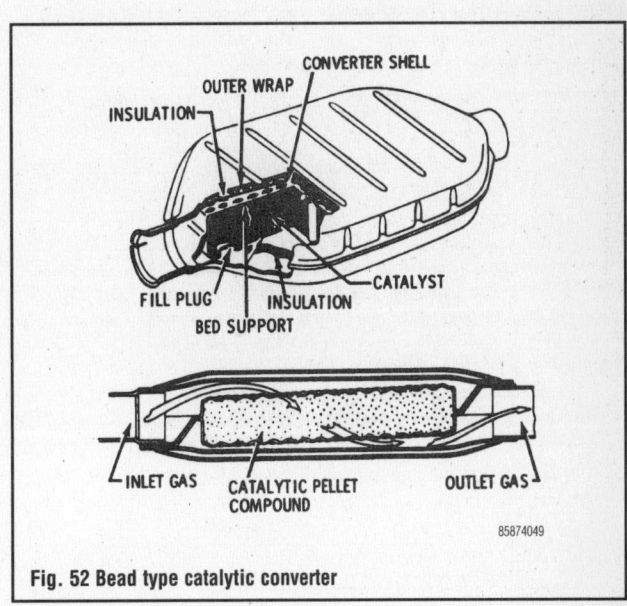

85874049

Fig. 52 Bead type catalytic converter

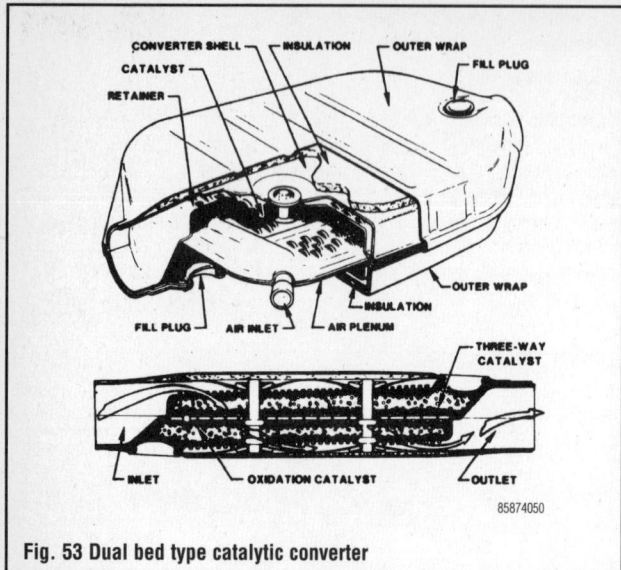

Fig. 53 Dual bed type catalytic converter

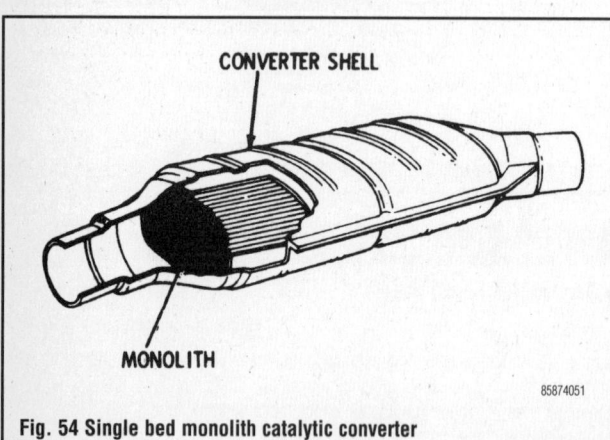

Fig. 54 Single bed monolith catalytic converter

There are essentially two types of catalytic converter: an oxidizing type is used on all 1975–80 models with the exception of those 1980 models built for Calif. It requires the addition of oxygen to spur the catalyst into reducing the engine's HC and CO emissions into H_2O and CO_2. Because of this need for oxygen, the AIR system is used with all these models.

The oxidizing catalytic converter, while effectively reducing HC and CO emissions, does little, if anything in the way of reducing NOx emissions. Thus, the three-way catalytic converter.

The three-way converter, unlike the oxidizing type, is capable of reducing HC, CO and NOx emissions; all at the same time. In theory, it seems impossible to reduce all three pollutants in one system since the reduction of HC and CO requires the addition of oxygen, while the reduction of NOx calls for the removal of oxygen. In actuality, the three-way system really can reduce all three pollutants, but only if the amount of oxygen in the exhaust system is precisely controlled. Due to this precise oxygen control requirement, the three-way converter system is used only in cars equipped with an oxygen sensor system (1980 Calif. cars and all 1981 and later models).

There are no service procedures required for the catalytic converter, although the converter body should be inspected occasionally for damage. Some models with the V-6 engine require a catalyst change at 30,000 mile intervals (consult your Owner's Manual).

PRECAUTIONS

1. Use only unleaded fuel.
2. Avoid prolonged idling; the engine should run no longer than 20 min. at curb idle and no longer than 10 min. at fast idle.
3. Do not disconnect any of the spark plug leads while the engine is running.
4. Make the engine compression checks as quickly as possible.

CATALYST TESTING

At the present time there is no known way to reliably test catalytic converter operation in the field. The only reliable test is a 12 hour and 40 min. soak test (CVS) which must be done in a laboratory.

An infrared HC/CO tester is not sensitive enough to measure the higher tailpipe emissions from a failing converter. Thus, a bad converter may allow enough emissions to escape so that the car is no longer in compliance with Federal or state standards, but will still not cause the needle on a tester to move off zero.

The chemical reactions which occur inside a catalytic converter generate a great deal of heat. Most converter problems can be traced to fuel or ignition system problems which cause unusually high emissions. As a result of the increased intensity of the chemical reactions, the converter literally burns itself up.

A completely failed converter might cause a tester to show a slight reading. As a result, it is occasionally possible to detect one of these.

As long as you avoid severe overheating and the use of leaded fuels it is reasonably safe to assume that the converter is working properly. If you are in doubt, take the car to a diagnostic center that has a tester.

Oxygen Sensor

➡**Some early models may include a maintenance reminder flag connected to the odometer which becomes visible in the instrument cluster at regular intervals, signaling the need for oxygen sensor replacement. To reset the maintenance warning flag, remove the lower steering column cover. The sensor reset cable is located to the left of the speedometer cluster. Pull on the sensor reset cable lightly to reset. Reinstall the lower steering cover.**

An oxygen sensor is used on all 1980 models built for Calif. and on all 1981 and later models. The sensor protrudes into the exhaust stream and monitors the oxygen content of the exhaust gases. The difference between the oxygen content of the exhaust gases and that of the outside air generates a voltage signal to the ECM. The ECM monitors this voltage and, depending upon the value of the signal received, issues a command to adjust for a rich or a lean condition.

No attempt should ever be made to measure the voltage output of the sensor. The current drain of any conventional voltmeter would be such that it would permanently damage the sensor. No jumpers, test leads or any other electrical connections should ever be made to the sensor. Use these tools ONLY on the ECM side of the wiring harness connector AFTER disconnecting it from the sensor.

REMOVAL & INSTALLATION

◆ **See Figures 55, 56 and 57**

The oxygen sensor must be replaced every 30,000 miles (48,000 km). The sensor may be difficult to remove when the engine temperature is below 120°F (49°C). Excessive removal force may damage the threads in the exhaust manifold or pipe; follow the removal procedure carefully.

1. Locate the oxygen sensor. On the V8 engines, it is on the front of the left side exhaust manifold, just above the point where it connects to the exhaust pipe. On the V6 engines, it is on the inside of the exhaust pipe where it bends toward the back of the car.

➡**On the V6 engine you may find it necessary to raise the front of the car and remove the oxygen sensor from underneath.**

2. Trace the wires leading from the oxygen sensor back to the first connector and then disconnect them (the connector on the V6 engine is attached to a bracket mounted on the right, rear of the engine block, while the connector on the V8 engine is attached to a bracket mounted on the top of the left side exhaust manifold).

3. Spray a commercial heat riser solvent onto the sensor threads and allow it to soak in for at least five minutes.

4. Carefully unscrew and remove the sensor.

To install:

5. First coat the new sensor's threads with G.M. anti-seize compound no. 5613695 or the equivalent.

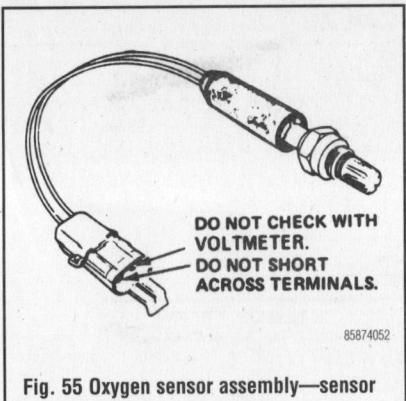

Fig. 55 Oxygen sensor assembly—sensor screws into exhaust manifold

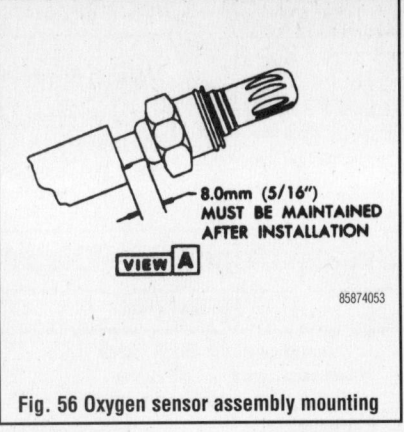

Fig. 56 Oxygen sensor assembly mounting

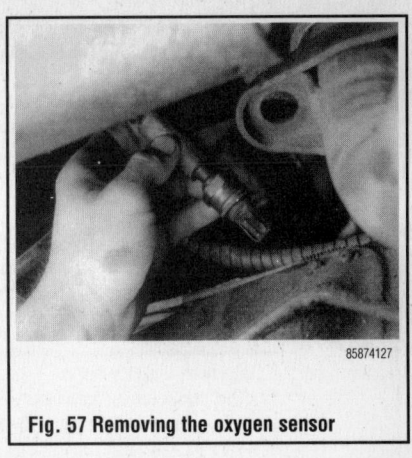

Fig. 57 Removing the oxygen sensor

➡The G.M. anti-seize compound is NOT a conventional anti-seize paste. The use of a regular paste may electrically insulate the sensor, rendering it useless. The threads MUST be coated with the proper electrically-conductive anti-seize compound.

6. Installation torque is 30 ft. lbs. (42 Nm.). Do not overtighten.
7. Reconnect the electrical connector. Be careful not to damage the electrical pigtail. Check the sensor boot for proper fit and installation.

DIESEL ENGINE EMISSION CONTROLS

Crankcase Ventilation

▶ **See Figures 58 and 59**

A Crankcase Depression Regulator Valve (CDRV) is used to regulate (meter) the flow of crankcase gases back into the engine to be burned. The CDRV is designed to limit vacuum in the crankcase as the gases are drawn from the valve covers through the CDRV and into the intake manifold (air crossover).

Fresh air enters the engine through the combination filter, check valve and oil fill cap. The fresh air mixes with blow-by gases and enters both valve covers. The gases pass through a filter installed on the valve covers and are drawn into connecting tubing.

Intake manifold vacuum acts against a spring loaded diaphragm to control the flow of crankcase gases. Higher intake vacuum levels pull the diaphragm closer to the top of the outlet tube. This reduces the amount of gases being drawn from the crankcase and decreases the vacuum level in the crankcase. As the intake vacuum decreases, the spring pushes the diaphragm away from the top of the outlet tube allowing more gases to flow to the intake manifold.

Do not allow any solvent to come in contact with the diaphragm of the Crankcase Depression Regulator Valve because the diaphragm will fail.

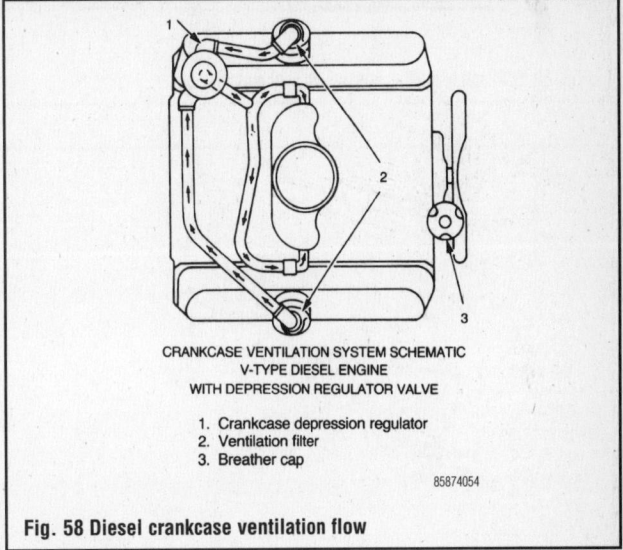

CRANKCASE VENTILATION SYSTEM SCHEMATIC
V-TYPE DIESEL ENGINE
WITH DEPRESSION REGULATOR VALVE

1. Crankcase depression regulator
2. Ventilation filter
3. Breather cap

Fig. 58 Diesel crankcase ventilation flow

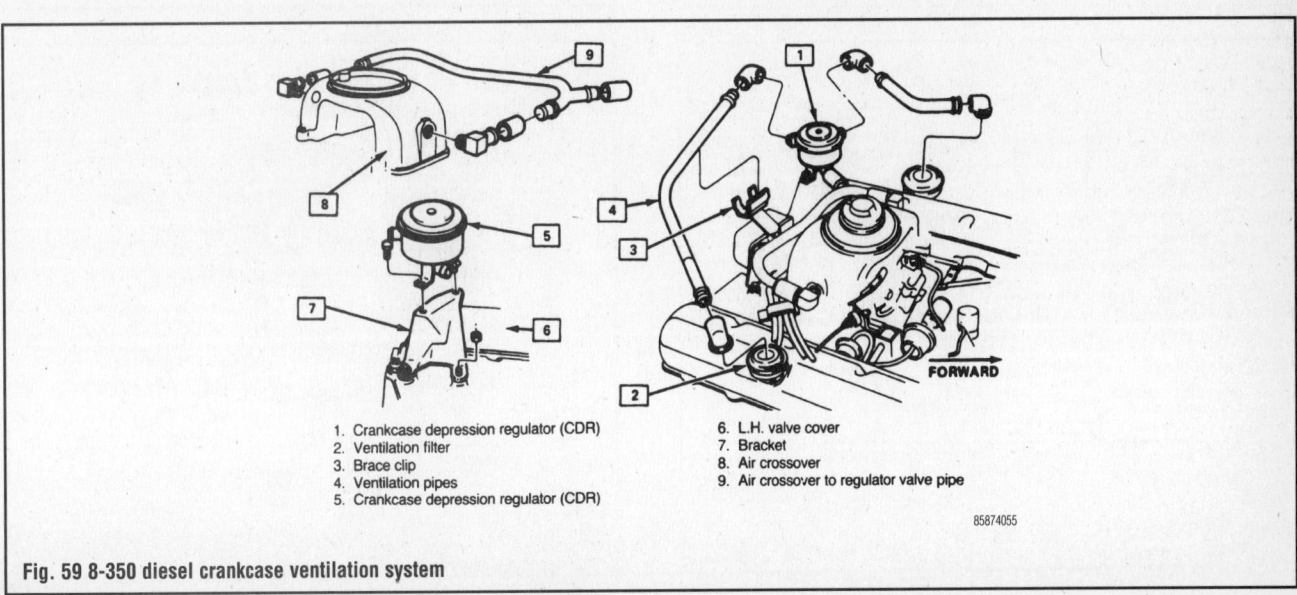

1. Crankcase depression regulator (CDR)
2. Ventilation filter
3. Brace clip
4. Ventilation pipes
5. Crankcase depression regulator (CDR)
6. L.H. valve cover
7. Bracket
8. Air crossover
9. Air crossover to regulator valve pipe

Fig. 59 8-350 diesel crankcase ventilation system

Exhaust Gas Recirculation (EGR) System

♦ **See Figures 60 thru 65**

To lower the formation of nitrogen oxides (NOx) in the exhaust, it is necessary to reduce combustion temperatures. This is done in the diesel, as in the gasoline engine, by introducing exhaust gases into the cylinders through the EGR valve.

FUNCTIONAL TESTS OF COMPONENTS

Vacuum Regulator Valve (VRV)

The Vacuum Regulator Valve is attached to the side of the injection pump and regulates vacuum in proportion to throttle angle. Vacuum from the vacuum pump is supplied to port A and vacuum at port B is reduced as the throttle is

EGR System diagnosis—Diesel Engine

Condition	Possible Causes	Correction
EGR valve will not open. Engine stalls on deceleration Engine runs rough on light throttle	Binding or stuck EGR valve. No vacuum to EGR valve. Control valve blocked or air flow restricted.	Replace EGR valve. Replace EGR valve. Check VRV, RVR, solenoid, T.C.C. Operation, Vacuum Pump and connecting hoses.
EGR valve will not close. (Heavy smoke on acceleration).	Binding or stuck EGR valve. Constant high vacuum to EGR valve.	Replace EGR valve. Check VRV, RVR, solenoid, and connecting hoses.
EGR valve opens partially.	Binding EGR valve. Low vacuum at EGR valve.	Replace EGR valve. Check VRV, RVR, solenoid, vacuum pump, and connecting hoses.

85874056

Fig. 60 EGR system diagnosis—diesel engine

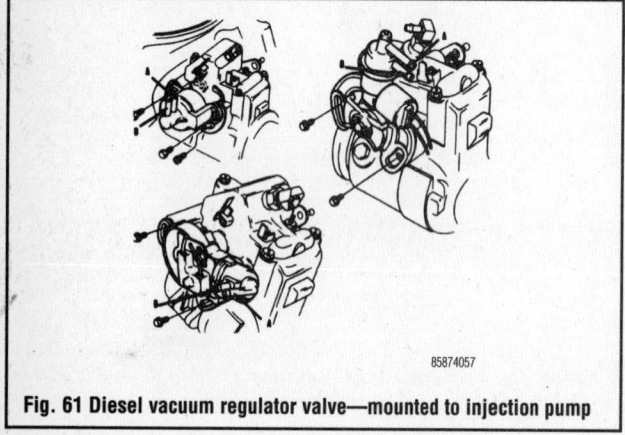

85874057

Fig. 61 Diesel vacuum regulator valve—mounted to injection pump

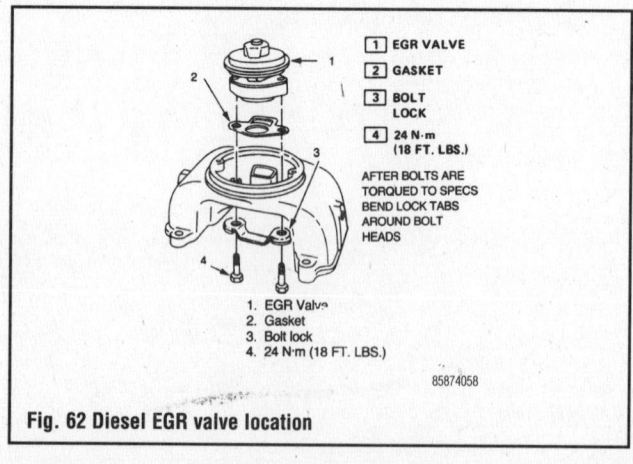

1 EGR VALVE
2 GASKET
3 BOLT LOCK
4 24 N·m (18 FT. LBS.)

AFTER BOLTS ARE TORQUED TO SPECS BEND LOCK TABS AROUND BOLT HEADS

1. EGR Valve
2. Gasket
3. Bolt lock
4. 24 N·m (18 FT. LBS.)

85874058

Fig. 62 Diesel EGR valve location

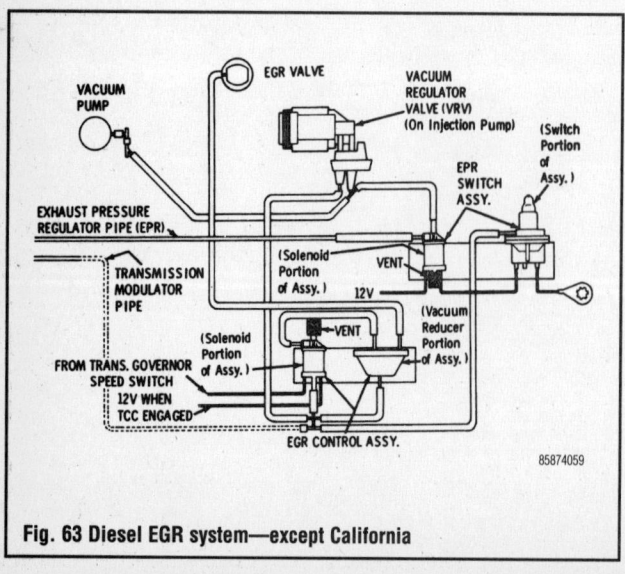

85874059

Fig. 63 Diesel EGR system—except California

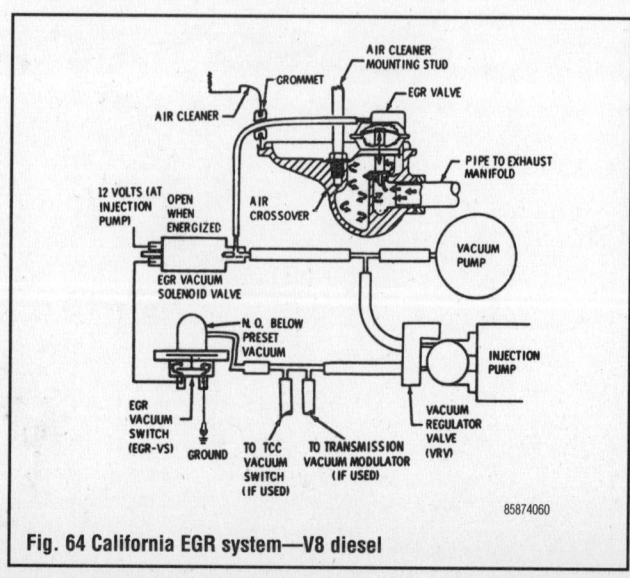

85874060

Fig. 64 California EGR system—V8 diesel

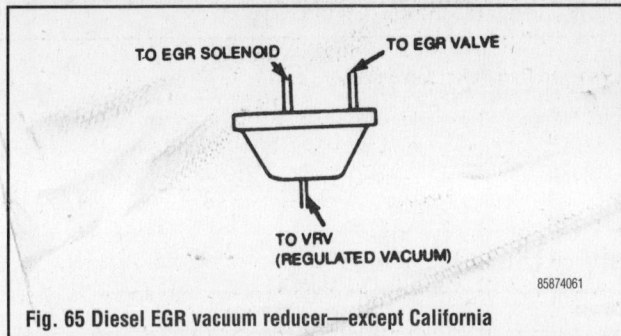

Fig. 65 Diesel EGR vacuum reducer—except California

opened. At closed throttle, the vacuum is 15 inches; at half throttle it is 6 inches; at wide open throttle there is no vacuum.

Exhaust Gas Recirculation (EGR) Valve

Apply vacuum to vacuum port. The valve should be fully open at 10.5 in. Hg and closed below 6 in. Hg.

Response Vacuum Reducer (RVR)

Connect a vacuum gage to the port marked **To EGR valve or T.C.C. solenoid**. Connect a hand operated vacuum pump to the VRV port. Draw a 50.66 kPa (15 inch) vacuum on the pump and the reading on the vacuum gauge should be lower than the vacuum pump reading as follows:
- 0.75 in. Hg—Except High Altitude
- 2.5 in. Hg—High Altitude

Torque Converter Clutch Operated Solenoid

When the torque converter clutch is engaged, an electrical signal energizes the solenoid allowing ports 1 and 3 to be interconnected. When the solenoid is not energized, port 1 is closed and ports 2 and 3 are interconnected.

SOLENOID ENERGIZED

- Ports 1 and 3 are connected.

SOLENOID DE-ENERGIZED

- Ports 2 and 3 are connected.

Engine Temperature Sensor (ETS)

OPERATION

◆ See Figure 66

The engine temperature sensor has two terminals. Twelve volts are applied to one terminal and the wire from the other terminal leads to the fast idle solenoid and Housing Pressure Cold Advance solenoid that is part of the injection pump.

The switch contacts are closed below 125°F (52°C). At the calibration point, the contacts are open, which turns off the solenoids.

Above Calibration

- Open circuit.

Below Calibration

- Closed circuit.

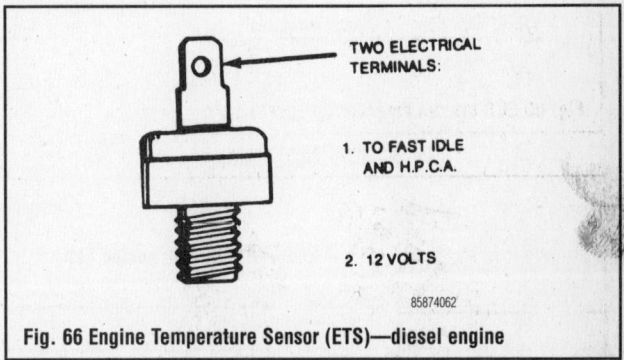

Fig. 66 Engine Temperature Sensor (ETS)—diesel engine

VACUUM DIAGRAMS

Following are vacuum diagrams for most of the engine and emissions package combinations covered by this manual. Because vacuum circuits will vary based on various engine and vehicle options, always refer first to the vehicle emission control information label, if present. Should the label be missing, or should vehicle be equipped with a different engine from the vehicle's original equipment, refer to the diagrams below for the same or similar configuration.

If you wish to obtain a replacement emissions label, most manufacturers make the labels available for purchase. The labels can usually be ordered from a local dealer.

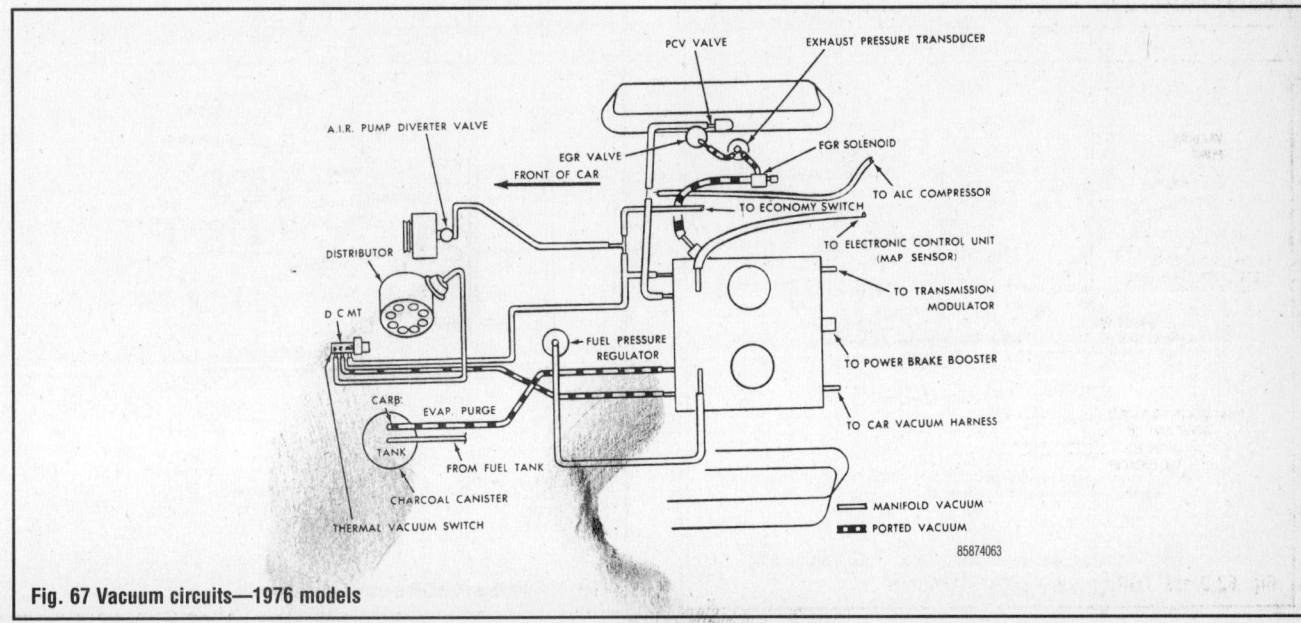

Fig. 67 Vacuum circuits—1976 models

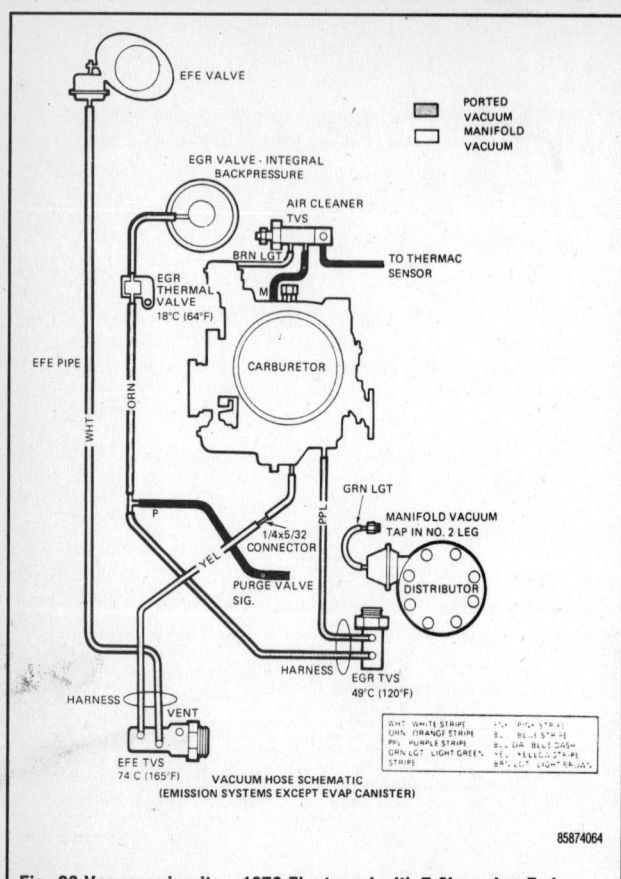

Fig. 68 Vacuum circuits—1979 Fleetwood with 7.0L engine Fed. (Carb.)

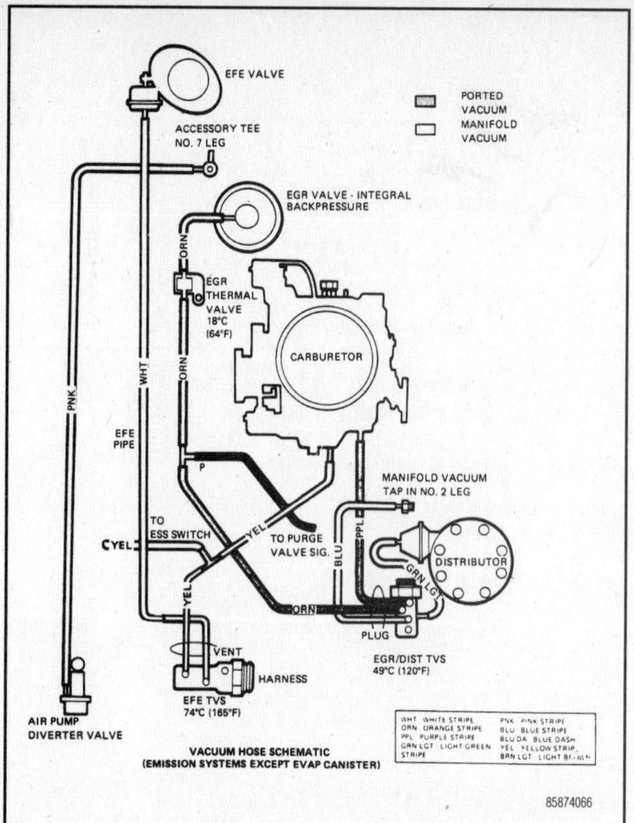

Fig. 70 Vacuum circuits—1979 Fleetwood with 7.0L engine Calif. (Carb.)

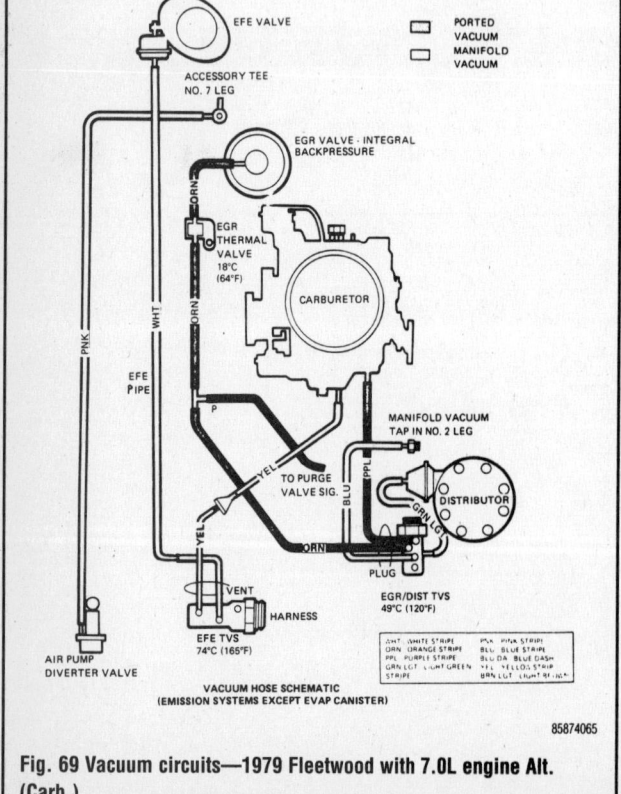

Fig. 69 Vacuum circuits—1979 Fleetwood with 7.0L engine Alt. (Carb.)

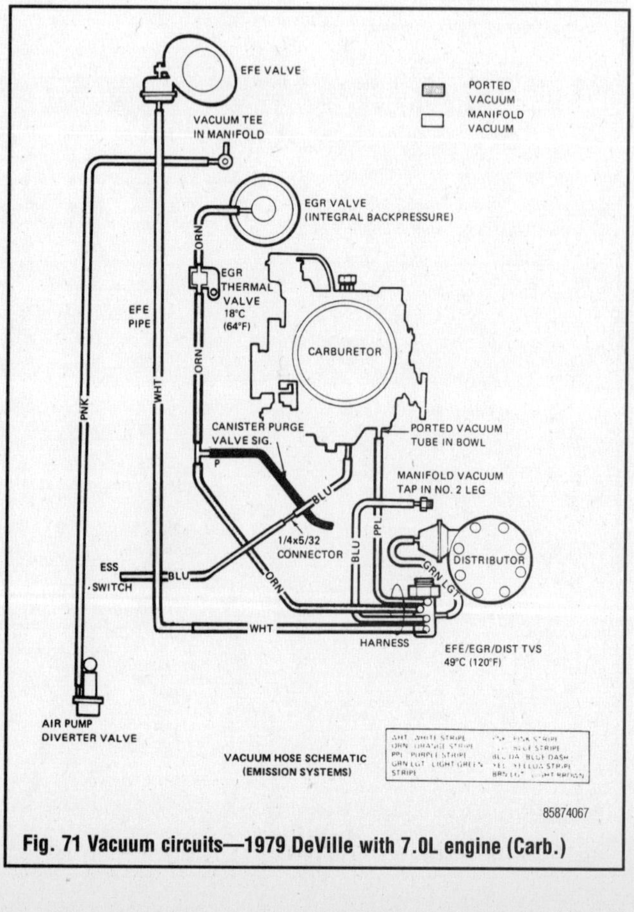

Fig. 71 Vacuum circuits—1979 DeVille with 7.0L engine (Carb.)

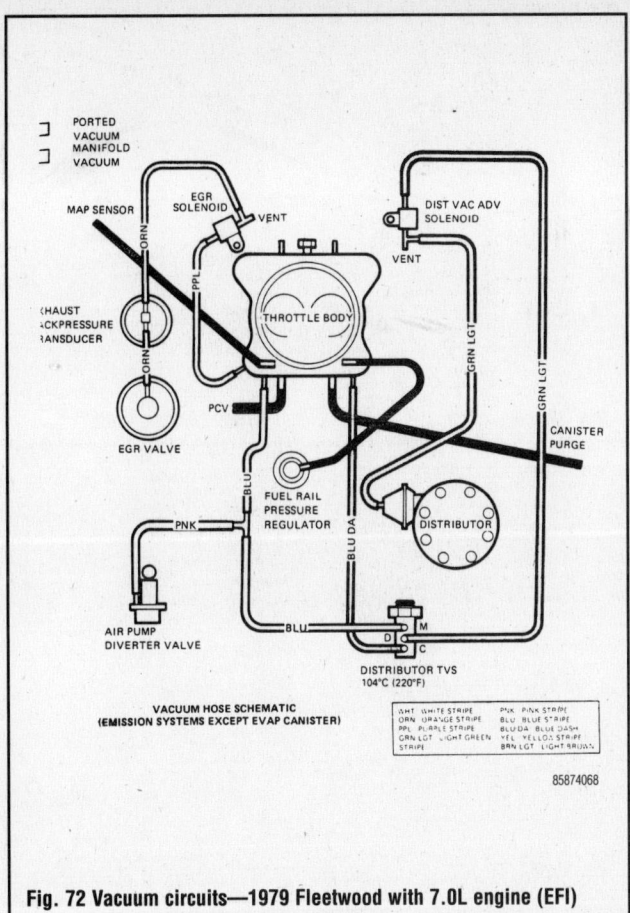

Fig. 72 Vacuum circuits—1979 Fleetwood with 7.0L engine (EFI)

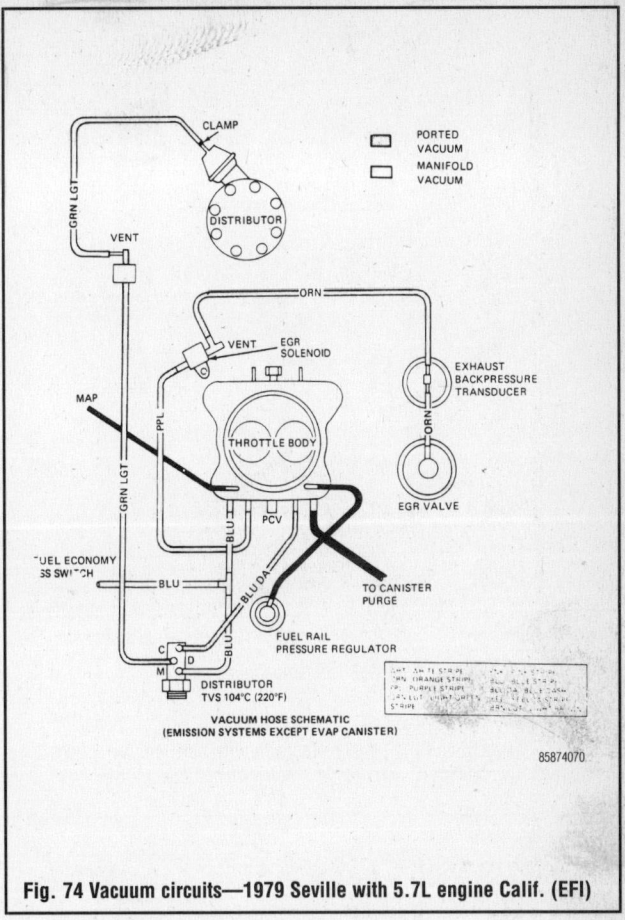

Fig. 74 Vacuum circuits—1979 Seville with 5.7L engine Calif. (EFI)

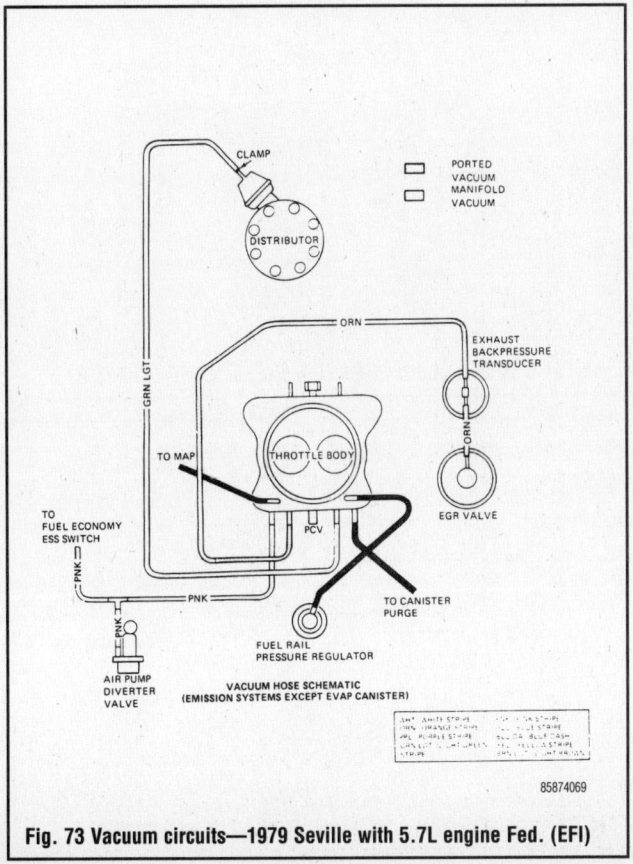

Fig. 73 Vacuum circuits—1979 Seville with 5.7L engine Fed. (EFI)

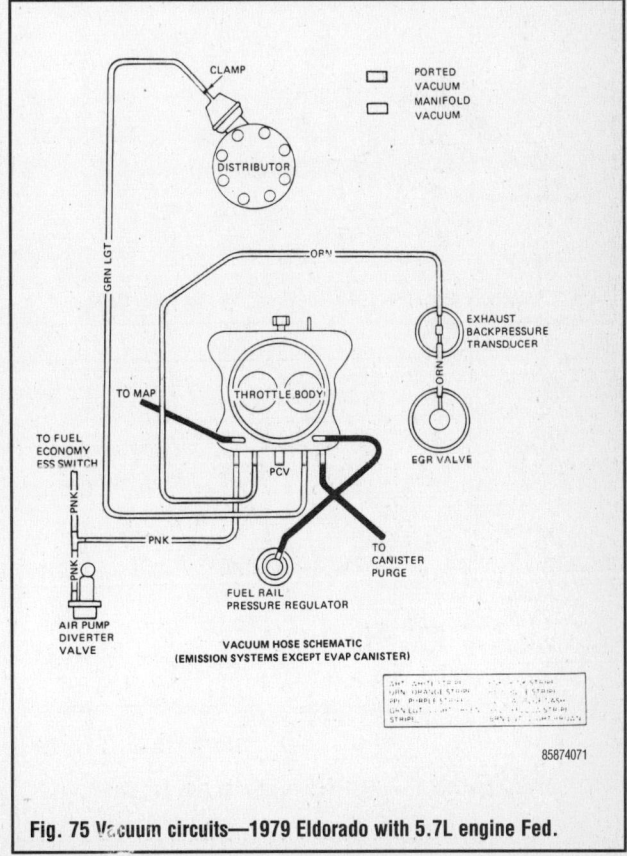

Fig. 75 Vacuum circuits—1979 Eldorado with 5.7L engine Fed.

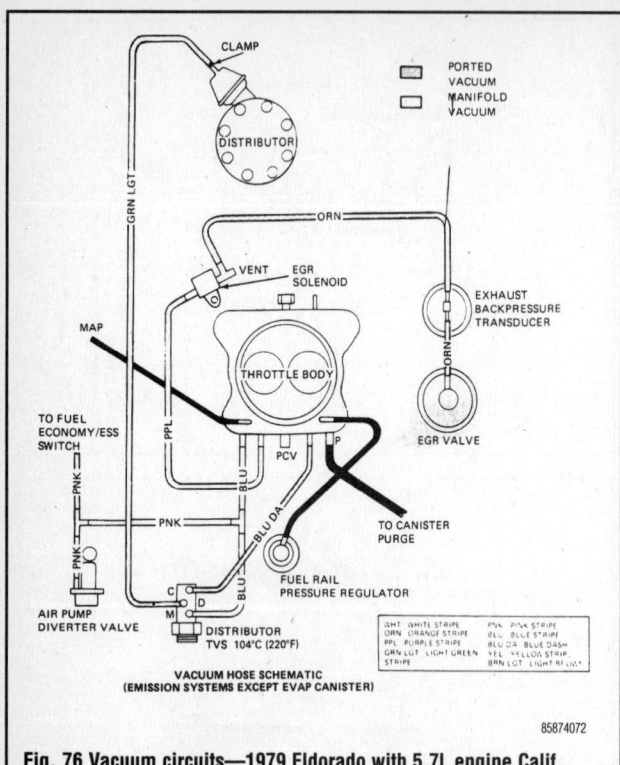

Fig. 76 Vacuum circuits—1979 Eldorado with 5.7L engine Calif.

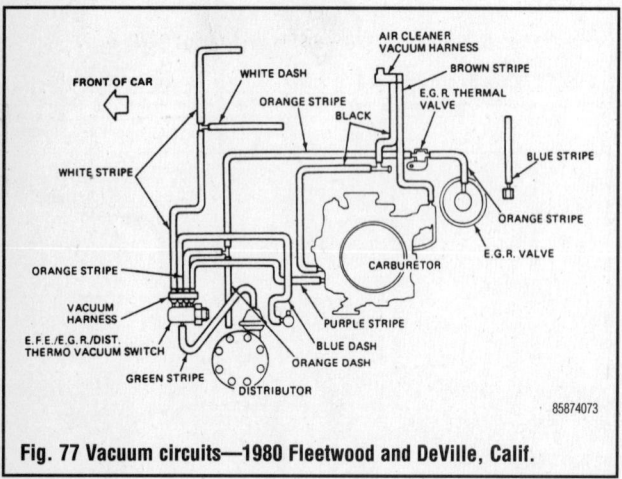

Fig. 77 Vacuum circuits—1980 Fleetwood and DeVille, Calif.

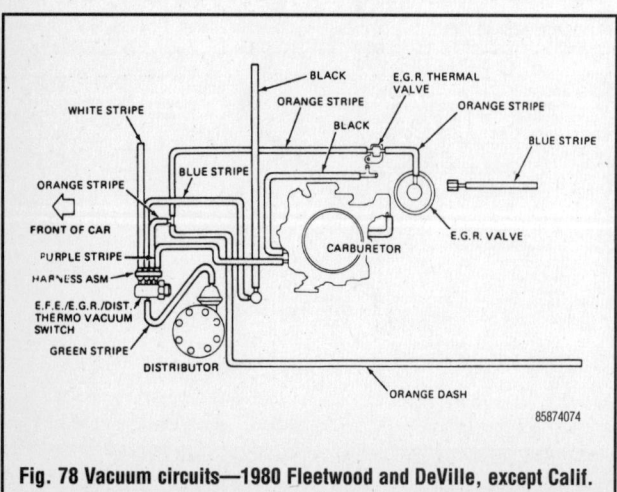

Fig. 78 Vacuum circuits—1980 Fleetwood and DeVille, except Calif.

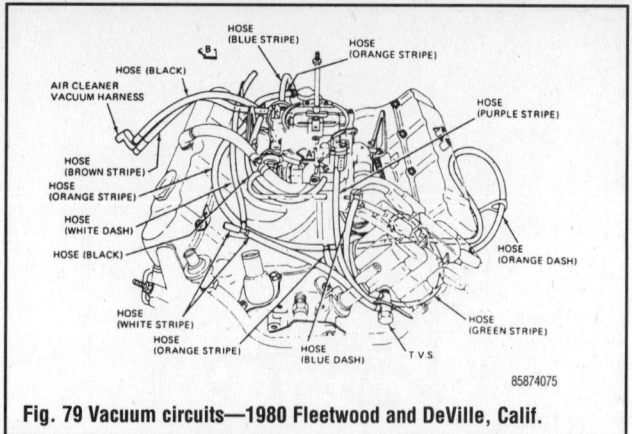

Fig. 79 Vacuum circuits—1980 Fleetwood and DeVille, Calif.

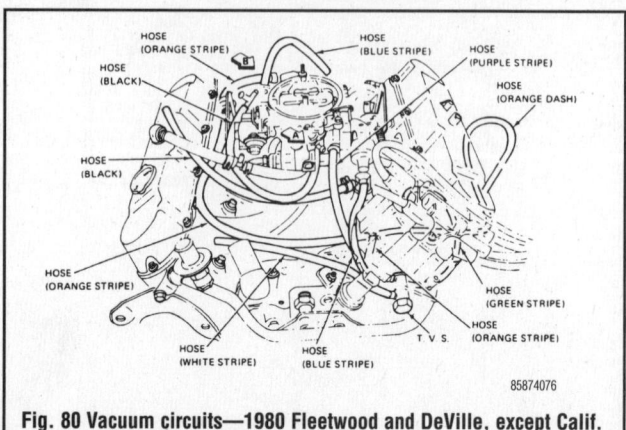

Fig. 80 Vacuum circuits—1980 Fleetwood and DeVille, except Calif.

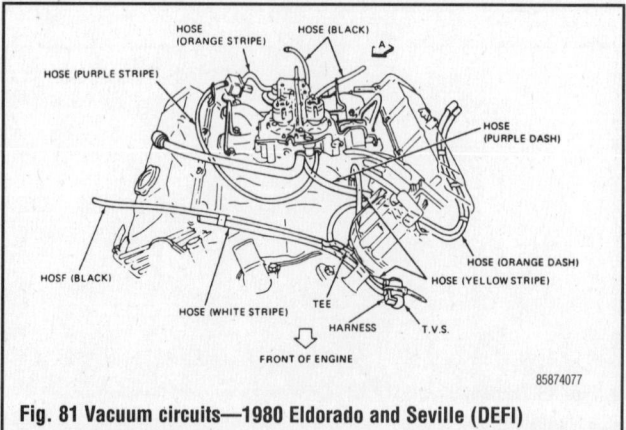

Fig. 81 Vacuum circuits—1980 Eldorado and Seville (DEFI)

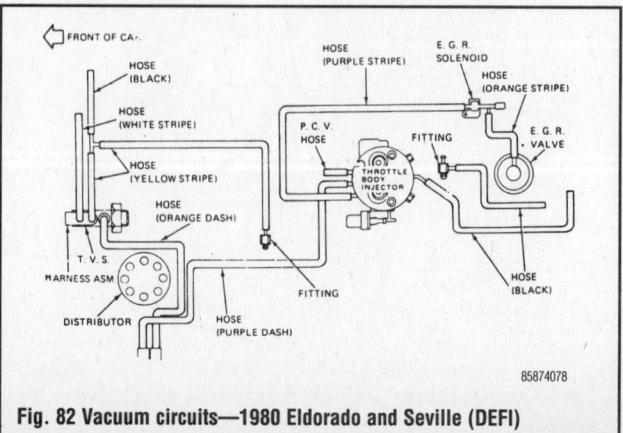

Fig. 82 Vacuum circuits—1980 Eldorado and Seville (DEFI)

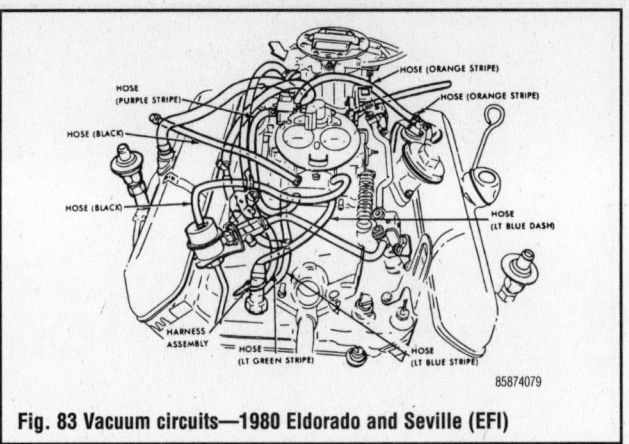

Fig. 83 Vacuum circuits—1980 Eldorado and Seville (EFI)

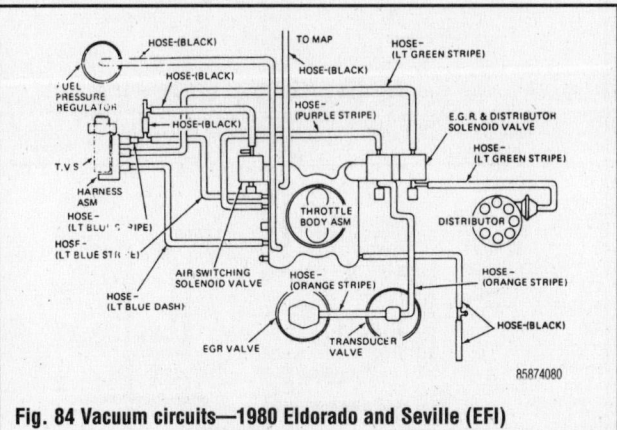

Fig. 84 Vacuum circuits—1980 Eldorado and Seville (EFI)

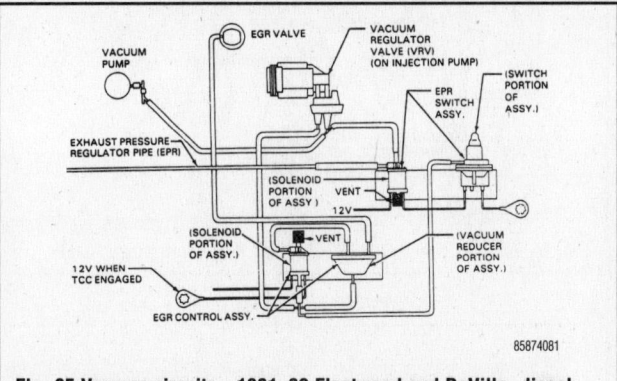

Fig. 85 Vacuum circuits—1981–82 Fleetwood and DeVille, diesel except Calif.

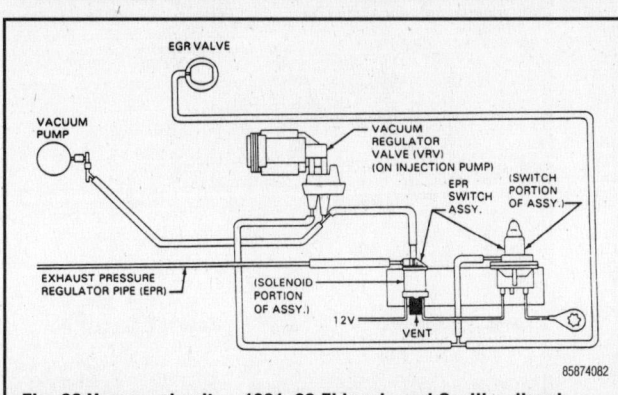

Fig. 86 Vacuum circuits—1981–82 Eldorado and Seville, diesel except Calif.

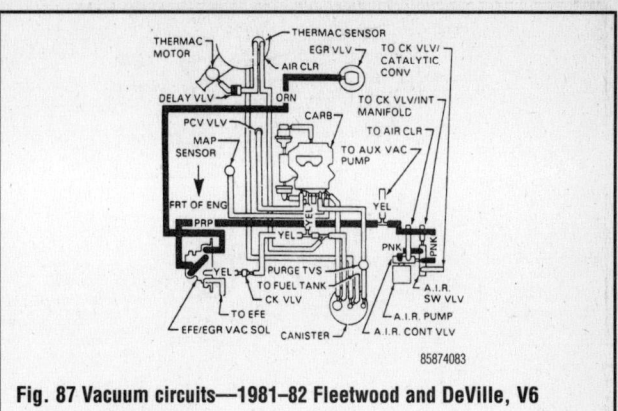

Fig. 87 Vacuum circuits—1981–82 Fleetwood and DeVille, V6 engine except Calif.

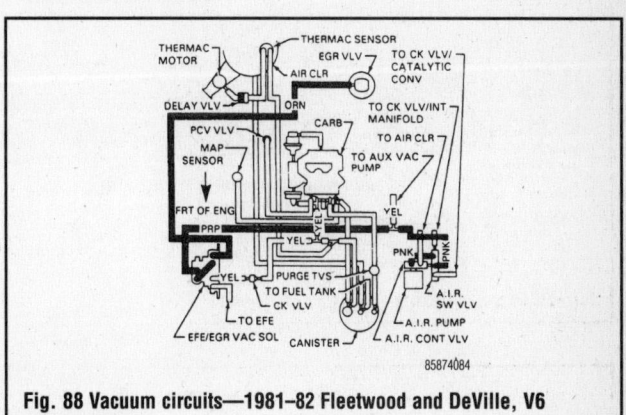

Fig. 88 Vacuum circuits—1981–82 Fleetwood and DeVille, V6 engine Calif.

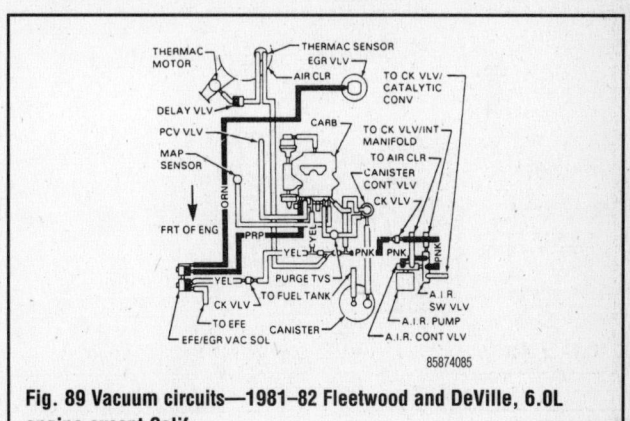

Fig. 89 Vacuum circuits—1981–82 Fleetwood and DeVille, 6.0L engine except Calif.

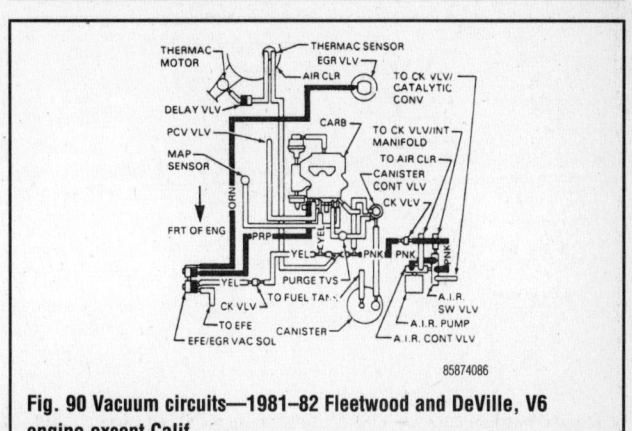

Fig. 90 Vacuum circuits—1981–82 Fleetwood and DeVille, V6 engine except Calif.

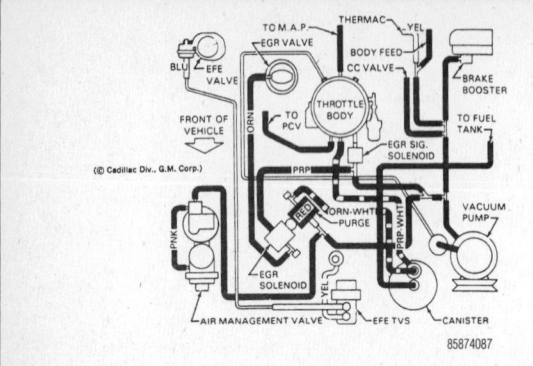

Fig. 91 Vacuum circuits—1981–82 Eldorado and Seville, V6 engine Calif.

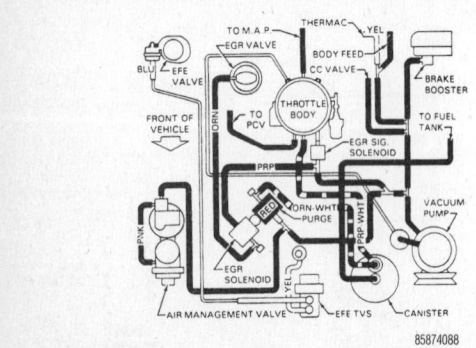

Fig. 92 Vacuum circuits—1981–82 Fleetwood and DeVille, 6.0L engine Calif.

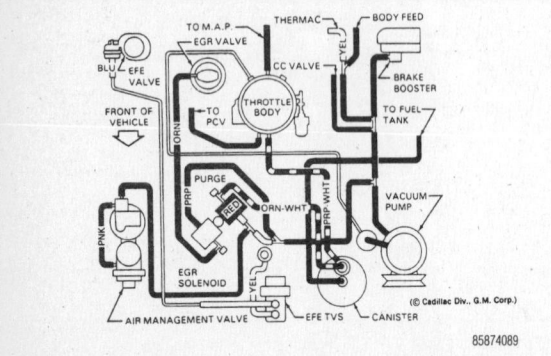

Fig. 93 Vacuum circuits—1981–82 Eldorado and Seville, 6.0L engine except Calif.

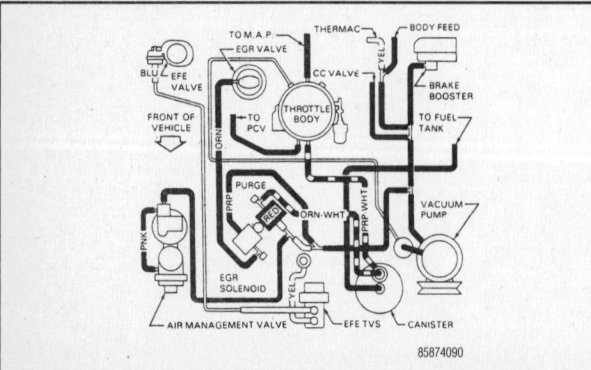

Fig. 94 Vacuum circuits—1981–82 Eldorado and Seville, 6.0L engine Calif.

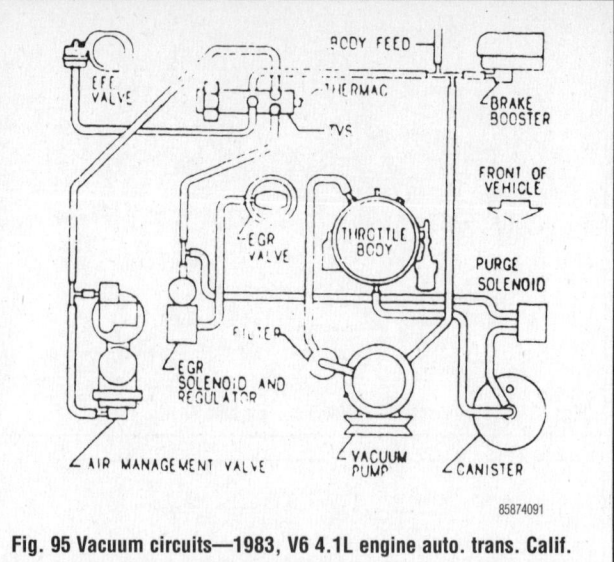

Fig. 95 Vacuum circuits—1983, V6 4.1L engine auto. trans. Calif.

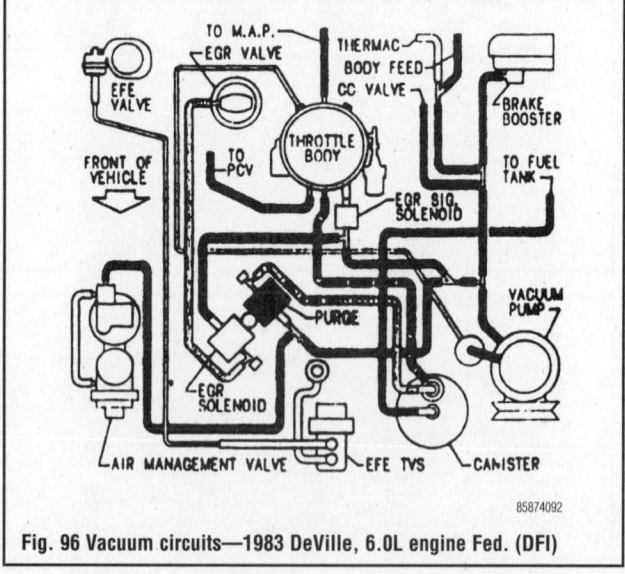

Fig. 96 Vacuum circuits—1983 DeVille, 6.0L engine Fed. (DFI)

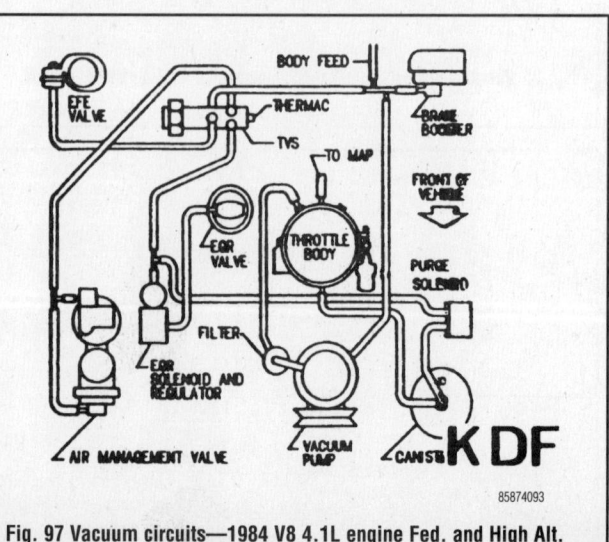

Fig. 97 Vacuum circuits—1984 V8 4.1L engine Fed. and High Alt. (DFI)

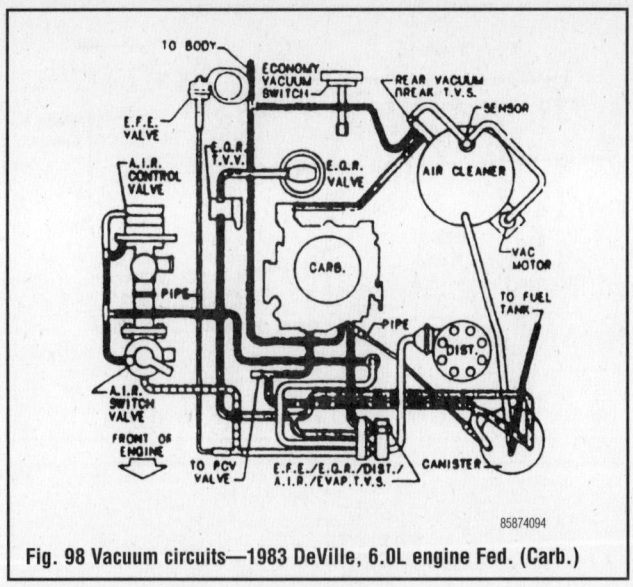

Fig. 98 Vacuum circuits—1983 DeVille, 6.0L engine Fed. (Carb.)

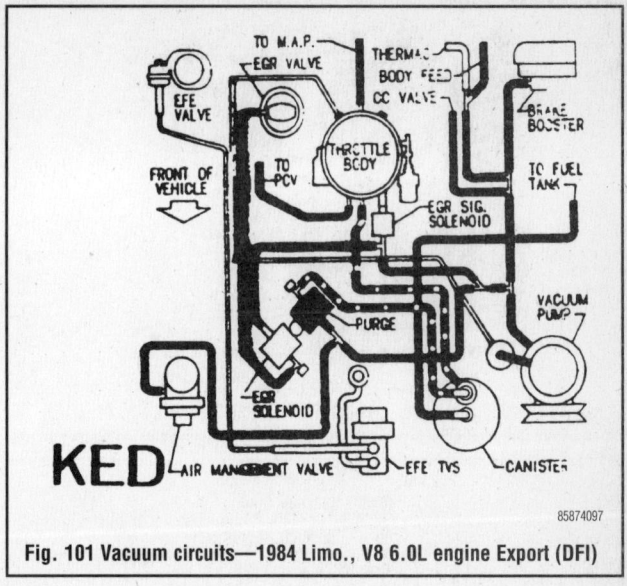

Fig. 101 Vacuum circuits—1984 Limo., V8 6.0L engine Export (DFI)

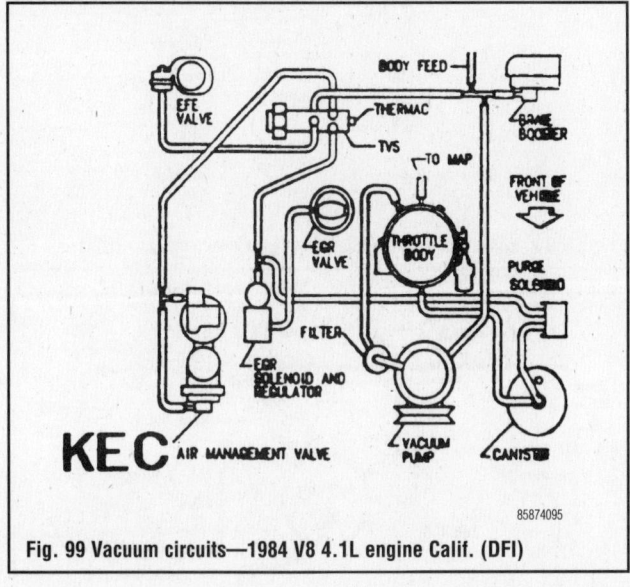

Fig. 99 Vacuum circuits—1984 V8 4.1L engine Calif. (DFI)

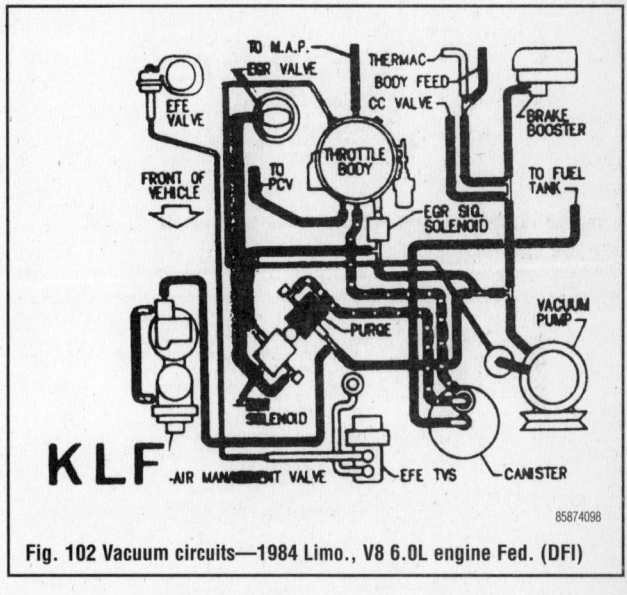

Fig. 102 Vacuum circuits—1984 Limo., V8 6.0L engine Fed. (DFI)

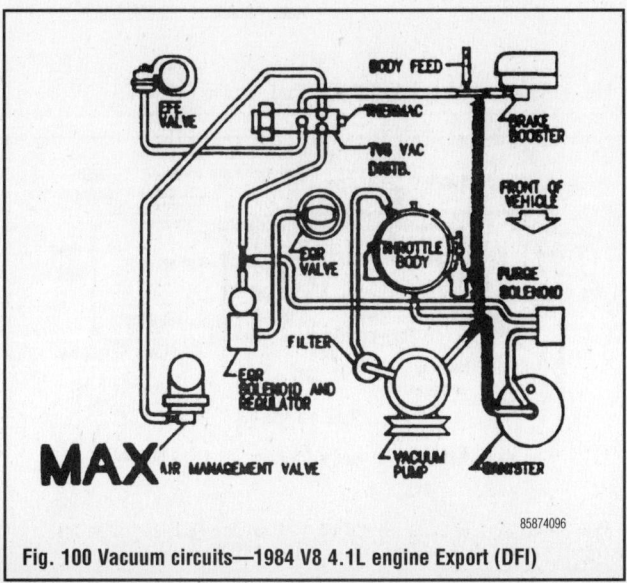

Fig. 100 Vacuum circuits—1984 V8 4.1L engine Export (DFI)

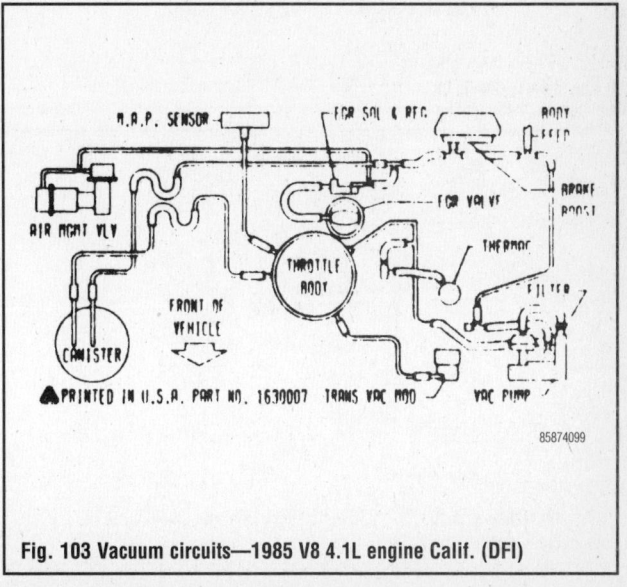

Fig. 103 Vacuum circuits—1985 V8 4.1L engine Calif. (DFI)

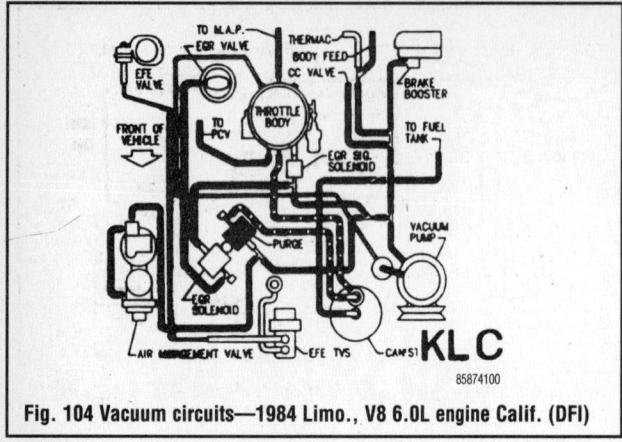

Fig. 104 Vacuum circuits—1984 Limo., V8 6.0L engine Calif. (DFI)

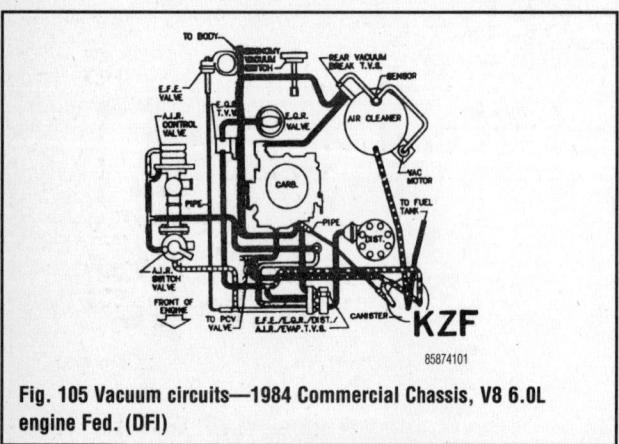

Fig. 105 Vacuum circuits—1984 Commercial Chassis, V8 6.0L engine Fed. (DFI)

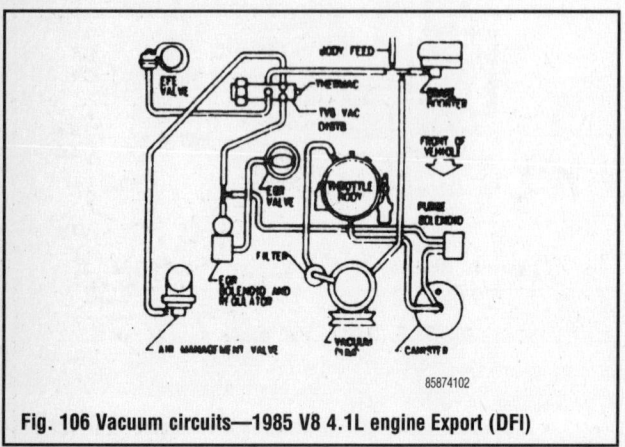

Fig. 106 Vacuum circuits—1985 V8 4.1L engine Export (DFI)

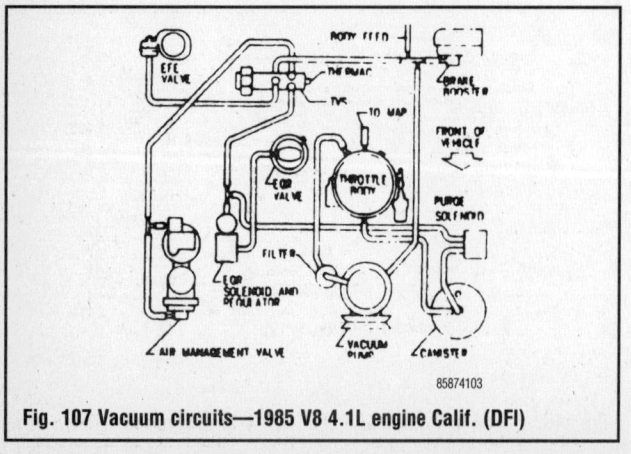

Fig. 107 Vacuum circuits—1985 V8 4.1L engine Calif. (DFI)

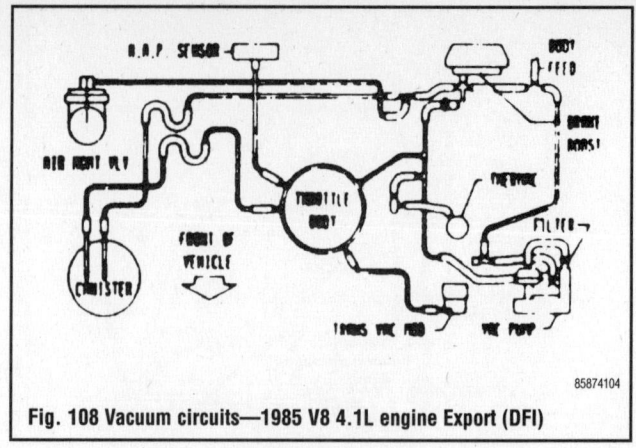

Fig. 108 Vacuum circuits—1985 V8 4.1L engine Export (DFI)

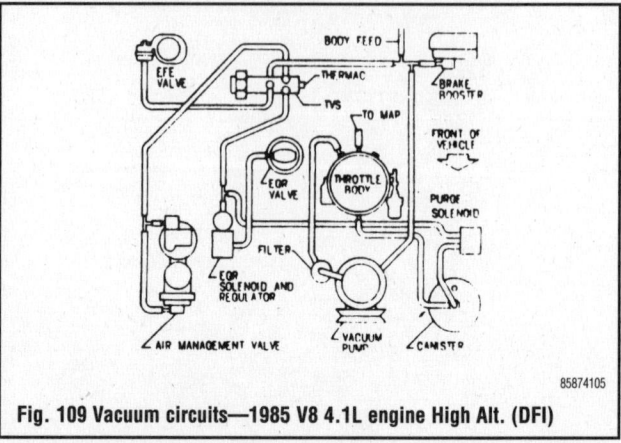

Fig. 109 Vacuum circuits—1985 V8 4.1L engine High Alt. (DFI)

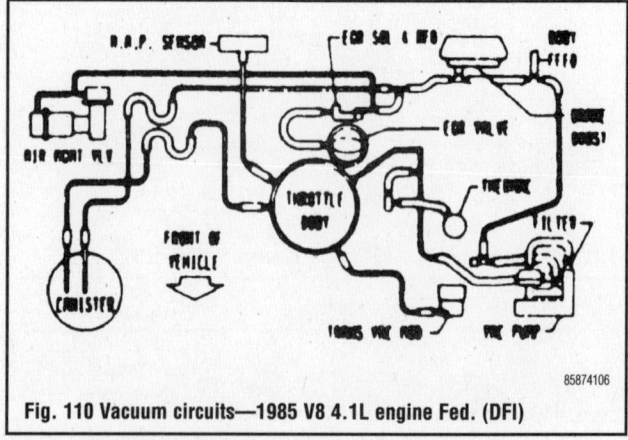

Fig. 110 Vacuum circuits—1985 V8 4.1L engine Fed. (DFI)

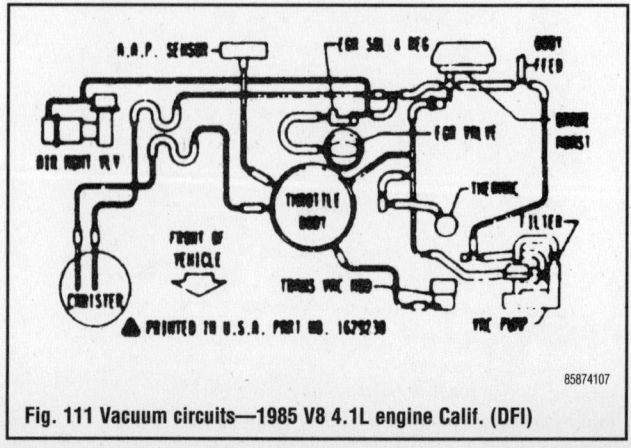

Fig. 111 Vacuum circuits—1985 V8 4.1L engine Calif. (DFI)

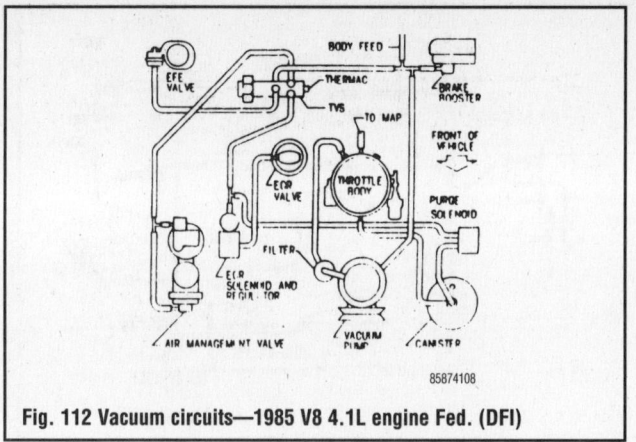

Fig. 112 Vacuum circuits—1985 V8 4.1L engine Fed. (DFI)

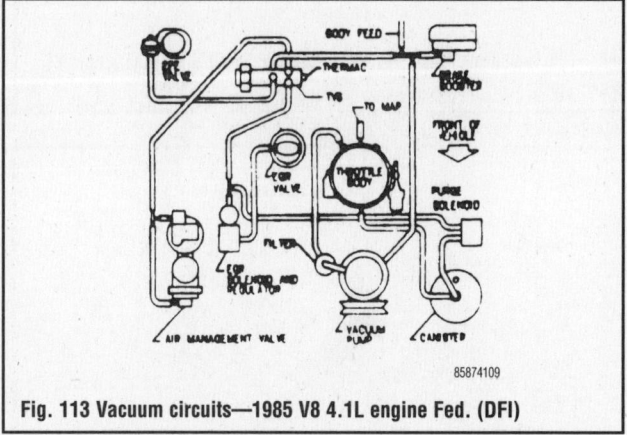

Fig. 113 Vacuum circuits—1985 V8 4.1L engine Fed. (DFI)

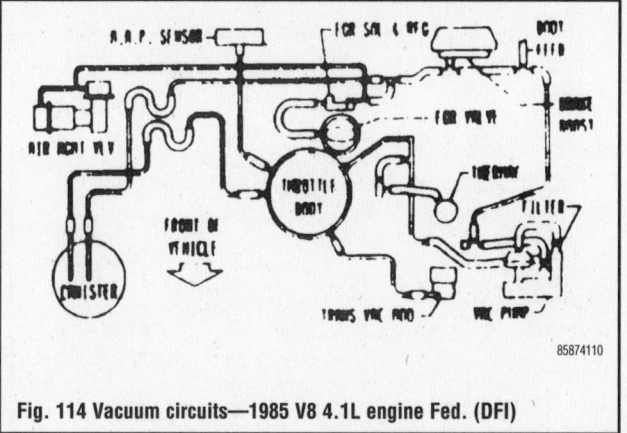

Fig. 114 Vacuum circuits—1985 V8 4.1L engine Fed. (DFI)

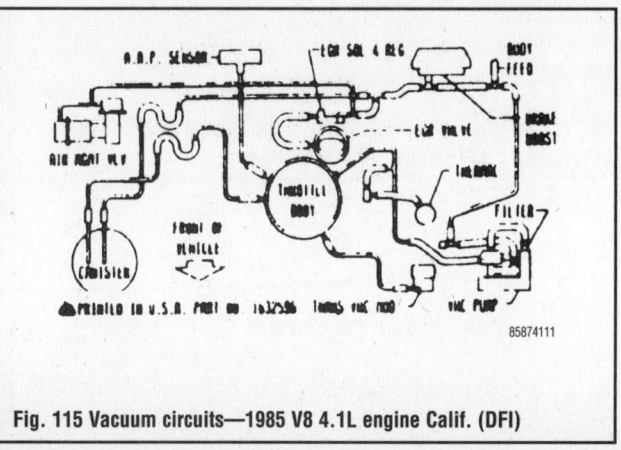

Fig. 115 Vacuum circuits—1985 V8 4.1L engine Calif. (DFI)

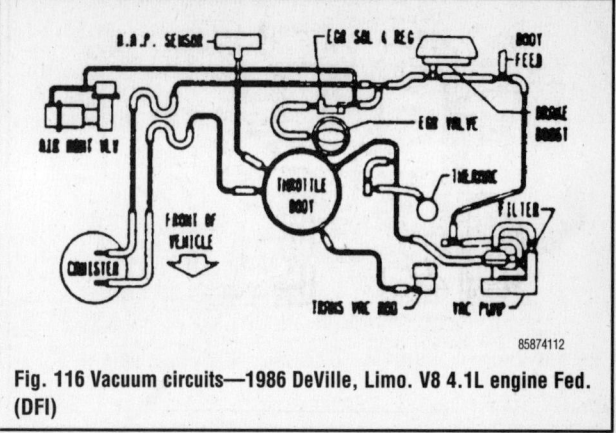

Fig. 116 Vacuum circuits—1986 DeVille, Limo. V8 4.1L engine Fed. (DFI)

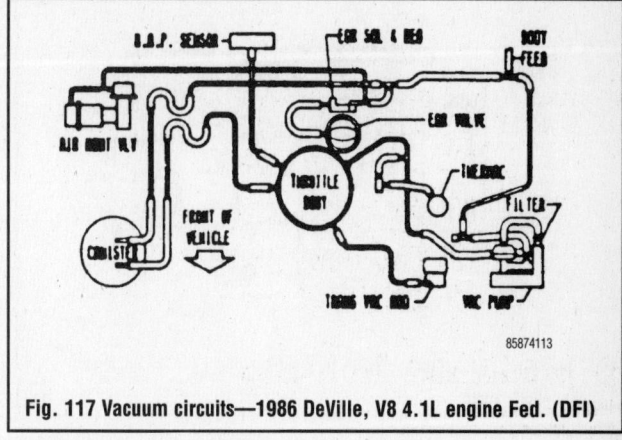

Fig. 117 Vacuum circuits—1986 DeVille, V8 4.1L engine Fed. (DFI)

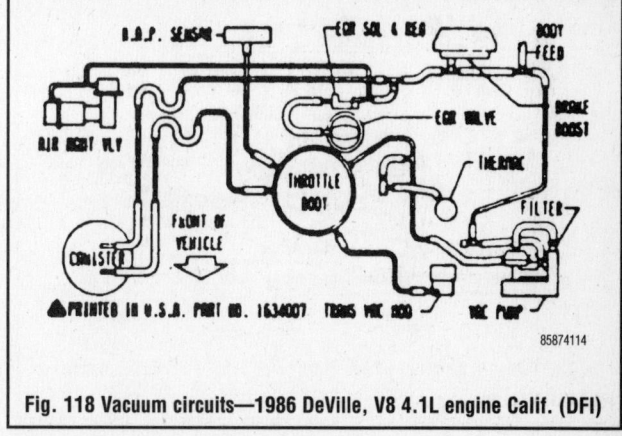

Fig. 118 Vacuum circuits—1986 DeVille, V8 4.1L engine Calif. (DFI)

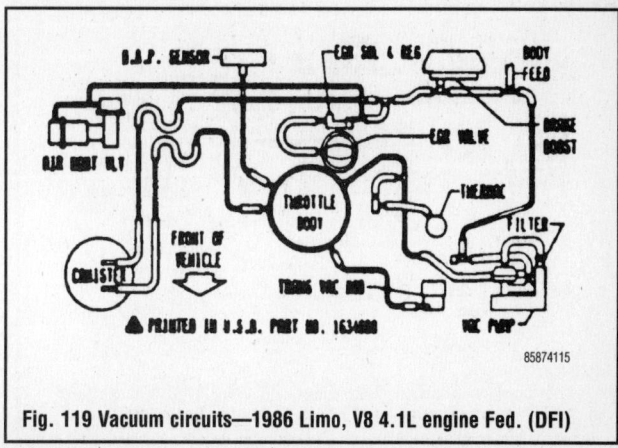

Fig. 119 Vacuum circuits—1986 Limo, V8 4.1L engine Fed. (DFI)

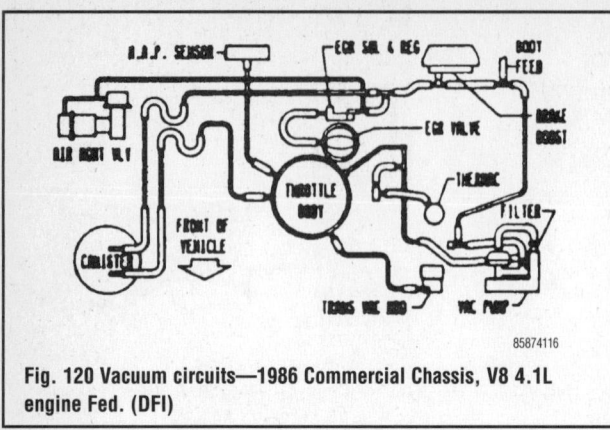

Fig. 120 Vacuum circuits—1986 Commercial Chassis, V8 4.1L engine Fed. (DFI)

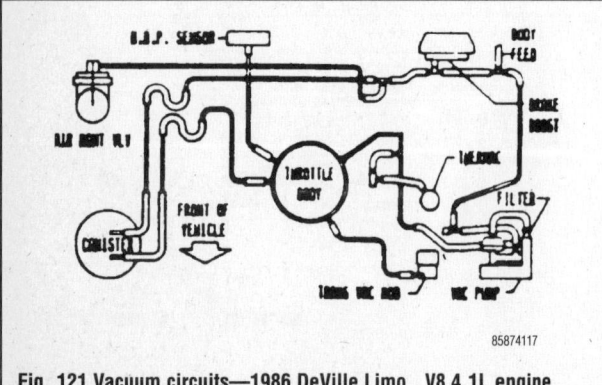

Fig. 121 Vacuum circuits—1986 DeVille Limo., V8 4.1L engine Export (DFI)

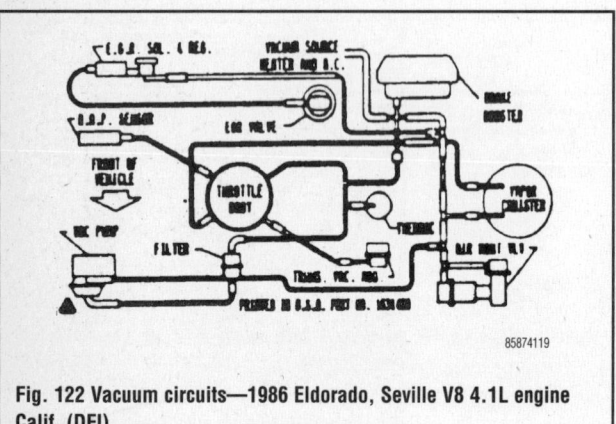

Fig. 122 Vacuum circuits—1986 Eldorado, Seville V8 4.1L engine Calif. (DFI)

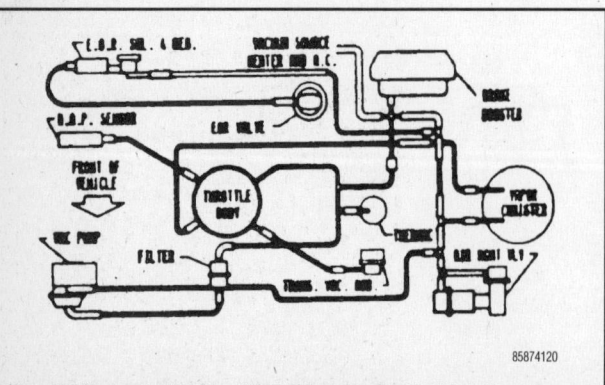

Fig. 123 Vacuum circuits—1986 Eldorado, Seville V8 4.1L engine Fed. (DFI)

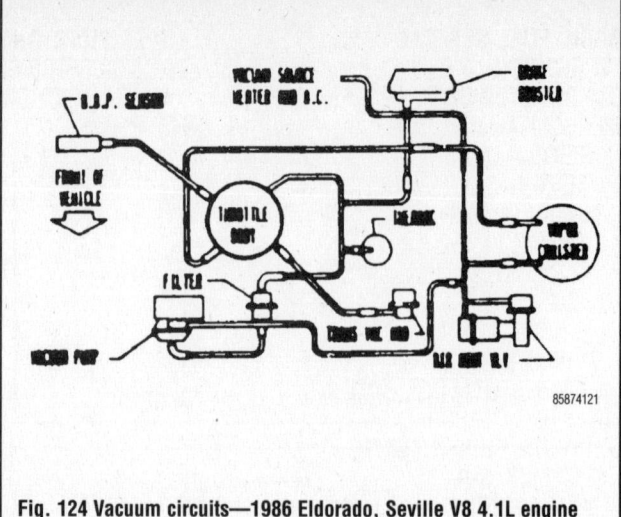

Fig. 124 Vacuum circuits—1986 Eldorado, Seville V8 4.1L engine Fed. (DFI)

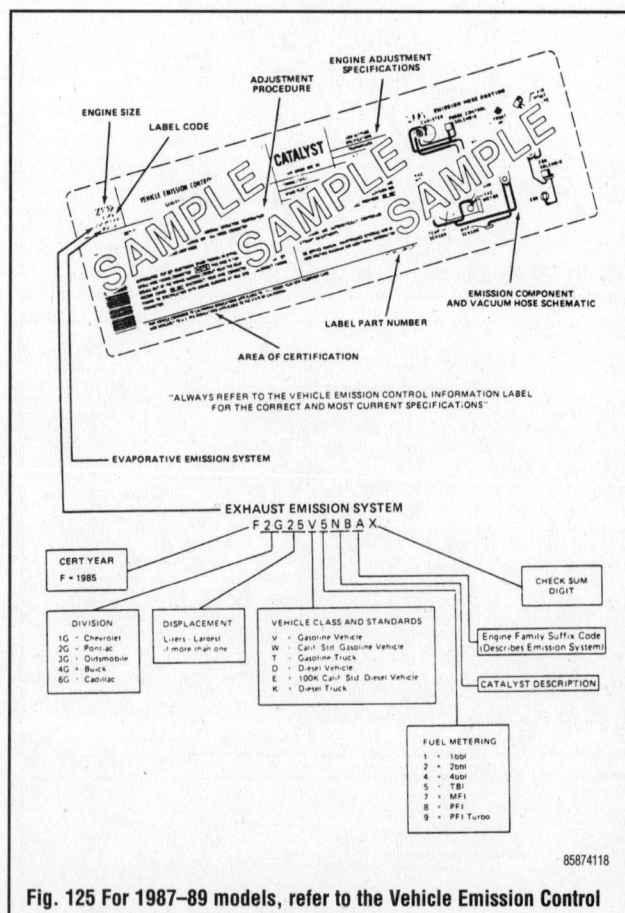

Fig. 125 For 1987–89 models, refer to the Vehicle Emission Control Information Label located under your hood

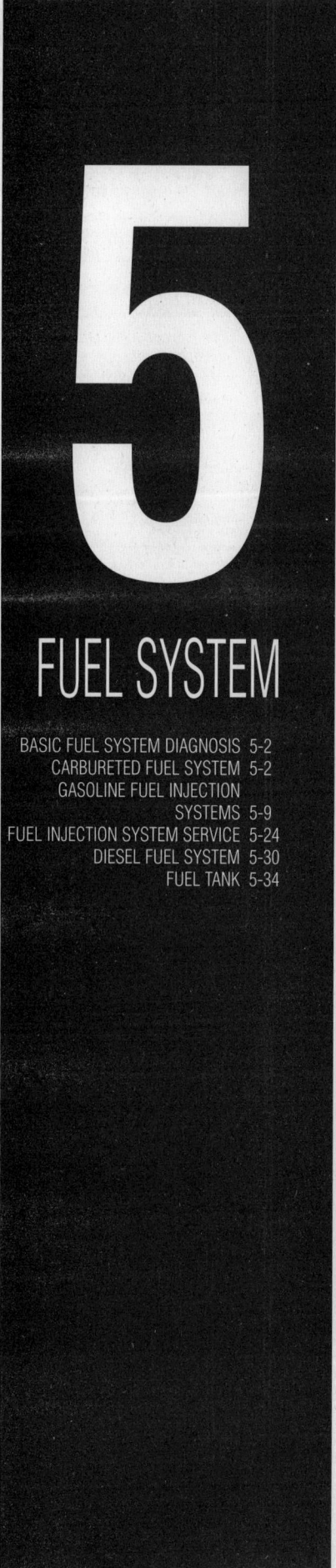

5
FUEL SYSTEM

BASIC FUEL SYSTEM DIAGNOSIS

When there is a problem starting or driving a vehicle, two of the most important checks involve the ignition and the fuel systems. The questions most mechanics attempt to answer first, "is there spark?" and "is there fuel?" will often lead to solving most basic problems. For ignition system diagnosis and testing, please refer to the information on engine electrical components and ignition systems found earlier in this manual. If the ignition system checks out (there is spark), then you must determine if the fuel system is operating properly (is there fuel?).

CARBURETED FUEL SYSTEM

Mechanical Fuel Pump

Fuel pumps used on all carbureted engines are of the single-action mechanical type. The fuel pump rocker arm is held in constant engagement with the eccentric on the camshaft by the rocker arm spring. As the end of the rocker arm which is in contact with the eccentric moves upward, the fuel link pulls the fuel diaphragm downward. The action of the diaphragm enlarges the fuel chamber, drawing fuel from the tank. Fuel flows to the carburetor only when the pressure in the outlet line is less than the pressure maintained by the diaphragm spring. The fuel pumps on all engines are not serviceable and must be replaced if defective.

REMOVAL & INSTALLATION

▶ **See Figure 1**

1. Locate the fuel pump on the side of the cylinder block and disconnect the fuel lines.
2. Remove the two pump mounting bolts.
3. Remove the pump and the gasket.

To install:

4. Use a new gasket when installing the pump.
5. Install the fuel lines, start the engine and check for leaks.

TESTING

The fuel line from the tank to the pump is the suction side of the system, while the line from the pump to the engine is the pressure side of the system. A leak on the pressure side, therefore, would be made apparently by dripping fuel, but a leak on the suction side would not be apparent except for the reduction of the volume of fuel on the pressure side.

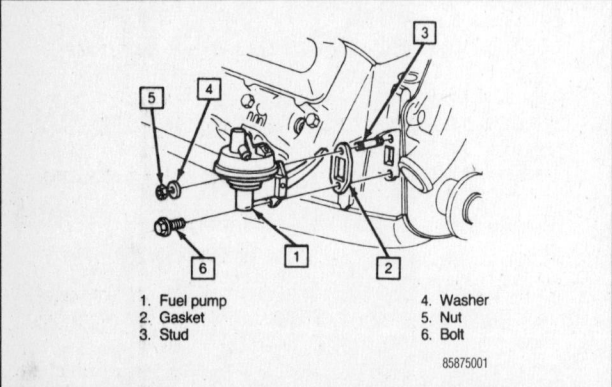

1. Fuel pump
2. Gasket
3. Stud
4. Washer
5. Nut
6. Bolt

85875001

Fig. 1 Common mechanical fuel pump—8-307 shown others similar

1. Tighten any loose line connections and look for bends or kinks.
2. Disconnect the fuel pipe at the carburetor. Disconnect the distributor-to-coil primary wire so that the engine can be cranked without firing. Place a container at the end of the pipe and crank the engine a few revolutions. If little or no gasoline flows from the open end of the pipe, the fuel pipe is clogged or the pump is defective.
3. If fuel flows from the pump in good volume from the pipe at the carburetor, check fuel pressure to be certain that the pump is operating within specified limits as follows:
   a. Attach a fuel pump pressure test gauge to the disconnected end of the pipe.

b. Run the engine at approximately 450–1000 rpm on the gasoline still remaining in the carburetor bowl. Note the reading on the pressure gauge.

c. If the pump is operating properly the pressure will be within the specifications listed in the Tune-Up Specifications chart found in Section 2. The pressure will remain constant between speeds of 450–1000 rpm. If the pressure is too low or too high at different speeds, the pump should be replaced.

➡**There are no adjustments that can be made on these fuel pumps.**

Carburetor

OPERATION

When the engine in your Cadillac is running, air/fuel mixture from the carburetor is being drawn into the engine by a partial vacuum which is created by the downward movement of the pistons on the intake stroke of the four-stroke cycle of the engine. The amount of air/fuel mixture that enters the engine is controlled by throttle plates in the bottom of the carburetor. When the engine is not running, the throttle plates are closed, completely blocking off the bottom of the carburetor from the inside of the engine. The throttle plates are connected, through the throttle linkage, to the gas pedal. What you are actually doing when you depress the gas pedal is opening up the throttle plates in the carburetor to admit more of the fuel/air mixture to the engine. The further you open the throttle plates in the carburetor, the higher the engine speed becomes.

As previously stated, when the engine is not running, the throttle plates in the carburetor remain closed. When the engine is idling, it is necessary to open the throttle plates slightly. To prevent having to keep your foot on the gas pedal when the engine is idling, an idle speed adjusting screw was added to the carburetor. This screw has the same effect as keeping your foot slightly depressed on the gas pedal. The idle speed adjusting screw contacts a lever, or, on most late model cars, a solenoid on the outside of the carburetor. When the screw is turned in, it opens the throttle plate or plates on the carburetor, raising the idle speed of the engine. This screw is called the curb idle adjusting screw and the procedures in this section will tell you how to adjust it.

Since it is difficult for the engine to draw the air/fuel mixture from the carburetor with the small amount of throttle plate opening that is present when the engine is idling, an idle mixture passage is provided in the carburetor. This passage delivers air/fuel mixture to the engine from a hole which is located in the bottom of the carburetor below the throttle plates. This idle mixture passage contains an adjusting screw which restricts the amount of air/fuel mixture that enters the engine at idle. The idle mixture screws are capped on late model cars due to emission control regulations.

MODEL IDENTIFICATION

General Motors Rochester carburetors are identified by their model code. The first number indicates the number of barrels, while one of the last letters indicates the type of choke used. These are **V** for the manifold mounted choke coil, **C** for the choke coil mounted in the carburetor body, and **E** for electric choke, also mounted on the carburetor. Model codes ending in **A** indicate an altitude-compensating carburetor. Four different carburetors have been used on Cadillacs since 1967: the Rochester 4MV 4 bbl. 1967–74; Rochester M4ME 4 bbl. 1975–80; the Rochester E4ME 4 bbl. 1980–84; and the E4MC in 1986.

REMOVAL & INSTALLATION

All Carburetors

1. Remove the air cleaner and its gasket.
2. Disconnect the fuel and vacuum lines from the carburetor.

3. Disconnect the choke coil rod, heated air line tube, or electrical connector.
4. Disconnect the throttle linkage.
5. Disconnect the throttle valve linkage if so equipped.
6. Disconnect the EGR line, if so equipped.
7. Remove the idle stop solenoid, if so equipped.
8. Remove the carburetor attaching nuts and/or bolts, gasket or insulator, and remove the carburetor.
9. Install the carburetor using the reverse of the removal procedure. Use a new gasket and fill the float bowl with gasoline to ease starting the engine.

PRELIMINARY CHECKS

All Carburetors

The following should be observed before attempting any adjustments.
1. Thoroughly warm the engine. If the engine is cold, be sure that it reaches operating temperature.
2. Check the torque of all carburetor mounting nuts and assembly screws. Also check the intake manifold-to-cylinder head bolts. If air is leaking at any of these points, any attempts at adjustment will inevitably lead to frustration.
3. Check the manifold heat control valve (if used) to be sure that it is free.
4. Check and adjust the choke as necessary.
5. Adjust the idle speed and mixture. If the mixture screws are capped, don't adjust them unless all other causes of rough idle have been eliminated. If any adjustments are performed that might possible change the idle speed or mixture, adjust the idle and mixture again when you are finished.

Before you make any carburetor adjustments make sure that the engine is in tune. Many problems which are thought to be carburetor-related can be traced to an engine which is simply out-of-tune. Any trouble in these areas will have symptoms like those of carburetor problems.

ADJUSTMENTS

Rochester 4MV-4 Bbl. Carburetor

The Rochester Quadrajet carburetor is a two stage, four-barrel downdraft carburetor. The designation MV refers to the type of choke system the carburetor is designed for. The MV model is equipped with a manifold thermostatic choke coil.

The primary side of the carburetor is equipped with 1⅜ diameter bores and a triple venturi with plain tube nozzles. During off idle and part throttle operation, the fuel is metered through tapered metering rods operating in specially designed jets positioned by a manifold vacuum responsive piston.

The secondary side of the carburetor contains two 2¼ in. bores. An air valve is used on the secondary side for metering control and supplements the primary bores.

The secondary air valve operates tapered metering rods which regulate the fuel in constant proportion to the air being supplied.

Accelerator Pump

1. Close the primary throttle valves by backing out the slow idle screw and making sure that the fast idle cam follower is off the steps of the fast idle cam.
2. Bend the secondary throttle closing tang away from the primary throttle lever.
3. With the pump in the appropriate hole in the pump lever, measure from the top of the choke valve wall to the top of the pump stem.
4. To adjust, bend the pump lever while supporting it with a screwdriver.
5. After adjusting, readjust the secondary throttle tang and the slow idle screw.

Idle Vent

After adjusting the accelerator pump rod as specified above, open the primary throttle valve enough to just close the idle vent. Measure from the top of the choke valve wall to the top of the pump plunger stem. If adjustment is necessary, bend the wire tang on the plump lever.

Float Level

With the air horn assembly upside down, measure the distance from the air horn gasket surface (gasket removed) to the top of the float at the toe.

➡ **Make sure the retaining pin is firmly held in place and that the tang of the float is firmly against the needle and seat assembly.**

Fast Idle

1. Position the fast idle lever on the high step of the fast idle cam. Disconnect and plug the vacuum hose at the EGR valve.
2. Be sure that the choke is wide open and the engine warm.
3. Turn the fast idle screw to gain the proper fast idle rpm.

Choke Rod

Position the cam follower on the second step of the fast idle cam, touching the high step. Close the choke valve directly. Gauge the clearance between the lower edge of the choke valve and the carburetor body. Bend the choke rod to obtain the specified clearance.

Air Valve Dashpot

◆ **See Figure 2**

Set the vacuum break diaphragm. Hold the air valve tightly closed. Gauge the clearance between the dashpot rod and the end of the slot in the air valve lever. Bend the rod to adjust. Remove the tape from the bleed purge hole.

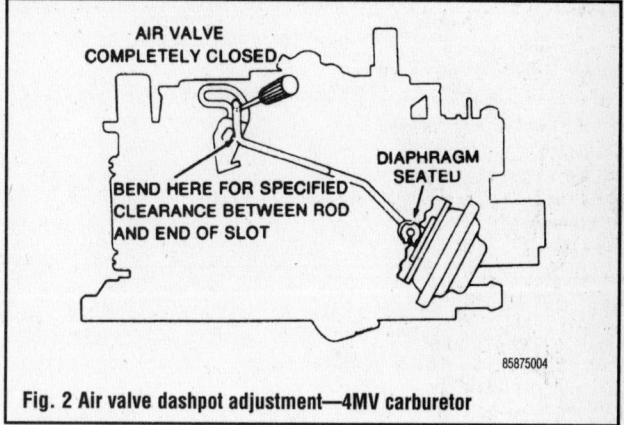

Fig. 2 Air valve dashpot adjustment—4MV carburetor

Choke Coil Rod

1. Close the choke valve by rotating the choke coil lever counterclockwise.
2. Disconnect the thermostatic coil rod from the upper lever.
3. Push down on the rod until it contacts the bracket of the coil.
4. The rod must fit in the notch of the upper lever.
5. If it does not, it must be bent on the curved portion just below the upper lever.

Vacuum Break

1. Fully seat the vacuum break diaphragm using an outside vacuum source.
2. Open the throttle valve enough to allow the fast idle cam follower to clear the fast idle cam.
3. The end of the vacuum break rod should be at the outer end of the slot in the vacuum break diaphragm plunger.
4. The specified clearance should register from the lower end of the choke valve to the inside air horn wall.
5. If the clearance is not correct, bend the vacuum break link.

Choke Unloader

Close the choke valve and secure it with a rubber band hooked to the vacuum break lever. Open the primary throttles all the way. Then measure the distance between the air horn and edge of the choke butterfly. Use the bottom side of the butterfly for this measurement. Bend the fast idle lever tang to achieve the proper opening of the choke.

Secondary Lockout

Completely open the choke valve and rotate the vacuum break lever clockwise. Bend the lever if the measurement between the lever and the secondary throttle exceeds specifications. Close the choke and gauge the distance between the lever and the secondary throttle shaft pin. Bend the lever to adjust.

Air Valve Spring

Remove all spring tension by loosening the locking screw and backing out the adjusting screw. Close the air valve and turn the adjusting screw in until the torsion spring touches the pin on the shaft, and then turn it the additional number of turns specified. Secure the locking screw.

Secondary Closing

This adjustment assures proper closing of the secondary throttle plates.
1. Set the idle as per instructions in the appropriate section. Make sure that the fast idle cam follower is not resting on the fast idle cam.
2. There should be 0.020 in. clearance between the secondary throttle actuating rod and the front of the slot on the secondary throttle lever with the closing tang on the throttle lever resting against the actuating lever.
3. Bend the tang on the primary throttle actuating rod to adjust.

Secondary Opening

1. Open the primary throttle valves until the actuating link contacts the upper tang on the secondary lever.
2. With two point-linkage, the bottom of the link should be in the center of the secondary lever slot.
3. With three point linkage, there should be 0.070 in. clearance between the link and the middle tang.
4. Bend the upper tang on the secondary lever to adjust as necessary.

ROCHESTER M4ME, E4ME, E4MC 4-BBL. CARBURETORS

♦ See Figures 3 thru 20

Float Level

1. Remove the air horn.
2. Hold the float retainer in place and lightly push down on the float against the needle.
3. Measure the gap between the casting surface and the top of the float at a point ³⁄₁₆ in. back from the float toe.
4. To adjust, remove the float and bend the float arm.
5. On CCC carburetors, if the float level varies more than ¹⁄₁₆ in. either way, adjust as follows:
    a. Level too high: Hold the float retainer firmly in place and push down on the center of the float body until the correct gap is attained.
    b. Level too low: Lift out the metering rods. Remove the solenoid connector screw. Turn the lean mixture solenoid screw clockwise counting the number of turns until the screw is lightly seated. Then, remove the screw. Lift the solenoid and connector from the float bowl. Remove the float and bend the arm to adjust. Install the float and check the adjustment. Install the

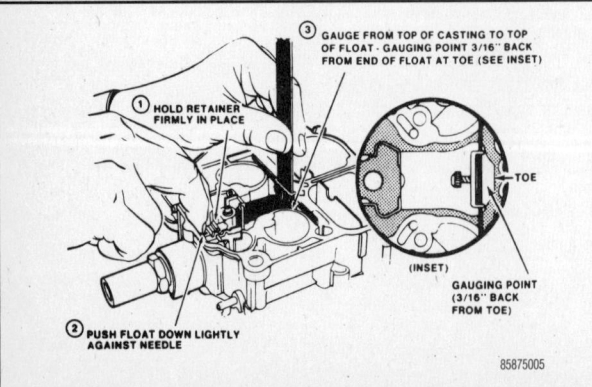

Fig. 3 Common quadrajet (4-bbl. carburetor) float level adjustment

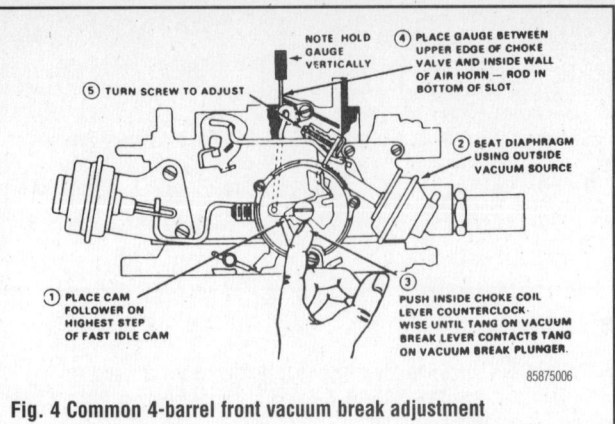

Fig. 4 Common 4-barrel front vacuum break adjustment

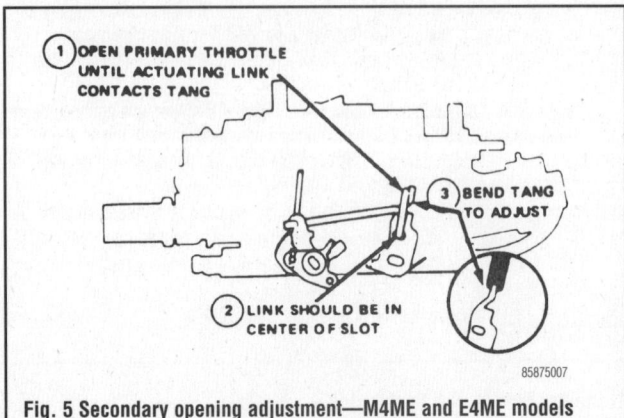

Fig. 5 Secondary opening adjustment—M4ME and E4ME models

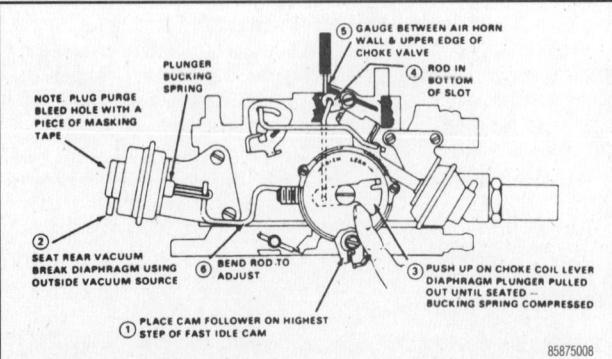

Fig. 6 4-barrel rear vacuum break adjustment (without adjusting screw)—through 1980 models

mixture screw to the exact number of turns noted earlier. Install all other parts.

1975–80 MODELS

1. Place the cam follower lever on the highest step of the fast idle cam.
2. Remove the choke cover and coil assembly from the choke housing.
3. Seat the front vacuum diaphragm using an outside vacuum source.
4. Push up on the inside choke coil lever until the tang on the vacuum break lever contacts the tang on the vacuum break plunger.
5. Place the proper size gauge between the upper edge of the choke plate and the inside of the air horn wall.
6. To adjust, turn the adjustment screw on the vacuum break plunger lever.
7. To adjust the secondary vacuum break, with the choke cover and coil removed, the cam follower on the highest step of the fast idle cam, tape over the bleed hole in the rear vacuum break diaphragm.
8. Seat the rear diaphragm using an outside vacuum source.

9. Close the choke by pushing up on the choke coil lever inside the choke housing. Make sure the choke rod is in the bottom of the slot in the choke lever.

10. Measure between the upper edge of the choke plate and the air horn wall with a wire type gauge.

11. To adjust, bend the vacuum break rod at the first bend near the diaphragm.

1981 AND LATER MODELS

The carburetors require special tools for adjustment. Service is best left to a professional mechanic.

Fast Idle Cam

1. Adjust the fast idle and place the cam follower on the second step of the fast idle cam.

2. Close the choke plate by pushing counterclockwise on the external choke

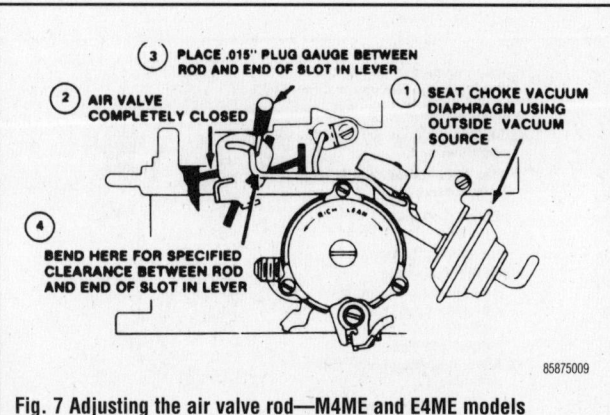

Fig. 7 Adjusting the air valve rod—M4ME and E4ME models

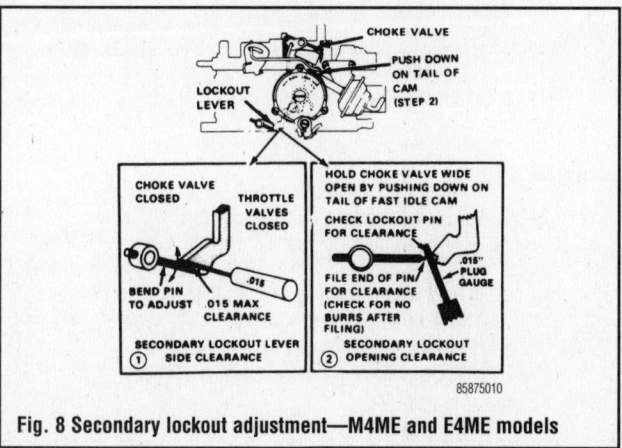

Fig. 8 Secondary lockout adjustment—M4ME and E4ME models

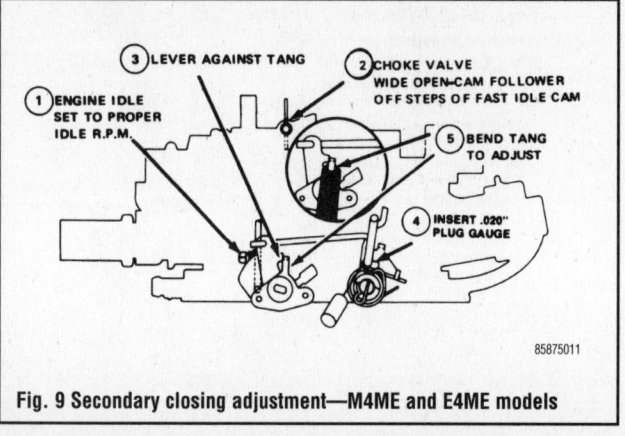

Fig. 9 Secondary closing adjustment—M4ME and E4ME models

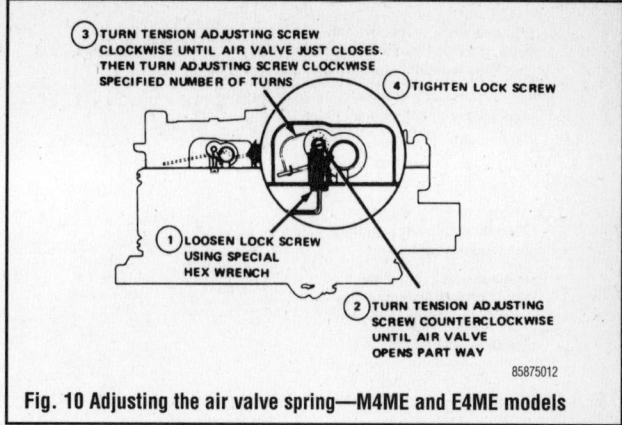

Fig. 10 Adjusting the air valve spring—M4ME and E4ME models

lever. On 1975–80 models, remove the coil assembly from the choke housing and push on the choke coil lever.

3. Measure between the upper edge of the choke plate and the air horn wall.

4. To adjust, 1975–80 models, bend the tang on the fast idle cam. Be sure that the tang rests against the cam after bending.

Choke Coil Lever

1. Remove the choke cover and thermostatic coil from the choke housing.

2. Push the coil tang counterclockwise until the choke plate is fully closed.

3. Insert a 0.120 in. gauge into the hole in the choke housing. The lower edge of the choke coil lever should just contact the side of the gauge.

4. Bend the choke rod to adjust, if necessary.

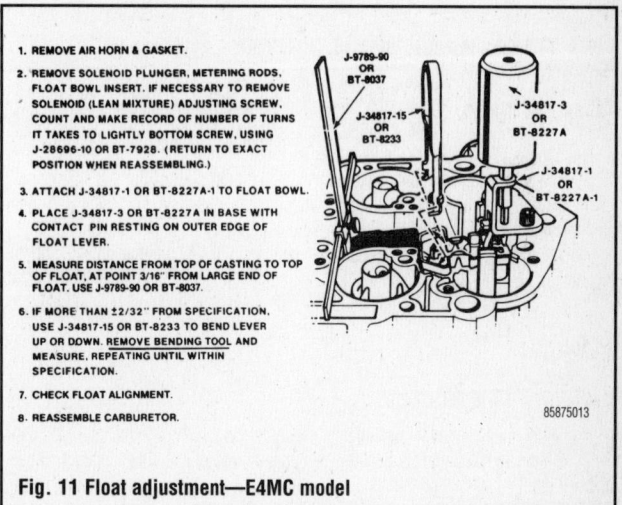

Fig. 11 Float adjustment—E4MC model

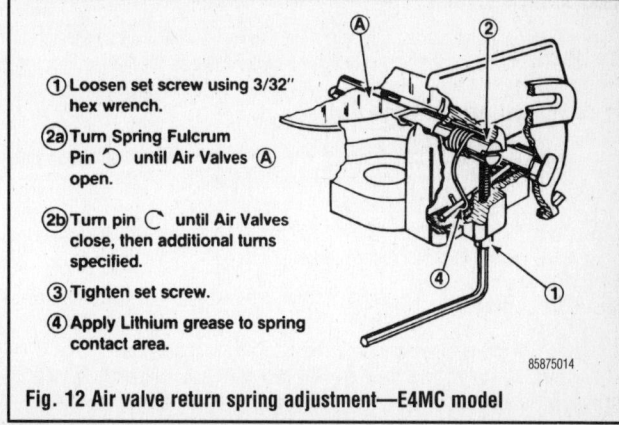

Fig. 12 Air valve return spring adjustment—E4MC model

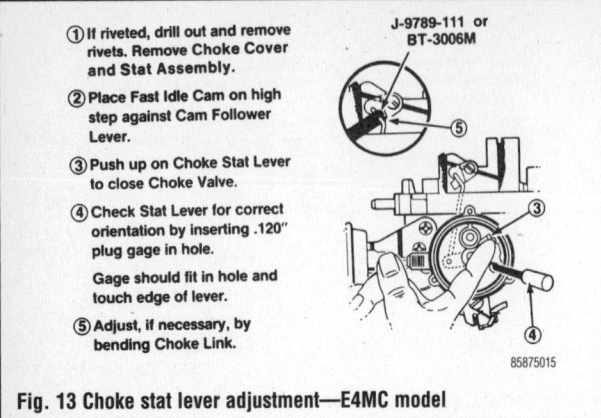

Fig. 13 Choke stat lever adjustment—E4MC model

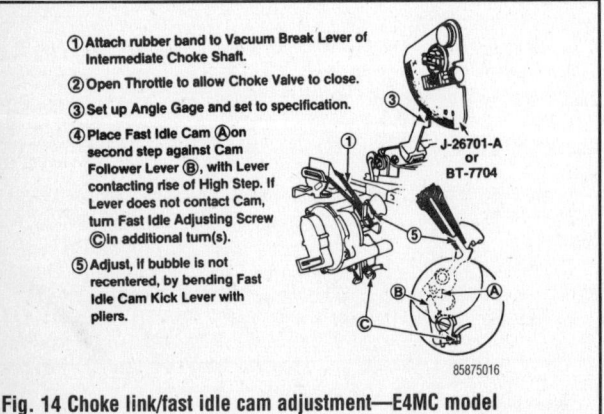

Fig. 14 Choke link/fast idle cam adjustment—E4MC model

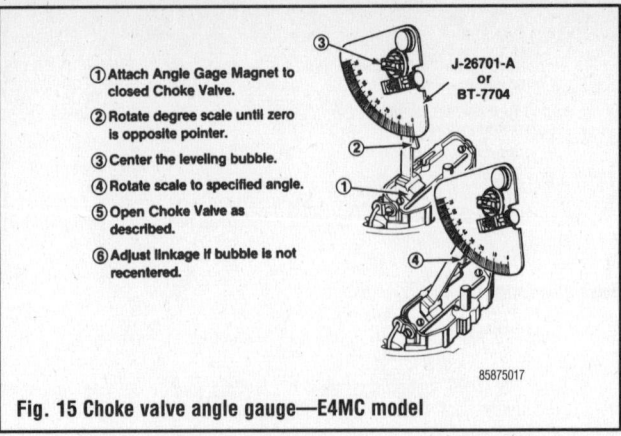

Fig. 15 Choke valve angle gauge—E4MC model

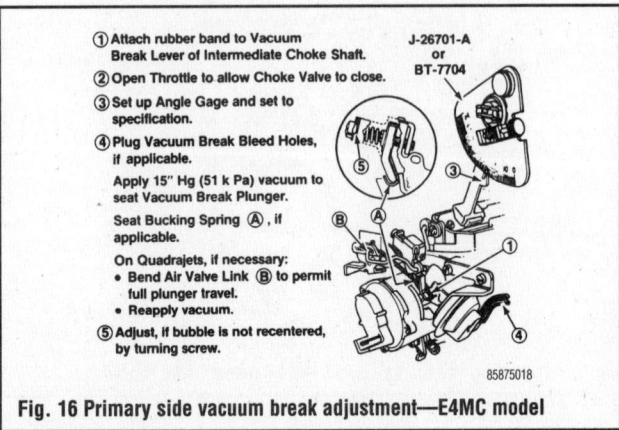

Fig. 16 Primary side vacuum break adjustment—E4MC model

Automatic Choke

1. Loosen the choke housing cover screws.
2. Place the fast idle cam follower on the highest step of the fast idle cam.
3. Rotate the cover and coil assembly counterclockwise until the choke plate just closes.
4. Align the index mark on the cover with the specified index point on the housing.
5. Tighten the retaining screws.

Unloader

THROUGH 1980 MODELS

1. With the choke plate completely closed, hold the throttle plates wide open.
2. Measure the distance between the upper edge of the choke plate and the airhorn wall.
3. Bend the tang on the fast idle lever to adjust.

1981 AND LATER MODELS

The unloader adjustment on these carburetors requires special tools and is quite complicated. Service here is best left to a professional mechanic.

Vacuum Break and Air Valve Rod

1. Using an outside vacuum source, seat the choke vacuum diaphragm. Put a piece of tape over the purge bleed hole if so equipped.
2. Close the air valve completely.
3. Insert the gauge between the rod and the end of the slot in the lever.
4. Bend the rod to adjust the clearance.

Secondary Lockout

1. Pull the choke wide open by pushing out on the choke lever.
2. Open the throttle until the end of the secondary actuating lever is opposite the toe of the lockout lever.

3. Measure the clearance between the lockout lever and the secondary lever.
4. Bend the lockout pin until the clearance is in accordance with the proper specifications.

Secondary Closing

1. Make sure that the idle speed is set to the proper specifications.
2. The choke valve should be wide open with the cam follower off of the steps of the fast idle cam.
3. There should be 0.020 in. clearance between the secondary throttle actuating rod and the front of the slot on the secondary throttle lever with the closing tang on the throttle lever resting against the actuating lever.
4. To adjust, bend the secondary closing tang on the primary throttle actuating rod.

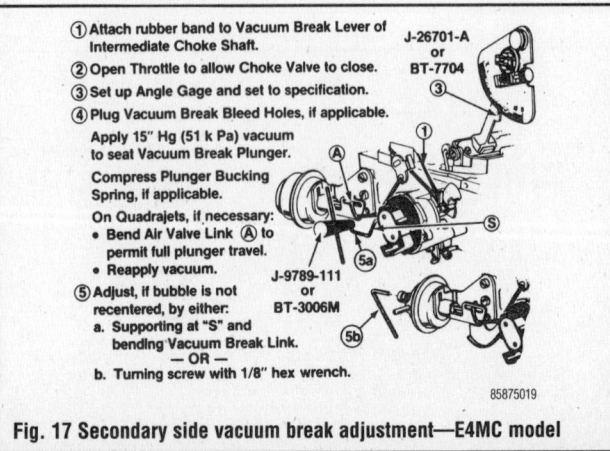

Fig. 17 Secondary side vacuum break adjustment—E4MC model

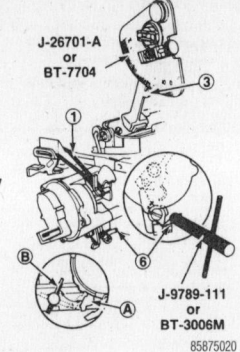

① Attach rubber band to Vacuum Break Lever of Intermediate Choke Shaft.
② Open Throttle to allow Choke Valve to close.
③ Set up Angle Gage and set to specification.
④ On Quadrajet, hold Secondary Throttle Lockout Lever Ⓐ away from pin Ⓑ.
⑤ Hold Throttle Lever in wide open position.
⑥ Adjust, if bubble is not recentered, by bending Fast Idle Lever.

Fig. 18 Unloader adjustment—E4MC model

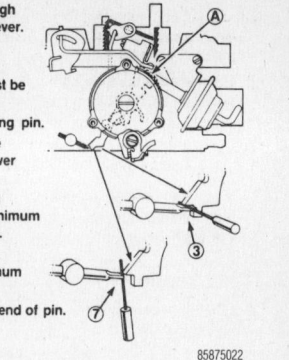

① Place Fast Idle Cam Ⓐ on high step against Cam Follower Lever.
② Hold Throttle Lever closed.
③ Gage the clearance between Lockout Lever and pin. It must be .015″ ±.005″.
④ Adjust, if necessary, by bending pin.
⑤ Push down on tail of Fast Idle Cam Ⓐ to move Lockout Lever away from pin.
⑥ Rotate Throttle Lever to bring Lockout Pin to position of minimum clearance with Lockout Lever.
⑦ Gage the clearance between Lockout Lever and pin. Minimum must be .015″.
⑧ Adjust, if necessary, by filing end of pin.

Fig. 20 Secondary throttle lockout adjustment—E4MC model

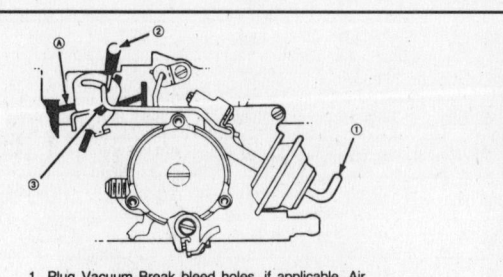

1. Plug Vacuum Break bleed holes, if applicable. Air Valves Ⓐ closed. Apply 15″ HG (51 k Pa) vacuum to seat Vacuum Breaker Plunger.
2. Gage the clearance between Air Valve Link and end of slot in lever.
3. Adjust, if necessary, by bending link.

Fig. 19 Air valve link adjustment (primary side)—E4MC model

Secondary Opening

1. Open the primary throttle valves until the actuating link contacts the upper tang on the secondary lever.
2. With the two point linkage, the bottom of the link should be in the center of the secondary lever slot.
3. With the three point linkage, there should be 0.070 in. clearance between the link and the middle tang.
4. To adjust, bend the upper tang on the secondary lever.

Air Valve Spring

To adjust the air valve spring windup, loosen the Allen head lockscrew and then turn the adjusting screw counterclockwise so as to remove all spring tension. With the air valve closed turn the adjusting screw clockwise the specified number of turns after the torsion spring contacts the pin on the shaft. Hold the adjusting screw in this position and tighten the lockscrew.

Carburetor Specifications (4MV)

Year	Carburetor Identification ①	Float Level (in.)	Air Valve Spring (turn)	Pump Rod (in.)	Primary Vacuum Break (in.)	Secondary Vacuum Break (in.)	Choke Rod (in.)	Choke Unloader (in.)	Fast Idle Speed (rpm)
'67	7036682 (4MV)	7/32	—	11/32	—	—	—	0.312	1725
	7036681 (4MV)	7/32	—	11/32	—	—	—	0.312	1725
'68	7016932 (4MV)	11/32	—	11/32	—	—	—	0.312	1925
	7016930 (4MV)	1/4	—	11/32	—	—	—	0.312	1925
'69	7016932 (4MV)	11/32	—	11/32	—	—	—	0.300	1925
	7016930 (4MV)	1/4	—	11/32	—	—	—	0.300	1925
'70	7047030 (4MV)	1/4	—	11/32	—	—	—	0.300	1925
'71	7041777 (4MV)	11/32	—	11/32	—	—	—	0.300	1925
	7041766 (4MV)	1/4	—	11/32	—	—	—	0.300	1925
'72	7047231 (4MV)	15/64	1/2	11/32	0.140	—	0.090	0.312	1925
	7047232 (4MV)	23/64	1/2	11/32	0.205	—	0.090	0.015	1925
'73	7046881 (4MV)	19/64	1/2	11/32	0.205	—	0.090	0.015	1925
	7047331 (4MV)	1/4	1/2	11/32	0.200	—	0.090	0.015	1925
	7047332 (4MV)	23/64	1/2	11/32	0.205	—	0.090	0.015	1925
'74	7044230 (4MV)	1/4	3/8	1/4	0.185	—	0.110	0.312	1400
	7044232 (4MV)	23/64	1/2	1/4	0.200	—	0.110	0.312	1400
	7044530 (4MV)	1/4	3/8	1/4	0.185	—	0.110	0.312	1400
	7044532 (4MV)	23/64	1/2	1/4	0.200	—	0.110	0.312	1400
	7044234 (4MV)	1/4	7/16	11/32	0.185	—	0.110	0.312	1400
	7044235 (4MV)	23/64	9/16	11/32	0.200	—	0.110	0.312	1400
	7044233 (4MV)	19/64	3/8	11/32	0.185	—	0.110	0.312	1400

① The carburetor identification number is stamped on the float blow, near the secondary throttle lever.

Carburetor Specifications (M4ME)

Year	Carburetor Identification ①	Float Level (in.)	Air Valve Spring (turn)	Pump Rod (in.)	Primary Vacuum Break (in.)	Secondary Vacuum Break (in.)	Choke Rod (in.)	Choke Unloader (in.)	Fast Idle Speed (rpm)
'75	7045230 (M4ME)	15/32	7/16	3/8	0.160	0.130	0.080	0.215	1250
	7044530 (M4ME)	15/32	1/2	3/8	0.230	0.230	0.080	0.215	1250
'76	7056232 (M4ME)	13/32	3/8	3/8	0.160	0.160	0.080	0.230	1400
	7056230 (M4ME)	13/32	3/8	3/8	0.160	0.160	0.080	0.230	1400
	7056530 (M4ME)	7/16	3/8	9/32	0.160	0.160	0.080	0.230	1400
'77	17057232 (M4ME)	13/32	1/2	3/8	0.140	0.140	0.080	0.230	1400
	17057233 (M4ME)	13/32	1/2	3/8	0.140	0.140	0.080	0.230	1400
	17057230 (M4ME)	13/32	1/2	7/16	0.140	0.140	0.080	0.230	1400
	17057231 (M4ME)	17/32	1/2	3/8	0.140	0.140	0.080	0.230	1400
	17057530 (M4ME)	13/32	1/2	7/16	0.150	0.150	0.080	0.230	1500
	17057533 (M4ME)	13/31	1/2	7/16	0.150	0.150	0.080	0.230	1500
'78	17058230 (M4ME)	13/32	1/2	3/8	0.150	0.165	0.080	0.230	1500
	17058232 (M4ME)	13/32	1/2	3/8	0.140	0.250	0.080	0.230	1400
	17058233 (M4ME)	13/32	1/2	3/8	0.140	0.250	0.080	0.230	1400
	17058533 (M4ME)	13/32	1/2	3/8	0.140	0.250	0.080	0.230	1400
	17058532 (M4ME)	13/32	1/2	3/8	0.140	0.250	0.080	0.230	1400
	17058530 (M4ME)	13/32	1/2	3/8	0.140	0.250	0.080	0.230	1400
	17058531 (M4ME)	13/32	1/2	3/8	0.140	0.250	0.080	0.230	1400
	17058535 (M4ME)	13/32	1/2	3/8	0.140	0.250	0.080	0.230	1400
'79	17059230 (M4ME)	13/32	1/2	9/32	0.142	0.234	0.083	0.142	1000
	17059232 (M4ME)	13/32	1/2	9/32	0.142	0.234	0.083	0.142	1500
	17059530 (M4ME)	13/32	1/2	9/32	0.149	0.164	0.083	0.142	1500
	17059532 (M4ME)	13/32	1/2	9/32	0.149	0.164	0.083	0.142	1500
'80	17080230 (M4ME)	7/16	1/2	9/32	0.149	0.136	0.083	0.220	1450
	17080530 (E4ME)	17/32	1/2	Fixed	0.142	0.400	0.083	0.260	1350
'81	17081248 (E4ME)	3/8	5/8	Fixed	0.164	0.136	0.139	0.243	②
	17081289 (E4ME)	13/32	5/8	Fixed	0.164	0.136	0.139	0.243	②
'82	17082246 (E4ME)	3/8	5/8	Fixed	0.149	0.149	0.139	0.195	②
	17082247 (E4ME)	13/32	5/8	Fixed	0.164	0.136	0.139	0.243	②
'83	17082266 (E4ME)	3/8	5/8	Fixed	0.149	0.149	0.071	0.195	②
	17082267 (E4ME)	3/8	5/8	Fixed	0.149	0.149	0.071	0.195	②

① The carburetor identification number is stamped on the float bowl, near the secondary throttle lever.
② See underhood decal.

85875C02

Carburetor Specifications (E4MC)

Year	Carburetor Identification ①	Float Level (in.)	Air Valve Spring (turn)	Pump Rod (in.)	Primary Vacuum Break (in./deg.)	Secondary Vacuum Break (in./deg.)	Secondary Opening (in.)	Choke Rod (in./deg.)	Choke Unloader (in./deg.)	Fast Idle Speed (rpm)
'86–'89	17086008 (E4MC)	11/32	1/2	Fixed	0.142/25	0.278/43	②	—/14°	0.220/35	③
	17086008 (E4MC)	14/32	1/2	Fixed	0.142/25	0.278/43	②	—/14°	0.220/35	③

① The carburetor identification number is stamped on the float bowl, near the secondary throttle lever.
② No measurement necessary on two point linkage; see text.
③ See underhood decal.

85875C03

GASOLINE FUEL INJECTION SYSTEMS

General Information

CADILLAC (DFI/EFI) INJECTION SYSTEMS

▶ **See Figures 21 and 22**

Cadillac has used two different types of fuel injection systems: Electronic Fuel Injection (EFI) and Digital Fuel Injection (DFI).

The EFI system is an indirect, or ported fuel injection system, on which each cylinder has its own fuel injector mounted behind the intake valve. The EFI system was used on 1977–79 Sevilles as standard equipment and on 1977–79 full size Cadillacs as an option.

The DFI system is a throttle body fuel injection system, on which two solenoid actuated fuel injectors are mounted in the throttle body and inject fuel down into the intake manifold. The DFI system, introduced on 1980 Sevilles, is used on 1980 6.0 liter (368 cu. in.) engines and all 1981 and later Cadillacs except the 252 cu. in. V6 engine and the 368 4 bbl. engine used in the limousine and commercial vehicles.

Both systems control the air/fuel mixture for combustion by monitoring selected engine operating conditions and electronically metering fuel requirements to meet those conditions.

The EFI system consists of four basic sub-systems: the fuel delivery system, the air induction system, the network of sensors, and the Electronic Control Unit (ECU). The DFI system includes the same sub-systems as the EFI, but uses a more detailed Electronic Control Module (ECM) and adds several more sub-systems. These include the electronic spark timing system (EST), idles speed control system (ISC), EGR (all) and charcoal canister (1981 and later) control system, modulated cylinder displacement (on cars so equipped), closed loop/open loop oxygen sensor system (1981 and later), and the failure operation circuit and diagnostics readout system.

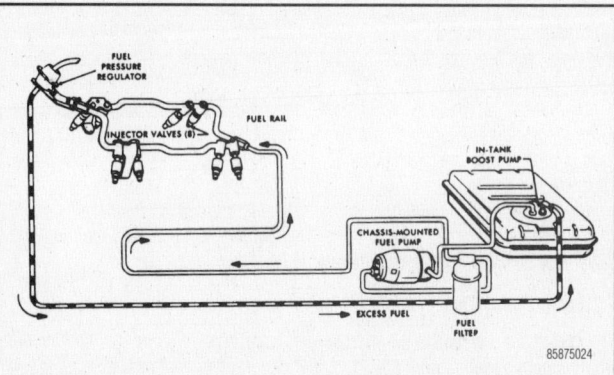

Fig. 21 Cadillac EFI system—each cylinder has its own fuel injector

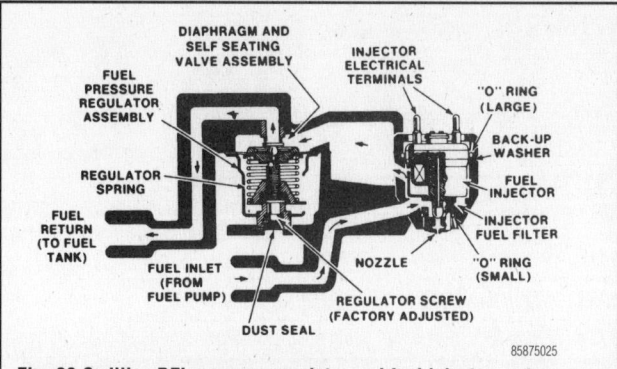

Fig. 22 Cadillac DFI pressure regulator and fuel injector system—both are contained in the throttle body

Fuel Delivery System

The EFI fuel delivery subsystem is made up of an in-tank fuel pump, a chassis mounted fuel pump, fuel filter, fuel pressure regulator, fuel rails, and an injector for each cylinder.

The DFI fuel delivery system consists of an in-tank fuel pump, fuel filter, fuel feed and return lines, and a TBI unit which includes fuel injectors and a pressure regulator.

ELECTRIC FUEL PUMPS

The electric fuel pump(s) are connected in parallel to the ECU/ECM and are activated by the ECU/ECM when the ignition is turned **ON** and the engine is cranking or operating. If the engine stalls or if the starter is not engaged, the fuel pumps will stop in about one second. The fuel is pumped from the fuel tank, through the supply line and the filter, through the pressure regulator, fuel rails (EFI) and to the injectors, with excess fuel being returned to the fuel tank. The fuel tank pump supplies fuel to the chassis mounted fuel pump or to the throttle body pressure regulator.

Vehicles with EFI have two electric fuel pumps; one is mounted in the fuel tank and is integral with the fuel level sending unit and the other, a chassis-mounted pump, is located in front of the rear axle either on the right or left side. The chassis mounted fuel pump is a constant-displacement, roller-vane pump with a check valve to prevent fuel from flowing back into the tank. This pump has a flow rate of 33 gallons per hour and maintains a minimum pressure of 39 psi. An internal relief valve opens at 55–95 psi to protect the system from excessive pressure. The pump is mounted under the vehicles except on the Eldorado, where it is mounted in front of the right rear wheel. A fuel filter is mounted on a bracket at the lower left front of the engine. On Seville models the fuel filter is mounted on the left side of the frame near the fuel pump.

Vehicles with DFI have one, in-tank, fuel pump. The fuel filter is located on the left side of the chassis just ahead of the rear axle.

FUEL FILTER

The fuel filter is located on a bracket on the lower left front of the engine or on the frame near the right rear wheel. The filter consists of a casing with an internal throwaway type paper filter element.

FUEL PRESSURE REGULATOR

The EFI fuel pressure regulator, located on the fuel rail at the front of the engine, maintains a constant 39 psi pressure across the fuel injectors. The DFI fuel pressure regulator is integral with the throttle body and cannot be serviced separately. The regulator contains an air chamber and fuel chamber separated by a spring-loaded diaphragm. The air chamber, on EFI systems, is connected by a hose to the throttle body assembly. The pressure in the air chamber of the regulator is identical to the pressure in the intake manifold. The changing manifold pressure and the spring control the action of the diaphragm valve, opening or closing an orifice in the fuel chamber of the regulator. At this point excess fuel is routed out of the regulator and back to the fuel tank.

FUEL INJECTOR

The fuel injector, on EFI systems, is a solenoid operated pintle valve that meters fuel to each cylinder. The injectors are controlled by an electronic pulse signal from the ECU. When energized, the valve opens for precisely the proper amount of time to spray the exact amount of fuel droplets required by the engine. When the injector is de-energized, it prevents any further fuel flow to the engine.

On the EFI engine, the injectors are located on the intake manifold above the intake valve of each cylinder. The eight injectors are divided into two groups of four each. Cylinders 1, 2, 7, and 8 form group 1 and the remaining injectors form group 2. All four injectors in each group are opened and closed simultaneously; the two groups operate alternately.

The DFI system uses two fuel injectors located in the throttle body. They are controlled by the electronic control module (ECM) and meter the atomized fuel into the throttle bore. Each injector contains a spring loaded ball valve controlled by a solenoid. When the ball valve is lifted from its seat by the solenoid plunger, fuel is fed through the atomizer/spray injector nozzle.

Air Induction System

The air induction system is made up of the throttle body assembly, idle speed control, and the intake manifold.

THROTTLE BODY

Air for combustion enters the throttle body and is controlled by the throttle valves which are connected to the accelerator pedal linkage, much like a conventional carburetor. The throttle body consists of a housing with two bores and two shaft mounted throttle valves. The throttle valves are pre-set slightly open when the throttle lever is resting against the idle stop position. The adjustment is not to be tampered with. An adjustable set screw on the front of the throttle body adjusts an idle bypass air passage incorporated within the throttle body and allows a regulated amount of air to bypass the throttle valves, adjusting warm engine idle speed.

A large port on top of the EFI throttle body contains the fast idle valve. Starting 1978 on EFI equipped Sevilles, a solenoid operated idle air compensator is added to provide more air to the engine when the air conditioner clutch is engaged at idle.

FAST IDLE VALVE

The EFI system fast idle valve, installed on the top of the throttle body, consists of a plastic body that houses an electric heater, a spring and plunger, and a temperature sensitive unit.

The fast idle valve is connected electrically to the fuel pump circuit through the ECU. When the engine is started cold, the open valve allows extra air to bypass the throttle valves.

The heater warms the thermal element which expands and forces the spring and plunger toward the air orifice, restricting the flow of extra air and gradually reducing the engine speed to the normal idle rpm. The fast idle valve has no effect after the thermal element reaches about 140°F. The rate at which the valve closes is a function of time and temperature. The warmer the air, the faster the valve closes. At 68°F (20°C) the valve will close in about 90 seconds and at -20°F (-29°C) the valve will require about 5 minutes to close.

IDLE SPEED CONTROL

The DFI idle speed control subsystem is controlled by the ECM. The system acts to control the engine idle speed using a small electric motor which, when used in conjunction with the throttle switch, adjusts idle speed by opening or closing the throttle valves. When the engine is cold, the idle speed motor opens the throttle valve to provide faster warm-up time, and as such acts as a fast idle device.

INTAKE MANIFOLD

The intake manifold is basically the same as those installed on carbureted engines. There are, however, a minor differences: On EFI systems only air travels through the intake manifold. There is a hole above each cylinder for injector installation. A port is made available for the installation of the air temperature sensor. There is no exhaust heat cross-over passage. The exhaust passage from the right cylinder head is for EGR only.

On the DFI system, both air and fuel travel through the intake manifold, much in the same manner as on a carbureted engine.

Engine Sensors

All the engine sensors are electrically connected to the Electronic Control Unit (ECU) or the Electronic Control Module (ECM). Each of the sensors operates independently, monitors a specific engine operating condition, and transmits this information via electronic signal to the ECU/ECM. The sensors continuously send information signals to the ECU/ECM while the ignition switch is in the On or Start position.

MANIFOLD ABSOLUTE PRESSURE (MAP) SENSOR

The manifold absolute pressure (MAP) sensor monitors pressure changes within the intake manifold which are the direct result of engine load, speed, and barometric pressure. As pressure in the intake manifold increases, additional fuel is required. The MAP sensor sends this information to the ECU/ECM so that the length of time the injectors are energized is increased or decreased accordingly.

The sensor is mounted within the electronic control unit. A manifold pressure line is routed with the engine harness and is connected to the front of the throttle body at one end to the MAP sensor at the other end.

THROTTLE POSITION SWITCH (TPS)

The throttle position switch (TPS) is mounted to the throttle body, connected to the throttle valve shaft, and monitors the opening or closing of the throttle valves. The switch senses the shaft movement and position and transmits electrical signals to the ECU/ECM. The ECU/ECM processes these signals to determine the fuel requirement for the engine.

MANIFOLD AIR TEMPERATURE SENSOR (MAT)

The MAT sensor is used on the DFI system and is installed in the intake manifold in front of the throttle body. This sensor measures the temperature of the air/fuel mixture in the intake manifold and provides this information to the ECM.

COOLANT TEMPERATURE SENSOR

This coolant temperature sensor is used on the DFI system and is installed in the right front corner of the engine directly below the thermostat. The sensor provides data to the ECM for fuel enrichment during cold operation, for idle speed control, ignition timing and EGR operation.

TEMPERATURE SENSORS

These sensors are used on the EFI system. The two air and coolant temperature sensors vary electrical current resistance as a function of temperature. Low temperatures provide low resistance and vice versa. Voltage changes across each sensor are monitored by the ECU.

The air temperature sensor is located on the rear of the intake manifold and is connected to the engine harness. The coolant temperature sensor is located on the heater hose fitting at the rear of the right cylinder head or on the right side of the block below the thermostat.

The sensors are identical and completely interchangeable.

SPEED SENSOR

On EFI systems the speed sensor is incorporated within the ignition distributor, and consists of two components. The first is a plastic housing containing two reed switches. The second is a rotor with two magnets attached to it and rotating with the distributor shaft.

The rotation of the magnets past the reed switches causes them to open and close, providing two signals: one for synchronization of the ECU and the proper injector group with the intake valve timing; and the engine rpm for fuel scheduling.

On DFI systems the engine speed signal pulses are picked up by an electronic module in the distributor. The pulses are sent to the ECM where they are used to calculate engine speed and spark advance.

OXYGEN SENSOR

The oxygen sensor system used on 1981 and later cars controls fuel injection quantity by monitoring the amount of oxygen present in the exhaust gases and sending this information to the ECM, which adjusts the amount of fuel injected to provide the ideal air/fuel mixture ratio (14.7:1). The oxygen sensor is attached to the exhaust system ahead of the catalytic converter. When the oxygen sensor system is controlling the air/fuel mixture, the DFI system is said to be in closed loop operation. When the oxygen sensor is not controlling the air/fuel mixture (engine cold, etc.) the DFI system is said to be in open loop operation.

BAROMETRIC PRESSURE (BARO) SENSOR

This unit senses ambient or barometric pressure and provides information to the ECM or ambient pressure changes due to altitude and/or weather. This sensor is used only on the DFI system and is mounted under the instrument panel near the right-hand A/C outlet. The sensor's atmospheric opening is covered by a foam filter.

ELECTRONIC CONTROL UNIT/MODULE (ECU/ECM)

The electronic control unit/module (ECU/ECM) located under the instrument panel or in the glove box is a pre-programmed computer. The ECU/ECM is electrically connected to the vehicle's power supply, all of the EFI/DFI system electrical components, plus the EGR activation solenoid and other emission controls by a harness routed through the firewall.

Cadillac Fuel Injection Application Chart

Model	Year	V8 Engines Cu In (Liters)	Type System
All	'75	500 (8.2)	①
SeVille	'76	350 (5.7)	Electronic Fuel Injection
All other	'76	425 (7.0)	②
SeVille	'77	350 (5.7)	Electronic Fuel Injection
All other	'77	425 (7.0)	②
SeVille ③	'78	350 (5.7)	Electronic Fuel Injection
DeVille and Fleetwood	'78	425 (7.0)	④
Eldorado ③ and Seville	'79	350 (5.7)	Electronic Fuel Injection
Deville and Fleetwood	'79	425 (7.0)	④
Seville ⑥	'80	350 (5.7)	Electronic Fuel Injection
Eldorado ⑥	'80	368 (6.0)	Digital Electronic Fuel Injection ⑩
SeVille ⑦	'81	350 (5.7)	Diesel Engine Standard
Deville ⑥ and Fleetwood	'81	368 (6.0)	Digital Fuel Injection ⑩
Eldorado, SeVille, Deville and Fleetwood	'82–'89	250 (4.1) 273 (4.5)	Digital Fuel Injection ⑩
Limosine ⑨	'82–'84	368 (6.0)	Digital Fuel Injection ⑩

① EFI available as an option on all 1975 Cadillacs, Except Fleetwood, Limosine and Commercial models.
② EFI standard on 1976–80 SeVille and optional on other models.
③ Diesel engine option available on 1978–79 SeVille—EFI not available on 1978 Eldorado—EFI was available on 1979 Eldorado.
④ EFI available only as optional equipment—standard equipment is a 4 bbl carburetor.
⑤ California only: EFI optional on SeVille and standard on Eldorado for 1980. EFI not available for 49 states in 1980. An optional 350 (5.7L) diesel available for 49 states on 1980 SeVille and Eldorado models.
⑥ Forty nine states: Digital Electronic Fuel Injection available on all 1980 Eldorado models.
⑦ Eldorado 368-V8 with DEFI or carburetor option is available.
⑧ DEVILLE and FLEETWOOD available with carburetor 252-V6 or 350-V8 diesel as options.
⑨ Commercial vehicles also available with carbureted 368-V8.
⑩ Digital Electronic Fuel Injection and Digital Fuel Injection are Cadillacs' names for throttle body fuel injection.

85875C04

When the ECU/ECM is energized by the turning ignition switch ON, it receives information from all of the engine sensors and activates the fuel pump(s), fast idle valve, fuel injectors, and emission control components.

The commands for proper air/fuel ratios for various driving and atmospheric conditions are designed into the ECU/ECM. As the electronic signals are received from the sensors, the ECU/ECM analyzes the signals and computes the exact fuel requirement for the engine. The ECU/ECM then causes the fuel injectors to open for a specific amount of time. The duration of time the injectors are open varies as the engine operating conditions change.

The electronic control units are calibrated differently depending on where the car is sold (California or 49 states) and in which vehicle the unit is installed. Each ECU/ECM is labeled for its intended use. The proper unit must be used for each application.

Troubleshooting

ELECTRONIC FUEL INJECTION (EFI) SYSTEM

1977–80 Models

➡ Because a special electronic tester is necessary to diagnose problems in the ECU, this section will deal with troubleshooting only mechanical and basic electrical problems of the EFI system. If the ECU is diagnosed as being the possible cause of a problem, the car should be taken to a Cadillac dealer where the special electronic tester and trained personal are available.

Before disconnecting any part of the fuel delivery system of EFI equipped vehicles, the pressure within the fuel lines must be bled off. Refer to steps 1–4 of the Chassis-Mounted Fuel Pump Removal for the proper procedure.

PROBLEM: Engine cranks but will not start.

POSSIBLE CAUSES:

➡**The following possible causes assume that the rest of the vehicle electrical system is functioning properly.**

• Blown 10 amp in-line fuel pump fuse (located under the instrument panel near the ECU wiring harness connectors) or, depending on year, a 20 amp fuse located in the fuse panel. To check, listen for the whine of the chassis-mounted fuel pump when the ignition key is turned to the On position. The fuel pump should only operate for one second before shutting off. Do not turn the ignition key to the Start position.

• Poor connection of the green wire at the fuel pump wiring harness near the ECU harness below the instrument panel. Check the operation of the fuel pump in the same manner as in the first POSSIBLE CAUSE above.

• Malfunction in the chassis-mounted pump.

• Open circuit in the purple wire between the starter solenoid and the ECU.

• Open circuit in the green wire between the alternator BAT terminal and the ECU.

• Poor connection at the engine coolant sensor or an open circuit in the wiring or the sensor, with the engine cold only. To check, connect an ohmmeter to the temperature sensor connector terminals. If the resistance in the sensor is greater than 1600 ohms, replace the sensor.

• Poor connection of the ECU wiring harness.

• Poor connection at the speed sensor on the distributor.

• The speed sensor trigger is stuck closed.

• The wide-open throttle section of the throttle position switch is shorted. To check, disconnect the switch; the engine should start.

• A restriction in the fuel delivery system.

PROBLEM: Hard starting.

POSSIBLE CAUSES:

• Open circuit in the engine coolant temperature sensor. This should occur only when the engine is cold or partially warm. The engine should start satisfactorily when hot.

• The wide-open-throttle section of the throttle position switch is shorted. To check, disconnect the switch; the engine should start.

• The fuel pressure regulator is malfunctioning.

• The chassis-mounted fuel pump is malfunctioning.

PROBLEM: Poor fuel economy.

POSSIBLE CAUSES:

• The manifold absolute air pressure sensor is disconnected or leaking.

• The vacuum hose at the fuel pressure regulator or throttle body is disconnected.

• The air temperature or coolant temperature sensors are malfunctioning. Check the coolant temperature sensor as outlined under "Engine cranks but will not start." Check the air temperature sensor by connecting an ohmmeter to the sensor connector terminals; if the sensor resistance is less than 700 ohms. Replace the sensor.

PROBLEM: Engine stalls after being started.

POSSIBLE CAUSES:

• A poor connection or open circuits in the black and yellow ignition signal wire between the fuse block and the ECU.

• A poor connection or open circuit in the wiring or body of the engine coolant temperature sensor; cold or warm engine only. Check as outlined under "Engine cranks but will not start."

• On 1978 and later Sevilles, a malfunctioning idle air compensator solenoid will cause stalling at idle.

PROBLEM: Rough idle.

POSSIBLE CAUSES:

• Disconnected, leaking, or pinched manifold absolute air pressure sensor vacuum hose.

• Poor connection or an open circuit in the air temperature sensor or wiring; cold engine only. Please refer to "Poor fuel economy."

• Poor connection or short in the sensor or wiring of the engine coolant temperature sensor. Please see "Engine cranks but will not start."

• Poor connection at the injectors.

PROBLEM: Fast idle condition is prolonged.

POSSIBLE CAUSES:

• Throttle position switch is in need of adjustment.

• Poor connection at the fast idle valve or an open circuit in the heating element.

• A vacuum leak in or around the throttle body.

PROBLEM: Hesitation of the engine under acceleration.

POSSIBLE CAUSES:

• Leaking, restricted, or disconnected manifold absolute air pressure sensor vacuum hose.

• Throttle position switch is in need of adjustment or is malfunctioning.

• Poor connection of the ECU wiring harness at the ECU.

• Poor connection at the EGR valve solenoid or solenoid stuck open; cold engine only.

• Intermittent malfunction of the speed sensor trigger at the distributor.

PROBLEM: High speed performance is poor.

POSSIBLE CAUSES:

• The wide-open-throttle section of the throttle position switch is in need of adjustment or the switch is malfunctioning.

• The fuel filter is blocked or restricted.

• The chassis-mounted fuel pump is malfunctioning.

• Intermittent malfunction of the speed sensor trigger.

• An open circuit in the purple wire between the starter solenoid and the ECU.

DIGITAL FUEL INJECTION (DFI) SYSTEM (EXCEPT 1986–88 ELDORADO AND SEVILLE)

▶ **See Figure 23**

The Digital Fuel Injection (DFI) system, is a speed density fuel system that accurately controls the air/fuel mixture into the engine in order to achieve desired performance and emission goals. The Manifold Absolute Pressure (MAP) sensor, Manifold Air Temperature (MAT) sensor, and the Barometric pressure sensor (BARO) are used to determine the density (amount) of air entering the engine.

The HEI distributor provides the engine with speed (rpm) information. All of this information is then fed to the Electronic Control Module (ECM) and the ECM performs a high speed digital computations to determine the proper amount of fuel necessary to achieve the desired air/fuel mixture.

Once the ECM has calculated how much fuel to deliver, it signals the fuel injectors to meter the fuel into the throttle body. When the combustion process has been completed, some Hydro Carbons (HC), Carbon Monoxide (CO) and Nitrous Oxides (NOx) result, therefore, each DFI engine has an emission system to reduce the amount of these gases into the exhaust stream.

The dual bed catalytic converter helps to convert each of these gases into a more inert gas, however, the conversion process is most efficient (lower emission levels) at an air fuel/mixture of 14.7:1.

Once the engine is warmed up, the ECM uses the input from the oxygen sensor to more precisely control the air/fuel mixture to 14.7:1. This correction process is known as closed loop operation.

Because a vehicle is driven under a wide range of operating conditions, the ECM must provide the correct quantity of fuel under all operating conditions. Therefore, additional sensors and switches are necessary to determine what operating conditions exist so that the ECM can provide an acceptable level of engine control and driveability under all operating conditions. The closed loop DFI operation provides the acceptable level of driveability and fuel economy while improving emission levels.

The following subsystems combine to form the DFI closed loop system:

• Fuel Delivery.

• Air Induction.

• Data Sensors.

• Electronic Control Module.

• Body Control Module.

• Electric Spark Timing.

• Idle Speed Control.

• Emission Controls.

• Closed Loop Fuel Control.

• System Diagnosis.

• Cruise Control.

• Torque Converter Clutch.

The 1985 and later models are also equipped with a Body Control Module (BCM) that is used to control various vehicle body functions based upon data sensors and switch inputs. The ECM and BCM exchange information to main-

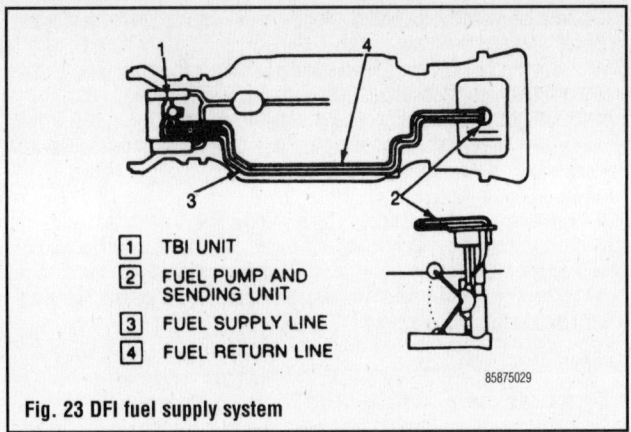

1. TBI UNIT
2. FUEL PUMP AND SENDING UNIT
3. FUEL SUPPLY LINE
4. FUEL RETURN LINE

85875029

Fig. 23 DFI fuel supply system

tain efficient operation of all vehicle functions. This transfer of information gives the BCM control over the ECM's self-diagnostic capabilities as well as its own.

Both the ECM and the BCM have the capability to diagnose faults with the various inputs and systems they control. When the ECM recognizes a problem, it lights a Service Soon telltale lamp on the instrument panel to alert the driver that a malfunction has occurred.

The digital fuel injection is performed by a pair of electronically actuated fuel metering valves, which, when actuated, spray a calculated quantity of fuel into the engine intake manifold. These valves or injectors are mounted on the throttle body above the throttle blades with the metering tip pointed into the throttle throats. Normally the injectors are alternately actuated .

Gasoline is supplied to the inlet of the injectors through the fuel lines and is maintained at a constant pressure across the injector inlets. When the solenoid-operated valves are energized, the injector ball valve moves to the full open position. Since the pressure differential across the valve is constant, the fuel quantity is changed by varying the time that the injector is held open.

The amount of air entering the engine is measured by monitoring the intake manifold absolute pressure (MAP), the intake manifold air temperature (MAT) and the engine speed (in rpm). This information allows the computer to compute the flow rate of air being inducted into the engine and, consequently, the flow rate of fuel required to achieve the desired air/fuel mixture for the particular engine operating condition.

➡ Some 1984–85 DFI equipped vehicles may experience an intermittent reduction of the power and or the engine stops running due to intermittent injector circuit operation. The trouble tree chart (DFI injector circuit test) can be used when attempting to diagnose such a condition. In some cases, it may be necessary to operate the vehicle and record the voltages as outlined, while the performance condition exists.

Fuel Supply System

The fuel supply system components provide fuel at the correct pressure for metering into the throttle bores by the injectors. The pressure regulator controls fuel pressure to a nominal 10.5 psi across the injectors. The fuel supply system is made up a fuel tank mounted electric pump, a full-flow fuel filter mounted on the vehicle frame, a fuel pressure regulator integral with the throttle body, fuel supply/return lines and two fuel injectors. The timing and amount of fuel supplied is controlled by the computer.

An electric, motor-driven, twin turbine-type pump is integral with the fuel tank float unit. It provides fuel at a positive pressure to the throttle body and fuel pressure regulator. The pump is specific for DFI application and is not repairable. However, the pump may be serviced separately from the fuel gauge unit.

Fuel pump operation is controlled by the fuel pump relay, located in the relay center. Operation of the relay is controlled by a signal from the computer. The fuel pump circuit is protected by a 10 amp fuse, located in the mini-fuse block. The computer turns the pump on with the ignition is turned to **ON** or **START**. However, if the engine is not cranked within one second after the ignition is turned on, the computer signal is removed and the pump turns off.

Fuel is pumped from the fuel tank through the supply line and the filter to the throttle body and pressure regulator. The injectors supply fuel to the engine in precisely timed bursts as a result of electrical signals from the computer. Excess fuel is returned to the fuel tank through the fuel return line.

The fuel tank incorporates a reservoir directly below the sending unit-in-tank pump assembly. The "bathtub" shaped reservoir is used to ensure a constant supply of fuel for the in-tank pump even at low fuel level and severe maneuvering conditions.

FUEL PUMP RELAY

When the key is first turned **ON** (key in the **RUN** position with the engine not running), the ECM will turn the fuel pump relay on for two seconds. This builds up the fuel pressure for cranking. If the engine is not started within two seconds, the ECM will shut off the fuel pump and wait until the engine starts. As soon as the engine is cranked, the ECM will turn the relay on a run the fuel pump.

OIL PRESSURE SWITCH

As a backup system to the fuel pump relay, the fuel pump can also be turned on by the oil pressure switch. The oil pressure switch has two circuits internally. One operates the oil pressure indicator lamp while the other is a normally closed open switch which closes when the oil pressure reaches about 4 psi. If the fuel pump relay fails, the oil pressure switch contacts will close and run the fuel pump.

An inoperative fuel pump relay can result in long cranking times, particularly if the engine is cold. The fuel pump relay inoperative will result in a code E20. The oil pressure switch acts as a backup to the relay to turn on the fuel pump as soon as the oil pressure reaches 4 psi.

An inoperative fuel pump would cause a no start condition. A fuel pump which does not provide enough pressure can result in poor performance.

Air Induction System

The air induction system consists of a throttle body and an intake manifold. Air for the combustion enters the throttle body and is distributed to each cylinder through the intake manifold. The throttle body contains a special distribution skirt below each injector to improve the fuel distribution.

The air flow rate is controlled by the throttle valves, which are connected to the accelerator linkage. The idle speed is determined by the position of the throttle valves and is controlled by the idle speed control (ISC).

Data Sensors

The purpose of the sensors is to supply electronic impulses to the ECM, which then computes the spark timing and fuel delivery rate necessary to maintain the desired air/fuel mixture. In doing so, the ECM controls the amount of fuel delivered to the engine.

MANIFOLD AIR TEMPERATURE (MAT) SENSOR

This sensor measures the temperature of the air/fuel mixture in the intake manifold and provides this information to the ECM. The sensor is a thermistor whose resistance changes as a function of temperature. When the temperature is low the resistance is high. When the temperature is high the resistance is low. This sensor is mounted in the intake manifold directly in front of the throttle body on the DeVille and Fleetwood. On the Eldorado and Seville, the sensor is located on the top right side of the engine near the alternator.

COOLANT TEMPERATURE SENSOR

The Coolant Temperature Sensor (CTS) is similar to the MAT sensor. This CTS provides coolant temperature information to the ECM for fuel enrichment, ignition timing, EGR operation, canister purge control, air management, EFE operation, idle speed control and closed loop fuel control. This sensor is located in the left front corner of the intake manifold on the DeVille and Fleetwood. On the Eldorado and Seville, it is located on the top left side of the engine near the distributor.

MANIFOLD ABSOLUTE PRESSURE (MAP) SENSOR

This sensor monitors the changes in the intake manifold pressure which result from engine load and speed changes. These pressure changes are supplied to the ECM in the form of electrical signals. As the intake manifold pressure increases, additional fuel is required. The MAP sensor sends information to the ECM and the ECM increases the injector on time (pulse width). When the manifold pressure decreases, the pulse width will be shortened.

On the DeVille and Fleetwood, the MAP sensor is mounted near the right rear side of the engine compartment. On the Eldorado and Seville, the MAP sensor is located on the top right side of the engine above the rear valve cover. On some models the MAP sensor may be located under the instrument panel near the right hand A/C outlet and electrically connected to the ECM.

BAROMETRIC PRESSURE (BARO) SENSOR

This sensor, senses the ambient or barometric pressure and provides information to the ECM on ambient pressure changes due to the altitude and to the weather. This sensor is usually mounted under the instrument panel near the right hand A/C outlet and sends an electrical signal to the ECM.

THROTTLE POSITION SENSOR (TPS)

The TPS sensor is a variable resistor mounted on the throttle body and is connected to the throttle valve shaft. Movement of the accelerator causes the throttle shaft to rotate and the throttle shaft rotation opens or closes the throttle blades. The sensor determines the shaft position (throttle angle) and transmits the appropriate electrical signal to the ECM.

The ECM processes these signals and uses the throttle angle information to operate the idle speed control system and to supply fuel enrichment as the throttle blades are opened.

VEHICLE SPEED SENSOR

The vehicle speed sensor informs the ECM as to how fast the vehicle is being driven. The ECM uses this signal for the logic required to operate the fuel economy data panel, the integral cruise control and the idle speed control system.

The speed sensor produces a very week signal. So therefore a vehicle speed sensor buffer is placed between the speed sensor and the ECM to amplify the speed signal. The speed sensor and the vehicle speed sensor buffer amplifier are located behind the speedometer cluster.

OXYGEN SENSOR

◆ See Figure 24

The oxygen sensor in the DFI system consists of a closed end Zirconia sensor placed in the engine exhaust gas stream This sensor generates a very weak voltage signal that varies with the oxygen content of the exhaust stream. As the oxygen content of the exhaust stream increases relative to the surrounding atmosphere, a lean fuel mixture is indicated by a low voltage output, as the oxygen content decreases, a rich fuel mixture is indicated by a rising voltage output from the sensor.

When the oxygen sensor is warm 392°F (200°C) The output voltage swings between 200 millivolts (lean mixture) and 800 millivolts (rich mixture). However, when the oxygen sensor is cold (below 392°F), the voltage output drops below this range and the response time of the sensor is much slower. The sensor cannot react quickly to rich-lean or lean-rich transitions; therefore, the sensor does not supply accurate information to the ECM. The output voltage may be read using a high impedance digital voltmeter.

➡**The high impedance digital voltmeter must a minimum 5 mega-ohm input impedance. Digital voltmeter's with a lower input impedance may cause an inaccurate reading or force the system to behave incorrectly.**

Some 1985 FWD DeVilles and Fleetwoods may experience a lean driveability condition and possibly ECM diagnostic codes 13 and or 45. Symptoms of a lean driveability condition can cause chuggle, surge sag, or reduced engine performance. This condition may be caused by a voltage difference between the oxygen sensor ground (engine block) and the ECM oxygen sensor ground reference, circuit 413, which connects to the generator bracket. Should a poor ground exist, the voltage difference between these two grounds is added to the oxygen sensor signal, falsely indicating a rich (high voltage) oxygen sensor signal to the ECM. The ECM compensates for a high oxygen sensor voltage by commanding a lean mixture.

If the generator stud has a black or brown single wire ring terminal on it, then the ECM oxygen sensor ground must be relocated. If the generator stud does nut have a black or brown single wire ring terminal on it, then the ECM oxygen sensor ground has been relocated. So proceed to the trouble code diagnosis if a code 13 or 45 is present.

ENGINE SPEED SENSOR

The engine speed sensor signal comes from the seven terminal HEI module in the distributor. Pulses from the distributor are sent to the ECM where the time between these pulses is used to calculate engine speed. The ECM adds the spark advance modifications to the signal and sends the signal back to the distributor.

POWER STEERING SWITCH

The power steering pressure switch is normally closed and opens when power steering pressure is detected. The power steering pressure switch receives 12 volts from the 10 amp solenoid fuse which is located in the relay center.

When high power steering pressures occur, the switch contacts are opened by the power steering oil pressure and the ECM reads 0 volts on the line which goes from the switch to the ECM. The ECM uses the power steering switch input to extend the ISC motor when high power steering loads occur, to help maintain and stable idle. Switch test code E.7.8 can be used to check the power steering pressure switch for proper operation.

PARK/NEUTRAL SWITCH

The park/neutral switch is part of the transmission neutral safety-backup switch Pin "A" of the six way weather pack connector on this switch is the park/neutral switch contacts. The park/neutral switch contacts are closed in park or neutral shorting the neutral safety-backup switch Pin "A" to ground. In any other gear range, pin "A" is open.

The ECM sends 12 volts to pin "A" of the neutral safety-backup switch. When the gear selector is in park or neutral, the 12 volt signal from the ECM is shorted to ground, resulting in 0 volts at the ECM. In reverse or forward gears the switch will be opened, resulting in 12 volts at the ECM.

The switch test code E.7.4 can be used to check the park/neutral switch for proper operation. An inoperative park/neutral switch could cause improper idle speed, cruise control or transmission converter clutch.

CRANK SIGNAL

The ECM looks at the starter solenoid to tell when the engine is cranking. It uses this to tell when the car is in the starting mode. If the crank signal is received by the ECM, a code 18 will be stored. Under these circumstances the vehicle may be difficult to start.

Electronic Control Module (ECM)

The Electronic Control Module, (ECM) or computer provides all computation and controls for the DFI system. Sensor inputs are fed into the computer from the various sensors. They are processed to produce the appropriate pulse duration for the injectors, the correct idle speed for the particular operating condition and the proper spark advance. Analog inputs from the sensors are converted to digital signals before processing. The computer assembly is mounted under the instrument panel and consists of various printed circuit boards mounted in a protective metal box. The computer receives power from the vehicle battery. When the ignition is set to the **ON** or **CRANK** position, the following information is received from the sensors:
- Engine coolant temperature
- Intake manifold air temperature
- Intake manifold absolute pressure
- Barometric pressure
- Engine speed
- Throttle position

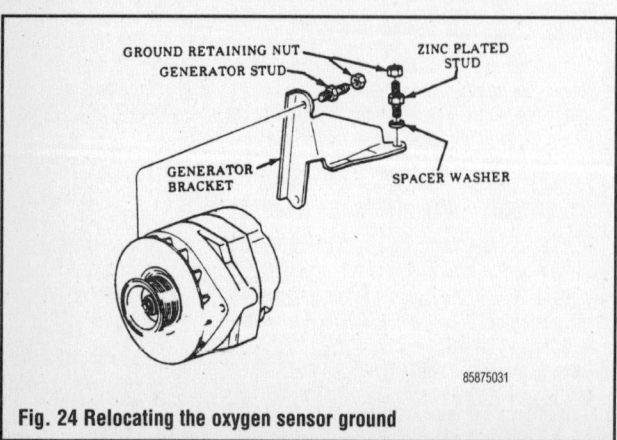

GROUND RETAINING NUT
GENERATOR STUD
ZINC PLATED STUD
GENERATOR BRACKET
SPACER WASHER

85875031

Fig. 24 Relocating the oxygen sensor ground

The following commands are transmitted by the ECM:
- Electric fuel pump activation
- Idle speed control
- Spark advance control
- Injection valve activation
- EGR solenoid activation

The desired air/fuel mixture for various driving and atmospheric conditions are programmed into the computer. As signals are received from the sensors, the computer processes the signals and computes the engine's fuel requirements. The computer issues commands to the injection valves to open for a specific time duration. The duration of the command pulses varies as the operating conditions change.

The digital electronic fuel injection system is activated when the ignition switch is turned to the **ON** position. The following events occur at this moment:
- The computer receives the ignition **ON** signal.
- The fuel pump is activated by the ECM. The pump will operate for approximately one second only, unless the engine is cranking or running.
- All engine sensors are activated and begin transmitting signals to the computer.
- The EGR solenoid is activated to block the vacuum signal to the EGR valve at coolant temperatures below 110°F (43°C).
- The CHECK ENGINE and COOLANT lights are illuminated as a functional check of the bulb and circuit.
- Operation of the fuel economy lamps begins.

The following events occur when the engine is started:
- The fuel pump is activated for continuous operation.
- The idle speed control motor will begin controlling idle speed, including fast idle speed, if the throttle switch is closed.
- The spark advance shifts from base (bypass) timing to the computer programmed spark curve.
- The fuel pressure regulator maintains the fuel pressure at 9–12 psi by returning excess fuel to the fuel tank.
- The computer alternately grounds each injector, precisely controlling the opening and closing time (pulse width) to deliver fuel to the engine.
- The following sensor signals are continuously received and processed by the computer:
- Engine coolant temperature
- Intake manifold air temperature
- Barometric pressure
- Intake manifold absolute air pressure
- Engine speed
- Throttle position changes

CENTRAL PROCESSING UNIT (CPU)

The digital signals received by the CPU are used to perform all mathematical computations and logic functions necessary to deliver the proper air/fuel mixture. The CPU also calculates the spark timing and idle speed information. The CPU commands the operation of emission controls, closed loop fuel control, cruise control and diagnostic system.

INPUT AND OUTPUT DEVICES

These integral devices of the ECM, convert the electrical signals received by the data sensors and change them over to digital signals for use by the CPU.

POWER SUPPLY

The main source of power for the ECM is from the battery, through the number one ignition circuit.

ECM MEMORY

There are three types of memory in the ECM and they are as follows:
- Programmable Read Only Memory (Prom) — The purpose of this memory is to contain the calibration information about each engine, transmission, body and rear axle ratio combination. If the battery voltage is lost for any reason, the PROM information is retained. The PROM chip can be easily changed if necessary.
- Read Only Memory (ROM) — The read only memory is programmed information that can be read only by the ECM. The read only memory program cannot be changed. If the battery voltage is lost at any time, the read only memory will be retained.
- Random Access Memory (RAM) — Random access memory acts as the scratch pad for the CPU. Information can be read into or out of the RAM mem-

ory hence it is called the scratch pad memory. The engine sensor information, diagnostic codes, and the results of calculations are temporarily stored here. If the battery voltage is removed, all the information in the Ram memory will be lost (this is similar to a hand held calculator when the switch is turned off).
- These three memory devices are all removable from the ECM unit.

To demonstrate how the ECM operates, the following is a list of events that will occur when the ignition switch is turned on:

1. The ECM receives the ignition on signal.
2. The fuel pump is activated by the ECM. The pump will operate for approximately one to two seconds only, unless the engine is being cranked or has started.
3. All engine sensors are activated and begin transmitting signals to the ECM.
4. The EGR solenoid is activated to block the vacuum signal to the EGR valve at a temperatures below 175°F (79°C).
5. The coolant light will be illuminated as a functional check of the bulb and the circuit.
6. The HEI bypass line is pulled down to 0 volts.

The following events are what occurs when the engine is being cranked.

7. The 12 volt crank signal is sent to the ECM.
8. The fuel pump is operating.
9. After a short series of prime pulses, injectors alternately deliver a fuel pulse on each distributor reference pulse.
10. The engine sensors continue to transmit signals to the ECM.
11. The Service Soon and Service Now lights are illuminated as a functional check of the bulb and circuit.
12. The other events are similar to the events which occur when the ignition switch is turned on.

The following events are what occurs when the engine is started.

13. The crank signal is removed from the ECM.
14. The injectors deliver fuel pulses alternately for each distributor reference pulse.
15. The HEI bypass line is pulled up to 5 volts and the HEI module receives spark advance signals from the ECM.
16. The ISC motor begins to control the idle speed if the throttle switch is closed.
17. The fuel pump operates continuously.
18. The pressure regulator maintains fuel pressure at 10.5 psi by returning excess fuel to the fuel tank.
19. The other events are similar to the events which occur when the ignition switch is turned on.

Body Control Module (BCM)

♦ See Figure 25

The BCM monitors and controls Electronic Climate Controls (ECC), rear defogger, outside temperature display, cooling fan control, fuel data display center display information, vacuum fluorescent display dimming, self diagnostics and retained accessory power system functions.

The BCM consists of input and output devices, CPU, power supply and memories that coincide with those of the ECM. The BCM exchanges information with the ECM to provide maximum reliability and improved serviceability of the body related systems.

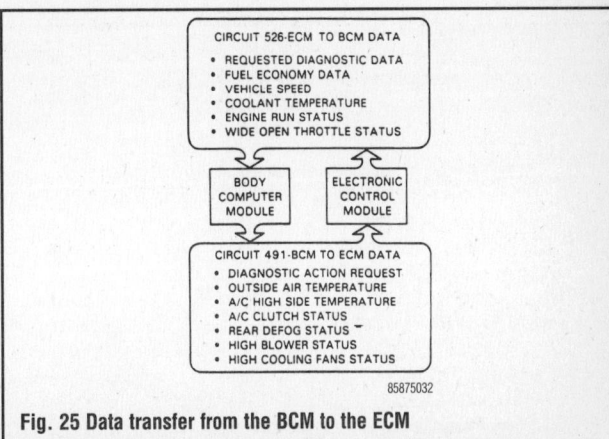

Fig. 25 Data transfer from the BCM to the ECM

Electronic Spark Timing (EST)

The EST type HEI distributor receives all spark timing information from the computer when the engine is running. The computer provides spark plug firing pulses based upon the various engine operating parameters. The electronic components for the electronic spark control system are integral with the computer. The two basic operating modes are cranking (or bypass) and normal engine operation.

When the engine is in the cranking/bypass mode, ignition timing occurs at a reference setting (distributor timing set point) regardless of other engine operating parameters. Under all other normal operating conditions, basic engine ignition timing is controlled by the computer and modified or added to, depending on particular conditions such as altitude and/or engine loading.

The HEI distributor communicates to the ECM through a four terminal connector which contains four circuits, these four circuits are as follows:
1. The distributor reference circuit.
2. The bypass circuit.
3. The EST circuit.
4. The ground circuit.

Whenever the pickup coil signals the HEI module to open the primary circuit, it also sends the spark timing signals to the ECM through the reference line.

When the voltage on the HEI bypass line is 0 volts (engine cranking), the HEI module is forced into the bypass mode which means that the HEI module provides spark advance at base timing and disregards the spark advance signal from the ECM. If the voltage on the HEI bypass line is 5 volts (engine running), the HEI module accepts the spark timing signal provided by the ECM.

Idle Speed Control System

The idle speed control system is controlled by the computer. The system acts to control engine idle speed in three ways; as a normal idle (rpm) control, as a fast idle device and as a "dashpot" on decelerations and throttle closing. The normal engine idle speed is programmed into the computer and no adjustments are possible. Under normal engine operating conditions, idle speed is maintained by monitoring idle speed in a closed loop fashion. To accomplish this loop, the computer periodically senses the engine idle speed and issues commands to the idle speed control in order to move the throttle stop, this maintaining the correct speed.

For engine starting, the throttle is either held open by the idle speed control for a longer (cold) or a shorter (hot) period to provide adequate engine warm-up prior to normal operation. When the engine is shut off, the throttle is opened by fully extending the idle speed control actuator to get ready for the next start.

Signal inputs for transmission gear, air conditioning compressor clutch (engaged or not engaged) and throttle (open or closed) are used to either increase or decrease throttle angle in response to these particular engine loadings.

Vehicle idle speed is controlled by an electrically driven actuator (idle speed control) which changes the throttle angle by acting as a movable idle stop. Inputs to the ISC actuator motor come from the ECM and are determined by the idle speed required for the particular operating condition. The electronic components for the ISC system are integral with the ECM. An integral part of the ISC is the throttle switch. The position of the switch determines whether the ISC should control idle speed or not. When the switch is closed, as determined by the throttle lever resting upon the end of the ISC actuator, the ECM will issue the appropriate commands to move the idle speed control to provide the programmed idle speed. When the throttle lever moves off the idle speed control actuator from idle, the throttle switch is opened. The computer than extends the actuator and stops sending idle speed commands and the driver controls the engine speed.

Diagnostic Procedure

The dash mounted Service Now and Service Soon telltale lights are used to inform you of detected system malfunctions or abnormalities. These malfunctions may be related to the various ECM inputs or controlled functions or to the ECM itself. The service telltale light that was illuminated by the fault occurrence will automatically go out if the fault clears. The fault is logged as an intermittent trouble code by the ECM; the ECM stores the trouble code associated with the detected failure until the diagnostic codes are cleared or until 50 ignition switch (on and off) cycles have occurred without any fault reappearing.

SERVICE TELLTALE OPERATION

Proper operation of the service telltale lights are as follows:
- Both lights are normally off (engine running or key on, engine nut running).
- A bulb check is performed; both bulbs turn on, when the ignition is in the **CRANK** position only. When the engine starts, both bulbs should go out.
- Depending on the trouble code set, either the Service Soon telltale light or the Service Now telltale light comes on and stays on while the malfunction (trouble code) is detected.
- If the malfunction is intermittent, the Service light that came on will go out when the malfunction is no longer detected. The light will come on each time the malfunction is again detected; the light may come on and go out again in the same key cycle. When a Service Soon malfunction is detected at the same time a Service Now malfunction is detected, only the Service Now telltale light comes on.
- Both service lights stay on when the system is displaying the diagnostic routine.

INTERMITTENT CODES VERSUS HARD FAILURES

The ECM may have two types of trouble codes stored in its memory:
- A code for a malfunction which is a hard failure. A hard failure turns on the appropriate service telltale light and keeps it on as long as the malfunction is present.
- A code intermittent malfunction which occurred within the last 50 ignition cycles. An intermittent failure will allow the service telltale light to turn off either when the malfunction clears up or when the key is next cycled to the OFF position.

The first pass of diagnostics, prefixed by ".E", will contain all history codes, both hard and intermittent. The second pass contains only the hard codes that are present and will be prefixed by ".E.E".

On the codes E12 through E51, the service telltale light will go out automatically if the malfunction clears. However the ECM stores the trouble associated with the detected failure until the diagnostic codes are cleared or until 50 ignition switch (ON/OFF) cycles have occurred without any fault reappearing. This condition is known as an intermittent failure.

When trouble code E30 or E48 is set, the Service Soon light will illuminate for the entire ignition cycle and system operation is not tested again until the next ignition cycle. This means that an intermittent malfunction will appear as a hard failure during the ignition cycle in which it occurs.

For codes E52 through E67, the service telltale lights will never come on. These codes indicate that a specific condition occurred of which you should be aware. Since many of these codes can be operator induced, a judgment must be made whether or not the code requires investigation. These codes will also be stored until the diagnostic system is cleared or until 50 ignition cycles have passed without any fault appearing.

Self-Diagnostic Features

TROUBLE CODES

In the process of controlling its various subsystems, the ECM and BCM continually monitor operating conditions for possible system malfunctions. By comparing system conditions against standard operating limits certain circuit and component malfunctions can be detected. A two digit numerical Trouble Code is stored in the computer memory when a problem is detected by this diagnostic system. These Trouble Codes can later be displayed by you as an aid in the system repair.

The occurrence of certain system malfunctions required that the vehicle operator be alerted to the problem so as to avoid prolonged operation of the vehicle under a degraded system performance. The computer controlled service telltale lights will be illuminated under these conditions which indicate that service is required.

If a particular malfunction would result in a unacceptable system operation, the self-diagnostics will attempt to minimize the effect by taking "Failsoft" action. "Failsoft" action refers to any specific attempt by the computer system to compensate for a detected problem. A typical "Failsoft" action would be substitution of a fixed input value when a sensor is detected to be open or shorted.

ECM/BCM SERVICE PRECAUTIONS

The ECM and BCM are designed to withstand normal current draws associated with vehicle operation, however care must be taken to avoid overloading any of these circuits. In testing for opens or shorts, do not ground or apply voltage to any of these circuits unless instructed to do so by the diagnostic procedures.

These circuits should be tested using a suitable high impedance multimeter J-34029A or J29125-A or equivalent, if they remain connected to the ECM or BCM. Power should never be removed or applied to the ECM or BCM with the key in **ON** position. Before removing or connecting battery cables, fuses or connectors always turn the ignition switch to the **OFF** position.

ENTERING DIAGNOSTIC MODE

▶ **See Figures 26 and 27**

To enter the diagnostic mode, proceed as follows:
1. Turn the ignition switch to the **ON** position.
2. Depress the OFF and WARMER buttons on the climate control panel (CCP) simultaneously and hold until "..." appears. Then "88" will be displayed, which indicates the beginning of the diagnostic readout.

➡**The purpose of illuminating the two display panels is to check that all segments of the displays are working. Diagnosis should not be attempted unless all segments appear as this could lead to misdiagnosis (code 34 could be code 31 with two segments inoperative, etc.). If any of the segments are inoperative, the affected display will need to be replaced.**

TROUBLE CODE DISPLAY

After the displays end the segment check, any Trouble Codes stored in computer memory will be displayed. If the Trouble Code (other than E51) are present, they will be displayed on the "Fuel Data Center" panel as follows:
1. Display of trouble codes will begin with an "8.8.8" on the "Fuel Data Center" panel approximately one second. Then this "..E" will be displayed which indicates the beginning of the ECM stored trouble codes. This first pass of the ECM codes includes all detected malfunctions whether they are currently present or not. If no ECM trouble codes are stored the "..E" display will be bypassed.

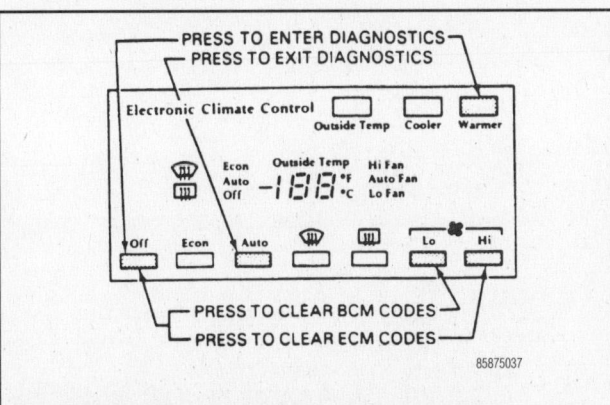

Fig. 26 Common DFI climate control panel (CCP) display

Fig. 27 Press to enter diagnostics—but read complete section first

2. Following the display of the "..E" the lowest numbered ECM code will be displayed for approximately two seconds. All ECM codes will be prefixed with an "E" (i.e. E12, E13, etc.).
3. Sequentially higher number ECM codes. if present will be displayed consecutively for two second intervals until the highest code present has been displayed.
4. The ".E.E" will then be displayed which indicates the beginning of the second pass of the ECM trouble codes. On the second pass, only hard trouble codes will be displayed. These are the codes which indicate a currently present malfunction. Codes which are displayed during the first pass but not during the second are intermittent the ".E.E" display will be bypassed.
5. When all the ECM codes have been displayed, the BCM codes will then be displayed in a similar fashion. The only exceptions during the BCM code display are:
    a. This "..F" precedes the first pass.
    b. BCM codes are prefixed by an "F".
    c. This ".F.F" precedes the second pass.
6. After all the ECM and BCM codes have been displayed or if no codes are present, code ".7.0" will be displayed. Code ".7.0" indicates that the system is ready for the next diagnostic feature to be selected.
7. If a code "E51" is currently being detected, it will be displayed continuously until the diagnostic mode is exited. During this display of code "E51", none of the other diagnostic features will be possible (i.e. switch tests. output cycling, etc.).

CLEARING THE TROUBLE CODES

Trouble codes are stored in the ECM's memory may be cleared (erased) by entering the diagnostic mode and then depressing the OFF and HI buttons on the climate control panel (CCP) simultaneously. Hold the buttons in until "E.0.0" appears. Trouble codes stored in the BCM's memory may be cleared by depressing the OFF and LO buttons simultaneously until the "F.0.0" appears. After the "E.0.0" or "F.0.0" is displayed, the ".7.0" will appear. With the ".7.0" is displayed turn the ignition off for at least 10 seconds before re-entering the diagnostic mode.

EXITING DIAGNOSTIC MODE

To get out of the diagnostic mode, depress the Auto button or turn the ignition switch OFF for 10 seconds. Trouble codes are not erased when this is done. The temperature setting will reappear in the display panel.

CLIMATE CONTROL IN DIAGNOSTIC MODE

Upon entering the diagnostic mode, the ECC will operate in whatever mode was being commanded just prior to depressing the OFF and WARMER buttons. Even through the display may change to the OFF mode just as the buttons are pushed, the prior operating mode is remembered and will resume after diagnostics is entered.

STATUS DISPLAY

While in the diagnostic mode, the mode indicators on the climate control panel (CCP) are used to indicate status of certain system operation modes. The different modes of operation are indicated by the status light either being turned on or turned off. A brief summary of each status light is provided below:
1. The AUTO status indicator is turned on whenever the ECM is operating in Closed Loop fuel control. This light should come on after the coolant and oxygen sensors have reached normal operating temperature.
2. The ECON status indicator is turned on whenever the oxygen sensor signal to the ECM indicates a RICH exhaust condition. This light should toggle between RICH and LEAN (flash on and off) during warm during warm steady throttle operation.
3. The OFF status indicator is turned on whenever the ECM senses that the throttle switch is closed. This light should be off whenever the throttle is applied.
4. The FRONT DEFOG status indicator is turned on whenever the ECM is commanding the VCC (viscous (torque) converter clutch) to engage. This light indicates whether the VCC is enabled or disabled by the ECM. Actual operation depends on the integrity of the VCC system.
5. The REAR DEFOG status indicator is turned on whenever the ECM senses that the 4th gear pressure switch is open. This light should only be on while in 4th gear operation.
6. The OUTSIDE TEMP status indicator is turned on whenever the BCM is

commanding the ECC (electronic comfort control) compressor clutch to engage. This light only indicates whether the clutch is enabled or disabled by the BCM. Actual operation depends on the integrity of the compressor clutch system.

➡️**The ECC is inhibited during diagnostic mode.**

7. The AUTO FAN status indicator is turned on whenever the feedback signal from the cooling fan control module to the BCM indicates that the fans are running. This light should be off whenever the fans are off.

➡️**"Fans Before Idle" is inhibited during the diagnostic mode.**

8. The HI-FAN status indicator is turned on whenever the BCM is commanding the UP-DOWN mode door to divert air flow up away from the heater outlet. This light will be off whenever the ECC system is in the HEATER or NORMAL PURGE modes.

9. The LO-FAN status indicator is turned on whenever the BCM is commanding the AC—DEF mode to divert air flow from the A/C outlets as in the A/C or NORMAL PURGE modes. This light will be off whenever the ECC system is in the HEATER, INTERMEDIATE, DEFROST and COLD PURGE modes.

10. The °F status indicator is turned on whenever the BCM senses that the refrigerant low pressure switch is open. The light will come on when the ambient temperature falls below approximately -5°F (-20°C) due to pressure temperature relationship of R-12. This light should remain off under all other conditions if the refrigerant system is fully charged and being controlled properly.

11. The °C status indicator is turned on whenever the BCM is commanding the heater water valve to block the coolant flow through the heater core. This light should remain off except when the air mix door is being commanded to the MAX A/C position (0%).

CODE .7.0

Code ".7.0" is a decision point. When code ".7.0" is displayed on the Data Center, you may select the diagnostic feature that you want to display. The following choices are available:

- ECM switch test.
- ECM data display.
- ECM output cycling.
- BCM data display.
- ECC program override.
- Cooling fans override.
- Exit the diagnostics or clear the codes and exit the diagnostics.

ECM SWITCH TEST SERIES

The engine must be running and Code ".7.0" must be displayed on the Data Center panel before the switch test can begin. To start the switch tests sequence depress and release the brake pedal; the switch test begins as the display switches from Code ".7.0" to Code "E.7.1."

➡️**If the display does not advance to Code "E.7.1", refer to diagnosis chart "E.7.1", because the ECM is not processing the brake signal.**

As each code is displayed, the associated switch must be cycled within 10 seconds or the code will be recorded in the ECM's memory as a failure. After the ECM recognizes a test as passing or after 10 seconds time-out elapses without the proper cycling being recognized, the display automatically advances to the next switch test code. The switch tests sequence is performed as follows:

1. With Code "E.7.1" displayed, depress and release the brake pedal again to test the cruise control brake circuit.

2. With Code "E.7.2" displayed. depress the throttle from the idle position to an open throttle position and then slowly release the throttle. While this action is being performed, the ECM checks the throttle switch for proper operation.

3. With Code "E.7.4" displayed and the brakes applied, shift the transmission lever into reverse and then neutral. This action checks the operation of the park neutral switch.

➡️**On vehicles without cruise control, codes E.7.5, E.7.6 and E.7.7 will be displayed but cannot be performed during the vehicle switch tests. When these codes are displayed during the switch tests, allow each code to reach its 10 second time out. After this time out has elapsed, the display will advance to the next code. Allow codes E.7.5, E.7.6 and E.7.7 to time out (30 seconds). Since these codes will be recorded as failures in the switch test sequence, a display E.0.0 will never be observed at the completion of the tests (see Step 9). To confirm proper**

operation of the remaining switch, Code E.7.8 must be observed as having advanced within 10 second time out. If the code cannot be advanced within its time out, it should be considered a failed test.

4. With Code "E.7.5" displayed, switch the cruise control instrument panel switch from OFF to ON and back to OFF to check the operation of this switch.

5. With Code "E.7.6" displayed and with the cruise instrument panel switch in the on position, depress and release the set coast button to check the operation of this switch.

6. With Code "E.7.7" displayed and with the cruise instrument panel switch in the on position, depress and release the resume/acceleration switch to check the operation of this switch.

7. With Code "E.7.8" displayed and the engine running, turn the wheels from straight ahead to the full right or left position and then return it to the straight ahead position. While this action is being performed, the ECM checks the power steering pressure switch for proper operation.

8. When the switch tests are completed, the ECM will now go back and display the switch codes which did not test properly. Each code which did not pass will be displayed beginning with the lowest number. The codes will not disappear until the affected switch circuit has been repaired and retested.

9. After the switch tests are completed and all circuits pass, the "Fuel Data Center" displays "E.0.0" and then returns to code ".7.0." The "E.0.0" indicates that all of the switch circuits are operating properly.

ECM Data Display

Code ".7.0" must be displayed on the "Data Center" panel before the diagnostics can begin to display the ECM data series. To display the ECM data information proceed as follows:

1. Depress the and release the Lo button on the climate control panel (CCP). The ECM data series will begin as the display switches from Code ".7.0" to Code "E.9.0". It is possible to leave the ECM data series at anytime and return to Code ".7.0" by clearing the ECM or BCM codes.

2. To advance the display, depress the Hi button on the climate control panel (CCP). To return to a lower number parameter or jump directly from E.9.0 to the end of the parameter list (P.1.3). depress the Lo button on the CCP.

3. When troubleshooting a malfunction, the ECM data display can be used to compare the vehicle with problems to a vehicle which is functioning properly. A brief summary of each parameter is provided below:

a. **P.0.1**—The throttle angle is displayed in degrees, the parameter range if from 10.0–90.0 degrees. The throttle angle displayed is actual indicated angle, not the throttle angle corrected by the ECM adaptive learning routine. A decimal point will appear before the last digit.

b. **P.0.2**—The map value is displayed in kilopascals (kPa), the parameter range is from 14–109.

c. **P.0.3**—The computed BARO value is displayed in kilopascals (kPa), the parameter range is from 61–103 kPa. BARO is calculated from the MAP reading taken at wide open throttle.

d. **P.0.4**—The coolant temperature is displayed in degrees Celsius (°C), the parameter display range is from -40 to +151°C.

e. **P.0.5**—The manifold air temperature is displayed in degrees Celsius (°C), the parameter display range is from -40 to +151°C.

f. **P.0.6**—The injector pulse width is displayed in milliseconds. A decimal point will appear before the last digit, the parameter display range is 0–99 ms.

g. **P.0.7**—The oxygen sensor voltage is displayed in volts, the display range is 0–1.14 volts. A decimal point will appear before the last two digits.

h. **P.0.8**—The spark advance value is displayed in degrees. This value will agree with a timing light on the engine (plus or minus 2 degrees) if the base timing has been adjusted properly. The parameter display range is from 0–52 degrees;.

i. **P.0.9**—The ignition cycle counter value is the number of times that the ignition has been cycled to the off since the ECM trouble code was last detected. After 50 ignition cycles without any malfunctions being detected, all stored ECM codes are cleared and the counter is reset to 0.

j. **P.1.0**—The battery voltage is read in volts. A decimal point will appear before the last digit. The parameter display range is from 0–25.5 volts.

k. **P.1.1**—The engine speed is displayed in rpm/10 (120 should be read at 1200 rpm). The parameter display range is 0–637 rpm; multiply the parameter by 10 to get rpm.

l. **P.1.2**—The vehicle speed is displayed in miles per hour (MPH). The parameter display range is 0–255 MPH.

m. **P.1.3**—The oxygen sensor cross counts is a counter that is incremented by one (1) each time the oxygen sensor "Crosses" the line from the rich to lean to lean to rich. Cross counts start at 0 increments to 255 where it rolls over and begins to increment again.

n. **P.1.4**—The fuel integrator is a record of how long the oxygen sensor has spent in the rich or lean voltage regions. The fuel integrator starts at 128 counts and resets to 128 counts on acceleration, deceleration and at heavy engine loads. If the fuel system is running to rich for current conditions, the integrator gets smaller to indicate less fuel is needed. If the fuel system is running too lean for current conditions, the integrator will get larger to indicate more fuel is needed. The parameter display range is from 0 (being a fuel system too rich, a lean command) to 255 (being a fuel system too lean, a rich command).

o. **P.1.5**—VCC volts is the voltage reading from the VCC temperature thermistor. The parameter display range is 0 volts (hot thermistor or circuit shorted) to 5.1 volts (cold thermistor or circuit open).

p. **P.1.6**—The ECM prom I.D. is displayed as a number up to three digits long which can be used to verify that the proper PROM was installed in the ECM.

4. When the ECM data display is initiated, the "Fuel Data Center" will display a parameter identification (i.e. P.0.1 or P.1.3) for one second and then a number will be displayed for nine seconds to indicate the parameter value. The display will continue to repeat this sequence of events until you decides to move another parameter.

ECM Output Cycling

◆ See Figure 28

This mode can be initiated after "E.9.5" is displayed on the "Fuel Data Center". The display of the "E.9.5" can be reached by depressing the Hi button while Code ".7.0" is displayed. The ECM output cycling mode, Code "E.9.6." turns the ECM's outputs on and off. To enter the output cycling mode, proceed as follows;

- The engine must be running.
- Turn the cruise instrument panel switch to the on position so that the cruise control outputs will cycle.
- Turn the engine off and within two seconds, turn the ignition on.
- Enter the diagnostics and display Code "E.9.5".
- Depress the accelerator pedal (throttle switch open) and release it (throttle switch closed). The ECM output cycling mode begins as the display switches from Code "E.9.5" to Code "E.9.6."
- It is possible to leave the ECM output cycling mode at any time and return to ".7.0" by clearing the ECM and BCM codes. If the display does not advance to Code "E.9.6", refer to Code "E.7.2" of the switch test.
- The output cycling mode will end automatically after two minutes of cycling and the display will switch from Code "E.9.6" to Code "E.9.5".
- The outputs will cycle on and off every three seconds until the two minute automatic shut off occurs. The only exception to this three second cycle is the

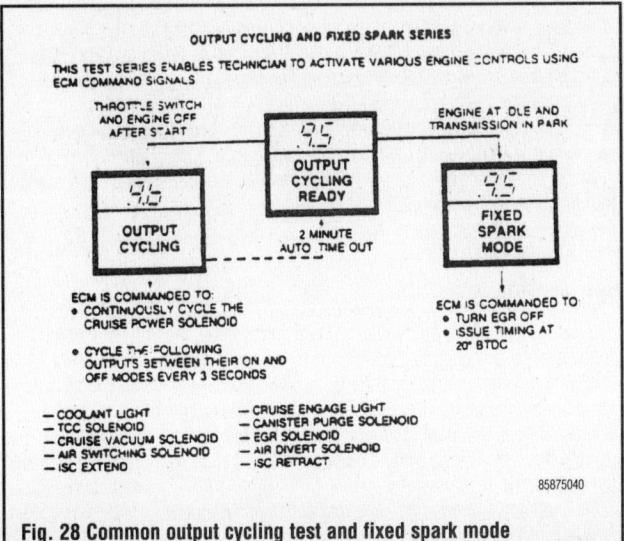

Fig. 28 Common output cycling test and fixed spark mode

cruise control power valve which cycles continuously. If additional output cycling is desired, recycle the throttle switch.

➡**The ECM has a "learning" capability. If the battery is disconnected the learning process has to begin all over again. A change may be noted in the vehicle's performance. To "teach" the ECM, insure the vehicle is at operating temperature and drive at part throttle, with moderate acceleration and idle conditions, until performance returns.**

Fixed Spark Mode Procedure (Set Timing)

To verify the proper adjustment of spark timing, the ECM will command a fixed 10 degrees of spark advance and disable the EGR operation whenever the following conditions are met:

- The engine must be running at warm (parameter "P.0.4" greater than 85°C.).
- The engine speed must be under 900 rpm.
- The transmission must be in Park.
- Exit diagnostics (press Auto) and jumper pins "A" (circuit #150) and "B" (circuit #451) in the ALDL connector. The service soon light may begin to flicker when pins "A" and "B" are jumped together.

BCM Data Display

Code ".7.0" must be displayed on the "Fuel Data Center" panel before the diagnostics can begin to display the BCM data series. To display the BCM data information proceed as follows:

1. Depress the and release the Outside Temp button on the climate control panel (CCP). The BCM data series will begin as the display switches from Code ".7.0" to Code "F.8.0". It is possible to leave the BCM data series at anytime and return to Code ".7.0" by clearing the ECM or BCM codes.

2. To advance the display, depress the Hi button on the climate control panel (CCP). To return to a lower number parameter or jump directly from "F.8.0" to the end of the parameter list ("P.3.1") depress the Lo button on the CCP.

3. When troubleshooting a malfunction, the BCM data display can be used to compare the vehicle with problems to a vehicle which is functioning properly. A brief summary of each parameter is provided below:

a. **P.2.0**—The commanded blower voltage is read in volts. A decimal point will appear before the last digit.

b. **P.2.1**—The coolant temperature is displayed in degrees Celsius (°C). This value is sent from the ECM to BCM.

c. **P.2.2**—The commanded air mix door position is displayed in percent (%). A value close to 0% represents a cold air mix and a value close to 100% represents a warm air mix.

d. **P.2.3**—The actual air mix door position is displayed in percent (%). This value should follow the commanded air mix door position (P.2.2) except when the door is commanded beyond its mechanical limits of travel.

e. **P.2.4**—The air delivery mode is displayed as a number from 0–7. Each number is a code which represents the following air delivery modes; 0 = Max A/C , 1 = A/C, 2 = Intermediate, 3 = heater, 4 = Off, 5 = Normal Purge, 6 = Cold Purge and 7 = Defrost.

f. **P.2.5**—The in car temperature is displayed in degrees Celsius (°C).

g. **P.2.6**—The actual outside temperature is displayed in degrees Celsius (°C). This value represents actual sensor temperature and is not restricted by the features used to minimize engine heat affects on the customer display value.

h. **P.2.7**—The high side temperature (condenser output) is displayed in degrees Celsius (°C).

i. **P.2.8**—The low side temperature (evaporator output) is displayed in degrees Celsius (°C).

j. **P.2.9**—The actual fuel level is read in gallons. A decimal point will appear before the last digit. The value represents actual sensor position and is not restricted by the features used to eliminate fuel slosh affects on the customer display value.

k. **P.3.0**—The ignition cycle counter value is the number of times that the ignition has been cycled to the off or start since a BCM trouble code was last detected. After 100 ignition cycles without any malfunctions being detected, all BCM codes are cleared and the counter is reset to 0.

l. **P.3.1**—The BCM prom I.D. is displayed as a number up to three digits long which can be used to verify that the proper PROM was installed in the BCM.

4. When the ECM data display is initiated, the "Fuel Data Center" will dis-

play a parameter check (i.e. P.2.0 or P.3.1) for one second and then a number will be displayed for nine seconds to indicate the parameter value. The display will continue to repeat this sequence of events until you decide to move another parameter.

ELECTRONIC COMFORT CONTROL (EEC)

During the display data on the "Fuel Data Center" (see BCM Data Display previously outlined in this section), the climate control panel (CCP) will display a two digit number which represents the ECC program number. This number represents various levels of heating and cooling effort. As "F.8.0" first appears on the "Fuel Data Center", the CCP will begin displaying the program number which is currently being used by the ECC system. As operating conditions change, this number will automatically change in response.

The automatic calculation of the program number can be bypassed by a manual override feature using the Warmer and Cooler buttons. While in the F.8.0 mode pressing the Warmer button will force the program number to increase at a controlled rate until the value of 100 is reached. The 100 represents the Max Heat mode of the ECC operation. Pressing the Cooler button will force the program number to decrease until the value of 0 is reached which represents the Max A/C mode.

This manual override of the automatic program number calculation will continue until the "F.8.0" mode is exited. This allows you to control the program number to any number from 0–100 and simultaneously observe the reaction of any of the BCM data parameters.

COOLING FAN OVERRIDE

Code ".7.0" must be displayed on the "Fuel Data Center" panel before the cooling fan override feature can be selected. This feature allows you to manually override the BCM's automatic control of the cooling fans speed. To manually command either "high fans" of "fans off", proceed as follows:

1. Depress and release the ECON button on the comfort control panel (CCP). The cooling fans override mode begins as the display switches from Code ".7.0" to code "F.8.5". It is possible to leave the cooling fans override mode at any time and return to ".7.0" by clearing the ECM and the BCM codes.

2. To command the "high fans" hold in the Hi button on the CCP. Fan speed should increase until the maximum speed is achieved. Releasing the Hi button will return the calculation of fan speed to automatic BCM control.

3. To command the "fans off" hold the Lo button on the CCP. The fan speed should decrease until the fans and completely stopped. Releasing the Lo button will return the calculation of fan speed to automatic BCM control.

➡ **Due to the varied Cadillac models covered in this section, some vehicles will use more sensors than others. A complete general diagnostic section is outlined. The steps and procedures can be altered as required (and necessary) to the specific model being diagnosed and the sensors with which it is equipped.**

1986–88 ELDORADO AND SEVILLE

Aboard these vehicles are several electronic components which can be controlled by you to provide valuable self-diagnostic information. These components are part of an electrical network, designed to control various engine and body subsystems. At the heart of the computer system is the Body Computer Module (BCM). The BCM is located in the middle of the instrument panel, behind the Driver Information Center display. It has climate control an internal microprocessor which is the center for communication with all the other components in the system. All system sensors and switches are monitored by the BCM or one of the four other major components that complete the computer system. These four components are:

1. Electronic Control Module (ECM).
2. Instrument Panel Cluster (IPC).
3. Programmer—Heating—Ventilation—A/C.
4. Climate Control/Driver Information Center.

A combination of inputs from these major components and the other sensors and switches communicate with the BCM, either as individual inputs, or on the common communications link called the data line. The various input to the BCM combine with program instructions within the system memory to provide accurate control over the many subsystems involved. When a subsystem circuit exceeds pre-programmed limits, a system malfunction is indicated and may provide certain backup functions. Control over the many subsystems from the

BCM is performed by controlling system outputs. This can be either direct or transmitted along the data line to one of the four other major components. The process of receiving, storing, testing, and controlling information is continuous. The data communication gives the BCM control over the ECM's self-diagnostic capabilities in addition to its own.

Between the BCM and the other four major components of the computer system, a communication process has been incorporated, which allows the devices to share information and thereby provide for additional control capability. In a method similar to that used by a telegraph system, the BCM's internal circuitry rapidly switches a circuit between 0 and 5 volts like a telegraph key. This process is used to convert information into a series of pulses which represents coded data messages understood by the other component. Also, much like a telegraph system, each major component has its own recognition code (address). so when a message is sent out on the data line, only the component or station that matches the assigned recognition code will pay attention, and the rest of the components or stations will ignore it.

Diagnostic Procedure

This section can be used to begin diagnosis of any complaint which does not directly relate to a specific subsystem or to obtain a detailed understanding of the vehicle self-diagnostic capabilities. As a starting point, ask yourself the following questions:

1. Is the Engine Control System telltale working? If this telltale fails to illuminate during crank, then the problem could be in the power supply circuits to the computer system.

2. Can Service Mode be accessed? If the display is not operating, self-diagnostics cannot be used.

3. Is there a Trouble Code displayed? If a trouble code is identified using the self-diagnostics, a problem has been detected by the system which can be corrected following the appropriately numbered code chart. Codes with a prefix of "E" are ECM codes. Codes with a prefix of "B" are BCM codes.

VISUAL INSPECTION

One of the most important checks, which must be done before any diagnostic activity, is a careful visual inspection of suspect wiring and components. This can often lead to fixing a problem without further steps. Inspect all vacuum hoses for pinches, cuts or disconnection's.

Be sure to inspect hoses that are difficult to see beneath the air cleaner. Inspect all the related wiring for bad connections (burned or chaffed spots, pinched wires, contact with sharp edges or hot exhaust manifolds). This visual inspection is very important. It must be done carefully and thoroughly.

1. The Engine Control System telltale is working.
2. Service Mode can be accessed.
3. No trouble codes are stored.
4. A careful visual check found no problems.

COMPUTER SYSTEM SERVICE PRECAUTIONS

The computer system is designated to withstand normal current draws associated with vehicle operation, however, care must be taken to avoid overloading any of these circuits. In testing for opens or shorts, do not ground or apply voltage to any of the circuits unless instructed to do so by the diagnostic procedures. These circuits should only be tested using the High Impedance Multimeter (J-29125A, J-34029A, or equivalent) if they remain connected to one of the computers. Power should never be removed or applied to one of the computers with the key in the ON position. Before removing or connecting battery cables, fuses or connectors always turn the ignition to the OFF position.

Self-Diagnostic Features

TROUBLE CODES

In the process of controlling the various subsystems, the ECM and BCM continually monitor operating conditions for possible system malfunctions. By comparing system conditions against standard operating limits certain circuit and component malfunctions can be detected. A three digit numerical Trouble Code is stored in computer memory when a problem is detected by this self diagnostic system. These Trouble Codes can later be displayed by you as an aid in system repair.

The occurrence of certain system malfunctions require that the vehicle operator be alerted to the problem so as to avoid prolonged operation of the vehicle under subnormal system performance. Computer controlled diagnostic messages and/or telltales will appear under these conditions which indicate that service is required.

If a particular malfunction would result in unacceptable system operation, the self-diagnostics will attempt to minimize the effect by taking "failsoft" action. "Failsoft" action refers to any specific attempt by the computer system to compensate for the detected problem. A typical failsoft action would be the substitution of a fixed input when a sensor is detected to be open or shorted.

ENTERING SERVICE MODE

To enter diagnostic mode, proceed as follows:
1. Turn the ignition **ON**.
2. Push the OFF and WARM buttons on the Climate Control Panel simultaneously and hold until the segment check appears on the Instrument Panel Cluster (IPC) and Climate Control Driver Information Center (CCDIC).

➡**Operating the vehicle in the Service Mode for extended time periods without the engine running or without a battery charger will cause the battery to run down and possibly relate false diagnostic information, or cause a no start condition. To ensure proper operation, attach a battery charger if vehicle is to be operated in Service Mode without engine running for periods longer than ½ hour.**

SEGMENT CHECK

The purpose of illuminating the IPC and CCDIC is to check that all segments of the vacuum fluorescent displays are working. On the IPC however, the turn signal indicators do not light during this check. Diagnosis should not be attempted unless all the CCDIC segments appear, as this could lead to misdiagnosis. If any portions or segments of the CCDIC display are inoperative, it must be replaced.

STATUS LIGHTS

While in the diagnostic service mode, the mode indicators on the Climate Control Panel (CCP) of the CCDIC are used to indicated the status of certain operating modes. The different modes of operation are indicted by the status light (turned on or turned off). A brief summary of each status light is provided below.
- 1. The OFF status indicator is turned on whenever the ECM is commanding the Viscous Converter Clutch (VCC) to engage. The light only indicated whether the VCC is enabled or disabled by the ECM. Actual operation depends on the integrity of the VCC system.
2. The AUTO status indicator is turned on whenever the ECM is operating in "closed loop" fuel control. This light should come on after the coolant and oxygen sensors have reached normal operating temperatures.
3. The ECON status indicator is turned on whenever the oxygen sensor signal to the ECM indicates a rich exhaust condition. This light should switch between rich and lean (flash on and off) during warm steady throttle operation.
4. The C status indicator is turned on whenever the ECM senses that the 3rd gear pressure switch is open. The light should be on while in 3rd gear operation.
5. The F status indicator is turned on whenever the ECM senses that the 3rd and 4th gear pressure switches are open. the light should be on while in 4th gear operation and the ECM had received a 3rd gear input signal.
6. The E status indicator is turned on whenever the ECM senses that the 4th gear pressure switch is open, but not the 3rd gear switch. The light should be on while in 4th gear operation and the ECM had not received a 3rd gear input signal.
7. The (front defog) status indicator is turned on whenever the BCM is commanding the ECC compressor clutch to engage. The light indicated whether the clutch is enabled or disabled by the BCM and actual operation depends on the integrity of the compressor clutch system.
8. The (rear defog) status indicator is turned on whenever the BCM senses that the low refrigerant pressure switch is open. The light should remain off if the refrigerant system is fully charged and being properly controlled. However, when the ambient temperature drops below approximately -5°F (-21°C), the light will come on due to the pressure-temperature relationship of R-12.
9. The LO Fan status indicator is turned on whenever the BCM is commanding the A/C-DEF mode door to divert air flow to the A/C outlets, as in the

A/C or normal purge modes. This light will be off whenever the ECC system is in the heater, intermediate, defrost and cold purge modes.
10. The NORM Fan Symbol status indicator is turned on whenever the BCM is commanding the heater water valve to block coolant flow through the heater core. the light should remain off except when the air mix door is being commanded to the max A/C position (0%).
11. The HI Fan Symbol status indicator is turned on whenever the BCM is commanding the UP-DOWN mode door to divert air flow up, away from the heater outlet. This light will be off whenever the ECC system is in the heater or normal purge mode.

TROUBLE CODE DISPLAY

After Service Mode is entered any trouble codes stored in computer memory will be displayed. ECM codes will be displayed first. If no ECM trouble codes are stored, a NO ECM CODES message will be displayed. All ECM codes will be prefixed with a "E" (i.e. EO13, EO14, etc.). The lowest numbered ECM code will be displayed first followed by progressively higher numbered codes present. Following the highest ECM code present or the NO ECM CODES message, BCM codes will be displayed. All BCM codes will be prefixed with a "B" (i.e. B110, B111, etc.). If no BCM Trouble Codes are stored "NO BCM CODES" message will be displayed. Any BCM and ECM codes displayed will also be accompanied by "Current" or "History". "History" indicated the failure was not present the last time the code was tested and "Current" indicated the fault still exists. At any time during the display of ECM or BCM codes, if the LO button on the CCP is depressed, the display of codes will be bypassed. At anytime during the display of trouble codes, it the Reset/Recall button on the Driver Information Center (DIC) is depressed the system will exit Service Mode and go back to normal vehicle operation.

CLIMATE CONTROL IN SERVICE MODE

Upon entering the Service Mode, the climate control will operate in whatever mode was being commanded just prior to depressing the OFF and WARM buttons. Even though the display may change just as the buttons are touched, the prior operating mode is remembered and will resume after Service Mode is entered. Extended Compressor at Idle (ECI) is not allowed while in the diagnostic mode. This allows observation of system parameters during normal compressor cycles.

OPERATING THE SERVICE MODE

After trouble codes have been displayed, the Service Mode can be used to perform several tests on different systems one at a time. Upon completion of code display, a specific system may bc selected for testing. Following the display of trouble codes, the first available system will be displayed (i.e. ECM?). While selecting a system to test, any of the following actions may be taken to control the display:
1. Depressing OFF button on the CCP will stop the system selection process and return the display to the beginning of the trouble code sequence.
2. Depressing the LO button on the CCP will display the next available system selection. This allows the display to be stepped through all system choices. This list of systems can be repeated following the end of the system list.
3. Depressing the HI button on the CCP will select the displayed system for testing.

SELECTING THE TEST TYPE

Having selected a system, the first available test type will be displayed (i.e. ECM DATA?). While selecting a specific test type, any of the following actions may be taken to control the display:
1. Depressing the OFF button on the CCP will stop the test type selection process and return the display to the next available system selection.
2. Depressing the LO button on the CCP will display the next available test type for the selected system. This allows the display to be stepped through all available test type choices. This list of test types can be repeated following the display of the last test type.
3. Depressing the HI button on the CCP will select the displayed test type. At this point the first of several specific tests will appear.

SELECTING THE TEST

Selection of the DATA?, INPUTS?, OUTPUTS? or OVERRIDE? test types will result in the first available test being displayed. If dashes ever appear, this test is not allowed with the engine running. Four characters of the display will contain a test code to identify the selection. The first two characters are letters which identify the system and test type (i.e. ED for ECM DATA) and the last two characters numerically identify the test (i.e. ED01 for Throttle Position). While selecting a specific test, any of the following actions may be taken to control the display:

1. Depressing the OFF button on the CCP will stop the test selection process and return the display to the next available test type for the selected system.

2. Depressing the LO button on the CCP will display the next smaller test number for the selected test type. If this button is pressed with the lowest test number displayed, the highest test number will then appear.

3. Depressing the HI button on the CCP will display the next larger test number for the selected test type. If this button is pressed with the highest test number displayed, the lowest test number will then appear.

SELECTING "CLEAR CODES?"

Selection of the CLEAR CODES? test type will result in the message CODES CLEAR being displayed alone with the selected system name. this message will appear for 3 seconds to indicated that all stored trouble codes have been erased from that system's memory. After 3 seconds the display will automatically return to the next available test type for the selected system.

SELECTING "SNAPSHOT?"

▶ See Figure 29

Selection of the SNAPSHOT? test type will result in the message SNAPSHOT TAKEN being displayed with the selected system name preceding it. This message will appear for 3 seconds to indicate that all system data and inputs have been stored in memory. After 3 seconds the display will automatically proceed to the first available snapshot test type (i.e. SNAP DATA). While selecting a snapshot test type, any of the following actions may be taken to control the display.

This ECM snapshot feature is included to assist in diagnosis of intermittent problems. The ECM snapshot selection will store one set of all of the ECM data parameter values and output status indications at the time that the snapshot is requested. To use the snapshot, enter the diagnostics and allow the Climate Control Drive Information Center (CCDIC) to idle at ECM SNAPSHOT. When intermittent condition occurs, or when the parameters are to be recorded, press HI and hold until the message ECM SNAPSHOT TAKEN appears. The ECM snapshot taken message indicates that the data is now stored for review.

1. Depressing the OFF button on the CCP will stop the test type selection process and return the display to the next available system selection.

2. Depressing the LO button will display the next available snapshot test type. this allows the display to be stepped through all available choices. This list of snapshot test types can be repeated following the display of the last choice.

3. Depressing the HI button with SNAP DATA? or SNAP INPUTS? displayed will select that test type. At this point the display is controlled as it would be for non-snapshot data and inputs displays, however, all values and status information represents memorized vehicle conditions.

4. Depressing the HI button with SNAPSHOT? displayed will again display the SNAPSHOT TAKEN message to indicate that new information has been stored in memory. Access to this information is obtained the same as previously described.

EXITING THE SERVICE MODE

To get out of the service mode, depress the Reset/Recall button on the DIC or turn the ignition switch off. Trouble codes are not erased when this is done.

Data Displays

Data displays are operated as defined under Operating The Service Mode. When troubleshooting a malfunction, the ECM and BCM data displayed can be used to compare the vehicle with problems to a vehicle which is functioning properly. A brief summary of each parameter is provided below:

ECM PARAMETERS

1. **ED01**—The throttle position (TPS) is displayed in degrees from -10–90 degrees.
2. **ED02**—The manifold air pressure (MAP) is displayed in kilopascals (kPa) from 14–109.
3. **ED03**—The computed barometric pressure (BARO) is displayed in kilopascals (kPa) from 61–103.
4. **ED04**—The coolant temperature is displayed in degrees Celsius (°C) from -40–151.
5. **ED05**—The manifold air temperature (MAT) sensor reading is displayed in degrees Celsius (°C) from -40° to +151°.
6. **ED06**—The fuel injector pulse width (ON time) is displayed in milliseconds (ms), from 0–99.
7. **ED07**—The oxygen sensor voltage is displayed in volts from 0–12.
8. **ED08**—The amount of spark advance is displayed in degrees, from 0–52.
9. **ED10**—The battery voltage is read in volts, from 0–25.5.
10. **ED11**—The engine speed is displayed in rpm from 0–6370.
11. **ED12**—The vehicle speed is displayed in miles per hour (MPH) from 0–159.
12. **ED18**—The oxygen sensor cross count is displayed as the number of times the O$_2$sensor crossed the reference line each second.
13. **ED19**—The fuel integrator is displayed in counts, from 88–160.
14. **ED26**—The viscous converter clutch (VCC) temperature is displayed as a voltage level at the ECM. The normal range is from 0–5.12 volts.
15. **ED98**—The ignition cycle counter valve is the number of times the ignition has been cycled to OFF since an ECM Trouble code was last detected. After 50 ignition cycles without any malfunction being detected, all stored ECM codes are cleared.

BCM PARAMETERS

1. **BD20**—The commanded blower voltage is read in volts from -3.3–18.
2. **BD21**—The coolant temperature is displayed in degrees Celsius (°C) from -40° to +151°. This value is sent from the ECM to the BCM. If this circuit malfunctions as determined by the ECM, the ECM will send the BCM a "Failsoft" value for display.
3. **BD22**—The commanded air mix door position is displayed in percent (%). A value close to 0% represents a cold air mix and a value close to 100% represents a warm air mix.
4. **BD23**—The actual air mix door position is displayed in percent (%). This value should follow the commanded air mix door position (BD22) except when the door is commanded beyond its mechanical limits of travel.
   a. 0 = MAX A/C.
   b. 1 = A/C.
   c. 2 = Intermediate.
   d. 3 = Heater.
   e. 4 = OFF.
   f. 5 = Normal Purge.
   g. 6 = Cold Purge.
   h. 7 = Front Defog.
5. **BD25**—The in-car temperature is displayed in degrees Celsius (°C), from -40° to +102°.
6. **BD26**—The actual outside temperature is displayed in degrees Celsius (°C), from -40° to +93°. This value represents actual sensor temperature and is not restricted by the features used to minimize engine heat affects on the customer display value.

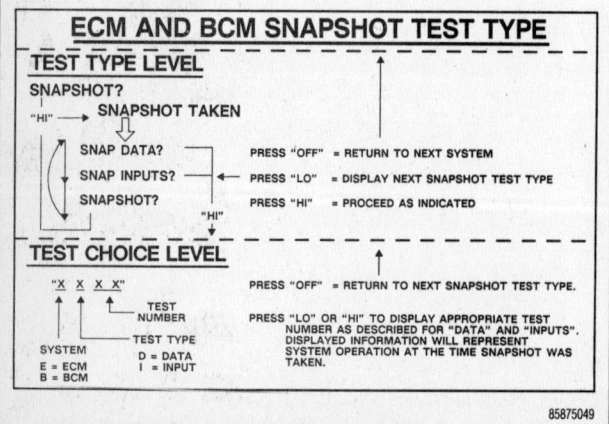

Fig. 29 Selecting SNAPSHOT-Eldorado and Seville

7. **BD27**—The high side temperature (condenser output) is displayed in degrees Celsius (°C) from -40° to +215°.

8. **BD28**—The low side temperature (evaporator input) is displayed in degrees Celsius (°C) from -40° to +93°.

9. **BD32**—The sun-load temperature sensor is displayed in degrees Celsius (°C) from -40° to +102°.

10. **BD40**—The actual fuel level is read in gallons between 0 and 19.0 (the display can read to 25.0). This value represents actual sensor position and is not restricted by the features used to eliminate fuel slosh effects on the customer display value.

11. **BD41**—The PRND 321 display in percent (%). PARK should display the highest percentage and 1 should display the lowest percentage.

12. **BD42**—The dimming potentiometer is displayed in percent (%). A value close to 0% represents maximum dimming and a value close to 100% represents maximum brightness.

13. **BD43**—The twilight delay potentiometer is displayed in percent (%). A value close to 0% represents minimum delay time and a value close to 100% represents maximum delay time.

14. **BD44**—The twilight photocell is displayed in percent (%). A value close to 0% represents daylight and value close to 100% represents darkness.

15. **BD50**—The battery voltage is read in volts between 0 and 16.

16. **BD51**—The generator field is displayed in percent (%). A value close to 0% represents minimum regulator on time and a value close to 100% represents maximum regulator on time.

17. **BD52**—The incandescent bulb reference is displayed in volts. With the parking lamps/headlamps OFF, the value is Zero (0) and with either parking or headlamps ON, the value is battery voltage.

18. **BD60**—The vehicle speed is displayed in miles per hour (MPH) from 0–100.

19. **BD61**—The engine speed is displayed in rpm from 0–63.

20. **BD70**—The cruise control servo position is displayed in percent (%) from 0–100. A value close to 0% represents at rest position and a value close to 100% represents wide open throttle.

21. **BD98**—The ignition cycle value is the number of times that the BCM has been turned OFF since a BCM trouble code was last detected. After 100 ignition cycles without any malfunction being detected, all BCM codes are cleared.

22. **BD99**—The BCM PROM I.D. is displayed as a number, up to four digits long, which can be used to verify that the proper PROM was installed in the BCM.

Input Displays

Input displays are operated as defined under Selecting the Test under the heading Operating The Service Mode. When troubleshooting a malfunction, the ECM, BCM, or IPC input display can be used to determine it the switch inputs can be properly interpreted. When one of the various input tests is selected, the state of the device is displayed as HI or LO. In general, the HI and LO refer to the input terminal voltage for that circuit. The display also indicates if the input changed state so that you can activate or deactivate any listed device and return to the display to see if it changed state. If a change of state occurred, an "X" will only appear once per selected input, although the HI/LO indication will continue to change as the input changes. Some tests are momentary and the "X" can be used as an indication of a change. The following is a list of ECM, BCM and IPC inputs:

ECM INPUT DISPLAYS

1. **EI71**—The brake switch display is LO when the brake pedal is depressed.

2. **EI72**—The throttle switch display is HI when the accelerator pedal is depressed.

3. **EI74**—The Park/Neutral (P/N) display is LO when the vehicle is in Park or Neutral.

4. **EI78**—The power steering pressure switch display is LO when power steering pressure (effort) is high, wheel in crimp position.

BCM INPUT DISPLAYS

1. **BI01**—The courtesy lamp panel switch display is LO when courtesy lights are on from switch.

2. **BI02**—The park lamp switch display is LO when the park lamp switch is in the OFF position.

3. **BI03**—The driver (front) door ajar switch display is LO when the driver (front) door is ajar.

4. **BI04**—The passenger (rear) door ajar switch display is LO when the passenger's (rear) door is ajar.

5. **BI05**—The door jamb switch display is LO when any door is open.

6. **BI06**—The door handle switch display is momentarily LO when either front outside door handle button is depressed.

7. **BI07**—The trunk open switch display is LO when the truck is open.

8. **BI08**—The low refrigerant pressure switch display is LO when the system is low on refrigerant.

9. **BI09**—The washer fluid level switch display is LO when the vehicle is low on washer fluid.

10. **BI30**—The TEMP/TIME switch display is LO when the button is depressed.

11. **BI41**—The cooling fan feedback display is LO when the cooling fans are running.

12. **BI51**—The generator feedback display is LO when there is a generator problem (or engine not running).

13. **BI71**—The cruise control brake switch display is HI when the cruise ON/OFF switch is ON and the brake pedal is not depressed (free state).

14. **BI75**—The cruise control ON/OFF switch display is HI when the switch is ON.

15. **BI76**—The cruise control SET/COAST switch display is HI when the cruise ON/OFF switch is ON and the SET/COAST switch is depressed.

16. **BI77**—The cruise control RESUME/ACCEL switch display is HI when the cruise ON/OFF switch is ON and the RESUME/ACCEL switch is pushed.

IPC INPUT DISPLAYS

1. **II78**—The headlamp switch display is HI whenever the headlamps are ON.

2. **II79**—The high beam switch display is LO as long as the lever is pulled in.

3. **II80**—The dimming sentinel switch display is LO whenever the system is on.

4. **II81**—The dimming sentinel photosensor display is HI whenever it senses light.

5. **II82**—The twilight enable switch display is LO whenever the system is ON.

Output Displays

Output displays are operated as defined under the heading Operating The Service Mode. When troubleshooting a malfunction, the ECM and BCM output cycling can be used to determine if the output tests can be actuated regardless of the inputs and normal program instructions. Once a test in outputs has been selected, the test will display HI and LO for three seconds in each state to indicated the command and output terminal voltage. A brief summary of each output is provided below:

ECM OUTPUT DISPLAYS

1. **EO00**—This test displays CYCLE NONE as no outputs are activated at this point.

2. **EO01**—The canister purge solenoid display will be LO when the solenoid is on (energized).

3. **EO02**—The viscous converter clutch (VCC) display will be LO when the solenoid is energized.

4. **EO03**—The EFE relay display will be LO when the relay is energized.

5. **EO04**—The EGR solenoid display will be LO when the solenoid is energized.

6. **EO05**—The air switch solenoid display will be LO when the solenoid is energized.

7. **EO06**—The air divert solenoid display will be LO when the solenoid is energized.

8. **EO07**—The ISC motor display will be LO when the plunger is retracting and HI during its extension.

9. **EO99**—This test displays CYCLE ALL as all outputs are cycled at this point.

BCM OUTPUT DISPLAYS

1. **BO00**—The NO OUTPUTS display will not display HI nor LO as this is a resting spot where no outputs will be cycled.

2. **BO01**—The cruise control vent solenoid display is HI when the vent solenoid is on (energized). The cruise ON/OFF switch must be on and the engine off for this output to cycle.

3. **BO02**—The cruise control vacuum solenoid display is HI when the vacuum solenoid is on (energized). The cruise ON/OFF switch must be ON and the engine OFF for this output to cycle.

4. **BO03**—The retained accessory power (RAP) relays display is LO when the relays are ON (energized).

5. **BO04**—The courtesy relay display is LO when the relay is ON (energized).

6. **BO05**—The twilight relays display is LO when the relays are ON (energized) with the lights ON.

7. **BO06**—The HI/LO beam relays display is LO when the relays are ON (energized) with the high beams ON.

Override Displays

Override displays are operated as defined under the heading Operating The Service Mode. When troubleshooting a malfunction, the BCM override feature allows testing of certain system functions regardless of normal program instructions.

Upon selecting a test, that function's current operation will be represented as a percentage of its full range and this value will be displayed on the ECC panel. The display will alternate between "—" for 1 second followed by he normal program value for 10 seconds. This alternating display is a reminder that the function is not currently being overridden.

Touching the WARM or COOL buttons on the ECC panel begins the override at which time the display will no longer alternate to "—". Touching the WARM button increases the value while the COOL button decreases the value. Upon release of the button, the display may either remain at the override value or automatically return to normal program control. This depends on which function is being overridden at the time. If the display remains at the override value, normal program control can be resumed in one of three ways:

1. Selection of another override test will cancel the current override.
2. Selection of another system will cancel the current override.
3. Overriding the value beyond either extreme (0 or 99) will display "—" momentarily and then jump to the opposite extreme. If the button is released while "—" is displayed, normal program control will resume and the display will again alternate.

The override test type is unique in that any other test type within the selected system may be active at the same time. After selecting an override test, touching the OFF button will allow selection of another test type and test, while at the

same time touching the WARM or COOL button, it is possible to monitor the effect of the override on different vehicle parameters.

4. **BS00**—This test will display "none" as no overrides are active at this point.

5. **BS01**—The program number override can be controlled from "0" (Max A/C) to "99" (Max heat). The display will hold the override value upon release of the buttons.

6. **BS02**—The vacuum fluorescent (VF) dimming override can be controlled from "0" (Max dim) to "99" (Max bright). The display will hold the override value upon release of the buttons.

7. **BS03**—The incandescent bulb-dimming override can be controlled from "0" (Max dim) to "99" (Max bright) if the park lamps have been turned on. The display will hold the override value upon release of the buttons.

8. **BS04**—The cooling fans override will control to "0" (fan OFF) or "99" (MAX fan) as long as the button is held. Normal control will resume upon release of the button.

9. **BS06**—The generator disable override will control to "0" (generator ON) or "99" (generator disabled) as long as the button is held. Normal control will resume upon release of the buttons.

Set Timing Mode

The set timing mode is used order tell the ECM NOT to advance the spark timing, but instead to allow it to remain at the base timing setting. This permits verification and setting of base spark timing. The ECM has a SET TIMING request line that goes to the ALDL connector terminal "B". The set timing mode is requested as follows:

1. Place the transmission in the Park (P) position and block the drive wheels. Start the engine and allow it to idle until the coolant temperature reaches 85⁻C.

2. Verify that the engine is idling at less than 900 rpm. If in the diagnostics mode, exit the diagnostics by pressing OFF on the CCDIC until the CCDIC is back in the standard climate control mode.

3. Using a suitable jumper wire, jumper pin **B** of the ALDL to pin **A** (internal ground).

   a. The ECM will command the BCM to display a message SET TIMING on the CCDIC.

   b. The engine will operate at base timing.

   c. Timing can now be checked with a standard timing light, it should be set to specification (usually 10 degrees BTDC).

4. To exit the SET TIMING mode, remove the ground from pin **B** of the ALDL connector and verify proper display operation.

FUEL INJECTION SYSTEM SERVICE

Fuel Pump

REMOVAL & INSTALLATION

Chassis-Mounted Fuel Pump (EFI System)

✳✳ CAUTION

Fuel is under high pressure; if the steps below are not followed, the fuel could spray out and result in a fire hazard and possible injury.

1. Disconnect the negative battery terminal.
2. Locate the pressure fitting in the fuel line and remove the protective cap.
3. Loosely install a special valve depressor (G.M. tool no. J-5420) on the fitting.
4. Wrap a towel around the fitting to block any spray and slowly tighten the tool until the pressure has been relieved.
5. Remove the tool and reinstall the protective cap.
6. Remove the fuel hoses from the pump.
7. Peel back the rubber boot and remove the two nuts, one from each electrical terminal. Remove the electrical leads.

➡**These nuts have metric threads.**

8. Remove the two screws and flat washers holding the fuel pump to the bracket and remove the pump assembly.

To install:

9. Install the fuel pump in the reverse order of removal.
10. Connect the green wire to the positive terminal on the pump and the black wire to the negative terminal. Check to make sure the fuel pump is resting evenly on its two mounts and not grounding against the bracket or frame.

In-Tank Fuel Pump (DFI and EFI Systems)

◆ See Figure 30

1. Disconnect the negative battery terminal, open the fuel tank filler door and disconnect the sending unit feed wire. Release the fuel pressure.

2. Siphon the fuel from the fuel tank. If the rear of the car is raised one foot higher than the front, more fuel can be taken out.

3. Raise the rear of the car and remove the screw securing the ground wire to the cross member.

4. Disconnect the fuel line, evaporative emission lines and the fuel return lines at the front of the tank.

5. Support the tank with a jack and wooden block and remove one screw on each side securing the fuel tank support straps to the body at the front of the tank.

6. Lower the jack and tank enough so that the fuel pump electrical lead can be disconnected. Disconnect the wire.

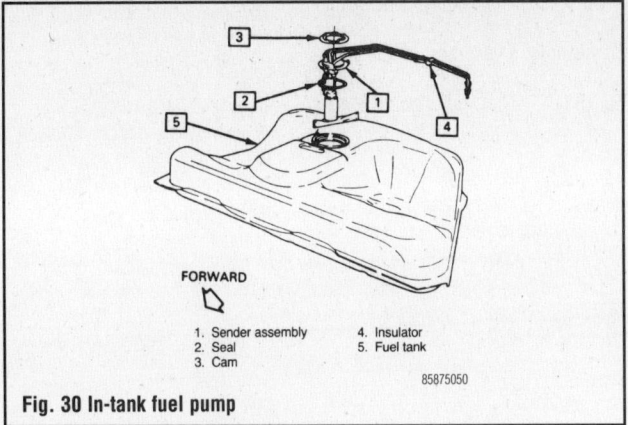

Fig. 30 In-tank fuel pump

1. Sender assembly
2. Seal
3. Cam
4. Insulator
5. Fuel tank

FORWARD

85875050

7. Remove the fuel tank from the car.
8. Remove the locknuts securing the fuel gauge tank unit and fuel pump feed wires to the tank unit.
9. Turn the cam locking ring counterclockwise with a soft non-ferrous punch and hammer. When the lock ring is disengaged, remove it and lift the gauge/pump unit from the tank.
10. Install in the reverse order of removal. Tighten the fuel tank retaining strap screws to 25 ft. lbs. (34 Nm).

Testing

1. Secure two sections of ⅜ in. x 10 in. (steel tubing), with a double-flare on one end of each section.
2. Install a flare nut on each section of tubing, then connect each of the sections into the flare nut-to-flare nut adapters, which are included in the Gauge Adapter tool No. J-29658–82.
3. Attach the pipe and the adapter assemblies to the Gage tool No. J-29658.
4. Raise and support the vehicle on jackstands.
5. Remove the air cleaner and plug the THERMAC vacuum port on the TBI.
6. Disconnect the fuel feed hose between the fuel tank and the filter, then secure the other ends of the ⅜ in. tubing into the fuel hoses with hose clamps.
7. Start the engine, check for leaks and observe the fuel pressure, it should be 9–13 psi.
8. Depressurize the fuel system, remove the testing tool, remove the plug from the THERMAC vacuum port, reconnect the fuel line, start the engine and check for fuel leaks.

EFI Component Service

ADJUSTMENTS

Idle Speed

➡Before low idle speed adjustment is made distributor vacuum advance hose(s) must be disconnected at the distributor and plugged. The hose must be disconnected at this location to include any calibrated leakage in balance of the system. Reset timing before making idle speed adjustment.

1. Disconnect parking brake hose at vacuum release cylinder and plug the hose. Set the parking brake and block the wheels. Disconnect the air leveling compressor hose at air cleaner and plug the hose.
2. Connect a tachometer, start and warm-up the engine to operating temperature.
3. Place the transmission in drive and turn the air conditioner off.
4. Loosen the lock nut on the idle bypass adjusting screw on the front of the throttle body.
5. Adjust the idle bypass adjusting screw to give 650 rpm.
6. Tighten the lock nut.
7. Turn off the engine and remove the tachometer.
8. Reconnect all hoses.

Throttle Position Switch

1. Loosen two throttle position switch mounting screws to permit rotation of the switch.
2. Hold the throttle valves in the idle position while performing step 3 and 4.
3. Turn the throttle position switch carefully counterclockwise until the end-stop has been reached.
4. Tighten throttle position switch mounting screws to 11 inch lbs. (1.2 Nm).
5. Check to insure that throttle valves close to the throttle stop. If not, repeat steps 2, 3 and 4.

REMOVAL & INSTALLATION

Electronic Control Unit/Module (ECM/ECU)

SEVILLE

1. Disconnect the negative battery cable.
2. Loosen the right-hand forward screw which secures the ECU cover to the ECU.
3. Remove the three remaining screws.
4. Remove the screws which secure the ECU to the instrument panel supports.
5. Carefully lower the ECU enough to disconnect three electrical connectors from the left hand side and the MAP hose from the front of the ECU.
6. Remove the ECU.
7. Installation is the reverse of removal.

EXCEPT ELDORADO AND SEVILLE

▶ See Figure 31

1. Disconnect the negative battery cable.
2. Remove the glove box liner.
3. Remove the ECU mounting screws and remove the ECU.
4. Disconnect the three electrical connectors (red, black and blue) and the MAP sensor hose.
5. Installation is the reverse of removal.

ELDORADO

1. Disconnect the negative battery cable.
2. Remove the three climate control outlet grilles right, left and center.
3. Working through the outlet openings, remove the three fasteners securing the pad to the instrument panel support.
4. Remove the screws securing the pad to the instrument panel horizontal support.
5. Pull the pad outward and disconnect the electrical connector from the windshield wiper switch.
6. Remove the pad.

➡To facilitate removal and/or installation place the shift lever in low range. Vehicles equipped with tilt wheel, place the wheel in the lowest position.

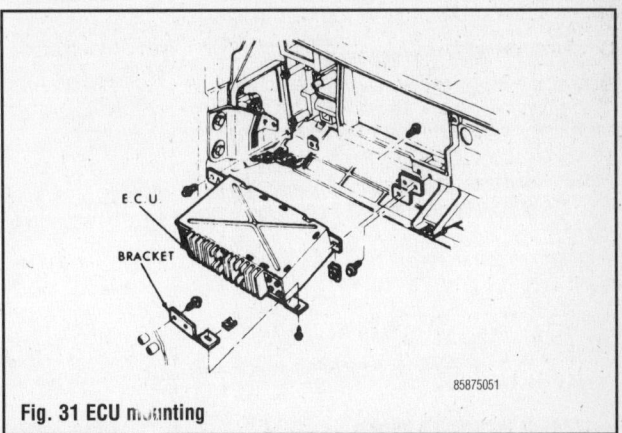

Fig. 31 ECU mounting

E.C.U.

BRACKET

85875051

7. Remove the MAP sensor hose.
8. Remove the mounting screws and then the ECU.
9. Remove the electrical connectors.
10. Installation is the reverse of removal.

Throttle Body Assembly

♦ **See Figures 32 thru 39**

1. Remove the air cleaner.
2. Disconnect the throttle return springs from the throttle lever.
3. Remove the retainer and remove the cruise control chain from the throttle lever on cars so equipped.
4. Remove the hairpin clip and disconnect the throttle cable.
5. Remove the rear throttle body mounting screws and position the throttle linkage out of the way.

6. Disconnect the throttle position switch electrical connector and fast idle valve electrical connector. Slide the fast idle valve wiring out of the notch in the throttle body.
7. Remove the vacuum hoses from the nipples on the throttle body. Use a backup wrench when removing the power brake vacuum line.
8. Remove the remaining throttle body mounting screws and remove the throttle body.
To install:
9. Remove the gasket material from the intake manifold and bottom of the throttle body.
10. The following parts are not included in a new throttle body assembly and should be removed as needed. Throttle position switch, fast idle valve seat, fast idle valve spring, fast idle valve, fast idle valve heater assembly, power brake vacuum fitting.
11. Installation is the reverse of removal.

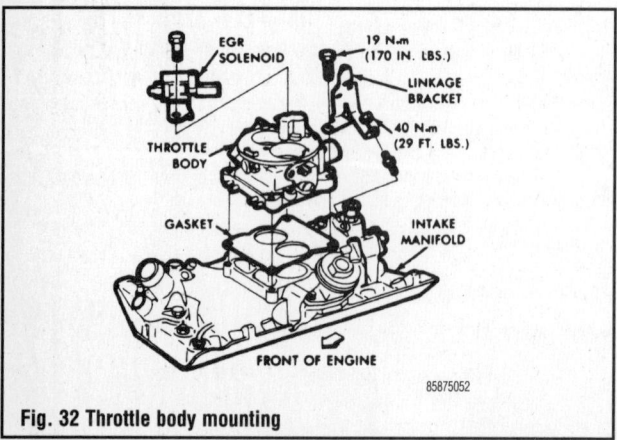

Fig. 32 Throttle body mounting

Fig. 33 View of the throttle body assembly

Fig. 34 Removing external pedal linkage

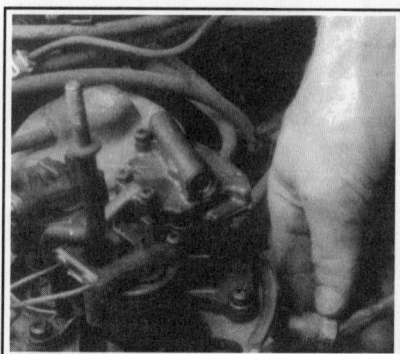

Fig. 35 Removing line from the throttle body

Fig. 36 Removing electrical connections from the throttle body

Fig. 37 Removing all necessary electrical connections

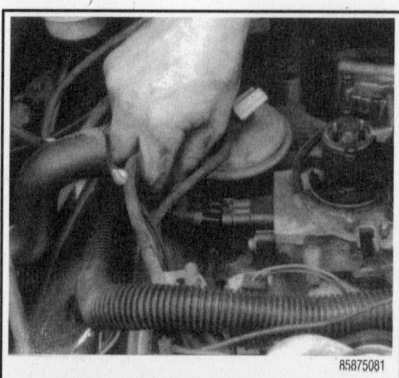

Fig. 38 Removing electrical connections from the side of the throttle body

Fig. 39 Removing the throttle body assembly

Fast Idle Valve

1. Remove the air cleaner and disconnect the electrical connector from the fast idle valve heater.
2. Remove the air cleaner stud.
3. Remove the fast idle valve heater by pushing down and twisting 90 degrees counterclockwise.
4. Remove the fast idle valve, spring and seat from the throttle body.
5. Installation is the reverse of removal.

Fuel Rail

EXCEPT SEVILLE

1. Remove and discard the hose clamp securing the pressure regulator hose to the front fuel rail.
2. Using a back-up wrench at the side rail fitting, remove the flare nut from each end of the fuel rail.
3. Disengage the front rail from the pressure regulator hose and remove it from the vehicle.
4. Installation is the reverse of removal.

Injection Valve

SEVILLE

1. Disconnect the electrical leads from all injectors on the fuel rail being removed and position the harness out of the way.
2. Remove the fuel inlet line from the fuel rail using a back-up wrench.
3. Remove the return hose and vacuum hose from the pressure regulator.
4. Disconnect the fuel rail from the fuel regulator.
5. Remove the screw holding each injector bracket to the intake manifold, and remove the brackets and grommets.
6. Remove the fuel rail and injectors from the engine as a complete unit.

➡Some injectors may stick in the fuel rail while others may remain in the manifold.

7. Remove the injectors from the fuel rail and from the intake as required.
8. Injection valves are sealed by O-rings at the fuel rail and intake manifold. Remove and discard all used O-rings.
9. Installation is the reverse of removal.

➡A conical shaped metal gasket should be used when servicing EFI fuel rail fittings. The gasket Part #1608786 or its equal is not required during production, but is needed during service procedures. This gasket should be inserted in the fuel rail inverted flare fitting each time a fitting is separated and reconnected in the field. These gaskets can not be re-used.

EXCEPT SEVILLE

1. Remove the front and rear fuel rails.
2. Remove the electrical conduit from the injector brackets (4 places on each side).
3. Disconnect the electrical leads from all injectors on the fuel rail being removed.
4. Remove the two screws holding each injector bracket to the intake manifold and remove the brackets and grommets.
5. Remove the fuel rail and injector from the engine as a unit. Some injectors may stick in the fuel rail while others may remain in the manifold.
6. Remove the injectors from the fuel rail and from the intake manifold as required.
7. Injection valves are sealed by O-rings at both fuel rail and intake manifold. Remove and discard all used O-rings.
8. Installation is the reverse of removal. Lubricate the new O-rings prior to installation.

Fuel Pressure Regulator

1. Remove the vacuum hose from the nipple on top of the pressure regulator.
2. Remove and discard clamps securing the flexible fuel hose connecting the regulator to the fuel rail. Remove the return line.
3. Remove one nut securing the pressure regulator to the bracket.

➡This nut has metric threads.

4. Work the regulator off the flexible fuel hose and out of the bracket.
5. Installation is the reverse of removal.

Throttle Position Switch

1. Remove the electrical connections from the switch.
2. Remove the two mounting screws and remove the switch from the throttle body.
3. Installation is the reverse of removal. Adjust the switch as necessary.

Coolant Temperature Sensor

1. Drain the radiator.

✳✳ CAUTION

When draining the coolant, keep in mind that cats and dogs are attracted by the ethylene glycol antifreeze, and are quite likely to drink any that is left in an uncovered container or in puddles on the ground. This will prove fatal in sufficient quantity. Always drain the coolant into a sealable container. Coolant should be reused unless it is contaminated or several years old.

2. Locate the water temperature sensor in the heater hose outlet at the rear of the right hand cylinder head.
3. Disconnect the electrical connector from the sensor.
4. Remove the sensor from the heater hose.
5. Installation is the reverse of removal.

Air Temperature Sensor

1. Locate the sensor at the right rear of the intake manifold.
2. Disconnect the sensor from its electrical connector.
3. Remove the sensor from the intake manifold.
4. Installation is the reverse of removal. Coat the sensors threads with a non-hardening sealer prior to reinstallation.

DFI Component Service

REMOVAL & INSTALLATION

Throttle Body

◗ See Figure 40

1. Remove the air cleaner.
2. Disconnect the following electrical connectors and position them out of the way, ISC-Idle Speed Control, TPS-Throttle Position Sensor, and both injectors.

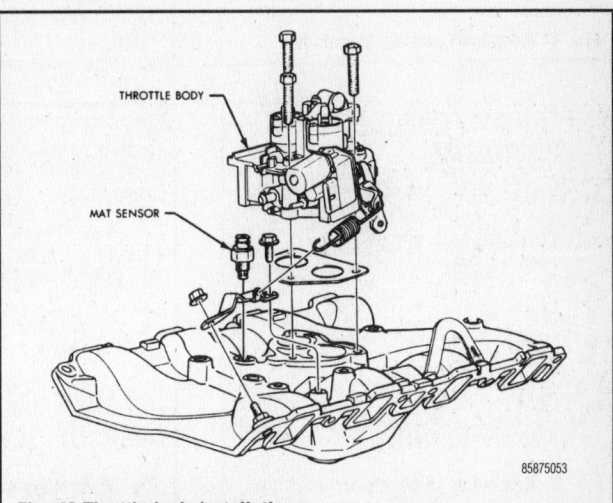

Fig. 40 Throttle body installation

3. Remove both throttle return springs, cruise control and throttle linkage and downshift cable.

4. Disconnect the following hoses and lines from the rear of the throttle body: fuel inlet and return line, brake booster line, MAP hose and the AIR hose.

➡**Use flare nut wrench on all fuel lines.**

5. Remove the PCV, EVAP, and EGR hoses from the front of the throttle body.

6. Remove the three throttle body mounting screws and remove the throttle body and gasket.

7. Installation is the reverse of removal. Check the adjustment of the TPS and ISC after reinstallation.

MAP Sensor

▶ **See Figure 41**

1. Remove the instrument panel lower cover.

2. Working under the extreme right hand side of the instrument panel, disconnect the MAP hose from the sensor.

3. Disconnect MAP sensor electrical connector, being careful not to damage small gauge wires on the sensor side.

➡**The MAP sensor has a female connector on the sensor side and a male connector on the harness. The BARO connector is reversed.**

4. Remove the one screw securing MAP sensor to the bracket and remove the sensor.

5. Installation is the reverse of removal.

BARO Sensor

1. Remove the instrument panel lower cover.
2. Remove the glove box liner.

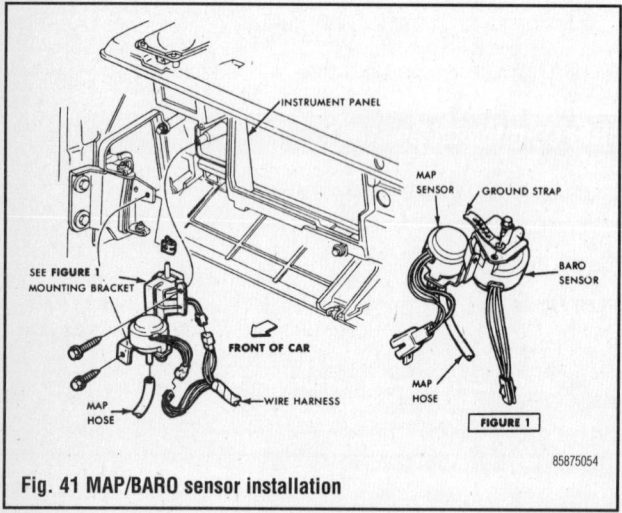

Fig. 41 MAP/BARO sensor installation

3. Disconnect the BARO sensor electrical connector. Be careful not to damage the small gauge wires on the sensor side.

4. Working through the glove box opening, remove one screw securing MAP/BARO bracket to the instrument panel.

5. Remove one screw securing the BARO sensor and ground strap to the bracket.

6. Installation is the reverse of removal.

Coolant Sensor

1. Drain the radiator coolant until the level is below the level of the sensor.

✳✳ CAUTION

When draining the coolant, keep in mind that cats and dogs are attracted by the ethylene glycol antifreeze, and are quite likely to drink any that is left in an uncovered container or in puddles on the ground. This will prove fatal in sufficient quantity. Always drain the coolant into a sealable container. Coolant should be reused unless it is contaminated or several years old.

2. Remove the alternator if necessary.
3. Disconnect the electrical pigtail and remove the sensor.
4. Installation is the reverse of removal.

Coat the sensor threads with a non-hardening sealer during reinstallation.

Throttle Position Sensor

▶ **See Figure 42**

➡**On later models, TPS removal is accomplished by simply removing the two screws and lifting off the sensor.**

1. Remove the electrical connector from the TPS sensor.

2. Remove the throttle body assembly from the intake manifold to gain access to the spot welds on the bottom side that hold the TPS attaching screws. Invert the throttle body. Support it to prevent damage to the injector electrical connections. Drill completely through the TPS screw access holes (2) in the base of the throttle body, using a $5/16$ in. drill bit.

3. Remove the two TPS attaching screws, lockwashers, and retainers. Then remove the TPS sensor from the throttle body, noting the location of the TPS lever in relation to the tang on the lever on the throttle shaft. Discard the TPS screws. New screws are supplied in service kits.

4. Installation is the reverse of removal. Adjust the TPS as necessary.

Fuel Injector

▶ **See Figures 43, 44 and 45**

✳✳ WARNING

When removing the injectors, be careful not to damage the electrical connector pins (on top of the injector), the injector fuel filter and the nozzle. The fuel injector is serviced as a complete assembly ONLY. The injector is an electrical component and should not be immersed in any kind of cleaner.

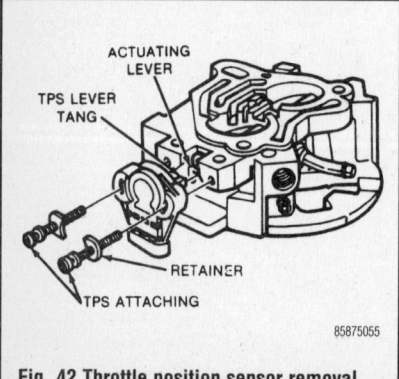

Fig. 42 Throttle position sensor removal on later models—DFI

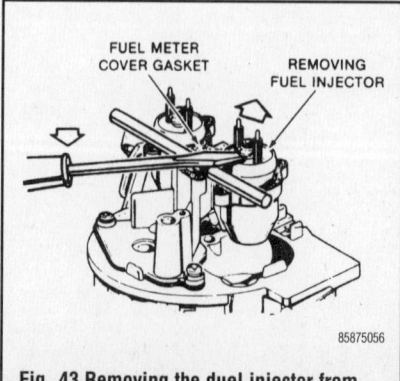

Fig. 43 Removing the duel injector from the throttle body—DFI

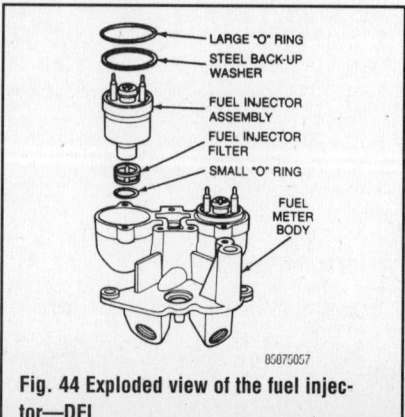

Fig. 44 Exploded view of the fuel injector—DFI

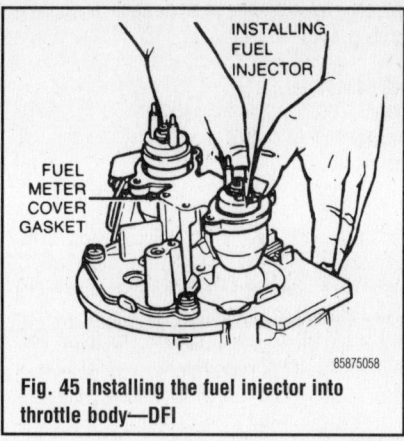

Fig. 45 Installing the fuel injector into throttle body—DFI

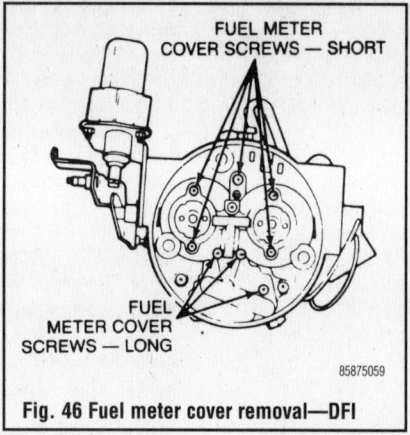

Fig. 46 Fuel meter cover removal—DFI

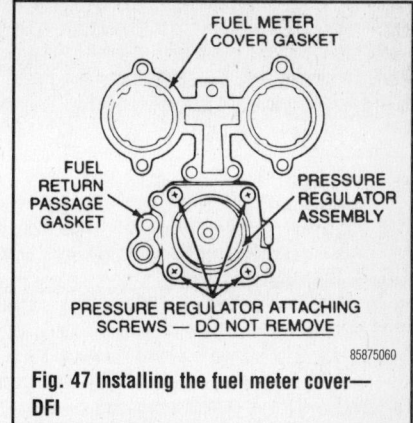

Fig. 47 Installing the fuel meter cover—DFI

1. Remove the air cleaner. Relieve the fuel pressure.
2. At the injector connector, squeeze the two tabs together and pull straight up.
3. Remove the fuel meter cover, but leave the cover gasket in position.
4. Using a small pry bar or tool No. J-26868, carefully lift the injector until it is free from the fuel meter body.
5. Remove the small O-ring from the nozzle end of the injector. Carefully rotate the injector's fuel filter back-and-forth to remove it from the base of the injector.

To install:

6. Discard the fuel meter cover gasket.
7. Remove the large O-ring and back-up washer from the counterbore of the fuel meter body injector cavity. Discard the O-rings.
8. With the large end facing the injector, fit the fuel filter onto the nozzle end of the injector. Use a twisting motion to seat the filter against the base of the injector.
9. Coat a new small O-ring with automatic transmission fluid and press it onto the nozzle end of the injector until it meets the fuel filter.
10. Position the back-up washer in the top counterbore of the fuel meter body injector cavity.
11. Coat a new large O-ring with automatic transmission fluid and position it directly above the back-up washer. The O-ring must be seated properly in the cavity and should be flush with the top of the fuel meter body casting surface.

➡The back-up washer and the large O-ring must be installed BEFORE the injector. Improper seating of the large O-ring will cause fuel leakage.

12. Install the injector into the cavity. The raised lug on the injector base must align with the cast notch in the fuel meter body cavity. Press the injector until it is fully seated in the cavity (the electrical terminals of the injector should be parallel to the throttle shaft).
13. Install the fuel meter cover.
14. Installation of the remaining components is in the reverse order of removal. Start the engine and check for any fuel leakage around the throttle body.

Pressure Regulator

1. Remove the air cleaner.
2. Remove the electrical connection on the injectors.
3. Remove the eight screws securing the pressure regulator assembly to the throttle body and remove the regulator.
4. Installation is the reverse of removal. Lubricate the new O-ring with Dexron®II® transmission fluid and install a new gasket.

Fuel Meter Cover

▶ See Figures 46 and 47

1. Remove the air cleaner.
2. Disconnect the electrical connector from the fuel injector.
3. Remove the fuel meter-to-fuel meter body screws and lockwashers.

➡When removing the fuel meter cover screws not the location of the two short screws.

4. Remove the fuel meter cover and discard the gasket.
5. To install, use a new gasket and reverse the removal procedures.

Fuel Meter Body

1. Remove the fuel inlet and outlet nuts and gaskets from the fuel meter body.
2. Remove the three screws and lockwashers. Remove the fuel meter body from the throttle body assembly.
3. Remove the fuel meter body insulator gasket.

➡Do not remove the center screw and staking at each end, holding the fuel distribution skirt in the throttle body. The skirt is an integral part of the throttle body and not serviced separately.

4. Installation is the reverse of removal.

Idle Speed Control (ISC) Motor

1. Disconnect the electrical connector.
2. Remove the two ISC mounting screws.
3. Remove the ISC control.
4. Installation is the reverse of removal. Adjust the ISC motor if necessary.

➡The idle speed control is specially calibrated at the factory and no attempt should be made to disassemble the unit. Do not immerse it in any type of cleaner. It must be removed before servicing or cleaning the throttle body. It is replaced only as an assembly.

CHECKS AND ADJUSTMENTS

Engine Idle Speed and Diagnostic Check

1. Remove the air cleaner, start the engine, and warm the engine up to normal operating temperature (upper radiator hose hot). Turn A/C off.
2. Connect a tachometer to the engine and connect the digital voltmeter as follows:
   a. (+) lead the TPS harness test point which connects to pin A, (0.8 blue dark wire).
   b. (-) lead to the TPS harness test point which connects to pin B, (0.8 black/white wire), circuit #4
   c. Select the 2V DC scale.
3. Open the set timing connect.
4. Retract the ISC motor by pressing the plunger (switch activated) in while the throttle is opened to approximately 1500 rpm. When the ISC motor fully retracts, disconnect the ISC connector, before releasing the throttle.
5. Jumper the ISC harness connector pins A and B together.
6. Under these conditions, the ISC plunger should not be touching the throttle lever. If contact is noted, adjust the ICS plunger (turn in) with pliers or suitable available special tool so that it is not touching the throttle lever.
7. The idle speed should now be 375 rpm (plus or minus 25 rpm) all

except Calif. Eldorado/Seville cars (Calif. Eldorado/Seville—400 rpm). Adjust throttle stop screw to proper rpm, if necessary. If the engine speed is not correct check that the throttle is not held off the minimum stop because of linkage preload. If necessary, adjust the throttle stop as described in the Minimum Air Rate Adjustment to obtain 375 rpm, all except Calif. Eldorado/Seville cars (Calif. Eldorado/Seville—400 rpm).

8. Digital voltmeter should indicate 0.50 volts plus or minus 0.05 volts. If necessary, adjust Throttle Position Sensor:

a. Remove throttle body assembly from the intake manifold to gain access to the spot welds on the bottom side holding the TPS attaching screws in place. Invert throttle body assembly and support the assembly to prevent damage to the injector electrical connections. Using a 5/16 in. drill bit, drill completely through TPS screw access holes in base of throttle body to be sure of removing the spot welds holding screws in place. Then loosen the screws just enough to permit rotation of the sensor.

b. With the engine idling at 375 rpm, all except non-Calif. Eldorado/Seville cars (Calif. Eldorado/Seville cars—400 rpm) loosen the TPS mounting screws and position the TPS lever so that the voltmeter reads 0.50 volt plus or minus 0.05 volts.

c. Tighten the TPS mounting screws with the sensor in this position. Recheck the voltmeter reading when the screws are tight to make sure that the adjustment has not changed.

9. Disconnect the test equipment, then engage all connections, including the set timing connector.

10. Turn the ignition off for 10 seconds. The ISC motor should move to its extended position.

11. The above procedure may have turned on the check engine light and may have set a trouble code. After the system is restored to normal operation, the check engine light will go out but the trouble code will remain as an intermittent problem. Enter diagnostics, clear the stored codes, and turn the ignition off for 10 seconds.

ISC Motor Adjustment

Adjustment of the ISC motor is necessary to establish the initial position of the motor after it has been replaced. ISC motor adjustment may also be necessary if the throttle pedal ratchets when the ignition is turned **OFF** or **ON**.

1. Remove the air cleaner, start the engine, and warm the engine up to normal operating temperature (upper radiator hose hot). Turn the A/C off.

2. Connect a tachometer to the engine.

3. Check the TPS adjustment as described in steps 2 through 7 in the TPS Adjustment section.

4. Unplug the set timing connector.

5. Disconnect the TPS connector.

6. Turn the ignition off for 10 seconds and observe the ISC plunger movement. It should fully extend.

7. When the ISC plunger is fully extended, disconnect the ISC connector. Jumper the ISC harness pins A and B together.

8. Reconnect the TPS and start the engine.

9. Under these conditions, engine idle speed should be 1500 rpm (plus or minus 100 rpm). If the engine speed is not correct, turn the ISC plunger to provide 1500 rpm.

10. Reconnect the ISC motor and repeat Steps 5–8. If the engine speed is too low, adjust the TPS as needed.

11. Disconnect the test equipment, then engage all wiring connections, including the set timing connector.

12. Turn the ignition off for 10 seconds. Start the engine and check the ISC motor for proper operation.

13. Turn the ignition off for 10 seconds. The ISC motor should move to its fully extended position.

14. The above procedure may have turned on the check engine light and may have set a trouble code. After the system is restored to its normal operation, the check engine light will go out but the trouble code will remain as an intermittent problem. Enter diagnostics, clear the stored codes, and turn the ignition off for 10 seconds.

Minimum Air Rate Adjustment

This adjustment should be performed only when the throttle body parts have been replaced or when required to do so by the TPS adjustment.

1. Remove the air cleaner, start the engine, and warm it up to normal operating temperature. Turn the A/C off.

2. Connect a tachometer to the engine.

3. Open the set timing connector.

4. Retract the ISC motor by pressing holding the plunger (switch-activated) in while the throttle is opened to approximately 1500 rpm. When the ISC motor fully retracts, disconnect the ISC connector before releasing the throttle.

5. Jumper the ISC harness connector pins A and B together.

6. Under these conditions, the ISC plunger should not be touching the throttle lever. If contact is noted, adjust the ISC motor as described under that heading.

7. The idle speed should now be 375 rpm (plus or minus 25 rpm) all except non-Calif. Eldorado/Seville cars (Calif. Eldorado/Seville—400 rpm). Adjust throttle stop screw to proper rpm, if necessary. If the engine speed is not correct check that the throttle is not held off the minimum stop because of linkage pre-load. If necessary, adjust the throttle stop as described in the Minimum Air Rate Adjustment to obtain 375 rpm-all except non-Calif. Eldorado/Seville cars (Calif. Eldorado/Seville—400 rpm).

8. Check the TPS adjustment as described under that heading.

9. Disconnect the test equipment, then engage all wiring connections, including the set timing connector.

10. Turn ignition off for 10 seconds. The ISC motor should move to its extended position.

11. The above procedure may have turned on the check engine light and may have set a trouble code. After the system is restored to normal operation, the check engine light will go out but the trouble code will remain as an intermittent problem. Enter diagnostics, clear the stored codes, and turn the ignition off for 10 seconds.

DIESEL FUEL SYSTEM

Fuel Supply Pump

REMOVAL & INSTALLATION

The diesel fuel supply pump is serviced in the same manner as the fuel pump on the gasoline engines.

▶ **See Figure 48**

Water in Fuel

Water is the worst enemy of the diesel fuel injection system. The injection pump, which is designed and constructed to extremely close tolerances, and the injectors can be easily damaged if enough water is forced through them in the fuel. Engine performance will also be drastically affected, and engine damage can occur.

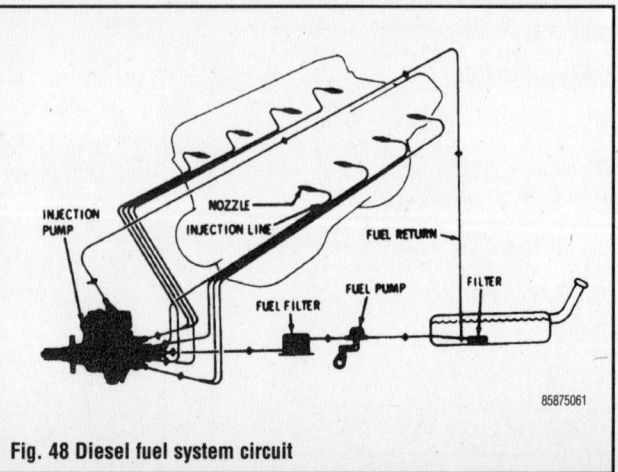

Fig. 48 Diesel fuel system circuit

Diesel fuel is much more susceptible than gasoline to water contamination. Diesel-engine cars are equipped with an indicator lamp system that turns on an instrument panel lamp if water (1–2 ½ gallons) is detected in the fuel tank. The lamp will come on for 2–5 seconds each time the ignition is turned on, assuring the driver the lamp is working. If there is water in the fuel, the light will come back on after a 15–20 second off delay, and then remain on.

PURGING THE FUEL TANK

Cars which have a Water in Fuel light may have the water removed from the tank with a siphon pump. The pump hose should be hooked up to the ¼ in. fuel return hose (the smaller of the two hoses) above the rear axle or under the hood near the fuel pump. Siphoning should continue until all water is removed from the tank. Use a clear plastic hose or observe the filter bowl on the siphon pump (if equipped) to determine when clear fuel begins to flow. Be sure to remove the cap on the fuel tank while purging. Replace the cap when finished. Discard the fuel filter and replace with a new filter.

Fuel Injection Pump

REMOVAL & INSTALLATION

▶ **See Figure 49**

1. Remove the air cleaner.
2. Remove the filters and pipes from the valve covers and air crossover.
3. Remove the air crossover and cap and intake manifold with screened covers (tool J-26996-1).
4. Disconnect the throttle rod and return spring.
5. Remove the bellcrank.
6. Remove the throttle and transmission cables from the intake manifold brackets.
7. Disconnect the fuel lines from the filter and remove the filter.
8. Disconnect the fuel inlet line at the pump.
9. Remove the rear A/C compressor brace and remove the fuel line.
10. Disconnect the fuel return line from the injection pump.
11. Remove the clamps and pull the fuel return lines from each injection nozzle.
12. Using two wrenches, disconnect the high pressure lines to the nozzles.
13. Remove the three injection pump retaining nuts with tool J-26987 or its equivalent.
14. Remove the pump and cap all lines and nozzles.

To install:

15. Remove the protective caps.
16. Line up the offset tang on the pump driveshaft with the pump driven gear and install the pump.
17. Install, but do not tighten the pump retaining nuts.
18. Connect the high pressure lines at the nozzles.
19. Using two wrenches, torque the high pressure line nuts to 25 ft. lbs. (34 Nm).
20. Connect the fuel return lines to the nozzles and pump.

21. Align the timing mark on the injection pump with the line on the timing mark adaptor and torque the mounting nuts to 35 ft. lbs. (47 Nm).

➡ **A ¾ in. open end wrench on the boss at the front of the injection pump will aid in rotating the pump to align the marks.**

22. Adjust the throttle rod:
    a. Remove the clip from the cruise control rod and remove the rod from the bellcrank.
    b. Loosen the locknut on the throttle rod a few turns, then shorten the rod several turns.
    c. Rotate the bellcrank to the full throttle stop, then lengthen the throttle rod until the injection pump lever contacts the injection pump full throttle stop, then release the bellcrank.
    d. Tighten the throttle rod locknut.
23. Install the fuel inlet line between the transfer pump and the filter.
24. Install the rear A/C compressor brace.
25. Install the bellcrank and clip.
26. Connect the throttle rod and return spring.
27. Adjust the transmission cable:
    a. Push the snap-lock to the disengaged position.
    b. Rotate the injection pump lever to the full throttle stop and hold it there.
    c. Push in the snap-lock until it is flush.
    d. Release the injection pump lever.
28. Start the engine and check for fuel leaks.
29. Remove the screened covers and install the air crossover.
30. Install the tubes in the air flow control valve in the air crossover and install the ventilation filters in the valve covers.
31. Install the air cleaner.
32. Start the engine and allow it to run for two minutes. Stop the engine, let it stand for two minutes, then restart. This permits the air to bleed off within the pump.

ADJUSTMENTS

Slow Idle Speed

▶ **See Figures 50 and 51**

1. Run the engine to normal operating temperature.
2. Insert the probe of a magnetic pickup tachometer into the timing indicator hole.
3. Set the parking brake and block the drive wheels.
4. Place the transmission in Drive and turn the A/C off.
5. Turn the slow idle screw on the injection pump to obtain the idle specification on the emission control label.

Fast Idle Solenoid

1. Set the parking brake and block the drive wheels.
2. Run the engine to normal operating temperature.
3. Place the transmission in Drive, disconnect the compressor clutch wire and turn the A/C on. On cars without A/C, disconnect the solenoid wire, and

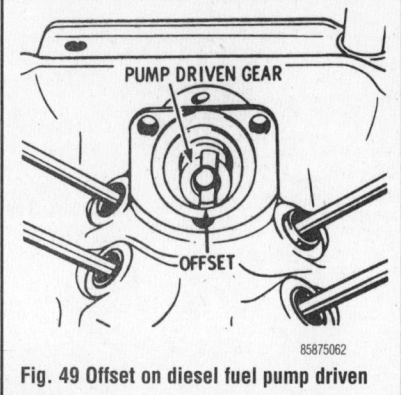

Fig. 49 Offset on diesel fuel pump driven gear

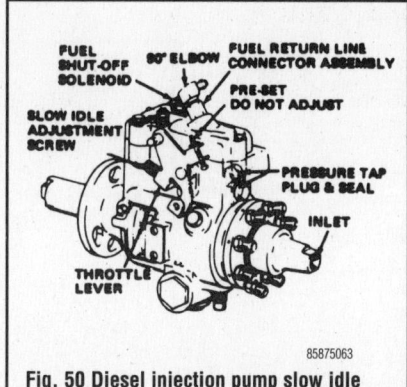

Fig. 50 Diesel injection pump slow idle screw—Roosa Master/Stanodyne pump

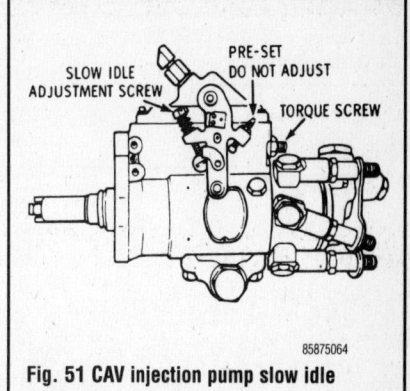

Fig. 51 CAV injection pump slow idle screw

connect jumper wires to the solenoid terminals. Ground one of the wires and connect the other to a 12 volt power source to activate the solenoid.

4. Adjust the fact idle solenoid plunger to obtain 650 rpm.

Cruise Control Servo Relay Rod

1. Turn the engine Off.
2. Adjust the rod to minimum slack then put the clip in the first free hole closest to the bellcrank, but within the servo bail.

Injection Timing

CHECKING

➥ **A special diesel timing meter is needed to check injection timing. There are a few variations of this meter, but the type desirable here uses a signal through a glow plug probe to determine combustion timing. The meter picks up the engine speed in RPM and the crankshaft position from the crankshaft balancer. This tool is available at automotive supply houses and from tool jobbers, and is the counterpart to a gasoline engine timing light, coupled with a tachometer. An intake manifold cover is also needed. The marks on the pump and adapter flange will normally be aligned within 0.030 in.**

1. Place the transmission shift lever in Park, apply the parking brake and block the rear wheels.
2. Start the engine and let it run at idle until fully warm. Shut off the engine.

➥ **If the engine is not allowed to completely warm up, the probe may soot up, causing incorrect timing readings.**

3. Remove the air cleaner assembly and carefully install cover J-26996-1. This cover over the intake is important. Disconnect the EGR valve hose.
4. Clean away all dirt from the engine probe holder (RPM counter) and the crankshaft balancer rim.
5. Clean the lens on both ends of the glow plug probe and clean the lens in the photoelectronic pick-up. Use a tooth pick to scrape the carbon from the combustion chamber side of the glow plug probe, then look through the probe to make sure it's clean. Cleanliness is crucial for accurate readings.
6. Install the probe into the crankshaft RPM counter (probe holder) on the engine front cover.
7. Remove the glow plug from No. 3 cylinder. Install the glow plug probe in the glow plug opening, and torque to 8 ft. lbs. (11 Nm).
8. Set the timing meter offset selector to **B** (99.5).
9. Connect the battery leads, red to positive, black to negative.
10. Disconnect the two-lead connector at the generator.
11. Start the engine. Adjust the engine RPM to the speed specified on the emissions control decal.
12. Observe the timing reading, then observe it again in 2 minutes. When the readings stabilize over the 2 minutes intervals, compare that final stabilized reading to the one specified on the emissions control decal. The timing reading will be an ATDC (After Top Dead Center) reading when set to specifications.
13. Disconnect the timing meter and install the removed glow plug, torquing it to 12 ft. lbs. (16 Nm).
14. Connect the generator two-lead connection.
15. Install the air cleaner assembly and connect the EGR valve hose.

ADJUSTMENT

1. Shut off the engine.
2. Note the relative position of the marks on the pump flange and the pump adaptor.
3. Loosen the nuts or bolts holding the pump to a point where the pump can just be rotated. Use a ¾ in. open-end wrench on the boss at the front of the injection pump.
4. Rotate the pump to the left to advance the timing and to the right to retard the timing. The width of the mark on the adaptor is equal to about 1 degree of timing. Move the pump the amount that is needed and tighten the pump retaining nuts to 18 ft. lbs.

5. Start the engine and recheck the timing as described earlier. Reset the timing if necessary.
6. Adjust the injection pump rod, reset the fast and curb idle speeds.

➥ **Wild needle fluctuations on the timing meter indicate a cylinder not firing properly. Correction of this condition must be made prior to adjusting the timing.**

7. If, after resetting the timing, the timing marks are far apart and the engine still runs poorly, the dynamic timing could still be off. It is possible that a malfunctioning cylinder will cause incorrect timing. If this occurs, it is essential that timing be checked in cylinders 2 or 3. If different timing exists between cylinders, try both positions to determine which timing works best.

Injection Nozzle

REMOVAL & INSTALLATION

◗ **See Figures 52, 53 and 54**

Lines Removed

1. Remove the fuel return line from the nozzle.
2. Remove the nozzle hold-down clamp and spacer using tool J-26952.
3. Cap the high pressure line and nozzle tip.

➥ **The nozzle tip is highly susceptible to damage and must be protected at all times.**

4. If an old nozzle is to be reinstalled, a new compression seal and carbon stop seal must be installed after removal of the used seals.
5. Remove the caps and install the nozzle, spacer and clamp. Torque to 25 ft. lbs. (34 Nm).
6. Replace return line, start the engine and check for leaks.

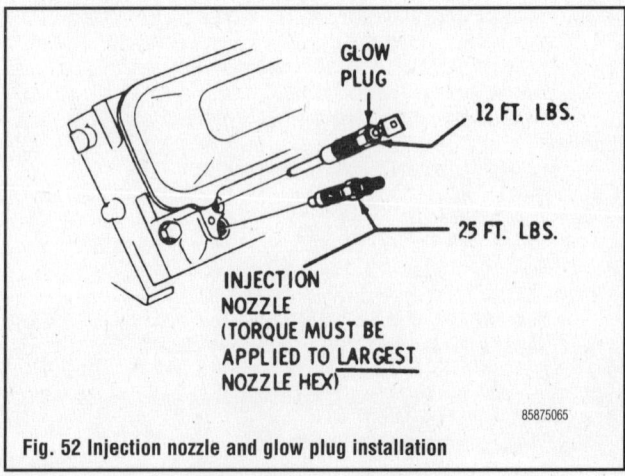

Fig. 52 Injection nozzle and glow plug installation

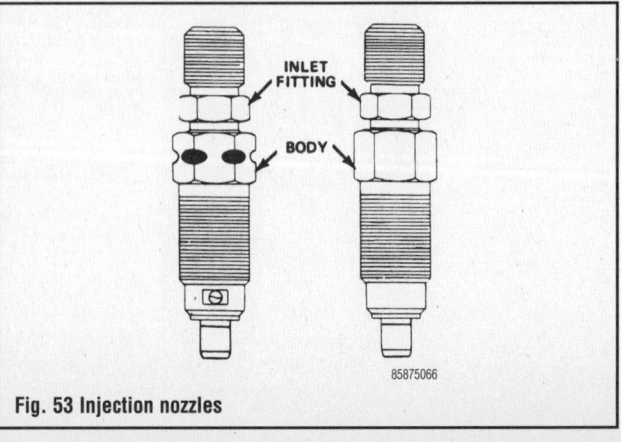

Fig. 53 Injection nozzles

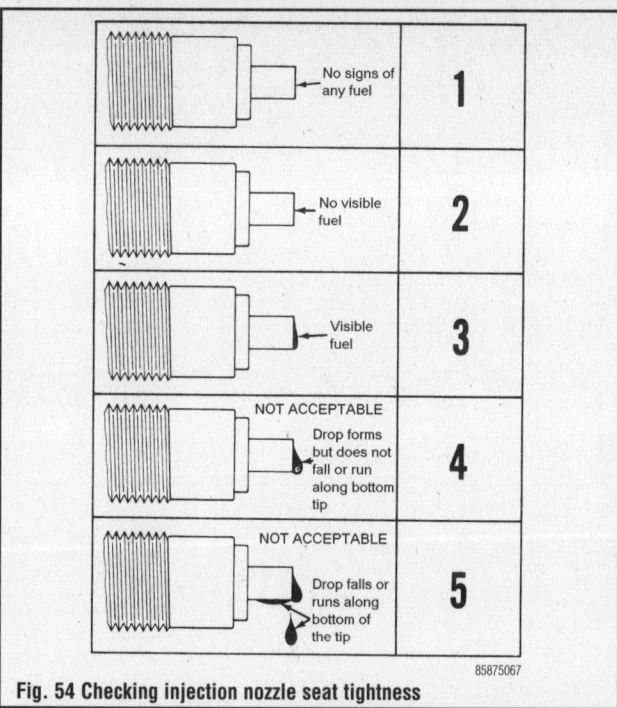

Fig. 54 Checking injection nozzle seat tightness

Injection Pump Adapter, Seal and New Timing Mark

REMOVAL & INSTALLATION

▶ **See Figures 55, 56 and 57**

1. Remove injection pump and lines as described earlier.
2. Remove the injection pump adapter.
3. Remove the seal from the adapter.

To install:

4. File the timing mark from the adapter. Do not file the mark off the pump.
5. Position the engine at TDC of No. 1 cylinder. Align the mark on the balancer with the zero mark on the indicator. The index is offset to the right when No. 1 is at TDC.
6. Apply a chassis lube to the seal areas. Install, but do not tighten the injection pump.
7. Install the new seal on the adapter using tool J-28425, or its equivalent.
8. Torque the adapter bolts to 25 ft. lbs. (34 Nm).
9. Install timing tool J-26896 into the injection pump adapter. Torque the tool, toward No. 1 cylinder to 50 ft. lbs. (68 Nm). Mark the injection pump adapter. Remove the tool.
10. Install the injection pump.

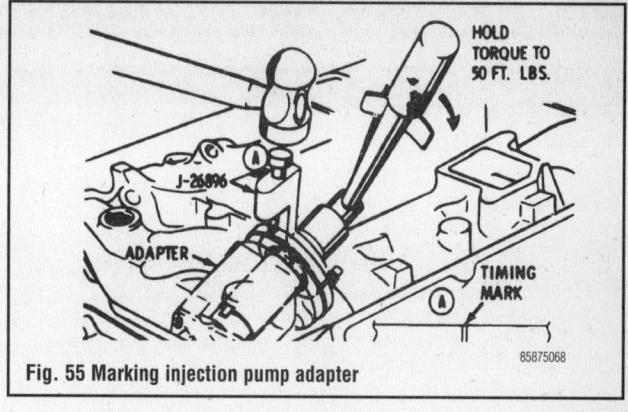

Fig. 55 Marking injection pump adapter

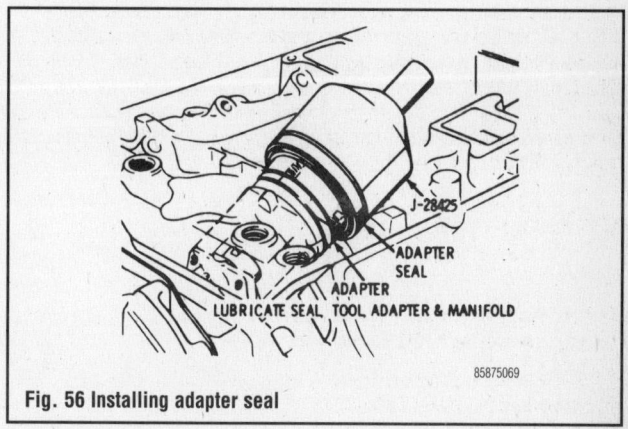

Fig. 56 Installing adapter seal

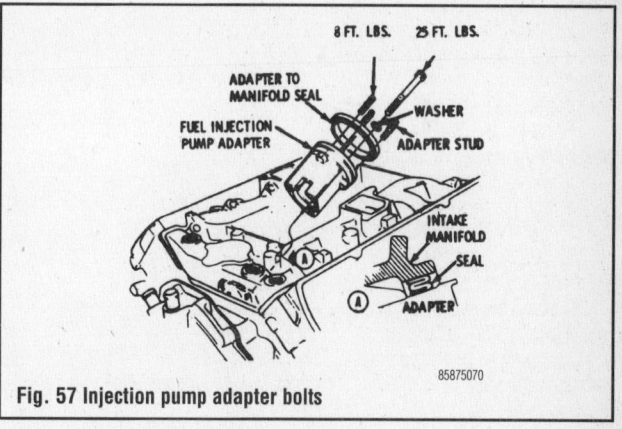

Fig. 57 Injection pump adapter bolts

FUEL TANK

Tank Assembly

REMOVAL & INSTALLATION

▶ **See Figure 58**

1. Drain tank.
2. Disconnect tank unit wire from connector in rear compartment.
3. Remove the ground wire retaining screw from the underbody.
4. Disconnect the hoses from the tank unit.
5. Support the fuel tank and disconnect the two fuel tank retaining straps.
6. Remove the tank from the car.
7. Remove the fuel gauge retaining cam, and remove the tank unit from the tank.
8. Installation is the reverse of removal. On California emissions-equipped cars, center the fuel filler pipe in the opening as required. Always replace the O-ring when the tank unit has been removed.

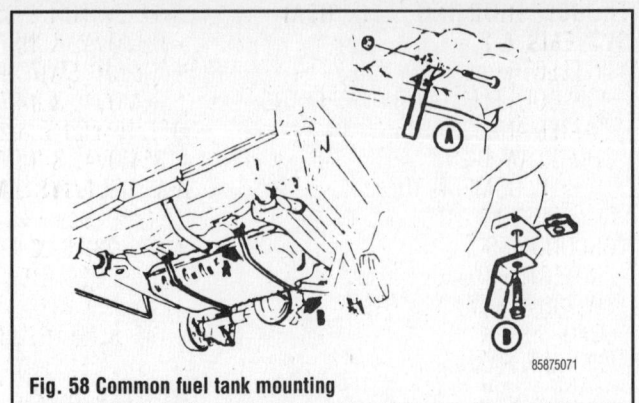

Fig. 58 Common fuel tank mounting

85875071

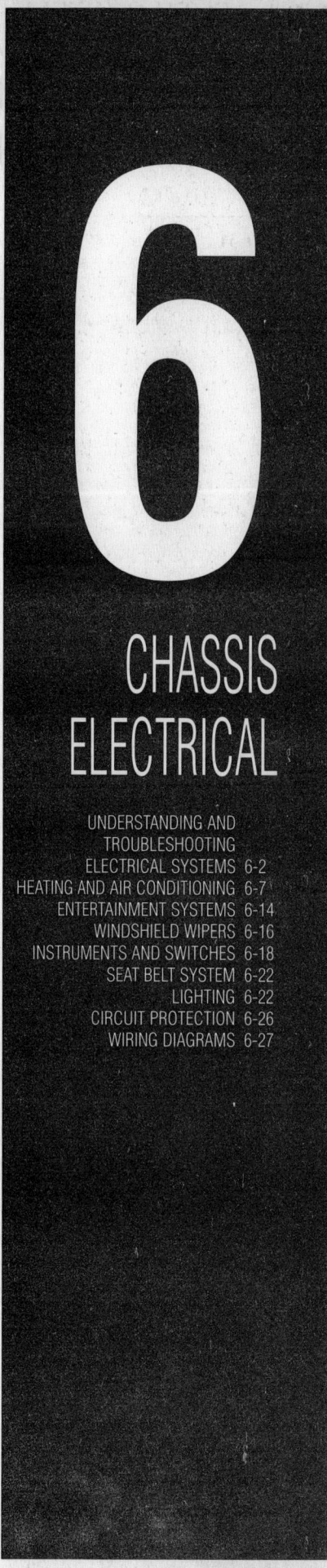

6

CHASSIS ELECTRICAL

UNDERSTANDING AND TROUBLESHOOTING ELECTRICAL SYSTEMS

Basic Electrical Theory

♦ **See Figure 1**

For any 12 volt, negative ground, electrical system to operate, the electricity must travel in a complete circuit. This simply means that current (power) from the positive (+) terminal of the battery must eventually return to the negative (-) terminal of the battery. Along the way, this current will travel through wires, fuses, switches and components. If, for any reason, the flow of current through the circuit is interrupted, the component fed by that circuit will cease to function properly.

Perhaps the easiest way to visualize a circuit is to think of connecting a light bulb (with two wires attached to it) to the battery—one wire attached to the negative (-) terminal of the battery and the other wire to the positive (+) terminal. With the two wires touching the battery terminals, the circuit would be complete and the light bulb would illuminate. Electricity would follow a path from the battery to the bulb and back to the battery. It's easy to see that with longer wires on our light bulb, it could be mounted anywhere. Further, one wire could be fitted with a switch so that the light could be turned on and off.

The normal automotive circuit differs from this simple example in two ways. First, instead of having a return wire from the bulb to the battery, the current travels through the frame of the vehicle. Since the negative (-) battery cable is attached to the frame (made of electrically conductive metal), the frame of the vehicle can serve as a ground wire to complete the circuit. Secondly, most automotive circuits contain multiple components which receive power from a single circuit. This lessens the amount of wire needed to power components on the vehicle.

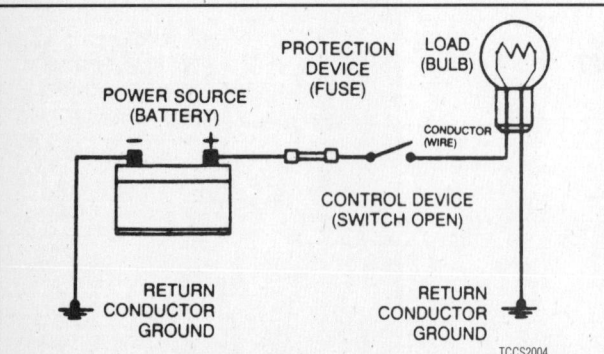

Fig. 1 This example illustrates a simple circuit. When the switch is closed, power from the positive (+) battery terminal flows through the fuse and the switch, and then to the light bulb. The light illuminates and the circuit is completed through the ground wire back to the negative (-) battery terminal. In reality, the two ground points shown in the illustration are attached to the metal frame of the vehicle, which completes the circuit back to the battery

HOW DOES ELECTRICITY WORK: THE WATER ANALOGY

Electricity is the flow of electrons—the subatomic particles that constitute the outer shell of an atom. Electrons spin in an orbit around the center core of an atom. The center core is comprised of protons (positive charge) and neutrons (neutral charge). Electrons have a negative charge and balance out the positive charge of the protons. When an outside force causes the number of electrons to unbalance the charge of the protons, the electrons will split off the atom and look for another atom to balance out. If this imbalance is kept up, electrons will continue to move and an electrical flow will exist.

Many people have been taught electrical theory using an analogy with water. In a comparison with water flowing through a pipe, the electrons would be the water and the wire is the pipe.

The flow of electricity can be measured much like the flow of water through a pipe. The unit of measurement used is amperes, frequently abbreviated as amps (a). You can compare amperage to the volume of water flowing through a pipe.

When connected to a circuit, an ammeter will measure the actual amount of current flowing through the circuit. When relatively few electrons flow through a circuit, the amperage is low. When many electrons flow, the amperage is high.

Water pressure is measured in units such as pounds per square inch (psi); The electrical pressure is measured in units called volts (v). When a voltmeter is connected to a circuit, it is measuring the electrical pressure.

The actual flow of electricity depends not only on voltage and amperage, but also on the resistance of the circuit. The higher the resistance, the higher the force necessary to push the current through the circuit. The standard unit for measuring resistance is an ohm. Resistance in a circuit varies depending on the amount and type of components used in the circuit. The main factors which determine resistance are:

• Material—some materials have more resistance than others. Those with high resistance are said to be insulators. Rubber materials (or rubber-like plastics) are some of the most common insulators used in vehicles as they have a very high resistance to electricity. Very low resistance materials are said to be conductors. Copper wire is among the best conductors. Silver is actually a superior conductor to copper and is used in some relay contacts, but its high cost prohibits its use as common wiring. Most automotive wiring is made of copper.

• Size—the larger the wire size being used, the less resistance the wire will have. This is why components which use large amounts of electricity usually have large wires supplying current to them.

• Length—for a given thickness of wire, the longer the wire, the greater the resistance. The shorter the wire, the less the resistance. When determining the proper wire for a circuit, both size and length must be considered to design a circuit that can handle the current needs of the component.

• Temperature—with many materials, the higher the temperature, the greater the resistance (positive temperature coefficient). Some materials exhibit the opposite trait of lower resistance with higher temperatures (negative temperature coefficient). These principles are used in many of the sensors on the engine.

OHM'S LAW

There is a direct relationship between current, voltage and resistance. The relationship between current, voltage and resistance can be summed up by a statement known as Ohm's law.

Voltage (E) is equal to amperage (I) times resistance (R): $E = I \times R$

Other forms of the formula are $R = E/I$ and $I = E/R$

In each of these formulas, E is the voltage in volts, I is the current in amps and R is the resistance in ohms. The basic point to remember is that as the resistance of a circuit goes up, the amount of current that flows in the circuit will go down, if voltage remains the same.

The amount of work that the electricity can perform is expressed as power. The unit of power is the watt (w). The relationship between power, voltage and current is expressed as:

Power (w) is equal to amperage (I) times voltage (E): $W = I \times E$

This is only true for direct current (DC) circuits; The alternating current formula is a tad different, but since the electrical circuits in most vehicles are DC type, we need not get into AC circuit theory.

Electrical Components

POWER SOURCE

Power is supplied to the vehicle by two devices: The battery and the alternator. The battery supplies electrical power during starting or during periods when the current demand of the vehicle's electrical system exceeds the output capacity of the alternator. The alternator supplies electrical current when the engine is running. Just not does the alternator supply the current needs of the vehicle, but it recharges the battery.

The Battery

In most modern vehicles, the battery is a lead/acid electrochemical device consisting of six 2 volt subsections (cells) connected in series, so that the unit is capable of producing approximately 12 volts of electrical pressure. Each subsection consists of a series of positive and negative plates held a short distance apart in a solution of sulfuric acid and water.

The two types of plates are of dissimilar metals. This sets up a chemical reaction, and it is this reaction which produces current flow from the battery when its positive and negative terminals are connected to an electrical load . The power removed from the battery is replaced by the alternator, restoring the battery to its original chemical state.

The Alternator

On some vehicles there isn't an alternator, but a generator. The difference is that an alternator supplies alternating current which is then changed to direct current for use on the vehicle, while a generator produces direct current. Alternators tend to be more efficient and that is why they are used.

Alternators and generators are devices that consist of coils of wires wound together making big electromagnets. One group of coils spins within another set and the interaction of the magnetic fields causes a current to flow. This current is then drawn off the coils and fed into the vehicles electrical system.

GROUND

Two types of grounds are used in automotive electric circuits. Direct ground components are grounded to the frame through their mounting points. All other components use some sort of ground wire which is attached to the frame or chassis of the vehicle. The electrical current runs through the chassis of the vehicle and returns to the battery through the ground (-) cable; if you look, you'll see that the battery ground cable connects between the battery and the frame or chassis of the vehicle.

➡ **It should be noted that a good percentage of electrical problems can be traced to bad grounds.**

PROTECTIVE DEVICES

▶ **See Figure 2**

It is possible for large surges of current to pass through the electrical system of your vehicle. If this surge of current were to reach the load in the circuit, the surge could burn it out or severely damage it. It can also overload the wiring, causing the harness to get hot and melt the insulation. To prevent this, fuses, circuit breakers and/or fusible links are connected into the supply wires of the electrical system. These items are nothing more than a built-in weak spot in the system. When an abnormal amount of current flows through the system, these protective devices work as follows to protect the circuit:

• Fuse—when an excessive electrical current passes through a fuse, the fuse "blows" (the conductor melts) and opens the circuit, preventing the passage of current.

• Circuit Breaker—a circuit breaker is basically a self-repairing fuse. It will open the circuit in the same fashion as a fuse, but when the surge subsides, the circuit breaker can be reset and does not need replacement.

• Fusible Link—a fusible link (fuse link or main link) is a short length of special, high temperature insulated wire that acts as a fuse. When an excessive electrical current passes through a fusible link, the thin gauge wire inside the link melts, creating an intentional open to protect the circuit. To repair the circuit, the link must be replaced. Some newer type fusible links are housed in plug-in modules, which are simply replaced like a fuse, while older type fusible links must be cut and spliced if they melt. Since this link is very early in the electrical path, it's the first place to look if nothing on the vehicle works, yet the battery seems to be charged and is properly connected.

✳✳ CAUTION

Always replace fuses, circuit breakers and fusible links with identically rated components. Under no circumstances should a component of higher or lower amperage rating be substituted.

SWITCHES & RELAYS

▶ **See Figures 3 and 4**

Switches are used in electrical circuits to control the passage of current. The most common use is to open and close circuits between the battery and the various electric devices in the system. Switches are rated according to the amount of amperage they can handle. If a sufficient amperage rated switch is not used in a circuit, the switch could overload and cause damage.

Some electrical components which require a large amount of current to operate use a special switch called a relay. Since these circuits carry a large amount of current, the thickness of the wire in the circuit is also greater. If this large wire were connected from the load to the control switch, the switch would have to carry the high amperage load and the fairing or dash would be twice as large to accommodate the increased size of the wiring harness. To prevent these problems, a relay is used.

Relays are composed of a coil and a set of contacts. When the coil has a current passed though it, a magnetic field is formed and this field causes the contacts to move together, completing the circuit. Most relays are normally open, preventing current from passing through the circuit, but they can take any electrical form depending on the job they are intended to do. Relays can be considered "remote control switches." They allow a smaller current to operate devices that require higher amperages. When a small current operates the coil, a larger current is allowed to pass by the contacts. Some common circuits which may use relays are the horn, headlights, starter, electric fuel pump and other high draw circuits.

LOAD

Every electrical circuit must include a "load" (something to use the electricity coming from the source). Without this load, the battery would attempt to deliver its entire power supply from one pole to another. This is called a "short circuit." All this electricity would take a short cut to ground and cause a great amount of damage to other components in the circuit by developing a tremendous amount of heat.

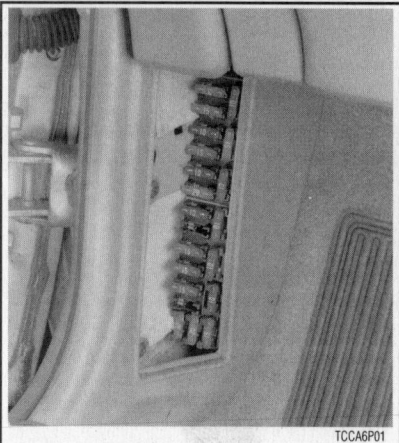

TCCA6P01

Fig. 2 Most vehicles use one or more fuse panels. This one is located on the driver's side kick panel

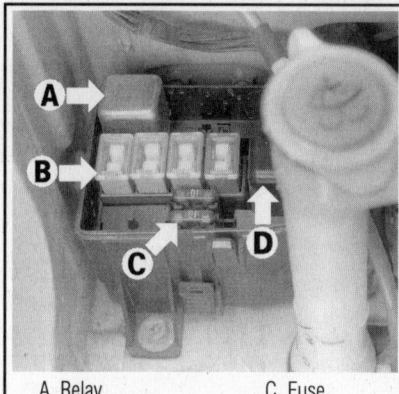

A. Relay
B. Fusible link
C. Fuse
D. Flasher

TCCA6P02

Fig. 3 The underhood fuse and relay panel usually contains fuses, relays, flashers and fusible links

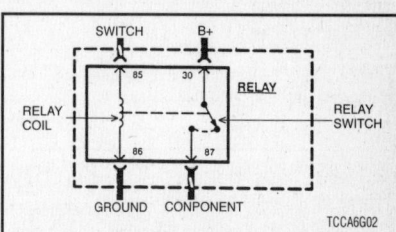

TCCA6G02

Fig. 4 Relays are composed of a coil and a switch. These two components are linked together so that when one operates, the other operates at the same time. The large wires in the circuit are connected from the battery to one side of the relay switch (B+) and from the opposite side of the relay switch to the load (component). Smaller wires are connected from the relay coil to the control switch for the circuit and from the opposite side of the relay coil to ground

This condition could develop sufficient heat to melt the insulation on all the surrounding wires and reduce a multiple wire cable to a lump of plastic and copper.

WIRING & HARNESSES

The average vehicle contains meters and meters of wiring, with hundreds of individual connections. To protect the many wires from damage and to keep them from becoming a confusing tangle, they are organized into bundles, enclosed in plastic or taped together and called wiring harnesses. Different harnesses serve different parts of the vehicle. Individual wires are color coded to help trace them through a harness where sections are hidden from view.

Automotive wiring or circuit conductors can be either single strand wire, multi-strand wire or printed circuitry. Single strand wire has a solid metal core and is usually used inside such components as alternators, motors, relays and other devices. Multi-strand wire has a core made of many small strands of wire twisted together into a single conductor. Most of the wiring in an automotive electrical system is made up of multi-strand wire, either as a single conductor or grouped together in a harness. All wiring is color coded on the insulator, either as a solid color or as a colored wire with an identification stripe. A printed circuit is a thin film of copper or other conductor that is printed on an insulator backing. Occasionally, a printed circuit is sandwiched between two sheets of plastic for more protection and flexibility. A complete printed circuit, consisting of conductors, insulating material and connectors for lamps or other components is called a printed circuit board. Printed circuitry is used in place of individual wires or harnesses in places where space is limited, such as behind instrument panels.

Since automotive electrical systems are very sensitive to changes in resistance, the selection of properly sized wires is critical when systems are repaired. A loose or corroded connection or a replacement wire that is too small for the circuit will add extra resistance and an additional voltage drop to the circuit.

The wire gauge number is an expression of the cross-section area of the conductor. Vehicles from countries that use the metric system will typically describe the wire size as its cross-sectional area in square millimeters. In this method, the larger the wire, the greater the number. Another common system for expressing wire size is the American Wire Gauge (AWG) system. As gauge number increases, area decreases and the wire becomes smaller. An 18 gauge wire is smaller than a 4 gauge wire. A wire with a higher gauge number will carry less current than a wire with a lower gauge number. Gauge wire size refers to the size of the strands of the conductor, not the size of the complete wire with insulator. It is possible, therefore, to have two wires of the same gauge with different diameters because one may have thicker insulation than the other.

It is essential to understand how a circuit works before trying to figure out why it doesn't. An electrical schematic shows the electrical current paths when a circuit is operating properly. Schematics break the entire electrical system down into individual circuits. In a schematic, usually no attempt is made to represent wiring and components as they physically appear on the vehicle; switches and other components are shown as simply as possible. Face views of harness connectors show the cavity or terminal locations in all multi-pin connectors to help locate test points.

CONNECTORS

▶ **See Figures 5 and 6**

Three types of connectors are commonly used in automotive applications—weatherproof, molded and hard shell.

TCCA6P03

Fig. 5 Hard shell (left) and weatherproof (right) connectors have replaceable terminals

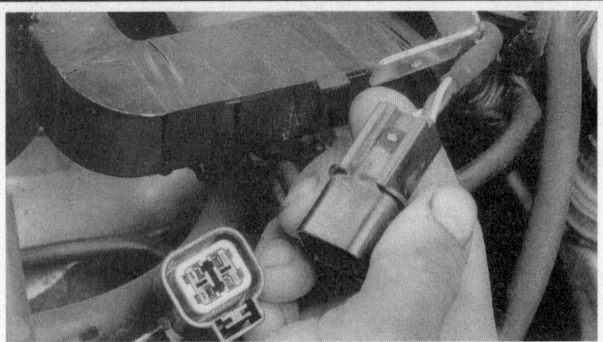

TCCA6P04

Fig. 6 Weatherproof connectors are most commonly used in the engine compartment or where the connector is exposed to the elements

• Weatherproof—these connectors are most commonly used where the connector is exposed to the elements. Terminals are protected against moisture and dirt by sealing rings which provide a weathertight seal. All repairs require the use of a special terminal and the tool required to service it. Unlike standard blade type terminals, these weatherproof terminals cannot be straightened once they are bent. Make certain that the connectors are properly seated and all of the sealing rings are in place when connecting leads.
• Molded—these connectors require complete replacement of the connector if found to be defective. This means splicing a new connector assembly into the harness. All splices should be soldered to insure proper contact. Use care when probing the connections or replacing terminals in them, as it is possible to create a short circuit between opposite terminals. If this happens to the wrong terminal pair, it is possible to damage certain components. Always use jumper wires between connectors for circuit checking and NEVER probe through weatherproof seals.
• Hard Shell—unlike molded connectors, the terminal contacts in hard-shell connectors can be replaced. Replacement usually involves the use of a special terminal removal tool that depresses the locking tangs (barbs) on the connector terminal and allows the connector to be removed from the rear of the shell. The connector shell should be replaced if it shows any evidence of burning, melting, cracks, or breaks. Replace individual terminals that are burnt, corroded, distorted or loose.

Test Equipment

Pinpointing the exact cause of trouble in an electrical circuit is most times accomplished by the use of special test equipment. The following describes different types of commonly used test equipment and briefly explains how to use them in diagnosis. In addition to the information covered below, the tool manufacturer's instructions booklet (provided with the tester) should be read and clearly understood before attempting any test procedures.

JUMPER WIRES

✳ CAUTION

Never use jumper wires made from a thinner gauge wire than the circuit being tested. If the jumper wire is of too small a gauge, it may overheat and possibly melt. Never use jumpers to bypass high resistance loads in a circuit. Bypassing resistances, in effect, creates a short circuit. This may, in turn, cause damage and fire. Jumper wires should only be used to bypass lengths of wire or to simulate switches.

Jumper wires are simple, yet extremely valuable, pieces of test equipment. They are basically test wires which are used to bypass sections of a circuit. Although jumper wires can be purchased, they are usually fabricated from lengths of standard automotive wire and whatever type of connector (alligator clip, spade connector or pin connector) that is required for the particular application being tested. In cramped, hard-to-reach areas, it is advisable to have insulated boots over the jumper wire terminals in order to prevent accidental grounding. It is also advisable to include a standard automotive fuse in any jumper wire. This is commonly referred to as a "fused jumper". By inserting an in-line fuse holder between a set of test leads, a fused jumper wire can be used for bypassing open circuits. Use a 5 amp fuse to provide protection against voltage spikes.

Jumper wires are used primarily to locate open electrical circuits, on either the ground (-) side of the circuit or on the power (+) side. If an electrical component fails to operate, connect the jumper wire between the component and a good ground. If the component operates only with the jumper installed, the ground circuit is open. If the ground circuit is good, but the component does not operate, the circuit between the power feed and component may be open. By moving the jumper wire successively back from the component toward the power source, you can isolate the area of the circuit where the open is located. When the component stops functioning, or the power is cut off, the open is in the segment of wire between the jumper and the point previously tested.

You can sometimes connect the jumper wire directly from the battery to the "hot" terminal of the component, but first make sure the component uses 12 volts in operation. Some electrical components, such as fuel injectors or sensors, are designed to operate on about 4 to 5 volts, and running 12 volts directly to these components will cause damage.

TEST LIGHTS

▶ **See Figure 7**

The test light is used to check circuits and components while electrical current is flowing through them. It is used for voltage and ground tests. To use a 12 volt test light, connect the ground clip to a good ground and probe wherever necessary with the pick. The test light will illuminate when voltage is detected. This does not necessarily mean that 12 volts (or any particular amount of voltage) is present; it only means that some voltage is present. It is advisable before using the test light to touch its ground clip and probe across the battery posts or terminals to make sure the light is operating properly.

✳✳ WARNING

Do not use a test light to probe electronic ignition, spark plug or coil wires. Never use a pick-type test light to probe wiring on computer controlled systems unless specifically instructed to do so. Any wire insulation that is pierced by the test light probe should be taped and sealed with silicone after testing.

Like the jumper wire, the 12 volt test light is used to isolate opens in circuits. But, whereas the jumper wire is used to bypass the open to operate the load, the 12 volt test light is used to locate the presence of voltage in a circuit. If the test light illuminates, there is power up to that point in the circuit; if the test light does not illuminate, there is an open circuit (no power). Move the test light in successive steps back toward the power source until the light in the handle illuminates. The open is between the probe and a point which was previously probed.

The self-powered test light is similar in design to the 12 volt test light, but contains a 1.5 volt penlight battery in the handle. It is most often used in place of a multimeter to check for open or short circuits when power is isolated from the circuit (continuity test).

The battery in a self-powered test light does not provide much current. A weak battery may not provide enough power to illuminate the test light even when a complete circuit is made (especially if there is high resistance in the cir-

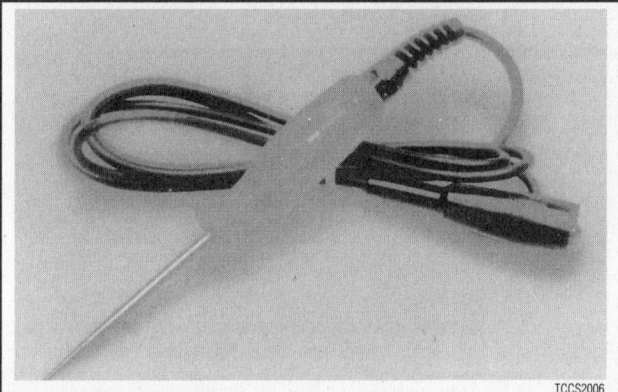

TCCS2006

Fig. 7 A 12 volt test light is used to detect the presence of voltage in a circuit

cuit). Always make sure that the test battery is strong. To check the battery, briefly touch the ground clip to the probe; if the light glows brightly, the battery is strong enough for testing.

➡**A self-powered test light should not be used on any computer controlled system or component. The small amount of electricity transmitted by the test light is enough to damage many electronic automotive components.**

MULTIMETERS

Multimeters are an extremely useful tool for troubleshooting electrical problems. They can be purchased in either analog or digital form and have a price range to suit any budget. A multimeter is a voltmeter, ammeter and ohmmeter (along with other features) combined into one instrument. It is often used when testing solid state circuits because of its high input impedance (usually 10 megaohms or more). A brief description of the multimeter main test functions follows:

• Voltmeter—the voltmeter is used to measure voltage at any point in a circuit, or to measure the voltage drop across any part of a circuit. Voltmeters usually have various scales and a selector switch to allow the reading of different voltage ranges. The voltmeter has a positive and a negative lead. To avoid damage to the meter, always connect the negative lead to the negative (-) side of the circuit (to ground or nearest the ground side of the circuit) and connect the positive lead to the positive (+) side of the circuit (to the power source or the nearest power source). Note that the negative voltmeter lead will always be black and that the positive voltmeter will always be some color other than black (usually red).

• Ohmmeter—the ohmmeter is designed to read resistance (measured in ohms) in a circuit or component. Most ohmmeters will have a selector switch which permits the measurement of different ranges of resistance (usually the selector switch allows the multiplication of the meter reading by 10, 100, 1,000 and 10,000). Some ohmmeters are "auto-ranging" which means the meter itself will determine which scale to use. Since the meters are powered by an internal battery, the ohmmeter can be used like a self-powered test light. When the ohmmeter is connected, current from the ohmmeter flows through the circuit or component being tested. Since the ohmmeter's internal resistance and voltage are known values, the amount of current flow through the meter depends on the resistance of the circuit or component being tested. The ohmmeter can also be used to perform a continuity test for suspected open circuits. In using the meter for making continuity checks, do not be concerned with the actual resistance readings. Zero resistance, or any ohm reading, indicates continuity in the circuit. Infinite resistance indicates an opening in the circuit. A high resistance reading where there should be none indicates a problem in the circuit. Checks for short circuits are made in the same manner as checks for open circuits, except that the circuit must be isolated from both power and normal ground. Infinite resistance indicates no continuity, while zero resistance indicates a dead short.

✳✳ WARNING

Never use an ohmmeter to check the resistance of a component or wire while there is voltage applied to the circuit.

• Ammeter—an ammeter measures the amount of current flowing through a circuit in units called amperes or amps. At normal operating voltage, most circuits have a characteristic amount of amperes, called "current draw" which can be measured using an ammeter. By referring to a specified current draw rating, then measuring the amperes and comparing the two values, one can determine what is happening within the circuit to aid in diagnosis. An open circuit, for example, will not allow any current to flow, so the ammeter reading will be zero. A damaged component or circuit will have an increased current draw, so the reading will be high. The ammeter is always connected in series with the circuit being tested. All of the current that normally flows through the circuit must also flow through the ammeter; if there is any other path for the current to follow, the ammeter reading will not be accurate. The ammeter itself has very little resistance to current flow and, therefore, will not affect the circuit, but it will measure current draw only when the circuit is closed and electricity is flowing. Excessive current draw can blow fuses and drain the battery, while a reduced current draw can cause motors to run slowly, lights to dim and other components to not operate properly.

Troubleshooting Electrical Systems

When diagnosing a specific problem, organized troubleshooting is a must. The complexity of a modern automotive vehicle demands that you approach any problem in a logical, organized manner. There are certain troubleshooting techniques, however, which are standard:

• Establish when the problem occurs. Does the problem appear only under certain conditions? Were there any noises, odors or other unusual symptoms? Isolate the problem area. To do this, make some simple tests and observations, then eliminate the systems that are working properly. Check for obvious problems, such as broken wires and loose or dirty connections. Always check the obvious before assuming something complicated is the cause.

• Test for problems systematically to determine the cause once the problem area is isolated. Are all the components functioning properly? Is there power going to electrical switches and motors. Performing careful, systematic checks will often turn up most causes on the first inspection, without wasting time checking components that have little or no relationship to the problem.

• Test all repairs after the work is done to make sure that the problem is fixed. Some causes can be traced to more than one component, so a careful verification of repair work is important in order to pick up additional malfunctions that may cause a problem to reappear or a different problem to arise. A blown fuse, for example, is a simple problem that may require more than another fuse to repair. If you don't look for a problem that caused a fuse to blow, a shorted wire (for example) may go undetected.

Experience has shown that most problems tend to be the result of a fairly simple and obvious cause, such as loose or corroded connectors, bad grounds or damaged wire insulation which causes a short. This makes careful visual inspection of components during testing essential to quick and accurate troubleshooting.

Testing

OPEN CIRCUITS

▶ See Figure 8

This test already assumes the existence of an open in the circuit and it is used to help locate the open portion.
1. Isolate the circuit from power and ground.
2. Connect the self-powered test light or ohmmeter ground clip to the ground side of the circuit and probe sections of the circuit sequentially.
3. If the light is out or there is infinite resistance, the open is between the probe and the circuit ground.
4. If the light is on or the meter shows continuity, the open is between the probe and the end of the circuit toward the power source.

SHORT CIRCUITS

→Never use a self-powered test light to perform checks for opens or shorts when power is applied to the circuit under test. The test light can be damaged by outside power.

1. Isolate the circuit from power and ground.
2. Connect the self-powered test light or ohmmeter ground clip to a good ground and probe any easy-to-reach point in the circuit.
3. If the light comes on or there is continuity, there is a short somewhere in the circuit.

4. To isolate the short, probe a test point at either end of the isolated circuit (the light should be on or the meter should indicate continuity).
5. Leave the test light probe engaged and sequentially open connectors or switches, remove parts, etc. until the light goes out or continuity is broken.
6. When the light goes out, the short is between the last two circuit components which were opened.

VOLTAGE

This test determines voltage available from the battery and should be the first step in any electrical troubleshooting procedure after visual inspection. Many electrical problems, especially on computer controlled systems, can be caused by a low state of charge in the battery. Excessive corrosion at the battery cable terminals can cause poor contact that will prevent proper charging and full battery current flow.
1. Set the voltmeter selector switch to the 20V position.
2. Connect the multimeter negative lead to the battery's negative (-) post or terminal and the positive lead to the battery's positive (+) post or terminal.
3. Turn the ignition switch **ON** to provide a load.
4. A well charged battery should register over 12 volts. If the meter reads below 11.5 volts, the battery power may be insufficient to operate the electrical system properly.

VOLTAGE DROP

▶ See Figure 9

When current flows through a load, the voltage beyond the load drops. This voltage drop is due to the resistance created by the load and also by small resistances created by corrosion at the connectors and damaged insulation on the wires. The maximum allowable voltage drop under load is critical, especially if there is more than one load in the circuit, since all voltage drops are cumulative.
1. Set the voltmeter selector switch to the 20 volt position.
2. Connect the multimeter negative lead to a good ground.
3. Operate the circuit and check the voltage prior to the first component (load).
4. There should be little or no voltage drop in the circuit prior to the first component. If a voltage drop exists, the wire or connectors in the circuit are suspect.
5. While operating the first component in the circuit, probe the ground side of the component with the positive meter lead and observe the voltage readings. A small voltage drop should be noticed. This voltage drop is caused by the resistance of the component.
6. Repeat the test for each component (load) down the circuit.
7. If a large voltage drop is noticed, the preceding component, wire or connector is suspect.

RESISTANCE

▶ See Figures 10 and 11

⁑ WARNING

Never use an ohmmeter with power applied to the circuit. The ohmmeter is designed to operate on its own power supply. The normal 12 volt electrical system voltage could damage the meter!

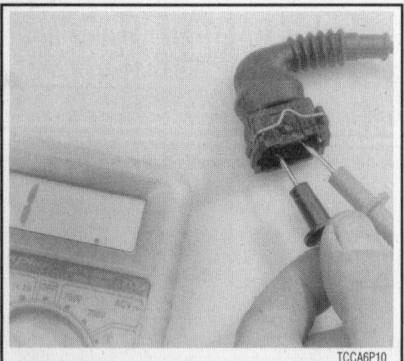
Fig. 8 The infinite reading on this multimeter indicates that the circuit is open

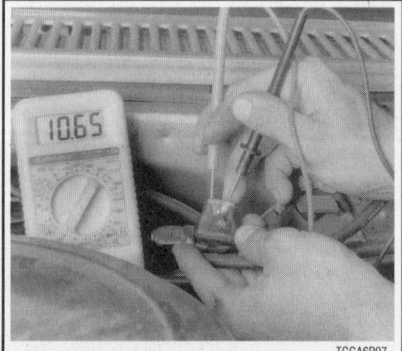
Fig. 9 This voltage drop test revealed high resistance (low voltage) in the circuit

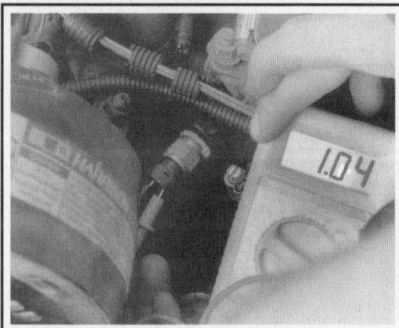
Fig. 10 Checking the resistance of a coolant temperature sensor with an ohmmeter. Reading is 1.04 kilohms

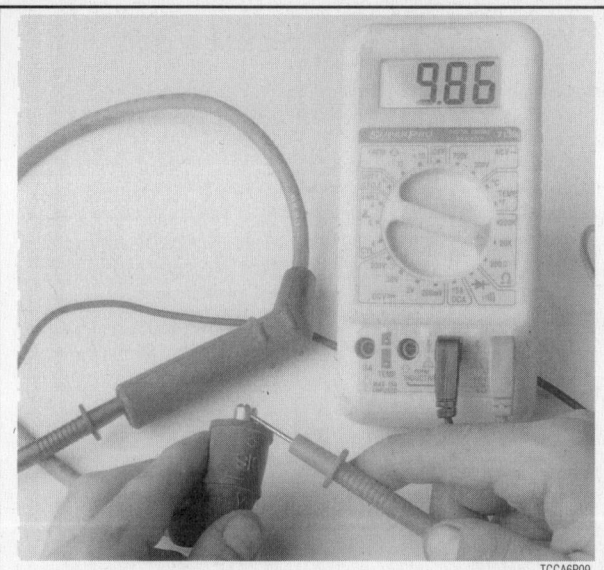

Fig. 11 Spark plug wires can be checked for excessive resistance using an ohmmeter

1. Isolate the circuit from the vehicle's power source.
2. Ensure that the ignition key is **OFF** when disconnecting any components or the battery.
3. Where necessary, also isolate at least one side of the circuit to be checked, in order to avoid reading parallel resistances. Parallel circuit resistances will always give a lower reading than the actual resistance of either of the branches.
4. Connect the meter leads to both sides of the circuit (wire or component) and read the actual measured ohms on the meter scale. Make sure the selector switch is set to the proper ohm scale for the circuit being tested, to avoid mis-reading the ohmmeter test value.

Wire and Connector Repair

Almost anyone can replace damaged wires, as long as the proper tools and parts are available. Wire and terminals are available to fit almost any need. Even the specialized weatherproof, molded and hard shell connectors are now available from aftermarket suppliers.

Be sure the ends of all the wires are fitted with the proper terminal hardware and connectors. Wrapping a wire around a stud is never a permanent solution and will only cause trouble later. Replace wires one at a time to avoid confusion. Always route wires exactly the same as the factory.

→If connector repair is necessary, only attempt it if you have the proper tools. Weatherproof and hard shell connectors require special tools to release the pins inside the connector. Attempting to repair these connectors with conventional hand tools will damage them.

HEATING AND AIR CONDITIONING

Blower Motor

REMOVAL & INSTALLATION

All Models Except Those Following

♦ See Figures 12, 13, 14, 15 and 16

1. Disconnect the negative battery cable.
2. Remove the rubber cooling hose from the nipple and the blower motor.
3. Disconnect the electrical connector(s).
4. Remove the screws that secure the motor to the case, then twist the motor and remove from the assembly.
5. To install, reverse the removal procedure. Use sealer as needed to make a water tight seal.

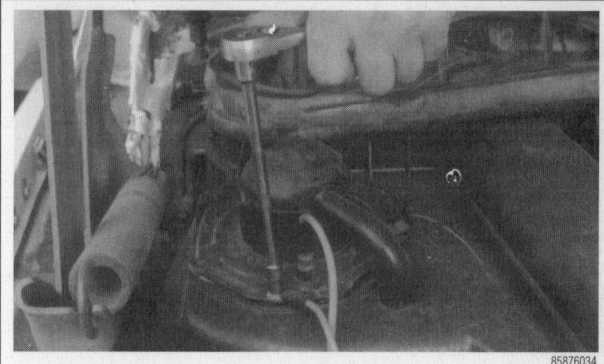

Fig. 12 Removing the blower motor retaining screws

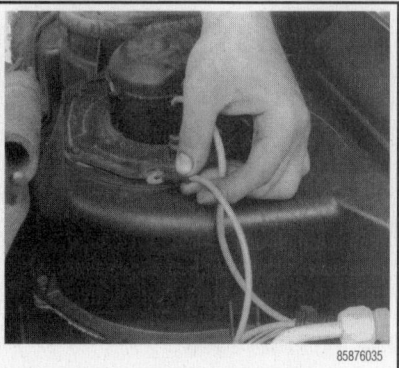

Fig. 13 Removing the blower motor ground strap

Fig. 14 Removing the blower motor electrical connection

Fig. 15 Removing the blower motor drain hose

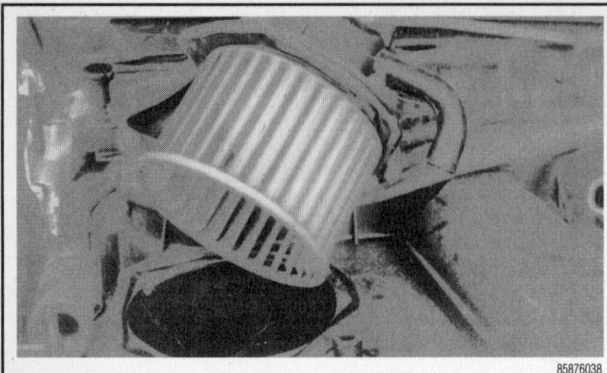

Fig. 16 Removing the blower motor assembly

1975–76 Fleetwood (Rear Unit)

♦ See Figure 17

➡The following applies to either the right or the left blower motor.

1. Remove the trim panel inside the luggage compartment.
2. Disconnect the double electrical connector at the motor.
3. Uncover and remove the five screws securing the blower motor to the housing.
4. Remove the blower motor and fan assembly.
5. To install, reverse the procedures above.

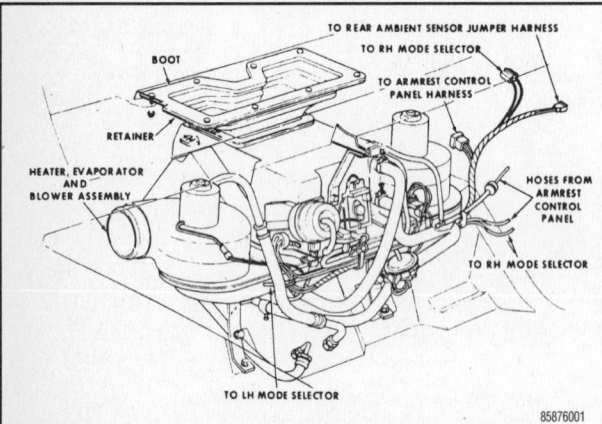

Fig. 17 Heater, evaporator and blower-rear unit—1975–76 Fleetwood

1979 Seville

1. Disconnect the negative battery cable.
2. Jack up the front of the car and support it on jackstands. Remove the right front wheel.
3. Remove the five screws securing the wheelhousing to the fender at the wheel opening.
4. Remove the two screws attaching the wheelhousing at the front.
5. Remove the three plastic retainers securing the wheel housing seal at the rear of the wheelwell, front of the wheelwell, at the fender, and forward of the wheelwell opening.
6. Remove the two screws behind the wheelwell securing the wheelhousing to the cowl brace.
7. Remove the battery and battery tray.
8. Remove the three screws and the retainer securing the wheelhousing to the radiator support under the horns.
9. Remove the wheelhousing damper upper mounting bolt and move the damper out of the way.
10. Remove the wheelhousing from the car. Some prying and bending may be necessary.
11. Remove the rubber cooling hose from the nipple and the blower motor.

12. Disconnect the electrical connector(s).
13. Remove the screws that secure the motor to the case, then twist the motor and remove from the assembly.
   To install:
14. Install the ground wire to the blower flange screw (at the 5 o'clock position).
15. Secure the capacitor to the blower flange screw (at the 5 o'clock position).
16. Place a bead of sealer around the opening where the blower will contact the case.
17. Guide the blower motor against the cowl and place on the locating dowel.
18. Install the five screws securing the blower to the case.
19. Install the right wheel house.
20. Reconnect the electrical connector lead to the motor.
21. Install the cooling hose on the motor and nipple.

1980–85 Seville

1. Disconnect the negative battery cable.
2. Disconnect and remove the Hi-Blower assembly.
3. Remove the blower motor assembly.
4. To install, reverse the above procedures, reseal the blower mounting surface with sealer.

1977–78 Eldorado

1. Disconnect the negative battery cable.
2. Jack up the front of the car and support it on jackstands. Remove the right front wheel.
3. Cut along the inside of the rectangular stamped bead on the right fender filler.
4. Unbolt and remove the blower motor.
5. To install, reverse the above procedures, fold the flap up and reseal the opening with sealer.

1979–85 Eldorado

1. Disconnect the negative battery cable.
2. Disconnect and remove the Hi-Blower assembly.
3. Remove the blower motor assembly.
4. To install, reverse the above procedures, reseal the blower mounting surface with sealer.

1986–89 Eldorado and Seville

♦ See Figure 18

1. Remove the air cleaner assembly.
2. Remove the strut tower brace.
3. Remove the wiring harness bracket.

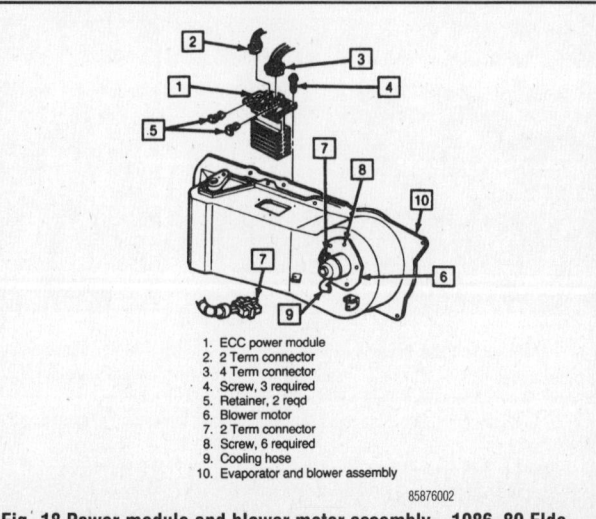

1. ECC power module
2. 2 Term connector
3. 4 Term connector
4. Screw, 3 required
5. Retainer, 2 reqd
6. Blower motor
7. 2 Term connector
8. Screw, 6 required
9. Cooling hose
10. Evaporator and blower assembly

Fig. 18 Power module and blower motor assembly—1986–89 Eldorado and Seville

4. Disconnect the heater electrical connector, the cooling hose and then remove the motor mounting screws.

5. Tilt the blower motor in its case and disconnect the fan from the motor. Be careful not to bend the fan blades.

6. Remove the blower motor.

7. Installation is in the reverse order of removal.

Heater Core Without Air Conditioning

REMOVAL & INSTALLATION

All 1967-71 Models

1. Drain the cooling system.
2. Disconnect the electrical connection to the blower motor.
3. Remove the blower motor mounting screws and remove the blower.
4. Remove the heater hoses from the fittings, leaving the clamps on the fittings.
5. Disconnect the cable to the temperature valve at the pivot assembly.
6. Remove the screws holding the bottom of the heater assembly to the cowl.
7. Remove the screws holding the top of the heater assembly to the cowl, then remove the assembly.
8. Remove the screws from each side of the heater core, securing the wire retaining clamps to the blower case, then remove the clamps.
9. Pull the core out of the case and remove the grommets from the inlet and outlet fitting.

To install:
10. Install the grommets and reposition the core into the case.
11. Install the screws to the on each side of the heater core and secure the wire to the blower case with the clamps.
12. Install the screws holding the top and bottom of the heater assembly to the cowl.
13. Connect the cable to the temperature valve at the pivot assembly.
14. Install the heater hoses to the fittings.
15. Install the blower motor mounting screws and wire connection.
16. Fill the cooling system.

✳✳ CAUTION

When draining the coolant, keep in mind that cats and dogs are attracted by the ethylene glycol antifreeze, and are quite likely to drink any that is left in an uncovered container or in puddles on the ground. This will prove fatal in sufficient quantity. Always drain the coolant into a sealable container. Coolant should be reused unless it is contaminated or several years old.

All 1972-76 Models

1. Drain the cooling system.
2. Remove the heater hoses from the core nipples. Plug the core nipples.
3. Remove the instrument panel top cover.
4. Remove the screws, then position the center ventilator duct and sleeve out of the way.
5. Remove the vacuum hoses from the diverter door and the defroster door vacuum actuators.
6. Unfasten the bowden cable from the temperature door and case, then move it out of the way.
7. Remove the screws securing the heater case to the cowl.
8. Work the heater case from its position under the instrument panel.
9. Remove the screws and clips securing the core to the heater case and lift out the core.

To install:
10. Install the grommets and reposition the core into the case.
11. Install the screws securing the heater case to the cowl.
12. Fasten the bowden cable to the temperature door and case.
13. Install the vacuum hoses to the diverter door and the defroster door vacuum actuators.
14. Install the center ventilator duct and sleeve with the retaining screws.
15. Install the instrument panel top cover.
16. Install the heater hoses from the core nipples.
17. Fill the cooling system

Heater Core With Air Conditioning

REMOVAL & INSTALLATION

1967-71 Models Except Eldorado

1. Drain the cooling system.
2. Remove the carburetor air cleaner.
3. Disconnect the vacuum hose assembly connectors from the servo vacuum valve and the control valve on the power servo unit.
4. Disconnect the vacuum hose from the power servo unit.
5. Disconnect the electrical connector from the power servo unit.
6. Remove the vacuum hoses and electrical connections from the master switch.
7. Disconnect the small diameter vacuum hose from the center port of the vacuum check valve.
8. Remove the screw securing the vacuum check valve mounting bracket to the heater air selector assembly, then position the check valve and bracket out of the way.
9. Disconnect the vacuum hose from the heater door vacuum power unit.
10. Disconnect the cable from the control valve on the power servo unit.
11. Remove the hoses from the heater inlet and outlet fittings.
12. Remove the screws securing the heater air selector to the cowl and remove the assembly from the engine compartment.
13. Remove the screws securing the heater core frame to the heater-air selector case, then remove the gasket from the case.
14. Pull the core frame, with the core attached, away from the heater-air selector case.
15. Remove the grommets from the inlet and outlet fittings.
16. Remove the corner screws securing the wire retaining clamps to the core frame.
17. Remove the clamps and the heater core.

To install:
18. Reposition the heater core to the frame and install the clamps.
19. Install the grommets to the inlet and outlet fittings.
20. Install the core frame, with the core attached, to the heater-air selector case.
21. Install the gasket to the case then install the screws securing the heater core frame to the heater-air selector case.
22. Install the screws securing the heater air selector to the cowl.
23. Install the hoses on the heater inlet and outlet fittings.
24. Connect the cable to the control valve on the power servo unit.
25. Connect the vacuum hose to the heater door vacuum power unit.
26. Install the screw securing the vacuum check valve mounting bracket to the heater air selector assembly.
27. Connect the small diameter vacuum hose to the center port of the vacuum check valve.
28. Install the vacuum hoses and electrical connections to the master switch.
29. Connect the electrical connector to the power servo unit.
30. Connect the vacuum hose to the power servo unit.
31. Connect the vacuum hose assembly connectors to the servo vacuum valve and the control valve on the power servo unit.
32. Install the carburetor air cleaner.
33. Fill the cooling system.

✳✳ CAUTION

When draining the coolant, keep in mind that cats and dogs are attracted by the ethylene glycol antifreeze, and are quite likely to drink any that is left in an uncovered container or in puddles on the ground. This will prove fatal in sufficient quantity. Always drain the coolant into a sealable container. Coolant should be reused unless it is contaminated or several years old.

1972-76 Models Except Eldorado and Seville

➡Air Cushion Restraint System (A.C.R.S.) is a driver restraint system. Before servicing any component turn ignition switch to LOCK, then disconnect the negative battery cable and tape terminal end to avoid accidental deployment.

1. Drain the cooling system.
2. Remove the heater hoses from the core nipples. Plug the core nipples.
3. Remove the instrument panel top cover.
4. Remove the right and left air conditioner outlet hoses, along with the center outlet connector.
5. Remove the screws securing the air conditioning distributor to the heater case and lift out the distributor.
6. Remove the defroster nozzle.
7. Remove the glove box.
8. Disconnect the vacuum hoses at the recirculator door, water valve, control head supply hose, and the programer (if so equipped).
9. Disconnect the aspirator hose from the in-car sensor.
10. Take off the instrument panel braces.
11. On the engine side cowl, remove the nuts securing the heater case to the cowl.
12. Work the heater case out from under the dash.
13. Remove the rubber seals from around the core nipples.
14. Remove the screw and clip from beneath the seal.
15. Take out the screws and clip from the opposite end of the core, then remove the core.

To install:

16. Reposition the core in the case, then install the screws and clip.
17. Install the rubber seals around the core nipples.
18. Position the heater case under the dash.
19. On the engine side cowl, install the nuts securing the heater case to the cowl.
20. Install the instrument panel braces.
21. Connect the aspirator hose to the in-car sensor.
22. Connect the vacuum hoses to the recirculator door, water valve, control head supply hose, and the programer (if so equipped).
23. Install the glove box.
24. Install the defroster nozzle.
25. Install the air conditioning distributor to the heater case with the retaining screws.
26. Install the right and left air conditioner outlet hoses, along with the center outlet connector.
27. Install the instrument panel top cover.
28. Install the heater hoses to the core nipples.
29. Fill the cooling system.

1977–89 Models Except Eldorado and Seville

♦ **See Figures 19 thru 31**

1. Disconnect the wiring from the blower, resistors, and thermostatic cycling switch.
2. Remove the right windshield washer nozzle.
3. Remove the right air inlet screen from the plenum.
4. Remove the two screws securing the thermostatic cycling switch to the module and carefully reposition the switch off the module cover.
5. Remove the 16 fasteners securing the module cover and remove it.
6. Remove the heater hoses from the core nipples. Plug the core nipples.
7. Remove one screw and retainer holding the core to the frame at the top.

8. Place the temperature door in the "MAX" hot position, then reach through the temperature housing and push the lower forward corner of the heater core away from the housing. This causes the core to snap out of the lower clamp. The core may not be removed in the vertical position.
9. To install, reverse the procedures above.

1967–71 Eldorado

1. Disconnect the negative battery cable and drain the cooling system.
2. Remove the rubber cooling hose from the nipple and the blower motor.
3. Disconnect the electrical connector(s).

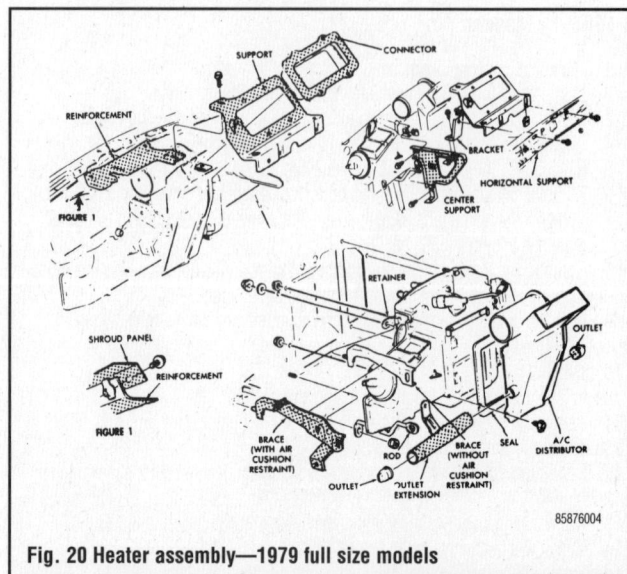
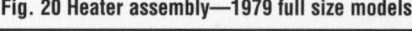

Fig. 20 Heater assembly—1979 full size models

Fig. 21 Removing the washer nozzle

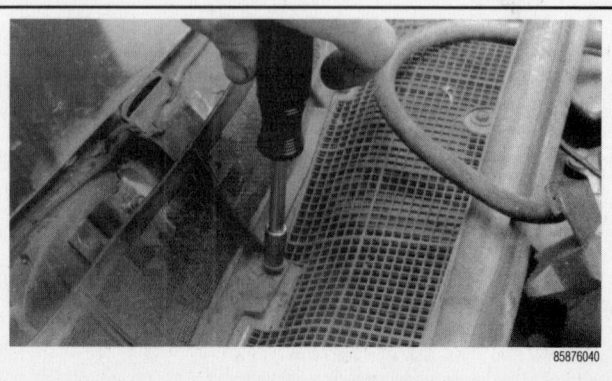

Fig. 22 Removing the air inlet screen retaining screws

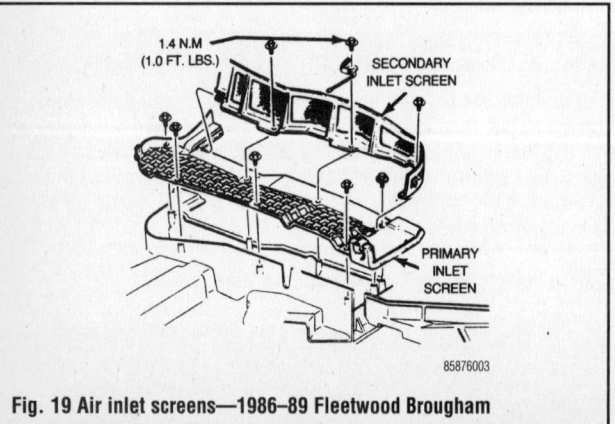

Fig. 19 Air inlet screens—1986–89 Fleetwood Brougham

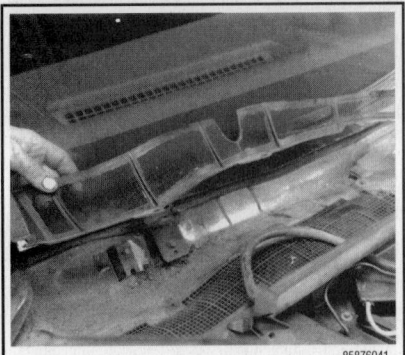

Fig. 23 Removing the air inlet screen retaining screws

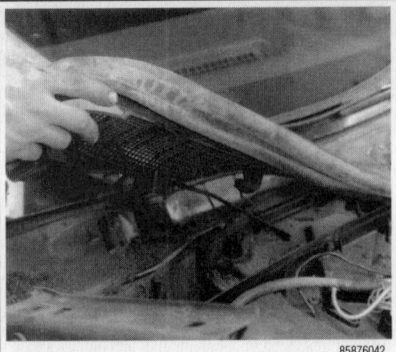

Fig. 24 Removing the air inlet screen assembly

Fig. 25 Removing heater and A/C components from a common heater case

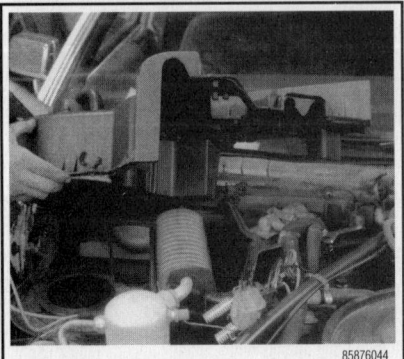

Fig. 26 Removing the module cover

Fig. 27 Removing the heater hose clamps

Fig. 28 Removing the heater hoses

Fig. 29 Removing the heater core retaining bracket screw

Fig. 30 Removing the heater core retaining bracket

Fig. 31 Removing the heater core

4. Remove the screws that secure the motor to the case, then twist the motor and remove from the assembly.

5. Remove the left cowl to fender shield strut rod.

6. Remove the heater hoses leaving the clamps on the fittings.

7. Disconnect the temperature cable and position it out of the way.

8. Disconnect the wire connector from the blower resistor.

9. Disconnect the vacuum hoses and position them out of the way.

10. Remove the 12 screws that secure heater blower assembly to the cowl.

11. Remove the heater blower assembly by pulling away from the cowl tipping the blower end downward.

12. Remove the four screws, two on each side of the heater core, that secure the wire retaining clamps to the heater blower case. Remove the clamps.

13. Pull the heater core out of the heater blower case.

To install:

14. Reposition the core in the case, then install the screws and clip.

15. Install the 12 screws that secure heater blower assembly to the cowl.

16. Connect the vacuum hoses.

17. Connect the wire connector to the blower resistor.

18. Connect the temperature cable.

19. Install the heater hoses.

20. Install the left cowl to fender shield strut rod.

21. Install the screws that secure the motor to the case.

22. Connect the electrical connector(s).

23. Install the rubber cooling hose to the nipple and the blower motor.

24. Connect the negative battery cable.

25. Fill the cooling system.

1972–76 Eldorado

➡Air Cushion Restraint System (A.C.R.S.) is a driver restraint system. Before servicing any component turn ignition switch to LOCK then disconnect the negative battery cable and tape terminal end to avoid accidental deployment.

1. Drain the cooling system.
2. Remove the heater hoses from the core nipples. Plug the core nipples.
3. Remove the instrument panel top cover.
4. Remove the right and left air conditioner outlet hoses, along with the center outlet connector.
5. Remove the screws securing the air conditioning distributor to the heater case and lift out the distributor.
6. Remove the defroster nozzle.
7. Remove the glove box.
8. Disconnect the vacuum hoses at the recirculator door, water valve, control head supply hose, and the programer (if so equipped).
9. Disconnect the aspirator hose from the in-car sensor.
10. Take off the instrument panel braces.
11. On the engine side cowl, remove the nuts securing the heater case to the cowl.
12. Work the heater case out from under the dash.
13. Remove the rubber seals from around the core nipples.
14. Remove the screw and clip from beneath the seal.
15. Take out the screws and clip from the opposite end of the core and remove the core.

To install:
16. Reposition the core in the case, then install the screws and clip.
17. Install the rubber seals around the core nipples.
18. Position the heater case under the dash.
19. On the engine side cowl, install the nuts securing the heater case to the cowl.
20. Install the instrument panel braces.
21. Connect the aspirator hose to the in-car sensor.
22. Connect the vacuum hoses to the recirculator door, water valve, control head supply hose, and the programer (if so equipped).
23. Install the glove box.
24. Install the defroster nozzle.
25. Install the air conditioning distributor to the heater case with the retaining screws.
26. Install the right and left air conditioner outlet hoses, along with the center outlet connector.
27. Install the instrument panel top cover.
28. Install the heater hoses to the core nipples.
29. Fill the cooling system.

1977–78 Eldorado

1. Drain the cooling system.
2. Remove the heater hoses from the core nipples. Plug the core nipples.
3. On the inside of the car, remove the air outlet grilles.
4. Remove the instrument panel fasteners from the inside of the grille opening.
5. Remove the four attaching screws from the instrument panel cross support and pull the panel pad outward. Disconnect the windshield wiper switch.
6. Remove the center air conditioning outlet support bracket.
7. Remove the left side air conditioning outlet hose from the air conditioning distributor.
8. Remove the center support attaching braces.
9. Remove the air conditioning distributor from the heater case.
10. Remove the defroster nozzle.
11. Remove the glove compartment liner.
12. Label and remove all vacuum and electrical connectors from the programmer.
13. Disconnect the vacuum hoses and position them out of the way.
14. Disconnect and remove the heater case.
15. Remove the rubber seal from around the heater core nipples.
16. Remove the screw and clip from beneath the seal.
17. Remove the core retaining screws and the clips, then remove the core.

To install:
18. Reposition the core in the case, then install the screws and clip.
19. Install the rubber seals around the core nipples.
20. Position the heater case under the dash.
21. Connect the vacuum hoses.
22. Connect all labeled vacuum and electrical connectors to the programmer.
23. Install the glove compartment liner.
24. Install the defroster nozzle.

25. Install the air conditioning distributor to the heater case.
26. Install the center support attaching braces.
27. Install the left side air conditioning outlet hose to the air conditioning distributor.
28. Install the center air conditioning outlet support bracket.
29. Connect the windshield wiper switch then install the four attaching screws to the instrument panel pad.
30. Install the instrument panel fasteners to the inside of the grille opening.
31. On the inside of the car, install the air outlet grilles.
32. Install the heater hoses and fill the cooling system.

1979–85 Eldorado

◆ See Figures 32 and 33

1. Drain the cooling system.
2. Remove the heater hoses from the core nipples. Plug the core nipples.
3. Remove the instrument panel top cover.
4. Remove the four defroster nozzle attaching screws at the cowl and the screw on the case, then remove the nozzle.
5. Label and disconnect the vacuum hoses.
6. Disconnect the electrical connector at the programer.
7. Under the hood, remove the heater case to cowl attaching screws.
8. Under the instrument panel, remove the heater case-to-cowl attaching screws.
9. Remove the heater case.
10. Remove the four case-to-core screws and remove the core.
11. To install, reverse the procedures above.

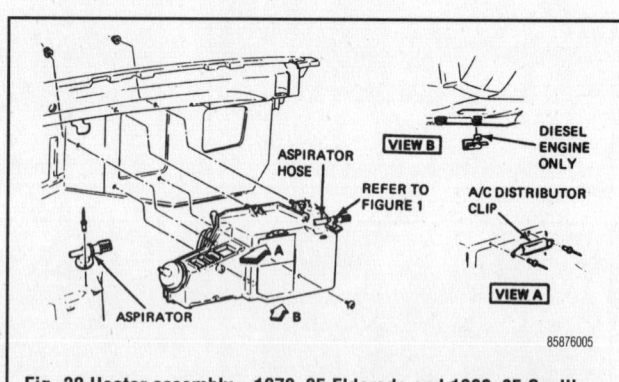

Fig. 32 Heater assembly—1979–85 Eldorado and 1980–85 Seville

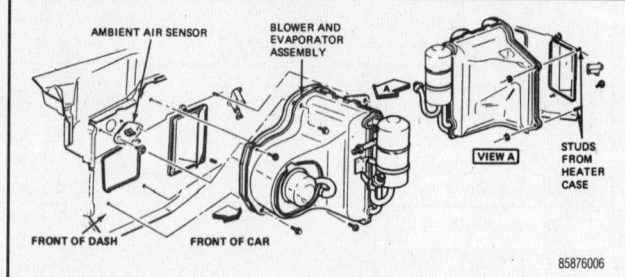

Fig. 33 Evaporator assembly—1979–85 Eldorado and 1980–85 Seville

1976–78 Seville

➡Air Cushion Restraint System (A.C.R.S.) is a driver restraint system. Before servicing any component turn ignition switch to LOCK then disconnect the negative battery cable and tape terminal end to avoid accidental deployment.

1. Disconnect the negative battery cable.
2. Drain the cooling system.
3. Remove the right hand wheel housing.
4. Disconnect the heater hoses from the core nipples. Plug the core nipples.

5. Remove the instrument panel right hand insert and appliqué.
6. Remove the fuel injection control unit.
7. Remove the radio, glove box door and glove box.
8. Remove the A/C programmer.
9. Remove the right hand lower instrument panel.
10. Remove the screws attaching the A/C distributor to the heater case and remove the distributor.
11. Remove the clips retaining the vacuum harness to the heater case and disconnect the vacuum hoses at the heater mode door. Remove the bulkhead grommet and defroster actuator. Position the vacuum harness out of the way.
12. From under the hood, remove the three nuts retaining the heater case to the cowl and remove the heater assembly from the cowl.
13. Disconnect the vacuum hose from the A/C mode door actuator and remove the heater assembly.
14. Remove the rubber seal from around the heater core pipes, then remove the screw and clip from beneath the seal.
15. Remove the screws from the opposite side of the core and remove the core.

To install:
16. Reposition the core in the case, then install the screws and clip.
17. Install the rubber seals around the core nipples.
18. Position the heater case under the dash.
19. On the engine side cowl, install the nuts securing the heater case to the cowl.
20. Connect the vacuum hose to the A/C mode door actuator.
21. Install the vacuum harness to the heater case and connect the vacuum hoses to the heater mode door. Reconnect the bulkhead grommet and defroster actuator.
22. Install the screws attaching the A/C distributor to the heater case and install the distributor.
23. Install the right hand lower instrument panel.
24. Install the A/C programmer.
25. Install the radio, glove box door and glove box.
26. Install the fuel injection control unit.
27. Install the instrument panel right hand insert and appliqué.
28. Connect the heater hoses to the core nipples.
29. Install the right hand wheel housing.
30. Fill the cooling system.
31. Connect the negative battery cable.

✳✳ CAUTION

When draining the coolant, keep in mind that cats and dogs are attracted by the ethylene glycol antifreeze, and are quite likely to drink any that is left in an uncovered container or in puddles on the ground. This will prove fatal in sufficient quantity. Always drain the coolant into a sealable container. Coolant should be reused unless it is contaminated or several years old.

1979 Seville

1. Drain the cooling system.
2. Remove the right side wheelhousing as outlined earlier in Blower Motor Removal for the 1979 Seville.
3. Remove the heater hoses from the core nipples. Plug the core nipples.
4. Remove the radio knobs, anti-rattle spring, control rings and both hex nuts.
5. Remove the ash tray.
6. Through the ash tray opening, remove the screw from behind the right side of the right hand instrument panel insert.
7. Close the ash tray door and remove the three instrument panel insert attaching screws.
8. Pull the insert out enough to disconnect the electrical connectors from the cigarette lighter and any other accessory switches.
9. Remove the mirror control cable clip from the back and remove the insert.
10. Remove the radio as outlined in Radio Removal & Installation.
11. Remove the door and the inner liner of the glove compartment.
12. Remove the litter receptacle.
13. Remove the screws which secure the recirculating air door actuator shroud to the right kick panel.

14. Disconnect the vacuum and electrical connectors from the air conditioning programer.
15. Remove the attaching screws and remove the programer.
16. Remove the right side lower instrument panel.
17. Remove the air conditioning distributor from the heater case.
18. Disconnect the vacuum harness at the heater case and disconnect the vacuum lines. Position the harness out of the way.
19. Under the hood, remove the three heater case attaching nuts from the cowl.
20. Inside the car, remove the heater case attaching screws.
21. Disconnect the vacuum hose from the air conditioning door actuator and remove the heater assembly.
22. Remove the seal around the water pipes along with the screw and the clip from beneath the seal.
23. Remove the two screws at the opposite ends of the core and remove the core.

To install:
24. Reposition the core and the two screws at the opposite ends.
25. Install the seal around the water pipes along with the screw and the clip from beneath the seal.
26. Install the heater case attaching screws and connect the vacuum hose to the air conditioning door actuator.
27. Under the hood, install the three heater case attaching nuts to the cowl.
28. Connect the vacuum harness at the heater case and connect the vacuum lines.
29. Install the air conditioning distributor to the heater case.
30. Install the right side lower instrument panel.
31. Install the programer.
32. Install the screws which secure the recirculating air door actuator shroud to the right kick panel.
33. Install the litter receptacle.
34. Install the door and the inner liner of the glove compartment.
35. Install the radio.
36. Install the mirror control cable clip to the back and install the insert.
37. Connect the electrical connectors to the cigarette lighter and any other accessory switches.
38. Install the three instrument panel attaching screws.
39. Through the ash tray opening, install the screw behind the right side of the right hand instrument panel insert.
40. Install the ash tray.
41. Install the radio knobs, anti-rattle spring, control rings and both hex nuts.
42. Install the heater hoses.
43. Install the right side wheelhousing as described in Blower Motor Removal for the 1979 Seville.
44. Fill the cooling system.

1980–85 Seville

1. Drain the cooling system.
2. Remove the heater hoses from the core nipples. Plug the core nipples.
3. Remove the instrument panel top cover.
4. Remove the four defroster nozzle attaching screws at the cowl and the screw on the case, then remove the nozzle.
5. Label and disconnect the vacuum hoses.
6. Disconnect the electrical connector at the programer.
7. Under the hood, remove the heater case to cowl attaching screws.
8. Under the instrument panel, remove the heater case-to-cowl attaching screws.
9. Remove the heater case.
10. Remove the four case-to-core screws and remove the core.

To install:
11. Install the four case-to-core screws and install the core.
12. Under the instrument panel, install the heater case-to-cowl attaching screws and install the heater case.
13. Under the hood, install the heater case to cowl attaching screws.
14. Connect the electrical connector at the programer.
15. Connect the vacuum hoses.
16. Install the four defroster nozzle attaching screws at the cowl and the screw on the case, then remove the nozzle.
17. Install the instrument panel top cover.
18. Install the heater hoses and fill the cooling system.

1986–89 Eldorado and Seville

1. Disconnect the negative battery cable.
2. Loosen the radiator drain plug and remove about half of the engine coolant.
3. Remove the glove box.
4. Remove the lower sound insulator from underneath the passenger side of the instrument panel.
5. Remove the programmer, the electronic control module and their mounting bracket.
6. Remove the module assembly heater core cover.
7. Tag and disconnect the inlet and outlet coolant hoses at the heater core. Be careful to plug the open ends of the hoses as coolant is likely to leak out.
8. Remove the two heater core mounting screws and lift out the core.
9. Installation is in the reverse order of removal.

Air Conditioning Components

REMOVAL & INSTALLATION

Repair or service of air conditioning components is not covered by this manual, because of the risk of personal injury or death, and because of the legal ramifications of servicing these components without the proper EPA certification and experience. Cost, personal injury or death, environmental damage, and legal considerations (such as the fact that it is a federal crime to vent refrigerant into the atmosphere), dictate that the A/C components on your vehicle should be serviced only by a Motor Vehicle Air Conditioning (MVAC) trained, and EPA certified automotive technician.

➡**If your vehicle's A/C system uses R-12 refrigerant and is in need of recharging, the A/C system can be converted over to R-134a refrigerant (less environmentally harmful and expensive). Refer to Section 1 for additional information on R-12 to R-134a conversions, and for additional considerations dealing with your vehicle's A/C system.**

Control Head

REMOVAL & INSTALLATION

1. Disconnect the negative battery cable.
2. Remove the radio knobs and the clock set knob (if so equipped).
3. Remove the instrument bezel retaining screws.
4. Pull the bezel outward to disconnect the defogger switch and the remote mirror control (if equipped).
5. Remove the instrument bezel.
6. Remove the control head-to-dash mounting screws and pull the head away from the dashboard.
7. Tag and disconnect the electrical connectors and/or the control cables. Remove the control head.
8. Installation is in the reverse order of removal.

ENTERTAINMENT SYSTEMS

The antenna trim must be adjusted on AM radios, when major repair has been done to the unit or the antenna changed. The trimmer screw is located behind the right side knob. Raise the antenna to its full height. Turn to a weak station around 1400 on the dial, and turn the volume down until barely audible. Turn the trimmer screw until the maximum volume is achieved.

Radio

REMOVAL & INSTALLATION

DeVille and Fleetwood

▸ **See Figure 34**

1967–73 VEHICLES

1. Remove the steering column lower cover.
2. Remove the defroster hose behind the radio.
3. Remove the radio knobs, washers and rings by pulling straight out.
4. Remove the nuts securing the control shafts to the panel.
5. Disconnect any wiring from the radio.
6. Remove the support bolts and remove the radio.
7. Installation is the reverse of removal.

1974–76 WITHOUT A.C.R.S

1. Remove the 4 screws each which secure the lower steering column cover to its reinforcement and the instrument panel support.

2. Take the lower cover off.
3. Unfasten the screws which secure the lower ash tray bracket, then remove the two screws from the left-hand ash tray bracket.
4. Unfasten the right-hand ash tray securing screws. Remove the ash tray assembly from the dash panel.
5. Remove the knobs, washers, outer rings, and shaft retaining nuts.
6. Remove the radio-to-dash panel lower support brace nut from the back of the radio.
7. Loosen, but don't remove, the screw which secures the brace to the support, and turn the brace clockwise.
8. Slide the radio back from the instrument panel. Detach the speaker connector, power connector, and antenna lead from it.
9. Turn the dial side of the radio (front) so that it is facing down, and lower the left side of the receiver. Withdraw it through the ash tray opening.
10. Installation is the reverse of removal.

1974–76 WITH A.C.R.S.

➡**Air Cushion Restraint System is a driver restraint system. Before servicing any component turn ignition switch to LOCK then disconnect the negative battery cable and tape terminal end to avoid accidental deployment.**

1. Turn the ignition switch to Lock.
2. Remove the negative (-) battery cable and tape its terminal end.
3. Remove the 3 screws which retain the glove box in the dash, but don't remove the two striker screws.
4. Remove the glove box partition screws, and set the glove box aside, without disconnecting the wiring.
5. Remove the tape storage compartment retaining screws and remove the compartment.
6. Remove the ash tray assembly retaining screws, pull the assembly out partway, unfasten the electrical leads, and remove the assembly.
7. Remove the knee restraint left trim screws.
8. Remove the screws, and loosen, but don't remove, the fifth screw (under the steering column) from the bottom of the knee restraint.
9. Remove the 4 knee restraint securing screws working from the tape storage compartment and ash tray openings.
10. Remove the knobs, washers, outer rings, and shaft retaining nuts.
11. Remove the radio-to-dash panel lower support brace nut from the back of the radio.
12. Loosen, but don't remove, the screw which secures the brace to the support, and turn the brace clockwise.

85876007

Fig. 34 Adjusting antenna trim

13. Through the knee restraint opening, disconnect the antenna lead, depress the locktabs and push the electrical connections upward to disengage them.

14. Clear the instrument panel support by turning the radio to the left. Slide the radio away from you, lower the front of the radio (dial), and withdraw it, front first, through the knee restraint opening.

15. Installation is the reverse of removal.

1977–89 VEHICLES

♦ See Figures 35 thru 46

1. Remove the radio knobs and anti-rattle springs.
2. Remove the two hex nuts securing the bezel to the radio.

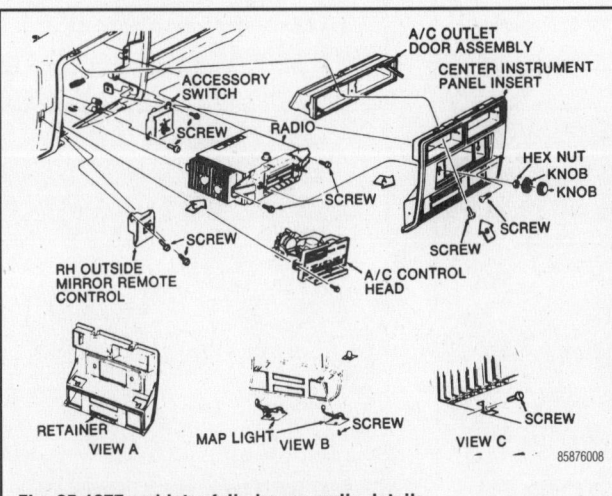
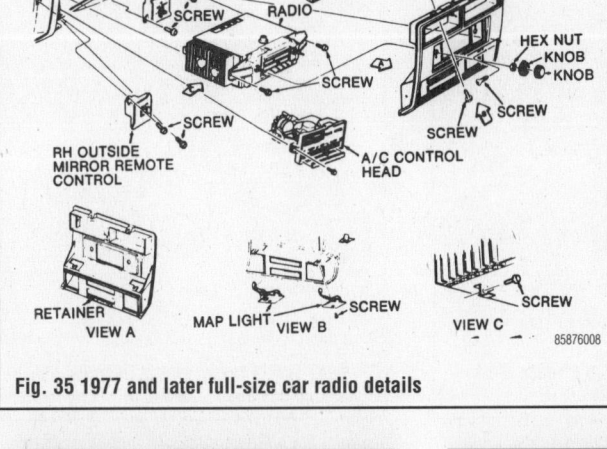

Fig. 35 1977 and later full-size car radio details

3. Remove the two center air conditioning outlet grilles. Remove the one screw in each outlet.
4. Remove the maplights and remove the center panel insert.
5. Unbolt and remove the radio from the panel.
6. Disconnect wiring.
7. Installation is the reverse of removal.

Eldorado

➡For 1967–76 Eldorado procedures please refer to the 1967–76 DeVille and Fleetwood procedures.

1977–78 VEHICLES

1. Remove the four screws attaching the steering column cover to the reinforcement.
2. Remove the four screws attaching the cover to the instrument panel cross support.
3. Remove the ash tray lower bracket screw.
4. Remove the two screws from the left side ash tray mounting bracket.
5. Working from the lower edge of the instrument panel, remove the ash tray right side attaching screw.
6. Remove the ash tray. Disconnect the bulb and the electrical connector.
7. Remove the radio knobs, the anti-rattle spring, the control rings and the retaining nuts.
8. Remove the brace nut at the rear of the radio.
9. Loosen the brace supporting screw and rotate the brace to the right.
10. Slide the radio from the instrument panel and disconnect the wiring.
11. Rotate the dial side downward and remove the radio through the ash tray opening.
12. Reverse to install.

1979–89 VEHICLES

♦ See Figure 47

1. Disconnect the negative battery cable.
2. Remove the screws from the top of the instrument panel center insert.

Fig. 36 Removing the trim panel retaining screws—radio removal

Fig. 37 Removing the radio outer knob

Fig. 38 Removing the radio inner knob

Fig. 39 Removing the radio assembly hex nuts

Fig. 40 Removing the A/C outlet grilles retainer clips

Fig. 41 Removing the A/C outlet grilles

Fig. 42 Removing the upper trim panel retaining screws

Fig. 43 Removing the radio trim panel—radio removal

Fig. 44 Removing the radio-to-dash side retaining bolts

Fig. 45 Removing the radio to dash lower retaining bolt

Fig. 46 Removing the radio electrical connections

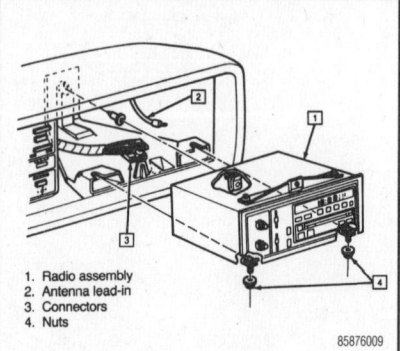

1. Radio assembly
2. Antenna lead-in
3. Connectors
4. Nuts

Fig. 47 Radio removal and installation—1986–89 Eldorado and Seville

3. Remove the radio knobs and remove the insert.
4. Remove the rear window defogger switch to gain access to the left side mounting screw if so equipped.
5. Remove the mounting screw.
6. Remove the radio and disconnect the wiring. Reverse to install.

Seville

1976–79 VEHICLES

1. Disconnect the negative battery ground.
2. Loosen the right forward screw which secures the fuel injection electrical control unit cover to the unit.
3. Remove the remaining three screws from the cover.
4. Remove the three screws which secure the unit to the panel supports.
5. Carefully lower the control unit enough to disconnect the three electrical connectors from the left hand side and the hose from the front of the unit. Remove the unit.
6. Remove the screw securing the climate control outlet extension to the heater case.

7. Disconnect the antenna.
8. Remove the radio support rod.
9. Remove the control knobs, anti-rattle springs, control rings and both hex nuts.

➡The control knobs on radios with 8-track are retained with 5/64 in. Allen screws.

10. Remove the radio. Installation is the reverse of removal.

1980–89 VEHICLES

1. Disconnect the negative battery cable.
2. Remove the screws from the top of the instrument panel center insert.
3. Remove the radio knobs and remove the insert.
4. Remove the rear window defogger switch to gain access to the left side mounting screw if so equipped.
5. Remove the mounting screw.
6. Remove the radio and disconnect the wiring. Reverse to install.

WINDSHIELD WIPERS

Blade and Arm

REMOVAL & INSTALLATION

◆ **See Figures 48 thru 53**

If the wiper assembly has a press-type release tab at the center, simply depress the tab and remove the blade. If the blade has no release tab, use a suitable tool to depress the spring at the center of the blade. This will release the entire assembly from the wiper arm. To install the assembly, position the blade over the pin at the tip of the arm and press until the spring retainer engages the groove in the pin.

To remove the element, either depress the release button or squeeze the spring retainer clip at the outer end of the blade and slide the element off. On installation, simply slide the new element in until it latches onto the blade.

➡Removal of the wiper arms on all models but the 1986 Eldorado and Seville requires the use of a special tool, G.M. J8966, or its equivalent. Versions of this tool are available in most auto parts stores. On the 1986 Eldorado and Seville, raise the arm, insert a suitable pin into the hole at the base of the arm until the spring tension is released and then remove the arm.

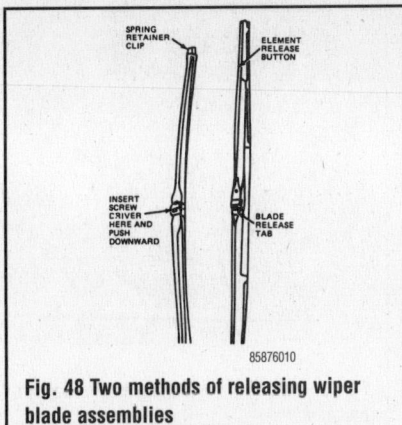

Fig. 48 Two methods of releasing wiper blade assemblies

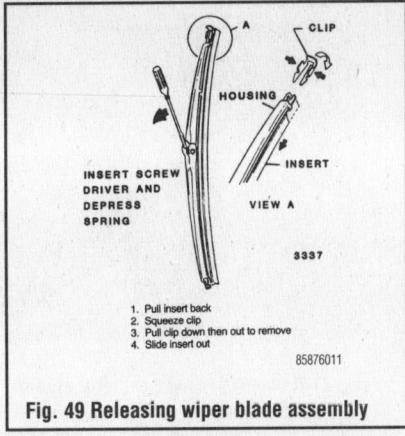

Fig. 49 Releasing wiper blade assembly

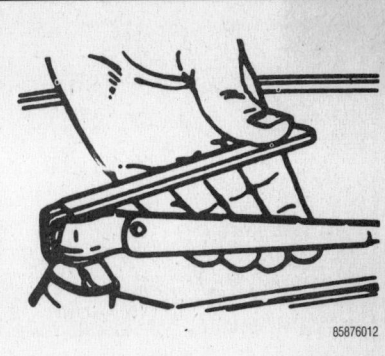

Fig. 50 Removing the wiper arm using special wiper arm tool

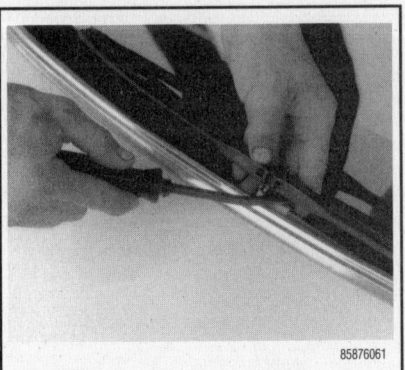

Fig. 51 Removing the wiper blade with insert

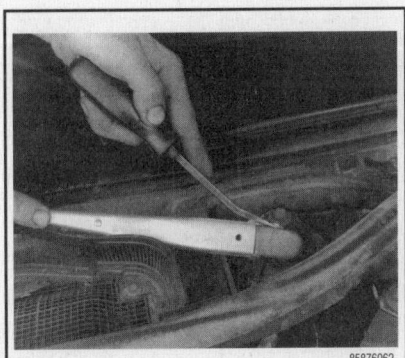

Fig. 52 Removing the wiper arm assembly

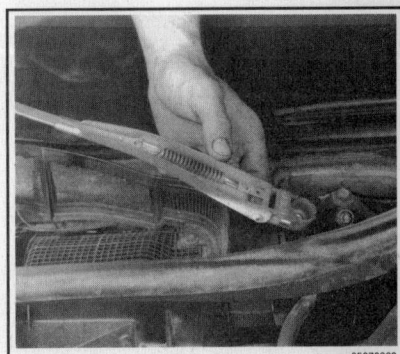

Fig. 53 View of the wiper arm—note key-way for correct installation

1. Insert the special tool under the base of the wiper arm and lever the arm off the linkage shaft.

➡On most later models, raising the hood will facilitate wiper arm removal.

2. Disconnect the washer hose from the arm (if so equipped). Remove the wiper arm.

3. Installation is in the reverse order of removal. The proper park position (when arms are at rest) is for the blades to be approximately 2 in. (50mm) above the lower molding of the windshield. Be sure that the wiper motor is in the park position before installing the arms.

Wiper Motor

REMOVAL & INSTALLATION

◆ See Figures 54 thru 60

1. Raise the hood and remove the cowl screen.
2. Loosen the transmission drive link-to-crank arm attaching nuts.
3. Remove the transmission drive link(s) from the motor crank arm.
4. Disconnect the wiring and washer hoses.
5. Remove the motor attaching screws.
6. Remove the motor while guiding the crank arm through the hole.
7. To install, reverse the removal procedure. The motor must be in the park position before assembling the crank arm to the transmission drive link(s).

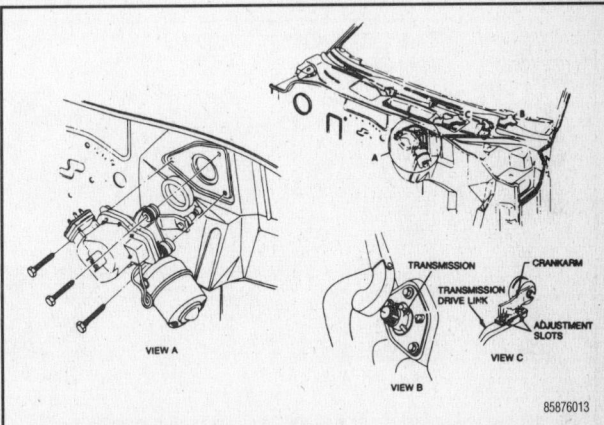

Fig. 54 Common wiper motor installation

Fig. 55 Mark all lines—wiper motor removal

Fig. 56 Removing electrical connection—wiper motor removal

Fig. 57 Removing the wiper motor assembly mounting bolts

Fig. 58 Removing the wiper motor assembly

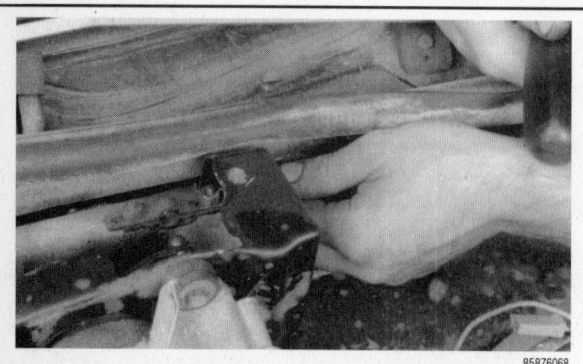

Fig. 59 View of the wiper motor-to-wiper transmission (linkage)

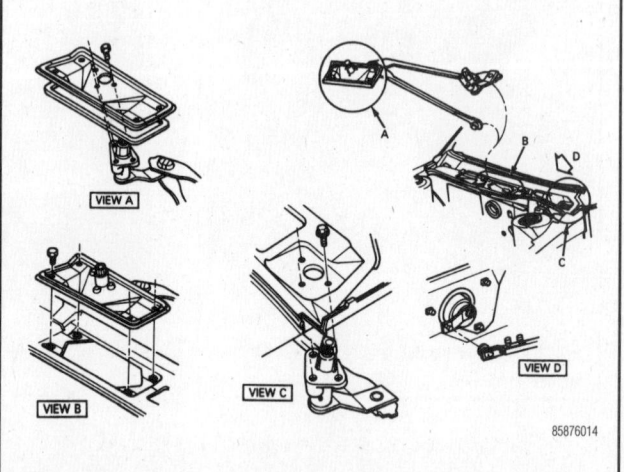

Fig. 61 Wiper linkage and transmission assembly—1986 Eldorado and Seville

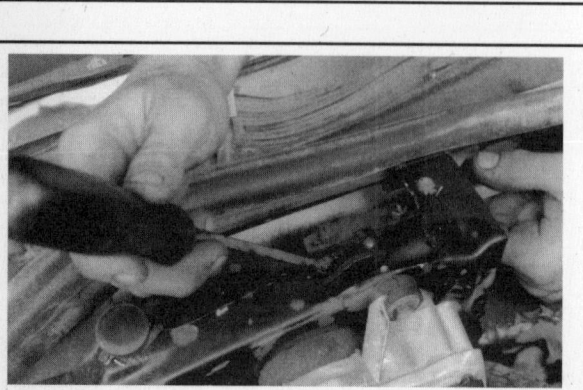

Fig. 60 Installing the wiper linkage to wiper motor assembly

Wiper Transmission (Linkage)

REMOVAL & INSTALLATION

▶ See Figures 61 and 62

1. Make sure the wipers are in the fully parked position.
2. Remove the cowl vent screen. On later models, it is necessary to raise the hood.
3. Remove the wiper arm and blade assemblies.
4. Loosen the nuts which attach the transmission drive links to the motor crank arm.
5. Disconnect the transmission drive links from the motor crank arm.
6. Remove the screws which attach the transmission to the body.
7. Remove the transmission and linkage assembly by guiding it through the plenum chamber opening.

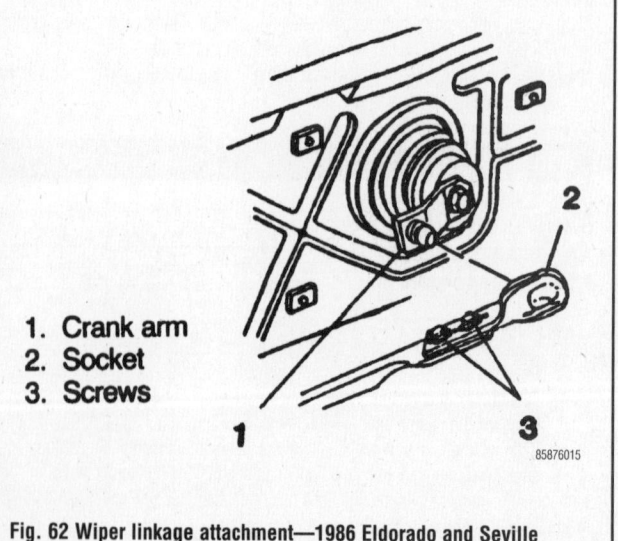

1. Crank arm
2. Socket
3. Screws

Fig. 62 Wiper linkage attachment—1986 Eldorado and Seville

To install:

8. Position the assembly in the plenum chamber through the opening. Loosely install the attaching screws.
9. Install the drive links on the motor crank arm and tighten the attaching nuts.

INSTRUMENTS AND SWITCHES

Instrument Cluster

REMOVAL & INSTALLATION

➡ Air Cushion Restraint System is a driver knee restraint system which is replaces the lower steering column cover assembly. Before servicing any component turn ignition switch to LOCK then disconnect the negative battery cable and tape terminal end to avoid accidental deployment.

All Except 1980–89 Seville and 1978–89 Eldorado

1. Disconnect the negative battery cable.
2. Remove the instrument panel insert.
3. With the shift lever in the Park position, remove the shift indicator cable and clip retaining screw from the steering column.
4. Remove the upper and lower cluster assembly retaining screws. Remove the screw directly above the steering column which retains the cluster to the speedometer mounting plate.
5. Pull the cluster outward, then disengage the speedometer cable and the electrical connections.
6. If equipped, disconnect the speed control sensor from the cluster assembly. Disengage other connectors as required.
7. Place the shift lever in the Low position, and if equipped with tilt wheel, place the wheel in its lowest position. Remove the cluster assembly from the dash.
8. Installation is the reverse of the removal procedure. Set the shift, indicator cable in the Neutral position and adjust the cable accordingly.

1980–81 Seville and 1978–81 Eldorado

1. Disconnect the negative battery cable.
2. Remove the top and bottom appliqué retaining screws.
3. Unsnap the portion of the appliqué trim below the steering column.
4. If equipped with tilt wheel, place in its lowest position and remove the appliqué panel.
5. Remove the cluster retaining screws. Pull the cluster outward, the disconnect the speedometer cable and printed circuit connectors. Remove the cluster.
6. Installation is the reverse of removal.

1982–85 Eldorado and Seville

1. Disconnect the negative battery cable.
2. Remove the left sound insulator.
3. Remove the instrument panel insert and appliqué trim from the instrument panel.
4. Place the shift lever in the **PARK** position and remove the shift indicator clip from the steering column.
5. Remove the steering column-to-upper mounting bracket nuts and lower the steering column.
6. Remove the upper steering column mounting bracket-to-cowl screws and lower the bracket.
7. Remove the cluster retaining screws. Pull the cluster outward, the disconnect the speedometer cable and printed circuit connectors. Remove the cluster.
8. To install, reverse the removal procedures. Be sure the shift indicator is properly aligned.

1986–89 Eldorado and Seville

1. Disconnect the negative battery cable. Remove the 7 screws located along the top and remove the instrument panel trim plate.
2. Remove the 4 mounting screws and the filter lens.
3. Remove the warning light lens screws and the lens. Remove the trip odometer reset button.
4. Remove the instrument panel cluster screws. Pull the cluster off the electrical connections and remove it. Using a pair of pliers, hold the retaining tabs at either end of the cluster board and remove the board.

5. To install the cluster, align it with the electrical connectors, push it into the instrument panel and reverse the removal procedures.

Speedometer Cable

REPLACEMENT

◗ See Figures 63 and 64

➡ Air Cushion Restraint System is a driver knee restraint system which replaces the lower steering column cover assembly. Before servicing any component turn the ignition switch to LOCK then disconnect the negative battery cable and tape terminal the end to avoid accidental deployment.

1. Disconnect the negative battery cable. Remove the lower steering column cover.
2. Reach behind the instrument cluster and push the speedometer cable casing toward the speedometer while depressing the retaining spring on the back of the instrument cluster case. Once the retaining spring has released, hold it in while pulling outward on the casing to disconnect the casing from the speedometer.
3. Remove the cable casing sealing plug from the dash panel. Then, pull the casing down from behind the dash and remove the cable.
4. If the cable is broken and cannot be entirely removed from the top, support the car securely, then unscrew the cable casing connector at the transmission. Pull the bottom part of the cable out, and then screw the connector back onto the transmission.
5. Lubricate the new cable with a speedometer cable grease. Insert it into the casing until it bottoms. Push inward while rotating it until the square portion at the bottom engages with the coupling in the transmission, permitting the cable to move in another inch or so. Then, reconnect the cable casing to the speedometer and install the sealing plug into the dash panel.

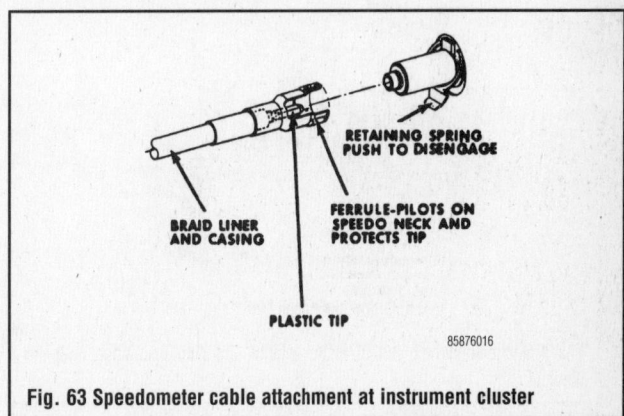

Fig. 63 Speedometer cable attachment at instrument cluster

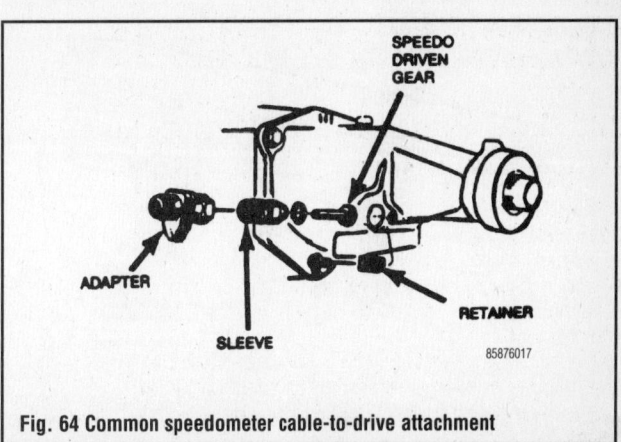

Fig. 64 Common speedometer cable-to-drive attachment

Ignition Switch

→All models made in 1969 and later are equipped with ignition switches which are mounted in the steering column. Removal and installation procedures for these models can be found in Section 8.

REMOVAL & INSTALLATION

1967-68 Models

1. Disconnect the battery ground cable. Put the ignition switch in the Accessory (ACC) position.
2. Insert a wire into the small hole in the face of the lock cylinder. Push in on the wire to depress the plunger. Continue turning the key until the cylinder can be removed from the switch.
3. Remove the switch bezel nut, and then pull the switch out from under the dash.
4. Go in from the front of the switch with a screwdriver and unsnap the theft resistant locking tangs on the connector, then unplug the connector.
5. Installation is in the reverse order of removal.

Wiper Switch

REMOVAL & INSTALLATION

♦ See Figures 65, 66 and 67

1967-73 Deville and Fleetwood

1. Disconnect the negative battery cable.
2. Open the left front door to gain access to the screw securing the control switch to the instrument panel extension on the door.
3. Loosen the screw securing the control switch to the extension.

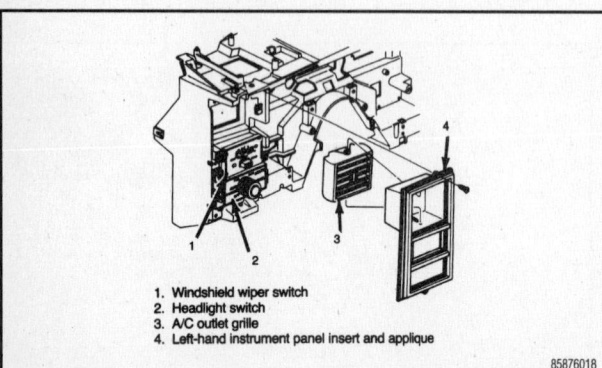

1. Windshield wiper switch
2. Headlight switch
3. A/C outlet grille
4. Left-hand instrument panel insert and applique

85876018

Fig. 65 Wiper switch installation—1979–85 Eldorado and 1980–85 Seville

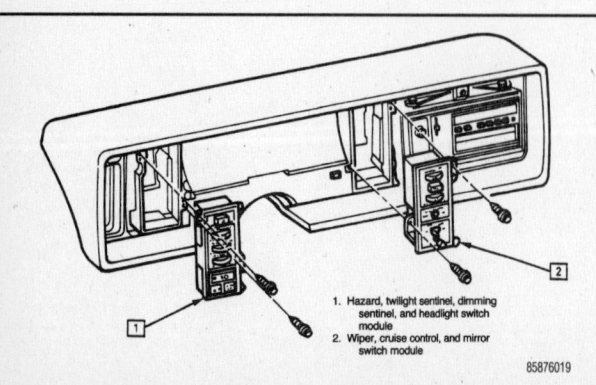

1. Hazard, twilight sentinel, dimming sentinel, and headlight switch module
2. Wiper, cruise control, and mirror switch module

85876019

Fig. 66 Switch modules used on the 1986–89 Eldorado and Seville

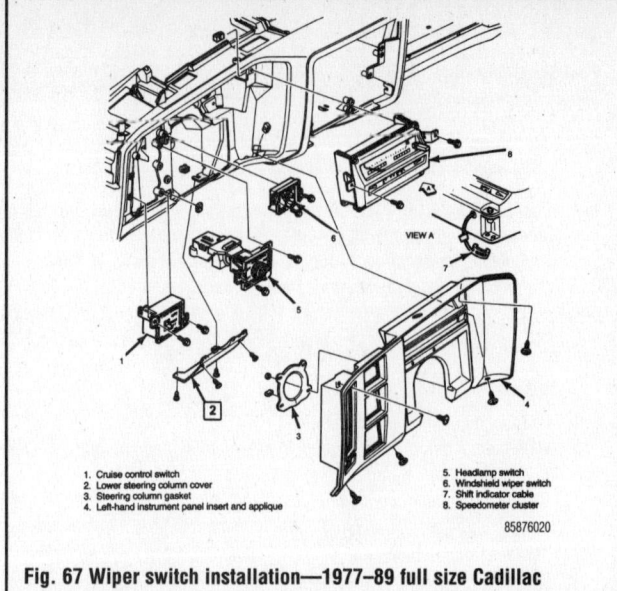

1. Cruise control switch
2. Lower steering column cover
3. Steering column gasket
4. Left-hand instrument panel insert and applique
5. Headlamp switch
6. Windshield wiper switch
7. Shift indicator cable
8. Speedometer cluster

85876020

Fig. 67 Wiper switch installation—1977–89 full size Cadillac

4. Pull the control switch out and disconnect the electrical connector.
5. To install, reverse the removal procedures.

1974–76 Deville/Fleetwood, 1974–78 Eldorado and 1976–79 Seville

1. Disconnect the negative battery cable.
2. Remove the left hand vent outlet grille as described below:
    a. Using tool, J-24612 or a thin-bladed screwdriver, compress the release tabs in the vent.
    b. Rotate the grille upward and remove the grille.
3. Working through the outlet opening, remove the screw(s) securing the switch to the instrument panel.
4. Pull the wiper switch and electrical connector out of the panel, then disconnect it from the harness.
5. To install, reverse the removal procedures.

1977–89 Deville and Fleetwood

1. Disconnect the negative battery cable.
2. Loosen the set screw in the left hand climate control door knob and remove the knob.
3. Remove the left hand vent outlet grille as described below:
    a. Using tool, J-24612-01 or a thin-bladed screwdriver, compress the release tabs in the vent.
    b. Rotate the grille upward and remove the grille.
4. Remove the 6 screws securing the bezel to the instrument panel.

→One screw is located inside of the climate control outlet.

5. Remove the 2 upper and lower screws in the lower steering column cover.
6. Disconnect the steering column seal on the lower surface and remove the bezel.
7. Remove the screw(s) securing the switch to the instrument panel.
8. Pull the wiper switch and electrical connector out of the panel, then disconnect it from the harness.
9. To install, reverse the removal procedures.

1979–85 Eldorado and 1980–85 Seville

1. Disconnect the negative battery cable.
2. Remove the 2 screws securing the insert appliqué to the instrument panel.
3. Remove the screw(s) securing the switch to the instrument panel.
4. Pull the wiper switch and electrical connector out of the panel, then disconnect it from the harness.
5. To install, reverse the removal procedures.

1986–89 Eldorado and Seville

➡The wiper control is located in a switch module on the instrument panel, to the right hand side of the steering column.

1. Remove the instrument panel trim plate.
   a. Disconnect the air conditioning vent.
   b. Remove the radio trim plate.
   c. Remove the seven screws and remove the trim plate.
2. Remove the two screws and pull the switch module out of the electrical connector in the instrument panel.
3. Installation is the reverse of removal.

Headlight Switch

REMOVAL & INSTALLATION

♦ See Figure 68

1967–79 Models

1. Disconnect the negative battery cable.
2. Remove the instrument panel bezel, retained on most model years with six screws (varies among models and years).
3. Pull the headlight control knob to the ON position.
4. Remove the screws (usually three) attaching the windshield wiper switch/light switch mounting plate to the instrument cluster and pull the assembly reward.
5. Depress the shaft retainer on the switch, then pull the knob and shaft assembly out.
6. Remove the ferrule nut and switch assembly from the mounting plate.
7. To install, reverse the removal procedures.

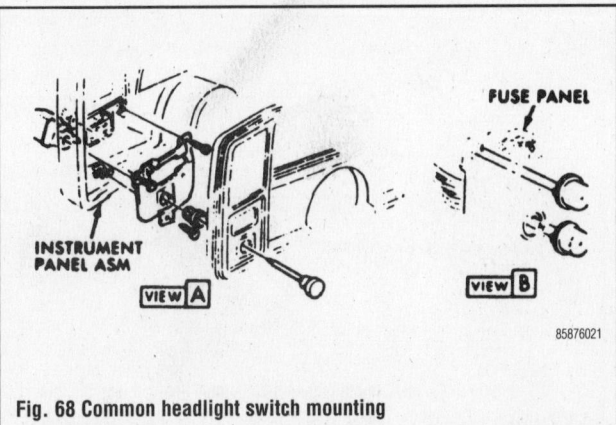

Fig. 68 Common headlight switch mounting

1980–84 Models

1. Disconnect the negative battery cable.
2. Pull the headlight control knob to the ON position.
3. Reaching up under the instrument panel, depress the switch shaft release button, then pull the shaft and the control knob out.
4. Remove the windshield wiper switch.
5. Remove the ferrule nut and the switch from the instrument panel.
6. Using a small pry bar, insert it into the side of the switch and pry the multi-contact electrical connector from the switch.
7. To install, reverse the removal procedures.

1985–89 Models Except 1986–89 Eldorado and Seville

1. Disconnect the negative battery cable.
2. For access, remove the steering column trim cover.

3. Remove the switch mounting screws.
4. Pull out the switch and disconnect the electrical connector.
5. To install, reverse the removal procedures.

1986–89 Eldorado and Seville

➡The headlight switch is located in a switch module on the instrument panel, to the left hand side of the steering column.

1. Remove the instrument panel trim plate.
   a. Disconnect the air conditioning vent.
   b. Remove the radio trim plate.
   c. Remove the seven screws and remove the trim plate.
2. Remove the two screws and pull the switch module out of the electrical connector in the instrument panel.
3. Installation is the reverse of removal.

Back-Up Light

REMOVAL & INSTALLATION

♦ See Figure 69

Except 1985–89 Eldorado and Seville

The switch is mounted on the steering column. Refer to Section 7 for Neutral Safety switch service procedures.
1. Disconnect the electrical connector at the switch.
2. Remove the clamp retaining screw and remove the switch.
To install:
3. Position the shift lever in the neutral gate notch.
4. Assemble the switch to the column by inserting the switch carrier tang in the shift slot and locate the switch up the column as far as the slot on the outer tube will allow, then fasten in position.
5. Remove the pin locator.
6. Attach the electrical connector.

1985–89 Eldorado and Seville

The back-up light/neutral safety switch on these models is mounted on the transmission and the procedure is located in Section 7.

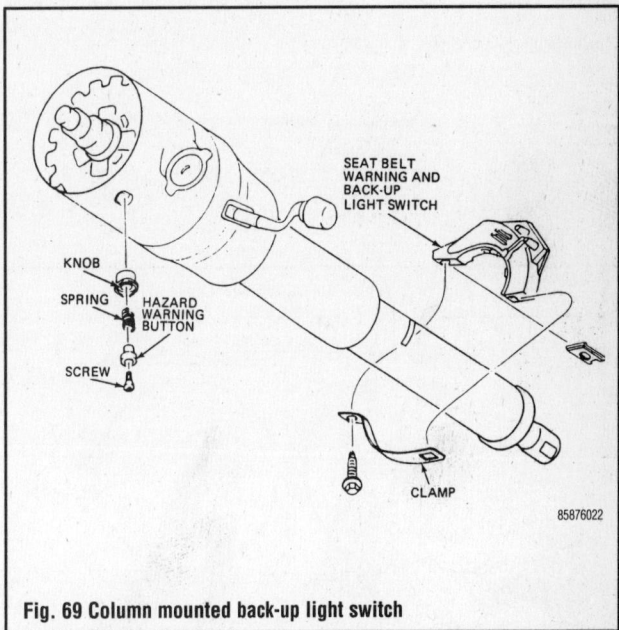

Fig. 69 Column mounted back-up light switch

SEAT BELT SYSTEM

Warning Buzzer and Light (1972–73)

Beginning January 1, 1972, all cars are required to have a warning system which operates a buzzer and a warning light if either the driver's or the right-hand front passenger's seat belts are not fastened when the seats are occupied and the car is in forward motion.

On Cadillac vehicles, this system consists of seat belt retractor switches, pressure sensitive front seat switches, a parking brake switch (manual transmission), or a transmission switch (automatic transmission), a warning light, and a buzzer.

The seat belt warning system is wired through the 20 amp "Gauges" fuse.

The warning light is located in the instrument cluster; and the buzzer, which is shared with the ignition key warning system, is taped to the instrument cluster wiring harness.

The warning system is activated when the ignition switch is ON, the front seats are occupied, and the seat belts are left in their retractors. Only when the front seat belts are extended and properly fastened will the warning light and buzzer stop.

Seat Belt/Starter Interlock (1974–75)

As required by law, all 1974 and some 1975 Cadillac passenger cars cannot be started until the front seat occupants are seated and have fastened their seat belts. If the proper sequence is not followed, the engine cannot be started.

If, after the car is started, the seat belts are unfastened, a warning buzzer and light will be activated in a similar manner to that described above for 1972–73 models.

The shoulder harness and lap belt are permanently fastened together, so that they both must be worn. The shoulder harness uses an inertia-lock reel to allow freedom of movement under normal driving conditions.

➡ **This type of reel locks up when the car decelerates rapidly, as during a crash or sudden stop.**

The lap belts use the same ratchet-type retractors that the 1972–73 models use. The switches for the interlock system have been removed from the lap belt retractors and placed in the belt buckles. The seat sensors remain the same as those used in 1972–73.

For ease of service, the car may be started from outside, by reaching in and turning the key, but without depressing the seat sensors.

In case of system failure, an over-ride switch is located under the hood. This is a one start switch and it must be reset each time it is used.

DISABLING THE INTERLOCK SYSTEM

Since the requirement for the interlock system was dropped during the 1975 model year, those systems installed on cars built earlier may now be legally disabled. The seat belt warning light is still required.

1. Disconnect the negative battery cable.
2. Locate the interlock harness connector under the left side of the instrument panel on or near the fuse block. It has orange, yellow, and green leads.
3. Cut and tape the ends of the green wire on the body side of the connector.
4. Remove the buzzer from the fuse block or connector.

LIGHTING

Headlights

REMOVAL & INSTALLATION

▸ **See Figures 70 thru 78**

1. Unscrew the Torx retaining screws and remove the headlight bezel.
2. Remove the headlight bulb retaining screws. These are the screws which hold the retaining ring for the bulb to the front of the car. Do not touch the two headlight aiming screws, at the top and the side of the retaining ring (these screws will have different heads), or the headlight aim will have to be re-adjusted.
3. Pull the bulb and ring forward, then separate them. Unplug the electrical connector from the rear of the bulb.
4. Plug the new bulb into the electrical connector. Install the bulb into the retaining ring and then install the ring and the bulb. Install the headlight bezel.

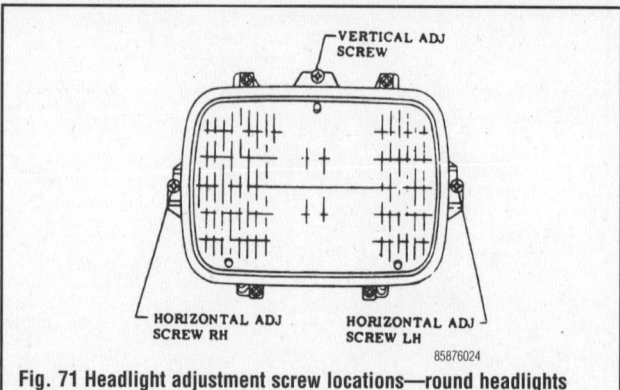

Fig. 71 Headlight adjustment screw locations—round headlights similar

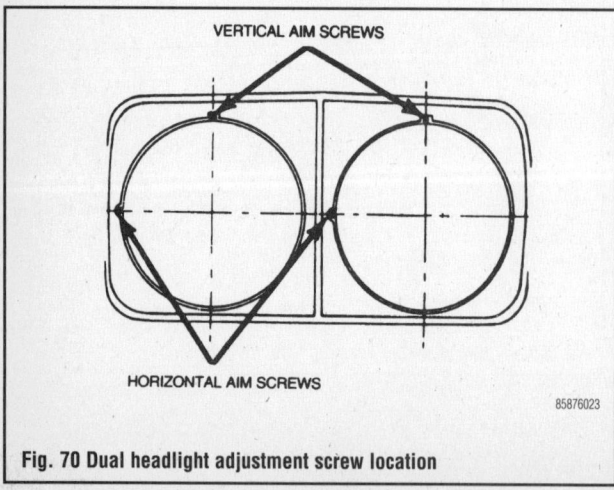

Fig. 70 Dual headlight adjustment screw location

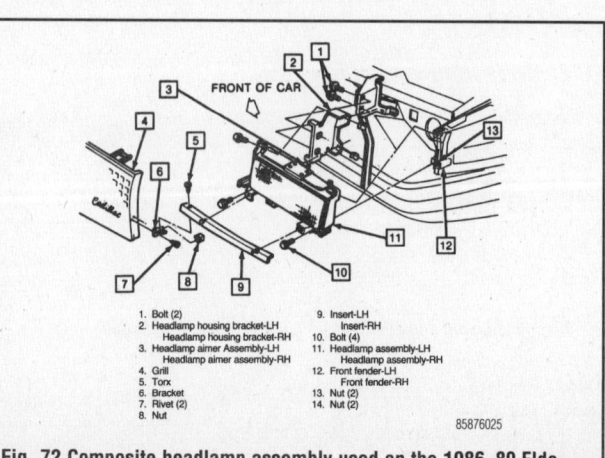

1. Bolt (2)
2. Headlamp housing bracket-LH
   Headlamp housing bracket-RH
3. Headlamp aimer Assembly-LH
   Headlamp aimer assembly-RH
4. Grill
5. Torx
6. Bracket
7. Rivet (2)
8. Nut
9. Insert-LH
   Insert-RH
10. Bolt (4)
11. Headlamp assembly-LH
    Headlamp assembly-RH
12. Front fender-LH
    Front fender-RH
13. Nut (2)
14. Nut (2)

Fig. 72 Composite headlamp assembly used on the 1986–89 Eldorado and Seville

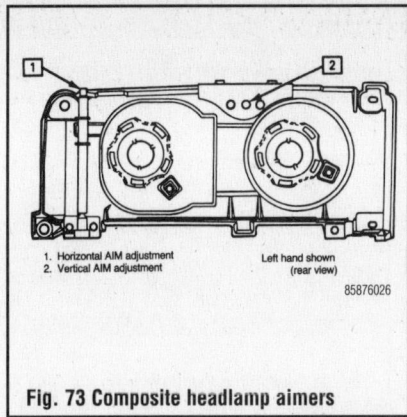

Fig. 73 Composite headlamp aimers

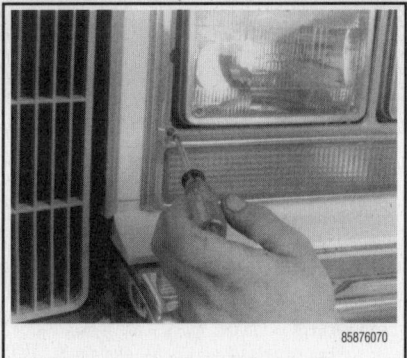

Fig. 74 Removing the headlight grille screws

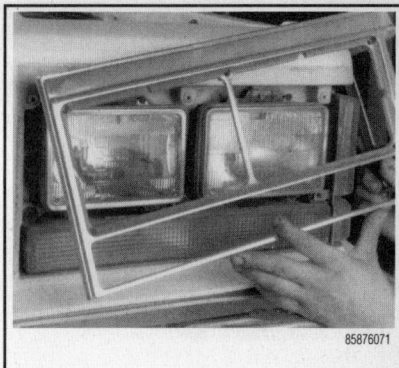

Fig. 75 Removing the headlight grille

Fig. 76 Removing the headlight bezel retaining screws

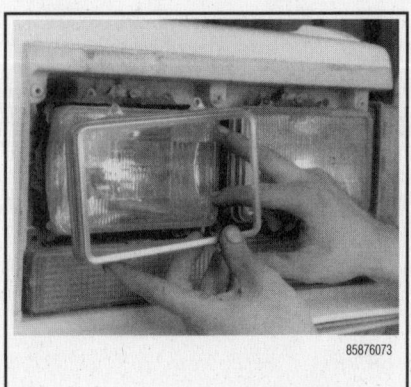

Fig. 77 Removing the headlight bezel

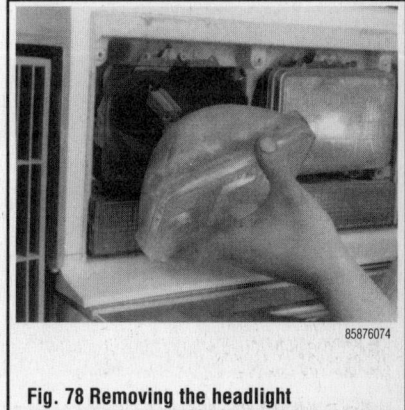

Fig. 78 Removing the headlight

HEADLIGHT AIMING

Except 1986–89 Eldorado and Seville

The headlights must be properly aimed to provide the best, safest road illumination. The lights should be checked for proper aim, and adjusted if necessary, after installing a new sealed beam unit or if the front end sheet metal has been replaced. Certain state and local authorities have requirements for headlight aiming; these should be checked before adjustment is made.

➡ The car's fuel tank should be about half full when adjusting the headlights. Tires should be properly inflated, and if a heavy load is normally carried in the car, it should remain there.

Horizontal and vertical aiming of each sealed beam unit is provided by two adjusting screws, which move the mounting ring in the body against the body of the coil spring. There is no adjustment for focus; this is done during headlight manufacturing.

1986–89 Eldorado and Seville

➡ These models are equipped with composite headlight assemblies. Due to the special tools required to adjust the aim (J-25300-1 Unit A Aimer; J-25300-2 Unit B Aimer and J-25300-203 Composite lamp Adapter), this procedure is best left to a qualified service technician.

1. Park the vehicle on level ground and set the parking brake.
2. Attach the three special tools mentioned in the NOTE above to the headlamps.
3. Rock the vehicle back-and-forth a few times.
4. Check that the fuel level is no more than a half tank and then set the aim. Vertical adjustment should be between 2 in. (50.8mm) UP and 2½ in. (63.5mm) DOWN. Horizontal adjustment should be between 4 in. (101mm) RIGHT and 4 in. (1016mm) LEFT.
5. Remove the special headlamp aiming tools.

Signal and Marker Lights

➡ Since the light housing capsules (on all late model vehicles) are constructed by means of sonic welding, the ONLY services which can be performed are the replacement of the bulbs or the housing themselves.

REMOVAL & INSTALLATION

Front Turn Signal and Parking Lights

1964–79 VEHICLES

1. Reach up under the fender and twist out the electrical socket from the rear of the housing.
2. Remove the housing-to-front fender extension screws and remove the housing (pull it rearward).
3. To install, reverse the removal procedures.

1980–89 VEHICLES

▶ See Figures 79 thru 86

1. Remove the headlight bezel mounting screws and the bezel.
2. Disconnect the twist lock socket from the lens housing.
3. Remove the parking light housing.

➡ To remove the bulb, turn the twist lock socket (at the rear of the housing) counterclockwise ¼ turn, then remove the socket with the bulb; replace the bulb if defective.

4. To install, reverse the removal procedures.

Side Marker Lights

1964–79 VEHICLES

1. Remove   headlight bezel mounting screws and the bezel.
2. Disconnect the twist lock socket from the lens housing.
3. Remove the marker light housing.

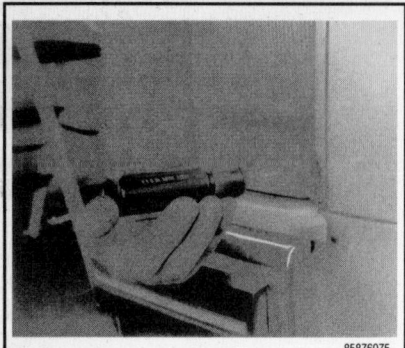

Fig. 79 Removing the lens housing retaining screws

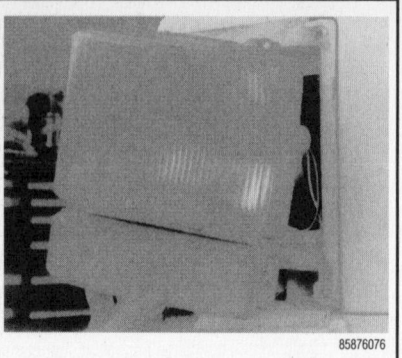

Fig. 80 Removing the lens housing

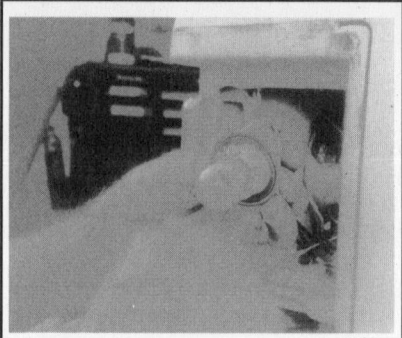

Fig. 81 Removing the bulb from the lens housing

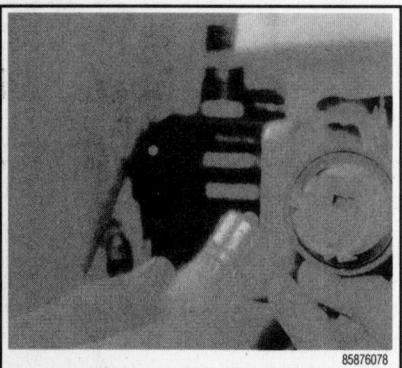

Fig. 82 Removing the parking light or turn signal bulb from a common socket

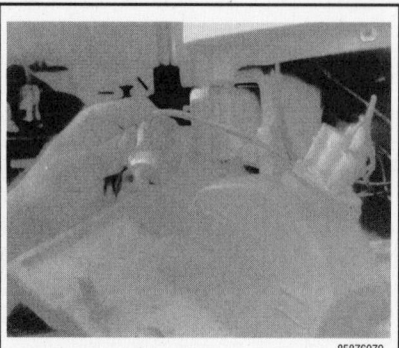

Fig. 83 Removing the side marker bulb from the lens housing

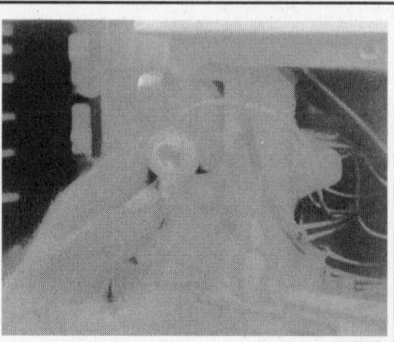

Fig. 84 Removing the side marker bulb from the socket

Fig. 85 Removing the lens housing retaining screw

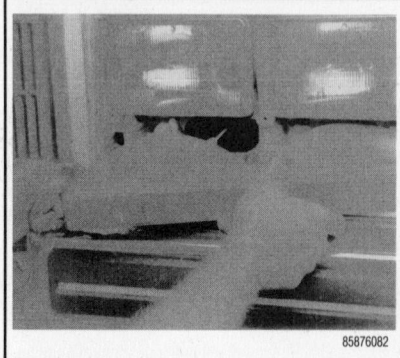

Fig. 86 Removing the lens housing

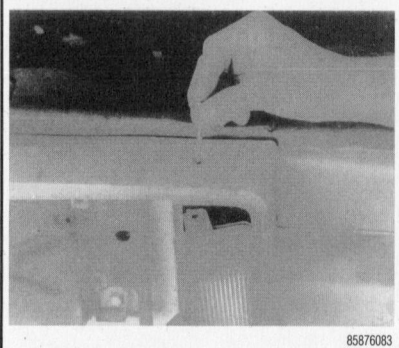

Fig. 87 Removing the reverse or back-up light housing screw

➡To remove the bulb, turn the twist lock socket (at the rear of the housing) counterclockwise ¼ turn, then remove the socket with the bulb; replace the bulb if defective.

   4. To install, reverse the removal procedures.

1980–89 VEHICHLES

   1. Remove the marker light housing screws and the housing.
   2. Disconnect the twist lock socket from the lens housing.

➡To remove the bulb, turn the twist lock socket (at the rear of the housing) counterclockwise ¼ turn, then remove the socket with the bulb; replace the bulb if defective.

   3. To install, reverse the removal procedures.

Rear Turn Signal, Brake and Parking Lights

▶ **See Figures 87 thru 98**

   1. Remove the tail light panel screws and the panel.
   2. Disconnect the twist lock socket from the lens housing.

➡To remove the bulb, turn the twist lock socket (at the rear of the housing) counterclockwise ¼ turn, then remove the socket with the bulb, replace the bulb if defective.

   3. To install, reverse the removal procedures.

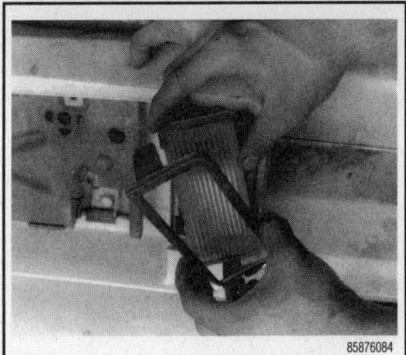

Fig. 88 Removing the reverse or back-up light housing assembly

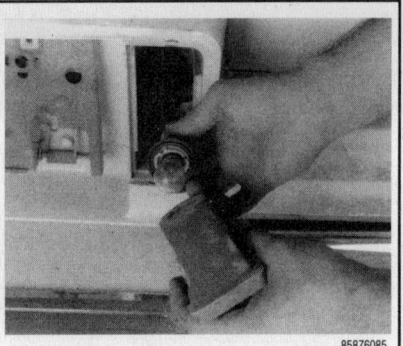

Fig. 89 Removing the reverse or back-up light from the housing

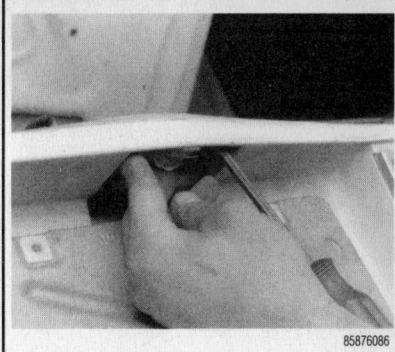

Fig. 90 Removing the license plate light housing screw

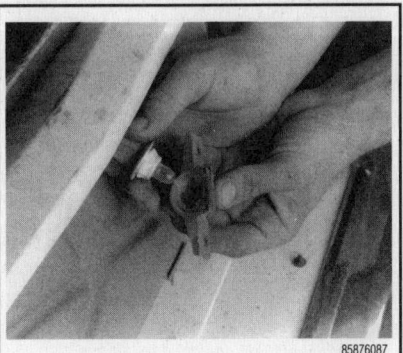

Fig. 91 Removing the license plate light housing

Fig. 92 Removing the tail light housing bezel retaining screw

Fig. 93 Removing the tail light housing bezel

Fig. 94 Removing the tail light housing screw

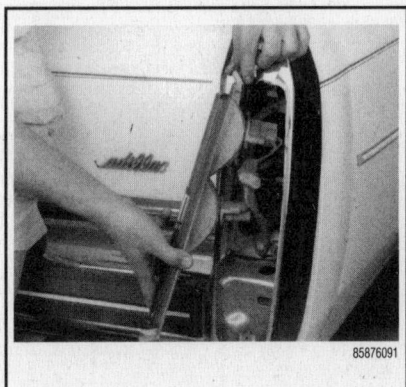

Fig. 95 Removing the tail light housing

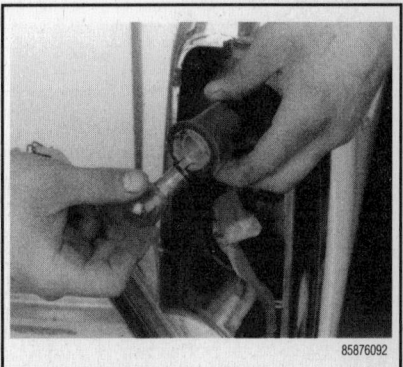

Fig. 96 Removing a common tail light or turn signal bulb

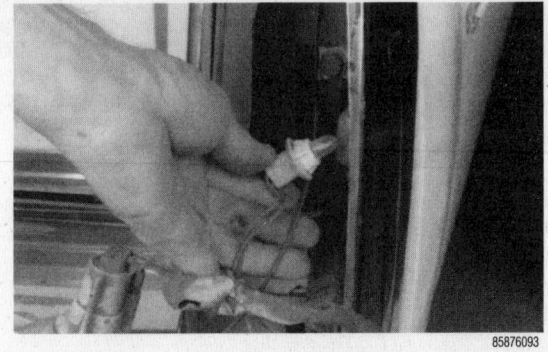

Fig. 97 Removing the side marker light from the housing

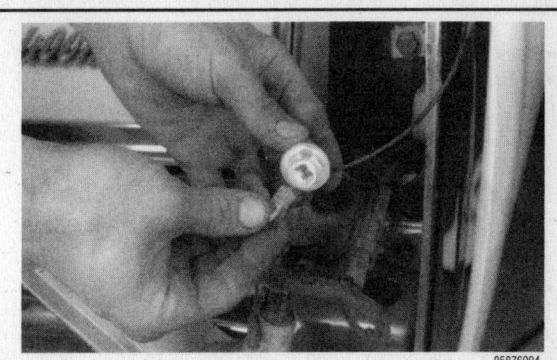

Fig. 98 Removing the side marker light from the socket

CIRCUIT PROTECTION

Fusible Links

All Cadillac models covered in this guide are equipped with fusible links in their electrical systems. The link itself is a piece of wire that is several gauges smaller than the supply wires to which they are connected. The link functions like a fuse in that it will "blow" (in the case of the link, melt) in the event of an overloaded or short circuit, thus protecting the rest of the circuit.

An example of a burned-out fusible link might be when headlights are operating and the rest of the car's electric's are dead, or vice versa. When a melted fusible link is found, the cause of the link failure should also be found and repaired. Some causes include short circuits, component failures, loose or poor connections, and overloaded circuits (often caused by improperly installed aftermarket accessories drawing too much current or overloading one circuit).

There are generally four fusible links installed on the cars covered here. Three are connected to the lower ends of the main supply wires that connect the starter solenoid, and the links are usually black or red in color. The fourth fusible link is connected to the "Bat" terminal of the alternator and controls the fuel injection circuit (if so equipped).

REPLACING FUSIBLE LINKS

1. Disconnect the negative battery cable.
2. Cut the wire next to the fusible link splice and remove the damaged fusible link and splice.
3. Strip about ½ in. (13mm) of insulation from the end of the new link and from the harness wire so that each will project halfway through the soldering sleeve.
4. Crimp a soldering sleeve over the stripped wire ends and carefully solder the joint. Cover the new joint tightly with a double layer of electrical tape.
5. Install a new link connector eye on the solenoid terminal. Connect the

negative battery terminal. To check the new link, simply feel and/or gently pull on each link. A good link will be intact and feel solid.

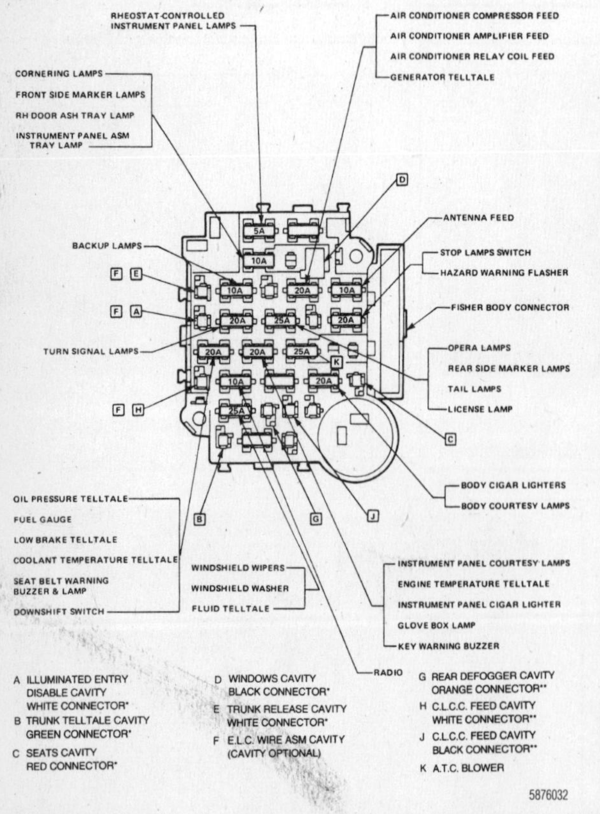

Fuses and Flashers

▶ **See Figures 99 and 100**

The fuse block on the models covered in this guide is located underneath the far left side of the instrument panel, up towards the floor mat. Two types of fuses have been used since 1967: the conventional type (cylindrical) fuse, found on 1967 through 1978 cars, and the new "Mini" fuses, found on 1978 and later models. The conventional fuses are held in the fuse block by small tangs, and are best removed with a small screwdriver or awl. The mini fuses are simply pushed into their respective places in the block.

To determine whether either type of fuse is blown, remove the suspect fuse and examine the element for a break. If the element (the strip of silver metal inside) is broken, replace the fuse with one of equal amperage. Some fuses have their amperage value molded into the fuse end, others (and all of the mini fuses) have a color coding system. See the fuse color chart for common amperage values.

The turn signal flasher is located under the dash to the right of the steering column on most models. The hazard flasher is under the dash, to the left of the steering column. On 1980 and later models, both the turn signal flasher and the hazard flasher are located at the lower left hand and the upper right hand cor-

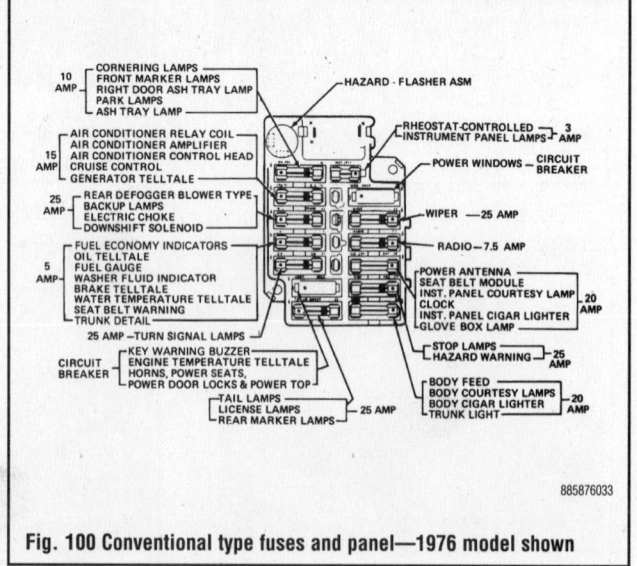

Fig. 100 Conventional type fuses and panel—1976 model shown

ners of the fuse block respectively. There is an inline fuse for the underhood/spotlamp circuit. The fuse box is marked to indicate fuse size and the circuit(s) protected.

Circuit Breakers

A circuit breaker in the light switch protects the headlight circuit. A separate 30 amp breaker mounted on the firewall protects the power window, seat, and power top circuits. Circuit breakers open and close rapidly to protect the circuit if current is excessive.

Buzzers, Relays and Flashers

The electrical protection devices are located in the convenience center, which is a swing down unit located under the instrument panel. All units are serviced by plug-in replacements.

Fig. 99 Fuse panel with mini-fuses—1980 full size Cadillac shown

WIRING DIAGRAMS

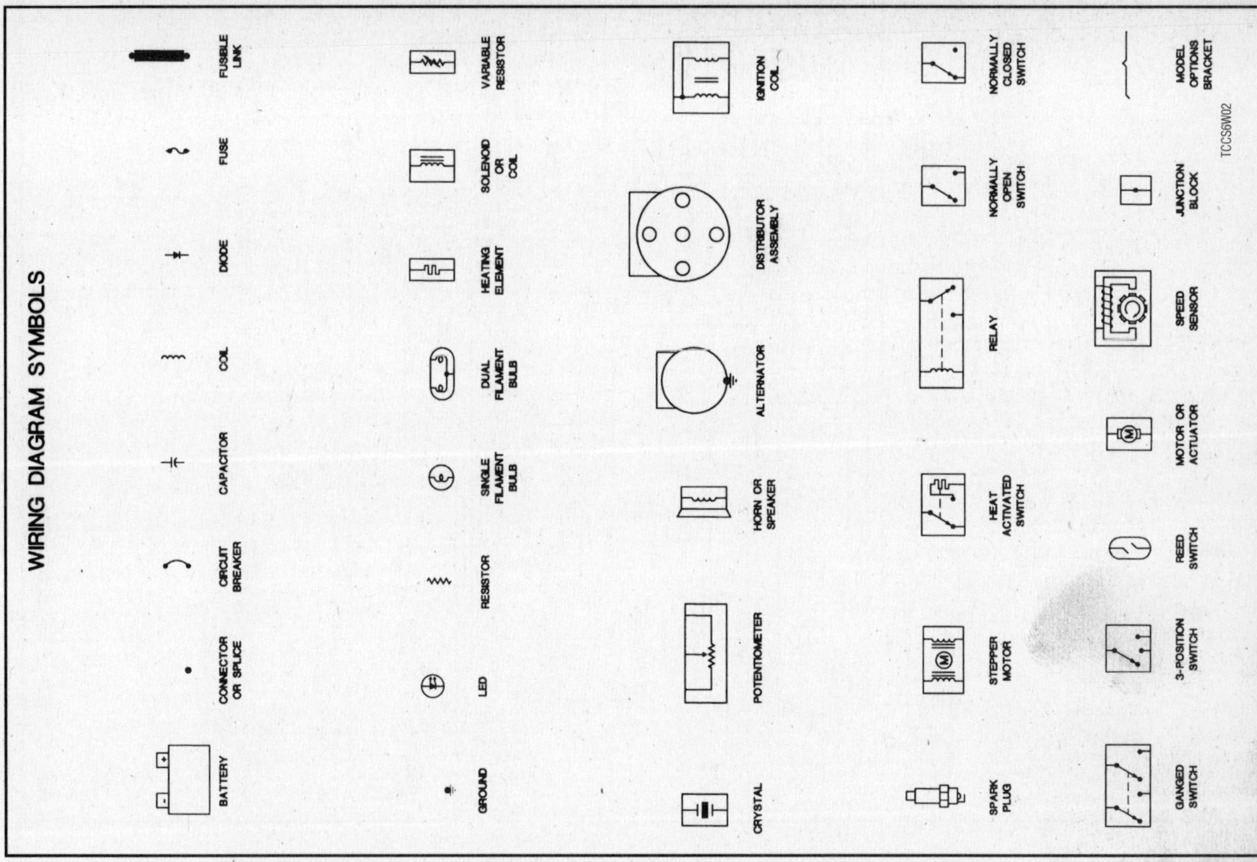

WIRING DIAGRAM SYMBOLS

FUSIBLE LINK · FUSE · DIODE · COIL · CAPACITOR · CIRCUIT BREAKER · CONNECTOR OR SPLICE · BATTERY

VARIABLE RESISTOR · SOLENOID OR COIL · HEATING ELEMENT · DUAL FILAMENT BULB · SINGLE FILAMENT BULB · POTENTIOMETER · RESISTOR · LED · GROUND

IGNITION COIL · DISTRIBUTOR ASSEMBLY · ALTERNATOR · HORN OR SPEAKER · STEPPER MOTOR · CRYSTAL · SPARK PLUG

NORMALLY CLOSED SWITCH · NORMALLY OPEN SWITCH · RELAY · HEAT ACTIVATED SWITCH · 3-POSITION SWITCH · GANGED SWITCH

MODEL OPTIONS BRACKET · JUNCTION BLOCK · SPEED SENSOR · MOTOR OR ACTUATOR · REED SWITCH

TCCS6W02

Common wiring diagram symbols

WIRE COLOR CHART

BLACK	BLK
BROWN	BRN
ORANGE	ORG
LIGHT GREEN	LT GRN
PINK	PNK
DARK BLUE	DK BLU
PURPLE	PPL
RED	RED
DARK GREEN	DK GRN
TAN	TAN
GRAY	GRY
WHITE	WHT
LIGHT BLUE	LT BLU
YELLOW	YEL

COMPONENT NAME · WIRE COLOR · SPLICE OR CONNECTOR · TERMINAL NUMBER · OTHER SYSTEM REFERENCE · MODEL OPTIONS BRACKET · CONDITIONS WHEN POWER IS APPLIED · BULB · CASE GROUND · GROUND

TCCS6W01

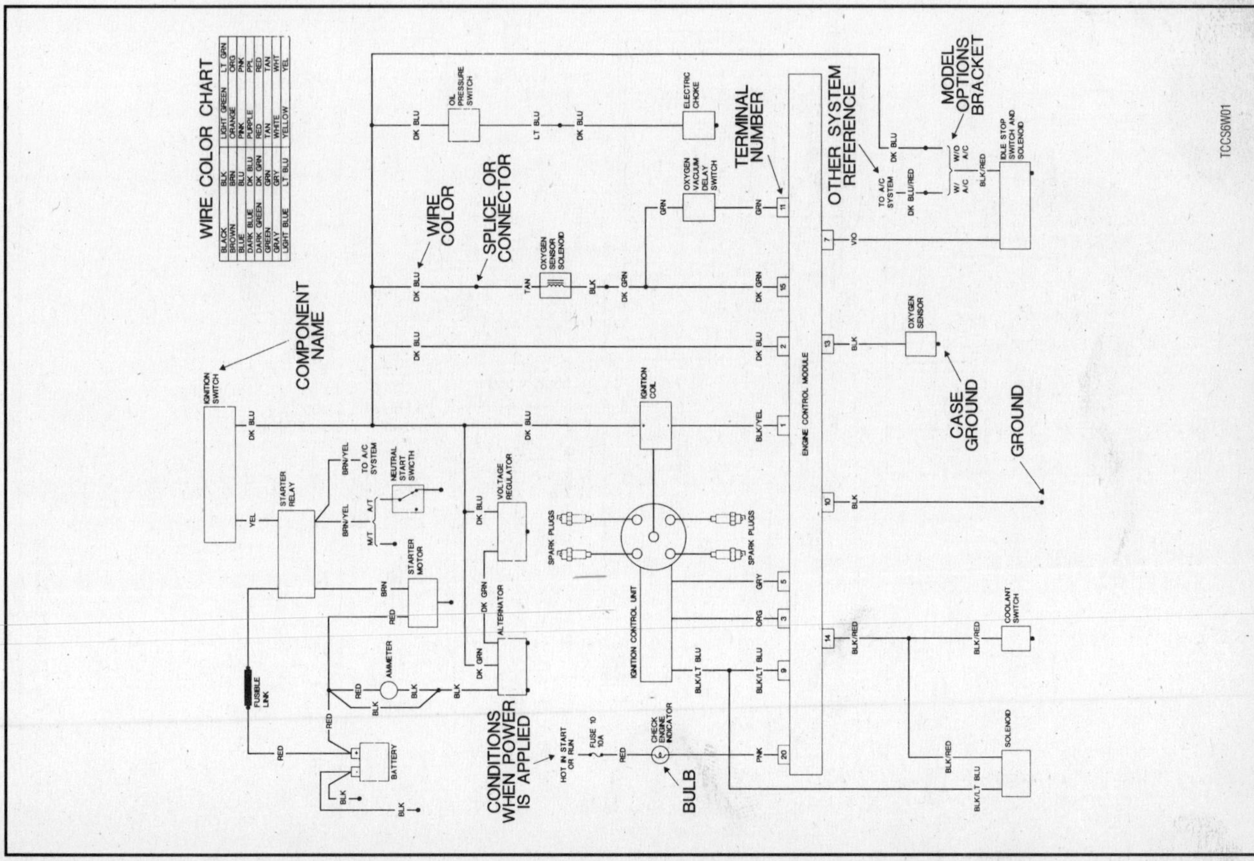

Sample diagram—how to read and interpret wiring

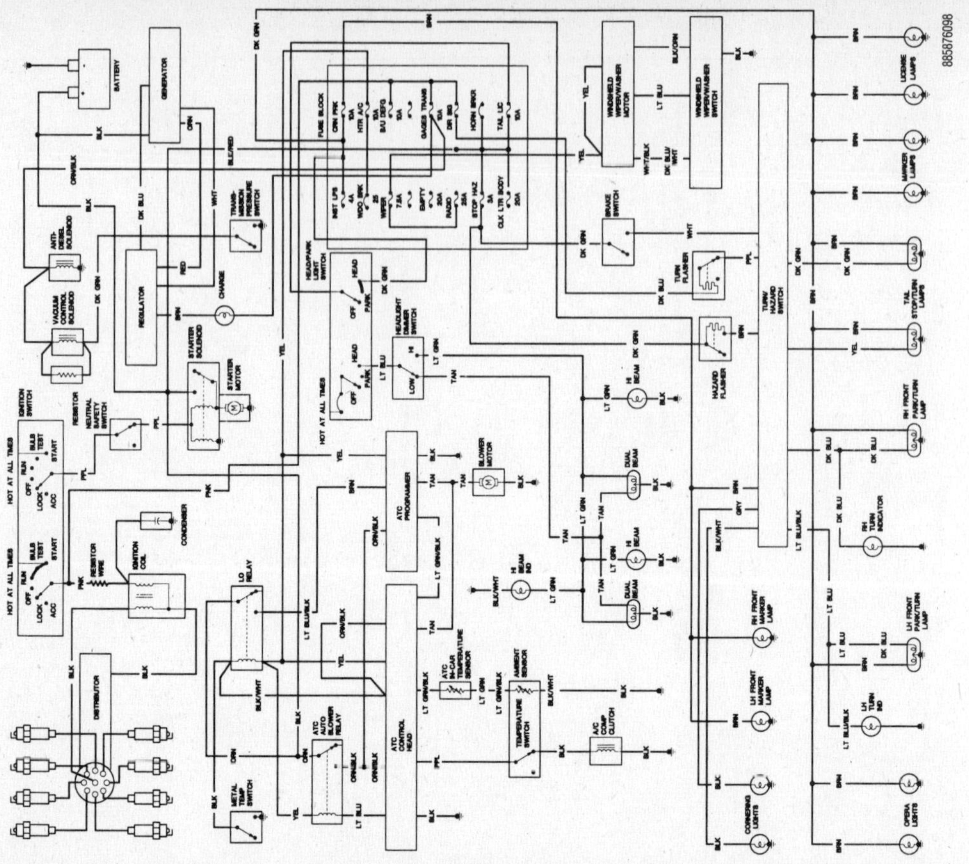

Fig. 102 1971-72 Cadillac DeVille

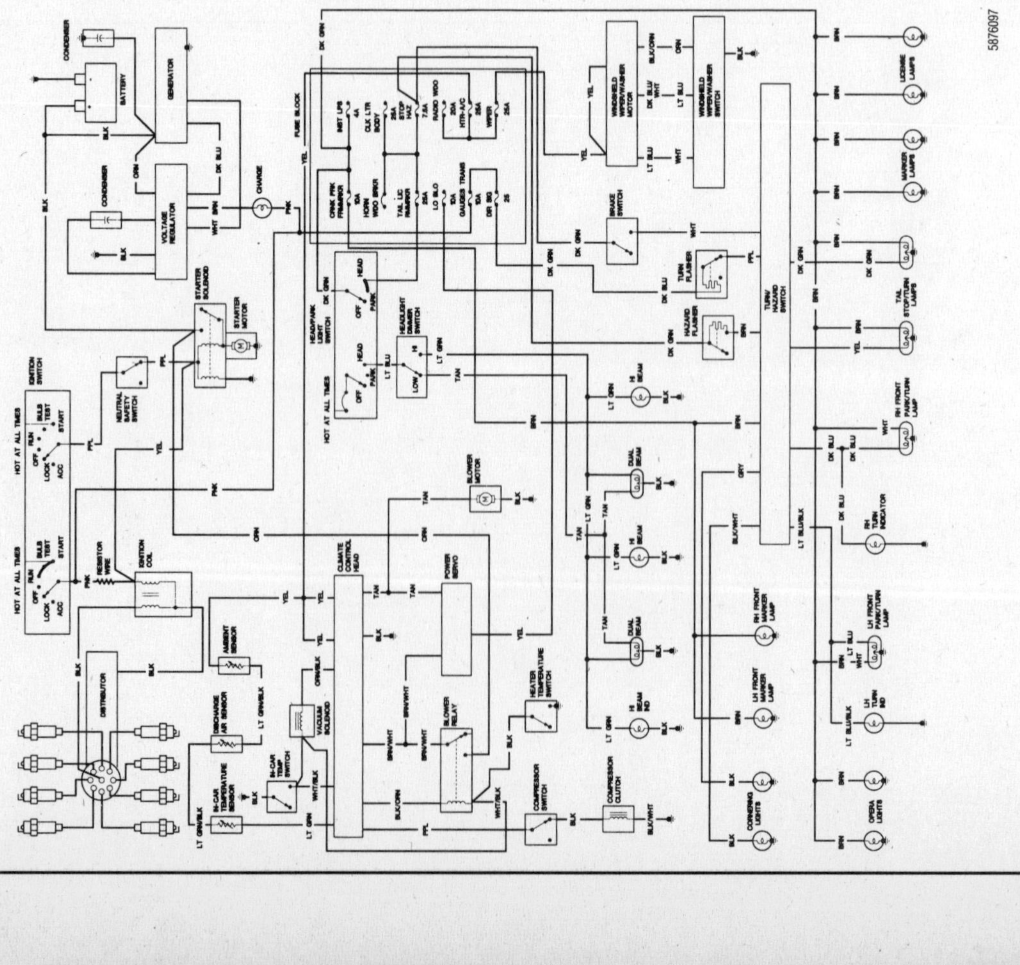

Fig. 101 1967-70 Cadillac DeVille

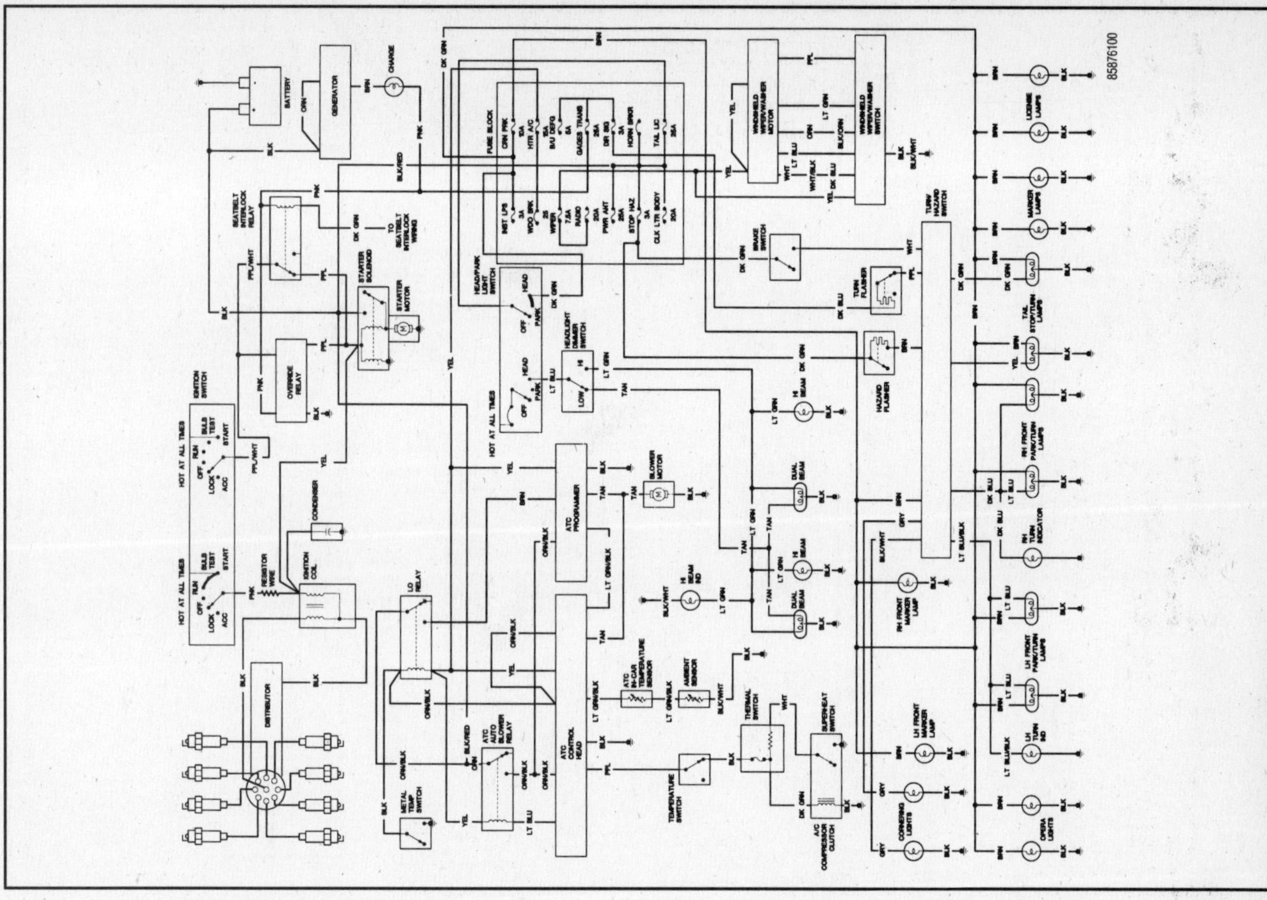

Fig. 104 1974 Cadillac DeVille

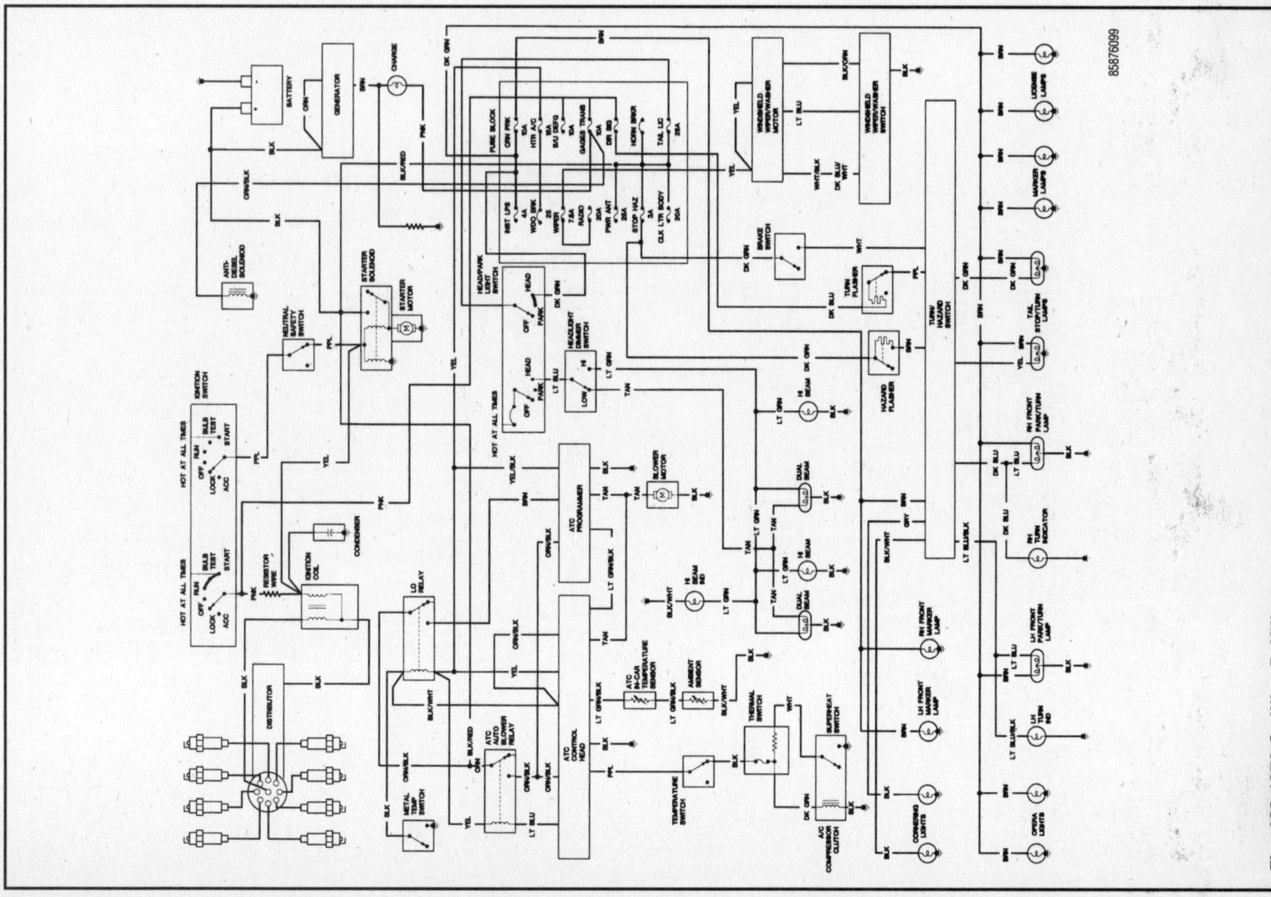

Fig. 103 1973 Cadillac DeVille

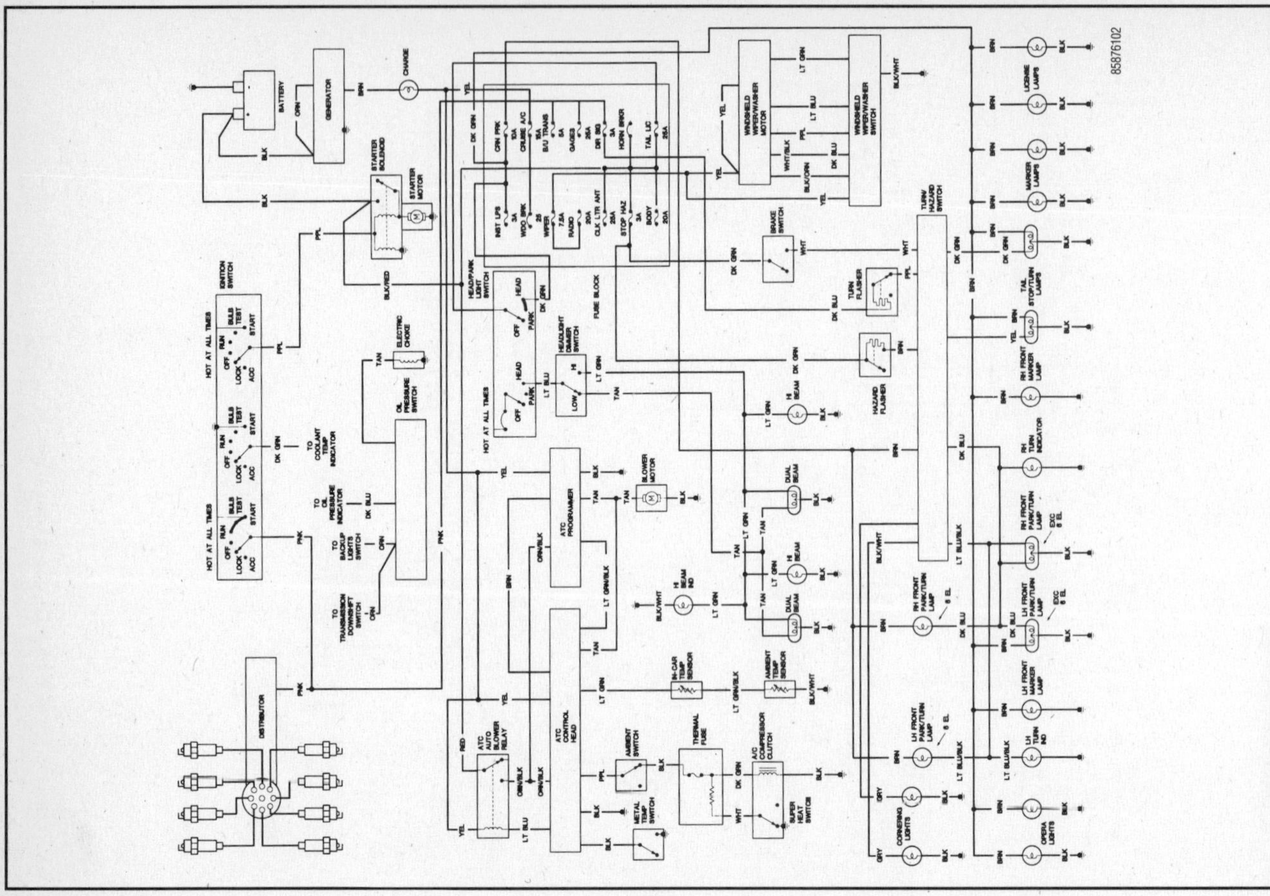

Fig. 106 1976 Cadillac DeVille

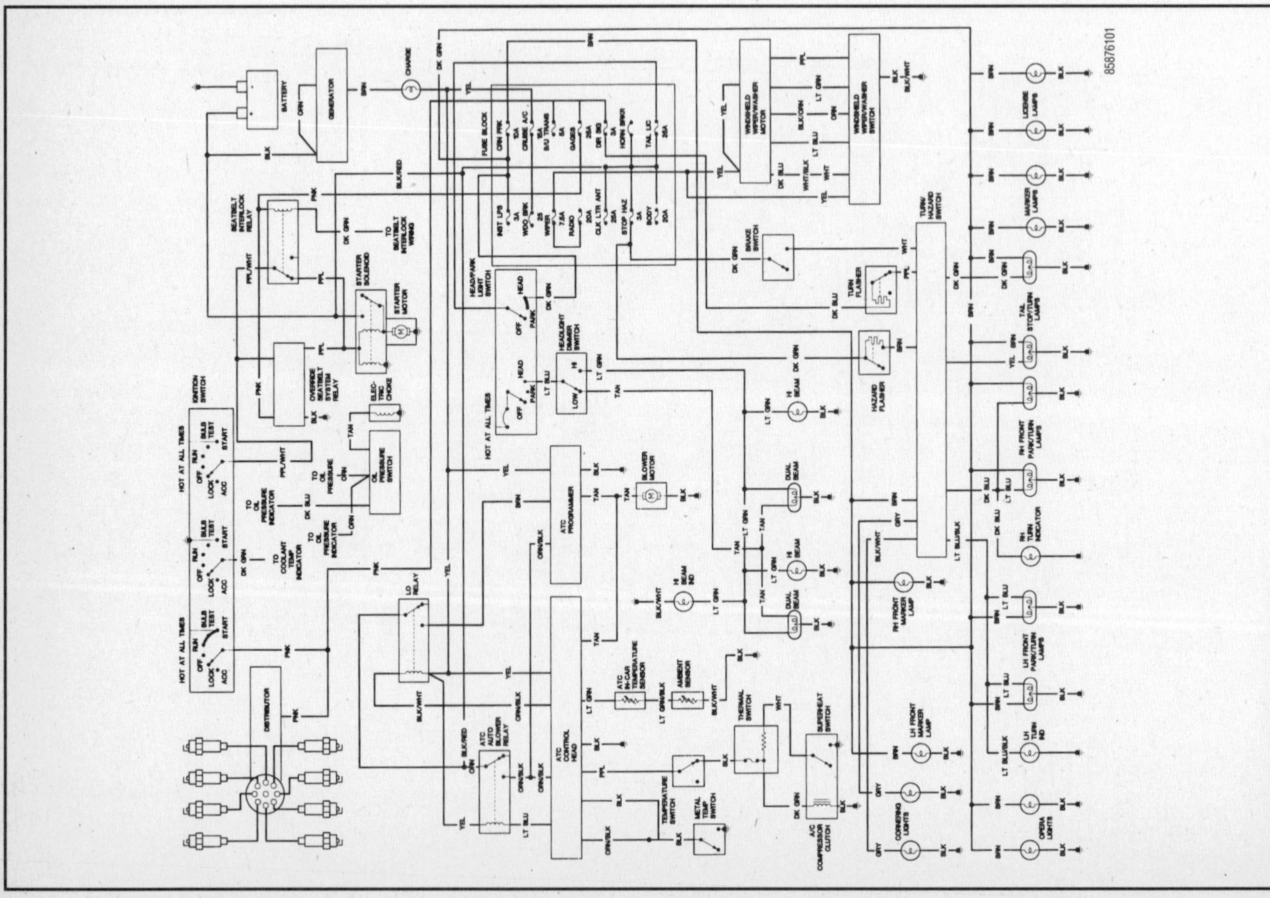

Fig. 105 1975 Cadillac DeVille

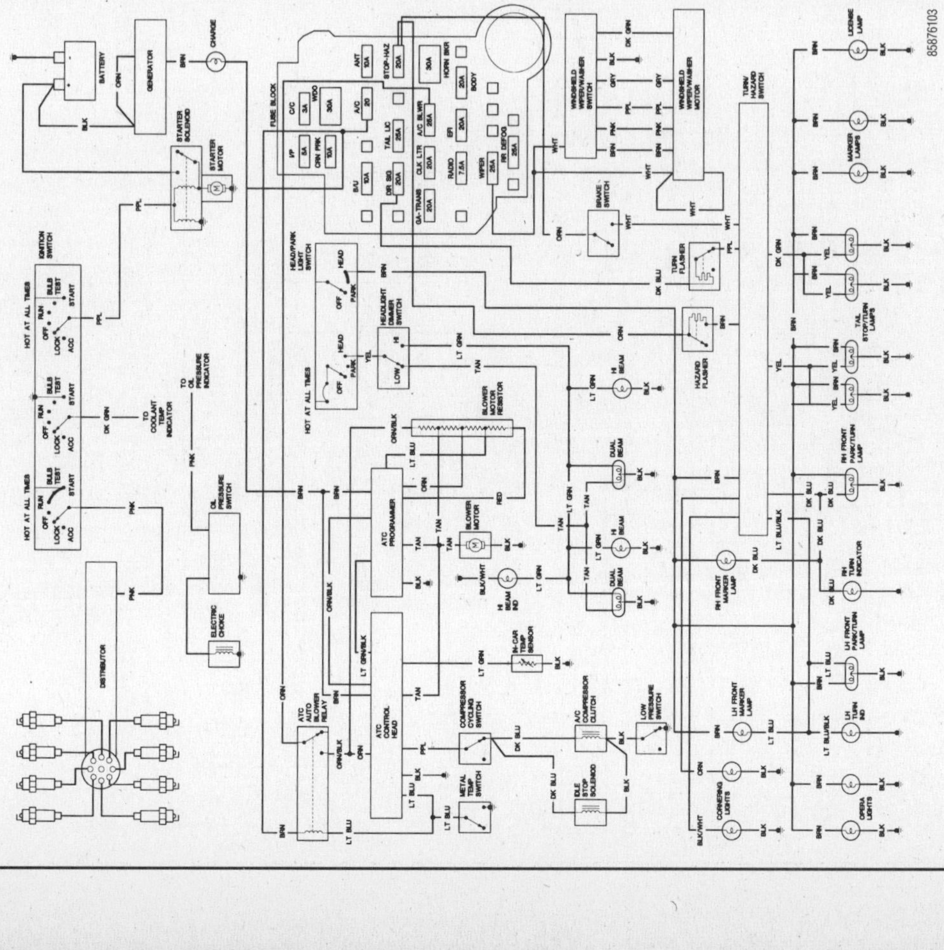

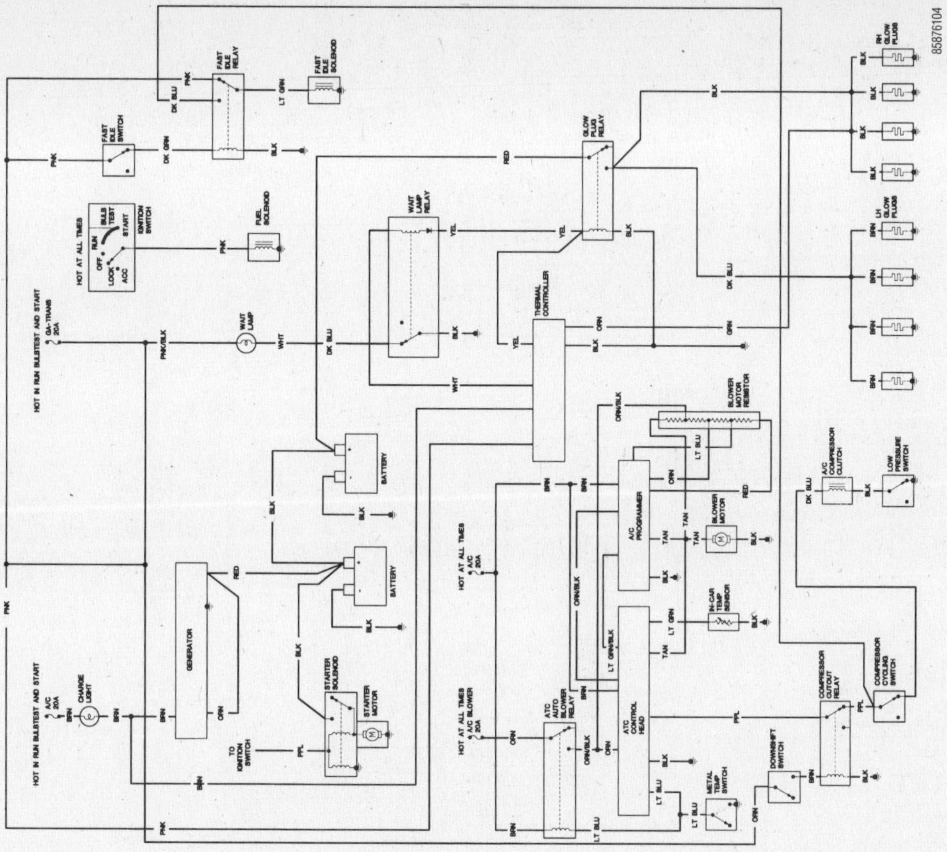

Fig. 108 1980 Cadillac DeVille and Fleetwood (diesel engine)

Fig. 107 1977-79 Cadillac DeVille and Fleetwood

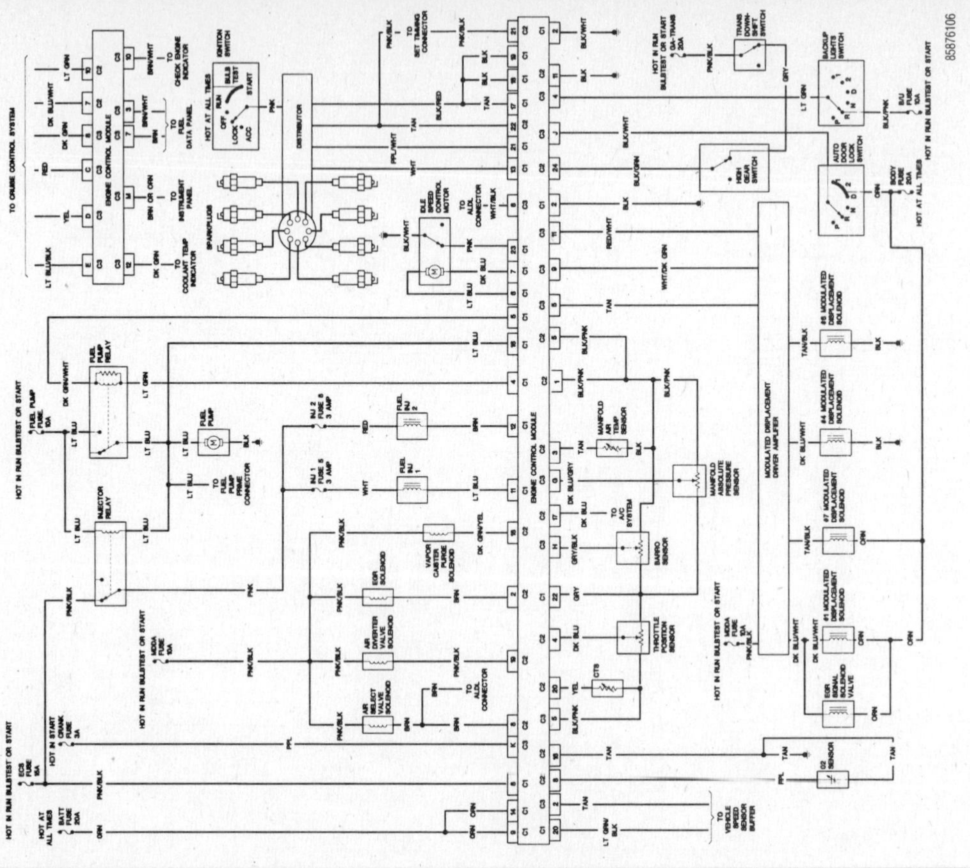

Fig. 110 1981 Cadillac DeVille and Fleetwood (V8 engine)

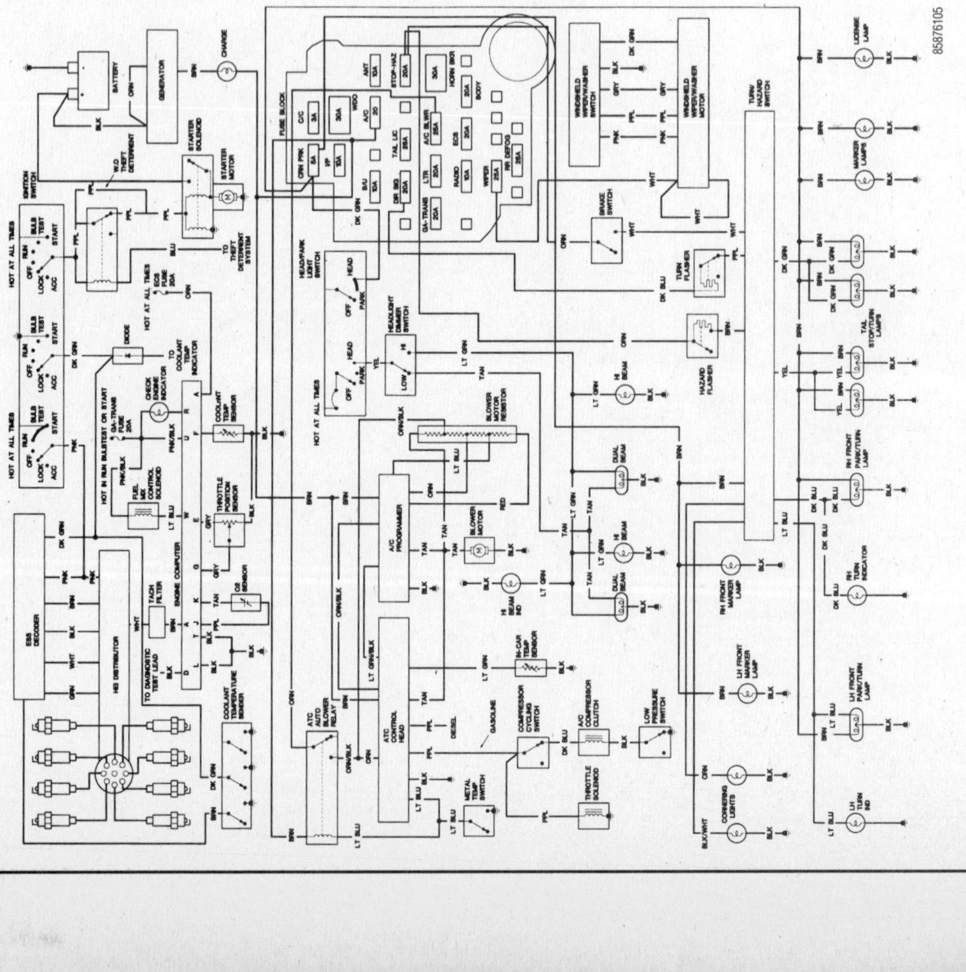

Fig. 109 1980 Cadillac DeVille and Fleetwood (gasoline engine)

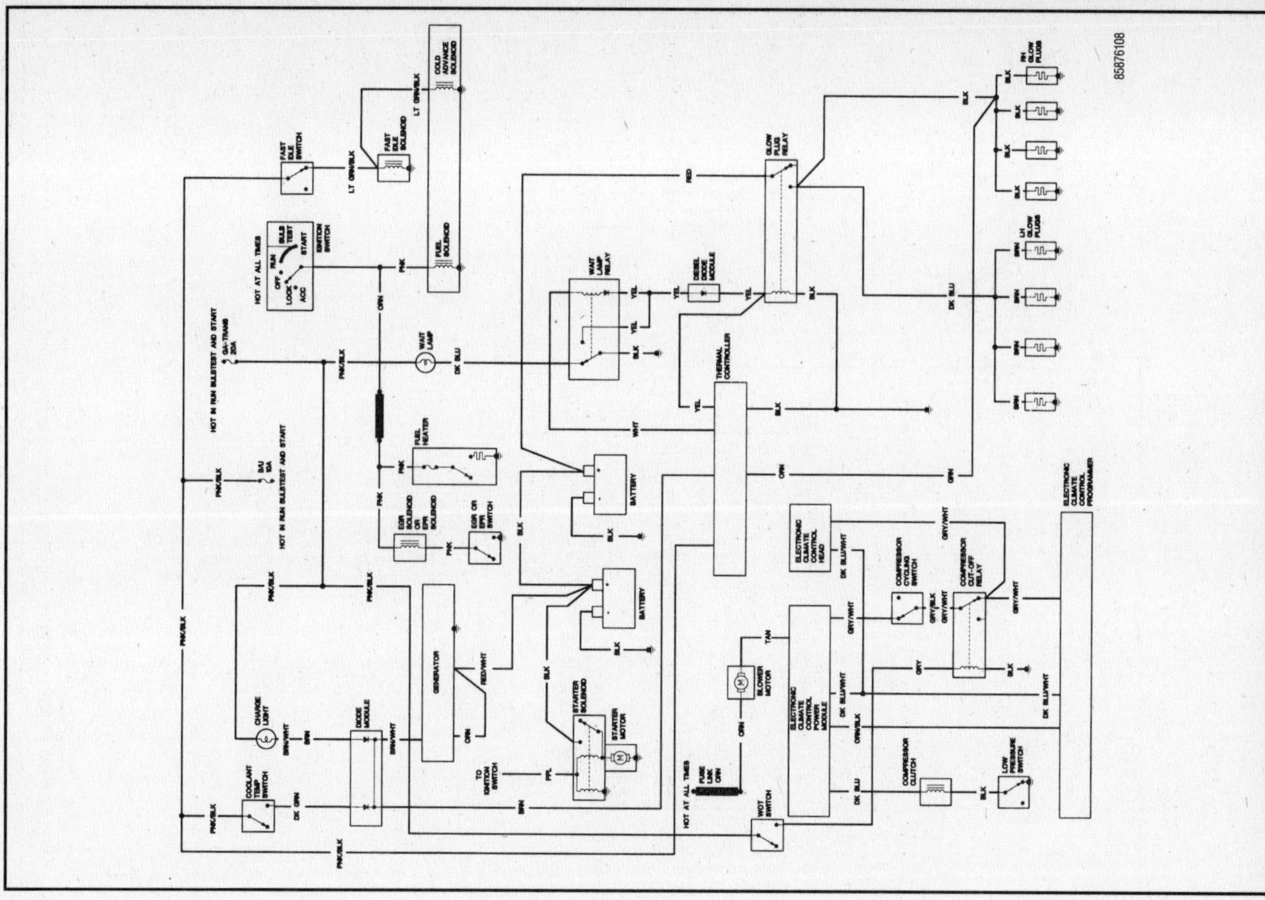

Fig. 112 1981 Cadillac DeVille and Fleetwood (diesel engine)

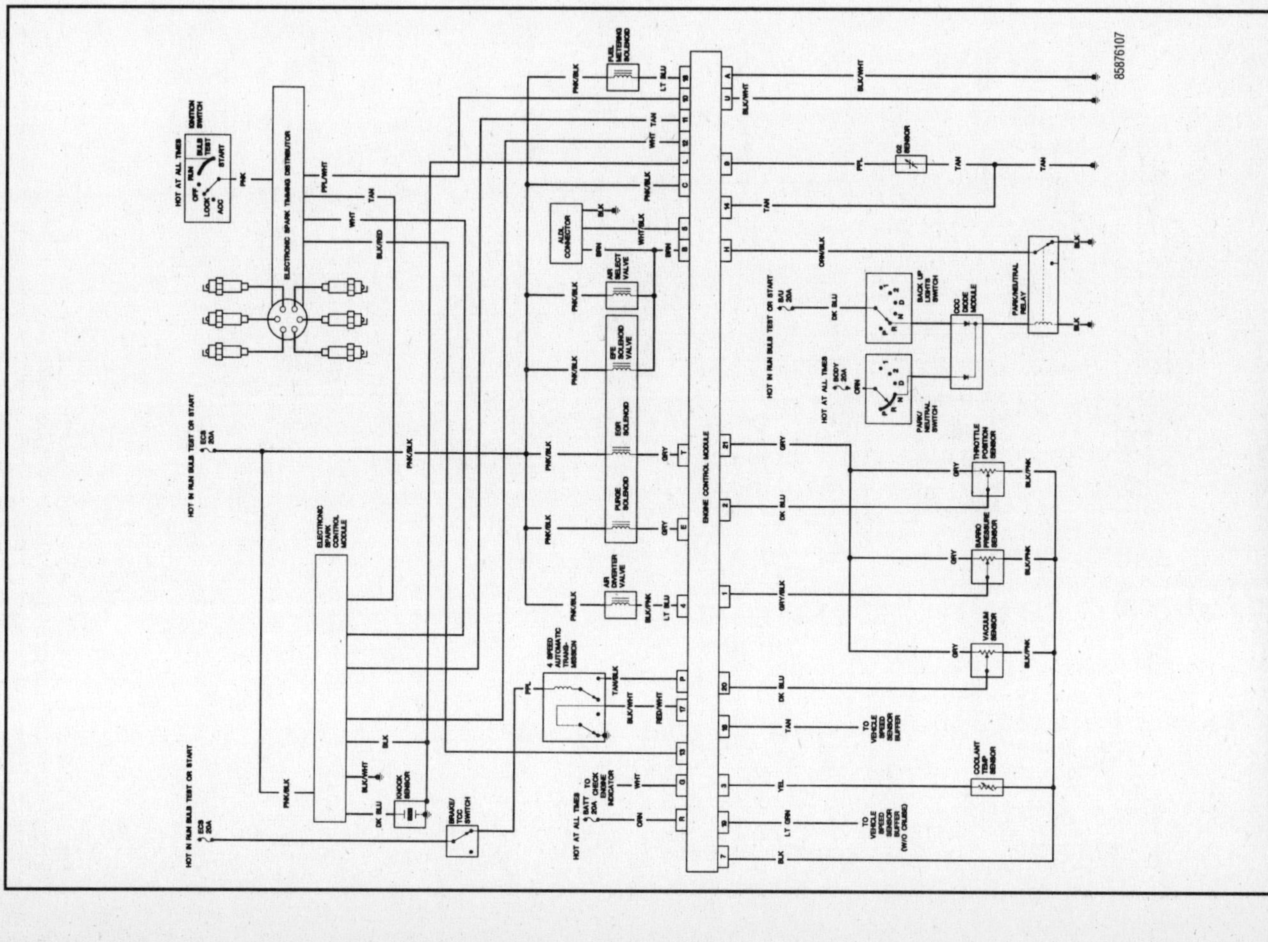

Fig. 111 1981 Cadillac DeVille and Fleetwood (V6 engine)

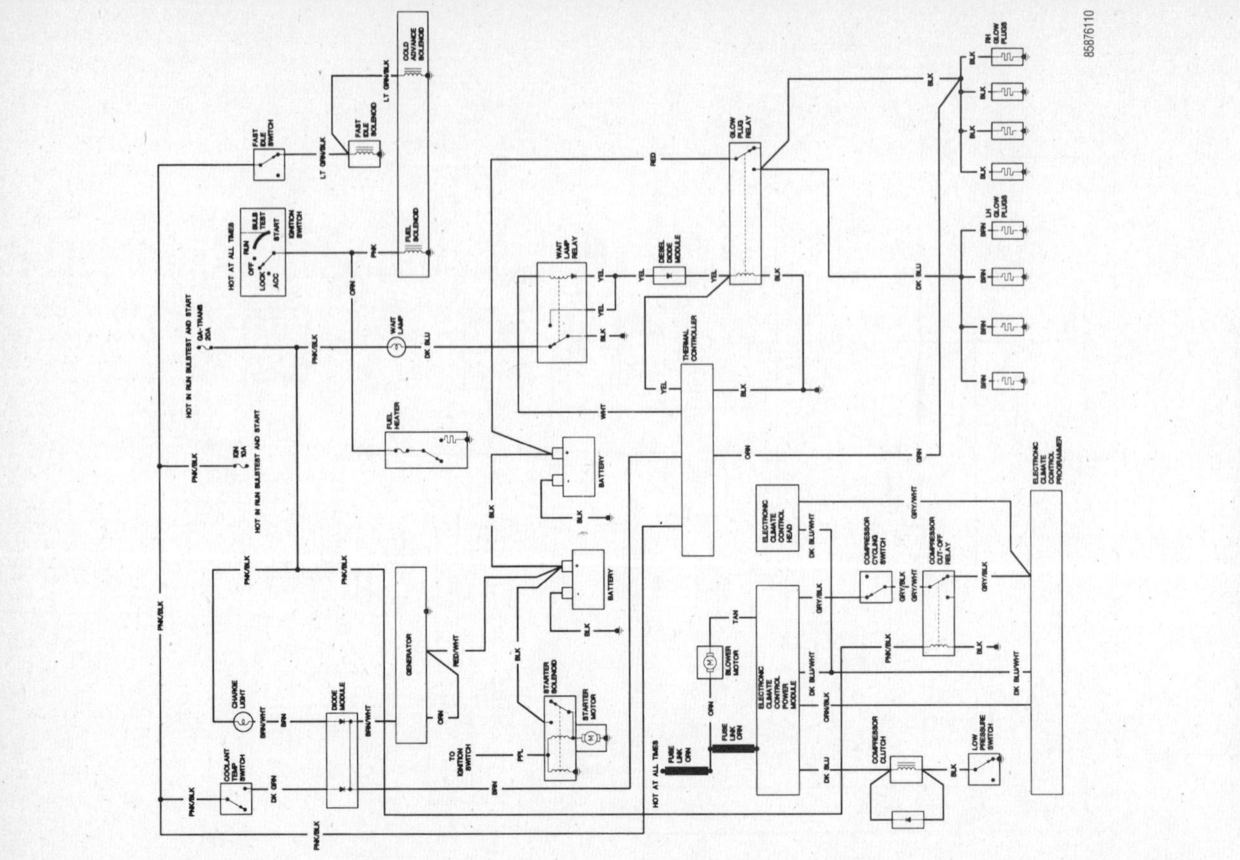

Fig. 114 1982 Cadillac DeVille and Fleetwood (diesel engine)

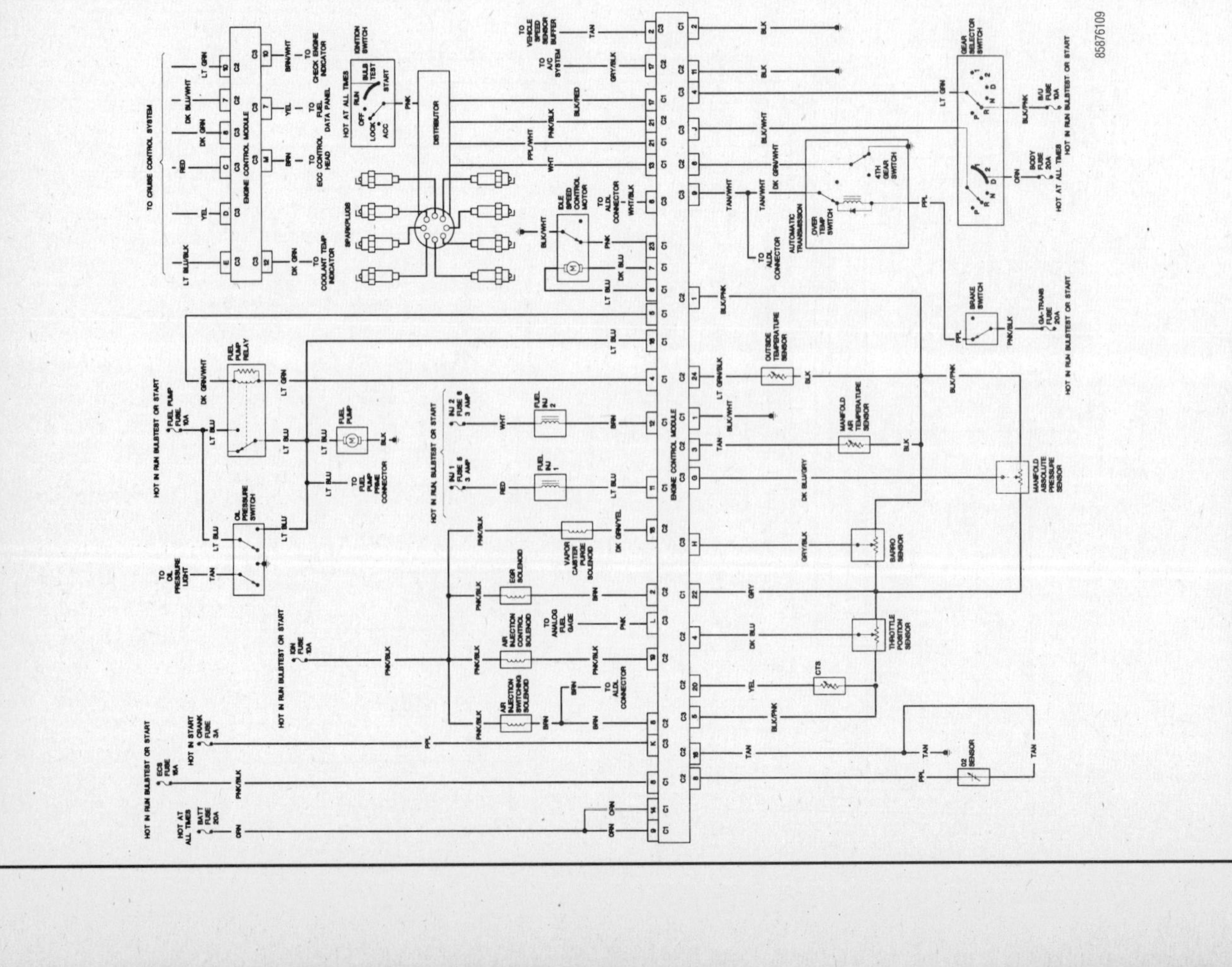

Fig. 113 1982 Cadillac DeVille and Fleetwood (V8 engine)

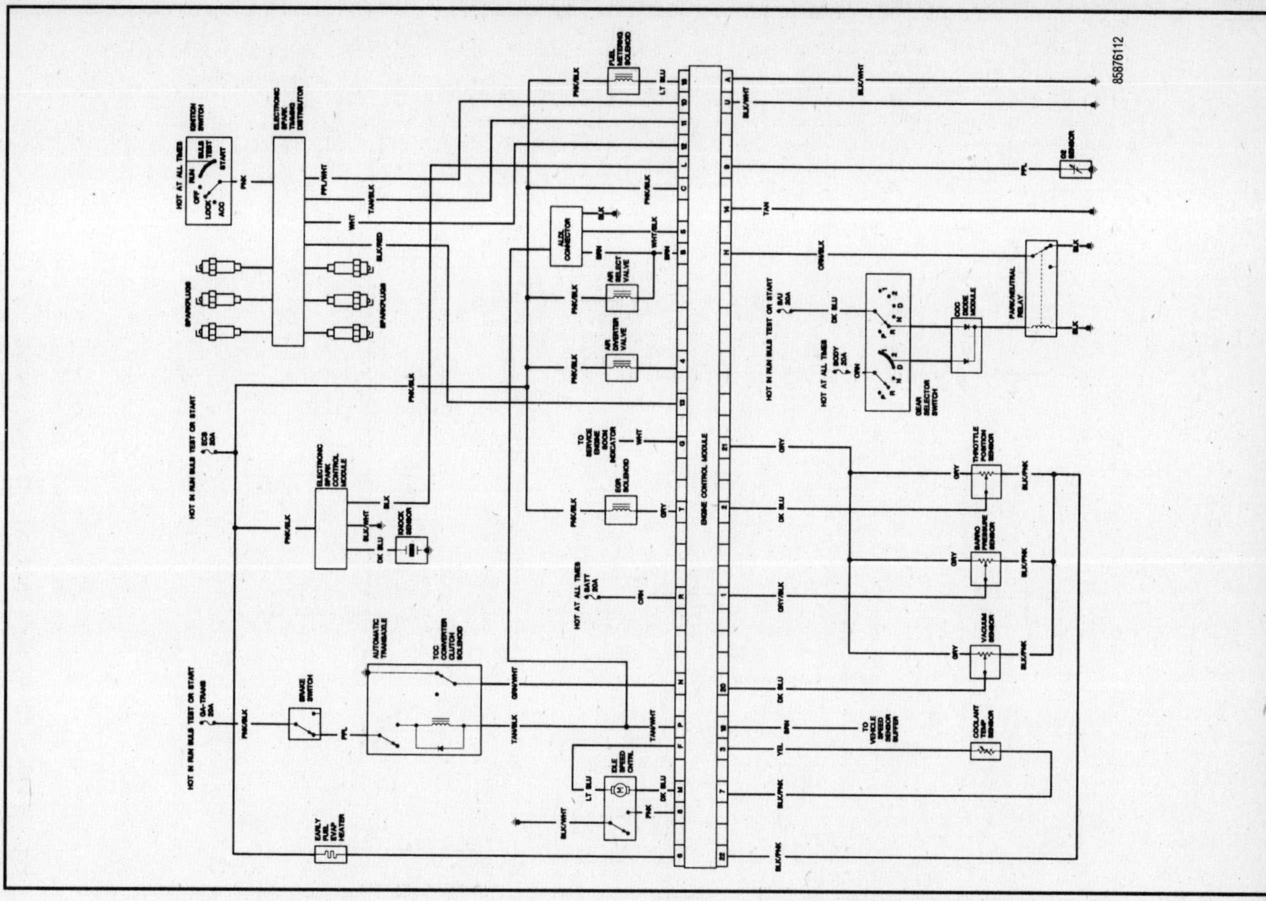

Fig. 116 1982 Cadillac DeVille and Fleetwood (V6 engine)

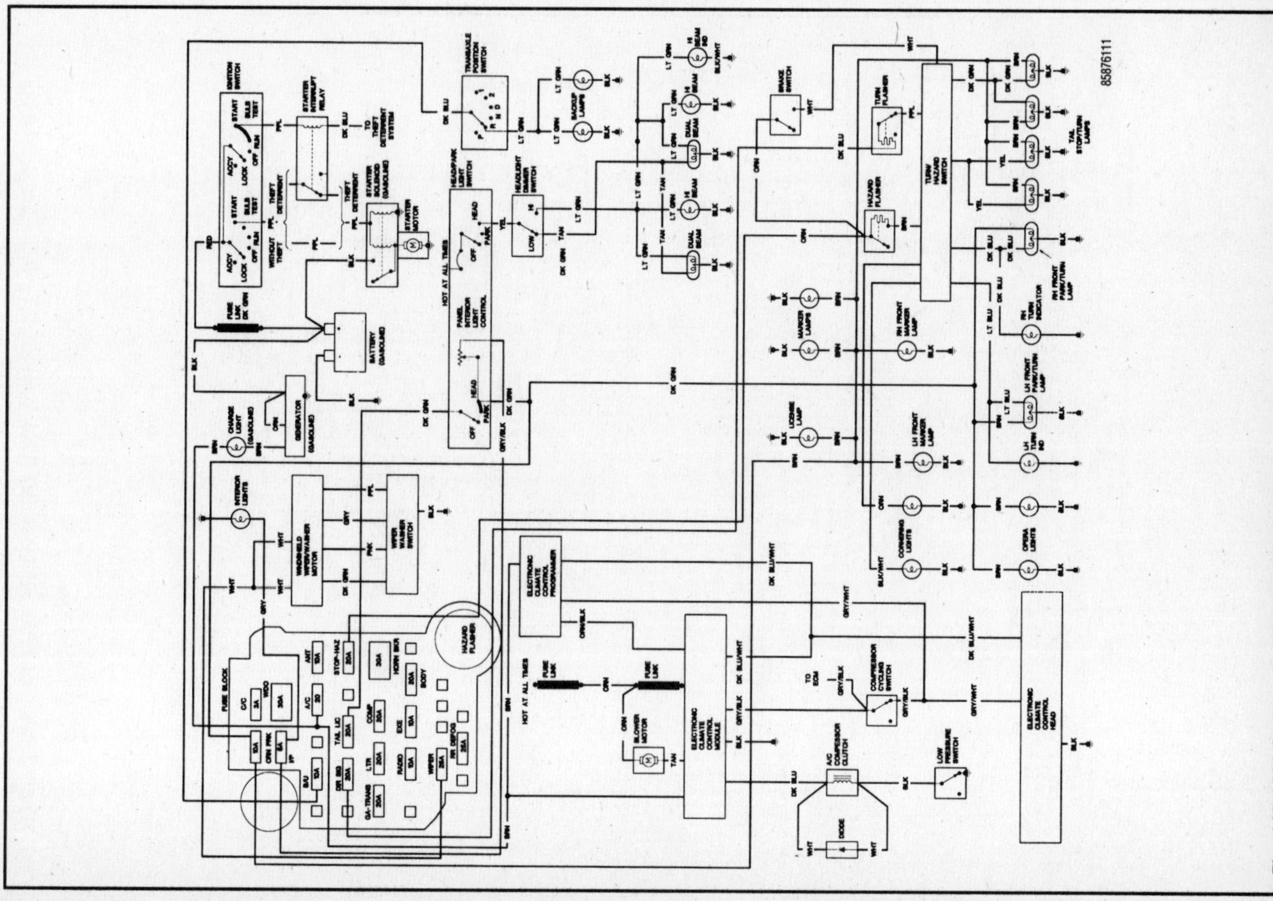

Fig. 115 1982 Cadillac DeVille and Fleetwood

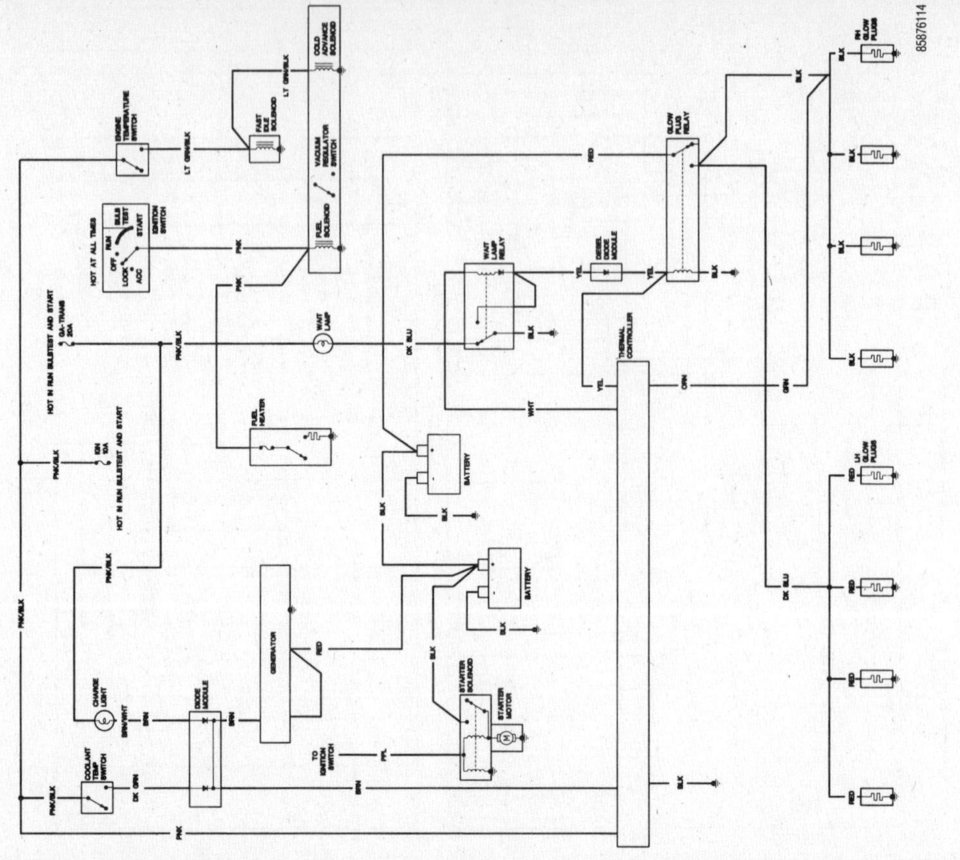

Fig. 118 1983 Cadillac DeVille and Fleetwood (diesel engine)

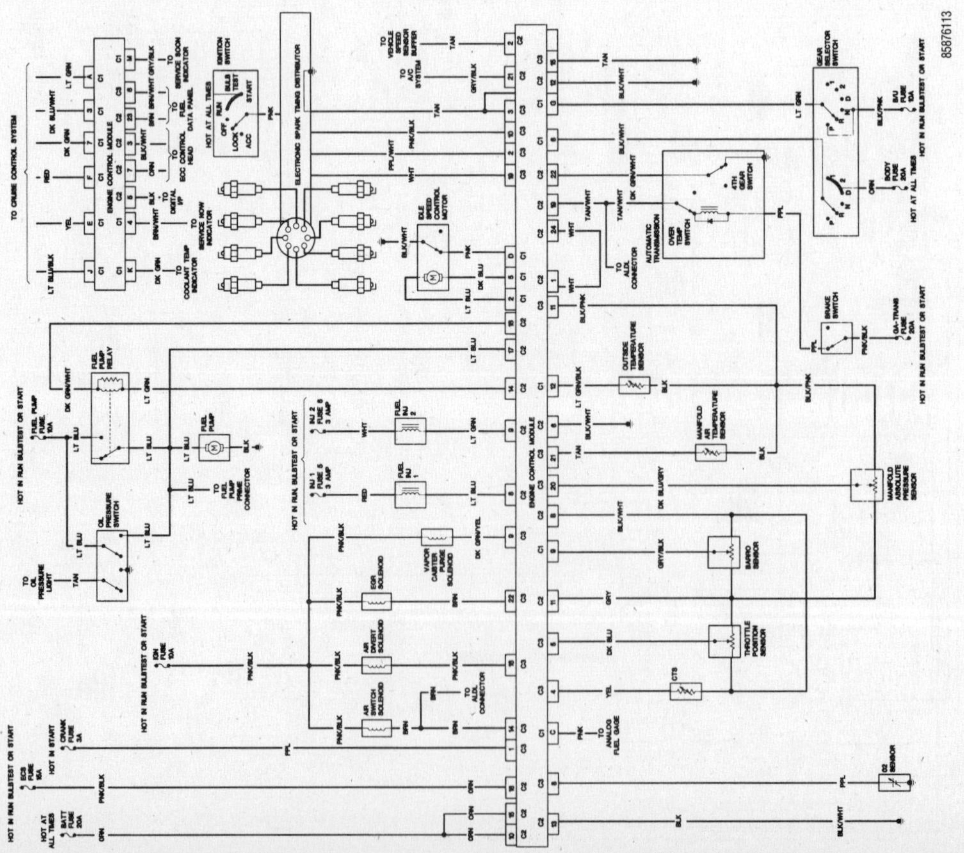

Fig. 117 1983 Cadillac DeVille and Fleetwood (V8 engine)

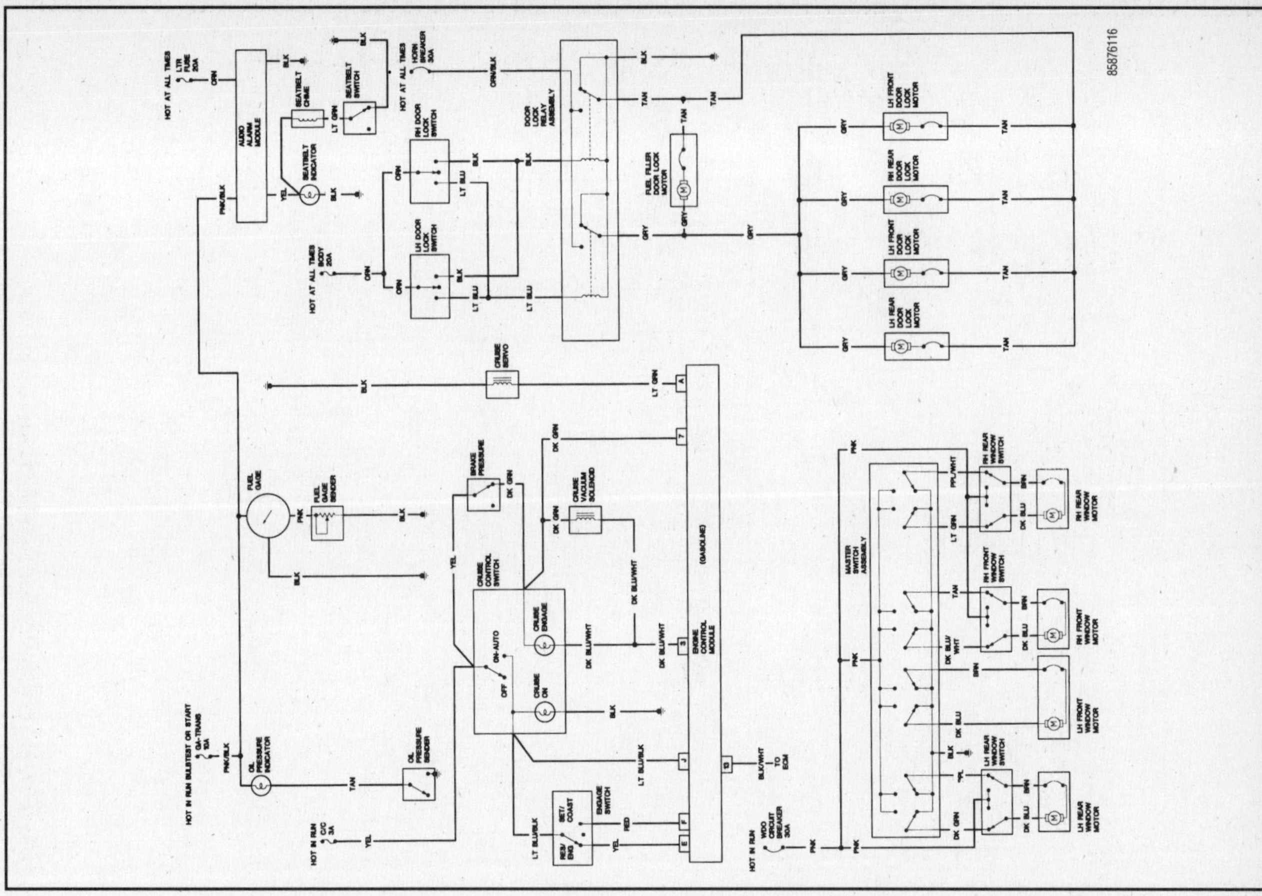

Fig. 120 1983 Cadillac DeVille and Fleetwood

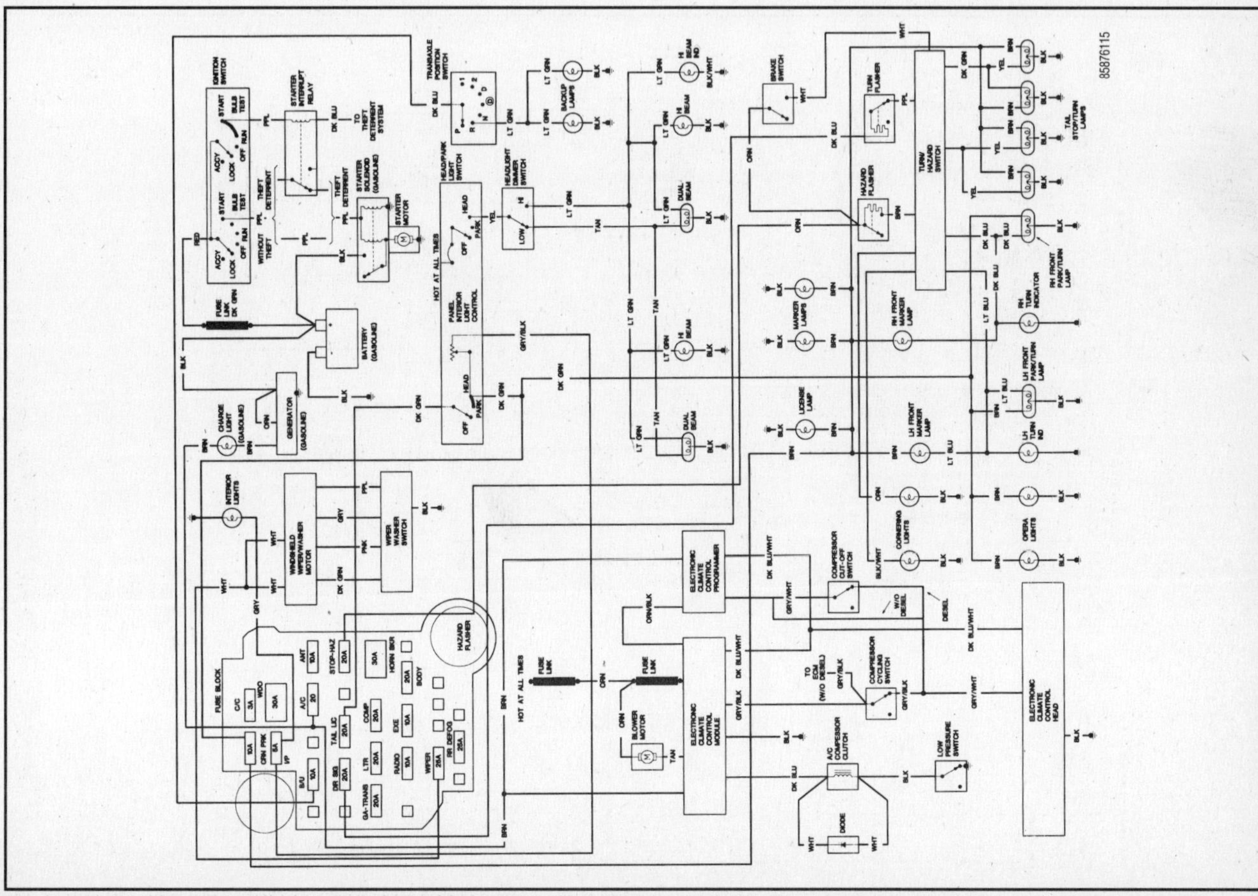

Fig. 119 1983 Cadillac DeVille and Fleetwood

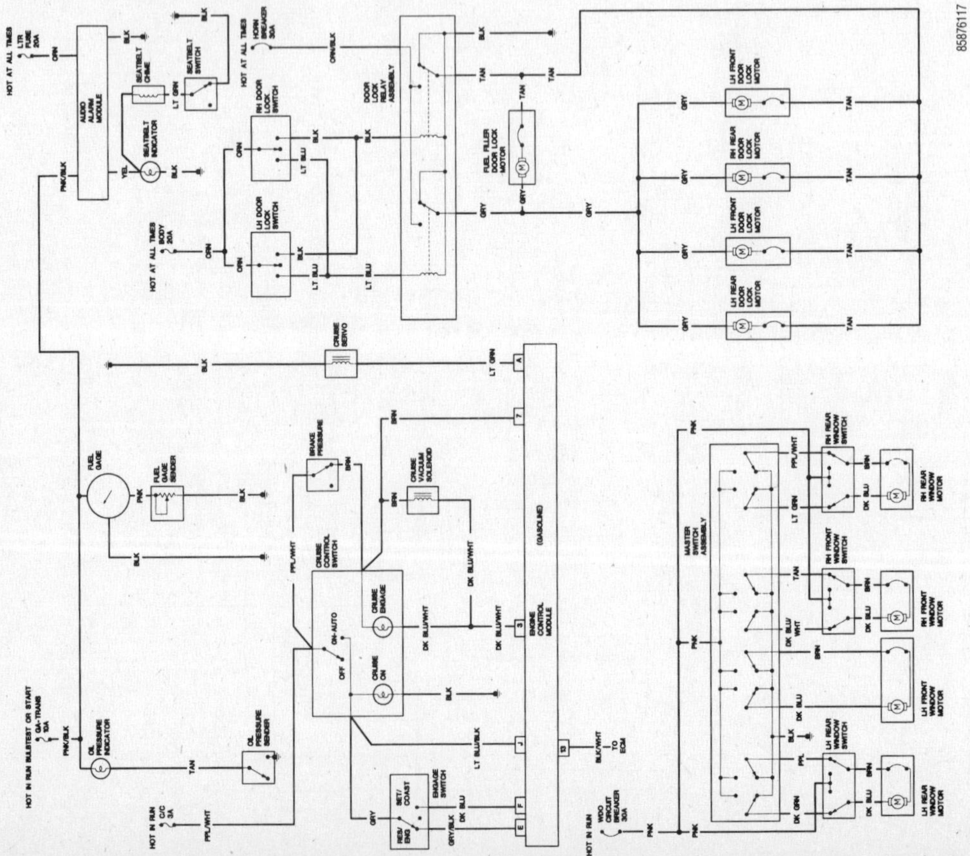

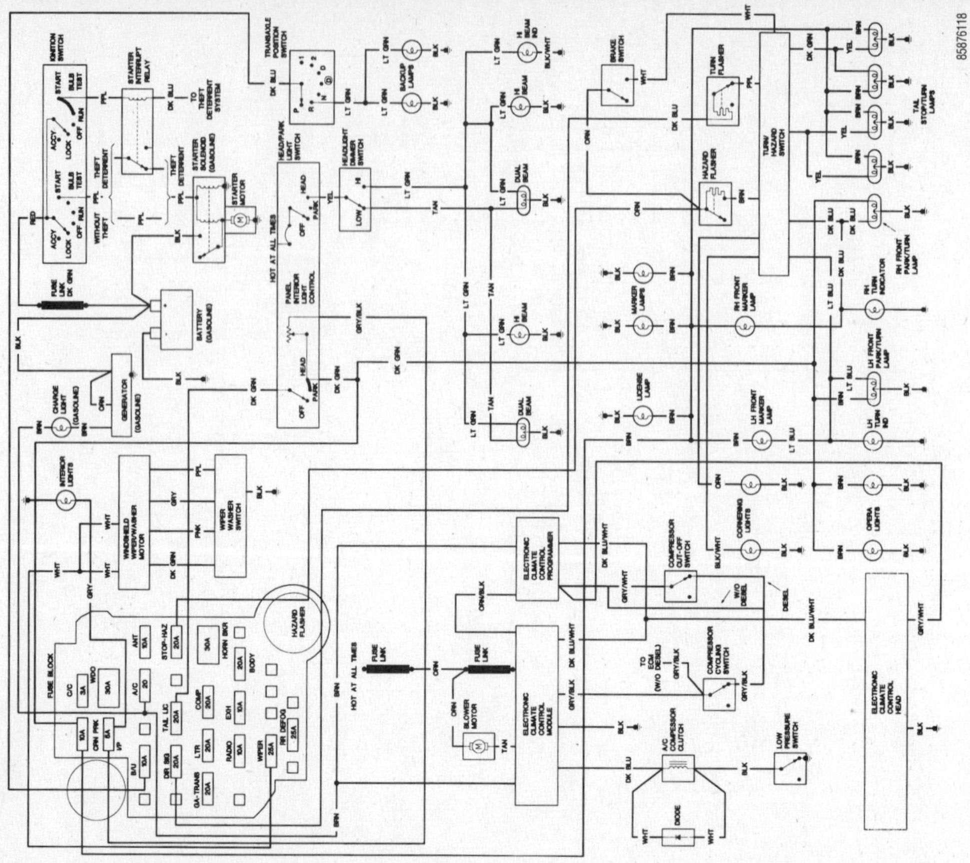

Fig. 122 1984 Cadillac DeVille and Fleetwood

Fig. 121 1984 Cadillac DeVille and Fleetwood

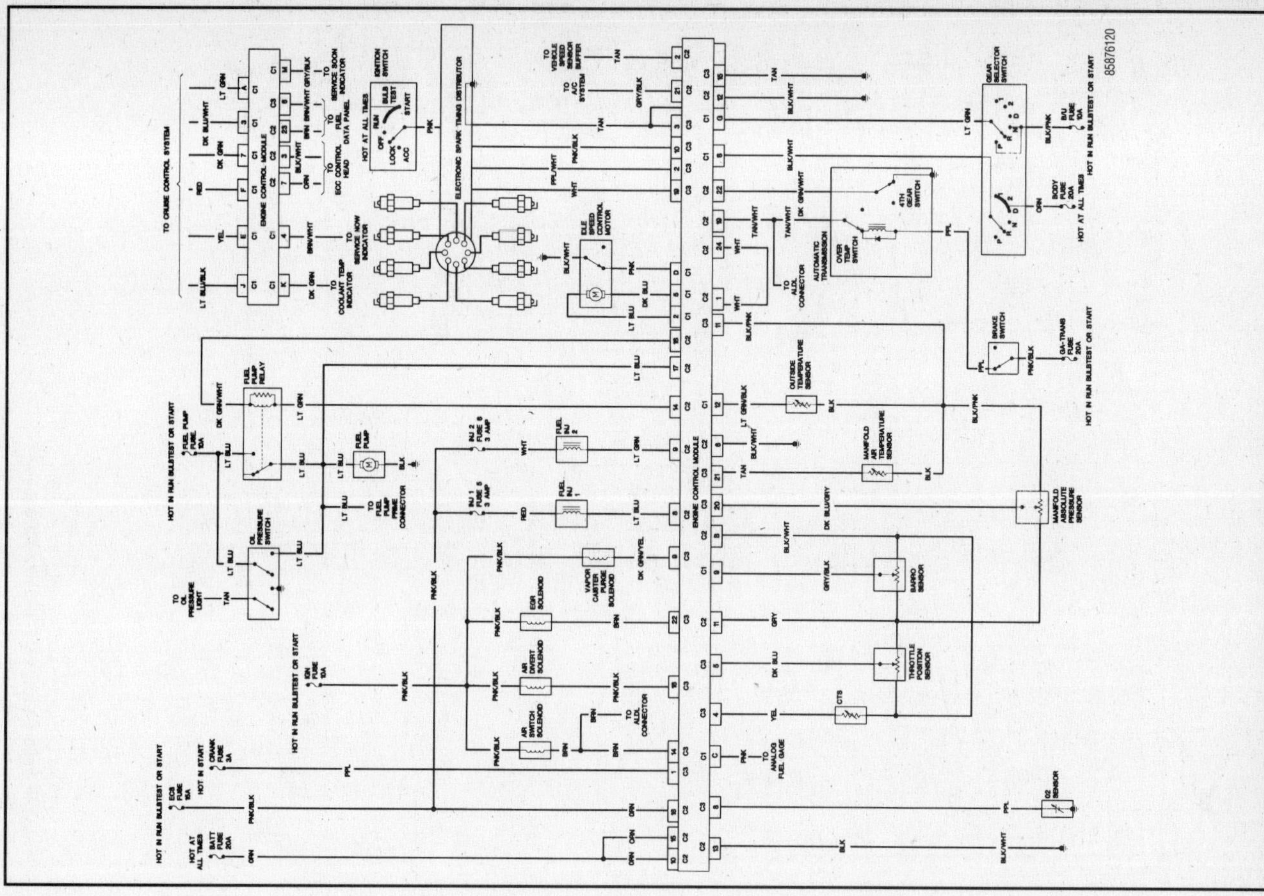

Fig. 124 1984 Cadillac DeVille and Fleetwood (V8 engine)

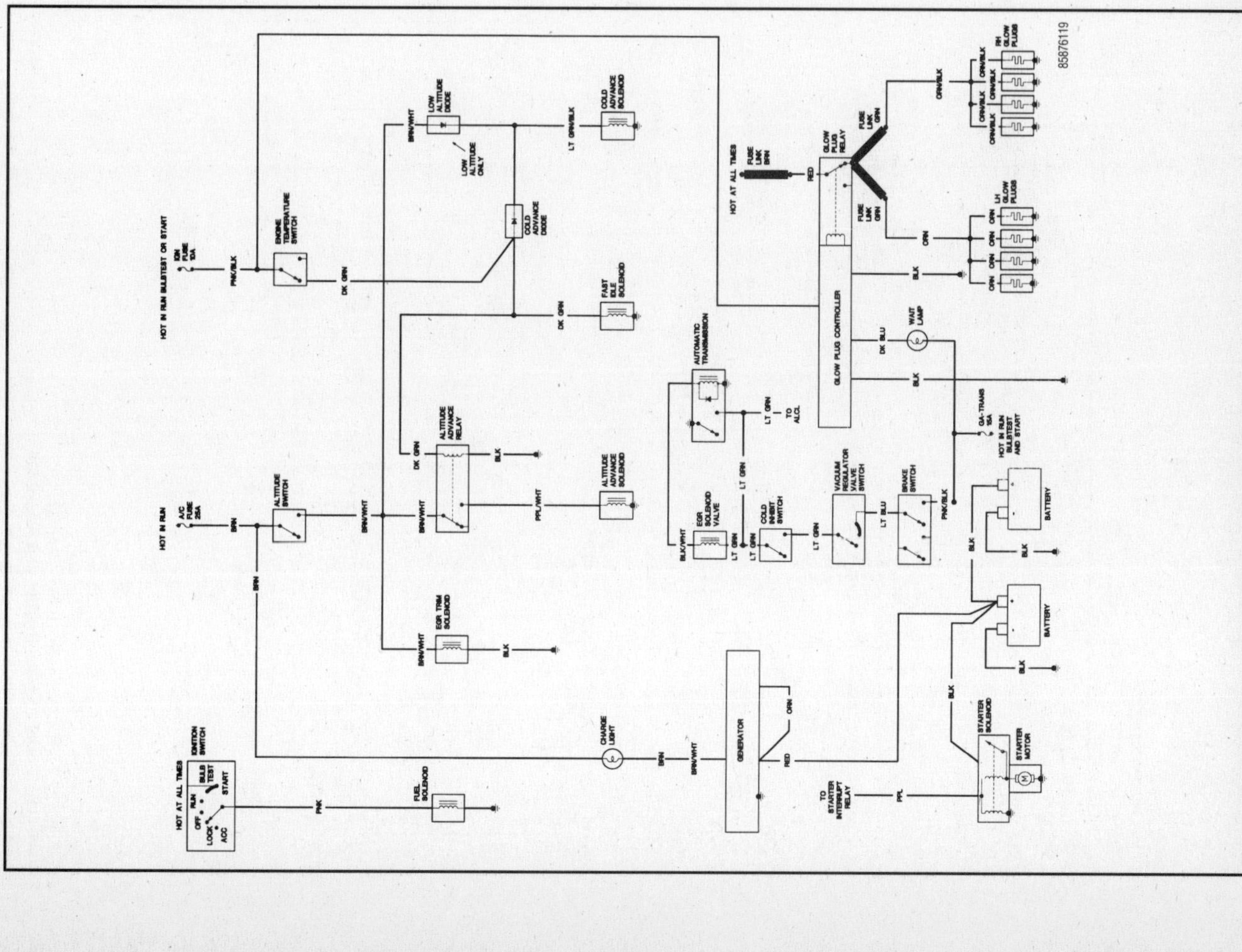

Fig. 123 1984 Cadillac DeVille and Fleetwood (diesel)

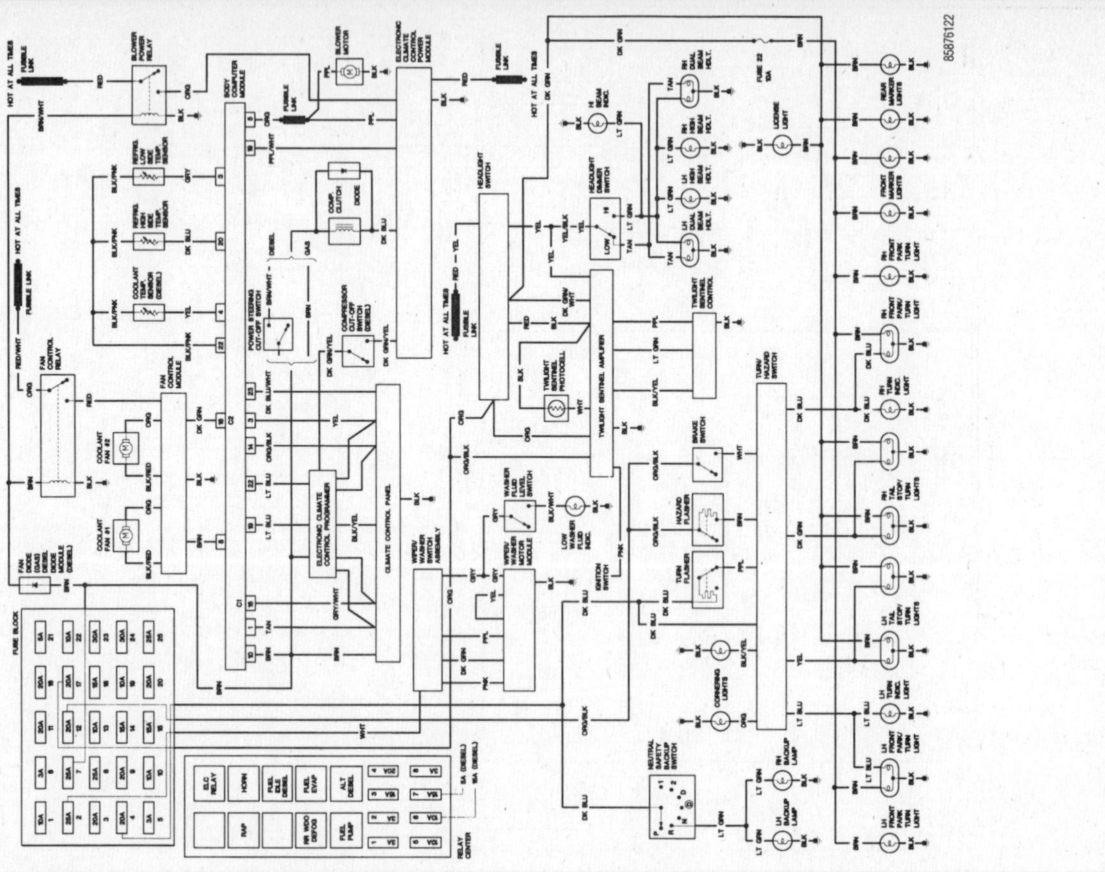

Fig. 126 1985 Cadillac DeVille and Fleetwood

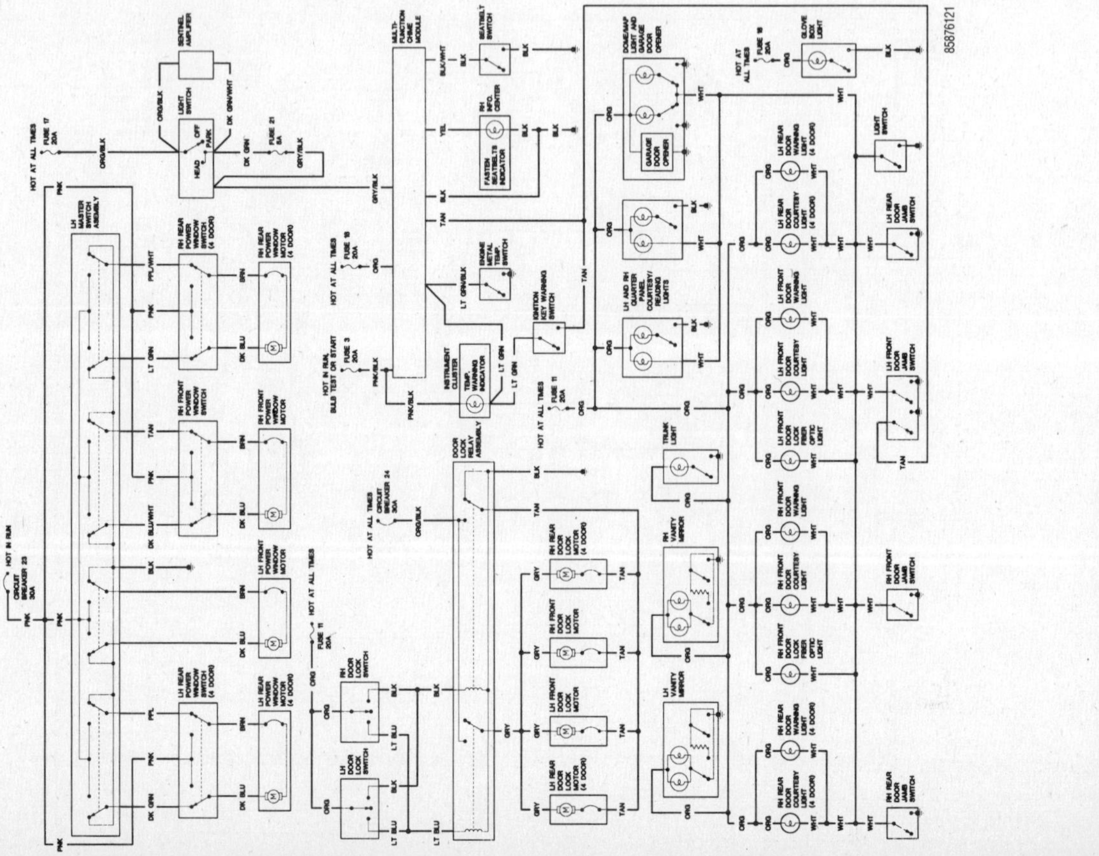

Fig. 125 1985 Cadillac DeVille and Fleetwood

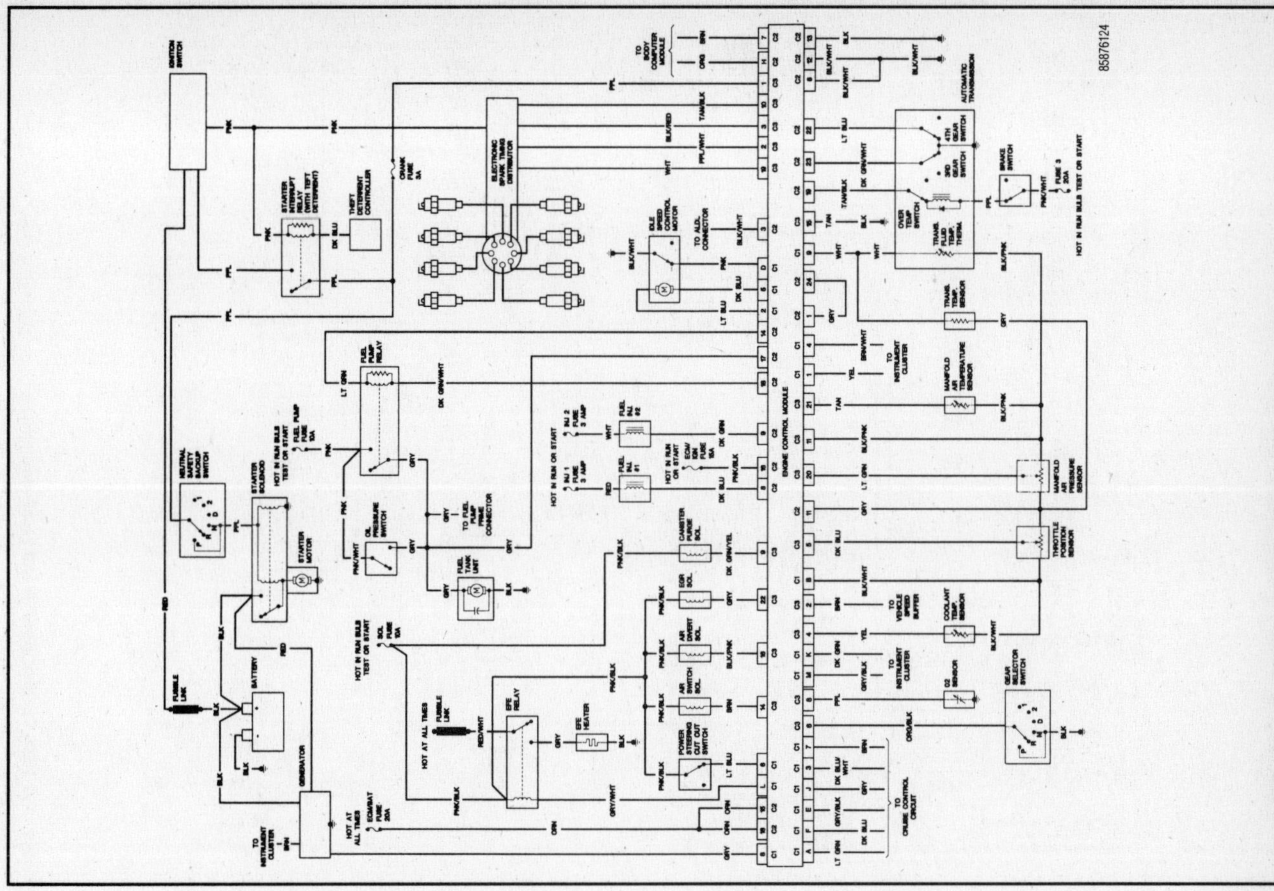

Fig. 128 1985 Cadillac DeVille and Fleetwood (gasoline engine)

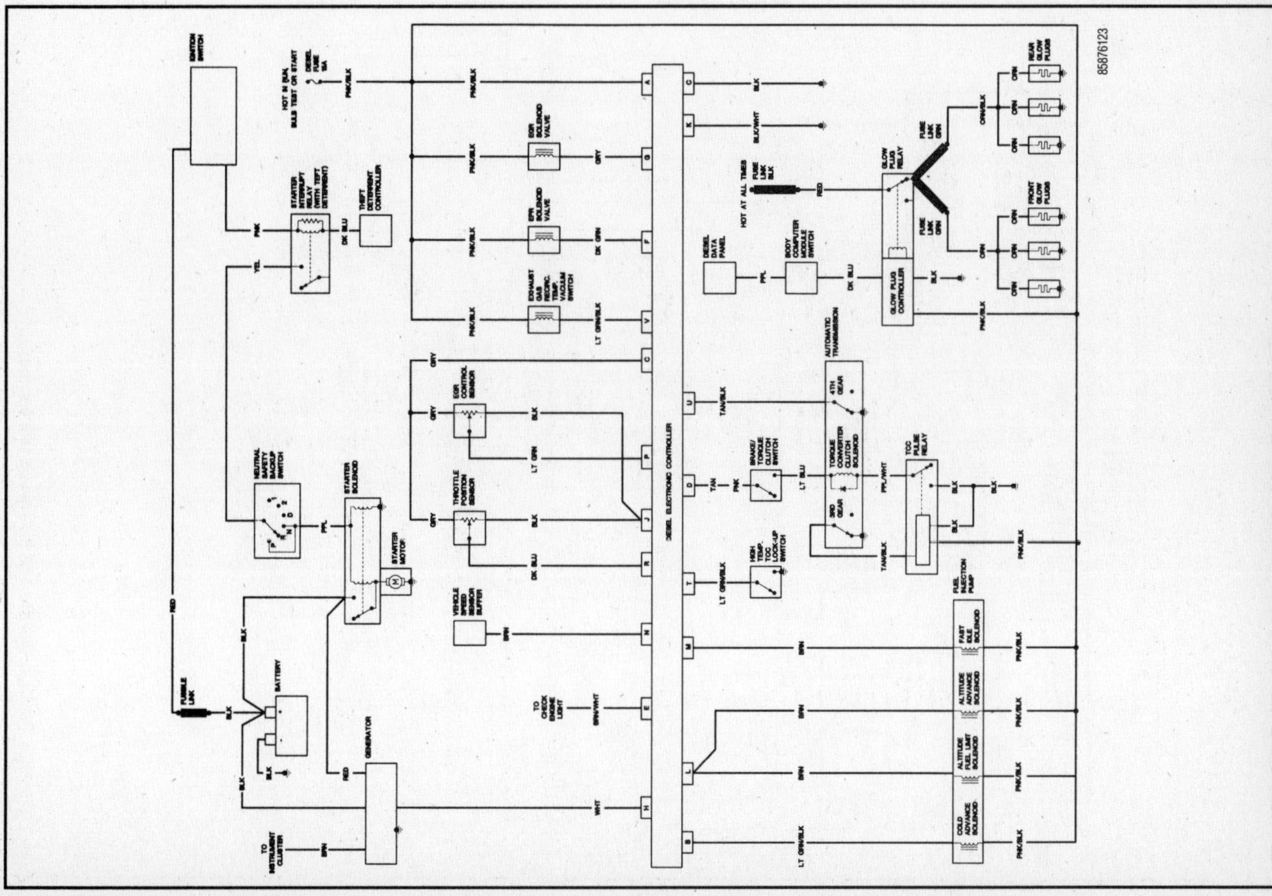

Fig. 127 1985 Cadillac DeVille and Fleetwood (diesel engine)

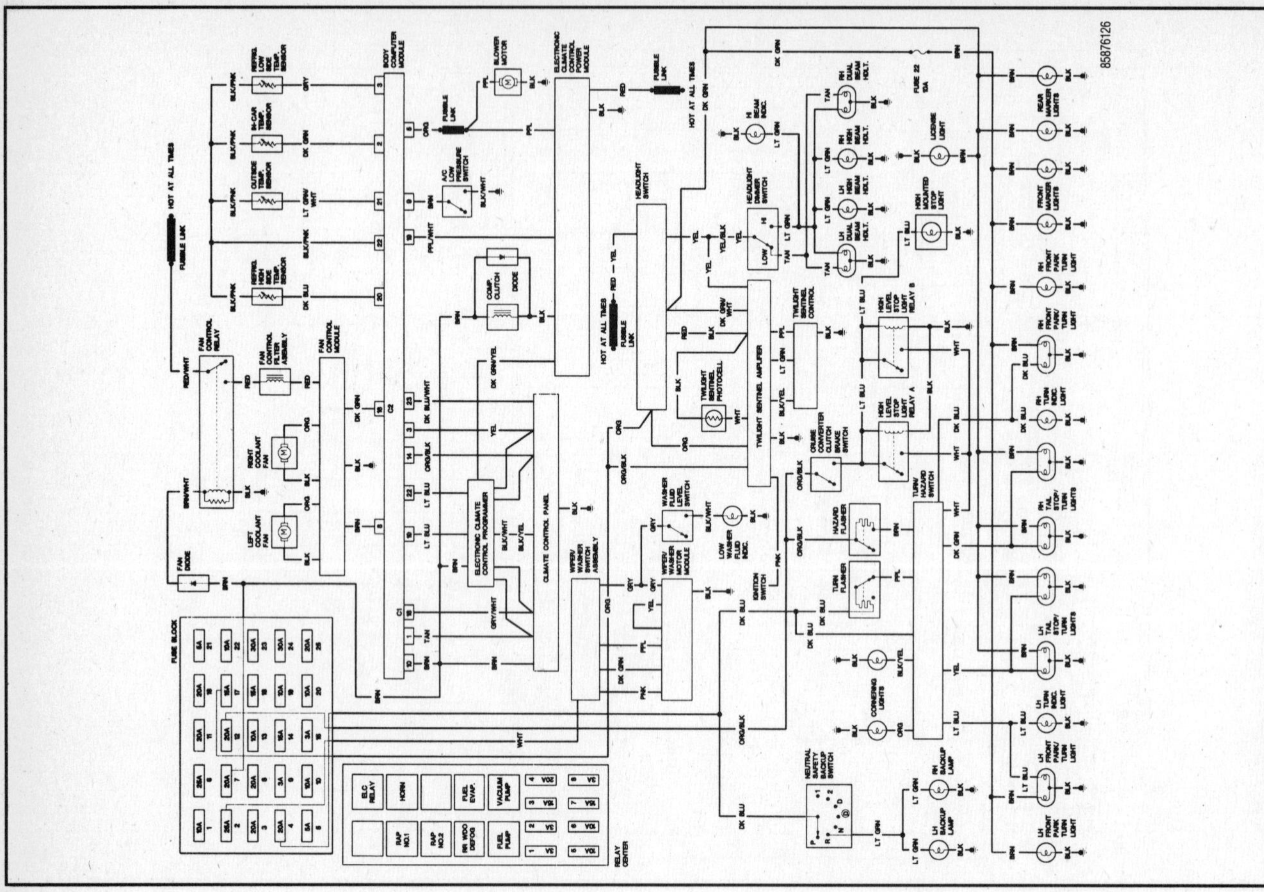

Fig. 130 1986 Cadillac DeVille and Fleetwood

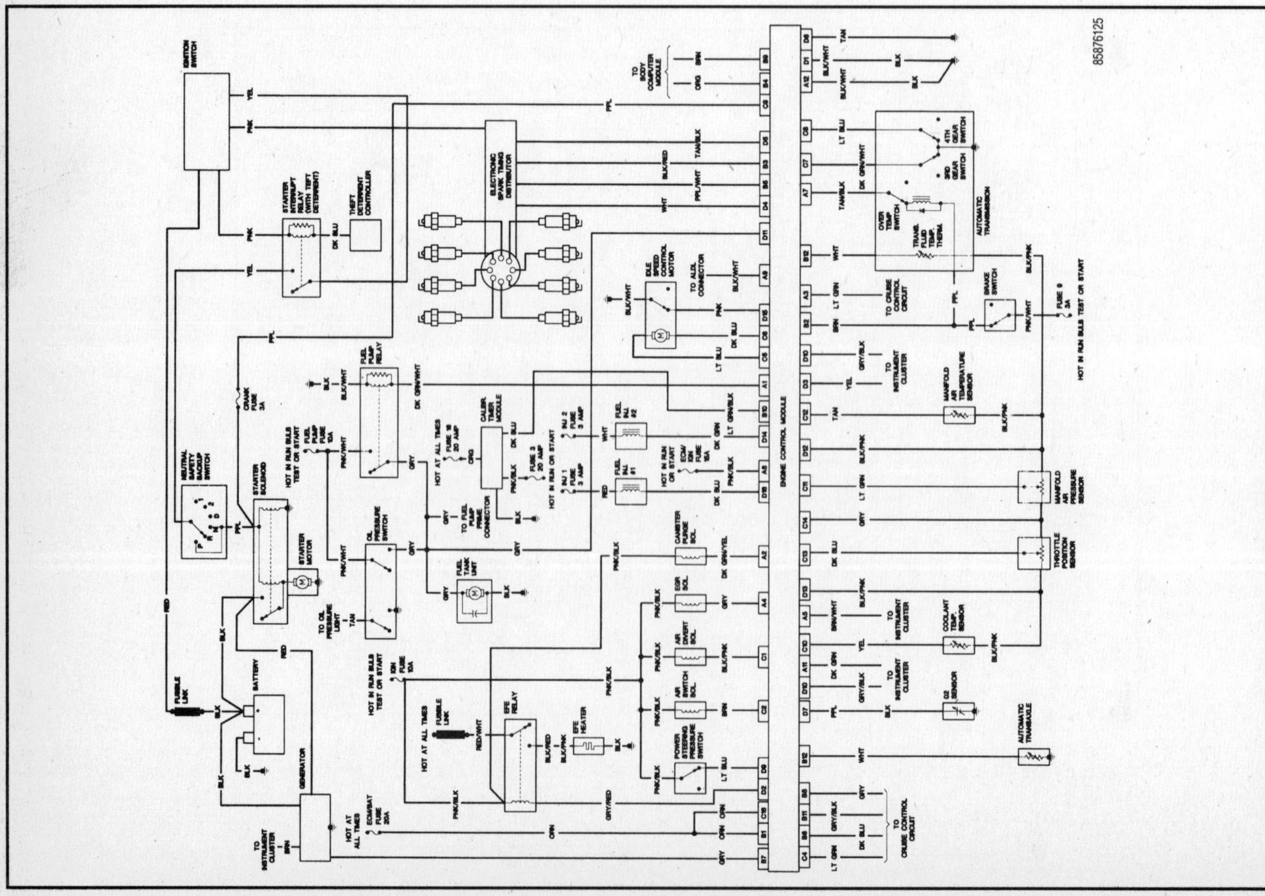

Fig. 129 1986 Cadillac DeVille and Fleetwood (V8 engine)

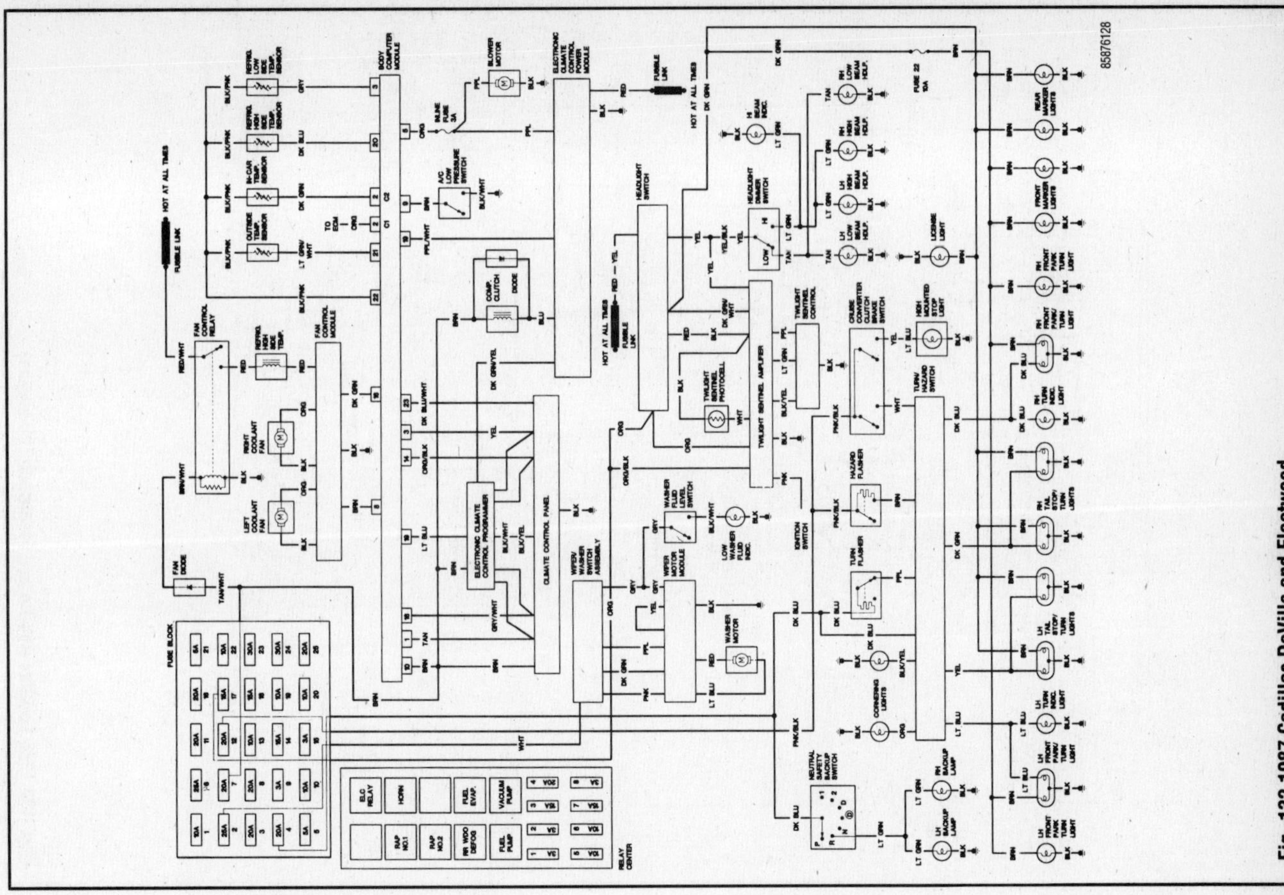

Fig. 132 1987 Cadillac DeVille and Fleetwood

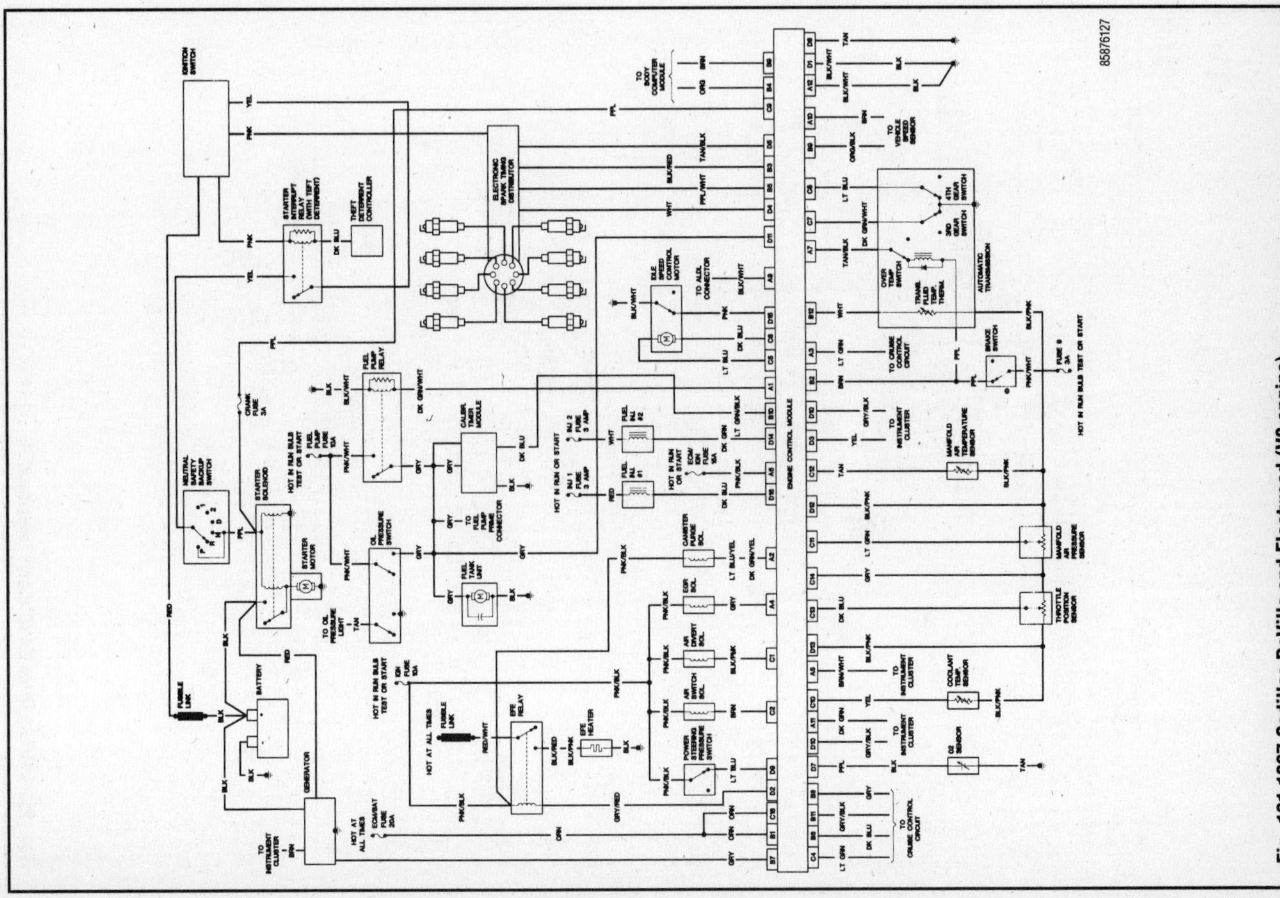

Fig. 131 1987 Cadillac DeVille and Fleetwood (V8 engine)

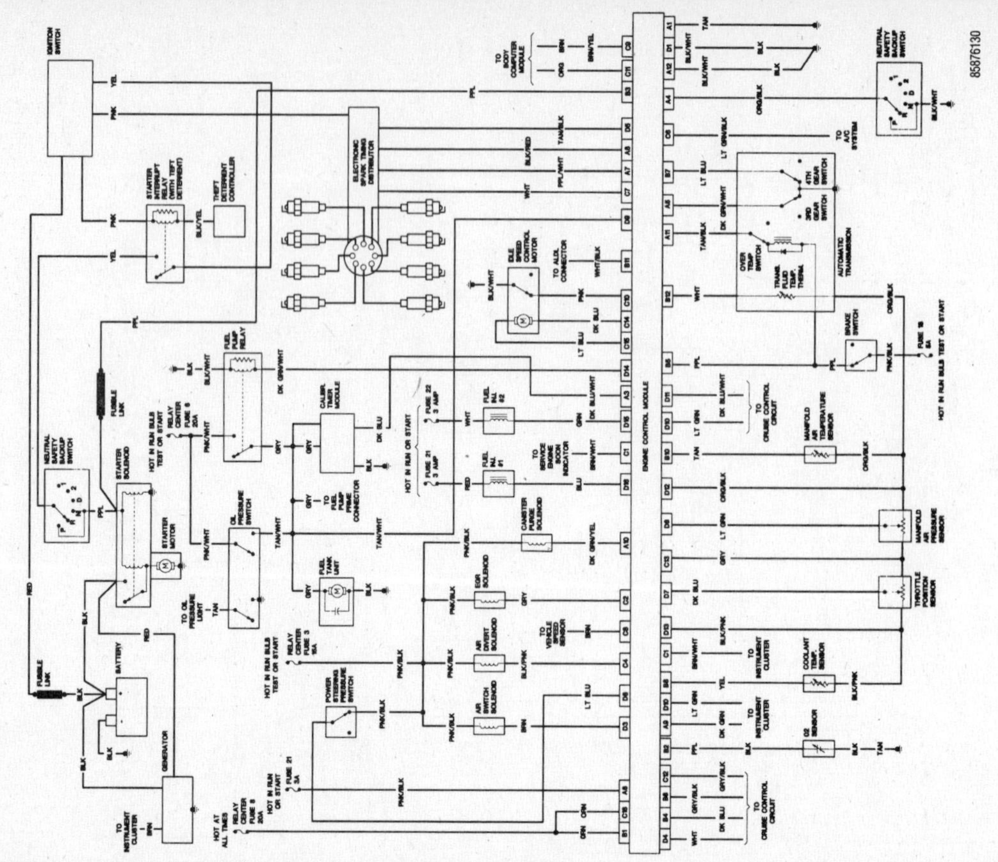

Fig. 134 1988 Cadillac DeVille and Fleetwood (V8 engine)

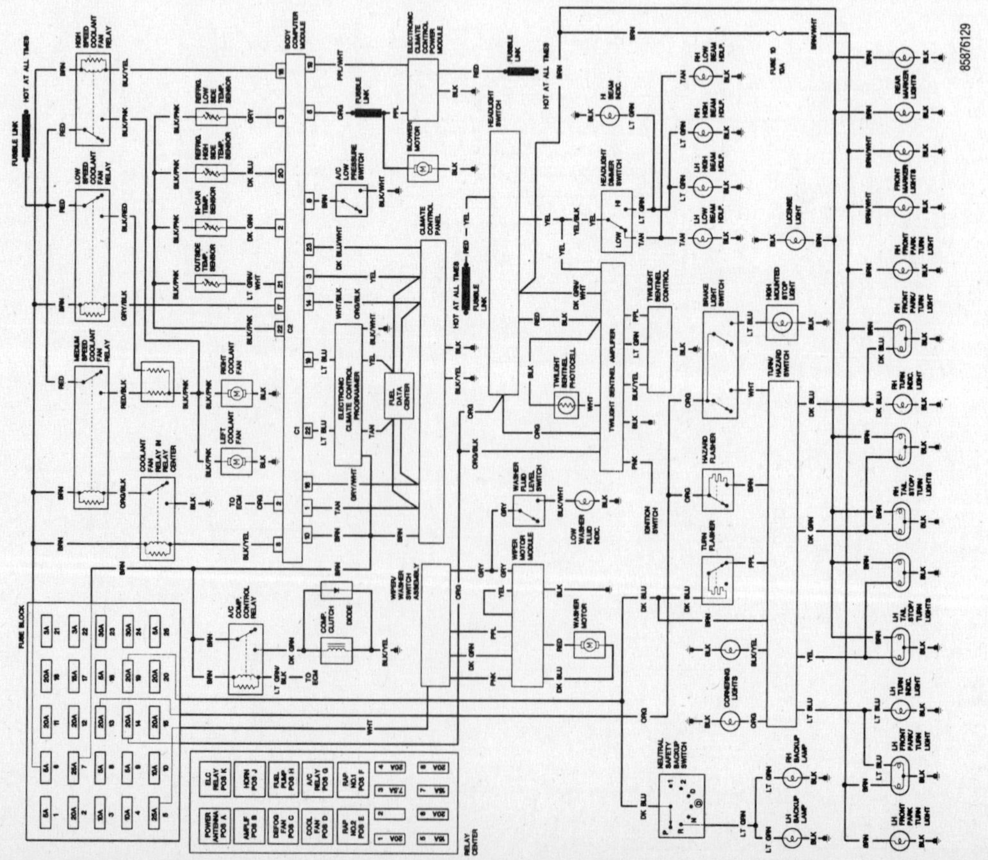

Fig. 133 1988 Cadillac DeVille and Fleetwood

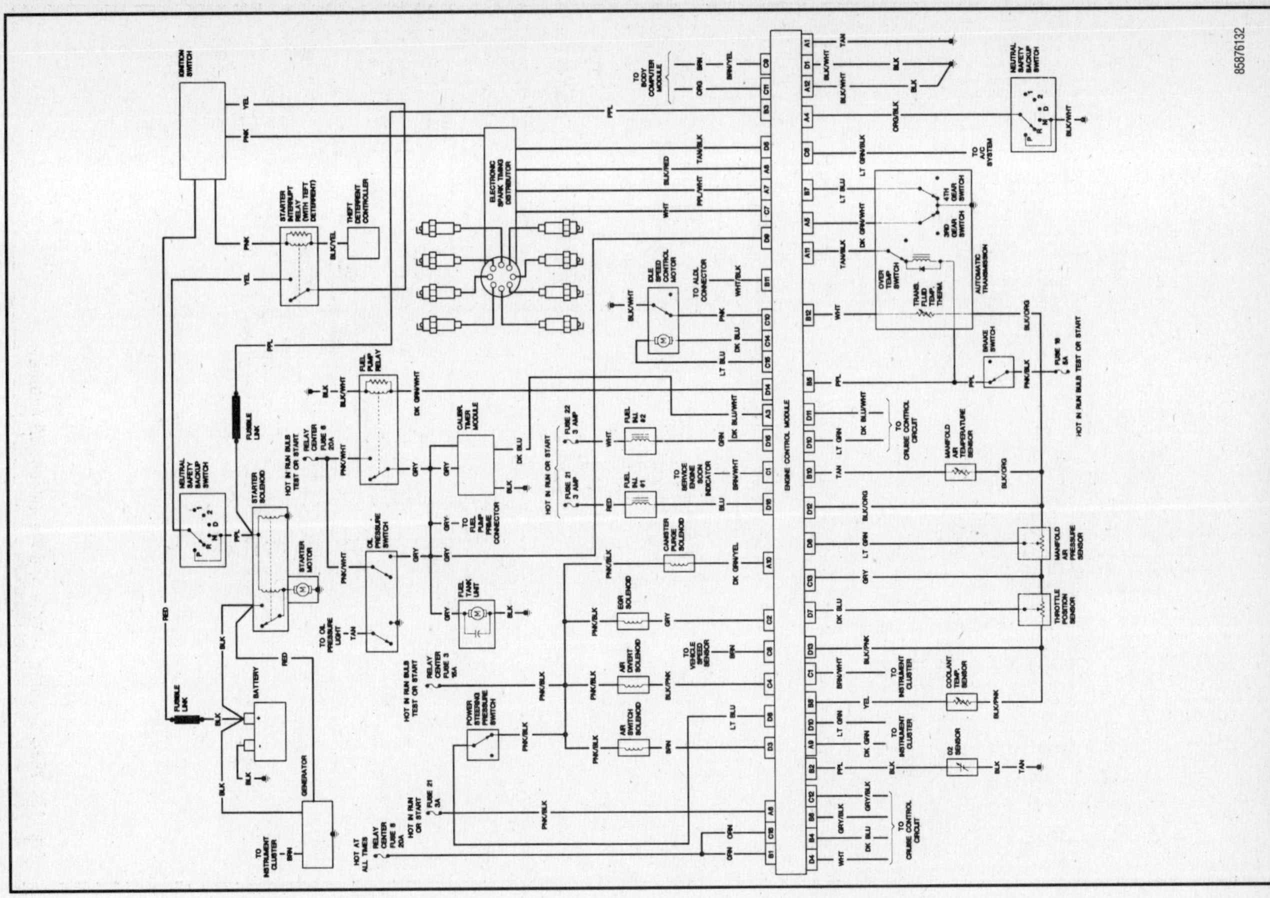

Fig. 136 1989 Cadillac DeVille and Fleetwood (V8 engine)

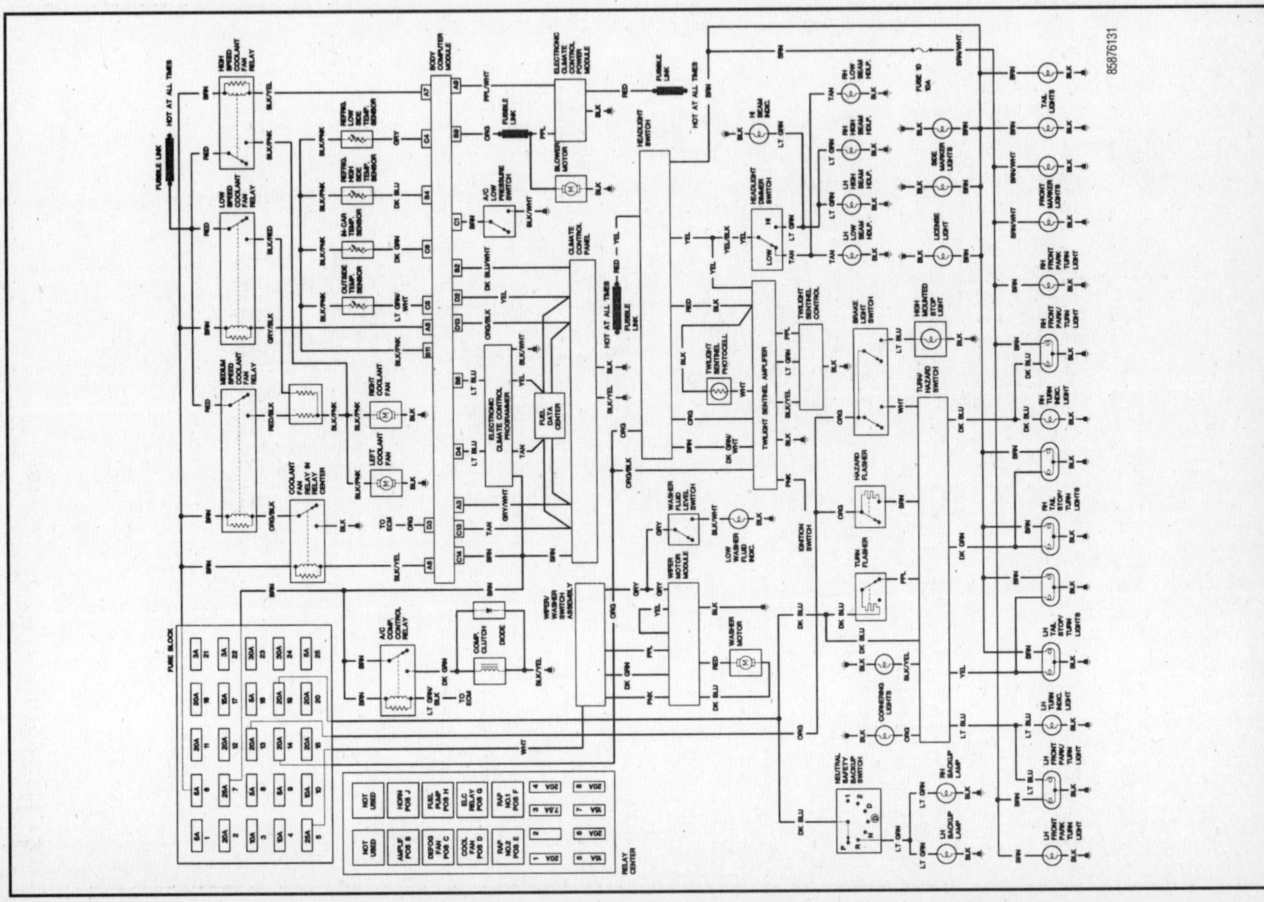

Fig. 135 1989 Cadillac DeVille and Fleetwood

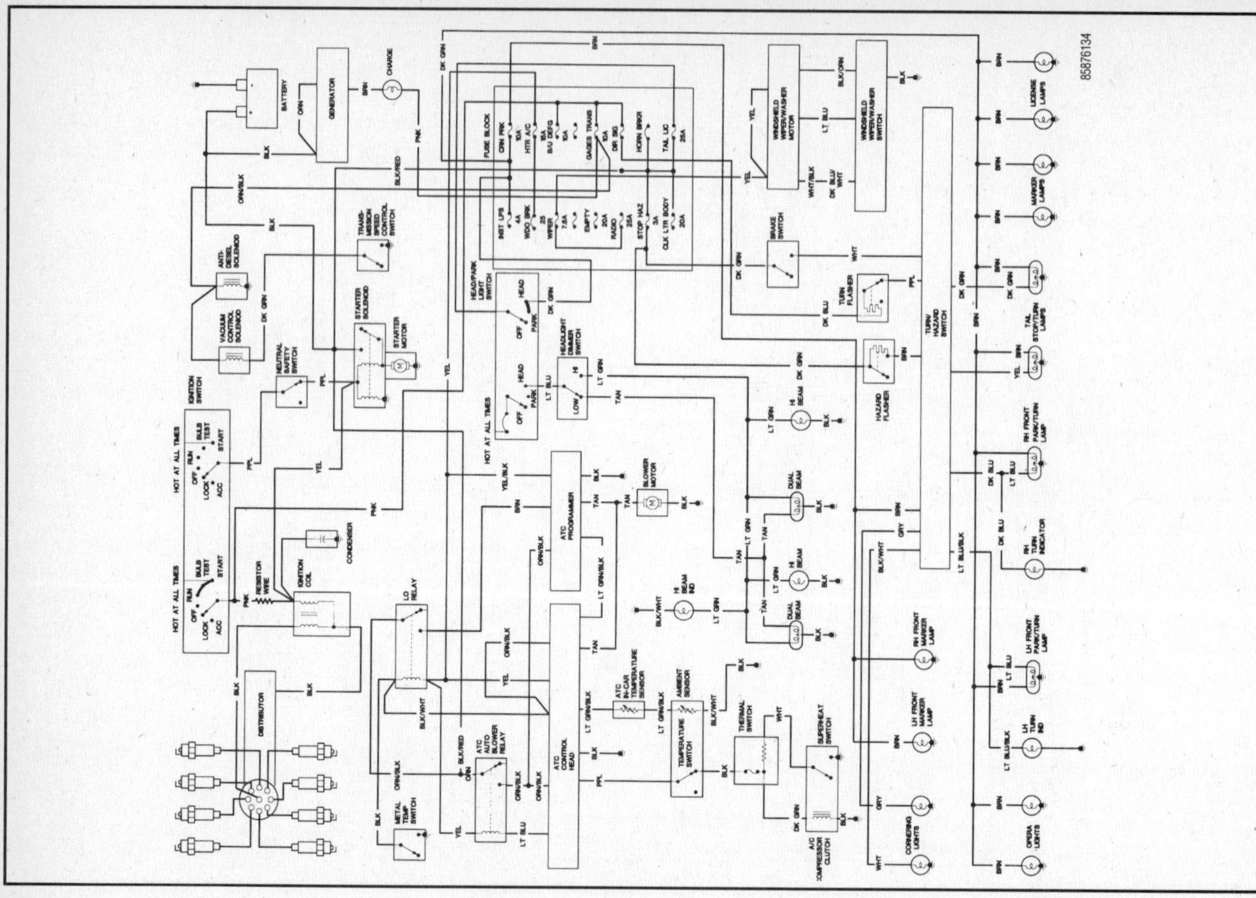

Fig. 138 1971-72 Cadillac Eldorado

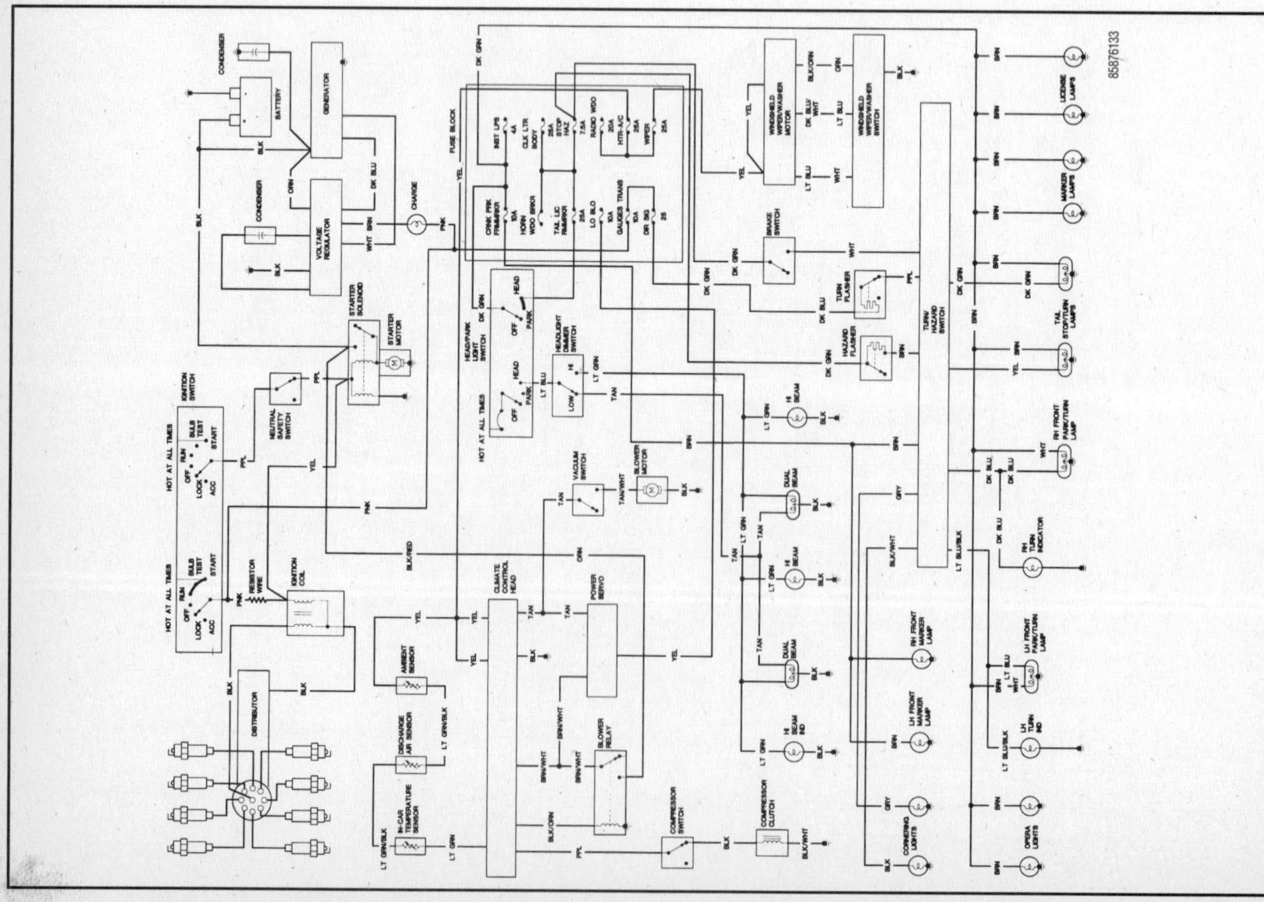

Fig. 137 1967-70 Cadillac Eldorado

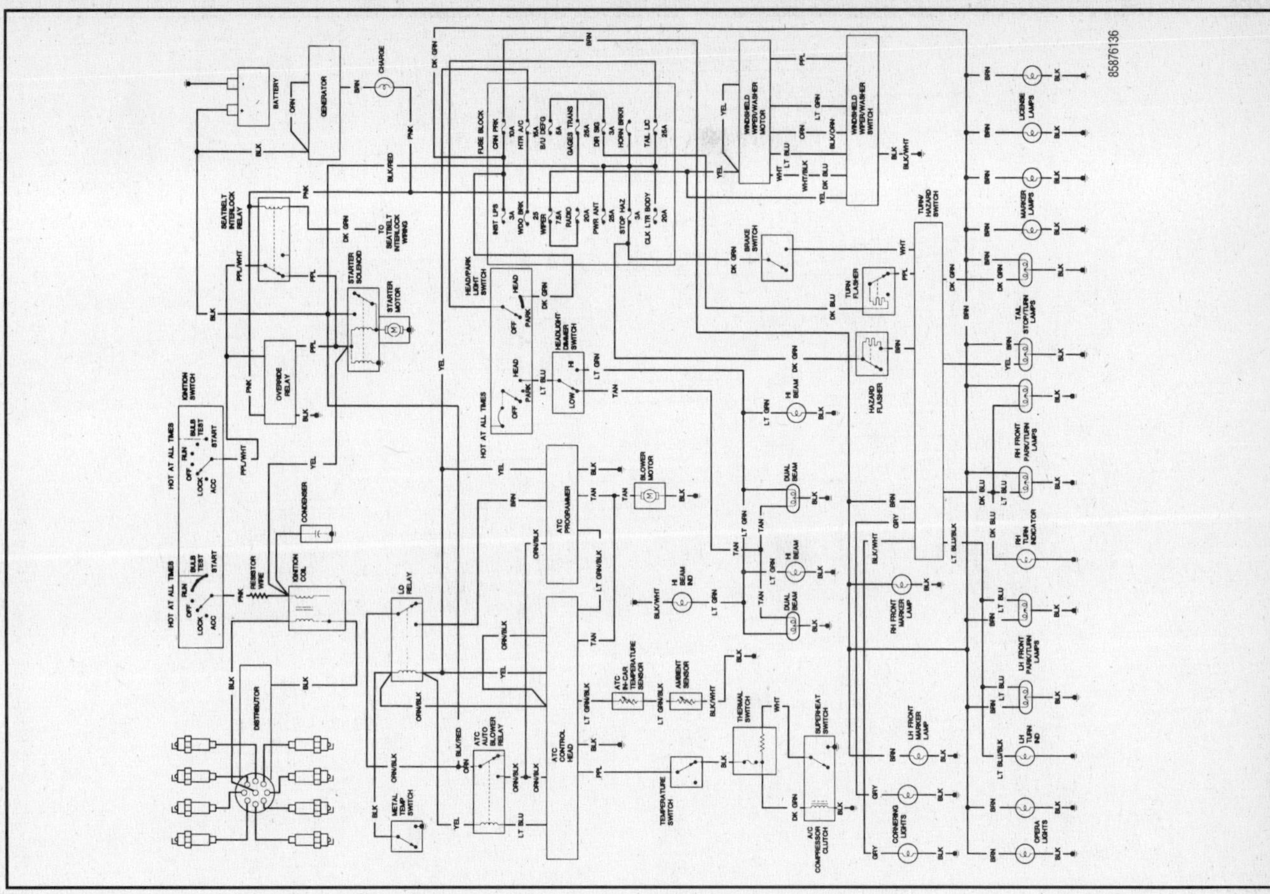

Fig. 140 1974 Cadillac Eldorado

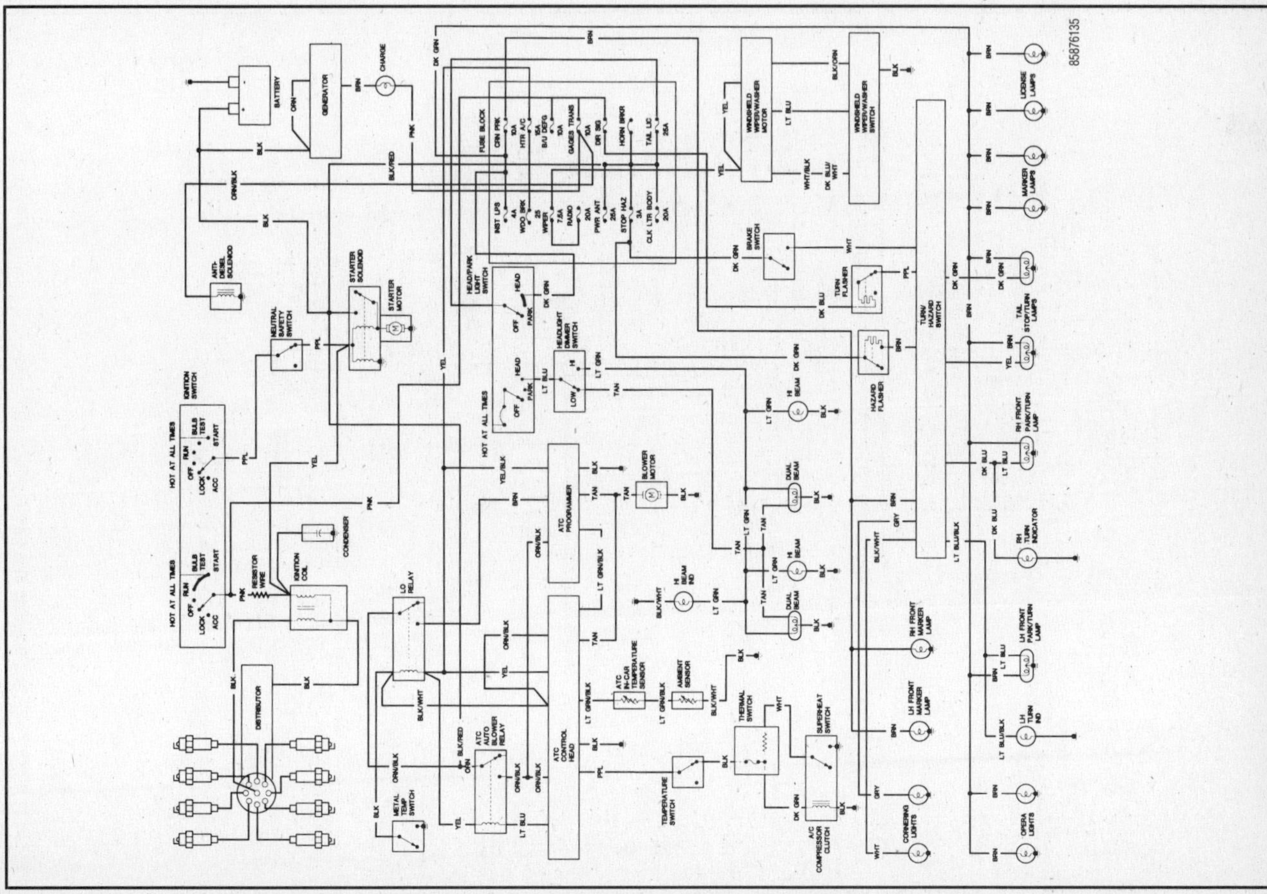

Fig. 139 1973 Cadillac Eldorado

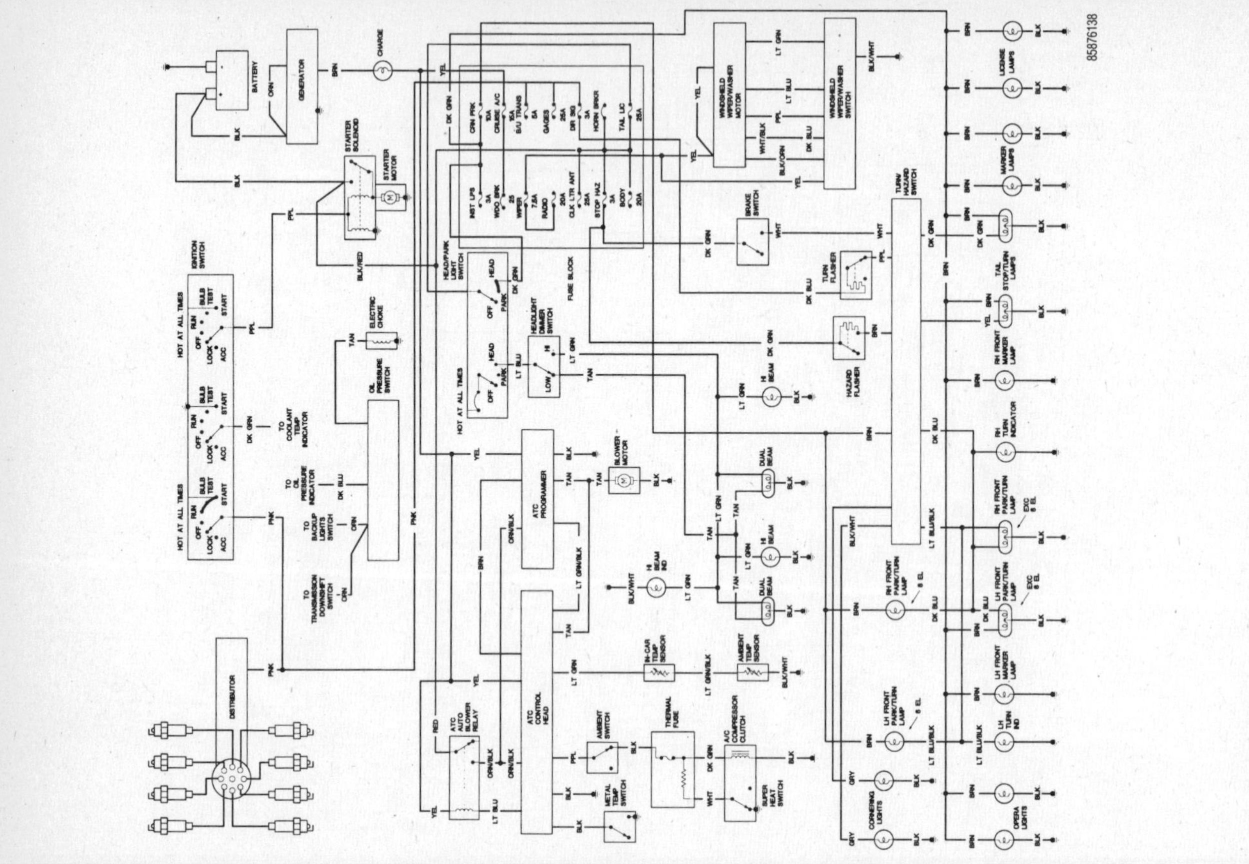

Fig. 142 1976 Cadillac Eldorado (V8 engine)

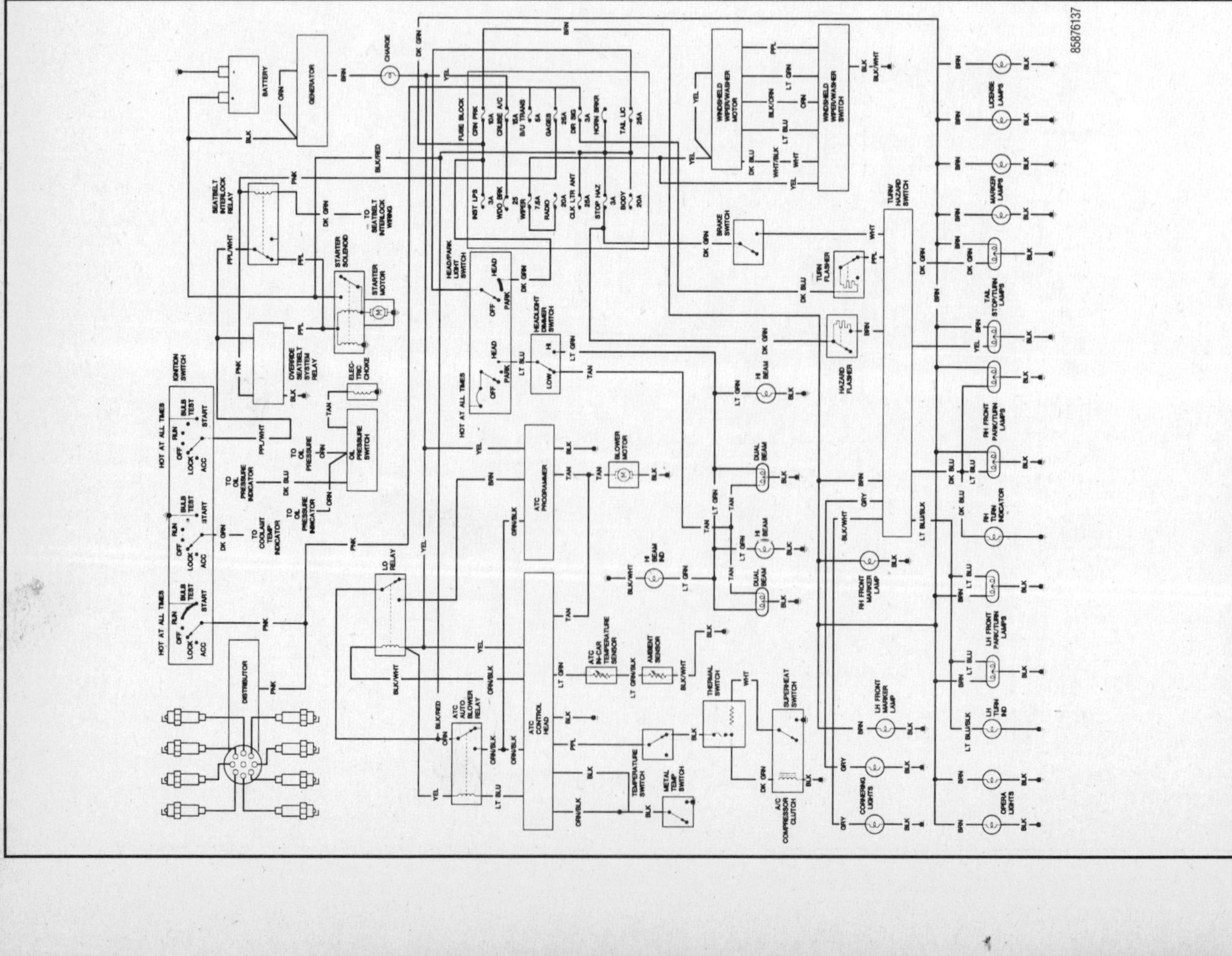

Fig. 141 1975 Cadillac Eldorado and Seville

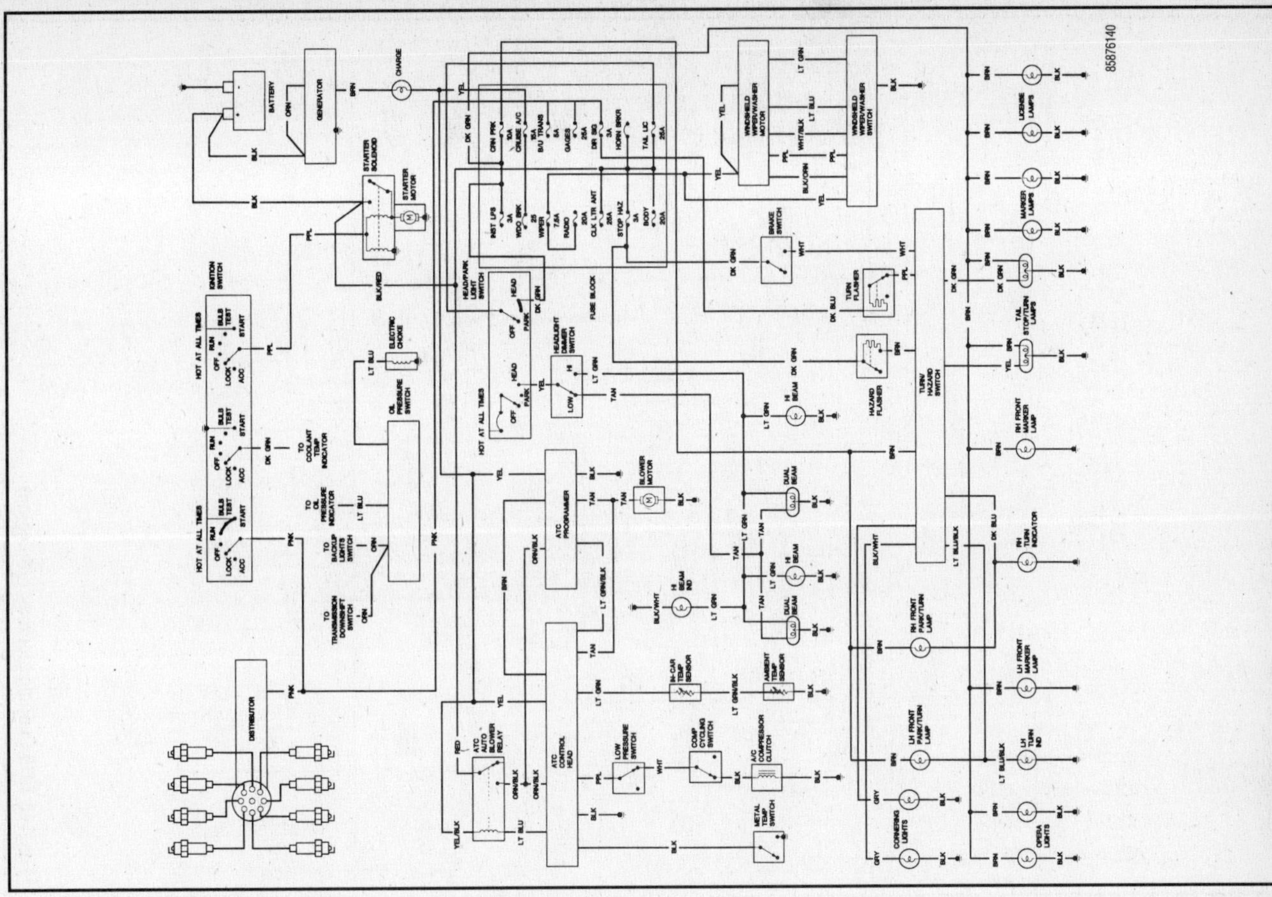

Fig. 144 1977 Cadillac Eldorado (V8 engine)

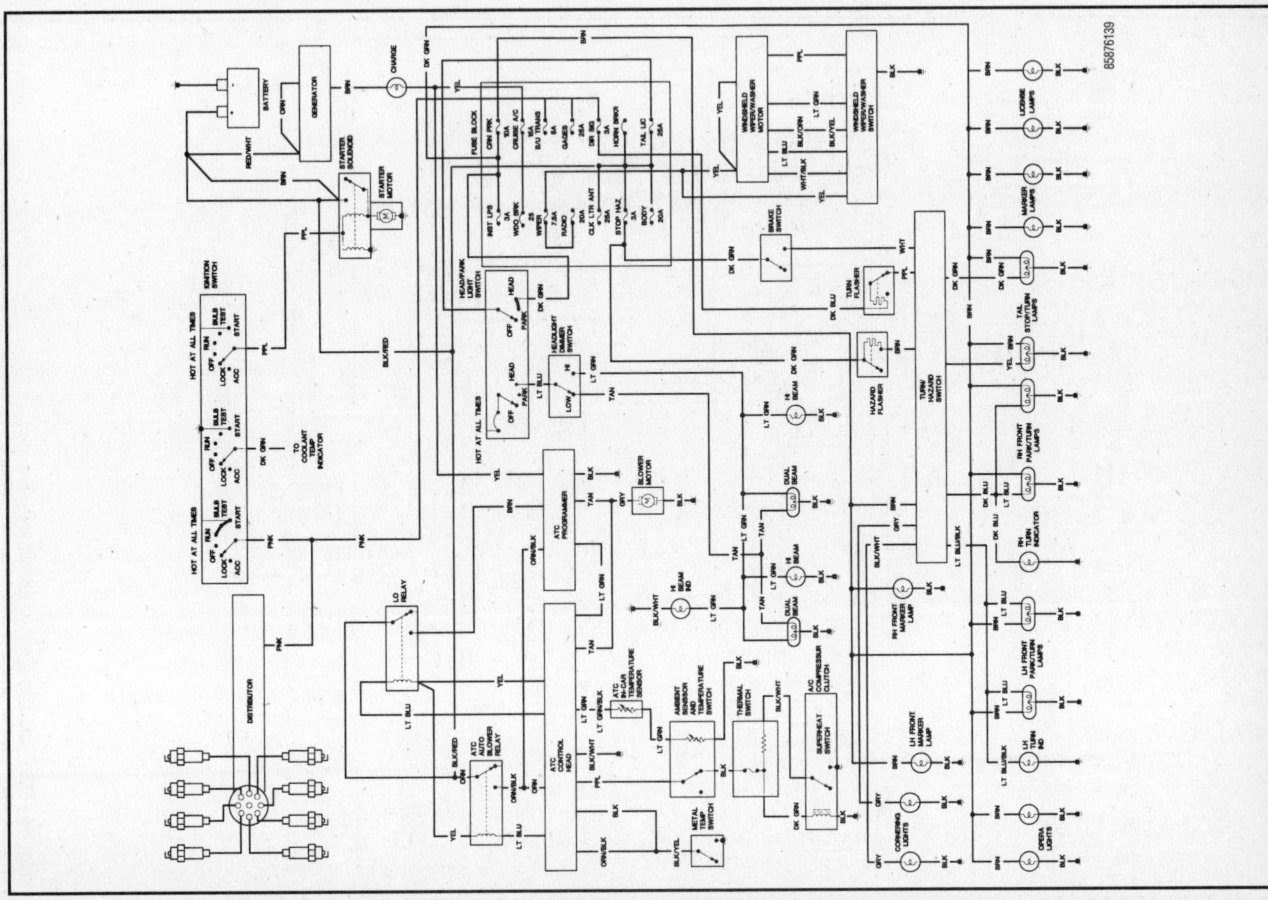

Fig. 143 1976 Cadillac Seville

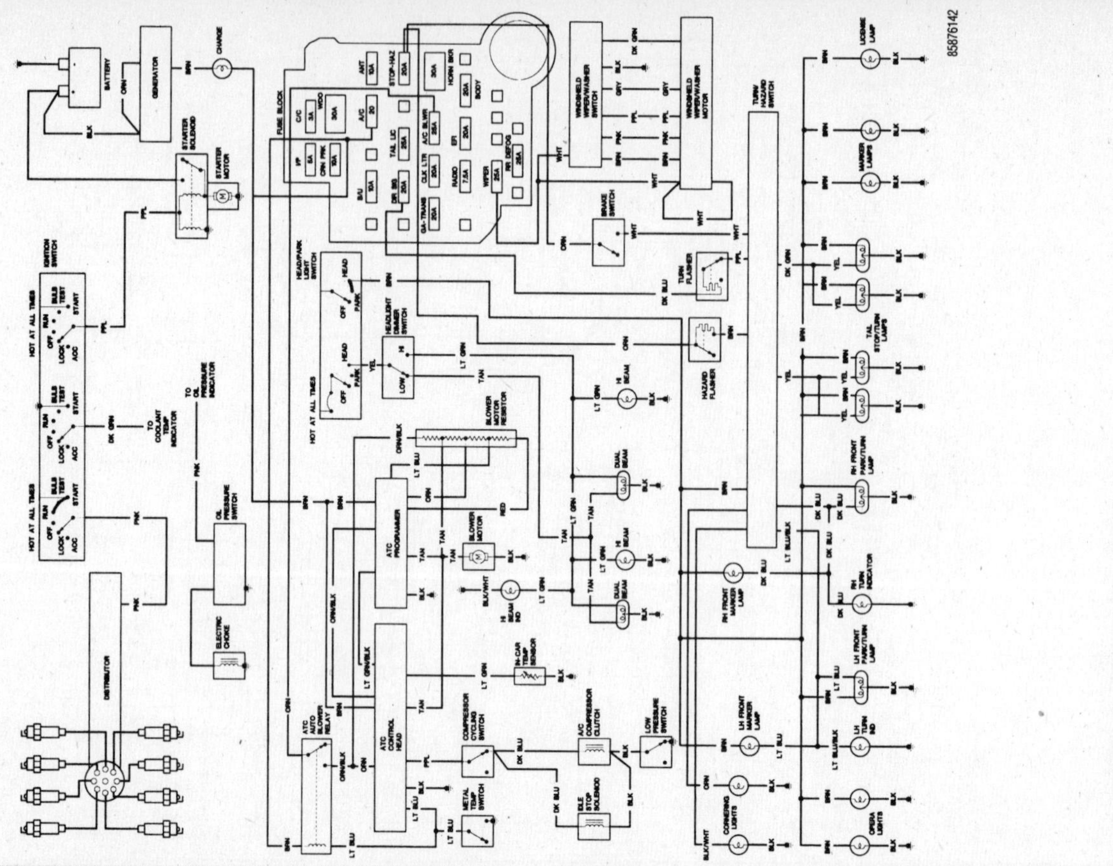

Fig. 146 1978 Cadillac Eldorado (V8 engine)

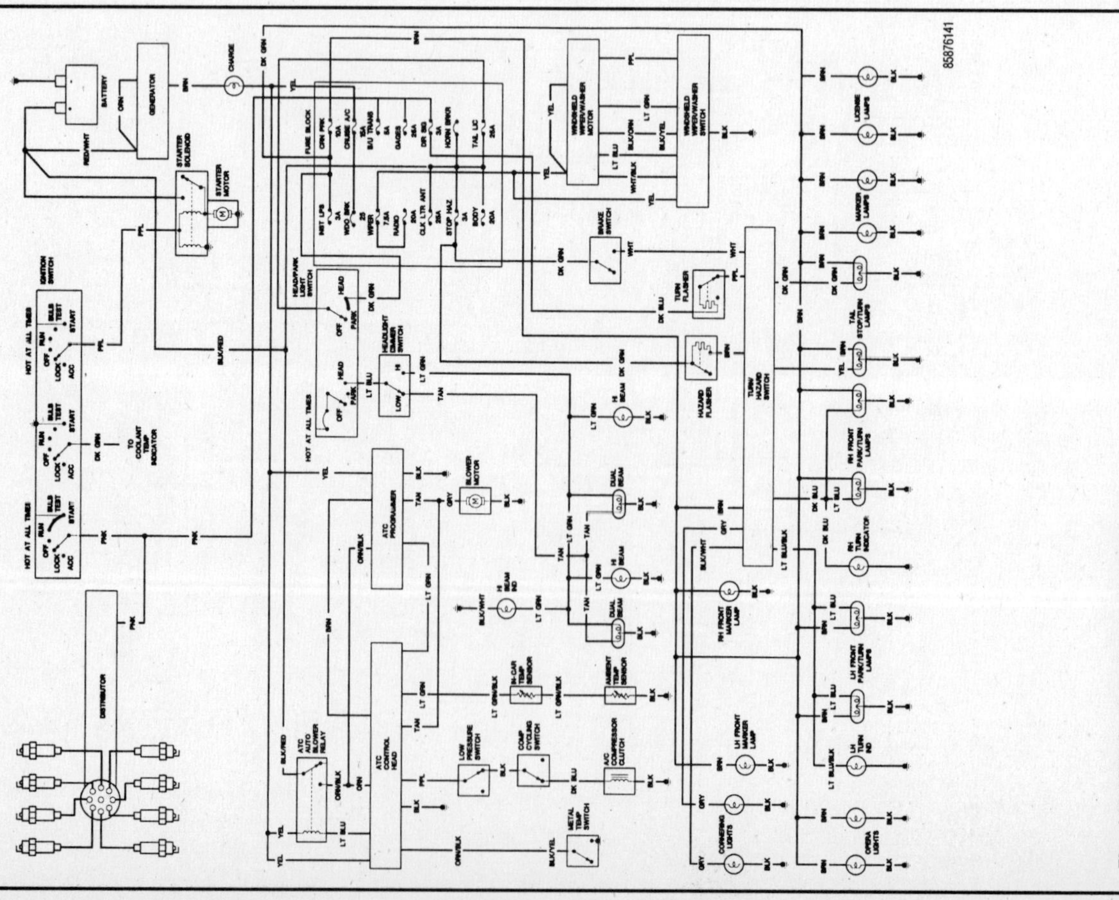

Fig. 145 1977 Cadillac Seville (V8 engine)

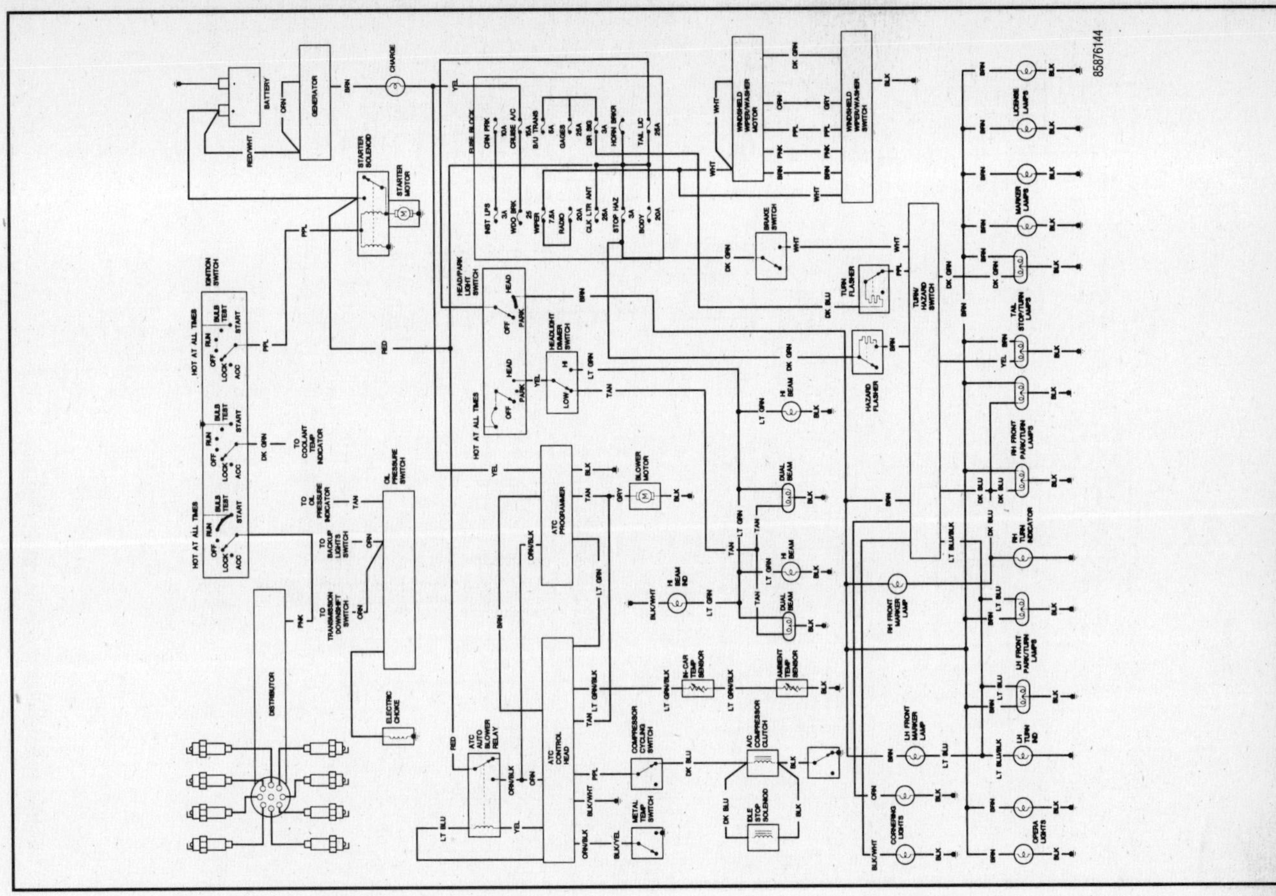

Fig. 148 1978 Cadillac Seville (V8 engine)

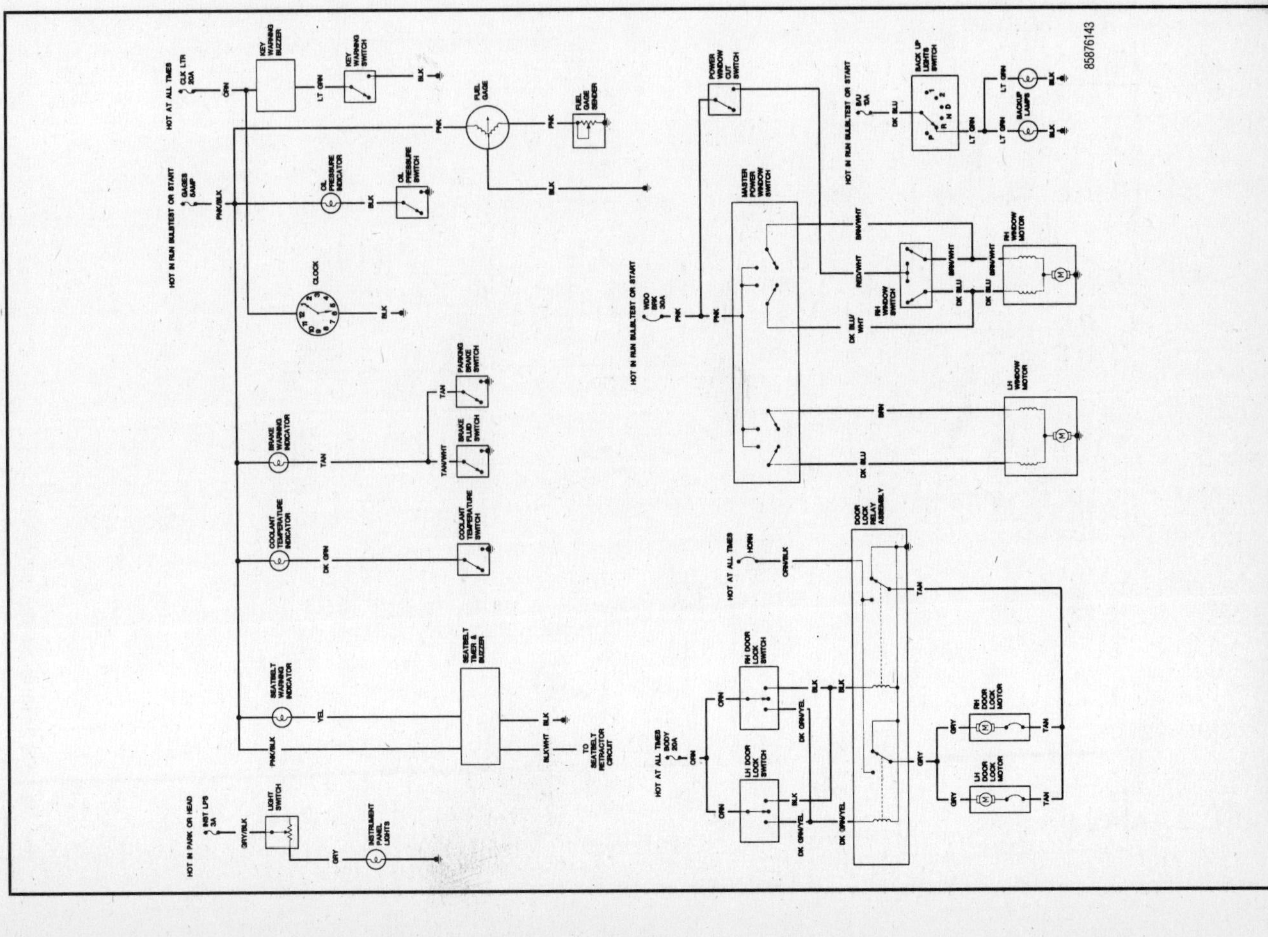

Fig. 147 1978 Cadillac Eldorado

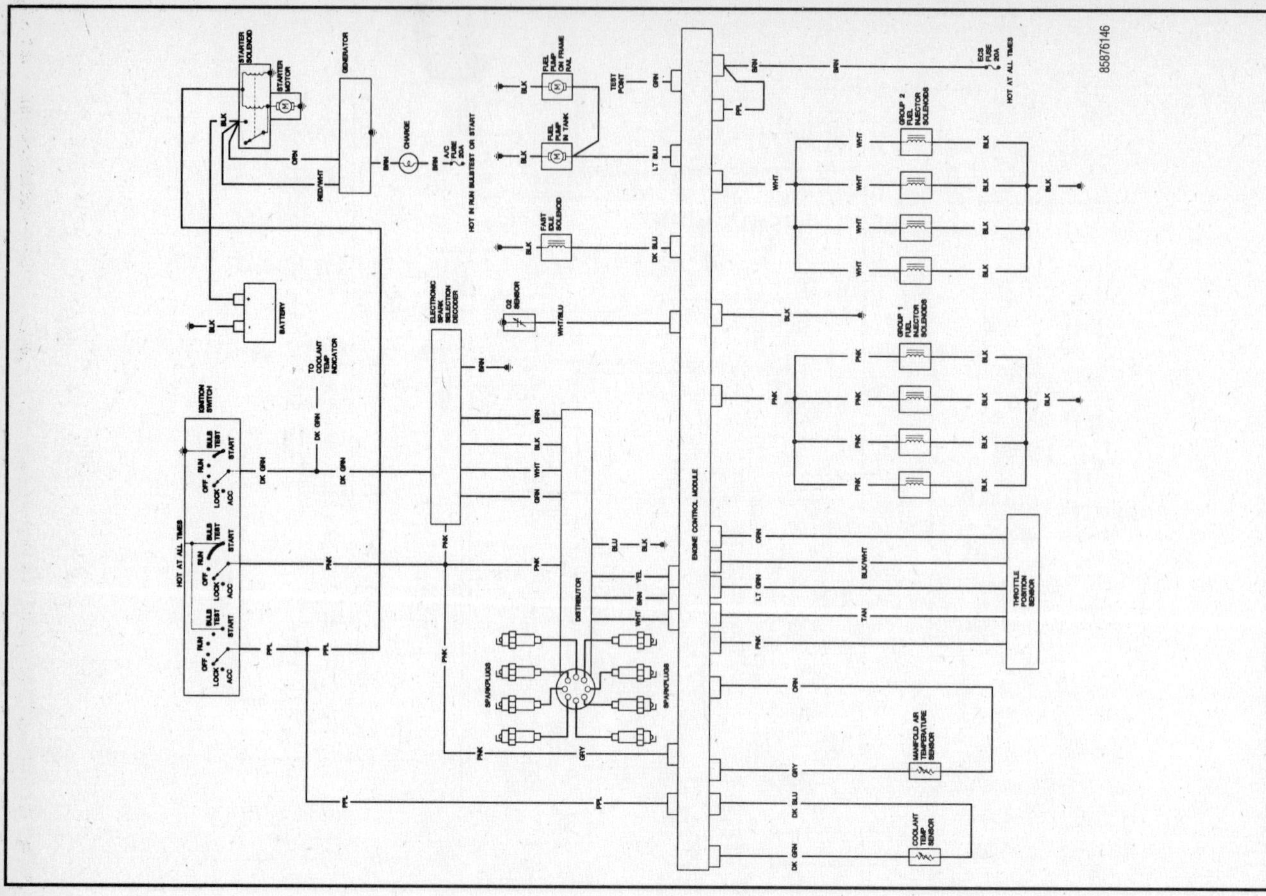

Fig. 150 1979 Cadillac Eldorado (V8 EFI engine)

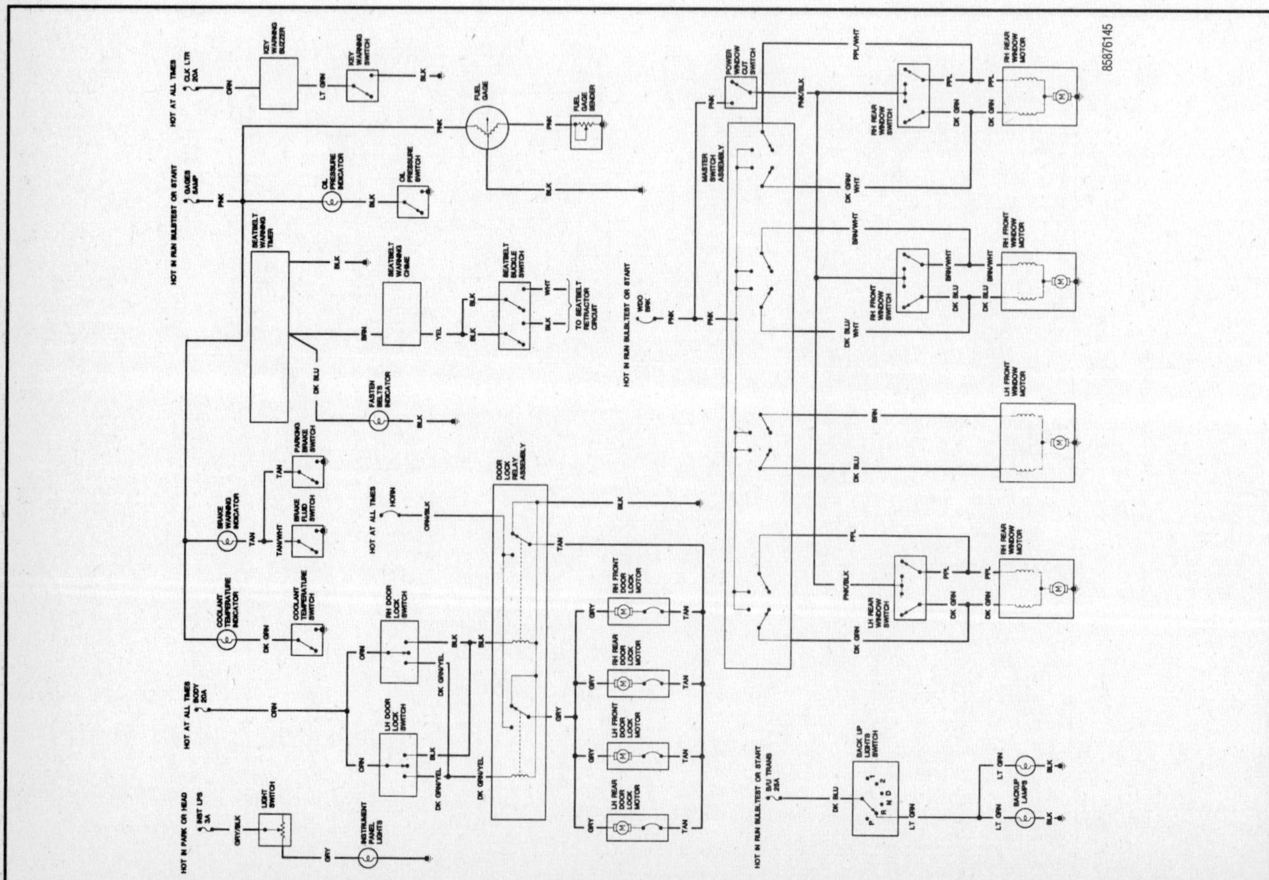

Fig. 149 1978 Cadillac Seville

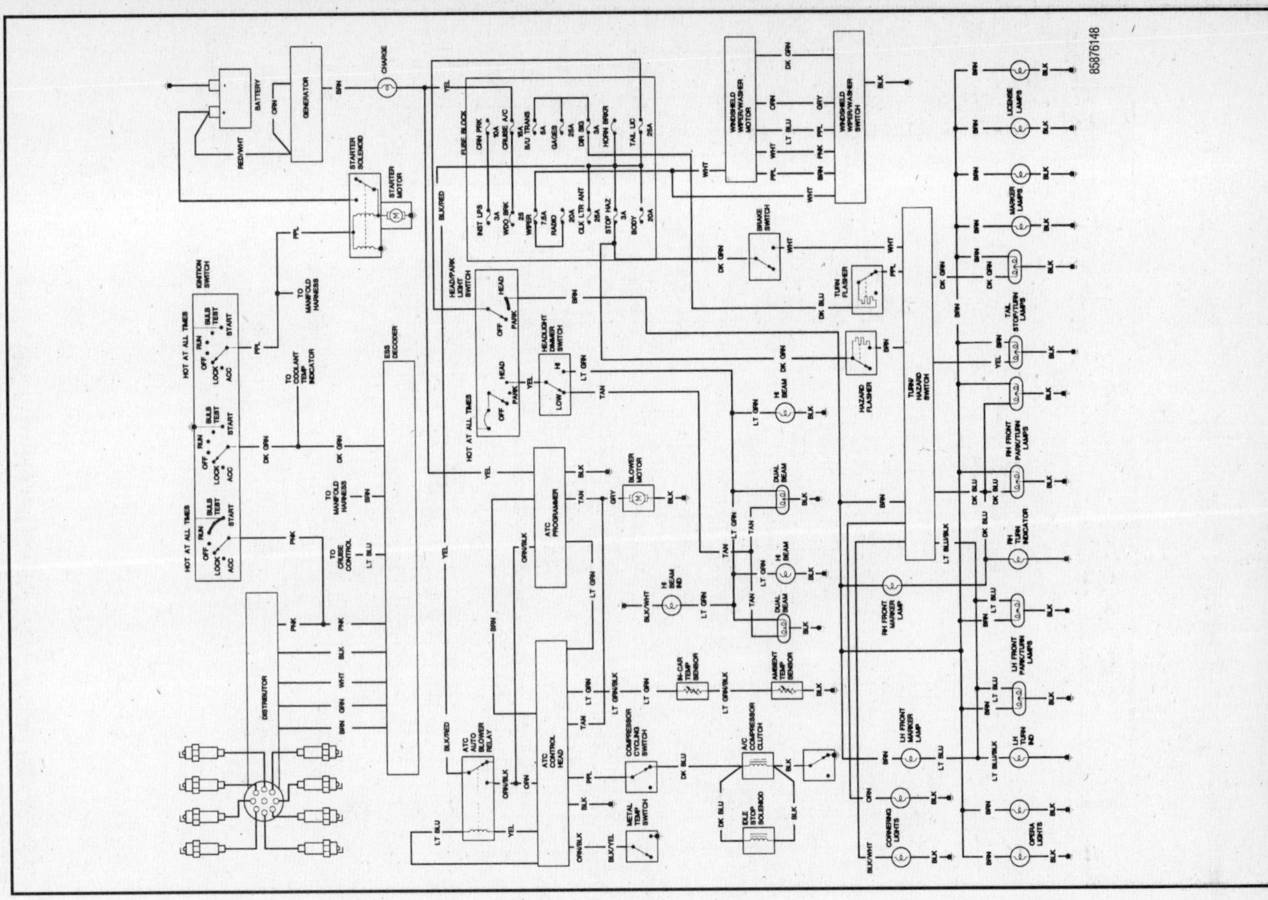

Fig. 152 1979 Cadillac Seville (V8 engine)

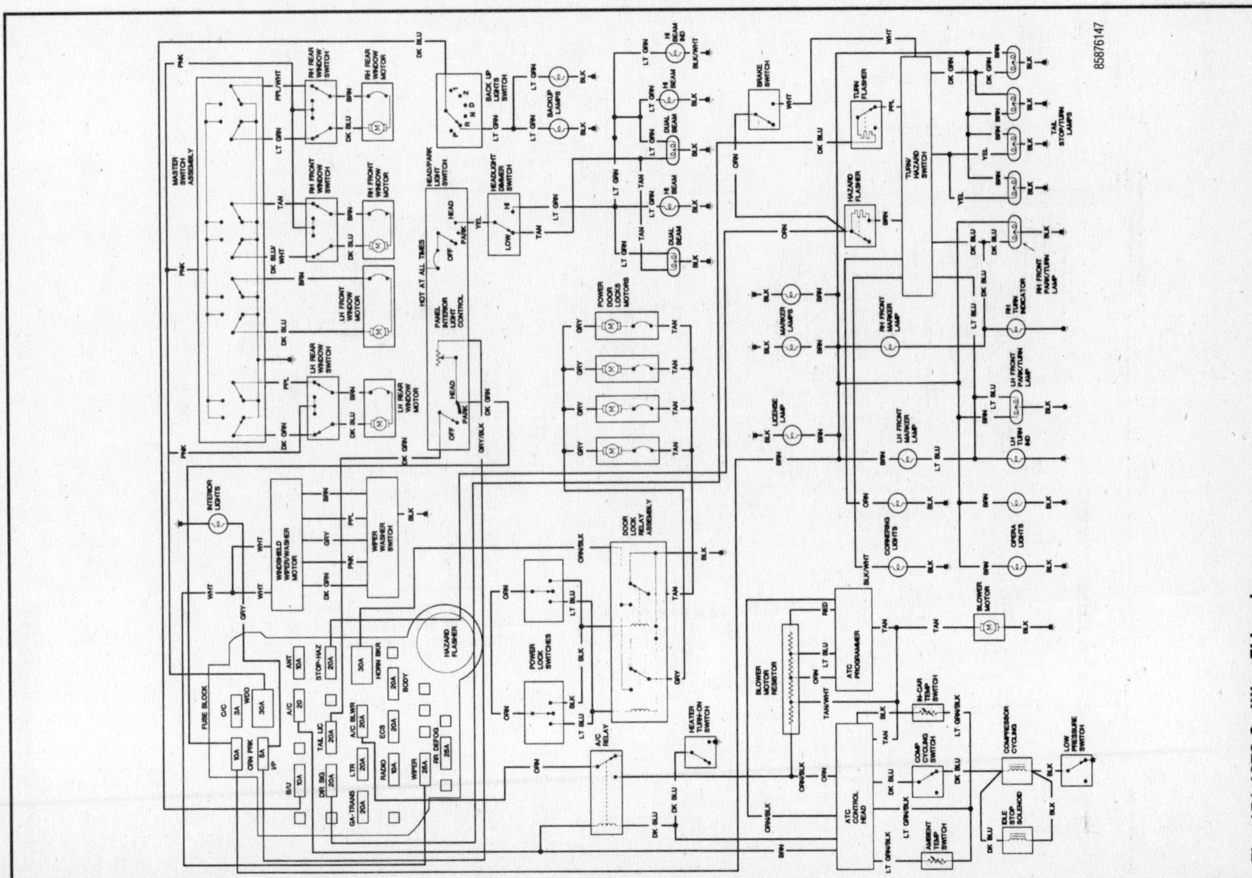

Fig. 151 1979 Cadillac Eldorado

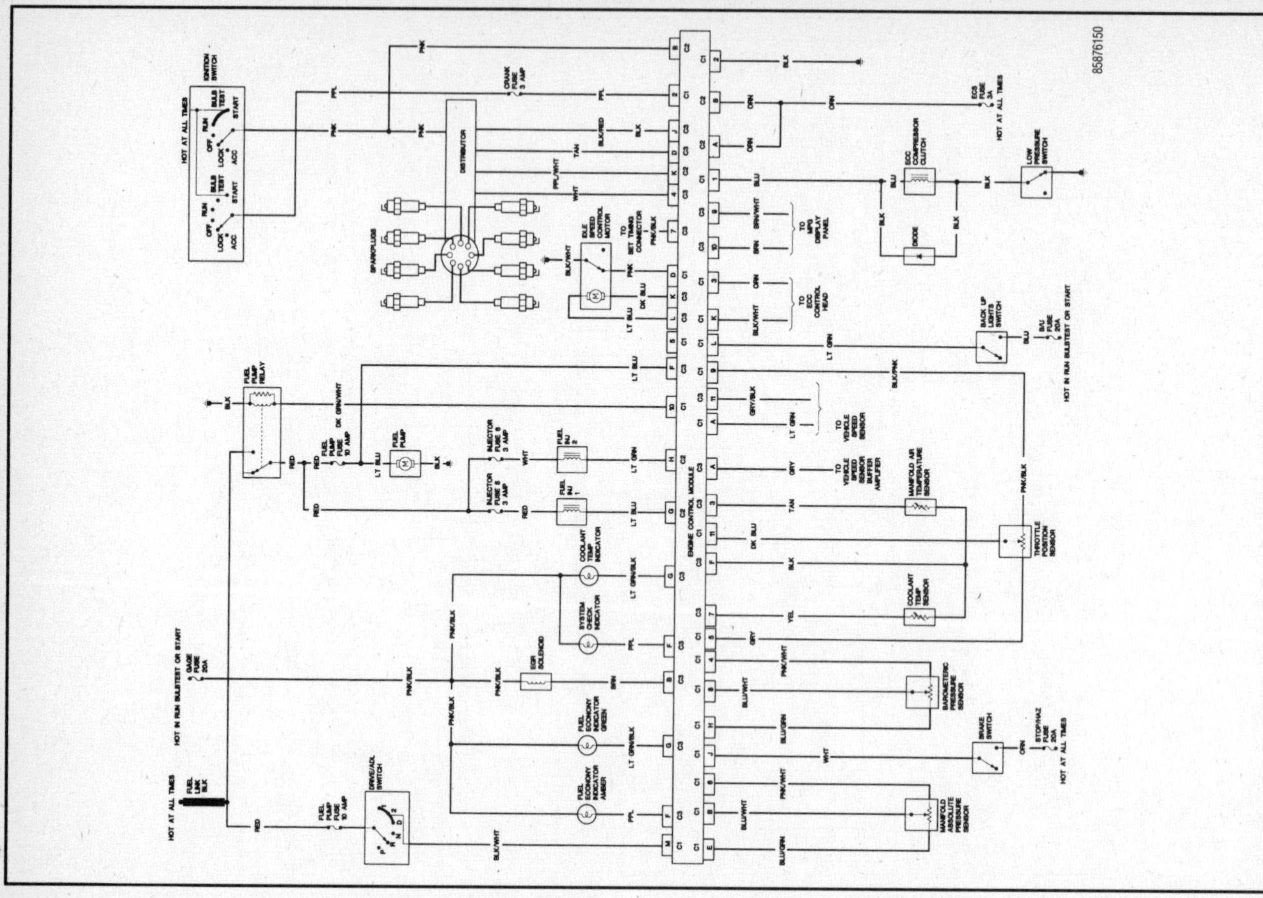

Fig. 154 1980 Cadillac Eldorado and Seville (V8 DFI engine)

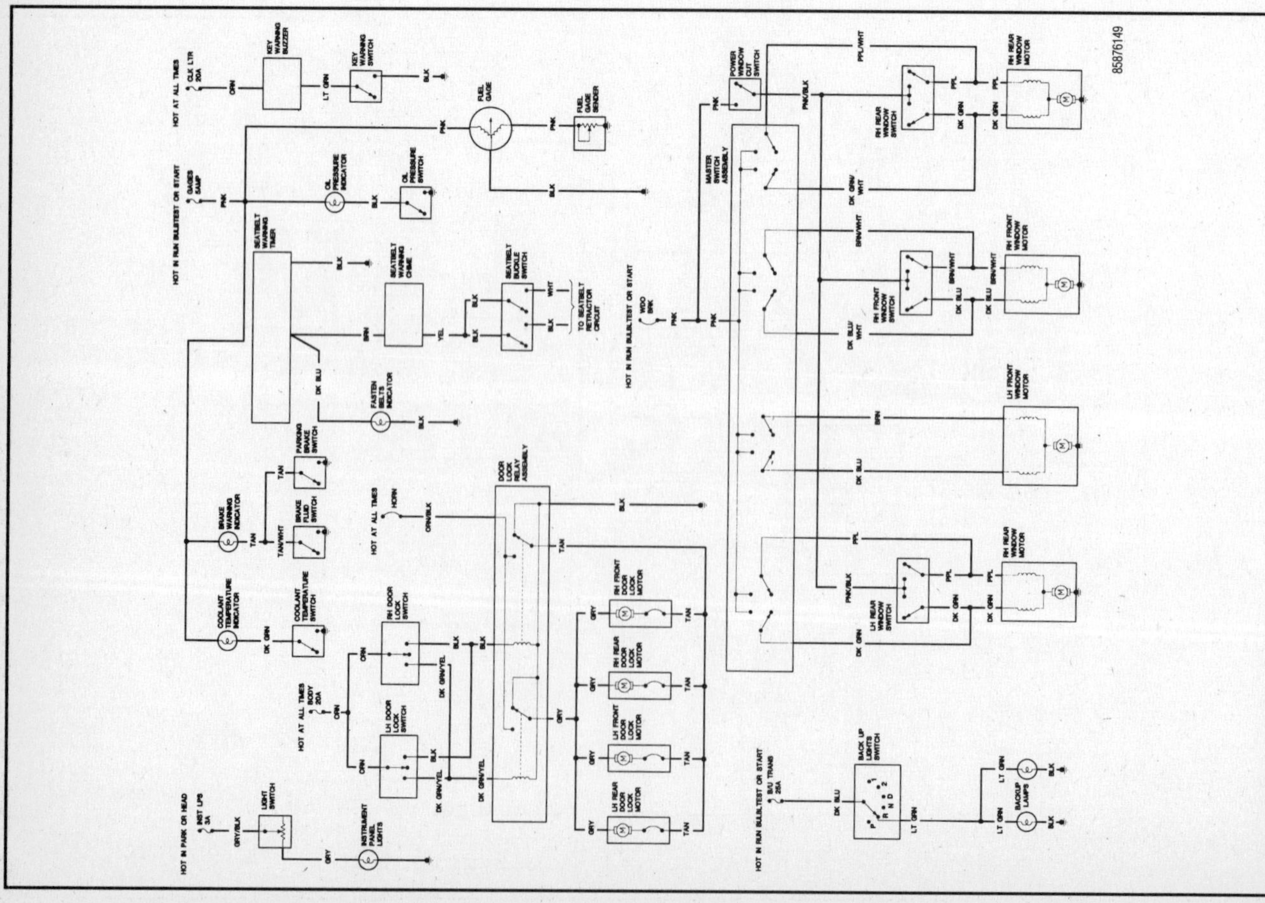

Fig. 153 1979 Cadillac Seville

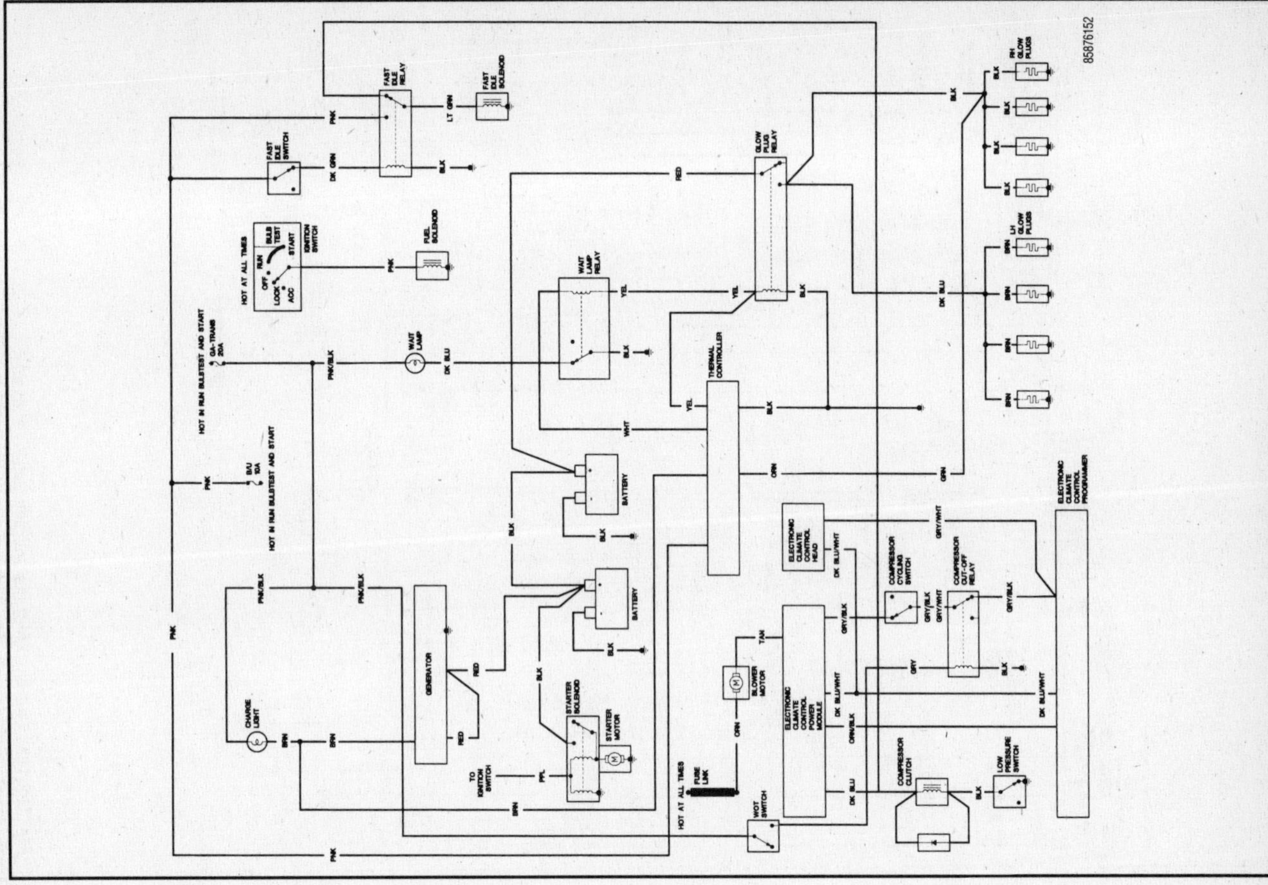

Fig. 156 1980 Cadillac Eldorado and Seville (diesel engine)

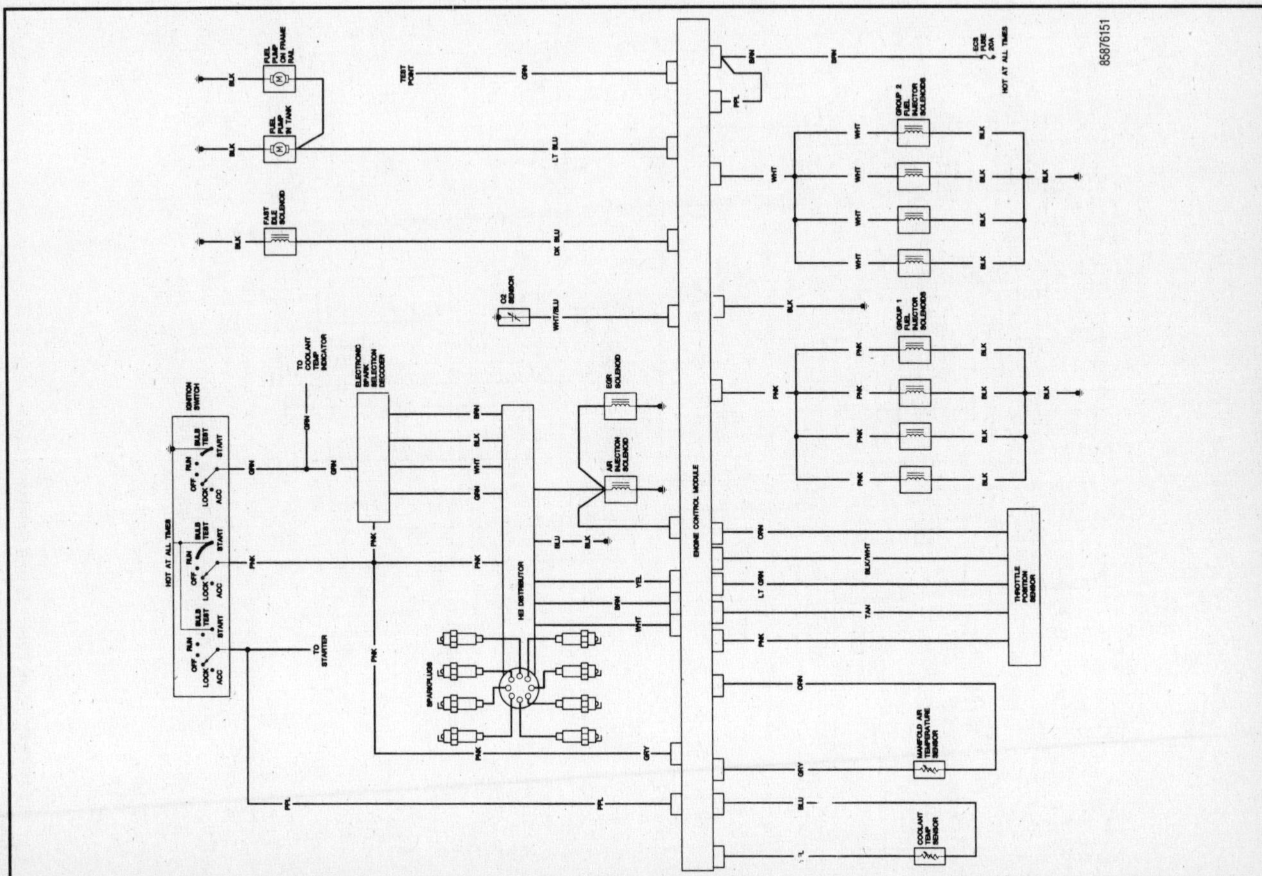

Fig. 155 1980 Cadillac Eldorado and Seville (V8 EFI engine)

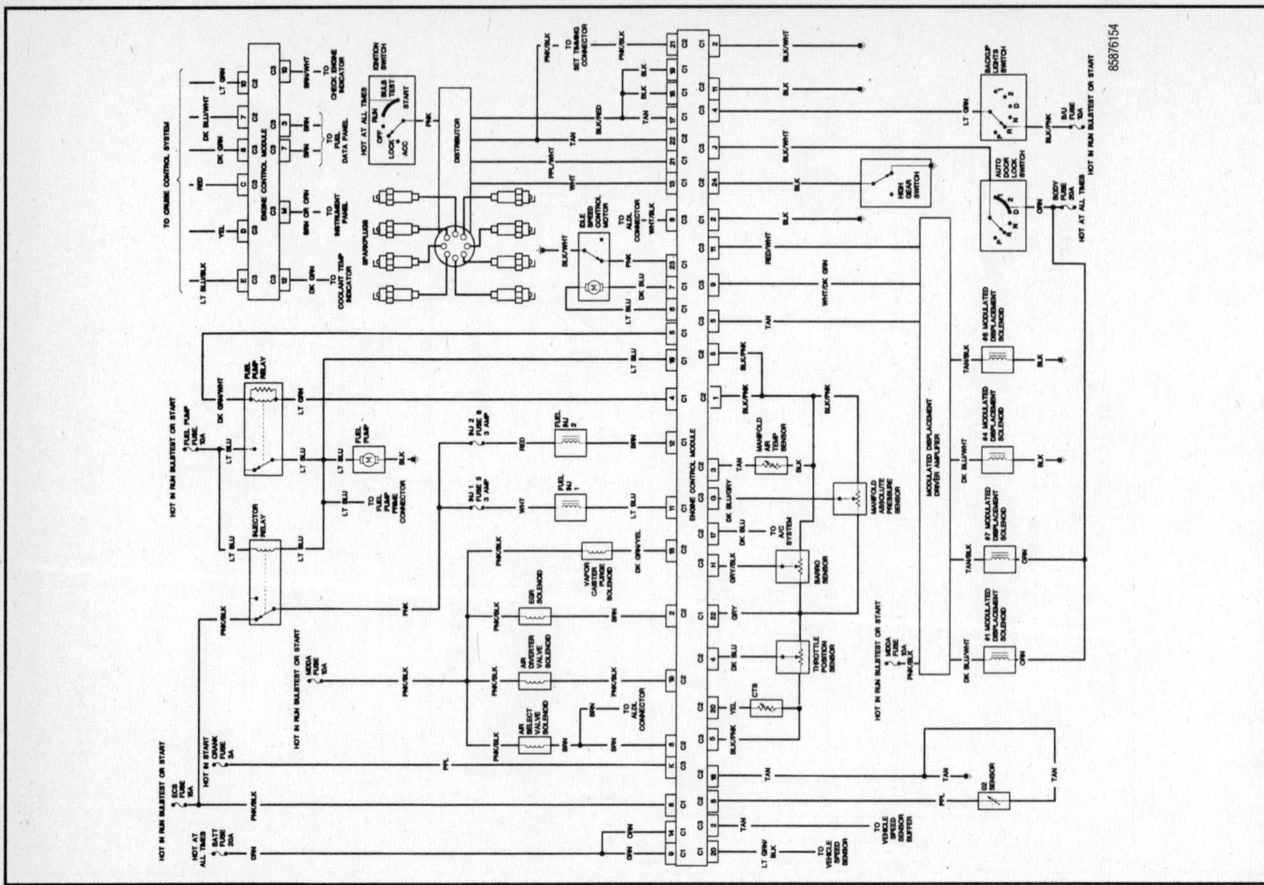

Fig. 158 1981 Cadillac Eldorado and Seville (V8 engine)

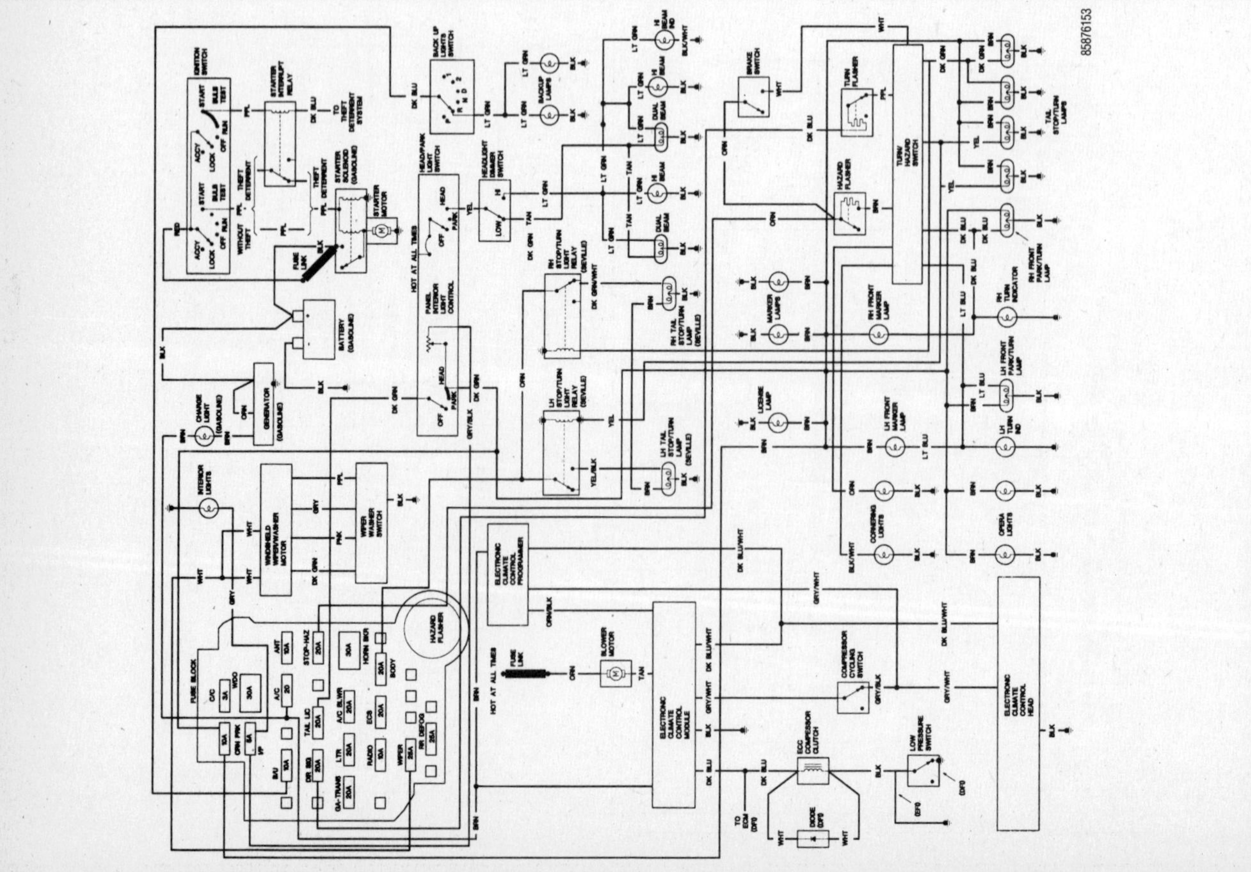

Fig. 157 1980 Cadillac Eldorado and Seville

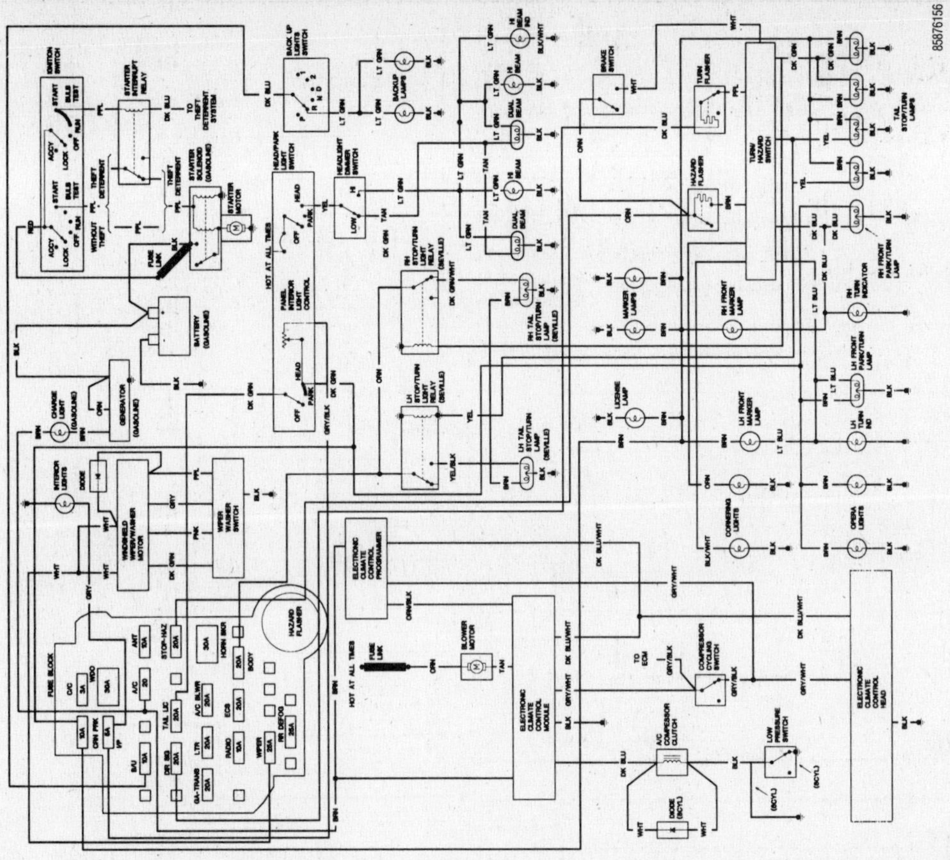

Fig. 160 1981 Cadillac Eldorado and Seville

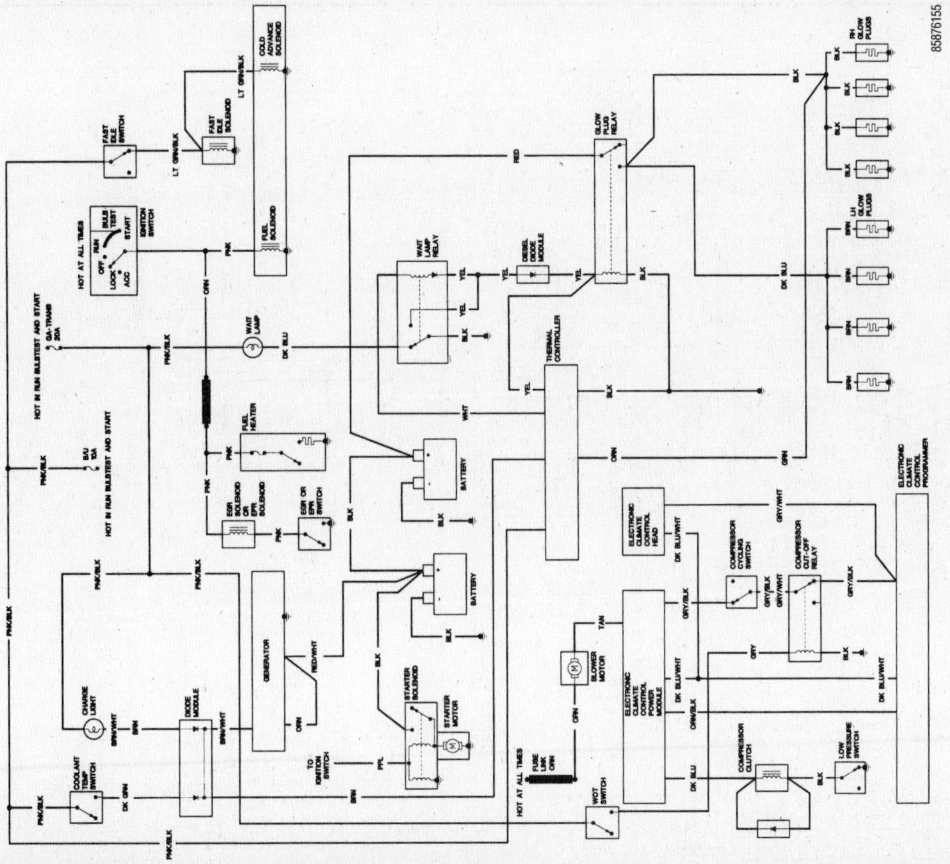

Fig. 159 1981 Cadillac Eldorado and Seville (diesel engine)

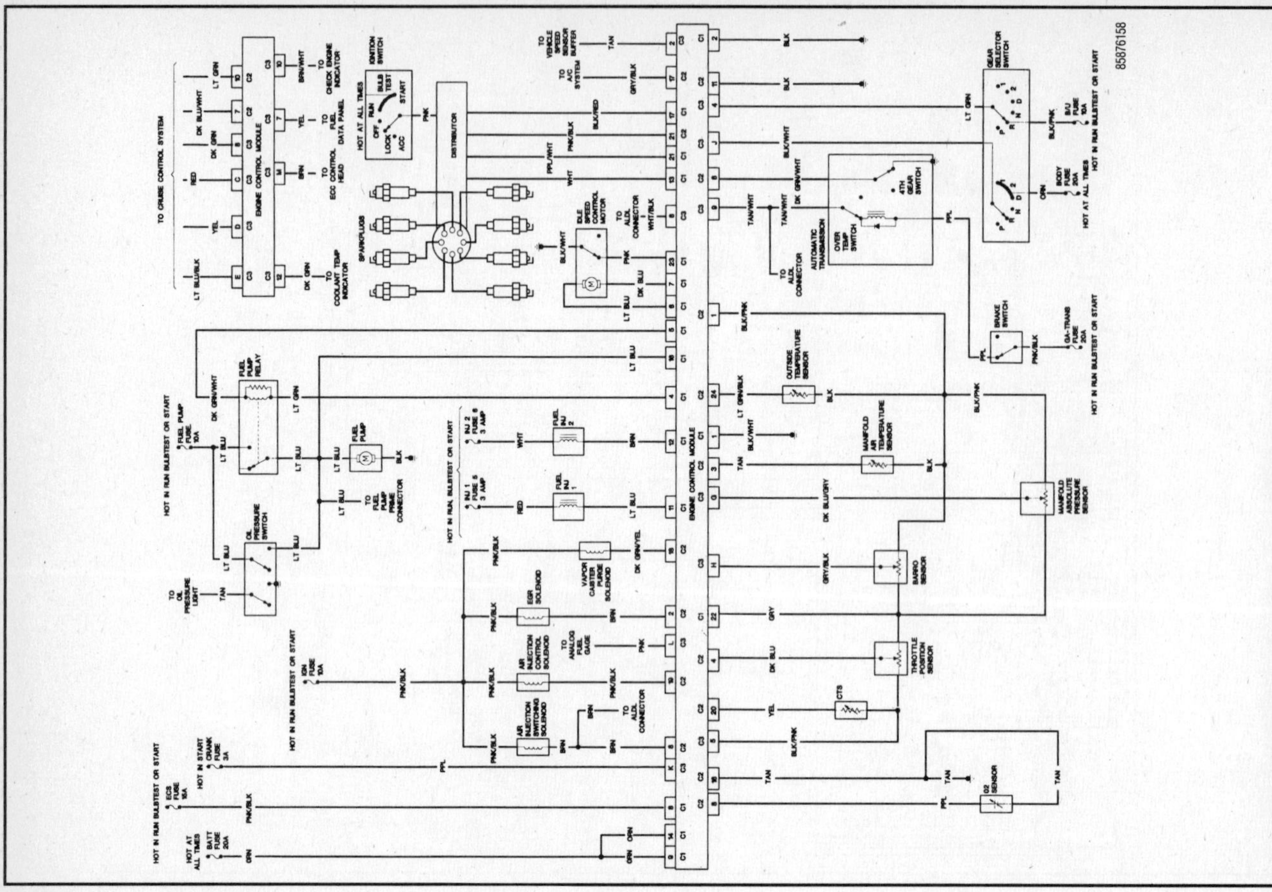

Fig. 162 1982 Cadillac Eldorado and Seville (V8 engine)

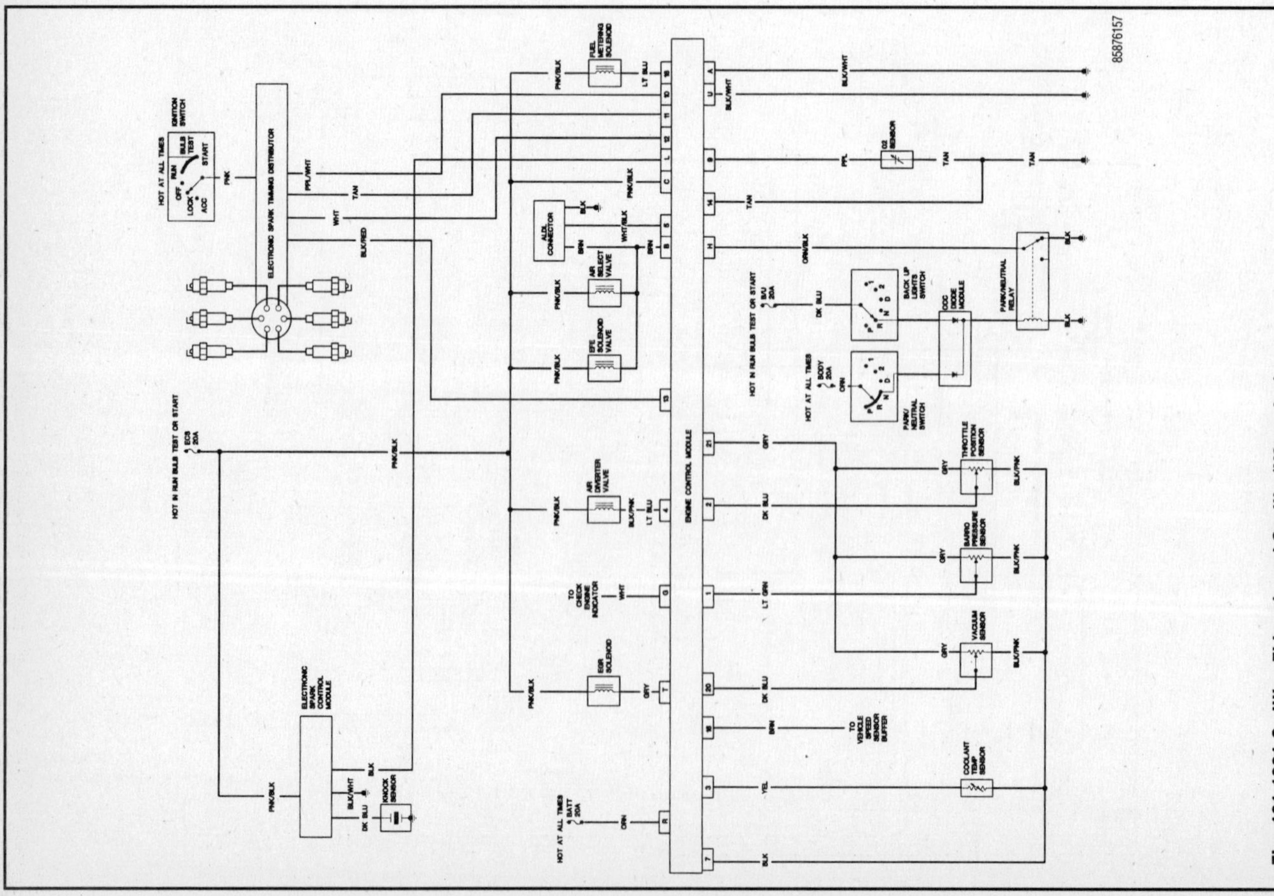

Fig. 161 1981 Cadillac Eldorado and Seville (V6 engine)

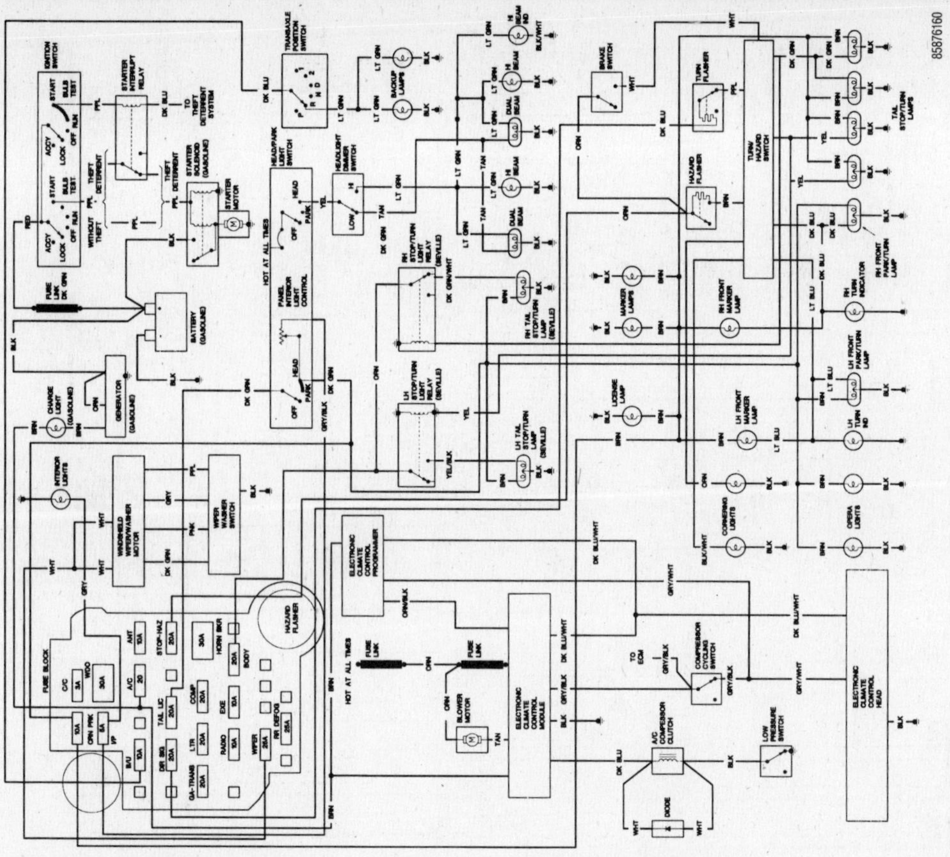

Fig. 164 1982 Cadillac Eldorado and Seville

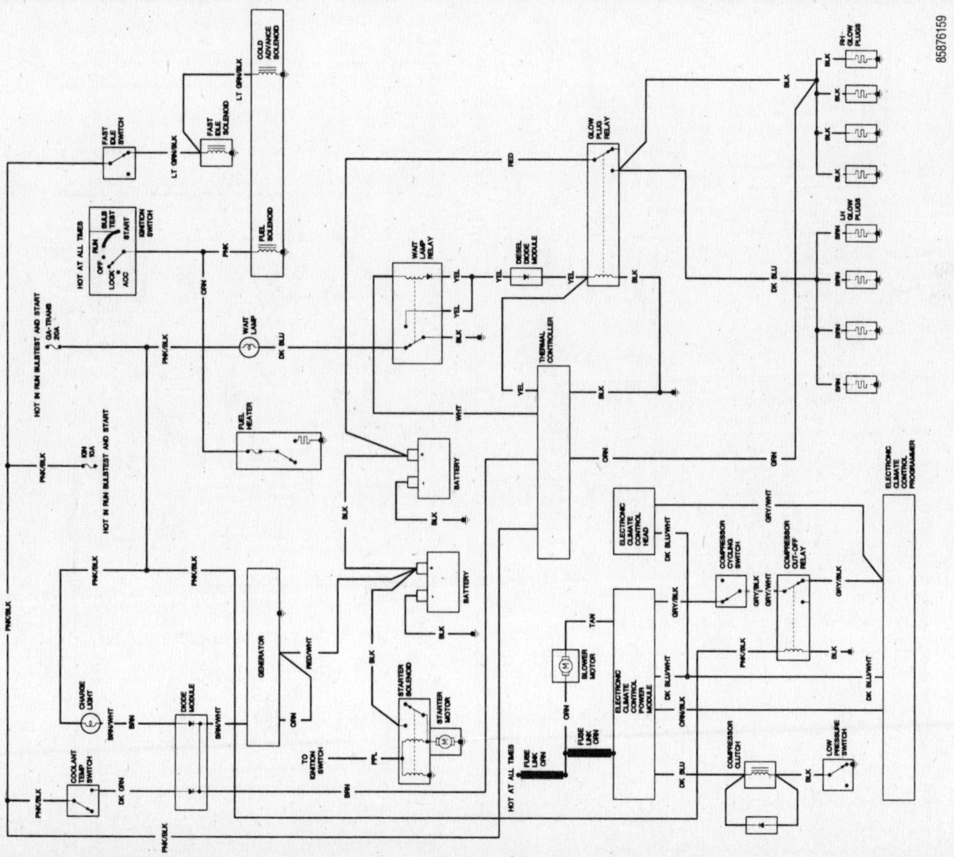

Fig. 163 1982 Cadillac Eldorado and Seville (diesel engine)

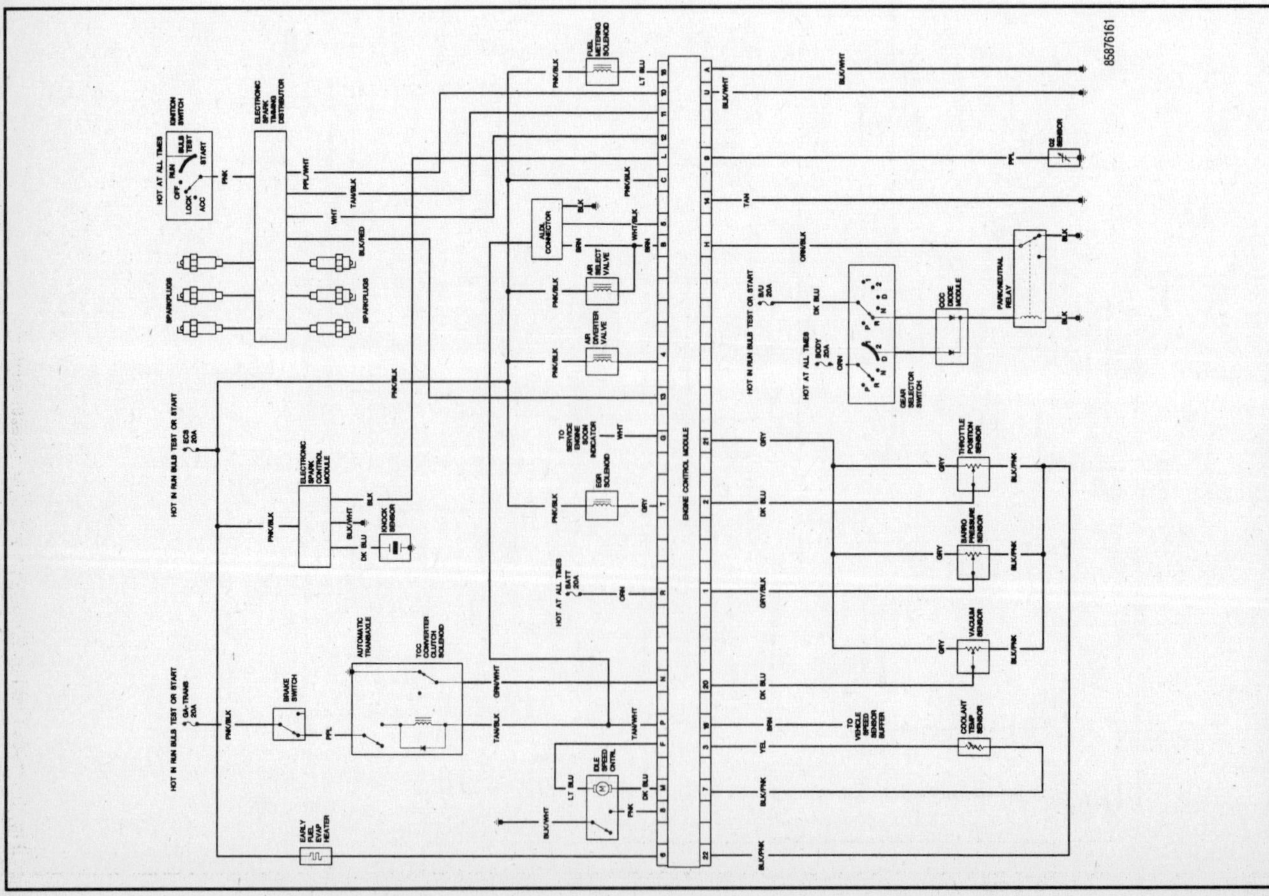

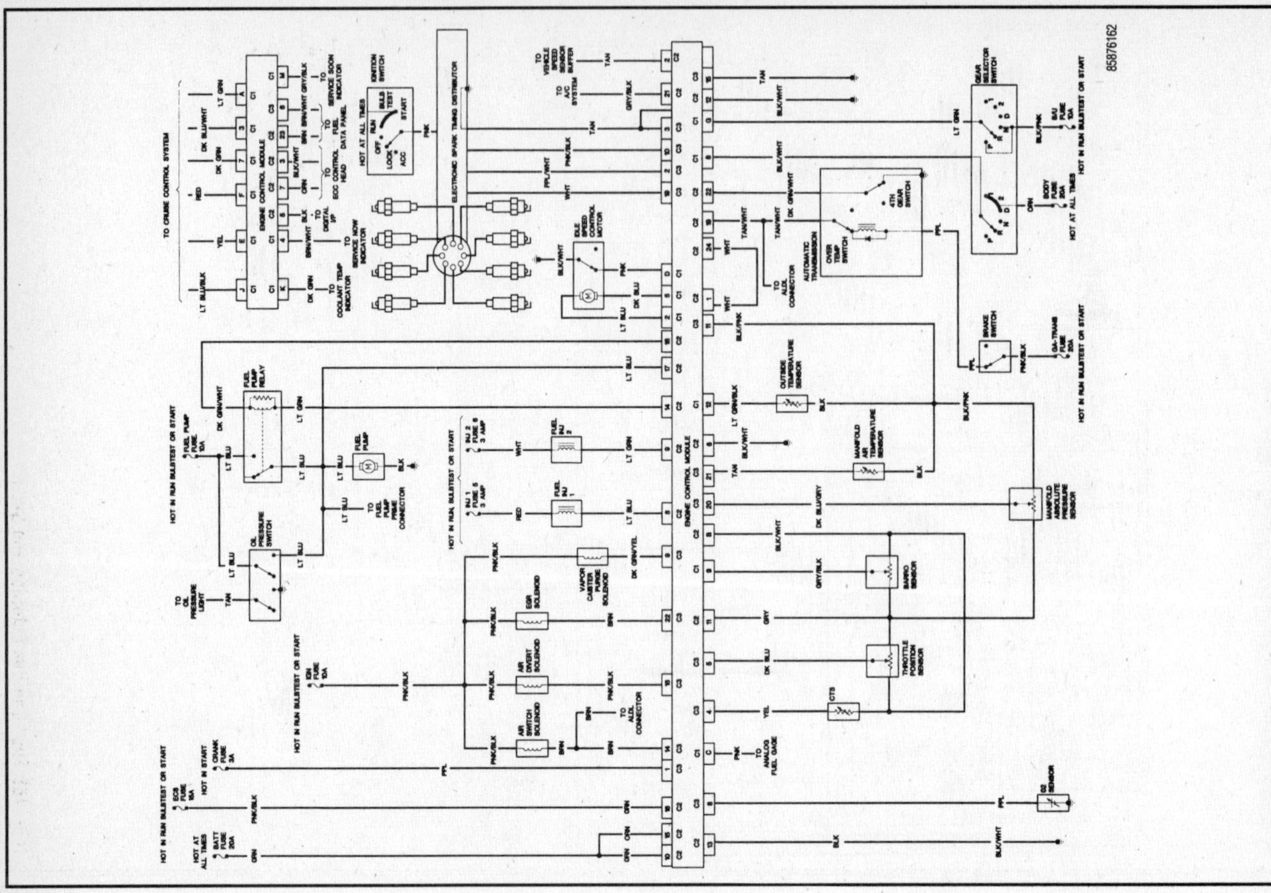

Fig. 166 1983 Cadillac Eldorado and Seville (V8 engine)

Fig. 165 1982 Cadillac Eldorado and Seville (V6 engine)

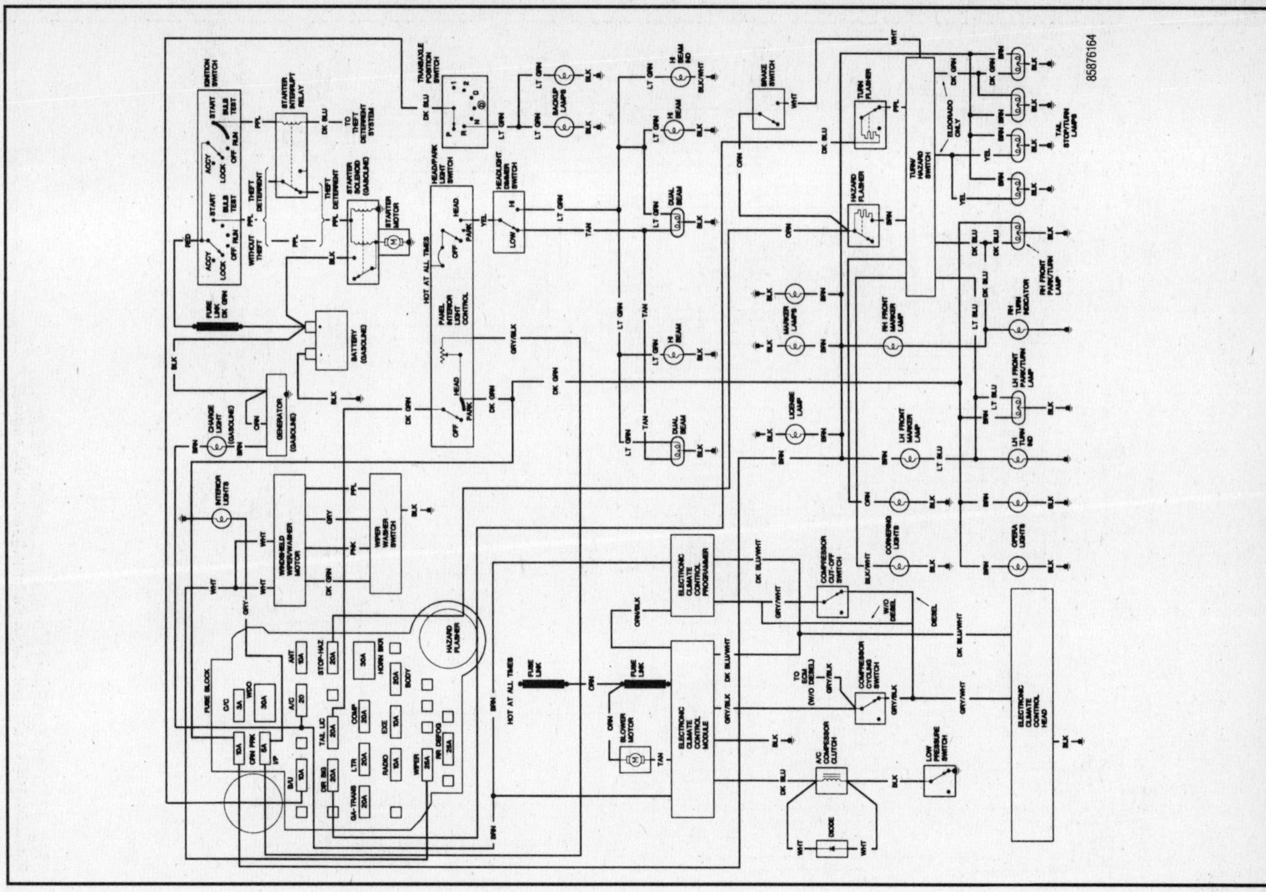

Fig. 168 1983 Cadillac Eldorado and Seville

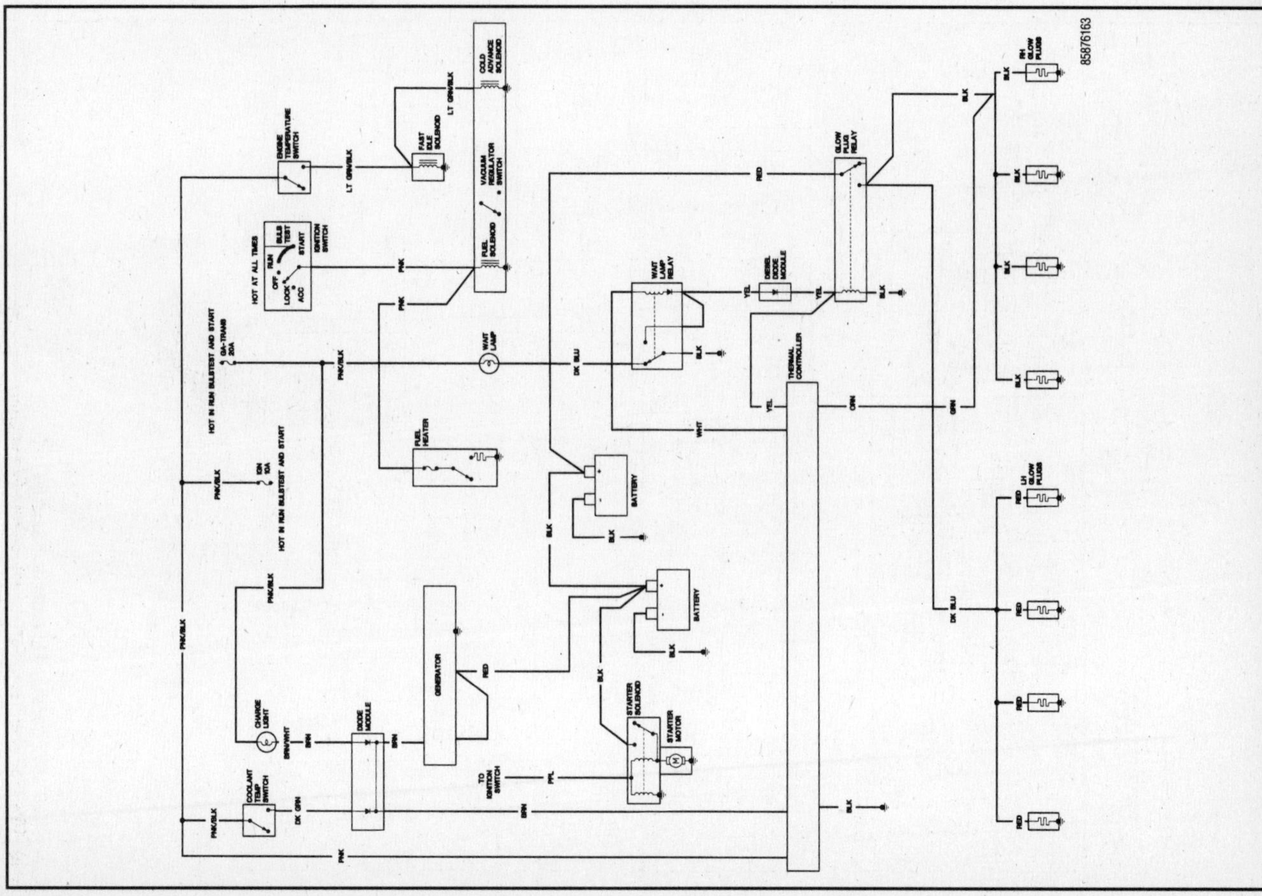

Fig. 167 1983 Cadillac Eldorado and Seville (diesel engine)

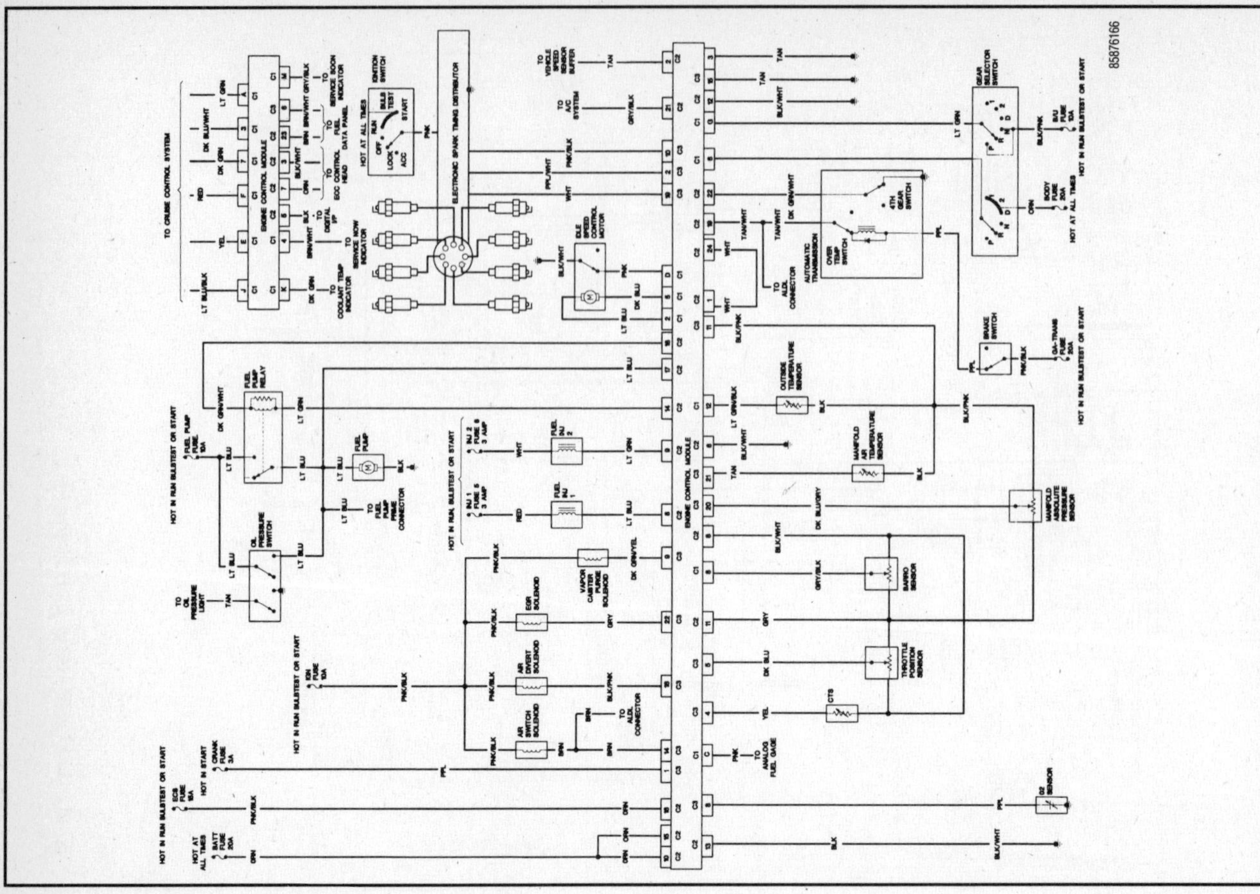

Fig. 170 1983 Cadillac Eldorado and Seville (V8 engine)

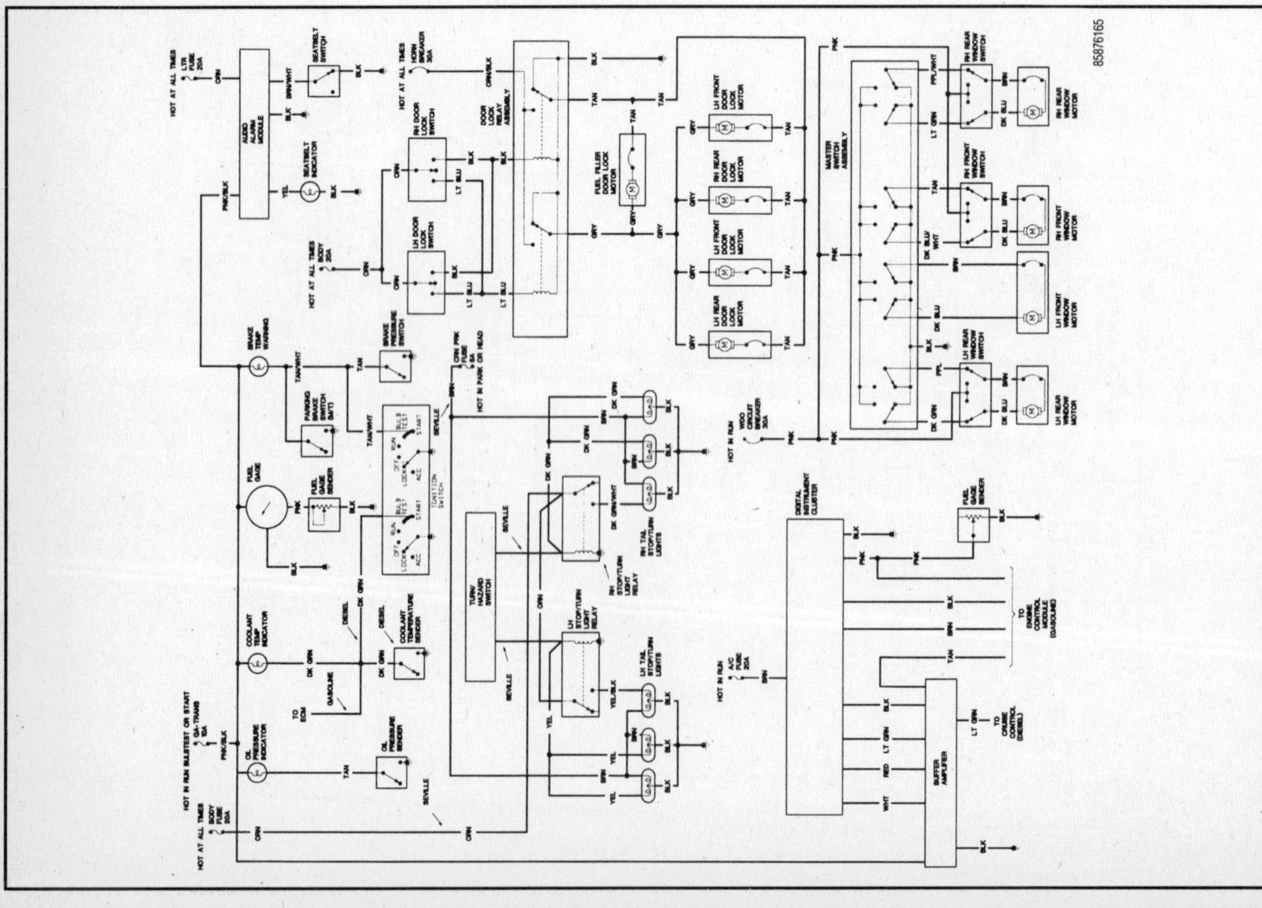

Fig. 169 1983 Cadillac Eldorado and Seville

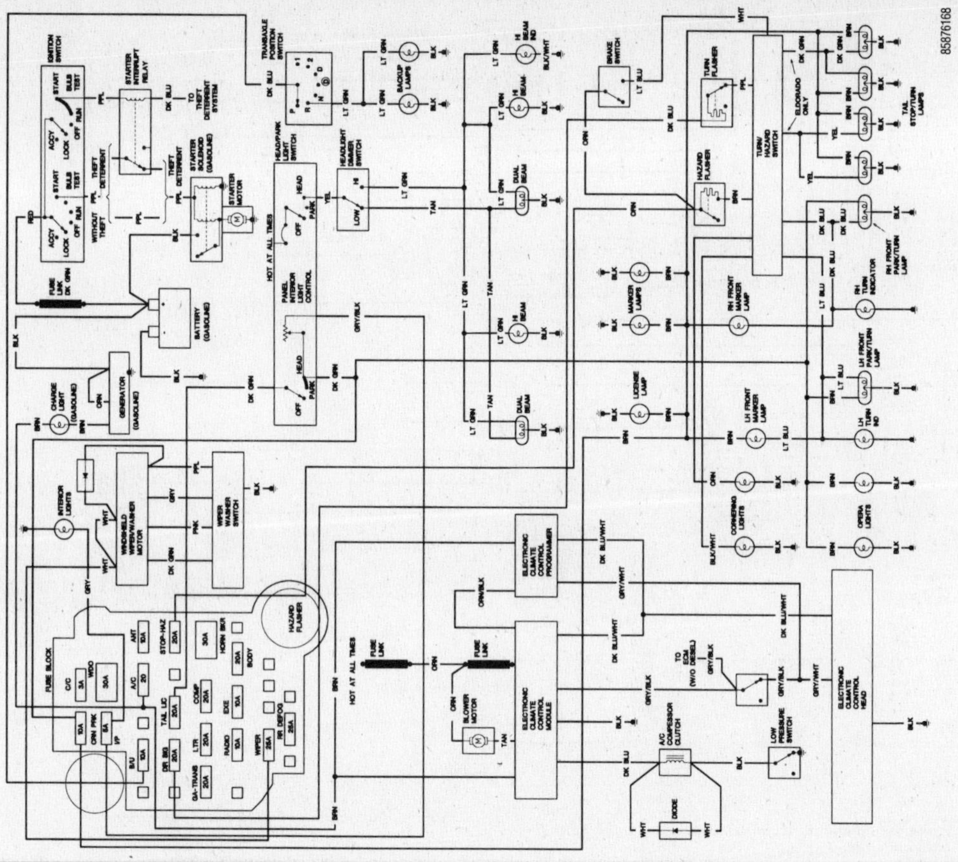

Fig. 172 1984 Cadillac Eldorado and Seville

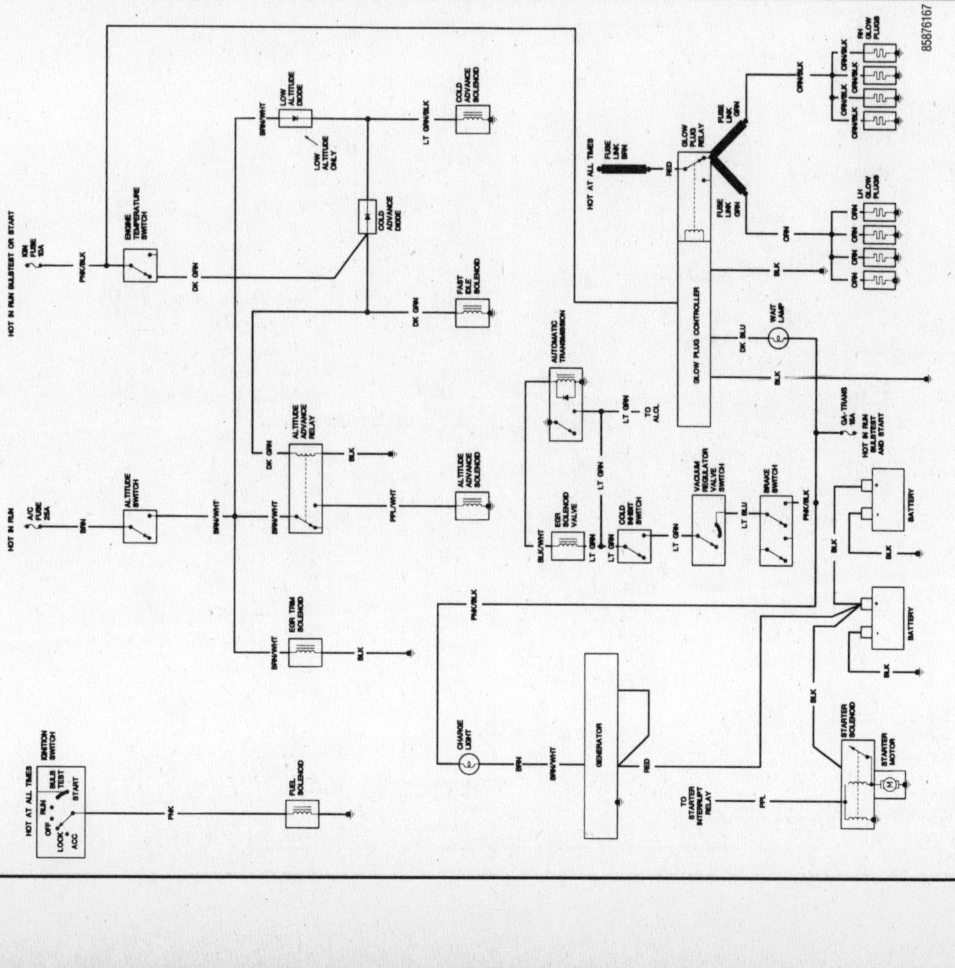

Fig. 171 1984 Cadillac Eldorado and Seville (diesel engine)

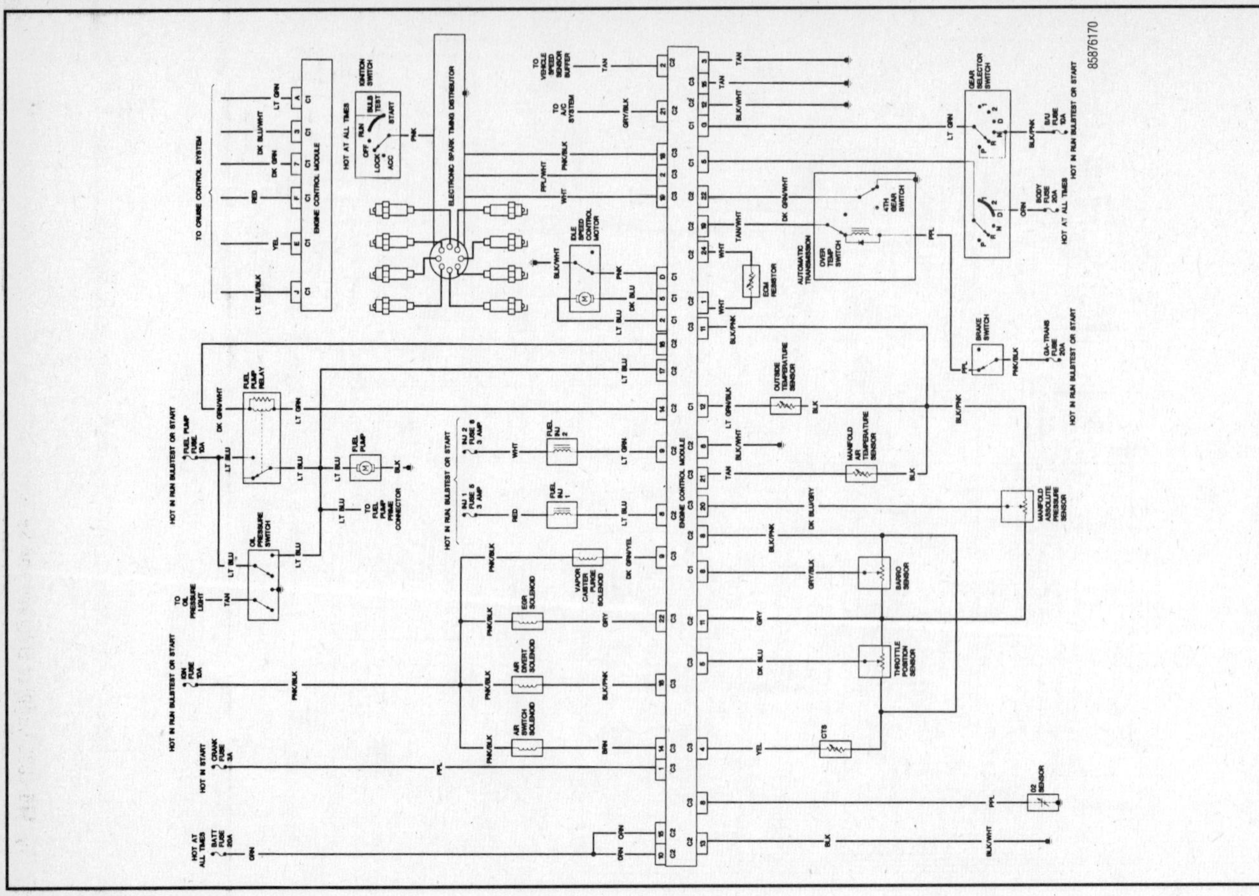

Fig. 174 1985 Cadillac Eldorado and Seville (V8 engine)

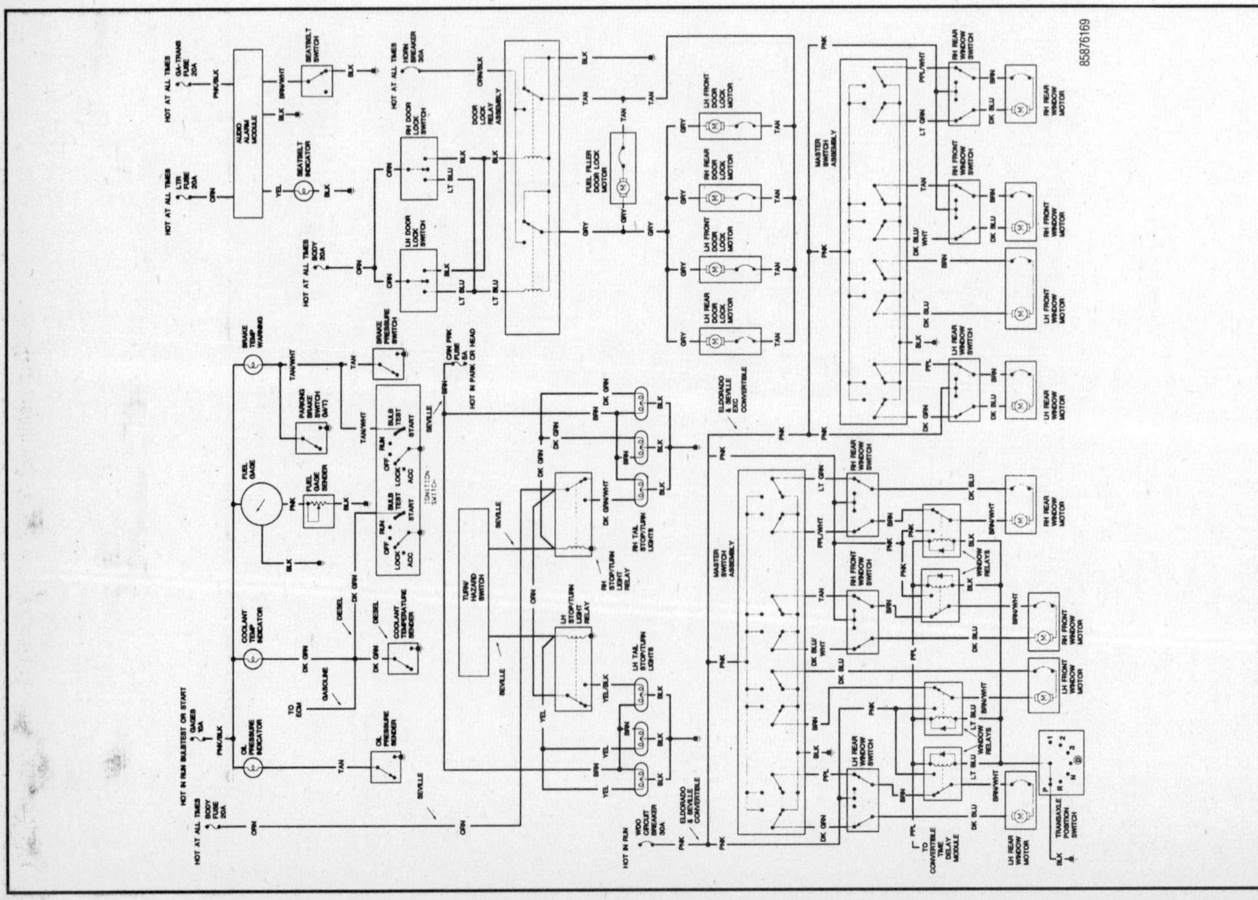

Fig. 173 1984 Cadillac Eldorado and Seville

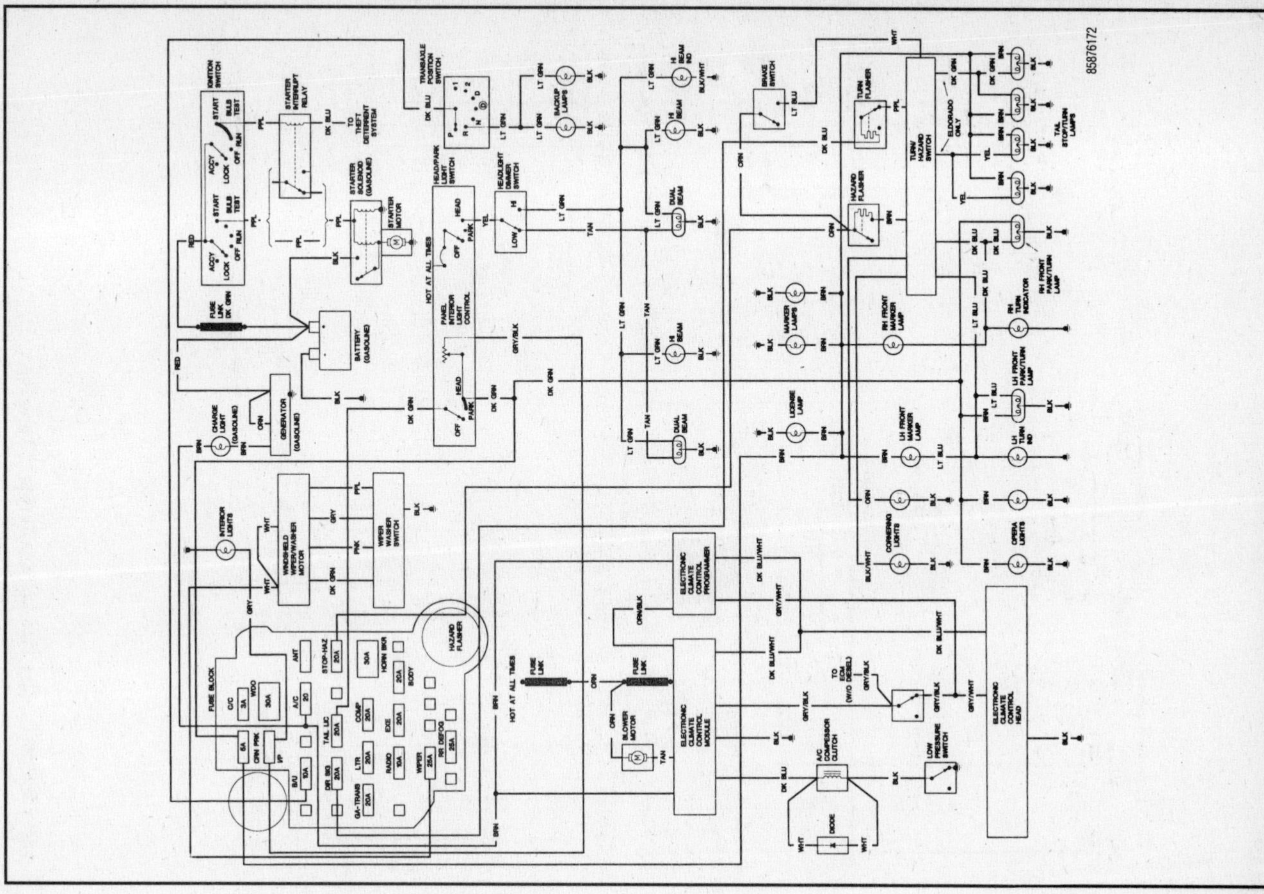

Fig. 176 1985 Cadillac Eldorado and Seville

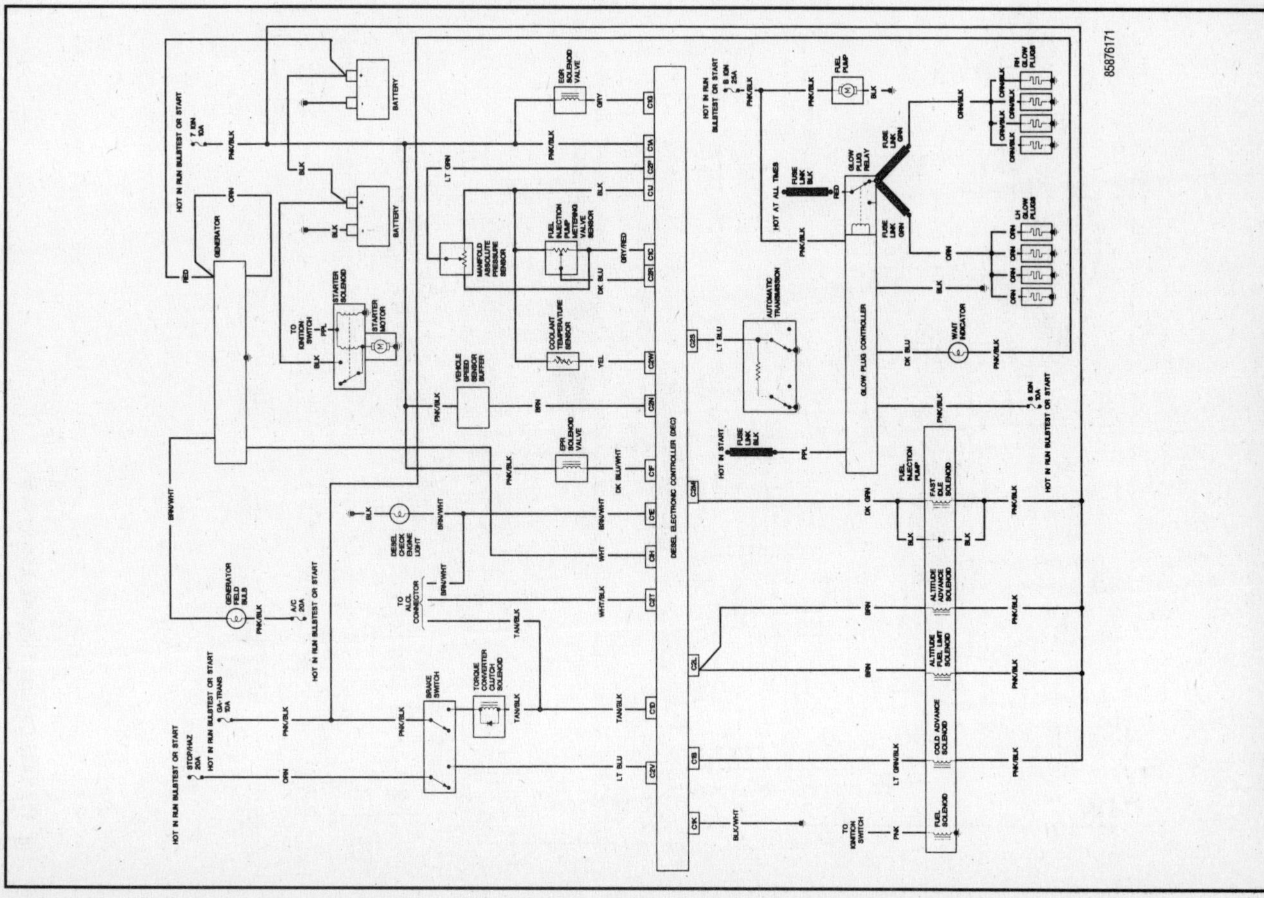

Fig. 175 1985 Cadillac Eldorado and Seville (V8 diesel engine)

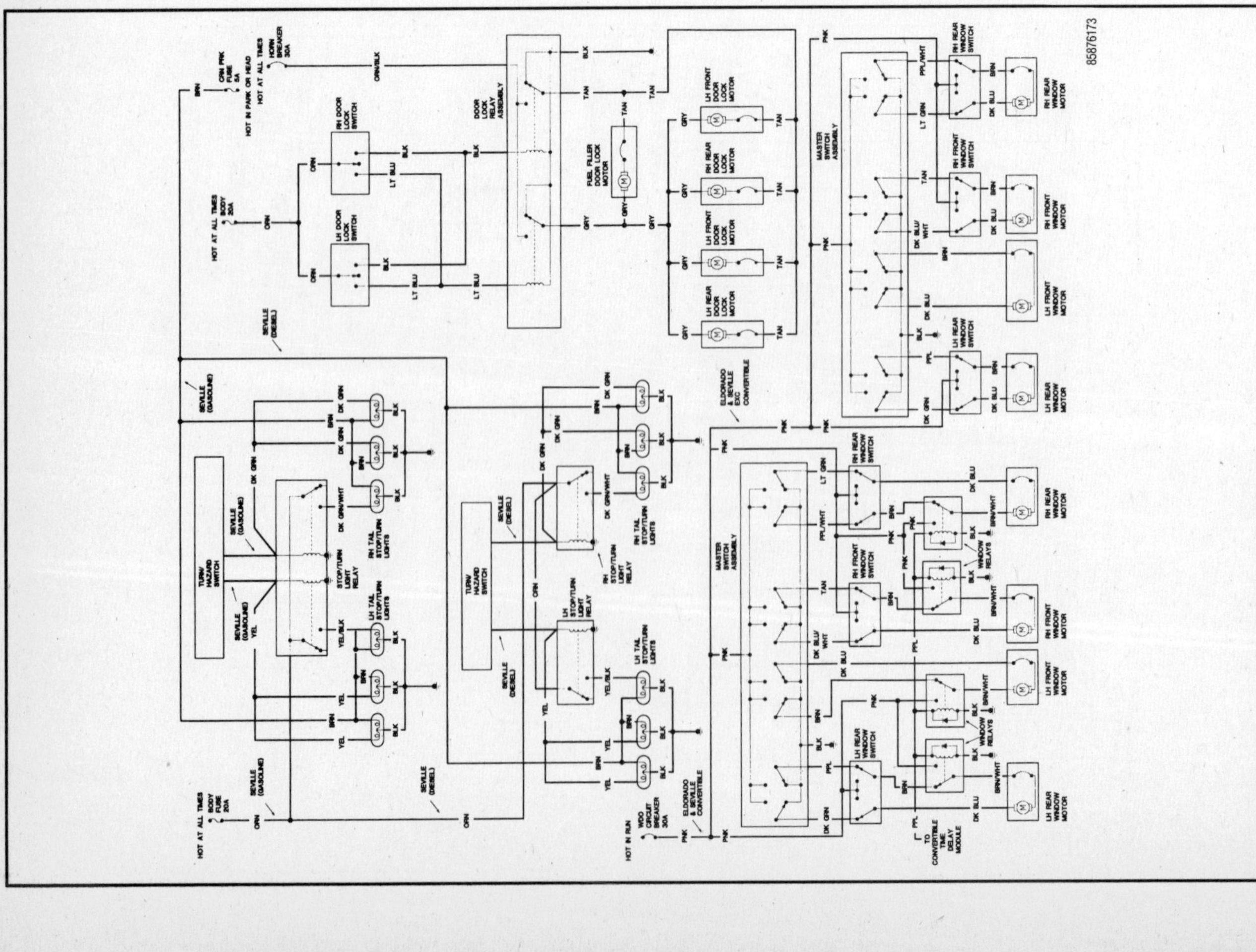

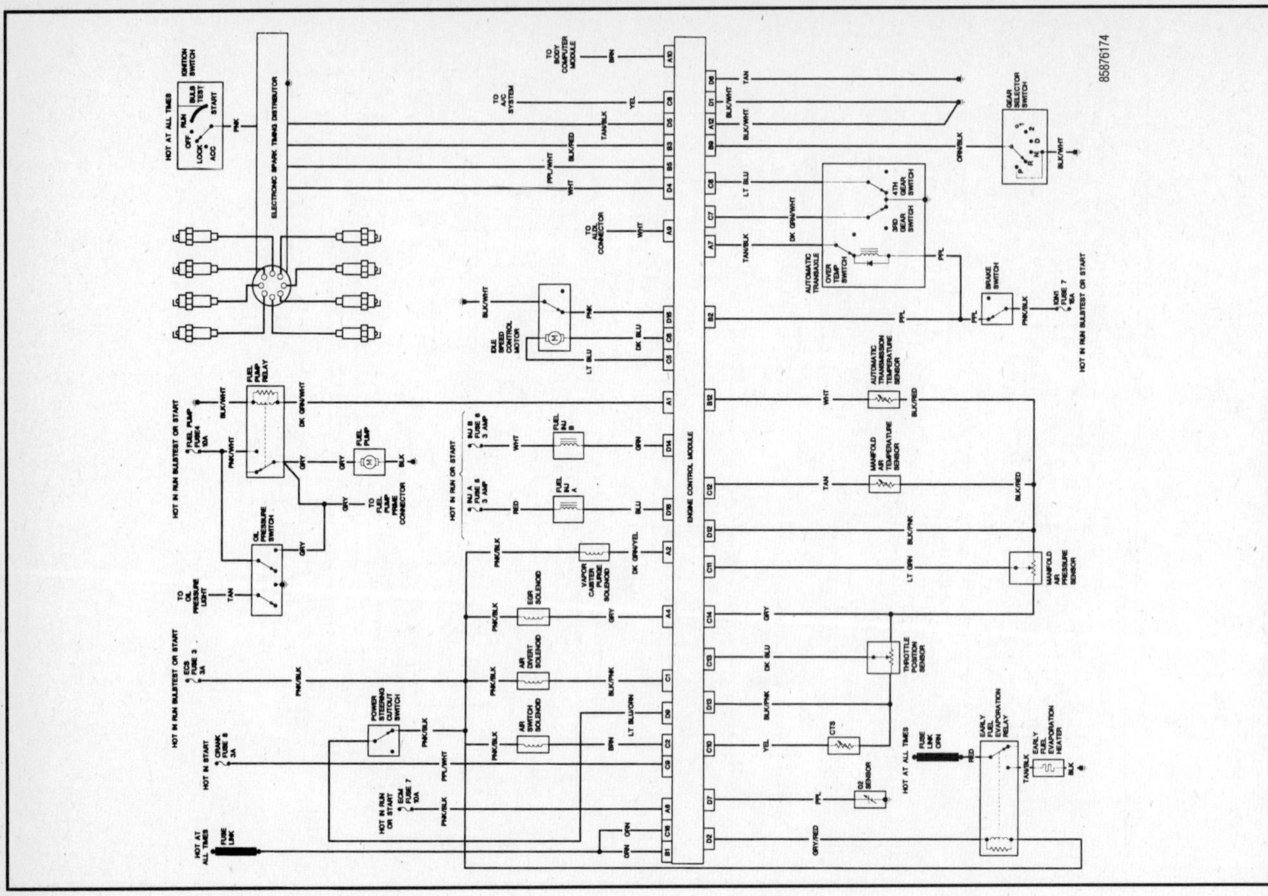

Fig. 178 1986 Cadillac Eldorado and Seville (V8 engine)

Fig. 177 1985 Cadillac Eldorado and Seville

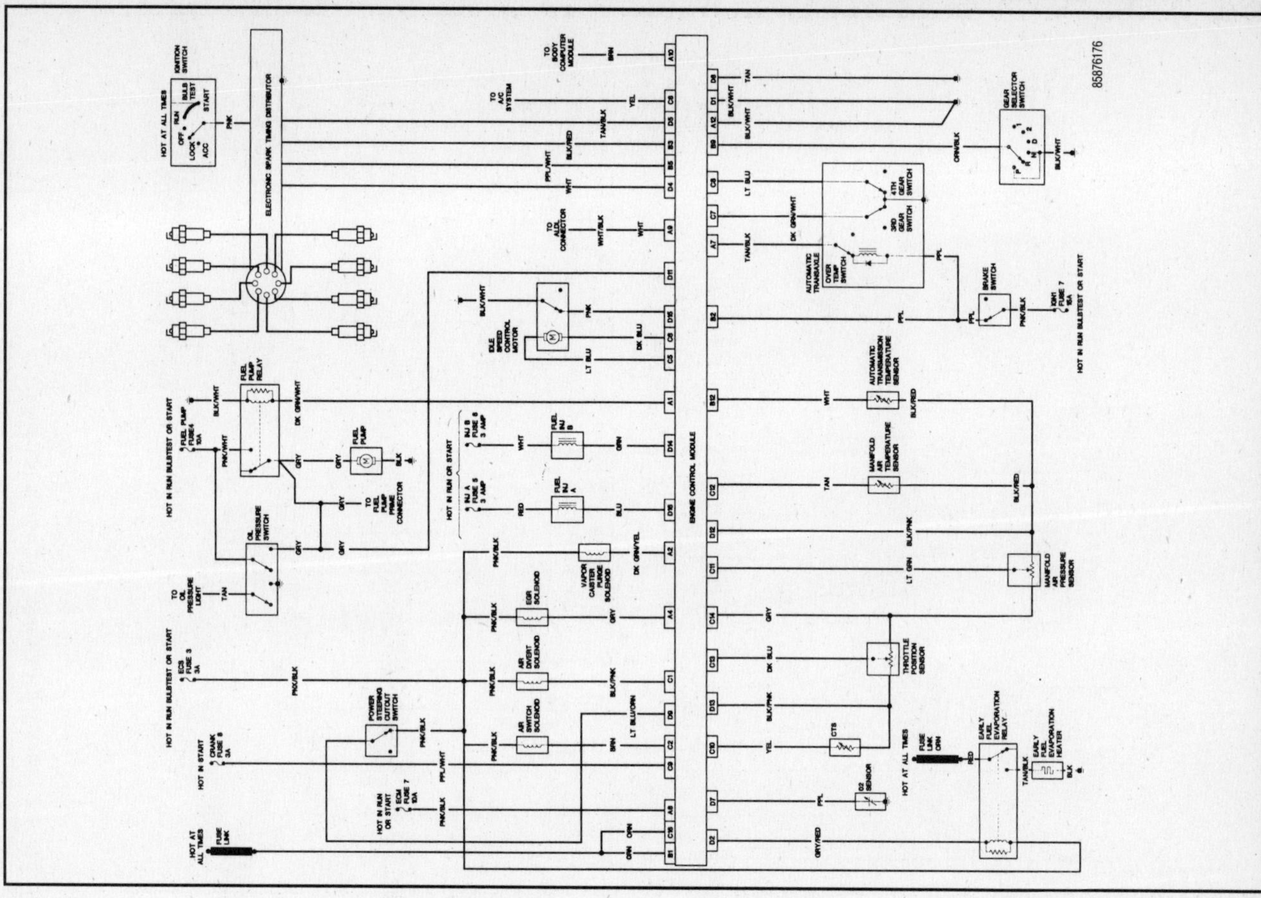

Fig. 180 1987 Cadillac Eldorado and Seville (V8 engine)

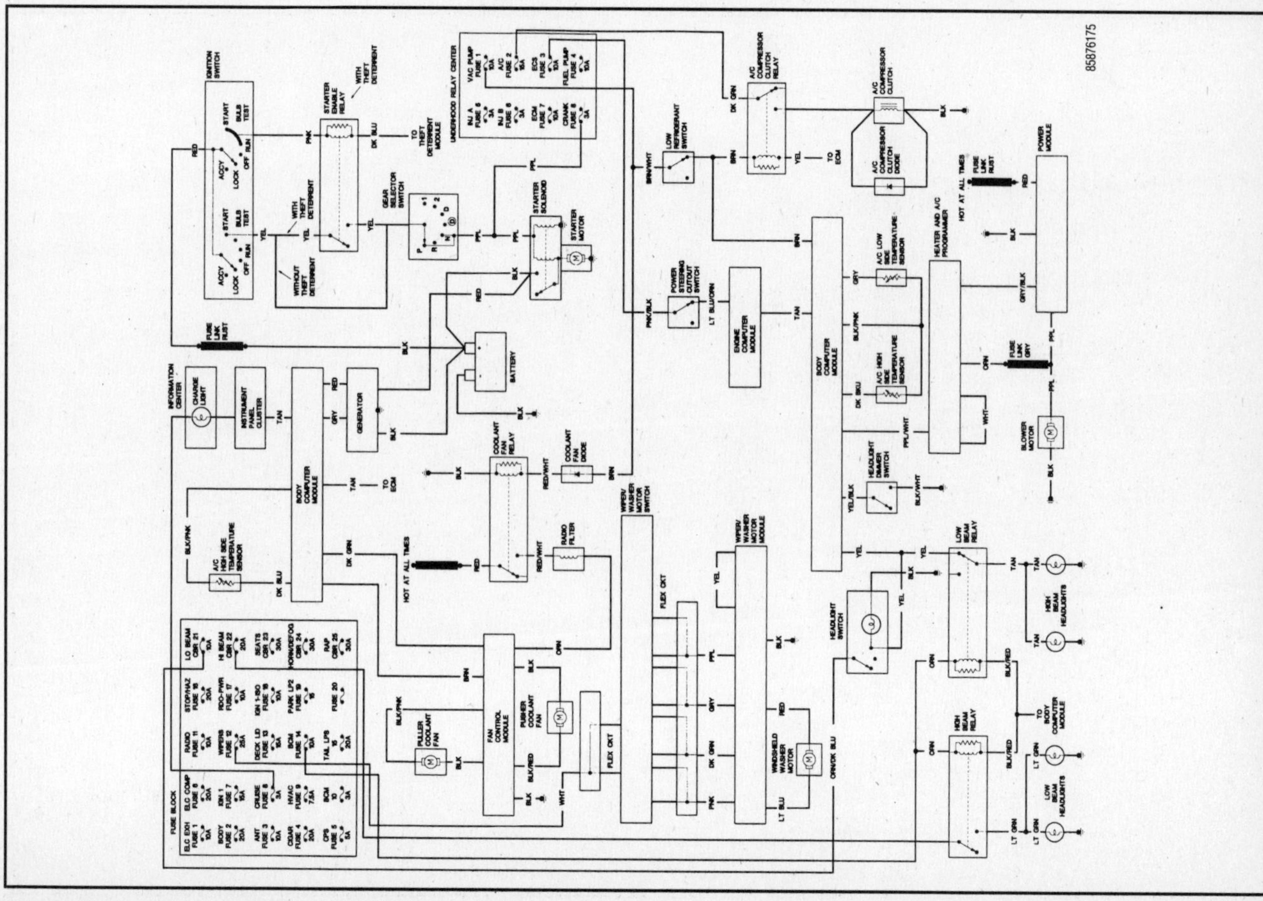

Fig. 179 1986 Cadillac Eldorado and Seville.

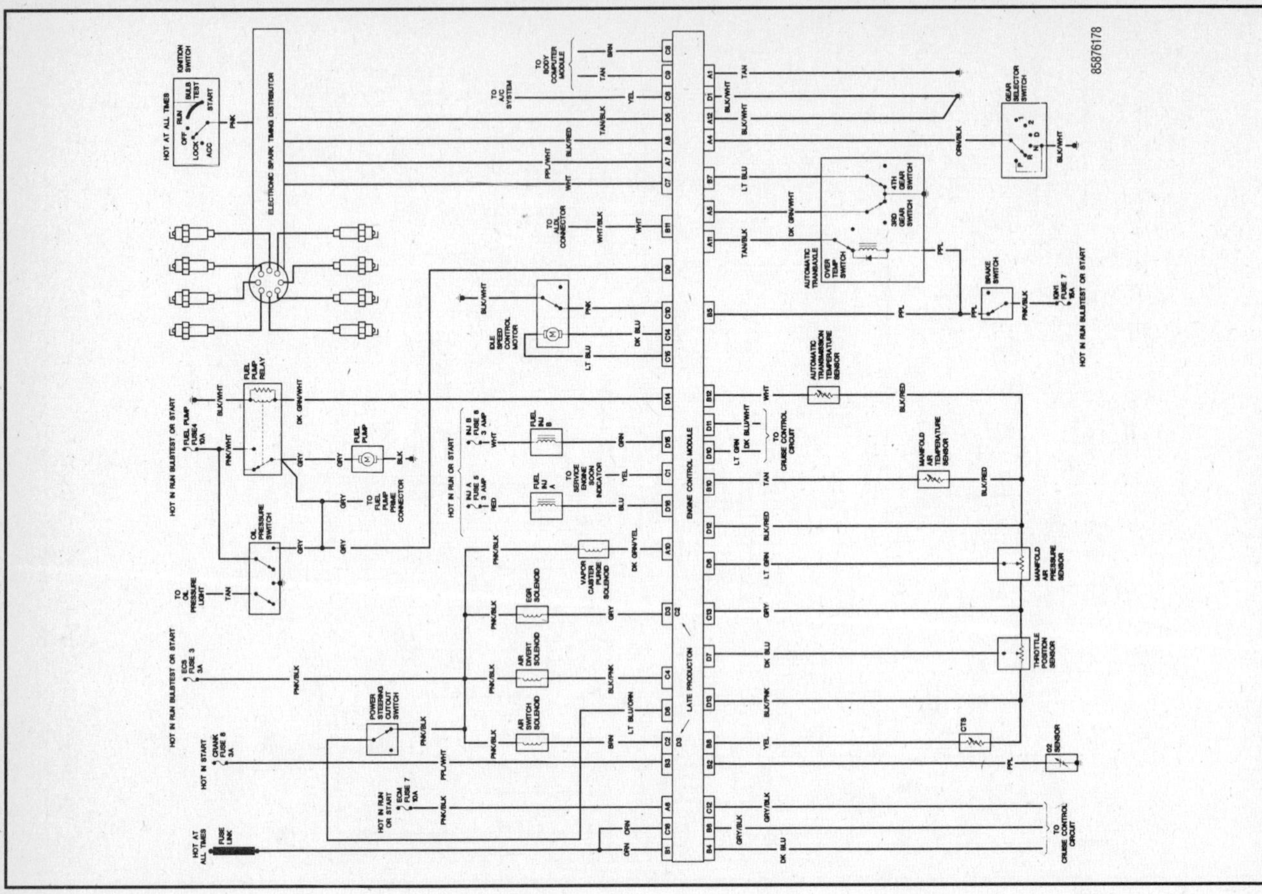

Fig. 182 1988 Cadillac Eldorado and Seville (V8 engine)

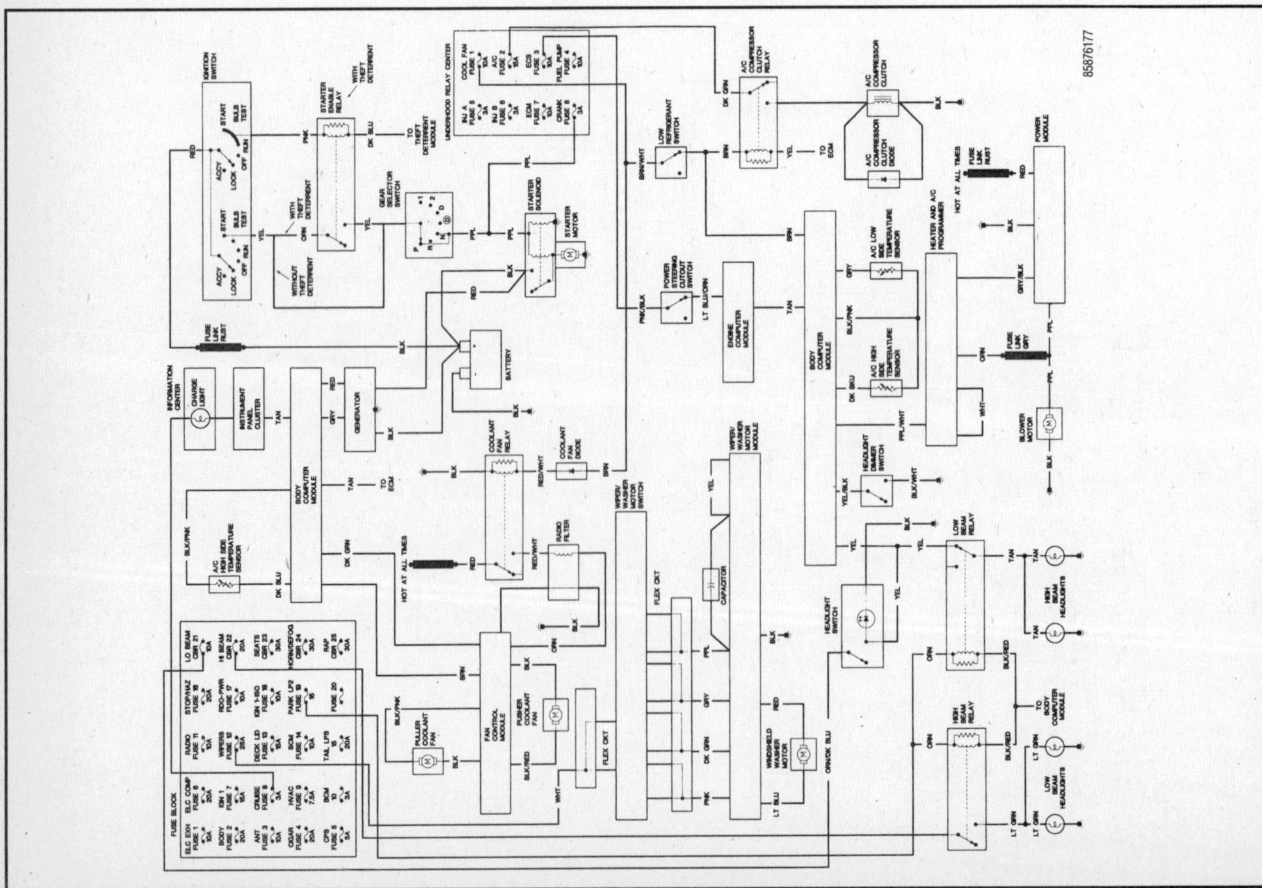

Fig. 181 1987 Cadillac Eldorado and Seville

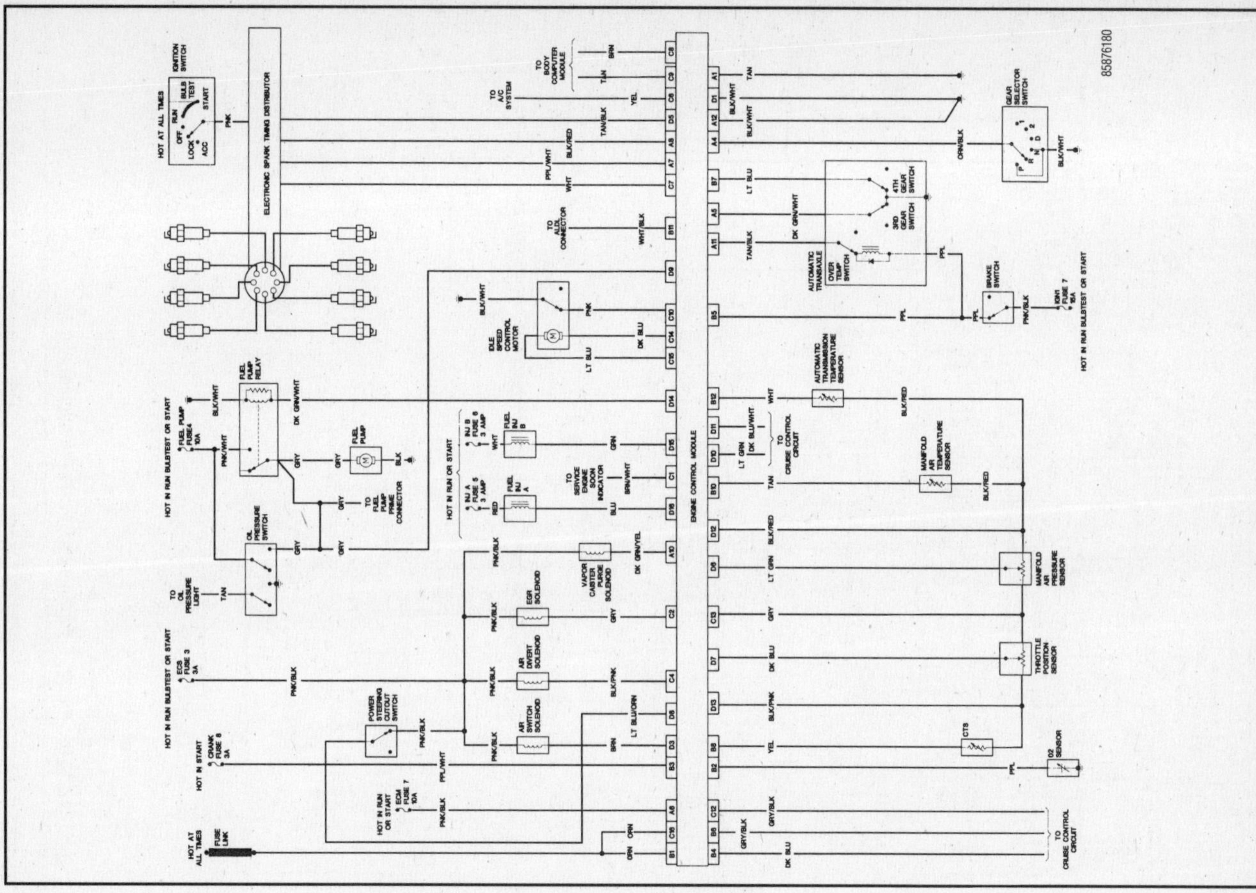

Fig. 184 1989 Cadillac Eldorado and Seville

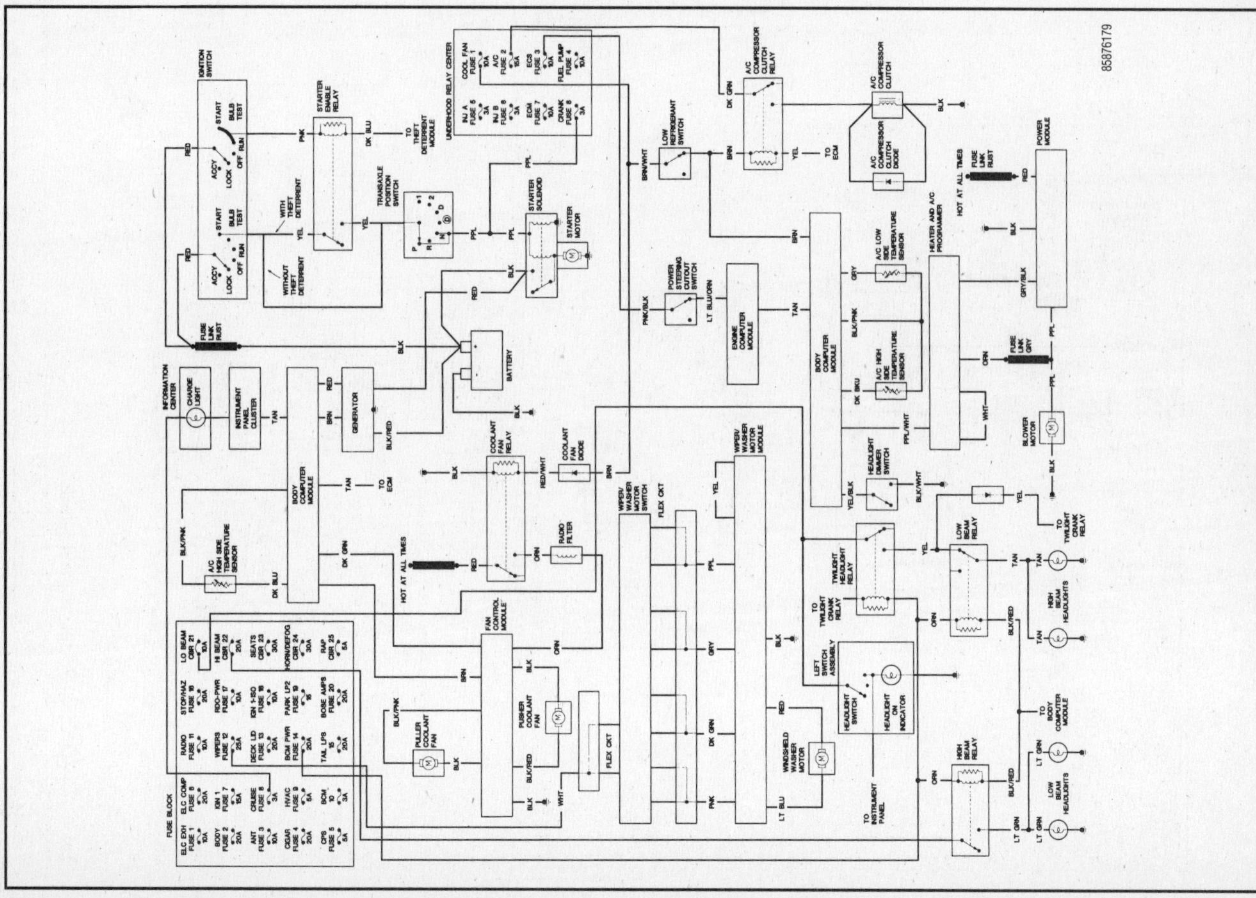

Fig. 183 1988 Cadillac Eldorado and Seville

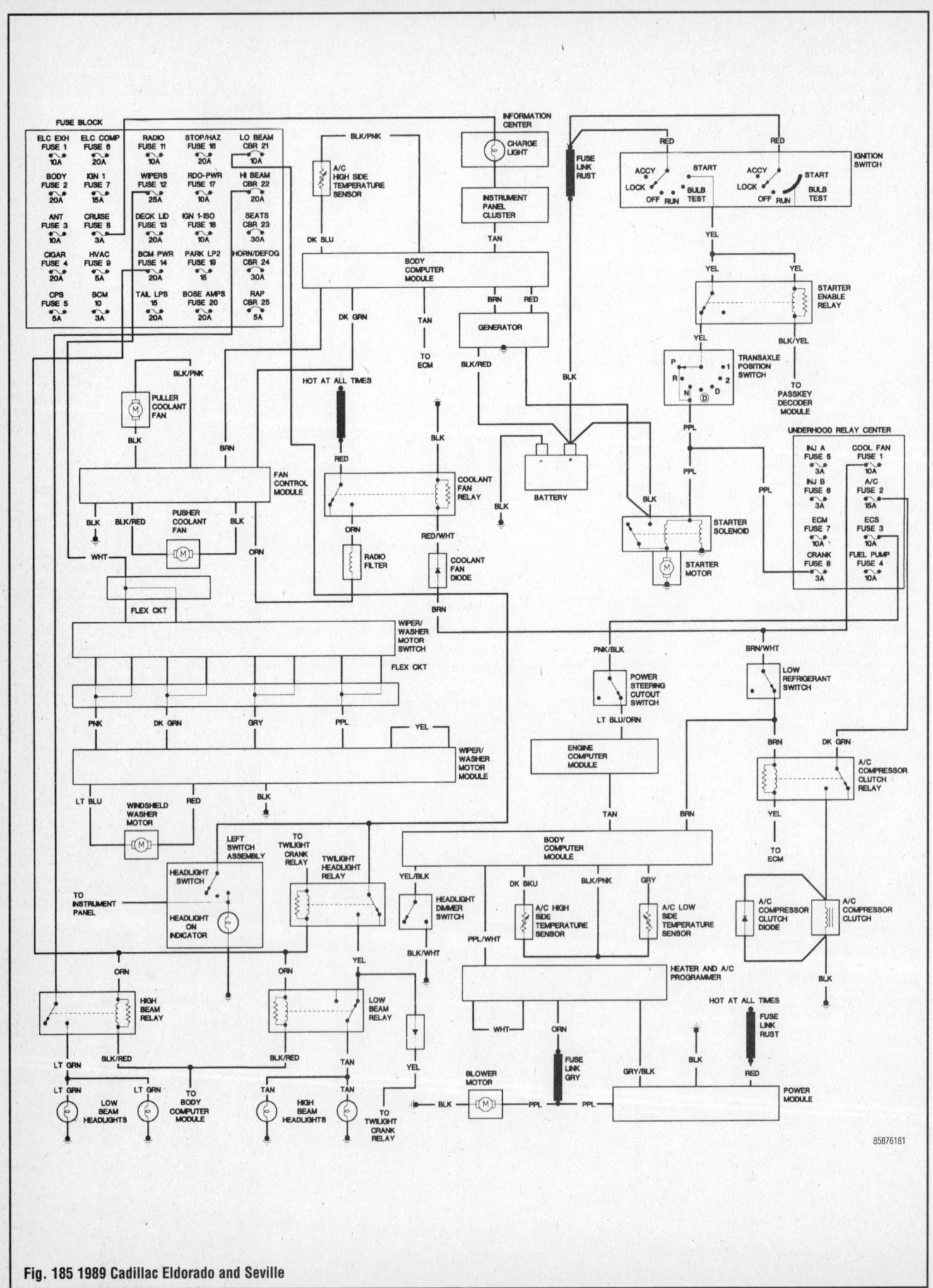

Fig. 185 1989 Cadillac Eldorado and Seville

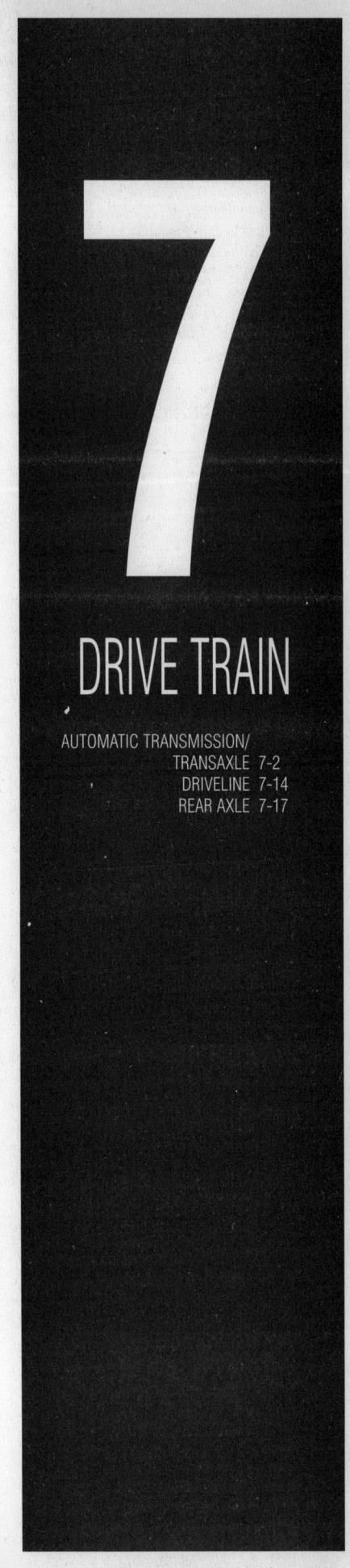

7

DRIVE TRAIN

AUTOMATIC TRANSMISSION/TRANSAXLE

Identification

General Motors Turbo Hydra-Matic automatic transmissions are used in all models covered in this guide. Through 1967–89, three basic transmission series have been used, covering four load capacities: the 200, which includes the 200C and 200–4R; the 350 including the 350C; and the 400, which includes the early model (1967–76) Turbo Hydra-Matic. There also have been two basic transaxle series used in the Eldorado and the front wheel drive Seville. The 325, which includes the 325–4L; and the 425, which includes the early model Turbo Hydra-Matic transaxle (1967–76) used in the Eldorado. 1986–89 front wheel drive models use the THM 440–T4 transaxle.

Adjustments

GASOLINE ENGINE MODELS

Shift Linkage/Cable

♦ See Figures 1, 2, 3 and 4

ALL MODELS EXCEPT 440–T4

1. Loosen the swivel screw on the shift linkage clamp.
2. Set the lever on the transmission into Neutral by moving it counterclockwise to the L1 detent, then clockwise three detent positions to Neutral.
3. Place the transmission selector lever (in the car) in Neutral as determined by the stop in the steering column. DO NOT use the indicator pointer for reference.
4. Tighten the shift linkage screw.
5. Check that the key cannot be removed and that the steering wheel is not locked when the key is in Run and the transmission is in Reverse. Check that the key can be removed and the transmission linkage is locked when the key is in Lock and the transmission is in Park. Be sure the car will start only in Park and Neutral. If it starts in any gear, the neutral start switch must be adjusted. Start the engine and check for proper shifting in all ranges.

440–T4

1. Move the console shift lever into the Neutral position.
2. Loosen the nut to the cable end pin at the transaxle manual lever arm. The transaxle cable must be assembled to the shift control assembly and installed in the control cable bracket.
3. Position the manual linkage lever arm in the Neutral position. Neutral may be found by rotating the manual lever clockwise from the Park position, through Reverse and into Neutral.

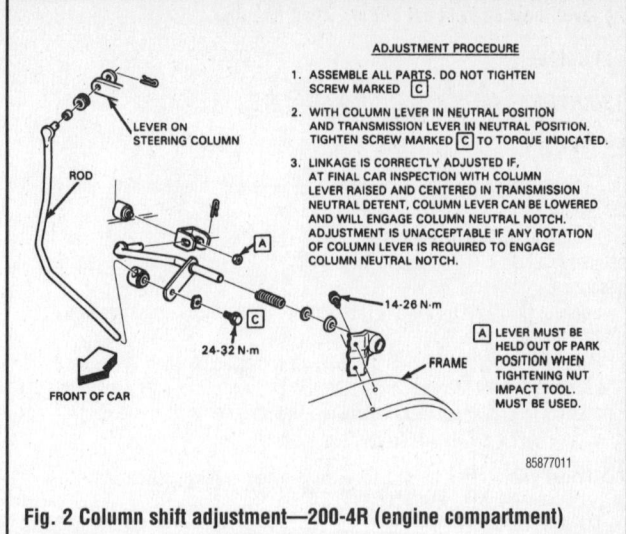

Fig. 2 Column shift adjustment—200-4R (engine compartment)

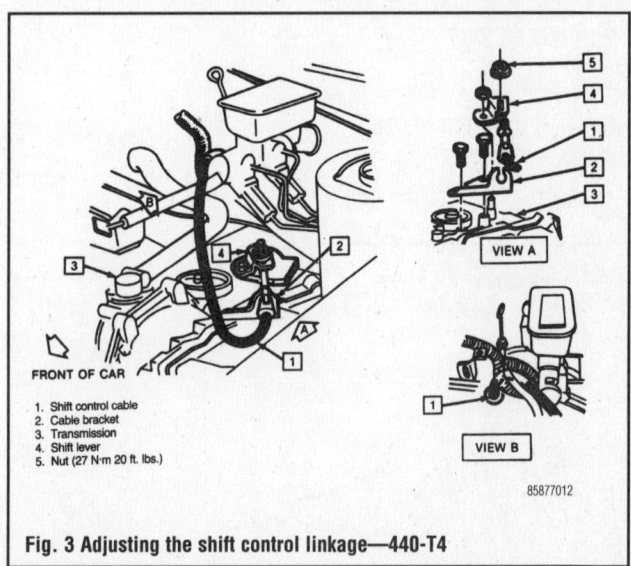

1. Shift control cable
2. Cable bracket
3. Transmission
4. Shift lever
5. Nut (27 N·m 20 ft. lbs.)

Fig. 3 Adjusting the shift control linkage—440-T4

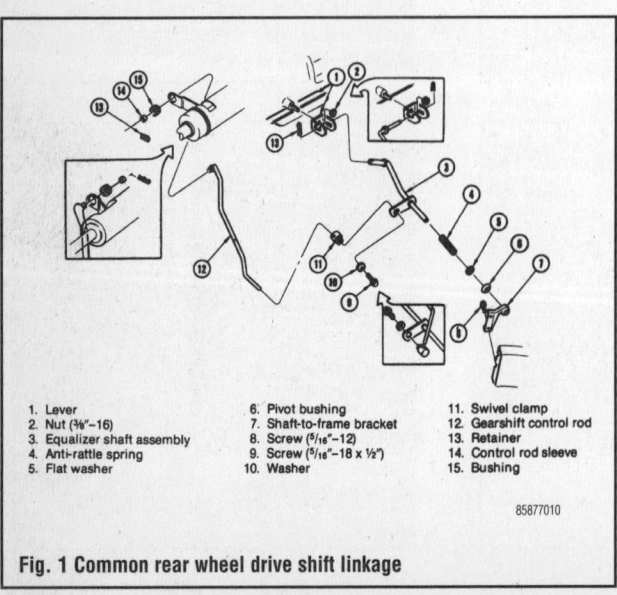

1. Lever	6. Pivot bushing	11. Swivel clamp
2. Nut (⅜"-16)	7. Shaft-to-frame bracket	12. Gearshift control rod
3. Equalizer shaft assembly	8. Screw (⁵⁄₁₆"-12)	13. Retainer
4. Anti-rattle spring	9. Screw (⁵⁄₁₆"-18 x ½")	14. Control rod sleeve
5. Flat washer	10. Washer	15. Bushing

Fig. 1 Common rear wheel drive shift linkage

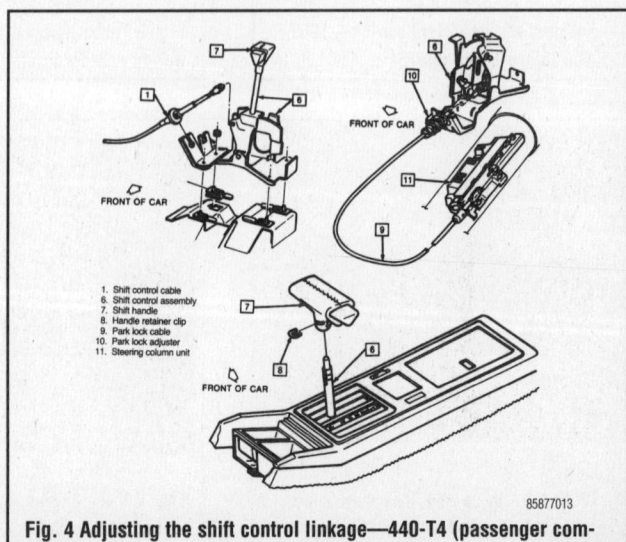

1. Shift control cable
6. Shift control assembly
7. Shift handle
8. Handle retainer clip
9. Park lock adjuster
10. Park lock adjuster
11. Steering column unit

Fig. 4 Adjusting the shift control linkage—440-T4 (passenger compartment)

4. With the cable end pin through the lever arm slot, hold the shift lever in the Neutral position and then tighten the nut on the cable end pin to 20 ft. lbs. (27 Nm).

➡The lever must be held out of Park when torquing.

Detent Cable

TURBO HYDRA-MATIC 350—THROUGH 1972

◆ **See Figure 5**

These transmissions utilize a downshift cable between the carburetor and the transmission.

1. Pry up on each side of the detent cable snap-lock with a small pry bar to release the lock. On cars equipped with a retaining screw, loosen the detent cable screw.
2. Squeeze the locking tabs and disconnect the snap-lock assembly from the throttle bracket.
3. Place the carburetor lever in the wide open throttle position. Make sure that the lever is against the wide open stop. On cars with Quadrajet carburetors, disengage the secondary lock-out before placing the lever in the wide open position.

➡The detent cable must be pulled through the detent position.

4. With the carburetor lever in the wide open position, push the snap-lock on the cable or else tighten the retaining screw.

➡Do not lubricate the detent cable.

TURBO HYDRA-MATIC 350—1973 AND LATER VEHICLES

◆ **See Figures 6, 7, 8, 9 and 10**

1. Stop the engine.
2. Locate the TV cable adjuster near the carburetor.

3. Depress and hold down the metal tab of the TV cable adjuster.
4. Move the slider until it stops against the fitting.
5. Release the adjuster tab.
6. Turn the carburetor lever to the full throttle stop position and release it.

➡By turning the carburetor lever to the full throttle stop, the TV cable will automatically adjust itself.

Detent Switch

◆ **See Figures 11, 12 and 13**

TURBO HYDRA-MATIC 400—1968 VEHICLES

1. Place the carburetor lever in the wide open position.
2. Position the automatic choke so that it is off.
3. Fully depress the switch plunger.
4. Adjust the switch mounting to obtain a distance of 0.05 in. (1.27mm) between the switch plunger and the throttle lever paddle.

TURBO HYDRA-MATIC 400—1969 AND LATER VEHICLES

Turbo Hydra-Matic 400 transmissions are equipped with an electrical detent, or downshift switch operated by the throttle linkage.

1. Pull the detent switch driver rearward until the hole in the switch body aligns with the hole in the driver. Insert a $\frac{3}{32}$ in. (2.38mm) diameter pin through the aligned holes to hold the driver in position.
2. Loosen the mounting bolt.
3. Press the switch plunger as far forward as possible. This will preset the switch for adjustment, which will occur on the first application of wide open throttle.
4. Tighten the mounting bolt and remove the pin.

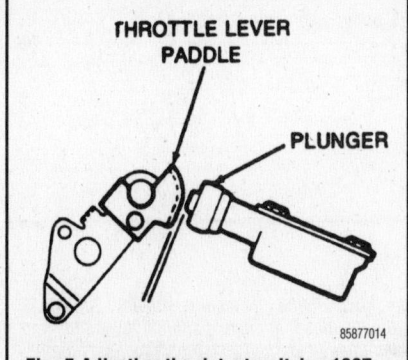

Fig. 5 Adjusting the detent switch—1967-72 Turbo Hydra-Matic 400

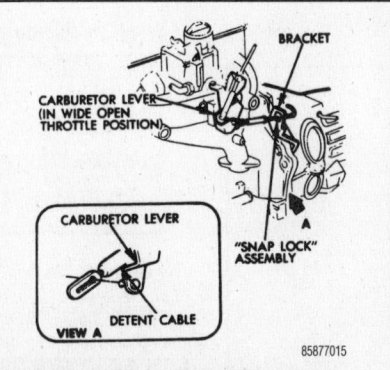

Fig. 6 Turbo Hydra-Matic 200 and 350 detent cable adjustment

Fig. 7 The detent (TV) cable is connected to the throttle lever on the carburetor or throttle body, as applicable

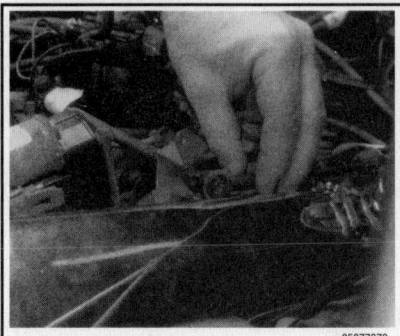

Fig. 8 Check linkage and mounting to carburetor or throttle body

Fig. 9 View of all transmission related linkage hardware

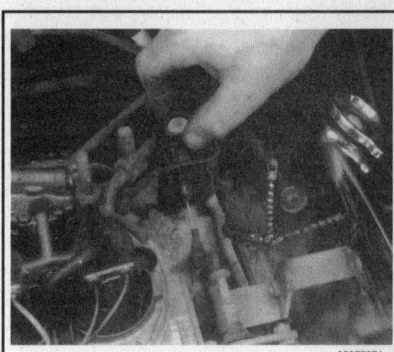

Fig. 10 Check linkage and mounting at this point

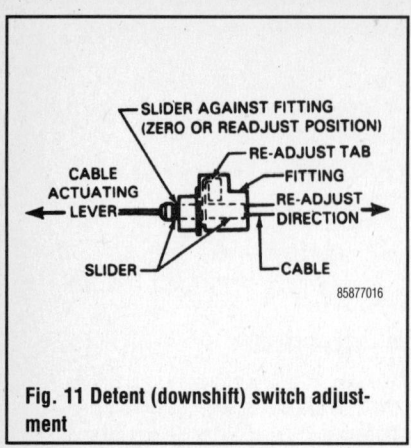

Fig. 11 Detent (downshift) switch adjustment

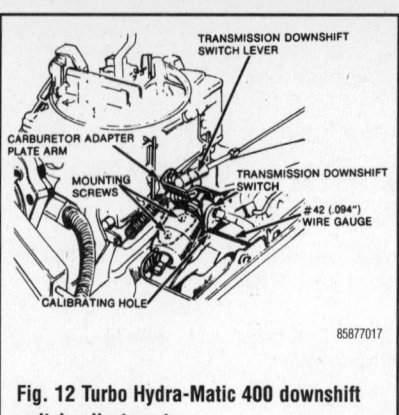

Fig. 12 Turbo Hydra-Matic 400 downshift switch adjustment

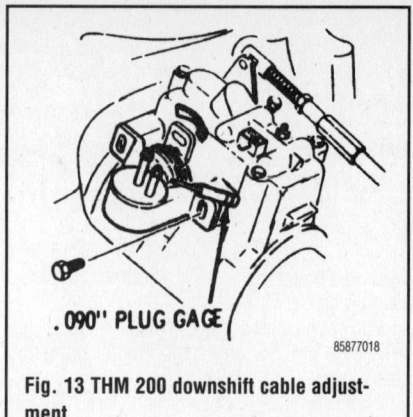

Fig. 13 THM 200 downshift cable adjustment

Throttle Valve (TV) Cable

▶ See Figures 14, 15 and 16

200–4R AND 440–T4

1. Check the transmission fluid level. The engine should be operating properly and the brakes should be adjusted. Check that the cable is connected at both ends.

2. Depress the adjustment tab on the upper end of the TV cable. While holding the tab down, move the slider through the fitting (away from the lever assembly) until it stops against the fitting.

3. Release the tab.

4. Rotate the cable actuating lever to the full throttle stop position. When doing this, the cable slider should ratchet out of the cable fitting toward the cable actuating lever.

5. Release the cable actuating assembly.

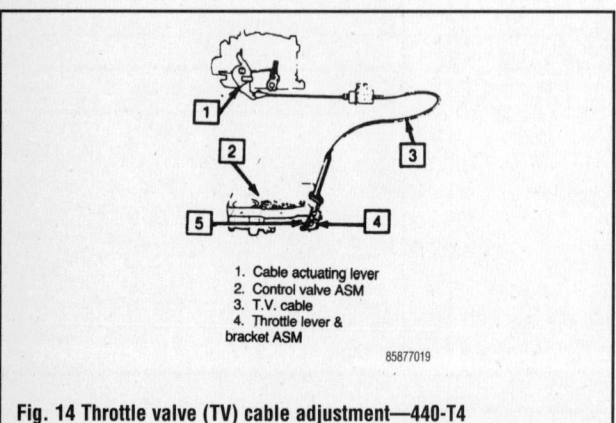

Fig. 14 Throttle valve (TV) cable adjustment—440-T4

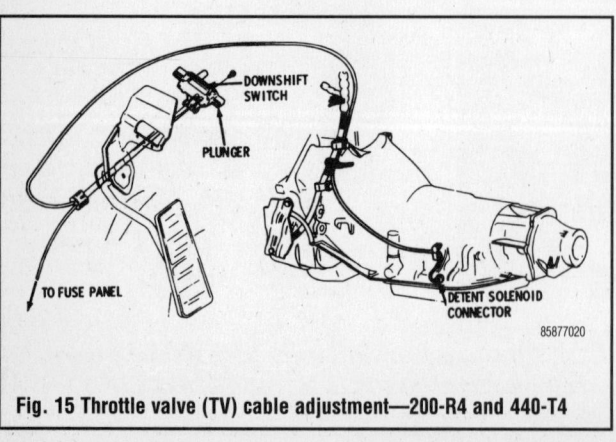

Fig. 15 Throttle valve (TV) cable adjustment—200-R4 and 440-T4

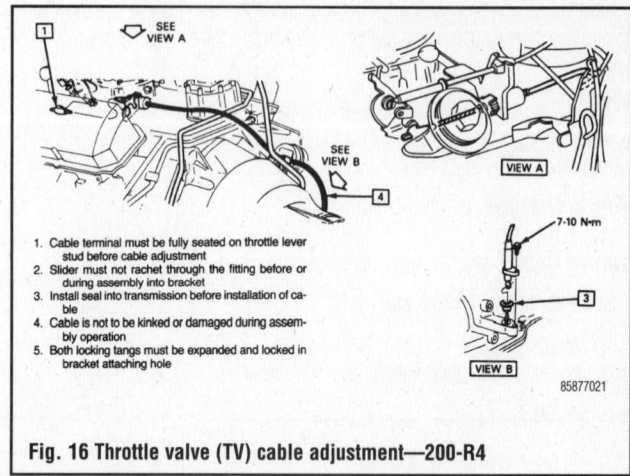

1. Cable terminal must be fully seated on throttle lever stud before cable adjustment
2. Slider must not rachet through the fitting before or during assembly into bracket
3. Install seal into transmission before installation of cable
4. Cable is not to be kinked or damaged during assembly operation
5. Both locking tangs must be expanded and locked in bracket attaching hole

Fig. 16 Throttle valve (TV) cable adjustment—200-R4

➡ Do not adjust the cable using the throttle pedal.

6. Check the cable for sticking and binding, at both cold and warm operating temperatures. Road test the vehicle.

DIESEL ENGINES MODELS

▶ See Figures 17, 18 and 19

➡ Before making any linkage adjustments, check the injection timing, and adjust if necessary. Also note that these adjustments should be performed together. The vacuum valve adjustment (THM 350's only) on 1979 and later models requires the use of several special tools.

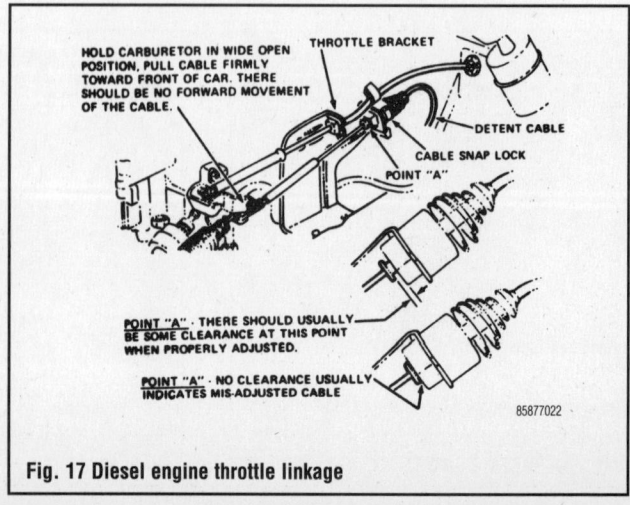

Fig. 17 Diesel engine throttle linkage

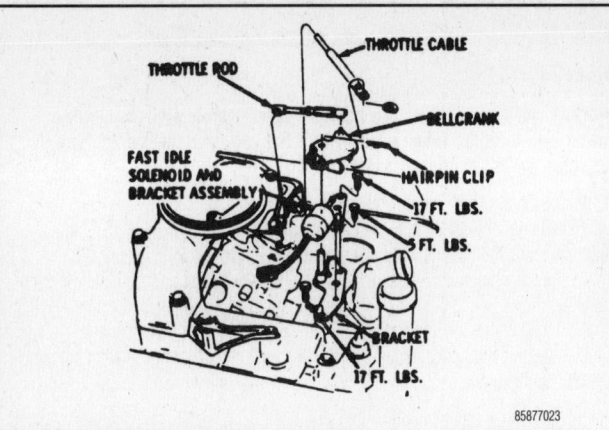

Fig. 18 Transmission vacuum valve adjustment—1978 diesel models

Throttle Rod

1. If equipped with cruise control, remove the clip from the control rod, then remove the rod from the bellcrank.

2. Remove the throttle valve cable (THM 200) or detent cable (THM 350) from the bellcrank.

3. Loosen the locknut on the throttle rod, then shorten the rod several turns.

4. Rotate the bellcrank to the full throttle stop, then lengthen the throttle rod until the injection pump lever contacts the injection pump full throttle stop. Release the bellcrank.

5. Tighten the throttle rod locknut.

6. Connect the throttle valve or detent cable and cruise control rod to the bellcrank. Adjust if necessary.

Throttle Valve (TV) or Detent Cable

Refer to the previous cable adjustment procedures for gasoline engines. Adjust according to the style of cable which is used.

Transmission Vacuum Valve

1978 MODELS

1. Remove the throttle rod from the bellcrank.

2. Loosen the transmission vacuum valve attaching bolts just enough to disengage the valve from the injection pump shaft.

3. Hold the injection pump lever against the full throttle stop.

4. Rotate the valve to the full throttle position, then insert a ³⁄₃₂ in. (2.38mm) diameter pin to hold the valve in the full throttle position.

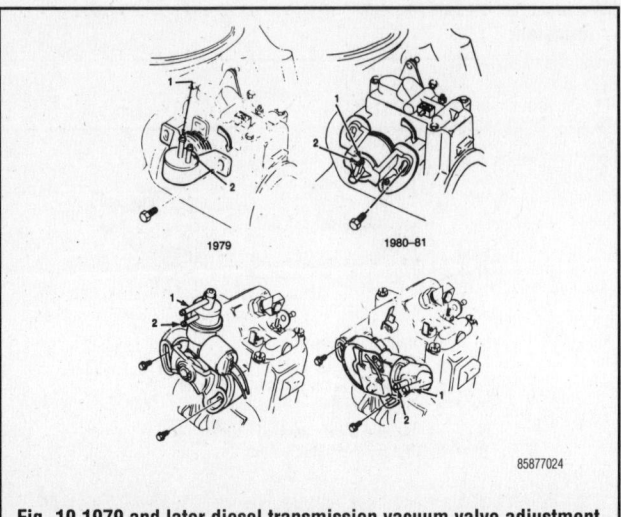

Fig. 19 1979 and later diesel transmission vacuum valve adjustment

5. Rotate the assembly clockwise until the injection pump lever is contacted.

6. While holding the assembly in contact with the lever, tighten the two bolts holding the vacuum valve to the pump, remove the pin and release the lever, then reconnect the throttle rod to the bellcrank.

1979 AND LATER MODELS

▶ See Figures 20, 21 and 22

1. Remove the air cleaner assembly.

2. Remove the air intake crossover from the intake manifold. Cover the intake manifold passages to prevent foreign material from entering the engine.

3. Disconnect the throttle rod from the injection pump throttle lever.

4. Loosen the transmission vacuum valve-to-injection pump bolts.

5. Mark and disconnect the vacuum lines from the vacuum valve.

6. Attach a carburetor angle gauge adapter (Kent-Moore tool J-26701-15 or its equivalent) to the injection pump throttle lever. Attach an angle gauge (J-26701 or its equivalent) to the gauge adapter.

7. Turn the throttle lever to the wide open throttle position. Set the angle gauge to zero degrees.

Year	Engine	Setting
1979	V8	49°
1980	V8	49–50°
1981	V8—Calif.	49–50°
1981	V8—non-Calif.	58°
1982	V8	58°

Fig. 20 Angle gauge settings

Year	In. Hg.
1979	8½–9
1980	7
1981 Calif.	7–8
1981 non-Calif.	8½–9
1982–83	10½

Fig. 21 Vacuum gauge readings

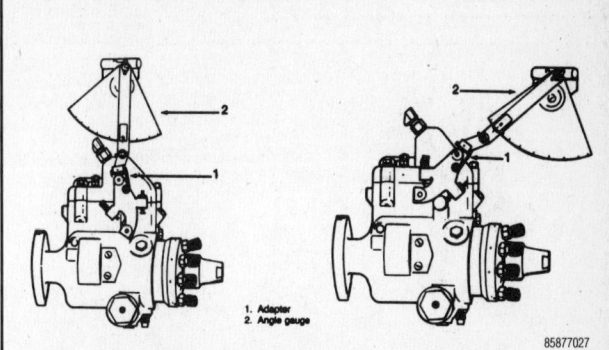

Fig. 22 Angle gauge installation (with adapter) for diesel vacuum valve adjustment—the gauge is positioned differently, depending on the type of throttle lever used

8. Center the bubble in the gauge level.

9. Set the angle gauge to the proper settings, according to the year and type of engine as indicated by the chart.

10. Attach a vacuum gauge to port 2 and a vacuum source (e.g. hand-held vacuum pump) to port 1 of the vacuum valve.

11. Apply 18–22 in. of vacuum to the valve. Slowly rotate the valve until the vacuum reading drops to the appropriate values, again as indicated by the vacuum gauge reading chart.

12. Tighten the vacuum valve retaining bolts.

13. Reconnect the original vacuum lines to the vacuum valve.

14. Remove the angle gauge and adapter.

15. Connect the throttle rod to the throttle lever.

16. Install the air intake crossover, using new gaskets.

17. Install the air cleaner assembly.

Neutral Safety Switch

REMOVAL & INSTALLATION

Except 1985–89 Eldorado and Seville

◆ See Figure 23

The neutral safety switch prevents the engine from being started in any transmission position except Neutral or Park. The switch is located on the upper side of the steering column under the instrument panel on column shift cars, and inside the shift console on floor shift models.

1. Remove the console for access on floor shift models.

2. Disconnect the electrical connectors.

3. Remove the neutral switch.

To install:

4. Place 1967–70 column shift lever models in Drive, and 1971 and later models in neutral. Locate the lever tang against the transmission selector plate on column shift models.

5. Align the slot in the contact support with the hole in the switch. Insert a ³⁄₃₂ in. (2.38mm) diameter pin in place. The switch is now aligned in Drive position.

➡1973 and later neutral safety switches have a shear-pin installed to aid in proper switch alignment so that insertion of a pin is unnecessary. Moving the shift lever from Neutral shears the pin.

6. Place the contact support drive slot over the drive tang. Install the switch mounting screws.

7. Remove the aligning pin. Connect the electrical wiring, and replace the console.

8. Set the parking brake and hold your foot on the service brake pedal. Check to see that the engine will start only in Park or Neutral.

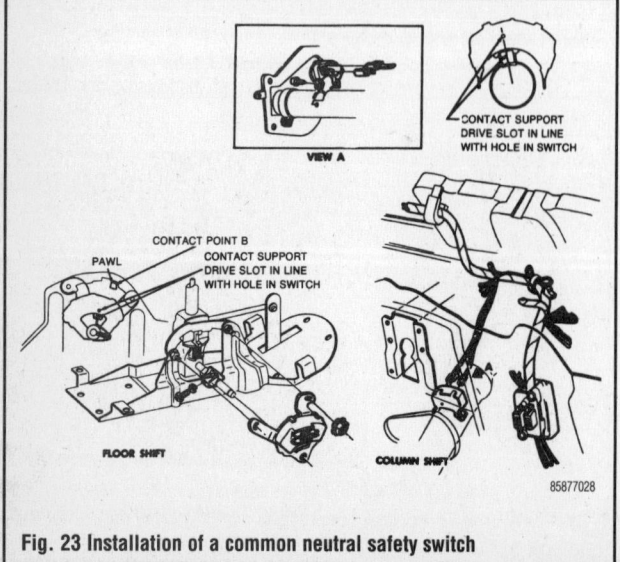

Fig. 23 Installation of a common neutral safety switch

ADJUSTMENT

◆ See Figure 24

➡1974 and later cars do not have a neutral safety switch. Instead, these cars have an interlock between the lock and the transmission selector, which is non-adjustable.

1. Place the shift lever in Neutral.

2. Move the switch until you can insert a gauge pin, ³⁄₃₂ in. (2.38mm) diameter, into the hole in the switch and through to the alignment hole.

3. Loosen the switch securing screws. Remove the console first, if necessary.

4. Tighten the screws and remove the pin.

5. Step on the brake pedal and check to see that the engine will only start in Neutral or Park.

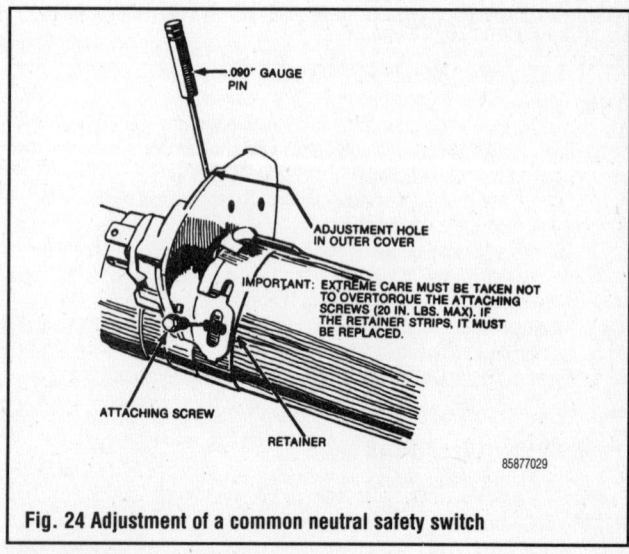

Fig. 24 Adjustment of a common neutral safety switch

1985–89 Eldorado and Seville

◆ See Figure 25

All neutral safety/back-up light switches come with a small plastic alignment pin installed. Leave this pin in place.

1. Place the shifter assembly in the Neutral position.

2. Remove the shifter lever-to-switch nut and the lever.

3. Disconnect the electrical connector from the neutral safety/back-up light switch.

4. Remove the neutral safety/back-up light switch-to-transaxle bolts and the switch from the vehicle.

To install:

5. Position the shifter shaft in the Neutral position.

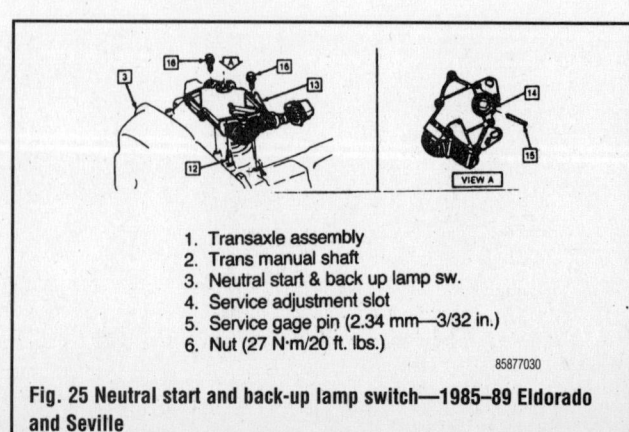

1. Transaxle assembly
2. Trans manual shaft
3. Neutral start & back up lamp sw.
4. Service adjustment slot
5. Service gage pin (2.34 mm—3/32 in.)
6. Nut (27 N·m/20 ft. lbs.)

Fig. 25 Neutral start and back-up lamp switch—1985–89 Eldorado and Seville

➡If using an old switch or the plastic pin (new switch) is broken, install a ³⁄₃₂ in. (2.38mm) diameter pin gauge (drill bit) into the neutral safety/back-up light switch; the switch is then locked into its Neutral position.

6. Align the flats of the shifter shaft and the neutral safety/back-up light, then, align the switch-to-tang on the transaxle. Torque the switch-to-transaxle bolts to 22 ft. lbs. (30 Nm). Remove the pin gauge.

7. To complete installation, reverse the removal procedures. Make sure that the engine starts only in the Park and Neutral positions.

Transmission/Transaxle

REMOVAL & INSTALLATION

Rear Wheel Drive Models

♦ **See Figures 26, 27 and 28**

1. Disconnect the negative battery cable.
2. Raise the car and make sure it is supported securely.
3. Disconnect the transmission linkage by removing the one nut from the shaft on the left side of the transmission.
4. Remove the speedometer drive cable.
5. Disconnect and cap the oil cooler pipes at the transmission. Plug the connector holes in the transmission.
6. Disconnect the vacuum modulator hose.
7. Remove the driveshaft.
8. Remove the lower flex plate housing cover.
9. Remove the three converter to flex plate attaching bolts. Rotate the converter and flexplate until the bolts can be reached for removal. A bolt in the end of the crankshaft balancer can be used to rotate the flexplate.

➡**Do not pry on the flexplate ring gear or transmission case to rotate the converter, as the flexplate or case may be damaged.**

10. Place a jack or other suitable device under the rear of the engine.
11. Remove the two nuts from the tunnel strap and remove the strap.
12. Remove the two rear engine mount to extension housing bolts.
13. Position a transmission jack under the transmission and raise just enough to take the load off the rear engine support, then remove the shim.
14. Remove the four bolts from the rear engine support and swivel the support out of the way. Allow the support to hang by the parking brake cable.
15. Disconnect the exhaust pipe from the exhaust manifold and remove the rear engine support cross member.
16. Remove the six transmission case to engine attaching bolts. If necessary lower the engine and transmission slightly to gain access to the upper attaching bolts.
17. Move the transmission towards the rear of the car, disengaging the transmission from the engine.
18. The converter weighs about 50 pounds. To prevent it from falling out and getting damaged, install a converter holding clamp Tool No. J-21366 on the front of the transmission case, and lower the transmission from the car.

To install:

19. Install the converter on the turbine shaft making certain that the converter drive hub is fully engaged with the pump gear tangs, and install the converter holding clamp on the front of the transmission case.
20. Align the front of the transmission case dowel holes with the dowels on the engine. Install the six transmission case to engine attaching bolts and tighten the bolts to 35 ft. lbs. (47 Nm).
21. Rotate the converter until two of the three weld nuts on the converter line up with the bolt holes in the flexplate.

➡**Make certain the converter rotates freely in this position and is not cocked and that the pilot in the center of the converter is properly seated in the crankshaft.**

22. Install the two flexplate to converter attaching bolts through the accessible holes in the flexplate and finger-tighten.

➡**The bolts must not be tightened at this time to assure proper alignment of the converter.**

23. Rotate the converter and install the third attaching bolt. Tighten all bolts to 35 ft. lbs. (47 Nm).
24. Lower the transmission carefully and install the two rear engine mount to extension housing bolts. Tighten the bolts to 55 ft. lbs. (75 Nm).
25. Install the exhaust pipe, rear engine support cross member and the tunnel strap.
26. The remainder of the installation is the reverse of removal. Add transmission fluid as required.

Front Wheel Drive Models

1967–85 VEHICLES

1. Open hood and disconnect negative battery cable (two cables on diesels).
2. Disconnect the speedometer cable at the transmission. Remove transmission oil dipstick tube.
3. Remove the air cleaner.
4. Disconnect the transmission throttle valve (TV/detent) cable at its upper end. Disconnect the linkage by removing one nut from shaft on left side of transmission, if so equipped.
5. Safely support the engine unit from underneath, or install an engine holding fixture between the cowl and radiator support.
6. Remove the top and two upper left final drive to transmission bolts.
7. Remove the remaining accessible engine-to-transmission bolts (5).
8. Jack up the car and safely support it with jackstands.
9. Remove the starter assembly.
10. Disconnect the transmission converter clutch connector.
11. Disconnect the transmission oil cooler lines and plug the openings.
12. Remove the flywheel inspection cover (loosen top left bolt). Matchmark the flywheel-to-converter relationship for later assembly.
13. Disconnect the exhaust Y-pipe connection to the left exhaust pipe at the manifold. On gasoline cars, disconnect the catalytic converter hanger bolts (2). On all, lower the exhaust system about 5 inches and support the system.
14. Remove the four bolts holding the second frame crossmember.
15. Position a hydraulic floor jack underneath the transmission, with a

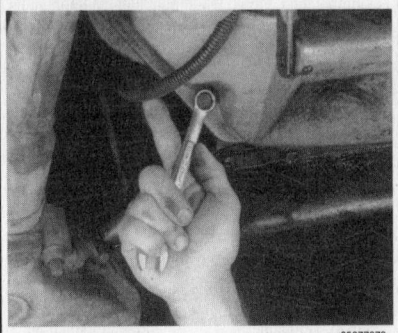
Fig. 26 Removing the transmission inspection cover bolts

Fig. 27 Removing the transmission inspection cover

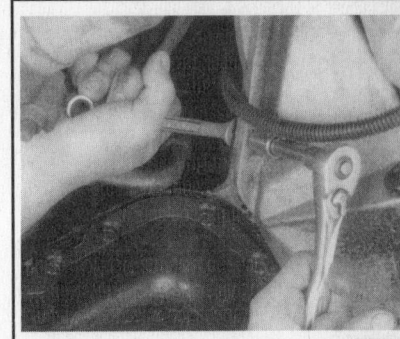
Fig. 28 Installing the transmission inspection cover bolts

wooden block on the jack pad to protect the transmission case. Jack up the transmission slightly.

16. Remove the three remaining final drive to transmission bolts.
17. Remove the converter-to-flywheel bolts.
18. Disconnect the shift linkage at the transmissions.
19. Remove the final drive support bracket bolt.
20. Remove the right transmission mount (through-bolt and three bracket bolts).
21. Remove the left transmission mount through-bolt. Remove the lower bracket-to-transmission bolt. Raise the transmission assembly about 2 inches for access to the two remaining upper bracket-to-transmission bolts. Remove the remaining transmission-to-engine bolt.
22. Carefully lower the transmission unit while disengaging the final drive.
23. Install a C-clamp or converter holding clamp in front of the torque converter (attached to the bell housing) to hold the converter in place. Remove the transmission from the car.

To install:

24. Install the transmission in the vehicle.
25. Reverse all the removal procedures.
26. Always replace the final drive-to-transmission gasket. Use care when engaging the final drive-to-transmission splines. Make sure the final drive-to-transmission mounting faces are in alignment with each other. After the splines are engaged, loosely install the two final drive-to-transmission lower attaching bolts. You can save time here by installing two engine-to-transmission bolts from above first to aid alignment.

After the final drive and transmission are mated align the transmission with the engine and install the remaining attaching bolts. Before the flywheel-to-converter bolts, make sure the weld nuts on the converter are flush with the flywheel and that the converter rotates freely by hand in this position. Then hand-start all three bolts and tighten finger-tight. This will insure proper converter alignment. Torque the transmission-to-engine bolts to 35 ft. lbs. (47 Nm), the final drive-to-transmission bolts to 30 ft. lbs. (41 Nm), and the final drive support bracket to final drive bolts to 35 ft. lbs. (47 Nm).

1986 AND LATER VEHICLES

▶ See Figure 29

1. Disconnect the negative battery cable.
2. Remove the air cleaner assembly.
3. Tag and disconnect the throttle valve (TV) cable at the transmission end and position it out of the way.
4. Disconnect and remove the cruise control servo and bracket assembly.
5. Tag and disconnect all electrical leads at the distributor, the oil pressure sending unit end at the transmission.
6. Remove the engine oil cooler line bracket. Wire the oil lines in their position so they do not become bent during transmission removal.
7. Disconnect the shift linkage bracket at the transmission. Disconnect the manual shift lever from the manual shaft. You needn't remove the cable from the lever or the bracket.
8. Remove the vacuum modulator.
9. Remove the TV cable support bracket and the engine oil cooler line bracket.
10. Remove the four bell housing-to-engine bolts in positions 2, 3, 4 and 5.
11. Disconnect the A.I.R. crossover pipe fitting and position it out of the way. Remove the radiator hose bracket.
12. Remove the transmission mount-to-bracket nuts.
13. Install an engine hoist to the engine lifting hooks and take the slack out so that the engine will be supported by the hoist.
14. Raise the front of the vehicle and support it on safety stands. Remove the front wheels.
15. Remove the right and left stabilizer link bolts and ball joint cotter pins and nuts. Separate both ball joints from the steering knuckles.
16. Remove the A/C splash shield. Remove the No. 1 cradle insulator mount cover.
17. Remove the hose connections and the rear mounting clip from the A.I.R. pipe end.
18. Tag and disconnect the vacuum hoses and wiring loom from the front of the engine cradle.
19. Remove the engine mount and dampener-to-engine cradle attachments, the transmission mount-to-engine cradle attachments and the wiring loom clip-to-transmission mount bracket.

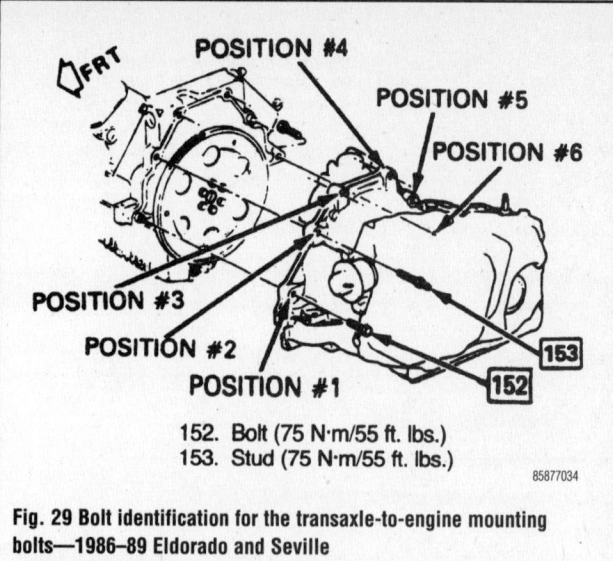

152. Bolt (75 N·m/55 ft. lbs.)
153. Stud (75 N·m/55 ft. lbs.)

85877034

Fig. 29 Bolt identification for the transaxle-to-engine mounting bolts—1986–89 Eldorado and Seville

20. Lower the vehicle.
21. Raise the transmission about 2 inches from the original position by means of the two left support hooks.
22. Raise the vehicle.
23. Remove the right front and left rear cradle-to-cradle bolts. Remove the left stabilizer mounting bolts.
24. Remove the No. 1 cradle mount insulator bolt and then remove the left cradle member.

➡ **When removing the left cradle member, separate the right front cover first.**

25. Remove the A.I.R. management valve and bracket assembly from the transmission mount bracket, then reposition the bracket-to-transmission stud bolts.
26. Lower the vehicle, then lower the transmission to its original position.
27. Remove the transmission mounting bracket and then raise the vehicle again.
28. Remove the right rear transmission mount-to-bracket and the engine-to-transmission brace bolts into the transmission. Disconnect the VSS connector.
29. Remove the flywheel covers and the torque converter bolts.
30. Position a transmission jack under the transmission to support it and then remove the remaining bell housing bolts.

➡ **When removing or installing the No. 6 bell housing bolt, it is necessary to use a 3 in. (76mm) long socket wrench extension to gain access to the bolt through the right side wheel housing.**

31. Disconnect and plug the oil cooler lines at the transmission.
32. Install drive axle boot seal protectors, then separate the halfshafts from the transmission and wire them out of the way.
33. Remove the transmission assembly.

To install:

34. Position the transmission and then install the lower bell housing bolts. Tighten all bolts and/or studs to 55 ft. lbs. (74 Nm).

➡ **When referring to the illustration, positions No. 2, 3 & 4 are studs. Positions No. 1, 5 & 6 are bolts (the bolt in position No. 6 is slightly longer than those in 1 and 5).**

35. Install the converter-to-flexplate bolts and tighten them to 46 ft. lbs. (63 Nm).
36. Install the flexplate splash shield and then attach and cooler lines to the transmission case. Tighten the cooler line fitting nuts to 15 ft. lbs. (21 Nm).
37. Installation of the remaining components is in the reverse order of removal. Please note the following points:
   a. Tighten the No. 1 insulator mount bolt to 74 ft. lbs. (100 Nm).
   b. Tighten all cradle-to-cradle mounting nuts to 74 ft. lbs. (100 Nm).
   c. Tighten the upper transaxle mounting bracket stud bolts to 74 ft. lbs. (100 Nm).

d. Tighten the side transaxle mounting bracket stud bolts to 50 ft. lbs. (70 Nm).

e. Tighten the rear (left) transaxle mounting nuts to 35 ft. lbs. (45 Nm).

f. Tighten the engine mount-to-cradle attachments to 35 ft. lbs. (45 Nm).

g. Tighten the right rear mounting bracket-to-transaxle mounting bolts to 50 ft. lbs. (70 Nm).

h. Tighten the right rear mounting bracket nuts to 35 ft. lbs. (45 Nm).

i. Tighten the stabilizer mounting bolts to 38 ft. lbs. (50 Nm).

j. Tighten the stabilizer link bolts to 13 ft. lbs. (17 Nm).

k. Tighten the ball joint nuts to 81 ft. lbs. (110 Nm).

l. Tighten the shift cable bracket-to-transaxle bolt to 18 ft. lbs. (24 Nm).

m. Check the transaxle fluid level.

n. Adjust the shift linkage and TV cable as previously described in this section.

Final Drive Unit

GENERAL INFORMATION

➡**A final drive unit is only used on front wheel drive models.**

The final drive unit is secured to the transmission by The final drive unit is secured to the transmission by six screws. It is held at the front by a support bracket which is attached to the engine block.

The 8 in. ring and pinion gear set is the hypoid type, having the pinion above the ring gear center. A splined transmission output shaft fits into and rotates the drive pinion gear. Two preloaded tapered roller bearings are used to support the drive pinion in the housing.

When the pinion nut is tightened, a spacer is compressed between the outer bearing and a shoulder on the pinion stem. This spacer allows bearing preload adjustment. The fore and aft position of the drive pinion is adjusted by the use of a measured shim placed between the drive pinion head and the inner bearing.

Torque from the drive pinion is transferred to the ring gear attached to the differential case. The case is held in the final drive housing by two tapered roller side bearings. Shims are used to adjust and maintain preload on the side bearings. Proper ring gear to pinion backlash is obtained by varying the shim thickness from side to side. Two side gears, inside the case, have splined bores for driving the output shafts. They are positioned to rotate in counterbored cavities in the case. Two pinion gears, also inside the case, have smooth bores and turn freely on the pinion cross shaft. The pinion gears are in constant mesh with the side gears and act as idler gears when wheels turn at different speeds. These gears are backed by steel thrust washers and the cross shaft is retained by a roll pin.

REMOVAL & INSTALLATION

▶ See Figure 30

1967–78 Eldorado

1. Disconnect the negative battery cable.
2. Unbolt the transmission filler tube bracket and remove the filler tube.
3. Remove screws A, B and the nut H.
4. Disconnect the transmission cooler lines from the final drive support bracket and slide the clip out of the way.
5. Remove the locknut, washer and long through-bolt holding the final drive support brace to the engine mount bracket.
6. Remove the right hand output shaft.

⁂ CAUTION

The shock absorbers act as rebound stops. Before performing the following Step, be sure that the right hand shock absorber lower sleeve cannot be dislodged from the stud.

7. Place jackstands under the front frame side rails and lower the hoist that was used when removing the right hand output shaft.
8. Remove the final drive cover and allow the lubricant to drain into a drain pan.
9. Remove the 6 screws holding the left hand drive axle to the output shaft. Compress the drive axle inner C.V. joint and hold it in this position to remove the final drive unit with the left hand output shaft installed.
10. Remove the bolt, washer, and nut holding the left tie strut to the frame

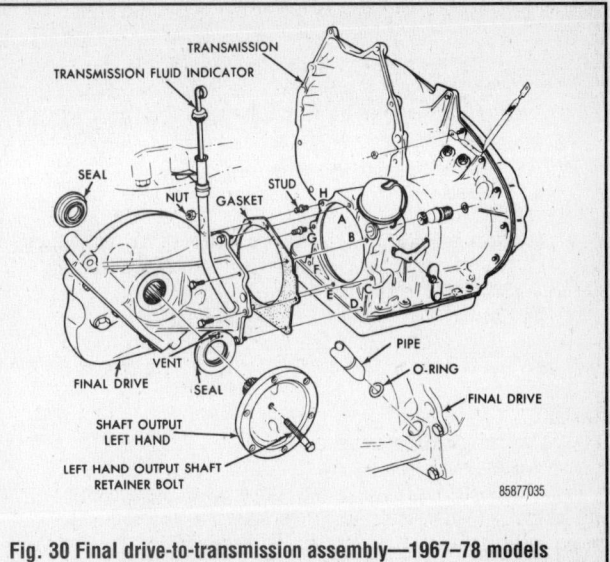

Fig. 30 Final drive-to-transmission assembly—1967–78 models

crossmember. Loosen the bolt holding the strut to the side rail and rotate the strut outboard until the strut is clear of the final drive area.

11. Remove the large through-bolt nut and washers, securing the final drive support bracket to the final drive.
12. Remove the final drive support bracket.
13. Remove the final drive cover and gasket(s).
14. Remove the final drive with a transmission lift and adapter. The adapter should have a rotating feature to ease removal and installation.
15. Place a drain pan under the transmission and remove screws C, D, E, F and nut G.
16. Disengage the final drive splines from the transmission and let the unit drain.
17. Remove the final drive unit from under the car by sliding the unit toward the front of the car and permitting the ring gear to rotate over the steering linkage. Lower the housing from the car.
18. Remove and discard the final drive-to-transmission gasket.

To install:

19. Positioning new gasket on transmission, install final drive unit, permitting ring gear to rotate up over steering linkage.
20. Align final drive splines with splines in transmission.
21. Align bolt studs G and H on transmission with holes in final drive.
22. Install bolts C, D, E and F and nut G finger-tight.
23. Install support bracket on final drive unit.
24. Install other support brackets.
25. Install bolt in fluid cooler lines, clamp and tighten to 8 ft. lbs. (11 Nm).
26. Tighten bolts C, D, E and F and nut G to 25 ft. lbs. (34 Nm).
27. Reposition left drive axle and install screws to 65 ft. lbs. (88 Nm).
28. Install right output shaft and axle.
29. Position final drive cover to final drive and install screws to 30 ft. lbs. (41 Nm), through 1973; 13 ft. lbs. (10 Nm) for 1974–78.
30. Fill final drive unit. Tighten lower shock.
31. Install wheels and tires, tightening nuts finger-tight.
32. Lower car and tighten wheel nuts to 105 ft. lbs. (142 Nm) through 1972; 130 ft. lbs. (176 Nm) for 1973–78.
33. Install bolts A and B and nut H, tightening to 25 ft. lbs. (34 Nm).
34. Install new O-ring on transmission filler tube, remove plug in filler tube hole and install filler tube.
35. Position the transmission cooler line clips and secure the support bracket with the screw.
36. Connect battery.
37. Check/add engine oil and transmission fluid. Start engine and add fluid as needed.
38. After running check the seals for leaks.

1979–85 Eldorado and 1980–85 Seville

▶ See Figure 31

1. Disconnect the negative battery cable and raise the car. Place jackstands underneath the front frame horns and the lower front post.

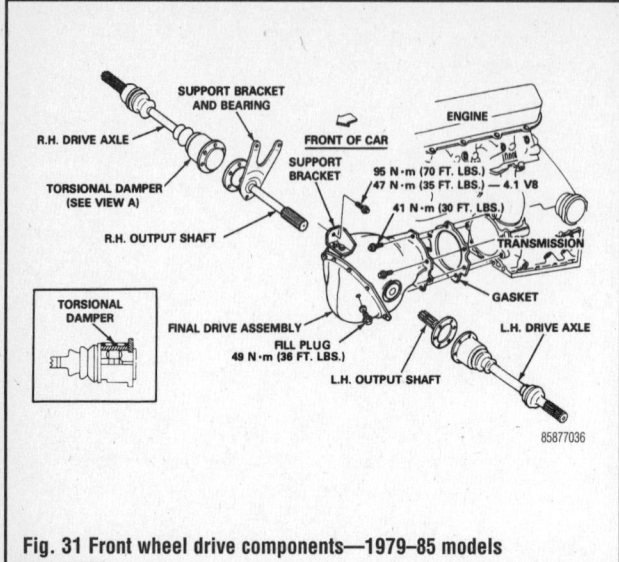

R.H. DRIVE AXLE

SUPPORT BRACKET
AND BEARING

FRONT OF CAR

ENGINE

SUPPORT
BRACKET

TORSIONAL DAMPER
(SEE VIEW A)

95 N·m (70 FT. LBS.)
47 N·m (35 FT. LBS.) — 4.1 V8

41 N·m (30 FT. LBS.)

R.H. OUTPUT SHAFT

TRANSMISSION

TORSIONAL
DAMPER

FINAL DRIVE ASSEMBLY

GASKET

FILL PLUG
49 N·m (36 FT. LBS.)

L.H. DRIVE AXLE

L.H. OUTPUT SHAFT

85877036

Fig. 31 Front wheel drive components—1979–85 models

2. Remove the frame brace attaching bolts and pivot the braces outward in order to gain access.

3. With a drain pan under the final drive cover, loosen the final drive cover screws and allow the fluid to drain. Remove the cover and gasket material.

4. Remove the screws on both sides attaching the output shaft to the drive axle. Separate the flanges of the shaft and axle to obtain clearance. The final drive assembly will be removed with the output shafts installed.

5. Remove the battery cable retaining screws from the right output shaft and the screws securing the support to the engine block. Rotate the support downward for clearance.

6. Remove the screws which attach the final drive shield to the transmission and the support bracket. Remove the shield.

7. Remove the remaining final drive screws.

8. Remove the final drive support-to-engine block attaching screws.

9. Using a puller, separate the steering linkage from the pitman arm. Push the linkage toward the front of the car.

10. Slide the final drive assembly forward, off the transmission shaft and remove the unit. Do not hold the unit by the output shafts as the seals or splines could easily be damaged.

To install:

11. Thoroughly clean all the gasket surfaces and position a new gasket on the final drive. Do not use a sealer on the gasket.

12. Align the final drive assembly, with the output shafts attached, to the transmission and install all the attaching screws except the one used to hold the shield. Torque in rotation to 30 ft. lbs. (41 Nm) in two steps.

13. Loosen the front support bracket screws and install the bracket to the engine block while holding the bracket flush on the housing pad. Torque to 50 ft. lbs. (68 Nm).

14. Install the final drive shield. Torque the drive-to-transmission screw to 30 ft. lbs. (41 Nm) and the bracket-to-housing screws to 34 ft. lbs. (46 Nm).

15. Align the right output shaft support with the attaching holes in the engine block. Do not allow the shaft and support assemblies to hang from the drive unit. By moving the flange end of the shaft up and down and installing the screws and washers loosely, locate the centered position. Torque the screws to 50 ft. lbs. (68 Nm).

16. Install the battery cable retainer.

17. Align the right drive axle to the output shaft and install the attaching screws. Torque the screws to 60 ft. lbs. (81 Nm). Repeat for the left side.

18. Position a new cover gasket or apply silicone sealer on the final drive cover. Install the cover and torque the screws to 7 ft. lbs. (9 Nm). Refill the unit. Torque the filler plug to 30 ft. lbs. (41 Nm)

19. Install the steering linkage to the pitman arm and torque to 60 ft. lbs. (81 Nm). If the cotter pin hole does not align properly, tighten the nut slightly. Do not loosen to align. Install a new cotter pin.

20. Install the frame braces and torque the nuts to 50 ft. lbs. (68 Nm).

21. Lower the car, connect the battery cable, start the car and check the transmission fluid. When the final drive has reached operating temperature, check it for leaks.

Halfshafts

Drive axles (halfshafts) on these front wheel drive models are flexible assemblies and consist of an axle shaft with an inner and outer constant velocity (CV) joint. The right halfshaft has a torsional damper mounted in the center. The inner constant velocity joint has complete flexibility, plus inward and outward movement. The outer constant velocity joint has complete flexibility but doesn't allow for inward and outward movement.

REMOVAL & INSTALLATION

1967–78 Eldorado

RIGHT DRIVE AXLE

1. Remove the negative battery cable and the wheel disc.

2. If the halfshaft is to be removed, release the cotter pin and loosen but do not remove the spindle nut.

3. Raise the car at the lower control arms.

4. Loosen but do not remove the right front shock absorber lower mounting nut. Then pry the shock absorber along the lower mounting stud until it reaches the nut. Do not remove the shock absorber from the lower mount.

5. To keep the torsion bar connectors from being damaged, cover them with a short length of rubber hose.

6. Remove the screws securing the halfshaft to the output shaft.

7. Position the inside end of the halfshaft toward the starter motor to gain access to the output shaft. Then remove the screw which supports the output shaft to the final drive housing.

8. Remove the two screws which support the right output shaft support to the engine.

9. Remove the output shaft, support and strut as an assembly in the following manner.

   a. Slide the output shaft outward to disengage the splines.

   b. Move the inside end of the assembly forward and downward until it is clear of the car.

10. If the halfshaft is to be removed, use the following procedure.

   a. Using a hammer and a wooden block tap the end of the halfshaft to unseat the axle at the hub.

➡**The spindle nut should be loosened but not removed.**

   b. Rotate the axle inward and toward the front of the car positioning the axle over the front crossmember and out from under the car.

✳ WARNING

Care must be exercised so that constant velocity joints do not turn to full extremes, and that seals are not damaged against shock absorber or stabilizer bar.

To install:

11. Carefully place right hand halfshaft assembly into lower control arm and enter outer race splines into knuckle.

12. Lubricate final drive output shaft seal with wheel bearing grease.

13. Install right hand output shaft into final drive and attach the support bolts to engine and brace. Torque the bolts to 50 ft. lbs. (68 Nm).

14. Install brace.

15. Move right hand halfshaft assembly toward front of car and align with right hand output shaft. Install attaching bolts and torque to 65 ft. lbs. (88 Nm).

16. Install washer and nut on halfshaft.

17. Remove the jack stands and lower the vehicle.

18. Tighten wheel lugs to 130 ft. lbs. (176 Nm); drive axle nut to 110 ft. lbs. (149 Nm). Install cotter pin.

➡**Align the hole by tightening the nut.**

LEFT DRIVE AXLE

1. Hoist car under the lower control arms.

2. Remove wheel and tire.

3. Remove halfshaft cotter pin, nut and washer.

4. Install a piece of rubber hose over lower control arm torsion bar connector.

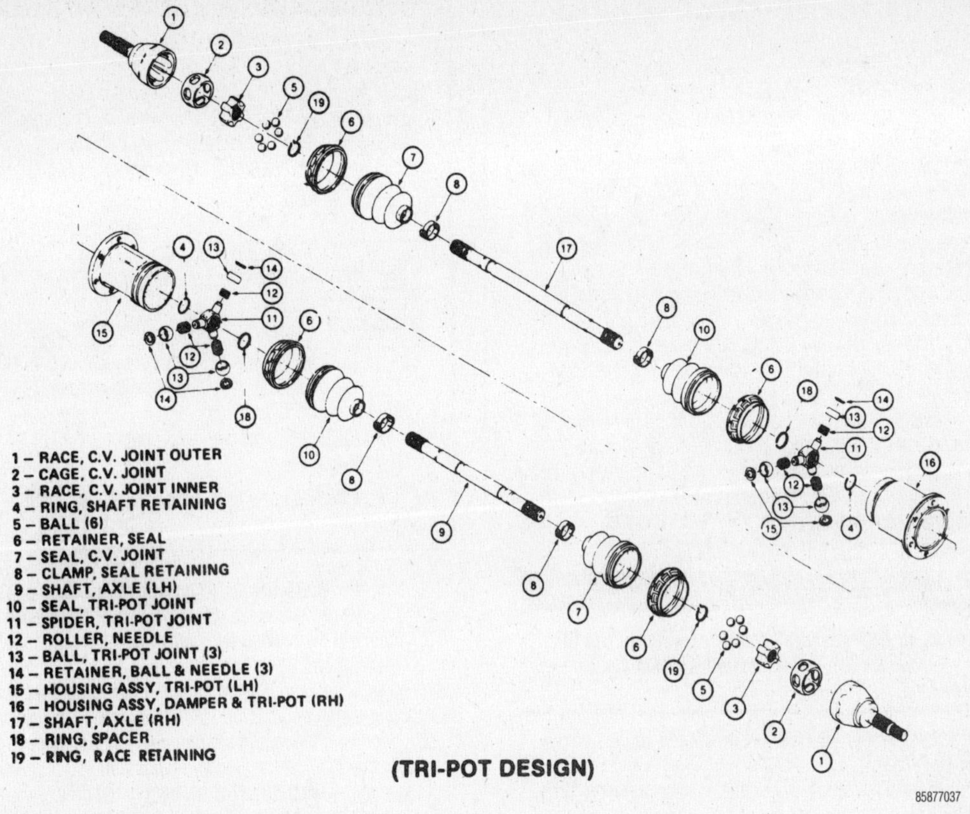

1 – RACE, C.V. JOINT OUTER
2 – CAGE, C.V. JOINT
3 – RACE, C.V. JOINT INNER
4 – RING, SHAFT RETAINING
5 – BALL (6)
6 – RETAINER, SEAL
7 – SEAL, C.V. JOINT
8 – CLAMP, SEAL RETAINING
9 – SHAFT, AXLE (LH)
10 – SEAL, TRI-POT JOINT
11 – SPIDER, TRI-POT JOINT
12 – ROLLER, NEEDLE
13 – BALL, TRI-POT JOINT (3)
14 – RETAINER, BALL & NEEDLE (3)
15 – HOUSING ASSY, TRI-POT (LH)
16 – HOUSING ASSY, DAMPER & TRI-POT (RH)
17 – SHAFT, AXLE (RH)
18 – RING, SPACER
19 – RING, RACE RETAINING
(TRI-POT DESIGN)
85877037

Fig. 32 Exploded view of the front halfshafts—1979–85

5. Remove six halfshaft-to-output shaft screws and washers.
6. Loosen upper shock mounting bolt.
7. Remove upper control arm ball joint cotter pin and nut.
8. Using hammer and brass drift, drive on knuckle until upper ball joint stud is free.
9. Remove brake hose bracket.
10. Tip upper part of knuckle and support outward so that brake hose is not damaged.
11. Carefully guide the halfshaft assembly outward. Remove left output shaft retaining bolt by installing two screws in the shaft flange to prevent shaft rotation. Pull the shaft straight out toward side of car.

➡Care must be exercised so that constant velocity joints do not turn to full extremes and that seals are not damaged against shock absorber or stabilizer bar.

12. To install, reverse removal procedure. Tighten output shaft retaining bolt to 50 ft. lbs. (68 Nm), upper ball joint stud nut to 60 ft. lbs. (81 Nm), upper shock absorber bolt to 75 ft. lbs. (102 Nm). Tighten wheel lug nuts to 130 ft. lbs. (176 Nm) Tighten halfshaft nut to 110 ft. lbs. (149 Nm).

J-28712 OR J-33162
RIGHT SHAFT
BOOT PROTECTOR
LEFT SHAFT
FRT
J-28468 OR J-33008
J-29794
J-2619-01
85877038

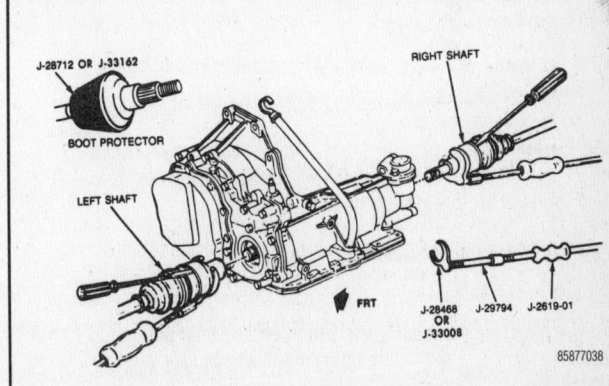

Fig. 33 Use a small prybar and the special tool shown to pull the halfshaft out of the transaxle—make sure to support the halfshaft at the center to avoid putting downward force on the outer joint

1979–85 Eldorado and 1980–85 Seville

➧ See Figures 32 and 33

RIGHT SIDE

1. Hoist car under lower control arms and remove the wheel.
2. Remove halfshaft cotter pin, retainer, nut and washer from the wheel hub.
3. Remove the oil filter.
4. Remove inner constant velocity joint attaching bolts.
5. Push inner constant velocity joint outward enough to disengage the right hand final drive output shaft, then move rearward.
6. Remove right hand output shaft bracket bolts to engine and final drive.
7. Remove right hand output shaft and halfshaft assembly.

To install:

WARNING

Care must be exercised so that constant velocity joints do not turn to full extremes, and that seals are not damaged against shock absorber or stabilizer bar.

8. Carefully place right hand halfshaft assembly into lower control arm and enter outer race splines into knuckle.
9. Lubricate final drive output shaft seal, with special seal lubricant.
10. Install right hand output shaft into final drive and attach the support bolts to engine and brace. Torque the bolts to 50 ft. lbs. (68 Nm).
11. Move right hand halfshaft assembly toward front of car and align with right hand output shaft. Install attaching bolts and torque to 60 ft. lbs. (81 Nm).

12. Install the oil filter.
13. Install washer and nut on Torque to 175 ft. lbs. (237 Nm), then install the retainer and cotter pin.
14. Remove floor stands and lower hoist.
15. Check engine oil level.

LEFT SIDE

1. Hoist car under lower control arms.
2. Remove wheel. Remove disc.
3. Remove halfshaft cotter pin, nut and washer.
4. Remove tie rod-end cotter pin and nut.
5. Remove the tie rod end from the knuckle with a puller.
6. Remove bolts from halfshaft assembly and left output shaft. Insert a spacer between the halfshaft and lower control arm.
7. Remove upper control arm ball joint cotter pin and nut.
8. Using hammer and brass drift, drive on knuckle until upper ball joint stud is free.
9. Using puller, remove lower ball joint from knuckle on 1979 models. Care must be exercised so that ball joint does not damage halfshaft seal.
10. Remove knuckle and support, so that the brake hose is not damaged on 1979 models, support the knuckle on 1980 and later models.
11. Carefully remove halfshaft assembly.
To install:

✳✳ WARNING

Care must be exercised so that constant velocity joints do not turn to full extremes and that seals are not damaged against shock absorber or stabilizer bar.

12. Carefully guide left hand halfshaft assembly onto lower control arm and into position on spacer.
13. Insert lower control ball joint stud into knuckle and attach nut on 1979 models. Do not torque.
14. Center left hand halfshaft assembly in opening of knuckle and insert upper ball joint stud.
15. Tighten the upper ball joint to 61 ft. lbs. (83 Nm) and the lower ball joint to 92 ft. lbs. (125 Nm).
16. Install the tie rod end and tighten to 40 ft. lbs. (54 Nm).

➡Always install new cotter pins after tightening ball stud nuts.

17. Install the halfshaft washer and nut, then tighten the retaining nut to 176 ft. lbs. (238 Nm).
18. Install the new halfshaft cotter pin through the castle nut.
19. Install the rotor, then install the tire and wheel assembly.
20. Remove the jackstands and lower the vehicle.

1986–89 Eldorado and Seville

♦ See Figure 34

➡To perform this procedure, you will need a special puller J-28733 or equivalent and new prevailing torque nut for each axle you need to remove.

1. Remove the prevailing torque hub nut and washer. Then, raise the vehicle and support it securely.
2. Remove the wheel and tire.
3. Remove the brake caliper and rotor.
4. Disconnect: the stabilizer bar at the control arm; the tie rod end at the steering knuckle and the lower ball joint stud at the steering knuckle. Then, use a prybar and screwdriver against a wood block (to protect the case) to pry the drive axle out of the transaxle case.
5. Use the special puller to force the drive axle out of the hub, and remove the axle from the car. Inspect the boot seals for damage and replace as necessary.
To install:
6. Position the drive axle ends into the steering knuckle and transaxle without fully seating them.
7. Refasten the lower ball joint stud to the steering knuckle and torque the

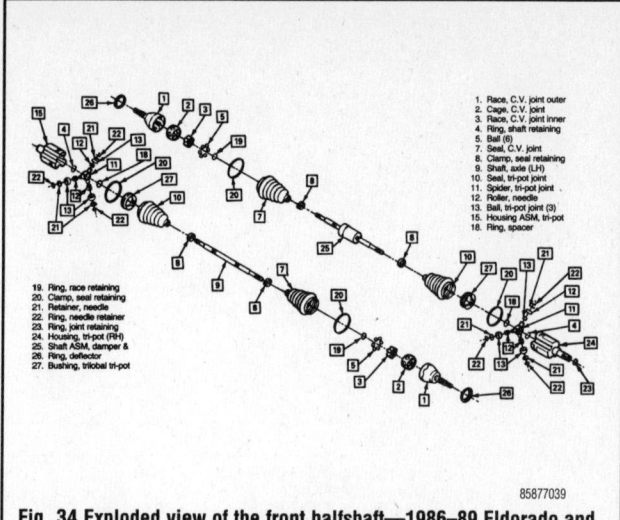

Fig. 34 Exploded view of the front halfshaft—1986–89 Eldorado and Seville

nut as described in Section 8. Reconnect the stabilizer bar to the lower control arm and the tie rod end to the steering knuckle, again referring to Section 8.
8. Reinstall the brake caliper with new mounting bolts.
9. Install a washer and new prevailing torque nut; torque the nut to 74 ft. lbs. (100 Nm). You can prevent the axle from turning when you torque the nut by inserting a small prybar into one of the slots in the brake rotor.
10. Seat the drive axle in the transaxle by positioning a screwdriver into the groove on the CV-joint housing and tapping the screwdriver with a hammer until the axle is seated. Grab the housing of the drive axle (not the driveshaft) and pull it outward to make sure the axle is properly seated.
11. Install the wheel and tire. Lower the vehicle. Then, final-torque the hub nut to 183 ft. lbs. (248 Nm).

CV-JOINT OVERHAUL

♦ See Figures 35, 36, 37 and 38

For all CV-joint overhaul procedures, please refer to the accompanying illustrations.

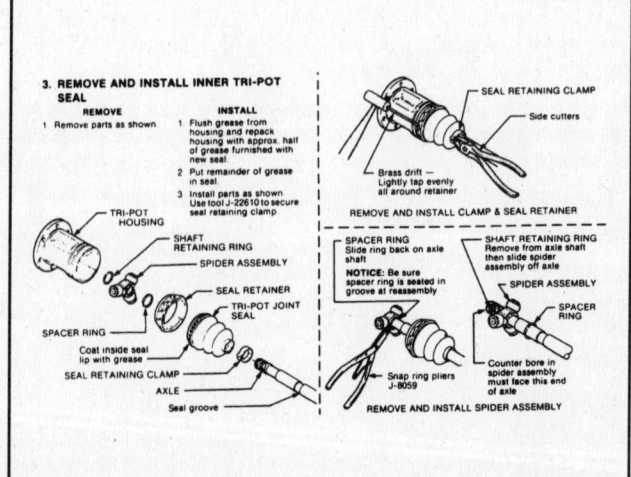

Fig. 35 Removal and installation of the inner CV-joint seal and assembly—1979–85 vehicles

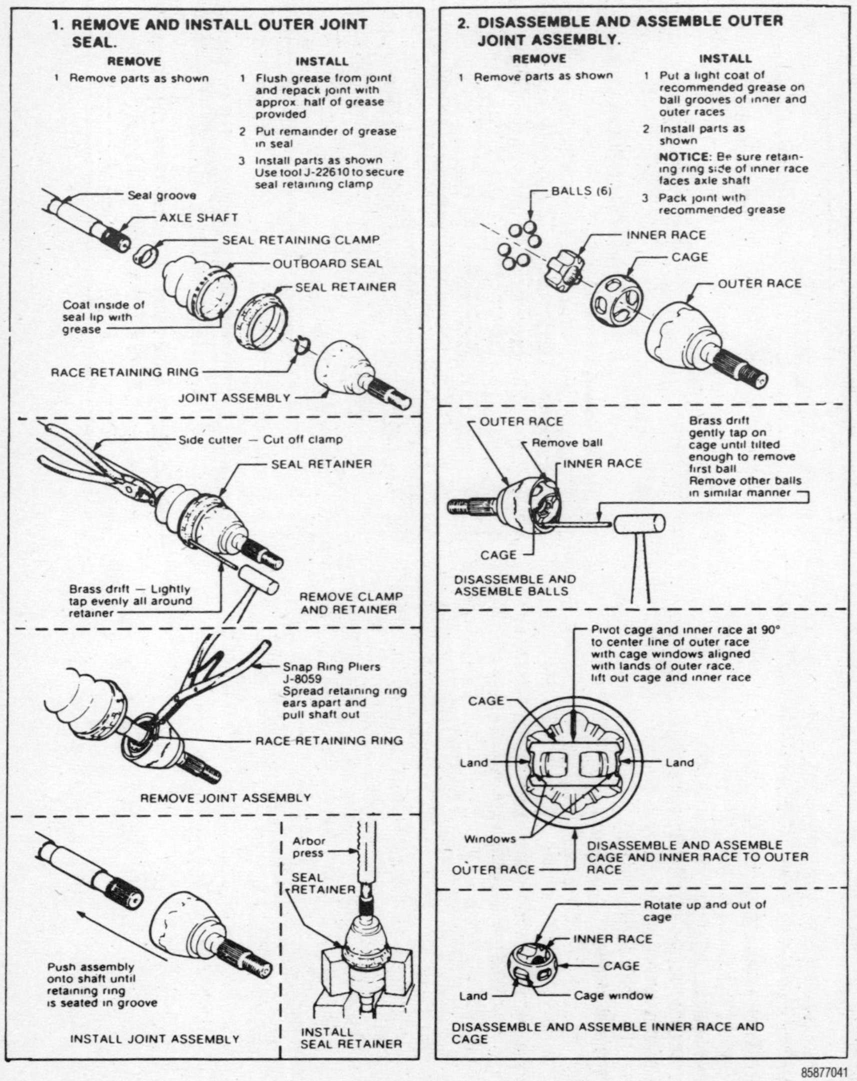

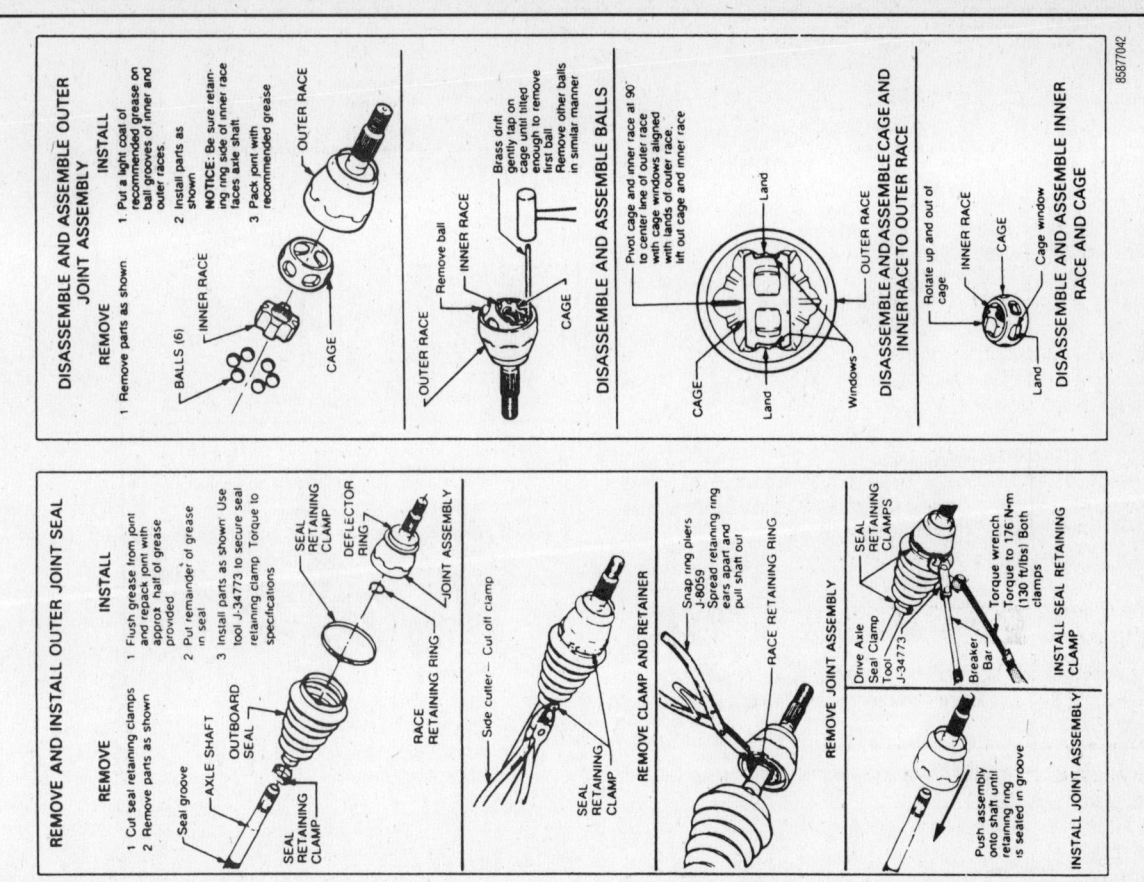

DISASSEMBLE AND ASSEMBLE OUTER JOINT ASSEMBLY

REMOVE
1 Remove parts as shown

INSTALL
1 Put a light coat of recommended grease on ball grooves of inner and outer races
2 Install parts as shown
NOTICE: Be sure retaining ring size of inner race faces axle shaft
3 Pack joint with recommended grease

OUTER RACE
BALLS (6)
INNER RACE
CAGE

Brass drift gently tap on cage until tilted enough to remove first ball Remove other balls in similar manner

OUTER RACE
Remove ball
INNER RACE
CAGE

DISASSEMBLE AND ASSEMBLE BALLS

Pivot cage and inner race at 90° to center line of outer race with cage windows aligned with lands of outer race lift out cage and inner race

OUTER RACE
CAGE
Land
Windows
Land

DISASSEMBLE AND ASSEMBLE CAGE AND INNER RACE TO OUTER RACE

INNER RACE
CAGE
Cage window

Rotate up and out of cage

Land

DISASSEMBLE AND ASSEMBLE INNER RACE AND CAGE

REMOVE AND INSTALL OUTER JOINT SEAL

REMOVE
1 Cut seal retaining clamps
2 Remove parts as shown

INSTALL
1 Flush grease from joint and repack joint with approx half of grease provided
2 Put remainder of grease in seal
3 Install parts as shown Use tool J-34773 to secure seal retaining clamp Torque to specifications

Seal groove
AXLE SHAFT
OUTBOARD SEAL
SEAL RETAINING CLAMP
SEAL RETAINING CLAMP
DEFLECTOR RING
JOINT ASSEMBLY

RACE RETAINING RING

Side cutter - Cut off clamp

SEAL RETAINING CLAMP

REMOVE CLAMP AND RETAINER

Snap ring pliers J-8059 Spread retaining ring ears apart and pull shaft out

RACE RETAINING RING

REMOVE JOINT ASSEMBLY

Push assembly onto shaft until retaining ring is seated in groove

INSTALL JOINT ASSEMBLY

SEAL RETAINING CLAMPS

Drive Axle Seal Clamp Tool J-34773

Breaker Bar

Torque wrench Torque to 176 N·m (130 ft/lbs) Both clamps

INSTALL SEAL RETAINING CLAMP

8587042

Fig. 37 Removal and installation of the outer CV-joint seal and assembly—1986-89 vehicles

2. DISASSEMBLE AND ASSEMBLE OUTER JOINT ASSEMBLY.

REMOVE
1 Remove parts as shown

INSTALL
1 Put a light coat of recommended grease on ball grooves of inner and outer races
2 Install parts as shown
NOTICE: Be sure retaining ring size of inner race faces axle shaft
3 Pack joint with recommended grease

BALLS (6)
INNER RACE
CAGE
OUTER RACE

Brass drift gently tap on cage until tilted enough to remove first ball Remove other balls in similar manner

OUTER RACE
Remove ball
INNER RACE
CAGE

DISASSEMBLE AND ASSEMBLE BALLS

Pivot cage and inner race at 90° to center line of outer race with cage windows aligned with lands of outer race lift out cage and inner race

Land
CAGE
OUTER RACE
Windows
Land

DISASSEMBLE AND ASSEMBLE CAGE AND INNER RACE TO OUTER RACE

INNER RACE
CAGE
Cage window

Rotate up and out of cage

Land

DISASSEMBLE AND ASSEMBLE INNER RACE AND CAGE

1. REMOVE AND INSTALL OUTER JOINT SEAL.

REMOVE
1 Remove parts as shown

INSTALL
1 Flush grease from joint and repack joint with approx half of grease provided
2 Put remainder of grease in seal
3 Install parts as shown Use tool J-22610 to secure seal retaining clamp

Seal groove
AXLE SHAFT
SEAL RETAINING CLAMP
OUTBOARD SEAL
SEAL RETAINER

Coat inside of seal lip with grease

RACE RETAINING RING

SEAL RETAINER
JOINT ASSEMBLY

Side cutter - Cut off clamp

SEAL RETAINER

REMOVE CLAMP AND RETAINER

Brass drift – Lightly tap evenly all around retainer

Snap Ring Pliers J-8059 Spread retaining ring ears apart and pull shaft out

RACE RETAINING RING

REMOVE JOINT ASSEMBLY

Arbor press

SEAL RETAINER

INSTALL SEAL RETAINER

Push assembly onto shaft until retaining ring is seated in groove

INSTALL JOINT ASSEMBLY

8587041

Fig. 36 Removal and installation of the outer CV-joint seal and assembly—1979-85 vehicles

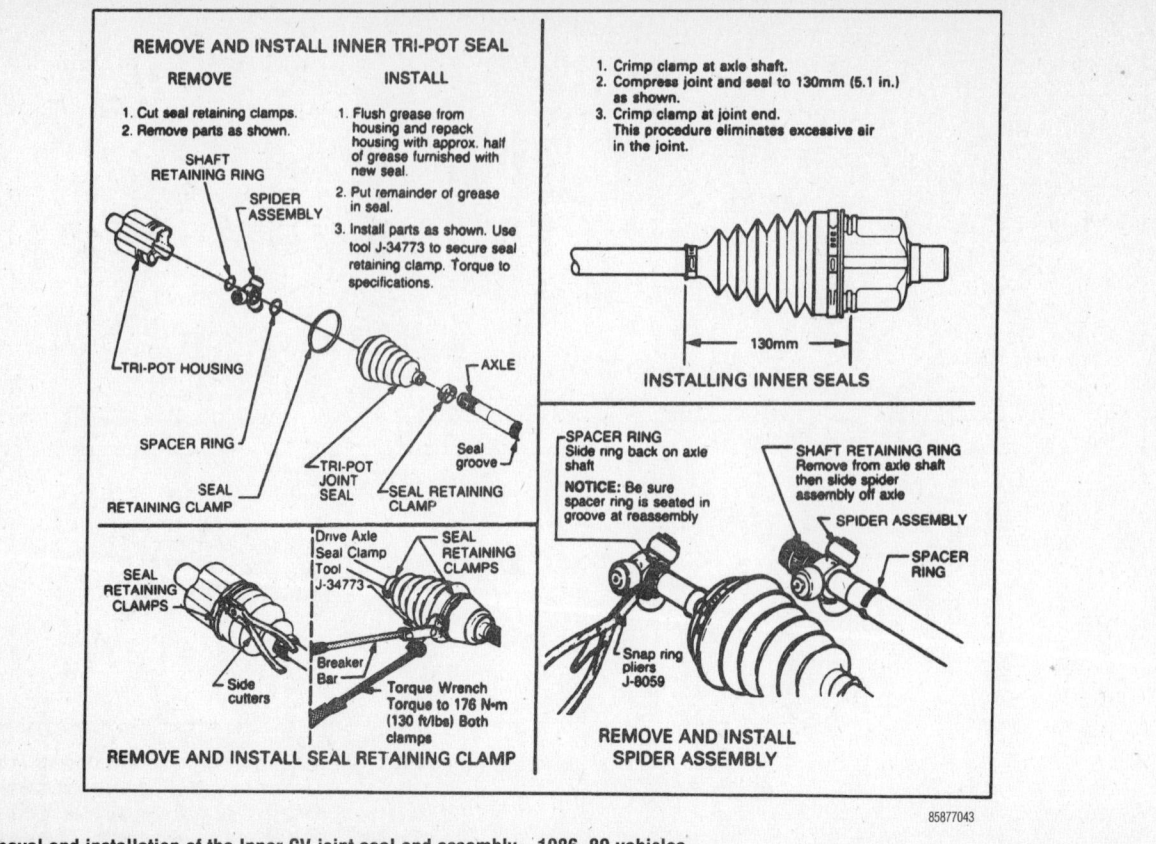

REMOVE AND INSTALL INNER TRI-POT SEAL

REMOVE

1. Cut seal retaining clamps.
2. Remove parts as shown.

SHAFT RETAINING RING
SPIDER ASSEMBLY
TRI-POT HOUSING
SPACER RING
AXLE
Seal groove
SEAL RETAINING CLAMP
TRI-POT JOINT SEAL
SEAL RETAINING CLAMP

INSTALL

1. Flush grease from housing and repack housing with approx. half of grease furnished with new seal.
2. Put remainder of grease in seal.
3. Install parts as shown. Use tool J-34773 to secure seal retaining clamp. Torque to specifications.

1. Crimp clamp at axle shaft.
2. Compress joint and seal to 130mm (5.1 in.) as shown.
3. Crimp clamp at joint end. This procedure eliminates excessive air in the joint.

130mm

INSTALLING INNER SEALS

SPACER RING
Slide ring back on axle shaft
NOTICE: Be sure spacer ring is seated in groove at reassembly

SHAFT RETAINING RING
Remove from axle shaft then slide spider assembly off axle

SPIDER ASSEMBLY
SPACER RING
Snap ring pliers J-8059

REMOVE AND INSTALL SPIDER ASSEMBLY

SEAL RETAINING CLAMPS
Side cutters
Drive Axle Seal Clamp Tool J-34773
SEAL RETAINING CLAMPS
Breaker Bar
Torque Wrench Torque to 176 N·m (130 ft/lbs) Both clamps

REMOVE AND INSTALL SEAL RETAINING CLAMP

85877043

Fig. 38 Removal and installation of the Inner CV-joint seal and assembly—1986–89 vehicles

DRIVELINE

Driveshaft and U-Joints

Driveshafts are used to transmit power from the transmission to the rear axle assembly. The Brougham, DeVille, and Seville use a one piece shaft, while the Limousine and Commercial Chassis use a two piece shaft.

A Single Cardan universal joint is used at the front of the shaft on the Seville, Limousine, and Commercial Chassis, while a Double Cardan constant velocity universal joint is used on the other models. All models use the Double Cardan constant velocity universal joint at the rear, and also at the center of the two piece shaft.

A Double Cardan joint consists of two single joints connected by a special link yoke. A ball and socket centering device is located between the crosses to maintain their relative positions, causing each cross to divide one half of the total angle cross the joint equally. Virtually all problems with driveshafts, caused by universal joint angles, are eliminated by use of the Double Cardan joint.

Each Driveshaft is installed in a similar manner. A universal joint and splined slip yoke are located at the front of the shaft, where they are held in alignment by a bushing in the rear of the transmission. The slip yoke permits fore and aft movement of the driveshaft as the rear axle assembly moves up and down. The spline is lubricated internally by transmission lubrication or grease. An oil seal at the transmission prevents leakage and protects the slip yoke from dust, dirt, and other harmful material. In addition, the two piece shaft has (on the front end of the rear section) an external splined slip yoke that fits into a splined coupling in the rear end of the front section. This slip spline has the same function as the slip yoke in allowing up and down movement of the rear axle. The two piece shaft is supported in the center by a center bearing support and bracket attached to the frame cross member. The rear of each driveshaft is attached to the rear axle assembly by means of a double flange connection with four bolts or by means of retaining straps.

REMOVAL & INSTALLATION

1. Raise the vehicle in the air and support it with jackstands.
2. Mark the relationship of the driveshaft to the differential flange so that they can be reassembled in the same position.
3. Disconnect the rear U-joint by removing the flange bolts, U-bolts or retaining straps.
4. To prevent the loss of the needle bearings, tape the bearing caps in place. If you are replacing the U-joint, this is not necessary.
5. Remove the driveshaft from the transmission by sliding it rearward. There will be some oil leakage from the rear of the transmission. It can be contained by placing a small plastic bag over the rear of the transmission and holding it in place with a rubber band.

To install:

6. Insert the front yoke into the transmission so that the driveshaft splines mesh with the transmission splines.
7. Using the reference marks made earlier, align the driveshaft with the differential flange and secure it with the U-bolts or retaining straps.

U-JOINT OVERHAUL

◆ See Figures 39 thru 45

❈❈❈ WARNING

NEVER clamp a driveshaft in a vise, as the tube is easily dented. Always clamp on one of the yokes, and support the shaft horizontally.

1. Remove the driveshaft as explained above and remove the snaprings from the ends of the bearing cup.
2. After removing the snaprings, place the driveshaft on the floor and place

KEY NO. PART NAME
0 – SHAFT ASSY PROPELLER
1 – YOKE ASSEMBLY, SLIP
2 – RING, RETAINING (BEARING)
3 – BEARING ASSEMBLY, UNIVERSAL JOINT
4 – SPIDER ASSEMBLY, UNIVERSAL JOINT
5 – TUBE ASSY, PROPELLER SHAFT
6 – BALL, CV JOINT
KEY NO. PART NAME
7 – YOKE, LINK
8 – SEAL, BALL STUD SUPPORT
9 – WASHER, BALL STUD SEAL
KEY NO. PART NAME
10 – SEAT, BALL STUD (3)
11 – WASHER, BALL STUD SEAT
12 – SPRING, BALL STUD SEAT
13 – YOKE, BALL STUD SUPPORT
ASSEMBLIES AND SERVICE KITS
JOINT ASSY SERVICE KIT, UNIVERSAL
YOKE ASSY SERVICE KIT, SUPPORT
JOINT SERVICE KIT, CV UNIVERSAL
BEARING ASSY SERV KIT, UNIV JOINT
SEVILLE
85877044

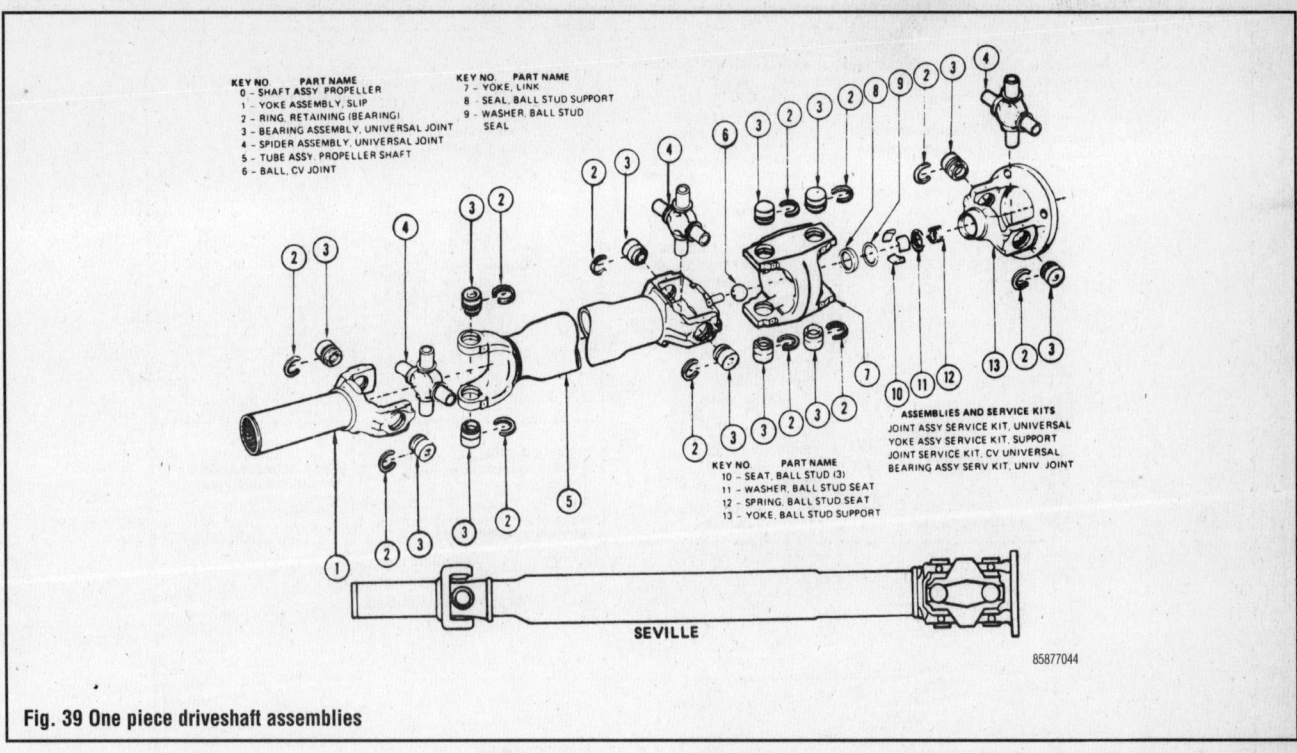

Fig. 39 One piece driveshaft assemblies

a large diameter socket under one of the bearing cups. Using a hammer and a drift, tap on the bearing opposite this one. This will push the trunnion through the yoke enough to force the bearing cup out of the yoke and into the socket. Repeat this procedure for the other bearing cups. If a hammer doesn't loosen the cups, they will have to be pressed out.

➡A Saginaw design driveshaft secures its U-joints in a different manner than the conventional snaprings of the Dana and Cleveland designs. Nylon material is injected through a small hole in the yoke and flows along a circular groove between the U-joint and the yoke thus creating a synthetic snapring. Disassembly of this Saginaw-type U-joint requires

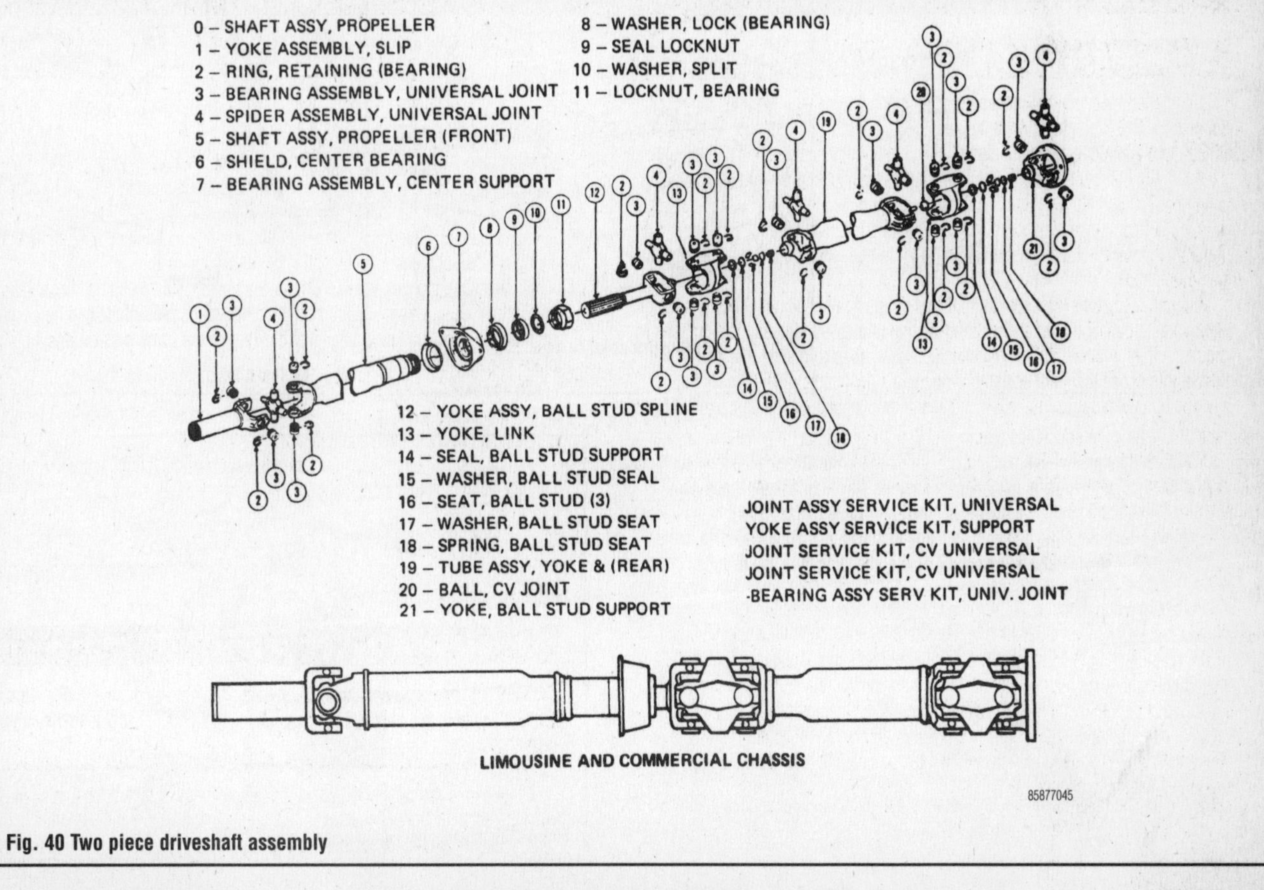

0 – SHAFT ASSY, PROPELLER
1 – YOKE ASSEMBLY, SLIP
2 – RING, RETAINING (BEARING)
3 – BEARING ASSEMBLY, UNIVERSAL JOINT
4 – SPIDER ASSEMBLY, UNIVERSAL JOINT
5 – SHAFT ASSY, PROPELLER (FRONT)
6 – SHIELD, CENTER BEARING
7 – BEARING ASSEMBLY, CENTER SUPPORT
8 – WASHER, LOCK (BEARING)
9 – SEAL LOCKNUT
10 – WASHER, SPLIT
11 – LOCKNUT, BEARING
12 – YOKE ASSY, BALL STUD SPLINE
13 – YOKE, LINK
14 – SEAL, BALL STUD SUPPORT
15 – WASHER, BALL STUD SEAL
16 – SEAT, BALL STUD (3)
17 – WASHER, BALL STUD SEAT
18 – SPRING, BALL STUD SEAT
19 – TUBE ASSY, YOKE & (REAR)
20 – BALL, CV JOINT
21 – YOKE, BALL STUD SUPPORT
JOINT ASSY SERVICE KIT, UNIVERSAL
YOKE ASSY SERVICE KIT, SUPPORT
JOINT SERVICE KIT, CV UNIVERSAL
JOINT SERVICE KIT, CV UNIVERSAL
BEARING ASSY SERV KIT, UNIV. JOINT
LIMOUSINE AND COMMERCIAL CHASSIS
85877045

Fig. 40 Two piece driveshaft assembly

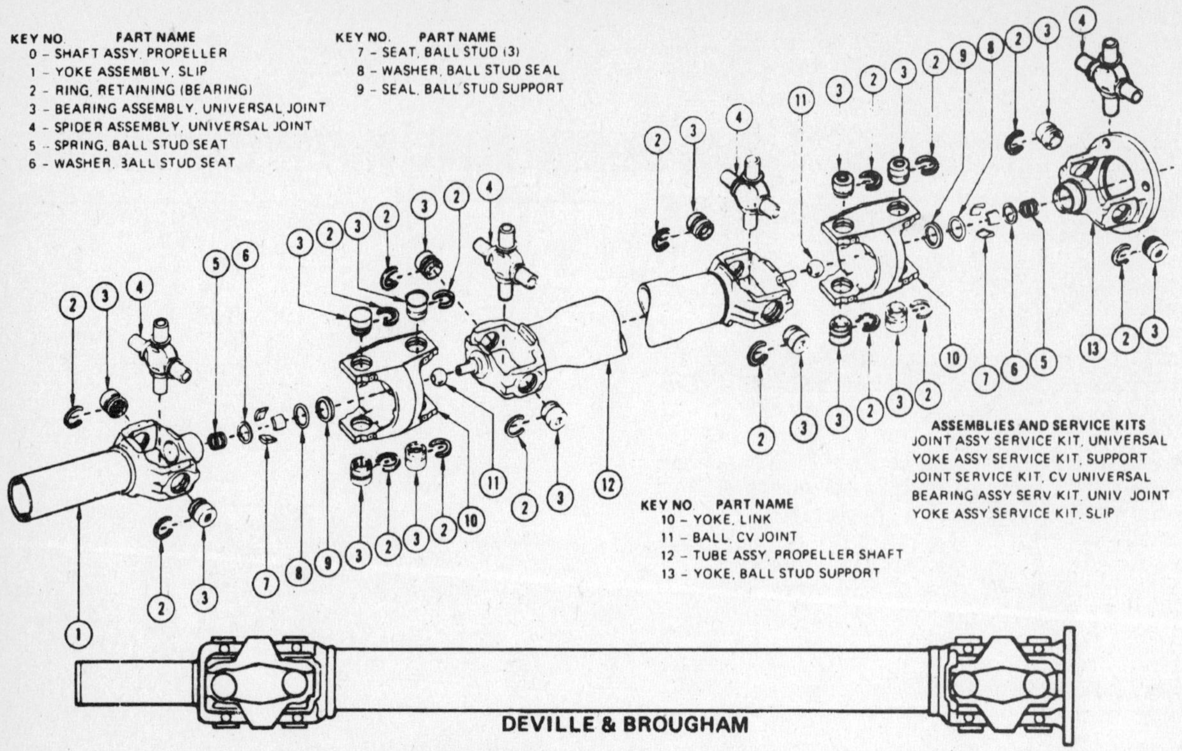

KEY NO.   PART NAME
0 – SHAFT ASSY, PROPELLER
1 – YOKE ASSEMBLY, SLIP
2 – RING, RETAINING (BEARING)
3 – BEARING ASSEMBLY, UNIVERSAL JOINT
4 – SPIDER ASSEMBLY, UNIVERSAL JOINT
5 – SPRING, BALL STUD SEAT
6 – WASHER, BALL STUD SEAT

KEY NO.   PART NAME
7 – SEAT, BALL STUD (3)
8 – WASHER, BALL STUD SEAL
9 – SEAL, BALL STUD SUPPORT

KEY NO.   PART NAME
10 – YOKE, LINK
11 – BALL, CV JOINT
12 – TUBE ASSY, PROPELLER SHAFT
13 – YOKE, BALL STUD SUPPORT

ASSEMBLIES AND SERVICE KITS
JOINT ASSY SERVICE KIT, UNIVERSAL
YOKE ASSY SERVICE KIT, SUPPORT
JOINT SERVICE KIT, CV UNIVERSAL
BEARING ASSY SERV KIT, UNIV JOINT
YOKE ASSY SERVICE KIT, SLIP

DEVILLE & BROUGHAM

85877046

Fig. 41 One piece driveshaft assemblies

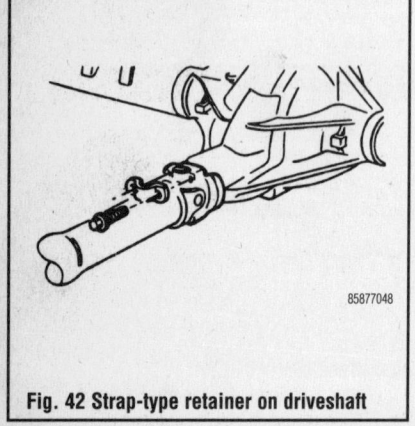

85877048

Fig. 42 Strap-type retainer on driveshaft

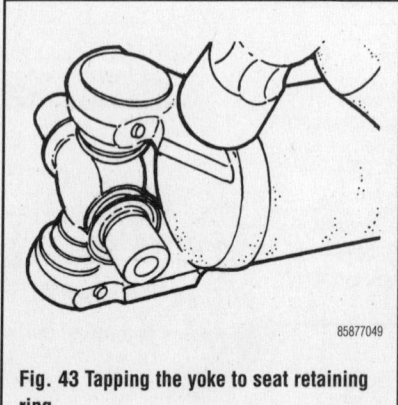

85877049

Fig. 43 Tapping the yoke to seat retaining ring

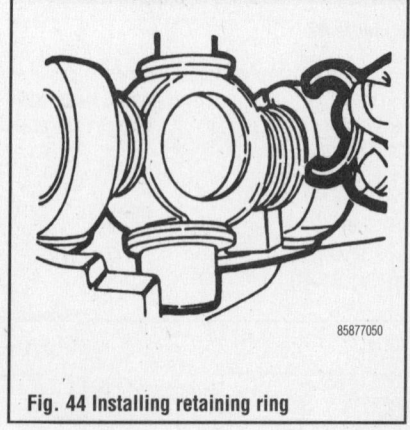

85877050

Fig. 44 Installing retaining ring

that the joint be pressed from the yoke. If a press is not available, it may be carefully hammered out using the same procedure (Step 2) as the Dana design although it may require more force to break the nylon ring. Either method, press or hammer, will damage the bearing cups and destroy the nylon rings. Replacement kits include new bearing cups and conventional metal snaprings to replace the original nylon type rings.

3. Using solvent, thoroughly clean the entire U-joint assembly. Inspect for excessive wear in the yoke bores and on the four ends of the trunnion. The needle bearings should not be scored, broken, or loose in their cups. Bearing cups may suffer slight distortion during removal and should be replaced.

4. Pack the bearings with chassis lube (lithium base) and completely fill each trunnion end with the same lubricant.

5. Place new dust seals on trunnions with cavity of seal toward end of trunnion. Care must be taken to avoid distortion of the seal. A suitable size socket and a vise can be used to press on the seal.

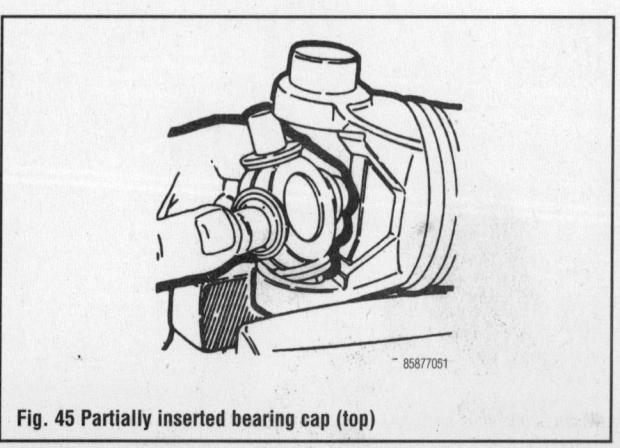

85877051

Fig. 45 Partially inserted bearing cap (top)

6. Insert one bearing cup about ¼ of the way into the yoke, then place the trunnion into yoke and bearing cup. Install another bearing cup and press both cups in, then install the snaprings. Snaprings on the Dana and Cleveland shafts must go on the outside of the yoke while the Saginaw shaft requires that rings go on the inside of the yoke. The gap in the Saginaw ring must face in toward the yoke. Once installed, the trunnion must move freely in yoke.

➡The Saginaw shaft uses two different size bearing cups (the ones with the groove) fit into the driveshaft yoke.

REAR AXLE

Identification

The rear axle number is located in the right or left axle tube adjacent to the axle carrier (differential). Anti-slip differentials are identified by a tag attached to the lower right section of the axle cover.

Determining Axle Ratio

▶ **See Figure 46**

An axle ratio is obtained by dividing the number of teeth on the drive pinion gear into the number of teeth on the ring gear. For instance on a 4.11 ratio, the driveshaft will turn 4.11 times for every turn of the rear wheel.

The most accurate way to determine the axle ratio is to drain the differential, remove the cover, and count the number of teeth on the ring and pinion.

An easier method is to jack and support the car so that both rear wheels are off the ground. Make a chalk mark on the rear wheel and the driveshaft. Block the front wheels and put the transmission in Neutral. Turn the rear wheel one complete revolution and count the number of turns made by the driveshaft. The number of driveshaft rotations is the axle ratio. More accuracy can be obtained by going more than one tire revolution and dividing the result by the number of tire rotations.

The axle ratio is also identified by the axle serial number prefix on the axle; the axle ratios are listed in dealer's parts books according to prefix number. Some axles have a tag on the cover.

Axle Shaft Bearings and Seals

▶ **See Figure 47**

Two types of axles are used on these models, the C and the non-C type. Axle shafts in the C type are retained by C-shaped locks, which fit grooves at the inner end of the shaft. Axle shafts in the non-C type are retained by the brake backing plate, which is bolted to the axle housing. Bearings in the C type axle consist on an outer race, bearing rollers, and a roller cage retained by snaprings. The non-C type axle uses a unit roller bearing (inner race, rollers, and outer race), which is pressed onto the shaft up to a shoulder. When servicing C or non-C type axles, it is imperative to determine the axle type before attempting any service. Before attempting any service to the drive axle or axle

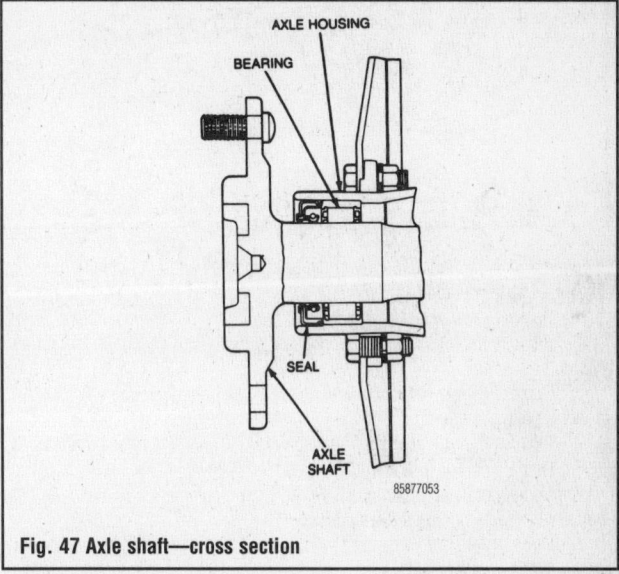

Fig. 47 Axle shaft—cross section

shafts, remove the axle carrier cover and visually determine if the axle shafts are retained by C-shaped locks at the inner end, or by the brake backing plate at the outer end.

REMOVAL & INSTALLATION

✳✳ CAUTION

Brake shoes may contain asbestos, which has been determined to be a cancer causing agent. Never clean the brake surfaces with compressed air! Avoid inhaling any dust from any brake surface! When cleaning brake surfaces, use a commercially available brake cleaning fluid.

Non C-Lock Type

▶ **See Figures 48 and 49**

Design allows for maximum axle shaft end-play of 0.022 in. (0.056mm), which can be measured with a dial indicator. If end-play is found to be excessive, the bearing should be replaced. Shimming the bearing is not recom-

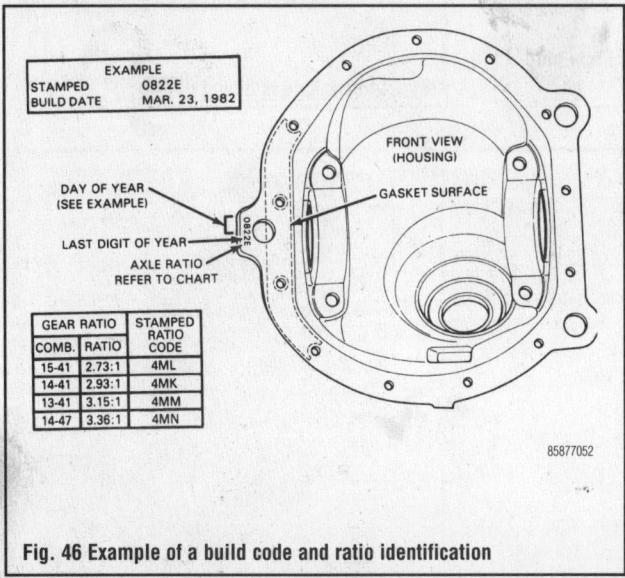

Fig. 46 Example of a build code and ratio identification

GEAR RATIO		STAMPED RATIO CODE
COMB.	RATIO	
15-41	2.73:1	4ML
14-41	2.93:1	4MK
13-41	3.15:1	4MM
14-47	3.36:1	4MN

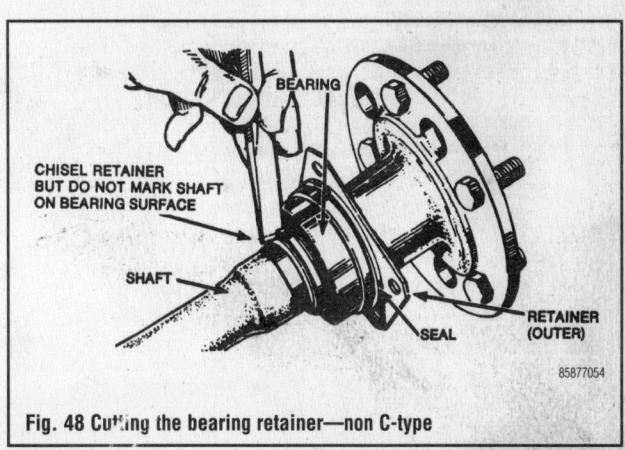

Fig. 48 Cutting the bearing retainer—non C-type

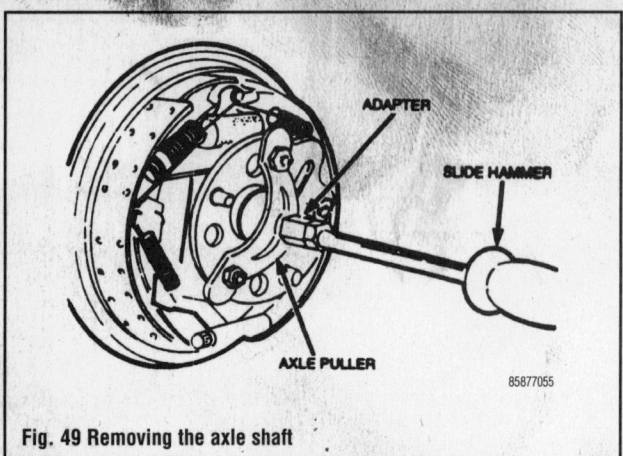

Fig. 49 Removing the axle shaft

mended as this ignores end-play of the bearing itself and could result in improper seating of the bearing.

1. Remove the wheel, tire and brake drum.
2. Remove the nuts holding the retainer plate to the backing plate. Disconnect the brake line.
3. Remove the retainer and install nuts, finger-tight, to prevent the brake backing plate from being dislodged.
4. Pull out the axle shaft and bearing assembly, using a slide hammer.
5. Using a chisel, nick the bearing retainer in three or four places. The retainer does not have to be cut, merely collapsed sufficiently, to allow the bearing retainer to be slid from the shaft.
6. Press off the bearing and install the new one by pressing it into position.
7. Press on the new retainer.

➡ **Do not attempt to press the bearing and the retainer on at the same time.**

8. Assemble the shaft and bearing in the housing being sure that the bearing is seated properly in the housing.
9. Install the retainer, drum, wheel and tire. Bleed the brakes.

C-Lock Type

▶ **See Figures 50 thru 63**

1. Raise the vehicle and remove the wheels.
2. If not done already, remove the differential cover.
3. Remove the differential pinion shaft lock-screw and the differential pinion shaft.
4. Push the flanged end of the axle shaft toward the center of the vehicle and remove the C-lock from the end of the shaft.
5. Remove the axle shaft from the housing, being careful not to damage the oil seal.
6. If necessary, remove the oil seal by inserting the button end of the axle shaft behind the steel case of the oil seal. Pry the seal loose from the bore.
7. Seat the legs of the bearing puller behind the bearing. Seat a washer against the bearing and hold it in place with a nut. Use a slide hammer to pull the bearing.
8. Pack the cavity between the seal lips with wheel bearing lubricant and lubricate a new wheel bearing with same.
9. Use a suitable driver and install the bearing until it bottoms against the tube. Install the oil seal.
10. Slide the axle shaft into place. Be sure that the splines on the shaft do not damage the oil seal. Make sure that the splines engage the differential side gear.
11. Install the axle shaft C-lock on the inner end of the axle shaft and push the shaft outward so that the C-lock seats in the differential side gear counterbore.
12. Position the differential pinion shaft through the case and pinions, aligning the hole in the case with the hole for the lockscrew.
13. Use a new gasket and install the carrier cover. Be sure that the gasket surfaces are clean before installing the gasket and cover.

Fig. 50 Installing axle bearing

Fig. 51 Installing axle seal

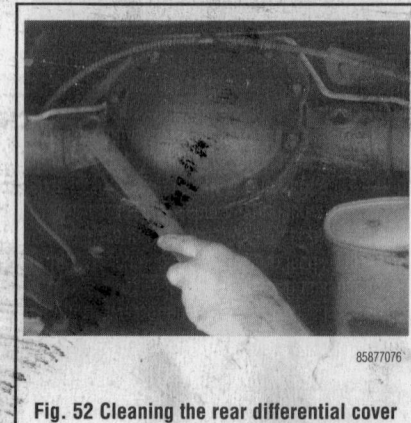

Fig. 52 Cleaning the rear differential cover

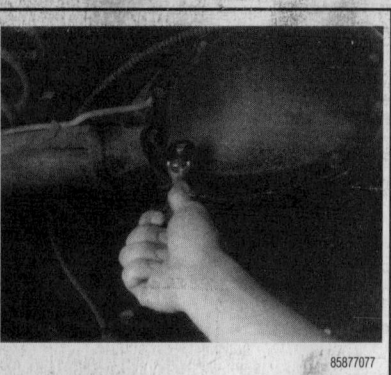

Fig. 53 Removing the rear differential cover bolts

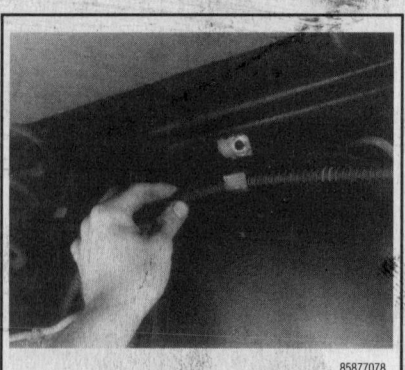

Fig. 54 Removing the rear differential cover related brackets

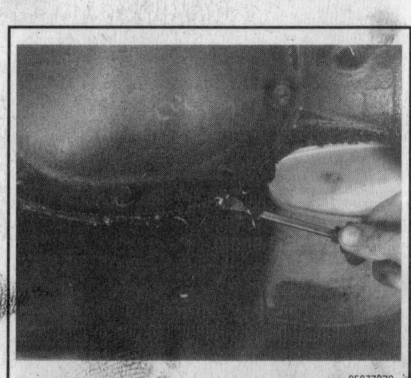

Fig. 55 Draining the rear differential assembly

Fig. 56 Removing the rear differential cover

Fig. 57 View of the rear differential assembly

Fig. 58 Removing the rear differential pinion shaft lock-screw

Fig. 59 View of the rear differential pinion shaft lock-screw

Fig. 60 Removing the rear differential pinion shaft

Fig. 61 Removing the C-lock from the end of the axle shaft

Fig. 62 Sliding the rear axle shaft outward

Fig. 63 Removing the rear axle shaft from the vehicle

14. Fill the axle with lubricant at the bottom of the filler hole.
15. Install the brake drum and wheel, then lower the car. Check for leaks and road test the car.

Pinion Seal

REMOVAL & INSTALLATION

▶ See Figure 64

1. Mark the driveshaft and the pinion yoke so they can be reassembled in the same position.

2. Disconnect the driveshaft from the rear axle pinion yoke and support the shaft up in the body tunnel by wiring the driveshaft to the exhaust pipe.
3. If joint bearings are not retained by a retainer strap, use a piece of tape to hold the bearings on their journals.
4. Remove the pinion seal.

To install:
5. Install the seal using an oil seal installer tool.
6. Install seal lubricant, 1050169 or equivalent, to the O.D. of the pinion yoke and sealing lip of the new seal.
7. Install the pinion yoke and tighten the nut to the same position as marked. While holding the pinion yoke, tighten the nut to 1/16 in. (1.59mm) beyond the alignment marks.

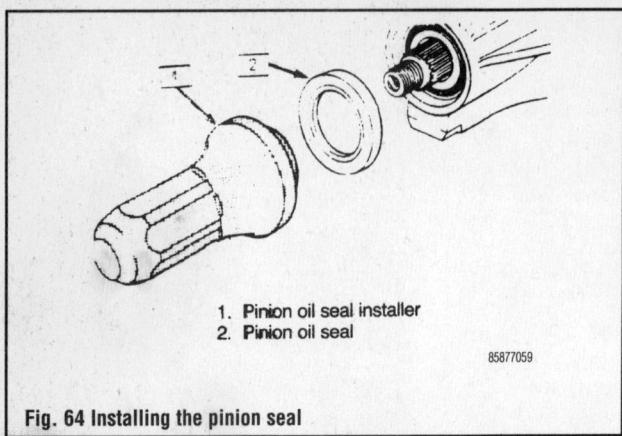

1. Pinion oil seal installer
2. Pinion oil seal

85877059

Fig. 64 Installing the pinion seal

Rear Axle Assembly

REMOVAL & INSTALLATION

♦ **See Figure 65**

1. Raise the car by the frame and place jackstands under the frame to support it safely. Place a support jack under the rear axle housing.
2. Disconnect the shock absorbers from the axle.
3. Mark the driveshaft and pinion yoke.
4. Move the driveshaft and support it out of the way.
5. Remove the brake line junction block bolt at the axle housing.
6. Disconnect the brake lines at the junction block.
7. Disconnect the upper control arms from the axle housing.
8. Lower the rear axle assembly on the support jack.
9. Remove the springs.
10. Remove the rear wheels and drums.
11. Remove the rear axle cover bolts and cover.
12. Remove the axle shafts. Refer to the Axle Shaft removal and installation procedure.
13. Disconnect the brake lines from the axle housing clips.
14. Remove the backing plates.

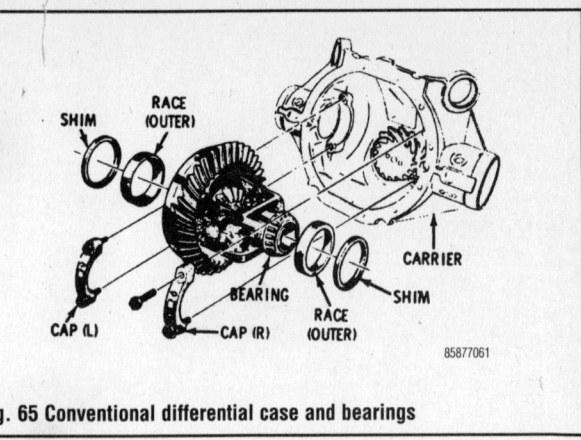

85877061

Fig. 65 Conventional differential case and bearings

15. Disconnect the lower control arms from the axle housing and remove the axle housing.

To install:

16. Place the rear axle housing into position and install the upper and lower control arms. Tighten the lower control arm-to-axle nuts to 90 ft. lbs. (122 Nm) and the bolts to 125 ft. lbs. (169 Nm). Tighten the upper control arm-to-axle nuts to 80 ft. lbs. (108 Nm) and the bolts to 90 ft. lbs. (122 Nm).
17. Install the backing plates.
18. Position the brake lines under the axle housing clips.
19. Install the axle shafts.
20. Install the rear axle cover and cover bolts and torque to 22 ft. lbs. (30 Nm).
21. Install the drums and wheels.
22. Raise the axle assembly on a support jack.
23. Install the springs.
24. Connect the brake lines at the junction block.
25. Install the brake line junction block bolt at the axle housing.
26. Install the driveshaft and tighten the strap bolts to 16 ft. lbs. (22 Nm).
27. Install the shock absorbers to the axle housing.
28. Fill with axle lubricant to a level flush with or within ¼ in. (6.35mm) of the filler hole.
29. Bleed the hydraulic brake system.
30. Lower the car.

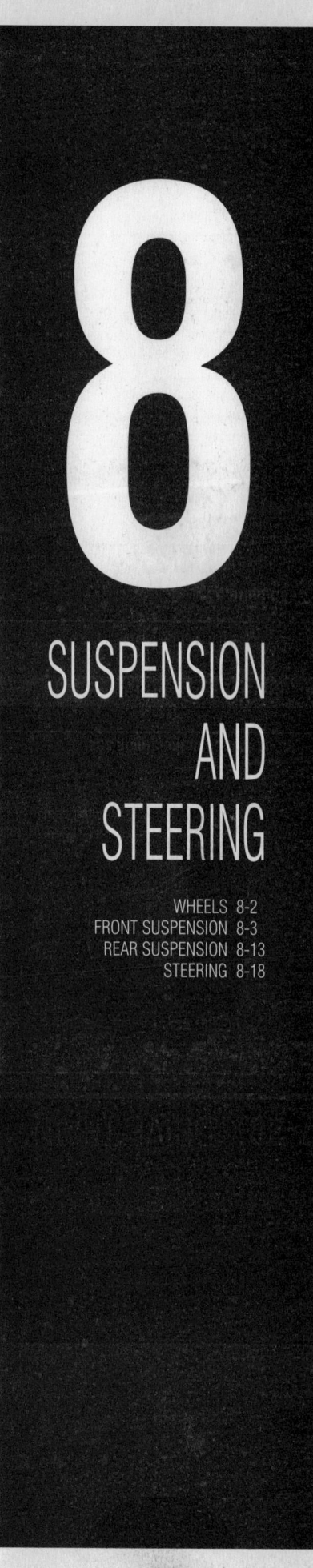

8

SUSPENSION
AND
STEERING

WHEELS

Wheels

REMOVAL & INSTALLATION

▶ **See Figures 1, 2 and 3**

1. Park the vehicle on a level surface.
2. Remove the jack, tire iron and, if necessary, the spare tire from their storage compartments.
3. Check the owner's manual or refer to Section 1 of this manual for the jacking points on your vehicle. Then, place the jack in the proper position.
4. If equipped with lug nut trim caps, remove them by either unscrewing or pulling them off the lug nuts, as appropriate. Consult the owner's manual, if necessary.
5. If equipped with a wheel cover or hub cap, insert the tapered end of the tire iron in the groove and pry off the cover.
6. Apply the parking brake and block the diagonally opposite wheel with a wheel chock or two.

➡ **Wheel chocks may be purchased at your local auto parts store, or a block of wood cut into wedges may be used. If possible, keep one or two of the chocks in your tire storage compartment, in case any of the tires has to be removed on the side of the road.**

7. If equipped with an automatic transmission/transaxle, place the selector lever in **P** or Park; with a manual transmission/transaxle, place the shifter in Reverse.
8. With the tires still on the ground, use the tire iron/wrench to break the lug nuts loose.

➡ **If a nut is stuck, never use heat to loosen it or damage to the wheel and bearings may occur. If the nuts are seized, one or two heavy hammer blows directly on the end of the bolt usually loosens the rust. Be careful, as continued pounding will likely damage the brake drum or rotor.**

9. Using the jack, raise the vehicle until the tire is clear of the ground. Support the vehicle safely using jackstands.
10. Remove the lug nuts, then remove the tire and wheel assembly.

To install:

11. Make sure the wheel and hub mating surfaces, as well as the wheel lug studs, are clean and free of all foreign material. Always remove rust from the wheel mounting surface and the brake rotor or drum. Failure to do so may cause the lug nuts to loosen in service.
12. Install the tire and wheel assembly and hand-tighten the lug nuts.
13. Using the tire wrench, tighten all the lug nuts, in a crisscross pattern, until they are snug.
14. Raise the vehicle and withdraw the jackstand, then lower the vehicle.
15. Using a torque wrench, tighten the lug nuts in a crisscross pattern. Check your owner's manual or refer to Section 1 of this manual for the proper tightening sequence.

⁂ WARNING

Do not overtighten the lug nuts, as this may cause the wheel studs to stretch or the brake disc (rotor) to warp.

16. If so equipped, install the wheel cover or hub cap. Make sure the valve stem protrudes through the proper opening before tapping the wheel cover into position.
17. If equipped, install the lug nut trim caps by pushing them or screwing them on, as applicable.
18. Remove the jack from under the vehicle, and place the jack and tire iron/wrench in their storage compartments. Remove the wheel chock(s).
19. If you have removed a flat or damaged tire, place it in the storage compartment of the vehicle and take it to your local repair station to have it fixed or replaced as soon as possible.

INSPECTION

Inspect the tires for lacerations, puncture marks, nails and other sharp objects. Repair or replace as necessary. Also check the tires for treadwear and air pressure as outlined in Check the wheel assemblies for dents, cracks, rust and metal fatigue. Repair or replace as necessary.

Wheel Lug Studs

REMOVAL & INSTALLATION

With Disc Brakes

▶ **See Figure 4**

1. Raise and support the appropriate end of the vehicle safely using jackstands, then remove the wheel.
2. Remove the brake pads and caliper. Support the caliper aside using wire or a coat hanger. For details, please refer to Section 9 of this manual.
3. Remove the outer wheel bearing and lift off the rotor. For details on wheel bearing removal, installation and adjustment, please refer to Section 1 of this manual.
4. Properly support the rotor using press bars, then drive the stud out using an arbor press.

➡ **If a press is not available, CAREFULLY drive the old stud out using a blunt drift. MAKE SURE the rotor is properly and evenly supported or it may be damaged.**

To install:

5. Clean the stud hole with a wire brush and start the new stud with a hammer and drift pin. Do not use any lubricant or thread sealer.
6. Finish installing the stud with the press.

Fig. 1 Place the jack at the proper lifting point on your vehicle

TCCA8P00

TCCA8P01

Fig. 2 Before jacking the vehicle, block the diagonally opposite wheel with one or, preferably, two chocks

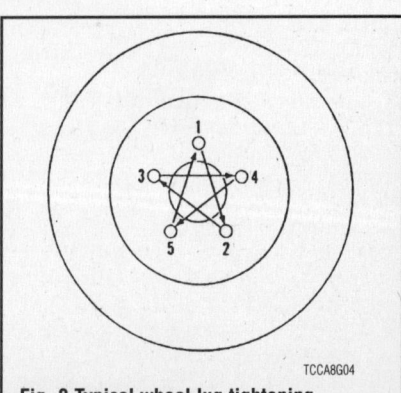

TCCA8G04

Fig. 3 Typical wheel lug tightening sequence

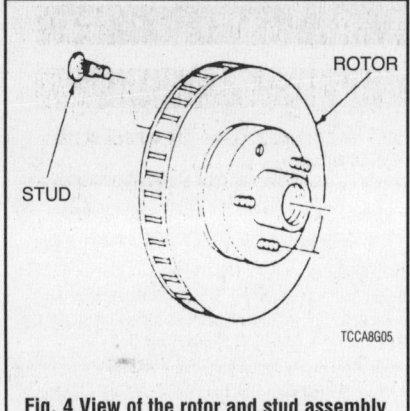

Fig. 4 View of the rotor and stud assembly

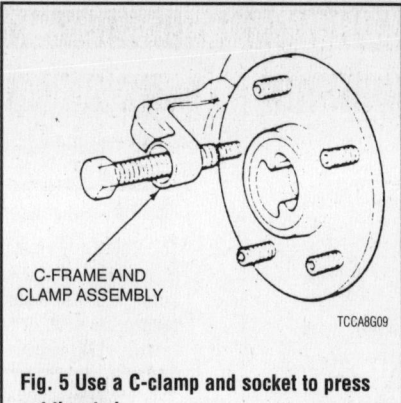

Fig. 5 Use a C-clamp and socket to press out the stud

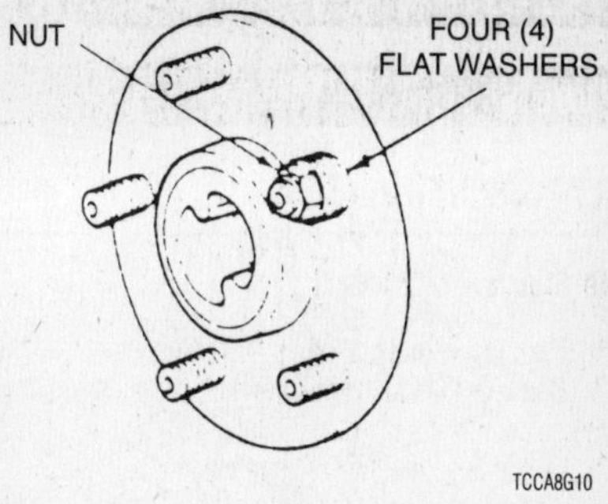

Fig. 6 Force the stud onto the axle flange using washers and a lug nut

➡️**If a press is not available, start the lug stud through the bore in the hub, then position about 4 flat washers over the stud and thread the lug nut. Hold the hub/rotor while tightening the lug nut, and the stud should be drawn into position. MAKE SURE THE STUD IS FULLY SEATED, then remove the lug nut and washers.**

7. Install the rotor and adjust the wheel bearings.
8. Install the brake caliper and pads.
9. Install the wheel, then remove the jackstands and carefully lower the vehicle.
10. Tighten the lug nuts to the proper torque.

With Drum Brakes

◆ **See Figures 5 and 6**

1. Raise the vehicle and safely support it with jackstands, then remove the wheel.

2. Remove the brake drum.
3. If necessary to provide clearance, remove the brake shoes, as outlined in Section 9 of this manual.
4. Using a large C-clamp and socket, press the stud from the axle flange.
5. Coat the serrated part of the stud with liquid soap and place it into the hole.

To install:

6. Position about 4 flat washers over the stud and thread the lug nut. Hold the flange while tightening the lug nut, and the stud should be drawn into position. MAKE SURE THE STUD IS FULLY SEATED, then remove the lug nut and washers.
7. If applicable, install the brake shoes.
8. Install the brake drum.
9. Install the wheel, then remove the jackstands and carefully lower the vehicle.
10. Tighten the lug nuts to the proper torque.

FRONT SUSPENSION

◆ **See Figures 7, 8 and 9**

The front suspension is designed to allow each wheel to compensate for changes in the road surface level without appreciably affecting the opposite wheel. Each wheel is independently connected to the frame by a steering knuckle, ball joint assemblies, upper and lower control arms. The control arms are specifically designed and positioned to allow the steering knuckles to move in a prescribed three dimensional arc. The front wheels are held in proper relationship to each other by two tie rods which are connected to steering arms on the knuckles and to an intermediate rod.

On rear wheel drive models coil chassis springs are mounted between the spring housings on the frame or front end sheet metal and the lower control arms. Front wheel drive models (through 1985) use torsion bars instead of coil springs. The front end of the torsion bar is attached to the lower control arm. The rear of the torsion bar is mounted into an adjustable arm in the torsion bar crossmember. The standing height of the car is controlled by the adjuster bolt and nut that positions the adjuster arm. Ride control is provided by double, direct acting, shock absorbers (mounted inside the coil springs on rear wheel drive models) and attached to the lower control arms by bolts and nuts. The upper portion of each shock absorber extends through the upper control arm frame bracket and is secured with two grommets, two grommet retainers and a nut. As of 1986, front wheel drive models are equipped with MacPherson-type struts. The struts, used on both sides, are a combination spring and shock absorber with the outer casing of the shock actually supporting the coil spring at the bottom and thus forming a major structural component of the suspension. The steering knuckle/wheel hub assembly is attached to the bottom of the strut. A strut mounting bearing at the top and a ball joint at the bottom allow the entire strut to rotate during cornering maneuvers.

Side roll of the front suspension is controlled by a spring steel stabilizer shaft. It is mounted in rubber bushings which are held to the frame side rails by brackets. The ends of the stabilizer are connected to the lower control arms by link bolts isolated by rubber grommets.

The upper control arm is attached to a cross shaft through isolating rubber bushings. The cross shaft, in turn, is bolted to frame brackets.

A ball joint assembly is riveted to the outer end of the upper arm. It is preloaded by a rubber spring to insure proper seating of the ball in the socket. The upper ball joint is attached to the steering knuckle by a torque prevailing nut.

The inner ends of the lower control arm have pressed-in bushings. Bolts, passing through the bushings, attach the arm to the frame. The lower ball joint assembly is a press fit in the arm and attaches to the steering knuckle with a torque prevailing nut.

Rubber grease seals are provided at ball socket assemblies to keep dirt and moisture from entering the joint and damaging bearing surfaces.

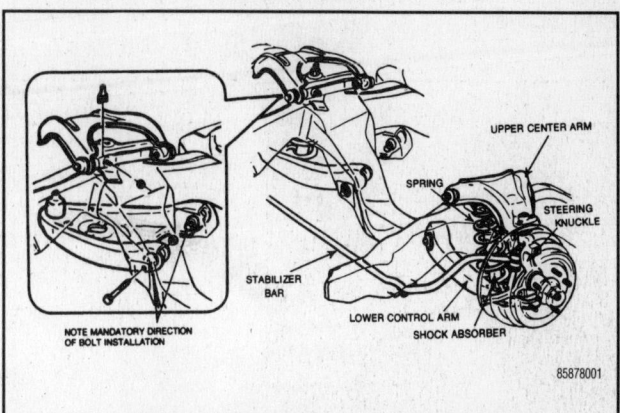

Fig. 7 Common front suspension on a rear wheel drive vehicle

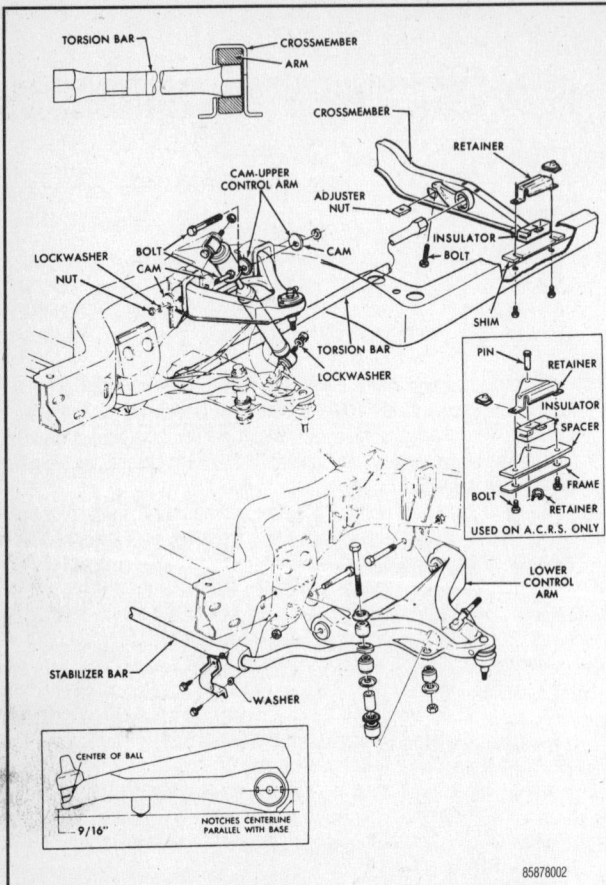

Fig. 8 Common front suspension on front wheel drive vehicles through 1985

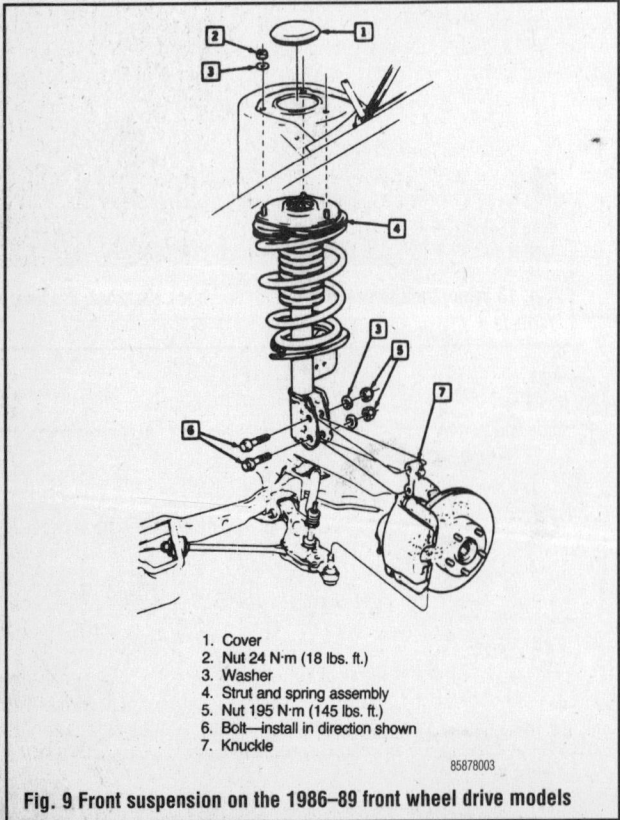

1. Cover
2. Nut 24 N·m (18 lbs. ft.)
3. Washer
4. Strut and spring assembly
5. Nut 195 N·m (145 lbs. ft.)
6. Bolt—install in direction shown
7. Knuckle

Fig. 9 Front suspension on the 1986–89 front wheel drive models

Coil Springs

REMOVAL & INSTALLATION

◆ See Figures 10 and 11

✲✲ CAUTION

The coil springs are under a considerable amount of tension. Be extremely careful when removing or installing them; they can exert enough force to cause serious injury. A coil spring compressor is recommended for removal and installation. This tool can usually be rented at tool rental shops.

1. Jack up the front end of the car, and support the car at the frame with jackstands so the control arms hang free.
2. Remove the shock absorber. Disconnect the stabilizer bar at the steering knuckle.
3. Support the inner end of the control arm with a floor jack.
4. Raise the jack enough to take the tension off the lower control arm pivot bolts.
5. Chain the spring to the lower control arm.
6. Remove first the rear, then the front pivot bolt.
7. Lower the jack, slowly and carefully, until all spring tension is released.
8. Note the way in which the spring is installed in relation to the drain holes on the control arm and remove it.

To install:

9. Position the spring to the control arm and raise it into place.
10. Install the pivot bolts and torque the nuts to 100 ft. lbs. (136 Nm).
11. Replace the shock absorber and stabilizer bar.

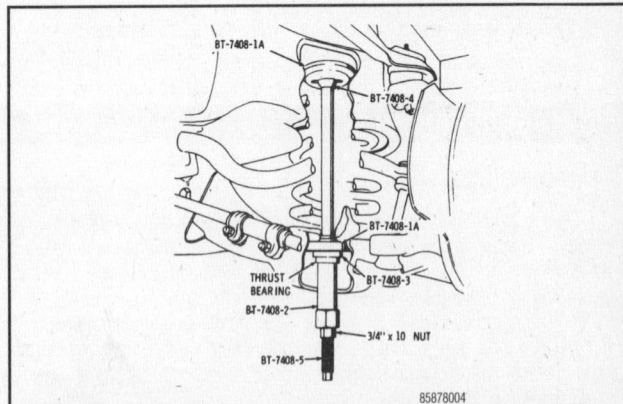

Fig. 10 Front coil spring removal—make sure the lock in the top of the spring compressor is in position whenever the tool is used

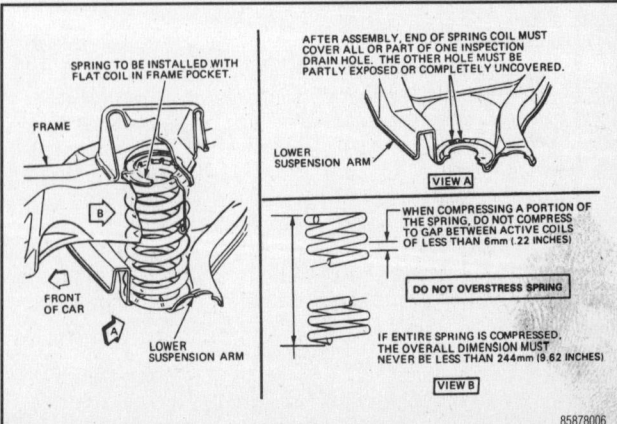

Fig. 11 Coil spring positioning on late model rear wheel drive models

Torsion Bars

REMOVAL & INSTALLATION

♦ See Figure 12

1. Jack up car and support so that front suspension hangs at full rebound.
2. Remove adjusting bolt from both torsion bar locknuts.
3. Install torsion bar remover and installer tool on torsion bar crossmember.
4. Tighten center bolt of tool until adjusting arm is raised high enough to permit removal of locknut. Remove locknut.
5. Repeat Steps 3 and 4 on other side of crossmember.
6. Remove parking brake cable guide at right side of underbody.
7. Remove torsion bar crossmember bolts and retainers from both sides. On 1974–76 models, remove the lock pins and retainers from either end of the crossmember.
8. Move crossmember toward side opposite the torsion bar being removed. One side of crossmember should clear frame at this point.
9. Lower the free end on the crossmember and drive it rearward until torsion bar is free. It may be necessary to loosen parking brake adjuster nut to gain slack in cable.

➡ **Although both torsion bars can be removed at this point, it is usually much easier to remove/install only one side at a time.**

10. Remove torsion bar from lower control arm.

➡ **Nicks or scratches in the torsion bar can cause its failure.**

To install:

11. Lubricate 3 in. (76mm) of each torsion bar end. Bars are marked **L** or **R** for left and right sides—do not interchange.
12. Slide torsion bar into lower control arm as far as it will go after installing the torsion bar seal.
13. Position adjusting arm in crossmember. Holding arm in place, slide torsion bar rearward until it is seated in adjusting arm. The torsion bars are stamped **L** for left and **R** for right. The stamped end is installed in the lower control arm.

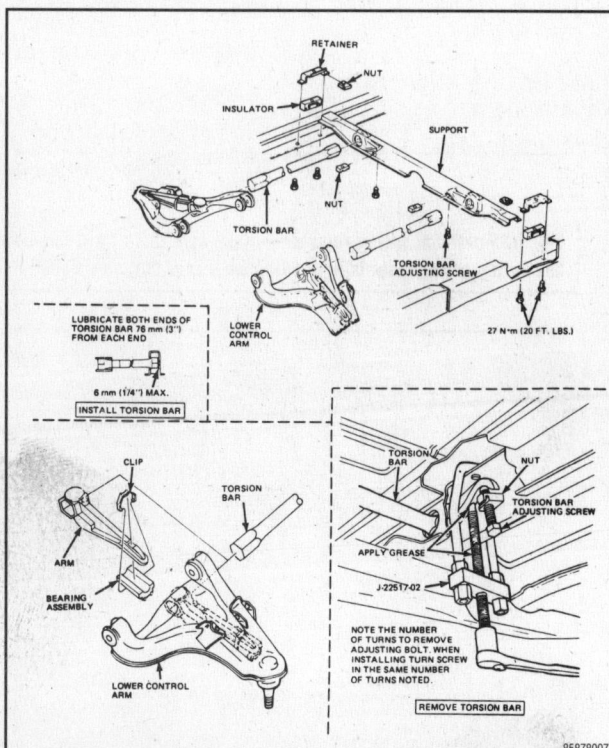

Fig. 12 Torsion bar removal and installation—front wheel drive models through 1985

14. Position crossmember to frame, then reverse the balance of the removal procedure.

Shock Absorbers

TESTING

♦ See Figure 13

The purpose of the shock absorber is simply to limit the motion of the spring during compression and rebound cycles. If the vehicle is not equipped with these motion dampers, the up and down motion would multiply until the vehicle was alternately trying to leap off the ground and to pound itself into the pavement.

Contrary to popular rumor, the shocks do not affect the ride height of the vehicle. This is controlled by other suspension components such as springs and tires. Worn shock absorbers can affect handling; if the front of the vehicle is rising or falling excessively, the "footprint" of the tires changes on the pavement and steering is affected.

The simplest test of the shock absorber is simply push down on one corner of the unladen vehicle and release it. Observe the motion of the body as it is released. In most cases, it will come up beyond it original rest position, dip back below it and settle quickly to rest. This shows that the damper is controlling the spring action. Any tendency to excessive pitch (up-and-down) motion or failure to return to rest within 2-3 cycles is a sign of poor function within the shock absorber. Oil-filled shocks may have a light film of oil around the seal, resulting from normal breathing and air exchange. This should NOT be taken as a sign of failure, but any sign of thick or running oil definitely indicates failure. Gas filled shocks may also show some film at the shaft; if the gas has leaked out, the shock will have almost no resistance to motion.

While each shock absorber can be replaced individually, it is recommended that they be changed as a pair (both front or both rear) to maintain equal response on both sides of the vehicle. Chances are quite good that if one has failed, its mate is weak also.

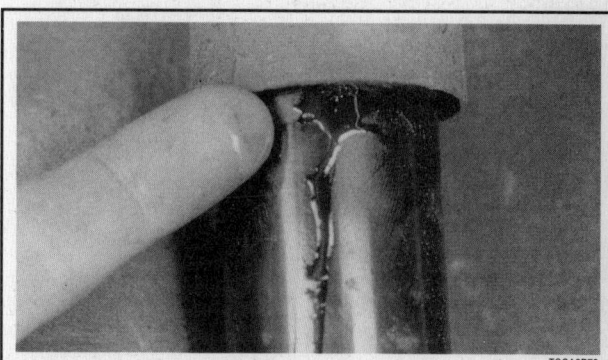

Fig. 13 When fluid is seeping out of the shock absorber, it's time to replace it

REMOVAL & INSTALLATION

♦ See Figures 14 and 15

1. Raise the car, and with an open end wrench hold the upper stem of the shock absorber from turning. Remove the upper stem retaining nut, retainer and grommet.
2. Remove the two bolts retaining the lower shock absorber pivot to the lower control arm, then pull the shock out through the bottom of the control arm.

To install:

3. With the lower retainer and the rubber grommet in place over the upper stem, install the shock (fully extended) back through the lower control arm.
4. Install the upper grommet, retainer and nut onto the upper stem.
5. Hold the upper stem from turning with an open end wrench, then tighten the retaining nut.
6. Reinstall the retainers on the lower end of the shock.

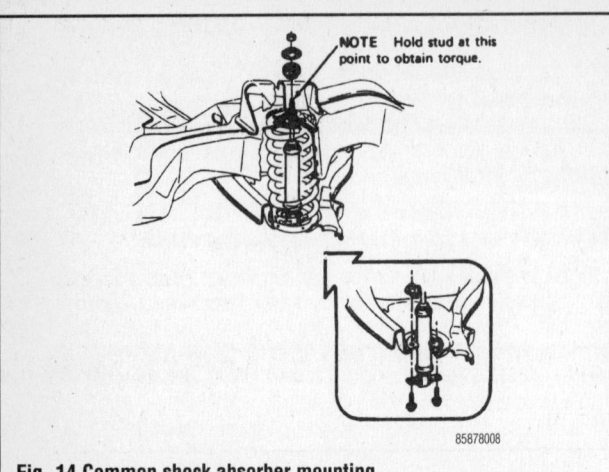

Fig. 14 Common shock absorber mounting

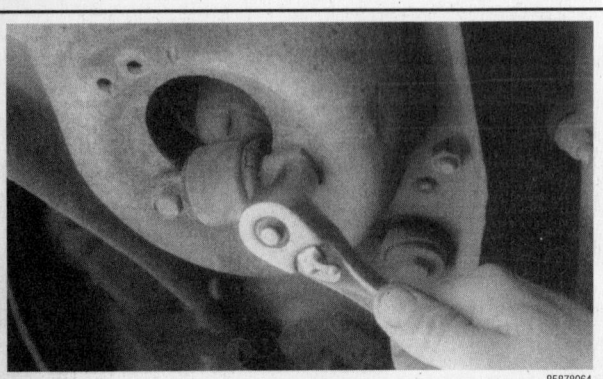

Fig. 15 Removing the lower front shock absorber mounting

MacPherson Struts

The struts retain the springs under tremendous pressure, even when removed from the vehicle. For this reason, several expensive special tools and substantial specialized knowledge are required to safely and effectively work on these components. If spring and shock absorber work is required, it is a good idea to remove the strut involved yourself, then take it to a repair facility which is fully equipped and familiar with MacPherson struts.

REMOVAL & INSTALLATION

1. Open the hood and remove the nuts attaching the top of the strut to the body.
2. Raise the vehicle and install jackstands under the cradle. Then, lower the vehicle so it rests on the jackstands and not on the control arms.

❈❈ CAUTION

Support all cars at the rear so that as components are removed, the weight will not shift, causing the car to fall off the supports.

3. Remove the tire and wheels related to the strut(s) involved.
4. Using a sharp tool, scribe the knuckle along the lower outboard radius of the strut. Then, scribe the strut flange on the inboard side, right along the curve of the knuckle. Finally, make a scribe mark across the strut/knuckle interface. These scribe marks will be used on reassembly to properly match the components.
5. Remove the brake line mounting bracket from the strut.

❈❈ WARNING

When working near the drive axles, make sure you don't permit the inner tri-pot joints to become overextended, as this could cause

undetectable damage. Also, make sure you do not scratch the spring coating, as this could result in premature failure of the spring.

6. Remove the strut-to-knuckle nuts and bolts, then carefully support the knuckle from the body with wire.
7. Remove the strut.

To install:

8. Install the strut, aligning all scribe marks to ensure it is in the proper position. Install the strut-to-knuckle nuts and bolts, then tighten just slightly.
9. Install the brake line bracket back onto the strut.
10. Install the nuts attaching the top of the strut to the body. Now, torque those nuts to 18 ft. lbs. (24 Nm). Torque the strut-to-knuckle bolts/nuts to 145 ft. lbs. (196 Nm).
11. Install the wheel, and torque the nuts to 100 ft. lbs. (136 Nm). Lower the car.

OVERHAUL

▶ **See Figures 16, 17, 18 and 19**

➡ There are five special tools that are required to complete this procedure, without them, strut overhaul is impossible. The tools are:

- J-3289-20 Holding fixture
- J-34013-47 Template
- J-34013-A Strut compressor
- J-34013-20 Clamp
- J-34013-38 Guiding rod

❈❈ WARNING

Care should be taken to avoid chipping or scratching the spring coating when handling the front suspension coil spring. Damage to the spring coating can cause premature spring failure.

1. Mount the strut assembly into the strut compressor (J-34013-A). Turn the compressor forcing screw until the spring is slightly compressed.
2. Using a socket wrench, hold the dampener shaft from turning while you remove the nut at the top of the dampener shaft.
3. Using the guiding rod (J-34013-38), remove the dampener shaft from the strut assembly.
4. Loosen the compressor screw while sliding the dampener rod out of the strut assembly. Continue loosening the screw until the strut dampener and spring can be removed.

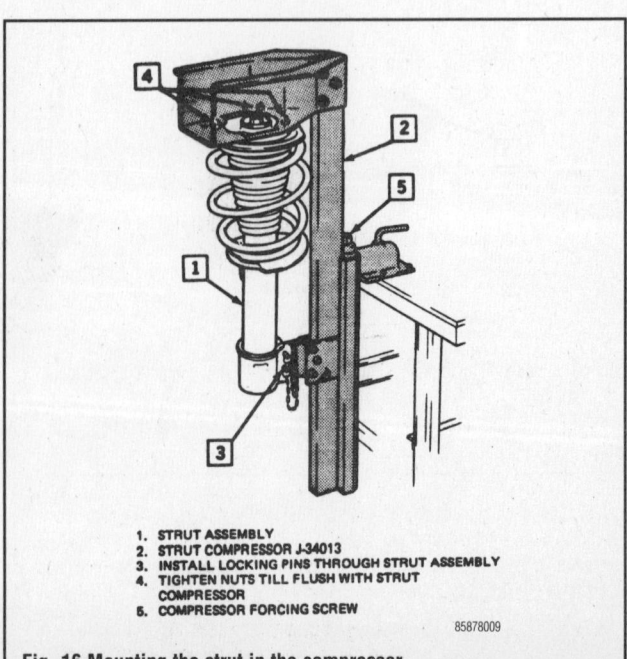

1. STRUT ASSEMBLY
2. STRUT COMPRESSOR J-34013
3. INSTALL LOCKING PINS THROUGH STRUT ASSEMBLY
4. TIGHTEN NUTS TILL FLUSH WITH STRUT COMPRESSOR
5. COMPRESSOR FORCING SCREW

Fig. 16 Mounting the strut in the compressor

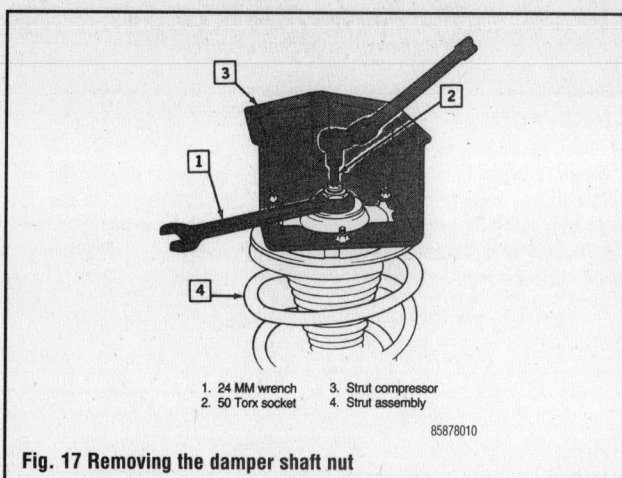

1. 24 MM wrench
2. 50 Torx socket
3. Strut compressor
4. Strut assembly

85878010

Fig. 17 Removing the damper shaft nut

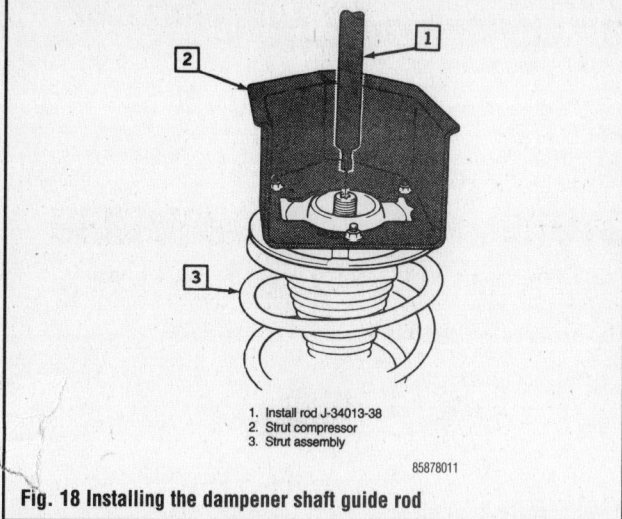

1. Install rod J-34013-38
2. Strut compressor
3. Strut assembly

85878011

Fig. 18 Installing the dampener shaft guide rod

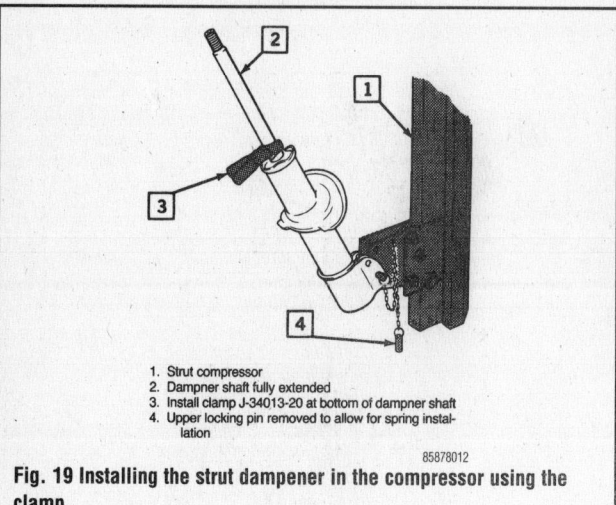

1. Strut compressor
2. Dampner shaft fully extended
3. Install clamp J-34013-20 at bottom of dampner shaft
4. Upper locking pin removed to allow for spring installation

85878012

Fig. 19 Installing the strut dampener in the compressor using the clamp

5. To install, position the strut dampener into the compressor with the clamp (J-34013-20) on the dampener shaft.

6. Position the spring over the strut in the correct manner, then move the assembly upright in the compressor and install the upper locking pin.

➡**The flat on the upper spring seat must face away from the centerline of the vehicle; or, when mounted in the compressor the spring seat will face the same direction as the steering knuckle mounting flange.**

7. Use the guiding rod once again and guide the dampener shaft into the strut body.

8. Turn the compressor screw clockwise while the guiding rod centers the shaft in the assembly.

9. Continue to turn the screw until the dampener shaft threads are visible through the top of the strut assembly, then install the washer and nut. Remove the clamp from the dampener shaft.

➡**Tighten the dampener shaft nut to 44 ft. lbs. (60 Nm) with a crow's foot line wrench while holding the shaft with a socket wrench.**

10. Remove the three nuts mounting the strut assembly into the compressor, then the two locking pins at the bottom of the compressor. Remove the strut assembly.

Upper Ball Joints

INSPECTION

➡**Before performing this inspection, make sure the wheel bearings are adjusted correctly and that the control arm bushings are in good condition. 1973 and later models covered in this manual are equipped with wear indicators on the lower ball joint. As long as the indicator extends below the ball stud seat, replacement is unnecessary; if only the lower ball joint is bad, however, both upper and lower ball joints should be replaced.**

1. Raise the car by placing the jack under the lower control arm at the spring seat.

2. Raise the car until there is a 1-2 in. (25–50mm) clearance under the wheel.

3. Insert a bar under the wheel and pry upward. If the wheel raises more than ⅛ in. (3mm), the ball joints are worn. Determine whether the upper or lower ball joint is worn by visual inspection while prying on the wheel.

REMOVAL & INSTALLATION

◆ **See Figures 20, 21, 22 and 23**

1976–79 Seville and 1977–86 Deville/Fleetwood

➡**On models other than those listed above, it is suggested that the entire upper control arm be replaced as an assembly.**

1. Raise the vehicle and support securely. Support the lower control arm securely. Remove the tire and wheel.

2. Remove the upper ball stud cotter pin and loosen the ball stud nut just one turn.

3. Procure a special tool designed to press out ball joints. These tools are available at most automotive parts stores. Locate the tool between the upper and lower ball joints, then press the joints out of the steering knuckle. Remove the tool.

4. Remove the ball joint stud nut, and separate the joint from the steering knuckle. Lift the upper arm up, then place a block of wood between the frame and the arm to support it.

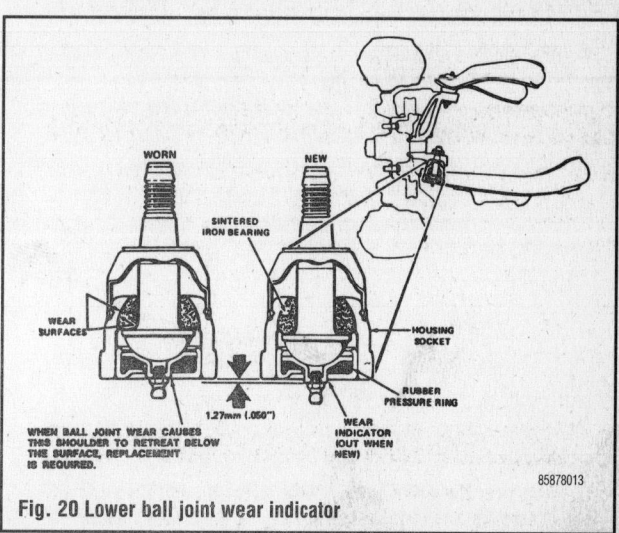

85878013

Fig. 20 Lower ball joint wear indicator

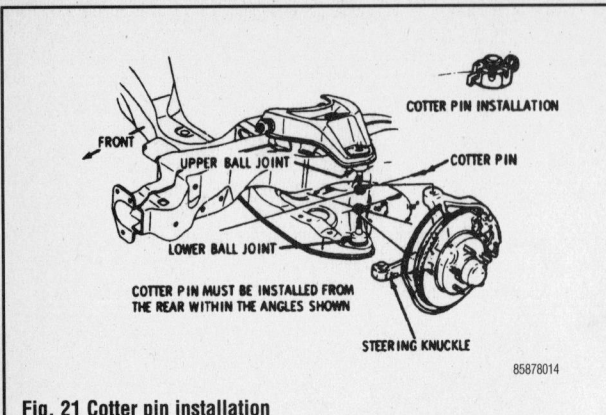

Fig. 21 Cotter pin installation

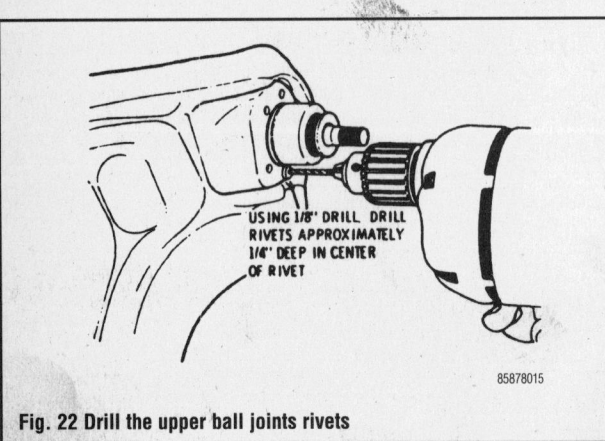

Fig. 22 Drill the upper ball joints rivets

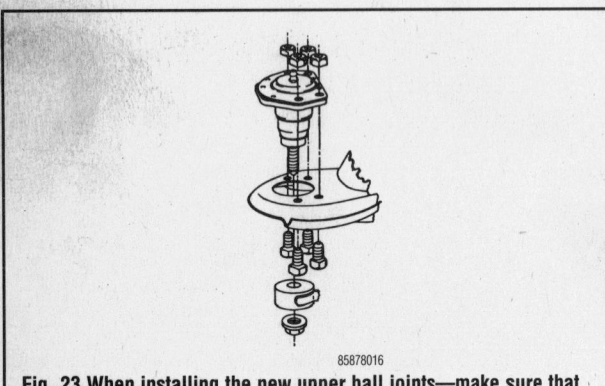

Fig. 23 When installing the new upper ball joints—make sure that the nuts are on the top

5. With the control arm in the raised position, drill a hole ¼ in. (6mm) deep into each rivet. Use a ⅛ in. (3mm) drill bit.

6. Use a ½ in. drill bit and drill off the heads of each rivet.

7. Punch out the rivets using a small punch, then remove the ball joint.

To install:

8. Install the new ball joint using fasteners that meet GM specifications. Bolts should come in from the bottom with the nuts going on top. Torque to 10 ft. lbs. (14 Nm).

9. Turn the ball stud cotter pin hole to the fore and aft position. Remove the block of wood from between the upper control arm and frame.

10. Clean and inspect the steering knuckle hole. Replace the steering knuckle if any out of roundness is noted.

11. Insert the ball stud into the steering knuckle, and install and torque the stud nut to 60 ft. lbs. (81 Nm). Install a new cotter pin. If nut must be turned to align cotter pin holes, tighten it further. Do not back off!

12. Install a lube fitting, and fill the joint with fresh grease.

13. Remove the lower control arm support (jack, etc.) and lower the car.

Lower Ball Joints

INSPECTION

→ Before performing this inspection, make sure the wheel bearings are adjusted correctly and that the control arm bushings are in good condition. 1973 and later models covered in this manual are equipped with wear indicators on the lower ball joint. As long as the indicator extends below the ball stud seat, replacement is unnecessary; if only the lower ball joint is bad, however, both upper and lower ball joints should be replaced.

1. Raise the car by placing the jack under the lower control arm at the spring seat.

2. Raise the car until there is a 1-2 in. (25–50mm) clearance under the wheel.

3. Insert a bar under the wheel and pry upward. If the wheel raises more than ⅛ in. (3mm), the ball joints are worn. Determine whether the upper or lower ball joint is worn by visual inspection while prying on the wheel.

REMOVAL & INSTALLATION

Except 1986–89 Eldorado/Seville

◆ **See Figures 24 and 25**

1. Raise the vehicle and support it securely. Support the lower control arm with a jack.

2. Remove the lower ball stud cotter pin, and loosen the ball stud nut just one turn.

3. Install a special tool designed for such work between the two ball studs, and press the stud downward in the steering knuckle. Remove the stud nut.

4. Pull the tire outward and at the same time upward, with your hands on the bottom (of the tire), to free the steering knuckle from the ball stud. The, remove the wheel.

5. Lift up on the upper control arm and place a block of wood between it and the frame. Be careful not to put any tension on the brake hose in doing this.

6. Pressed-in ball joints:

a. Press the ball joint out of the lower control arm with a tool made for that purpose. You may have to disconnect the tie rod at the steering knuckle to do this.

b. To install, position the new ball joint, with the vent in the rubber boot facing inward, onto the lower control arm. Press the joint fully into the control arm with a tool designed for this.

7. Riveted ball joints:

a. With the control arm in the raised position, drill a hole ¼ in. (6mm) deep into each rivet. Use a ⅛ in. (3mm) drill bit.

b. Use a ½ in. drill bit and drill off the heads of each rivet.

c. Punch out the rivets using a small punch, then remove the ball joint.

d. Install the new ball joint using fasteners that meet GM specifications. Bolts should come in from the bottom with the nuts going on top. Torque to 10 ft. lbs. (14 Nm).

8. Turn the ball stud cotter pin hole so it is fore and aft.

9. Remove the block of wood holding the upper control arm out of the way, and inspect the tapered hole in the steering knuckle. Remove any dirt from the

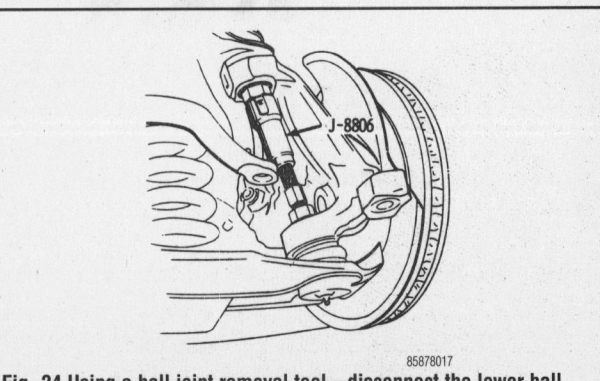

Fig. 24 Using a ball joint removal tool—disconnect the lower ball joint

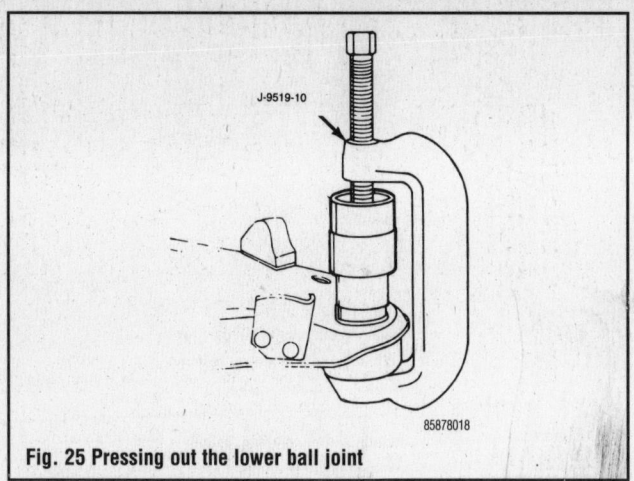

Fig. 25 Pressing out the lower ball joint

hole. If the hole is out of round or there is other noticeable damage, replace the entire steering knuckle.

1986–89 Eldorado and Seville

▶ See Figure 26

1. Raise the vehicle and support it under the cradle in a secure manner, so the control arms will hang free.
2. Remove the wheel.
3. Remove the stabilizer bar insulators, retainers, spacer, and bolt.
4. Using a ¼ in. drill bit for the first pass, and a ½ in. bit for the second, drill out the three rivets retaining the joint. Remove the cotter pin and nut and remove the ball joint.
   To install:
5. Install in reverse order, replacing the ball joint mounting rivets with bolts and torque them to 50 ft. lbs. (68 Nm).
6. Insert the ball joint stud into the steering knuckle, and install the nut. Torque the nut to 7 ft. lbs. (9 Nm) then turn it an additional 180 degrees while watching the required torque. It must reach at least 48 ft. lbs. (65 Nm). The nut may be turned as much as 1/16 turn more to install the cotter pin. Install the cotter pin. Reverse the remaining procedures to complete the installation.

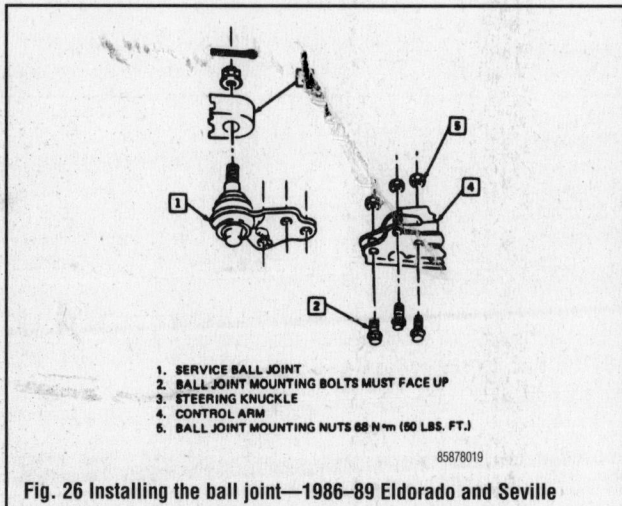

1. SERVICE BALL JOINT
2. BALL JOINT MOUNTING BOLTS MUST FACE UP
3. STEERING KNUCKLE
4. CONTROL ARM
5. BALL JOINT MOUNTING NUTS 68 N·m (50 LBS. FT.)

Fig. 26 Installing the ball joint—1986–89 Eldorado and Seville

Sway Bar

REMOVAL & INSTALLATION

▶ See Figure 27

1. Jack up the front end of the car and safely support it with jackstands.

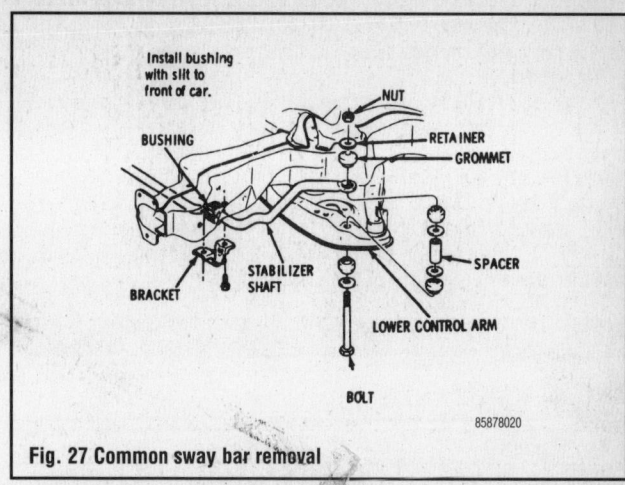

Fig. 27 Common sway bar removal

2. Disconnect each side of the sway bar linkage by removing the nut from the link bolt. Pull the bolt from the linkage, then remove the retainers, grommets and spacer.
3. Remove the bracket-to-frame or body bolts on both sides of the car and remove the sway bar, rubber bushings and brackets.
4. To install, reverse the above procedure. Make sure the rubber bushings are installed squarely in the bracket with the slit in the bushings facing the front of the car. Torque the sway bar link nuts to 13 ft. lbs. (18 Nm).

Upper Control Arm

REMOVAL & INSTALLATION

▶ See Figure 28

1. Raise the vehicle on a hoist.
2. Support the outer end of the lower control arm with a jack.

❊❊ CAUTION

Leave the jack in place during removal and installation, in order to keep the spring and control arm positioned.

3. Remove the wheel. Remove the shock absorber.
4. Separate the upper ball joint from the steering knuckle as described above under Upper Ball Joint Replacement.
5. Remove the control arm shaft-to-frame nuts.

➡ Tape the shims together and identify them so that they can be installed in the positions from which they were removed.

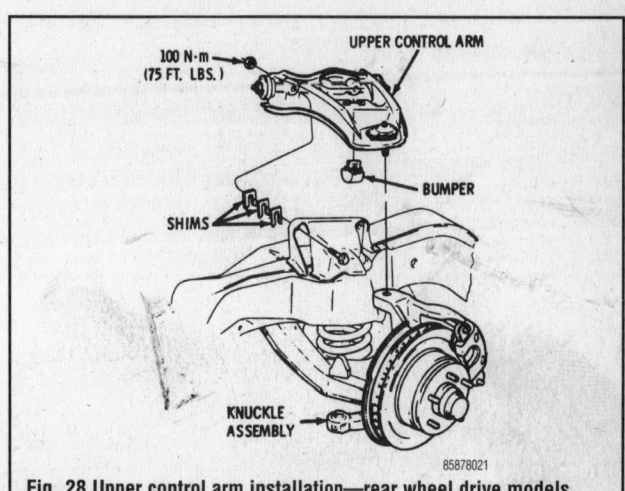

Fig. 28 Upper control arm installation—rear wheel drive models shown, other models similar

6. Remove the bolts which attach the control arm shaft to the frame and remove the control arm. Note the positions of the bolts.

To install:

7. Install in the reverse order of removal. Make sure that the shaft-to-frame bolts are installed in the same position they were in before removal and that the shims are in their original positions. Use free running nuts (not locknuts) to pull serrated bolts through the frame. Then install the locknuts. Tighten the thinner shim pack first. After the car has been lowered to the ground, bounce the front end to center the bushings, then tighten the bushing collar bolts to 45 ft. lbs. (61 Nm). Tighten the shaft-to-frame bolts to 90 ft. lbs. (122 Nm). The control arm shaft nuts are tightened to 75 ft. lbs. (102 Nm).

Lower Control Arm

REMOVAL & INSTALLATION

▶ **See Figure 29**

Except 1986–89 Eldorado/Seville

1. Remove the spring or torsion bar as described earlier.
2. Remove the ball stud from the steering knuckle as described earlier.
3. Remove the control arm pivot bolts and the control arm.
4. To install, reverse the above procedure. If any bolts are to be replaced, do so with bolts of equal strengthened quality.

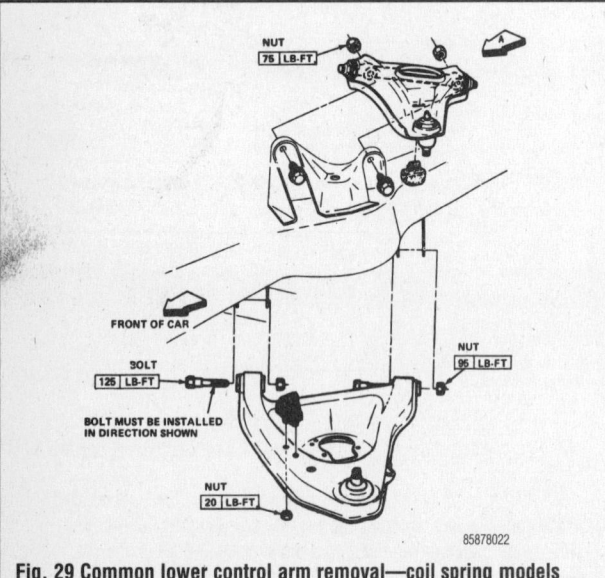

Fig. 29 Common lower control arm removal—coil spring models

1986–89 Eldorado and Seville

▶ **See Figures 30 and 31**

✳✳ WARNING

Throughout this procedure, take care not to overextend the tri-pot joints. Overextension could result in separation of internal components, resulting in eventual failure of the joint. The damage done would not be readily detectable. You will need a 90 degree angle torque wrench J-35551 or equivalent.

1. Raise the car and support it by the cradle on jackstands. Remove the tire and wheel.
2. Disconnect the stabilizer shaft insulator, retainers, spacer, and bolt from the control arm.
3. Disconnect the lower ball joint from the knuckle.
4. Remove the control arm bushing bolt and front nut, retainer, and insulator. Then, remove the control arm from the frame.

To install:

5. Install the control arm back onto the frame with the bushing bolt and front nut, retainer, and insulator, but do not tighten them at this time.

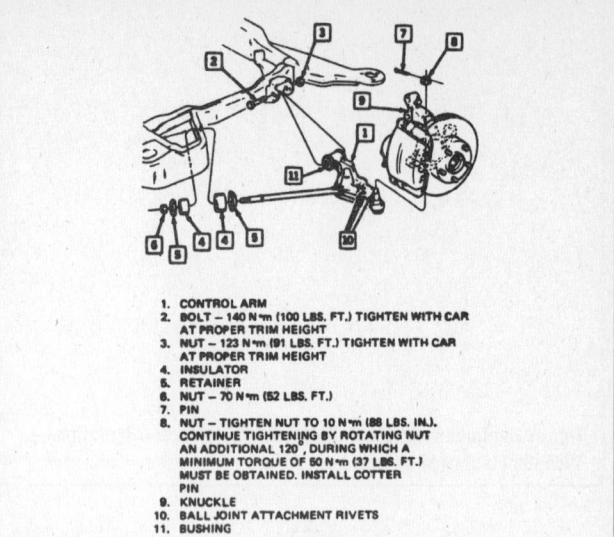

1. CONTROL ARM
2. BOLT — 140 N·m (100 LBS. FT.) TIGHTEN WITH CAR AT PROPER TRIM HEIGHT
3. NUT — 123 N·m (91 LBS. FT.) TIGHTEN WITH CAR AT PROPER TRIM HEIGHT
4. INSULATOR
5. RETAINER
6. NUT — 70 N·m (52 LBS. FT.)
7. PIN
8. NUT — TIGHTEN NUT TO 10 N·m (88 LBS. IN.). CONTINUE TIGHTENING BY ROTATING NUT AN ADDITIONAL 120°, DURING WHICH A MINIMUM TORQUE OF 50 N·m (37 LBS. FT.) MUST BE OBTAINED. INSTALL COTTER PIN
9. KNUCKLE
10. BALL JOINT ATTACHMENT RIVETS
11. BUSHING

Fig. 30 Lower control arm and steering knuckle—1986–89 Eldorado and Seville

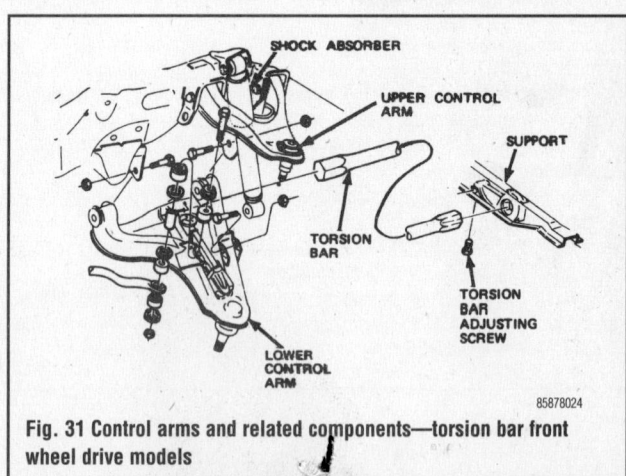

Fig. 31 Control arms and related components—torsion bar front wheel drive models

6. Connect the lower ball joint to the knuckle.
7. Connect the stabilizer shaft insulator, retainers, spacer, and bolt. Tighten the shaft nut/bolt to 13 ft. lbs. (18 Nm).
8. Insert the ball joint stud into the steering knuckle, and install the nut. Torque the nut to 7 ft. lbs. (9 Nm); then turn it an additional 180 degrees while watching the required torque. Torque must reach at least 48 ft. lbs. (65 Nm) in that 180 degrees. Install the cotter pin.
9. Install the tire and wheel, then lower the car to the ground, leaving it unsupported by any jacking equipment. Torque the wheel nuts to 100 ft. lbs. (136 Nm). Then, torque the control arm bushing bolt to 100 ft. lbs. (136 Nm), or if it is a nut, to 91 ft. lbs. (123 Nm). Torque the retaining nut to 52 ft. lbs. (70 Nm).

Steering Knuckle

REMOVAL & INSTALLATION

Rear Wheel Drive Models

▶ **See Figure 32**

1. Siphon some fluid from the brake master cylinder.
2. Raise and support the vehicle on jackstands.
3. Remove the wheel and tire assembly.

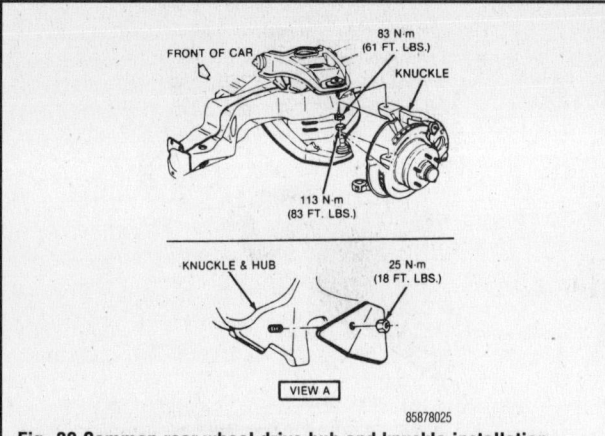

Fig. 32 Common rear wheel drive hub and knuckle installation—1986–89 Fleetwood shown

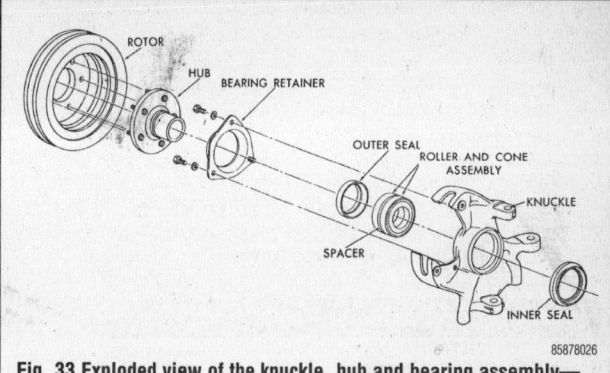

Fig. 33 Exploded view of the knuckle, hub and bearing assembly—Eldorado through 1978

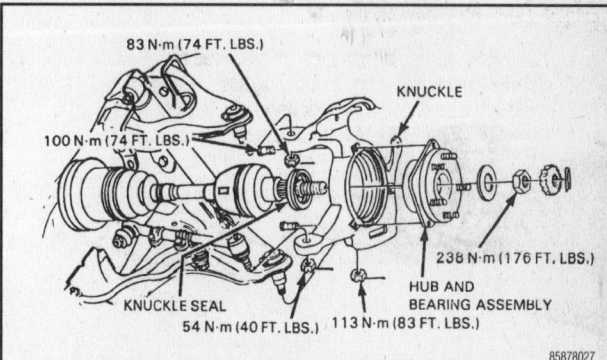

Fig. 34 Exploded view of the knuckle, hub and bearing assembly—1979–85 Eldorado and 1980–85 Seville

4. Remove the caliper from the steering knuckle and support on a wire.

5. Remove the splash shield.

6. Remove the grease cup, the cotter pin, the castle nut and the hub assembly.

7. Remove the 3 bolts holding the shield to the steering knuckle.

8. Using the ball joint removal tool J-6627, disconnect the tie rod from the steering knuckle.

9. Using ball joint removal tool J-23742, disconnect the ball joints from the steering knuckle.

10. Place a floor jack under the lower control arm (near the spring seat) and disconnect the ball joint from the steering knuckle.

11. Raise the upper control arm and disconnect the ball joint from the steering knuckle.

12. Remove the steering knuckle from the vehicle.

To install:

13. Place the steering knuckle into position and insert the upper and lower ball joints.

14. Install the stud nuts and torque the upper nut to 61 ft. lbs. (83 Nm) and the lower nut to 83 ft. lbs. (112 Nm).

15. Install the splash shield.

16. Install the hub and rotor assembly.

17. Install the outer bearing, then install the spindle washer and nut. Adjust the front wheel bearing.

18. Install the brake caliper.

19. Install the wheel and tire assembly.

20. Lower the car.

21. Check the front wheel alignment and reset as necessary.

Front Knuckle, Hub and Bearing Assembly

REMOVAL & INSTALLATION

Front Wheel Drive Models

THROUGH 1985

▶ See Figures 33 and 34

➡The 1980–85 Sevilles and the Eldorados through 1985 use sealed wheel bearings which require no adjustment or lubrication.

1. Remove hub cap, loosen wheel nuts, remove drive axle cotter pin and loosen drive axle nut.

2. Jack up car and place jackstands under lower control arms.

3. Remove axle nut, then remove the wheel and tire assembly.

4. Remove brake hose and caliper.

➡Matchmark disc and hub, then remove the disc.

5. Remove the upper ball joint cotter pin and loosen stud nut.

6. Strike steering knuckle near upper joint to separate it from taper.

7. Cover the lower control arm torsion bar connector with a short piece of rubber hose to avoid damaging the inboard tri-pot joint seal when the hub and knuckle are removed.

8. Remove tie rod end cotter pin and nut.

9. Separate tie rod end from steering knuckle using a tie rod splitter.

10. Remove lower ball joint cotter pin and stud nut.

11. Disconnect lower ball joint.

12. Remove hub, backing plate and steering knuckle as an assembly.

To install:

13. Guide the knuckle assembly over the drive axle, install the lower joint stud into the knuckle and attach the nut, but do not tighten at this time.

14. Install the tie rod end stud into the knuckle and attach the nut. Do not tighten at this time.

15. Install the upper ball joint stud into the knuckle, install the nut loosely, do not tighten at this time.

16. Align the disc and hub, then install the disc on the hub. Install one or two nuts on the hub to prevent the disc from falling off.

17. Install the caliper.

18. On some models it may be necessary to remove the upper ball joint nut to install the brake hose clip on the stud. Be careful not to twist the brake hose during caliper installation.

19. Tighten the upper ball joint nut to 60 ft. lbs. (81 Nm) and install a new cotter pin. Bend the cotter pin against the flats on the nut.

20. Tighten the tie rod end nut to 40 ft. lbs. (54 Nm).

21. Tighten the lower ball joint nut to 80 ft. lbs. (108 Nm) and install a new cotter pin. Bend the cotter pin against the flats on the nut.

22. Install the drive axle washer and nut but do not tighten at this time.

23. Remove the nuts holding the disc on the hub and install the wheel and tire. Tighten the wheel nuts until they are snug, do not tighten at this time.

24. Raise the car, remove the jackstands and lower the car.

25. Tighten the wheel lug nuts to 130 ft. lbs. (176 Nm) through 1978, or to 100 ft. lbs. (136 Nm) for 1979–85 vehicles.

26. Install the drive axle nut and install a new cotter pin. Tighten drive axle nut to 110 ft. lbs. (149 Nm) through 1978, or to 175 ft. lbs. (237 Nm) for 1979–85 vehicles.

1986–89 VEHICLES

◆ See Figures 35 and 36

➡ To perform this procedure you will need a front hub spindle remover GM tool No. J-28733 or equivalent and a hub seal installer GM tool No. J-34657 or equivalent.

1. Raise the vehicle, then position jackstands under its cradle. Lower the vehicle so the jackstands support it and the control arms are free. Remove the front wheel.

2. Use a drift inserted through one of the slots in the rotor and a caliper slot to keep the rotor from turning. Then, remove the hub nut and washer.

3. Remove the caliper and caliper support, then remove the rotor.

4. Use the spindle remover to force the drive axle out of the hub.

5. Remove the hub and bearings retaining bolts, then remove the hub and bearing assembly. Remove the seal by driving it toward the center of the car, then cutting it off the drive axle.

To install:

6. Lubricate the lip of a new seal with wheel bearing grease and install it with a seal driver.

7. The remainder of installation is the reverse of removal. Keep in mind the following points:

   a. Torque the hub and bearing retaining bolts to 70 ft. lbs. (95 Nm).

   b. Install the caliper with new mounting bolts.

   c. Install the hub nut and washer part way with the vehicle in the air.

Install the wheel, then raise the vehicle, remove the jackstands, and lower it to the floor. Final torque the hub nut to 180 ft. lbs. (244 Nm).

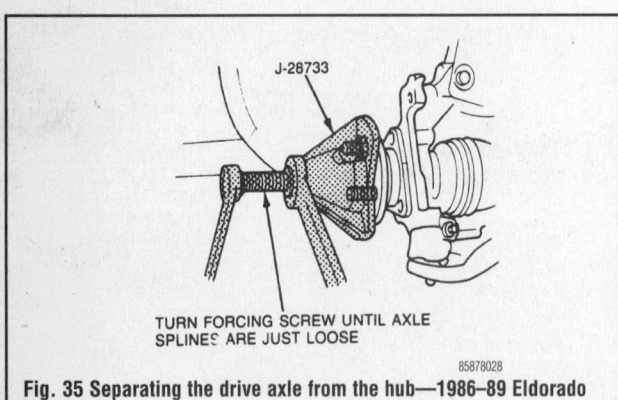

TURN FORCING SCREW UNTIL AXLE SPLINES ARE JUST LOOSE

85878028

Fig. 35 Separating the drive axle from the hub—1986–89 Eldorado and Seville

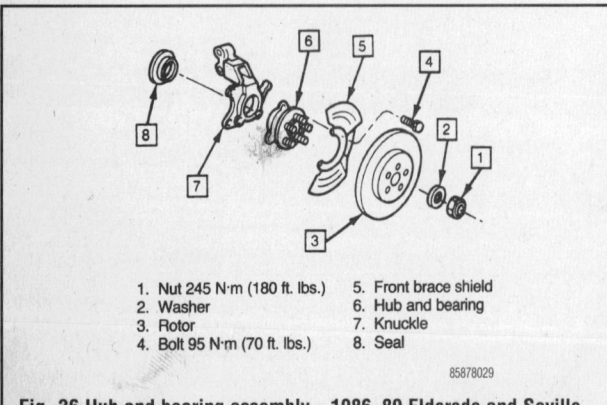

1. Nut 245 N·m (180 ft. lbs.)	5. Front brace shield
2. Washer	6. Hub and bearing
3. Rotor	7. Knuckle
4. Bolt 95 N·m (70 ft. lbs.)	8. Seal

85878029

Fig. 36 Hub and bearing assembly—1986–89 Eldorado and Seville

Wheel Alignment

If the tires are worn unevenly, if the vehicle is not stable on the highway or if the handling seems uneven in spirited driving, the wheel alignment should be checked. If an alignment problem is suspected, first check for improper tire inflation and other possible causes. These can be worn suspension or steering components, accident damage or even unmatched tires. If any worn or damaged components are found, they must be replaced before the wheels can be properly aligned. Wheel alignment requires very expensive equipment and involves minute adjustments which must be accurate; it should only be performed by a trained technician. Take your vehicle to a properly equipped shop.

Following is a description of the alignment angles which are adjustable on most vehicles and how they affect vehicle handling. Although these angles can apply to both the front and rear wheels, usually only the front suspension is adjustable.

CASTER

◆ See Figure 37

Looking at a vehicle from the side, caster angle describes the steering axis rather than a wheel angle. The steering knuckle is attached to a control arm or strut at the top and a control arm at the bottom. The wheel pivots around the line between these points to steer the vehicle. When the upper point is tilted back, this is described as positive caster. Having a positive caster tends to make the wheels self-centering, increasing directional stability. Excessive positive caster makes the wheels hard to steer, while an uneven caster will cause a pull to one side. Overloading the vehicle or sagging rear springs will affect caster, as will raising the rear of the vehicle. If the rear of the vehicle is lower than normal, the caster becomes more positive.

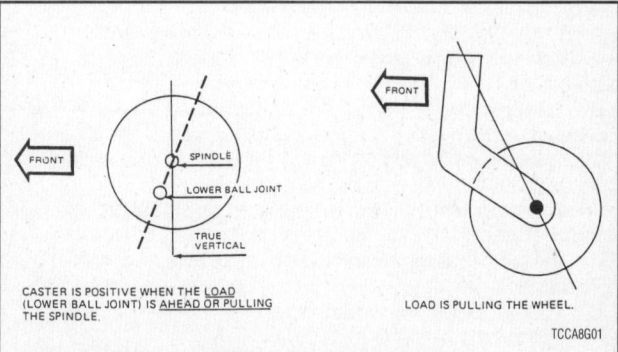

CASTER IS POSITIVE WHEN THE LOAD (LOWER BALL JOINT) IS AHEAD OR PULLING THE SPINDLE.

LOAD IS PULLING THE WHEEL.

TCCA8G01

Fig. 37 Caster affects straight-line stability. Caster wheels used on shopping carts, for example, employ positive caster

CAMBER

◆ See Figure 38

Looking from the front of the vehicle, camber is the inward or outward tilt of the top of wheels. When the tops of the wheels are tilted in, this is negative camber; if they are tilted out, it is positive. In a turn, a slight amount of negative camber helps maximize contact of the tire with the road. However, too much negative camber compromises straight-line stability, increases bump steer and torque steer.

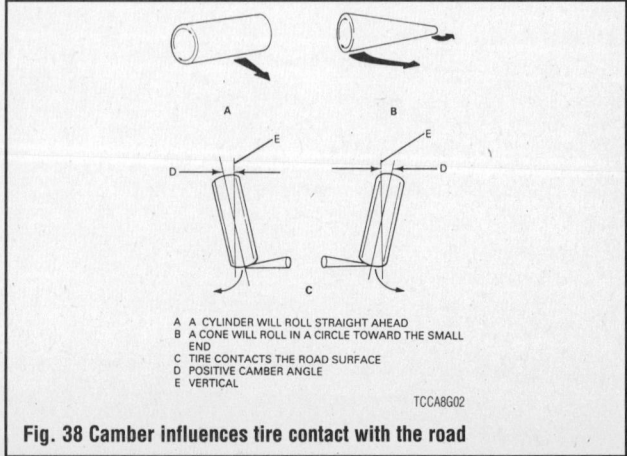

A A CYLINDER WILL ROLL STRAIGHT AHEAD
B A CONE WILL ROLL IN A CIRCLE TOWARD THE SMALL END
C TIRE CONTACTS THE ROAD SURFACE
D POSITIVE CAMBER ANGLE
E VERTICAL

TCCA8G02

Fig. 38 Camber influences tire contact with the road

TOE

♦ **See Figure 39**

Looking down at the wheels from above the vehicle, toe angle is the distance between the front of the wheels, relative to the distance between the back of the wheels. If the wheels are closer at the front, they are said to be toed-in or to have negative toe. A small amount of negative toe enhances directional stability and provides a smoother ride on the highway.

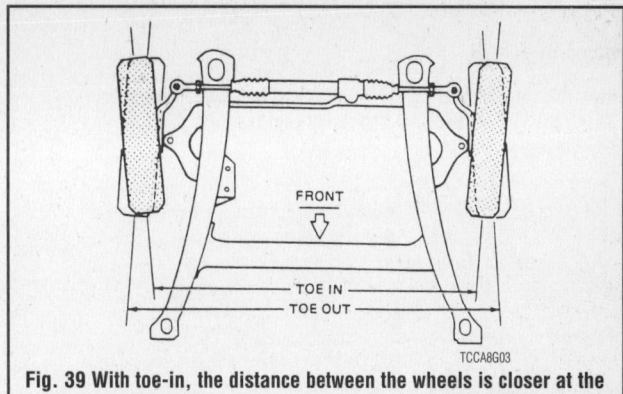

Fig. 39 With toe-in, the distance between the wheels is closer at the front than at the rear

REAR SUSPENSION

♦ **See Figures 40, 41, 42 and 43**

The full size Cadillac models use a four-link rear suspension system. The axle housing is connected to the frame by two upper and lower control arms with rubber bushings at each end of the arm. Two coil springs support the weight of the car in the rear. They are retained between seats in the frame and brackets axle housing and the frame. A rubber insulator is used on the upper side. Shock absorbers are mounted between the axle housing and the frame.

The Commercial Chassis and 1976–79 Seville models are semi-elliptical leaf springs to support the rear axle. Shock absorbers are mounted between the axle housing and the frame.

The rear suspension on the 1967–70 Eldorado models consists of two single leaf, semi-elliptical springs, two vertical and two horizontal shock absorbers.

The 1971–78 models use a four-link, coil spring suspension. The rear axle is a straight, hollow tube design. The spindles are pressed and bolted to the axle flanges and taper roller bearings are used.

The 1979–85 Eldorado and the 1980–85 Seville utilize an independent rear suspension system, incorporating a relatively long control arm for a minimum camber change. The hub and wheel bearing is one unit which requires no periodic maintenance or adjustment.

The 1986–89 Eldorado and Seville utilize an independent, transverse mounted leaf spring rear suspension system. All components are attached to a center crossmember assembly which is attached to the vehicle's body at four points. Each rear wheel is connected to the crossmember assembly through the

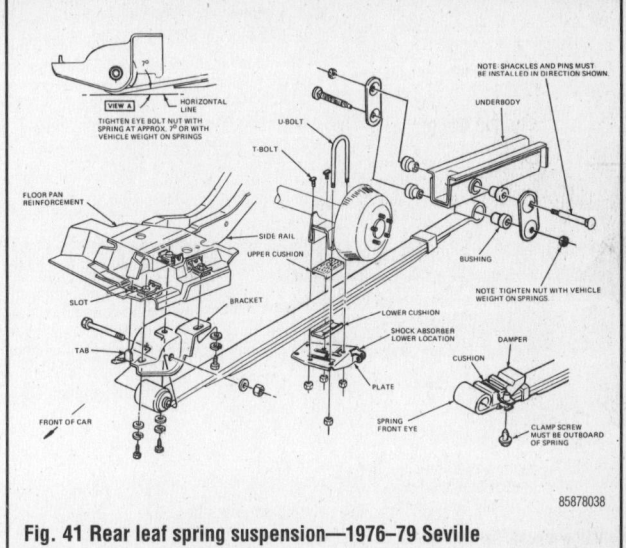

Fig. 41 Rear leaf spring suspension—1976–79 Seville

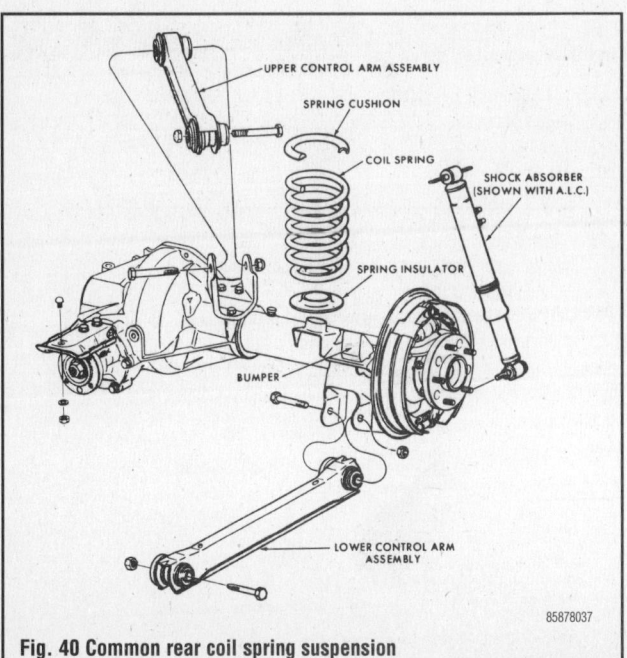

Fig. 40 Common rear coil spring suspension

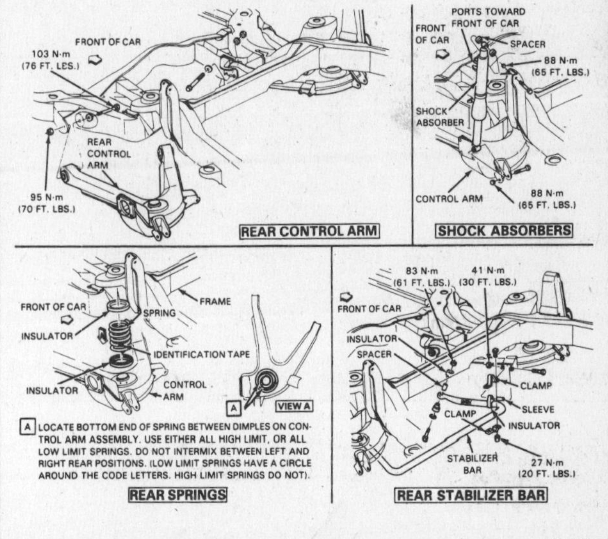

Fig. 42 Independent rear suspension—1979–85 Eldorado and 1980–85 Seville

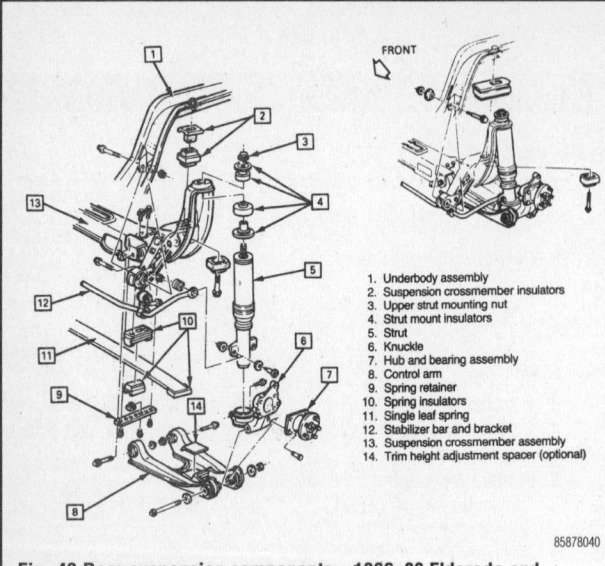

FRONT

1. Underbody assembly
2. Suspension crossmember insulators
3. Upper strut mounting nut
4. Strut mount insulators
5. Strut
6. Knuckle
7. Hub and bearing assembly
8. Control arm
9. Spring retainer
10. Spring insulators
11. Single leaf spring
12. Stabilizer bar and bracket
13. Suspension crossmember assembly
14. Trim height adjustment spacer (optional)

85878040

Fig. 43 Rear suspension components—1986–89 Eldorado and Seville

suspension knuckle using an air-adjustable strut and lower control arm configuration. The transverse mounted spring is a single leaf design constructed of a lightweight composite material. The hub and bearing is a single, non-serviceable unit which requires no periodic maintenance.

Coil Springs

REMOVAL & INSTALLATION

DeVille and Fleetwood

1. Raise and support the car.
2. Place a jack under the differential housing.
3. Remove the wheels.
4. If the car has level control, disconnect the link at the overtravel lever and position it in its center location.
5. Remove the shock absorber lower retaining nuts and washers.

❊ CAUTION

The shock absorbers act as stops for the suspension. Make certain that both the axle and the frame are supported before continuing.

6. Disconnect the brake line retaining clip from the axle and frame, but do not disconnect the brake line. This should allow enough slack as the axle is lowered to eliminate the need for disconnecting and reconnecting the brake line. If enough slack cannot be obtained, disconnect the brake line from the hose and plug both openings. Be sure to bleed the brakes after installation.
7. Disconnect rear U-joint and wire the driveshaft out of the way. Do not allow the driveshaft to hang unsupported.
8. Remove nuts and bolts that secure both upper control arms to the axle brackets.
9. Lower rear axle assembly slowly until the springs are free and remove the springs.

❊ CAUTION

Do not allow the differential to twist as it is lowered, since the spring may fly out!

To install:

10. Tape the upper rubber insulator to the top of the spring and position the upper end of the LH rear spring coil toward the left frame side rail and position the upper end of the RH rear spring coil toward the right frame side rail.

11. Seat the bottom of the spring on the rear axle.
12. Raise the rear axle, being careful to engage the axle in the upper control arms and install the pivot bolts. Tighten the nut securing the control arm to the rear axle to 70 ft. lbs. (95 Nm) On Limousine or Commercial Chassis tighten to 83 ft. lbs. (112 Nm).
13. Install the cable in the clip at the center of the rear crossmember. and connect the cable to the C-connector.
14. Slide the cable through the hole and connect the left hand parking brake cable to equalizer and install the clips.
15. Place a jackstand under the nose carrier.
16. Remove the wire from the driveshaft and connect the shaft to the pinion shaft.
17. Install the lower control arm to axle bolts and torque to 122 ft. lbs. (165 Nm) On Limousine or Commercial Chassis tighten to 100 ft. lbs. (136 Nm).
18. If equipped with ELC, connect the link to the height sensor arm.
19. Install one bolt securing the junction block to the top of the rear axle and secure the brake lines in the clips.
20. If equipped with ELC, position the stabilizer bar on the car and install the two bolts and washer on each side of the car securing the stabilizer bar to the lower control arms.
21. Install the shock absorbers.
22. Remove the jackstands and lower the car.

1971–78 Eldorado

1. Raise the car under the tube assembly and support it with stands at the frame lift points. Do not remove the jack.
2. Disconnect the brake line clips.
3. Disconnect the shock absorber at the lower mount.
4. Install a spring compressor and finger-tighten the nuts.
5. Disconnect the control arm at the tube assembly.
6. Lower the jack (supporting the control arm, not the frame) and remove the spring.

❊ WARNING

Do not stretch the brake hose.

To install:

7. Place the insulator on top of the spring and install the spring. The top end of the spring should point to the right side of the car.
8. Hoist the tube assembly and connect the shock absorber.

➡ **For 1979–85 Eldorado and 1980–85 Seville procedures please refer to Rear Control Arm and Coil Spring removal and installation in this section.**

Leaf Springs

REMOVAL & INSTALLATION

Commercial Chassis

1. Jack up car and support it on jackstands at frame side rails.
2. Support axle housing with jackstands.
3. Disconnect shock absorber from U-bolt plate.
4. Remove front spring eye bolt.
5. Remove U-bolt plate nuts, plate and insulators.
6. Disconnect rear shackle links and lower spring.
7. To install, reverse removal procedure. Tighten shackle nuts to 70 ft. lbs. (95 Nm), U-bolt nuts to 45 ft. lbs. (61 Nm), and lower shock nuts to 50 ft. lbs. (68 Nm). The car must be lowered to the ground before tightening the U-bolt nuts.

1977–79 Seville

1. Raise the rear of the car and support it so the axle can be raised or lowered. Raise the axle so that all tension is relieved from the spring.
2. Disconnect the rear automatic leveling valve over-travel lever from its link and hold the lever in the exhaust position (down) to deflate the shock absorbers.

3. Disconnect the lower half of the shock absorbers and move them out of the way.

4. Loosen the parking brake adjustment at the equalizer and remove the parking brake cable clip from the front retaining bracket on the spring. Remove the cable clamps from the under side of the springs.

5. Loosen the spring front eye bushing-to-retaining bracket bolt.

6. Remove the bolts retaining the front spring bracket to the underbody.

7. Lower the axle enough to permit access to the front eye bolt and remove the bracket from the spring.

➡ **The front eye bushing can be replaced at this time.**

8. Remove the U-bolt and T-bolt nuts retaining the lower spring plate to the axle and stabilizer bar brackets.

9. Remove the upper and lower spring pads and spring plate.

10. Support the spring with a jackstand and remove the two nuts from the rear shackle.

11. Separate the shackle and remove the spring from the vehicle.

To install:

12. If the spring is being replaced, remove the spring damper for installation on the new spring by removing the clamp bolt and bending the bottom half of the clamp down about 2 in. (50mm). Slide the clamp rearward over the damper and remove the damper from the spring.

13. Position the spring damper on the new spring and position it ⅛ in. (3mm) from the front spring eye. Slide the clamp forward over the damper and position the clamp at the second leaf of the spring.

➡ **The clamp must face upward and the nut must be on the outside of the spring. Install the clamp bolt pointing up and tighten to 20 ft. lbs. (27 Nm). Do not tighten any of the attaching hardware to specifications until Step 25 (when all components are in position). Allow the retaining nuts and bolts to remain only finger-tight.**

14. Position the front eye of the spring to the front mounting bracket and install the attaching bolt and washer with the bolt head on the inside. Bolt torque will be 105 ft. lbs. (142 Nm).

15. Install the upper shackle bushings in the frame. Position the shackles to the bushings, then install the bolt and nut. Torque will be 50 ft. lbs. (68 Nm).

16. Install the bushing halves in the rear spring eye and install the spring to the shackle. Lower shackle bolt and nut torque will be 50 ft. lbs. (68 Nm).

17. Raise the front end of the spring and position the bracket to the underbody. Make sure the tab on the bracket is aligned in the slot in the underbody.

18. Install the screws retaining the front spring bracket to the underbody. Torque will be 30 ft. lbs. (41 Nm).

19. Position the spring upper cushion between the spring and the axle bracket so the cushion ribs align with the bracket locating ribs.

20. Position the lower mounting plate over the locating dowel on the lower spring pad and install the retaining nuts. Torque will be 45 ft. lbs. (61 Nm).

21. Position the stabilizer brackets to the lower spring plate. Retaining bolts and nut torque will be 30 ft. lbs. (41 Nm).

22. Connect the rear shock absorber mount to the lower spring bracket. Torque will be 45 ft. lbs. (61 Nm).

23. Install the parking brake cable under the leaf spring, then secure it at the front of the spring with the wire clip and clamp. Adjust the parking brake cable.

24. Connect the rear leveling over-travel lever to its link.

25. Tighten all of the attaching hardware to the specified torques.

26. Lower the vehicle.

1967–70 Eldorado

1. Raise the car. Support the rear axle at center with hydraulic jack. Remove the rear wheel from side being worked on.

2. Remove the nut that secures the automatic level control link to the axle bracket, then remove link.

3. Remove the nut that secures the front of spring to frame bracket.

➡ **Do not remove bolt now.**

4. Remove the two nuts at rear shackle outer link and remove the link.

5. Remove the four nuts and lockwashers that secure the center spring clamp to the rear axle and position it out of the way.

6. Lower the hydraulic jack until axle is free from the spring. Remove the rear shackle assembly from the spring and body.

7. Remove the bolt from the front of the spring and remove the spring.

8. Installation is the reverse of the removal procedure. Tighten all of the attaching hardware to the specified torques.

Single Transverse Leaf Spring

REMOVAL & INSTALLATION

➡ **See Figures 44 and 45**

1986–89 Eldorado and Seville

1. Raise the car and support it securely by the frame. Remove the tire and wheel from the side on which you wish to draw out the spring.

2. If you are working on the left side, and the car has Electronic Level Control (ELC), disconnect the ELC height sensor link.

3. If the car has a stabilizer bar, disconnect the mounting bolt at the strut.

4. Reinstall two wheel nuts opposite each other to hold the rotor onto the hub/bearing assembly.

5. Remove and suspend the brake caliper.

6. Loosen but DO NOT REMOVE the knuckle pivot bolt on the outboard end of the control arm.

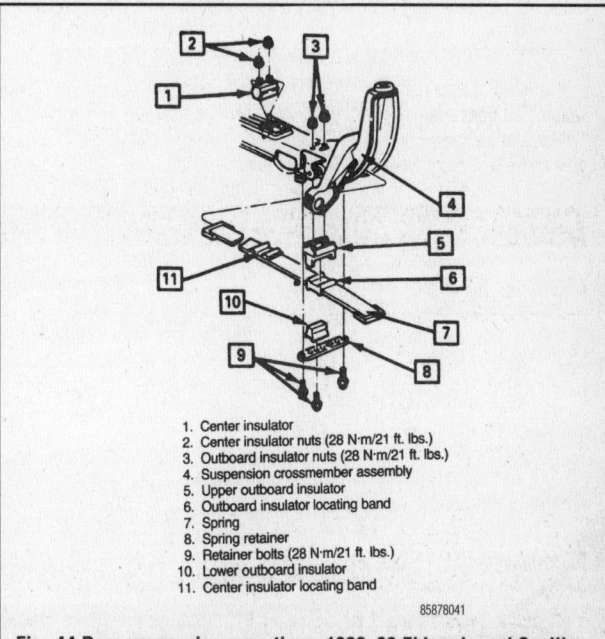

1. Center insulator
2. Center insulator nuts (28 N·m/21 ft. lbs.)
3. Outboard insulator nuts (28 N·m/21 ft. lbs.)
4. Suspension crossmember assembly
5. Upper outboard insulator
6. Outboard insulator locating band
7. Spring
8. Spring retainer
9. Retainer bolts (28 N·m/21 ft. lbs.)
10. Lower outboard insulator
11. Center insulator locating band

85878041

Fig. 44 Rear suspension mounting—1986–89 Eldorado and Seville

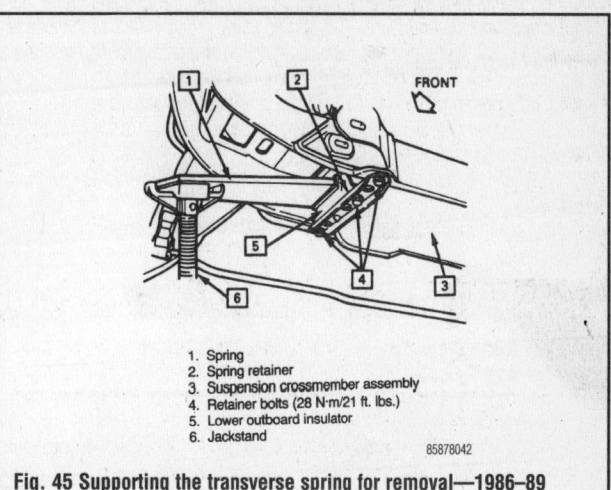

1. Spring
2. Spring retainer
3. Suspension crossmember assembly
4. Retainer bolts (28 N·m/21 ft. lbs.)
5. Lower outboard insulator
6. Jackstand

85878042

Fig. 45 Supporting the transverse spring for removal—1986–89 Eldorado and Seville

7. Remove the strut rod cap, mounting nut, retainer, and upper insulator. Then, compress the strut by hand and remove the lower insulator.

8. Remove the inner control arm nuts. Support the knuckle and control arm with a floorjack, then remove the inner control arm bolts. Remove the control arm, knuckle, strut, hub/bearing, and rotor as an assembly.

9. Using a jackstand capable of suspending the entire weight of the car, suspend the outer end of the spring securely.

※ CAUTION

Make sure the jackstand is square under the spring so that the stand will not shift, or personal injury could result.

10. Gradually and cautiously lower the car until its weight compresses the spring so there is no weight on the spring retainer. Then, remove the retainer mounting bolts, the retainer, and the lower insulator from that side of the car. Raise the car slowly until the jackstand is free of downward pressure from the spring and remove it.

11. Draw the spring out of the rear suspension. Remove the upper spring insulators as necessary.

To install:

12. Install any insulators that required replacement. Upper outboard insulators must be installed so that the molded arrow points toward the vehicle centerline. Torque the center and outboard insulator nuts to 21 ft. lbs. (28 Nm).

13. Position the spring into the crossmember. Make sure the outboard and center insulator locating bands are centered on the insulators.

14. Follow Step 9 and the caution above to support the outer end of the spring with a jackstand. Then, carefully and gradually lower the car until its weight will permit easy installation of the spring retainer.

15. Install the lower insulator and spring retainer and torque the bolts to 21 ft. lbs. (28 Nm). Raise the vehicle carefully and when the spring is clear, remove the jackstand.

16. Position the assembled control arm, knuckle, strut, hub and bearing and rotor assembly into the crossmember assembly and install the inner control arm bolts and nuts JUST HAND TIGHT!

17. Install the lower strut insulator and position the strut rod into the suspension support assembly.

18. Install the upper strut insulator, retainer, and nut. Torque the upper strut nut to 65 ft. lbs. (88 Nm), the knuckle pivot bolt to 59 ft. lbs. (80 Nm) and the inner control arm bolts to 66 ft. lbs. (89 Nm).

19. Install the strut rod cap. Install the stabilizer mounting bolt if the car has a stabilizer bar. Torque this bolt to 43 ft. lbs. (58 Nm).

20. Remove the two wheel nuts retaining the brake rotor. Install the remaining parts in reverse of the removal procedure. Have the rear end alignment checked and adjusted, if necessary.

Rear Control Arm and Coil Spring

REMOVAL & INSTALLATION

1979–85 Eldorado and 1980–85 Seville

♦ See Figure 46

1. Raise the car and remove the wheel.
2. Remove the bolt from each side which secures the front of the stabilizer bar to the control arm.
3. Remove the inner bolt and loosen the outer bolt from each side of the stabilized link.
4. Position the bottom parts of the link to one side and remove the stabilizer bar.
5. Disconnect the brake line bracket from the control arm.
6. Remove about ⅔ of the fluid from the front master cylinder.
7. Loosen the parking brake tension at the cable equalizer.
8. Remove the cable from the parking brake and remove the cable bracket from the caliper or brake drum backing plate.
9. Remove the return spring, lock nut, lever and the anti-friction washer on disc brakes. The lever must be held while removing the nut.
10. Install and tighten a 7 in. (178mm) C-clamp on the caliper to bottom the cylinder pistons.

11. Disconnect the brake line from the brake and plug the openings to prevent the entrance of dirt.

12. With a ⅜ in. Allen wrench, remove the two caliper mounting bolts and remove the caliper, pads and rotor. On drum brakes, remove the hub and bearing assembly and remove the brake backing plate, along with the brake shoes.

13. If working on the left side, snap the Electronic Level Control (ELC) link off the control arm.

14. Support the bottom of the control arm with a floor jack.

15. Remove the ELC line at the shock.

16. Remove the shock absorber.

17. Lower the control arm to relieve tension on the spring. Remove the spring and the insulators.

18. Remove the two control arm mounting bolts and remove the control arm.

To install:

19. Position the control arm to the frame brackets and install the two mounting bolts and nuts. Tighten to 75 ft. lbs. (9 Nm).

20. Install the spring with the upper and lower insulator.

21. Using a floor jack, compress the spring until the shock absorber can be installed, secure to the brackets on the control arm and frame with the two mounting bolts and nuts. Tighten to 60 ft. lbs. (81 Nm) and remove the floor jack.

22. Connect the ELC air line to the shock connector.

23. If working on the left hand side of the control arm, snap on the ELC link to its ball pivot at the control arm and snap the locking tab in place.

24. Install the rotor on the hub aligning the marks made during disassembly.

25. Install the brake caliper.

26. Install the wheel and tighten the lug nuts to 100 ft. lbs. (136 Nm).

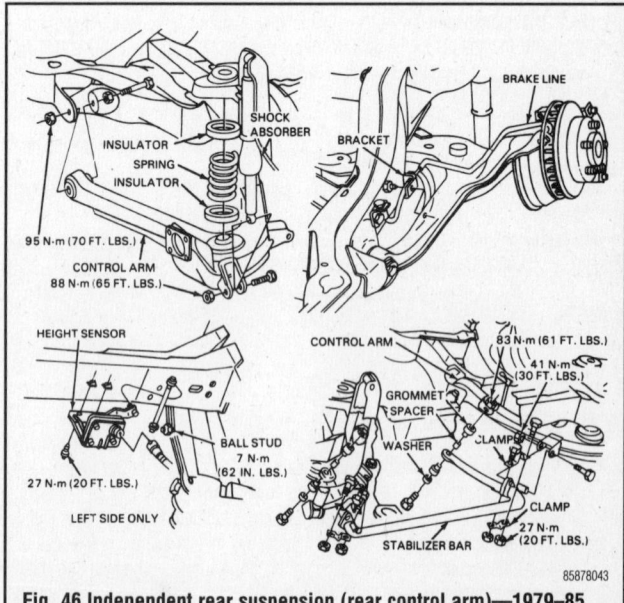

Fig. 46 Independent rear suspension (rear control arm)—1979–85 Eldorado and 1980–85 Seville

Shock Absorbers

TESTING

Refer to the shock absorber testing procedure in the front suspension portion of this section.

REMOVAL & INSTALLATION

♦ See Figures 47, 48 and 49

➡Examine the shock absorbers following the testing procedure given for front shocks.

Purge a new shock of air by repeatedly extending it in its normal position and compressing it while inverted.

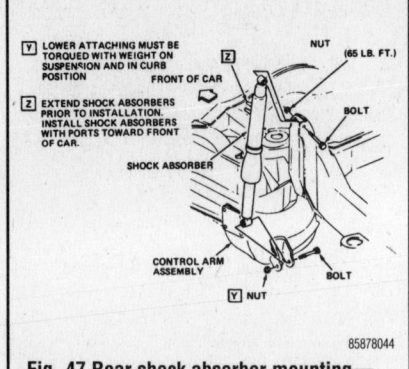

Fig. 47 Rear shock absorber mounting—1979–85 Eldorado and 1980–85 Seville

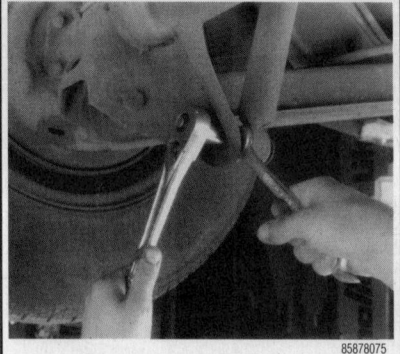

Fig. 48 Removing the lower mounting nut on the rear shock absorber

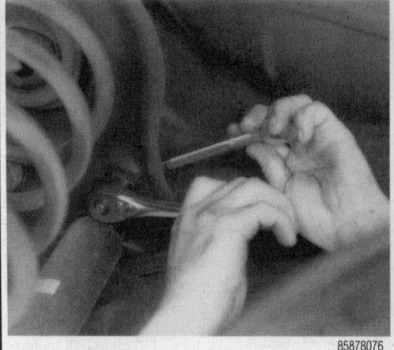

Fig. 49 Removing the upper mounting on the rear shock absorber

1. Raise the rear of the vehicle, then support both the frame and the axle with separate jackstands.

2. If the vehicle is equipped with Electronic Level Control, remove the air lines at the shocks.

✳✳ WARNING

The shocks act as rebound stops for the rear suspension and under no circumstances should the rear end be raised excessively high while disconnecting the shocks, unless both the rear axle and the frame are supported.

3. Remove the upper retaining bolts and nuts. To do this, bend a ½ in. box end wrench, to form a 45 degree angle at a point one inch from the center of the box diameter. This is used to hold the upper mounting nut.

4. Remove the lower retaining nut while holding the stem by the grommet to keep the stem from turning. Pull the shock off.

5. Installation is the reverse of removal.

Damper Strut

REMOVAL & INSTALLATION

♦ See Figure 50

1986–89 Eldorado and Seville

1. Raise and support the vehicle on safety stands. Remove the wheel and tire assembly.

2. Disconnect the Electronic Level Control (ELC) height sensor link if the left strut is to be removed.

3. Reinstall two wheel nuts in order to hold the rotor on the hub and bearing assembly.

4. Remove the stabilizer bar mounting bolt at the strut, if so equipped.

5. Remove the brake caliper without disconnecting the hydraulic lines and wire it out of the way.

6. Loosen the knuckle pivot bolt on the outer end of the control arm. Do not remove it!

7. Remove the upper strut rod cap, mounting nut, retainer and insulator.

8. Compress the strut by hand and remove the lower insulator.

9. Rotate the strut and knuckle assembly outward by pivoting on the knuckle pivot bolt.

10. Remove the knuckle pinch bolt. Remove the strut from the knuckle. Inspect the upper and lower strut insulators for cuts, cracks, tears or other damage. Replace if necessary.

To install:

11. Position the strut in the knuckle so that it is fully seated with the tang on the strut bottomed in the knuckle slot.

12. Install the knuckle pinch bolt and tighten to 40 ft. lbs. (55 Nm).

13. Install the lower insulator on the strut, then position the strut rod in the suspension crossmember assembly.

14. Install the upper insulator and retainer. Tighten the nut upper strut nut to 65 ft. lbs. (88 Nm). Tighten the knuckle pivot bolt to 59 ft. lbs. (80 Nm).

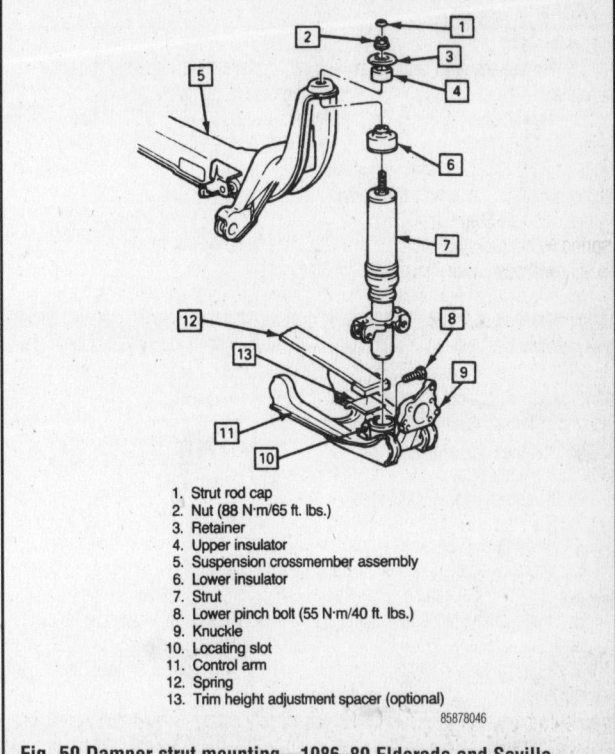

1. Strut rod cap
2. Nut (88 N·m/65 ft. lbs.)
3. Retainer
4. Upper insulator
5. Suspension crossmember assembly
6. Lower insulator
7. Strut
8. Lower pinch bolt (55 N·m/40 ft. lbs.)
9. Knuckle
10. Locating slot
11. Control arm
12. Spring
13. Trim height adjustment spacer (optional)

Fig. 50 Damper strut mounting—1986–89 Eldorado and Seville

15. Install the strut rod cap and the stabilizer bar mounting bolt. Tighten the bolt to 43 ft. lbs. (58 Nm).

16. Installation of the remaining components is in the reverse order of removal.

Hub and Bearing Assembly

REMOVAL & INSTALLATION

♦ See Figure 51

1986–89 Eldorado and Seville

1. Raise the vehicle and support it on safety stands. Remove the wheel and tire assembly.

2. Remove the brake caliper without disconnecting the hydraulic lines and wire it out of the way.

3. Remove the rotor retainers if the car is equipped with them. These may be discarded after removal.

4. Remove the rotor.

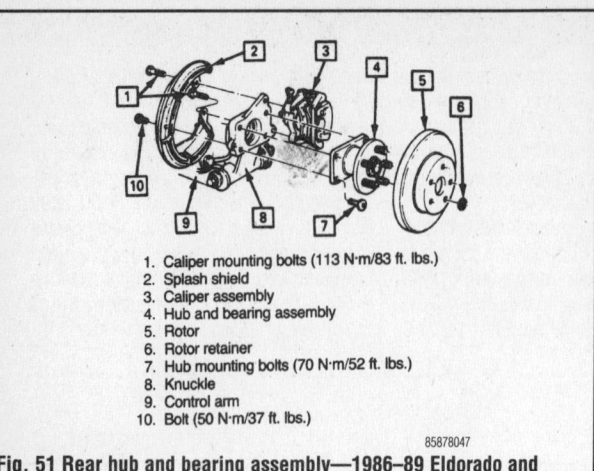

1. Caliper mounting bolts (113 N·m/83 ft. lbs.)
2. Splash shield
3. Caliper assembly
4. Hub and bearing assembly
5. Rotor
6. Rotor retainer
7. Hub mounting bolts (70 N·m/52 ft. lbs.)
8. Knuckle
9. Control arm
10. Bolt (50 N·m/37 ft. lbs.)

85878047

Fig. 51 Rear hub and bearing assembly—1986–89 Eldorado and Seville

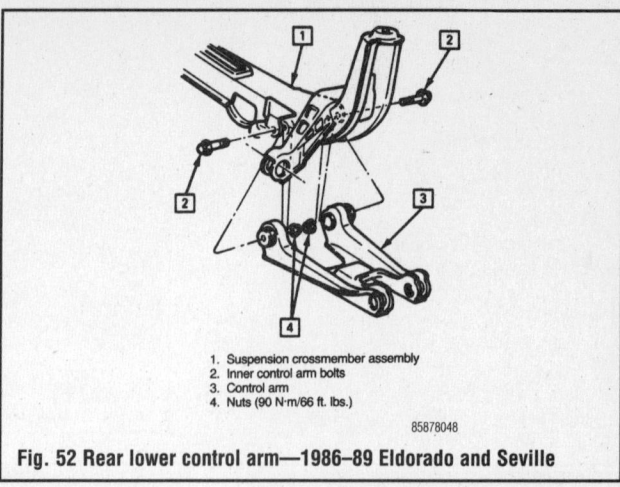

1. Suspension crossmember assembly
2. Inner control arm bolts
3. Control arm
4. Nuts (90 N·m/66 ft. lbs.)

85878048

Fig. 52 Rear lower control arm—1986–89 Eldorado and Seville

5. Remove the four hub mounting bolts and pull off the hub and bearing assembly.

To install:

6. Position the hub and bearing assembly on the knuckle and tighten the bolts to 52 ft. lbs. (70 Nm).

7. Install the rotor and the caliper.

➡ **Be sure to use new mounting bolts when installing the brake caliper.**

8. Install the wheel and lower the vehicle.

Lower Control Arm and Knuckle

REMOVAL & INSTALLATION

♦ **See Figures 52 and 53**

1986–89 Eldorado and Seville

1. Raise the vehicle and support it on safety stands. Remove the wheel.
2. If removing the left side control arm, disconnect the Electronic Level Control (ELC) height sensor link.
3. If equipped with a rear stabilizer bar, remove the bar mounting bolt at the strut.
4. Reinstall two wheel bolts to hold the rotor in place on the hub and bearing assembly.
5. Remove the brake caliper without disconnecting the hydraulic lines and suspend it out of the way.
6. Loosen the knuckle pivot bolt on the outer end of the control arm. DO NOT REMOVE THE PIVOT BOLT AT THIS TIME!
7. Remove the strut rod cap, mounting nut, retainer and the upper insulator.
8. Carefully compress the strut with your hand, then remove the lower insulator.
9. Remove the knuckle pivot bolt while supporting the knuckle. Remove the knuckle, strut, hub and bearing and rotor as an assembly.
10. Remove the two inner mounting bolts, then lift out the lower control arm.

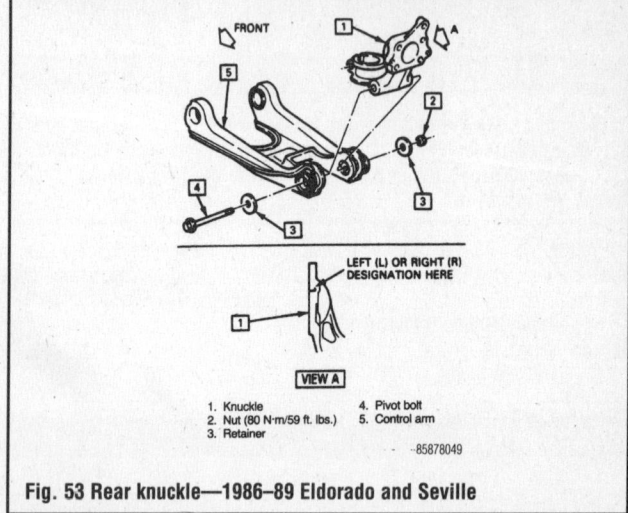

1. Knuckle
2. Nut (80 N·m/59 ft. lbs.)
3. Retainer
4. Pivot bolt
5. Control arm

85878049

Fig. 53 Rear knuckle—1986–89 Eldorado and Seville

To install:

11. Position the control arm and install both inner mounting bolts. DO NOT TIGHTEN THE BOLTS!
12. Position the knuckle, strut, hub and bearing, and the rotor assembly on the control arm, then install the pivot bolt. DO NOT TIGHTEN THE PIVOT BOLT!
13. Install the lower strut insulator and position the strut rod in the crossmember assembly.
14. Install the upper strut insulator, retainer and nut.
15. Now you may tighten all the bolts. Tighten the upper strut nut to 65 ft. lbs. (88 Nm); the knuckle pivot bolt to 59 ft. lbs. (80 Nm); and the two inner control arm bolts to 66 ft. lbs. (90 Nm).
16. Install the strut rod cap and the stabilizer bar mounting bolt. Tighten it to 43 ft. lbs. (58 Nm).
17. Remove the two wheel nuts and install the brake caliper using new mounting bolts. Connect the ELC height sensor link, install the wheel and lower the car.

STEERING

Steering Wheel

REMOVAL & INSTALLATION

♦ **See Figures 54 thru 62**

➡ **For 1974–76 models equipped with an Air Cushion Restraint System (ACRS) perform the special procedure following, prior to removing steering wheel.**

Special Procedure For Cars With A.C.R.S.

Some 1974–76 models have an Air Cushion Restraint System (ACRS). One of the elements of this complex system is an air cushion module. The steering wheel can be removed in the manner described in this section after the module has been removed.

To remove the module:

1. Turn the ignition lock to the LOCK position.
2. Disconnect the battery ground cable and tape the end to prevent any possibility of a complete circuit.

3. Remove the 4 module-to-steering wheel screws. A special tool is available to do this.

4. Lift up the module and disconnect the horn wire.

5. Disconnect the module wire connector. A special tool is available to do this, too.

To install the module:

6. Hold the module with the emblem in the lower right corner.

7. Loop the air cushion harness clockwise from the 11 o'clock position to the 6 o'clock position.

8. Install the module connector by pushing it onto the column circuit firmly. Check that it is fully seated.

9. Install the horn wire.

10. Position the module, making sure that the wiring is still in place, and install the 4 screws. Torque them to 40 inch lbs. (4.5 Nm).

11. Reconnect the battery ground cable.

12. Turn the ignition lock to any position other than LOCK and check that the restraint indicator light operates correctly.

✴✴ CAUTION

The driver air cushion module should always be carried with the vinyl cover away from all parts of one's body and should always be laid on a flat surface with the vinyl side up. This is necessary so that a free space is provided to allow the air cushion to expand in case of accidental deployment. Do not attempt to repair any portion of the module. The module must be serviced as a unit. Attempting repairs such as soldering wires, changing covers, etc. may cause accidental inflation or impair operation of the driver module and cause serious injury. Do not dispose of a module in any way. The highly flammable material in the module can cause serious burns if ignited. Modules must be exchanged at an authorized dealer's parts department.

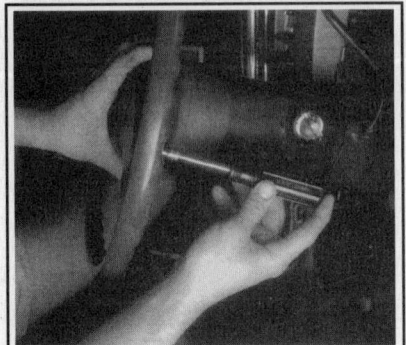

Fig. 54 Removing the horn pad retaining screws

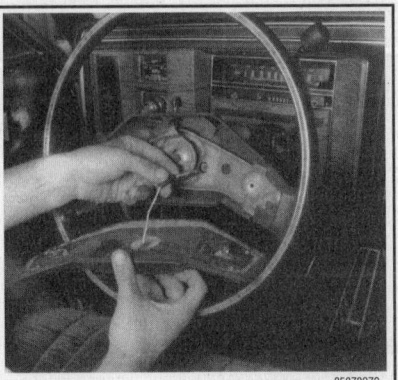

Fig. 55 Removing the horn wire

Fig. 56 Removing the tilt plate assembly

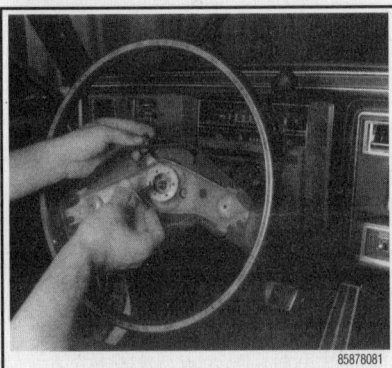

Fig. 57 Removing the tilt plate assembly bolt

Fig. 58 Removing the steering wheel nut

Fig. 59 View of the steering wheel retaining nut

Fig. 60 Removing the steering wheel with a puller

Fig. 61 Mark the steering wheel before removing the wheel

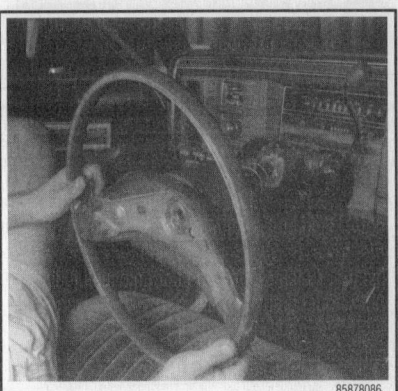

Fig. 62 Removing the steering wheel

All Non-Tilt Wheels

1. Disconnect the negative battery cable.
2. Remove the center pad assembly, either by removing the screws or by gently prying the pad off. Lift up on the pad and disconnect the horn wire by pushing in on the insulator and turning counterclockwise.
3. Remove the steering wheel nut retainer and attaching nut. Using a puller, remove the steering wheel.

To install:

4. Align the marks on the wheel hub to the marks on the steering shaft.
5. Install the steering wheel, retainer and nut, then torque the nut to 30 ft. lbs. (41 Nm).

➡**When the mark on the steering wheel hub and the steering shaft are lined up, the wheel spokes should be horizontal as the car is driven straight ahead. If they are not horizontal it may be necessary to adjust the tie rod ends until the steering wheel is properly aligned.**

6. Install the horn wire in the cam tower, push in and turn clockwise. Align the pad assembly into position and either press into place or install the screws. Connect the negative battery cable.

Tilt and Telescope Wheels

EXCEPT 1986–89 ELDORADO AND SEVILLE

1. Remove the negative battery cable.
2. Remove the pad assembly by either removing the screws or prying the pad off. Disconnect the bayonet-type connector at the horn wire by pushing in and turning counterclockwise.
3. Push the locking lever counterclockwise until the full release position is obtained.
4. Scribe a mark on the plate assembly where the two attaching screws attach the plate assembly to the locking lever. Remove the two screws.
5. Unscrew the plate assembly and remove.
6. Remove the steering wheel nut retainer and nut. Using a puller, remove the wheel.

To install:

7. Install a 5/16 in. x 18 set screw into the upper shaft at the full extended position and lock.
8. Install the steering wheel, aligning the scribe mark on the hub with the slash mark on the end of the shaft. Make sure that the unattached end of the horn upper contact assembly is seated flush against the top of the horn contact assembly.
9. Install the nut on the upper steering shaft, along with the nut retainer. Torque to 30 ft. lbs. (41 Nm).
10. Remove the set screw installed in Step 7.
11. Install the plate assembly and finger-tighten the retainer(s).
12. Position the locking lever in the vertical position and move the lever counterclockwise until the holes in the plate align with the holes in the lever. Install the attaching screws.
13. Align the pad assembly with the holes in the steering wheel and install the retaining screws. Connect the negative battery cable. Check to see that the locking lever securely locks the wheel travel and that the wheel travel is free in the unlocked position.

1986–89 ELDORADO AND SEVILLE

◆ **See Figure 63**

1. Remove the two screws retaining the steering wheel horn pad.
2. Remove the horn pad, then disconnect the horn and cruise control wiring electrical leads.
3. Remove the three screws from the telescope adjusting lever.
4. Remove the steering shaft telescope adjuster assembly by unscrewing it from the steering shaft.
5. Remove the telescope lever.
6. Scribe a mark on the steering shaft and the steering wheel boss.
7. Install a wheel puller and remove the steering wheel.

To install:

8. Align the scribe mark on the steering wheel boss so that it is within one serration of the mark on the steering shaft. Slide the steering wheel all the way on and tighten the nut to 35 ft. lbs. (47 Nm).
9. Pull the steering shaft all the way out so that it is fully extended.

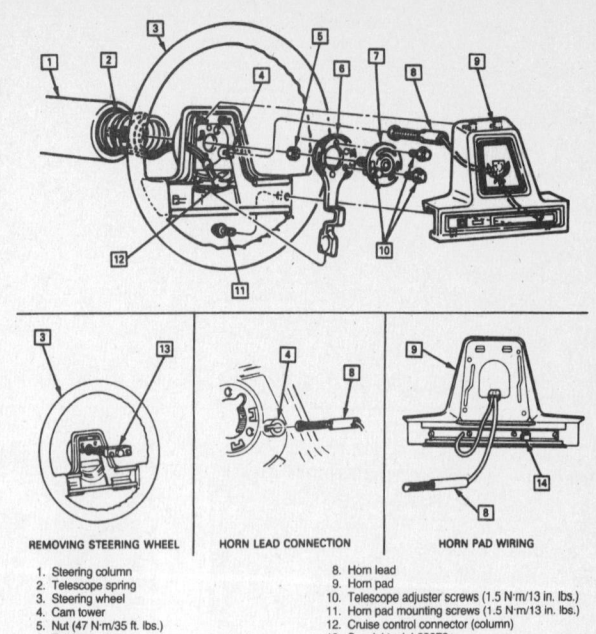

Fig. 63 Steering pad and horn pad removal—1986–89 Eldorado and Seville

1. Steering column
2. Telescope spring
3. Steering wheel
4. Cam tower
5. Nut (47 N·m/35 ft. lbs.)
6. Telescope lever
7. Telescope adjuster
8. Horn lead
9. Horn pad
10. Telescope adjuster screws (1.5 N·m/13 in. lbs.)
11. Horn pad mounting screws (1.5 N·m/13 in. lbs.)
12. Cruise control connector (column)
13. Special tool J-23072
14. Cruise control connector (horn pad)

85878052

10. Install the telescope lever so that it is in the 5 o'clock position.
11. Thread the telescope adjuster assembly onto the steering shaft until it is finger-tight.
12. Install the three mounting screws for the telescoping adjusting lever. Move the lever all the way to the right. The steering wheel should move in and out freely. Move the lever all the way to the left. The steering wheel should be locked in position with the lever approximately 1/4 in. (5mm) from the left side of the shroud opening. The lever must not come in contact with the shroud when it is in the fully locked position.
13. If the steering wheel does not operate as above, loosen the lever mounting screws, rotate the lever to the proper position and tighten the screws.
14. Connect the horn lead and the cruise control wiring.
15. Install the steering wheel horn pad.

Turn Signal Switch

REMOVAL & INSTALLATION

◆ **See Figure 64**

➡**On 1974–76 models equipped with an Air Cushion Restraint System (ACRS) be sure to follow the special procedures listed under steering wheel removal.**

Standard Column

1. Disconnect the negative battery cable.
2. Remove the steering wheel.
3. Insert a thin screwdriver into the lockplate and remove the lockplate cover assembly.
4. Install a spring compressor onto the steering shaft. Tighten the tool to compress the lockplate and the spring. Remove the snapring from the groove in the shaft.

✳✳ CAUTION

When the snapring is removed do not allow the shaft to slide out the bottom of the column!

5. Remove the lockplate, then slide the turn signal cam along with the upper bearing preload spring and the thrust washer off the upper steering shaft.

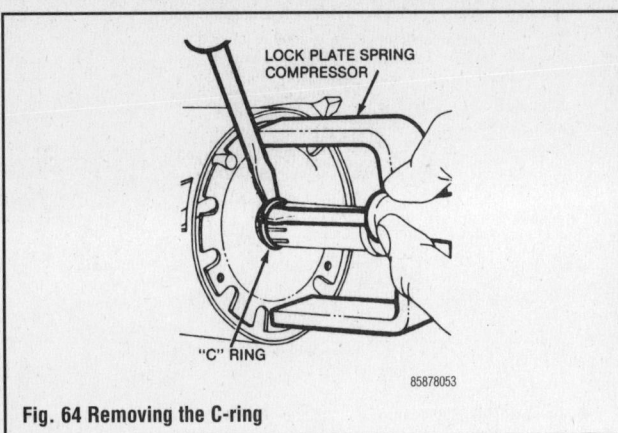

LOCK PLATE SPRING
COMPRESSOR

"C" RING

85878053

Fig. 64 Removing the C-ring

6. Remove the steering column lower cover.

7. Unscrew the turn signal lever and remove it from the column.

8. On cars with cruise control:

a. Disconnect the cruise control wire from the harness near the bottom of the column.

b. Remove the harness protector from the cruise control wire.

c. Remove the turn signal lever. Do not remove the wire from the column.

9. Remove the two vertical bolts at the steering column upper support. Remove the shim packs. Keep the shims in order for reinstallation.

10. Remove the four screws securing the column upper mounting bracket to the column and remove the bracket.

11. Disconnect the turn signal wiring and remove the wires from the plastic protector.

12. Remove the turn signal switch mounting screws.

13. Slide the switch connector out of the bracket on the steering column.

14. If the switch is known to be bad, cut the wires and discard the switch. Tape the connector of the new switch to the old wires, and pull the new harness down through the steering column while removing the old wires.

15. If the original switch is to be reused, wrap the tape around the wire and connector, then pull the harness up through the column. It may be helpful to attach a length of wire or string to the harness connector before pulling it up through the column to facilitate installation.

16. After freeing the switch wiring protector from its mounting, pull the turn signal switch straight up and remove the switch, switch harness, and the connector from the column.

To install:

17. Install the turn signal switch, feeding the harness, connector and harness protector down through the housing.

18. Position the turn signal switch in the neutral position and install the three screws securing the switch to the upper housing.

19. On cars equipped with cruise control perform the following:

a. Connect the cruise control harness to piano wire or equivalent, and feed the harness into the turn signal lever opening. Gently pull the wire and feed the harness through the steering column into position.

b. Remove the tape from the turn signal wire harness.

c. Remove the piano wire from the harness connector.

d. Position the turn signal lever on the turn signal switch and install the one screw.

20. Position the turn signal switch wiring protector over the upper bracket mounting boss on the upper steering column.

21. Position the steering column upper mounting bracket over the turn signal wiring harness protector and secure the bracket to the column with the four screws.

22. Install the turn signal switch connector in the bracket on the steering column upper jacket.

23. Install the hazard warning switch knob.

24. Install the thrust washer on the steering shaft.

25. Install the upper bearing preload spring and turn signal canceling cam.

26. Install the lock plate with the large flat on the plate aligned with the large flat on the steering shaft.

27. Place a new snapring on the upper end of the steering shaft.

28. Install a spring compressor J–23131, on the steering shaft.

29. Compress the lock plate and spring. Next slide the new snapring down until the ring locks in the groove in the upper end of the shaft. Remove the spring compressor tool.

30. Position the plastic lock ring cover on the upper end of the shaft and snap the three fingers over the lock plate assembly. Turn the shaft to make certain the cover does not contact the upper housing assembly. Install the shift lever.

31. Install the steering wheel.

32. Install the steering column.

Tilt and Telescopic Columns

1. Disconnect the battery and remove the steering wheel.

2. Remove the rubber sleeve bumper from the steering shaft.

3. Remove the plastic retainer with a screwdriver, disengaging the tabs on the retainer from the C-ring.

4. Compress the upper steering shaft pre-load spring with a spring compressor and remove the C-ring. When installing the spring compressor, pull the upper shaft up about 1 in. (25mm) and turn the ignition to the LOCK position to hold the shaft in place.

5. Remove the spring compressor, then remove the upper steering shaft lock plate, horn contact carrier and the preload spring.

6. Remove the steering column lower cover.

7. Unscrew and remove the turn signal lever. If equipped with cruise control:

a. Disconnect the cruise control wire from the harness near the bottom of the steering column.

b. Slide the protector off the cruise control wire. On 1977 and later models, remove the lever attaching screw and carefully pull the lever out enough to allow the removal of the turn signal switch.

8. Remove the two nuts and shim packs from the upper column support. Keep the shims together as a unit for reinstallation.

9. Remove the bracket from the steering column by removing the two attaching screws from each side.

10. Disconnect the turn signal wiring harness from the car harness and remove the wires from the plastic protector.

11. Remove the turn signal switch retaining screws and pull the switch up out of the steering column.

12. If the switch is to be replaced, cut the wires from the switch and tape the new switch connector to the old wires. Carefully pull the new harness down through the column as the old wires are removed.

13. If the old switch is to be reused, tape the connector to the wires and carefully pull the harness up out of the column.

To install:

14. Feed the wiring harness down through the steering column to replace the old switch.

15. Secure the switch in the steering column.

16. Install the upper shaft preload spring.

17. Install the lock plate and carrier assembly. Make sure that the flat on the lower end of the steering shaft is pointing up and that the small plastic tab on the carrier is up or nearest the top of the column. The flat surface of the lock plate must be installed facing down against the turn signal switch.

18. Install the spring compressor, depress the preload spring and lock plate, then install the C-ring with the wide side toward the keyway.

19. Remove the spring compressor and install the plastic retainer on the C-ring.

20. Install the rubber sleeve bumper over the steering shaft and install the steering wheel.

21. Install the turn signal lever. If the vehicle is equipped with cruise control: On 1977 and later models, secure the lever to the switch with the retaining screw and install the wiring harness.

22. Remove the tape from the end of the harness, then connect the switch and cruise control, if so equipped, to the car harness.

23. Cover both harnesses with the plastic protector and position it to the column. The turn signal connector slides on the tabs of the column.

24. Position the steering column upper bracket over the turn signal switch harness plastic protector.

25. Install the mounting bracket nuts and shims in their original positions.

26. Install the steering column lower cover.

Ignition Switch

REPLACEMENT

1. Disconnect the negative battery terminal.
2. Position the lock cylinder in the LOCK position.
3. Remove the steering column lower cover.
4. Loosen the two nuts on upper steering column, allowing the column to drop.

✳✳ WARNING

Do not remove the nuts, as the column may bend under its own weight.

5. Disconnect the ignition switch connector at the switch.
6. Remove the two screws securing the ignition switch to the steering column. Remove the switch.
To install:
7. Assemble the ignition switch on the actuator rod and adjust it to the LOCK position, as follows:
   a. Standard Column — Hold the switch actuating rod stationary with one hand while moving the switch toward the bottom of the column until the switch reaches the end of its travel (ACC position). Back off one detent, then, with the key also in the LOCK position, tighten the two switch mounting screws to 35 inch lbs. (4 Nm).
   b. Tilt column — Hold the switch actuating rod stationary with one hand while moving the switch toward the upper end of the column until the switch reaches the end of its travel (ACC position). Back off one detent, then, with the key also in the LOCK position, tighten the two switch mounting screws to 35 inch lbs. (4 Nm).
8. Connect the wires, tighten the two steering column nuts, install the lower cover and reconnect the battery.

Ignition Lock Cylinder

REMOVAL & INSTALLATION

▶ **See Figures 65 and 66**

➡ **On 1974–76 models, equipped with an Air Cushion Restraint System (ACRS) perform the special procedure for removing the air cushion module from the steering wheel, if necessary, prior to removing the lock cylinder.**

Standard Steering Column

1. Remove the steering wheel.
2. Remove the lockplate cover assembly.
3. After compressing the lockplate spring, remove the snapring from the groove in the shaft.

✳✳ CAUTION

When the snapring is removed do not allow the shaft to slide out the bottom of the column.

4. Remove the lockplate, then slide the turn signal cam and the upper bearing preload spring off the upper steering shaft.
5. Remove the thrust washer from the shaft.
6. Remove the hazard warning switch from the column along with the turn signal lever.
7. Use the following procedure if the car is equipped with cruise control.
   a. Attach a piece of stiff wire to the connector on the cruise control switch harness.
   b. Gently pull the harness up and out of the column.
8. Remove the turn signal switch mounting screws.
9. Slide the switch connector out of the bracket on the steering column.
10. After freeing the switch wiring protector from its mounting, pull the turn signal switch straight up and remove the switch, switch harness and the connector from the column.

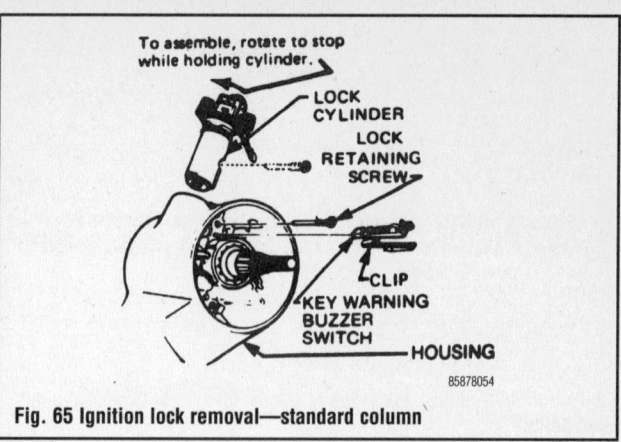

Fig. 65 Ignition lock removal—standard column

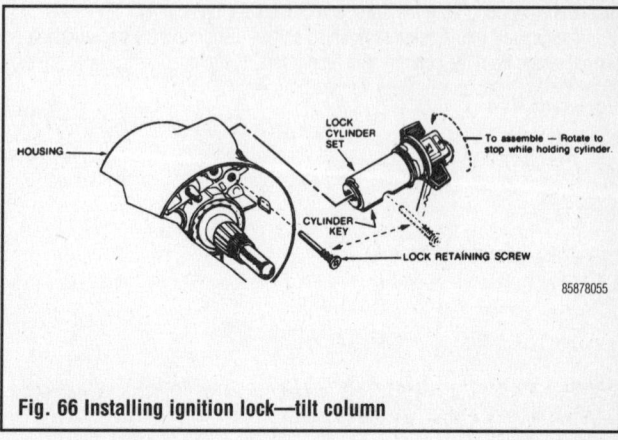

Fig. 66 Installing ignition lock—tilt column

11. Turn the ignition switch to **ON** or **RUN**, then insert a small drift pin into the slot next to the switch mounting screw boss. Push the lock cylinder tab and remove the lock cylinder.
12. Installation is the reverse of the removal procedure.

Tilt Column

1. Remove the steering wheel.
2. Remove the rubber sleeve bumper from the steering shaft.
3. Using an appropriate tool, remove the plastic retainer.
4. Using a spring compressor, depress the upper steering shaft spring and remove the C-ring. Release the steering shaft lockplate, the horn contact carrier, and the upper steering shaft preload spring.
5. Remove the four screws which hold the upper mounting bracket, then remove the bracket.
6. Slide the harness connector out of the bracket on the steering column. Tape the upper part of the harness and connector.
7. Disconnect the hazard button and position the shift bowl in Park. Remove the turn signal lever from the column.
8. Use the following procedure for cars with cruise control.
   a. Remove the harness protector from the harness.
   b. Attach a piece of piano wire to the switch harness connector.
   c. Before removing the turn signal lever, loop a piece of piano wire and insert it into the turn signal lever opening. Using the wire, pull the cruise control harness out through the opening.
   d. Pull the rest of the harness up through and out of the column.
   e. Remove the guide wire from the connector and secure the wire to the column.
   f. Remove the turn signal level.
9. Pull the turn signal switch up until the end connector is within the shift bowl. Remove the hazard flasher lever. Allow the switch to hang.
10. Place the ignition key in the run position.
11. Depress the center of the lock cylinder retaining tab with a small prytool, then remove the lock cylinder. On some model remove the lock cylinder retaining screw.

To install:

12. When assembling the lock cylinder, rotate the key to the stop position while holding the cylinder and push the cylinder in all the way.

13. Install the retaining screw on those models so equipped, and tighten to 40 inch lbs. (4.5 Nm).

14. Install all components in the reverse of the removal procedure order. Check switch for proper operation.

Steering Column

REMOVAL & INSTALLATION

1. Disconnect the negative battery cable.

➡ **If necessary to remove the steering wheel, be sure to use a steering wheel puller.**

2. Remove the nut/bolt from the upper intermediate shaft coupling, then separate the coupling from the lower end of the steering column.

3. If equipped with a column mounted shifter, disconnect the transmission control linkage from the column shift tube levers. If equipped with a floor shifter, disconnect the back drive linkage.

4. At the steering column assembly, disconnect all of the electrical connectors.

5. Remove the floor pan cover-to-floor screws, the floor seal and the cover.

6. Remove the steering column bracket-to-instrument panel nuts. If equipped with an automatic transmission, disconnect the shift position indicator pointer.

➡ **Once the steering column has been removed from the vehicle, be careful not to drop it (especially on its' end), lean on it or damage it in any way; the column is very susceptible to damage.**

7. To install, reverse the removal procedures.

Tie Rod Ends

REMOVAL & INSTALLATION

Except 1986–89 Eldorado and Seville

▶ **See Figures 67 thru 72**

1. Remove the cotter pins and nuts from the tie rod end studs.

2. Tap on the steering arm near the tie rod end (use another hammer as backing) and pull down on the tie rod, if necessary, to free it.

➡ **DO NOT tap directly on the steering arm using the hammer; instead, position the second hammer across the arm and tap lightly on the second hammer head.**

3. Remove the inner stud in the same manner as the outer.

4. Loosen the clamp bolts and unscrew the ends (count the number of turns—install the same amount of turns to keep adjustment close as possible) if they are being replaced.

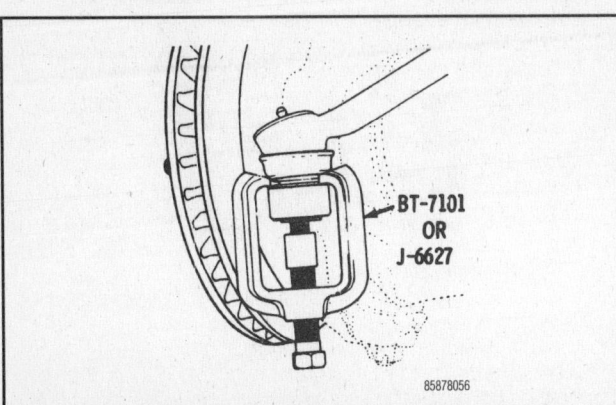

Fig. 67 Disconnecting steering linkage using puller or ball joint tool

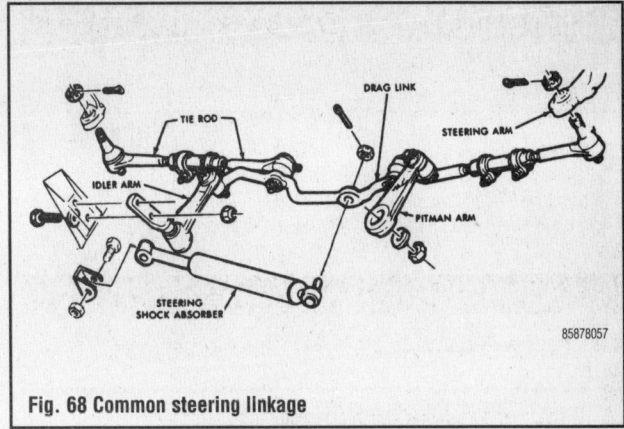

Fig. 68 Common steering linkage

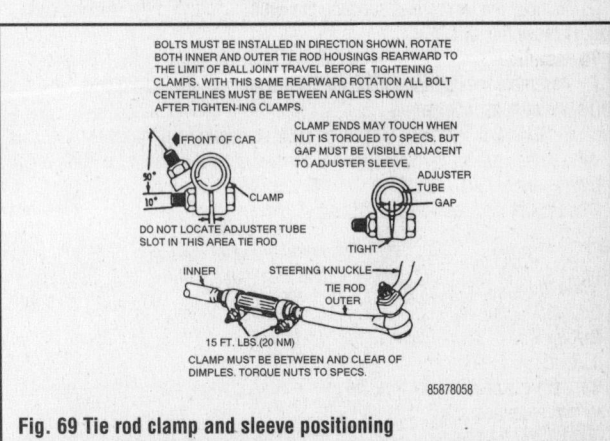

Fig. 69 Tie rod clamp and sleeve positioning

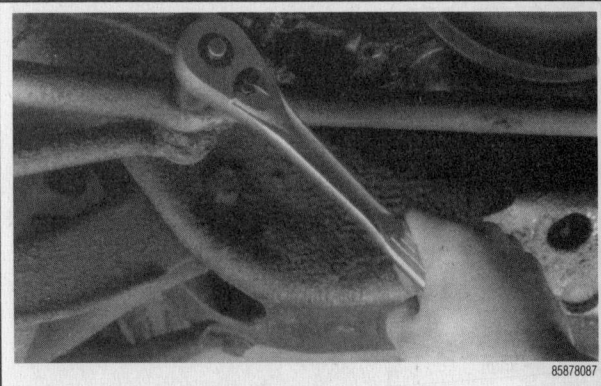
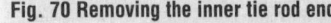

Fig. 70 Removing the inner tie rod end

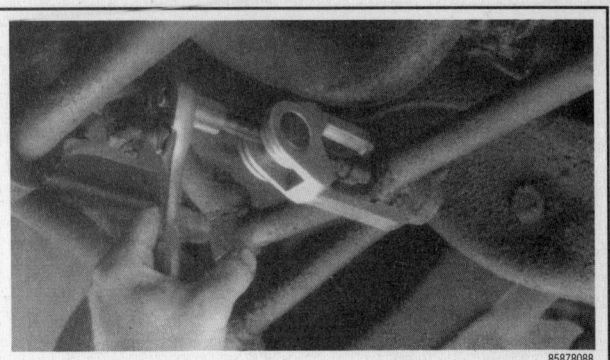

Fig. 71 Removing the inner tie rod from steering linkage with special tool

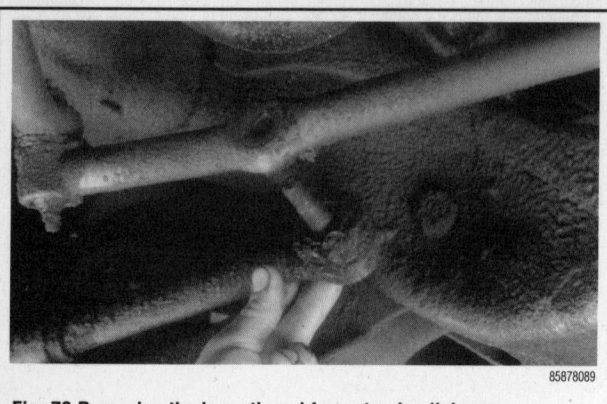

Fig. 72 Removing the inner tie rod from steering linkage

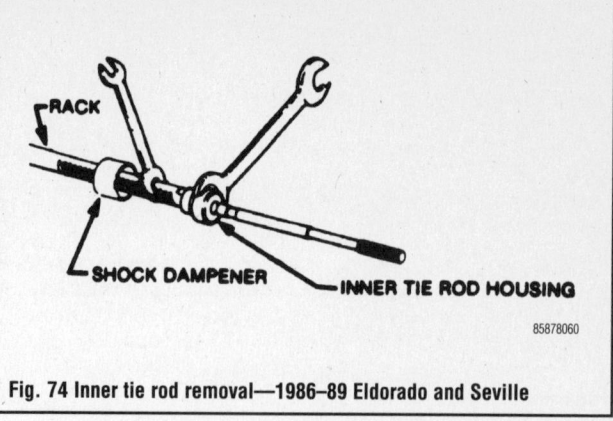

Fig. 74 Inner tie rod removal—1986–89 Eldorado and Seville

To install:

5. Lubricate the tie rod end threads with chassis grease if they were removed. Install each end assembly an equal distance from the sleeve.

6. Ensure that the tie rod end stud threads and nut are clean. Install new seals, then install the studs into the steering arms and relay rod.

7. Install the stud nuts. Tighten the inner and outer end nuts to 35 ft. lbs. (47 Nm). Install new cotter pins.

8. Adjust the toe-in to specifications.

➡Before tightening the sleeve clamps, ensure that the clamps are positioned so that adjusting sleeve slot is covered by the clamp. Never back nut off to insert cotter pin; always tighten it until the pin can fit through the castellations.

1986–89 Eldorado and Seville

▶ See Figures 73 and 74

OUTER TIE ROD

1. Loosen the tie rod jam nut.
2. Use a tie rod puller or equivalent and remove the tie rod end from the steering knuckle.
3. Remove the outer tie rod.

To install:

4. Thread the outer tie rod onto the inner rod, DO NOT tighten the jam nut yet.
5. Press the outer tie rod end into the steering knuckle.
6. Adjust toe-in by turning the outer tie rod, then tighten the jam nut to 50 ft. lbs. (70 Nm).

INNER TIE ROD

1. Remove the outer tie rod as detailed above.
2. Remove the shock dampener ring from the inner tie rod housing and slide it back onto the steering rack.
3. Position an open-end wrench on the rack flat so as to prevent damage when removing the tie rod.

4. Turn the inner tie rod housing counterclockwise until it separates from the rack. Remove the tie rod.

To install:

5. Bottom the tie rod assembly on the rack.
6. Tighten the housing by using a wrench on the rack flat.
7. Support the rack and housing, then stake the tie rod housing to the rack flat. Stake both sides.
8. Check the stake by attempting to pass a 0.010 in. (0.25mm) feeler gauge between the rack and housing stake on both sides. It should not pass through.
9. Slide the shock dampener over the inner tie rod housing until it engages.
10. Install the outer tie rod.

Rack and Pinion Assembly

REMOVAL & INSTALLATION

▶ See Figure 75

1986–89 Eldorado and Seville

1. Raise the front of the vehicle and support it on safety stands. Remove the wheel and tire assembly.
2. Disconnect the intermediate shaft lower coupling.

✳✳ CAUTION

Failure to disconnect the intermediate shaft from the rack and pinion stub shaft can result in damage to the steering gear and/or intermediate shaft that can cause loss of steering control!

3. Disconnect both tie rod ends at the steering knuckles.
4. Disconnect the line retainer.
5. Disconnect and plug the outlet and pressure hose.

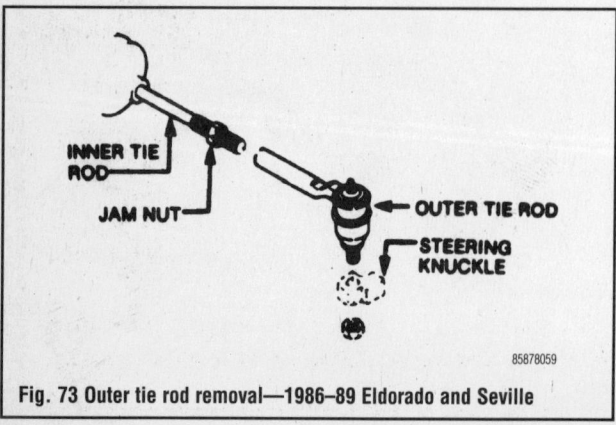

Fig. 73 Outer tie rod removal—1986–89 Eldorado and Seville

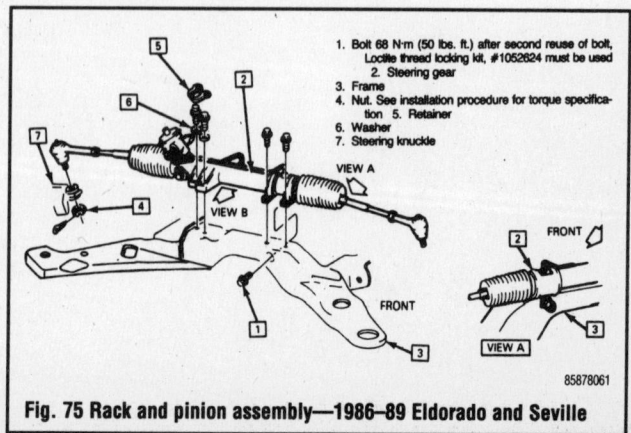

Fig. 75 Rack and pinion assembly—1986–89 Eldorado and Seville

6. Tag and disconnect the pressure switch electrical lead.

7. Remove the five rack and pinion assembly mounting bolts.

8. Remove the rack assembly by sliding out to the side.

To install:

9. Slide the rack assembly into position and tighten the mounting bolts to 50 ft. lbs. (68 Nm).

10. Install the outlet and pressure hose. Tighten the fitting to 20 ft. lbs. (27 Nm).

11. Install the tie rod ends and tighten the nut to 7.5 ft. lbs. (10 Nm). Tighten the nut an additional ⅓ of a turn (two flats of the nut).

➡**When tightening the tie rod end nut in Step 12, a minimum torque of 33 ft. lbs. (45 Nm) must be obtained. If you find this to be impossible, check for stripped threads. If the threads are satisfactory, replacement of the tie rod end and/or the steering knuckle will most likely be required.**

12. After tightening the tie rod end nut to specifications, align the slot in the nut with the cotter pin hole in the shaft. This is done by TIGHTENING ONLY! Never align the slot and the hole by loosening the nut!

13. Connect the intermediate shaft lower coupling to the rack stub shaft and tighten the bolt to 30 ft. lbs. (50 Nm).

14. Reconnect the pressure switch. Install the wheel and tire assembly, then lower the car.

15. Bleed the power steering system as detailed later in this section.

Power Steering Pump

REMOVAL & INSTALLATION

▶ **See Figures 76 and 77**

1. Remove the hoses at the pump and tape the openings shut to prevent contamination. Position the disconnected lines in a raised position to prevent leakage.

2. Remove the pump belt.

3. Loosen the retaining bolts and any braces, and remove the pump.

To install:

4. Install the pump on the engine with the retaining bolts hand-tight.

5. Connect and tighten the hose fittings.

6. Refill the pump with fluid and bleed by turning the pulley counterclockwise (viewed from the front). Stop the bleeding when air bubbles no longer appear.

7. Install the pump belt on the pulley and adjust the tension as described in Section 1.

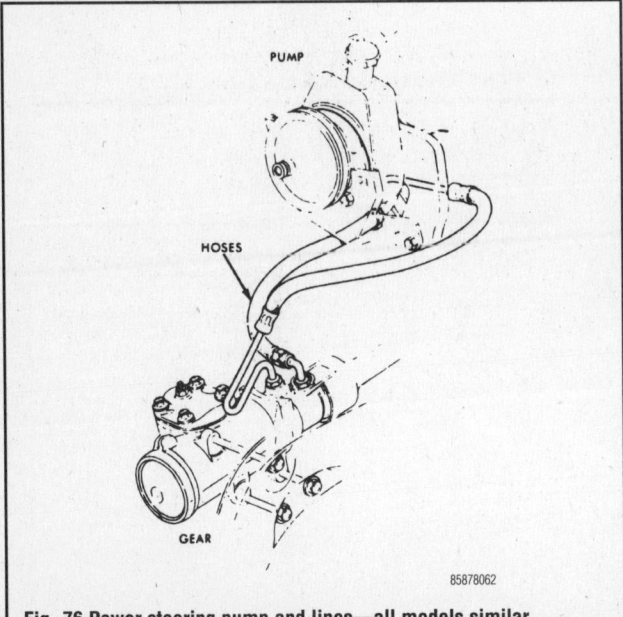

Fig. 76 Power steering pump and lines—all models similar

Fig. 77 View of power steering pump and gear steering box

SYSTEM BLEEDING

1. Fill the fluid reservoir.

2. Let the fluid stand undisturbed for two minutes, then crank the engine for about two seconds. Refill reservoir if necessary.

3. Repeat Steps 1 and 2 above until the fluid level remains constant after cranking the engine.

4. Raise the front of the car until the wheels are off the ground, then start the engine. Increase the engine speed to about 1,500 rpm.

5. Turn the wheels to the left and right, checking the fluid level and refilling if necessary. If the oil is extremely foamy, allow the car to stand a few minutes with the engine off, then repeat the above procedure.

Power Steering Gearbox

REMOVAL & INSTALLATION

▶ **See Figure 78**

Except 1986–89 Eldorado and Seville

1. Remove the coupling shield from the steering shaft (if so equipped).

2. Disconnect the hoses from the gearbox and cap or plug the hose fittings.

3. Jack up the front end of the car and support it with jackstands.

4. Remove the pitman shaft nut, then disconnect the pitman shaft using a puller (it is a press-fit).

5. Remove the three bolts attaching the gearbox to the frame side rail and remove the gearbox.

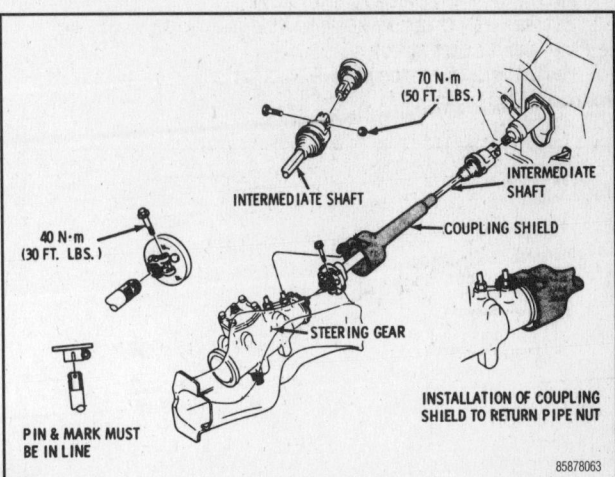

Fig. 78 Power steering gearbox, coupling shield and intermediate shaft

→ If the mounting threads are stripped, do not repair; replace the housing.

To install:

6. Before installing the gearbox, apply a sodium fiber grease to the gearbox mounting pads to prevent squeaks between the gear housing and the frame. Note that the flat on the gearbox lower shaft must index with the flat in the coupling flange. Make sure there is a minimum of 0.040 in. (1mm) clearance between the coupling hub and the steering gearbox upper seal.

7. Reverse the removal procedure for installation. Before tightening the gearbox-to-frame bolts, shift the gearbox as necessary to place it in the same plane as the steering shaft so that the flexible coupling is not distorted. Torque the gearbox-to-frame bolts to 80 ft. lbs. (108 Nm), and the pitman shaft nut to 185 ft. lbs. (251 Nm).

8. After connecting the hoses to the pump add GM Power Steering Fluid or an equivalent to bring the fluid level to the full COLD mark. Bleed the system by running the engine at idle for 30 seconds then at a fast idle for one minute BEFORE turning the steering wheel. Then, with the engine still running, turn the steering wheel through its full travel two or three times. Recheck the oil level and top up if necessary.

TORQUE SPECIFICATIONS

Component	U.S.	Metric
Brake caliper-to-knuckle	38 ft. lbs.	51 Nm
Control arm mounting nut (front)	140 ft. lbs.	190 Nm
Control arm mounting nut (rear)	90 ft. lbs.	123 Nm
Idler arm-to-frame	61 ft. lbs.	83 Nm
Pitman shaft nut	185 ft. lbs.	250 Nm
Tie rod adjuster clamp nut	14 ft. lbs.	19 Nm
Tie rod pivot to steering knuckle	35 ft. lbs.	48 Nm
Idler arm to intermediate rod	40 ft. lbs.	54 Nm
Pitman arm to intermediate rod	45 ft. lbs.	60 Nm
Tie rod to intermediate rod	40 ft. lbs.	54 Nm

85878C01

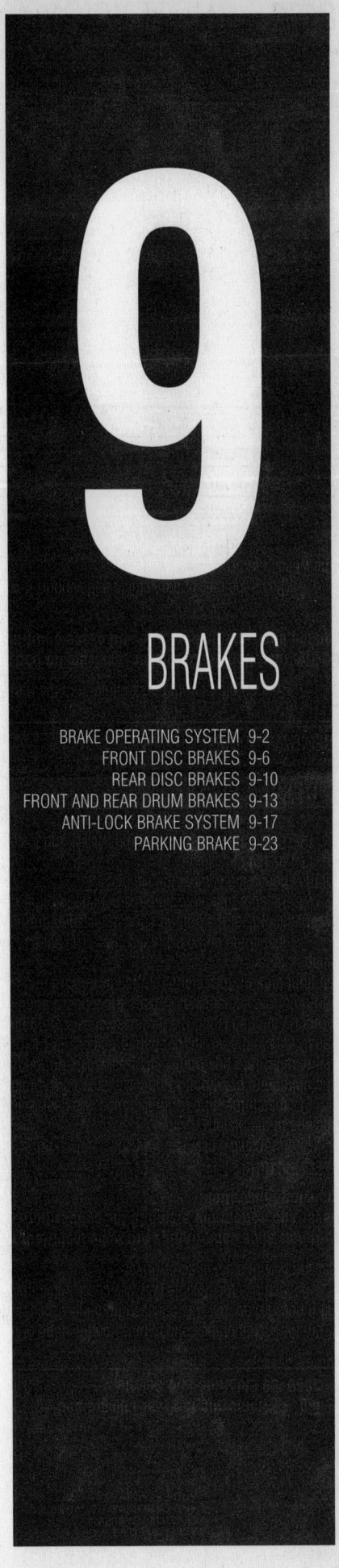

9

BRAKES

BRAKE OPERATING SYSTEM

Basic Operating Principles

Hydraulic systems are used to actuate the brakes of all modern automobiles. The system transports the power required to force the frictional surfaces of the braking system together from the pedal to the individual brake units at each wheel. A hydraulic system is used for two reasons.

First, fluid under pressure can be carried to all parts of an automobile by small pipes and flexible hoses without taking up a significant amount of room or posing routing problems.

Second, a great mechanical advantage can be given to the brake pedal end of the system, and the foot pressure required to actuate the brakes can be reduced by making the surface area of the master cylinder pistons smaller than that of any of the pistons in the wheel cylinders or calipers.

The master cylinder consists of a fluid reservoir along with a double cylinder and piston assembly. Double type master cylinders are designed to separate the front and rear braking systems hydraulically in case of a leak. The master cylinder coverts mechanical motion from the pedal into hydraulic pressure within the lines. This pressure is translated back into mechanical motion at the wheels by either the wheel cylinder (drum brakes) or the caliper (disc brakes).

Steel lines carry the brake fluid to a point on the vehicle's frame near each of the vehicle's wheels. The fluid is then carried to the calipers and wheel cylinders by flexible tubes in order to allow for suspension and steering movements.

In drum brake systems, each wheel cylinder contains two pistons, one at either end, which push outward in opposite directions and force the brake shoe into contact with the drum.

In disc brake systems, the cylinders are part of the calipers. At least one cylinder in each caliper is used to force the brake pads against the disc.

All pistons employ some type of seal, usually made of rubber, to minimize fluid leakage. A rubber dust boot seals the outer end of the cylinder against dust and dirt. The boot fits around the outer end of the piston on disc brake calipers, and around the brake actuating rod on wheel cylinders.

The hydraulic system operates as follows: When at rest, the entire system, from the piston(s) in the master cylinder to those in the wheel cylinders or calipers, is full of brake fluid. Upon application of the brake pedal, fluid trapped in front of the master cylinder piston(s) is forced through the lines to the wheel cylinders. Here, it forces the pistons outward, in the case of drum brakes, and inward toward the disc, in the case of disc brakes. The motion of the pistons is opposed by return springs mounted outside the cylinders in drum brakes, and by spring seals, in disc brakes.

Upon release of the brake pedal, a spring located inside the master cylinder immediately returns the master cylinder pistons to the normal position. The pistons contain check valves and the master cylinder has compensating ports drilled in it. These are uncovered as the pistons reach their normal position. The piston check valves allow fluid to flow toward the wheel cylinders or calipers as the pistons withdraw. Then, as the return springs force the brake pads or shoes into the released position, the excess fluid reservoir through the compensating ports. It is during the time the pedal is in the released position that any fluid that has leaked out of the system will be replaced through the compensating ports.

Dual circuit master cylinders employ two pistons, located one behind the other, in the same cylinder. The primary piston is actuated directly by mechanical linkage from the brake pedal through the power booster. The secondary piston is actuated by fluid trapped between the two pistons. If a leak develops in front of the secondary piston, it moves forward until it bottoms against the front of the master cylinder, and the fluid trapped between the pistons will operate the rear brakes. If the rear brakes develop a leak, the primary piston will move forward until direct contact with the secondary piston takes place, and it will force the secondary piston to actuate the front brakes. In either case, the brake pedal moves farther when the brakes are applied, and less braking power is available.

All dual circuit systems use a switch to warn the driver when only half of the brake system is operational. This switch is usually located in a valve body which is mounted on the firewall or the frame below the master cylinder. A hydraulic piston receives pressure from both circuits, each circuit's pressure being applied to one end of the piston. When the pressures are in balance, the piston remains stationary. When one circuit has a leak, however, the greater pressure in that circuit during application of the brakes will push the piston to one side, closing the switch and activating the brake warning light.

In disc brake systems, this valve body also contains a metering valve and, in some cases, a proportioning valve. The metering valve keeps pressure from

traveling to the disc brakes on the front wheels until the brake shoes on the rear wheels have contacted the drums, ensuring that the front brakes will never be used alone. The proportioning valve controls the pressure to the rear brakes to lessen the chance of rear wheel lock-up during very hard braking.

Warning lights may be tested by depressing the brake pedal and holding it while opening one of the wheel cylinder bleeder screws. If this does not cause the light to go on, substitute a new lamp, make continuity checks, and, finally, replace the switch as necessary.

The hydraulic system may be checked for leaks by applying pressure to the pedal gradually and steadily. If the pedal sinks very slowly to the floor, the system has a leak. This is not to be confused with a springy or spongy feel due to the compression of air within the lines. If the system leaks, there will be a gradual change in the position of the pedal with a constant pressure.

Check for leaks along all lines and at wheel cylinders. If no external leaks are apparent, the problem is inside the master cylinder.

DISC BRAKES

Instead of the traditional expanding brakes that press outward against a circular drum, disc brake systems utilize a disc (rotor) with brake pads positioned on either side of it. An easily-seen analogy is the hand brake arrangement on a bicycle. The pads squeeze onto the rim of the bike wheel, slowing its motion. Automobile disc brakes use the identical principle but apply the braking effort to a separate disc instead of the wheel.

The disc (rotor) is a casting, usually equipped with cooling fins between the two braking surfaces. This enables air to circulate between the braking surfaces making them less sensitive to heat buildup and more resistant to fade. Dirt and water do not drastically affect braking action since contaminants are thrown off by the centrifugal action of the rotor or scraped off the by the pads. Also, the equal clamping action of the two brake pads tends to ensure uniform, straight line stops. Disc brakes are inherently self-adjusting. There are three general types of disc brake:

1. A fixed caliper.
2. A floating caliper.
3. A sliding caliper.

The fixed caliper design uses two pistons mounted on either side of the rotor (in each side of the caliper). The caliper is mounted rigidly and does not move.

The sliding and floating designs are quite similar. In fact, these two types are often lumped together. In both designs, the pad on the inside of the rotor is moved into contact with the rotor by hydraulic force. The caliper, which is not held in a fixed position, moves slightly, bringing the outside pad into contact with the rotor. There are various methods of attaching floating calipers. Some pivot at the bottom or top, and some slide on mounting bolts. In any event, the end result is the same.

DRUM BRAKES

Drum brakes employ two brake shoes mounted on a stationary backing plate. These shoes are positioned inside a circular drum which rotates with the wheel assembly. The shoes are held in place by springs. This allows them to slide toward the drums (when they are applied) while keeping the linings and drums in alignment. The shoes are actuated by a wheel cylinder which is mounted at the top of the backing plate. When the brakes are applied, hydraulic pressure forces the wheel cylinder's actuating links outward. Since these links bear directly against the top of the brake shoes, the tops of the shoes are then forced against the inner side of the drum. This action forces the bottoms of the two shoes to contact the brake drum by rotating the entire assembly slightly (known as servo action). When pressure within the wheel cylinder is relaxed, return springs pull the shoes back away from the drum.

Most modern drum brakes are designed to self-adjust themselves during application when the vehicle is moving in reverse. This motion causes both shoes to rotate very slightly with the drum, rocking an adjusting lever, thereby causing rotation of the adjusting screw. Some drum brake systems are designed to self-adjust during application whenever the brakes are applied. This on-board adjustment system reduces the need for maintenance adjustments and keeps both the brake function and pedal feel satisfactory.

Applications

All models covered in this manual are equipped with front disc brakes except the 1967–68 DeVille and Fleetwood, 1967 Eldorado, and 1976 Seville. On these models front disc brakes may have been ordered optionally to replace the front drum brakes. The 1976 and later Eldorado and the 1977 and later Seville models are equipped with four wheel disc brakes as standard equipment. Rear disc brakes are available optionally on the DeVille and Fleetwood.

Beginning in 1976, Hydro-boost is installed on the Fleetwood limousine models and the Commercial Chassis models. It is also used on all diesel engine equipped models. Hydro-boost is a hydraulically-assisted power brake booster. The power steering pump provides the hydraulic fluid pressure to operate both the power brake booster and the power steering gear.

Adjustments

DISC BRAKES

There is no adjustment provision on hydraulic disc brakes; they are inherently self-adjusting.

DRUM BRAKES

▶ **See Figures 1 and 2**

➡**Drum brakes are self-adjusting, but provision is made for manual adjustment as follows:**

1. Jack up the rear of the car and support it with jackstands.
2. The inner sides of the brake backing plates have a lanced area, oblong in shape. Knock this area out with a punch—you will have to remove the brake drum to clean out any metal pieces that will be deposited by the punch, and you will have to purchase rubber plugs at a GM dealer or auto supply store to plug the punched holes in the backing plates. Many cars will already have the holes punched and plugs installed.
3. Turn the star-shaped adjusting screw inside the drum with a brake spoon, until the wheel can just be turned by hand. Do this to both wheels until there is equal drag on each wheel.
4. Insert a brake adjusting spoon into the hole, along with a small screwdriver to hold the adjuster lever away from the sprocket. Back off each adjusting screw about 25 notches or to a very slight drag. If you still hear and feel the brake shoes dragging slightly when you turn the wheels by hand, back off another one or two notches. If there is still excess drag on the drums, the parking brake cables could be excessively tight.
5. Install the rubber plugs into the adjusting holes. Check the parking brake adjustment.

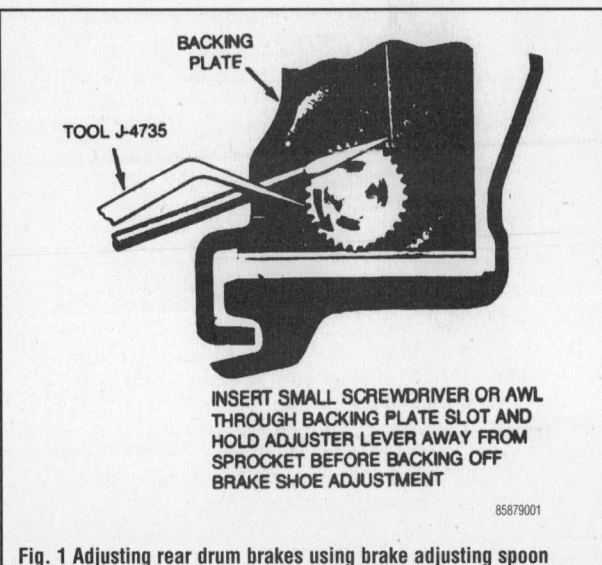

BACKING PLATE

TOOL J-4735

INSERT SMALL SCREWDRIVER OR AWL THROUGH BACKING PLATE SLOT AND HOLD ADJUSTER LEVER AWAY FROM SPROCKET BEFORE BACKING OFF BRAKE SHOE ADJUSTMENT

85879001

Fig. 1 Adjusting rear drum brakes using brake adjusting spoon

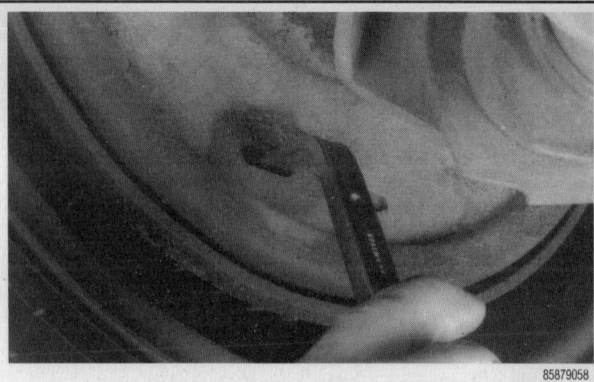

85879058

Fig. 2 Rear drum brake adjustment—with brake tool

Brake Light Switch

REMOVAL & INSTALLATION

When the brake pedal is in the fully released position, the stop light switch plunger should be fully depressed against the pedal arm. The switch is adjusted by moving it in or out.

1. Disconnect the stop light switch electrical connector(s).
2. Remove the switch from the bracket.

To install:

3. Make sure that the tubular clip is in the brake pedal mounting bracket.
4. Depress the brake pedal and insert the switch into the tubular clip until it seats on the clip; a click will be hard.
5. Pull the brake pedal fully rearward, against the pedal stop, until the clicking sounds can no longer be heard; the switch is adjusting itself in the bracket.
6. Release the brake pedal, then pull the pedal rearward again to assure that the adjustment is complete.

Master Cylinder

REMOVAL & INSTALLATION

▶ **See Figures 3, 4, 5 and 6**

The master cylinder can be removed without removing the power vacuum cylinder from the car.

1. Clean the area around the master cylinder.
2. Disconnect the hydraulic lines at the master cylinder. Plug or tape the ends of the lines to prevent dirt from entering and to prevent fluid from leaking out.
3. Remove the master cylinder attaching nuts and remove the master cylinder.
4. Drain the master cylinder.

✳✳ WARNING

Be careful to keep brake fluid away from all body paint-the fluid acts like paint remover, and a few drops will quickly bubble any paint with which it comes in contact.

5. Installation is the reverse of the removal procedure. Bleed the master cylinder, brake system and adjust the brake system.
6. To bleed the master cylinder before installing it in the car. Do so in the following manner:
   a. Install plugs in the outlet ports.
   b. Place the unit in a vise with the front end tilted slightly downward. DO NOT OVERTIGHTEN the vise.
   c. Fill both reservoirs with clean fluid.
   d. Using a smooth, round rod push in on the primary piston.
   e. Release the pressure on the rod and watch for air bubbles in the fluid. Keep repeating this until the bubbles disappear.
   f. Loosen the vise and position the cylinder so the front end is tilted slightly upward. Repeat steps **d** and **e**.
   g. Place the diaphragm cover on the reservoir.

Power Brake Booster

REMOVAL & INSTALLATION

▶ **See Figure 7**

1. Disconnect the vacuum hose from the vacuum check valve.
2. Unbolt the master cylinder and carefully move it aside without disconnecting the hydraulic lines.

➡ **If sufficient booster clearance cannot be obtained, it will be necessary to disconnect the hydraulic lines from the master cylinder, then remove the master cylinder.**

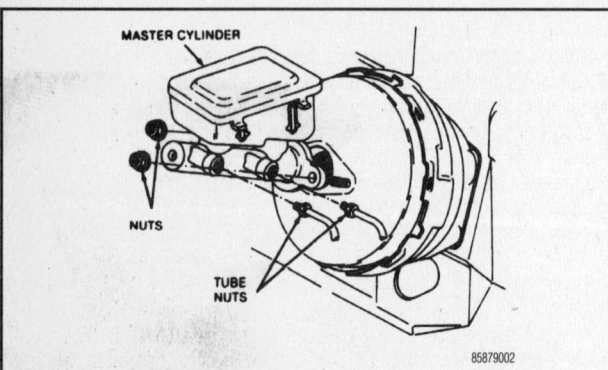

Fig. 3 Common master cylinder mounting—unit is secured to the driver's side of the firewall

3. Disconnect the pushrod at the brake pedal assembly.
4. Remove the booster-to-cowl nuts and lockwashers and the booster from engine compartment.
5. To install, reverse the removal procedures. Torque the booster-to-cowl and the master cylinder-to-booster mounting nuts to 28 ft. lbs. (38 Nm).

➡ **Make sure to check the operation of the stop lights. Allow the engine vacuum to build before applying the brakes. Bleed the hydraulic system if the lines were disconnected from the master cylinder.**

Combination Valve

The combination valve used on Cadillac models is a three-function valve. It serves as a metering valve, balance valve, and brake warning switch. There are two different valves, one manufactured by Bendix and one manufactured by Kelsey-Hayes. Both valves serve the same function and differ only in minor details. In any case, all combination valves are non-adjustable and must be replaced if they are found to be defective.

REMOVAL & INSTALLATION

▶ **See Figures 8 and 9**

1. Disconnect the negative battery cable.
2. Disconnect the electrical lead from the switch.
3. Place rags under the unit to absorb any spilled brake fluid.
4. Clean any dirt from the hydraulic lines and the switch/valve assembly. Disconnect the hydraulic lines from the assembly. If necessary, loosen the line connections at the master cylinder. Tape the open line ends to prevent the entrance of dirt.
5. Remove the mounting screws and remove the switch/valve assembly.

Fig. 4 Removing the brake lines from the master cylinder

Fig. 5 Removing the master cylinder mounting nuts

Fig. 6 Removing the master cylinder from the power brake booster assembly

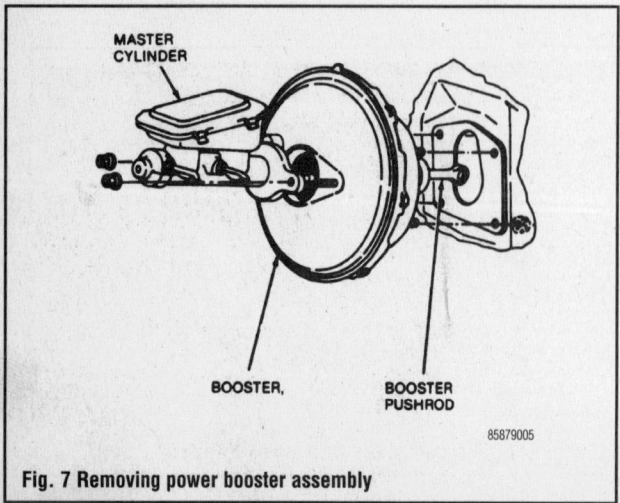

Fig. 7 Removing power booster assembly

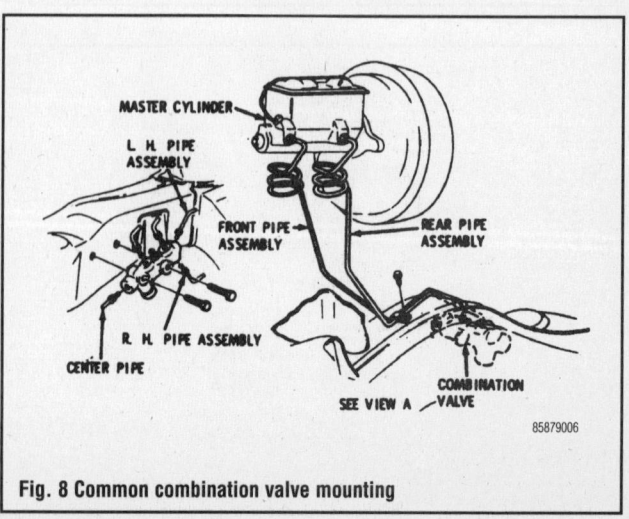

Fig. 8 Common combination valve mounting

To install:

6. Make sure that the new unit is clean and free of dust and lint. If in doubt, wash the new unit in clean brake fluid.

7. Place the new unit in position and install it to its mounting bracket with screws.

8. Remove the tape from the hydraulic lines and connect them to the unit. If necessary, tighten the line connections at the master cylinder.

9. Connect the electrical lead.

10. Connect the negative battery cable.

11. Bleed the brake systems.

Brake Bleeding

The hydraulic brake system must be bled any time one of the lines is disconnected or any time air enters the system. If the brake pedal feels spongy upon application, and goes almost to the floor but regains height when pumped, air has entered the system. It must be bled out. Check for leaks that would have allowed the entry of air and repair them before bleeding the system. If air was introduced at the master cylinder (reservoir level dropped too low or fittings were disconnected), then bleeding must begin at the master cylinder assembly. Some cylinders are equipped with bleeder screws, while others must be bled through the fittings (by loosening and tightening them while the brake pedal is depressed). Once the master cylinder is purged of air, the wheel points should be bled in the correct sequence: right rear wheel cylinder, left rear, right front, and left front.

MANUAL BLEEDING

▶ **See Figures 10, 11 and 12**

This method of bleeding requires two people, one to depress the brake pedal and the other to open the bleeder screws.

1. Clean the top of the master cylinder, remove the cover and fill the reservoirs with clean fluid. To prevent squirting fluid, replace the cover.

➡**IMPORTANT: On cars with front disc brakes, it will be necessary to hold in the metering valve pin during the bleeding procedure. The metering valve is located beneath the master cylinder and the pin is situated under the rubber boot on the end of the valve housing. This may be taped in or held by an assistant.**

✳ CAUTION

Never reuse brake fluid which has been bled from the system!

2. Fill the master cylinder with brake fluid.

3. Install a box-end wrench on the bleeder screw on the right rear wheel.

4. Attach a length of small diameter, clean vinyl tubing to the bleeder screw. Submerge the other end of the rubber tubing in a glass jar partially filled with clean brake fluid. Make sure the rubber tube fits on the bleeder screw snugly or you may be squirted with brake fluid when the bleeder screw is opened.

5. Have your friend slowly depress the brake pedal. As this is done, open the bleeder screw half a turn and allow the fluid to run through the tube. Close the bleeder screw, then return the brake pedal to its fully released position.

6. Repeat this procedure until no bubbles appear in the jar. Refill the master cylinder.

7. Repeat this procedure on the left rear, right front, and left front wheels, in that order. Periodically refill the master cylinder so it does not run dry.

8. If the brake warning light is on, depress the brake pedal firmly. If there is no air in the system, the light will go out.

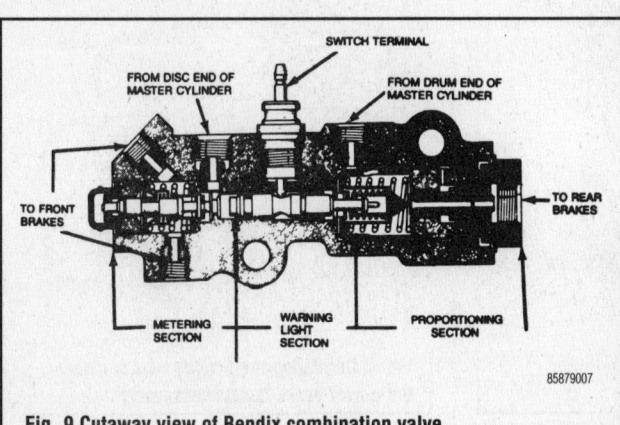

Fig. 9 Cutaway view of Bendix combination valve

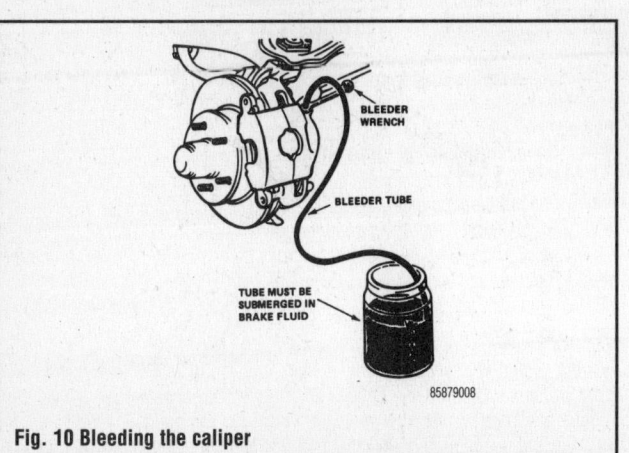

Fig. 10 Bleeding the caliper

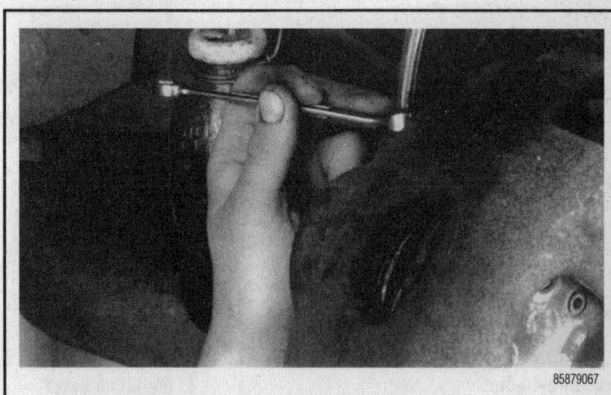

Fig. 11 Bleeding the front brakes at the caliper

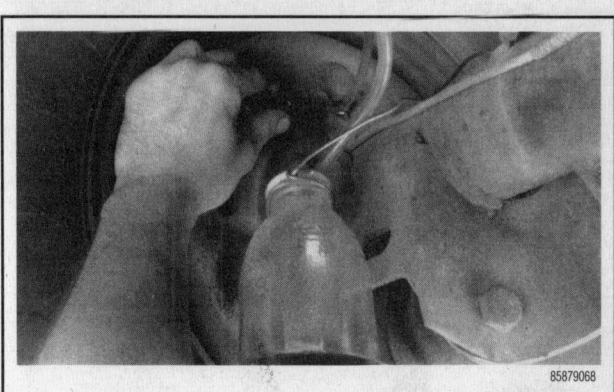

Fig. 12 Bleeding the rear brakes at the wheel cylinder

FRONT DISC BRAKES

❄❄ CAUTION

Brake shoes may contain asbestos, which has been determined to be a cancer causing agent. Never clean the brake surfaces with compressed air! Avoid inhaling any dust from any brake surface! When cleaning brake surfaces, use a commercially available brake cleaning fluid.

Brake Pads

INSPECTION

◗ See Figures 13 and 14

Brake pads should be inspected at least once a year or at 7,500 miles, whichever occurs first. Check both ends of the outboard shoe, looking in at each end of the caliper; then check the lining thickness on the inboard shoe, looking down through the inspection hole. Lining should be more than 0.020 in. (0.051mm) thick above the rivet (so that the lining is thicker than the metal backing). Keep in mind that any applicable state inspection standards that are more stringent take precedence. All four pads must be replaced if one shows excessive wear.

➡️All 1979 and later models have a wear indicator that makes a noise when the linings wear to a degree where replacement is necessary. The spring clip is an integral part of the inboard shoe and lining. When the brake pad reaches a certain degree of wear, the clip will contact the rotor and produce a warning noise.

REMOVAL & INSTALLATION

◗ See Figures 15 thru 20

1. Siphon off ⅔ of the brake fluid from the master cylinder.

➡️The insertion of the thicker replacement pads will push the caliper piston back into its bore and will cause a full master cylinder to overflow.

2. Jack the car up and support it with jackstands. Remove the wheel(s).
3. Install a C-clamp on the caliper so that the solid side of the clamp rests against the back of the caliper and the screw end rests against the metal part of the outboard pad.
4. Tighten the clamp until the caliper moves enough to bottom the piston in its bore. Remove the clamp.
5. Remove the two Allen head caliper mounting bolts enough to allow the caliper to be pulled off the disc.
6. Remove the inboard pad and dislodge the outboard pad. Place the caliper where it won't be supported by the brake hose (hang it by a wire hook from the frame).
7. Remove the pad support spring clip from the piston.
8. Remove the two bolt ear sleeves and the four rubber bushings from the ears.
9. Brake pads should be replaced when they are worn to within ⅟₃₂ in. (0.80mm) of the rivet heads.

To install:
10. Check the inside of the caliper for leakage and the condition of the piston dust boot.

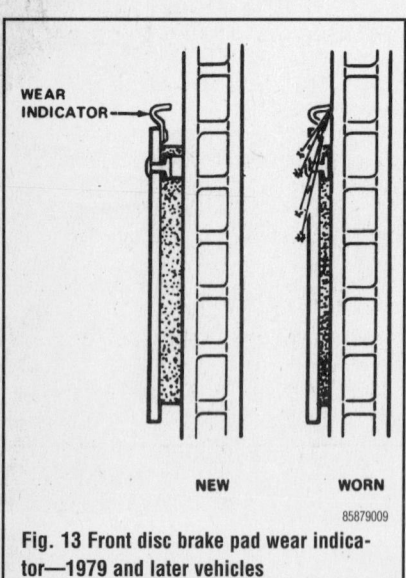

Fig. 13 Front disc brake pad wear indicator—1979 and later vehicles

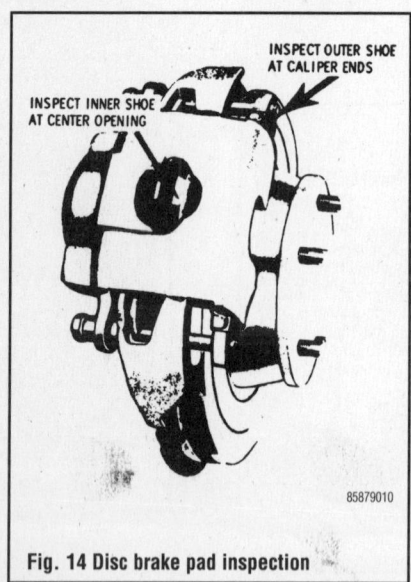

Fig. 14 Disc brake pad inspection

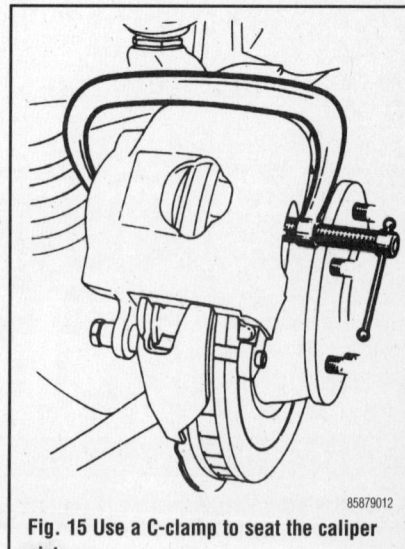

Fig. 15 Use a C-clamp to seat the caliper piston

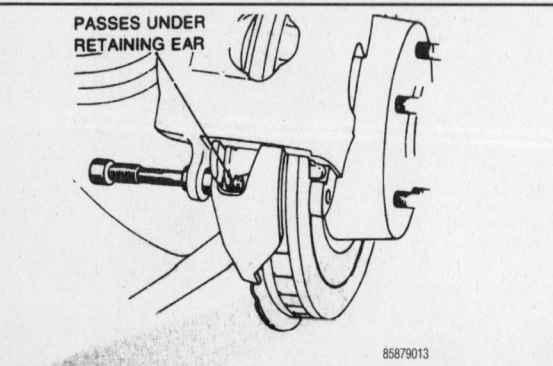

Fig. 16 The Allen head caliper bolts must go under the pad retaining ears

11. Lubricate the two new sleeves and four bushings with a silicone spray.
12. Install the bushings in each caliper ear. Install the two sleeves in the two inboard ears.
13. If the piston was not fully bottomed during removal there may not be sufficient clearance for new pad insulation. If necessary, install the pad support spring clip and the old pad into the center of the piston. You will then push this pad down to get the piston flat against the caliper. Use a C-clamp or a large pair of channel-type pliers to carefully depress the piston back into the bore. Make sure the piston boot is not pinched or otherwise damaged. DO NOT attempt to force the piston any further then necessary to insert the new pads.

➡️If the piston will not slide easily back into the bore DO NOT force it. Have an assistant hold the caliper and loosen the bleeder valve to relieve pressure, while you carefully press the old pad (in order to push on the piston) and slowly insert the piston until it is flush with the

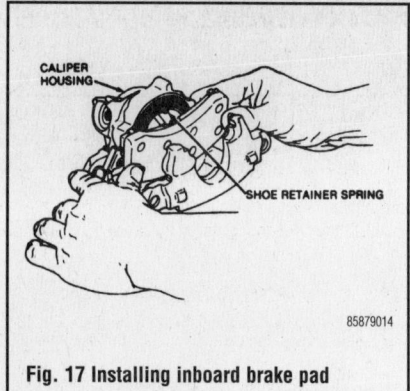

Fig. 17 Installing inboard brake pad

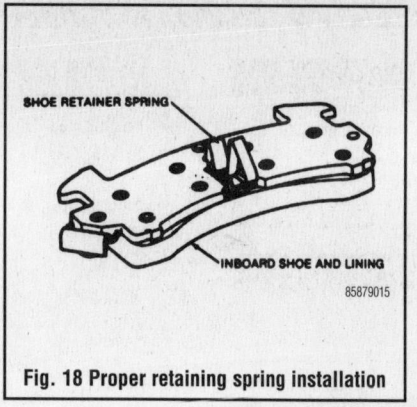

Fig. 18 Proper retaining spring installation

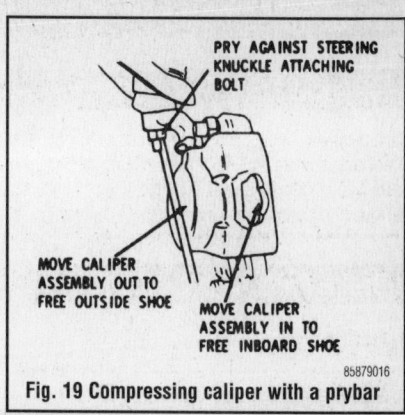

Fig. 19 Compressing caliper with a prybar

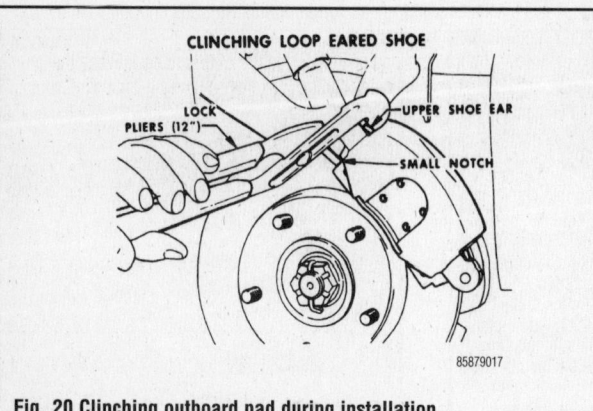

Fig. 20 Clinching outboard pad during installation

caliper surface. When it is flush, immediately close the bleeder valve so that no air gets into the system. Once the brakes are installed, the caliper should be properly bled to assure no air was drawn into the system.

14. Position the outboard shoe with the ears of the shoes over the caliper ears and the tab at the bottom engaged in the caliper cutout notch.

➡On models with wear sensors, make sure the wear sensor is toward the rear of the caliper.

15. With the two shoes in position, place the caliper over the brake disc and align the holes in the caliper with those of the mounting bracket.

✳✳ CAUTION

Make certain that the brake hose is not twisted or kinked.

16. Install the mounting bracket bolts through the sleeves in the inboard caliper ears and through the mounting bracket, making sure that the ends of the bolts pass under the retaining ears of the inboard shoe.

➡When installing the caliper on 1986–89 Eldorados and Sevilles, NEW caliper mounting bolts must be used.

17. Tighten the bolts into the bracket and tighten to 35 ft. lbs. (47 Nm) except for 1986–89 vehicles which should be tightened to 63 ft. lbs. (85 Nm). Bend over the outer pad ears.

18. Install the front wheel and lower the car.

19. Add fluid to the master cylinder reservoirs so that they are ¼ in. from the top.

20. Test the brake pedal by pumping it to obtain a hard pedal. Check the fluid level again and add fluid as necessary. Do not move the vehicle until a hard pedal is obtained. Bleed the brakes if necessary.

Brake Caliper

REMOVAL & INSTALLATION

▶ See Figures 21 thru 28

1. Raise the car and support it on jackstands.
2. Remove the tire and wheel assembly from the side on which the caliper is being removed.
3. Disconnect the brake hose at the support bracket. Tape the end of the line to prevent contamination.
4. Remove the two caliper retaining bolts and lift off the caliper.
5. Remove the brake pads and identify them as inboard or outboard if they are being reused.
6. Remove the U-shaped retainer from the hose fitting and pull the hose from the bracket. Remove the caliper assembly.

To install:

7. Install the brake pads. If the same pads are being reused, return them to their original places (outboard or inboard) as marked during removal. New pads will usually have an arrow on the back indicating the direction of disc rotation. Install caliper assembly and install retaining bolts.
8. Install the brake hose into the caliper, passing the female end through the support bracket.
9. Make sure that the tube line is clean and connect the brake line nut to the caliper.
10. Install the hose fitting into the support bracket and install the U-shaped

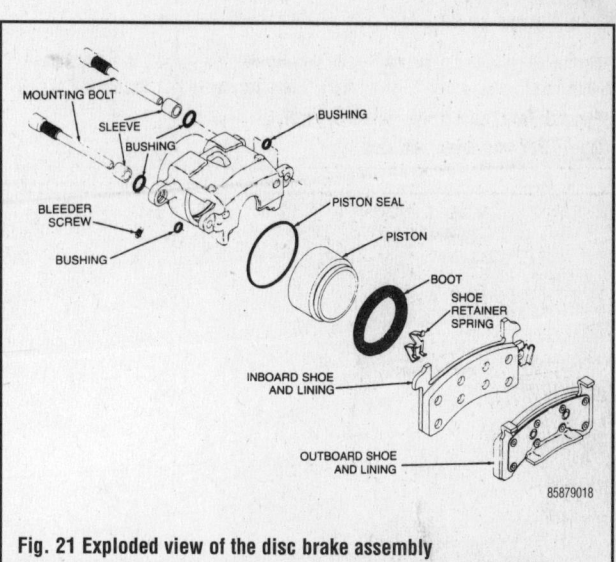

Fig. 21 Exploded view of the disc brake assembly

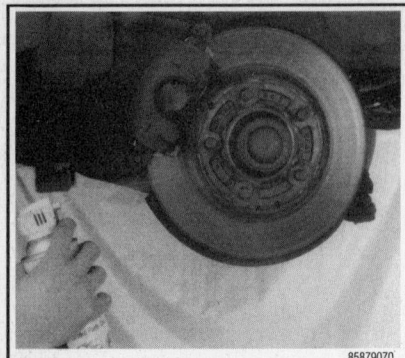

Fig. 22 Cleaning the disc brake caliper and rotor

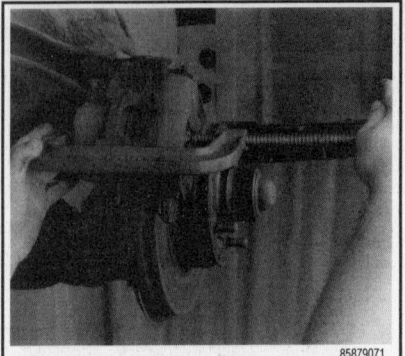

Fig. 23 Compressing the disc brake caliper with C-clamp

Fig. 24 Removing the disc brake caliper bolts or pins

Fig. 25 View of the disc brake caliper bolts or pins

Fig. 26 Removing the disc brake caliper from the brake rotor

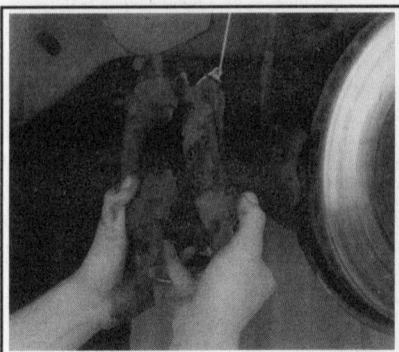

Fig. 27 Support the caliper before removing the outboard pad . . .

retainer. Turn the steering wheel from side to side to make sure that the hose doesn't interfere with the tire. If it does, turn the hose end one or two points in the bracket until the interference is eliminated.

11. After performing the above check, install the steel tube connector and tighten it.

12. Bleed the brakes.

13. Install the wheels and lower the car.

OVERHAUL

▶ See Figures 29 thru 34

➡Some vehicles may be equipped dual piston calipers. The procedure to overhaul the caliper is essentially the same with the exception of multiple pistons, O-rings and dust boots.

1. Remove the caliper from the vehicle and place on a clean workbench.

❋❋❋ CAUTION

NEVER place your fingers in front of the pistons in an attempt to catch or protect the pistons when applying compressed air. This could result in personal injury!

➡Depending upon the vehicle, there are two different ways to remove the piston from the caliper. Refer to the brake pad replacement procedure to make sure you have the correct procedure for your vehicle.

2. The first method is as follows:

a. Stuff a shop towel or a block of wood into the caliper to catch the piston.

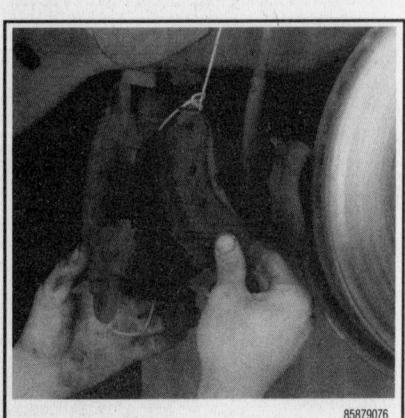

Fig. 28 . . . and the inboard pad

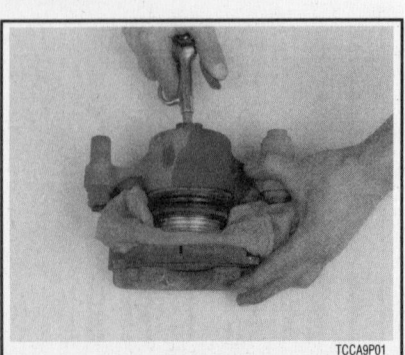

Fig. 29 For some types of calipers, use compressed air to drive the piston out of the caliper, but make sure to keep your fingers clear

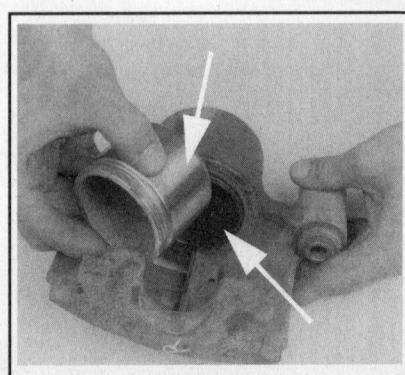

Fig. 30 Withdraw the piston from the caliper bore

Fig. 31 Use a prytool to carefully pry around the edge of the boot . . .

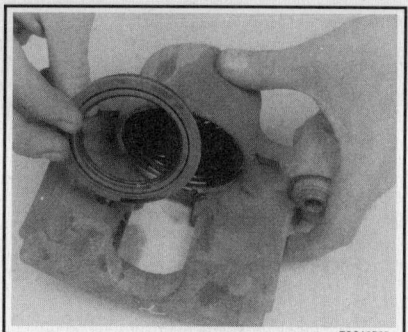

Fig. 32 . . . then remove the boot from the caliper housing, taking care not to score or damage the bore

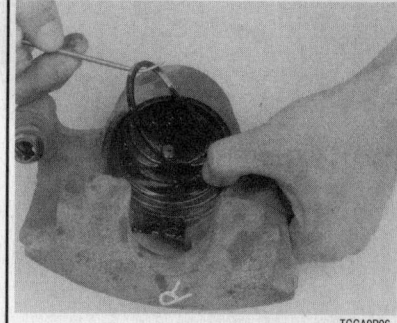

Fig. 33 Use extreme caution when removing the piston seal; DO NOT scratch the caliper bore

b. Remove the caliper piston using compressed air applied into the caliper inlet hole. Inspect the piston for scoring, nicks, corrosion and/or worn or damaged chrome plating. The piston must be replaced if any of these conditions are found.

3. For the second method, you must rotate the piston to retract it from the caliper.

4. If equipped, remove the anti-rattle clip.

5. Use a prytool to remove the caliper boot, being careful not to scratch the housing bore.

6. Remove the piston seals from the groove in the caliper bore.

7. Carefully loosen the brake bleeder valve cap and valve from the caliper housing.

8. Inspect the caliper bores, pistons and mounting threads for scoring or excessive wear.

9. Use crocus cloth to polish out light corrosion from the piston and bore.

10. Clean all parts with denatured alcohol and dry with compressed air.

To assemble:

11. Lubricate and install the bleeder valve and cap.

12. Install the new seals into the caliper bore grooves, making sure they are not twisted.

13. Lubricate the piston bore.

14. Install the pistons and boots into the bores of the calipers and push to the bottom of the bores.

15. Use a suitable driving tool to seat the boots in the housing.

16. Install the caliper in the vehicle.

17. Install the wheel and tire assembly, then carefully lower the vehicle.

18. Properly bleed the brake system.

Brake Disc (Rotor)

REMOVAL & INSTALLATION

1. Raise the car, support it with jackstands, and remove the wheel and tire assembly.

2. Remove the brake caliper as previously outlined.

3. Remove the dust cap and remove the wheel bearing nut after removing the cotter pin.

4. Remove the wheel bearing, hub, and disc assembly from the spindle.

5. Installation is the reverse order of removal. Adjust the wheel bearing as outlined in this section.

INSPECTION

▶ See Figures 35 and 36

1. Check the disc for any obvious defects such as excessive rust, chipping, or deep scoring. Light scoring is normal on disc brakes.

2. Make sure there is no wheel bearing play and then check the disc for runout as follows:

3. Install a dial indicator on the caliper so that its feeler will contact the disc about one inch below its outer edge.

4. Turn the disc and observe the runout reading. If the reading exceeds 0.002 in. (0.051mm), the disc should be replaced.

➡ All brake rotors (disc) have a minimum thickness dimension cast into them, on the hub between the lugs. This is the minimum wear dimension and not a refinish dimension. Do not reuse a brake rotor that will not meet specifications. Replace with a new rotor.

Refinishing of brake rotors can be handled at machine shops equipped for brake work.

Wheel Bearings

REAR WHEEL DRIVE MODELS

Properly adjusted bearings have a slightly loose feeling. Wheel bearings must never be preloaded. Preloading will damage the bearings and eventually the spindles. If the bearings are too loose, they should be cleaned, inspected, and then adjusted.

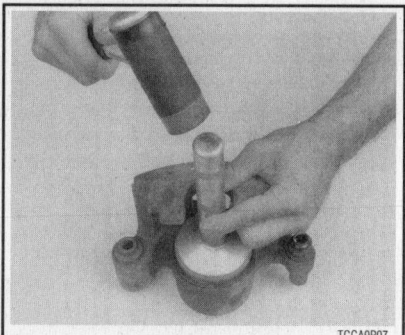

Fig. 34 Use the proper size driving tool and a mallet to properly seal the boots in the caliper housing

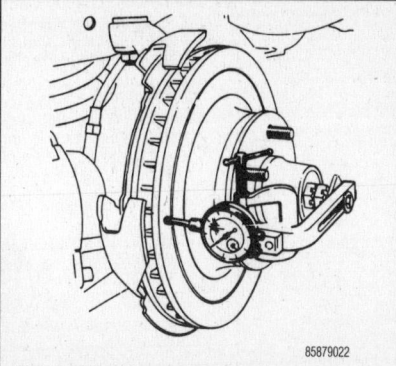

Fig. 35 Checking brake disc runout with a dial indicator

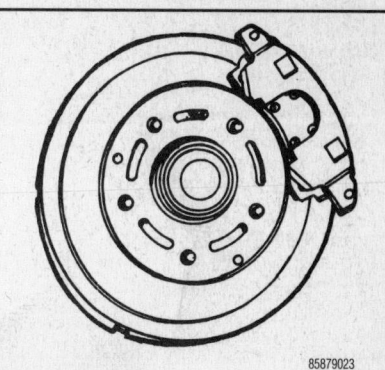

Fig. 36 Discard dimension (.965) stamped on disc hub

Hold the tire at the top and bottom and move the wheel in and out of the spindle. If the movement is greater than 0.005 in. (0.127mm), the bearings are too loose.

Adjustment

▶ **See Figure 37**

1. Raise and support the car by the lower control arm.
2. Remove the hub cap, then remove the dust cap from the hub.
3. Remove the cotter pin and spindle nut.
4. Spin the wheel forward by hand. Tighten the nut until snug to fully seat the bearings.
5. Back off the nut ¼–½ turn until it is just loose, then tighten it finger-tight.
6. Loosen the nut until either hole in the spindle lines up with a slot in the nut and then insert the cotter pin. This may appear to be too loose, but it is the correct adjustment.
7. Proper adjustment creates 0.001–0.005 in. (0.0254–0.127) of end play.

Removal & Installation

1. Remove the hub and disc assembly.
2. Remove the outer roller bearing assembly from the hub. The inner bearing assembly can be removed after prying out the inner seal. Discard the seal.

To install:

3. Wash all parts in solvent and check for excessive wear or damage.
4. To replace the outer or inner race, knock out the old race with a hammer and brass drift. New races must be installed squarely and evenly to avoid damage.
5. Pack the bearings with a high melting point bearing lubricant.
6. Lightly grease the spindle and the inside of the hub.
7. Place the inner bearing in the hub race and install a new grease seal.
8. Carefully install the hub and disc assembly.
9. Install the outer wheel bearing.
10. Install the washer and nut and adjust the bearings according to the procedure outlined above.
11. Install the caliper and torque the mounting bolts to 35 ft. lbs. (47 Nm).
12. Install the dust cap and the wheel and tire assembly, then lower the car to the ground.

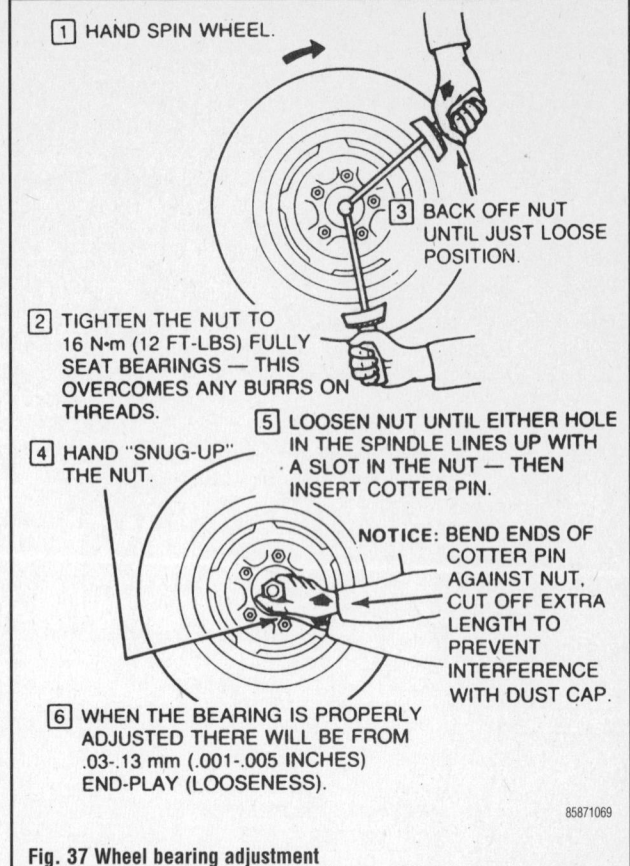

Fig. 37 Wheel bearing adjustment

REAR DISC BRAKES

▶ **See Figures 38 and 39**

⚠ CAUTION

Brake shoes may contain asbestos, which has been determined to be a cancer causing agent. Never clean the brake surfaces with compressed air! Avoid inhaling any dust from any brake surface! When cleaning brake surfaces, use a commercially available brake cleaning fluid.

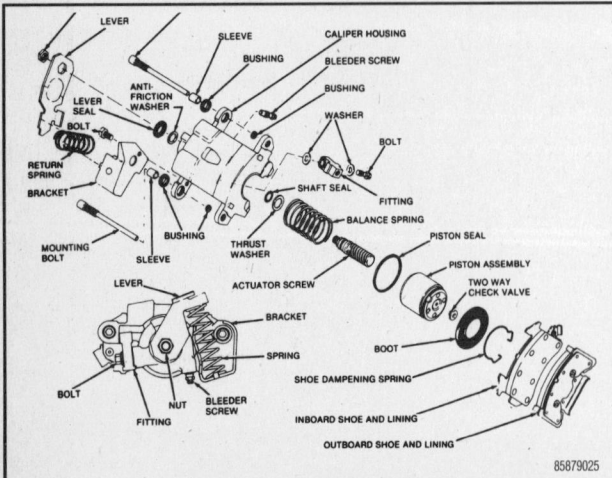

Fig. 38 Rear disc brake caliper and parking brake assembly— 1967–85 vehicles

Rear hydraulic disc brakes are available as standard equipment on the Eldorado and Seville models and as an option on some Full Size models. The brakes are almost identical in design and operation to the front disc brakes, with the exception of the parking brake mechanism that is built into the rear brake calipers. When the parking brake is applied, the lever turns the actuator screw which is threaded into a nut in the piston assembly. This causes the piston to move outward and the caliper to slide inward mechanically, forcing the linings against the brake disc. The piston assembly contains a self-adjusting mechanism for the parking brake.

With the exception of those on the 1986–89 Eldorado and Seville, the rear disc brakes are serviced by following procedures detailed in the Front Disc Brake section. As for the 1986–89 Eldorado and Seville, any procedures which are different from those pertaining to the front brakes are detailed below.

Disc Brake Pads

REMOVAL & INSTALLATION

▶ **See Figures 40 thru 45**

1. Siphon off ⅔ of the brake fluid from the master cylinder.

➡**The insertion of the thicker replacement pads will push the caliper piston back into its bore and will cause a full master cylinder to overflow.**

2. Raise the rear of the vehicle and support it with safety stands. Remove the wheel and tire assembly.
3. Remove the caliper as detailed later in this section.
4. Remove the outboard brake shoe and lining by unsnapping the shoe springs from the caliper holes.

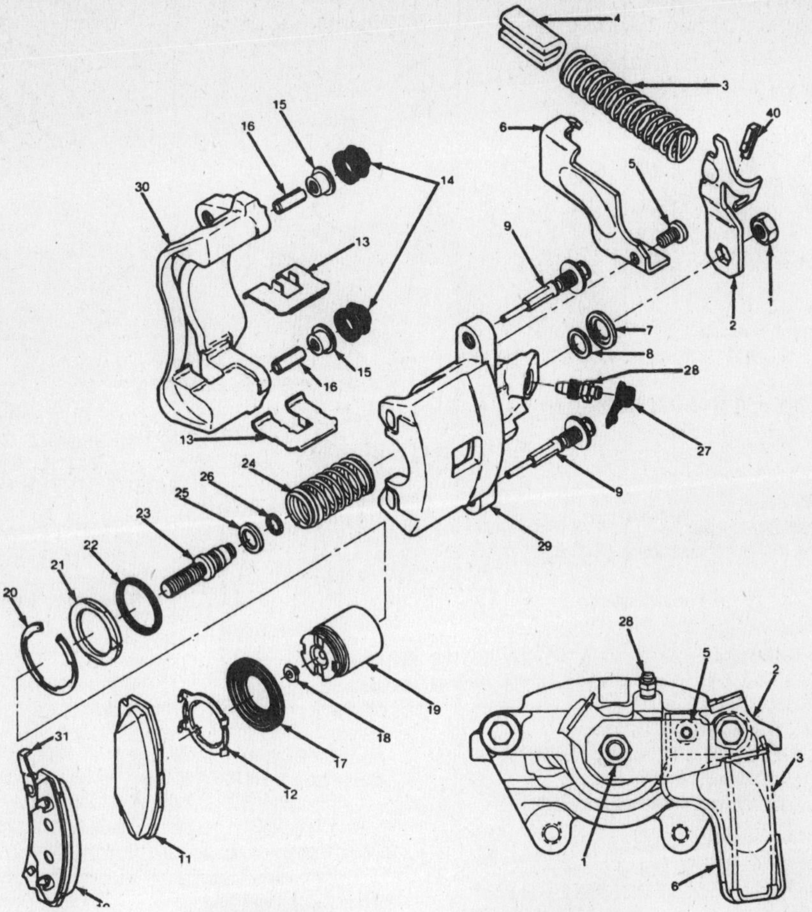

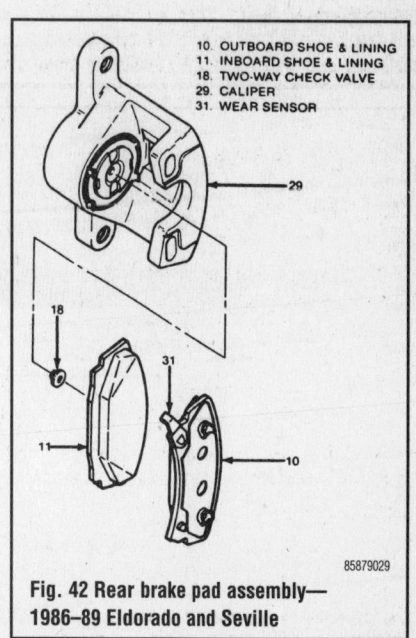

1. NUT
2. PARK BRAKE LEVER
3. RETURN SPRING
4. DAMPER
5. BOLT
6. BRACKET
7. LEVER SEAL
8. ANTI-FRICTION WASHER

9. MOUNTING BOLT
10. OUTBOARD SHOE & LINING
11. INBOARD SHOE & LINING
12. SHOE RETAINER
13. INSULATOR
14. BOLT BOOT
15. SUPPORT BUSHING
16. BUSHING

17. CALIPER PISTON BOOT
18. TWO-WAY CHECK VALVE
19. PISTON ASSEMBLY
20. RETAINER
21. PISTON LOCATOR
22. PISTON SEAL
23. ACTUATOR SCREW
24. BALANCE SPRING & RETAINER

25. THRUST WASHER
26. SHAFT SEAL
27. CAP
28. BLEEDER VALVE
29. CALIPER HOUSING
30. BRACKET
31. WEAR SENSOR
40. RETAINING CLIP

85879026

Fig. 39 Exploded view of the rear disc brake caliper—1986–89 Eldorado and Seville

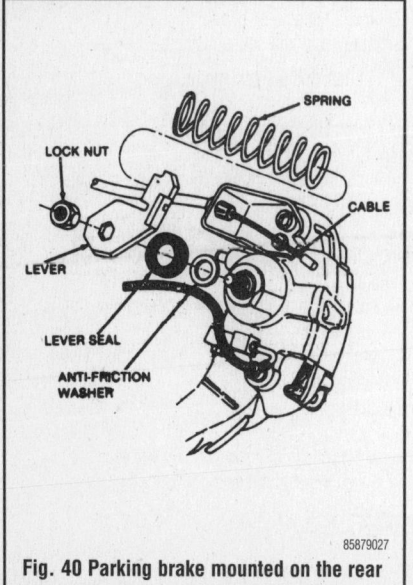

85879027

Fig. 40 Parking brake mounted on the rear disc brake caliper—1967–85 vehicles

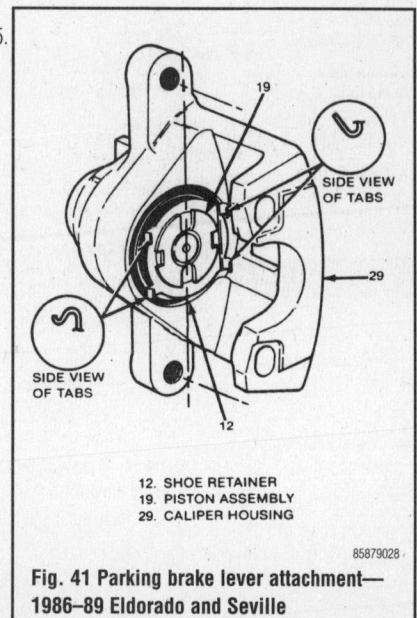

12. SHOE RETAINER
19. PISTON ASSEMBLY
29. CALIPER HOUSING

85879028

Fig. 41 Parking brake lever attachment—1986–89 Eldorado and Seville

10. OUTBOARD SHOE & LINING
11. INBOARD SHOE & LINING
18. TWO-WAY CHECK VALVE
29. CALIPER
31. WEAR SENSOR

85879029

Fig. 42 Rear brake pad assembly—1986–89 Eldorado and Seville

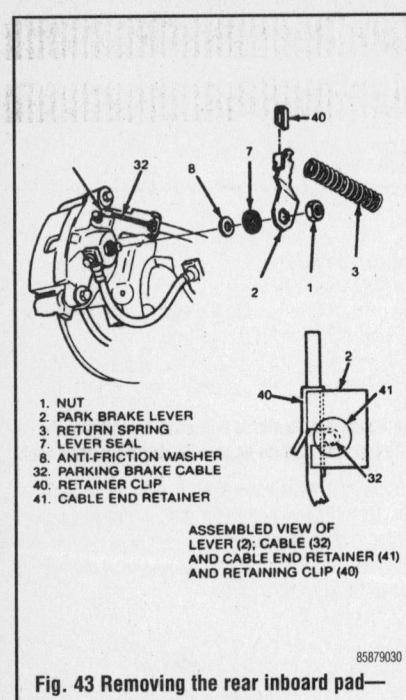

1. NUT
2. PARK BRAKE LEVER
3. RETURN SPRING
7. LEVER SEAL
8. ANTI-FRICTION WASHER
32. PARKING BRAKE CABLE
40. RETAINER CLIP
41. CABLE END RETAINER

ASSEMBLED VIEW OF
LEVER (2); CABLE (32)
AND CABLE END RETAINER (41)
AND RETAINING CLIP (40)

Fig. 43 Removing the rear inboard pad—1986–89 Eldorado and Seville

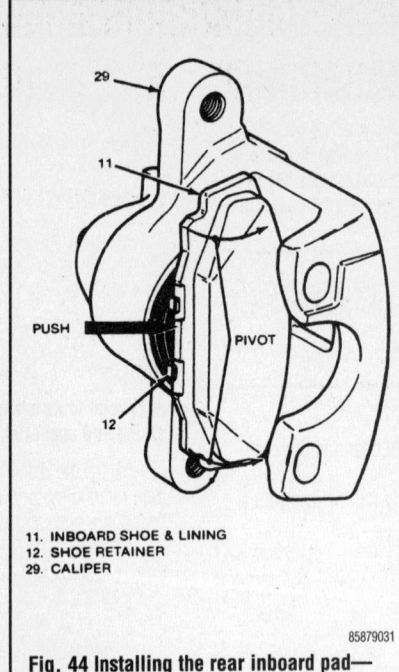
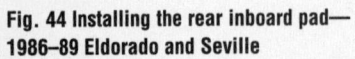

11. INBOARD SHOE & LINING
12. SHOE RETAINER
29. CALIPER

Fig. 44 Installing the rear inboard pad—1986–89 Eldorado and Seville

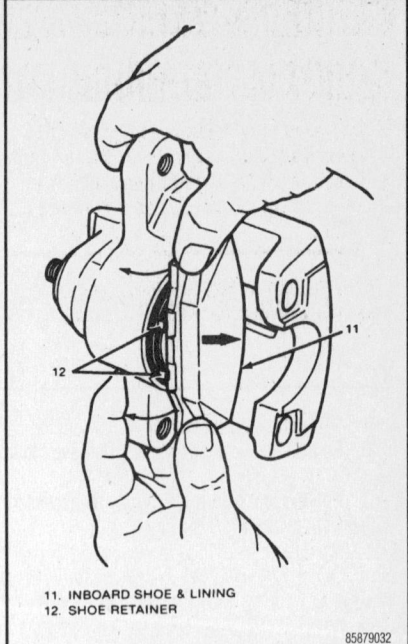

11. INBOARD SHOE & LINING
12. SHOE RETAINER

Fig. 45 Positioning the piston and pad retainer—1986–89 Eldorado and Seville

From the inside of the caliper, press on the edge of the inboard brake shoe and tilt it outward so that it is released from the shoe retainer.

6. Remove the flexible two way check valve from the end of the piston assembly with a small screwdriver.

➡️**If new shoes and linings are to be installed, remove the parking brake lever and bottom the piston in the caliper bore as shown in the accompanying illustration.**

To install:

7. Lubricate a new two way check valve with silicone fluid and press it into the end of the piston.

8. Install the inboard brake shoe. Make sure that the shoe retainer and the piston are positioned right. The tabs on the retainer are different; rotate the retainer into position if necessary. The buttons on the backing of the shoe must engage the larger, D-shaped notches in the piston. The piston will be properly aligned when the larger notches are aligned with the caliper mounting bolt holes as shown. Engage the inboard edge of the shoe with the straight tabs on the retainer, press downward and snap the shoe under the S-shaped tabs.

9. Install the outboard brake shoe. The shoe is properly installed when the wear sensor is at the trailing edge of the shoe during forward rotation.

10. Be sure to snap both shoe springs into the caliper holes so that the back of the shoe is flat against the caliper.

11. Install the caliper.

12. Bleed the brakes, install the wheels and lower the vehicle.

Brake Caliper

REMOVAL & INSTALLATION

1. Siphon off ⅔ of the brake fluid from the master cylinder.

➡️**The insertion of the thicker replacement pads will push the caliper piston back into its bore and will cause a full master cylinder to overflow.**

2. Raise the rear of the vehicle and support it with safety stands. Remove the wheel and tire assembly.

3. Reinstall two lug nuts to keep the rotor from turning.

4. Remove the retaining clip from the parking brake actuator lever.

5. Disconnect the parking brake cable and spring from the lever.

6. While holding the parking brake lever in place, remove the lock nut. Remove the lever, lever seal and the anti-friction washer.

7. If the caliper is to be overhauled or replaced, remove the bolt attaching the brake line inlet fitting.

8. Remove the caliper mounting bolts and then remove the caliper from the rotor and mounting bracket.

9. Check the lever seal and the anti-friction washer for wear and replace if worn.

10. Check the mounting bolts for any wear or damage, replace if necessary. Check the bolt boots, support bushings and caliper piston boot for any wear, cracking or other damage, replace as necessary.

11. Replace the insulators.

To install:

12. Coat the entire shaft of the caliper mounting bolts with a thin film of silicone grease.

13. Slide the caliper over the rotor and into the mounting bracket. Make sure that the new insulators are in position. Tighten the mounting bolts to 63 ft. lbs. (85 Nm).

14. If you disconnected the inlet fitting, install it and tighten to 32 ft. lbs. (44 Nm). Use two NEW copper washers.

15. Lubricate the parking brake lever seal with silicone grease and then install it and the anti-friction washer.

16. Install the lever onto the actuator screw hex properly. Tighten the nut to 35 ft. lbs. (48 Nm) while holding the lever in position and then rotate the lever back against the stop on the caliper.

17. Install the spring with the damper and then connect the parking brake cable.

18. Install the retaining clip onto the lever so that it prevents the parking brake cable from sliding out of the slot in the lever.

19. Adjust the parking brake cable by tightening the cable at the adjuster until the lever begins to move off the stop on the caliper. Loosen the adjustment just enough so that the lever moves back against the stop. Apply and release the parking brake three times to verify proper adjustment.

20. Remove the two lug nuts and then replace the wheels. Lower the vehicle.

21. Bleed the brake system and recheck the fluid level.

FRONT AND REAR DRUM BRAKES

❊ CAUTION

Brake shoes may contain asbestos which has been determined to be a cancer causing agent. Never clean the brake surfaces with compressed air! Avoid inhaling any dust from any brake surface! When cleaning brake surfaces, use a commercially available brake cleaning fluid.

Brake Drum

REPLACEMENT

1. Raise and support the car.
2. Remove the wheel or wheels. Remove the front wheel bearings, if necessary.
3. Pull the brake drum off. It may be necessary to gently tap the rear edges of the drum to start it off the studs.
4. If extreme resistance to removal is encountered, it will be necessary to retract the adjusting screw. Knock out the access hole in the brake drum and turn the adjuster to retract the linings away from the drum.
5. Install a replacement hole cover before reinstalling drum.
6. Install the drums in the same position on the hub as removed. Adjust front wheel bearings, if necessary.

INSPECTION

1. Check the drums for any cracks, scores, grooves, or an out-of-round condition. Replace if cracked. Slight scores can be removed with fine emery cloth while extensive scoring requires turning the drum on a lathe.
2. Never have a drum turned more than 0.060 in. (1.524mm).

Brake Shoes

REMOVAL & INSTALLATION

◆ See Figures 46 thru 62

1. Raise the car and support it on jackstands.
2. Slacken the parking brake cable.
3. Remove the rear wheel and brake drum. The front wheel and drum may be removed as a unit by removing the spindle nut and cotter pin.
4. Free the brake shoe return springs, actuator pull-back spring, hold-down pins and springs, along with the actuator assembly.

➡Special tools available from auto supply stores will ease removal of the spring and anchor pin, but the job may still be done with common hand tools.

5. On the rear wheels, disconnect the adjusting mechanism and spring, then remove the primary shoe. The primary shoe has a shorter lining than the secondary and is mounted at the front of the wheel.
6. Disconnect the parking brake lever from the secondary shoe and remove the shoe. Front wheel shoes may be removed together.

To install:
7. Clean and inspect all brake parts.
8. Check the wheel cylinders for seal condition and leaking.
9. Repack wheel bearings and replace the seals.
10. Inspect the replacement shoes for nicks or burrs, lubricate the backing plate contact points, brake cable and levers, and adjusting screws and then assemble.
11. Make sure that the right and left-hand adjusting screws are not mixed. You can prevent this by working on one side at a time. This will also provide you with a reference for reassembly. The star wheel should be nearest to the secondary shoe when correctly installed.
12. Reverse all removal procedures. When completed, make an initial adjustment as previously described.

➡Maintenance procedures for the metallic lining option are the same as those for standard linings. Do not substitute these linings in standard drums, unless they have been honed to a 20 micro-inch finish and equipped with special heat-resistant springs.

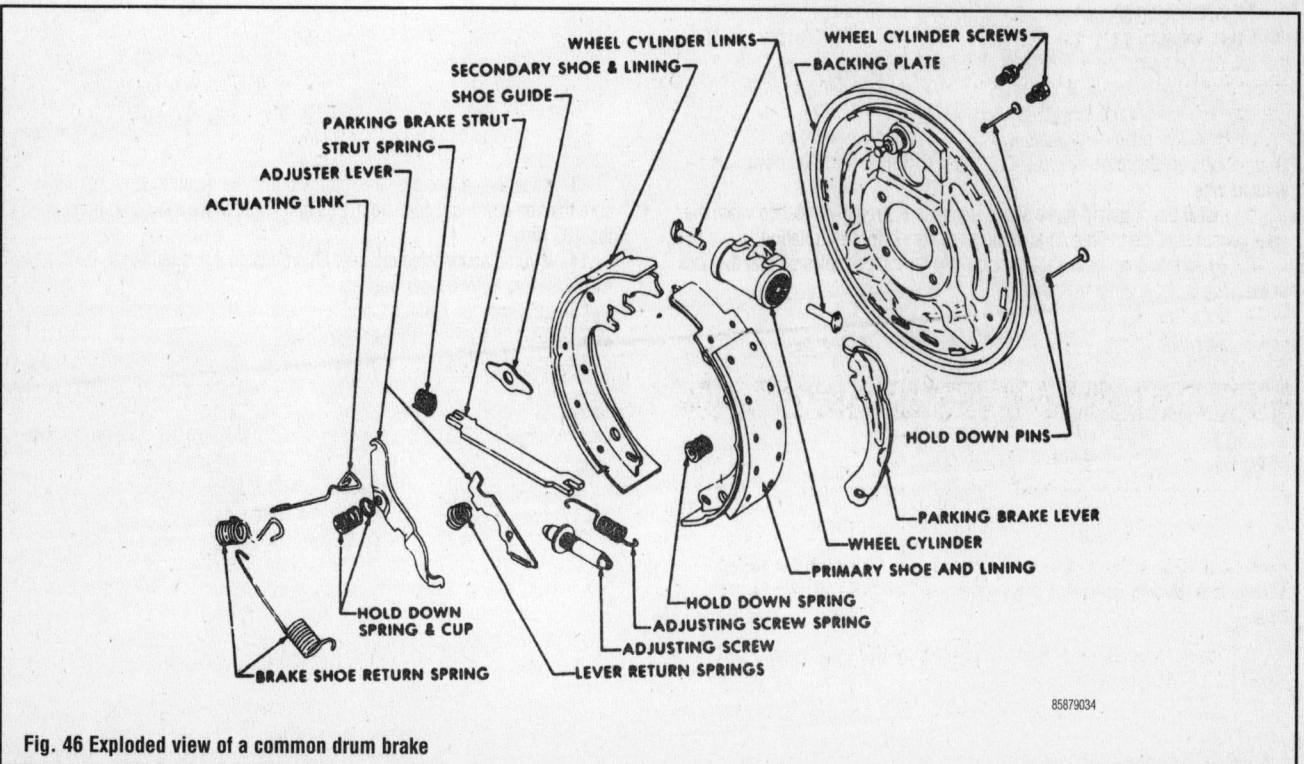

WHEEL CYLINDER LINKS
WHEEL CYLINDER SCREWS
SECONDARY SHOE & LINING
BACKING PLATE
SHOE GUIDE
PARKING BRAKE STRUT
STRUT SPRING
ADJUSTER LEVER
ACTUATING LINK
HOLD DOWN PINS
PARKING BRAKE LEVER
WHEEL CYLINDER
PRIMARY SHOE AND LINING
HOLD DOWN SPRING & CUP
HOLD DOWN SPRING
ADJUSTING SCREW SPRING
ADJUSTING SCREW
LEVER RETURN SPRINGS
BRAKE SHOE RETURN SPRING

85879034

Fig. 46 Exploded view of a common drum brake

Fig. 47 Removing the brake drum

Fig. 48 View of a drum brake system

Fig. 49 Cleaning the brake shoes before removal

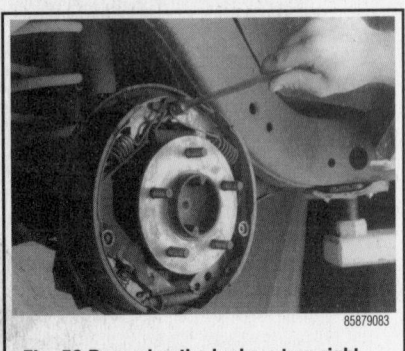

Fig. 50 Removing the brake return right spring with special brake tool

Fig. 51 Removing the brake return spring

Fig. 52 Removing the brake return left spring with special brake tool

Fig. 53 Removing the brake self-adjuster actuating link

Fig. 54 Removing the brake shoe guide

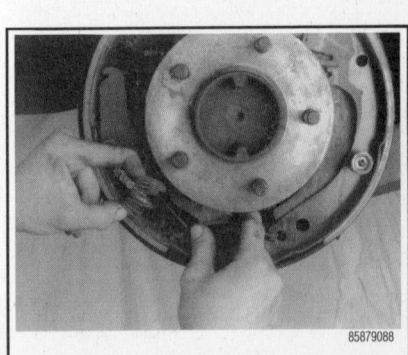

Fig. 55 Removing the brake self-adjuster return spring

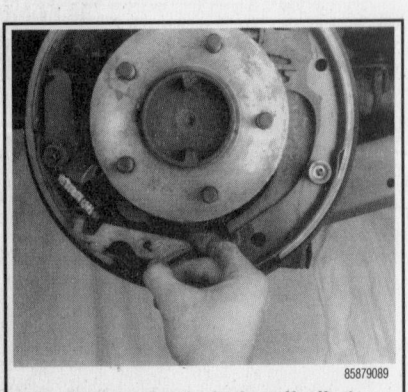

Fig. 56 Removing the brake self-adjuster lever

Fig. 57 Removing the brake hold-down spring

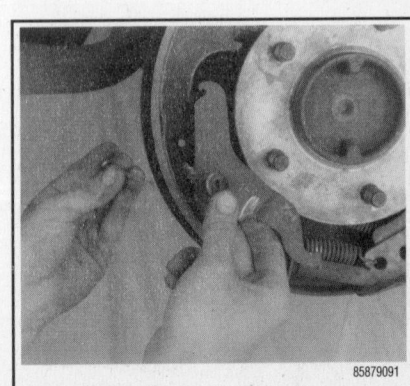

Fig. 58 Removing the brake hold-down spring and cup

Fig. 59 Removing the brake shoes

Fig. 60 Removing the parking brake strut

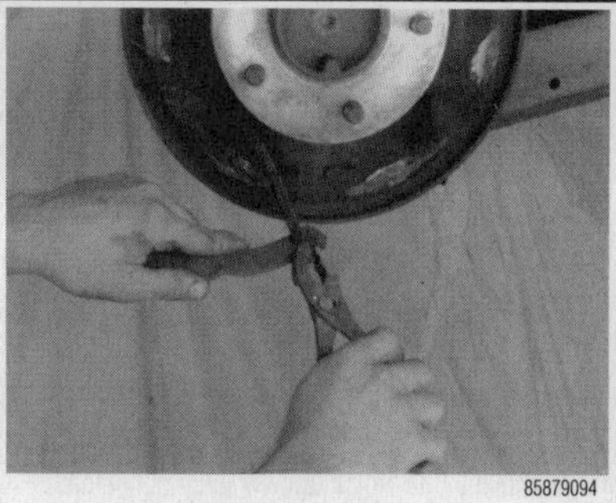

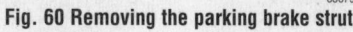

Fig. 61 Removing the parking brake cable from the parking brake lever

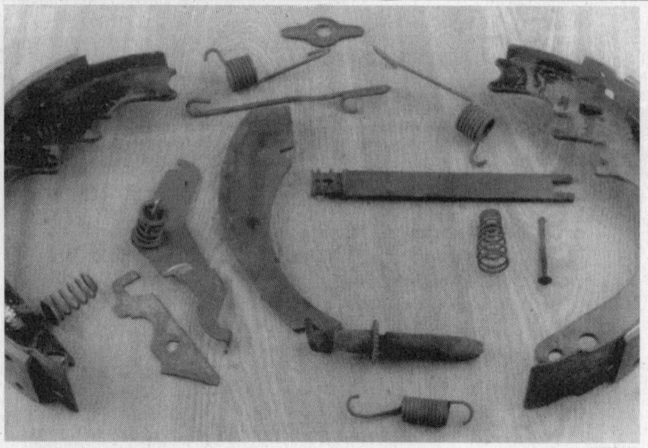

Fig. 62 View of the brake shoes, brake springs and hardware

Wheel Cylinders

REMOVAL & INSTALLATION

▶ **See Figures 63 thru 68**

1. Clean away all dirt, crud and foreign material from around wheel cylinder. It is important that dirt be kept away from the brake line when the cylinder is disconnected.

2. Disconnect the inlet tube line.

3. Wheel cylinders are retained by two types of fasteners. One type uses a round retainer with locking clips, which attaches to the wheel cylinder on the back side of the brake backing plate. The other type simply uses two bolts, which screw into the wheel cylinder from the back side of the backing plate.

4. To remove the round retainer-type cylinders, insert two awls or pins into the access slots between the wheel cylinder pilot and the retainer locking tabs. Bend both tabs away simultaneously. The wheel cylinder can be removed, as the retainer is released.

Fig. 63 Removing the wheel cylinder retaining bolts

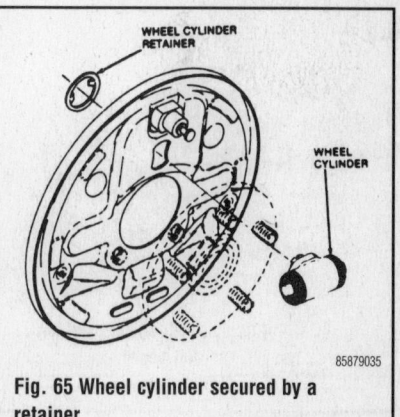

Fig. 64 Removing the wheel cylinder

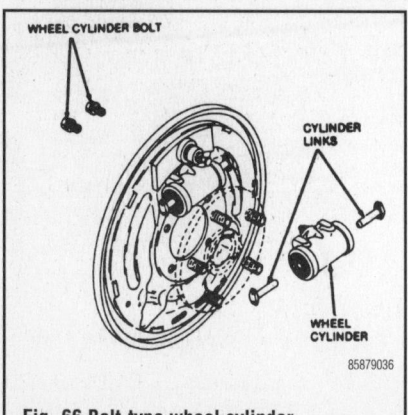

Fig. 65 Wheel cylinder secured by a retainer

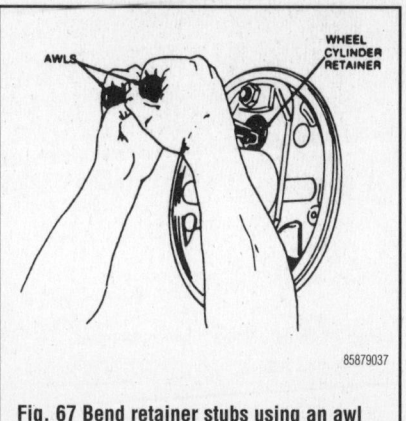

Fig. 66 Bolt-type wheel cylinder

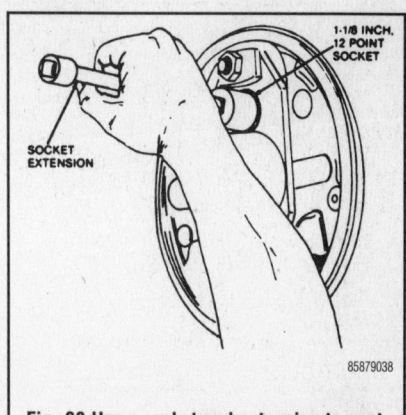

Fig. 67 Bend retainer stubs using an awl

Fig. 68 Use a socket and extension to seat

5. To remove bolted cylinders, loosen and remove the retaining bolts from the back side of the backing plate, then remove the cylinder.

6. Installation is the reverse of the removal procedures. To install the retainer-type cylinder, position the wheel cylinder and hold it in place, then drive the retainer into place using a socket. Bleed and adjust the brake system.

OVERHAUL

♦ **See Figures 69 thru 78**

Wheel cylinder overhaul kits may be available, but often at little or no savings over a reconditioned wheel cylinder. It often makes sense with these components to substitute a new or reconditioned part instead of attempting an overhaul.

If no replacement is available, or you would prefer to overhaul your wheel cylinders, the following procedure may be used. When rebuilding and

installing wheel cylinders, avoid getting any contaminants into the system. Always use clean, new, high quality brake fluid. If dirty or improper fluid has been used, it will be necessary to drain the entire system, flush the system with proper brake fluid, replace all rubber components, then refill and bleed the system.

1. Remove the wheel cylinder from the vehicle and place on a clean workbench.

2. First remove and discard the old rubber boots, then withdraw the pistons. Piston cylinders are equipped with seals and a spring assembly, all located behind the pistons in the cylinder bore.

3. Remove the remaining inner components, seals and spring assembly. Compressed air may be useful in removing these components. If no compressed air is available, be VERY careful not to score the wheel cylinder bore when removing parts from it. Discard all components for which replacements were supplied in the rebuild kit.

4. Wash the cylinder and metal parts in denatured alcohol or clean brake fluid.

✲✲ WARNING

Never use a mineral-based solvent such as gasoline, kerosene or paint thinner for cleaning purposes. These solvents will swell rubber components and quickly deteriorate them.

5. Allow the parts to air dry or use compressed air. Do not use rags for cleaning, since lint will remain in the cylinder bore.

6. Inspect the piston and replace it if it shows scratches.

7. Lubricate the cylinder bore and seals using clean brake fluid.

8. Position the spring assembly.

9. Install the inner seals, then the pistons.

10. Insert the new boots into the counterbores by hand. Do not lubricate the boots.

11. Install the wheel cylinder.

Fig. 69 Remove the outer boots from the wheel cylinder

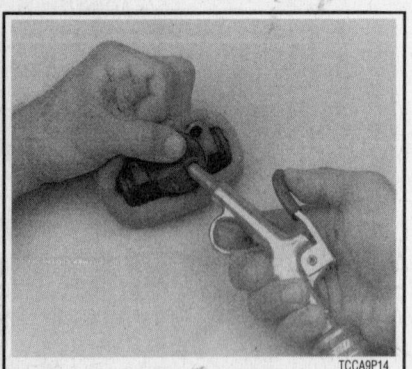
Fig. 70 Compressed air can be used to remove the pistons and seals

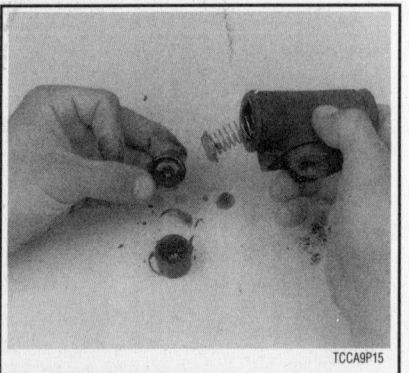
Fig. 71 Remove the pistons, cup seals and spring from the cylinder

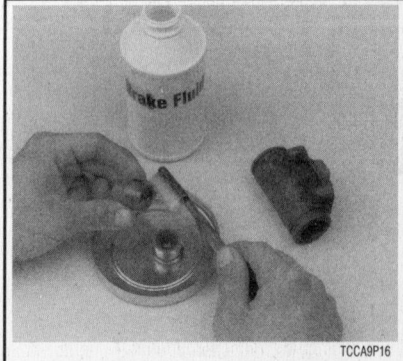
Fig. 72 Use brake fluid and a soft brush to clean the pistons . . .

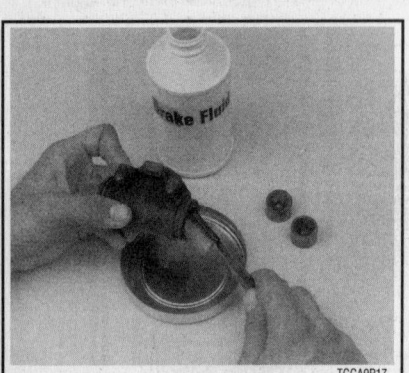
Fig. 73 . . . and the bore of the wheel cylinder

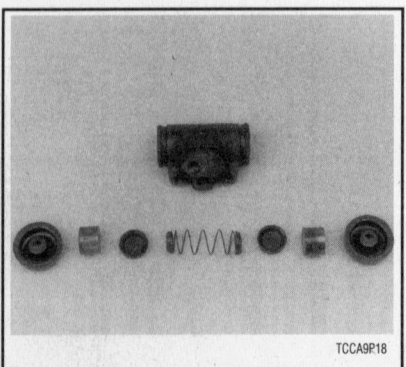
Fig. 74 Once cleaned and inspected, the wheel cylinder is ready for assembly

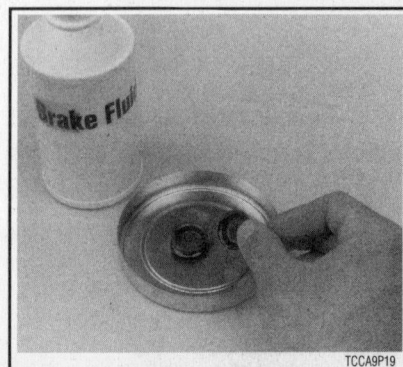
Fig. 75 Lubricate the cup seals with brake fluid

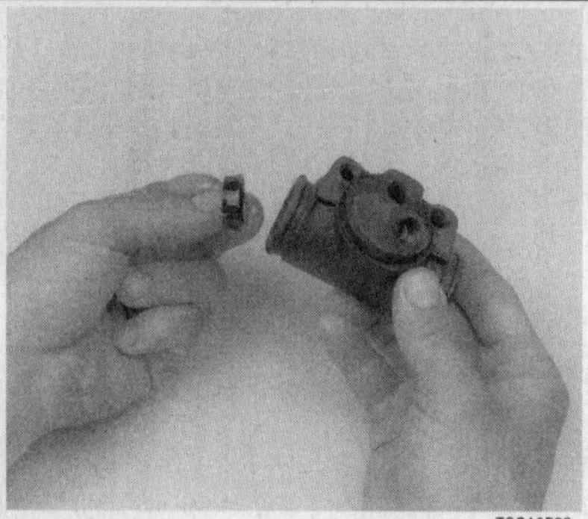

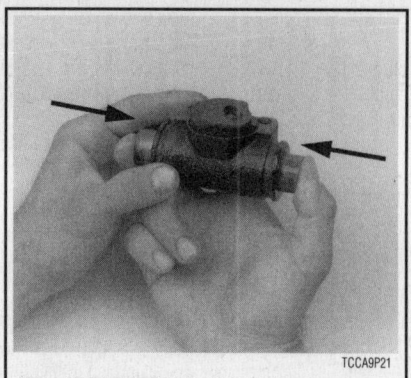

Fig. 76 Install the spring, then the cup seals in the bore

TCCA9P20

Fig. 77 Lightly lubricate the pistons, then install them

TCCA9P21

Fig. 78 The boots can now be installed over the wheel cylinder ends

TCCA9P22

ANTI-LOCK BRAKE SYSTEM

General Information

The Anti-Lock Brake System (ABS) used on the 1988–89 models works on all 4 wheels. A combination of wheel speed sensors and a microprocessor can determine when a wheel is about to lock-up and adjust the brake pressure to maintain better braking. This system helps the driver maintain the control of the vehicle under heavy braking conditions.

✳✳ CAUTION

Some procedures in this section require that hydraulic lines, hoses and fitting be disconnected for inspection or testing purposes. Before disconnecting any hydraulic lines, hoses or fittings, BE SURE THAT THE ACCUMULATOR IS FULLY DEPRESSURIZED as described in this section. Failure to depressurize the hydraulic accumulator may result in personal injury!

SYSTEM OPERATIONS

Normal and Anti-Lock Braking

Under normal driving conditions the Anti-Lock brake system functions the same as a standard brake system. However, during the detection of wheel lock-up a slight bump or a kick-back will be felt in the brake pedal. This bump felt in the pedal will be followed by a series of short pulsation's which occur in rapid succession. The brake pedal pulsations will continue until there is no longer a need for the anti-lock function or until the car is stopped. A slight chirping noise may be heard during brake applications with anti-lock. This noise is normal and indicates that the anti-lock system is being used. When the anti-lock system is being used, the brake pedal may rise even as the brakes are being applied. This is normal. Maintaining a constant force on the pedal will provide the shortest stopping distance.

Anti-Lock Warning Light

Vehicles equipped with the Anti-Lock Brake System (ABS) will have an amber warning light in the instrument panel marked "ANTI-LOCK". This warning light will illuminate if a malfunction in the anti-lock brake system is detected by the electronic controller. In case of an electronic malfunction, the controller will turn on the "ANTI-LOCK" warning light and shut-down the anti-lock braking function. If the "ANTI-LOCK" warning light and the red "BRAKE" warning light come on at the same time, there may be something wrong with the hydraulic brake system. If ONLY the "ANTI-LOCK" light is on, normal braking with full assist is operational.

The "ANTI-LOCK" light will turn on during the starting of the engine and will usually stay on for approximately 3 seconds after the ignition switch is returned to the **RUN** position. In some cases the "ANTI-LOCK" light may stay on as long as 30 seconds. This may be normal operation. If the light stays on longer than 30 seconds after starting the engine, or comes on and stays on while driving, the brake system should be inspected for a malfunction.

Brake System Warning Light

If a condition in the brake system which reduces the braking ability, the driver will be warned by a "BRAKE" warning light which will illuminate on the instrument panel cluster (IPC). On all models, the "BRAKE" light is controlled by inputs to the Body Computer Module (BCM). When necessary, the BCM utilizes serial data communication to the command the IPC to turn on the "BRAKE" light. This occurs when:
- Parking brake is not fully released
- Low brake fluid
- Low accumulator pressure
- Instrument panel cluster segment check

SYSTEM COMPONENTS

▶ See Figures 79 thru 84

The Anti-Lock brake system consists of a pump motor assembly, fluid accumulator, pressure switch, fluid reservoir with an integral filter, hydraulic booster/master cylinder, 4 wheel speed sensors, Electronic Brake Control Module (EBCM), and a valve block assembly. A wiring harness with specific fuses and relays connects the major system components to the EBCM which controls the Anti-Lock brake system.

Electronic Brake Control Module

The EBCM microcomputer monitors the speed of each wheel to determine if any of the wheels are beginning to lock-up. If lock-up of a wheel is detected, the brake pressures are automatically adjusted to provide for maximum braking without wheel lock.

The EBCM is a separate computer used exclusively for control of the Anti-Lock brake system and is located in the trunk compartment on the left wheel-

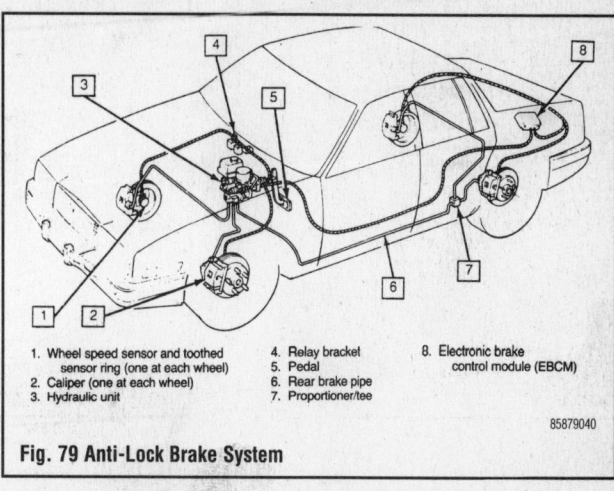

1. Wheel speed sensor and toothed sensor ring (one at each wheel)
2. Caliper (one at each wheel)
3. Hydraulic unit
4. Relay bracket
5. Pedal
6. Rear brake pipe
7. Proportioner/tee
8. Electronic brake control module (EBCM)

85879040

Fig. 79 Anti-Lock Brake System

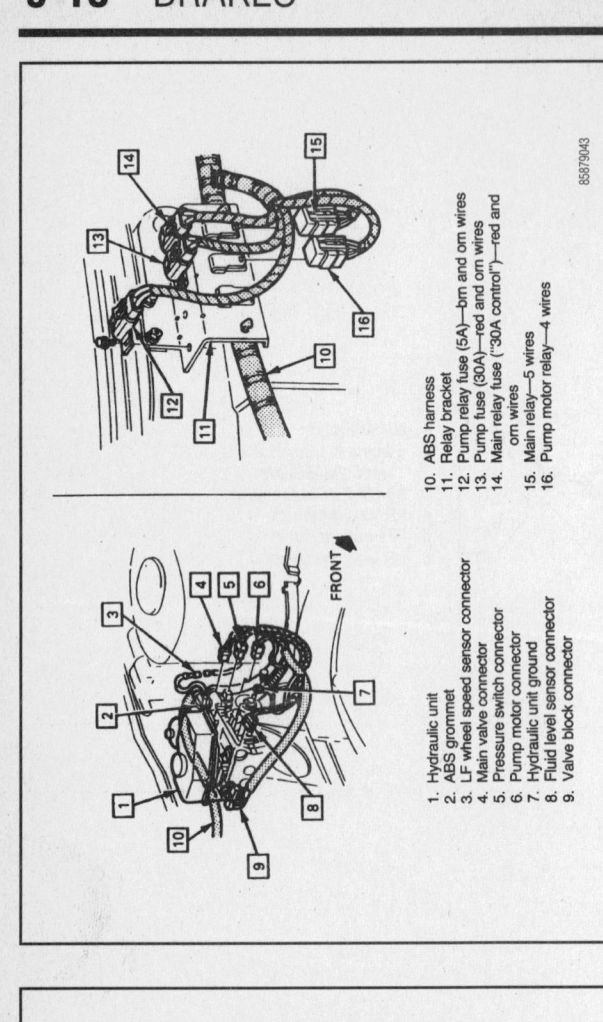

1. Hydraulic unit
2. ABS grommet
3. LF wheel speed sensor connector
4. Main valve connector
5. Pressure switch connector
6. Pump motor connector
7. Hydraulic unit ground
8. Fluid level sensor connector
9. Valve block connector
10. ABS harness
11. Relay bracket
12. Pump relay fuse (5A)—bm and om wires
13. Pump fuse (30A)—red and om wires
14. Main relay fuse ("30A control")—red and om wires
15. Main relay—5 wires
16. Pump motor relay—4 wires

Fig. 82 Underhood components—Anti-Lock Brake System

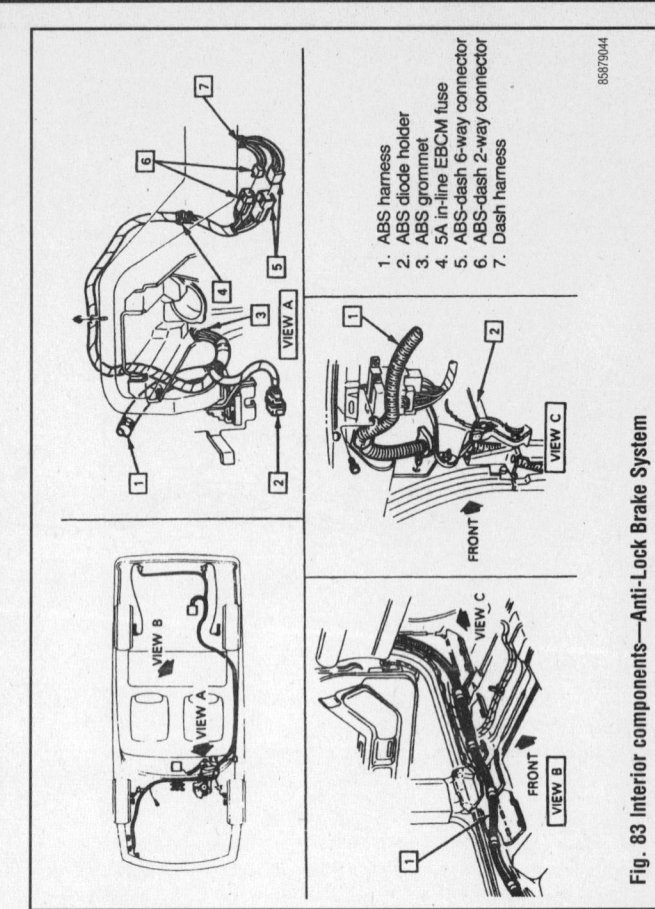

1. ABS harness
2. ABS diode holder
3. ABS grommet
4. 5A in-line EBCM fuse
5. ABS-dash 6-way connector
6. ABS-dash 2-way connector
7. Dash harness

Fig. 83 Interior components—Anti-Lock Brake System

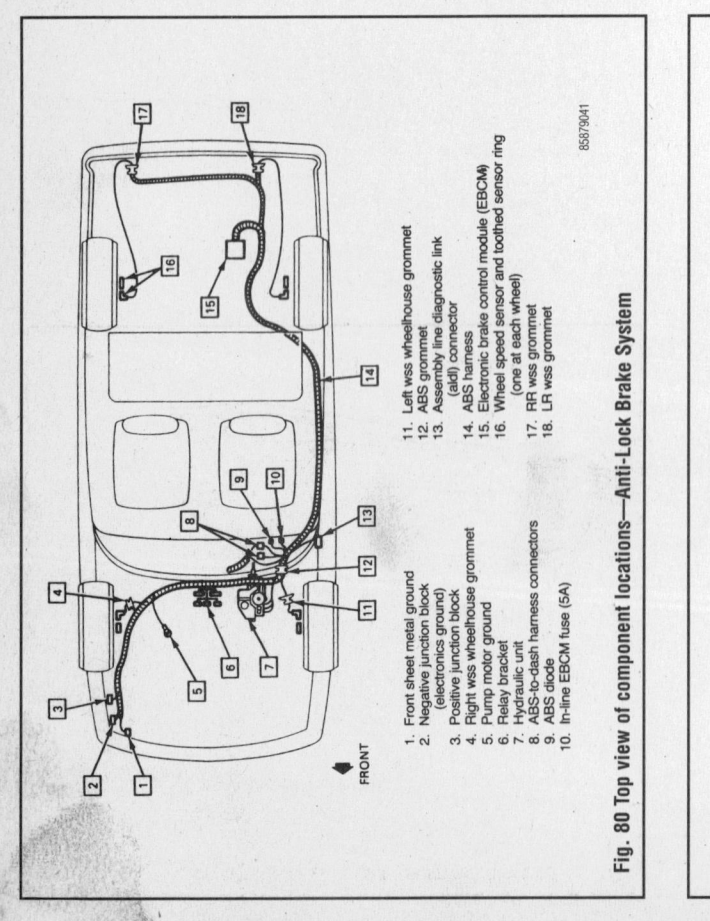

1. Front sheet metal ground
2. Negative junction block (electronics ground)
3. Positive junction block
4. Right wss wheelhouse grommet
5. Pump motor ground
6. Relay bracket
7. Hydraulic unit
8. ABS diode
9. ABS-to-dash harness connectors
10. In-line EBCM fuse (5A)
11. Left wss wheelhouse grommet
12. ABS grommet
13. Assembly line diagnostic link (aldl) connector
14. ABS harness
15. Electronic brake control module (EBCM)
16. Wheel speed sensor and toothed sensor ring (one at each wheel)
17. RR wss grommet
18. LR wss grommet

Fig. 80 Top view of component locations—Anti-Lock Brake System

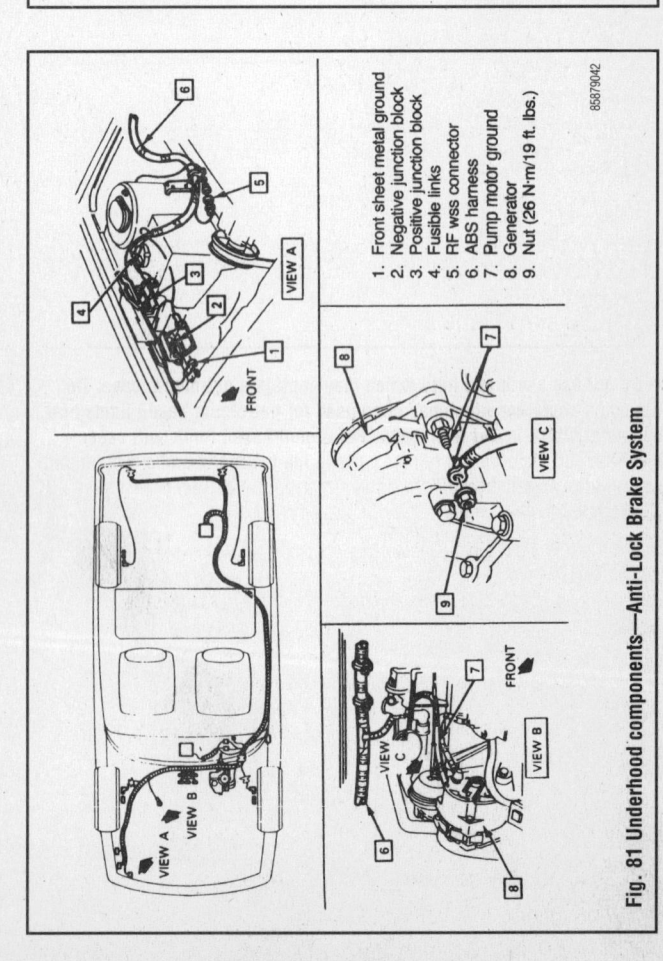

1. Front sheet metal ground
2. Negative junction block
3. Positive junction block
4. Fusible links
5. RF wss connector
6. ABS harness
7. Pump motor ground
8. Generator
9. Nut (26 N·m/19 ft. lbs.)

Fig. 81 Underhood components—Anti-Lock Brake System

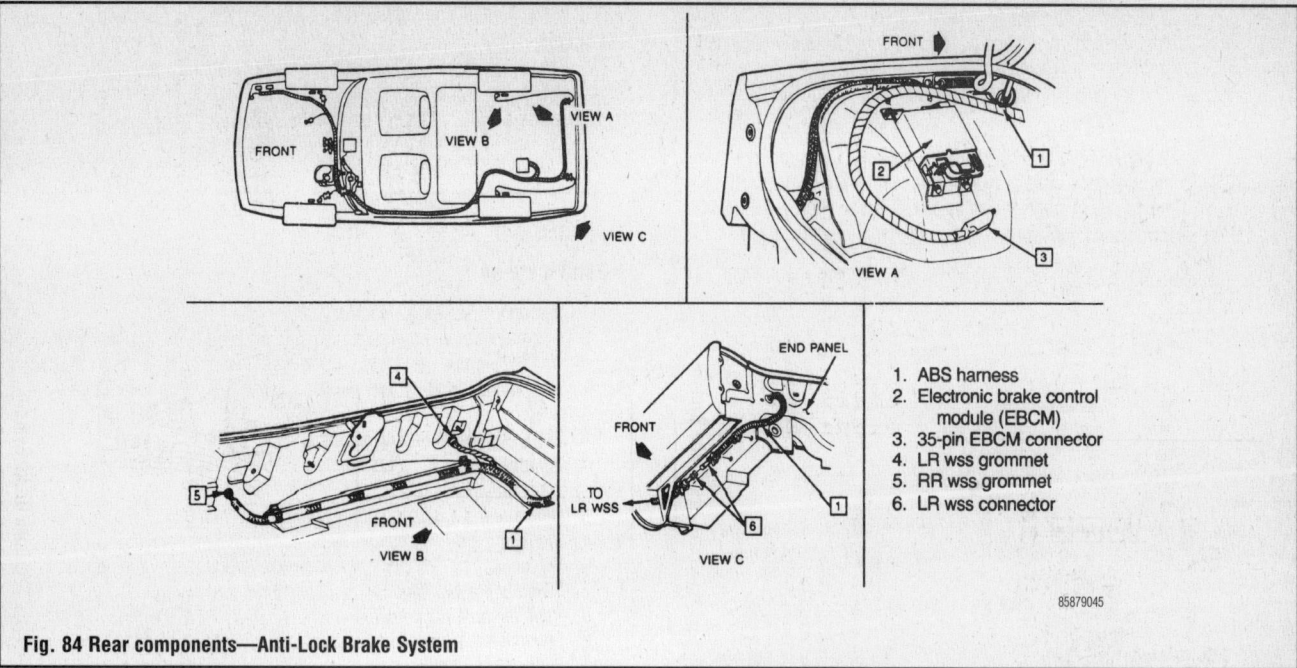

Fig. 84 Rear components—Anti-Lock Brake System

1. ABS harness
2. Electronic brake control module (EBCM)
3. 35-pin EBCM connector
4. LR wss grommet
5. RR wss grommet
6. LR wss connector

house. The EBCM provides outputs to the hydraulic unit and the "ANTI-LOCK" warning light based on the controller logic and the EBCM inputs.

Hydraulic Unit

The anti-lock brake system utilizes an integral hydraulic unit, mounted on the cowl, which functions as brake booster and master cylinder. In addition, the hydraulic unit provides brake fluid pressure modulation for each of the individual wheel circuits as required during anti-lock braking. The hydraulic unit consists of several independent components:

- Booster/master cylinder assembly
- Valve block
- Hydraulic accumulator
- Fluid level sensor
- Pump/motor assembly
- Pressure switch

Component Replacement

CHECKING AND ADDING BRAKE FLUID

➡ **Do not use any brake fluid which may contain a petroleum base. Do not use a container which has been used for petroleum based fluids or a container which is wet with water. Petroleum based fluids will cause swelling and distortion of rubber parts in the hydraulic brake system and water will mix with brake fluid, lowering the fluid boiling point. Keep all fluid containers capped to prevent contamination.**

The plastic fluid reservoir, on the ABS hydraulic unit, has a label marking the proper "FULL" level. The hydraulic accumulator must be depressurized when checking the brake fluid level. Use the following procedure to check the brake fluid level.

1. With the ignition switch **OFF**, depressurize the hydraulic accumulator by applying the brake pedal approximately 25 times using a pedal force of approximately 50 lbs. (222 N). A noticeable change in the pedal feel will occur when the accumulator is depressurized. Continue to apply the pedal several times after this change in pedal feel occurs.
2. Inspect the fluid level.
3. Thoroughly clean the reservoir cap and surrounding area prior to cap removal to avoid contamination of the reservoir.
4. Fill the reservoir to the "FULL" mark using DOT–3 brake fluid. Use of DOT–5 silicone fluid is not allowed, as internal damage to the pump components may result.

BLEEDING BRAKE SYSTEM

Pressure Bleeding

◆ **See Figure 85**

FRONT BRAKES

1. With the ignition **OFF**, depressurize the hydraulic accumulator by pumping the brake pedal a minimum of 25 times using a pedal force of approximately 50 lbs. (222 N).
2. Remove the reservoir cap.
3. Install the pressure bleeder adapter J–35789 or equivalent.
4. Attach the bleeder equipment to bleeder adapter. Charge the pressure bleeder to approximately 20 psi (138 kPa).
5. Connect a transparent hose to either front caliper bleed screw. Submerge the free end of the hose in a clear glass container which is partially filled with clean brake fluid.
6. With the pressure bleeder turned on, open the caliper bleed screw ½–¾ turn and allow the fluid to flow into the container. Leave the caliper bleed screw open until clear, bubble-free fluid flows from the hose.

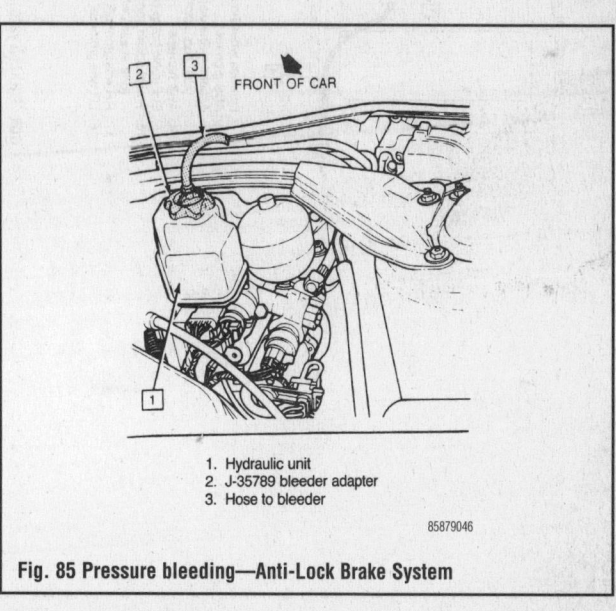

1. Hydraulic unit
2. J-35789 bleeder adapter
3. Hose to bleeder

Fig. 85 Pressure bleeding—Anti-Lock Brake System

7. Repeat Step 6 at the other front caliper.

8. After bleeding at both front calipers, remove the pressure bleeding equipment and bleeder adapter.

9. Remove excess brake fluid from the reservoir to bring the fluid level to the "FULL" mark.

➡**Do not remove brake fluid from the reservoir using a syringe or other instrument which is contaminated with water, petroleum based fluids or any other foreign material. Contamination of the brake fluid may result in impaired system operation, property damage or personal injury.**

10. Install the reservoir cap. Turn the ignition **ON** and allow the pump to charge the accumulator.

REAR BRAKES

1. Turn the ignition **ON** and allow the system to charge. (The pump motor will stop when the system is charged.)

2. Attach a bleeder hose to 1 rear bleeder valve. Submerge the other end of the hose in a container of clean brake fluid.

3. With the ignition **ON**, have an assistant slightly depress the brake pedal and hold it.

4. Open the caliper bleed screw ½–¾ turn and allow brake fluid to flow into the container. Leave the caliper bleed screw open until it is clear, bubble-free fluid flows from the hose.

5. When air-free brake fluid flows from the bleeder hose, close the caliper bleed screw.

6. Check the brake fluid level periodically during the bleeding procedure. Do not allow the fluid level to drop below the reservoir seam line.

7. Repeat Steps 2–5 on the other rear bleeder valve.

8. After bleeding is completed, depressurize the accumulator and fill the fluid reservoir to the "FULL" mark.

❊❊ CAUTION

Do not move the vehicle until a firm brake pedal is obtained. Failure to obtain a firm brake pedal may result in a brake system failure and personal injury.

Manual Bleeding

The front hydraulic system may be manually bled using conventional bleeding methods. The rear brakes can not be bled using conventional methods and should be pressure bled.

1. With the ignition **OFF**, depressurize the hydraulic accumulator by pumping the brake pedal a minimum of 25 times using a pedal force of approximately 50 lbs. (222 N).

❊❊ CAUTION

Failure to depressurize the hydraulic accumulator, prior to performing this operation may result in personal injury and/or damage to the painted surfaces!

2. Connect a transparent hose to the caliper bleed screw. Submerge the free end of the hose in a clear glass container, which is partially filled with clean, fresh brake fluid.

3. Slowly pump the brake pedal several times, using full strokes of the pedal and allowing approximately 5 seconds between pedal strokes. After 2 or 3 strokes, continue to hold pressure on the pedal, keeping it at the bottom of its travel.

4. With pressure on the pedal, open the bleed screw ½–¾ turn. Leave bleed screw open until fluid no longer flows from the hose. Tighten the bleed screw and release the pedal.

5. Repeat this procedure until clear, bubble-free fluid flows from the hose.

6. Repeat all steps at each of the calipers.

ADJUSTMENT

Front Wheel Speed Sensor

1. Loosen the front wheel speed sensor mounting bracket bolts so that the bracket is snug to the knuckle but can be moved by hand.

2. Using a feeler gauge, adjust the sensor (between the tip of the sensor and

one of the teeth on the toothed sensor ring) to 0.020 in. (0.50mm) by moving the bracket.

3. Tighten the mounting bracket bolts to 19 ft. lbs. (26 Nm).

4. After tightening the bolts, check the sensor gap to be sure that it was not disturbed while tightening the bracket bolts.

REMOVAL & INSTALLATION

Hydraulic Unit

◗ See Figure 86

1. Disconnect the negative battery cable.

2. Depressurize the accumulator by applying and releasing the brake pedal a minimum of 25 times using approximately 50 lbs. (222 N) force on the pedal. A noticeable change in pedal feel will occur when the accumulator is completely discharged.

3. Label and disconnect all electrical connections to the unit.

4. Remove the pump bolt and move the energy unit to the side to gain access to the brake lines.

5. Disconnect the 3 lines connected to the valve block. Use a second wrench to prevent the line from twisting.

6. Disconnect the line attaching the hydraulic unit to the combination valve.

7. From the inside of the car, disconnect the pushrod from the brake pedal.

8. Push the dust boot forward, past the hex on the pushrod.

9. Separate the pushrod halves by unthreading the 2 pieces.

10. Remove the 2 unit-to-pushrod bracket bolts and remove the hydraulic unit.

➡**The front half of the pushrod will remain locked into the hydraulic unit.**

To install:

11. Position the hydraulic unit to the support bracket.

12. Install the support bracket bolts and torque them to 37 ft. lbs. (50 Nm).

13. Thread the 2 halves of the pushrod together and tighten.

14. Reposition the dust boot.

15. Connect the line from the combination valve to the hydraulic unit.

16. Connect the 3 lines to the valve block, reposition the energy unit as necessary.

17. Install all the electrical connections to the unit.

18. Connect the negative battery cable.

19. Bleed the brake system.

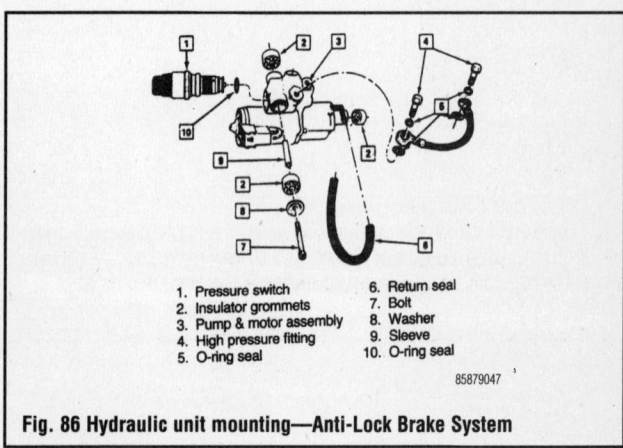

1. Pressure switch	6. Return seal
2. Insulator grommets	7. Bolt
3. Pump & motor assembly	8. Washer
4. High pressure fitting	9. Sleeve
5. O-ring seal	10. O-ring seal

85879047

Fig. 86 Hydraulic unit mounting—Anti-Lock Brake System

Pump and Motor Assembly

◗ See Figure 87

1. Disconnect the negative battery cable.

2. Depressurize the accumulator by applying and releasing the brake pedal a minimum of 25 times using approximately 50 lbs. (222 N) force on the pedal. A noticeable change in pedal feel will occur when the accumulator is completely discharged.

3. Disconnect the electrical connector from the pressure switch and the electric motor. Remove the fluid from the reservoir.

➡**Do not remove brake fluid from the reservoir using a syringe or other instrument which is contaminated with water, petroleum based fluids or**

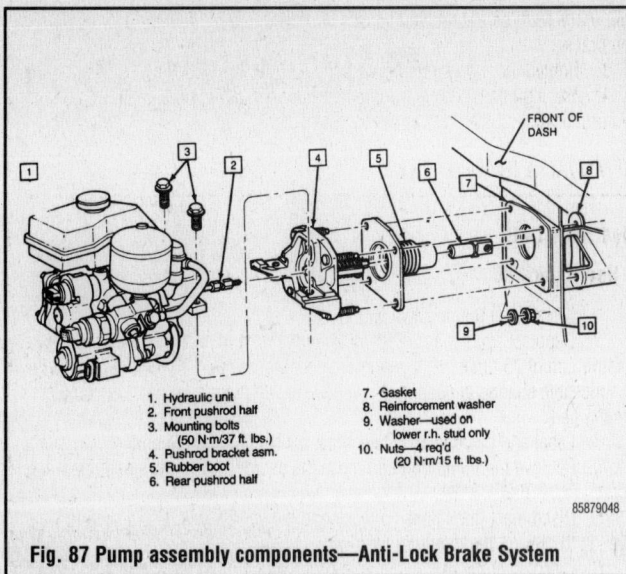

1. Hydraulic unit
2. Front pushrod half
3. Mounting bolts
   (50 N·m/37 ft. lbs.)
4. Pushrod bracket asm.
5. Rubber boot
6. Rear pushrod half
7. Gasket
8. Reinforcement washer
9. Washer—used on
   lower r.h. stud only
10. Nuts—4 req'd
    (20 N·m/15 ft. lbs.)

85879048

Fig. 87 Pump assembly components—Anti-Lock Brake System

any other foreign material. Contamination of the brake fluid may result in impaired system operation, property damage or personal injury.

4. Remove the hydraulic accumulator and O-ring.
5. Disconnect the high pressure hose fitting connected to the pump.
6. Remove the pressure hose assembly and O-rings.
7. Disconnect the wire clip then, pull the return hose fitting out of the pump body.
8. Remove the bolt attaching the pump and motor assembly to the main body.
9. Remove the pump and motor assembly by sliding it off of the locating pin.

➡ **Replace the insulators if damaged or deteriorated.**

To install:
10. Position the pump and motor assembly to the main body.
11. Install the bolt attaching the pump and motor assembly to the main body.
12. Connect the pressure hose assembly.
13. Connect the return hose and fitting into the pump body. Install the wire clip.
14. Install the bolt, O-rings and fitting of the high pressure hose to the pump assembly.
15. Connect the electrical connector to the pump motor.
16. Connect the negative battery cable.

Valve Block Assembly

♦ **See Figure 88**

1. Disconnect the negative battery cable.
2. Depressurize the accumulator by applying and releasing the brake pedal a minimum of 25 times using approximately 50 lbs. (222 N) force on the pedal. A noticeable change in pedal feel will occur when the accumulator is completely discharged.

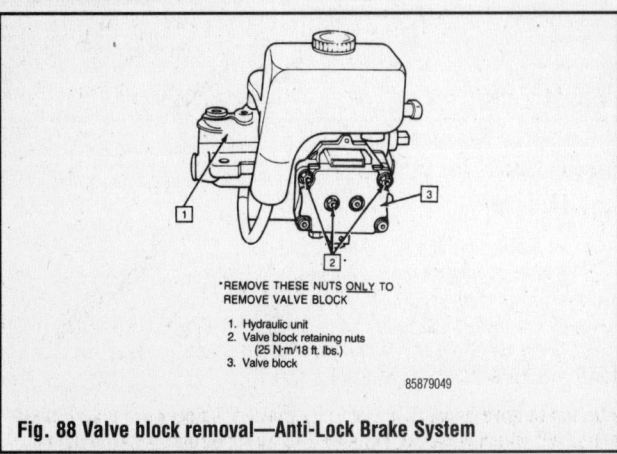

*REMOVE THESE NUTS ONLY TO
REMOVE VALVE BLOCK

1. Hydraulic unit
2. Valve block retaining nuts
   (25 N·m/18 ft. lbs.)
3. Valve block

85879049

Fig. 88 Valve block removal—Anti-Lock Brake System

3. Remove the hydraulic unit.
4. Remove the 3 nuts and washers.
5. Remove the valve block assembly and O-rings by sliding the valve block off of the studs.

To install:
6. Lubricate the O-rings with brake fluid.
7. Install the valve block and O-rings onto the master cylinder body.
8. Install the 3 nuts and washers removed in Step 4.
9. Install the hydraulic unit.
10. Install the negative battery cable.
11. Refill and bleed the system.

Pressure Warning Switch

1. Disconnect the negative battery cable.
2. Depressurize the accumulator by applying and releasing the brake pedal a minimum of 25 times using approximately 50 lbs. (222 N) force on the pedal. A noticeable change in pedal feel will occur when the accumulator is completely discharged.
3. Disconnect the electrical connector from the pressure/warning switch.
4. Remove the pressure/warning switch using special tool No. J–35804.
5. Remove the O-ring from the switch.

To install:
6. Lubricate the O-ring with clean brake fluid.
7. Install the O-ring on the pressure/warning switch.
8. Install the switch and tighten to 15 ft. lbs. (20 Nm) using special tool No. J–35804.
9. Connect the electrical connector to the pressure/warning switch.
10. Connect the negative battery cable.
11. Turn the ignition to the **ON** position. The "Brake" light should go out within 30 seconds and the pump motor should turn off within 40 seconds.
12. Check for leakage around the switch.

Hydraulic Accumulator

1. Disconnect the negative battery cable.
2. Depressurize the accumulator by applying and releasing the brake pedal a minimum of 25 times using approximately 50 lbs. (222 N) force on the pedal. A noticeable change in pedal feel will occur when the accumulator is completely discharged.
3. Unscrew the hydraulic accumulator from the hydraulic unit.
4. Remove the O-ring from the accumulator.

To install:
5. Lubricate a new O-ring with clean brake fluid and install it on the accumulator.
6. Install the accumulator and tighten to 30 ft. lbs. (40 Nm).
7. Connect the negative battery cable.
8. Turn the ignition to the **ON** position. The "Brake" light should go out within 30 seconds and the pump motor should turn off within 40 seconds.
9. Check for leakage around the accumulator.

Brake Fluid Reservoir and Seal

1. Disconnect the negative battery cable.
2. Depressurize the accumulator by applying and releasing the brake pedal a minimum of 25 times using approximately 50 lbs. (222 N) force on the pedal. A noticeable change in pedal feel will occur when the accumulator is completely discharged.
3. Remove the return hose and drain the brake fluid into a container and discard the fluid.
4. Disconnect the electrical connectors from the fluid level sensor assembly.
5. Remove the reservoir to block mounting bolt.
6. Remove the reservoir by carefully prying between the reservoir and the master cylinder.

To install:
7. Lubricate the seals with clean brake fluid.
8. Install the seals and O-ring into the master cylinder body.
9. Push the reservoir into the master cylinder until it is fully seated.
10. Install the reservoir to valve block mounting bracket bolt.
11. Connect the electrical connectors to the reservoir cap.
12. Connect the sump hose to the reservoir.
13. Refill the reservoir with clean brake fluid.
14. Connect the negative battery cable.

Wheel Speed Sensor

FRONT BRAKES

▶ See Figure 89

1. Disconnect the sensor connector from the underhood area near the strut tower.
2. Raise the vehicle and support on safety stands.
3. Disengage the sensor cable grommet from the wheel house pass-through hose and remove the sensor cable from the retaining brackets.
4. To remove the sensor (without the mounting bracket):
   a. Remove the sensor mounting bolt.
   b. Remove the sensor from the vehicle.
5. To remove the sensor (with the mounting bracket):
   a. Remove the mounting bracket bolts.
   b. Remove the assembly from the vehicle.
   c. If necessary, remove the sensor from the mounting bracket.

To install:
6. If the mounting bracket was removed from the knuckle, install the mounting bracket and bolts. Install the bracket bolts finger tight. Do not tighten at this time.
7. If the sensor was removed from the mounting bracket, thoroughly coat the sensor with anti-corrosion compound (GM P/N 1052856) or equivalent in all areas where the sensor contacts the mounting bracket. Install the sensor in the mounting bracket and tighten to 9 ft. lbs. (12 Nm).

➡**Failure to coat the sensor with anti-corrosion compound prior to installation in the bracket will result in reduced sensor life.**

8. Route the sensor cable and install in the retainers. Install the wheel-house pass-through grommet.

➡**Proper installation of the wheel speed sensor cables is critical to continued system operation. Be sure that the cables are installed in retainers. Failure to install the cables in the retainers may result in contact with moving parts and/or over-extension of the cables, resulting in circuit damage.**

9. If the mounting bracket was loosened or removed, adjust the front sensor gap.
10. Lower the vehicle.
11. Connect the wheel speed sensor connector underhood.

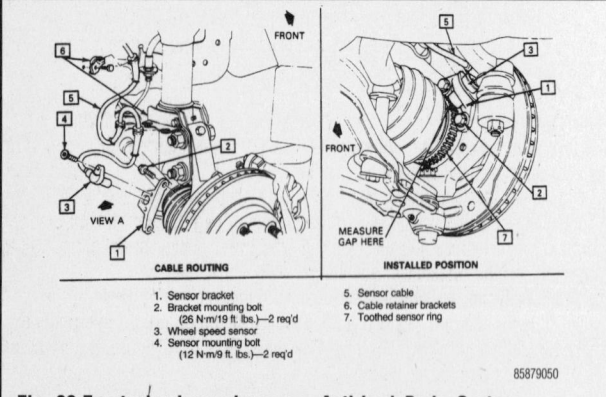

1. Sensor bracket
2. Bracket mounting bolt (26 N·m/19 ft. lbs.)—2 req'd
3. Wheel speed sensor
4. Sensor mounting bolt (12 N·m/9 ft. lbs.)—2 req'd
5. Sensor cable
6. Cable retainer brackets
7. Toothed sensor ring

85879050

Fig. 89 Front wheel speed sensor—Anti-Lock Brake System

REAR BRAKES

▶ See Figure 90

1. Raise the vehicle and support on safety stands.
2. Disconnect the sensor connector and remove the sensor cable from the retainer brackets.
3. Remove the sensor mounting bolt and remove the sensor from the vehicle.
To install:
4. Position the sensor in the knuckle and install the mounting bolt. Tighten mounting bolt to 9 ft. lbs. (12 Nm).
5. Install the wheel speed sensor cable in the retainers.

➡**Proper installation of the wheel speed sensor cables is critical to continued system operation. Be sure that the cables are installed in retainers. Failure to install the cables in the retainers may result in contact with moving parts and/or over-extension of the cables, resulting in circuit damage.**

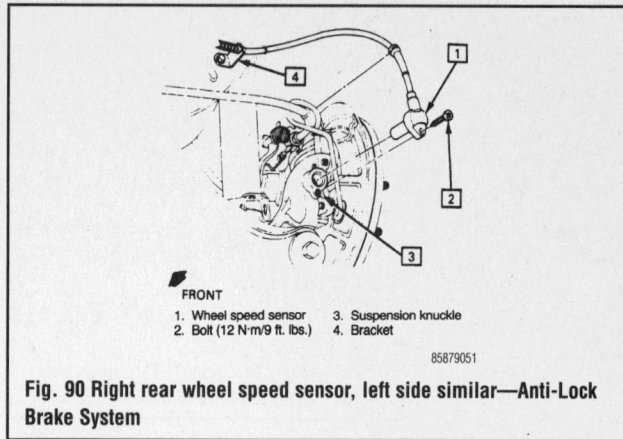

FRONT
1. Wheel speed sensor
2. Bolt (12 N·m/9 ft. lbs.)
3. Suspension knuckle
4. Bracket

85879051

Fig. 90 Right rear wheel speed sensor, left side similar—Anti-Lock Brake System

6. Connect the wheel speed sensor connector.

Diagnosis and Testing

ABS SELF-DIAGNOSIS

The system is equipped with a self-diagnostic capability, which may be used to assist in isolation of the ABS fault. This feature includes trouble codes which could be displayed by the EBCM through flashing of the amber "ANTI-LOCK" light in the instrument panel cluster (IPC). In order to access and understand any ABS trouble code which may be present, it is necessary to enter the ABS diagnostic mode and read the trouble codes.

Displaying ABS Trouble Codes

➡**The EBCM will store any failure codes which set in the non-volatile memory. These codes will remain stored in the EBCM until they are erased. Unplugging the EBCM, disconnecting the battery cables, or turning OFF the ignition switch will not clear the trouble codes from memory.**

Only certain ABS malfunctions will cause the EBCM to store diagnostic trouble codes. Failures which cause the system to set a code will generally involve wheel speed sensors, the main valve or the inlet and outlet valves. Conditions affecting the pump/motor assembly, the accumulator, pressure switch and fluid level sensor will not generally cause an ABS trouble code to set.

The EBCM can display these trouble codes only when a request is made by entering ABS diagnostic mode.

Reading ABS Trouble Codes

▶ See Figures 91, 92 and 93

1. Turn the ignition **ON** and allow the pump to charge the accumulator. If the accumulator is discharged, the "BRAKE" and "ANTI-LOCK" light will remain on for up to 30 seconds.
2. Turn the ignition **OFF**.
3. With the ignition switch **OFF**, place a jumper between the Assembly Line Diagnostic Link (ALDL) terminals **G** and **A**, or simply jumper between ALDL terminal **G** and body ground.
4. Turn the ignition switch to **RUN** and count the "ANTI-LOCK" light flashes. Record the trouble code.

➡**If the light turns on for 4 seconds and then turns off and remains off, no trouble codes are present.**

5. To check for additional trouble codes, leave the ignition switch in **RUN** and disconnect the jumper from the ALDL terminal **G**, then re-install the jumper at ALDL terminal **G**.
6. Repeat Step 5 until no addition trouble codes are displayed.

Clearing ABS Trouble Codes

The ABS trouble codes should not be cleared until repairs are completed. The EBCM will not allow ABS codes to clear unless all the codes have been read.

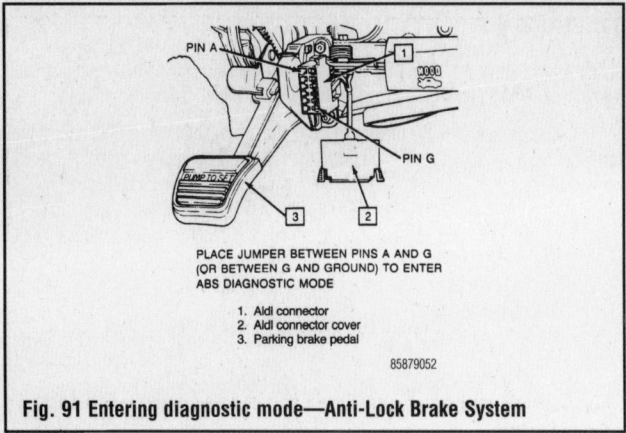

PLACE JUMPER BETWEEN PINS A AND G
(OR BETWEEN G AND GROUND) TO ENTER
ABS DIAGNOSTIC MODE

1. Aldl connector
2. Aldl connector cover
3. Parking brake pedal

85879052

Fig. 91 Entering diagnostic mode—Anti-Lock Brake System

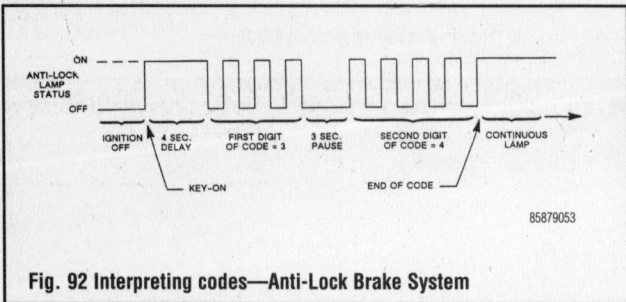

85879053

Fig. 92 Interpreting codes—Anti-Lock Brake System

ABS Code	System	ABS Code	System
11	EBCM	45	2 SENSOR (LF)
12	EBCM	46	2 SENSORS (RF)
21	MAIN VALVE	47	2 SENSORS (REAR)
22	LF INLET VALVE	48	3 SENSORS
23	LF OUTLET VALVE	51	LF OUTLET VALVE
24	RF INLET VALVE	52	RF OUTLET VALVE
25	RF OUTLET VALVE	53	REAR OUTLET VALVE
26	REAR INLET VALVE	54	REAR OUTLET VALVE
27	REAR OUTLET VALVE	55	LF WHEEL SPEED SENSOR
31	LF WHEEL SPEED SENSOR	56	RF WHEEL SPEED SENSOR
32	RF WHEEL SPEED SENSOR	57	RR WHEEL SPEED SENSOR
33	RR WHEEL SPEED SENSOR	58	LR WHEEL SPEED SENSOR
34	LR WHEEL SPEED SENSOR	61	EBCM LOOP CKT
35	LF WHEEL SPEED SENSOR	71	LF OUTLET VALVE
36	RF WHEEL SPEED SENSOR	72	RF OUTLET VALVE
37	RR WHEEL SPEED SENSOR	73	REAR OUTLET VALVE
38	LR WHEEL SPEED SENSOR	74	REAR OUTLET VALVE
41	LF WHEEL SPEED SENSOR	75	LF WHEEL SPEED SENSOR
42	RF WHEEL SPEED SENSOR	76	RF WHEEL SPEED SENSOR
43	RR WHEEL SPEED SENSOR	77	RR WHEEL SPEED SENSOR
44	LR WHEEL SPEED SENSOR	78	LR WHEEL SPEED SENSOR

85879054

Fig. 93 ABS Code Identification

The ABS trouble codes are cleared by driving the vehicle at a speed greater than 18 mph. After attempting to clear the codes, check that all codes are cleared by attempting to read the codes. If the codes did not clear, repeat the read-out procedure and drive the vehicle again at a speed greater than 18 mph.

NOTE ON INTERMITTENTS

As with virtually any electronic system, intermittent failures in the anti-lock brake system may be difficult to accurately diagnose. The ABS trouble codes which may be stored by the EBCM are not specifically designated as "Current" or "History" codes, as are BCM and ECM codes. These codes, however, can be helpful in diagnosing intermittent conditions.

If an intermittent condition is being diagnosed, the ABS self-diagnostic system can be used in the following manner to help isolate the suspect circuit:

1. First, display and clear any ABS trouble codes which may be present in the EBCM.

2. Then test drive the vehicle, attempting to repeat the failure condition. A description of the driving circumstances under which the failure occurs, if available, can be helpful in duplicating the condition.

3. After duplicating the condition, stop the vehicle and display any ABS trouble codes which may have been stored.

4. If no trouble codes were stored, it may become necessary to use symptom diagnosis.

5. If the system malfunction is not repeated during the test drive, a good description of vehicle behavior may be helpful in locating a "most probable" component or circuit.

6. Most intermittent problems are caused by faulty electrical connections or wiring. When an intermittent failure is encountered, check suspect circuits for:

• Poor mating of connector halves or terminals not fully seated in the connector body (backed out).

• Improperly formed or damaged terminals. All connector terminals in a problem circuit should be carefully reformed to increase contact tension.

• Poor terminal to wire connection. This requires removing the terminal from the connector body to inspect.

Most failures of the anti-lock brake system will disable anti-lock function for the entire ignition cycle, even if the fault clears before key-off. There are a few failure conditions, however, which will allow the ABS operation to resume during the ignition cycle in which a failure occurred if the failure conditions are no longer present.

The following conditions may result in intermittent operation of the "BRAKE" and "ANTI-LOCK" lamps. All other failures will cause at least one of the two warning lamps to remain on until the ignition switch is turned off and then back on. Circuits involving these inputs to the EBCM should be investigated if a complaint of intermittent warning system operation is encountered.

• Low system voltage

If low system voltage is detected at the EBCM, the ABS will turn on the "ANTI-LOCK" lamp until normal system voltage is achieved. Once normal voltage is seen at the EBCM, normal operation resumes.

• Low brake fluid

A low brake fluid condition will cause the ABS to turn on the "BRAKE" and "ANTI-LOCK" lamps. When the fluid level sensor again indicates an acceptable fluid level, normal operation will resume.

• Low accumulator pressure

Low accumulator pressure will cause both the "BRAKE" and "ANTI-LOCK" lamps to turn on. Once normal operating pressure is achieved, the lamps will be turned off and the system will operate normally.

Additionally, any condition which results in interruption of power to the EBCM or hydraulic unit may cause the warning lamps to turn on intermittently. These circuits include the main relay, main relay fuse, EBCM fuse, pump motor relay and fuses and related wiring.

PARKING BRAKE

All models are equipped with a foot-operated ratchet-type parking brake. A cable assembly connects this pedal to an intermediate cable by means of an equalizer. Adjustment is made at the equalizer. The intermediate cable connects with two rear cables and each of these cables enters a rear wheel.

Cables

REMOVAL & INSTALLATION

▶ See Figures 94, 95, 96 and 97

Front Cable

1. Raise the front of the vehicle and support it on safety stands.

2. Disconnect the front cable from the intermediate cable at the adjuster.

3. Disengage the cable housing retainer at the point where the cable passes through the underbody.

4. Lower the vehicle and remove the left side dash close-out panel.

5. Disconnect the cable at the pedal assembly and remove the cable.

To install:

6. Position the cable in the car and install the cable end in the pedal assembly.

7. Install the left dash close-out panel.

8. Raise and support the vehicle again.

9. Connect the front cable to the intermediate cable and adjust the parking brake.

Intermediate Cable

1. Raise the front of the vehicle and support it on safety stands.

2. Disconnect the front cable from the intermediate cable at the adjuster.

3. Remove the adjuster from the cable.
4. Disconnect the intermediate cable and both rear cables at the equalizer.
5. Remove the cable from the vehicle.

To install:

6. Position the intermediate cable through the retainers.
7. Reconnect all cables to the equalizer.
8. Connect the intermediate cable to the front cable at the adjuster. Adjust the parking brake.

Rear Cables

1. Raise the front of the vehicle and support it on safety stands.
2. Loosen the cable at the adjuster.
3. Disconnect all cables at the equalizer.
4. Disengage the cable housing retainer from the rear suspension cross-member assembly.
5. Remove the cable from the caliper assembly and then remove the cable.

To install:

6. Position the cables in the retainers.
7. Install the cable in the caliper assembly.
8. Reconnect all cables at the equalizer.
9. Adjust the parking brake.

ADJUSTMENT

Rear Drum Brakes

The need for parking brake adjustment is indicated if the parking brake pedal travel is more than 15 clicks under heavy foot pressure.

1. Depress the parking brake pedal exactly 4 ratchet clicks.
2. Jack up the car and safely support it with jackstands.
3. Tighten the adjusting nut until the left rear wheel can just be turned rearward using two hands, but is locked when forward rotation is attempted.
4. With the mechanism totally disengaged, the rear wheels should turn freely in either direction with no brake drag.

➡ **It is very important that the parking brake cables are not adjusted too tightly causing brake drag.**

5. Remove the jackstands and lower the car.

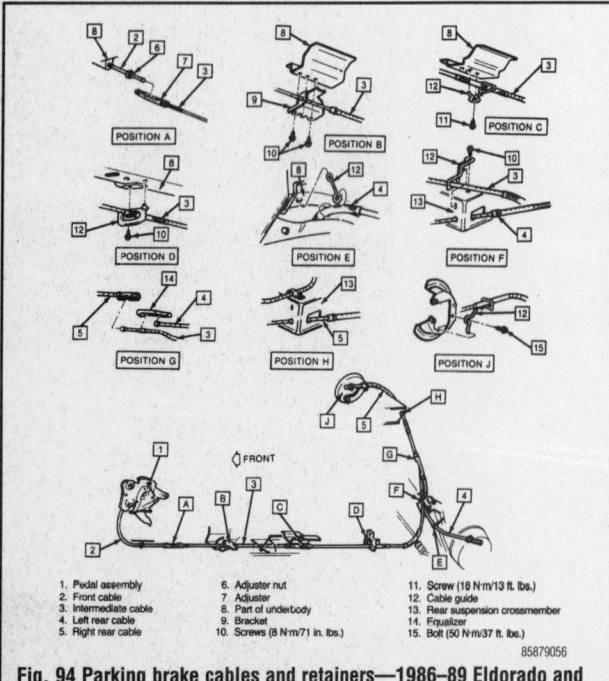

1. Pedal assembly
2. Front cable
3. Intermediate cable
4. Left rear cable
5. Right rear cable
6. Adjuster nut
7. Adjuster
8. Part of underbody
9. Bracket
10. Screws (8 N·m/71 in. lbs.)
11. Screw (18 N·m/13 ft. lbs.)
12. Cable guide
13. Rear suspension crossmember
14. Equalizer
15. Bolt (50 N·m/37 ft. lbs.)

85879056

Fig. 94 Parking brake cables and retainers—1986–89 Eldorado and Seville

Rear Disc Brakes

➡ **For adjustment on 1986–89 Eldorado and Sevilles, please refer to the Rear Disc Brake Caliper (removal and installation) section.**

1. Lubricate the parking brake cables at the underbody rub points and at the equalizer hooks. Make sure there is free movement at all cables, and that the parking brake pedal is in the fully released position.
2. Jack up the rear of the car and support it with jackstands.
3. Hold the brake cable stud from turning and tighten the equalizer nut until all cable slack is removed.
4. Make sure the caliper levers are against the stops on the caliper housings after tightening the equalizer nut.
5. If the levers are off the stops, loosen the cable until the levers return to the stops.
6. Operate the parking brake pedal several times to check the adjustment. When the cable is adjusted, the parking brake pedal should travel 4–5 inches (102–127 Nm) with about 125 pounds of force on the pedal.
7. After the adjustment, the levers must be on the caliper stops. Back off the brake adjustment if necessary to keep the levers on the stops. Remove the jackstands and lower the car.

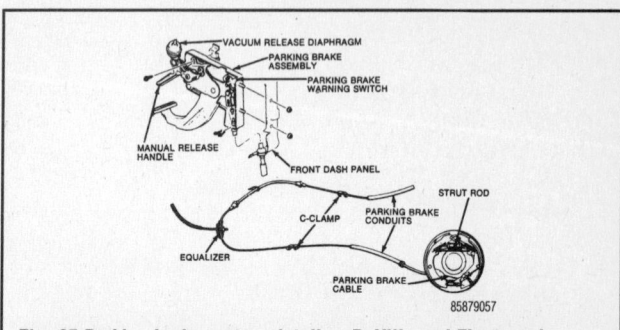

85879057

Fig. 95 Parking brake system details—DeVille and Fleetwood

85879103

Fig. 96 Removing the parking brake cable from the brake backing plate

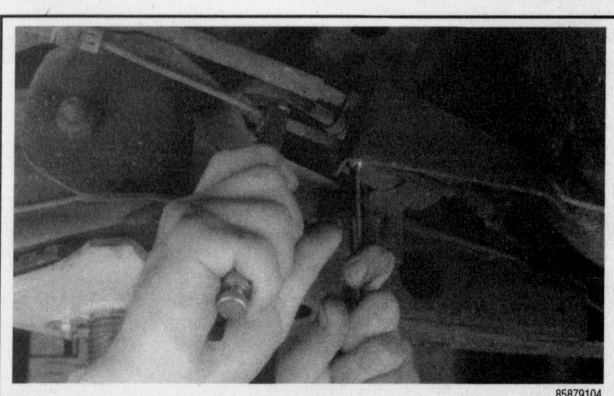

85879104

Fig. 97 Common parking brake adjustment

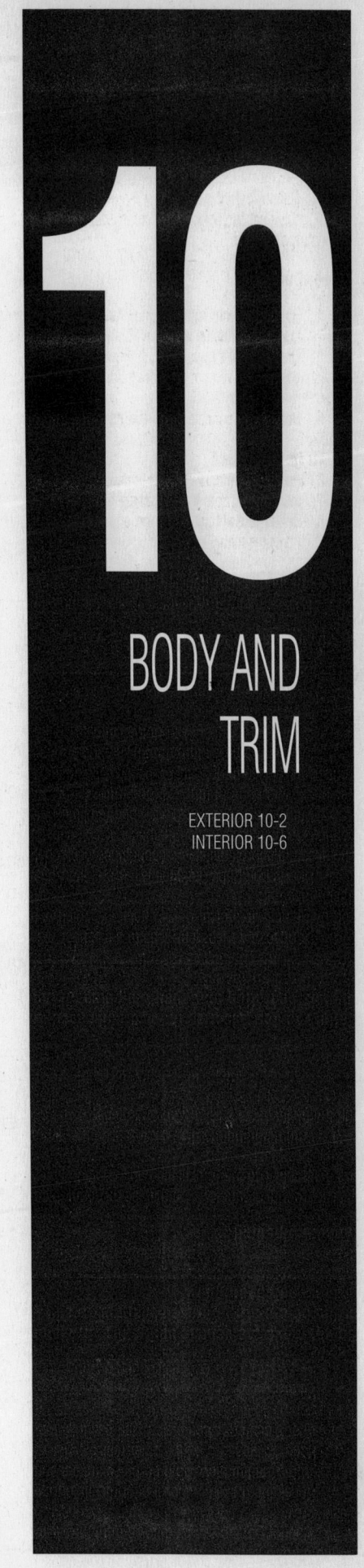

10

BODY AND TRIM

EXTERIOR

Doors

REMOVAL & INSTALLATION

On some models, when removing the door only, it is recommended that the door be removed from the hinges because of the easier access to the door side hinge bolts.

1. Prior to loosening any hinge bolts, mark the position of the hinge on the door to ease adjustment when reinstalling the door on the hinge.
2. On doors equipped with power operated components, remove the trim and detach the inner panel water deflector enough to disconnect the wire harness from the components (remove the negative battery cable, first). Detach the rubber conduit and the wiring harness from the door.
3. With the aid of a helper, support the door in the open position and remove the upper and lower hinge to door hinge pillar attaching bolts.
4. Installation is the reverse of removal. Prior to reinstalling the door to the body, clean off old sealer at the hinge attaching areas and supply a coat of heavy bodied sealer to the surface of the hinge that mates to the pillar or body to prevent corrosion. Adjust the door as necessary.

ADJUSTMENT

Front

Door adjustments are provided through the use of floating anchor plates in the door and front body hinge pillars. When checking the door for alignment and prior to making any adjustment, mark the location and remove the door lock striker from the body to allow the door to hang freely on its hinges.

1. Adjust the door up and down and/or fore and aft at the body hinge pillar attachments.
2. Adjust the door in and out at the door hinge pillar attachments.

Rear

In or out and up or down adjustment is available at the door side hinge attaching bolts. Fore or aft and a slight up or down adjustment is available at the body side center pillar hinge attaching bolts.

Hood

REMOVAL & INSTALLATION

▶ **See Figures 1, 2 and 3**

Except 1986–89 Eldorado and Seville

1. Scribe the hinge locations on the underside of the hood panel to aid in the positioning of the hood when it is reinstalled.

2. Remove the screws and washers securing the hinge assemblies to the hood panel. On the Eldorado and Seville, remove the two screws from the side of the hood panel, one on each side, also disconnect the gas cylinder retaining clip if so equipped.
3. Remove the hood with the aid of a helper, using care to avoid damage to the finish. Stand the hood on its rear corners or its side, using protective supports, otherwise sheet metal damage may result.

To install:

4. With the aid of a helper, place the hood in position so that the hinges line up with the scribe marks made during removal, then install the attaching washers and screws at each hinge assembly and tighten.
5. Carefully close the hood and check the alignment of the hood at the fender and grille front end panel opening.
6. Adjust the hood latch mechanism and/or hood panel, if necessary.

1986–89 Eldorado and Seville

▶ **See Figure 4**

1. Scribe the hinge locations on the underside of the hood panel to aid in the positioning of the hood when it is reinstalled.
2. Remove the four screws.
3. Disconnect the two top gas spring clips.
4. Remove the hood with the aid of a helper, using care to avoid damage to the finish. Do not stand the hood on its rear corners. The hood must be positioned so that it rests on its side, using protective supports, otherwise sheet metal damage may result.

To install:

5. With the aid of a helper, place the hood in position so that the hinges line up with the scribe marks made during removal, then install the attaching washers and screws at each hinge assembly and tighten.
6. Install the two gas spring clips.
7. Carefully close the hood, then check the alignment of the hood at the fender and grille front end panel opening.
8. Adjust the hood latch mechanism and/or hood panel, if necessary.

ADJUSTMENT

Except 1986–89 Eldorado and Seville

1. Loosen the hood attaching screws at each hood hinge. Elongated holes in each hinge provide fore and aft adjustment of the hood.
2. Tighten the hinge to hood attaching screws on the both sides.
3. Adjust the rubber bumpers so that the hood panel is flush with the fenders.
4. Adjust the hood latch mechanism, if necessary.

1986–89 Eldorado and Seville

1. Loosen the hood attaching bolts at each hood hinge. Oversized holes in the hinge provide for fore and aft adjustment of the hood.

85870032

Fig. 1 Mark the hood hinges before hood removal

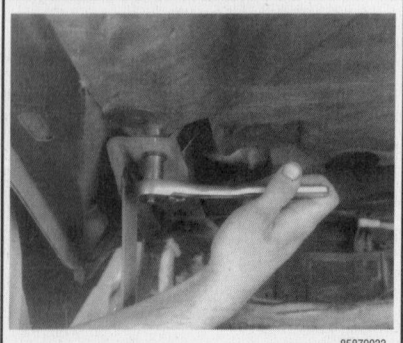

85870033

Fig. 2 Removing the hood retaining bolts

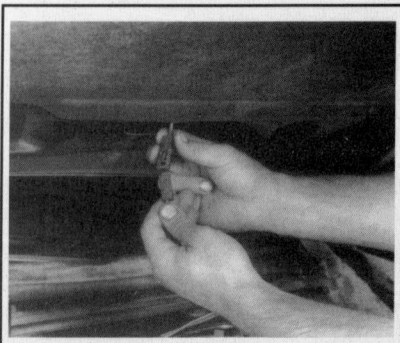

85870034

Fig. 3 Disconnect the hood light connection before removing the hood

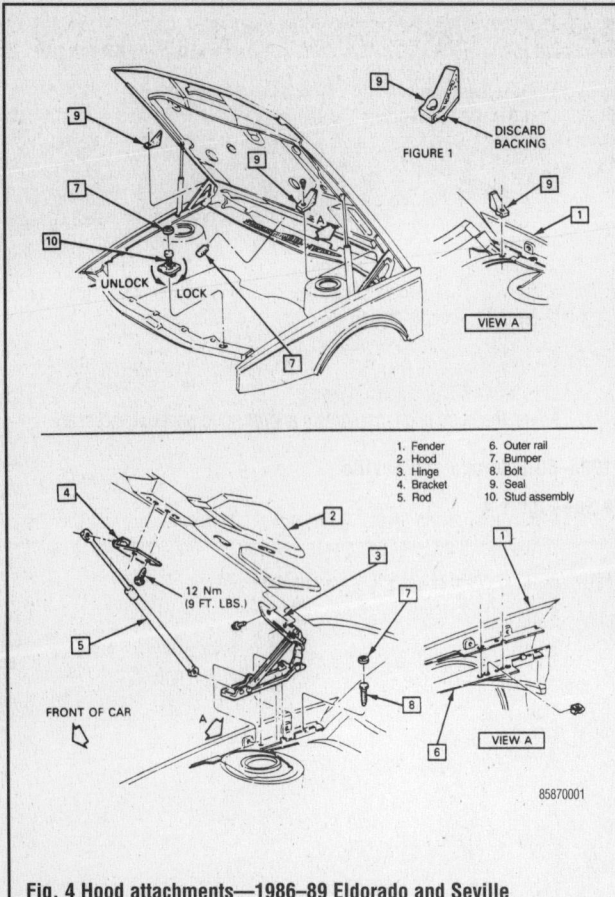

1. Fender
2. Hood
3. Hinge
4. Bracket
5. Rod
6. Outer rail
7. Bumper
8. Bolt
9. Seal
10. Stud assembly

12 Nm (9 FT. LBS.)

FRONT OF CAR

85870001

Fig. 4 Hood attachments—1986–89 Eldorado and Seville

2. Tighten the hinge to hood attaching screws on the both sides.
3. Adjust the rubber bumpers so that the hood panel is flush with the fenders.
4. Adjust the hood latch mechanism, if necessary.

➡After the hood alignment is performed, sufficient load must remain on the front and rear center hood stop bumpers to eliminate hood flutter. This can be achieved by lowering the primary latch an additional ⅛ inch (3.175mm) for front flutter. For rear flutter the rear center bumper must be adjusted.

Trunk Lid

REMOVAL & INSTALLATION

1. Prop the lid open and place protective coverings along the edges of the rear compartment opening to prevent damage to the painted surfaces.
2. Where necessary, disengage any wire harnesses or vacuum assist mechanisms that may interfere with lid removal.
3. Mark the location of the hinge strap attaching bolts to the lid.
4. While a helper supports the lid, remove the attaching bolts securing the hinges to the lid and remove the lid.
5. To install align the lid with the scribed marks and reverse the removal procedure.

ALIGNMENT

Fore/aft and up/down adjustments of the lid assembly is controlled by the hinge strap to lid attaching bolts. Some styles have rubber bumpers at the rear outboard corners of the lid. These bumpers can be adjusted to raise or lower the rear corners of the deck lid.

Grille

REMOVAL & INSTALLATION

Except 1980–89 Eldorado and Seville

1. On 1979 and later models, remove the right and left filler panels. Early models used retaining screws, later models used plastic retainers.
2. Remove the grille retaining screws.
3. On models equipped with the Guide-Matic, disconnect the support rod. Remove the grille from the vehicle.
4. Installation is the reverse of the removal procedure.

1980–89 Eldorado and Seville

▶ **See Figure 5**

1. Remove the front end sheet metal cross panel, or radiator support panel.
2. Remove the grille retaining screws or locking pin retainers and remove the grille.
3. Installation is the reverse of removal.

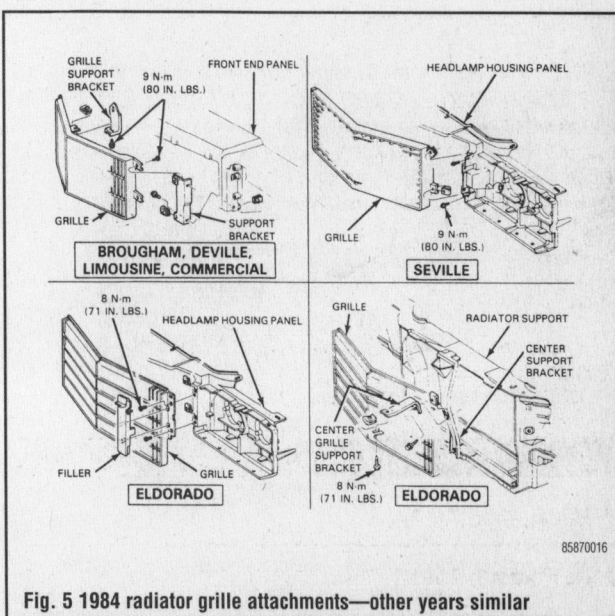

85870016

Fig. 5 1984 radiator grille attachments—other years similar

Outside Mirrors

REMOVAL & INSTALLATION

▶ **See Figures 6 and 7**

1. It may be necessary to remove the trim panel on the some models and any support brackets present.
2. Remove the sound absorber or water deflector as necessary.
3. Detach any cable retainer tabs from the door.
4. Remove the wire connectors, if so equipped.
5. Remove the mirror retaining nuts and remove the mirror.
6. Installation is the reverse of removal.

➡Replacement mirror glass is available. It comes with an adhesive back which may be pressed into place.

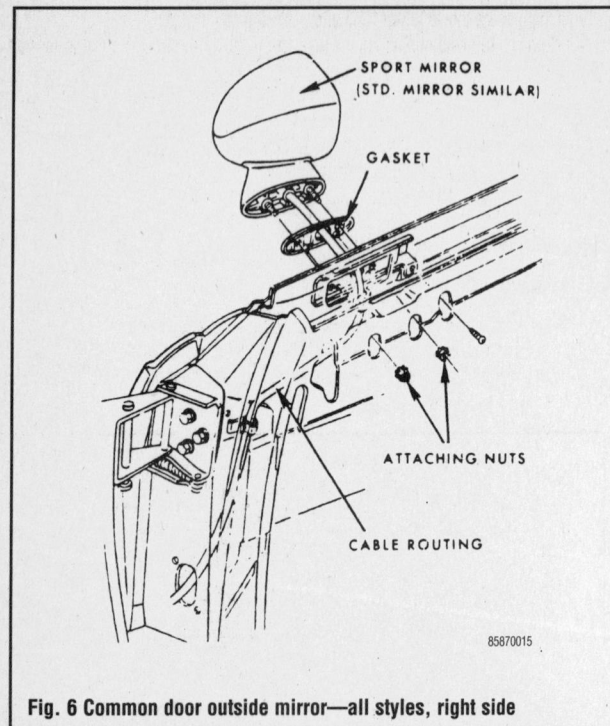

Fig. 6 Common door outside mirror—all styles, right side

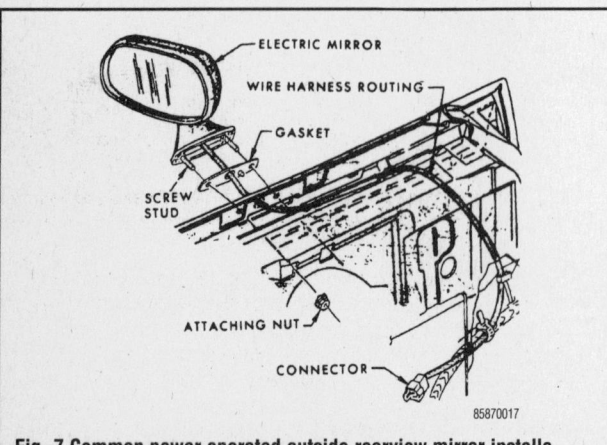

Fig. 7 Common power operated outside rearview mirror installation—left side shown, right side similar

Power Antenna

REMOVAL & INSTALLATION

1967–81 Models Except Eldorado and Seville

▶ See Figure 8

1. Lower the antenna.
2. Disconnect the negative battery cable.
3. Disconnect the electrical connector and the antenna lead cable from the support tube.
4. Remove the two screws which secure the upper antenna mounting bracket to the fender.
5. Remove the bolt and washers securing the antenna to the right fender antenna mounting bracket and grommet, then remove the antenna and splash shield from the car.
6. The escutcheon may be removed by depressing the lock tabs and pushing the escutcheon out through the top of the fender.
7. Installation is the reverse of removal.

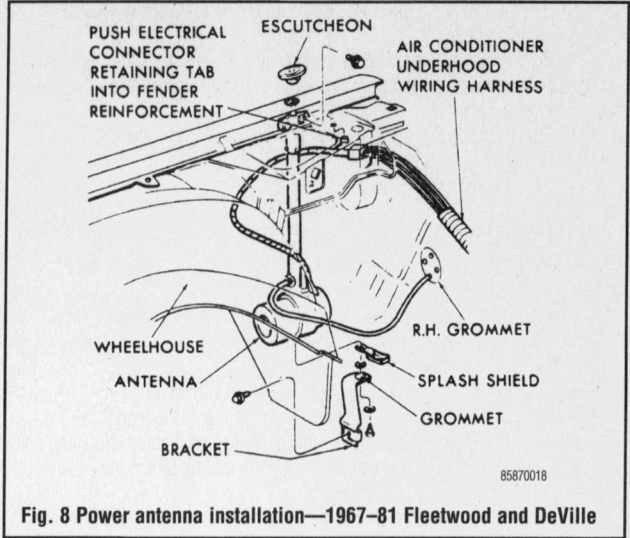

Fig. 8 Power antenna installation—1967–81 Fleetwood and DeVille

1982–89 Models Except Eldorado and Seville

▶ See Figure 9

1. Turn the wheels all the way to the right.
2. Raise the hood and disconnect the negative battery cable.
3. Disconnect the antenna wiring harness and lead connectors.
4. Remove the antenna harness retaining strap.
5. Remove the escutcheon and two upper fender to antenna bolts.
6. Remove the lower half of the wheel housing.
7. Remove the one bolt retaining the antenna assembly to the inner fender.
8. Remove the two bolts holding the lower fender support and remove the support.
9. Remove the one bolt holding the antenna brackets together.
10. Attach a guide wire (must be at least four feet) to the top of the existing antenna.
11. Remove the antenna.
12. Installation is the reverse of removal. Secure the wiring with a new retaining strap.

1967–78 Eldorado

1. Lower the antenna.
2. Disconnect the negative battery cable.
3. Disconnect the electrical connector and the antenna lead cable from the support tube.

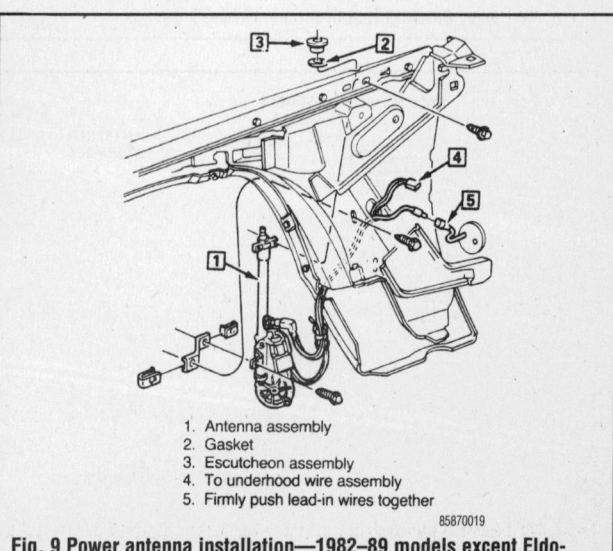

1. Antenna assembly
2. Gasket
3. Escutcheon assembly
4. To underhood wire assembly
5. Firmly push lead-in wires together

Fig. 9 Power antenna installation—1982–89 models except Eldorado and Seville

4. Remove the two screws which secure the upper antenna mounting bracket to the fender.

5. Remove the bolt and washers securing the antenna to the right fender antenna mounting bracket and grommet, then remove the antenna and splash shield from the car.

6. The escutcheon may be removed by depressing the lock tabs and pushing the escutcheon out through the top of the fender.

7. Installation is the reverse of removal.

1976–79 Seville

▶ See Figure 10

1. Raise the hood and disconnect the negative battery cable.
2. Remove the three retainers which secure the access plate to the left hand wheelhouse.
3. Disconnect the antenna lead and electrical connector.
4. Remove the antenna escutcheon from the top of the fender.
5. Loosen the screw securing the antenna to the wheelhouse mounting bracket.
6. Slide the antenna and grommet from the mounting bracket and remove through the wheelhouse access port.
7. Installation is the reverse of removal. Make sure the two drain holes in the bottom of the antenna housing and the two drain holes in the base of the mast are open.

1979–82 Eldorado and 1980–82 Seville

▶ See Figure 11

1. Raise the hood and disconnect the negative battery cable.
2. Support the front of the hood to the radiator support bracket and remove the right hand hood hinge.

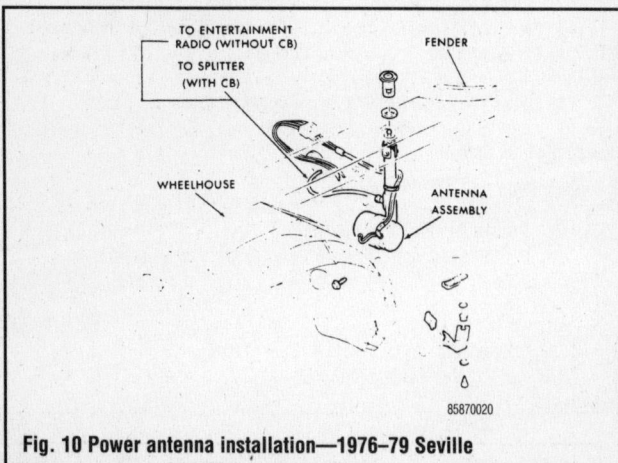

Fig. 10 Power antenna installation—1976–79 Seville

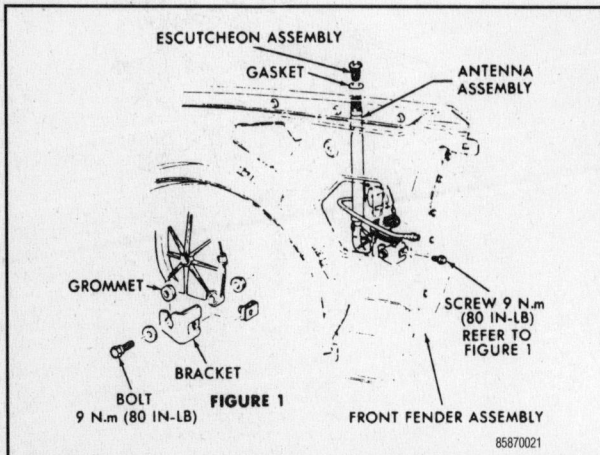

Fig. 11 Power antenna installation—1979–82 Eldorado and 1980–82 Seville

3. Disconnect the antenna lead and electrical connector.
4. Remove the one screw from inside the right door, securing the antenna to the fender.
5. Hold the antenna in position and remove the escutcheon securing the antenna support tube to the fender.
6. Remove the antenna through the hood hinge opening.
7. Remove the mounting bracket.
8. Installation is the reverse of removal.

1983–85 Eldorado and Seville

▶ See Figure 12

1. Raise the hood and disconnect the negative battery cable.
2. Disconnect the antenna lead and electrical connector.
3. Remove the escutcheon from the fender and the two upper attaching bolts.

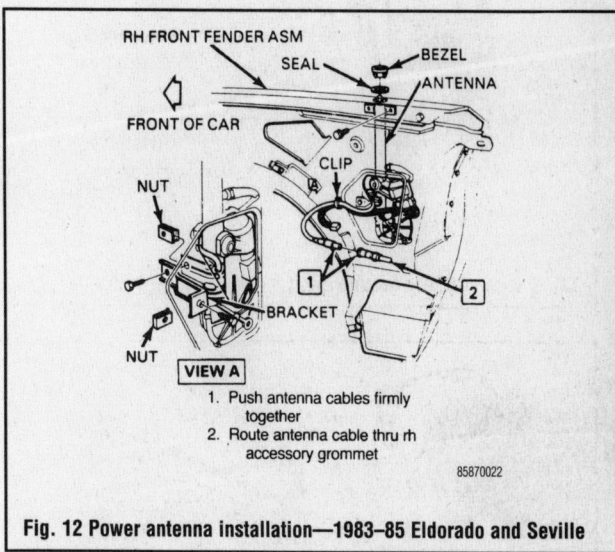

Fig. 12 Power antenna installation—1983–85 Eldorado and Seville

4. Support the hood and remove the right hand hood support. Circle the washer bolt area with a grease pencil for proper hood alignment upon reassembly.
5. Remove the one screw from the inner fender.
6. Remove the antenna through the inner fender hole.
7. Installation is the reverse of removal.

1986–89 Eldorado and Seville

▶ See Figure 13

1. Disconnect the negative battery cable.
2. Remove the right hand sound insulating panel.

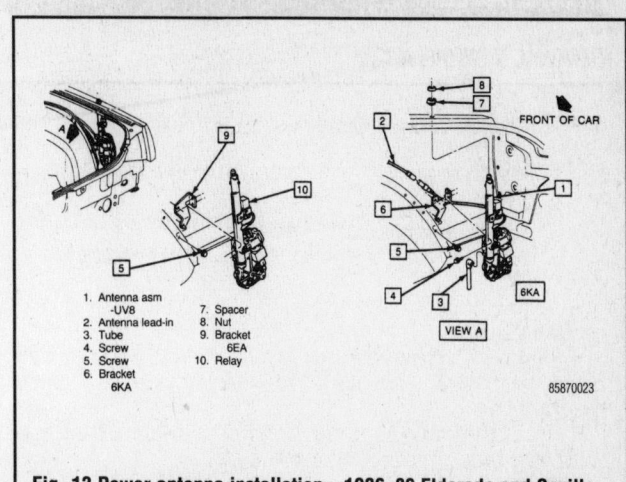

Fig. 13 Power antenna installation—1986–89 Eldorado and Seville

3. Disconnect the antenna lead from the radio.
4. Disconnect the electrical connector from the antenna motor.
5. Remove the rear portion of the wheel opening shield and push aside.
6. Remove the one screw from the top of the antenna tube.

7. Remove the two screws from the lower mounting bracket.
8. Remove the grommet from the body.
9. Remove the antenna assembly with the lead and wire harness.
10. Installation is the reverse of removal.

INTERIOR

Door Panels

REMOVAL & INSTALLATION

1. Remove all door inside handles.
2. Remove the door inside locking rod knob.
3. On styles with door pull handles, remove the screws inserted through the handle into the door panel.
4. On styles with remote control mirror assemblies, remove the remote mirror escutcheon and disengage the end of the mirror control cable from the escutcheon.
5. On styles equipped with switch cover plate in the door armrest, remove the screws securing the cover plate, then disconnect the switches and cigar lighter, if so equipped, from the harness connectors.
6. Remove the remote control cover plates and remove the exposed screws securing the cover plate to the door inner panel.
7. On styles with integral armrest, remove the screws inserted through the pull cup into the armrest hanger support. On some styles it may be necessary to remove the screws behind the armrest deflector or courtesy lamp remote control cover plate. On styles with armrest applied after the door trim installation, remove the armrest to door inner panel attaching screws.
8. On styles with two piece trim panels, disengage the retainer clips at the front and rear of the upper trim panel. Remove the upper trim panel by lifting upward and sliding slightly rearward to disengage the front door inner panel at the beltline.
9. On styles with electric switches located in the door trim panel, disconnect the wire harness at the switch assembly.
10. To remove the lower trim panel, remove the attaching screws along the upper edge of the lower trim panel. Then starting at a lower corner, insert a pry type tool between the door inner panel and the trim panel and disengage the retaining clips down both sides and across the bottom. On styles with courtesy lamps or reading lamps located in the trim panel, disconnect the wire harness at the lamp assembly.
11. On styles with one piece trim panels, remove all the clips around the perimeter of the trim panel. Push the trim panel downward and outboard to disengage it from the door inner panel at the beltline. Disconnect any courtesy lamp wire harnesses, if so equipped and remove the trim panel from the door.
12. Installation is the reverse of removal. On styles with adjustable trim supports at the beltline, the door trim panel can be adjusted in or out so as not to restrict door window operation.

Door Locks

REMOVAL & INSTALLATION

1. Remove all door trim, then detach the insulator pad and inner panel water deflector enough for access to lock.
2. On rear doors so equipped, the stationary window and the ventilator assembly will have to be removed for access to the lock.
3. Disengage the inside handle and power lock connecting rods as required. On front doors with electric locks, remove the electric lock actuator as required. On some styles it may be necessary to remove the inside handle and then remove the lock and connecting rod as a unit.
4. Disengage the locking rod on rear door locks with the remote lock button. On doors with the locking button directly above the lock, the locking rod is removed with the lock.
5. Remove the lock attaching screws and remove the lock through the access hole. On some front door models, slide the lock down to clear the door frame extension.
6. To install, first install the spring clips to the lock assembly, then reverse the removal procedure.

Front Door Regulator

REMOVAL & INSTALLATION

Fleetwood Brougham and DeVille

▶ See Figure 14

1. Remove all door trim and detach the insulator pad and inner panel water deflector enough for access to lock.
2. With the glass in the full up position, tape the glass to the door upper frame with cloth back tape.
3. Remove the lower sash channel bolts.
4. Punch out the center of the regulator rivets and drill out the rivets using a ¼ inch (6.35mm) drill bit.

✳✳ CAUTION

If electric motor removal from the regulator is required, it is important to follow the procedure outlined in this section. The regulator lift arm is under tension from the counterbalance spring and can cause personal injury if the sector gear is not locked into position.

5. Disconnect the electrical harness where applicable and remove the regulator through the access hole in the inner panel.
6. To install reverse the removal procedure. Use ¼ inch x 0.0500 inch aluminum peel type rivets to attach the regulator to the inner door panel.

Eldorado and Seville

▶ See Figures 15, 16, 17 and 18

1. Tape the glass in the full up position.
2. Remove the trim panel, sound absorber pad and water deflector.
3. On 1986–89 Sevilles, remove the inner panel cam by sliding off of the roller of the regulator.
4. Drill out the two regulator retaining rivets using a ¼ inch (6.35mm) drill bit.

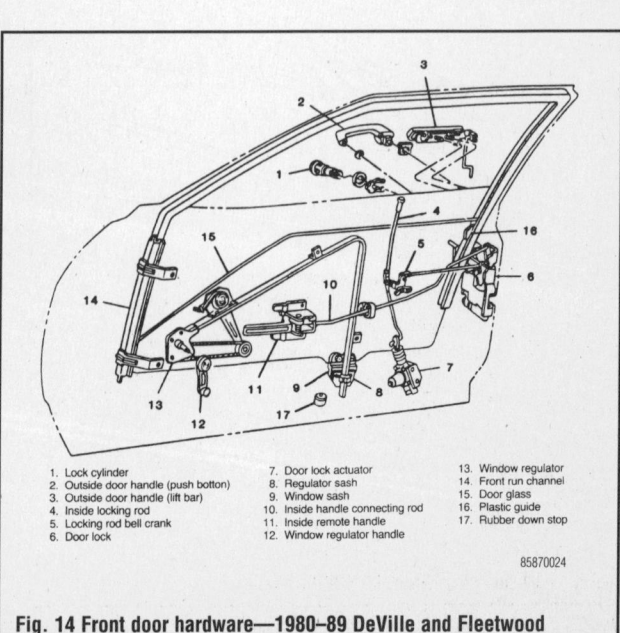

1. Lock cylinder
2. Outside door handle (push botton)
3. Outside door handle (lift bar)
4. Inside locking rod
5. Locking rod bell crank
6. Door lock
7. Door lock actuator
8. Regulator sash
9. Window sash
10. Inside handle connecting rod
11. Inside remote handle
12. Window regulator handle
13. Window regulator
14. Front run channel
15. Door glass
16. Plastic guide
17. Rubber down stop

85870024

Fig. 14 Front door hardware—1980–89 DeVille and Fleetwood

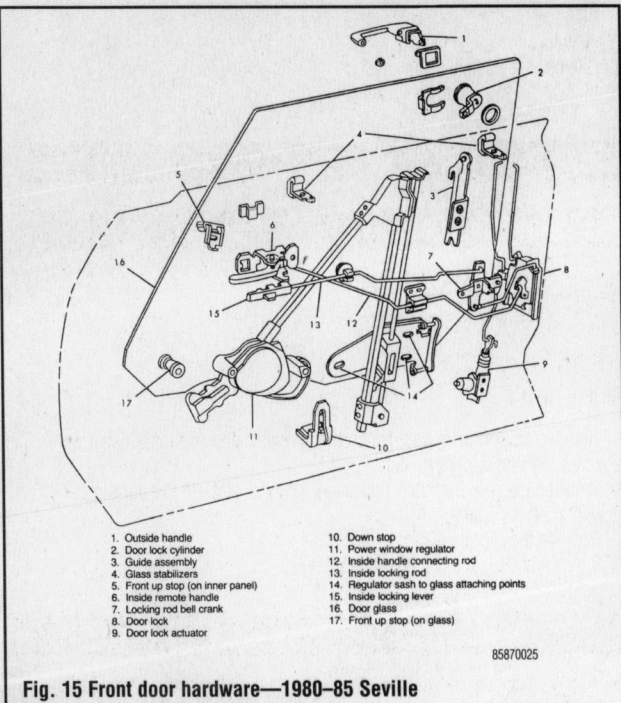

1. Outside handle
2. Door lock cylinder
3. Guide assembly
4. Glass stabilizers
5. Front up stop (on inner panel)
6. Inside remote handle
7. Locking rod bell crank
8. Door lock
9. Door lock actuator
10. Down stop
11. Power window regulator
12. Inside handle connecting rod
13. Inside locking rod
14. Regulator sash to glass attaching points
15. Inside locking lever
16. Door glass
17. Front up stop (on glass)

85870025

Fig. 15 Front door hardware—1980–85 Seville

✳✳ CAUTION

If electric motor removal from the regulator is required, it is important to follow the procedure outlined in this section. The regulator lift arm is under tension from the counterbalance spring and can cause personal injury if the sector gear is not locked into position.

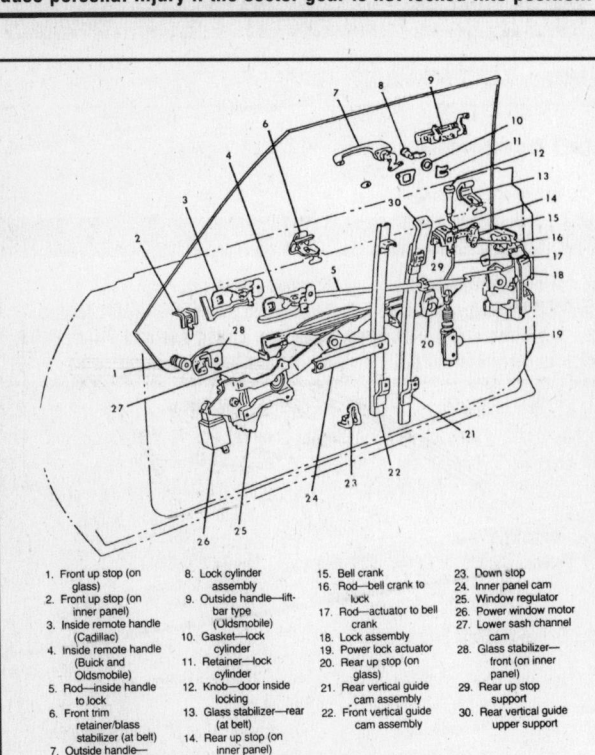

1. Front up stop (on glass)
2. Front up stop (on inner panel)
3. Inside remote handle (Cadillac)
4. Inside remote handle (Buick and Oldsmobile)
5. Rod—inside handle to lock
6. Front trim retainer/glass stabilizer (at belt)
7. Outside handle—push-button type (Buick and Cadillac)
8. Lock cylinder assembly
9. Outside handle—liftbar type (Oldsmobile)
10. Gasket—lock cylinder
11. Retainer—lock cylinder
12. Knob—door inside locking
13. Glass stabilizer—rear (at belt)
14. Rear up stop (on inner panel)
15. Bell crank
16. Rod—bell crank to lock
17. Rod—actuator to bell crank
18. Lock assembly
19. Power lock actuator
20. Rear up stop (on glass)
21. Rear vertical guide cam assembly
22. Front vertical guide cam assembly
23. Down stop
24. Inner panel cam
25. Window regulator
26. Power window motor
27. Lower sash channel cam
28. Glass stabilizer—front (on inner panel)
29. Rear up stop support
30. Rear vertical guide upper support

85870026

Fig. 16 Front door hardware—1979–85 Eldorado

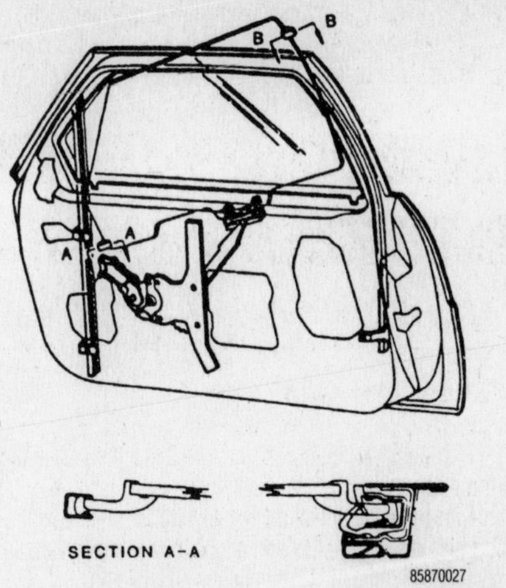

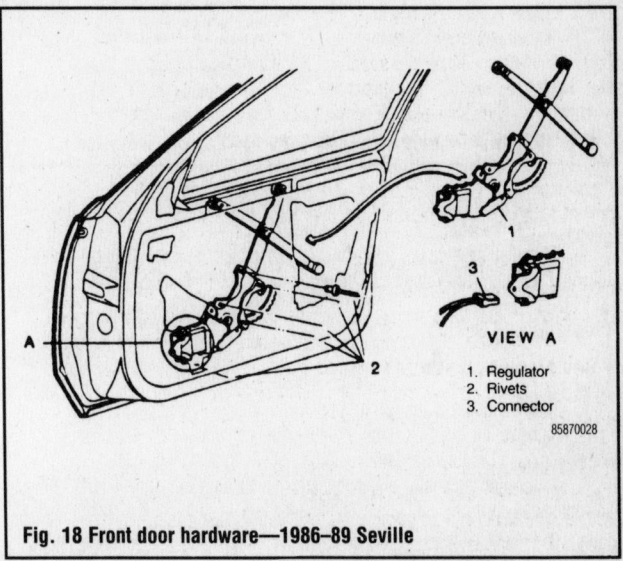

SECTION A-A

85870027

Fig. 17 Front door hardware—1986–89 Eldorado

1. Regulator
2. Rivets
3. Connector

VIEW A

85870028

Fig. 18 Front door hardware—1986–89 Seville

5. Disconnect the wire connector from the regulator motor.
6. Remove the regulator.
7. To install reverse the removal procedure. Use ¼ inch x ⅝ inch aluminum peel type rivets to attach the regulator.

Rear Door Regulator

REMOVAL & INSTALLATION

Fleetwood Brougham and DeVille

▶ See Figure 19

1. Remove all door trim and detach the insulator pad and inner panel water deflector enough for access to lock.
2. With the glass in the full up position, tape the glass to the door upper frame with cloth back tape.
3. Remove the lower sash channel bolts.
4. Punch out the center of the regulator rivets and drill out the rivets using a ¼ inch (6.35mm) drill bit.

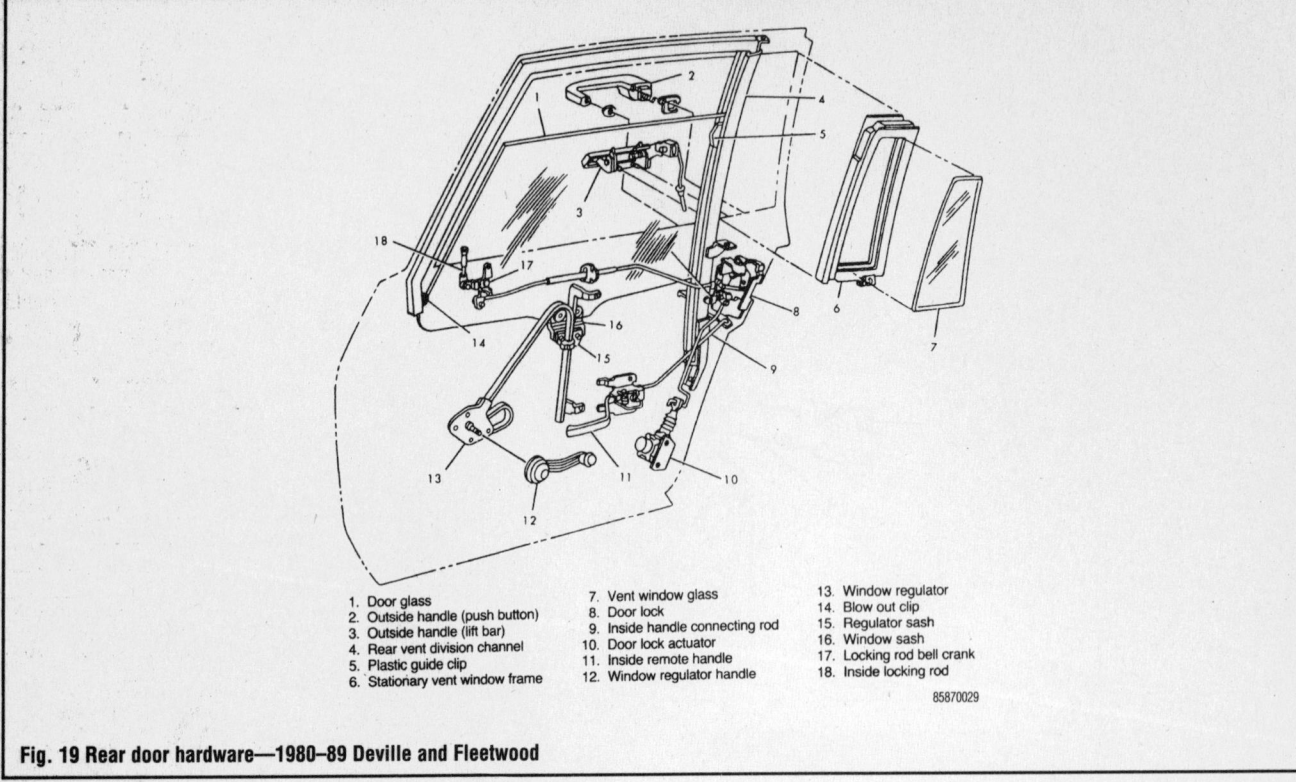

1. Door glass
2. Outside handle (push button)
3. Outside handle (lift bar)
4. Rear vent division channel
5. Plastic guide clip
6. Stationary vent window frame
7. Vent window glass
8. Door lock
9. Inside handle connecting rod
10. Door lock actuator
11. Inside remote handle
12. Window regulator handle
13. Window regulator
14. Blow out clip
15. Regulator sash
16. Window sash
17. Locking rod bell crank
18. Inside locking rod

85870029

Fig. 19 Rear door hardware—1980–89 Deville and Fleetwood

5. Disconnect the electrical harness where applicable and remove the regulator through the access hole in the inner panel.
6. To install reverse the removal procedure. Use ¼ inch x 0.0500 inch aluminum peel type rivets to attach the regulator to the inner door panel.

Eldorado and Seville

▶ **See Figures 20 and 21**

1. Tape the glass in the full up position.
2. Remove the trim panel, sound absorber pad and water deflector.
3. Remove the lock module assembly.
4. Punch out the center of the regulator rivets and drill out the rivets uing a ¼ inch (6.35mm) drill bit.
5. Disconnect the electrical harness where applicable and remove the regulator.

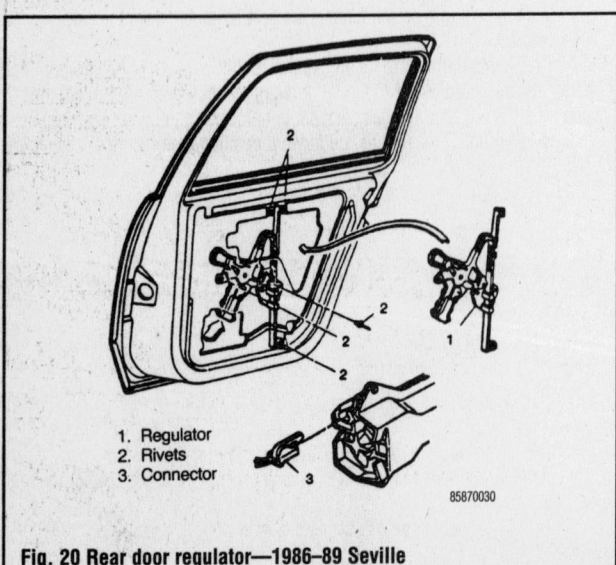

1. Regulator
2. Rivets
3. Connector

85870030

Fig. 20 Rear door regulator—1986–89 Seville

6. To install reverse the removal procedure. Use ¼ inch x ⅝ inch aluminum peel type rivets to attach the regulator to the inner door panel.

Electric Window Motor

REMOVAL & INSTALLATION

Except Tape Drive Regulators

1. Remove the regulator.

※※ **CAUTION**

The following step must be performed when the regulator is removed from the door. The regulator lift arms are under tension from the counterbalance spring and can cause serious injury if the motor is removed without locking the sector gear in position.

2. Drill a hole through the regulator sector gear and back plate and install a screw and nut to lock the sector gear into position. Do not drill the hole closer than ½ in to the edge of the sector gear or backplate.
3. Remove the rivets holding the motor to the regulator using a ³⁄₁₆ inch (4.76mm) drill bit.
   To install:
4. Install the motor to the regulator using ³⁄₁₆ inch rivets.
5. Install the regulator.

Tape Drive Regulators

1. Remove the trim panel, sound absorber pad and water deflector.
2. Disconnect the harness at the motor.
3. Tape the window to the frame with pieces of cloth backed body tape to prevent the glass from dropping when the regulator motor is removed.

※※ **CAUTION**

Unless the glass is taped or blocked in the up position, personal injury and/or glass damage may result.

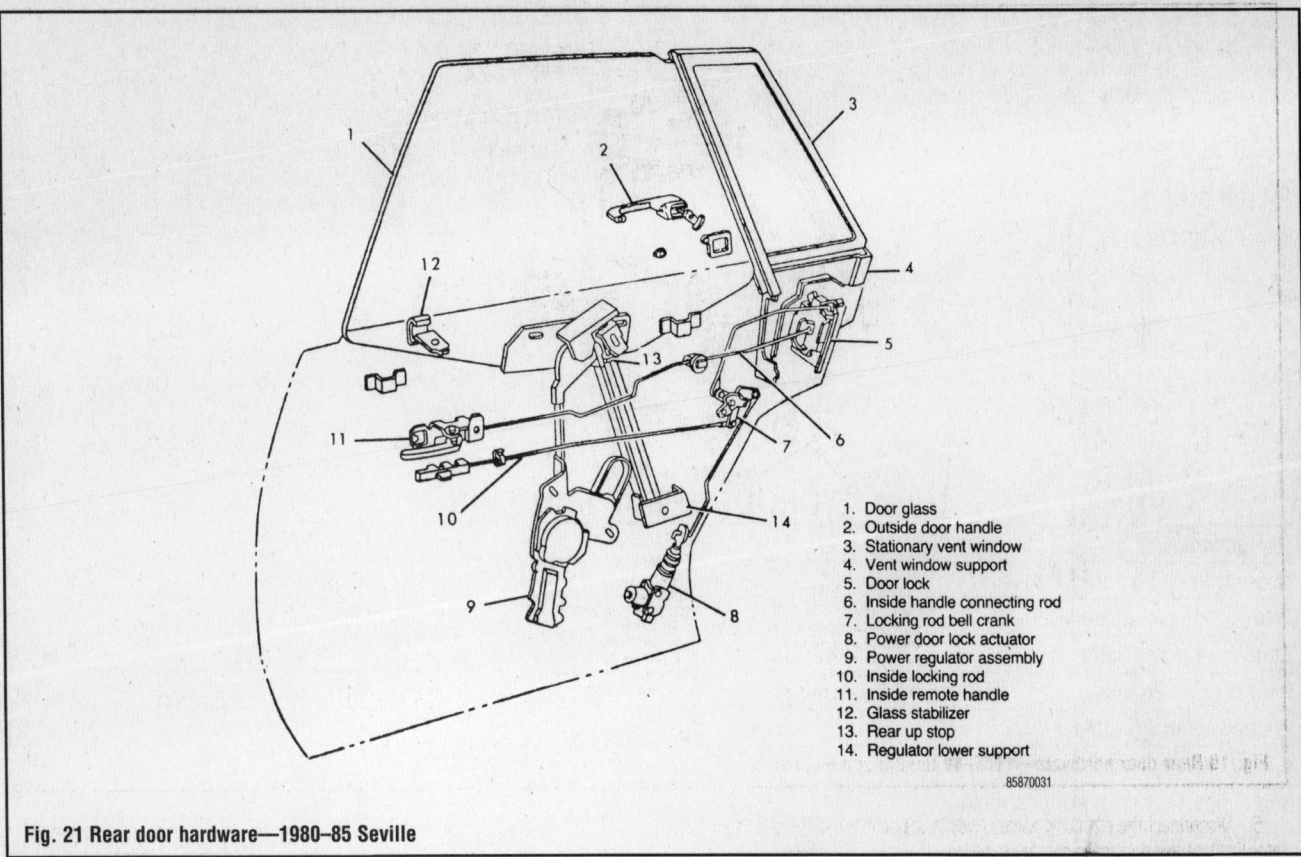

1. Door glass
2. Outside door handle
3. Stationary vent window
4. Vent window support
5. Door lock
6. Inside handle connecting rod
7. Locking rod bell crank
8. Power door lock actuator
9. Power regulator assembly
10. Inside locking rod
11. Inside remote handle
12. Glass stabilizer
13. Rear up stop
14. Regulator lower support

85870031

Fig. 21 Rear door hardware—1980–85 Seville

4. The front doors have locating dimples in the inner panel to locate the motor to regulator attaching bolts. Using a ¾ inch (19mm) hole saw, drill the three holes at the locating dimples.

5. Remove the motor attaching bolts, disconnect the wire connector and remove the motor through the access hole.

To install:

6. Lubricate the motor drive gear and regulator sector teeth. Attach the motor to the regulator and make sure the drive gear properly engages the sector gear teeth before installing the motor attaching bolts. Tighten the attaching bolts to 125 inch lbs. (14 Nm).

7. Use waterproof tape to seal any holes outside the water deflector sealing area and install the trim.

Inside Rear View Mirror

REMOVAL & INSTALLATION

The rearview mirror is attached to a support by a retaining screw. The support is secured to the windshield glass by the supplier using a plastic-polyvinyl butyl adhesive.

Seats

REMOVAL & INSTALLATION

All seat assemblies are secured to the floor pan by either nuts installed on the floor pan anchor plate studs, or bolts installed into the anchor nuts or plates in the floor pan.

All electrically operated seats and seats equipped with a cigar lighter, courtesy lamps etc., have a ground wire secured to the seat frame and under one of the seat adjuster to floor pan attaching bolts or nuts.

1. On models so equipped, remove the shoulder belt guide loop inner attaching screw; then carefully lift the upper portion of the guide loop enough to slide the shoulder strap webbing out of the loop.

2. Operate the seat to the full forward position. If the six way power seat is operable, operate the seat to the full forward and upward position. Where necessary to gain access to the adjuster to floor pan attaching bolts or nuts, remove the adjuster foot covers.

3. On full width and split seats where the front inner seat belts go through the seat assembly, remove the inner seat belt to floor pan anchor plate attaching bolts.

4. Remove the adjuster rear foot covers and track covers, where present; then remove the adjuster to floor pan rear attaching nuts or bolts. Operate the seat to the full rearward position. Remove the adjuster foot covers and track covers where present; then remove the adjuster to floor pan front attaching nuts or bolts.

5. On seats having any electrical equipment such as power adjusters, power reclining seat back, cigar lighter, etc., tilt the seat rearward and disconnect the feed wire connector.

6. With the aid of a helper, remove the seat assembly from the car.

To install:

7. Check that both adjusters are parallel and in phase with each other. If not operate the power adjusters to the full forward position then disconnect the cable from the adjuster that has reached its full forward position. Operate the other adjuster until it reaches its full forward position then reconnect the cable. Check the operation of both adjusters.

8. Tighten the seat adjuster to floor pan attaching bolts or nuts to 18–24 ft. lbs. (24–33 Nm).

Power Seat Motor

REMOVAL & INSTALLATION

Two Way Type

1. If operable, operate the seat to the midway position.

2. Remove the seat adjuster-to-floor pan attaching nuts and bolts, then tilt the seat rearward.

3. On the full width seat, disconnect both power drive cables from the motor.

4. Disconnect the feed wire harness from the actuator motor.

5. Remove the screws that secure the motor support to the seat bottom frame and remove the motor with the attached support from the seat frame.

6. Remove the screws securing the motor support bracket and remove the motor assembly.

7. Installation is the reverse of removal.

Six Way Seats

TRANSMISSION TYPE

1. Remove the seat assembly with the attached adjusters, motor and transmission, then place upside down on a clean, protected surface.

2. Disconnect the motor feed wires from the motor control relay.

3. Remove the two motor support attaching screws; then remove the three screws attaching the transmission to the motor. Move the motor outboard (away from the transmission) enough to disengage the motor from the rubber coupling.

4. To install, reverse the removal procedure making sure the rubber coupling is properly engaged at both the motor and transmission. Secure the seat harness correctly and check operation.

3 MOTOR DIRECT DRIVE TYPE

1. Remove the seat assembly with the attached adjusters, motor and transmission, then place upside down on a clean, protected surface.

2. Disconnect the motor wire harness connector at the motor.

3. Remove the screw securing the motor assembly support to the motor mounting bracket on the adjuster.

4. Carefully disengage the drive cables from the adjusters, remove the nut from the motor stabilizer rod and remove the motor assembly from the adjusters. The drive cables may be removed from the motor.

5. Installation is the reverse of removal. Make sure the adjusters are in phase with each other. If necessary, remove one cable and adjust one gearnut to align with the other.

TORQUE SPECIFICATIONS

Component	U.S.	Metric
Door striker adjustment bolt	35–45 ft. lbs.	48–60 Nm
Power door lock actuator	90–125 inch lbs.	10–14 Nm
Front door hinge bolts	21 ft. lbs.	29 Nm
Rear door hinge bolts	21 ft. lbs.	29 Nm
Window channel retainer	90–125 inch lbs.	10–14 Nm
Window-to-regulator sash bolts	60 inch lbs.	7 Nm
Seat adjuster-to-seat bottom frame	21 ft. lbs.	28 Nm
Seat adjuster-to-floor pan	24 ft. lbs.	32 Nm
Seat belt retractor bolt	35 ft. lbs.	48 Nm
Seat belt anchor bolt	35 ft. lbs.	48 Nm
Bumper bolts	20 ft. lbs.	27 Nm
Energy absorbing unit-to-reinforcement	20 ft. lbs.	27 Nm

85870C01

GLOSSARY

AIR/FUEL RATIO: The ratio of air-to-gasoline by weight in the fuel mixture drawn into the engine.

AIR INJECTION: One method of reducing harmful exhaust emissions by injecting air into each of the exhaust ports of an engine. The fresh air entering the hot exhaust manifold causes any remaining fuel to be burned before it can exit the tailpipe.

ALTERNATOR: A device used for converting mechanical energy into electrical energy.

AMMETER: An instrument, calibrated in amperes, used to measure the flow of an electrical current in a circuit. Ammeters are always connected in series with the circuit being tested.

AMPERE: The rate of flow of electrical current present when one volt of electrical pressure is applied against one ohm of electrical resistance.

ANALOG COMPUTER: Any microprocessor that uses similar (analogous) electrical signals to make its calculations.

ARMATURE: A laminated, soft iron core wrapped by a wire that converts electrical energy to mechanical energy as in a motor or relay. When rotated in a magnetic field, it changes mechanical energy into electrical energy as in a generator.

ATMOSPHERIC PRESSURE: The pressure on the Earth's surface caused by the weight of the air in the atmosphere. At sea level, this pressure is 14.7 psi at 32°F (101 kPa at 0°C).

ATOMIZATION: The breaking down of a liquid into a fine mist that can be suspended in air.

AXIAL PLAY: Movement parallel to a shaft or bearing bore.

BACKFIRE: The sudden combustion of gases in the intake or exhaust system that results in a loud explosion.

BACKLASH: The clearance or play between two parts, such as meshed gears.

BACKPRESSURE: Restrictions in the exhaust system that slow the exit of exhaust gases from the combustion chamber.

BAKELITE: A heat resistant, plastic insulator material commonly used in printed circuit boards and transistorized components.

BALL BEARING: A bearing made up of hardened inner and outer races between which hardened steel balls roll.

BALLAST RESISTOR: A resistor in the primary ignition circuit that lowers voltage after the engine is started to reduce wear on ignition components.

BEARING: A friction reducing, supportive device usually located between a stationary part and a moving part.

BIMETAL TEMPERATURE SENSOR: Any sensor or switch made of two dissimilar types of metal that bend when heated or cooled due to the different expansion rates of the alloys. These types of sensors usually function as an on/off switch.

BLOWBY: Combustion gases, composed of water vapor and unburned fuel, that leak past the piston rings into the crankcase during normal engine operation. These gases are removed by the PCV system to prevent the buildup of harmful acids in the crankcase.

BRAKE PAD: A brake shoe and lining assembly used with disc brakes.

BRAKE SHOE: The backing for the brake lining. The term is, however, usually applied to the assembly of the brake backing and lining.

BUSHING: A liner, usually removable, for a bearing; an anti-friction liner used in place of a bearing.

CALIPER: A hydraulically activated device in a disc brake system, which is mounted straddling the brake rotor (disc). The caliper contains at least one piston and two brake pads. Hydraulic pressure on the piston(s) forces the pads against the rotor.

CAMSHAFT: A shaft in the engine on which are the lobes (cams) which operate the valves. The camshaft is driven by the crankshaft, via a belt, chain or gears, at one half the crankshaft speed.

CAPACITOR: A device which stores an electrical charge.

CARBON MONOXIDE (CO): A colorless, odorless gas given off as a normal byproduct of combustion. It is poisonous and extremely dangerous in confined areas, building up slowly to toxic levels without warning if adequate ventilation is not available.

CARBURETOR: A device, usually mounted on the intake manifold of an engine, which mixes the air and fuel in the proper proportion to allow even combustion.

CATALYTIC CONVERTER: A device installed in the exhaust system, like a muffler, that converts harmful byproducts of combustion into carbon dioxide and water vapor by means of a heat-producing chemical reaction.

CENTRIFUGAL ADVANCE: A mechanical method of advancing the spark timing by using flyweights in the distributor that react to centrifugal force generated by the distributor shaft rotation.

CHECK VALVE: Any one-way valve installed to permit the flow of air, fuel or vacuum in one direction only.

CHOKE: A device, usually a moveable valve, placed in the intake path of a carburetor to restrict the flow of air.

CIRCUIT: Any unbroken path through which an electrical current can flow. Also used to describe fuel flow in some instances.

CIRCUIT BREAKER: A switch which protects an electrical circuit from overload by opening the circuit when the current flow exceeds a predetermined level. Some circuit breakers must be reset manually, while most reset automatically.

COIL (IGNITION): A transformer in the ignition circuit which steps up the voltage provided to the spark plugs.

COMBINATION MANIFOLD: An assembly which includes both the intake and exhaust manifolds in one casting.

COMBINATION VALVE: A device used in some fuel systems that routes fuel vapors to a charcoal storage canister instead of venting them into the atmosphere. The valve relieves fuel tank pressure and allows fresh air into the tank as the fuel level drops to prevent a vapor lock situation.

COMPRESSION RATIO: The comparison of the total volume of the cylinder and combustion chamber with the piston at BDC and the piston at TDC.

CONDENSER: 1. An electrical device which acts to store an electrical charge, preventing voltage surges. 2. A radiator-like device in the air conditioning system in which refrigerant gas condenses into a liquid, giving off heat.

CONDUCTOR: Any material through which an electrical current can be transmitted easily.

CONTINUITY: Continuous or complete circuit. Can be checked with an ohmmeter.

COUNTERSHAFT: An intermediate shaft which is rotated by a mainshaft and transmits, in turn, that rotation to a working part.

CRANKCASE: The lower part of an engine in which the crankshaft and related parts operate.

CRANKSHAFT: The main driving shaft of an engine which receives reciprocating motion from the pistons and converts it to rotary motion.

CYLINDER: In an engine, the round hole in the engine block in which the piston(s) ride.

CYLINDER BLOCK: The main structural member of an engine in which is found the cylinders, crankshaft and other principal parts.

CYLINDER HEAD: The detachable portion of the engine, usually fastened to the top of the cylinder block and containing all or most of the combustion chambers. On overhead valve engines, it contains the valves and their operating parts. On overhead cam engines, it contains the camshaft as well.

DEAD CENTER: The extreme top or bottom of the piston stroke.

DETONATION: An unwanted explosion of the air/fuel mixture in the combustion chamber caused by excess heat and compression, advanced timing, or an overly lean mixture. Also referred to as "ping".

DIAPHRAGM: A thin, flexible wall separating two cavities, such as in a vacuum advance unit.

DIESELING: A condition in which hot spots in the combustion chamber cause the engine to run on after the key is turned off.

DIFFERENTIAL: A geared assembly which allows the transmission of motion between drive axles, giving one axle the ability to turn faster than the other.

DIODE: An electrical device that will allow current to flow in one direction only.

DISC BRAKE: A hydraulic braking assembly consisting of a brake disc, or rotor, mounted on an axle, and a caliper assembly containing, usually two brake pads which are activated by hydraulic pressure. The pads are forced against the sides of the disc, creating friction which slows the vehicle.

DISTRIBUTOR: A mechanically driven device on an engine which is responsible for electrically firing the spark plug at a predetermined point of the piston stroke.

DOWEL PIN: A pin, inserted in mating holes in two different parts allowing those parts to maintain a fixed relationship.

DRUM BRAKE: A braking system which consists of two brake shoes and one or two wheel cylinders, mounted on a fixed backing plate, and a brake drum, mounted on an axle, which revolves around the assembly.

DWELL: The rate, measured in degrees of shaft rotation, at which an electrical circuit cycles on and off.

ELECTRONIC CONTROL UNIT (ECU): Ignition module, module, amplifier or igniter. See Module for definition.

ELECTRONIC IGNITION: A system in which the timing and firing of the spark plugs is controlled by an electronic control unit, usually called a module. These systems have no points or condenser.

END-PLAY: The measured amount of axial movement in a shaft.

ENGINE: A device that converts heat into mechanical energy.

EXHAUST MANIFOLD: A set of cast passages or pipes which conduct exhaust gases from the engine.

FEELER GAUGE: A blade, usually metal, or precisely predetermined thickness, used to measure the clearance between two parts.

FIRING ORDER: The order in which combustion occurs in the cylinders of an engine. Also the order in which spark is distributed to the plugs by the distributor.

FLOODING: The presence of too much fuel in the intake manifold and combustion chamber which prevents the air/fuel mixture from firing, thereby causing a no-start situation.

FLYWHEEL: A disc shaped part bolted to the rear end of the crankshaft. Around the outer perimeter is affixed the ring gear. The starter drive engages the ring gear, turning the flywheel, which rotates the crankshaft, imparting the initial starting motion to the engine.

FOOT POUND (ft. lbs. or sometimes, ft.lb.): The amount of energy or work needed to raise an item weighing one pound, a distance of one foot.

FUSE: A protective device in a circuit which prevents circuit overload by breaking the circuit when a specific amperage is present. The device is constructed around a strip or wire of a lower amperage rating than the circuit it is designed to protect. When an amperage higher than that stamped on the fuse is present in the circuit, the strip or wire melts, opening the circuit.

GEAR RATIO: The ratio between the number of teeth on meshing gears.

GENERATOR: A device which converts mechanical energy into electrical energy.

HEAT RANGE: The measure of a spark plug's ability to dissipate heat from its firing end. The higher the heat range, the hotter the plug fires.

HUB: The center part of a wheel or gear.

HYDROCARBON (HC): Any chemical compound made up of hydrogen and carbon. A major pollutant formed by the engine as a byproduct of combustion.

HYDROMETER: An instrument used to measure the specific gravity of a solution.

INCH POUND (inch lbs.; sometimes in.lb. or in. lbs.): One twelfth of a foot pound.

INDUCTION: A means of transferring electrical energy in the form of a magnetic field. Principle used in the ignition coil to increase voltage.

INJECTOR: A device which receives metered fuel under relatively low pressure and is activated to inject the fuel into the engine under relatively high pressure at a predetermined time.

INPUT SHAFT: The shaft to which torque is applied, usually carrying the driving gear or gears.

INTAKE MANIFOLD: A casting of passages or pipes used to conduct air or a fuel/air mixture to the cylinders.

JOURNAL: The bearing surface within which a shaft operates.

KEY: A small block usually fitted in a notch between a shaft and a hub to prevent slippage of the two parts.

MANIFOLD: A casting of passages or set of pipes which connect the cylinders to an inlet or outlet source.

MANIFOLD VACUUM: Low pressure in an engine intake manifold formed just below the throttle plates. Manifold vacuum is highest at idle and drops under acceleration.

MASTER CYLINDER: The primary fluid pressurizing device in a hydraulic system. In automotive use, it is found in brake and hydraulic clutch systems and is pedal activated, either directly or, in a power brake system, through the power booster.

MODULE: Electronic control unit, amplifier or igniter of solid state or integrated design which controls the current flow in the ignition primary circuit based on input from the pick-up coil. When the module opens the primary circuit, high secondary voltage is induced in the coil.

NEEDLE BEARING: A bearing which consists of a number (usually a large number) of long, thin rollers.

OHM: (Ω) The unit used to measure the resistance of conductor-to-electrical flow. One ohm is the amount of resistance that limits current flow to one ampere in a circuit with one volt of pressure.

OHMMETER: An instrument used for measuring the resistance, in ohms, in an electrical circuit.

OUTPUT SHAFT: The shaft which transmits torque from a device, such as a transmission.

OVERDRIVE: A gear assembly which produces more shaft revolutions than that transmitted to it.

OVERHEAD CAMSHAFT (OHC): An engine configuration in which the camshaft is mounted on top of the cylinder head and operates the valve either directly or by means of rocker arms.

OVERHEAD VALVE (OHV): An engine configuration in which all of the valves are located in the cylinder head and the camshaft is located in the cylinder block. The camshaft operates the valves via lifters and pushrods.

OXIDES OF NITROGEN (NOx): Chemical compounds of nitrogen produced as a byproduct of combustion. They combine with hydrocarbons to produce smog.

OXYGEN SENSOR: Use with the feedback system to sense the presence of oxygen in the exhaust gas and signal the computer which can reference the voltage signal to an air/fuel ratio.

PINION: The smaller of two meshing gears.

PISTON RING: An open-ended ring with fits into a groove on the outer diameter of the piston. Its chief function is to form a seal between the piston and cylinder wall. Most automotive pistons have three rings: two for compression sealing; one for oil sealing.

PRELOAD: A predetermined load placed on a bearing during assembly or by adjustment.

PRIMARY CIRCUIT: the low voltage side of the ignition system which consists of the ignition switch, ballast resistor or resistance wire, bypass, coil, electronic control unit and pick-up coil as well as the connecting wires and harnesses.

PRESS FIT: The mating of two parts under pressure, due to the inner diameter of one being smaller than the outer diameter of the other, or vice versa; an interference fit.

RACE: The surface on the inner or outer ring of a bearing on which the balls, needles or rollers move.

REGULATOR: A device which maintains the amperage and/or voltage levels of a circuit at predetermined values.

RELAY: A switch which automatically opens and/or closes a circuit.

RESISTANCE: The opposition to the flow of current through a circuit or electrical device, and is measured in ohms. Resistance is equal to the voltage divided by the amperage.

RESISTOR: A device, usually made of wire, which offers a preset amount of resistance in an electrical circuit.

RING GEAR: The name given to a ring-shaped gear attached to a differential case, or affixed to a flywheel or as part of a planetary gear set.

ROLLER BEARING: A bearing made up of hardened inner and outer races between which hardened steel rollers move.

ROTOR: 1. The disc-shaped part of a disc brake assembly, upon which the brake pads bear; also called, brake disc. 2. The device mounted atop the distributor shaft, which passes current to the distributor cap tower contacts.

SECONDARY CIRCUIT: The high voltage side of the ignition system, usually above 20,000 volts. The secondary includes the ignition coil, coil wire, distributor cap and rotor, spark plug wires and spark plugs.

SENDING UNIT: A mechanical, electrical, hydraulic or electro-magnetic device which transmits information to a gauge.

SENSOR: Any device designed to measure engine operating conditions or ambient pressures and temperatures. Usually electronic in nature and designed to send a voltage signal to an on-board computer, some sensors may operate as a simple on/off switch or they may provide a variable voltage signal (like a potentiometer) as conditions or measured parameters change.

SHIM: Spacers of precise, predetermined thickness used between parts to establish a proper working relationship.

SLAVE CYLINDER: In automotive use, a device in the hydraulic clutch system which is activated by hydraulic force, disengaging the clutch.

SOLENOID: A coil used to produce a magnetic field, the effect of which is to produce work.

SPARK PLUG: A device screwed into the combustion chamber of a spark ignition engine. The basic construction is a conductive core inside of a ceramic insulator, mounted in an outer conductive base. An electrical charge from the spark plug wire travels along the conductive core and jumps a preset air gap to a grounding point or points at the end of the conductive base. The resultant spark ignites the fuel/air mixture in the combustion chamber.

SPLINES: Ridges machined or cast onto the outer diameter of a shaft or inner diameter of a bore to enable parts to mate without rotation.

TACHOMETER: A device used to measure the rotary speed of an engine, shaft, gear, etc., usually in rotations per minute.

THERMOSTAT: A valve, located in the cooling system of an engine, which is closed when cold and opens gradually in response to engine heating, controlling the temperature of the coolant and rate of coolant flow.

TOP DEAD CENTER (TDC): The point at which the piston reaches the top of its travel on the compression stroke.

TORQUE: The twisting force applied to an object.

TORQUE CONVERTER: A turbine used to transmit power from a driving member to a driven member via hydraulic action, providing changes in drive ratio and torque. In automotive use, it links the driveplate at the rear of the engine to the automatic transmission.

TRANSDUCER: A device used to change a force into an electrical signal.

TRANSISTOR: A semi-conductor component which can be actuated by a small voltage to perform an electrical switching function.

TUNE-UP: A regular maintenance function, usually associated with the replacement and adjustment of parts and components in the electrical and fuel systems of a vehicle for the purpose of attaining optimum performance.

TURBOCHARGER: An exhaust driven pump which compresses intake air and forces it into the combustion chambers at higher than atmospheric pressures. The increased air pressure allows more fuel to be burned and results in increased horsepower being produced.

VACUUM ADVANCE: A device which advances the ignition timing in response to increased engine vacuum.

VACUUM GAUGE: An instrument used to measure the presence of vacuum in a chamber.

VALVE: A device which control the pressure, direction of flow or rate of flow of a liquid or gas.

VALVE CLEARANCE: The measured gap between the end of the valve stem and the rocker arm, cam lobe or follower that activates the valve.

VISCOSITY: The rating of a liquid's internal resistance to flow.

VOLTMETER: An instrument used for measuring electrical force in units called volts. Voltmeters are always connected parallel with the circuit being tested.

WHEEL CYLINDER: Found in the automotive drum brake assembly, it is a device, actuated by hydraulic pressure, which, through internal pistons, pushes the brake shoes outward against the drums.

MASTER

INDEX